Data Mining: Concepts and Techniques

Second Edition

The Morgan Kaufmann Series in Data Management Systems
Series Editor: Jim Gray, Microsoft Research

Data Mining: Concepts and Techniques, Second Edition
Jiawei Han and Micheline Kamber

Querying XML: XQuery, XPath, and SQL/XML in context
Jim Melton and Stephen Buxton

Foundations of Multidimensional and Metric Data Structures
Hanan Samet

Database Modeling and Design: Logical Design, Fourth Edition
Toby J. Teorey, Sam S. Lightstone and Thomas P. Nadeau

Joe Celko's SQL for Smarties: Advanced SQL Programming, Third Edition
Joe Celko

Moving Objects Databases
Ralf Guting and Markus Schneider

Joe Celko's SQL Programming Style
Joe Celko

Data Mining: Practical Machine Learning Tools and Techniques, Second Edition
Ian Witten and Eibe Frank

Fuzzy Modeling and Genetic Algorithms for Data Mining and Exploration
Earl Cox

Data Modeling Essentials, Third Edition
Graeme C. Simsion and Graham C. Witt

Location-Based Services
Jochen Schiller and Agnès Voisard

Database Modeling with Microsft® Visio for Enterprise Architects
Terry Halpin, Ken Evans, Patrick Hallock, Bill Maclean

Designing Data-Intensive Web Applications
Stephano Ceri, Piero Fraternali, Aldo Bongio, Marco Brambilla, Sara Comai, and Maristella Matera

Mining the Web: Discovering Knowledge from Hypertext Data
Soumen Chakrabarti

Advanced SQL:II 1999—Understanding Object-Relational and Other Advanced Features
Jim Melton

Database Tuning: Principles, Experiments, and Troubleshooting Techniques
Dennis Shasha and Philippe Bonnet

SQL:1999—Understanding Relational Language Components
Jim Melton and Alan R. Simon

Information Visualization in Data Mining and Knowledge Discovery
Edited by Usama Fayyad, Georges G. Grinstein, and Andreas Wierse

Transactional Information Systems: Theory, Algorithms, and Practice of Concurrency Control and Recovery
Gerhard Weikum and Gottfried Vossen

Spatial Databases: With Application to GIS
Philippe Rigaux, Michel Scholl, and Agnes Voisard

Information Modeling and Relational Databases: From Conceptual Analysis to Logical Design
Terry Halpin

Component Database Systems
Edited by Klaus R. Dittrich and Andreas Geppert

Managing Reference Data in Enterprise Databases: Binding Corporate Data to the Wider World
Malcolm Chisholm

Data Mining: Concepts and Techniques
Jiawei Han and Micheline Kamber

Understanding SQL and Java Together: A Guide to SQLJ, JDBC, and Related Technologies
Jim Melton and Andrew Eisenberg

Database: Principles, Programming, and Performance, Second Edition
Patrick and Elizabeth O'Neil

The Object Data Standard: ODMG 3.0
Edited by R. G. G. Cattell and Douglas K. Barry

Data on the Web: From Relations to Semistructured Data and XML
Serge Abiteboul, Peter Buneman, and Dan Suciu

Data Mining: Practical Machine Learning Tools and Techniques with Java Implementations
Ian Witten and Eibe Frank

Joe Celko's SQL for Smarties: Advanced SQL Programming, Second Edition
Joe Celko

Joe Celko's Data and Databases: Concepts in Practice
Joe Celko

Developing Time-Oriented Database Applications in SQL
Richard T. Snodgrass

Web Farming for the Data Warehouse
Richard D. Hackathorn

Management of Heterogeneous and Autonomous Database Systems
Edited by Ahmed Elmagarmid, Marek Rusinkiewicz, and Amit Sheth

Object-Relational DBMSs: Tracking the Next Great Wave, Second Edition
Michael Stonebraker and Paul Brown,with Dorothy Moore

A Complete Guide to DB2 Universal Database
Don Chamberlin

Universal Database Management: A Guide to Object/Relational Technology
Cynthia Maro Saracco

Readings in Database Systems, Third Edition
Edited by Michael Stonebraker and Joseph M. Hellerstein

Understanding SQL's Stored Procedures: A Complete Guide to SQL/PSM
Jim Melton

Principles of Multimedia Database Systems
V. S. Subrahmanian

Principles of Database Query Processing for Advanced Applications
Clement T. Yu and Weiyi Meng

Advanced Database Systems
Carlo Zaniolo, Stefano Ceri, Christos Faloutsos, Richard T. Snodgrass, V. S. Subrahmanian, and Roberto Zicari

Principles of Transaction Processing
Philip A. Bernstein and Eric Newcomer

Using the New DB2: IBMs Object-Relational Database System
Don Chamberlin

Distributed Algorithms
Nancy A. Lynch

Active Database Systems: Triggers and Rules For Advanced Database Processing
Edited by Jennifer Widom and Stefano Ceri

Migrating Legacy Systems: Gateways, Interfaces, & the Incremental Approach
Michael L. Brodie and Michael Stonebraker

Atomic Transactions
Nancy Lynch, Michael Merritt, William Weihl, and Alan Fekete

Query Processing for Advanced Database Systems
Edited by Johann Christoph Freytag, David Maier, and Gottfried Vossen

Transaction Processing: Concepts and Techniques
Jim Gray and Andreas Reuter

Building an Object-Oriented Database System: The Story of O_2
Edited by François Bancilhon, Claude Delobel, and Paris Kanellakis

Database Transaction Models for Advanced Applications
Edited by Ahmed K. Elmagarmid

A Guide to Developing Client/Server SQL Applications
Setrag Khoshafian, Arvola Chan, Anna Wong, and Harry K. T. Wong

The Benchmark Handbook for Database and Transaction Processing Systems, Second Edition
Edited by Jim Gray

Camelot and Avalon: A Distributed Transaction Facility
Edited by Jeffrey L. Eppinger, Lily B. Mummert, and Alfred Z. Spector

Readings in Object-Oriented Database Systems
Edited by Stanley B. Zdonik and David Maier

Data Mining: Concepts and Techniques

Second Edition

Jiawei Han

University of Illinois at Urbana-Champaign

Micheline Kamber

Morgan Kaufmann Publishers

An imprint of Elsevier

Data Mining: Concepts and Techniques, 2/e
Han and Kamber

Morgan Kaufmann Publishers
An imprint of Elsevier
500 Sansome Street, Suite 400, San Francisco, CA 94111

Original ISBN: 978-1-55860-901-3

First Printed in India 2006
Reprinted 2006
Reprinted 2007 (thrice)
Reprinted 2008 (six times)
Reprinted 2009 (six times)
Reprinted 2010

Indian Reprint ISBN: 978-81-312-0535-8

Registered Office: Gate No. 3, Building No.A-1, 2 Industrial Area, Kalkaji, New Delhi 110 019.
Corporate Office: 14th Floor, Building No. 10B, DLF Cyber City, Phase-II, Gurgaon-122 002, Haryana, India.

Printed and bound at Rajkamal Electric Press, Kundli, Haryana.

Dedication

To Y. Dora and Lawrence for your love and encouragement

J.H.

To Erik, Kevan, Kian, and Mikael for your love and inspiration

M.K.

Contents

Foreword

We are deluged by data—scientific data, medical data, demographic data, financial data, and marketing data. People have no time to look at this data. Human attention has become the precious resource. So, we must find ways to automatically analyze the data, to automatically classify it, to automatically summarize it, to automatically discover and characterize trends in it, and to automatically flag anomalies. This is one of the most active and exciting areas of the database research community. Researchers in areas including statistics, visualization, artificial intelligence, and machine learning are contributing to this field. The breadth of the field makes it difficult to grasp the extraordinary progress over the last few decades.

Six years ago, Jiawei Han's and Micheline Kamber's seminal textbook organized and presented Data Mining. It heralded a golden age of innovation in the field. This revision of their book reflects that progress; more than half of the references and historical notes are to recent work. The field has matured with many new and improved algorithms, and has broadened to include many more datatypes: streams, sequences, graphs, time-series, geospatial, audio, images, and video. We are certainly not at the end of the golden age—indeed research and commercial interest in data mining continues to grow—but we are all fortunate to have this modern compendium.

The book gives quick introductions to database and data mining concepts with particular emphasis on data analysis. It then covers in a chapter-by-chapter tour the concepts and techniques that underlie classification, prediction, association, and clustering. These topics are presented with examples, a tour of the best algorithms for each problem class, and with pragmatic rules of thumb about when to apply each technique. The Socratic presentation style is both very readable and very informative. I certainly learned a lot from reading the first edition and got re-educated and updated in reading the second edition.

Jiawei Han and Micheline Kamber have been leading contributors to data mining research. This is the text they use with their students to bring them up to speed on the field. The field is evolving very rapidly, but this book is a quick way to learn the basic ideas, and to understand where the field is today. I found it very informative and stimulating, and believe you will too.

Jim Gray
Microsoft Research
San Francisco, CA, USA

Preface

Our capabilities of both generating and collecting data have been increasing rapidly. Contributing factors include the computerization of business, scientific, and government transactions; the widespread use of digital cameras, publication tools, and bar codes for most commercial products; and advances in data collection tools ranging from scanned text and image platforms to satellite remote sensing systems. In addition, popular use of the World Wide Web as a global information system has flooded us with a tremendous amount of data and information. This explosive growth in stored or transient data has generated an urgent need for new techniques and automated tools that can intelligently assist us in transforming the vast amounts of data into useful information and knowledge.

This book explores the concepts and techniques of *data mining*, a promising and flourishing frontier in data and information systems and their applications. Data mining, also popularly referred to as *knowledge discovery from data (KDD)*, is the automated or convenient extraction of patterns representing knowledge implicitly stored or captured in large databases, data warehouses, the Web, other massive information repositories, or data streams.

Data mining is a multidisciplinary field, drawing work from areas including database technology, machine learning, statistics, pattern recognition, information retrieval, neural networks, knowledge-based systems, artificial intelligence, high-performance computing, and data visualization. We present techniques for the discovery of patterns hidden *in large data sets*, focusing on issues relating to their feasibility, usefulness, effectiveness, and scalability. As a result, this book is not intended as an introduction to database systems, machine learning, statistics, or other such areas, although we do provide the background necessary in these areas in order to facilitate the reader's comprehension of their respective roles in data mining. Rather, the book is a comprehensive introduction to data mining, presented with effectiveness and scalability issues in focus. It should be useful for computing science students, application developers, and business professionals, as well as researchers involved in any of the disciplines listed above.

Data mining emerged during the late 1980s, made great strides during the 1990s, and continues to flourish into the new millennium. This book presents an overall picture of the field, introducing interesting data mining techniques and systems and discussing applications and research directions. An important motivation for writing this book was the need to build an organized framework for the study of data mining—a challenging task, owing to the extensive multidisciplinary nature of this fast-developing field. We hope that this book will encourage people with different backgrounds and experiences to exchange their views regarding data mining so as to contribute toward the further promotion and shaping of this exciting and dynamic field.

Organization of the Book

Since the publication of the first edition of this book, great progress has been made in the field of data mining. Many new data mining methods, systems, and applications have been developed. This new edition substantially revises the first edition of the book, with numerous enhancements and a reorganization of the technical contents of the entire book. In addition, several new chapters are included to address recent developments on mining complex types of data, including stream data, sequence data, graph structured data, social network data, and multirelational data.

The chapters are described briefly as follows, with emphasis on the new material.

Chapter 1 provides an introduction to the multidisciplinary field of data mining. It discusses the evolutionary path of database technology, which has led to the need for data mining, and the importance of its applications. It examines the types of data to be mined, including relational, transactional, and data warehouse data, as well as complex types of data such as data streams, time-series, sequences, graphs, social networks, multirelational data, spatiotemporal data, multimedia data, text data, and Web data. The chapter presents a general classification of data mining tasks, based on the different kinds of knowledge to be mined. In comparison with the first edition, two new sections are introduced: Section 1.7 is on data mining primitives, which allow users to interactively communicate with data mining systems in order to direct the mining process, and Section 1.8 discusses the issues regarding how to integrate a data mining system with a database or data warehouse system. These two sections represent the condensed materials of Chapter 4, "*Data Mining Primitives, Languages and Architectures,*" in the first edition. Finally, major challenges in the field are discussed.

Chapter 2 introduces techniques for preprocessing the data before mining. This corresponds to Chapter 3 of the first edition. Because data preprocessing precedes the construction of data warehouses, we address this topic here, and then follow with an introduction to data warehouses in the subsequent chapter. This chapter describes various statistical methods for descriptive data summarization, including measuring both central tendency and dispersion of data. The description of data cleaning methods has been enhanced. Methods for data integration and transformation and data reduction are discussed, including the use of concept hierarchies for dynamic and static discretization. The automatic generation of concept hierarchies is also described.

Chapters 3 and 4 provide a solid introduction to data warehouse, OLAP (On-Line Analytical Processing), and data generalization. These two chapters correspond to Chapters 2 and 5 of the first edition, but with substantial enhancement regarding data warehouse implementation methods. **Chapter 3** introduces the basic concepts, architectures and general implementations of data warehouse and on-line analytical processing, as well as the relationship between data warehousing and data mining. **Chapter 4** takes a more in-depth look at data warehouse and OLAP technology, presenting a detailed study of methods of data cube computation, including the recently developed star-cubing and high-dimensional OLAP methods. Further explorations of data warehouse and OLAP are discussed, such as discovery-driven cube exploration, multifeature cubes for complex data mining queries, and cube gradient analysis. Attribute-oriented induction, an alternative method for data generalization and concept description, is also discussed.

Chapter 5 presents methods for mining frequent patterns, associations, and correlations in transactional and relational databases and data warehouses. In addition to introducing the basic concepts, such as market basket analysis, many techniques for frequent itemset mining are presented in an organized way. These range from the basic Apriori algorithm and its variations to more advanced methods that improve on efficiency, including the frequent-pattern growth approach, frequent-pattern mining with vertical data format, and mining closed frequent itemsets. The chapter also presents techniques for mining multilevel association rules, multidimensional association rules, and quantitative association rules. In comparison with the previous edition, this chapter has placed greater emphasis on the generation of meaningful association and correlation rules. Strategies for constraint-based mining and the use of interestingness measures to focus the rule search are also described.

Chapter 6 describes methods for data classification and prediction, including decision tree induction, Bayesian classification, rule-based classification, the neural network technique of backpropagation, support vector machines, associative classification, *k*-nearest neighbor classifiers, case-based reasoning, genetic algorithms, rough set theory, and fuzzy set approaches. Methods of regression are introduced. Issues regarding accuracy and how to choose the best classifier or predictor are discussed. In comparison with the corresponding chapter in the first edition, the sections on rule-based classification and support vector machines are new, and the discussion of measuring and enhancing classification and prediction accuracy has been greatly expanded.

Cluster analysis forms the topic of **Chapter 7**. Several major data clustering approaches are presented, including partitioning methods, hierarchical methods, density-based methods, grid-based methods, and model-based methods. New sections in this edition introduce techniques for clustering high-dimensional data, as well as for constraint-based cluster analysis. Outlier analysis is also discussed.

Chapters 8 to 10 treat advanced topics in data mining and cover a large body of materials on recent progress in this frontier. These three chapters now replace our previous single chapter on advanced topics. **Chapter 8** focuses on the mining of stream data, time-series data, and sequence data (covering both transactional sequences and biological sequences). The basic data mining techniques (such as frequent-pattern mining, classification, clustering, and constraint-based mining) are extended for these types of data. **Chapter 9** discusses methods for graph and structural pattern mining, social network analysis and multirelational data mining. **Chapter 10** presents methods for mining object, spatial, multimedia, text, and Web data, which cover a great deal of new progress in these areas.

Finally, in **Chapter 11**, we summarize the concepts presented in this book and discuss applications and trends in data mining. New material has been added on data mining for biological and biomedical data analysis, other scientific applications, intrusion detection, and collaborative filtering. Social impacts of data mining, such as privacy and data security issues, are discussed, in addition to challenging research issues. Further discussion of ubiquitous data mining has also been added.

The **Appendix** provides an introduction to Microsoft's OLE DB for Data Mining (OLEDB for DM).

Throughout the text, italic font is used to emphasize terms that are defined, while bold font is used to highlight or summarize main ideas. Sans serif font is used for reserved words. Bold italic font is used to represent multidimensional quantities.

This book has several strong features that set it apart from other texts on data mining. It presents a very broad yet in-depth coverage from the spectrum of data mining, especially regarding several recent research topics on data stream mining, graph mining, social network analysis, and multirelational data mining. The chapters preceding the advanced topics are written to be as self-contained as possible, so they may be read in order of interest by the reader. All of the major methods of data mining are presented. Because we take a database point of view to data mining, the book also presents many important topics in data mining, such as scalable algorithms and multidimensional OLAP analysis, that are often overlooked or minimally treated in other books.

To the Instructor

This book is designed to give a broad, yet detailed overview of the field of data mining. It can be used to teach an *introductory* course on data mining at an advanced undergraduate level or at the first-year graduate level. In addition, it can also be used to teach an *advanced* course on data mining.

If you plan to use the book to teach an introductory course, you may find that the materials in Chapters 1 to 7 are essential, among which Chapter 4 may be omitted if you do not plan to cover the implementation methods for data cubing and on-line analytical processing in depth. Alternatively, you may omit some sections in Chapters 1 to 7 and use Chapter 11 as the final coverage of applications and trends on data mining.

If you plan to use the book to teach an advanced course on data mining, you may use Chapters 8 through 11. Moreover, additional materials and some recent research papers may supplement selected themes from among the advanced topics of these chapters.

Individual chapters in this book can also be used for tutorials or for special topics in related courses, such as database systems, machine learning, pattern recognition, and intelligent data analysis.

Each chapter ends with a set of exercises, suitable as assigned homework. The exercises are either short questions that test basic mastery of the material covered, longer questions that require analytical thinking, or implementation projects. Some exercises can also be used as research discussion topics. The bibliographic notes at the end of each chapter can be used to find the research literature that contains the origin of the concepts and methods presented, in-depth treatment of related topics, and possible extensions. Extensive teaching aids are available from the book's websites, such as lecture slides, reading lists, and course syllabi.

To the Student

We hope that this textbook will spark your interest in the young yet fast-evolving field of data mining. We have attempted to present the material in a clear manner, with careful explanation of the topics covered. Each chapter ends with a summary describing the main points. We have included many figures and illustrations throughout the text in order to make the book more enjoyable and reader-friendly. Although this book was designed as a textbook, we have tried to organize it so that it will also be useful to you as a reference book or handbook, should you later decide to perform in-depth research in the related fields or pursue a career in data mining.

What do you need to know in order to read this book?

- You should have some knowledge of the concepts and terminology associated with database systems, statistics, and machine learning. However, we do try to provide enough background of the basics in these fields, so that if you are not so familiar with these fields or your memory is a bit rusty, you will not have trouble following the discussions in the book.
- You should have some programming experience. In particular, you should be able to read pseudo-code and understand simple data structures such as multidimensional arrays.

To the Professional

This book was designed to cover a wide range of topics in the field of data mining. As a result, it is an excellent handbook on the subject. Because each chapter is designed to be as stand-alone as possible, you can focus on the topics that most interest you. The book can be used by application programmers and information service managers who wish to learn about the key ideas of data mining on their own. The book would also be useful for technical data analysis staff in banking, insurance, medicine, and retailing industries who are interested in applying data mining solutions to their businesses. Moreover, the book may serve as a comprehensive survey of the data mining field, which may also benefit researchers who would like to advance the state-of-the-art in data mining and extend the scope of data mining applications.

The techniques and algorithms presented are of practical utility. Rather than selecting algorithms that perform well on small "toy" data sets, the algorithms described in the book are geared for the discovery of patterns and knowledge hidden in large, real data sets. In Chapter 11, we briefly discuss data mining systems in commercial use, as well as promising research prototypes. Algorithms presented in the book are illustrated in pseudo-code. The pseudo-code is similar to the C programming language, yet is designed so that it should be easy to follow by programmers unfamiliar with C or C++. If you wish to implement any of the algorithms, you should find the translation of our pseudo-code into the programming language of your choice to be a fairly straightforward task.

Book Websites with Resources

The book has a website at *www.cs.uiuc.edu/~hanj/bk2* and another with Morgan Kaufmann Publishers at *www.mkp.com/datamining2e*. These websites contain many supplemental materials for readers of this book or anyone else with an interest in data mining. The resources include:

- **Slide presentations per chapter.** Lecture notes in Microsoft PowerPoint slides are available for each chapter.
- **Artwork of the book.** This may help you to make your own slides for your classroom teaching.
- **Instructors' manual.** This complete set of answers to the exercises in the book is available only to instructors from the publisher's website.
- **Course syllabi and lecture plan.** These are given for undergraduate and graduate versions of introductory and advanced courses on data mining, which use the text and slides.
- **Supplemental reading lists with hyperlinks.** Seminal papers for supplemental reading are organized per chapter.
- **Links to data mining data sets and software.** We will provide a set of links to data mining data sets and sites containing interesting data mining software packages, such as IlliMine from the University of Illinois at Urbana-Champaign (*http://illimine.cs.uiuc.edu*).
- **Sample assignments, exams, course projects.** A set of sample assignments, exams, and course projects will be made available to instructors from the publisher's website.
- **Table of contents of the book in PDF.**
- **Errata on the different printings of the book.** We welcome you to point out any errors in the book. Once the error is confirmed, we will update this errata list and include acknowledgment of your contribution.

Comments or suggestions can be sent to *hanj@cs.uiuc.edu*. We would be happy to hear from you.

Acknowledgments for the First Edition of the Book

We would like to express our sincere thanks to all those who have worked or are currently working with us on data mining–related research and/or the DBMiner project, or have provided us with various support in data mining. These include Rakesh Agrawal, Stella Atkins, Yvan Bedard, Binay Bhattacharya, (Yandong) Dora Cai, Nick Cercone, Surajit Chaudhuri, Sonny H. S. Chee, Jianping Chen, Ming-Syan Chen, Qing Chen, Qiming Chen, Shan Cheng, David Cheung, Shi Cong, Son Dao, Umeshwar Dayal, James Delgrande, Guozhu Dong, Carole Edwards, Max Egenhofer, Martin Ester, Usama Fayyad, Ling Feng, Ada Fu, Yongjian Fu, Daphne Gelbart, Randy Goebel, Jim Gray, Robert Grossman, Wan Gong, Yike Guo, Eli Hagen, Howard Hamilton, Jing He, Larry Henschen, Jean Hou, Mei-Chun Hsu, Kan Hu, Haiming Huang, Yue Huang, Julia Itskevitch, Wen Jin, Tiko Kameda, Hiroyuki Kawano, Rizwan Kheraj, Eddie Kim, Won Kim, Krzysztof Koperski, Hans-Peter Kriegel, Vipin Kumar, Laks V. S. Lakshmanan, Joyce Man Lam, James Lau, Deyi Li, George (Wenmin) Li, Jin Li, Ze-Nian Li, Nancy Liao, Gang Liu, Junqiang Liu, Ling Liu, Alan (Yijun) Lu, Hongjun Lu, Tong Lu, Wei Lu, Xuebin Lu, Wo-Shun Luk, Heikki Mannila, Runying Mao, Abhay Mehta, Gabor Melli, Alberto Mendelzon, Tim Merrett, Harvey Miller, Drew Miners, Behzad Mortazavi-Asl, Richard Muntz, Raymond T. Ng, Vicent Ng, Shojiro Nishio, Beng-Chin Ooi, Tamer Ozsu, Jian Pei, Gregory Piatetsky-Shapiro, Helen Pinto, Fred Popowich, Amynmohamed Rajan, Peter Scheuermann, Shashi Shekhar, Wei-Min Shen, Avi Silberschatz, Evangelos Simoudis, Nebojsa Stefanovic, Yin Jenny Tam, Simon Tang, Zhaohui Tang, Dick Tsur, Anthony K. H. Tung, Ke Wang, Wei Wang, Zhaoxia Wang, Tony Wind, Lara Winstone, Ju Wu, Betty (Bin) Xia, Cindy M. Xin, Xiaowei Xu, Qiang Yang, Yiwen Yin, Clement Yu, Jeffrey Yu, Philip S. Yu, Osmar R. Zaiane, Carlo Zaniolo, Shuhua Zhang, Zhong Zhang, Yvonne Zheng, Xiaofang Zhou, and Hua Zhu. We are also grateful to Jean Hou, Helen Pinto, Lara Winstone, and Hua Zhu for their help with some of the original figures in this book, and to Eugene Belchev for his careful proofreading of each chapter.

We also wish to thank Diane Cerra, our Executive Editor at Morgan Kaufmann Publishers, for her enthusiasm, patience, and support during our writing of this book, as well as Howard Severson, our Production Editor, and his staff for their conscientious efforts regarding production. We are indebted to all of the reviewers for their invaluable feedback. Finally, we thank our families for their wholehearted support throughout this project.

Acknowledgments for the Second Edition of the Book

We would like to express our grateful thanks to all of the previous and current members of the Data Mining Group at UIUC, the faculty and students in the Data and Information Systems (DAIS) Laboratory in the Department of Computer Science, the University of Illinois at Urbana-Champaign, and many friends and colleagues, whose constant support and encouragement have made our work on this edition a rewarding experience. These include Gul Agha, Rakesh Agrawal, Loretta Auvil, Peter Bajcsy, Geneva Belford, Deng Cai, Y. Dora Cai, Roy Cambell, Kevin C.-C. Chang, Surajit Chaudhuri, Chen Chen, Yixin Chen, Yuguo Chen, Hong Cheng, David Cheung, Shengnan Cong, Gerald DeJong, AnHai Doan, Guozhu Dong, Charios Ermopoulos, Martin Ester, Christos Faloutsos, Wei Fan, Jack C. Feng, Ada Fu, Michael Garland, Johannes Gehrke, Hector Gonzalez, Mehdi Harandi, Thomas Huang, Wen Jin, Chulyun Kim, Sangkyum Kim, Won Kim, Won-Young Kim, David Kuck, Young-Koo Lee, Harris Lewin, Xiaolei Li, Yifan Li, Chao Liu, Han Liu, Huan Liu, Hongyan Liu, Lei Liu, Ying Lu, Klara Nahrstedt, David Padua, Jian Pei, Lenny Pitt, Daniel Reed, Dan Roth, Bruce Schatz, Zheng Shao, Marc Snir, Zhaohui Tang, Bhavani M. Thuraisingham, Josep Torrellas, Peter Tzvetkov, Benjamin W. Wah, Haixun Wang, Jianyong Wang, Ke Wang, Muyuan Wang, Wei Wang, Michael Welge, Marianne Winslett, Ouri Wolfson, Andrew Wu, Tianyi Wu, Dong Xin, Xifeng Yan, Jiong Yang, Xiaoxin Yin, Hwanjo Yu, Jeffrey X. Yu, Philip S. Yu, Maria Zemankova, ChengXiang Zhai, Yuanyuan Zhou, and Wei Zou. Deng Cai and ChengXiang Zhai have contributed to the text mining and Web mining sections, Xifeng Yan to the graph mining section, and Xiaoxin Yin to the multirelational data mining section. Hong Cheng, Charios Ermopoulos, Hector Gonzalez, David J. Hill, Chulyun Kim, Sangkyum Kim, Chao Liu, Hongyan Liu, Kasif Manzoor, Tianyi Wu, Xifeng Yan, and Xiaoxin Yin have contributed to the proofreading of the individual chapters of the manuscript.

We also which to thank Diane Cerra, our Publisher at Morgan Kaufmann Publishers, for her constant enthusiasm, patience, and support during our writing of this book. We are indebted to Alan Rose, the book Production Project Manager, for his tireless and ever prompt communications with us to sort out all details of the production process. We are grateful for the invaluable feedback from all of the reviewers. Finally, we thank our families for their wholehearted support throughout this project.

Introduction

This book is an introduction to a young and promising field called *data mining* and *knowledge discovery from data*. The material in this book is presented from a database perspective, where emphasis is placed on basic data mining concepts and techniques for uncovering interesting data patterns hidden in *large data sets*. The implementation methods discussed are particularly oriented toward the development of *scalable* and *efficient* data mining tools. In this chapter, you will learn how data mining is part of the natural evolution of database technology, why data mining is important, and how it is defined. You will learn about the general architecture of data mining systems, as well as gain insight into the kinds of data on which mining can be performed, the types of patterns that can be found, and how to tell which patterns represent useful knowledge. You will study data mining primitives, from which data mining query languages can be designed. Issues regarding how to integrate a data mining system with a database or data warehouse are also discussed. In addition to studying a classification of data mining systems, you will read about challenging research issues for building data mining tools of the future.

1.1 What Motivated Data Mining? Why Is It Important?

Necessity is the mother of invention. —Plato

Data mining has attracted a great deal of attention in the information industry and in society as a whole in recent years, due to the wide availability of huge amounts of data and the imminent need for turning such data into useful information and knowledge. The information and knowledge gained can be used for applications ranging from market analysis, fraud detection, and customer retention, to production control and science exploration.

Data mining can be viewed as a result of the natural evolution of information technology. The database system industry has witnessed an evolutionary path in the development of the following functionalities (Figure 1.1): *data collection and database creation, data management* (including data storage and retrieval, and database

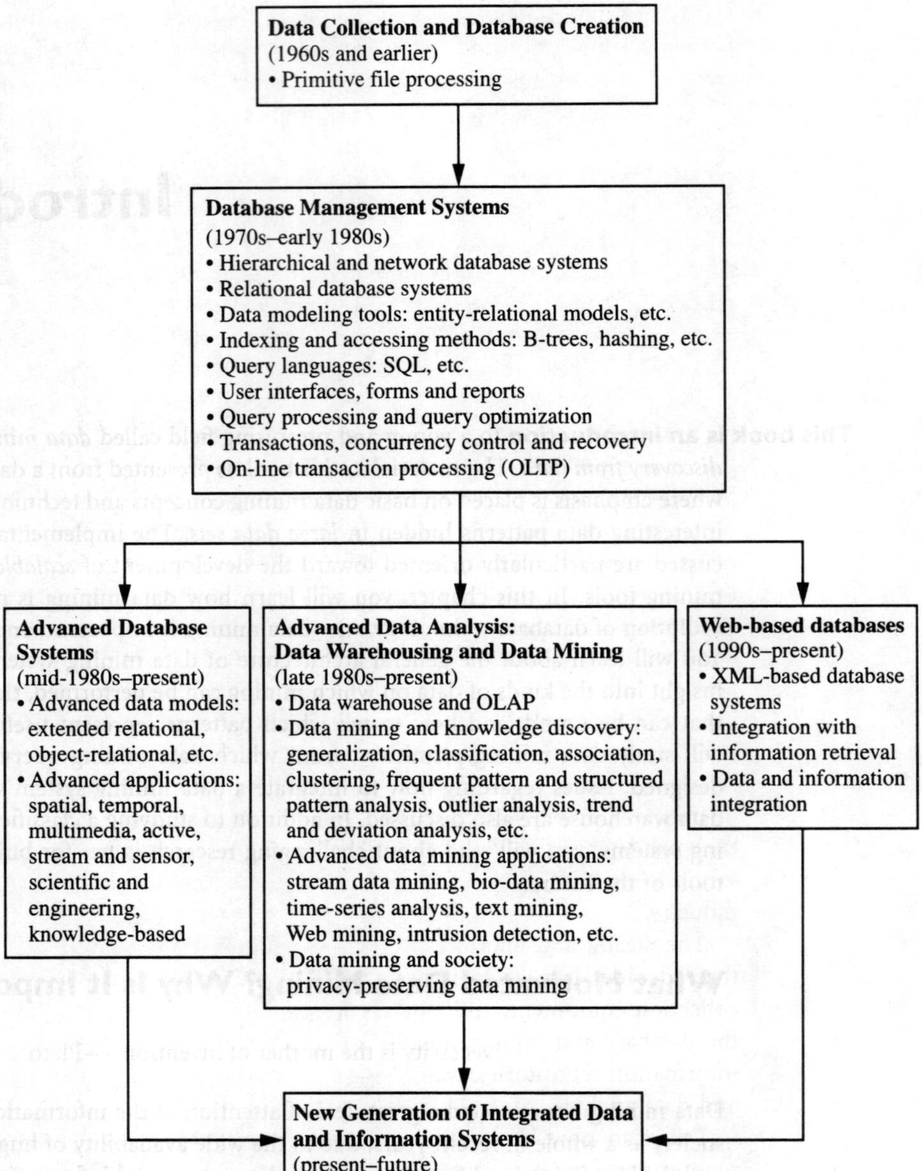

Figure 1.1 The evolution of database system technology.

transaction processing), and *advanced data analysis* (involving data warehousing and data mining). For instance, the early development of data collection and database creation mechanisms served as a prerequisite for later development of effective mechanisms for data storage and retrieval, and query and transaction processing. With numerous database systems offering query and transaction processing as common practice, advanced data analysis has naturally become the next target.

Since the 1960s, database and information technology has been evolving systematically from primitive file processing systems to sophisticated and powerful database systems. The research and development in database systems since the 1970s has progressed from early hierarchical and network database systems to the development of relational database systems (where data are stored in relational table structures; see Section 1.3.1), data modeling tools, and indexing and accessing methods. In addition, users gained convenient and flexible data access through query languages, user interfaces, optimized query processing, and transaction management. Efficient methods for **on-line transaction processing (OLTP)**, where a query is viewed as a read-only transaction, have contributed substantially to the evolution and wide acceptance of relational technology as a major tool for efficient storage, retrieval, and management of large amounts of data.

Database technology since the mid-1980s has been characterized by the popular adoption of relational technology and an upsurge of research and development activities on new and powerful database systems. These promote the development of advanced data models such as extended-relational, object-oriented, object-relational, and deductive models. Application-oriented database systems, including spatial, temporal, multimedia, active, stream, and sensor, and scientific and engineering databases, knowledge bases, and office information bases, have flourished. Issues related to the distribution, diversification, and sharing of data have been studied extensively. Heterogeneous database systems and Internet-based global information systems such as the World Wide Web (WWW) have also emerged and play a vital role in the information industry.

The steady and amazing progress of computer hardware technology in the past three decades has led to large supplies of powerful and affordable computers, data collection equipment, and storage media. This technology provides a great boost to the database and information industry, and makes a huge number of databases and information repositories available for transaction management, information retrieval, and data analysis.

Data can now be stored in many different kinds of databases and information repositories. One data repository architecture that has emerged is the **data warehouse** (Section 1.3.2), a repository of multiple heterogeneous data sources organized under a unified schema at a single site in order to facilitate management decision making. Data warehouse technology includes data cleaning, data integration, and **on-line analytical processing (OLAP)**, that is, analysis techniques with functionalities such as summarization, consolidation, and aggregation as well as the ability to view information from different angles. Although OLAP tools support multidimensional analysis and decision making, additional data analysis tools are required for in-depth analysis, such as

Figure 1.2 We are data rich, but information poor.

data classification, clustering, and the characterization of data changes over time. In addition, huge volumes of data can be accumulated beyond databases and data warehouses. Typical examples include the World Wide Web and *data streams*, where data flow in and out like streams, as in applications like video surveillance, telecommunication, and sensor networks. The effective and efficient analysis of data in such different forms becomes a challenging task.

The abundance of data, coupled with the need for powerful data analysis tools, has been described as a *data rich but information poor* situation. The fast-growing, tremendous amount of data, collected and stored in large and numerous data repositories, has far exceeded our human ability for comprehension without powerful tools (Figure 1.2). As a result, data collected in large data repositories become "data tombs"—data archives that are seldom visited. Consequently, important decisions are often made based not on the information-rich data stored in data repositories, but rather on a decision maker's intuition, simply because the decision maker does not have the tools to extract the valuable knowledge embedded in the vast amounts of data. In addition, consider expert system technologies, which typically rely on users or domain experts to *manually* input knowledge into knowledge bases. Unfortunately, this procedure is prone to biases and errors, and is extremely time-consuming and costly. Data mining tools perform data analysis and may uncover important data patterns, contributing greatly to business strategies, knowledge bases, and scientific and medical research. The widening gap between data and information calls for a systematic development of *data mining tools* that will turn data tombs into "golden nuggets" of knowledge.

1.2 So, What Is Data Mining?

Simply stated, **data mining** refers to *extracting or "mining" knowledge from large amounts of data.* The term is actually a misnomer. Remember that the mining of gold from rocks or sand is referred to as *gold* mining rather than rock or sand mining. Thus, data mining should have been more appropriately named "knowledge mining from data," which is unfortunately somewhat long. "Knowledge mining," a shorter term, may not reflect the emphasis on mining from large amounts of data. Nevertheless, mining is a vivid term characterizing the process that finds a small set of precious nuggets from a great deal of raw material (Figure 1.3). Thus, such a misnomer that carries both "data" and "mining" became a popular choice. Many other terms carry a similar or slightly different meaning to data mining, such as **knowledge mining from data, knowledge extraction, data/pattern analysis, data archaeology**, and **data dredging.**

Many people treat data mining as a synonym for another popularly used term, **Knowledge Discovery from Data**, or KDD. Alternatively, others view data mining as simply an

Figure 1.3 Data mining—searching for knowledge (interesting patterns) in your data.

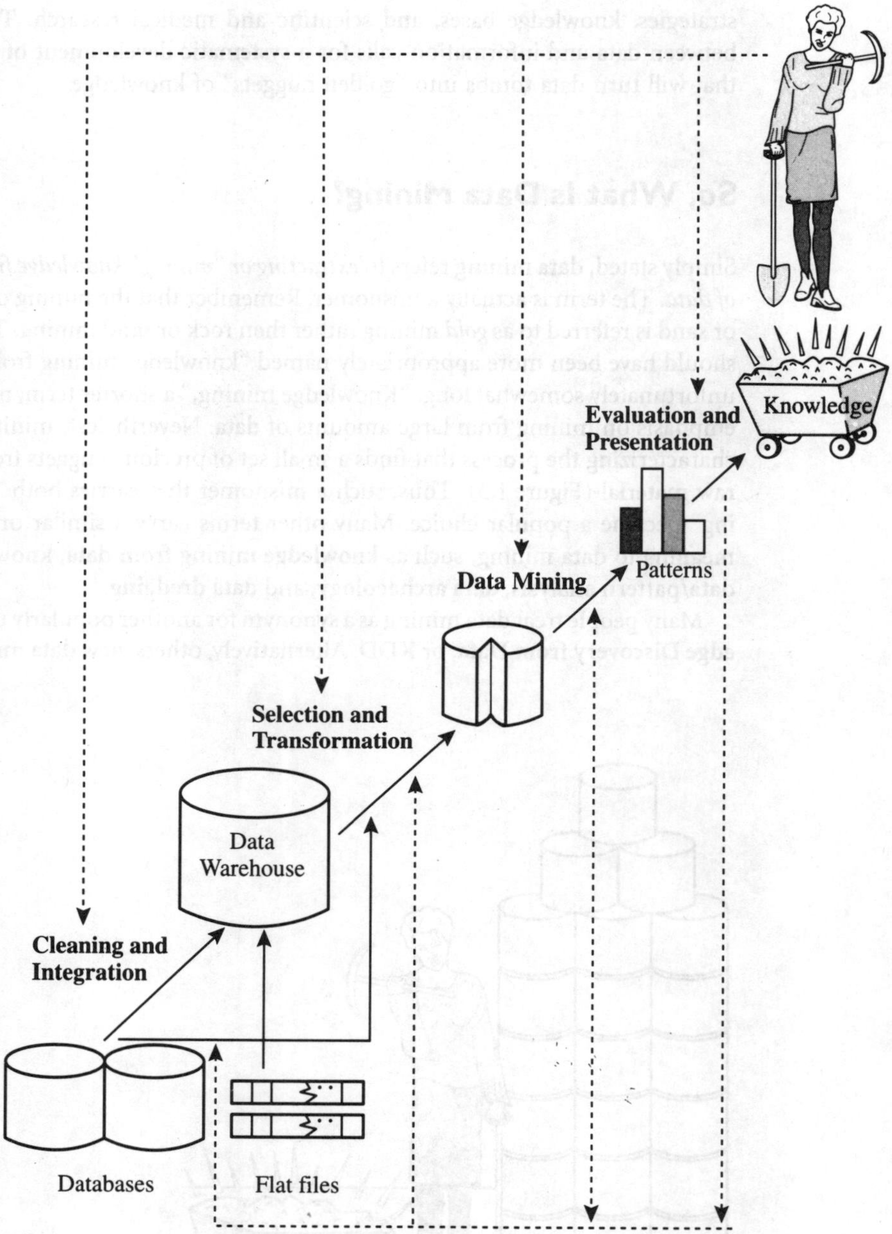

Figure 1.4 Data mining as a step in the process of knowledge discovery.

essential step in the process of knowledge discovery. Knowledge discovery as a process is depicted in Figure 1.4 and consists of an iterative sequence of the following steps:

1. **Data cleaning** (to remove noise and inconsistent data)
2. **Data integration** (where multiple data sources may be combined)[1]
3. **Data selection** (where data relevant to the analysis task are retrieved from the database)
4. **Data transformation** (where data are transformed or consolidated into forms appropriate for mining by performing summary or aggregation operations, for instance)[2]
5. **Data mining** (an essential process where intelligent methods are applied in order to extract data patterns)
6. **Pattern evaluation** (to identify the truly interesting patterns representing knowledge based on some **interestingness measures**; Section 1.5)
7. **Knowledge presentation** (where visualization and knowledge representation techniques are used to present the mined knowledge to the user)

Steps 1 to 4 are different forms of data preprocessing, where the data are prepared for mining. The data mining step may interact with the user or a knowledge base. The interesting patterns are presented to the user and may be stored as new knowledge in the knowledge base. Note that according to this view, data mining is only one step in the entire process, albeit an essential one because it uncovers hidden patterns for evaluation.

We agree that data mining is a step in the knowledge discovery process. However, in industry, in media, and in the database research milieu, the term data mining is becoming more popular than the longer term of knowledge discovery from data. Therefore, in this book, we choose to use the term data mining. We adopt a broad view of data mining functionality: data mining is the process of discovering interesting knowledge from large amounts of data stored in databases, data warehouses, or other information repositories.

Based on this view, the architecture of a typical data mining system may have the following major components (Figure 1.5):

- **Database, data warehouse, World Wide Web, or other information repository:** This is one or a set of databases, data warehouses, spreadsheets, or other kinds of information repositories. Data cleaning and data integration techniques may be performed on the data.
- **Database or data warehouse server:** The database or data warehouse server is responsible for fetching the relevant data, based on the user's data mining request.

[1] A popular trend in the information industry is to perform data cleaning and data integration as a preprocessing step, where the resulting data are stored in a data warehouse.

[2] Sometimes data transformation and consolidation are performed before the data selection process, particularly in the case of data warehousing. *Data reduction* may also be performed to obtain a smaller representation of the original data without sacrificing its integrity.

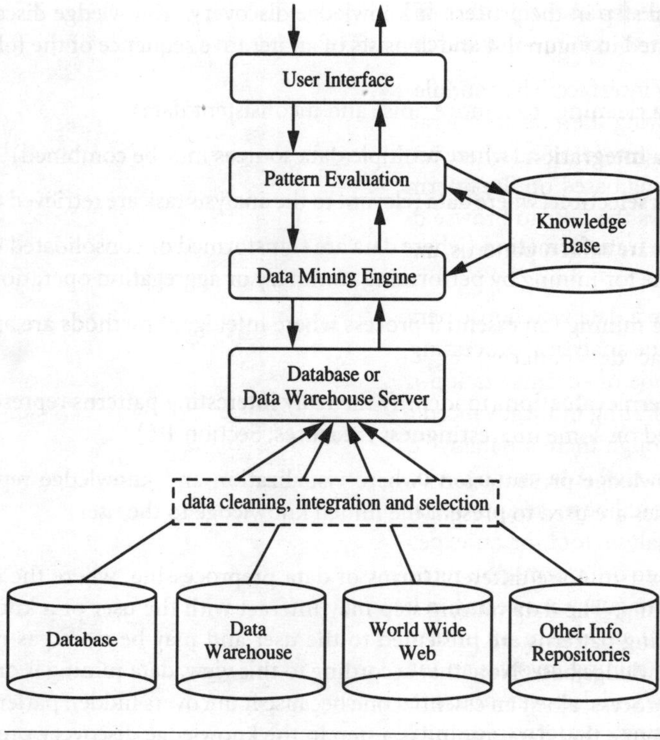

Figure 1.5 Architecture of a typical data mining system.

- **Knowledge base:** This is the domain knowledge that is used to guide the search or evaluate the interestingness of resulting patterns. Such knowledge can include **concept hierarchies,** used to organize attributes or attribute values into different levels of abstraction. Knowledge such as user beliefs, which can be used to assess a pattern's interestingness based on its unexpectedness, may also be included. Other examples of domain knowledge are additional interestingness constraints or thresholds, and metadata (e.g., describing data from multiple heterogeneous sources).
- **Data mining engine:** This is essential to the data mining system and ideally consists of a set of functional modules for tasks such as characterization, association and correlation analysis, classification, prediction, cluster analysis, outlier analysis, and evolution analysis.
- **Pattern evaluation module:** This component typically employs interestingness measures (Section 1.5) and interacts with the data mining modules so as to *focus* the search toward interesting patterns. It may use interestingness thresholds to filter out discovered patterns. Alternatively, the pattern evaluation module may be integrated with the mining module, depending on the implementation of the data mining method used. For efficient data mining, it is highly recommended to push

the evaluation of pattern interestingness as deep as possible into the mining process so as to confine the search to only the interesting patterns.

- **User interface:** This module communicates between users and the data mining system, allowing the user to interact with the system by specifying a data mining query or task, providing information to help focus the search, and performing exploratory data mining based on the intermediate data mining results. In addition, this component allows the user to browse database and data warehouse schemas or data structures, evaluate mined patterns, and visualize the patterns in different forms.

From a data warehouse perspective, data mining can be viewed as an advanced stage of on-line analytical processing (OLAP). However, data mining goes far beyond the narrow scope of summarization-style analytical processing of data warehouse systems by incorporating more advanced techniques for data analysis.

Although there are many "data mining systems" on the market, not all of them can perform true data mining. A data analysis system that does not handle large amounts of data should be more appropriately categorized as a machine learning system, a statistical data analysis tool, or an experimental system prototype. A system that can only perform data or information retrieval, including finding aggregate values, or that performs deductive query answering in large databases should be more appropriately categorized as a database system, an information retrieval system, or a deductive database system.

Data mining involves an integration of techniques from multiple disciplines such as database and data warehouse technology, statistics, machine learning, high-performance computing, pattern recognition, neural networks, data visualization, information retrieval, image and signal processing, and spatial or temporal data analysis. We adopt a database perspective in our presentation of data mining in this book. That is, emphasis is placed on *efficient* and *scalable* data mining techniques. For an algorithm to be **scalable**, its running time should grow approximately linearly in proportion to the size of the data, given the available system resources such as main memory and disk space. By performing data mining, interesting knowledge, regularities, or high-level information can be extracted from databases and viewed or browsed from different angles. The discovered knowledge can be applied to decision making, process control, information management, and query processing. Therefore, data mining is considered one of the most important frontiers in database and information systems and one of the most promising interdisciplinary developments in the information technology.

1.3 Data Mining—On What Kind of Data?

In this section, we examine a number of different data repositories on which mining can be performed. In principle, data mining should be applicable to any kind of data repository, as well as to transient data, such as data streams. Thus the scope of our examination of data repositories will include relational databases, data warehouses, transactional databases, advanced database systems, flat files, data streams, and the

World Wide Web. Advanced database systems include object-relational databases and specific application-oriented databases, such as spatial databases, time-series databases, text databases, and multimedia databases. The challenges and techniques of mining may differ for each of the repository systems.

Although this book assumes that readers have basic knowledge of information systems, we provide a brief introduction to each of the major data repository systems listed above. In this section, we also introduce the fictitious *AllElectronics* store, which will be used to illustrate concepts throughout the text.

1.3.1 Relational Databases

A database system, also called a **database management system (DBMS)**, consists of a collection of interrelated data, known as a **database**, and a set of software programs to manage and access the data. The software programs involve mechanisms for the definition of database structures; for data storage; for concurrent, shared, or distributed data access; and for ensuring the consistency and security of the information stored, despite system crashes or attempts at unauthorized access.

A **relational database** is a collection of **tables**, each of which is assigned a unique name. Each table consists of a set of **attributes** (*columns* or *fields*) and usually stores a large set of **tuples** (*records* or *rows*). Each tuple in a relational table represents an object identified by a unique *key* and described by a set of attribute values. A semantic data model, such as an **entity-relationship** (ER) data model, is often constructed for relational databases. An ER data model represents the database as a set of entities and their relationships.

Consider the following example.

Example 1.1 **A relational database for *AllElectronics*.** The *AllElectronics* company is described by the following relation tables: *customer, item, employee,* and *branch*. Fragments of the tables described here are shown in Figure 1.6.

- The relation *customer* consists of a set of attributes, including a unique customer identity number (*cust_ID*), customer name, address, age, occupation, annual income, credit information, category, and so on.
- Similarly, each of the relations *item*, *employee*, and *branch* consists of a set of attributes describing their properties.
- Tables can also be used to represent the relationships between or among multiple relation tables. For our example, these include *purchases* (customer purchases items, creating a sales transaction that is handled by an employee), *items_sold* (lists the items sold in a given transaction), and *works_at* (employee works at a branch of *AllElectronics*).

■

Relational data can be accessed by **database queries** written in a relational query language, such as SQL, or with the assistance of graphical user interfaces. In the latter, the user may employ a menu, for example, to specify attributes to be included in the query, and the constraints on these attributes. A given query is transformed into a set of *customer*

cust_ID	*name*	*address*	*age*	*income*	*credit_info*	*category*	...
C1	Smith, Sandy	1223 Lake Ave., Chicago, IL	31	$78000	1	3	...
...	...	...	...	...	...	...	...

item

item_ID	*name*	*brand*	*category*	*type*	*price*	*place_made*	*supplier*	*cost*
I3	hi-res-TV	Toshiba	high resolution	TV	$988.00	Japan	NikoX	$600.00
I8	Laptop	Dell	laptop	computer	$1369.00	USA	Dell	$983.00
...	...	...	...	...	...	...	...	...

employee

empl_ID	*name*	*category*	*group*	*salary*	*commission*
E55	Jones, Jane	home entertainment	manager	$118,000	2%
...	...	...	...	...	...

branch

branch_ID	*name*	*address*
B1	City Square	396 Michigan Ave., Chicago, IL
...	...	...

purchases

trans_ID	*cust_ID*	*empl_ID*	*date*	*time*	*method_paid*	*amount*
T100	C1	E55	03/21/2005	15:45	Visa	$1357.00
...	...	...	...	...	...	...

items_sold

trans_ID	*item_ID*	*qty*
T100	I3	1
T100	I8	2
...	...	...

works_at

empl_ID	*branch_ID*
E55	B1
...	...

Figure 1.6 Fragments of relations from a relational database for *AllElectronics*.

relational operations, such as join, selection, and projection, and is then optimized for efficient processing. A query allows retrieval of specified subsets of the data. Suppose that your job is to analyze the *AllElectronics* data. Through the use of relational queries, you can ask things like "Show me a list of all items that were sold in the last quarter." Relational languages also include aggregate functions such as sum, avg (average), count, max (maximum), and min (minimum). These allow you to ask things like "Show me the total sales of the last month, grouped by branch," or "How many sales transactions occurred in the month of December?" or "Which sales person had the highest amount of sales?"

When data mining is applied to relational databases, we can go further by *searching for trends or data patterns*. For example, data mining systems can analyze customer data to predict the credit risk of new customers based on their income, age, and previous credit information. Data mining systems may also detect deviations, such as items whose sales are far from those expected in comparison with the previous year. Such deviations can then be further investigated (e.g., has there been a change in packaging of such items, or a significant increase in price?).

Relational databases are one of the most commonly available and rich information repositories, and thus they are a major data form in our study of data mining.

1.3.2 Data Warehouses

Suppose that *AllElectronics* is a successful international company, with branches around the world. Each branch has its own set of databases. The president of *AllElectronics* has asked you to provide an analysis of the company's sales per item type per branch for the third quarter. This is a difficult task, particularly since the relevant data are spread out over several databases, physically located at numerous sites.

If *AllElectronics* had a data warehouse, this task would be easy. A **data warehouse** is a repository of information collected from multiple sources, stored under a unified schema, and that usually resides at a single site. Data warehouses are constructed via a process of data cleaning, data integration, data transformation, data loading, and periodic data refreshing. This process is discussed in Chapters 2 and 3. Figure 1.7 shows the typical framework for construction and use of a data warehouse for *AllElectronics*.

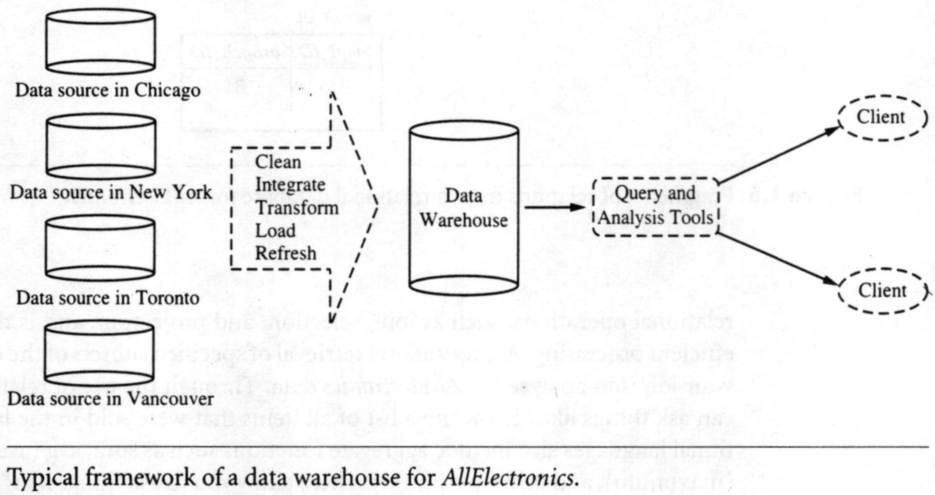

Figure 1.7 Typical framework of a data warehouse for *AllElectronics*.

To facilitate decision making, the data in a data warehouse are *organized around major subjects*, such as customer, item, supplier, and activity. The data are stored to provide information from a *historical perspective* (such as from the past 5–10 years) and are typically *summarized*. For example, rather than storing the details of each sales transaction, the data warehouse may store a summary of the transactions per item type for each store or, summarized to a higher level, for each sales region.

A data warehouse is usually modeled by a multidimensional database structure, where each **dimension** corresponds to an attribute or a set of attributes in the schema, and each **cell** stores the value of some aggregate measure, such as *count* or *sales_amount*. The actual physical structure of a data warehouse may be a relational data store or a **multidimensional data cube**. A data cube provides a multidimensional view of data and allows the precomputation and fast accessing of summarized data.

Example 1.2 **A data cube for *AllElectronics*.** A data cube for summarized sales data of *AllElectronics* is presented in Figure 1.8(a). The cube has three dimensions: *address* (with city values *Chicago, New York, Toronto, Vancouver*), *time* (with quarter values *Q1, Q2, Q3, Q4*), and *item* (with item type values *home entertainment, computer, phone, security*). The aggregate value stored in each cell of the cube is *sales_amount* (in thousands). For example, the total sales for the first quarter, *Q1*, for items relating to security systems in Vancouver is $400,000, as stored in cell ⟨*Vancouver, Q1, security*⟩. Additional cubes may be used to store aggregate sums over each dimension, corresponding to the aggregate values obtained using different SQL group-bys (e.g., the total sales amount per city and quarter, or per city and item, or per quarter and item, or per each individual dimension). ■

"I have also heard about data marts. What is the difference between a data warehouse and a data mart?" you may ask. A data warehouse collects information about subjects that span an *entire organization*, and thus its scope is *enterprise-wide*. A **data mart**, on the other hand, is a department subset of a data warehouse. It focuses on selected subjects, and thus its scope is *department-wide*.

By providing multidimensional data views and the precomputation of summarized data, data warehouse systems are well suited for **on-line analytical processing**, or **OLAP**. OLAP operations use background knowledge regarding the domain of the data being studied in order to allow the presentation of data at *different levels of abstraction*. Such operations accommodate different user viewpoints. Examples of OLAP operations include **drill-down** and **roll-up**, which allow the user to view the data at differing degrees of summarization, as illustrated in Figure 1.8(b). For instance, we can drill down on sales data summarized by *quarter* to see the data summarized by *month*. Similarly, we can roll up on sales data summarized by *city* to view the data summarized by *country*.

Although data warehouse tools help support data analysis, additional tools for data mining are required to allow more in-depth and automated analysis. An overview of data warehouse and OLAP technology is provided in Chapter 3. Advanced issues regarding data warehouse and OLAP implementation and data generalization are discussed in Chapter 4.

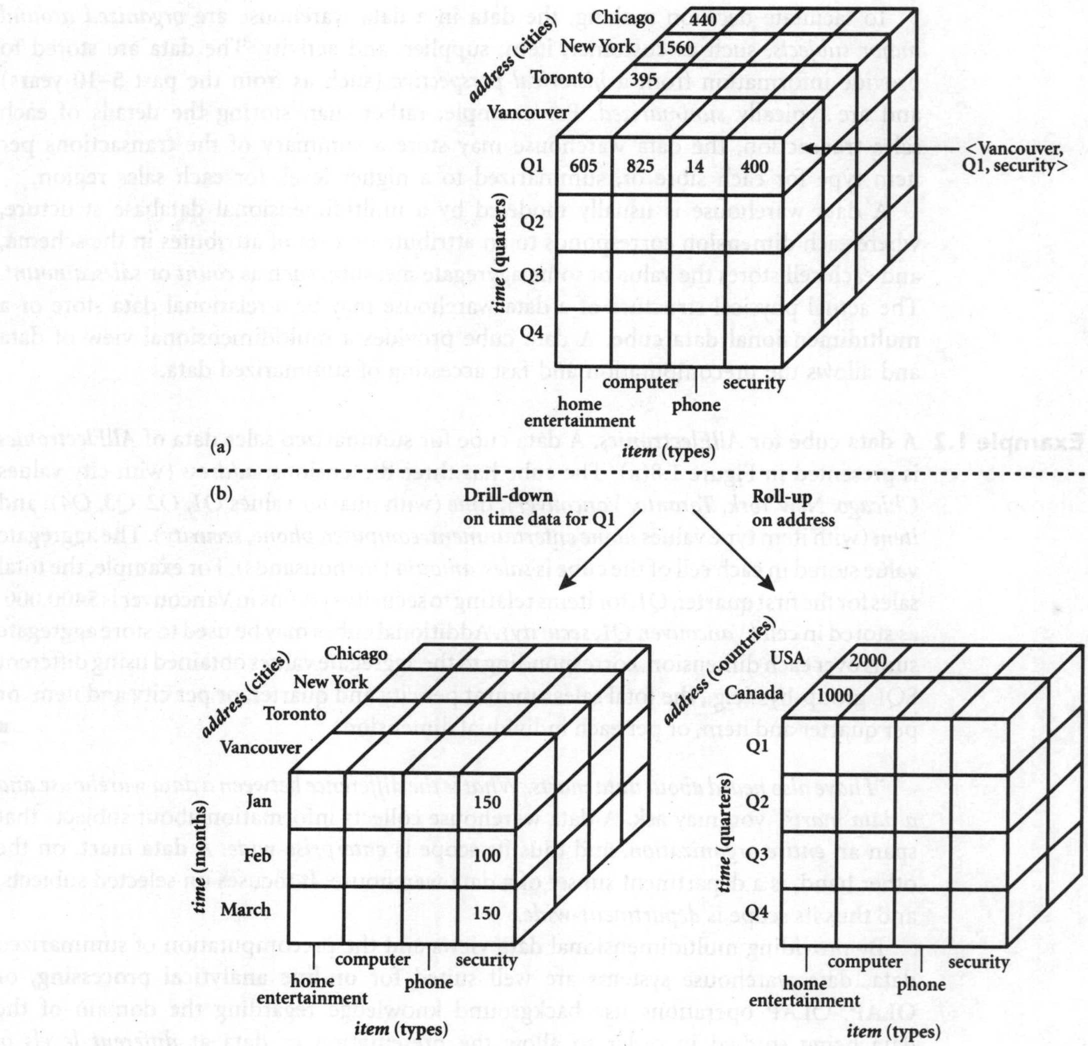

Figure 1.8 A multidimensional data cube, commonly used for data warehousing, (a) showing summarized data for *AllElectronics* and (b) showing summarized data resulting from drill-down and roll-up operations on the cube in (a). For improved readability, only some of the cube cell values are shown.

1.3.3 Transactional Databases

In general, a transactional database consists of a file where each record represents a transaction. A transaction typically includes a unique transaction identity number (*trans_ID*) and a list of the items making up the transaction (such as items purchased in a store).

trans_ID	*list of item_IDs*
T100	I1, I3, I8, I16
T200	I2, I8
...	...

Figure 1.9 Fragment of a transactional database for sales at *AllElectronics*.

The transactional database may have additional tables associated with it, which contain other information regarding the sale, such as the date of the transaction, the customer ID number, the ID number of the salesperson and of the branch at which the sale occurred, and so on.

Example 1.3 A transactional database for *AllElectronics*. Transactions can be stored in a table, with one record per transaction. A fragment of a transactional database for *AllElectronics* is shown in Figure 1.9. From the relational database point of view, the *sales* table in Figure 1.9 is a nested relation because the attribute *list of item_IDs* contains a set of *items*. Because most relational database systems do not support nested relational structures, the transactional database is usually either stored in a flat file in a format similar to that of the table in Figure 1.9 or unfolded into a standard relation in a format similar to that of the *items_sold* table in Figure 1.6. ■

As an analyst of the *AllElectronics* database, you may ask, "Show me all the items purchased by Sandy Smith" or "How many transactions include item number I3?" Answering such queries may require a scan of the entire transactional database.

Suppose you would like to dig deeper into the data by asking, "Which items sold well together?" This kind of *market basket data analysis* would enable you to bundle groups of items together as a strategy for maximizing sales. For example, given the knowledge that printers are commonly purchased together with computers, you could offer an expensive model of printers at a discount to customers buying selected computers, in the hopes of selling more of the expensive printers. A regular data retrieval system is not able to answer queries like the one above. However, data mining systems for transactional data can do so by identifying *frequent itemsets*, that is, sets of items that are frequently sold together. The mining of such frequent patterns for transactional data is discussed in Chapter 5.

1.3.4 Advanced Data and Information Systems and Advanced Applications

Relational database systems have been widely used in business applications. With the progress of database technology, various kinds of advanced data and information systems have emerged and are undergoing development to address the requirements of new applications.

The new database applications include handling spatial data (such as maps), engineering design data (such as the design of buildings, system components, or integrated circuits), hypertext and multimedia data (including text, image, video, and audio data), time-related data (such as historical records or stock exchange data), stream data (such as video surveillance and sensor data, where data flow in and out like streams), and the World Wide Web (a huge, widely distributed information repository made available by the Internet). These applications require efficient data structures and scalable methods for handling complex object structures; variable-length records; semistructured or unstructured data; text, spatiotemporal, and multimedia data; and database schemas with complex structures and dynamic changes.

In response to these needs, advanced database systems and specific application-oriented database systems have been developed. These include object-relational database systems, temporal and time-series database systems, spatial and spatiotemporal database systems, text and multimedia database systems, heterogeneous and legacy database systems, data stream management systems, and Web-based global information systems.

While such databases or information repositories require sophisticated facilities to efficiently store, retrieve, and update large amounts of complex data, they also provide fertile grounds and raise many challenging research and implementation issues for data mining. In this section, we describe each of the advanced database systems listed above.

Object-Relational Databases

Object-relational databases are constructed based on an object-relational data model. This model extends the relational model by providing a rich data type for handling complex objects and object orientation. Because most sophisticated database applications need to handle complex objects and structures, object-relational databases are becoming increasingly popular in industry and applications.

Conceptually, the object-relational data model inherits the essential concepts of **object-oriented databases**, where, in general terms, each entity is considered as an **object**. Following the *AllElectronics* example, objects can be individual employees, customers, or items. Data and code relating to an object are *encapsulated* into a single unit. Each object has associated with it the following:

- A set of **variables** that describe the objects. These correspond to attributes in the entity-relationship and relational models.
- A set of **messages** that the object can use to communicate with other objects, or with the rest of the database system.
- A set of **methods**, where each method holds the code to implement a message. Upon receiving a message, the method returns a value in response. For instance, the method for the message *get_photo*(*employee*) will retrieve and return a photo of the given employee object.

Objects that share a common set of properties can be grouped into an **object class**. Each object is an **instance** of its class. Object classes can be organized into class/subclass hierarchies so that each class represents properties that are common to objects in that class. For instance, an *employee* class can contain variables like *name, address*, and *birthdate*. Suppose that the class, *sales_person*, is a subclass of the class, *employee*. A *sales_person* object would inherit all of the variables pertaining to its superclass of *employee*. In addition, it has all of the variables that pertain specifically to being a salesperson (e.g., *commission*). Such a class inheritance feature benefits information sharing.

For data mining in object-relational systems, techniques need to be developed for handling complex object structures, complex data types, class and subclass hierarchies, property inheritance, and methods and procedures.

Temporal Databases, Sequence Databases, and Time-Series Databases

A **temporal database** typically stores relational data that include time-related attributes. These attributes may involve several timestamps, each having different semantics. A **sequence database** stores sequences of ordered events, with or without a concrete notion of time. Examples include customer shopping sequences, Web click streams, and biological sequences. A **time-series database** stores sequences of values or events obtained over repeated measurements of time (e.g., hourly, daily, weekly). Examples include data collected from the stock exchange, inventory control, and the observation of natural phenomena (like temperature and wind).

Data mining techniques can be used to find the characteristics of object evolution, or the trend of changes for objects in the database. Such information can be useful in decision making and strategy planning. For instance, the mining of banking data may aid in the scheduling of bank tellers according to the volume of customer traffic. Stock exchange data can be mined to uncover trends that could help you plan investment strategies (e.g., when is the best time to purchase *AllElectronics* stock?). Such analyses typically require defining multiple granularity of time. For example, time may be decomposed according to fiscal years, academic years, or calendar years. Years may be further decomposed into quarters or months.

Spatial Databases and Spatiotemporal Databases

Spatial databases contain spatial-related information. Examples include geographic (map) databases, very large-scale integration (VLSI) or computed-aided design databases, and medical and satellite image databases. Spatial data may be represented in **raster format**, consisting of *n*-dimensional bit maps or pixel maps. For example, a 2-D satellite image may be represented as raster data, where each pixel registers the rainfall in a given area. Maps can be represented in **vector format**, where roads, bridges, buildings, and lakes are represented as unions or overlays of basic geometric constructs, such as points, lines, polygons, and the partitions and networks formed by these components.

Geographic databases have numerous applications, ranging from forestry and ecology planning to providing public service information regarding the location of telephone and electric cables, pipes, and sewage systems. In addition, geographic databases are commonly used in vehicle navigation and dispatching systems. An example of such a system for taxis would store a city map with information regarding one-way streets, suggested routes for moving from region A to region B during rush hour, and the location of restaurants and hospitals, as well as the current location of each driver.

"What kind of data mining can be performed on spatial databases?" you may ask. Data mining may uncover patterns describing the characteristics of houses located near a specified kind of location, such as a park, for instance. Other patterns may describe the climate of mountainous areas located at various altitudes, or describe the change in trend of metropolitan poverty rates based on city distances from major highways. The relationships among a set of spatial objects can be examined in order to discover which subsets of objects are spatially auto-correlated or associated. Clusters and outliers can be identified by spatial cluster analysis. Moreover, spatial classification can be performed to construct models for prediction based on the relevant set of features of the spatial objects. Furthermore, "spatial data cubes" may be constructed to organize data into multidimensional structures and hierarchies, on which OLAP operations (such as drill-down and roll-up) can be performed.

A spatial database that stores spatial objects that change with time is called a **spatiotemporal database**, from which interesting information can be mined. For example, we may be able to group the trends of moving objects and identify some strangely moving vehicles, or distinguish a bioterrorist attack from a normal outbreak of the flu based on the geographic spread of a disease with time.

Text Databases and Multimedia Databases

Text databases are databases that contain word descriptions for objects. These word descriptions are usually not simple keywords but rather long sentences or paragraphs, such as product specifications, error or bug reports, warning messages, summary reports, notes, or other documents. Text databases may be highly unstructured (such as some Web pages on the World Wide Web). Some text databases may be somewhat structured, that is, *semistructured* (such as e-mail messages and many HTML/XML Web pages), whereas others are relatively well structured (such as library catalogue databases). Text databases with highly regular structures typically can be implemented using relational database systems.

"What can data mining on text databases uncover?" By mining text data, one may uncover general and concise descriptions of the text documents, keyword or content associations, as well as the clustering behavior of text objects. To do this, standard data mining methods need to be integrated with information retrieval techniques and the construction or use of hierarchies specifically for text data (such as dictionaries and thesauruses), as well as discipline-oriented term classification systems (such as in biochemistry, medicine, law, or economics).

Multimedia databases store image, audio, and video data. They are used in applications such as picture content-based retrieval, voice-mail systems, video-on-demand systems, the World Wide Web, and speech-based user interfaces that recognize spoken commands. Multimedia databases must support large objects, because data objects such as video can require gigabytes of storage. Specialized storage and search techniques are also required. Because video and audio data require real-time retrieval at a steady and predetermined rate in order to avoid picture or sound gaps and system buffer overflows, such data are referred to as **continuous-media data**.

For multimedia data mining, storage and search techniques need to be integrated with standard data mining methods. Promising approaches include the construction of multimedia data cubes, the extraction of multiple features from multimedia data, and similarity-based pattern matching.

Heterogeneous Databases and Legacy Databases

A **heterogeneous database** consists of a set of interconnected, autonomous component databases. The components communicate in order to exchange information and answer queries. Objects in one component database may differ greatly from objects in other component databases, making it difficult to assimilate their semantics into the overall heterogeneous database.

Many enterprises acquire legacy databases as a result of the long history of information technology development (including the application of different hardware and operating systems). A **legacy database** is a group of *heterogeneous databases* that combines different kinds of data systems, such as relational or object-oriented databases, hierarchical databases, network databases, spreadsheets, multimedia databases, or file systems. The heterogeneous databases in a legacy database may be connected by intra- or inter-computer networks.

Information exchange across such databases is difficult because it would require precise transformation rules from one representation to another, considering diverse semantics. Consider, for example, the problem in exchanging information regarding student academic performance among different schools. Each school may have its own computer system and use its own curriculum and grading system. One university may adopt a quarter system, offer three courses on database systems, and assign grades from A+ to F, whereas another may adopt a semester system, offer two courses on databases, and assign grades from 1 to 10. It is very difficult to work out precise course-to-grade transformation rules between the two universities, making information exchange difficult. Data mining techniques may provide an interesting solution to the information exchange problem by performing statistical data distribution and correlation analysis, and transforming the given data into higher, more generalized, conceptual levels (such as *fair*, *good*, or *excellent* for student grades), from which information exchange can then more easily be performed.

Data Streams

Many applications involve the generation and analysis of a new kind of data, called **stream data**, where data flow in and out of an observation platform (or window) dynamically. Such data streams have the following unique features: *huge or possibly infinite volume, dynamically changing, flowing in and out in a fixed order, allowing only one or a small* *number of scans, and demanding fast (often real-time) response time.* Typical examples of data streams include various kinds of scientific and engineering data, time-series data, and data produced in other dynamic environments, such as power supply, network traffic, stock exchange, telecommunications, Web click streams, video surveillance, and weather or environment monitoring.

Because data streams are normally not stored in any kind of data repository, effective and efficient management and analysis of stream data poses great challenges to researchers. Currently, many researchers are investigating various issues relating to the development of data stream management systems. A typical query model in such a system is the *continuous query model,* where predefined queries constantly evaluate incoming streams, collect aggregate data, report the current status of data streams, and respond to their changes.

Mining data streams involves the efficient discovery of general patterns and dynamic changes within stream data. For example, we may like to detect intrusions of a computer network based on the anomaly of message flow, which may be discovered by clustering data streams, dynamic construction of stream models, or comparing the current frequent patterns with that at a certain previous time. Most stream data reside at a rather low level of abstraction, whereas analysts are often more interested in higher and multiple levels of abstraction. Thus, multilevel, multidimensional on-line analysis and mining should be performed on stream data as well.

The World Wide Web

The World Wide Web and its associated distributed information services, such as Yahoo!, Google, America Online, and AltaVista, provide rich, worldwide, on-line information services, where data objects are linked together to facilitate interactive access. Users seeking information of interest traverse from one object via links to another. Such systems provide ample opportunities and challenges for data mining. For example, understanding user access patterns will not only help improve system design (by providing efficient access between highly correlated objects), but also leads to better marketing decisions (e.g., by placing advertisements in frequently visited documents, or by providing better customer/user classification and behavior analysis). Capturing user access patterns in such distributed information environments is called **Web usage mining (or Weblog mining)**.

Although Web pages may appear fancy and informative to human readers, they can be highly unstructured and lack a predefined schema, type, or pattern. Thus it is difficult for computers to understand the semantic meaning of diverse Web pages and structure them in an organized way for systematic information retrieval and data mining. Web services that provide keyword-based searches without understanding the context behind the Web pages can only offer limited help to users. For example, a Web search based on a single keyword may return hundreds of Web page pointers containing the keyword, but most of the pointers will be very weakly related to what the user wants to find. Data mining can often provide additional help here than Web search services. For example, **authoritative Web page analysis** based on linkages among Web pages can help rank Web pages based on their importance, influence, and topics. **Automated Web page clustering and classification** help group and arrange Web pages in a multidimensional manner based on their contents. **Web community analysis** helps identify hidden Web social networks and communities and observe their evolution. Web mining is the development of scalable and effective Web data analysis and mining methods. It may help us learn about the distribution of information on the Web in general, characterize and classify Web pages, and uncover Web dynamics and the association and other relationships among different Web pages, users, communities, and Web-based activities.

Data mining in advanced database and information systems is discussed in Chapters 8 to 10.

1.4 Data Mining Functionalities—What Kinds of Patterns Can Be Mined?

We have observed various types of databases and information repositories on which data mining can be performed. Let us now examine the kinds of data patterns that can be mined.

Data mining functionalities are used to specify the kind of patterns to be found in data mining tasks. In general, data mining tasks can be classified into two categories: **descriptive** and **predictive**. Descriptive mining tasks characterize the general properties of the data in the database. Predictive mining tasks perform inference on the current data in order to make predictions.

In some cases, users may have no idea regarding what kinds of patterns in their data may be interesting, and hence may like to search for several different kinds of patterns in parallel. Thus it is important to have a data mining system that can mine multiple kinds of patterns to accommodate different user expectations or applications. Furthermore, data mining systems should be able to discover patterns at various granularity (i.e., different levels of abstraction). Data mining systems should also allow users to specify hints to guide or focus the search for interesting patterns. Because some patterns may not hold for all of the data in the database, a measure of certainty or "trustworthiness" is usually associated with each discovered pattern.

Data mining functionalities, and the kinds of patterns they can discover, are described below.

1.4.1 Concept/Class Description: Characterization and Discrimination

Data can be associated with classes or concepts. For example, in the *AllElectronics* store, classes of items for sale include *computers* and *printers*, and concepts of customers include *bigSpenders* and *budgetSpenders*. It can be useful to describe individual classes and concepts in summarized, concise, and yet precise terms. Such descriptions of a class or a concept are called **class/concept descriptions**. These descriptions can be derived via (1) *data characterization*, by summarizing the data of the class under study (often called

the target class) in general terms, or (2) *data discrimination*, by comparison of the target class with one or a set of comparative classes (often called the **contrasting classes**), or (3) both data characterization and discrimination.

Data characterization is a summarization of the general characteristics or features of a target class of data. The data corresponding to the user-specified class are typically collected by a database query. For example, to study the characteristics of software products whose sales increased by 10% in the last year, the data related to such products can be collected by executing an SQL query.

There are several methods for effective data summarization and characterization. Simple data summaries based on statistical measures and plots are described in Chapter 2. The data cube–based OLAP roll-up operation (Section 1.3.2) can be used to perform user-controlled data summarization along a specified dimension. This process is further detailed in Chapters 3 and 4, which discuss data warehousing. An *attribute-oriented induction* technique can be used to perform data generalization and characterization without step-by-step user interaction. This technique is described in Chapter 4.

The output of data characterization can be presented in various forms. Examples include **pie charts, bar charts, curves, multidimensional data cubes,** and **multidimensional tables**, including crosstabs. The resulting descriptions can also be presented as **generalized relations** or in rule form (called **characteristic rules**). These different output forms and their transformations are discussed in Chapter 4.

Example 1.4 **Data characterization.** A data mining system should be able to produce a description summarizing the characteristics of customers who spend more than $1,000 a year at *AllElectronics*. The result could be a general profile of the customers, such as they are 40–50 years old, employed, and have excellent credit ratings. The system should allow users to drill down on any dimension, such as on *occupation* in order to view these customers according to their type of employment. ■

Data discrimination is a comparison of the general features of target class data objects with the general features of objects from one or a set of contrasting classes. The target and contrasting classes can be specified by the user, and the corresponding data objects retrieved through database queries. For example, the user may like to compare the general features of software products whose sales increased by 10% in the last year with those whose sales decreased by at least 30% during the same period. The methods used for data discrimination are similar to those used for data characterization.

"*How are discrimination descriptions output?*" The forms of output presentation are similar to those for characteristic descriptions, although discrimination descriptions should include comparative measures that help distinguish between the target and contrasting classes. Discrimination descriptions expressed in rule form are referred to as **discriminant rules.**

Example 1.5 **Data discrimination.** A data mining system should be able to compare two groups of *AllElectronics* customers, such as those who shop for computer products regularly (more than two times a month) versus those who rarely shop for such products (i.e., less than three times a year). The resulting description provides a general comparative profile of the customers, such as 80% of the customers who frequently purchase computer products are between 20 and 40 years old and have a university education, whereas 60% of the customers who infrequently buy such products are either seniors or youths, and have no university degree. Drilling down on a dimension, such as *occupation*, or adding new dimensions, such as *income_level*, may help in finding even more discriminative features between the two classes. ■

Concept description, including characterization and discrimination, is described in Chapter 4.

1.4.2 Mining Frequent Patterns, Associations, and Correlations

Frequent patterns, as the name suggests, are patterns that occur frequently in data. There are many kinds of frequent patterns, including itemsets, subsequences, and substructures. A *frequent itemset* typically refers to a set of items that frequently appear together in a transactional data set, such as milk and bread. A frequently occurring subsequence, such as the pattern that customers tend to purchase first a PC, followed by a digital camera, and then a memory card, is a *(frequent) sequential pattern*. A substructure can refer to different structural forms, such as graphs, trees, or lattices, which may be combined with itemsets or subsequences. If a substructure occurs frequently, it is called a *(frequent) structured pattern*. Mining frequent patterns leads to the discovery of interesting associations and correlations within data.

Example 1.6 **Association analysis.** Suppose, as a marketing manager of *AllElectronics*, you would like to determine which items are frequently purchased together within the same transactions. An example of such a rule, mined from the *AllElectronics* transactional database, is

$$buys(X, \text{"computer"}) \Rightarrow buys(X, \text{"software"}) \; [support = 1\%, confidence = 50\%]$$

where X is a variable representing a customer. A **confidence**, or certainty, of 50% means that if a customer buys a computer, there is a 50% chance that she will buy software as well. A 1% **support** means that 1% of all of the transactions under analysis showed that computer and software were purchased together. This association rule involves a single attribute or predicate (i.e., *buys*) that repeats. Association rules that contain a single predicate are referred to as **single-dimensional association rules**. Dropping the predicate notation, the above rule can be written simply as "*computer* $\Rightarrow$ *software* [1%, 50%]".

Suppose, instead, that we are given the *AllElectronics* relational database relating to purchases. A data mining system may find association rules like

$$age(X, \text{"20...29"}) \wedge income(X, \text{"20K...29K"}) \Rightarrow buys(X, \text{"CD player"})$$
$$[support = 2\%, confidence = 60\%]$$

The rule indicates that of the *AllElectronics* customers under study, 2% are 20 to 29 years of age with an income of 20,000 to 29,000 and have purchased a CD player at *AllElectronics*. There is a 60% probability that a customer in this age and income group will purchase a CD player. Note that this is an association between more than one attribute, or predicate (i.e., *age, income*, and *buys*). Adopting the terminology used in multidimensional databases, where each attribute is referred to as a dimension, the above rule can be referred to as a **multidimensional association rule**. ■

Typically, association rules are discarded as uninteresting if they do not satisfy both a **minimum support threshold** and a **minimum confidence threshold**. Additional analysis can be performed to uncover interesting statistical **correlations** between associated attribute-value pairs.

Frequent itemset mining is the simplest form of frequent pattern mining. The mining of frequent patterns, associations, and correlations is discussed in Chapter 5, where particular emphasis is placed on efficient algorithms for frequent itemset mining. Sequential pattern mining and structured pattern mining are considered advanced topics. They are discussed in Chapters 8 and 9, respectively.

1.4.3 Classification and Prediction

Classification is the process of finding a **model** (or function) that describes and distinguishes data classes or concepts, for the purpose of being able to use the model to predict the class of objects whose class label is unknown. The derived model is based on the analysis of a set of **training data** (i.e., data objects whose class label is known).

"How is the derived model presented?" The derived model may be represented in various forms, such as *classification (IF-THEN) rules, decision trees, mathematical formulae*, or *neural networks* (Figure 1.10). A **decision tree** is a flow-chart-like tree structure, where each node denotes a test on an attribute value, each branch represents an outcome of the test, and tree leaves represent classes or class distributions. Decision trees can easily be converted to classification rules. A **neural network**, when used for classification, is typically a collection of neuron-like processing units with weighted connections between the units. There are many other methods for constructing classification models, such as naïve Bayesian classification, support vector machines, and k-nearest neighbor classification.

Whereas classification predicts categorical (discrete, unordered) labels, **prediction** models continuous-valued functions. That is, it is used to predict missing or unavailable *numerical data values* rather than class labels. Although the term *prediction* may refer to both numeric prediction and class label prediction, in this book we use it to refer primarily to numeric prediction. **Regression analysis** is a statistical methodology that is most often used for numeric prediction, although other methods exist as well. Prediction also encompasses the identification of distribution *trends* based on the available data.

Classification and prediction may need to be preceded by **relevance analysis**, which attempts to identify attributes that do not contribute to the classification or prediction process. These attributes can then be excluded.

Example 1.7 **Classification and prediction.** Suppose, as sales manager of *AllElectronics*, you would like to classify a large set of items in the store, based on three kinds of responses to a

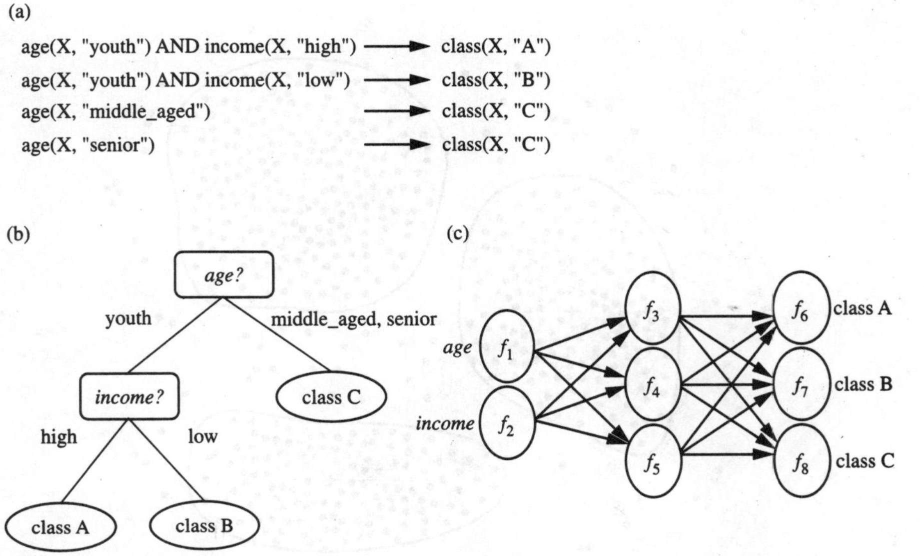

Figure 1.10 A classification model can be represented in various forms, such as (a) IF-THEN rules, (b) a decision tree, or a (c) neural network.

sales campaign: *good response*, *mild response*, and *no response*. You would like to derive a model for each of these three classes based on the descriptive features of the items, such as *price*, *brand*, *place_made*, *type*, and *category*. The resulting classification should maximally distinguish each class from the others, presenting an organized picture of the data set. Suppose that the resulting classification is expressed in the form of a decision tree. The decision tree, for instance, may identify *price* as being the single factor that best distinguishes the three classes. The tree may reveal that, after *price*, other features that help further distinguish objects of each class from another include *brand* and *place_made*. Such a decision tree may help you understand the impact of the given sales campaign and design a more effective campaign for the future.

Suppose instead, that rather than predicting categorical response labels for each store item, you would like to predict the amount of revenue that each item will generate during an upcoming sale at *AllElectronics*, based on previous sales data. This is an example of (numeric) prediction because the model constructed will predict a continuous-valued function, or ordered value. ■

Chapter 6 discusses classification and prediction in further detail.

1.4.4 Cluster Analysis

"*What is cluster analysis?*" Unlike classification and prediction, which analyze class-labeled data objects, clustering analyzes data objects without consulting a known class label.

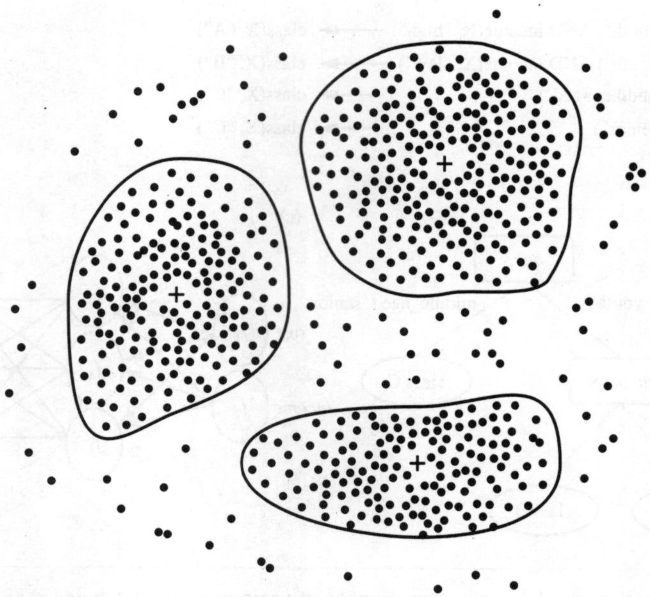

Figure 1.11 A 2-D plot of customer data with respect to customer locations in a city, showing three data clusters. Each cluster "center" is marked with a "+".

In general, the class labels are not present in the training data simply because they are not known to begin with. Clustering can be used to generate such labels. The objects are clustered or grouped based on the principle of *maximizing the intraclass similarity and minimizing the interclass similarity*. That is, clusters of objects are formed so that objects within a cluster have high similarity in comparison to one another, but are very dissimilar to objects in other clusters. Each cluster that is formed can be viewed as a class of objects, from which rules can be derived. Clustering can also facilitate **taxonomy formation**, that is, the organization of observations into a hierarchy of classes that group similar events together.

Example 1.8 Cluster analysis. Cluster analysis can be performed on *AllElectronics* customer data in order to identify homogeneous subpopulations of customers. These clusters may represent individual target groups for marketing. Figure 1.11 shows a 2-D plot of customers with respect to customer locations in a city. Three clusters of data points are evident. ■

Cluster analysis forms the topic of Chapter 7.

1.4.5 Outlier Analysis

A database may contain data objects that do not comply with the general behavior or model of the data. These data objects are **outliers**. Most data mining methods discard outliers as noise or exceptions. However, in some applications such as fraud detection, the rare events can be more interesting than the more regularly occurring ones. The analysis of outlier data is referred to as **outlier mining.**

Outliers may be detected using statistical tests that assume a distribution or probability model for the data, or using distance measures where objects that are a substantial distance from any other cluster are considered outliers. Rather than using statistical or distance measures, deviation-based methods identify outliers by examining differences in the main characteristics of objects in a group.

Example 1.9 Outlier analysis. Outlier analysis may uncover fraudulent usage of credit cards by detecting purchases of extremely large amounts for a given account number in comparison to regular charges incurred by the same account. Outlier values may also be detected with respect to the location and type of purchase, or the purchase frequency. ■

Outlier analysis is also discussed in Chapter 7.

1.4.6 Evolution Analysis

Data **evolution analysis** describes and models regularities or trends for objects whose behavior changes over time. Although this may include characterization, discrimination, association and correlation analysis, classification, prediction, or clustering of *time-related* data, distinct features of such an analysis include time-series data analysis, sequence or periodicity pattern matching, and similarity-based data analysis.

Example 1.10 Evolution analysis. Suppose that you have the major stock market (time-series) data of the last several years available from the New York Stock Exchange and you would like to invest in shares of high-tech industrial companies. A data mining study of stock exchange data may identify stock evolution regularities for overall stocks and for the stocks of particular companies. Such regularities may help predict future trends in stock market prices, contributing to your decision making regarding stock investments. ■

Data evolution analysis is discussed in Chapter 8.

1.5 Are All of the Patterns Interesting?

A data mining system has the potential to generate thousands or even millions of patterns, or rules.

"So," you may ask, *"are all of the patterns interesting?"* Typically not—only a small fraction of the patterns potentially generated would actually be of interest to any given user.

This raises some serious questions for data mining. You may wonder, *"What makes a pattern interesting? Can a data mining system generate all of the interesting patterns? Can a data mining system generate only interesting patterns?"*

To answer the first question, a pattern is **interesting** if it is (1) *easily understood* by humans, (2) *valid* on new or test data with some degree of *certainty*, (3) potentially *useful*, and (4) *novel*. A pattern is also interesting if it validates a hypothesis that the user *sought to confirm*. An interesting pattern represents **knowledge**.

Several **objective measures of pattern interestingness** exist. These are based on the structure of discovered patterns and the statistics underlying them. An objective measure for association rules of the form $X \Rightarrow Y$ is rule **support**, representing the percentage of transactions from a transaction database that the given rule satisfies. This is taken to be the probability $P(X \cup Y)$, where $X \cup Y$ indicates that a transaction contains both X and Y, that is, the union of itemsets X and Y. Another objective measure for association rules is **confidence**, which assesses the degree of certainty of the detected association. This is taken to be the conditional probability $P(Y|X)$, that is, the probability that a transaction containing X also contains Y. More formally, support and confidence are defined as

$$support(X \Rightarrow Y) = P(X \cup Y).$$
$$confidence(X \Rightarrow Y) = P(Y|X).$$

In general, each interestingness measure is associated with a threshold, which may be controlled by the user. For example, rules that do not satisfy a confidence threshold of, say, 50% can be considered uninteresting. Rules below the threshold likely reflect noise, exceptions, or minority cases and are probably of less value.

Although objective measures help identify interesting patterns, they are insufficient unless combined with subjective measures that reflect the needs and interests of a particular user. For example, patterns describing the characteristics of customers who shop frequently at *AllElectronics* should interest the marketing manager, but may be of little interest to analysts studying the same database for patterns on employee performance. Furthermore, many patterns that are interesting by objective standards may represent common knowledge and, therefore, are actually uninteresting. **Subjective interestingness measures** are based on user beliefs in the data. These measures find patterns interesting if they are **unexpected** (contradicting a user's belief) or offer strategic information on which the user can act. In the latter case, such patterns are referred to as **actionable**. Patterns that are **expected** can be interesting if they confirm a hypothesis that the user wished to validate, or resemble a user's hunch.

The second question—*"Can a data mining system generate all of the interesting patterns?"*—refers to the **completeness** of a data mining algorithm. It is often unrealistic and inefficient for data mining systems to generate all of the possible patterns. Instead, user-provided constraints and interestingness measures should be used to focus the search. For some mining tasks, such as association, this is often sufficient to ensure the completeness of the algorithm. Association rule mining is an example where the use of constraints and interestingness measures can ensure the completeness of mining. The methods involved are examined in detail in Chapter 5.

Finally, the third question—*"Can a data mining system generate only interesting patterns?"*—is an optimization problem in data mining. It is highly desirable for data mining systems to generate only interesting patterns. This would be much more efficient for users and data mining systems, because neither would have to search through the patterns generated in order to identify the truly interesting ones. Progress has been made in this direction; however, such optimization remains a challenging issue in data mining.

Measures of pattern interestingness are essential for the efficient discovery of patterns of value to the given user. Such measures can be used after the data mining step in order to rank the discovered patterns according to their interestingness, filtering out the uninteresting ones. More importantly, such measures can be used to guide and constrain the discovery process, improving the search efficiency by pruning away subsets of the pattern space that do not satisfy prespecified interestingness constraints. Such constraint-based mining is described in Chapter 5 (with respect to association mining) and Chapter 7 (with respect to clustering).

Methods to assess pattern interestingness, and their use to improve data mining efficiency, are discussed throughout the book, with respect to each kind of pattern that can be mined.

1.6 Classification of Data Mining Systems

Data mining is an interdisciplinary field, the confluence of a set of disciplines, including database systems, statistics, machine learning, visualization, and information science (Figure 1.12). Moreover, depending on the data mining approach used, techniques from other disciplines may be applied, such as neural networks, fuzzy and/or rough set theory, knowledge representation, inductive logic programming, or high-performance computing. Depending on the kinds of data to be mined or on the given data mining application, the data mining system may also integrate techniques from spatial data analysis, information retrieval, pattern recognition, image analysis, signal processing, computer graphics, Web technology, economics, business, bioinformatics, or psychology.

Because of the diversity of disciplines contributing to data mining, data mining research is expected to generate a large variety of data mining systems. Therefore, it is necessary to provide a clear classification of data mining systems, which may help potential users distinguish between such systems and identify those that best match their needs. Data mining systems can be categorized according to various criteria, as follows:

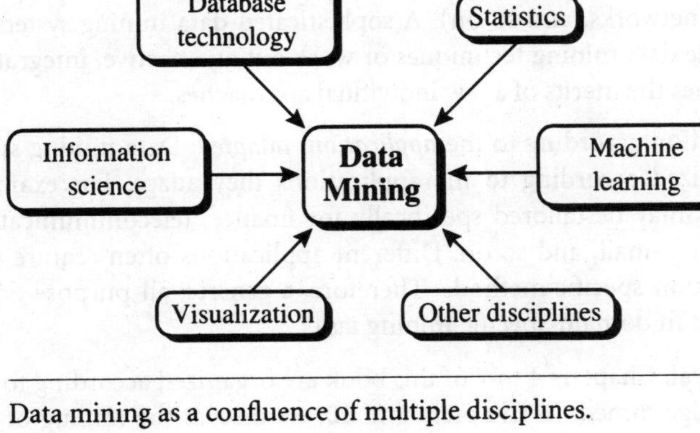

Figure 1.12 Data mining as a confluence of multiple disciplines.

Classification according to the *kinds of databases* mined: A data mining system can be classified according to the kinds of databases mined. Database systems can be classified according to different criteria (such as data models, or the types of data or applications involved), each of which may require its own data mining technique. Data mining systems can therefore be classified accordingly.

For instance, if classifying according to data models, we may have a relational, transactional, object-relational, or data warehouse mining system. If classifying according to the special types of data handled, we may have a spatial, time-series, text, stream data, multimedia data mining system, or a World Wide Web mining system.

Classification according to the *kinds of knowledge* mined: Data mining systems can be categorized according to the kinds of knowledge they mine, that is, based on data mining functionalities, such as characterization, discrimination, association and correlation analysis, classification, prediction, clustering, outlier analysis, and evolution analysis. A comprehensive data mining system usually provides multiple and/or integrated data mining functionalities.

Moreover, data mining systems can be distinguished based on the granularity or levels of abstraction of the knowledge mined, including generalized knowledge (at a high level of abstraction), primitive-level knowledge (at a raw data level), or knowledge at multiple levels (considering several levels of abstraction). An advanced data mining system should facilitate the discovery of knowledge at multiple levels of abstraction.

Data mining systems can also be categorized as those that mine data regularities (commonly occurring patterns) versus those that mine data irregularities (such as exceptions, or outliers). In general, concept description, association and correlation analysis, classification, prediction, and clustering mine data regularities, rejecting outliers as noise. These methods may also help detect outliers.

Classification according to the *kinds of techniques* utilized: Data mining systems can be categorized according to the underlying data mining techniques employed. These techniques can be described according to the degree of user interaction involved (e.g., autonomous systems, interactive exploratory systems, query-driven systems) or the methods of data analysis employed (e.g., database-oriented or data warehouse–oriented techniques, machine learning, statistics, visualization, pattern recognition, neural networks, and so on). A sophisticated data mining system will often adopt multiple data mining techniques or work out an effective, integrated technique that combines the merits of a few individual approaches.

Classification according to the *applications adapted*: Data mining systems can also be categorized according to the applications they adapt. For example, data mining systems may be tailored specifically for finance, telecommunications, DNA, stock markets, e-mail, and so on. Different applications often require the integration of application-specific methods. Therefore, a generic, all-purpose data mining system may not fit domain-specific mining tasks.

In general, Chapters 4 to 7 of this book are organized according to the various kinds of knowledge mined. In Chapters 8 to 10, we discuss the mining of complex types of data on a variety of advanced database systems. Chapter 11 describes major data mining applications as well as typical commercial data mining systems. Criteria for choosing a data mining system are also provided.

1.7 Data Mining Task Primitives

Each user will have a **data mining task** in mind, that is, some form of data analysis that he or she would like to have performed. A data mining task can be specified in the form of a **data mining query**, which is input to the data mining system. A data mining query is defined in terms of **data mining task primitives**. These primitives allow the user to *interactively* communicate with the data mining system during discovery in order to direct the mining process, or examine the findings from different angles or depths. The data mining primitives specify the following, as illustrated in Figure 1.13.

- The set of *task-relevant data* to be mined: This specifies the portions of the database or the set of data in which the user is interested. This includes the database attributes or data warehouse dimensions of interest (referred to as the *relevant attributes or dimensions*).
- The *kind of knowledge* to be mined: This specifies the *data mining functions* to be performed, such as characterization, discrimination, association or correlation analysis, classification, prediction, clustering, outlier analysis, or evolution analysis.
- The *background knowledge* to be used in the discovery process: This knowledge about the domain to be mined is useful for guiding the knowledge discovery process and for evaluating the patterns found. *Concept hierarchies* are a popular form of background knowledge, which allow data to be mined at multiple levels of abstraction. An example of a concept hierarchy for the attribute (or dimension) *age* is shown in Figure 1.14. User beliefs regarding relationships in the data are another form of background knowledge.
- The *interestingness measures and thresholds* for pattern evaluation: They may be used to guide the mining process or, after discovery, to evaluate the discovered patterns. Different kinds of knowledge may have different interestingness measures. For example, interestingness measures for association rules include *support* and *confid*[illegible] Rules whose support and confidence values are below user-specified thresh[illegible] considered uninteresting.
- The expected *representation for visualizing* the discovered patterns: T[illegible] form in which discovered patterns are to be displayed, which may in[illegible] charts, graphs, decision trees, and cubes.

A **data mining query language** can be designed to inco[illegible] allowing users to flexibly interact with data mining systems. H[illegible] language provides a foundation on which user-friendly grap[illegible]

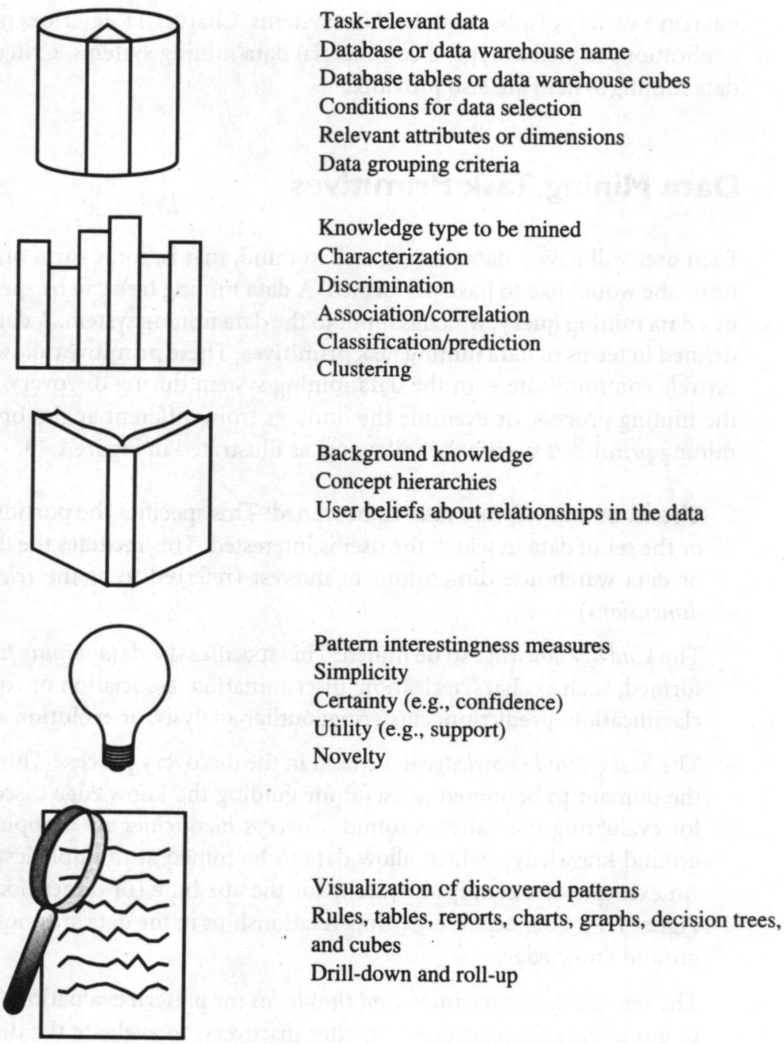

Figure 1.13 Primitives for specifying a data mining task.

This facilitates a data mining system's communication with other information systems and its integration with the overall information processing environment.

Designing a comprehensive data mining language is challenging because data mining ...s a wide spectrum of tasks, from data characterization to evolution analysis. Each ...s different requirements. The design of an effective data mining query language ... a deep understanding of the power, limitation, and underlying mechanisms of ...us kinds of data mining tasks.

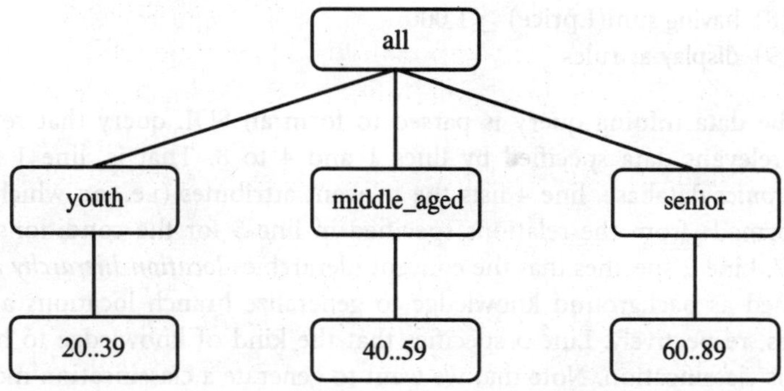

Figure 1.14 A concept hierarchy for the attribute (or dimension) *age*. The root node represents the most general abstraction level, denoted as all.

There are several proposals on data mining languages and standards. In this book, we use a data mining query language known as DMQL (Data Mining Query Language), which was designed as a teaching tool, based on the above primitives. Examples of its use to specify data mining queries appear throughout this book. The language adopts an SQL-like syntax, so that it can easily be integrated with the relational query language, SQL. Let's look at how it can be used to specify a data mining task.

Example 1.11 **Mining classification rules.** Suppose, as a marketing manager of *AllElectronics*, you would like to classify customers based on their buying patterns. You are especially interested in those customers whose salary is no less than \$40,000, and who have bought more than \$1,000 worth of items, each of which is priced at no less than \$100. In particular, you are interested in the customer's age, income, the types of items purchased, the purchase location, and where the items were made. You would like to view the resulting classification in the form of rules. This data mining query is expressed in DMQL[3] as follows, where each line of the query has been enumerated to aid in our discussion.

(1) use database AllElectronics_db
(2) use hierarchy location_hierarchy for T.branch, age_hierarchy for C.age
(3) mine classification as promising_customers
(4) in relevance to C.age, C.income, I.type, I.place_made, T.branch
(5) from customer C, item I, transaction T
(6) where I.item_ID = T.item_ID and C.cust_ID = T.cust_ID
    and C.income $\geq$ 40,000 and I.price $\geq$ 100
(7) group by T.cust_ID

[3]Note that in this book, query language keywords are displayed in sans serif font.

(8) having sum(I.price) $\geq$ 1,000
(9) display as rules

The data mining query is parsed to form an SQL query that retrieves the set of task-relevant data specified by lines 1 and 4 to 8. That is, line 1 specifies the *AllElectronics* database, line 4 lists the relevant attributes (i.e., on which mining is to be performed) from the relations specified in line 5 for the conditions given in lines 6 and 7. Line 2 specifies that the concept hierarchies *location_hierarchy* and *age_hierarchy* be used as background knowledge to generalize branch locations and customer age values, respectively. Line 3 specifies that the kind of knowledge to be mined for this task is classification. Note that we want to generate a classification model for "promising_customers" versus "non_promising_customers." In classification, often, an attribute may be specified as the **class label attribute**, whose values *explicitly* represent the classes. However, in this example, the two classes are *implicit*. That is, the specified data are retrieved and considered examples of "promising_customers," whereas the remaining customers in the customer table are considered as "non-promising_customers." Classification is performed based on this training set. Line 9 specifies that the mining results are to be displayed as a set of rules. Several detailed classification methods are introduced in Chapter 6. ■

There is no standard data mining query language as of yet; however, researchers and industry have been making good progress in this direction. Microsoft's OLE DB for Data Mining (described in the appendix of this book) includes DMX, an XML-styled data mining language. Other standardization efforts include PMML (Programming data Model Markup Language) and CRISP-DM (CRoss-Industry Standard Process for Data Mining).

1.8 Integration of a Data Mining System with a Database or Data Warehouse System

Section 1.2 outlined the major components of the architecture for a typical data mining system (Figure 1.5). A good system architecture will facilitate the data mining system to make best use of the software environment, accomplish data mining tasks in an efficient and timely manner, interoperate and exchange information with other information systems, be adaptable to users' diverse requirements, and evolve with time.

A critical question in the design of a data mining (DM) system is how to integrate or *couple* the DM system with a database (DB) system and/or a data warehouse (DW) system. If a DM system works as a stand-alone system or is embedded in an application program, there are no DB or DW systems with which it has to communicate. This simple scheme is called *no coupling*, where the main focus of the DM design rests on developing effective and efficient algorithms for mining the available data sets. However, when a DM system works in an environment that requires it to communicate with other information system components, such as DB and DW systems, possible integration schemes include *no coupling, loose coupling, semitight coupling,* and *tight coupling.* We examine each of these schemes, as follows:

- **No coupling:** *No coupling* means that a DM system will not utilize any function of a DB or DW system. It may fetch data from a particular source (such as a file system), process data using some data mining algorithms, and then store the mining results in another file.

  Such a system, though simple, suffers from several drawbacks. First, a DB system provides a great deal of flexibility and efficiency at storing, organizing, accessing, and processing data. Without using a DB/DW system, a DM system may spend a substantial amount of time finding, collecting, cleaning, and transforming data. In DB and/or DW systems, data tend to be well organized, indexed, cleaned, integrated, or consolidated, so that finding the task-relevant, high-quality data becomes an easy task. Second, there are many tested, scalable algorithms and data structures implemented in DB and DW systems. It is feasible to realize efficient, scalable implementations using such systems. Moreover, most data have been or will be stored in DB/DW systems. Without any coupling of such systems, a DM system will need to use other tools to extract data, making it difficult to integrate such a system into an information processing environment. Thus, no coupling represents a poor design.

- **Loose coupling:** *Loose coupling* means that a DM system will use some facilities of a DB or DW system, fetching data from a data repository managed by these systems, performing data mining, and then storing the mining results either in a file or in a designated place in a database or data warehouse.

  Loose coupling is better than no coupling because it ca[...] any portion of data stored in databases or data warehouses by using query [...] indexing, and other system facilities. It incurs some advantages of the [...] ncy, and other features provided by such systems. However, ma[...] mining systems are main memory-based. Because mining d[...] uctures and query optimization methods provided by D[...] cult for loose coupling to achieve high scalability a[...] data sets.

- **Semitight coupling:** *Semiti*[...] ng a DM system to a DB/DW system, effic[...] data mining primitives (identified by [...] mining functions) can be provided [...] lude sorting, indexing, aggregation, [...] omputation of some essential statistical m[...] ndard deviation, and so on. Moreover, some [...] esults can be precomputed and stored in the [...] nediate mining results are either precomputed or [...] design will enhance the performance of a DM system.

- **Tight coupling:** *Tight coupling* [...] stem is smoothly integrated into the DB/DW system. The data [...] m is treated as one functional component of an information system. Data mining queries and functions are optimized based on mining query analysis, data structures, indexing schemes, and query processing methods of a DB or DW system. With further technology advances, DM, DB, and DW systems will evolve and integrate together as one information system with multiple functionalities. This will provide a uniform information processing environment.

This approach is highly desirable because it facilitates efficient implementations of data mining functions, high system performance, and an integrated information processing environment.

With this analysis, it is easy to see that a data mining system should be coupled with a DB/DW system. Loose coupling, though not efficient, is better than no coupling because it uses both data and system facilities of a DB/DW system. Tight coupling is highly desirable, but its implementation is nontrivial and more research is needed in this area. Semitight coupling is a compromise between loose and tight coupling. It is important to identify commonly used data mining primitives and provide efficient implementations of such primitives in DB or DW systems.

1.9 Major Issues in Data Mining

The scope of this book addresses major issues in data mining regarding mining methodology, user interaction, performance, and diverse data types. These issues are introduced below:

Mining methodology and user interaction issues: These reflect the kinds of knowledge mined, the ability to mine knowledge at multiple granularities, the use of domain knowledge, ad hoc mining, and knowledge visualization.

- *Mining different kinds of knowledge in databases:* Because different users can be interested in different kinds of knowledge, data mining should cover a wide spectrum of data analysis and knowledge discovery tasks, including data characterization, discrimination, association and correlation analysis, classification, prediction, clustering, outlier analysis, and evolution analysis (which includes trend and similarity analysis). These tasks may use the same database in different ways and require the development of numerous data mining techniques.
- *Interactive mining of knowledge at multiple levels of abstraction:* Because it is difficult to know exactly what can be discovered within a database, the data mining process should be *interactive*. For databases containing a huge amount of data, appropriate sampling techniques can first be applied to facilitate interactive data exploration. Interactive mining allows users to focus the search for patterns, providing and refining data mining requests based on returned results. Specifically, knowledge should be mined by drilling down, rolling up,

and pivoting through the data space and knowledge space interactively, similar to what OLAP can do on data cubes. In this way, the user can interact with the data mining system to view data and discovered patterns at multiple granularities and from different angles.

- *Incorporation of background knowledge:* Background knowledge, or information regarding the domain under study, may be used to guide the discovery process and allow discovered patterns to be expressed in concise terms and at different levels of abstraction. Domain knowledge related to databases, such as integrity constraints and deduction rules, can help focus and speed up a data mining process, or judge the interestingness of discovered patterns.

- *Data mining query languages and ad hoc data mining:* Relational query languages (such as SQL) allow users to pose ad hoc queries for data retrieval. In a similar vein, high-level data mining query languages need to be developed to allow users to describe ad hoc data mining tasks by facilitating the specification of the relevant sets of data for analysis, the domain knowledge, the kinds of knowledge to be mined, and the conditions and constraints to be enforced on the discovered patterns. Such a language should be integrated with a database or data warehouse query language and optimized for efficient and flexible data mining.

- *Presentation and visualization of data mining results:* Discovered knowledge should be expressed in high-level languages, visual representations, or other expressive forms so that the knowledge can be easily understood and directly usable by humans. This is especially crucial if the data mining system is to be interactive. This requires the system to adopt expressive knowledge representation techniques, such as trees, tables, rules, graphs, charts, crosstabs, matrices, or curves.

- *Handling noisy or incomplete data:* The data stored in a database may reflect noise, exceptional cases, or incomplete data objects. When mining data regularities, these objects may confuse the process, causing the knowledge model constructed to overfit the data. As a result, the accuracy of the discovered patterns can be poor. Data cleaning methods and data analysis methods that can handle noise are required, as well as outlier mining methods for the discovery and analysis of exceptional cases.

- *Pattern evaluation—the interestingness problem:* A data mining system can uncover thousands of patterns. Many of the patterns discovered may be uninteresting to the given user, either because they represent common knowledge or lack novelty. Several challenges remain regarding the development of techniques to assess the interestingness of discovered patterns, particularly with regard to subjective measures that estimate the value of patterns with respect to a given user class, based on user beliefs or expectations. The use of interestingness measures or user-specified constraints to guide the discovery process and reduce the search space is another active area of research.

Performance issues: These include efficiency, scalability, and parallelization of data mining algorithms.

- *Efficiency and scalability of data mining algorithms:* To effectively extract information from a huge amount of data in databases, data mining algorithms must be efficient and scalable. In other words, the running time of a data mining algorithm must be predictable and acceptable in large databases. From a database perspective on knowledge discovery, efficiency and scalability are key issues in the implementation of data mining systems. Many of the issues discussed above under *mining methodology and user interaction* must also consider efficiency and scalability.
- *Parallel, distributed, and incremental mining algorithms:* The huge size of many databases, the wide distribution of data, and the computational complexity of some data mining methods are factors motivating the development of **parallel and distributed data mining algorithms.** Such algorithms divide the data into partitions, which are processed in parallel. The results from the partitions are then merged. Moreover, the high cost of some data mining processes promotes the need for **incremental** data mining algorithms that incorporate database updates without having to mine the entire data again "from scratch." Such algorithms perform knowledge modification incrementally to amend and strengthen what was previously discovered.

Issues relating to the diversity of database types:

- *Handling of relational and complex types of data:* Because relational databases and data warehouses are widely used, the development of efficient and effective data mining systems for such data is important. However, other databases may contain complex data objects, hypertext and multimedia data, spatial data, temporal data, or transaction data. It is unrealistic to expect one system to mine all kinds of data, given the diversity of data types and different goals of data mining. Specific data mining systems should be constructed for mining specific kinds of data. Therefore, one may expect to have different data mining systems for different kinds of data.
- *Mining information from heterogeneous databases and global information systems:* Local- and wide-area computer networks (such as the Internet) connect many sources of data, forming huge, distributed, and heterogeneous databases. The discovery of knowledge from different sources of structured, semistructured, or unstructured data with diverse data semantics poses great challenges to data mining. Data mining may help disclose high-level data regularities in multiple heterogeneous databases that are unlikely to be discovered by simple query systems and may improve information exchange and interoperability in heterogeneous databases. Web mining, which uncovers interesting knowledge about Web contents, Web structures, Web usage, and Web dynamics, becomes a very challenging and fast-evolving field in data mining.

The above issues are considered major requirements and challenges for the further evolution of data mining technology. Some of the challenges have been addressed in recent data mining research and development, *to a certain extent*, and are now considered *requirements*, while others are still at the research stage. The issues, however, continue to stimulate further investigation and improvement. Additional issues relating to applications, privacy, and the social impacts of data mining are discussed in Chapter 11, the final chapter of this book.

1.10 Summary

- **Database technology** has evolved from primitive file processing to the development of database management systems with query and transaction processing. Further progress has led to the increasing demand for efficient and effective advanced data analysis tools. This need is a result of the explosive growth in data collected from applications, including business and management, government administration, science and engineering, and environmental control.

- **Data mining** is the task of discovering interesting patterns from large amounts of data, where the data can be stored in databases, data warehouses, or other information repositories. It is a young interdisciplinary field, drawing from areas such as database systems, data warehousing, statistics, machine learning, data visualization, information retrieval, and high-performance computing. Other contributing areas include neural networks, pattern recognition, spatial data analysis, image databases, signal processing, and many application fields, such as business, economics, and bioinformatics.

- A **knowledge discovery process** includes data cleaning, data integration, data selection, data transformation, data mining, pattern evaluation, and knowledge presentation.

- The **architecture** of a typical data mining system includes a database and/or data warehouse and their appropriate servers, a data mining engine and pattern evaluation module (both of which interact with a knowledge base), and a graphical user interface. **Integration** of the data mining components, as a whole, with a database or data warehouse system can involve either no coupling, loose coupling, semitight coupling, or tight coupling. A well-designed data mining system should offer tight or semitight coupling with a database and/or data warehouse system.

- Data patterns can be mined from many different kinds of **databases**, such as relational databases, data warehouses, and transactional, and object-relational databases. Interesting data patterns can also be extracted from other kinds of **information repositories**, including spatial, time-series, sequence, text, multimedia, and legacy databases, data streams, and the World Wide Web.

- A **data warehouse** is a repository for long-term storage of data from multiple sources, organized so as to facilitate management decision making. The data are stored under a unified schema and are typically summarized. Data warehouse systems provide some data analysis capabilities, collectively referred to as **OLAP (on-line analytical processing)**.

- **Data mining functionalities** include the discovery of concept/class descriptions, associations and correlations, classification, prediction, clustering, trend analysis, outlier and deviation analysis, and similarity analysis. Characterization and discrimination are forms of data summarization.
- A pattern represents **knowledge** if it is easily understood by humans; valid on test data with some degree of certainty; and potentially useful, novel, or validates a hunch about which the user was curious. Measures of **pattern interestingness**, either *objective* or *subjective*, can be used to guide the discovery process.
- **Data mining systems can be classified** according to the kinds of databases mined, the kinds of knowledge mined, the techniques used, or the applications adapted.
- We have studied five **primitives** for specifying a data mining task in the form of a **data mining query**. These primitives are the specification of task-relevant data (i.e., the data set to be mined), the kind of knowledge to be mined, background knowledge (typically in the form of concept hierarchies), interestingness measures, and knowledge presentation and visualization techniques to be used for displaying the discovered patterns.
- **Data mining query languages** can be designed to support ad hoc and interactive data mining. A data mining query language, such as DMQL, should provide commands for specifying each of the data mining primitives. Such query languages are SQL-based and may eventually form a standard on which graphical user interfaces for data mining can be based.
- Efficient and effective data mining in large databases poses numerous requirements and great challenges to researchers and developers. The issues involved include data mining methodology, user interaction, performance and scalability, and the processing of a large variety of data types. Other issues include the exploration of data mining applications and their social impacts.

Exercises

1.1 What is *data mining*? In your answer, address the following:

(a) Is it another hype?

(b) Is it a simple transformation of technology developed from databases, statistics, and machine learning?

(c) Explain how the evolution of database technology led to data mining.

(d) Describe the steps involved in data mining when viewed as a process of knowledge discovery.

1.2 Present an example where data mining is crucial to the success of a business. What *data mining functions* does this business need? Can they be performed alternatively by data query processing or simple statistical analysis?

1.3 Suppose your task as a software engineer at *Big University* is to design a data mining system to examine the university course database, which contains the following information: the name, address, and status (e.g., undergraduate or graduate) of each student, the courses taken, and the cumulative grade point average (GPA). Describe the *architecture* you would choose. What is the purpose of each component of this architecture?

1.4 How is a *data warehouse* different from a database? How are they similar?

1.5 Briefly describe the following *advanced database systems* and applications: object-relational databases, spatial databases, text databases, multimedia databases, stream data, the World Wide Web.

1.6 Define each of the following *data mining functionalities*: characterization, discrimination, association and correlation analysis, classification, prediction, clustering, and evolution analysis. Give examples of each data mining functionality, using a real-life database with which you are familiar.

1.7 What is the difference between discrimination and classification? Between characterization and clustering? Between classification and prediction? For each of these pairs of tasks, how are they similar?

1.8 Based on your observation, describe another possible kind of knowledge that needs to be discovered by data mining methods but has not been listed in this chapter. Does it require a mining methodology that is quite different from those outlined in this chapter?

1.9 List and describe the five *primitives* for specifying a data mining task.

1.10 Describe why *concept hierarchies* are useful in data mining.

1.11 *Outliers* are often discarded as noise. However, one person's garbage could be another's treasure. For example, exceptions in credit card transactions can help us detect the fraudulent use of credit cards. Taking fraudulence detection as an example, propose two methods that can be used to detect outliers and discuss which one is more reliable.

1.12 Recent applications pay special attention to spatiotemporal data streams. A *spatiotemporal data stream* contains spatial information that changes over time, and is in the form of stream data (i.e., the data flow in and out like possibly infinite streams).

(a) Present three application examples of spatiotemporal data streams.

(b) Discuss what kind of interesting knowledge can be mined from such data streams, with limited time and resources.

(c) Identify and discuss the major challenges in spatiotemporal data mining.

(d) Using one application example, sketch a method to mine one kind of knowledge from such stream data efficiently.

1.13 Describe the differences between the following approaches for the integration of a data mining system with a database or data warehouse system: *no coupling*, *loose coupling*, *semitight coupling,* and *tight coupling.* State which approach you think is the most popular, and why.

1.14 Describe three challenges to data mining regarding *data mining methodology* and *user interaction issues.*

1.15 What are the major challenges of mining a huge amount of data (such as billions of tuples) in comparison with mining a small amount of data (such as a few hundred tuple data set)?

1.16 Outline the major research challenges of data mining in one specific application domain, such as stream/sensor data analysis, spatiotemporal data analysis, or bioinformatics.

Bibliographic Notes

The book *Knowledge Discovery in Databases,* edited by Piatetsky-Shapiro and Frawley [PSF91], is an early collection of research papers on knowledge discovery from data. The book *Advances in Knowledge Discovery and Data Mining,* edited by Fayyad, Piatetsky-Shapiro, Smyth, and Uthurusamy [FPSSe96], is a collection of later research results on knowledge discovery and data mining. There have been many data mining books published in recent years, including *Predictive Data Mining* by Weiss and Indurkhya [WI98], *Data Mining Solutions: Methods and Tools for Solving Real-World Problems* by Westphal and Blaxton [WB98], *Mastering Data Mining: The Art and Science of Customer Relationship Management* by Berry and Linoff [BL99], *Building Data Mining Applications for CRM* by Berson, Smith, and Thearling [BST99], *Data Mining: Practical Machine Learning Tools and Techniques with Java Implementations* by Witten and Frank [WF05], *Principles of Data Mining (Adaptive Computation and Machine Learning)* by Hand, Mannila, and Smyth [HMS01], *The Elements of Statistical Learning* by Hastie, Tibshirani, and Friedman [HTF01], *Data Mining: Introductory and Advanced Topics* by Dunham [Dun03], *Data Mining: Multimedia, Soft Computing, and Bioinformatics* by Mitra and Acharya [MA03], and *Introduction to Data Mining* by Tan, Steinbach and Kumar [TSK05]. There are also books containing collections of papers on particular aspects of knowledge discovery, such as *Machine Learning and Data Mining: Methods and Applications* edited by Michalski, Brakto, and Kubat [MBK98], and *Relational Data Mining* edited by Dzeroski and Lavrac [De01], as well as many tutorial notes on data mining in major database, data mining, and machine learning conferences.

KDnuggets News, moderated by Piatetsky-Shapiro since 1991, is a regular, free electronic newsletter containing information relevant to data mining and knowledge discovery. The *KDnuggets* website, located at *www.kdnuggets.com,* contains a good collection of information relating to data mining.

The data mining community started its first international conference on knowledge discovery and data mining in 1995 [Fe95]. The conference evolved from the four international workshops on knowledge discovery in databases, held from 1989 to 1994 [PS89, PS91a, FUe93, Fe94]. ACM-SIGKDD, a Special Interest Group on Knowledge Discovery in Databases, was set up under ACM in 1998. In 1999, ACM-SIGKDD organized the fifth international conference on knowledge discovery and data mining (KDD'99). The IEEE Computer Science Society has organized its annual data mining conference, International Conference on Data Mining (ICDM), since 2001. SIAM (Society on Industrial and Applied Mathematics) has organized its annual data mining conference, SIAM Data Mining conference (SDM), since 2002. A dedicated journal, *Data Mining and Knowledge Discovery*, published by Kluwers Publishers, has been available since 1997. ACM-SIGKDD also publishes a biannual newsletter, *SIGKDD Explorations*. There are a few other international or regional conferences on data mining, such as the Pacific Asian Conference on Knowledge Discovery and Data Mining (PAKDD), the European Conference on Principles and Practice of Knowledge Discovery in Databases (PKDD), and the International Conference on Data Warehousing and Knowledge Discovery (DaWaK).

Research in data mining has also been published in books, conferences, and journals on databases, statistics, machine learning, and data visualization. References to such sources are listed below.

Popular textbooks on database systems include *Database Systems: The Complete Book* by Garcia-Molina, Ullman, and Widom [GMUW02], *Database Management Systems* by Ramakrishnan and Gehrke [RG03], *Database System Concepts* by Silberschatz, Korth, and Sudarshan [SKS02], and *Fundamentals of Database Systems* by Elmasri and Navathe [EN03]. For an edited collection of seminal articles on database systems, see *Readings in Database Systems* by Hellerstein and Stonebraker [HS05]. Many books on data warehouse technology, systems, and applications have been published in the last several years, such as *The Data Warehouse Toolkit: The Complete Guide to Dimensional Modeling* by Kimball and M. Ross [KR02], *The Data Warehouse Lifecycle Toolkit: Expert Methods for Designing, Developing, and Deploying Data Warehouses* by Kimball, Reeves, Ross, et al. [KRRT98], *Mastering Data Warehouse Design: Relational and Dimensional Techniques* by Imhoff, Galemmo, and Geiger [IGG03], *Building the Data Warehouse* by Inmon [Inm96], and *OLAP Solutions: Building Multidimensional Information Systems* by Thomsen [Tho97]. A set of research papers on materialized views and data warehouse implementations were collected in *Materialized Views: Techniques, Implementations, and Applications* by Gupta and Mumick [GM99]. Chaudhuri and Dayal [CD97] present a comprehensive overview of data warehouse technology.

Research results relating to data mining and data warehousing have been published in the proceedings of many international database conferences, including the *ACM-SIGMOD International Conference on Management of Data (SIGMOD)*, the *International Conference on Very Large Data Bases (VLDB)*, the *ACM SIGACT-SIGMOD-SIGART Symposium on Principles of Database Systems (PODS)*, the *International Conference on Data Engineering (ICDE)*, the *International Conference on Extending Database Technology (EDBT)*, the *International Conference on Database Theory (ICDT)*, the *International Conference on Information and Knowledge Management (CIKM)*, the *International Conference on Database and Expert Systems Applications (DEXA)*, and the *International Symposium on Database Systems for Advanced Applications (DASFAA)*. Research in data mining is also published in major database journals, such as *IEEE Transactions on Knowledge and Data Engineering (TKDE)*, *ACM Transactions on Database Systems (TODS)*, *Journal of*

ACM (JACM), *Information Systems*, *The VLDB Journal*, *Data and Knowledge Engineering*, *International Journal of Intelligent Information Systems (JIIS)*, and *Knowledge and Information Systems (KAIS)*.

Many effective data mining methods have been developed by statisticians and pattern recognition researchers, and introduced in a rich set of textbooks. An overview of classification from a statistical pattern recognition perspective can be found in *Pattern Classification* by Duda, Hart, Stork [DHS01]. There are also many textbooks covering different topics in statistical analysis, such as *Mathematical Statistics: Basic Ideas and Selected Topics*, by Bickel and Doksum [BD01], *The Statistical Sleuth: A Course in Methods of Data Analysis* by Ramsey and Schafer [RS01], *Applied Linear Statistical Models* by Neter, Kutner, Nachtsheim, and Wasserman [NKNW96], *An Introduction to Generalized Linear Models* by Dobson [Dob05], *Applied Statistical Time Series Analysis* by Shumway [Shu88], and *Applied Multivariate Statistical Analysis* by Johnson and Wichern [JW05].

Research in statistics is published in the proceedings of several major statistical conferences, including *Joint Statistical Meetings*, *International Conference of the Royal Statistical Society*, and *Symposium on the Interface: Computing Science and Statistics*. Other sources of publication include the *Journal of the Royal Statistical Society*, *The Annals of Statistics*, *Journal of American Statistical Association*, *Technometrics*, and *Biometrika*.

Textbooks and reference books on machine learning include *Machine Learning, An Artificial Intelligence Approach*, Vols. 1–4, edited by Michalski et al. [MCM83, MCM86, KM90, MT94], *C4.5: Programs for Machine Learning* by Quinlan [Qui93], *Elements of Machine Learning* by Langley [Lan96], and *Machine Learning* by Mitchell [Mit97]. The book *Computer Systems That Learn: Classification and Prediction Methods from Statistics, Neural Nets, Machine Learning, and Expert Systems* by Weiss and Kulikowski [WK91] compares classification and prediction methods from several different fields. For an edited collection of seminal articles on machine learning, see *Readings in Machine Learning* by Shavlik and Dietterich [SD90].

Machine learning research is published in the proceedings of several large machine learning and artificial intelligence conferences, including the *International Conference on Machine Learning (ML)*, the *ACM Conference on Computational Learning Theory (COLT)*, the *International Joint Conference on Artificial Intelligence (IJCAI)*, and the *American Association of Artificial Intelligence Conference (AAAI)*. Other sources of publication include major machine learning, artificial intelligence, pattern recognition, and knowledge system journals, some of which have been mentioned above. Others include *Machine Learning (ML)*, *Artificial Intelligence Journal (AI)*, *IEEE Transactions on Pattern Analysis and Machine Intelligence (PAMI)*, and *Cognitive Science*.

Pioneering work on data visualization techniques is described in *The Visual Display of Quantitative Information* [Tuf83], *Envisioning Information* [Tuf90], and *Visual Explanations: Images and Quantities, Evidence and Narrative* [Tuf97], all by Tufte, in addition to *Graphics and Graphic Information Processing* by Bertin [Ber81], *Visualizing Data* by Cleveland [Cle93], and *Information Visualization in Data Mining and Knowledge Discovery* edited by Fayyad, Grinstein, and Wierse [FGW01]. Major conferences and symposiums on visualization include *ACM Human Factors in Computing Systems (CHI)*, *Visualization*, and the *International Symposium on Information Visualization*. Research on visualization is also published in *Transactions on Visualization and Computer Graphics*, *Journal of Computational and Graphical Statistics*, and *IEEE Computer Graphics and Applications*.

The DMQL data mining query language was proposed by Han, Fu, Wang, et al. [HFW$^+$96] for the *DBMiner* data mining system. Other examples include *Discovery Board* (formerly *Data Mine*) by Imielinski, Virmani, and Abdulghani [IVA96], and MSQL by Imielinski and Virmani [IV99]. MINE RULE, an SQL-like operator for mining single-dimensional association rules, was proposed by Meo, Psaila, and Ceri [MPC96] and extended by Baralis and Psaila [BP97]. Microsoft Corporation has made a major data mining standardization effort by proposing OLE DB for Data Mining (DM) [Cor00] and the DMX language [TM05, TMK05]. An introduction to the data mining language primitives of DMX can be found in the appendix of this book. Other standardization efforts include PMML (Programming data Model Markup Language) [Ras04], described at *www.dmg.org*, and CRISP-DM (CRoss-Industry Standard Process for Data Mining), described at *www.crisp-dm.org*.

Architectures of data mining systems have been discussed by many researchers in conference panels and meetings. The recent design of data mining languages, such as [BP97, IV99, Cor00, Ras04], the proposal of on-line analytical mining, such as [Han98], and the study of optimization of data mining queries, such as [NLHP98, STA98, LNHP99], can be viewed as steps toward the tight integration of data mining systems with database systems and data warehouse systems. For relational or object-relational systems, data mining primitives as proposed by Sarawagi, Thomas, and Agrawal [STA98] may be used as building blocks for the efficient implementation of data mining in such database systems.

2 Data Preprocessing

Today's real-world databases are highly susceptible to noisy, missing, and inconsistent data due to their typically huge size (often several gigabytes or more) and their likely origin from multiple, heterogenous sources. Low-quality data will lead to low-quality mining results. *"How can the data be preprocessed in order to help improve the quality of the data and, consequently, of the mining results? How can the data be preprocessed so as to improve the efficiency and ease of the mining process?"*

There are a number of data preprocessing techniques. *Data cleaning* can be applied to remove noise and correct inconsistencies in the data. *Data integration* merges data from multiple sources into a coherent data store, such as a data warehouse. *Data transformations*, such as normalization, may be applied. For example, normalization may improve the accuracy and efficiency of mining algorithms involving distance measurements. *Data reduction* can reduce the data size by aggregating, eliminating redundant features, or clustering, for instance. These techniques are not mutually exclusive; they may work together. For example, data cleaning can involve transformations to correct wrong data, such as by transforming all entries for a *date* field to a common format. Data processing techniques, when applied before mining, can substantially improve the overall quality of the patterns mined and/or the time required for the actual mining.

In this chapter, we introduce the basic concepts of data preprocessing in Section 2.1. Section 2.2 presents *descriptive data summarization*, which serves as a foundation for data preprocessing. Descriptive data summarization helps us study the general characteristics of the data and identify the presence of noise or outliers, which is useful for successful data cleaning and data integration. The methods for data preprocessing are organized into the following categories: *data cleaning* (Section 2.3), *data integration and transformation* (Section 2.4), and *data reduction* (Section 2.5). Concept hierarchies can be used in an alternative form of data reduction where we replace low-level data (such as raw values for *age*) with higher-level concepts (such as *youth*, *middle-aged*, or *senior*). This form of data reduction is the topic of Section 2.6, wherein we discuss the automatic eneration of concept hierarchies from numerical data using data discretization techniques. The automatic generation of concept hierarchies from categorical data is also described.

2.1 Why Preprocess the Data?

Imagine that you are a manager at *AllElectronics* and have been charged with analyzing the company's data with respect to the sales at your branch. You immediately set out to perform this task. You carefully inspect the company's database and data warehouse, identifying and selecting the attributes or dimensions to be included in your analysis, such as *item*, *price*, and *units_sold*. Alas! You notice that several of the attributes for various tuples have no recorded value. For your analysis, you would like to include information as to whether each item purchased was advertised as on sale, yet you discover that this information has not been recorded. Furthermore, users of your database system have reported errors, unusual values, and inconsistencies in the data recorded for some transactions. In other words, the data you wish to analyze by data mining techniques are **incomplete** (lacking attribute values or certain attributes of interest, or containing only aggregate data), **noisy** (containing errors, or *outlier* values that deviate from the expected), and **inconsistent** (e.g., containing discrepancies in the department codes used to categorize items). Welcome to the real world!

Incomplete, noisy, and inconsistent data are commonplace properties of large real-world databases and data warehouses. Incomplete data can occur for a number of reasons. Attributes of interest may not always be available, such as customer information for sales transaction data. Other data may not be included simply because it was not considered important at the time of entry. Relevant data may not be recorded due to a misunderstanding, or because of equipment malfunctions. Data that were inconsistent with other recorded data may have been deleted. Furthermore, the recording of the history or modifications to the data may have been overlooked. Missing data, particularly for tuples with missing values for some attributes, may need to be inferred.

There are many possible reasons for noisy data (having incorrect attribute values). The data collection instruments used may be faulty. There may have been human or computer errors occurring at data entry. Errors in data transmission can also occur. There may be technology limitations, such as limited buffer size for coordinating synchronized data transfer and consumption. Incorrect data may also result from inconsistencies in naming conventions or data codes used, or inconsistent formats for input fields, such as *date*. Duplicate tuples also require data cleaning.

Data cleaning routines work to "clean" the data by filling in missing values, smoothing noisy data, identifying or removing outliers, and resolving inconsistencies. If users believe the data are dirty, they are unlikely to trust the results of any data mining that has been applied to it. Furthermore, dirty data can cause confusion for the mining procedure, resulting in unreliable output. Although most mining routines have some procedures for dealing with incomplete or noisy data, they are not always robust. Instead, they may concentrate on avoiding overfitting the data to the function being modeled. Therefore, a useful preprocessing step is to run your data through some data cleaning routines. Section 2.3 discusses methods for cleaning up your data.

Getting back to your task at *AllElectronics*, suppose that you would like to include data from multiple sources in your analysis. This would involve integrating multiple databases, data cubes, or files, that is, **data integration**. Yet some attributes representing a given concept may have different names in different databases, causing inconsistencies and redundancies. For example, the attribute for customer identification may be referred to as *customer_id* in one data store and *cust_id* in another. Naming inconsistencies may also occur for attribute values. For example, the same first name could be registered as "Bill" in one database, but "William" in another, and "B." in the third. Furthermore, you suspect that some attributes may be inferred from others (e.g., annual revenue). Having a large amount of redundant data may slow down or confuse the knowledge discovery process. Clearly, in addition to data cleaning, steps must be taken to help avoid redundancies during data integration. Typically, data cleaning and data integration are performed as a preprocessing step when preparing the data for a data warehouse. Additional data cleaning can be performed to detect and remove redundancies that may have resulted from data integration.

Getting back to your data, you have decided, say, that you would like to use a distance-based mining algorithm for your analysis, such as neural networks, nearest-neighbor classifiers, or clustering.[1] Such methods provide better results if the data to be analyzed have been *normalized*, that is, scaled to a specific range such as [0.0, 1.0]. Your customer data, for example, contain the attributes *age* and *annual salary*. The *annual salary* attribute usually takes much larger values than *age*. Therefore, if the attributes are left unnormalized, the distance measurements taken on *annual salary* will generally outweigh distance measurements taken on *age*. Furthermore, it would be useful for your analysis to obtain aggregate information as to the sales per customer region—something that is not part of any precomputed data cube in your data warehouse. You soon realize that **data transformation** operations, such as normalization and aggregation, are additional data preprocessing procedures that would contribute toward the success of the mining process. Data integration and data transformation are discussed in Section 2.4.

"Hmmm," you wonder, as you consider your data even further. *"The data set I have selected for analysis is HUGE, which is sure to slow down the mining process. Is there any way I can reduce the size of my data set, without jeopardizing the data mining results?"* **Data reduction** obtains a reduced representation of the data set that is much smaller in volume, yet produces the same (or almost the same) analytical results. There are a number of strategies for data reduction. These include *data aggregation* (e.g., building a data cube), *attribute subset selection* (e.g., removing irrelevant attributes through correlation analysis), *dimensionality reduction* (e.g., using encoding schemes such as minimum length encoding or wavelets), and *numerosity reduction* (e.g., "replacing" the data by alternative, smaller representations such as clusters or parametric models). Data reduction is the topic of Section 2.5. Data can also be "reduced" by *generalization* with the use of concept hierarchies, where low-level concepts, such as *city* for customer location, are replaced with higher-level concepts, such as *region* or *province_or_state*. A concept hierarchy organizes the concepts into varying levels of abstraction. *Data discretization* is

[1] Neural networks and nearest-neighbor classifiers are described in Chapter 6, and clustering is discussed in Chapter 7.

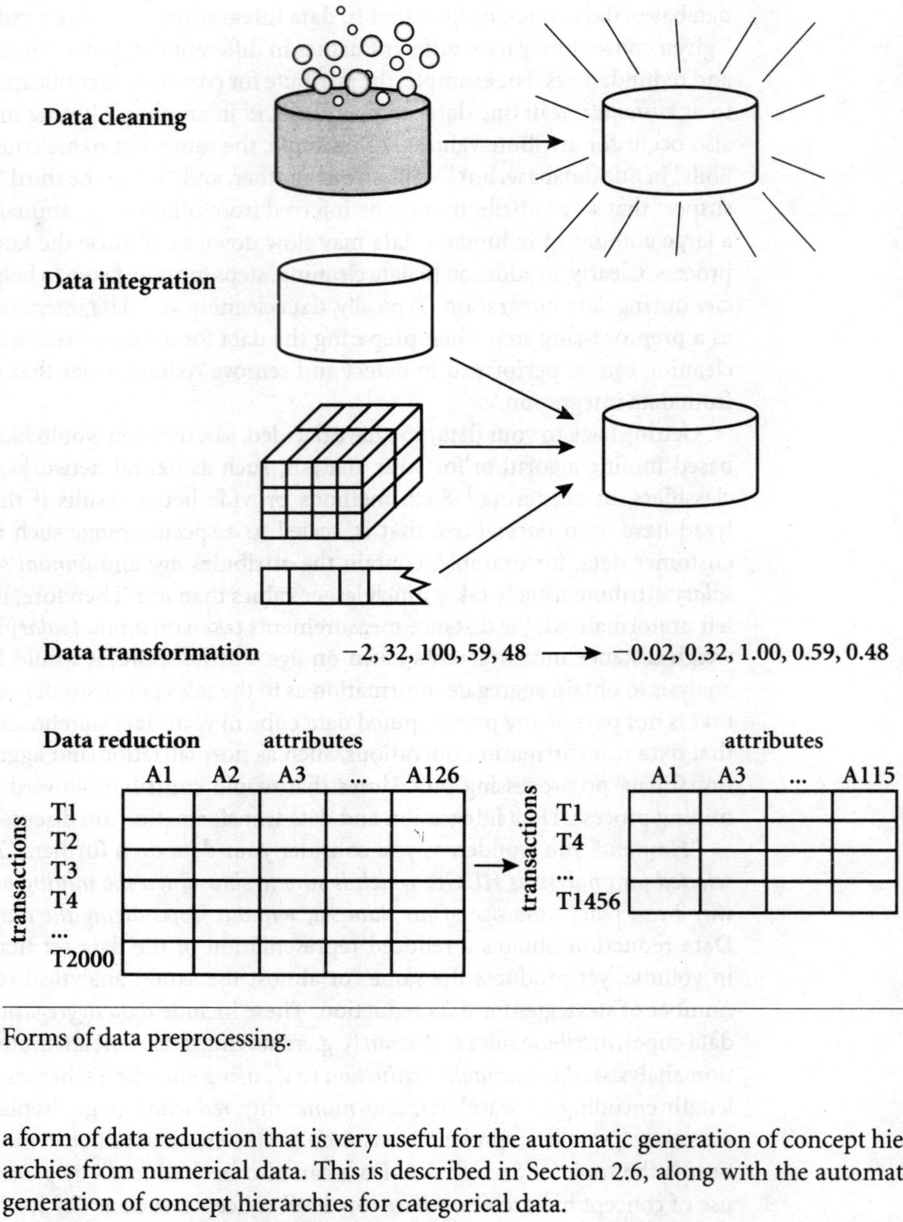

Figure 2.1 Forms of data preprocessing.

a form of data reduction that is very useful for the automatic generation of concept hierarchies from numerical data. This is described in Section 2.6, along with the automatic generation of concept hierarchies for categorical data.

Figure 2.1 summarizes the data preprocessing steps described here. Note that the above categorization is not mutually exclusive. For example, the removal of redundant data may be seen as a form of data cleaning, as well as data reduction.

In summary, real-world data tend to be dirty, incomplete, and inconsistent. Data preprocessing techniques can improve the quality of the data, thereby helping to improve the accuracy and efficiency of the subsequent mining process. Data preprocessing is an important step in the knowledge discovery process, because quality decisions must be based on quality data. Detecting data anomalies, rectifying them early, and reducing the data to be analyzed can lead to huge payoffs for decision making.

2.2 Descriptive Data Summarization

For data preprocessing to be successful, it is essential to have an overall picture of your data. Descriptive data summarization techniques can be used to identify the typical properties of your data and highlight which data values should be treated as noise or outliers. Thus, we first introduce the basic concepts of descriptive data summarization before getting into the concrete workings of data preprocessing techniques.

For many data preprocessing tasks, users would like to learn about data characteristics regarding both central tendency and dispersion of the data. Measures of central tendency include *mean, median, mode,* and *midrange,* while measures of data dispersion include *quartiles, interquartile range (IQR),* and *variance.* These descriptive statistics are of great help in understanding the distribution of the data. Such measures have been studied extensively in the statistical literature. From the data mining point of view, we need to examine how they can be computed efficiently in large databases. In particular, it is necessary to introduce the notions of *distributive measure, algebraic measure,* and *holistic measure.* Knowing what kind of measure we are dealing with can help us choose an efficient implementation for it.

2.2.1 Measuring the Central Tendency

In this section, we look at various ways to measure the central tendency of data. The most common and most effective numerical measure of the "center" of a set of data is the *(arithmetic) mean.* Let $x_1, x_2, \ldots, x_N$ be a set of N values or observations, such as for some attribute, like *salary.* The mean of this set of values is

$$\bar{x} = \frac{\sum_{i=1}^{N} x_i}{N} = \frac{x_1 + x_2 + \cdots + x_N}{N}. \tag{2.1}$$

This corresponds to the built-in aggregate function, *average* (**avg()** in SQL), provided in relational database systems.

A **distributive measure** is a measure (i.e., function) that can be computed for a given data set by partitioning the data into smaller subsets, computing the measure for each subset, and then merging the results in order to arrive at the measure's value for the original (entire) data set. Both **sum()** and **count()** are distributive measures because they can be computed in this manner. Other examples include **max()** and **min()**. An **algebraic measure** is a measure that can be computed by applying an algebraic function to one or more distributive measures. Hence, *average* (or **mean()**) is an algebraic measure because it can be computed by **sum()/count()**. When computing data cubes[2], **sum()** and **count()** are typically saved in precomputation. Thus, the derivation of *average* for data cubes is straightforward.

Sometimes, each value x_i in a set may be associated with a weight w_i, for $i = 1,\ldots,N$. The weights reflect the significance, importance, or occurrence frequency attached to their respective values. In this case, we can compute

$$\bar{x} = \frac{\sum_{i=1}^{N} w_i x_i}{\sum_{i=1}^{N} w_i} = \frac{w_1x_1 + w_2x_2 + \cdots + w_Nx_N}{w_1 + w_2 + \cdots + w_N}. \tag{2.2}$$

This is called the **weighted arithmetic mean** or the **weighted average**. Note that the weighted average is another example of an algebraic measure.

Although the mean is the single most useful quantity for describing a data set, it is not always the best way of measuring the center of the data. A major problem with the *mean* is its sensitivity to extreme (e.g., outlier) values. Even a small number of extreme values can corrupt the mean. For example, the mean salary at a company may be substantially pushed up by that of a few highly paid managers. Similarly, the average score of a class in an exam could be pulled down quite a bit by a few very low scores. To offset the effect caused by a small number of extreme values, we can instead use the **trimmed mean**, which is the mean obtained after chopping off values at the high and low extremes. For example, we can sort the values observed for *salary* and remove the top and bottom 2% before computing the mean. We should avoid trimming too large a portion (such as 20%) at both ends as this can result in the loss of valuable information.

For skewed (asymmetric) data, a better measure of the center of data is the *median*. Suppose that a given data set of N distinct values is sorted in numerical order. If N is odd, then the **median** is the *middle value* of the ordered set; otherwise (i.e., if N is even), the median is the average of the middle two values.

A **holistic measure** is a measure that must be computed on the entire data set as a whole. It cannot be computed by partitioning the given data into subsets and merging the values obtained for the measure in each subset. The median is an example of a holistic measure. Holistic measures are much more expensive to compute than distributive measures such as those listed above.

We can, however, easily *approximate* the median value of a data set. Assume that data are grouped in intervals according to their x_i data values and that the frequency (i.e., number of data values) of each interval is known. For example, people may be grouped according to their annual salary in intervals such as 10–20K, 20–30K, and so on. Let the interval that contains the median frequency be the *median interval*. We can approximate the median of the entire data set (e.g., the median salary) by interpolation using the formula:

$$median = L_1 + \left(\frac{N/2 - (\sum freq)_l}{freq_{median}}\right) width, \tag{2.3}$$

[2] Data cube computation is described in detail in Chapters 3 and 4.

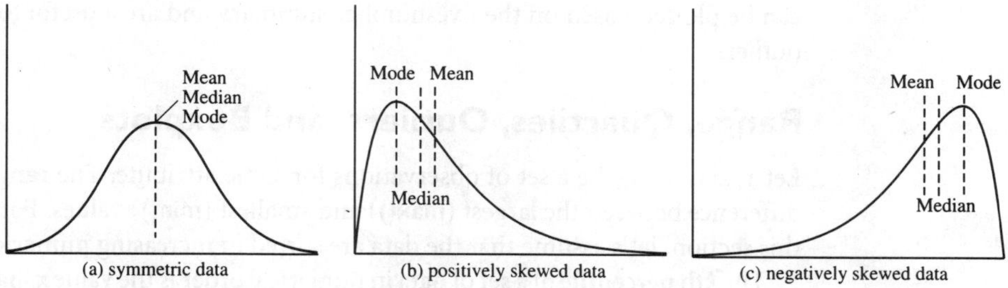

Figure 2.2 Mean, median, and mode of symmetric versus positively and negatively skewed data.

where L_1 is the lower boundary of the median interval, N is the number of values in the entire data set, $(\sum freq)_l$ is the sum of the frequencies of all of the intervals that are lower than the median interval, $freq_{median}$ is the frequency of the median interval, and $width$ is the width of the median interval.

Another measure of central tendency is the *mode*. The **mode** for a set of data is the value that occurs most frequently in the set. It is possible for the greatest frequency to correspond to several different values, which results in more than one mode. Data sets with one, two, or three modes are respectively called **unimodal, bimodal**, and **trimodal.** In general, a data set with two or more modes is **multimodal**. At the other extreme, if each data value occurs only once, then there is no mode.

For unimodal frequency curves that are moderately skewed (asymmetrical), we have the following empirical relation:

$$mean - mode = 3 \times (mean - median). \tag{2.4}$$

This implies that the mode for unimodal frequency curves that are moderately skewed can easily be computed if the mean and median values are known.

In a unimodal frequency curve with perfect symmetric data distribution, the mean, median, and mode are all at the same center value, as shown in Figure 2.2(a). However, data in most real applications are not symmetric. They may instead be either positively skewed, where the mode occurs at a value that is smaller than the median (Figure 2.2(b)), or negatively skewed, where the mode occurs at a value greater than the median (Figure 2.2(c)).

The **midrange** can also be used to assess the central tendency of a data set. It is the average of the largest and smallest values in the set. This algebraic measure is easy to compute using the SQL aggregate functions, **max()** and **min()**.

2.2.2 Measuring the Dispersion of Data

The degree to which numerical data tend to spread is called the **dispersion**, or **variance** of the data. The most common measures of data dispersion are *range*, the *five-number summary* (based on *quartiles*), the *interquartile range*, and the *standard deviation*. Boxplots can be plotted based on the five-number summary and are a useful tool for identifying outliers.

Range, Quartiles, Outliers, and Boxplots

Let $x_1, x_2, \ldots, x_N$ be a set of observations for some attribute. The **range** of the set is the difference between the largest (**max()**) and smallest (**min()**) values. For the remainder of this section, let's assume that the data are sorted in increasing numerical order.

The **kth percentile** of a set of data in numerical order is the value x_i having the property that k percent of the data entries lie at or below x_i. The *median* (discussed in the previous subsection) is the 50th percentile.

The most commonly used percentiles other than the median are **quartiles.** The **first quartile**, denoted by Q_1, is the 25th percentile; the **third quartile**, denoted by Q_3, is the 75th percentile. The quartiles, including the median, give some indication of the center, spread, and shape of a distribution. The distance between the first and third quartiles is a simple measure of spread that gives the range covered by the middle half of the data. This distance is called the **interquartile range** (IQR) and is defined as

$$IQR = Q_3 - Q_1. \tag{2.5}$$

Based on reasoning similar to that in our analysis of the median in Section 2.2.1, we can conclude that Q_1 and Q_3 are holistic measures, as is IQR.

No single numerical measure of spread, such as IQR, is very useful for describing skewed distributions. The spreads of two sides of a skewed distribution are unequal (Figure 2.2). Therefore, it is more informative to also provide the two quartiles Q_1 and Q_3, along with the median. A common rule of thumb for identifying suspected **outliers** is to single out values falling at least $1.5 \times IQR$ above the third quartile or below the first quartile.

Because Q_1, the median, and Q_3 together contain no information about the endpoints (e.g., tails) of the data, a fuller summary of the shape of a distribution can be obtained by providing the lowest and highest data values as well. This is known as the *five-number summary.* The **five-number summary** of a distribution consists of the median, the quartiles Q_1 and Q_3, and the smallest and largest individual observations, written in the order *Minimum*, Q_1, *Median*, Q_3, *Maximum*.

Boxplots are a popular way of visualizing a distribution. A boxplot incorporates the five-number summary as follows:

- Typically, the ends of the box are at the quartiles, so that the box length is the interquartile range, IQR.
- The median is marked by a line within the box.
- Two lines (called *whiskers*) outside the box extend to the smallest (*Minimum*) and largest (*Maximum*) observations.

When dealing with a moderate number of observations, it is worthwhile to plot potential outliers individually. To do this in a boxplot, the whiskers are extended to

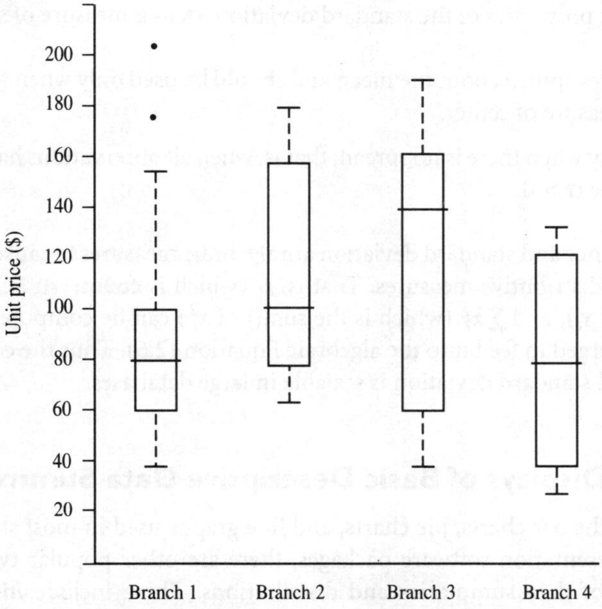

Figure 2.3 Boxplot for the unit price data for items sold at four branches of *AllElectronics* during a given time period.

the extreme low and high observations *only if* these values are less than $1.5 \times IQR$ beyond the quartiles. Otherwise, the whiskers terminate at the most extreme observations occurring within $1.5 \times IQR$ of the quartiles. The remaining cases are plotted individually. Boxplots can be used in the comparisons of several sets of compatible data. Figure 2.3 shows boxplots for unit price data for items sold at four branches of *AllElectronics* during a given time period. For branch 1, we see that the median price of items sold is \$80, Q_1 is \$60, Q_3 is \$100. Notice that two outlying observations for this branch were plotted individually, as their values of 175 and 202 are more than 1.5 times the IQR here of 40. The efficient computation of boxplots, or even *approximate boxplots* (based on approximates of the five-number summary), remains a challenging issue for the mining of large data sets.

Variance and Standard Deviation

The variance of N observations, $x_1, x_2, \ldots, x_N$, is

$$\sigma^2 = \frac{1}{N}\sum_{i=1}^{N}(x_i - \bar{x})^2 = \frac{1}{N}\left[\sum x_i^2 - \frac{1}{N}\left(\sum x_i\right)^2\right], \tag{2.6}$$

where $\bar{x}$ is the mean value of the observations, as defined in Equation (2.1). The standard deviation, σ, of the observations is the square root of the variance, σ^2.

The basic properties of the standard deviation, σ, as a measure of spread are

- σ measures spread about the mean and should be used only when the mean is chosen as the measure of center.
- $\sigma = 0$ only when there is no spread, that is, when all observations have the same value. Otherwise $\sigma > 0$.

The variance and standard deviation are algebraic measures because they can be computed from distributive measures. That is, N (which is **count()** in SQL), $\sum x_i$ (which is the **sum()** of x_i), and $\sum x_i^2$ (which is the **sum()** of x_i^2) can be computed in any partition and then merged to feed into the algebraic Equation (2.6). Thus the computation of the variance and standard deviation is scalable in large databases.

2.2.3 Graphic Displays of Basic Descriptive Data Summaries

Aside from the bar charts, pie charts, and line graphs used in most statistical or graphical data presentation software packages, there are other popular types of graphs for the display of data summaries and distributions. These include *histograms, quantile plots, q-q plots, scatter plots,* and *loess curves.* Such graphs are very helpful for the visual inspection of your data.

Plotting **histograms, or frequency histograms,** is a graphical method for summarizing the distribution of a given attribute. A histogram for an attribute A partitions the data distribution of A into disjoint subsets, or *buckets.* Typically, the width of each bucket is uniform. Each bucket is represented by a rectangle whose height is equal to the count or relative frequency of the values at the bucket. If A is categoric, such as *automobile_model* or *item_type,* then one rectangle is drawn for each known value of A, and the resulting graph is more commonly referred to as a **bar chart.** If A is numeric, the term *histogram* is preferred. Partitioning rules for constructing histograms for numerical attributes are discussed in Section 2.5.4. In an equal-width histogram, for example, each bucket represents an equal-width range of numerical attribute A.

Figure 2.4 shows a histogram for the data set of Table 2.1, where buckets are defined by equal-width ranges representing \$20 increments and the frequency is the count of items sold. Histograms are at least a century old and are a widely used univariate graphical method. However, they may not be as effective as the quantile plot, q-q plot, and boxplot methods for comparing groups of univariate observations.

A **quantile plot** is a simple and effective way to have a first look at a univariate data distribution. First, it displays all of the data for the given attribute (allowing the user to assess both the overall behavior and unusual occurrences). Second, it plots quantile information. The mechanism used in this step is slightly different from the percentile computation discussed in Section 2.2.2. Let x_i, for $i = 1$ to N, be the data sorted in increasing order so that x_1 is the smallest observation and x_N is the largest. Each observation, x_i, is paired with a percentage, f_i, which indicates that approximately $100f_i\%$ of the data are below or equal to the value, x_i. We say "approximately" because

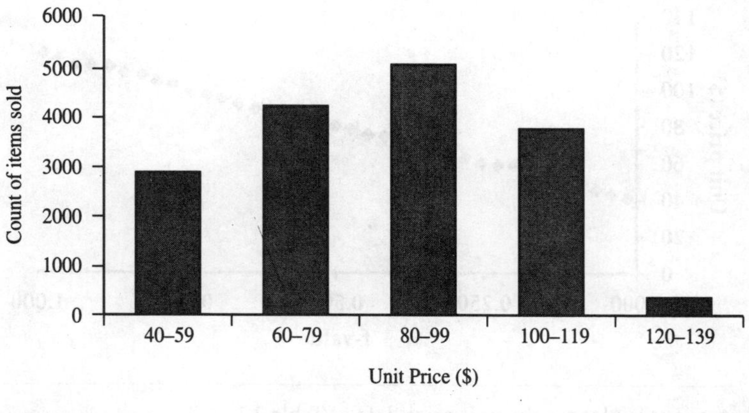

Figure 2.4 A histogram for the data set of Table 2.1.

Table 2.1 A set of unit price data for items sold at a branch of *AllElectronics*.

Unit price ($)	*Count of items sold*
40	275
43	300
47	250
..	..
74	360
75	515
78	540
..	..
115	320
117	270
120	350

there may not be a value with exactly a fraction, f_i, of the data below or equal to x_i. Note that the 0.25 quantile corresponds to quartile Q_1, the 0.50 quantile is the median, and the 0.75 quantile is Q_3.

Let

$$f_i = \frac{i - 0.5}{N}. \tag{2.7}$$

These numbers increase in equal steps of $1/N$, ranging from $1/2N$ (which is slightly above zero) to $1 - 1/2N$ (which is slightly below one). On a quantile plot, x_i is graphed against f_i. This allows us to compare different distributions based on their quantiles. For example, given the quantile plots of sales data for two different time periods, we can

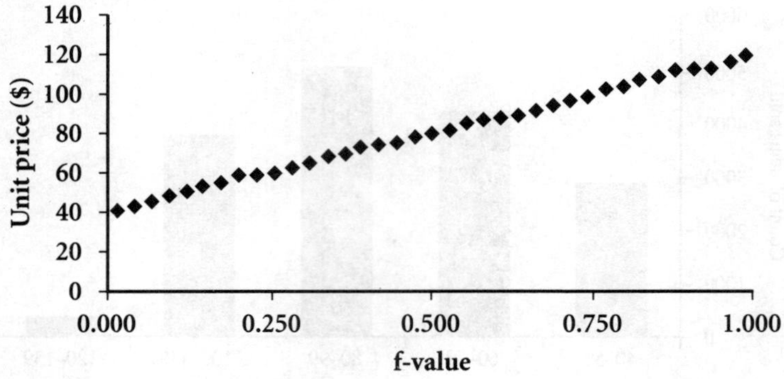

Figure 2.5 A quantile plot for the unit price data of Table 2.1.

compare their Q_1, median, Q_3, and other f_i values at a glance. Figure 2.5 shows a quantile plot for the *unit price* data of Table 2.1.

A **quantile-quantile plot**, or **q-q plot**, graphs the quantiles of one univariate distribution against the corresponding quantiles of another. It is a powerful visualization tool in that it allows the user to view whether there is a shift in going from one distribution to another.

Suppose that we have two sets of observations for the variable *unit price*, taken from two different branch locations. Let $x_1, \ldots, x_N$ be the data from the first branch, and $y_1, \ldots, y_M$ be the data from the second, where each data set is sorted in increasing order. If $M = N$ (i.e., the number of points in each set is the same), then we simply plot y_i against x_i, where y_i and x_i are both $(i-0.5)/N$ quantiles of their respective data sets. If $M < N$ (i.e., the second branch has fewer observations than the first), there can be only M points on the q-q plot. Here, y_i is the $(i-0.5)/M$ quantile of the y data, which is plotted against the $(i-0.5)/M$ quantile of the x data. This computation typically involves interpolation.

Figure 2.6 shows a quantile-quantile plot for *unit price* data of items sold at two different branches of *AllElectronics* during a given time period. Each point corresponds to the same quantile for each data set and shows the unit price of items sold at branch 1 versus branch 2 for that quantile. For example, here the lowest point in the left corner corresponds to the 0.03 quantile. (To aid in comparison, we also show a straight line that represents the case of when, for each given quantile, the unit price at each branch is the same. In addition, the darker points correspond to the data for Q_1, the median, and Q_3, respectively.) We see that at this quantile, the unit price of items sold at branch 1 was slightly less than that at branch 2. In other words, 3% of items sold at branch 1 were less than or equal to \$40, while 3% of items at branch 2 were less than or equal to \$42. At the highest quantile, we see that the unit price of items at branch 2 was slightly less than that at branch 1. In general, we note that there is a shift in the distribution of branch 1 with respect to branch 2 in that the unit prices of items sold at branch 1 tend to be lower than those at branch 2.

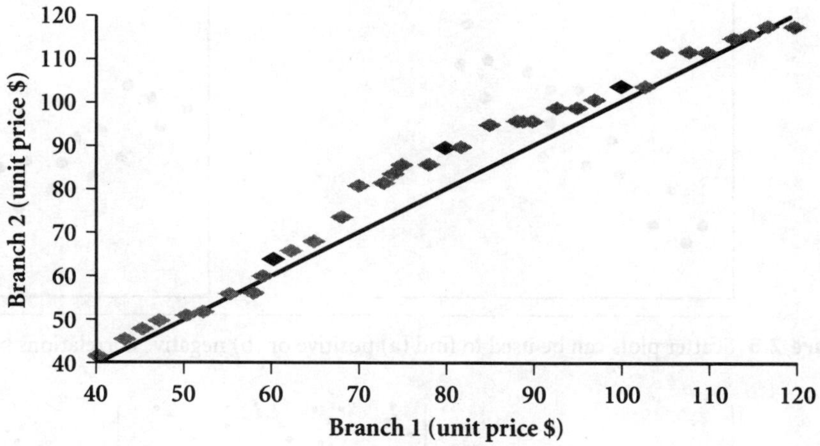

Figure 2.6 A quantile-quantile plot for unit price data from two different branches.

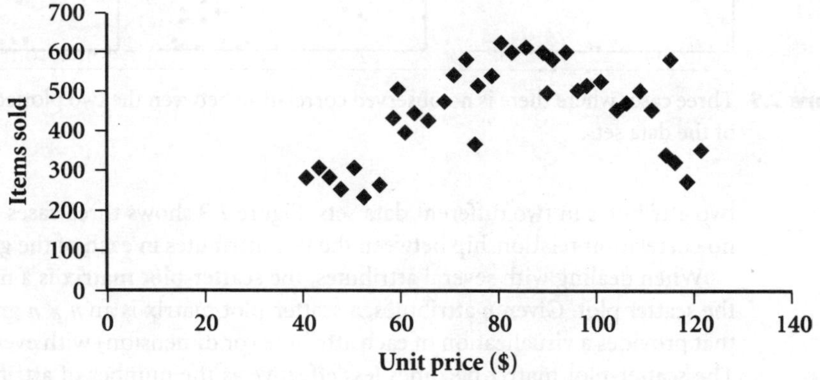

Figure 2.7 A scatter plot for the data set of Table 2.1.

A **scatter plot** is one of the most effective graphical methods for determining if there appears to be a relationship, pattern, or trend between two numerical attributes. To construct a scatter plot, each pair of values is treated as a pair of coordinates in an algebraic sense and plotted as points in the plane. Figure 2.7 shows a scatter plot for the set of data in Table 2.1. The scatter plot is a useful method for providing a first look at bivariate data to see clusters of points and outliers, or to explore the possibility of correlation relationships.[3] In Figure 2.8, we see examples of positive and negative correlations between

[3] A statistical test for correlation is given in Section 2.4.1 on data integration (Equation (2.8)).

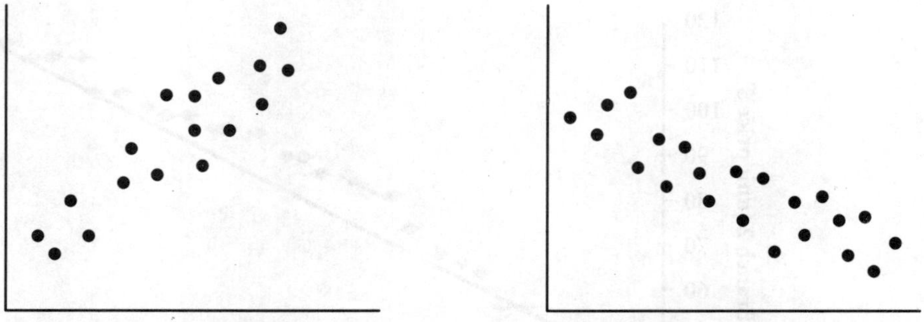

Figure 2.8 Scatter plots can be used to find (a) positive or (b) negative correlations between attributes.

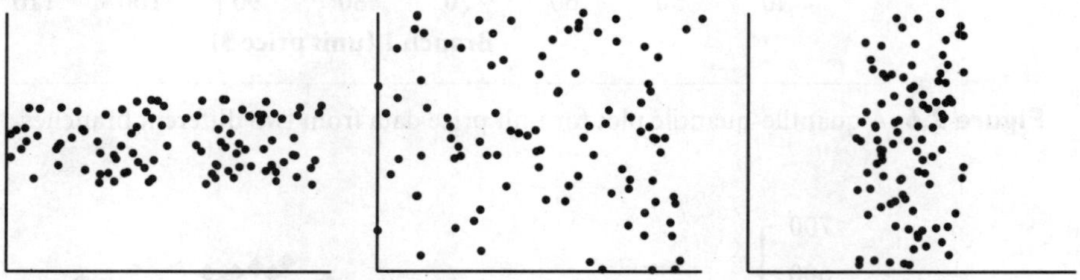

Figure 2.9 Three cases where there is no observed correlation between the two plotted attributes in each of the data sets.

two attributes in two different data sets. Figure 2.9 shows three cases for which there is no correlation relationship between the two attributes in each of the given data sets.

When dealing with several attributes, the **scatter-plot matrix** is a useful extension to the scatter plot. Given n attributes, a scatter-plot matrix is an $n \times n$ grid of scatter plots that provides a visualization of each attribute (or dimension) with every other attribute. The scatter-plot matrix becomes less effective as the number of attributes under study grows. In this case, user interactions such as zooming and panning become necessary to help interpret the individual scatter plots effectively.

A **loess curve** is another important exploratory graphic aid that adds a smooth curve to a scatter plot in order to provide better perception of the pattern of dependence. The word *loess* is short for "local regression." Figure 2.10 shows a loess curve for the set of data in Table 2.1.

To fit a loess curve, values need to be set for two parameters—α, a smoothing parameter, and λ, the degree of the polynomials that are fitted by the regression. While α can be any positive number (typical values are between 1/4 and 1), λ can be 1 or 2. The goal in choosing α is to produce a fit that is as smooth as possible without unduly distorting the underlying pattern in the data. The curve becomes smoother as α increases. There may be some lack of fit, however, indicating possible "missing" data patterns. If α is very small, the underlying pattern is tracked, yet overfitting of the data may occur where local "wiggles" in the curve may not be supported by the data. If the underlying pattern of the data has a

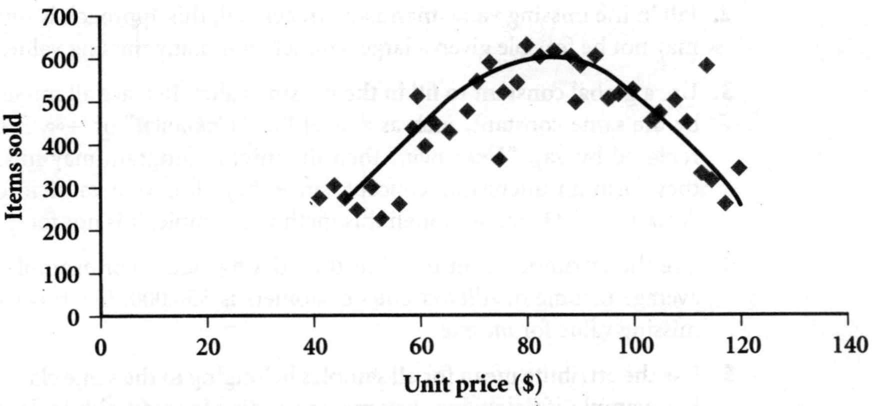

Figure 2.10 A loess curve for the data set of Table 2.1.

"gentle" curvature with no local maxima and minima, then local linear fitting is usually sufficient ($\lambda = 1$). However, if there are local maxima or minima, then local quadratic fitting ($\lambda = 2$) typically does a better job of following the pattern of the data and maintaining local smoothness.

In conclusion, descriptive data summaries provide valuable insight into the overall behavior of your data. By helping to identify noise and outliers, they are especially useful for data cleaning.

2.3 Data Cleaning

Real-world data tend to be incomplete, noisy, and inconsistent. *Data cleaning* (or *data cleansing*) routines attempt to fill in missing values, smooth out noise while identifying outliers, and correct inconsistencies in the data. In this section, you will study basic methods for data cleaning. Section 2.3.1 looks at ways of handling missing values. Section 2.3.2 explains data smoothing techniques. Section 2.3.3 discusses approaches to data cleaning as a process.

2.3.1 Missing Values

Imagine that you need to analyze *AllElectronics* sales and customer data. You note that many tuples have no recorded value for several attributes, such as customer *income*. How can you go about filling in the missing values for this attribute? Let's look at the following methods:

1. **Ignore the tuple**: This is usually done when the class label is missing (assuming the mining task involves classification). This method is not very effective, unless the tuple contains several attributes with missing values. It is especially poor when the percentage of missing values per attribute varies considerably.

2. **Fill in the missing value manually**: In general, this approach is time-consuming and may not be feasible given a large data set with many missing values.
3. **Use a global constant to fill in the missing value**: Replace all missing attribute values by the same constant, such as a label like "*Unknown*" or $-\infty$. If missing values are replaced by, say, "*Unknown,*" then the mining program may mistakenly think that they form an interesting concept, since they all have a value in common—that of "*Unknown.*" Hence, although this method is simple, it is not foolproof.
4. **Use the attribute mean to fill in the missing value**: For example, suppose that the average income of *AllElectronics* customers is \$56,000. Use this value to replace the missing value for *income*.
5. **Use the attribute mean for all samples belonging to the same class as the given tuple**: For example, if classifying customers according to *credit_risk*, replace the missing value with the average *income* value for customers in the same credit risk category as that of the given tuple.
6. **Use the most probable value to fill in the missing value**: This may be determined with regression, inference-based tools using a Bayesian formalism, or decision tree induction. For example, using the other customer attributes in your data set, you may construct a decision tree to predict the missing values for *income*. Decision trees, regression, and Bayesian inference are described in detail in Chapter 6.

Methods 3 to 6 bias the data. The filled-in value may not be correct. Method 6, however, is a popular strategy. In comparison to the other methods, it uses the most information from the present data to predict missing values. By considering the values of the other attributes in its estimation of the missing value for *income*, there is a greater chance that the relationships between *income* and the other attributes are preserved.

It is important to note that, in some cases, a missing value may not imply an error in the data! For example, when applying for a credit card, candidates may be asked to supply their driver's license number. Candidates who do not have a driver's license may naturally leave this field blank. Forms should allow respondents to specify values such as "not applicable". Software routines may also be used to uncover other null values, such as "don't know", "?", or "none". Ideally, each attribute should have one or more rules regarding the *null* condition. The rules may specify whether or not nulls are allowed, and/or how such values should be handled or transformed. Fields may also be intentionally left blank if they are to be provided in a later step of the business process. Hence, although we can try our best to clean the data after it is seized, good design of databases and of data entry procedures should help minimize the number of missing values or errors in the first place.

2.3.2 Noisy Data

"*What is noise?*" Noise is a random error or variance in a measured variable. Given a numerical attribute such as, say, *price*, how can we "smooth" out the data to remove the noise? Let's look at the following data smoothing techniques:

Sorted data for *price* (in dollars): 4, 8, 15, 21, 21, 24, 25, 28, 34

Partition into (equal-frequency) bins:

Bin 1: 4, 8, 15
Bin 2: 21, 21, 24
Bin 3: 25, 28, 34

Smoothing by bin means:

Bin 1: 9, 9, 9
Bin 2: 22, 22, 22
Bin 3: 29, 29, 29

Smoothing by bin boundaries:

Bin 1: 4, 4, 15
Bin 2: 21, 21, 24
Bin 3: 25, 25, 34

Figure 2.11 Binning methods for data smoothing.

1. **Binning:** Binning methods smooth a sorted data value by consulting its "neighborhood," that is, the values around it. The sorted values are distributed into a number of "buckets," or *bins*. Because binning methods consult the neighborhood of values, they perform *local* smoothing. Figure 2.11 illustrates some binning techniques. In this example, the data for *price* are first sorted and then partitioned into *equal-frequency* bins of size 3 (i.e., each bin contains three values). In **smoothing by bin means**, each value in a bin is replaced by the mean value of the bin. For example, the mean of the values 4, 8, and 15 in Bin 1 is 9. Therefore, each original value in this bin is replaced by the value 9. Similarly, **smoothing by bin medians** can be employed, in which each bin value is replaced by the bin median. In **smoothing by bin boundaries**, the minimum and maximum values in a given bin are identified as the *bin boundaries*. Each bin value is then replaced by the closest boundary value. In general, the larger the width, the greater the effect of the smoothing. Alternatively, bins may be *equal-width*, where the interval range of values in each bin is constant. Binning is also used as a discretization technique and is further discussed in Section 2.6.
2. **Regression:** Data can be smoothed by fitting the data to a function, such as with regression. *Linear regression* involves finding the "best" line to fit two attributes (or variables), so that one attribute can be used to predict the other. *Multiple linear regression* is an extension of linear regression, where more than two attributes are involved and the data are fit to a multidimensional surface. Regression is further described in Section 2.5.4, as well as in Chapter 6.

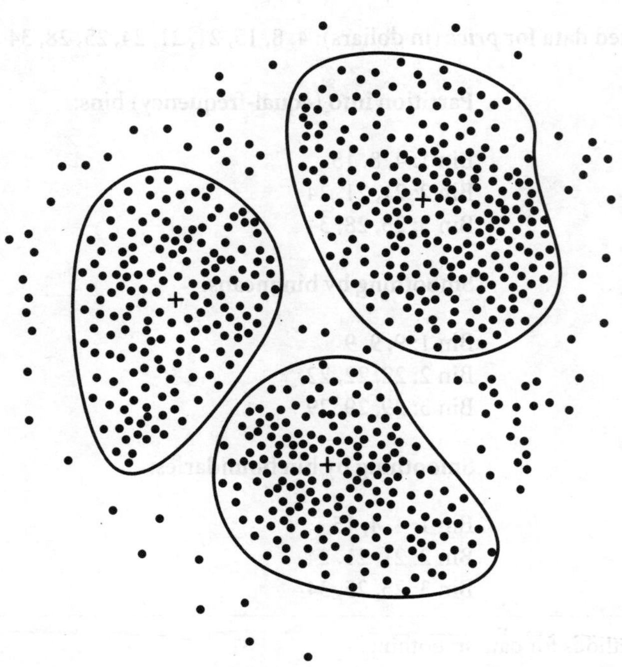

Figure 2.12 A 2-D plot of customer data with respect to customer locations in a city, showing three data clusters. Each cluster centroid is marked with a "+", representing the average point in space for that cluster. Outliers may be detected as values that fall outside of the sets of clusters.

3. **Clustering:** Outliers may be detected by clustering, where similar values are organized into groups, or "clusters." Intuitively, values that fall outside of the set of clusters may be considered outliers (Figure 2.12). Chapter 7 is dedicated to the topic of clustering and outlier analysis.

Many methods for data smoothing are also methods for data reduction involving discretization. For example, the binning techniques described above reduce the number of distinct values per attribute. This acts as a form of data reduction for logic-based data mining methods, such as decision tree induction, which repeatedly make value comparisons on sorted data. Concept hierarchies are a form of data discretization that can also be used for data smoothing. A concept hierarchy for *price*, for example, may map real *price* values into *inexpensive*, *moderately_priced*, and *expensive*, thereby reducing the number of data values to be handled by the mining process. Data discretization is discussed in Section 2.6. Some methods of classification, such as neural networks, have built-in data smoothing mechanisms. Classification is the topic of Chapter 6.

2.3.3 Data Cleaning as a Process

Missing values, noise, and inconsistencies contribute to inaccurate data. So far, we have looked at techniques for handling missing data and for smoothing data. *"But data cleaning is a big job. What about data cleaning as a process? How exactly does one proceed in tackling this task? Are there any tools out there to help?"*

The first step in data cleaning as a process is *discrepancy detection*. Discrepancies can be caused by several factors, including poorly designed data entry forms that have many optional fields, human error in data entry, deliberate errors (e.g., respondents not wanting to divulge information about themselves), and data decay (e.g., outdated addresses). Discrepancies may also arise from inconsistent data representations and the inconsistent use of codes. Errors in instrumentation devices that record data, and system errors, are another source of discrepancies. Errors can also occur when the data are (inadequately) used for purposes other than originally intended. There may also be inconsistencies due to data integration (e.g., where a given attribute can have different names in different databases).[4]

"So, how can we proceed with discrepancy detection?" As a starting point, use any knowledge you may already have regarding properties of the data. Such knowledge or "data about data" is referred to as **metadata**. For example, what are the domain and data type of each attribute? What are the acceptable values for each attribute? What is the range of the length of values? Do all values fall within the expected range? Are there any known dependencies between attributes? The descriptive data summaries presented in Section 2.2 are useful here for grasping data trends and identifying anomalies. For example, values that are more than two standard deviations away from the mean for a given attribute may be flagged as potential outliers. In this step, you may write your own scripts and/or use some of the tools that we discuss further below. From this, you may find noise, outliers, and unusual values that need investigation.

As a data analyst, you should be on the lookout for the inconsistent use of codes and any inconsistent data representations (such as "2004/12/25" and "25/12/2004" for *date*). **Field overloading** is another source of errors that typically results when developers squeeze new attribute definitions into unused (bit) portions of already defined attributes (e.g., using an unused bit of an attribute whose value range uses only, say, 31 out of 32 bits).

The data should also be examined regarding unique rules, consecutive rules, and null rules. A **unique rule** says that each value of the given attribute must be different from all other values for that attribute. A **consecutive rule** says that there can be no missing values between the lowest and highest values for the attribute, and that all values must also be unique (e.g., as in check numbers). A **null rule** specifies the use of blanks, question marks, special characters, or other strings that may indicate the null condition (e.g., where a value for a given attribute is not available), and how such values should be handled. As mentioned in Section 2.3.1, reasons for missing values may include (1) the person originally asked to provide a value for the attribute refuses and/or finds

[4]Data integration and the removal of redundant data that can result from such integration are further described in Section 2.4.1.

that the information requested is not applicable (e.g., a *license-number* attribute left blank by nondrivers); (2) the data entry person does not know the correct value; or (3) the value is to be provided by a later step of the process. The null rule should specify how to record the null condition, for example, such as to store zero for numerical attributes, a blank for character attributes, or any other conventions that may be in use (such as that entries like "don't know" or "?" should be transformed to blank).

There are a number of different commercial tools that can aid in the step of discrepancy detection. **Data scrubbing tools** use simple domain knowledge (e.g., knowledge of postal addresses, and spell-checking) to detect errors and make corrections in the data. These tools rely on parsing and fuzzy matching techniques when cleaning data from multiple sources. **Data auditing tools** find discrepancies by analyzing the data to discover rules and relationships, and detecting data that violate such conditions. They are variants of data mining tools. For example, they may employ statistical analysis to find correlations, or clustering to identify outliers. They may also use the descriptive data summaries that were described in Section 2.2.

Some data inconsistencies may be corrected manually using external references. For example, errors made at data entry may be corrected by performing a paper trace. Most errors, however, will require *data transformations*. This is the second step in data cleaning as a process. That is, once we find discrepancies, we typically need to define and apply (a series of) transformations to correct them.

Commercial tools can assist in the data transformation step. **Data migration tools** allow simple transformations to be specified, such as to replace the string *"gender"* by *"sex"*. **ETL (extraction/transformation/loading) tools** allow users to specify transforms through a graphical user interface (GUI). These tools typically support only a restricted set of transforms so that, often, we may also choose to write custom scripts for this step of the data cleaning process.

The two-step process of discrepancy detection and data transformation (to correct discrepancies) iterates. This process, however, is error-prone and time-consuming. Some transformations may introduce more discrepancies. Some *nested discrepancies* may only be detected after others have been fixed. For example, a typo such as "20004" in a year field may only surface once all date values have been converted to a uniform format. Transformations are often done as a batch process while the user waits without feedback. Only after the transformation is complete can the user go back and check that no new anomalies have been created by mistake. Typically, numerous iterations are required before the user is satisfied. Any tuples that cannot be automatically handled by a given transformation are typically written to a file without any explanation regarding the reasoning behind their failure. As a result, the entire data cleaning process also suffers from a lack of interactivity.

New approaches to data cleaning emphasize increased interactivity. Potter's Wheel, for example, is a publicly available data cleaning tool (see *http://control.cs.berkeley.edu/abc*) that integrates discrepancy detection and transformation. Users gradually build a series of transformations by composing and debugging individual transformations, one step at a time, on a spreadsheet-like interface. The transformations can be specified graphically or by providing examples. Results are shown immediately on the records that are visible on the screen. The user can choose to undo the transformations, so that transformations that introduced additional errors can be "erased." The tool performs discrepancy checking automatically in the background on the latest transformed view of the data. Users can gradually develop and refine transformations as discrepancies are found, leading to more effective and efficient data cleaning.

Another approach to increased interactivity in data cleaning is the development of declarative languages for the specification of data transformation operators. Such work focuses on defining powerful extensions to SQL and algorithms that enable users to express data cleaning specifications efficiently.

As we discover more about the data, it is important to keep updating the metadata to reflect this knowledge. This will help speed up data cleaning on future versions of the same data store.

2.4 Data Integration and Transformation

Data mining often requires data integration—the merging of data from multiple data stores. The data may also need to be transformed into forms appropriate for mining. This section describes both data integration and data transformation.

2.4.1 Data Integration

It is likely that your data analysis task will involve *data integration*, which combines data from multiple sources into a coherent data store, as in data warehousing. These sources may include multiple databases, data cubes, or flat files.

There are a number of issues to consider during data integration. *Schema integration* and *object matching* can be tricky. How can equivalent real-world entities from multiple data sources be matched up? This is referred to as the **entity identification problem.** For example, how can the data analyst or the computer be sure that *customer_id* in one database and *cust_number* in another refer to the same attribute? Examples of metadata for each attribute include the name, meaning, data type, and range of values permitted for the attribute, and null rules for handling blank, zero, or null values (Section 2.3). Such metadata can be used to help avoid errors in schema integration. The metadata may also be used to help transform the data (e.g., where data codes for *pay_type* in one database may be *"H"* and "*S*", and *1* and *2* in another). Hence, this step also relates to data cleaning, as described earlier.

Redundancy is another important issue. An attribute (such as *annual revenue*, for instance) may be redundant if it can be "derived" from another attribute or set of attributes. Inconsistencies in attribute or dimension naming can also cause redundancies in the resulting data set.

Some redundancies can be detected by **correlation analysis.** Given two attributes, such analysis can measure how strongly one attribute implies the other, based on the available data. For numerical attributes, we can evaluate the correlation between two attributes, *A* and *B*, by computing the **correlation coefficient** (also known as *Pearson's product moment coefficient*, named after its inventer, Karl Pearson). This is

$$r_{A,B} = \frac{\sum_{i=1}^{N}(a_i - \bar{A})(b_i - \bar{B})}{N\sigma_A\sigma_B} = \frac{\sum_{i=1}^{N}(a_ib_i) - N\bar{A}\bar{B}}{N\sigma_A\sigma_B}, \tag{2.8}$$

where N is the number of tuples, a_i and b_i are the respective values of A and B in tuple i, $\bar{A}$ and $\bar{B}$ are the respective mean values of A and B, σ_A and σ_B are the respective standard deviations of A and B (as defined in Section 2.2.2), and $\Sigma(a_ib_i)$ is the sum of the AB cross-product (that is, for each tuple, the value for A is multiplied by the value for B in that tuple). Note that $-1 \leq r_{A,B} \leq +1$. If $r_{A,B}$ is greater than 0, then A and B are positively correlated, meaning that the values of A increase as the values of B increase. The higher the value, the stronger the correlation (i.e., the more each attribute implies the other). Hence, a higher value may indicate that A (or B) may be removed as a redundancy. If the resulting value is equal to 0, then A and B are independent and there is no correlation between them. If the resulting value is less than 0, then A and B are negatively correlated, where the values of one attribute increase as the values of the other attribute decrease. This means that each attribute discourages the other. Scatter plots can also be used to view correlations between attributes (Section 2.2.3).

Note that correlation does not imply causality. That is, if A and B are correlated, this does not necessarily imply that A causes B or that B causes A. For example, in analyzing a demographic database, we may find that attributes representing the number of hospitals and the number of car thefts in a region are correlated. This does not mean that one causes the other. Both are actually causally linked to a third attribute, namely, *population*.

For categorical (discrete) data, a correlation relationship between two attributes, A and B, can be discovered by a χ^2 (**chi-square**) test. Suppose A has c distinct values, namely $a_1, a_2, \ldots a_c$. B has r distinct values, namely $b_1, b_2, \ldots b_r$. The data tuples described by A and B can be shown as a **contingency table,** with the c values of A making up the columns and the r values of B making up the rows. Let (A_i, B_j) denote the event that attribute A takes on value a_i and attribute B takes on value b_j, that is, where $(A = a_i, B = b_j)$. Each and every possible (A_i, B_j) joint event has its own cell (or slot) in the table. The χ^2 value (also known as the *Pearson* χ^2 *statistic*) is computed as:

$$\chi^2 = \sum_{i=1}^{c}\sum_{j=1}^{r}\frac{(o_{ij} - e_{ij})^2}{e_{ij}}, \tag{2.9}$$

where o_{ij} is the *observed frequency* (i.e., actual count) of the joint event (A_i, B_j) and e_{ij} is the *expected frequency* of (A_i, B_j), which can be computed as

$$e_{ij} = \frac{count(A = a_i) \times count(B = b_j)}{N}, \tag{2.10}$$

where N is the number of data tuples, $count(A = a_i)$ is the number of tuples having value a_i for A, and $count(B = b_j)$ is the number of tuples having value b_j for B. The sum in Equation (2.9) is computed over all of the $r \times c$ cells. Note that the cells that contribute the most to the χ^2 value are those whose actual count is very different from that expected.

Table 2.2 A 2×2 contingency table for the data of Example 2.1. Are *gender* and *preferred_Reading* correlated?

	male	*female*	Total
fiction	250 (90)	200 (360)	450
non_fiction	50 (210)	1000 (840)	1050
Total	300	1200	1500

The χ^2 statistic tests the hypothesis that A and B are independent. The test is based on a significance level, with $(r-1) \times (c-1)$ degrees of freedom. We will illustrate the use of this statistic in an example below. If the hypothesis can be rejected, then we say that A and B are statistically related or associated.

Let's look at a concrete example.

Example 2.1 **Correlation analysis of categorical attributes using χ^2.** Suppose that a group of 1,500 people was surveyed. The gender of each person was noted. Each person was polled as to whether their preferred type of reading material was fiction or nonfiction. Thus, we have two attributes, *gender* and *preferred_reading*. The observed frequency (or count) of each possible joint event is summarized in the contingency table shown in Table 2.2, where the numbers in parentheses are the expected frequencies (calculated based on the data distribution for both attributes using Equation (2.10)).

Using Equation (2.10), we can verify the expected frequencies for each cell. For example, the expected frequency for the cell (male, fiction) is

$$e_{11} = \frac{count(male) \times count(fiction)}{N} = \frac{300 \times 450}{1500} = 90,$$

and so on. Notice that in any row, the sum of the expected frequencies must equal the total observed frequency for that row, and the sum of the expected frequencies in any column must also equal the total observed frequency for that column. Using Equation (2.9) for χ^2 computation, we get

$$\begin{aligned}\chi^2 &= \frac{(250-90)^2}{90} + \frac{(50-210)^2}{210} + \frac{(200-360)^2}{360} + \frac{(1000-840)^2}{840} \\ &= 284.44 + 121.90 + 71.11 + 30.48 = 507.93.\end{aligned}$$

For this 2×2 table, the degrees of freedom are $(2-1)(2-1) = 1$. For 1 degree of freedom, the χ^2 value needed to reject the hypothesis at the 0.001 significance level is 10.828 (taken from the table of upper percentage points of the χ^2 distribution, typically available from any textbook on statistics). Since our computed value is above this, we can reject the hypothesis that *gender* and *preferred_reading* are independent and conclude that the two attributes are (strongly) correlated for the given group of people. ■

In addition to detecting redundancies between attributes, duplication should also be detected at the tuple level (e.g., where there are two or more identical tuples for a given unique data entry case). The use of denormalized tables (often done to improve performance by avoiding joins) is another source of data redundancy. Inconsistencies often arise between various duplicates, due to inaccurate data entry or updating some but not all of the occurrences of the data. For example, if a purchase order database contains attributes for the purchaser's name and address instead of a key to this information in a purchaser database, discrepancies can occur, such as the same purchaser's name appearing with different addresses within the purchase order database.

A third important issue in data integration is the *detection and resolution of data value conflicts*. For example, for the same real-world entity, attribute values from different sources may differ. This may be due to differences in representation, scaling, or encoding. For instance, a *weight* attribute may be stored in metric units in one system and British imperial units in another. For a hotel chain, the *price* of rooms in different cities may involve not only different currencies but also different services (such as free breakfast) and taxes. An attribute in one system may be recorded at a lower level of abstraction than the "same" attribute in another. For example, the *total_sales* in one database may refer to one branch of *All_Electronics*, while an attribute of the same name in another database may refer to the total sales for *All_Electronics* stores in a given region.

When matching attributes from one database to another during integration, special attention must be paid to the *structure* of the data. This is to ensure that any attribute functional dependencies and referential constraints in the source system match those in the target system. For example, in one system, a *discount* may be applied to the order, whereas in another system it is applied to each individual line item within the order. If this is not caught before integration, items in the target system may be improperly discounted.

The semantic heterogeneity and structure of data pose great challenges in data integration. Careful integration of the data from multiple sources can help reduce and avoid redundancies and inconsistencies in the resulting data set. This can help improve the accuracy and speed of the subsequent mining process.

2.4.2 Data Transformation

In *data transformation*, the data are transformed or consolidated into forms appropriate for mining. Data transformation can involve the following:

- **Smoothing**, which works to remove noise from the data. Such techniques include binning, regression, and clustering.
- **Aggregation**, where summary or aggregation operations are applied to the data. For example, the daily sales data may be aggregated so as to compute monthly and annual total amounts. This step is typically used in constructing a data cube for analysis of the data at multiple granularities.
- **Generalization** of the data, where low-level or "primitive" (raw) data are replaced by higher-level concepts through the use of concept hierarchies. For example, categorical

attributes, like *street*, can be generalized to higher-level concepts, like *city* or *country*. Similarly, values for numerical attributes, like *age*, may be mapped to higher-level concepts, like *youth, middle-aged*, and *senior*.

- **Normalization,** where the attribute data are scaled so as to fall within a small specified range, such as −1.0 to 1.0, or 0.0 to 1.0.
- **Attribute construction** (or *feature construction*), where new attributes are constructed and added from the given set of attributes to help the mining process.

Smoothing is a form of data cleaning and was addressed in Section 2.3.2. Section 2.3.3 on the data cleaning process also discussed ETL tools, where users specify transformations to correct data inconsistencies. Aggregation and generalization serve as forms of data reduction and are discussed in Sections 2.5 and 2.6, respectively. In this section, we therefore discuss normalization and attribute construction.

An attribute is normalized by scaling its values so that they fall within a small specified range, such as 0.0 to 1.0. Normalization is particularly useful for classification algorithms involving neural networks, or distance measurements such as nearest-neighbor classification and clustering. If using the neural network backpropagation algorithm for classification mining (Chapter 6), normalizing the input values for each attribute measured in the training tuples will help speed up the learning phase. For distance-based methods, normalization helps prevent attributes with initially large ranges (e.g., *income*) from outweighing attributes with initially smaller ranges (e.g., binary attributes). There are many methods for data normalization. We study three: *min-max normalization, z-score normalization*, and *normalization by decimal scaling*.

Min-max normalization performs a linear transformation on the original data. Suppose that min_A and max_A are the minimum and maximum values of an attribute, A. Min-max normalization maps a value, v, of A to v' in the range $[new\_min_A, new\_max_A]$ by computing

$$v' = \frac{v - min_A}{max_A - min_A}(new\_max_A - new\_min_A) + new\_min_A. \tag{2.11}$$

Min-max normalization preserves the relationships among the original data values. It will encounter an "out-of-bounds" error if a future input case for normalization falls outside of the original data range for A.

Example 2.2 Min-max normalization. Suppose that the minimum and maximum values for the attribute *income* are \$12,000 and \$98,000, respectively. We would like to map *income* to the range [0.0, 1.0]. By min-max normalization, a value of \$73,600 for *income* is transformed to $\frac{73,600-12,000}{98,000-12,000}(1.0-0)+0 = 0.716$. ■

In **z-score normalization** (or *zero-mean normalization*), the values for an attribute, A, are normalized based on the mean and standard deviation of A. A value, v, of A is normalized to v' by computing

$$v' = \frac{v - \bar{A}}{\sigma_A}, \tag{2.12}$$

where $\bar{A}$ and σ_A are the mean and standard deviation, respectively, of attribute A. This method of normalization is useful when the actual minimum and maximum of attribute A are unknown, or when there are outliers that dominate the min-max normalization.

Example 2.3 **z-score normalization** Suppose that the mean and standard deviation of the values for the attribute *income* are \$54,000 and \$16,000, respectively. With z-score normalization, a value of \$73,600 for *income* is transformed to $\frac{73,600-54,000}{16,000} = 1.225$. ■

Normalization by decimal scaling normalizes by moving the decimal point of values of attribute A. The number of decimal points moved depends on the maximum absolute value of A. A value, v, of A is normalized to v' by computing

$$v' = \frac{v}{10^j}, \tag{2.13}$$

where j is the smallest integer such that $Max(|v'|) < 1$.

Example 2.4 **Decimal scaling.** Suppose that the recorded values of A range from -986 to 917. The maximum absolute value of A is 986. To normalize by decimal scaling, we therefore divide each value by 1,000 (i.e., $j = 3$) so that -986 normalizes to -0.986 and 917 normalizes to 0.917. ■

Note that normalization can change the original data quite a bit, especially the latter two methods shown above. It is also necessary to save the normalization parameters (such as the mean and standard deviation if using z-score normalization) so that future data can be normalized in a uniform manner.

In **attribute construction**,[5] new attributes are constructed from the given attributes and added in order to help improve the accuracy and understanding of structure in high-dimensional data. For example, we may wish to add the attribute *area* based on the attributes *height* and *width*. By combining attributes, attribute construction can discover missing information about the relationships between data attributes that can be useful for knowledge discovery.

2.5 Data Reduction

Imagine that you have selected data from the *AllElectronics* data warehouse for analysis. The data set will likely be huge! Complex data analysis and mining on huge amounts of data can take a long time, making such analysis impractical or infeasible.

[5] In the machine learning literature, attribute construction is known as *feature construction*.

Data reduction techniques can be applied to obtain a reduced representation of the data set that is much smaller in volume, yet closely maintains the integrity of the original data. That is, mining on the reduced data set should be more efficient yet produce the same (or almost the same) analytical results.

Strategies for data reduction include the following:

1. **Data cube aggregation**, where aggregation operations are applied to the data in the construction of a data cube.
2. **Attribute subset selection**, where irrelevant, weakly relevant, or redundant attributes or dimensions may be detected and removed.
3. **Dimensionality reduction**, where encoding mechanisms are used to reduce the data set size.
4. **Numerosity reduction**, where the data are replaced or estimated by alternative, smaller data representations such as parametric models (which need store only the model parameters instead of the actual data) or nonparametric methods such as clustering, sampling, and the use of histograms.
5. **Discretization and concept hierarchy generation**, where raw data values for attributes are replaced by ranges or higher conceptual levels. Data discretization is a form of numerosity reduction that is very useful for the automatic generation of concept hierarchies. Discretization and concept hierarchy generation are powerful tools for data mining, in that they allow the mining of data at multiple levels of abstraction. We therefore defer the discussion of discretization and concept hierarchy generation to Section 2.6, which is devoted entirely to this topic.

Strategies 1 to 4 above are discussed in the remainder of this section. The computational time spent on data reduction should not outweigh or "erase" the time saved by mining on a reduced data set size.

2.5.1 Data Cube Aggregation

Imagine that you have collected the data for your analysis. These data consist of the *AllElectronics* sales per quarter, for the years 2002 to 2004. You are, however, interested in the annual sales (total per year), rather than the total per quarter. Thus the data can be *aggregated* so that the resulting data summarize the total sales per year instead of per quarter. This aggregation is illustrated in Figure 2.13. The resulting data set is smaller in volume, without loss of information necessary for the analysis task.

Data cubes are discussed in detail in Chapter 3 on data warehousing. We briefly introduce some concepts here. Data cubes store multidimensional aggregated information. For example, Figure 2.14 shows a data cube for multidimensional analysis of sales data with respect to annual sales per item type for each *AllElectronics* branch. Each cell holds an aggregate data value, corresponding to the data point in multidimensional space. (For readability, only some cell values are shown.) Concept

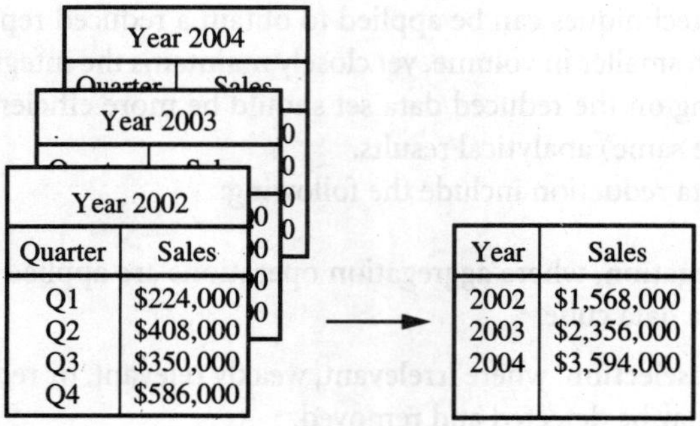

Figure 2.13 Sales data for a given branch of *AllElectronics* for the years 2002 to 2004. On the left, the sales are shown per quarter. On the right, the data are aggregated to provide the annual sales.

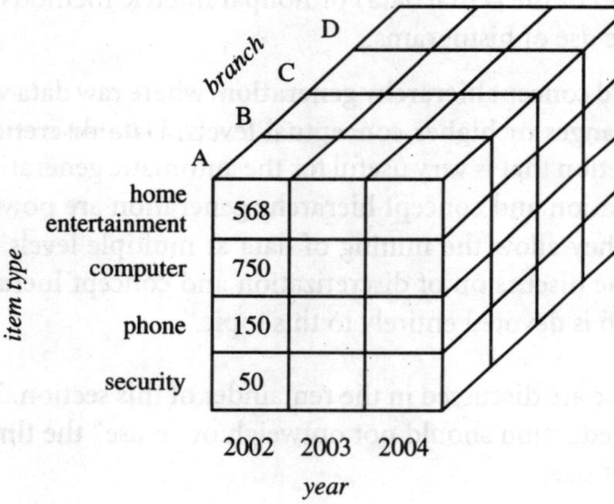

Figure 2.14 A data cube for sales at *AllElectronics*.

hierarchies may exist for each attribute, allowing the analysis of data at multiple levels of abstraction. For example, a hierarchy for *branch* could allow branches to be grouped into regions, based on their address. Data cubes provide fast access to precomputed, summarized data, thereby benefiting on-line analytical processing as well as data mining.

The cube created at the lowest level of abstraction is referred to as the *base cuboid.* The base cuboid should correspond to an individual entity of interest, such as *sales* or *customer.* In other words, the lowest level should be usable, or useful for the analysis. A cube at the highest level of abstraction is the *apex cuboid.* For the sales data of Figure 2.14, the apex cuboid would give one total—the total *sales* for all three years, for all item types, and for all branches. Data cubes created for varying levels of abstraction are often referred to as *cuboids*, so that a data cube may instead refer to a *lattice of cuboids*. Each higher level of abstraction further reduces the resulting data size. When replying to data mining requests, the *smallest* available cuboid relevant to the given task should be used. This issue is also addressed in Chapter 3.

2.5.2 Attribute Subset Selection

Data sets for analysis may contain hundreds of attributes, many of which may be irrelevant to the mining task or redundant. For example, if the task is to classify customers as to whether or not they are likely to purchase a popular new CD at *AllElectronics* when notified of a sale, attributes such as the customer's telephone number are likely to be irrelevant, unlike attributes such as *age* or *music_taste*. Although it may be possible for a domain expert to pick out some of the useful attributes, this can be a difficult and time-consuming task, especially when the behavior of the data is not well known (hence, a reason behind its analysis!). Leaving out relevant attributes or keeping irrelevant attributes may be detrimental, causing confusion for the mining algorithm employed. This can result in discovered patterns of poor quality. In addition, the added volume of irrelevant or redundant attributes can slow down the mining process.

Attribute subset selection[6] reduces the data set size by removing irrelevant or redundant attributes (or dimensions). The goal of attribute subset selection is to find a minimum set of attributes such that the resulting probability distribution of the data classes is as close as possible to the original distribution obtained using all attributes. Mining on a reduced set of attributes has an additional benefit. It reduces the number of attributes appearing in the discovered patterns, helping to make the patterns easier to understand.

"How can we find a 'good' subset of the original attributes?" For n attributes, there are 2^n possible subsets. An exhaustive search for the optimal subset of attributes can be prohibitively expensive, especially as n and the number of data classes increase. Therefore, heuristic methods that explore a reduced search space are commonly used for attribute subset selection. These methods are typically **greedy** in that, while searching through attribute space, they always make what looks to be the best choice at the time. Their strategy is to make a locally optimal choice in the hope that this will lead to a globally optimal solution. Such greedy methods are effective in practice and may come close to estimating an optimal solution.

The "best" (and "worst") attributes are typically determined using tests of statistical significance, which assume that the attributes are independent of one another. Many

[6] In machine learning, attribute subset selection is known as *feature subset selection*.

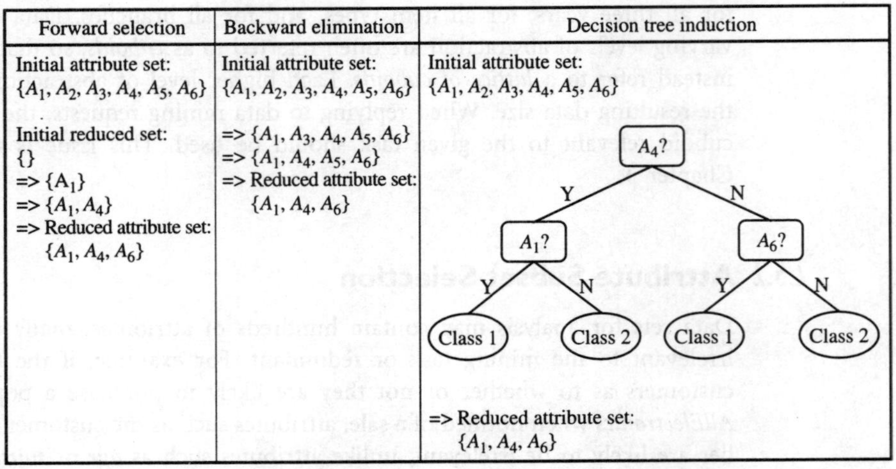

Figure 2.15 Greedy (heuristic) methods for attribute subset selection.

other attribute evaluation measures can be used, such as the *information gain* measure used in building decision trees for classification.[7]

Basic heuristic methods of attribute subset selection include the following techniques, some of which are illustrated in Figure 2.15.

1. **Stepwise forward selection:** The procedure starts with an empty set of attributes as the reduced set. The best of the original attributes is determined and added to the reduced set. At each subsequent iteration or step, the best of the remaining original attributes is added to the set.
2. **Stepwise backward elimination:** The procedure starts with the full set of attributes. At each step, it removes the worst attribute remaining in the set.
3. **Combination of forward selection and backward elimination:** The stepwise forward selection and backward elimination methods can be combined so that, at each step, the procedure selects the best attribute and removes the worst from among the remaining attributes.
4. **Decision tree induction:** Decision tree algorithms, such as ID3, C4.5, and CART, were originally intended for classification. Decision tree induction constructs a flowchart-like structure where each internal (nonleaf) node denotes a test on an attribute, each branch corresponds to an outcome of the test, and each external (leaf) node denotes a

[7] The information gain measure is described in detail in Chapter 6. It is briefly described in Section 2.6.1 with respect to attribute discretization.

class prediction. At each node, the algorithm chooses the "best" attribute to partition the data into individual classes.

When decision tree induction is used for attribute subset selection, a tree is constructed from the given data. All attributes that do not appear in the tree are assumed to be irrelevant. The set of attributes appearing in the tree form the reduced subset of attributes.

The stopping criteria for the methods may vary. The procedure may employ a threshold on the measure used to determine when to stop the attribute selection process.

2.5.3 Dimensionality Reduction

In *dimensionality reduction*, data encoding or transformations are applied so as to obtain a reduced or "compressed" representation of the original data. If the original data can be *reconstructed* from the compressed data without any loss of information, the data reduction is called **lossless**. If, instead, we can reconstruct only an approximation of the original data, then the data reduction is called **lossy**. There are several well-tuned algorithms for string compression. Although they are typically lossless, they allow only limited manipulation of the data. In this section, we instead focus on two popular and effective methods of lossy dimensionality reduction: *wavelet transforms* and *principal components analysis*.

Wavelet Transforms

The **discrete wavelet transform** (DWT) is a linear signal processing technique that, when applied to a data vector $\boldsymbol{X}$, transforms it to a numerically different vector, $\boldsymbol{X}'$, of **wavelet coefficients**. The two vectors are of the same length. When applying this technique to data reduction, we consider each tuple as an n-dimensional data vector, that is, $\boldsymbol{X} = (x_1, x_2, \ldots, x_n)$, depicting n measurements made on the tuple from n database attributes.[8]

"How can this technique be useful for data reduction if the wavelet transformed data are of the same length as the original data?" The usefulness lies in the fact that the wavelet transformed data can be truncated. A compressed approximation of the data can be retained by storing only a small fraction of the strongest of the wavelet coefficients. For example, all wavelet coefficients larger than some user-specified threshold can be retained. All other coefficients are set to 0. The resulting data representation is therefore very sparse, so that operations that can take advantage of data sparsity are computationally very fast if performed in wavelet space. The technique also works to remove noise without smoothing out the main features of the data, making it effective for data cleaning as well. Given a set of coefficients, an approximation of the original data can be constructed by applying the *inverse* of the DWT used.

[8] In our notation, any variable representing a vector is shown in bold italic font; measurements depicting the vector are shown in italic font.

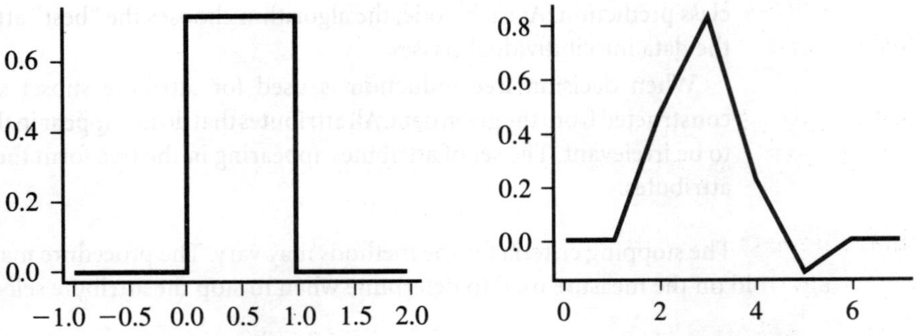

(a) Haar-2 (b) Daubechies-4

Figure 2.16 Examples of wavelet families. The number next to a wavelet name is the number of *vanishing moments* of the wavelet. This is a set of mathematical relationships that the coefficients must satisfy and is related to the number of coefficients.

The DWT is closely related to the *discrete Fourier transform (DFT)*, a signal processing technique involving sines and cosines. In general, however, the DWT achieves better lossy compression. That is, if the same number of coefficients is retained for a DWT and a DFT of a given data vector, the DWT version will provide a more accurate approximation of the original data. Hence, for an equivalent approximation, the DWT requires less space than the DFT. Unlike the DFT, wavelets are quite localized in space, contributing to the conservation of local detail.

There is only one DFT, yet there are several families of DWTs. Figure 2.16 shows some wavelet families. Popular wavelet transforms include the Haar-2, Daubechies-4, and Daubechies-6 transforms. The general procedure for applying a discrete wavelet transform uses a hierarchical *pyramid algorithm* that halves the data at each iteration, resulting in fast computational speed. The method is as follows:

1. The length, L, of the input data vector must be an integer power of 2. This condition can be met by padding the data vector with zeros as necessary ($L \geq n$).
2. Each transform involves applying two functions. The first applies some data smoothing, such as a sum or weighted average. The second performs a weighted difference, which acts to bring out the detailed features of the data.
3. The two functions are applied to pairs of data points in X, that is, to all pairs of measurements (x_{2i}, x_{2i+1}). This results in two sets of data of length $L/2$. In general, these represent a smoothed or low-frequency version of the input data and the high-frequency content of it, respectively.
4. The two functions are recursively applied to the sets of data obtained in the previous loop, until the resulting data sets obtained are of length 2.
5. Selected values from the data sets obtained in the above iterations are designated the wavelet coefficients of the transformed data.

Equivalently, a matrix multiplication can be applied to the input data in order to obtain the wavelet coefficients, where the matrix used depends on the given DWT. The matrix must be **orthonormal**, meaning that the columns are unit vectors and are mutually orthogonal, so that the matrix inverse is just its transpose. Although we do not have room to discuss it here, this property allows the reconstruction of the data from the smooth and smooth-difference data sets. By factoring the matrix used into a product of a few sparse matrices, the resulting *"fast DWT"* algorithm has a complexity of $O(n)$ for an input vector of length n.

Wavelet transforms can be applied to multidimensional data, such as a data cube. This is done by first applying the transform to the first dimension, then to the second, and so on. The computational complexity involved is linear with respect to the number of cells in the cube. Wavelet transforms give good results on sparse or skewed data and on data with ordered attributes. Lossy compression by wavelets is reportedly better than JPEG compression, the current commercial standard. Wavelet transforms have many real-world applications, including the compression of fingerprint images, computer vision, analysis of time-series data, and data cleaning.

Principal Components Analysis

In this subsection we provide an intuitive introduction to principal components analysis as a method of dimesionality reduction. A detailed theoretical explanation is beyond the scope of this book.

Suppose that the data to be reduced consist of tuples or data vectors described by n attributes or dimensions. **Principal components analysis,** or **PCA** (also called the Karhunen-Loeve, or K-L, method), searches for k n-dimensional orthogonal vectors that can best be used to represent the data, where $k \leq n$. The original data are thus projected onto a much smaller space, resulting in dimensionality reduction. Unlike attribute subset selection, which reduces the attribute set size by retaining a subset of the initial set of attributes, PCA "combines" the essence of attributes by creating an alternative, smaller set of variables. The initial data can then be projected onto this smaller set. PCA often reveals relationships that were not previously suspected and thereby allows interpretations that would not ordinarily result.

The basic procedure is as follows:

1. The input data are normalized, so that each attribute falls within the same range. This step helps ensure that attributes with large domains will not dominate attributes with smaller domains.

2. PCA computes k orthonormal vectors that provide a basis for the normalized input data. These are unit vectors that each point in a direction perpendicular to the others. These vectors are referred to as the *principal components*. The input data are a linear combination of the principal components.

3. The principal components are sorted in order of decreasing "significance" or strength. The principal components essentially serve as a new set of axes for the

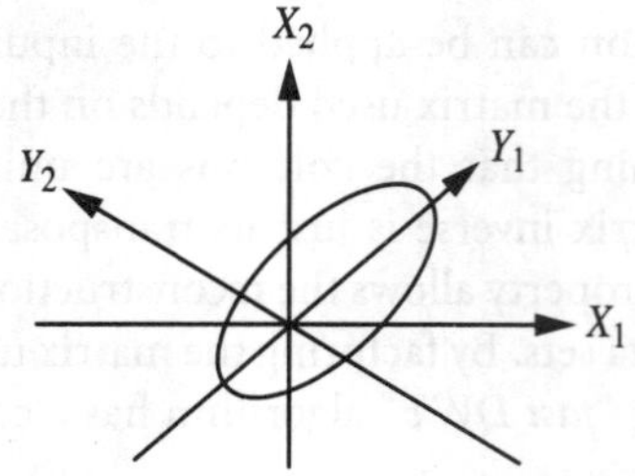

Figure 2.17 Principal components analysis. Y_1 and Y_2 are the first two principal components for the given data.

data, providing important information about variance. That is, the sorted axes are such that the first axis shows the most variance among the data, the second axis shows the next highest variance, and so on. For example, Figure 2.17 shows the first two principal components, Y_1 and Y_2, for the given set of data originally mapped to the axes X_1 and X_2. This information helps identify groups or patterns within the data.

4. Because the components are sorted according to decreasing order of "significance," the size of the data can be reduced by eliminating the weaker components, that is, those with low variance. Using the strongest principal components, it should be possible to reconstruct a good approximation of the original data.

PCA is computationally inexpensive, can be applied to ordered and unordered attributes, and can handle sparse data and skewed data. Multidimensional data of more than two dimensions can be handled by reducing the problem to two dimensions. Principal components may be used as inputs to multiple regression and cluster analysis. In comparison with wavelet transforms, PCA tends to be better at handling sparse data, whereas wavelet transforms are more suitable for data of high dimensionality.

2.5.4 Numerosity Reduction

"Can we reduce the data volume by choosing alternative, 'smaller' forms of data representation?" Techniques of *numerosity reduction* can indeed be applied for this purpose. These techniques may be parametric or nonparametric. For *parametric methods*, a model is used to estimate the data, so that typically only the data parameters need to be stored, instead of the actual data. (Outliers may also be stored.) Log-linear models, which estimate discrete multidimensional probability distributions, are an example. *Nonparametric methods* for storing reduced representations of the data include histograms, clustering, and sampling.

Let's look at each of the numerosity reduction techniques mentioned above.

Regression and Log-Linear Models

Regression and log-linear models can be used to approximate the given data. In (simple) **linear regression**, the data are modeled to fit a straight line. For example, a random variable, y (called a *response variable*), can be modeled as a linear function of another random variable, x (called a *predictor variable*), with the equation

$$y = wx + b, \tag{2.14}$$

where the variance of y is assumed to be constant. In the context of data mining, x and y are numerical database attributes. The coefficients, w and b (called *regression coefficients*), specify the slope of the line and the Y-intercept, respectively. These coefficients can be solved for by the *method of least squares*, which minimizes the error between the actual line separating the data and the estimate of the line. **Multiple linear regression** is an extension of (simple) linear regression, which allows a response variable, y, to be modeled as a linear function of two or more predictor variables.

Log-linear models approximate discrete multidimensional probability distributions. Given a set of tuples in n dimensions (e.g., described by n attributes), we can consider each tuple as a point in an n-dimensional space. Log-linear models can be used to estimate the probability of each point in a multidimensional space for a set of discretized attributes, based on a smaller subset of dimensional combinations. This allows a higher-dimensional data space to be constructed from lower-dimensional spaces. Log-linear models are therefore also useful for dimensionality reduction (since the lower-dimensional points together typically occupy less space than the original data points) and data smoothing (since aggregate estimates in the lower-dimensional space are less subject to sampling variations than the estimates in the higher-dimensional space).

Regression and log-linear models can both be used on sparse data, although their application may be limited. While both methods can handle skewed data, regression does exceptionally well. Regression can be computationally intensive when applied to high-dimensional data, whereas log-linear models show good scalability for up to 10 or so dimensions. Regression and log-linear models are further discussed in Section 6.11.

Histograms

Histograms use binning to approximate data distributions and are a popular form of data reduction. Histograms were introduced in Section 2.2.3. A **histogram** for an attribute, A, partitions the data distribution of A into disjoint subsets, or *buckets*. If each bucket represents only a single attribute-value/frequency pair, the buckets are called *singleton buckets*. Often, buckets instead represent continuous ranges for the given attribute.

Example 2.5 **Histograms.** The following data are a list of prices of commonly sold items at *AllElectronics* (rounded to the nearest dollar). The numbers have been sorted: 1, 1, 5, 5, 5, 5, 5, 8, 8, 10, 10, 10, 10, 12, 14, 14, 14, 15, 15, 15, 15, 15, 15, 18, 18, 18, 18, 18, 18, 18, 18, 20, 20, 20, 20, 20, 20, 20, 21, 21, 21, 21, 25, 25, 25, 25, 25, 28, 28, 30, 30, 30.

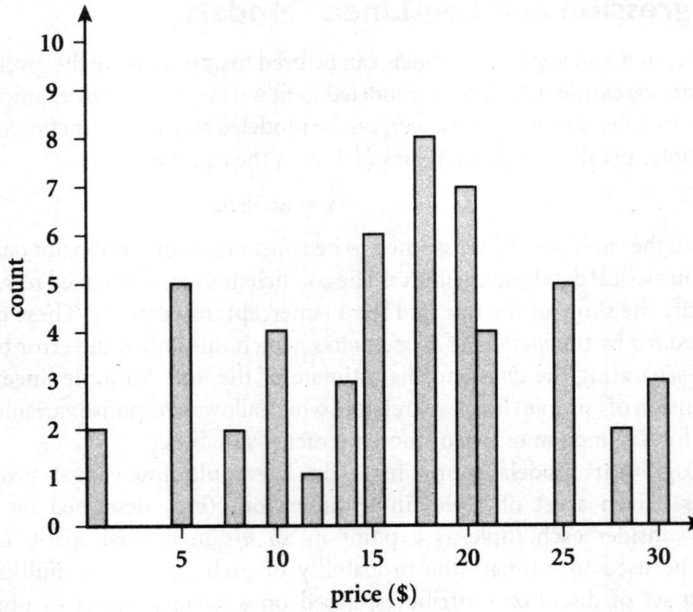

Figure 2.18 A histogram for *price* using singleton buckets—each bucket represents one price-value/frequency pair.

Figure 2.18 shows a histogram for the data using singleton buckets. To further reduce the data, it is common to have each bucket denote a continuous range of values for the given attribute. In Figure 2.19, each bucket represents a different $10 range for *price*. ■

"How are the buckets determined and the attribute values partitioned?" There are several partitioning rules, including the following:

- **Equal-width:** In an equal-width histogram, the width of each bucket range is uniform (such as the width of $10 for the buckets in Figure 2.19).
- **Equal-frequency** (or equidepth): In an equal-frequency histogram, the buckets are created so that, roughly, the frequency of each bucket is constant (that is, each bucket contains roughly the same number of contiguous data samples).
- **V-Optimal:** If we consider all of the possible histograms for a given number of buckets, the V-Optimal histogram is the one with the least variance. Histogram variance is a weighted sum of the original values that each bucket represents, where bucket weight is equal to the number of values in the bucket.
- **MaxDiff:** In a MaxDiff histogram, we consider the difference between each pair of adjacent values. A bucket boundary is established between each pair for pairs having the $\beta - 1$ largest differences, where β is the user-specified number of buckets.

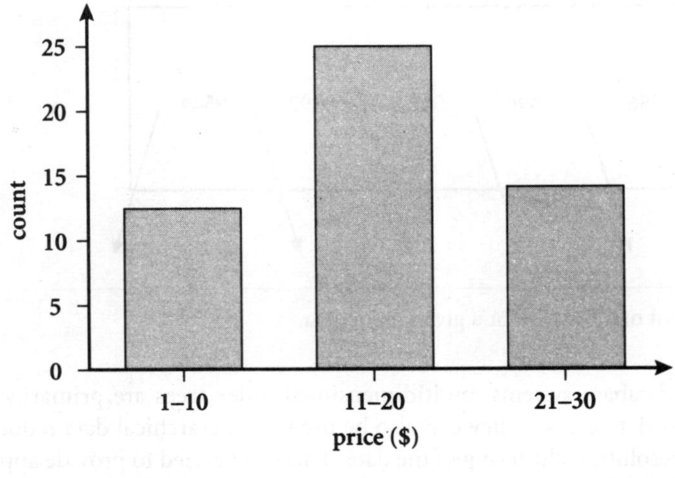

Figure 2.19 An equal-width histogram for *price*, where values are aggregated so that each bucket has a uniform width of $10.

V-Optimal and MaxDiff histograms tend to be the most accurate and practical. Histograms are highly effective at approximating both sparse and dense data, as well as highly skewed and uniform data. The histograms described above for single attributes can be extended for multiple attributes. *Multidimensional histograms* can capture dependencies between attributes. Such histograms have been found effective in approximating data with up to five attributes. More studies are needed regarding the effectiveness of multidimensional histograms for very high dimensions. Singleton buckets are useful for storing outliers with high frequency.

Clustering

Clustering techniques consider data tuples as objects. They partition the objects into groups or *clusters*, so that objects within a cluster are "similar" to one another and "dissimilar" to objects in other clusters. Similarity is commonly defined in terms of how "close" the objects are in space, based on a distance function. The "quality" of a cluster may be represented by its *diameter*, the maximum distance between any two objects in the cluster. *Centroid distance* is an alternative measure of cluster quality and is defined as the average distance of each cluster object from the cluster centroid (denoting the "average object," or average point in space for the cluster). Figure 2.12 of Section 2.3.2 shows a 2-D plot of customer data with respect to customer locations in a city, where the centroid of each cluster is shown with a "+". Three data clusters are visible.

In data reduction, the cluster representations of the data are used to replace the actual data. The effectiveness of this technique depends on the nature of the data. It is much more effective for data that can be organized into distinct clusters than for smeared data.

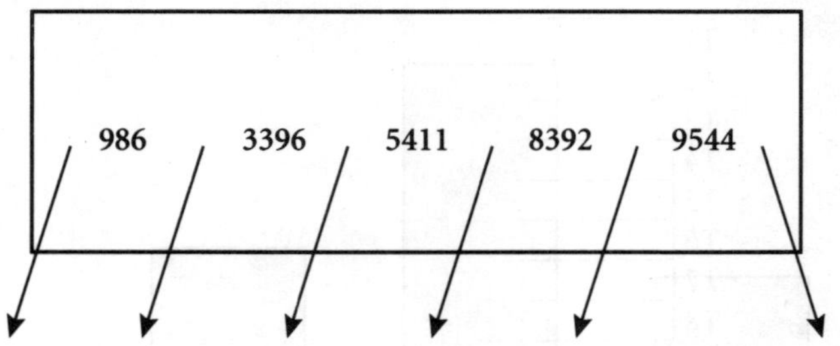

Figure 2.20 The root of a B+-tree for a given set of data.

In database systems, **multidimensional index trees** are primarily used for providing fast data access. They can also be used for hierarchical data reduction, providing a multiresolution clustering of the data. This can be used to provide approximate answers to queries. An index tree recursively partitions the multidimensional space for a given set of data objects, with the root node representing the entire space. Such trees are typically balanced, consisting of internal and leaf nodes. Each parent node contains keys and pointers to child nodes that, collectively, represent the space represented by the parent node. Each leaf node contains pointers to the data tuples they represent (or to the actual tuples).

An index tree can therefore store aggregate and detail data at varying levels of resolution or abstraction. It provides a hierarchy of clusterings of the data set, where each cluster has a label that holds for the data contained in the cluster. If we consider each child of a parent node as a bucket, then an index tree can be considered as a *hierarchical histogram*. For example, consider the root of a B+-tree as shown in Figure 2.20, with pointers to the data keys 986, 3396, 5411, 8392, and 9544. Suppose that the tree contains 10,000 tuples with keys ranging from 1 to 9999. The data in the tree can be approximated by an equal-frequency histogram of six buckets for the key ranges 1 to 985, 986 to 3395, 3396 to 5410, 5411 to 8391, 8392 to 9543, and 9544 to 9999. Each bucket contains roughly 10,000/6 items. Similarly, each bucket is subdivided into smaller buckets, allowing for aggregate data at a finer-detailed level. The use of multidimensional index trees as a form of data reduction relies on an ordering of the attribute values in each dimension. Two-dimensional or multidimensional index trees include R-trees, quad-trees, and their variations. They are well suited for handling both sparse and skewed data.

There are many measures for defining clusters and cluster quality. Clustering methods are further described in Chapter 7.

Sampling

Sampling can be used as a data reduction technique because it allows a large data set to be represented by a much smaller random sample (or subset) of the data. Suppose that a large data set, *D*, contains *N* tuples. Let's look at the most common ways that we could sample *D* for data reduction, as illustrated in Figure 2.21.

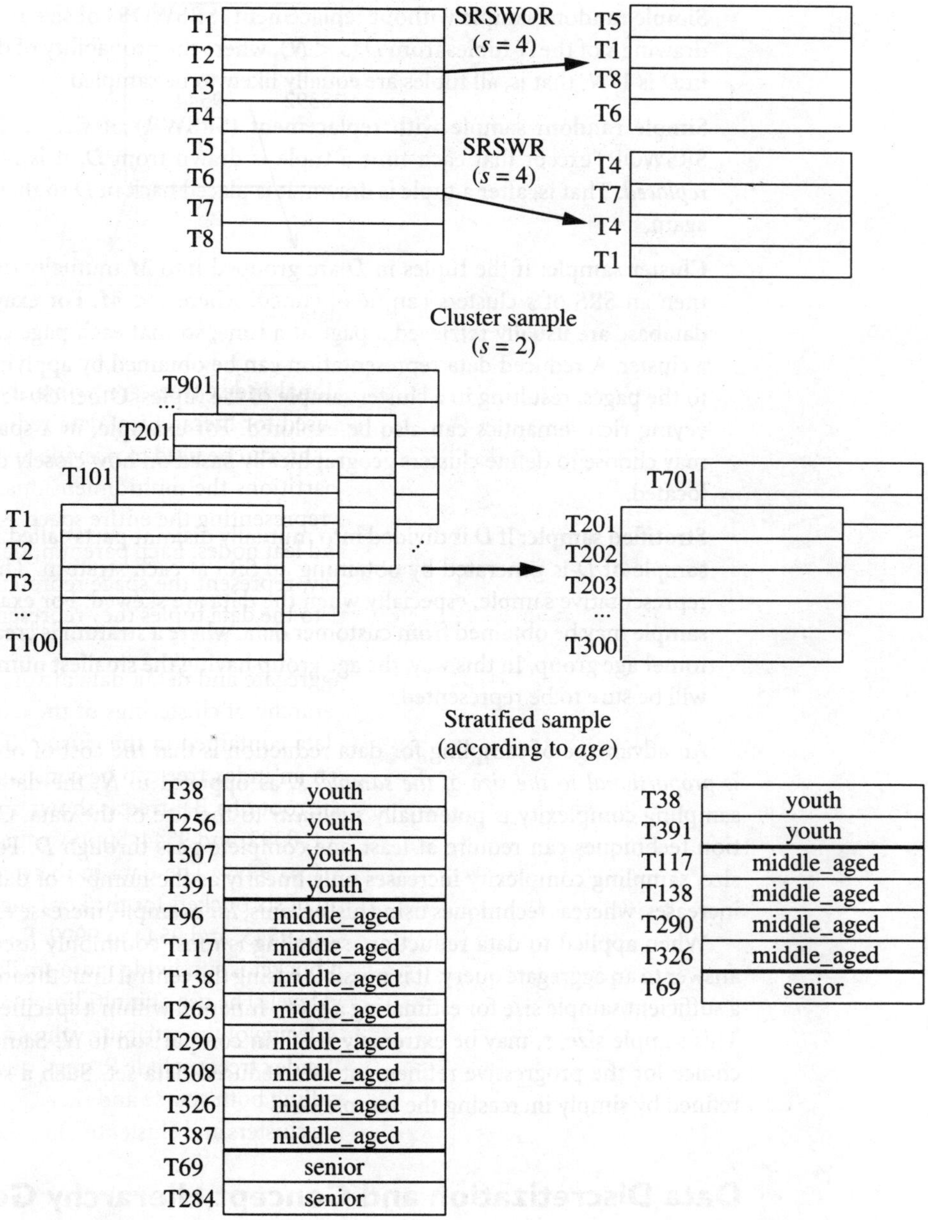

Figure 2.21 Sampling can be used for data reduction.

- **Simple random sample without replacement (SRSWOR) of size** s: This is created by drawing s of the N tuples from D ($s < N$), where the probability of drawing any tuple in D is $1/N$, that is, all tuples are equally likely to be sampled.
- **Simple random sample with replacement (SRSWR) of size** s: This is similar to SRSWOR, except that each time a tuple is drawn from D, it is recorded and then *replaced*. That is, after a tuple is drawn, it is placed back in D so that it may be drawn again.
- **Cluster sample**: If the tuples in D are grouped into M mutually disjoint "clusters," then an SRS of s clusters can be obtained, where $s < M$. For example, tuples in a database are usually retrieved a page at a time, so that each page can be considered a cluster. A reduced data representation can be obtained by applying, say, SRSWOR to the pages, resulting in a cluster sample of the tuples. Other clustering criteria conveying rich semantics can also be explored. For example, in a spatial database, we may choose to define clusters geographically based on how closely different areas are located.
- **Stratified sample:** If D is divided into mutually disjoint parts called *strata*, a stratified sample of D is generated by obtaining an SRS at each stratum. This helps ensure a representative sample, especially when the data are skewed. For example, a stratified sample may be obtained from customer data, where a stratum is created for each customer age group. In this way, the age group having the smallest number of customers will be sure to be represented.

An advantage of sampling for data reduction is that the cost of obtaining a sample *is proportional to the size of the sample*, s, as opposed to N, the data set size. Hence, sampling complexity is potentially *sublinear* to the size of the data. Other data reduction techniques can require at least one complete pass through D. For a fixed sample size, sampling complexity increases only linearly as the number of data dimensions, n, increases, whereas techniques using histograms, for example, increase exponentially in n.

When applied to data reduction, sampling is most commonly used to estimate the answer to an aggregate query. It is possible (using the central limit theorem) to determine a sufficient sample size for estimating a given function within a specified degree of error. This sample size, s, may be extremely small in comparison to N. Sampling is a natural choice for the progressive refinement of a reduced data set. Such a set can be further refined by simply increasing the sample size.

2.6 Data Discretization and Concept Hierarchy Generation

Data discretization techniques can be used to reduce the number of values for a given continuous attribute by dividing the range of the attribute into intervals. Interval labels can then be used to replace actual data values. Replacing numerous values of a continuous attribute by a small number of interval labels thereby reduces and simplifies the original data. This leads to a concise, easy-to-use, knowledge-level representation of mining results.

Discretization techniques can be categorized based on how the discretization is performed, such as whether it uses class information or which direction it proceeds (i.e., top-down vs. bottom-up). If the discretization process uses class information, then we say it is *supervised discretization*. Otherwise, it is *unsupervised*. If the process starts by first finding one or a few points (called *split points* or *cut points*) to split the entire attribute range, and then repeats this recursively on the resulting intervals, it is called *top-down discretization* or *splitting*. This contrasts with *bottom-up discretization* or *merging*, which starts by considering all of the continuous values as potential split-points, removes some by merging neighborhood values to form intervals, and then recursively applies this process to the resulting intervals. Discretization can be performed recursively on an attribute to provide a hierarchical or multiresolution partitioning of the attribute values, known as a concept hierarchy. Concept hierarchies are useful for mining at multiple levels of abstraction.

A concept hierarchy for a given numerical attribute defines a discretization of the attribute. Concept hierarchies can be used to reduce the data by collecting and replacing low-level concepts (such as numerical values for the attribute *age*) with higher-level concepts (such as *youth, middle-aged*, or *senior*). Although detail is lost by such data generalization, the generalized data may be more meaningful and easier to interpret. This contributes to a consistent representation of data mining results among multiple mining tasks, which is a common requirement. In addition, mining on a reduced data set requires fewer input/output operations and is more efficient than mining on a larger, ungeneralized data set. Because of these benefits, discretization techniques and concept hierarchies are typically applied before data mining as a preprocessing step, rather than during mining. An example of a concept hierarchy for the attribute *price* is given in Figure 2.22. More than one concept hierarchy can be defined for the same attribute in order to accommodate the needs of various users.

Manual definition of concept hierarchies can be a tedious and time-consuming task for a user or a domain expert. Fortunately, several discretization methods can be used to automatically generate or dynamically refine concept hierarchies for numerical attributes. Furthermore, many hierarchies for categorical attributes are

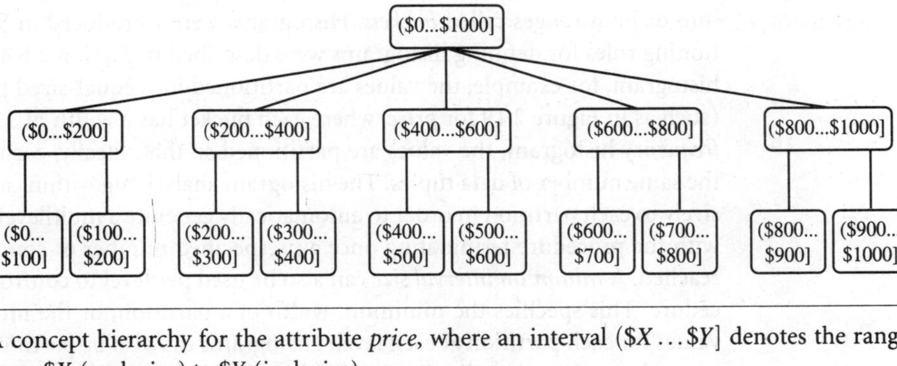

Figure 2.22 A concept hierarchy for the attribute *price*, where an interval ($\$X \ldots \$Y$] denotes the range from $\$X$ (exclusive) to $\$Y$ (inclusive).

implicit within the database schema and can be automatically defined at the schema definition level.

Let's look at the generation of concept hierarchies for numerical and categorical data.

2.6.1 Discretization and Concept Hierarchy Generation for Numerical Data

It is difficult and laborious to specify concept hierarchies for numerical attributes because of the wide diversity of possible data ranges and the frequent updates of data values. Such manual specification can also be quite arbitrary.

Concept hierarchies for numerical attributes can be constructed automatically based on data discretization. We examine the following methods: *binning*, *histogram analysis*, *entropy-based discretization*, χ^2*-merging*, *cluster analysis*, and *discretization by intuitive partitioning*. In general, each method assumes that the values to be discretized are sorted in ascending order.

Binning

Binning is a top-down splitting technique based on a specified number of bins. Section 2.3.2 discussed binning methods for data smoothing. These methods are also used as discretization methods for numerosity reduction and concept hierarchy generation. For example, attribute values can be discretized by applying equal-width or equal-frequency binning, and then replacing each bin value by the bin mean or median, as in *smoothing by bin means* or *smoothing by bin medians*, respectively. These techniques can be applied recursively to the resulting partitions in order to generate concept hierarchies. Binning does not use class information and is therefore an unsupervised discretization technique. It is sensitive to the user-specified number of bins, as well as the presence of outliers.

Histogram Analysis

Like binning, histogram analysis is an unsupervised discretization technique because it does not use class information. Histograms partition the values for an attribute, A, into disjoint ranges called *buckets*. Histograms were introduced in Section 2.2.3. Partitioning rules for defining histograms were described in Section 2.5.4. In an *equal-width* histogram, for example, the values are partitioned into equal-sized partitions or ranges (such as in Figure 2.19 for *price*, where each bucket has a width of \$10). With an *equal-frequency* histogram, the values are partitioned so that, ideally, each partition contains the same number of data tuples. The histogram analysis algorithm can be applied recursively to each partition in order to automatically generate a multilevel concept hierarchy, with the procedure terminating once a prespecified number of concept levels has been reached. A *minimum interval size* can also be used per level to control the recursive procedure. This specifies the minimum width of a partition, or the minimum number of values for each partition at each level. Histograms can also be partitioned based on cluster analysis of the data distribution, as described below.

Entropy-Based Discretization

Entropy is one of the most commonly used discretization measures. It was first introduced by Claude Shannon in pioneering work on information theory and the concept of information gain. Entropy-based discretization is a supervised, top-down splitting technique. It explores class distribution information in its calculation and determination of split-points (data values for partitioning an attribute range). To discretize a numerical attribute, A, the method selects the value of A that has the minimum entropy as a split-point, and recursively partitions the resulting intervals to arrive at a hierarchical discretization. Such discretization forms a concept hierarchy for A.

Let D consist of data tuples defined by a set of attributes and a class-label attribute. The class-label attribute provides the class information per tuple. The basic method for entropy-based discretization of an attribute A within the set is as follows:

1. Each value of A can be considered as a potential interval boundary or split-point (denoted *split_point*) to partition the range of A. That is, a split-point for A can partition the tuples in D into two subsets satisfying the conditions $A \leq split\_point$ and $A > split\_point$, respectively, thereby creating a binary discretization.
2. Entropy-based discretization, as mentioned above, uses information regarding the class label of tuples. To explain the intuition behind entropy-based discretization, we must take a glimpse at classification. Suppose we want to classify the tuples in D by partitioning on attribute A and some split-point. Ideally, we would like this partitioning to result in an exact classification of the tuples. For example, if we had two classes, we would hope that all of the tuples of, say, class C_1 will fall into one partition, and all of the tuples of class C_2 will fall into the other partition. However, this is unlikely. For example, the first partition may contain many tuples of C_1, but also some of C_2. How much more information would we still need for a perfect classification, after this partitioning? This amount is called the *expected information requirement* for classifying a tuple in D based on partitioning by A. It is given by

$$Info_A(D) = \frac{|D_1|}{|D|}Entropy(D_1) + \frac{|D_2|}{|D|}Entropy(D_2), \tag{2.15}$$

where D_1 and D_2 correspond to the tuples in D satisfying the conditions $A \leq split\_point$ and $A > split\_point$, respectively; $|D|$ is the number of tuples in D, and so on. The entropy function for a given set is calculated based on the class distribution of the tuples in the set. For example, given m classes, $C_1, C_2, \ldots, C_m$, the entropy of D_1 is

$$Entropy(D_1) = -\sum_{i=1}^{m} p_i \log_2(p_i), \tag{2.16}$$

where p_i is the probability of class C_i in D_1, determined by dividing the number of tuples of class C_i in D_1 by $|D_1|$, the total number of tuples in D_1. Therefore, when selecting a split-point for attribute A, we want to pick the attribute value that gives the minimum expected information requirement (i.e., $\min(Info_A(D))$). This would result in the minimum amount of expected information (still) required to perfectly classify the tuples after partitioning by $A \leq split\_point$ and $A > split\_point$. This is equivalent to the attribute-value pair with the maximum information gain (the further details of which are given in Chapter 6 on classification.) Note that the value of $Entropy(D_2)$ can be computed similarly as in Equation (2.16).

"But our task is discretization, not classification!", you may exclaim. This is true. We use the split-point to partition the range of A into two intervals, corresponding to $A \leq split\_point$ and $A > split\_point$.

3. The process of determining a split-point is recursively applied to each partition obtained, until some stopping criterion is met, such as when the minimum information requirement on all candidate split-points is less than a small threshold, ε, or when the number of intervals is greater than a threshold, *max_interval*.

Entropy-based discretization can reduce data size. Unlike the other methods mentioned here so far, entropy-based discretization uses class information. This makes it more likely that the interval boundaries (split-points) are defined to occur in places that may help improve classification accuracy. The entropy and information gain measures described here are also used for decision tree induction. These measures are revisited in greater detail in Section 6.3.2.

Interval Merging by χ^2 Analysis

ChiMerge is a χ^2-based discretization method. The discretization methods that we have studied up to this point have all employed a top-down, splitting strategy. This contrasts with ChiMerge, which employs a bottom-up approach by finding the best neighboring intervals and then merging these to form larger intervals, recursively. The method is supervised in that it uses class information. The basic notion is that for accurate discretization, the relative class frequencies should be fairly consistent within an interval. Therefore, if two adjacent intervals have a very similar distribution of classes, then the intervals can be merged. Otherwise, they should remain separate.

ChiMerge proceeds as follows. Initially, each distinct value of a numerical attribute A is considered to be one interval. χ^2 tests are performed for every pair of adjacent intervals. Adjacent intervals with the least χ^2 values are merged together, because low χ^2 values for a pair indicate similar class distributions. This merging process proceeds recursively until a predefined stopping criterion is met.

The χ^2 statistic was introduced in Section 2.4.1 on data integration, where we explained its use to detect a correlation relationship between two categorical attributes (Equation (2.9)). Because ChiMerge treats intervals as discrete categories, Equation (2.9) can be applied. The χ^2 statistic tests the hypothesis that two adjacent intervals for a given attribute are independent of the class. Following the method in Example 2.1, we can construct a contingency table for our data. The contingency table has two columns (representing the two adjacent intervals) and m rows, where m is the number of distinct classes. Applying Equation (2.9) here, the cell value o_{ij} is the count of tuples in the ith interval and j^{th} class. Similarly, the expected frequency of o_{ij} is e_{ij} = (number of tuples in interval *i*) × (number of tuples in class *j*)/*N*, where *N* is the total number of data tuples. Low χ^2 values for an interval pair indicate that the intervals are independent of the class and can, therefore, be merged.

The stopping criterion is typically determined by three conditions. First, merging stops when χ^2 values of all pairs of adjacent intervals exceed some threshold, which is determined by a specified significance level. A too (or very) high value of significance level for the χ^2 test may cause overdiscretization, whereas a too (or very) low value may lead to underdiscretization. Typically, the significance level is set between 0.10 and 0.01. Second, the number of intervals cannot be over a prespecified *max-interval*, such as 10 to 15. Finally, recall that the premise behind ChiMerge is that the relative class frequencies should be fairly consistent within an interval. In practice, some inconsistency is allowed, although this should be no more than a prespecified threshold, such as 3%, which may be estimated from the training data. This last condition can be used to remove irrelevant attributes from the data set.

Cluster Analysis

Cluster analysis is a popular data discretization method. A clustering algorithm can be applied to discretize a numerical attribute, *A*, by partitioning the values of *A* into clusters or groups. Clustering takes the distribution of *A* into consideration, as well as the closeness of data points, and therefore is able to produce high-quality discretization results. Clustering can be used to generate a concept hierarchy for *A* by following either a top-down splitting strategy or a bottom-up merging strategy, where each cluster forms a node of the concept hierarchy. In the former, each initial cluster or partition may be further decomposed into several subclusters, forming a lower level of the hierarchy. In the latter, clusters are formed by repeatedly grouping neighboring clusters in order to form higher-level concepts. Clustering methods for data mining are studied in Chapter 7.

Discretization by Intuitive Partitioning

Although the above discretization methods are useful in the generation of numerical hierarchies, many users would like to see numerical ranges partitioned into relatively uniform, easy-to-read intervals that appear intuitive or "natural." For example, annual salaries broken into ranges like ($50,000, $60,000] are often more desirable than ranges like ($51,263.98, $60,872.34], obtained by, say, some sophisticated clustering analysis.

The **3-4-5 rule** can be used to segment numerical data into relatively uniform, natural-seeming intervals. In general, the rule partitions a given range of data into 3, 4, or 5 relatively equal-width intervals, recursively and level by level, based on the value range at the most significant digit. We will illustrate the use of the rule with an example further below. The rule is as follows:

- If an interval covers 3, 6, 7, or 9 distinct values at the most significant digit, then partition the range into 3 intervals (3 equal-width intervals for 3, 6, and 9; and 3 intervals in the grouping of 2-3-2 for 7).

- If it covers 2, 4, or 8 distinct values at the most significant digit, then partition the range into 4 equal-width intervals.
- If it covers 1, 5, or 10 distinct values at the most significant digit, then partition the range into 5 equal-width intervals.

The rule can be recursively applied to each interval, creating a concept hierarchy for the given numerical attribute. Real-world data often contain extremely large positive and/or negative outlier values, which could distort any top-down discretization method based on minimum and maximum data values. For example, the assets of a few people could be several orders of magnitude higher than those of others in the same data set. Discretization based on the maximal asset values may lead to a highly biased hierarchy. Thus the top-level discretization can be performed based on the range of data values representing the majority (e.g., 5th percentile to 95th percentile) of the given data. The extremely high or low values beyond the top-level discretization will form distinct interval(s) that can be handled separately, but in a similar manner.

The following example illustrates the use of the 3-4-5 rule for the automatic construction of a numerical hierarchy.

Example 2.6 **Numeric concept hierarchy generation by intuitive partitioning.** Suppose that profits at different branches of *AllElectronics* for the year 2004 cover a wide range, from −\$351,976.00 to \$4,700,896.50. A user desires the automatic generation of a concept hierarchy for *profit*. For improved readability, we use the notation $(l...r]$ to represent the interval $(l, r]$. For example, (−\$1,000,000...\$0] denotes the range from −\$1,000,000 (exclusive) to \$0 (inclusive).

Suppose that the data within the 5th percentile and 95th percentile are between −\$159,876 and \$1,838,761. The results of applying the 3-4-5 rule are shown in Figure 2.23.

1. Based on the above information, the minimum and maximum values are $MIN =$ −\$351,976.00, and $MAX =$ \$4,700,896.50. The low (5th percentile) and high (95th percentile) values to be considered for the top or first level of discretization are $LOW =$ −\$159,876, and $HIGH =$ \$1,838,761.
2. Given LOW and HIGH, the most significant digit (*msd*) is at the million dollar digit position (i.e., $msd =$ 1,000,000). Rounding LOW down to the million dollar digit, we get $LOW' =$ −\$1,000,000; rounding $HIGH$ up to the million dollar digit, we get $HIGH' =$ +\$2,000,000.
3. Since this interval ranges over three distinct values at the most significant digit, that is, (2,000,000 − (−1,000,000))/1,000,000 = 3, the segment is partitioned into three equal-width subsegments according to the 3-4-5 rule: (−\$1,000,000...\$0], (\$0...\$1,000,000], and (\$1,000,000...\$2,000,000]. This represents the top tier of the hierarchy.

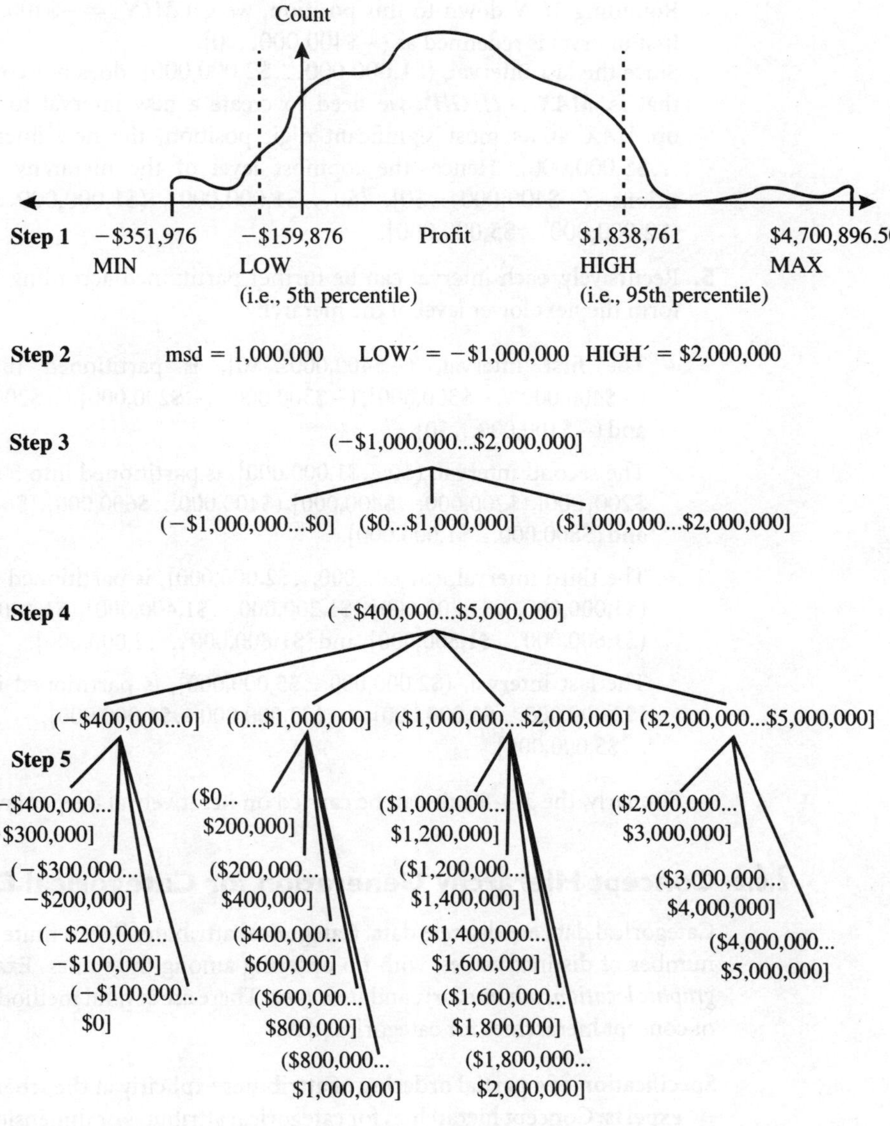

Figure 2.23 Automatic generation of a concept hierarchy for *profit* based on the 3-4-5 rule.

4. We now examine the MIN and MAX values to see how they "fit" into the first-level partitions. Since the first interval (−\$1,000,000 . . . \$0] covers the *MIN* value, that is, $LOW' < MIN$, we can adjust the left boundary of this interval to make the interval smaller. The most significant digit of *MIN* is the hundred thousand digit position.

Rounding *MIN* down to this position, we get $MIN' = -\$400{,}000$. Therefore, the first interval is redefined as (−$400,000...0].
Since the last interval, ($1,000,000...$2,000,000], does not cover the *MAX* value, that is, $MAX > HIGH'$, we need to create a new interval to cover it. Rounding up *MAX* at its most significant digit position, the new interval is ($2,000,000 ...$5,000,000]. Hence, the topmost level of the hierarchy contains four partitions, (−$400,000...$0], ($0...$1,000,000], ($1,000,000...$2,000,000], and ($2,000,000...$5,000,000].

5. Recursively, each interval can be further partitioned according to the 3-4-5 rule to form the next lower level of the hierarchy:

- The first interval, (−$400,000...$0], is partitioned into 4 subintervals: (−$400,000...−$300,000], (−$300,000...−$200,000], (−$200,000...−$100,000], and (−$100,000...$0].
- The second interval, ($0...$1,000,000], is partitioned into 5 subintervals: ($0...$200, 000], ($200,000...$400,000], ($400,000...$600,000], ($600,000...$800,000], and ($800,000...$1,000,000].
- The third interval, ($1,000,000...$2,000,000], is partitioned into 5 subintervals: ($1,000,000...$1,200,000], ($1,200,000...$1,400,000], ($1,400,000...$1,600,000], ($1,600,000...$1,800,000], and ($1,800,000...$2,000,000].
- The last interval, ($2,000,000...$5,000,000], is partitioned into 3 subintervals: ($2,000,000...$3,000,000], ($3,000,000...$4,000,000], and ($4,000,000 ...$5,000,000].

Similarly, the 3-4-5 rule can be carried on iteratively at deeper levels, as necessary. ■

2.6.2 Concept Hierarchy Generation for Categorical Data

Categorical data are discrete data. Categorical attributes have a finite (but possibly large) number of distinct values, with no ordering among the values. Examples include *geographic location, job category*, and *item type*. There are several methods for the generation of concept hierarchies for categorical data.

Specification of a partial ordering of attributes explicitly at the schema level by users or experts: Concept hierarchies for categorical attributes or dimensions typically involve a group of attributes. A user or expert can easily define a concept hierarchy by specifying a partial or total ordering of the attributes at the schema level. For example, a relational database or a dimension *location* of a data warehouse may contain the following group of attributes: *street, city, province_or_state*, and *country*. A hierarchy can be defined by specifying the total ordering among these attributes at the schema level, such as *street* < *city* < *province_or_state* < *country*.

Specification of a portion of a hierarchy by explicit data grouping: This is essentially the manual definition of a portion of a concept hierarchy. In a large database, it is unrealistic to define an entire concept hierarchy by explicit value enumeration. On the contrary, we can easily specify explicit groupings for a small portion of intermediate-level data. For example, after specifying that *province* and *country* form a hierarchy at the schema level, a user could define some intermediate levels manually, such as "{*Alberta, Saskatchewan, Manitoba*} ⊂ *prairies_Canada*" and "{*British Columbia, prairies_Canada*} ⊂ *Western_Canada*".

Specification of a *set of attributes*, but not of their partial ordering: A user may specify a set of attributes forming a concept hierarchy, but omit to explicitly state their partial ordering. The system can then try to automatically generate the attribute ordering so as to construct a meaningful concept hierarchy. "*Without knowledge of data semantics, how can a hierarchical ordering for an arbitrary set of categorical attributes be found?*" Consider the following observation that since higher-level concepts generally cover several subordinate lower-level concepts, an attribute defining a high concept level (e.g., *country*) will usually contain a smaller number of distinct values than an attribute defining a lower concept level (e.g., *street*). Based on this observation, a concept hierarchy can be automatically generated based on the number of distinct values per attribute in the given attribute set. The attribute with the most distinct values is placed at the lowest level of the hierarchy. The lower the number of distinct values an attribute has, the higher it is in the generated concept hierarchy. This heuristic rule works well in many cases. Some local-level swapping or adjustments may be applied by users or experts, when necessary, after examination of the generated hierarchy.

Let's examine an example of this method.

Example 2.7 Concept hierarchy generation based on the number of distinct values per attribute. Suppose a user selects a set of location-oriented attributes, *street, country, province_or_state*, and *city*, from the *AllElectronics* database, but does not specify the hierarchical ordering among the attributes.

A concept hierarchy for *location* can be generated automatically, as illustrated in Figure 2.24. First, sort the attributes in ascending order based on the number of distinct values in each attribute. This results in the following (where the number of distinct values per attribute is shown in parentheses): *country* (15), *province_or_state* (365), *city* (3567), and *street* (674,339). Second, generate the hierarchy from the top down according to the sorted order, with the first attribute at the top level and the last attribute at the bottom level. Finally, the user can examine the generated hierarchy, and when necessary, modify it to reflect desired semantic relationships among the attributes. In this example, it is obvious that there is no need to modify the generated hierarchy. ■

Note that this heuristic rule is not foolproof. For example, a time dimension in a database may contain 20 distinct years, 12 distinct months, and 7 distinct days of the week. However, this does not suggest that the time hierarchy should be "*year* < *month* < *days_of_the_week*", with *days_of_the_week* at the top of the hierarchy.

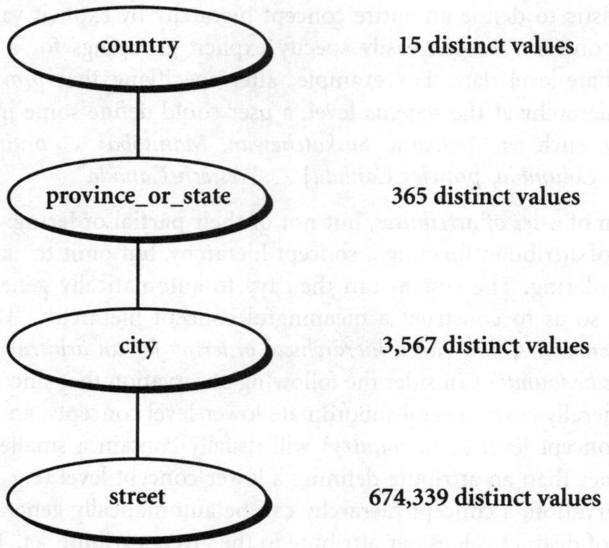

Figure 2.24 Automatic generation of a schema concept hierarchy based on the number of distinct attribute values.

Specification of only a partial set of attributes: Sometimes a user can be sloppy when defining a hierarchy, or have only a vague idea about what should be included in a hierarchy. Consequently, the user may have included only a small subset of the relevant attributes in the hierarchy specification. For example, instead of including all of the hierarchically relevant attributes for *location*, the user may have specified only *street* and *city*. To handle such partially specified hierarchies, it is important to embed data semantics in the database schema so that attributes with tight semantic connections can be pinned together. In this way, the specification of one attribute may trigger a whole group of semantically tightly linked attributes to be "dragged in" to form a complete hierarchy. Users, however, should have the option to override this feature, as necessary.

Example 2.8 **Concept hierarchy generation using prespecified semantic connections.** Suppose that a data mining expert (serving as an administrator) has pinned together the five attributes *number, street, city, province_or_state*, and *country*, because they are closely linked semantically regarding the notion of *location*. If a user were to specify only the attribute *city* for a hierarchy defining *location*, the system can automatically drag in all of the above five semantically related attributes to form a hierarchy. The user may choose to drop any of these attributes, such as *number* and *street*, from the hierarchy, keeping *city* as the lowest conceptual level in the hierarchy. ■

2.7 Summary

- **Data preprocessing** is an important issue for both data warehousing and data mining, as real-world data tend to be incomplete, noisy, and inconsistent. Data preprocessing includes data cleaning, data integration, data transformation, and data reduction.
- **Descriptive data summarization** provides the analytical foundation for data preprocessing. The basic statistical measures for data summarization include *mean, weighted mean, median*, and *mode* for measuring the central tendency of data, and *range, quartiles, interquartile range, variance*, and *standard deviation* for measuring the dispersion of data. Graphical representations, such as *histograms, boxplots, quantile plots, quantile-quantile plots, scatter plots*, and *scatter-plot matrices*, facilitate visual inspection of the data and are thus useful for data preprocessing and mining.
- **Data cleaning** routines attempt to fill in missing values, smooth out noise while identifying outliers, and correct inconsistencies in the data. Data cleaning is usually performed as an iterative two-step process consisting of discrepancy detection and data transformation.
- **Data integration** combines data from multiple sources to form a coherent data store. Metadata, correlation analysis, data conflict detection, and the resolution of semantic heterogeneity contribute toward smooth data integration.
- **Data transformation** routines convert the data into appropriate forms for mining. For example, attribute data may be **normalized** so as to fall between a small range, such as 0.0 to 1.0.
- **Data reduction** techniques such as data cube aggregation, attribute subset selection, dimensionality reduction, numerosity reduction, and discretization can be used to obtain a reduced representation of the data while minimizing the loss of information content.
- **Data discretization and automatic generation of concept hierarchies** for numerical data can involve techniques such as binning, histogram analysis, entropy-based discretization, χ^2 analysis, cluster analysis, and discretization by intuitive partitioning. For categorical data, concept hierarchies may be generated based on the number of distinct values of the attributes defining the hierarchy.
- Although numerous methods of data preprocessing have been developed, data preprocessing remains an active area of research, due to the huge amount of inconsistent or dirty data and the complexity of the problem.

Exercises

2.1 *Data quality* can be assessed in terms of accuracy, completeness, and consistency. Propose two other dimensions of data quality.

2.2 Suppose that the values for a given set of data are grouped into intervals. The intervals and corresponding frequencies are as follows.

age	*frequency*
1–5	200
5–15	450
15–20	300
20–50	1500
50–80	700
80–110	44

Compute an *approximate median* value for the data.

2.3 Give three additional commonly used statistical measures (i.e., not illustrated in this chapter) for the characterization of *data dispersion*, and discuss how they can be computed efficiently in large databases.

2.4 Suppose that the data for analysis includes the attribute *age*. The *age* values for the data tuples are (in increasing order) 13, 15, 16, 16, 19, 20, 20, 21, 22, 22, 25, 25, 25, 25, 30, 33, 33, 35, 35, 35, 35, 36, 40, 45, 46, 52, 70.

(a) What is the *mean* of the data? What is the *median*?

(b) What is the *mode* of the data? Comment on the data's modality (i.e., bimodal, trimodal, etc.).

(c) What is the *midrange* of the data?

(d) Can you find (roughly) the first quartile ($Q1$) and the third quartile ($Q3$) of the data?

(e) Give the *five-number summary* of the data.

(f) Show a *boxplot* of the data.

(g) How is a *quantile-quantile plot* different from a *quantile plot*?

2.5 In many applications, new data sets are incrementally added to the existing large data sets. Thus an important consideration for computing descriptive data summary is whether a measure can be computed efficiently in incremental manner. Use *count, standard deviation*, and *median* as examples to show that a distributive or algebraic measure facilitates efficient incremental computation, whereas a holistic measure does not.

2.6 In real-world data, tuples with *missing values* for some attributes are a common occurrence. Describe various methods for handling this problem.

2.7 Using the data for *age* given in Exercise 2.4, answer the following.

(a) Use *smoothing by bin means* to smooth the data, using a bin depth of 3. Illustrate your steps. Comment on the effect of this technique for the given data.

(b) How might you determine *outliers* in the data?

(c) What other methods are there for *data smoothing*?

2.8 Discuss issues to consider during *data integration*.

2.9 Suppose a hospital tested the age and body fat data for 18 randomly selected adults with the following result:

age	23	23	27	27	39	41	47	49	50
%fat	9.5	26.5	7.8	17.8	31.4	25.9	27.4	27.2	31.2

age	52	54	54	56	57	58	58	60	61
%fat	34.6	42.5	28.8	33.4	30.2	34.1	32.9	41.2	35.7

(a) Calculate the mean, median, and standard deviation of *age* and *%fat*.

(b) Draw the boxplots for *age* and *%fat*.

(c) Draw a *scatter plot* and a *q-q plot* based on these two variables.

(d) Normalize the two variables based on *z-score normalization*.

(e) Calculate the *correlation coefficient* (Pearson's product moment coefficient). Are these two variables positively or negatively correlated?

2.10 What are the value ranges of the following *normalization methods*?

(a) min-max normalization

(b) z-score normalization

(c) normalization by decimal scaling

2.11 Use the two methods below to *normalize* the following group of data:
200, 300, 400, 600, 1000

(a) min-max normalization by setting $min = 0$ and $max = 1$

(b) z-score normalization

2.12 Using the data for *age* given in Exercise 2.4, answer the following:

(a) Use min-max normalization to transform the value 35 for *age* onto the range [0.0, 1.0].

(b) Use z-score normalization to transform the value 35 for *age*, where the standard deviation of *age* is 12.94 years.

(c) Use normalization by decimal scaling to transform the value 35 for *age*.

(d) Comment on which method you would prefer to use for the given data, giving reasons as to why.

2.13 Use a flowchart to summarize the following procedures for *attribute subset selection*:

(a) stepwise forward selection

(b) stepwise backward elimination

(c) a combination of forward selection and backward elimination

2.14 Suppose a group of 12 *sales price* records has been sorted as follows:
5, 10, 11, 13, 15, 35, 50, 55, 72, 92, 204, 215
Partition them into three bins by each of the following methods:

(a) equal-frequency (equidepth) partitioning
(b) equal-width partitioning
(c) clustering

2.15 Using the data for *age* given in Exercise 2.4,

(a) Plot an equal-width histogram of width 10.
(b) Sketch examples of each of the following sampling techniques: SRSWOR, SRSWR, cluster sampling, stratified sampling. Use samples of size 5 and the strata "youth," "middle-aged," and "senior."

2.16 [Contributed by Chen Chen] The *median* is one of the most important holistic measures in data analysis. Propose several methods for median approximation. Analyze their respective complexity under different parameter settings and decide to what extent the real value can be approximated. Moreover, suggest a heuristic strategy to balance between accuracy and complexity and then apply it to all methods you have given.

2.17 [Contributed by Deng Cai] It is important to define or select similarity measures in data analysis. However, there is no commonly accepted subjective similarity measure. Using different similarity measures may deduce different results. Nonetheless, some apparently different similarity measures may be equivalent after some transformation.

Suppose we have the following two-dimensional data set:

	A_1	A_2
x_1	1.5	1.7
x_2	2	1.9
x_3	1.6	1.8
x_4	1.2	1.5
x_5	1.5	1.0

(a) Consider the data as two-dimensional data points. Given a new data point, $x = (1.4, 1.6)$ as a query, rank the database points based on similarity with the query using (1) Euclidean distance (Equation 7.5), and (2) cosine similarity (Equation 7.16).
(b) Normalize the data set to make the norm of each data point equal to 1. Use Euclidean distance on the transformed data to rank the data points.

2.18 ChiMerge [Ker92] is a supervised, bottom-up (i.e., merge-based) *data discretization* method. It relies on χ^2 analysis: adjacent intervals with the least χ^2 values are merged together until the stopping criterion is satisfied.

(a) Briefly describe how ChiMerge works.

(b) Take the IRIS data set, obtained from *http://www.ics.uci.edu/~mlearn/MLRepository.html* (UC-Irvine Machine Learning Data Repository), as a data set to be discretized. Perform data discretization for each of the four numerical attributes using the ChiMerge method. (Let the stopping criteria be: *max-interval* = 6.) You need to write a small program to do this to avoid clumsy numerical computation. Submit your simple analysis and your test results: split points, final intervals, and your documented source program.

2.19 Propose an algorithm, in pseudo-code or in your favorite programming language, for the following:

(a) The automatic generation of a concept hierarchy for categorical data based on the number of distinct values of attributes in the given schema

(b) The automatic generation of a concept hierarchy for numerical data based on the *equal-width* partitioning rule

(c) The automatic generation of a concept hierarchy for numerical data based on the *equal-frequency* partitioning rule

2.20 Robust data loading poses a challenge in database systems because the input data are often dirty. In many cases, an input record may have several missing values and some records could be *contaminated* (i.e., with some data values out of range or of a different data type than expected). Work out an automated *data cleaning and loading* algorithm so that the erroneous data will be marked and contaminated data will not be mistakenly inserted into the database during data loading.

Bibliographic Notes

Data preprocessing is discussed in a number of textbooks, including English [Eng99], Pyle [Pyl99], Loshin [Los01], Redman [Red01], and Dasu and Johnson [DJ03]. More specific references to individual preprocessing techniques are given below.

Methods for descriptive data summarization have been studied in the statistics literature long before the onset of computers. Good summaries of statistical descriptive data mining methods include Freedman, Pisani, and Purves [FPP97], and Devore [Dev95]. For statistics-based visualization of data using boxplots, quantile plots, quantile-quantile plots, scatter plots, and loess curves, see Cleveland [Cle93].

For discussion regarding data quality, see Redman [Red92], Wang, Storey, and Firth [WSF95], Wand and Wang [WW96], Ballou and Tayi [BT99], and Olson [Ols03]. Potter's Wheel (*http://control.cs.berkeley.edu/abc*), the interactive data cleaning tool described in Section 2.3.3, is presented in Raman and Hellerstein [RH01]. An example of the development of declarative languages for the specification of data transformation operators is given in Galhardas, Florescu, Shasha, et al. [GFS+01]. The handling of missing attribute values is discussed in Friedman [Fri77], Breiman, Friedman, Olshen, and Stone [BFOS84], and Quinlan [Qui89]. A method for the detection of outlier or "garbage" patterns in a handwritten character database is given in Guyon, Matic, and Vapnik [GMV96]. Binning and data normalization are treated in many texts, including Kennedy, Lee, Van Roy, et al. [KLV+98], Weiss and Indurkhya [WI98], and Pyle [Pyl99]. Systems that include attribute (or feature) construction include BACON by Langley, Simon, Bradshaw, and Zytkow [LSBZ87], Stagger by Schlimmer [Sch86], FRINGE by Pagallo [Pag89], and AQ17-DCI by Bloedorn and Michalski [BM98]. Attribute construction is also described in Liu and Motoda [LM98], [Le98]. Dasu, Johnson, Muthukrishnan, and Shkapenyuk [DJMS02] developed a system called Bellman wherein they propose a set of methods for building a data quality browser by mining on the structure of the database.

A good survey of data reduction techniques can be found in Barbará, Du Mouchel, Faloutos, et al. [BDF+97]. For algorithms on data cubes and their precomputation, see Sarawagi and Stonebraker [SS94], Agarwal, Agrawal, Deshpande, et al. [AAD+96], Harinarayan, Rajaraman, and Ullman [HRU96], Ross and Srivastava [RS97], and Zhao, Deshpande, and Naughton [ZDN97]. Attribute subset selection (or *feature subset selection*) is described in many texts, such as Neter, Kutner, Nachtsheim, and Wasserman [NKNW96], Dash and Liu [DL97], and Liu and Motoda [LM98, LM98b]. A combination forward selection and backward elimination method was proposed in Siedlecki and Sklansky [SS88]. A wrapper approach to attribute selection is described in Kohavi and John [KJ97]. Unsupervised attribute subset selection is described in Dash, Liu, and Yao [DLY97]. For a description of wavelets for dimensionality reduction, see Press, Teukolosky, Vetterling, and Flannery [PTVF96]. A general account of wavelets can be found in Hubbard [Hub96]. For a list of wavelet software packages, see Bruce, Donoho, and Gao [BDG96]. Daubechies transforms are described in Daubechies [Dau92]. The book by Press et al. [PTVF96] includes an introduction to singular value decomposition for principal components analysis. Routines for PCA are included in most statistical software packages, such as SAS (*www.sas.com/SASHome.html*).

An introduction to regression and log-linear models can be found in several textbooks, such as James [Jam85], Dobson [Dob90], Johnson and Wichern [JW92], Devore [Dev95], and Neter et al. [NKNW96]. For log-linear models (known as *multiplicative models* in the computer science literature), see Pearl [Pea88]. For a general introduction to histograms, see Barbará et al. [BDF+97] and Devore and Peck [DP97]. For extensions of single attribute histograms to multiple attributes, see Muralikrishna and DeWitt [MD88] and Poosala and Ioannidis [PI97]. Several references to clustering algorithms are given in Chapter 7 of this book, which is devoted to the topic. A survey of multidimensional indexing structures is given in Gaede and Günther [GG98]. The use of multidimensional index trees for data aggregation is discussed in Aoki [Aok98]. Index trees include R-trees (Guttman [Gut84]), quad-trees (Finkel and Bentley [FB74]), and their variations. For discussion on sampling and data mining, see Kivinen and Mannila [KM94] and John and Langley [JL96].

There are many methods for assessing attribute relevance. Each has its own bias. The information gain measure is biased toward attributes with many values. Many alternatives have been proposed, such as gain ratio (Quinlan [Qui93]), which considers the probability of each attribute value. Other relevance measures include the gini index (Breiman, Friedman, Olshen, and Stone [BFOS84]), the χ^2 contingency table statistic, and the uncertainty coefficient (Johnson and Wichern [JW92]). For a comparison of attribute selection measures for decision tree induction, see Buntine and Niblett [BN92]. For additional methods, see Liu and Motoda [LM98b], Dash and Liu [DL97], and Almuallim and Dietterich [AD91].

Liu, Hussain, Tan, and Dash [LHTD02] performed a comprehensive survey of data discretization methods. Entropy-based discretization with the C4.5 algorithm is described in Quinlan [Qui93]. In Catlett [Cat91], the D-2 system binarizes a numerical feature recursively. ChiMerge by Kerber [Ker92] and Chi2 by Liu and Setiono [LS95] are methods for the automatic discretization of numerical attributes that both employ the χ^2 statistic. Fayyad and Irani [FI93] apply the minimum description length principle to determine the number of intervals for numerical discretization. Concept hierarchies and their automatic generation from categorical data are described in Han and Fu [HF94]

3 Data Warehouse and OLAP Technology: An Overview

Data warehouses generalize and consolidate data in multidimensional space. The construction of data warehouses involves data cleaning, data integration, and data transformation and can be viewed as an important preprocessing step for data mining. Moreover, data warehouses provide *on-line analytical processing (OLAP)* tools for the interactive analysis of multidimensional data of varied granularities, which facilitates effective data generalization and data mining. Many other data mining functions, such as association, classification, prediction, and clustering, can be integrated with OLAP operations to enhance interactive mining of knowledge at multiple levels of abstraction. Hence, the data warehouse has become an increasingly important platform for data analysis and on-line analytical processing and will provide an effective platform for data mining. Therefore, data warehousing and OLAP form an essential step in the knowledge discovery process. This chapter presents an overview of data warehouse and OLAP technology. Such an overview is essential for understanding the overall data mining and knowledge discovery process.

In this chapter, we study a well-accepted definition of the data warehouse and see why more and more organizations are building data warehouses for the analysis of their data. In particular, we study the *data cube*, a multidimensional data model for data warehouses and OLAP, as well as OLAP operations such as roll-up, drill-down, slicing, and dicing. We also look at data warehouse architecture, including steps on data warehouse design and construction. An overview of data warehouse implementation examines general strategies for efficient data cube computation, OLAP data indexing, and OLAP query processing. Finally, we look at *on-line-analytical mining*, a powerful paradigm that integrates data warehouse and OLAP technology with that of data mining.

3.1 What Is a Data Warehouse?

Data warehousing provides architectures and tools for business executives to systematically organize, understand, and use their data to make strategic decisions. Data warehouse systems are valuable tools in today's competitive, fast-evolving world. In the last several years, many firms have spent millions of dollars in building enterprise-wide data warehouses. Many people feel that with competition mounting in every industry, data warehousing is the latest must-have marketing weapon—a way to retain customers by learning more about their needs.

"*Then, what exactly is a data warehouse?*" Data warehouses have been defined in many ways, making it difficult to formulate a rigorous definition. Loosely speaking, a data warehouse refers to a database that is maintained separately from an organization's operational databases. Data warehouse systems allow for the integration of a variety of application systems. They support information processing by providing a solid platform of consolidated historical data for analysis.

According to William H. Inmon, a leading architect in the construction of data warehouse systems, "A data warehouse is a subject-oriented, integrated, time-variant, and nonvolatile collection of data in support of management's decision making process" [Inm96]. This short, but comprehensive definition presents the major features of a data warehouse. The four keywords, *subject-oriented, integrated, time-variant,* and *nonvolatile,* distinguish data warehouses from other data repository systems, such as relational database systems, transaction processing systems, and file systems. Let's take a closer look at each of these key features.

- **Subject-oriented**: A data warehouse is organized around major subjects, such as customer, supplier, product, and sales. Rather than concentrating on the day-to-day operations and transaction processing of an organization, a data warehouse focuses on the modeling and analysis of data for decision makers. Hence, data warehouses typically provide a simple and concise view around particular subject issues by excluding data that are not useful in the decision support process.

- **Integrated:** A data warehouse is usually constructed by integrating multiple heterogeneous sources, such as relational databases, flat files, and on-line transaction records. Data cleaning and data integration techniques are applied to ensure consistency in naming conventions, encoding structures, attribute measures, and so on.

- **Time-variant**: Data are stored to provide information from a historical perspective (e.g., the past 5–10 years). Every key structure in the data warehouse contains, either implicitly or explicitly, an element of time.
- **Nonvolatile:** A data warehouse is always a physically separate store of data transformed from the application data found in the operational environment. Due to this separation, a data warehouse does not require transaction processing, recovery, and concurrency control mechanisms. It usually requires only two operations in data accessing: *initial loading of data* and *access of data*.

In sum, a data warehouse is a semantically consistent data store that serves as a physical implementation of a decision support data model and stores the information on which an enterprise needs to make strategic decisions. A data warehouse is also often viewed as an architecture, constructed by integrating data from multiple heterogeneous sources to support structured and/or ad hoc queries, analytical reporting, and decision making.

Based on this information, we view *data warehousing* as the *process of constructing and using data warehouses*. The construction of a data warehouse requires data cleaning, data integration, and data consolidation. The utilization of a data warehouse often necessitates a collection of *decision support* technologies. This allows "knowledge workers" (e.g., managers, analysts, and executives) to use the warehouse to quickly and conveniently obtain an overview of the data, and to make sound decisions based on information in the warehouse. Some authors use the term "data warehousing" to refer only to the process of data warehouse *construction*, while the term "warehouse DBMS" is used to refer to the *management and utilization* of data warehouses. We will not make this distinction here.

"*How are organizations using the information from data warehouses?*" Many organizations use this information to support business decision-making activities, including (1) increasing customer focus, which includes the analysis of customer buying patterns (such as buying preference, buying time, budget cycles, and appetites for spending); (2) repositioning products and managing product portfolios by comparing the performance of sales by quarter, by year, and by geographic regions in order to fine-tune production strategies; (3) analyzing operations and looking for sources of profit; and (4) managing the customer relationships, making environmental corrections, and managing the cost of corporate assets.

Data warehousing is also very useful from the point of view of *heterogeneous database integration*. Many organizations typically collect diverse kinds of data and maintain large databases from multiple, heterogeneous, autonomous, and distributed information sources. To integrate such data, and provide easy and efficient access to it, is highly desirable, yet challenging. Much effort has been spent in the database industry and research community toward achieving this goal.

The traditional database approach to heterogeneous database integration is to build **wrappers** and **integrators** (or **mediators**), on top of multiple, heterogeneous databases. When a query is posed to a client site, a metadata dictionary is used to translate the query into queries appropriate for the individual heterogeneous sites involved. These queries are then mapped and sent to local query processors. The results returned from the different sites are integrated into a global answer set. This **query-driven approach** requires complex information filtering and integration processes, and competes for resources with processing at local sources. It is inefficient and potentially expensive for frequent queries, especially for queries requiring aggregations.

Data warehousing provides an interesting alternative to the traditional approach of heterogeneous database integration described above. Rather than using a query-driven approach, data warehousing employs an **update-driven** approach in which information from multiple, heterogeneous sources is integrated in advance and stored in a warehouse for direct querying and analysis. Unlike on-line transaction processing databases, data warehouses do not contain the most current information. However, a data warehouse brings high performance to the integrated heterogeneous database system because data are copied, preprocessed, integrated, annotated, summarized, and restructured into one semantic data store. Furthermore, query processing in data warehouses does not interfere with the processing at local sources. Moreover, data warehouses can store and integrate historical information and support complex multidimensional queries. As a result, data warehousing has become popular in industry.

3.1.1 Differences between Operational Database Systems and Data Warehouses

Because most people are familiar with commercial relational database systems, it is easy to understand what a data warehouse is by comparing these two kinds of systems.

The major task of on-line operational database systems is to perform on-line transaction and query processing. These systems are called **on-line transaction processing (OLTP)** systems. They cover most of the day-to-day operations of an organization, such as purchasing, inventory, manufacturing, banking, payroll, registration, and accounting. Data warehouse systems, on the other hand, serve users or knowledge workers in the role of data analysis and decision making. Such systems can organize and present data in various formats in order to accommodate the diverse needs of the different users. These systems are known as **on-line analytical processing (OLAP)** systems.

The major distinguishing features between OLTP and OLAP are summarized as follows:

- **Users and system orientation**: An OLTP system is *customer-oriented* and is used for transaction and query processing by clerks, clients, and information technology professionals. An OLAP system is *market-oriented* and is used for data analysis by knowledge workers, including managers, executives, and analysts.
- **Data contents**: An OLTP system manages current data that, typically, are too detailed to be easily used for decision making. An OLAP system manages large amounts of historical data, provides facilities for summarization and aggregation, and stores and manages information at different levels of granularity. These features make the data easier to use in informed decision making.
- **Database design:** An OLTP system usually adopts an entity-relationship (ER) data model and an application-oriented database design. An OLAP system typically adopts either a *star* or *snowflake* model (to be discussed in Section 3.2.2) and a subject-oriented database design.
- **View:** An OLTP system focuses mainly on the current data within an enterprise or department, without referring to historical data or data in different organizations. In contrast, an OLAP system often spans multiple versions of a database schema, due to the evolutionary process of an organization. OLAP systems also deal with information that originates from different organizations, integrating information from many data stores. Because of their huge volume, OLAP data are stored on multiple storage media.
- **Access patterns:** The access patterns of an OLTP system consist mainly of short, atomic transactions. Such a system requires concurrency control and recovery mechanisms. However, accesses to OLAP systems are mostly read-only operations (because most

Table 3.1 Comparison between OLTP and OLAP systems.

Feature	*OLTP*	*OLAP*
Characteristic	operational processing	informational processing
Orientation	transaction	analysis
User	clerk, DBA, database professional	knowledge worker (e.g., manager, executive, analyst)
Function	day-to-day operations	long-term informational requirements, decision support
DB design	ER based, application-oriented	star/snowflake, subject-oriented
Data	current; guaranteed up-to-date	historical; accuracy maintained over time
Summarization	primitive, highly detailed	summarized, consolidated
View	detailed, flat relational	summarized, multidimensional
Unit of work	short, simple transaction	complex query
Access	read/write	mostly read
Focus	data in	information out
Operations	index/hash on primary key	lots of scans
Number of records accessed	tens	millions
Number of users	thousands	hundreds
DB size	100 MB to GB	100 GB to TB
Priority	high performance, high availability	high flexibility, end-user autonomy
Metric	transaction throughput	query throughput, response time

NOTE: Table is partially based on [CD97].

data warehouses store historical rather than up-to-date information), although many could be complex queries.

Other features that distinguish between OLTP and OLAP systems include database size, frequency of operations, and performance metrics. These are summarized in Table 3.1.

3.1.2 But, Why Have a Separate Data Warehouse?

Because operational databases store huge amounts of data, you may wonder, *"why not perform on-line analytical processing directly on such databases instead of spending additional time and resources to construct a separate data warehouse?"* A major reason for such a separation is to help promote the *high performance of both systems.* An operational database is designed and tuned from known tasks and workloads, such as indexing and hashing using primary keys, searching for particular records, and optimizing "canned" queries. On the other hand, data warehouse queries are often complex. They involve the computation of large groups of data at summarized levels, and may require the use of special data organization, access, and implementation methods based on multidimensional views. Processing OLAP queries in operational databases would substantially degrade the performance of operational tasks.

Moreover, an operational database supports the concurrent processing of multiple transactions. Concurrency control and recovery mechanisms, such as locking and logging, are required to ensure the consistency and robustness of transactions. An OLAP query often needs read-only access of data records for summarization and aggregation. Concurrency control and recovery mechanisms, if applied for such OLAP operations, may jeopardize the execution of concurrent transactions and thus substantially reduce the throughput of an OLTP system.

Finally, the separation of operational databases from data warehouses is based on the different structures, contents, and uses of the data in these two systems. Decision support requires historical data, whereas operational databases do not typically maintain historical data. In this context, the data in operational databases, though abundant, is usually far from complete for decision making. Decision support requires consolidation (such as aggregation and summarization) of data from heterogeneous sources, resulting in high-quality, clean, and integrated data. In contrast, operational databases contain only detailed raw data, such as transactions, which need to be consolidated before analysis. Because the two systems provide quite different functionalities and require different kinds of data, it is presently necessary to maintain separate databases. However, many vendors of operational relational database management systems are beginning to optimize such systems to support OLAP queries. As this trend continues, the separation between OLTP and OLAP systems is expected to decrease.

3.2 A Multidimensional Data Model

Data warehouses and OLAP tools are based on a **multidimensional data model**. This model views data in the form of a *data cube*. In this section, you will learn how data cubes model *n*-dimensional data. You will also learn about concept hierarchies and how they can be used in basic OLAP operations to allow interactive mining at multiple levels of abstraction.

3.2.1 From Tables and Spreadsheets to Data Cubes

"*What is a data cube?*" A **data cube** allows data to be modeled and viewed in multiple dimensions. It is defined by dimensions and facts.

In general terms, **dimensions** are the perspectives or entities with respect to which an organization wants to keep records. For example, *AllElectronics* may create a *sales* data warehouse in order to keep records of the store's sales with respect to the dimensions *time*, *item*, *branch*, and *location*. These dimensions allow the store to keep track of things like monthly sales of items and the branches and locations

Table 3.2 A 2-D view of sales data for *AllElectronics* according to the dimensions *time* and *item*, where the sales are from branches located in the city of Vancouver. The measure displayed is *dollars_sold* (in thousands).

location = "Vancouver"				
	item (type)			
time *(quarter)*	*home entertainment*	*computer*	*phone*	*security*
Q1	605	825	14	400
Q2	680	952	31	512
Q3	812	1023	30	501
Q4	927	1038	38	580

at which the items were sold. Each dimension may have a table associated with it, called a **dimension table**, which further describes the dimension. For example, a dimension table for *item* may contain the attributes *item_name, brand,* and *type.* Dimension tables can be specified by users or experts, or automatically generated and adjusted based on data distributions.

A multidimensional data model is typically organized around a central theme, like *sales,* for instance. This theme is represented by a fact table. **Facts** are numerical measures. Think of them as the quantities by which we want to analyze relationships between dimensions. Examples of facts for a sales data warehouse include *dollars_sold* (sales amount in dollars), *units_sold* (number of units sold), and *amount_budgeted.* The **fact table** contains the names of the *facts,* or measures, as well as keys to each of the related dimension tables. You will soon get a clearer picture of how this works when we look at multidimensional schemas.

Although we usually think of cubes as 3-D geometric structures, in data warehousing the data cube is *n*-dimensional. To gain a better understanding of data cubes and the multidimensional data model, let's start by looking at a simple 2-D data cube that is, in fact, a table or spreadsheet for sales data from *AllElectronics.* In particular, we will look at the *AllElectronics* sales data for items sold per quarter in the city of Vancouver. These data are shown in Table 3.2. In this 2-D representation, the sales for Vancouver are shown with respect to the *time* dimension (organized in quarters) and the *item* dimension (organized according to the types of items sold). The fact or measure displayed is *dollars_sold* (in thousands).

Now, suppose that we would like to view the sales data with a third dimension. For instance, suppose we would like to view the data according to *time* and *item,* as well as *location* for the cities Chicago, New York, Toronto, and Vancouver. These 3-D data are shown in Table 3.3. The 3-D data of Table 3.3 are represented as a series of 2-D tables. Conceptually, we may also represent the same data in the form of a 3-D data cube, as in Figure 3.1.

Table 3.3 A 3-D view of sales data for *AllElectronics*, according to the dimensions *time*, *item*, and *location*. The measure displayed is *dollars_sold* (in thousands).

	location = "Chicago"				**location** = "New York"				**location** = "Toronto"				**location** = "Vancouver"			
	item				**item**				**item**				**item**			
time	*home ent.*	*comp.*	*phone*	*sec.*	*home ent.*	*comp.*	*phone*	*sec.*	*home ent.*	*comp.*	*phone*	*sec.*	*home ent.*	*comp.*	*phone*	*sec.*
Q1	854	882	89	623	1087	968	38	872	818	746	43	591	605	825	14	400
Q2	943	890	64	698	1130	1024	41	925	894	769	52	682	680	952	31	512
Q3	1032	924	59	789	1034	1048	45	1002	940	795	58	728	812	1023	30	501
Q4	1129	992	63	870	1142	1091	54	984	978	864	59	784	927	1038	38	580

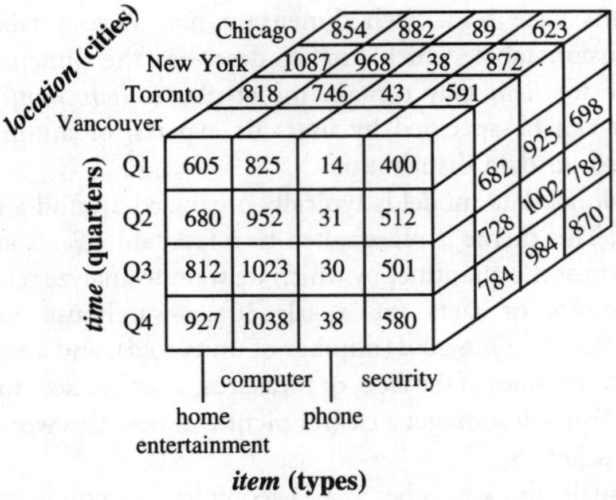

Figure 3.1 A 3-D data cube representation of the data in Table 3.3, according to the dimensions *time*, *item*, and *location*. The measure displayed is *dollars_sold* (in thousands).

Suppose that we would now like to view our sales data with an additional fourth dimension, such as *supplier*. Viewing things in 4-D becomes tricky. However, we can think of a 4-D cube as being a series of 3-D cubes, as shown in Figure 3.2. If we continue in this way, we may display any n-D data as a series of $(n-1)$-D "cubes." The data cube is a metaphor for multidimensional data storage. The actual physical storage of such data may differ from its logical representation. The important thing to remember is that data cubes are n-dimensional and do not confine data to 3-D.

The above tables show the data at different degrees of summarization. In the data warehousing research literature, a data cube such as each of the above is often referred to

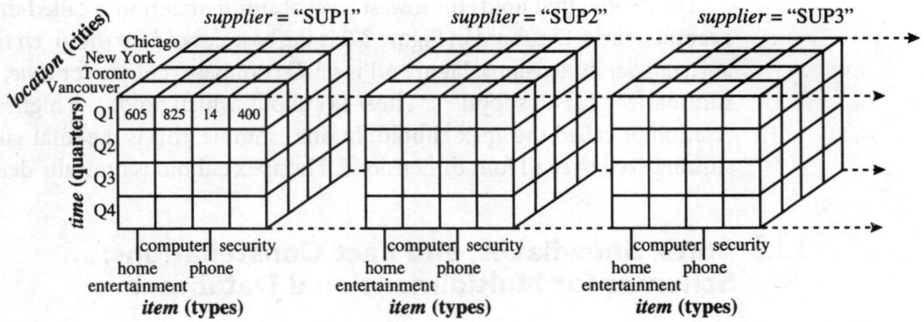

Figure 3.2 A 4-D data cube representation of sales data, according to the dimensions *time, item, location,* and *supplier*. The measure displayed is *dollars_sold* (in thousands). For improved readability, only some of the cube values are shown.

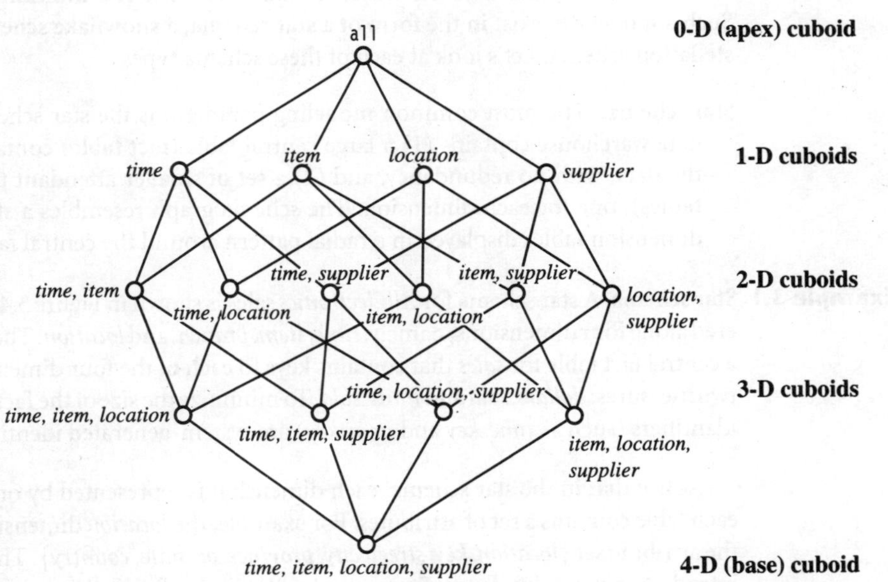

Figure 3.3 Lattice of cuboids, making up a 4-D data cube for the dimensions *time, item, location,* and *supplier*. Each cuboid represents a different degree of summarization.

as a **cuboid**. Given a set of dimensions, we can generate a cuboid for each of the possible subsets of the given dimensions. The result would form a *lattice* of cuboids, each showing the data at a different level of summarization, or **group by**. The lattice of cuboids is then referred to as a data cube. Figure 3.3 shows a lattice of cuboids forming a data cube for the dimensions *time, item, location,* and *supplier*.

The cuboid that holds the lowest level of summarization is called the **base cuboid.** For example, the 4-D cuboid in Figure 3.2 is the base cuboid for the given *time, item, location,* and *supplier* dimensions. Figure 3.1 is a 3-D (nonbase) cuboid for *time, item,* and *location,* summarized for all suppliers. The 0-D cuboid, which holds the highest level of summarization, is called the **apex cuboid.** In our example, this is the total sales, or *dollars_sold,* summarized over all four dimensions. The apex cuboid is typically denoted by **all.**

3.2.2 Stars, Snowflakes, and Fact Constellations: Schemas for Multidimensional Databases

The entity-relationship data model is commonly used in the design of relational databases, where a database schema consists of a set of entities and the relationships between them. Such a data model is appropriate for on-line transaction processing. A data warehouse, however, requires a concise, subject-oriented schema that facilitates on-line data analysis.

The most popular data model for a data warehouse is a **multidimensional model.** Such a model can exist in the form of a **star schema,** a **snowflake schema,** or a **fact constellation schema.** Let's look at each of these schema types.

Star schema: The most common modeling paradigm is the star schema, in which the data warehouse contains (1) a large central table (**fact table**) containing the bulk of the data, with no redundancy, and (2) a set of smaller attendant tables (**dimension tables**), one for each dimension. The schema graph resembles a starburst, with the dimension tables displayed in a radial pattern around the central fact table.

Example 3.1 **Star schema.** A star schema for *AllElectronics* sales is shown in Figure 3.4. Sales are considered along four dimensions, namely, *time, item, branch,* and *location.* The schema contains a central fact table for *sales* that contains keys to each of the four dimensions, along with two measures: *dollars_sold* and *units_sold.* To minimize the size of the fact table, dimension identifiers (such as *time_key* and *item_key*) are system-generated identifiers. ■

Notice that in the star schema, each dimension is represented by only one table, and each table contains a set of attributes. For example, the *location* dimension table contains the attribute set {*location_key, street, city, province_or_state, country*}. This constraint may introduce some redundancy. For example, "*Vancouver*" and "*Victoria*" are both cities in the Canadian province of British Columbia. Entries for such cities in the *location* dimension table will create redundancy among the attributes *province_or_state* and *country,* that is, (..., *Vancouver, British Columbia, Canada*) and (..., *Victoria, British Columbia, Canada*). Moreover, the attributes within a dimension table may form either a hierarchy (total order) or a lattice (partial order).

Snowflake schema: The snowflake schema is a variant of the star schema model, where some dimension tables are *normalized,* thereby further splitting the data into additional tables. The resulting schema graph forms a shape similar to a snowflake.

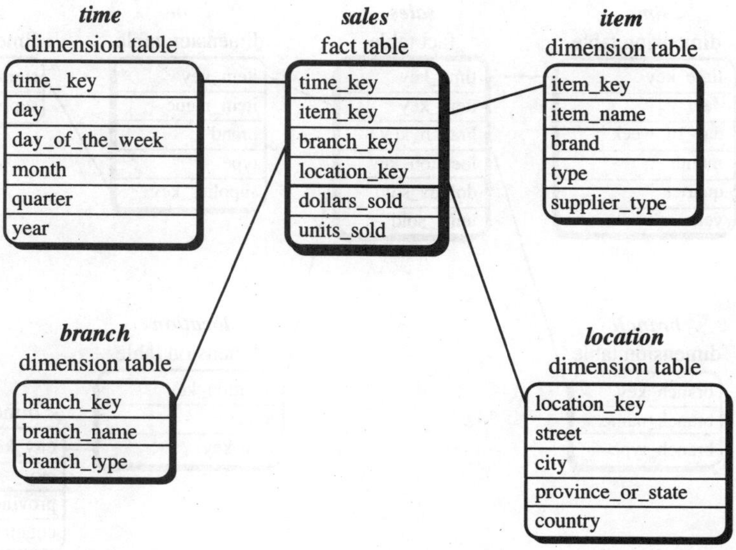

Figure 3.4 Star schema of a data warehouse for sales.

The major difference between the snowflake and star schema models is that the dimension tables of the snowflake model may be kept in normalized form to reduce redundancies. Such a table is easy to maintain and saves storage space. However, this saving of space is negligible in comparison to the typical magnitude of the fact table. Furthermore, the snowflake structure can reduce the effectiveness of browsing, since more joins will be needed to execute a query. Consequently, the system performance may be adversely impacted. Hence, although the snowflake schema reduces redundancy, it is not as popular as the star schema in data warehouse design.

Example 3.2 Snowflake schema. A snowflake schema for *AllElectronics* sales is given in Figure 3.5. Here, the *sales* fact table is identical to that of the star schema in Figure 3.4. The main difference between the two schemas is in the definition of dimension tables. The single dimension table for *item* in the star schema is normalized in the snowflake schema, resulting in new *item* and *supplier* tables. For example, the *item* dimension table now contains the attributes *item_key, item_name, brand, type*, and *supplier_key*, where *supplier_key* is linked to the *supplier* dimension table, containing *supplier_key* and *supplier_type* information. Similarly, the single dimension table for *location* in the star schema can be normalized into two new tables: *location* and *city*. The *city_key* in the new *location* table links to the *city* dimension. Notice that further normalization can be performed on *province_or_state* and *country* in the snowflake schema shown in Figure 3.5, when desirable. ■

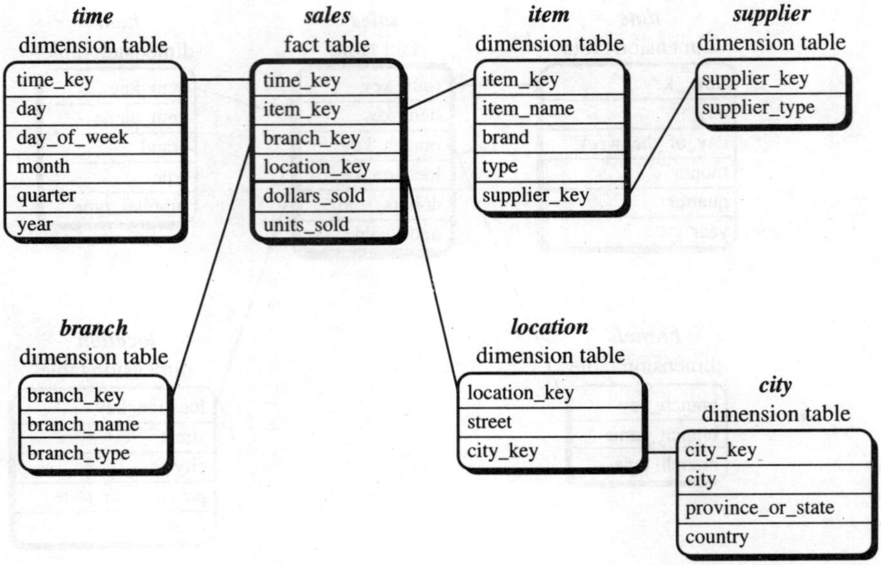

Figure 3.5 Snowflake schema of a data warehouse for sales.

Fact constellation: Sophisticated applications may require multiple fact tables to *share* dimension tables. This kind of schema can be viewed as a collection of stars, and hence is called a **galaxy schema** or a **fact constellation**.

Example 3.3 **Fact constellation.** A fact constellation schema is shown in Figure 3.6. This schema specifies two fact tables, *sales* and *shipping*. The *sales* table definition is identical to that of the star schema (Figure 3.4). The *shipping* table has five dimensions, or keys: *item_key, time_key, shipper_key, from_location*, and *to_location*, and two measures: *dollars_cost* and *units_shipped*. A fact constellation schema allows dimension tables to be shared between fact tables. For example, the dimensions tables for *time, item*, and *location* are shared between both the *sales* and *shipping* fact tables. ■

In data warehousing, there is a distinction between a data warehouse and a data mart. A data warehouse collects information about subjects that span the *entire organization*, such as *customers, items, sales, assets*, and *personnel*, and thus its scope is *enterprise-wide*. For data warehouses, the fact constellation schema is commonly used, since it can model multiple, interrelated subjects. A **data mart**, on the other hand, is a department subset of the data warehouse that focuses on selected subjects, and thus its scope is *department-wide*. For data marts, the *star* or *snowflake* schema are commonly used, since both are geared toward modeling single subjects, although the star schema is more popular and efficient.

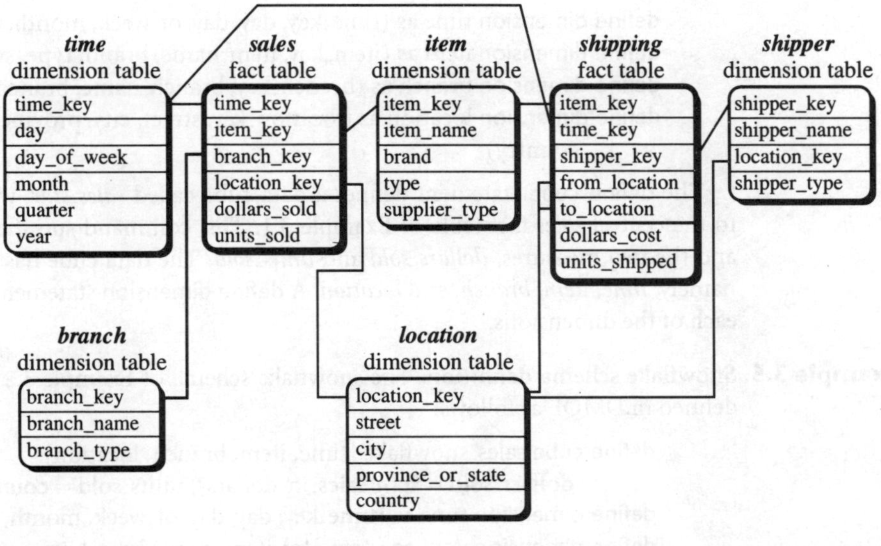

Figure 3.6 Fact constellation schema of a data warehouse for sales and shipping.

3.2.3 Examples for Defining Star, Snowflake, and Fact Constellation Schemas

"How can I define a multidimensional schema for my data?" Just as relational query languages like SQL can be used to specify relational queries, a **data mining query language** can be used to specify data mining tasks. In particular, we examine how to define data warehouses and data marts in our SQL-based data mining query language, DMQL.

Data warehouses and data marts can be defined using two language primitives, one for *cube definition* and one for *dimension definition*. The *cube definition* statement has the following syntax:

define cube ⟨cube_name⟩ [⟨dimension_list⟩]: ⟨measure_list⟩

The *dimension definition* statement has the following syntax:

define dimension ⟨dimension_name⟩ as (⟨attribute_or_dimension_list⟩)

Let's look at examples of how to define the star, snowflake, and fact constellation schemas of Examples 3.1 to 3.3 using DMQL. DMQL keywords are displayed in sans serif font.

Example 3.4 **Star schema definition.** The star schema of Example 3.1 and Figure 3.4 is defined in DMQL as follows:

define cube sales_star [time, item, branch, location]:
dollars_sold = sum(sales_in_dollars), units_sold = count(*)

```
define dimension time as (time_key, day, day_of_week, month, quarter, year)
define dimension item as (item_key, item_name, brand, type, supplier_type)
define dimension branch as (branch_key, branch_name, branch_type)
define dimension location as (location_key, street, city, province_or_state,
        country)
```

The **define cube** statement defines a data cube called *sales_star*, which corresponds to the central *sales* fact table of Example 3.1. This command specifies the dimensions and the two measures, *dollars_sold* and *units_sold*. The data cube has four dimensions, namely, *time, item, branch*, and *location*. A **define dimension** statement is used to define each of the dimensions. ■

Example 3.5 **Snowflake schema definition.** The snowflake schema of Example 3.2 and Figure 3.5 is defined in DMQL as follows:

```
define cube sales_snowflake [time, item, branch, location]:
        dollars_sold = sum(sales_in_dollars), units_sold = count(*)
define dimension time as (time_key, day, day_of_week, month, quarter, year)
define dimension item as (item_key, item_name, brand, type, supplier
        (supplier_key, supplier_type))
define dimension branch as (branch_key, branch_name, branch_type)
define dimension location as (location_key, street, city
        (city_key, city, province_or_state, country))
```

This definition is similar to that of *sales_star* (Example 3.4), except that, here, the *item* and *location* dimension tables are normalized. For instance, the *item* dimension of the *sales_star* data cube has been normalized in the *sales_snowflake* cube into two dimension tables, *item* and *supplier*. Note that the dimension definition for *supplier* is specified within the definition for *item*. Defining *supplier* in this way implicitly creates a *supplier_key* in the *item* dimension table definition. Similarly, the *location* dimension of the *sales_star* data cube has been normalized in the *sales_snowflake* cube into two dimension tables, *location* and *city*. The dimension definition for *city* is specified within the definition for *location*. In this way, a *city_key* is implicitly created in the *location* dimension table definition. ■

Finally, a fact constellation schema can be defined as a set of interconnected cubes. Below is an example.

Example 3.6 **Fact constellation schema definition.** The fact constellation schema of Example 3.3 and Figure 3.6 is defined in DMQL as follows:

```
define cube sales [time, item, branch, location]:
        dollars_sold = sum(sales_in_dollars), units_sold = count(*)
define dimension time as (time_key, day, day_of_week, month, quarter, year)
define dimension item as (item_key, item_name, brand, type, supplier_type)
define dimension branch as (branch_key, branch_name, branch_type)
define dimension location as (location_key, street, city, province_or_state,
        country)
```

> **define cube** shipping [time, item, shipper, from_location, to_location]:
> dollars_cost = sum(cost_in_dollars), units_shipped = count(*)
> **define dimension** time **as** time **in cube** sales
> **define dimension** item **as** item **in cube** sales
> **define dimension** shipper **as** (shipper_key, shipper_name, location **as** location **in cube** sales, shipper_type)
> **define dimension** from_location **as** location **in cube** sales
> **define dimension** to_location **as** location **in cube** sales

A **define cube** statement is used to define data cubes for *sales* and *shipping*, corresponding to the two fact tables of the schema of Example 3.3. Note that the *time*, *item*, and *location* dimensions of the *sales* cube are shared with the *shipping* cube. This is indicated for the *time* dimension, for example, as follows. Under the **define cube** statement for *shipping*, the statement "**define dimension** *time* **as** *time* **in cube** *sales*" is specified. ■

3.2.4 Measures: Their Categorization and Computation

"How are measures computed?" To answer this question, we first study how measures can be categorized.[1] Note that a *multidimensional point* in the data cube space can be defined by a set of dimension-value pairs, for example, ⟨*time* = *"Q1"*, *location* = *"Vancouver"*, *item* = *"computer"*⟩. A data cube **measure** is a numerical function that can be evaluated at each point in the data cube space. A measure value is computed for a given point by aggregating the data corresponding to the respective dimension-value pairs defining the given point. We will look at concrete examples of this shortly.

Measures can be organized into three categories (i.e., distributive, algebraic, holistic), based on the kind of aggregate functions used.

Distributive: An aggregate function is *distributive* if it can be computed in a distributed manner as follows. Suppose the data are partitioned into *n* sets. We apply the function to each partition, resulting in *n* aggregate values. If the result derived by applying the function to the *n* aggregate values is the same as that derived by applying the function to the entire data set (without partitioning), the function can be computed in a distributed manner. For example, **count()** can be computed for a data cube by first partitioning the cube into a set of subcubes, computing **count()** for each subcube, and then summing up the counts obtained for each subcube. Hence, **count()** is a distributive aggregate function. For the same reason, **sum()**, **min()**, and **max()** are distributive aggregate functions. A measure is *distributive* if it is obtained by applying a distributive aggregate function. Distributive measures can be computed efficiently because they can be computed in a distributive manner.

[1] This categorization was briefly introduced in Chapter 2 with regards to the computation of measures for descriptive data summaries. We reexamine it here in the context of data cube measures.

Algebraic: An aggregate function is *algebraic* if it can be computed by an algebraic function with *M* arguments (where *M* is a bounded positive integer), each of which is obtained by applying a distributive aggregate function. For example, **avg()** (average) can be computed by **sum()/count()**, where both **sum()** and **count()** are distributive aggregate functions. Similarly, it can be shown that **min_N()** and **max_N()** (which find the *N* minimum and *N* maximum values, respectively, in a given set) and **standard_deviation()** are algebraic aggregate functions. A measure is *algebraic* if it is obtained by applying an algebraic aggregate function.

Holistic: An aggregate function is *holistic* if there is no constant bound on the storage size needed to describe a subaggregate. That is, there does not exist an algebraic function with *M* arguments (where *M* is a constant) that characterizes the computation. Common examples of holistic functions include **median()**, **mode()**, and **rank()**. A measure is *holistic* if it is obtained by applying a holistic aggregate function.

Most large data cube applications require efficient computation of distributive and algebraic measures. Many efficient techniques for this exist. In contrast, it is difficult to compute holistic measures efficiently. Efficient techniques to *approximate* the computation of some holistic measures, however, do exist. For example, rather than computing the exact **median()**, Equation (2.3) of Chapter 2 can be used to estimate the approximate median value for a large data set. In many cases, such techniques are sufficient to overcome the difficulties of efficient computation of holistic measures.

Example 3.7 Interpreting measures for data cubes. Many measures of a data cube can be computed by relational aggregation operations. In Figure 3.4, we saw a star schema for *AllElectronics* sales that contains two measures, namely, *dollars_sold* and *units_sold*. In Example 3.4, the *sales_star* data cube corresponding to the schema was defined using DMQL commands. *"But how are these commands interpreted in order to generate the specified data cube?"*

Suppose that the relational database schema of *AllElectronics* is the following:

time(time_key, day, day_of_week, month, quarter, year)
item(item_key, item_name, brand, type, supplier_type)
branch(branch_key, branch_name, branch_type)
location(location_key, street, city, province_or_state, country)
sales(time_key, item_key, branch_key, location_key, number_of_units_sold, price)

The DMQL specification of Example 3.4 is translated into the following SQL query, which generates the required *sales_star* cube. Here, the **sum** aggregate function, is used to compute both *dollars_sold* and *units_sold*:

```
select s.time_key, s.item_key, s.branch_key, s.location_key,
        sum(s.number_of_units_sold * s.price), sum(s.number_of_units_sold)
from time t, item i, branch b, location l, sales s,
where s.time_key = t.time_key and s.item_key = i.item_key
        and s.branch_key = b.branch_key and s.location_key = l.location_key
group by s.time_key, s.item_key, s.branch_key, s.location_key
```

The cube created in the above query is the base cuboid of the *sales_star* data cube. It contains all of the dimensions specified in the data cube definition, where the granularity of each dimension is at the **join key** level. A join key is a key that links a fact table and a dimension table. The fact table associated with a base cuboid is sometimes referred to as the **base fact table**.

By changing the **group by** clauses, we can generate other cuboids for the *sales_star* data cube. For example, instead of grouping by *s.time_key*, we can group by *t.month*, which will sum up the measures of each group by month. Also, removing "**group by** *s.branch_key*" will generate a higher-level cuboid (where sales are summed for all branches, rather than broken down per branch). Suppose we modify the above SQL query by removing *all* of the **group by** clauses. This will result in obtaining the total sum of *dollars_sold* and the total count of *units_sold* for the given data. This zero-dimensional cuboid is the apex cuboid of the *sales_star* data cube. In addition, other cuboids can be generated by applying selection and/or projection operations on the base cuboid, resulting in a lattice of cuboids as described in Section 3.2.1. Each cuboid corresponds to a different degree of summarization of the given data. ■

Most of the current data cube technology confines the measures of multidimensional databases to *numerical data*. However, measures can also be applied to other kinds of data, such as spatial, multimedia, or text data. This will be discussed in future chapters.

3.2.5 Concept Hierarchies

A **concept hierarchy** defines a sequence of mappings from a set of low-level concepts to higher-level, more general concepts. Consider a concept hierarchy for the dimension *location*. City values for *location* include Vancouver, Toronto, New York, and Chicago. Each city, however, can be mapped to the province or state to which it belongs. For example, Vancouver can be mapped to British Columbia, and Chicago to Illinois. The provinces and states can in turn be mapped to the country to which they belong, such as Canada or the USA. These mappings form a concept hierarchy for the dimension *location*, mapping a set of low-level concepts (i.e., cities) to higher-level, more general concepts (i.e., countries). The concept hierarchy described above is illustrated in Figure 3.7.

Many concept hierarchies are implicit within the database schema. For example, suppose that the dimension *location* is described by the attributes *number, street, city, province_or_state, zipcode*, and *country*. These attributes are related by a total order, forming a concept hierarchy such as "*street* $<$ *city* $<$ *province_or_state* $<$ *country*". This hierarchy is shown in Figure 3.8(a). Alternatively, the attributes of a dimension may be organized in a partial order, forming a lattice. An example of a partial order for the *time* dimension based on the attributes *day, week, month, quarter*, and *year* is "*day* $<$ $\{$*month* $<$*quarter; week*$\}$ $<$ *year*".[2] This lattice structure is shown in Figure 3.8(b). A concept hierarchy

[2] Since a *week* often crosses the boundary of two consecutive months, it is usually not treated as a lower abstraction of *month*. Instead, it is often treated as a lower abstraction of *year*, since a year contains approximately 52 weeks.

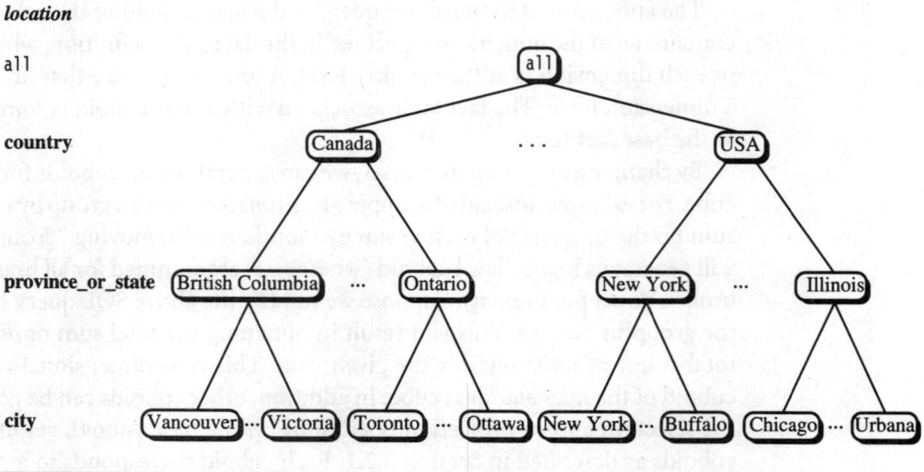

Figure 3.7 A concept hierarchy for the dimension *location*. Due to space limitations, not all of the nodes of the hierarchy are shown (as indicated by the use of "ellipsis" between nodes).

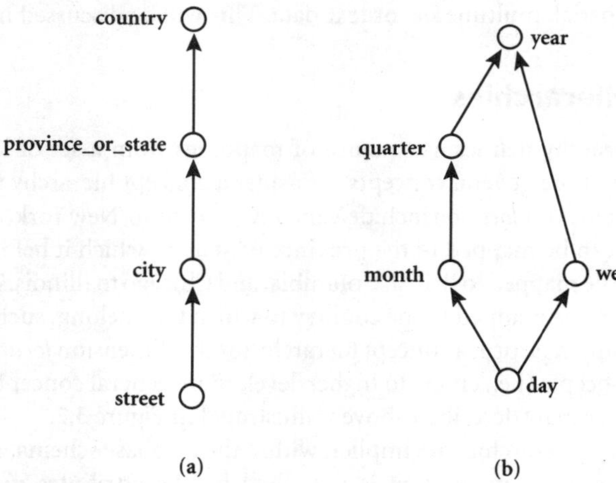

Figure 3.8 Hierarchical and lattice structures of attributes in warehouse dimensions: (a) a hierarchy for *location*; (b) a lattice for *time*.

that is a total or partial order among attributes in a database schema is called a **schema hierarchy**. Concept hierarchies that are common to many applications may be predefined in the data mining system, such as the concept hierarchy for *time*. Data mining systems should provide users with the flexibility to tailor predefined hierarchies according to their particular needs. For example, users may like to define a fiscal year starting on April 1 or an academic year starting on September 1.

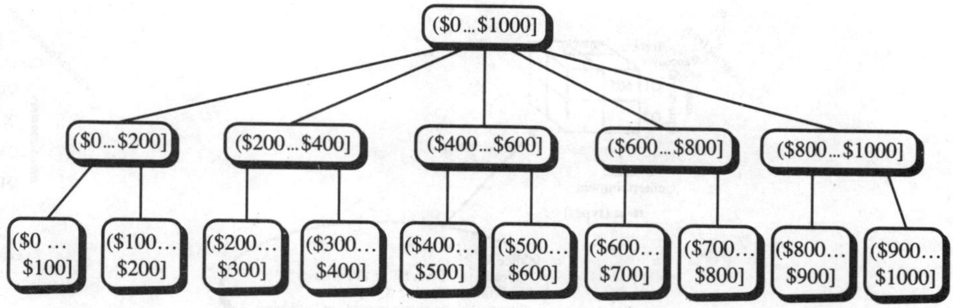

Figure 3.9 A concept hierarchy for the attribute *price*.

Concept hierarchies may also be defined by discretizing or grouping values for a given dimension or attribute, resulting in a **set-grouping hierarchy**. A total or partial order can be defined among groups of values. An example of a set-grouping hierarchy is shown in Figure 3.9 for the dimension *price*, where an interval ($\$X \ldots \$Y]$ denotes the range from $\$X$ (exclusive) to $\$Y$ (inclusive).

There may be more than one concept hierarchy for a given attribute or dimension, based on different user viewpoints. For instance, a user may prefer to organize *price* by defining ranges for *inexpensive, moderately_priced*, and *expensive.*

Concept hierarchies may be provided manually by system users, domain experts, or knowledge engineers, or may be automatically generated based on statistical analysis of the data distribution. The automatic generation of concept hierarchies is discussed in Chapter 2 as a preprocessing step in preparation for data mining.

Concept hierarchies allow data to be handled at varying levels of abstraction, as we shall see in the following subsection.

3.2.6 OLAP Operations in the Multidimensional Data Model

"How are concept hierarchies useful in OLAP?" In the multidimensional model, data are organized into multiple dimensions, and each dimension contains multiple levels of abstraction defined by concept hierarchies. This organization provides users with the flexibility to view data from different perspectives. A number of OLAP data cube operations exist to materialize these different views, allowing interactive querying and analysis of the data at hand. Hence, OLAP provides a user-friendly environment for interactive data analysis.

Example 3.8 **OLAP operations.** Let's look at some typical OLAP operations for multidimensional data. Each of the operations described below is illustrated in Figure 3.10. At the center of the figure is a data cube for *AllElectronics* sales. The cube contains the dimensions *location, time,* and *item*, where *location* is aggregated with respect to city values, *time* is aggregated with respect to quarters, and *item* is aggregated with respect to item types. To

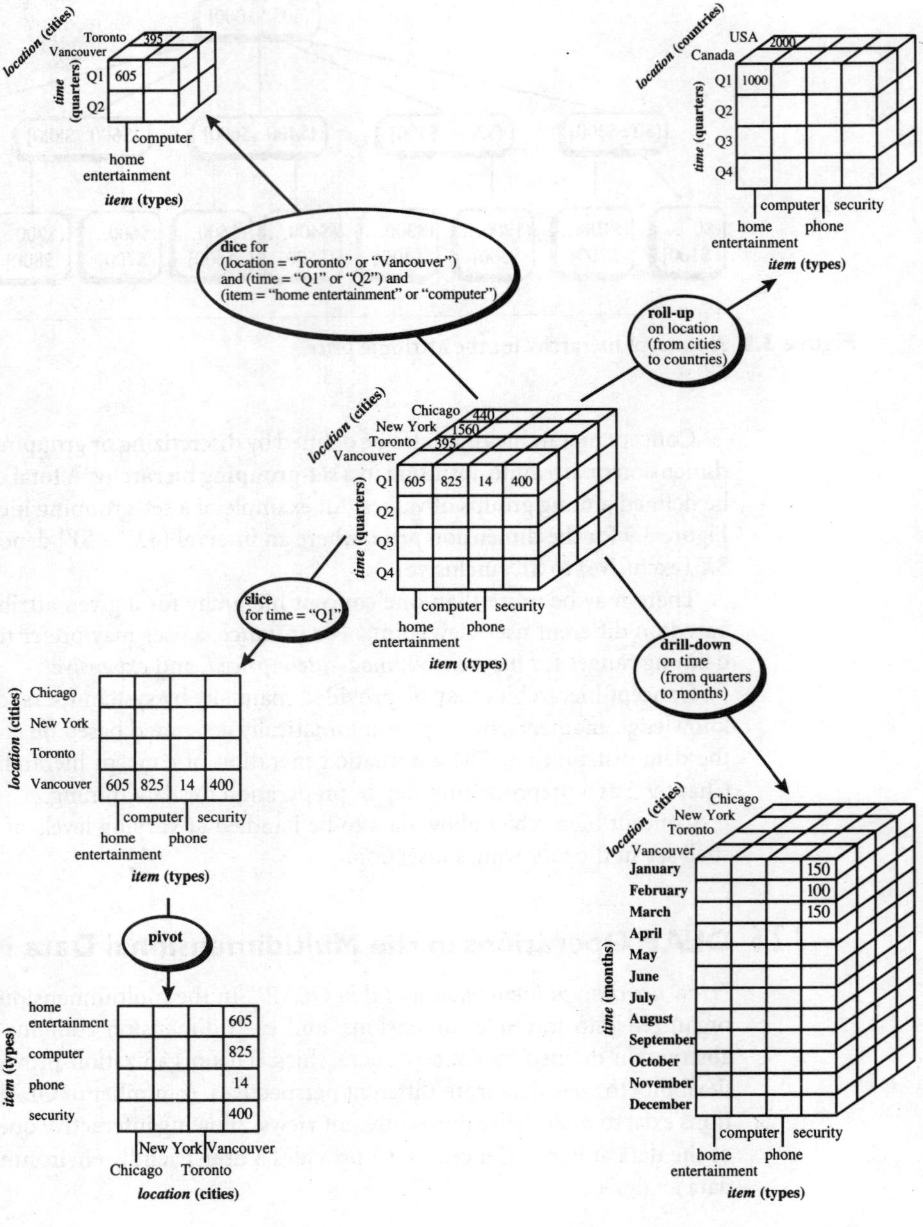

Figure 3.10 Examples of typical OLAP operations on multidimensional data.

aid in our explanation, we refer to this cube as the central cube. The measure displayed is *dollars_sold* (in thousands). (For improved readability, only some of the cubes' cell values are shown.) The data examined are for the cities Chicago, New York, Toronto, and Vancouver.

Roll-up: The roll-up operation (also called the *drill-up* operation by some vendors) performs aggregation on a data cube, either by *climbing up a concept hierarchy* for a dimension or by *dimension reduction.* Figure 3.10 shows the result of a roll-up operation performed on the central cube by climbing up the concept hierarchy for *location* given in Figure 3.7. This hierarchy was defined as the total order "*street* < *city* < *province_or_state* < *country*." The roll-up operation shown aggregates the data by ascending the *location* hierarchy from the level of *city* to the level of *country*. In other words, rather than grouping the data by city, the resulting cube groups the data by country.

When roll-up is performed by dimension reduction, one or more dimensions are removed from the given cube. For example, consider a sales data cube containing only the two dimensions *location* and *time*. Roll-up may be performed by removing, say, the *time* dimension, resulting in an aggregation of the total sales by location, rather than by location and by time.

Drill-down: Drill-down is the reverse of roll-up. It navigates from less detailed data to more detailed data. Drill-down can be realized by either *stepping down a concept hierarchy* for a dimension or *introducing additional dimensions.* Figure 3.10 shows the result of a drill-down operation performed on the central cube by stepping down a concept hierarchy for *time* defined as "*day* < *month* < *quarter* < *year*." Drill-down occurs by descending the *time* hierarchy from the level of *quarter* to the more detailed level of *month*. The resulting data cube details the total sales per month rather than summarizing them by quarter.

Because a drill-down adds more detail to the given data, it can also be performed by adding new dimensions to a cube. For example, a drill-down on the central cube of Figure 3.10 can occur by introducing an additional dimension, such as *customer_group*.

Slice and dice: The *slice* operation performs a selection on one dimension of the given cube, resulting in a subcube. Figure 3.10 shows a slice operation where the sales data are selected from the central cube for the dimension *time* using the criterion *time* = "*Q1*". The *dice* operation defines a subcube by performing a selection on two or more dimensions. Figure 3.10 shows a dice operation on the central cube based on the following selection criteria that involve three dimensions: (*location* = "*Toronto*" or "*Vancouver*") and (*time* = "*Q1*" or "*Q2*") and (*item* = "*home entertainment*" or "*computer*").

Pivot (rotate): *Pivot* (also called *rotate*) is a visualization operation that rotates the data axes in view in order to provide an alternative presentation of the data. Figure 3.10 shows a pivot operation where the *item* and *location* axes in a 2-D slice are rotated.

Other examples include rotating the axes in a 3-D cube, or transforming a 3-D cube into a series of 2-D planes.

Other OLAP operations: Some OLAP systems offer additional drilling operations. For example, **drill-across** executes queries involving (i.e., across) more than one fact table. The **drill-through** operation uses relational SQL facilities to drill through the bottom level of a data cube down to its back-end relational tables.

Other OLAP operations may include ranking the top *N* or bottom *N* items in lists, as well as computing moving averages, growth rates, interests, internal rates of return, depreciation, currency conversions, and statistical functions. ■

OLAP offers analytical modeling capabilities, including a calculation engine for deriving ratios, variance, and so on, and for computing measures across multiple dimensions. It can generate summarizations, aggregations, and hierarchies at each granularity level and at every dimension intersection. OLAP also supports functional models for forecasting, trend analysis, and statistical analysis. In this context, an OLAP engine is a powerful data analysis tool.

OLAP Systems versus Statistical Databases

Many of the characteristics of OLAP systems, such as the use of a multidimensional data model and concept hierarchies, the association of measures with dimensions, and the notions of roll-up and drill-down, also exist in earlier work on statistical databases (SDBs). A **statistical database** is a database system that is designed to support statistical applications. Similarities between the two types of systems are rarely discussed, mainly due to differences in terminology and application domains.

OLAP and SDB systems, however, have distinguishing differences. While SDBs tend to focus on socioeconomic applications, OLAP has been targeted for business applications. Privacy issues regarding concept hierarchies are a major concern for SDBs. For example, given summarized socioeconomic data, it is controversial to allow users to view the corresponding low-level data. Finally, unlike SDBs, OLAP systems are designed for handling huge amounts of data efficiently.

3.2.7 A Starnet Query Model for Querying Multidimensional Databases

The querying of multidimensional databases can be based on a **starnet model**. A starnet model consists of radial lines emanating from a central point, where each line represents a concept hierarchy for a dimension. Each abstraction level in the hierarchy is called a **footprint**. These represent the granularities available for use by OLAP operations such as drill-down and roll-up.

Example 3.9 **Starnet.** A starnet query model for the *AllElectronics* data warehouse is shown in Figure 3.11. This starnet consists of four radial lines, representing concept hierarchies

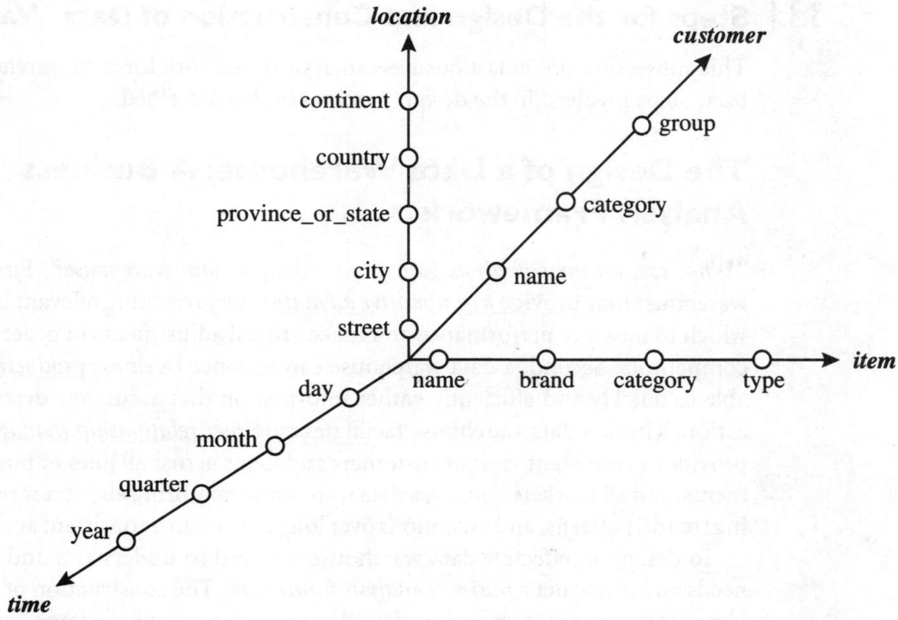

Figure 3.11 Modeling business queries: a starnet model.

for the dimensions *location, customer, item*, and *time*, respectively. Each line consists of footprints representing abstraction levels of the dimension. For example, the *time* line has four footprints: "day," "month," "quarter," and "year." A concept hierarchy may involve a single attribute (like *date* for the *time* hierarchy) or several attributes (e.g., the concept hierarchy for *location* involves the attributes *street, city, province_or_state*, and *country*). In order to examine the item sales at *AllElectronics*, users can roll up along the *time* dimension from *month* to *quarter*, or, say, drill down along the *location* dimension from *country* to *city*. Concept hierarchies can be used to **generalize** data by replacing low-level values (such as "day" for the *time* dimension) by higher-level abstractions (such as "year"), or to **specialize** data by replacing higher-level abstractions with lower-level values. ■

3.3 Data Warehouse Architecture

In this section, we discuss issues regarding data warehouse architecture. Section 3.3.1 gives a general account of how to design and construct a data warehouse. Section 3.3.2 describes a three-tier data warehouse architecture. Section 3.3.3 describes back-end tools and utilities for data warehouses. Section 3.3.4 describes the metadata repository. Section 3.3.5 presents various types of warehouse servers for OLAP processing.

3.3.1 Steps for the Design and Construction of Data Warehouses

This subsection presents a business analysis framework for data warehouse design. The basic steps involved in the design process are also described.

The Design of a Data Warehouse: A Business Analysis Framework

"*What can business analysts gain from having a data warehouse?*" First, having a data warehouse may provide a *competitive advantage* by presenting relevant information from which to measure performance and make critical adjustments in order to help win over competitors. Second, a data warehouse can enhance business *productivity* because it is able to quickly and efficiently gather information that accurately describes the organization. Third, a data warehouse facilitates *customer relationship management* because it provides a consistent view of customers and items across all lines of business, all departments, and all markets. Finally, a data warehouse may bring about *cost reduction* by tracking trends, patterns, and exceptions over long periods in a consistent and reliable manner.

To design an effective data warehouse we need to understand and analyze business needs and construct a *business analysis framework*. The construction of a large and complex information system can be viewed as the construction of a large and complex building, for which the owner, architect, and builder have different views. These views are combined to form a complex framework that represents the top-down, business-driven, or owner's perspective, as well as the bottom-up, builder-driven, or implementor's view of the information system.

Four different views regarding the design of a data warehouse must be considered: the *top-down view*, the *data source view*, the *data warehouse view*, and the *business query view*.

- The **top-down view** allows the selection of the relevant information necessary for the data warehouse. This information matches the current and future business needs.
- The **data source view** exposes the information being captured, stored, and managed by operational systems. This information may be documented at various levels of detail and accuracy, from individual data source tables to integrated data source tables. Data sources are often modeled by traditional data modeling techniques, such as the entity-relationship model or CASE (computer-aided software engineering) tools.
- The **data warehouse view** includes fact tables and dimension tables. It represents the information that is stored inside the data warehouse, including precalculated totals and counts, as well as information regarding the source, date, and time of origin, added to provide historical context.
- Finally, the **business query view** is the perspective of data in the data warehouse from the viewpoint of the end user.

Building and using a data warehouse is a complex task because it requires *business skills, technology skills*, and *program management skills*. Regarding *business skills*, building a data warehouse involves understanding how such systems store and manage their data, how to build **extractors** that transfer data from the operational system to the data warehouse, and how to build **warehouse refresh software** that keeps the data warehouse reasonably up-to-date with the operational system's data. Using a data warehouse involves understanding the significance of the data it contains, as well as understanding and translating the business requirements into queries that can be satisfied by the data warehouse. Regarding *technology skills*, data analysts are required to understand how to make assessments from quantitative information and derive facts based on conclusions from historical information in the data warehouse. These skills include the ability to discover patterns and trends, to extrapolate trends based on history and look for anomalies or paradigm shifts, and to present coherent managerial recommendations based on such analysis. Finally, *program management skills* involve the need to interface with many technologies, vendors, and end users in order to deliver results in a timely and cost-effective manner.

The Process of Data Warehouse Design

A data warehouse can be built using a *top-down approach*, a *bottom-up approach*, or a *combination of both*. The **top-down approach** starts with the overall design and planning. It is useful in cases where the technology is mature and well known, and where the business problems that must be solved are clear and well understood. The **bottom-up approach** starts with experiments and prototypes. This is useful in the early stage of business modeling and technology development. It allows an organization to move forward at considerably less expense and to evaluate the benefits of the technology before making significant commitments. In the **combined approach**, an organization can exploit the planned and strategic nature of the top-down approach while retaining the rapid implementation and opportunistic application of the bottom-up approach.

From the software engineering point of view, the design and construction of a data warehouse may consist of the following steps: *planning, requirements study, problem analysis, warehouse design, data integration and testing*, and finally *deployment of the data warehouse*. Large software systems can be developed using two methodologies: the *waterfall method* or the *spiral method*. The **waterfall method** performs a structured and systematic analysis at each step before proceeding to the next, which is like a waterfall, falling from one step to the next. The **spiral method** involves the rapid generation of increasingly functional systems, with short intervals between successive releases. This is considered a good choice for data warehouse development, especially for data marts, because the turnaround time is short, modifications can be done quickly, and new designs and technologies can be adapted in a timely manner.

In general, the warehouse design process consists of the following steps:

1. Choose a *business process* to model, for example, orders, invoices, shipments, inventory, account administration, sales, or the general ledger. If the business

process is organizational and involves multiple complex object collections, a data warehouse model should be followed. However, if the process is departmental and focuses on the analysis of one kind of business process, a data mart model should be chosen.

2. Choose the *grain* of the business process. The grain is the fundamental, atomic level of data to be represented in the fact table for this process, for example, individual transactions, individual daily snapshots, and so on.
3. Choose the *dimensions* that will apply to each fact table record. Typical dimensions are time, item, customer, supplier, warehouse, transaction type, and status.
4. Choose the *measures* that will populate each fact table record. Typical measures are numeric additive quantities like *dollars_sold* and *units_sold*.

Because data warehouse construction is a difficult and long-term task, its implementation scope should be clearly defined. The goals of an initial data warehouse implementation should be *specific, achievable,* and *measurable.* This involves determining the time and budget allocations, the subset of the organization that is to be modeled, the number of data sources selected, and the number and types of departments to be served.

Once a data warehouse is designed and constructed, the initial deployment of the warehouse includes initial installation, roll-out planning, training, and orientation. Platform upgrades and maintenance must also be considered. Data warehouse administration includes data refreshment, data source synchronization, planning for disaster recovery, managing access control and security, managing data growth, managing database performance, and data warehouse enhancement and extension. Scope management includes controlling the number and range of queries, dimensions, and reports; limiting the size of the data warehouse; or limiting the schedule, budget, or resources.

Various kinds of data warehouse design tools are available. **Data warehouse development tools** provide functions to define and edit metadata repository contents (such as schemas, scripts, or rules), answer queries, output reports, and ship metadata to and from relational database system catalogues. **Planning and analysis tools** study the impact of schema changes and of refresh performance when changing refresh rates or time windows.

3.3.2 A Three-Tier Data Warehouse Architecture

Data warehouses often adopt a three-tier architecture, as presented in Figure 3.12.

1. The bottom tier is a **warehouse database server** that is almost always a relational database system. Back-end tools and utilities are used to feed data into the bottom tier from operational databases or other external sources (such as customer profile information provided by external consultants). These tools and utilities perform data extraction, cleaning, and transformation (e.g., to merge similar data from different

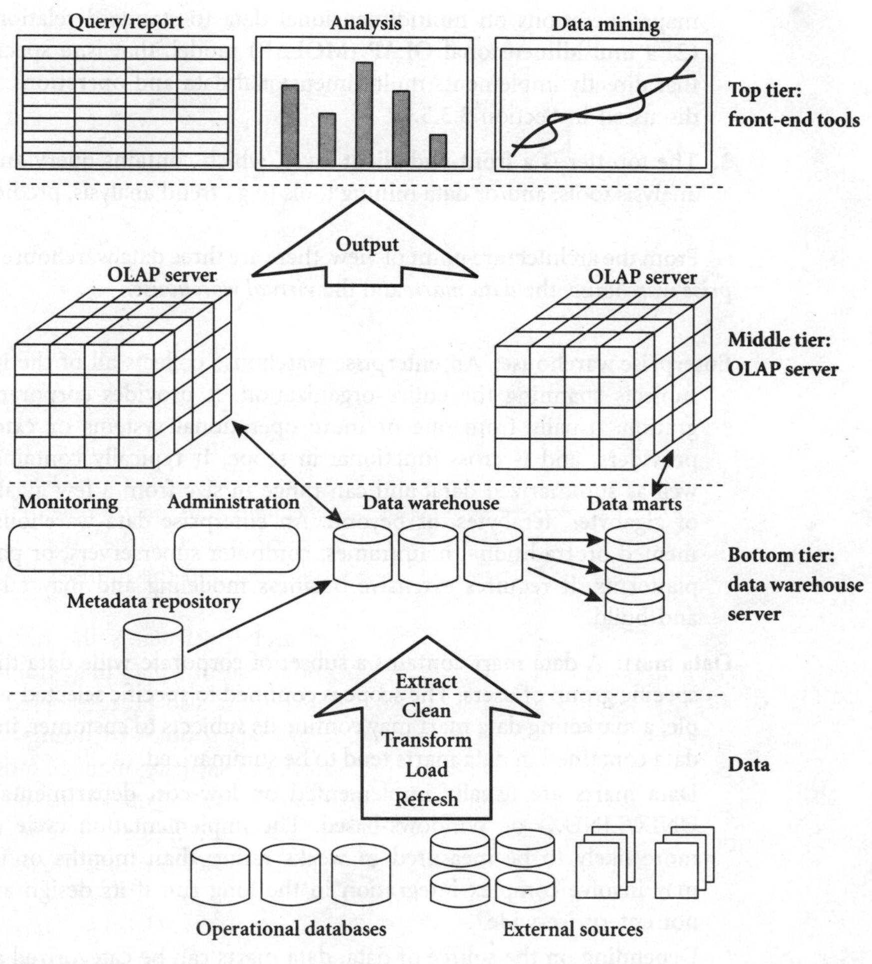

Figure 3.12 A three-tier data warehousing architecture.

sources into a unified format), as well as load and refresh functions to update the data warehouse (Section 3.3.3). The data are extracted using application program interfaces known as gateways. A gateway is supported by the underlying DBMS and allows client programs to generate SQL code to be executed at a server. Examples of gateways include ODBC (Open Database Connection) and OLEDB (Open Linking and Embedding for Databases) by Microsoft and JDBC (Java Database Connection). This tier also contains a metadata repository, which stores information about the data warehouse and its contents. The metadata repository is further described in Section 3.3.4.

2. The middle tier is an **OLAP server** that is typically implemented using either (1) a **relational OLAP (ROLAP)** model, that is, an extended relational DBMS that

maps operations on multidimensional data to standard relational operations; or (2) a **multidimensional OLAP (MOLAP)** model, that is, a special-purpose server that directly implements multidimensional data and operations. OLAP servers are discussed in Section 3.3.5.

3. The top tier is a **front-end client layer**, which contains query and reporting tools, analysis tools, and/or data mining tools (e.g., trend analysis, prediction, and so on).

From the architecture point of view, there are three data warehouse models: the *enterprise warehouse*, the *data mart*, and the *virtual warehouse*.

Enterprise warehouse: An enterprise warehouse collects all of the information about subjects spanning the entire organization. It provides corporate-wide data integration, usually from one or more operational systems or external information providers, and is cross-functional in scope. It typically contains detailed data as well as summarized data, and can range in size from a few gigabytes to hundreds of gigabytes, terabytes, or beyond. An enterprise data warehouse may be implemented on traditional mainframes, computer superservers, or parallel architecture platforms. It requires extensive business modeling and may take years to design and build.

Data mart: A data mart contains a subset of corporate-wide data that is of value to a specific group of users. The scope is confined to specific selected subjects. For example, a marketing data mart may confine its subjects to customer, item, and sales. The data contained in data marts tend to be summarized.

Data marts are usually implemented on low-cost departmental servers that are UNIX/LINUX- or Windows-based. The implementation cycle of a data mart is more likely to be measured in weeks rather than months or years. However, it may involve complex integration in the long run if its design and planning were not enterprise-wide.

Depending on the source of data, data marts can be categorized as independent or dependent. *Independent* data marts are sourced from data captured from one or more operational systems or external information providers, or from data generated locally within a particular department or geographic area. *Dependent* data marts are sourced directly from enterprise data warehouses.

Virtual warehouse: A virtual warehouse is a set of views over operational databases. For efficient query processing, only some of the possible summary views may be materialized. A virtual warehouse is easy to build but requires excess capacity on operational database servers.

"*What are the pros and cons of the top-down and bottom-up approaches to data warehouse development?*" The top-down development of an enterprise warehouse serves as a systematic solution and minimizes integration problems. However, it is expensive, takes a long time to develop, and lacks flexibility due to the difficulty in achieving consistency and consensus for a common data model for the entire organization. The bottom-up approach to the design, development, and deployment of independent data marts provides flexibility, low cost, and rapid return of investment. It, however, can lead to problems when integrating various disparate data marts into a consistent enterprise data warehouse.

A recommended method for the development of data warehouse systems is to implement the warehouse in an incremental and evolutionary manner, as shown in Figure 3.13. First, a high-level corporate data model is defined within a reasonably short period (such as one or two months) that provides a corporate-wide, consistent, integrated view of data among different subjects and potential usages. This high-level model, although it will need to be refined in the further development of enterprise data warehouses and departmental data marts, will greatly reduce future integration problems. Second, independent data marts can be implemented in parallel with the enterprise warehouse based on the same corporate data model set as above. Third, distributed data marts can be constructed to integrate different data marts via hub servers. Finally, a **multitier data warehouse** is constructed where the enterprise warehouse is the sole custodian of all warehouse data, which is then distributed to the various dependent data marts.

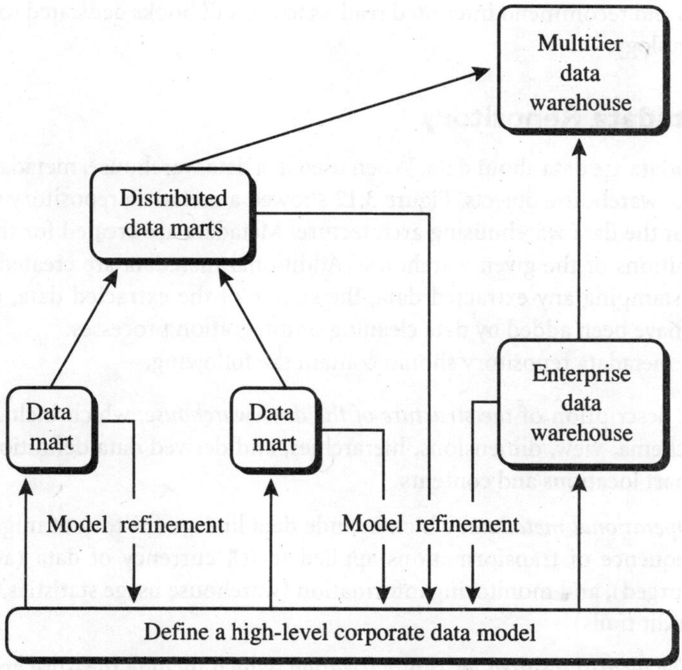

Figure 3.13 A recommended approach for data warehouse development.

3.3.3 Data Warehouse Back-End Tools and Utilities

Data warehouse systems use back-end tools and utilities to populate and refresh their data (Figure 3.12). These tools and utilities include the following functions:

- **Data extraction,** which typically gathers data from multiple, heterogeneous, and external sources
- **Data cleaning,** which detects errors in the data and rectifies them when possible
- **Data transformation,** which converts data from legacy or host format to warehouse format
- **Load,** which sorts, summarizes, consolidates, computes views, checks integrity, and builds indices and partitions
- **Refresh,** which propagates the updates from the data sources to the warehouse

Besides cleaning, loading, refreshing, and metadata definition tools, data warehouse systems usually provide a good set of data warehouse management tools.

Data cleaning and data transformation are important steps in improving the quality of the data and, subsequently, of the data mining results. They are described in Chapter 2 on Data Preprocessing. Because we are mostly interested in the aspects of data warehousing technology related to data mining, we will not get into the details of the remaining tools and recommend interested readers to consult books dedicated to data warehousing technology.

3.3.4 Metadata Repository

Metadata are data about data. When used in a data warehouse, metadata are the data that define warehouse objects. Figure 3.12 showed a metadata repository within the bottom tier of the data warehousing architecture. Metadata are created for the data names and definitions of the given warehouse. Additional metadata are created and captured for timestamping any extracted data, the source of the extracted data, and missing fields that have been added by data cleaning or integration processes.

A metadata repository should contain the following:

- A description of *the structure of the data warehouse,* which includes the warehouse schema, view, dimensions, hierarchies, and derived data definitions, as well as data mart locations and contents
- *Operational metadata,* which include data lineage (history of migrated data and the sequence of transformations applied to it), currency of data (active, archived, or purged), and monitoring information (warehouse usage statistics, error reports, and audit trails)
- *The algorithms used for summarization,* which include measure and dimension definition algorithms, data on granularity, partitions, subject areas, aggregation, summarization, and predefined queries and reports

- *The mapping from the operational environment to the data warehouse*, which includes source databases and their contents, gateway descriptions, data partitions, data extraction, cleaning, transformation rules and defaults, data refresh and purging rules, and security (user authorization and access control)
- *Data related to system performance*, which include indices and profiles that improve data access and retrieval performance, in addition to rules for the timing and scheduling of refresh, update, and replication cycles
- *Business metadata*, which include business terms and definitions, data ownership information, and charging policies

A data warehouse contains different levels of summarization, of which metadata is one type. Other types include current detailed data (which are almost always on disk), older detailed data (which are usually on tertiary storage), lightly summarized data and highly summarized data (which may or may not be physically housed).

Metadata play a very different role than other data warehouse data and are important for many reasons. For example, metadata are used as a directory to help the decision support system analyst locate the contents of the data warehouse, as a guide to the mapping of data when the data are transformed from the operational environment to the data warehouse environment, and as a guide to the algorithms used for summarization between the current detailed data and the lightly summarized data, and between the lightly summarized data and the highly summarized data. Metadata should be stored and managed persistently (i.e., on disk).

3.3.5 Types of OLAP Servers: ROLAP versus MOLAP versus HOLAP

Logically, OLAP servers present business users with multidimensional data from data warehouses or data marts, without concerns regarding how or where the data are stored. However, the physical architecture and implementation of OLAP servers must consider data storage issues. Implementations of a warehouse server for OLAP processing include the following:

Relational OLAP (ROLAP) servers: These are the intermediate servers that stand in between a relational back-end server and client front-end tools. They use a *relational or extended-relational DBMS* to store and manage warehouse data, and OLAP middleware to support missing pieces. ROLAP servers include optimization for each DBMS back end, implementation of aggregation navigation logic, and additional tools and services. ROLAP technology tends to have greater scalability than MOLAP technology. The DSS server of Microstrategy, for example, adopts the ROLAP approach.

Multidimensional OLAP (MOLAP) servers: These servers support multidimensional views of data through *array-based multidimensional storage engines*. They map multidimensional views directly to data cube array structures. The advantage of using a data cube is that it allows fast indexing to precomputed summarized data. Notice that with multidimensional data stores, the storage utilization may be low if the data set is sparse. In such cases, sparse matrix compression techniques should be explored (Chapter 4). Many MOLAP servers adopt a two-level storage representation to handle dense and sparse data sets: denser subcubes are identified and stored as array structures, whereas sparse subcubes employ compression technology for efficient storage utilization.

Hybrid OLAP (HOLAP) servers: The hybrid OLAP approach combines ROLAP and MOLAP technology, benefiting from the greater scalability of ROLAP and the faster computation of MOLAP. For example, a HOLAP server may allow large volumes of detail data to be stored in a relational database, while aggregations are kept in a separate MOLAP store. The Microsoft SQL Server 2000 supports a hybrid OLAP server.

Specialized SQL servers: To meet the growing demand of OLAP processing in relational databases, some database system vendors implement specialized SQL servers that provide advanced query language and query processing support for SQL queries over star and snowflake schemas in a read-only environment.

"*How are data actually stored in ROLAP and MOLAP architectures?*" Let's first look at ROLAP. As its name implies, ROLAP uses relational tables to store data for on-line analytical processing. Recall that the fact table associated with a base cuboid is referred to as a *base fact table.* The base fact table stores data at the abstraction level indicated by the join keys in the schema for the given data cube. Aggregated data can also be stored in fact tables, referred to as **summary fact tables.** Some summary fact tables store both base fact table data and aggregated data, as in Example 3.10. Alternatively, separate summary fact tables can be used for each level of abstraction, to store only aggregated data.

Example 3.10 **A ROLAP data store.** Table 3.4 shows a summary fact table that contains both base fact data and aggregated data. The schema of the table is "⟨*record_identifier (RID), item, ..., day, month, quarter, year, dollars_sold*⟩", where *day, month, quarter,* and *year* define the date of sales, and *dollars_sold* is the sales amount. Consider the tuples with an *RID* of 1001 and 1002, respectively. The data of these tuples are at the base fact level, where the date of sales is October 15, 2003, and October 23, 2003, respectively. Consider the tuple with an *RID* of 5001. This tuple is at a more general level of abstraction than the tuples 1001

Table 3.4 Single table for base and summary facts.

RID	*item*	...	*day*	*month*	*quarter*	*year*	*dollars_sold*
1001	TV	...	15	10	Q4	2003	250.60
1002	TV	...	23	10	Q4	2003	175.00
...	...	...	...	...	...	...	...
5001	TV	...	all	10	Q4	2003	45,786.08
...	...	...	...	...	...	...	...

and 1002. The *day* value has been generalized to **all**, so that the corresponding *time* value is October 2003. That is, the *dollars_sold* amount shown is an aggregation representing the entire month of October 2003, rather than just October 15 or 23, 2003. The special value **all** is used to represent subtotals in summarized data. ■

MOLAP uses multidimensional array structures to store data for on-line analytical processing. This structure is discussed in the following section on data warehouse implementation and, in greater detail, in Chapter 4.

Most data warehouse systems adopt a client-server architecture. A relational data store always resides at the data warehouse/data mart server site. A multidimensional data store can reside at either the database server site or the client site.

3.4 Data Warehouse Implementation

Data warehouses contain huge volumes of data. OLAP servers demand that decision support queries be answered in the order of seconds. Therefore, it is crucial for data warehouse systems to support highly efficient cube computation techniques, access methods, and query processing techniques. In this section, we present an overview of methods for the efficient implementation of data warehouse systems.

3.4.1 Efficient Computation of Data Cubes

At the core of multidimensional data analysis is the efficient computation of aggregations across many sets of dimensions. In SQL terms, these aggregations are referred to as **group-by**'s. Each group-by can be represented by a *cuboid*, where the set of group-by's forms a lattice of cuboids defining a data cube. In this section, we explore issues relating to the efficient computation of data cubes.

The compute cube Operator and the Curse of Dimensionality

One approach to cube computation extends SQL so as to include a **compute cube** operator. The **compute cube** operator computes aggregates over all subsets of the dimensions specified in the operation. This can require excessive storage space, especially for large numbers of dimensions. We start with an intuitive look at what is involved in the efficient computation of data cubes.

Example 3.11 **A data cube is a lattice of cuboids.** Suppose that you would like to create a data cube for *AllElectronics* sales that contains the following: *city, item, year*, and *sales_in_dollars*. You would like to be able to analyze the data, with queries such as the following:

- "*Compute the sum of sales, grouping by city and item.*"
- "*Compute the sum of sales, grouping by city.*"
- "*Compute the sum of sales, grouping by item.*"

What is the total number of cuboids, or group-by's, that can be computed for this data cube? Taking the three attributes, *city, item*, and *year*, as the dimensions for the data cube, and *sales_in_dollars* as the measure, the total number of cuboids, or group-by's, that can be computed for this data cube is $2^3 = 8$. The possible group-by's are the following: {(*city, item, year*), (*city, item*), (*city, year*), (*item, year*), (*city*), (*item*), (*year*), ()}, where () means that the group-by is empty (i.e., the dimensions are not grouped). These group-by's form a lattice of cuboids for the data cube, as shown in Figure 3.14. The **base cuboid** contains all three dimensions, *city, item*, and *year*. It can return the total sales for any combination of the three dimensions. The **apex cuboid**, or 0-D cuboid, refers to the case where the group-by is empty. It contains the total sum of all sales. The base cuboid is the least generalized (most specific) of the cuboids. The apex cuboid is the most generalized (least specific) of the cuboids, and is often denoted as **all**. If we start at the apex cuboid and explore downward in the lattice, this is equivalent to drilling down within the data cube. If we start at the base cuboid and explore upward, this is akin to rolling up. ■

An SQL query containing no group-by, such as "compute the sum of total sales," is a *zero-dimensional operation*. An SQL query containing one group-by, such as "compute the sum of sales, group by city," is a *one-dimensional operation*. A cube operator on *n* dimensions is equivalent to a collection of **group by** statements, one for each subset

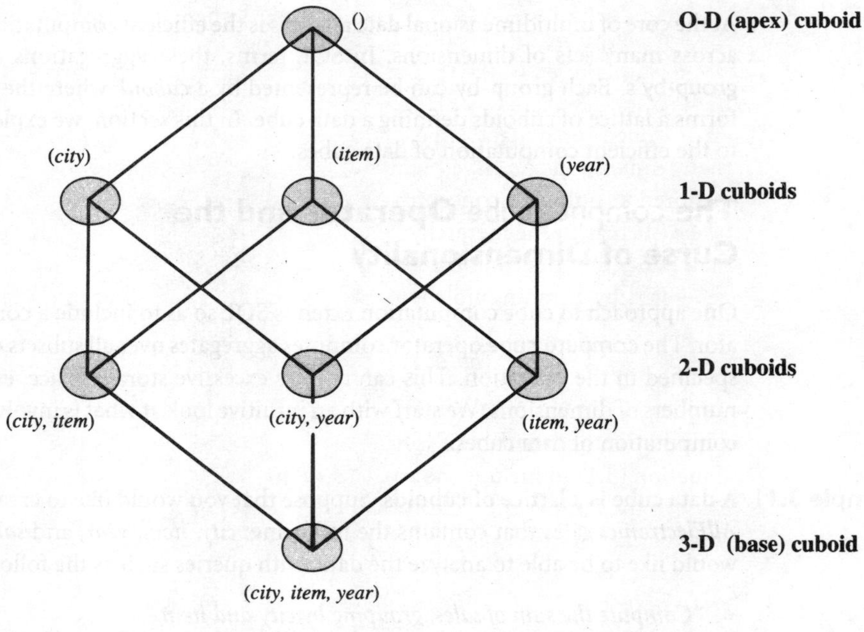

Figure 3.14 Lattice of cuboids, making up a 3-D data cube. Each cuboid represents a different group-by. The base cuboid contains the three dimensions *city, item*, and *year*.

of the n dimensions. Therefore, the cube operator is the n-dimensional generalization of the **group by** operator.

Based on the syntax of DMQL introduced in Section 3.2.3, the data cube in Example 3.11 could be defined as

define cube sales_cube [city, item, year]: **sum**(sales_in_dollars)

For a cube with n dimensions, there are a total of 2^n cuboids, including the base cuboid. A statement such as

compute cube sales_cube

would explicitly instruct the system to compute the sales aggregate cuboids for all of the eight subsets of the set $\{city, item, year\}$, including the empty subset. A cube computation operator was first proposed and studied by Gray et al. [GCB+97].

On-line analytical processing may need to access different cuboids for different queries. Therefore, it may seem like a good idea to compute all or at least some of the cuboids in a data cube in advance. Precomputation leads to fast response time and avoids some redundant computation. Most, if not all, OLAP products resort to some degree of precomputation of multidimensional aggregates.

A major challenge related to this precomputation, however, is that the required storage space may explode if all of the cuboids in a data cube are precomputed, especially when the cube has many dimensions. The storage requirements are even more excessive when many of the dimensions have associated concept hierarchies, each with multiple levels. This problem is referred to as the **curse of dimensionality**. The extent of the curse of dimensionality is illustrated below.

"*How many cuboids are there in an* n*-dimensional data cube?*" If there were no hierarchies associated with each dimension, then the total number of cuboids for an n-dimensional data cube, as we have seen above, is 2^n. However, in practice, many dimensions do have hierarchies. For example, the dimension *time* is usually not explored at only one conceptual level, such as *year*, but rather at multiple conceptual levels, such as in the hierarchy "*day < month < quarter < year*". For an n-dimensional data cube, the total number of cuboids that can be generated (including the cuboids generated by climbing up the hierarchies along each dimension) is

$$Total\ number\ of\ cuboids = \prod_{i=1}^{n}(L_i + 1), \tag{3.1}$$

where L_i is the number of levels associated with dimension i. One is added to L_i in Equation (3.1) to include the *virtual* top level, **all**. (Note that generalizing to **all** is equivalent to the removal of the dimension.) This formula is based on the fact that, at most, one abstraction level in each dimension will appear in a cuboid. For example, the time dimension as specified above has 4 conceptual levels, or 5 if we include the virtual level **all**. If the cube has 10 dimensions and each dimension has 5 levels (including **all**), the total number of cuboids that can be generated is $5^{10} \approx 9.8 \times 10^6$. The size of each cuboid also depends on the *cardinality* (i.e., number of distinct values) of each dimension. For example, if the *AllElectronics* branch in each city sold every item, there would be

$|city| \times |item|$ tuples in the *city-item* group-by alone. As the number of dimensions, number of conceptual hierarchies, or cardinality increases, the storage space required for many of the group-by's will grossly exceed the (fixed) size of the input relation.

By now, you probably realize that it is unrealistic to precompute and materialize all of the cuboids that can possibly be generated for a data cube (or from a base cuboid). If there are many cuboids, and these cuboids are large in size, a more reasonable option is *partial materialization*, that is, to materialize only *some* of the possible cuboids that can be generated.

Partial Materialization: Selected Computation of Cuboids

There are three choices for data cube materialization given a base cuboid:

1. **No materialization:** Do not precompute any of the "nonbase" cuboids. This leads to computing expensive multidimensional aggregates on the fly, which can be extremely slow.

2. **Full materialization:** Precompute all of the cuboids. The resulting lattice of computed cuboids is referred to as the *full cube*. This choice typically requires huge amounts of memory space in order to store all of the precomputed cuboids.

3. **Partial materialization:** Selectively compute a proper subset of the whole set of possible cuboids. Alternatively, we may compute a subset of the cube, which contains only those cells that satisfy some user-specified criterion, such as where the tuple count of each cell is above some threshold. We will use the term *subcube* to refer to the latter case, where only some of the cells may be precomputed for various cuboids. Partial materialization represents an interesting trade-off between storage space and response time.

The partial materialization of cuboids or subcubes should consider three factors: (1) identify the subset of cuboids or subcubes to materialize; (2) exploit the materialized cuboids or subcubes during query processing; and (3) efficiently update the materialized cuboids or subcubes during load and refresh.

The selection of the subset of cuboids or subcubes to materialize should take into account the queries in the workload, their frequencies, and their accessing costs. In addition, it should consider workload characteristics, the cost for incremental updates, and the total storage requirements. The selection must also consider the broad context of physical database design, such as the generation and selection of indices. Several OLAP products have adopted heuristic approaches for cuboid and subcube selection. A popular approach is to materialize the set of cuboids on which other frequently referenced cuboids are based. Alternatively, we can compute an *iceberg cube*, which is a data cube that stores only those cube cells whose aggregate value (e.g., count) is above some minimum support threshold. Another common strategy is to materialize a *shell cube*. This involves precomputing the cuboids for only a small number of dimensions (such as 3 to 5) of a data cube. Queries on additional combinations of the dimensions can be computed on-the-fly. Because our aim in this chapter is to provide a solid introduction and overview of data warehousing for data mining, we defer our detailed discussion of cuboid selection and computation to Chapter 4, which studies data warehouse and OLAP implementation in greater depth.

Once the selected cuboids have been materialized, it is important to take advantage of them during query processing. This involves several issues, such as how to determine the relevant cuboid(s) from among the candidate materialized cuboids, how to use available index structures on the materialized cuboids, and how to transform the OLAP operations onto the selected cuboid(s). These issues are discussed in Section 3.4.3 as well as in Chapter 4.

Finally, during load and refresh, the materialized cuboids should be updated efficiently. Parallelism and incremental update techniques for this operation should be explored.

3.4.2 Indexing OLAP Data

To facilitate efficient data accessing, most data warehouse systems support index structures and materialized views (using cuboids). General methods to select cuboids for materialization were discussed in the previous section. In this section, we examine how to index OLAP data by *bitmap indexing* and *join indexing*.

The **bitmap indexing** method is popular in OLAP products because it allows quick searching in data cubes. The bitmap index is an alternative representation of the *record_ID (RID)* list. In the bitmap index for a given attribute, there is a distinct bit vector, ***Bv***, for each value *v* in the domain of the attribute. If the domain of a given attribute consists of *n* values, then *n* bits are needed for each entry in the bitmap index (i.e., there are *n* bit vectors). If the attribute has the value *v* for a given row in the data table, then the bit representing that value is set to 1 in the corresponding row of the bitmap index. All other bits for that row are set to 0.

Example 3.12 **Bitmap indexing.** In the *AllElectronics* data warehouse, suppose the dimension *item* at the top level has four values (representing item types): *"home entertainment," "computer," "phone,"* and *"security."* Each value (e.g., *"computer"*) is represented by a bit vector in the bitmap index table for *item*. Suppose that the cube is stored as a relation table with 100,000 rows. Because the domain of *item* consists of four values, the bitmap index table requires four bit vectors (or lists), each with 100,000 bits. Figure 3.15 shows a base (data) table containing the dimensions *item* and *city*, and its mapping to bitmap index tables for each of the dimensions. ■

Bitmap indexing is advantageous compared to hash and tree indices. It is especially useful for low-cardinality domains because comparison, join, and aggregation operations are then reduced to bit arithmetic, which substantially reduces the processing time. Bitmap indexing leads to significant reductions in space and I/O since a string of characters can be represented by a single bit. For higher-cardinality domains, the method can be adapted using compression techniques.

The **join indexing** method gained popularity from its use in relational database query processing. Traditional indexing maps the value in a given column to a list of rows having

Base table

RID	*item*	*city*
R1	H	V
R2	C	V
R3	P	V
R4	S	V
R5	H	T
R6	C	T
R7	P	T
R8	S	T

Item bitmap index table

RID	H	C	P	S
R1	1	0	0	0
R2	0	1	0	0
R3	0	0	1	0
R4	0	0	0	1
R5	1	0	0	0
R6	0	1	0	0
R7	0	0	1	0
R8	0	0	0	1

City bitmap index table

RID	V	T
R1	1	0
R2	1	0
R3	1	0
R4	1	0
R5	0	1
R6	0	1
R7	0	1
R8	0	1

Note: H for "home entertainment, " C for "computer, " P for "phone, " S for "security, " V for "Vancouver, " T for "Toronto."

Figure 3.15 Indexing OLAP data using bitmap indices.

that value. In contrast, join indexing registers the joinable rows of two relations from a relational database. For example, if two relations $R(RID, A)$ and $S(B, SID)$ join on the attributes A and B, then the join index record contains the pair (RID, SID), where RID and SID are record identifiers from the R and S relations, respectively. Hence, the join index records can identify joinable tuples without performing costly join operations. Join indexing is especially useful for maintaining the relationship between a foreign key[3] and its matching primary keys, from the joinable relation.

The star schema model of data warehouses makes join indexing attractive for cross-table search, because the linkage between a fact table and its corresponding dimension tables comprises the foreign key of the fact table and the primary key of the dimension table. Join indexing maintains relationships between attribute values of a dimension (e.g., within a dimension table) and the corresponding rows in the fact table. Join indices may span multiple dimensions to form **composite join indices.** We can use join indices to identify subcubes that are of interest.

Example 3.13 **Join indexing.** In Example 3.4, we defined a star schema for *AllElectronics* of the form "*sales_star* [*time, item, branch, location*]: *dollars_sold* = sum (*sales_in_dollars*)". An example of a join index relationship between the *sales* fact table and the dimension tables for *location* and *item* is shown in Figure 3.16. For example, the "*Main Street*" value in the *location* dimension table joins with tuples T57, T238, and T884 of the *sales* fact table. Similarly, the "*Sony-TV*" value in the *item* dimension table joins with tuples T57 and T459 of the *sales* fact table. The corresponding join index tables are shown in Figure 3.17.

[3]A set of attributes in a relation schema that forms a primary key for another relation schema is called a foreign key.

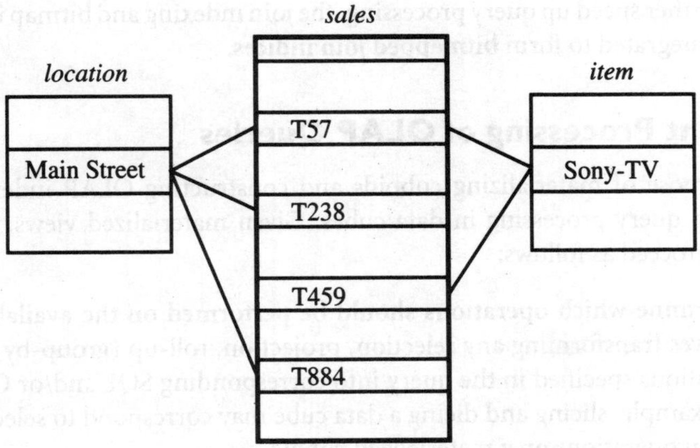

Figure 3.16 Linkages between a *sales* fact table and dimension tables for *location* and *item*.

Join index table for *location/sales*

location	*sales_key*
...	...
Main Street	T57
Main Street	T238
Main Street	T884
...	...

Join index table for *item/sales*

item	*sales_key*
...	...
Sony-TV	T57
Sony-TV	T459
...	...

Join index table linking two dimensions *location/item/sales*

location	*item*	*sales_key*
...	...	...
Main Street	Sony-TV	T57
...	...	...

Figure 3.17 Join index tables based on the linkages between the *sales* fact table and dimension tables for *location* and *item* shown in Figure 3.16.

Suppose that there are 360 time values, 100 items, 50 branches, 30 locations, and 10 million sales tuples in the *sales_star* data cube. If the *sales* fact table has recorded sales for only 30 items, the remaining 70 items will obviously not participate in joins. If join indices are not used, additional I/Os have to be performed to bring the joining portions of the fact table and dimension tables together. ■

To further speed up query processing, the join indexing and bitmap indexing methods can be integrated to form **bitmapped join indices.**

3.4.3 Efficient Processing of OLAP Queries

The purpose of materializing cuboids and constructing OLAP index structures is to speed up query processing in data cubes. Given materialized views, query processing should proceed as follows:

1. **Determine which operations should be performed on the available cuboids:** This involves transforming any selection, projection, roll-up (group-by), and drill-down operations specified in the query into corresponding SQL and/or OLAP operations. For example, slicing and dicing a data cube may correspond to selection and/or projection operations on a materialized cuboid.
2. **Determine to which materialized cuboid(s) the relevant operations should be applied:** This involves identifying all of the materialized cuboids that may potentially be used to answer the query, pruning the above set using knowledge of "dominance" relationships among the cuboids, estimating the costs of using the remaining materialized cuboids, and selecting the cuboid with the least cost.

Example 3.14 **OLAP query processing.** Suppose that we define a data cube for *AllElectronics* of the form "*sales_cube* [*time, item, location*]: sum(*sales_in_dollars*)". The dimension hierarchies used are "*day* < *month* < *quarter* < *year*" for *time*, "*item_name* < *brand* < *type*" for *item*, and "*street* < *city* < *province_or_state* < *country*" for *location*.

Suppose that the query to be processed is on {*brand, province_or_state*}, with the selection constant "*year* = *2004*". Also, suppose that there are four materialized cuboids available, as follows:

- cuboid 1: {*year, item_name, city*}
- cuboid 2: {*year, brand, country*}
- cuboid 3: {*year, brand, province_or_state*}
- cuboid 4: {*item_name, province_or_state*} where *year* = *2004*

"*Which of the above four cuboids should be selected to process the query?*" Finer-granularity data cannot be generated from coarser-granularity data. Therefore, cuboid 2 cannot be used because *country* is a more general concept than *province_or_state*. Cuboids 1, 3, and 4 can be used to process the query because (1) they have the same set or a superset of the dimensions in the query, (2) the selection clause in the query can imply the selection in the cuboid, and (3) the abstraction levels for the *item* and *location* dimensions in these cuboids are at a finer level than *brand* and *province_or_state*, respectively.

"*How would the costs of each cuboid compare if used to process the query?*" It is likely that using cuboid 1 would cost the most because both *item_name* and *city* are at a lower level than the *brand* and *province_or_state* concepts specified in the query. If there are not many *year* values associated with *items* in the cube, but there are several *item_names* for each *brand*, then cuboid 3 will be smaller than cuboid 4, and thus cuboid 3 should be chosen to process the query. However, if efficient indices are available for cuboid 4, then cuboid 4 may be a better choice. Therefore, some cost-based estimation is required in order to decide which set of cuboids should be selected for query processing. ■

Because the storage model of a MOLAP server is an *n*-dimensional array, the front-end multidimensional queries are mapped directly to server storage structures, which provide direct addressing capabilities. The straightforward array representation of the data cube has good indexing properties, but has poor storage utilization when the data are sparse. For efficient storage and processing, sparse matrix and data compression techniques should therefore be applied. The details of several such methods of cube computation are presented in Chapter 4.

The storage structures used by dense and sparse arrays may differ, making it advantageous to adopt a two-level approach to MOLAP query processing: use array structures for dense arrays, and sparse matrix structures for sparse arrays. The two-dimensional dense arrays can be indexed by B-trees.

To process a query in MOLAP, the dense one- and two-dimensional arrays must first be identified. Indices are then built to these arrays using traditional indexing structures. The two-level approach increases storage utilization without sacrificing direct addressing capabilities.

"Are there any other strategies for answering queries quickly?" Some strategies for answering queries quickly concentrate on providing *intermediate feedback* to the users. For example, in **on-line aggregation**, a data mining system can display "what it knows so far" instead of waiting until the query is fully processed. Such an approximate answer to the given data mining query is periodically refreshed and refined as the computation process continues. Confidence intervals are associated with each estimate, providing the user with additional feedback regarding the reliability of the answer so far. This promotes interactivity with the system—the user gains insight as to whether or not he or she is probing in the "right" direction without having to wait until the end of the query. While on-line aggregation does not improve the total time to answer a query, the overall data mining process should be quicker due to the increased interactivity with the system.

Another approach is to employ **top *N* queries**. Suppose that you are interested in finding only the best-selling items among the millions of items sold at *AllElectronics*. Rather than waiting to obtain a list of all store items, sorted in decreasing order of sales, you would like to see only the top *N*. Using statistics, query processing can be optimized to return the top *N* items, rather than the whole sorted list. This results in faster response time while helping to promote user interactivity and reduce wasted resources.

The goal of this section was to provide an overview of data warehouse implementation. Chapter 4 presents a more advanced treatment of this topic. It examines the efficient computation of data cubes and processing of OLAP queries in greater depth, providing detailed algorithms.

3.5 From Data Warehousing to Data Mining

"How do data warehousing and OLAP relate to data mining?" In this section, we study the usage of data warehousing for information processing, analytical processing, and data mining. We also introduce on-line analytical mining (OLAM), a powerful paradigm that integrates OLAP with data mining technology.

3.5.1 Data Warehouse Usage

Data warehouses and data marts are used in a wide range of applications. Business executives use the data in data warehouses and data marts to perform data analysis and make strategic decisions. In many firms, data warehouses are used as an integral part of a *plan-execute-assess* "closed-loop" feedback system for enterprise management. Data warehouses are used extensively in banking and financial services, consumer goods and retail distribution sectors, and controlled manufacturing, such as demand-based production.

Typically, the longer a data warehouse has been in use, the more it will have evolved. This evolution takes place throughout a number of phases. Initially, the data warehouse is mainly used for generating reports and answering predefined queries. Progressively, it is used to analyze summarized and detailed data, where the results are presented in the form of reports and charts. Later, the data warehouse is used for strategic purposes, performing multidimensional analysis and sophisticated slice-and-dice operations. Finally, the data warehouse may be employed for knowledge discovery and strategic decision making using data mining tools. In this context, the tools for data warehousing can be categorized into *access and retrieval tools, database reporting tools, data analysis tools*, and *data mining tools.*

Business users need to have the means to know what exists in the data warehouse (through metadata), how to access the contents of the data warehouse, how to examine the contents using analysis tools, and how to present the results of such analysis.

There are three kinds of data warehouse applications: *information processing, analytical processing*, and *data mining*:

- **Information processing** supports querying, basic statistical analysis, and reporting using crosstabs, tables, charts, or graphs. A current trend in data warehouse information processing is to construct low-cost Web-based accessing tools that are then integrated with Web browsers.
- **Analytical processing** supports basic OLAP operations, including slice-and-dice, drill-down, roll-up, and pivoting. It generally operates on historical data in both summarized and detailed forms. The major strength of on-line analytical processing over information processing is the multidimensional data analysis of data warehouse data.
- **Data mining** supports knowledge discovery by finding hidden patterns and associations, constructing analytical models, performing classification and prediction, and presenting the mining results using visualization tools.

"How does data mining relate to information processing and on-line analytical processing?" Information processing, based on queries, can find useful information. However, answers to such queries reflect the information directly stored in databases or computable by aggregate functions. They do not reflect sophisticated patterns or regularities buried in the database. Therefore, information processing is not data mining.

On-line analytical processing comes a step closer to data mining because it can derive information summarized at multiple granularities from user-specified subsets of a data warehouse. Such descriptions are equivalent to the class/concept descriptions discussed in Chapter 1. Because data mining systems can also mine generalized class/concept descriptions, this raises some interesting questions: *"Do OLAP systems perform data mining? Are OLAP systems actually data mining systems?"*

The functionalities of OLAP and data mining can be viewed as disjoint: OLAP is a data summarization/aggregation *tool* that helps simplify data analysis, while data mining allows the *automated discovery* of implicit patterns and interesting knowledge hidden in large amounts of data. OLAP tools are targeted toward simplifying and supporting interactive data analysis, whereas the goal of data mining tools is to automate as much of the process as possible, while still allowing users to guide the process. In this sense, data mining goes one step beyond traditional on-line analytical processing.

An alternative and broader view of data mining may be adopted in which data mining covers both data description and data modeling. Because OLAP systems can present general descriptions of data from data warehouses, OLAP functions are essentially for user-directed data summary and comparison (by drilling, pivoting, slicing, dicing, and other operations). These are, though limited, data mining functionalities. Yet according to this view, data mining covers a much broader spectrum than simple OLAP operations because it performs not only data summary and comparison but also association, classification, prediction, clustering, time-series analysis, and other data analysis tasks.

Data mining is not confined to the analysis of data stored in data warehouses. It may analyze data existing at more detailed granularities than the summarized data provided in a data warehouse. It may also analyze transactional, spatial, textual, and multimedia data that are difficult to model with current multidimensional database technology. In this context, data mining covers a broader spectrum than OLAP with respect to data mining functionality and the complexity of the data handled.

Because data mining involves more automated and deeper analysis than OLAP, data mining is expected to have broader applications. Data mining can help business managers find and reach more suitable customers, as well as gain critical business insights that may help drive market share and raise profits. In addition, data mining can help managers understand customer group characteristics and develop optimal pricing strategies accordingly, correct item bundling based not on intuition but on actual item groups derived from customer purchase patterns, reduce promotional spending, and at the same time increase the overall net effectiveness of promotions.

3.5.2 From On-Line Analytical Processing to On-Line Analytical Mining

In the field of data mining, substantial research has been performed for data mining on various platforms, including transaction databases, relational databases, spatial databases, text databases, time-series databases, flat files, data warehouses, and so on.

On-line analytical mining (OLAM) (also called **OLAP mining**) integrates on-line analytical processing (OLAP) with data mining and mining knowledge in multidimensional databases. Among the many different paradigms and architectures of data mining systems, OLAM is particularly important for the following reasons:

- **High quality of data in data warehouses:** Most data mining tools need to work on integrated, consistent, and cleaned data, which requires costly data cleaning, data integration, and data transformation as preprocessing steps. A data warehouse constructed by such preprocessing serves as a valuable source of high-quality data for OLAP as well as for data mining. Notice that data mining may also serve as a valuable tool for data cleaning and data integration as well.
- **Available information processing infrastructure surrounding data warehouses:** Comprehensive information processing and data analysis infrastructures have been or will be systematically constructed surrounding data warehouses, which include accessing, integration, consolidation, and transformation of multiple heterogeneous databases, ODBC/OLE DB connections, Web-accessing and service facilities, and reporting and OLAP analysis tools. It is prudent to make the best use of the available infrastructures rather than constructing everything from scratch.
- **OLAP-based exploratory data analysis:** Effective data mining needs exploratory data analysis. A user will often want to traverse through a database, select portions of relevant data, analyze them at different granularities, and present knowledge/results in different forms. On-line analytical mining provides facilities for data mining on different subsets of data and at different levels of abstraction, by drilling, pivoting, filtering, dicing, and slicing on a data cube and on some intermediate data mining results. This, together with data/knowledge visualization tools, will greatly enhance the power and flexibility of exploratory data mining.
- **On-line selection of data mining functions:** Often a user may not know what kinds of knowledge she would like to mine. By integrating OLAP with multiple data mining functions, on-line analytical mining provides users with the flexibility to select desired data mining functions and swap data mining tasks dynamically.

Architecture for On-Line Analytical Mining

An OLAM server performs analytical mining in data cubes in a similar manner as an OLAP server performs on-line analytical processing. An integrated OLAM and OLAP architecture is shown in Figure 3.18, where the OLAM and OLAP servers both accept user on-line queries (or commands) via a graphical user interface API and work with the data cube in the data analysis via a cube API. A metadata directory is used to

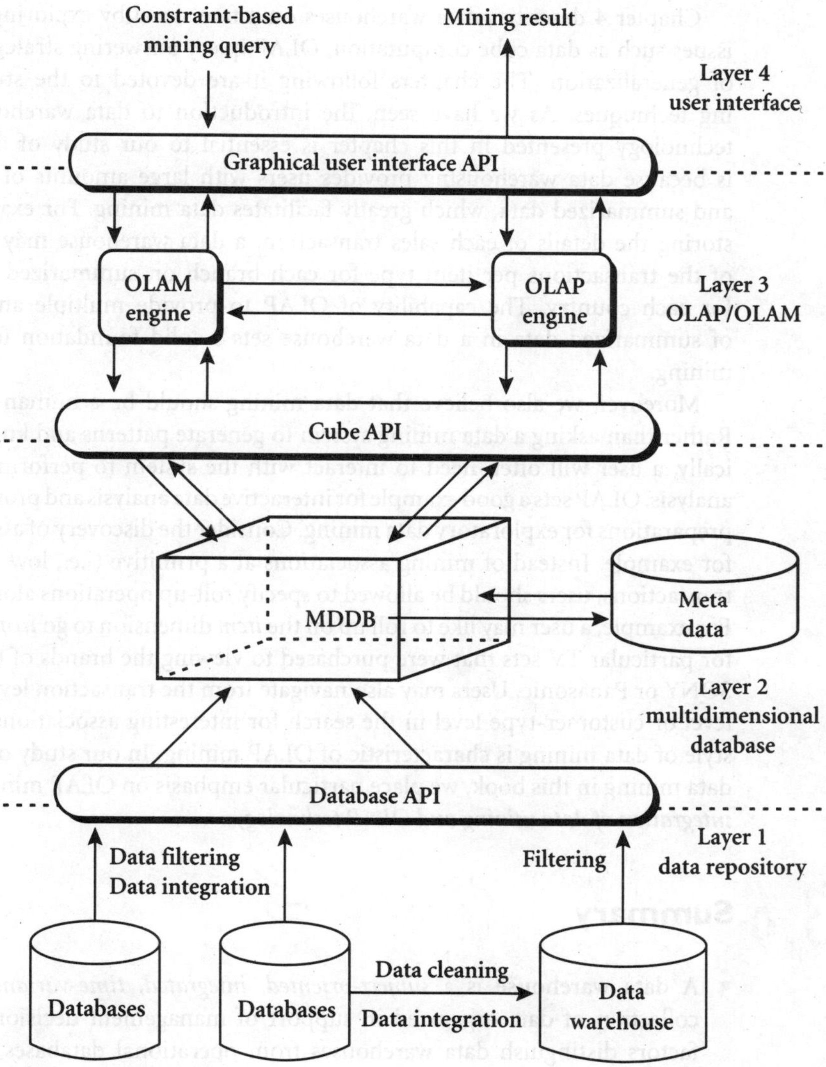

Figure 3.18 An integrated OLAM and OLAP architecture.

guide the access of the data cube. The data cube can be constructed by accessing and/or integrating multiple databases via an MDDB API and/or by filtering a data warehouse via a database API that may support OLE DB or ODBC connections. Since an OLAM server may perform multiple data mining tasks, such as concept description, association, classification, prediction, clustering, time-series analysis, and so on, it usually consists of multiple integrated data mining modules and is more sophisticated than an OLAP server.

Chapter 4 describes data warehouses on a finer level by exploring implementation issues such as data cube computation, OLAP query answering strategies, and methods of generalization. The chapters following it are devoted to the study of data mining techniques. As we have seen, the introduction to data warehousing and OLAP technology presented in this chapter is essential to our study of data mining. This is because data warehousing provides users with large amounts of clean, organized, and summarized data, which greatly facilitates data mining. For example, rather than storing the details of each sales transaction, a data warehouse may store a summary of the transactions per item type for each branch or, summarized to a higher level, for each country. The capability of OLAP to provide multiple and dynamic views of summarized data in a data warehouse sets a solid foundation for successful data mining.

Moreover, we also believe that data mining should be a human-centered process. Rather than asking a data mining system to generate patterns and knowledge automatically, a user will often need to interact with the system to perform exploratory data analysis. OLAP sets a good example for interactive data analysis and provides the necessary preparations for exploratory data mining. Consider the discovery of association patterns, for example. Instead of mining associations at a primitive (i.e., low) data level among transactions, users should be allowed to specify roll-up operations along any dimension. For example, a user may like to roll up on the *item* dimension to go from viewing the data for particular TV sets that were purchased to viewing the brands of these TVs, such as SONY or Panasonic. Users may also navigate from the transaction level to the customer level or customer-type level in the search for interesting associations. Such an OLAP-style of data mining is characteristic of OLAP mining. In our study of the principles of data mining in this book, we place particular emphasis on OLAP mining, that is, on the *integration of data mining and OLAP technology*.

3.6 Summary

- A **data warehouse** is a *subject-oriented, integrated, time-variant*, and *nonvolatile* collection of data organized in support of management decision making. Several factors distinguish data warehouses from operational databases. Because the two systems provide quite different functionalities and require different kinds of data, it is necessary to maintain data warehouses separately from operational databases.
- A **multidimensional data model** is typically used for the design of corporate *data warehouses* and *departmental data marts*. Such a model can adopt a *star schema, snowflake schema*, or *fact constellation schema*. The core of the *multidimensional model* is the **data cube**, which consists of a large set of *facts* (or *measures*) and a number of *dimensions*. Dimensions are the entities or perspectives with respect to which an organization wants to keep records and are hierarchical in nature.
- A data cube consists of a **lattice of cuboids**, each corresponding to a different degree of summarization of the given multidimensional data.

- **Concept hierarchies** organize the values of attributes or dimensions into gradual levels of abstraction. They are useful in mining at multiple levels of abstraction.

- **On-line analytical processing (OLAP)** can be performed in data warehouses/marts using the multidimensional data model. Typical OLAP operations include *roll-up*, *drill-*(*down, across, through*), *slice-and-dice*, *pivot* (*rotate*), as well as statistical operations such as ranking and computing moving averages and growth rates. OLAP operations can be implemented efficiently using the data cube structure.

- Data warehouses often adopt a **three-tier architecture**. The bottom tier is a *warehouse database server*, which is typically a relational database system. The middle tier is an *OLAP server*, and the top tier is a *client*, containing query and reporting tools.

- A data warehouse contains **back-end tools and utilities** for populating and refreshing the warehouse. These cover data extraction, data cleaning, data transformation, loading, refreshing, and warehouse management.

- Data warehouse **metadata** are data defining the warehouse objects. A metadata repository provides details regarding the warehouse structure, data history, the algorithms used for summarization, mappings from the source data to warehouse form, system performance, and business terms and issues.

- OLAP servers may use **relational OLAP (ROLAP)**, or **multidimensional OLAP (MOLAP)**, or **hybrid OLAP (HOLAP)**. A ROLAP server uses an extended relational DBMS that maps OLAP operations on multidimensional data to standard relational operations. A MOLAP server maps multidimensional data views directly to array structures. A HOLAP server combines ROLAP and MOLAP. For example, it may use ROLAP for historical data while maintaining frequently accessed data in a separate MOLAP store.

- **Full materialization** refers to the computation of all of the cuboids in the lattice defining a data cube. It typically requires an excessive amount of storage space, particularly as the number of dimensions and size of associated concept hierarchies grow. This problem is known as the **curse of dimensionality**. Alternatively, **partial materialization** is the selective computation of a subset of the cuboids or subcubes in the lattice. For example, an **iceberg cube** is a data cube that stores only those cube cells whose aggregate value (e.g., **count**) is above some minimum support threshold.

- OLAP query processing can be made more efficient with the use of indexing techniques. In **bitmap indexing**, each attribute has its own bitmap index table. Bitmap indexing reduces join, aggregation, and comparison operations to bit arithmetic. **Join indexing** registers the joinable rows of two or more relations from a relational database, reducing the overall cost of OLAP join operations. **Bitmapped join indexing**, which combines the bitmap and join index methods, can be used to further speed up OLAP query processing.

- Data warehouses are used for *information processing* (querying and reporting), *analytical processing* (which allows users to navigate through summarized and detailed data by OLAP operations), and *data mining* (which supports knowledge discovery). OLAP-based data mining is referred to as **OLAP mining**, or on-line analytical mining (OLAM), which emphasizes the interactive and exploratory nature of OLAP mining.

Exercises

3.1 State why, for the integration of multiple heterogeneous information sources, many companies in industry prefer the *update-driven approach* (which constructs and uses data warehouses), rather than the *query-driven approach* (which applies wrappers and integrators). Describe situations where the query-driven approach is preferable over the update-driven approach.

3.2 Briefly compare the following concepts. You may use an example to explain your point(s).

(a) Snowflake schema, fact constellation, starnet query model

(b) Data cleaning, data transformation, refresh

(c) Enterprise warehouse, data mart, virtual warehouse

3.3 Suppose that a data warehouse consists of the three dimensions *time, doctor*, and *patient*, and the two measures *count* and *charge*, where *charge* is the fee that a doctor charges a patient for a visit.

(a) Enumerate three classes of schemas that are popularly used for modeling data warehouses.

(b) Draw a schema diagram for the above data warehouse using one of the schema classes listed in (a).

(c) Starting with the base cuboid [*day, doctor, patient*], what specific *OLAP operations* should be performed in order to list the total fee collected by each doctor in 2004?

(d) To obtain the same list, write an SQL query assuming the data are stored in a relational database with the schema *fee* (*day, month, year, doctor, hospital, patient, count, charge*).

3.4 Suppose that a data warehouse for *Big University* consists of the following four dimensions: *student, course, semester*, and *instructor*, and two measures *count* and *avg_grade*. When at the lowest conceptual level (e.g., for a given student, course, semester, and instructor combination), the *avg_grade* measure stores the actual course grade of the student. At higher conceptual levels, *avg_grade* stores the average grade for the given combination.

(a) Draw a *snowflake schema* diagram for the data warehouse.

(b) Starting with the base cuboid [*student, course, semester, instructor*], what specific *OLAP operations* (e.g., roll-up from *semester* to *year*) should one perform in order to list the average grade of *CS* courses for each *Big University* student.

(c) If each dimension has five levels (including all), such as "*student* < *major* < *status* < *university* < all", how many cuboids will this cube contain (including the base and apex cuboids)?

3.5 Suppose that a data warehouse consists of the four dimensions, *date, spectator, location*, and *game*, and the two measures, *count* and *charge*, where *charge* is the fare that a spectator pays when watching a game on a given date. Spectators may be students, adults, or seniors, with each category having its own charge rate.

(a) Draw a *star schema* diagram for the data warehouse.

(b) Starting with the base cuboid [*date, spectator, location, game*], what specific *OLAP operations* should one perform in order to list the total charge paid by student spectators at GM_Place in 2004?

(c) *Bitmap indexing* is useful in data warehousing. Taking this cube as an example, briefly discuss advantages and problems of using a bitmap index structure.

3.6 A data warehouse can be modeled by either a *star schema* or a *snowflake schema*. Briefly describe the similarities and the differences of the two models, and then analyze their advantages and disadvantages with regard to one another. Give your opinion of which might be more empirically useful and state the reasons behind your answer.

3.7 Design a data warehouse for a regional weather bureau. The weather bureau has about 1,000 probes, which are scattered throughout various land and ocean locations in the region to collect basic weather data, including air pressure, temperature, and precipitation at each hour. All data are sent to the central station, which has collected such data for over 10 years. Your design should facilitate efficient querying and on-line analytical processing, and derive general weather patterns in multidimensional space.

3.8 A popular data warehouse implementation is to construct a multidimensional database, known as a data cube. Unfortunately, this may often generate a huge, yet very sparse multidimensional matrix. Present an example illustrating such a huge and sparse data cube.

3.9 Regarding the *computation of measures* in a data cube:

(a) Enumerate three categories of measures, based on the kind of aggregate functions used in computing a data cube.

(b) For a data cube with the three dimensions *time, location*, and *item*, which category does the function *variance* belong to? Describe how to compute it if the cube is partitioned into many chunks.
Hint: The formula for computing *variance* is $\frac{1}{N}\sum_{i=1}^{N}(x_i - \bar{x}_i)^2$, where $\bar{x}_i$ is the average of N x_is.

(c) Suppose the function is "*top 10 sales*". Discuss how to efficiently compute this measure in a data cube.

3.10 Suppose that we need to record three measures in a data cube: **min**, **average**, and **median**. Design an efficient computation and storage method for each measure given that the cube allows data to be *deleted incrementally* (i.e., in small portions at a time) from the cube.

3.11 In data warehouse technology, a multiple dimensional view can be implemented by a relational database technique (*ROLAP*), or by a multidimensional database technique (*MOLAP*), or by a hybrid database technique (*HOLAP*).

(a) Briefly describe each implementation technique.

(b) For each technique, explain how each of the following functions may be implemented:

i. The generation of a data warehouse (including aggregation)

ii. Roll-up

iii. Drill-down

iv. Incremental updating

Which implementation techniques do you prefer, and why?

3.12 Suppose that a data warehouse contains 20 dimensions, each with about five levels of granularity.

(a) Users are mainly interested in four particular dimensions, each having three frequently accessed levels for rolling up and drilling down. How would you design a data cube structure to efficiently support this preference?

(b) At times, a user may want to *drill through* the cube, down to the raw data for one or two particular dimensions. How would you support this feature?

3.13 A data cube, C, has n dimensions, and each dimension has exactly p distinct values in the base cuboid. Assume that there are no concept hierarchies associated with the dimensions.

(a) What is the *maximum number of cells* possible in the base cuboid?

(b) What is the *minimum number of cells* possible in the base cuboid?

(c) What is the *maximum number of cells* possible (including both base cells and aggregate cells) in the data cube, C?

(d) What is the *minimum number of cells* possible in the data cube, C?

3.14 What are the differences between the three main types of data warehouse usage: *information processing*, *analytical processing*, and *data mining*? Discuss the motivation behind *OLAP mining* (*OLAM*).

Bibliographic Notes

There are a good number of introductory level textbooks on data warehousing and OLAP technology, including Kimball and Ross [KR02], Imhoff, Galemmo, and Geiger [IGG03], Inmon [Inm96], Berson and Smith [BS97b], and Thomsen [Tho97].

Chaudhuri and Dayal [CD97] provide a general overview of data warehousing and OLAP technology. A set of research papers on materialized views and data warehouse implementations were collected in *Materialized Views: Techniques, Implementations, and Applications* by Gupta and Mumick [GM99].

The history of decision support systems can be traced back to the 1960s. However, the proposal of the construction of large data warehouses for multidimensional data analysis is credited to Codd [CCS93], who coined the term *OLAP* for *on-line analytical processing*. The OLAP council was established in 1995. Widom [Wid95] identified several research problems in data warehousing. Kimball and Ross [KR02] provide an overview of the deficiencies of SQL regarding the ability to support comparisons that are common in the business world and present a good set of application cases that require data warehousing and OLAP technology. For an overview of OLAP systems versus statistical databases, see Shoshani [Sho97].

Gray, Chauduri, Bosworth et al. [GCB+97] proposed the data cube as a relational aggregation operator generalizing group-by, crosstabs, and subtotals. Harinarayan, Rajaraman, and Ullman [HRU96] proposed a greedy algorithm for the partial materialization of cuboids in the computation of a data cube. Sarawagi and Stonebraker [SS94] developed a chunk-based computation technique for the efficient organization of large multidimensional arrays. Agarwal, Agrawal, Deshpande, et al. [AAD+96] proposed several methods for the efficient computation of multidimensional aggregates for ROLAP servers. A chunk-based multiway array aggregation method for data cube computation in MOLAP was proposed in Zhao, Deshpande, and Naughton [ZDN97]. Ross and Srivastava [RS97] pointed out the problem of the curse of dimensionality in cube materialization and developed a method for computing sparse data cubes. Iceberg queries were first described in Fang, Shivakumar, Garcia-Molina, et al. [FSGM+98]. BUC, an efficient bottom-up method for computing iceberg cubes was introduced by Beyer and Ramakrishnan [BR99]. References for the further development of cube computation methods are given in the Bibliographic Notes of Chapter 4. The use of join indices to speed up relational query processing was proposed by Valduriez [Val87]. O'Neil and Graefe [OG95] proposed a bitmapped join index method to speed up OLAP-based query processing. A discussion of the performance of bitmapping and other nontraditional index techniques is given in O'Neil and Quass [OQ97].

For work regarding the selection of materialized cuboids for efficient OLAP query processing, see Chaudhuri and Dayal [CD97], Harinarayan, Rajaraman, and Ullman [HRU96], and Sristava, Dar, Jagadish, and Levy [SDJL96]. Methods for cube size estimation can be found in Deshpande, Naughton, Ramasamy, et al. [DNR+97], Ross and Srivastava [RS97], and Beyer and Ramakrishnan [BR99]. Agrawal, Gupta, and Sarawagi [AGS97] proposed operations for modeling multidimensional databases. Methods for answering queries quickly by on-line aggregation are described in Hellerstein, Haas, and Wang [HHW97] and Hellerstein, Avnur, Chou, et al. [HAC+99]. Techniques for estimating the top N queries are proposed in Carey and Kossman [CK98] and Donjerkovic and Ramakrishnan [DR99]. Further studies on intelligent OLAP and discovery-driven exploration of data cubes are presented in the Bibliographic Notes of Chapter 4.

4 Data Cube Computation and Data Generalization

Data generalization is a process that abstracts a large set of task-relevant data in a database from a relatively low conceptual level to higher conceptual levels. Users like the ease and flexibility of having large data sets summarized in concise and succinct terms, at different levels of granularity, and from different angles. Such data descriptions help provide an overall picture of the data at hand.

Data warehousing and OLAP perform data generalization by summarizing data at varying levels of abstraction. An overview of such technology was presented in Chapter 3. From a data analysis point of view, data generalization is a form of *descriptive data mining*, which describes data in a concise and summarative manner and presents interesting general properties of the data. In this chapter, we look at descriptive data mining in greater detail. Descriptive data mining differs from *predictive data mining*, which analyzes data in order to construct one or a set of models and attempts to predict the behavior of new data sets. Predictive data mining, such as classification, regression analysis, and trend analysis, is covered in later chapters.

This chapter is organized into three main sections. The first two sections expand on notions of data warehouse and OLAP implementation presented in the previous chapter, while the third presents an alternative method for data generalization. In particular, Section 4.1 shows how to efficiently compute data cubes at varying levels of abstraction. It presents an in-depth look at specific methods for data cube computation. Section 4.2 presents methods for further exploration of OLAP and data cubes. This includes discovery-driven exploration of data cubes, analysis of cubes with sophisticated features, and cube gradient analysis. Finally, Section 4.3 presents another method of data generalization, known as *attribute-oriented induction*.

4.1 Efficient Methods for Data Cube Computation

Data cube computation is an essential task in data warehouse implementation. The precomputation of all or part of a data cube can greatly reduce the response time and enhance the performance of on-line analytical processing. However, such computation is challenging because it may require substantial computational time and storage space. This section explores efficient methods for data cube computation. Section 4.1.1 introduces general concepts and computation strategies relating to cube materialization. Sections 4.1.2 to 4.1.5 detail specific computation algorithms, namely, MultiWay array aggregation, BUC, Star-Cubing, the computation of shell fragments, and the computation of cubes involving complex measures.

4.1.1 A Road Map for the Materialization of Different Kinds of Cubes

Data cubes facilitate the on-line analytical processing of multidimensional data. *"But how can we compute data cubes in advance, so that they are handy and readily available for query processing?"* This section contrasts full cube materialization (i.e., precomputation) versus various strategies for partial cube materialization. For completeness, we begin with a review of the basic terminology involving data cubes. We also introduce a cube cell notation that is useful for describing data cube computation methods.

Cube Materialization: Full Cube, Iceberg Cube, Closed Cube, and Shell Cube

Figure 4.1 shows a 3-D data cube for the dimensions *A*, *B*, and *C*, and an aggregate measure, *M*. A data cube is a lattice of cuboids. Each cuboid represents a group-by. *ABC* is the base cuboid, containing all three of the dimensions. Here, the aggregate measure, *M*, is computed for each possible combination of the three dimensions. The base cuboid is the least generalized of all of the cuboids in the data cube. The most generalized cuboid is the apex cuboid, commonly represented as all. It contains one value—it aggregates measure *M* for all of the tuples stored in the base cuboid. To drill down in the data cube, we move from the apex cuboid, downward in the lattice. To

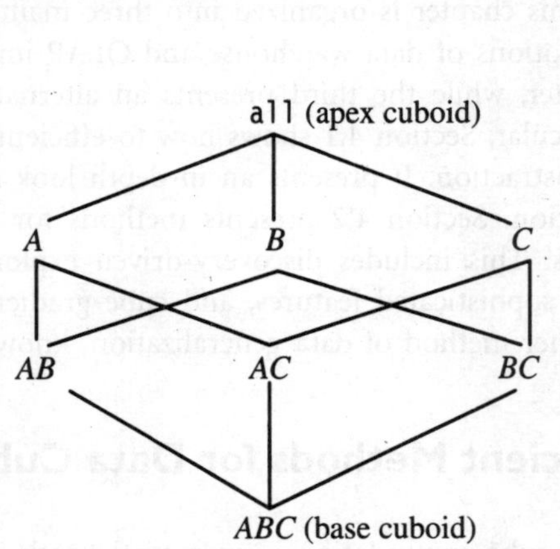

Figure 4.1 Lattice of cuboids, making up a 3-D data cube with the dimensions *A*, *B*, and *C* for some aggregate measure, *M*.

roll up, we move from the base cuboid, upward. For the purposes of our discussion in this chapter, we will always use the term data cube to refer to a lattice of cuboids rather than an individual cuboid.

A cell in the base cuboid is a **base cell.** A cell from a nonbase cuboid is an **aggregate** cell. An aggregate cell aggregates over one or more dimensions, where each aggregated dimension is indicated by a "$*$" in the cell notation. Suppose we have an n-dimensional data cube. Let $a = (a_1, a_2, \ldots, a_n, \textit{measures})$ be a cell from one of the cuboids making up the data cube. We say that a is an ***m*-dimensional cell** (that is, from an m-dimensional cuboid) if exactly m ($m \leq n$) values among $\{a_1, a_2, \ldots, a_n\}$ are *not* "$*$". If $m = n$, then a is a base cell; otherwise, it is an aggregate cell (i.e., where $m < n$).

Example 4.1 **Base and aggregate cells.** Consider a data cube with the dimensions *month, city,* and *customer_group*, and the measure *price*. (*Jan*, $*$, $*$, 2800) and ($*$, *Toronto*, $*$, 1200) are 1-D cells, (*Jan*, $*$, *Business*, 150) is a 2-D cell, and (*Jan*, *Toronto*, *Business*, 45) is a 3-D cell. Here, all base cells are 3-D, whereas 1-D and 2-D cells are aggregate cells. ■

An ancestor-descendant relationship may exist between cells. In an n-dimensional data cube, an i-D cell $a = (a_1, a_2, \ldots, a_n, \textit{measures}_a)$ is an **ancestor** of a j-D cell $b = (b_1, b_2, \ldots, b_n, \textit{measures}_b)$, and b is a **descendant** of a, if and only if (1) $i < j$, and (2) for $1 \leq m \leq n$, $a_m = b_m$ whenever $a_m \neq$ "$*$". In particular, cell a is called a **parent** of cell b, and b is a **child** of a, if and only if $j = i + 1$ and b is a descendant of a.

Example 4.2 **Ancestor and descendant cells.** Referring to our previous example, 1-D cell $a =$ (*Jan*, $*$, $*$, 2800), and 2-D cell $b =$ (*Jan*, $*$, *Business*, 150), are *ancestors* of 3-D cell $c =$ (*Jan*, *Toronto*, *Business*, 45); c is a *descendant* of both a and b; b is a *parent* of c, and c is a *child* of b. ■

In order to ensure fast on-line analytical processing, it is sometimes desirable to precompute the **full cube** (i.e., all the cells of all of the cuboids for a given data cube). This, however, is exponential to the number of dimensions. That is, a data cube of n dimensions contains 2^n cuboids. There are even more cuboids if we consider concept hierarchies for each dimension.[1] In addition, the size of each cuboid depends on the cardinality of its dimensions. Thus, precomputation of the full cube can require huge and often excessive amounts of memory.

Nonetheless, full cube computation algorithms are important. **Individual** cuboids may be stored on secondary storage and accessed when necessary. Alternatively, we can use such algorithms to compute smaller cubes, consisting of a subset of the given set of dimensions, or a smaller range of possible values for some of the dimensions. In such cases, the smaller cube is a full cube for the given subset of dimensions and/or dimension values. A thorough understanding of full cube computation methods will

[1] Equation (3.1) gives the total number of cuboids in a data cube where each dimension has an associated concept hierarchy.

help us develop efficient methods for computing partial cubes. Hence, it is important to explore scalable methods for computing all of the cuboids making up a data cube, that is, for full materialization. These methods must take into consideration the limited amount of main memory available for cuboid computation, the total size of the computed data cube, as well as the time required for such computation.

Partial materialization of data cubes offers an interesting trade-off between storage space and response time for OLAP. Instead of computing the full cube, we can compute only a subset of the data cube's cuboids, or subcubes consisting of subsets of cells from the various cuboids.

Many cells in a cuboid may actually be of little or no interest to the data analyst. Recall that each cell in a full cube records an aggregate value. Measures such as *count*, *sum*, or *sales_in_dollars* are commonly used. For many cells in a cuboid, the measure value will be zero. When the product of the cardinalities for the dimensions in a cuboid is large relative to the number of nonzero-valued tuples that are stored in the cuboid, then we say that the cuboid is **sparse**. If a cube contains many sparse cuboids, we say that the cube is **sparse**.

In many cases, a substantial amount of the cube's space could be taken up by a large number of cells with very low measure values. This is because the cube cells are often quite sparsely distributed within a multiple dimensional space. For example, a customer may only buy a few items in a store at a time. Such an event will generate only a few nonempty cells, leaving most other cube cells empty. In such situations, it is useful to materialize only those cells in a cuboid (group-by) whose measure value is above some minimum threshold. In a data cube for sales, say, we may wish to materialize only those cells for which $count \geq 10$ (i.e., where at least 10 tuples exist for the cell's given combination of dimensions), or only those cells representing $sales \geq \$100$. This not only saves processing time and disk space, but also leads to a more focused analysis. The cells that cannot pass the threshold are likely to be too trivial to warrant further analysis. Such partially materialized cubes are known as **iceberg cubes**. The minimum threshold is called the **minimum support threshold**, or *minimum support(min_sup)*, for short. By materializing only a fraction of the cells in a data cube, the result is seen as the "tip of the iceberg," where the "iceberg" is the potential full cube including all cells. An iceberg cube can be specified with an SQL query, as shown in the following example.

Example 4.3 Iceberg cube.

```
compute cube sales_iceberg as
select month, city, customer_group, count(*)
from salesInfo
cube by month, city, customer_group
having count(*) >= min_sup
```

The **compute cube** statement specifies the precomputation of the iceberg cube, *sales_iceberg*, with the dimensions *month*, *city*, and *customer_group*, and the aggregate measure **count()**. The input tuples are in the *salesInfo* relation. The **cube by** clause specifies that aggregates (group-by's) are to be formed for each of the possible subsets of the given dimensions. If we were computing the full cube, each group-by would correspond to a cuboid in the data cube lattice. The constraint specified in the **having** clause is known as the **iceberg condition**. Here, the iceberg measure is *count*. Note that the iceberg cube computed for Example 4.3 could be used to answer group-by queries on any combination of the specified dimensions of the form **having count(*)** $>= v$, where $v \geq min\_sup$. Instead of *count*, the iceberg condition could specify more complex measures, such as *average*.

If we were to omit the **having** clause of our example, we would end up with the full cube. Let's call this cube *sales_cube*. The iceberg cube, *sales_iceberg*, excludes all the cells of *sales_cube* whose count is less than *min_sup*. Obviously, if we were to set the minimum support to 1 in *sales_iceberg*, the resulting cube would be the full cube, *sales_cube*. ■

A naïve approach to computing an iceberg cube would be to first compute the full cube and then prune the cells that do not satisfy the iceberg condition. However, this is still prohibitively expensive. An efficient approach is to compute only the iceberg cube directly without computing the full cube. Sections 4.1.3 and 4.1.4 discuss methods for efficient iceberg cube computation.

Introducing iceberg cubes will lessen the burden of computing trivial aggregate cells in a data cube. However, we could still end up with a large number of uninteresting cells to compute. For example, suppose that there are 2 base cells for a database of 100 dimensions, denoted as $\{(a_1, a_2, a_3, \ldots, a_{100}) : 10, (a_1, a_2, b_3, \ldots, b_{100}) : 10\}$, where each has a cell count of 10. If the minimum support is set to 10, there will still be an impermissible number of cells to compute and store, although most of them are not interesting. For example, there are $2^{101} - 6$ distinct aggregate cells,[2] like $\{(a_1, a_2, a_3, a_4, \ldots, a_{99}, *) : 10, \ldots, (a_1, a_2, *, a_4, \ldots, a_{99}, a_{100}) : 10, \ldots, (a_1, a_2, a_3, *, \ldots, *, *) : 10\}$, but most of them do not contain much new information. If we ignore all of the aggregate cells that can be obtained by replacing some constants by $*$'s while keeping the same measure value, there are only three distinct cells left: $\{(a_1, a_2, a_3, \ldots, a_{100}) : 10, (a_1, a_2, b_3, \ldots, b_{100}) : 10, (a_1, a_2, *, \ldots, *) : 20\}$. That is, out of $2^{101} - 6$ distinct aggregate cells, only 3 really offer new information.

To systematically compress a data cube, we need to introduce the concept of *closed coverage*. A cell, c, is a *closed cell* if there exists no cell, d, such that d is a specialization (descendant) of cell c (that is, where d is obtained by replacing a $*$ in c with a non-$*$ value), and d has the same measure value as c. A **closed cube** is a data cube consisting of only closed cells. For example, the three cells derived above are the three closed cells of the data cube for the data set: $\{(a_1, a_2, a_3, \ldots, a_{100}) : 10, (a_1, a_2, b_3, \ldots, b_{100}) : 10\}$. They form the lattice of a closed cube as shown in Figure 4.2. Other nonclosed cells can be derived from their corresponding closed cells in this lattice. For example, "$(a_1, *, *, \ldots, *) : 20$" can be derived from "$(a_1, a_2, *, \ldots, *) : 20$" because the former is a generalized nonclosed cell of the latter. Similarly, we have "$(a_1, a_2, b_3, *, \ldots, *) : 10$".

Another strategy for partial materialization is to precompute only the cuboids involving a small number of dimensions, such as 3 to 5. These cuboids form a cube

[2]The proof is left as an exercise for the reader.

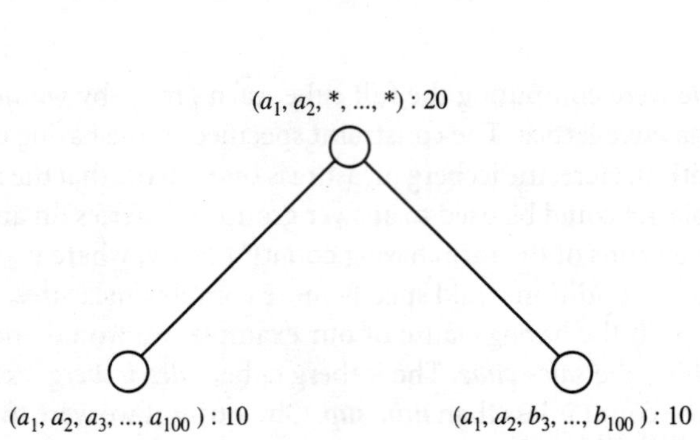

Figure 4.2 Three closed cells forming the lattice of a closed cube.

shell for the corresponding data cube. Queries on additional combinations of the dimensions will have to be computed on the fly. For example, we could compute all cuboids with 3 dimensions or less in an n-dimensional data cube, resulting in a cube shell of size 3. This, however, can still result in a large number of cuboids to compute, particularly when n is large. Alternatively, we can choose to precompute only portions or *fragments* of the cube shell, based on cuboids of interest. Section 4.1.5 discusses a method for computing such **shell fragments** and explores how they can be used for efficient OLAP query processing.

General Strategies for Cube Computation

With different kinds of cubes as described above, we can expect that there are a good number of methods for efficient computation. In general, there are two basic data structures used for storing cuboids. Relational tables are used as the basic data structure for the implementation of relational OLAP (ROLAP), while multidimensional arrays are used as the basic data structure in multidimensional OLAP (MOLAP). Although ROLAP and MOLAP may each explore different cube computation techniques, some optimization "tricks" can be shared among the different data representations. The following are general optimization techniques for the efficient computation of data cubes.

Optimization Technique 1: Sorting, hashing, and grouping. Sorting, hashing, and grouping operations should be applied to the dimension attributes in order to reorder and cluster related tuples.

In cube computation, aggregation is performed on the tuples (or cells) that share the same set of dimension values. Thus it is important to explore sorting, hashing, and grouping operations to access and group such data together to facilitate computation of such aggregates.

For example, to compute total sales by *branch*, *day*, and *item*, it is more efficient to sort tuples or cells by *branch*, and then by *day*, and then group them according to the *item* name. Efficient implementations of such operations in large data sets have been extensively studied in the database research community. Such implementations can be extended to data cube computation.

This technique can also be further extended to perform **shared-sorts** (i.e., sharing sorting costs across multiple cuboids when sort-based methods are used), or to perform **shared-partitions** (i.e., sharing the partitioning cost across multiple cuboids when hash-based algorithms are used).

Optimization Technique 2: Simultaneous aggregation and caching intermediate results. In cube computation, it is efficient to compute higher-level aggregates from previously computed lower-level aggregates, rather than from the base fact table. Moreover, simultaneous aggregation from cached intermediate computation results may lead to the reduction of expensive disk I/O operations.

For example, to compute sales by *branch*, we can use the intermediate results derived from the computation of a lower-level cuboid, such as sales by *branch* and *day*. This technique can be further extended to perform **amortized scans** (i.e., computing as many cuboids as possible at the same time to amortize disk reads).

Optimization Technique 3: Aggregation from the smallest child, when there exist multiple child cuboids. When there exist multiple child cuboids, it is usually more efficient to compute the desired parent (i.e., more generalized) cuboid from the smallest, previously computed child cuboid.

For example, to compute a sales cuboid, C_{branch}, when there exist two previously computed cuboids, $C_{\{branch,year\}}$ and $C_{\{branch,item\}}$, it is obviously more efficient to compute C_{branch} from the former than from the latter if there are many more distinct items than distinct years.

Many other optimization tricks may further improve the computational efficiency. For example, *string dimension attributes can be mapped to integers with values ranging from zero to the cardinality of the attribute.* However, the following optimization technique plays a particularly important role in iceberg cube computation.

Optimization Technique 4: The Apriori pruning method can be explored to compute iceberg cubes efficiently. The **Apriori property**,[3] in the context of data cubes, states as follows: *If a given cell does not satisfy minimum support, then no descendant (i.e., more specialized or detailed version) of the cell will satisfy minimum support either.* This property can be used to substantially reduce the computation of iceberg cubes.

Recall that the specification of iceberg cubes contains an iceberg condition, which is a constraint on the cells to be materialized. A common iceberg condition is that the cells must satisfy a *minimum support* threshold, such as a minimum count or sum. In this situation, the Apriori property can be used to prune away the exploration of the descendants of the cell. For example, if the count of a cell, *c*, in a cuboid is less than a minimum support threshold, *v*, then the count of any of *c*'s descendant cells in the lower-level cuboids can never be greater than or equal to *v*, and thus can be pruned. In other words, if a condition (e.g., the iceberg condition specified in a **having** clause)

[3]The Apriori property was proposed in the Apriori algorithm for association rule mining by R. Agrawal and R. Srikant [AS94]. Many algorithms in association rule mining have adopted this property. Association rule mining is the topic of Chapter 5.

is violated for some cell c, then every descendant of c will also violate that condition. Measures that obey this property are known as **antimonotonic**.[4] This form of pruning was made popular in association rule mining, yet also aids in data cube computation by cutting processing time and disk space requirements. It can lead to a more focused analysis because cells that cannot pass the threshold are unlikely to be of interest.

In the following subsections, we introduce several popular methods for efficient cube computation that explore some or all of the above optimization strategies. Section 4.1.2 describes the *multiway array aggregation* (MultiWay) method for computing full cubes. The remaining sections describe methods for computing iceberg cubes. Section 4.1.3 describes a method known as BUC, which computes iceberg cubes from the apex cuboid, downward. Section 4.1.4 describes the Star-Cubing method, which integrates top-down and bottom-up computation. Section 4.1.5 describes a minimal cubing approach that computes shell fragments for efficient high-dimensional OLAP. Finally, Section 4.1.6 describes a method for computing iceberg cubes with complex measures, such as *average*. To simplify our discussion, we exclude the cuboids that would be generated by climbing up any existing hierarchies for the dimensions. Such kinds of cubes can be computed by extension of the discussed methods. Methods for the efficient computation of closed cubes are left as an exercise for interested readers.

4.1.2 Multiway Array Aggregation for Full Cube Computation

The **Multiway Array Aggregation** (or simply **MultiWay**) method computes a full data cube by using a multidimensional array as its basic data structure. It is a typical MOLAP approach that uses direct array addressing, where dimension values are accessed via the position or index of their corresponding array locations. Hence, MultiWay cannot perform any value-based reordering as an optimization technique. A different approach is developed for the array-based cube construction, as follows:

1. Partition the array into chunks. A **chunk** is a subcube that is small enough to fit into the memory available for cube computation. **Chunking** is a method for dividing an n-dimensional array into small n-dimensional chunks, where each chunk is stored as an object on disk. The chunks are compressed so as to remove wasted space resulting from empty array cells (i.e., cells that do not contain any valid data, whose cell count is zero). For instance, "*chunkID + offset*" can be used as a cell addressing mechanism **to compress a sparse array structure** and when searching for cells within a chunk. Such a compression technique is powerful enough to handle sparse cubes, both on disk and in memory.
2. Compute aggregates by visiting (i.e., accessing the values at) cube cells. The order in which cells are visited can be optimized so as to *minimize the number of times that each cell must be revisited*, thereby reducing memory access and storage costs. The trick is

[4] **Antimonotone** is based on *condition violation*. This differs from **monotone**, which is based on *condition satisfaction*.

to exploit this ordering so that partial aggregates can be computed simultaneously, and any unnecessary revisiting of cells is avoided.

Because this chunking technique involves "overlapping" some of the aggregation computations, it is referred to as **multiway array aggregation.** It performs **simultaneous aggregation**—that is, it computes aggregations simultaneously on multiple dimensions.

We explain this approach to array-based cube construction by looking at a concrete example.

Example 4.4 **Multiway array cube computation.** Consider a 3-D data array containing the three dimensions *A*, *B*, and *C*. The 3-D array is partitioned into small, memory-based chunks. In this example, the array is partitioned into 64 chunks as shown in Figure 4.3. Dimension *A* is organized into four equal-sized partitions, a_0, a_1, a_2, and a_3. Dimensions *B* and *C* are similarly organized into four partitions each. Chunks 1, 2, ..., 64 correspond to the subcubes $a_0b_0c_0$, $a_1b_0c_0$, ..., $a_3b_3c_3$, respectively. Suppose that the cardinality of the dimensions *A*, *B*, and *C* is 40, 400, and 4000, respectively. Thus, the size of the array for each dimension, *A*, *B*, and *C*, is also 40, 400, and 4000, respectively. The size of each partition in *A*, *B*, and *C* is therefore 10, 100, and 1000, respectively. Full materialization of the corresponding data cube involves the computation of all of the cuboids defining this cube. The resulting full cube consists of the following cuboids:

- The base cuboid, denoted by *ABC* (from which all of the other cuboids are directly or indirectly computed). This cube is already computed and corresponds to the given 3-D array.
- The 2-D cuboids, *AB*, *AC*, and *BC*, which respectively correspond to the group-by's *AB*, *AC*, and *BC*. These cuboids must be computed.
- The 1-D cuboids, *A*, *B*, and *C*, which respectively correspond to the group-by's *A*, *B*, and *C*. These cuboids must be computed.
- The 0-D (apex) cuboid, denoted by **all**, which corresponds to the group-by (); that is, there is no group-by here. This cuboid must be computed. It consists of one value. If, say, the data cube measure is **count**, then the value to be computed is simply the total count of all of the tuples in *ABC*.

Let's look at how the multiway array aggregation technique is used in this computation. There are many possible orderings with which chunks can be read into memory for use in cube computation. Consider the ordering labeled from 1 to 64, shown in Figure 4.3. Suppose we would like to compute the b_0c_0 chunk of the *BC* cuboid. We allocate space for this chunk in *chunk memory.* By scanning chunks 1 to 4 of *ABC*, the b_0c_0 chunk is computed. That is, the cells for b_0c_0 are aggregated over a_0 to a_3. The chunk memory can then be assigned to the next chunk, b_1c_0, which completes its aggregation after the scanning of the next four chunks of *ABC*: 5 to 8. Continuing

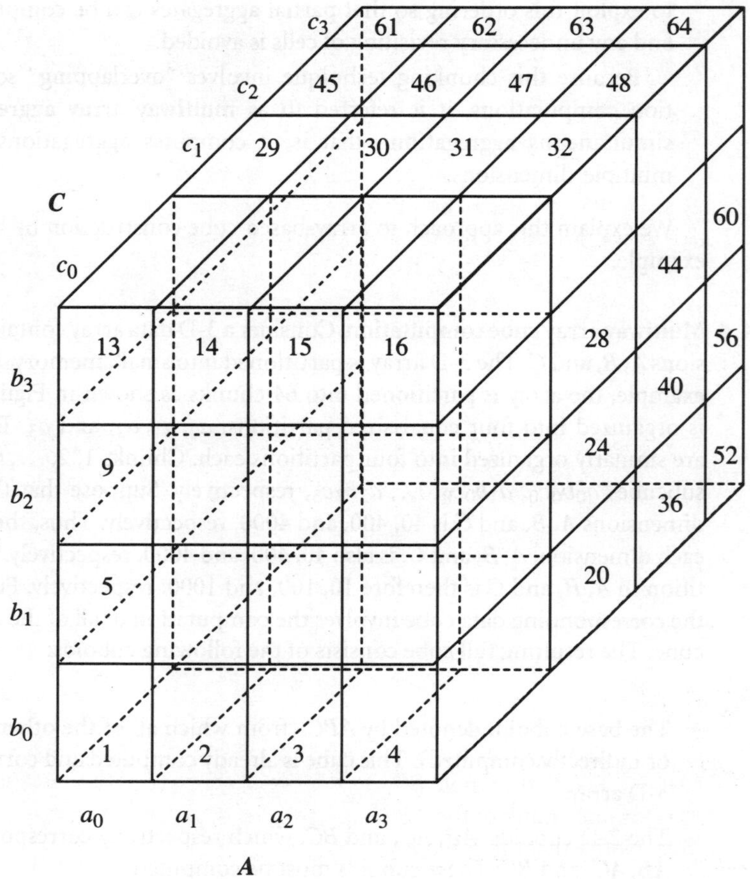

Figure 4.3 A 3-D array for the dimensions *A*, *B*, and *C*, organized into 64 *chunks*. Each chunk is small enough to fit into the memory available for cube computation.

in this way, the entire *BC* cuboid can be computed. Therefore, only *one* chunk of *BC* needs to be in memory, at a time, for the computation of all of the chunks of *BC*.

In computing the *BC* cuboid, we will have scanned each of the 64 chunks. *"Is there a way to avoid having to rescan all of these chunks for the computation of other cuboids, such as AC and AB?"* The answer is, most definitely—*yes*. This is where the "multiway computation" or "simultaneous aggregation" idea comes in. For example, when chunk 1 (i.e., $a_0b_0c_0$) is being scanned (say, for the computation of the 2-D chunk b_0c_0 of *BC*, as described above), all of the other 2-D chunks relating to $a_0b_0c_0$ can be simultaneously computed. That is, when $a_0b_0c_0$ is being scanned, each of the three chunks, b_0c_0, a_0c_0, and a_0b_0, on the three 2-D aggregation planes, *BC*, *AC*, and *AB*, should be computed then as well. In other words, multiway computation simultaneously aggregates to each of the 2-D planes while a 3-D chunk is in memory.

Now let's look at how different orderings of chunk scanning and of cuboid computation can affect the overall data cube computation efficiency. Recall that the size of the dimensions A, B, and C is 40, 400, and 4000, respectively. Therefore, the largest 2-D plane is BC (of size $400 \times 4000 = 1,600,000$). The second largest 2-D plane is AC (of size $40 \times 4000 = 160,000$). AB is the smallest 2-D plane (with a size of $40 \times 400 = 16,000$).

Suppose that the chunks are scanned in the order shown, from chunk 1 to 64. By scanning in this order, one chunk of the largest 2-D plane, BC, is *fully* computed for each row scanned. That is, b_0c_0 is fully aggregated after scanning the row containing chunks 1 to 4; b_1c_0 is fully aggregated after scanning chunks 5 to 8, and so on. In comparison, the complete computation of one chunk of the second largest 2-D plane, AC, requires scanning 13 chunks, given the ordering from 1 to 64. That is, a_0c_0 is fully aggregated only after the scanning of chunks 1, 5, 9, and 13. Finally, the complete computation of one chunk of the smallest 2-D plane, AB, requires scanning 49 chunks. For example, a_0b_0 is fully aggregated after scanning chunks 1, 17, 33, and 49. Hence, AB requires the longest scan of chunks in order to complete its computation. To avoid bringing a 3-D chunk into memory more than once, the minimum memory requirement for holding all relevant 2-D planes in chunk memory, according to the chunk ordering of 1 to 64, is as follows: 40×400 (for the whole AB plane) + 40×1000 (for one row of the AC plane) + 100×1000 (for one chunk of the BC plane) = $16,000 + 40,000 + 100,000 = 156,000$ memory units.

Suppose, instead, that the chunks are scanned in the order 1, 17, 33, 49, 5, 21, 37, 53, and so on. That is, suppose the scan is in the order of first aggregating toward the AB plane, and then toward the AC plane, and lastly toward the BC plane. The minimum memory requirement for holding 2-D planes in chunk memory would be as follows: 400×4000 (for the whole BC plane) + 40×1000 (for one row of the AC plane) + 10×100 (for one chunk of the AB plane) = 1,600,000 + 40,000 + 1000 = 1,641,000 memory units. Notice that this is *more than 10 times* the memory requirement of the scan ordering of 1 to 64.

Similarly, we can work out the minimum memory requirements for the multiway computation of the 1-D and 0-D cuboids. Figure 4.4 shows the most efficient ordering and the least efficient ordering, based on the minimum memory requirements for the data cube computation. The most efficient ordering is the chunk ordering of 1 to 64. ■

Example 4.4 assumes that there is enough memory space for *one-pass* cube computation (i.e., to compute all of the cuboids from one scan of all of the chunks). If there is insufficient memory space, the computation will require more than one pass through the 3-D array. In such cases, however, the basic principle of ordered chunk computation remains the same. MultiWay is most effective when the product of the cardinalities of dimensions is moderate and the data are not too sparse. When the dimensionality is high or the data are very sparse, the in-memory arrays become too large to fit in memory, and this method becomes infeasible.

With the use of appropriate sparse array compression techniques and careful ordering of the computation of cuboids, it has been shown by experiments that MultiWay array cube computation is significantly faster than traditional ROLAP (relationa record-based)

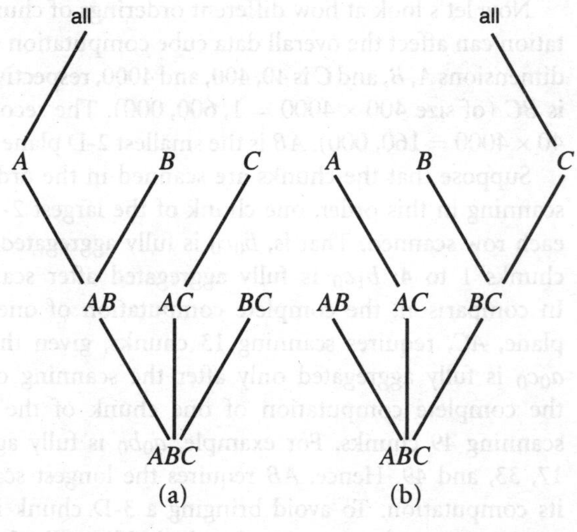

Figure 4.4 Two orderings of multiway array aggregation for computation of the 3-D cube of Example 4.4: (a) most efficient ordering of array aggregation (minimum memory requirements = 156,000 memory units); (b) least efficient ordering of array aggregation (minimum memory requirements = 1,641,000 memory units).

computation. Unlike ROLAP, the array structure of MultiWay does not require saving space to store search keys. Furthermore, MultiWay uses direct array addressing, which is faster than the key-based addressing search strategy of ROLAP. For ROLAP cube computation, instead of cubing a table directly, it can be faster to convert the table to an array, cube the array, and then convert the result back to a table. However, this observation works only for cubes with a relatively small number of dimensions because the number of cuboids to be computed is exponential to the number of dimensions.

"What would happen if we tried to use MultiWay to compute iceberg cubes?" Remember that the Apriori property states that if a given cell does not satisfy minimum support, then neither will any of its descendants. Unfortunately, MultiWay's computation starts from the base cuboid and progresses upward toward more generalized, ancestor cuboids. It cannot take advantage of Apriori pruning, which requires a parent node to be computed before its child (i.e., more specific) nodes. For example, if the count of a cell *c* in, say, *AB*, does not satisfy the minimum support specified in the iceberg condition, then we cannot prune away computation of *c*'s ancestors in the *A* or *B* cuboids, because the count of these cells may be greater than that of *c*.

4.1.3 BUC: Computing Iceberg Cubes from the Apex Cuboid Downward

BUC is an algorithm for the computation of sparse and iceberg cubes. Unlike MultiWay, BUC constructs the cube from the apex cuboid toward the base cuboid. This allows BUC to share data partitioning costs. This order of processing also allows BUC to prune during construction, using the Apriori property.

Figure 4.1 shows a lattice of cuboids, making up a 3-D data cube with the dimensions *A*, *B*, and *C*. The apex (0-D) cuboid, representing the concept all (that is, (∗, ∗, ∗)), is at the top of the lattice. This is the most aggregated or generalized level. The 3-D base cuboid, *ABC*, is at the bottom of the lattice. It is the least aggregated (most detailed or specialized) level. This representation of a lattice of cuboids, with the apex at the top and the base at the bottom, is commonly accepted in data warehousing. It consolidates the notions of *drill-down* (where we can move from a highly aggregated cell to lower, more detailed cells) and *roll-up* (where we can move from detailed, low-level cells to higher-level, more aggregated cells).

BUC stands for "Bottom-Up Construction." However, according to the lattice convention described above and used throughout this book, the order of processing of BUC is actually top-down! The authors of BUC view a lattice of cuboids in the reverse order, with the apex cuboid at the bottom and the base cuboid at the top. In that view, BUC does bottom-up construction. However, because we adopt the application worldview where *drill-down* refers to drilling from the apex cuboid down toward the base cuboid, the exploration process of BUC is regarded as top-down. BUC's exploration for the computation of a 3-D data cube is shown in Figure 4.5.

The BUC algorithm is shown in Figure 4.6. We first give an explanation of the algorithm and then follow up with an example. Initially, the algorithm is called with the input relation (set of tuples). BUC aggregates the entire input (line 1) and writes

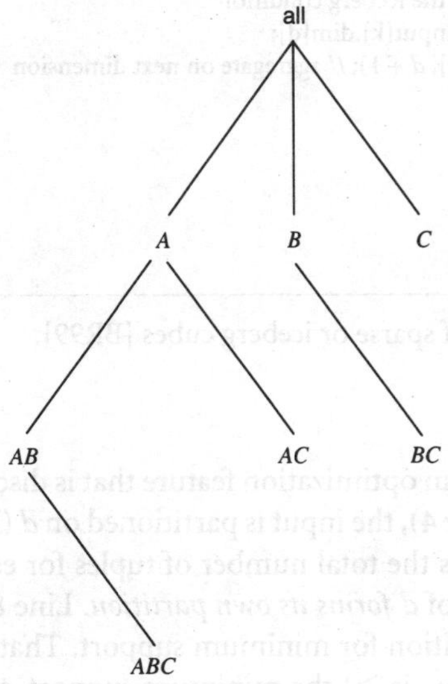

Figure 4.5 BUC's exploration for the computation of a 3-D data cube. Note that the computation starts from the apex cuboid.

Algorithm: BUC. Algorithm for the computation of sparse and iceberg cubes.

Input:

- *input*: the relation to aggregate;
- *dim*: the starting dimension for this iteration.

Globals:

- constant *numDims*: the total number of dimensions;
- constant *cardinality[numDims]*: the cardinality of each dimension;
- constant *min_sup*: the minimum number of tuples in a partition in order for it to be output;
- *outputRec*: the current output record;
- *dataCount[numDims]*: stores the size of each partition. *dataCount[i]* is a list of integers of size *cardinality[i]*.

Output: Recursively output the iceberg cube cells satisfying the minimum support.

Method:

```
(1)  Aggregate(input); // Scan input to compute measure, e.g., count. Place result in outputRec.
(2)  if input.count() == 1 then // Optimization
         WriteAncestors(input[0], dim); return;
     endif
(3)  write outputRec;
(4)  for (d = dim; d < numDims; d++) do //Partition each dimension
(5)      C = cardinality[d];
(6)      Partition(input, d, C, dataCount[d]); //create C partitions of data for dimension d
(7)      k = 0;
(8)      for (i = 0; i < C; i++) do // for each partition (each value of dimension d)
(9)          c = dataCount[d][i];
(10)         if c >= min_sup then // test the iceberg condition
(11)             outputRec.dim[d] = input[k].dim[d];
(12)             BUC(input[k...k+c], d+1); // aggregate on next dimension
(13)         endif
(14)         k +=c;
(15)     endfor
(16)     outputRec.dim[d] = all;
(17) endfor
```

Figure 4.6 BUC algorithm for the computation of sparse or iceberg cubes [BR99].

the resulting total (line 3). (Line 2 is an optimization feature that is discussed later in our example.) For each dimension d (line 4), the input is partitioned on d (line 6). On return from Partition(), *dataCount* contains the total number of tuples for each distinct value of dimension d. Each distinct value of *d forms its own partition.* Line 8 iterates through each partition. Line 10 tests the partition for minimum support. That is, if the number of tuples in the partition satisfies (i.e., is $\geq$) the minimum support, then the partition becomes the input relation for a recursive call made to BUC, which computes the iceberg cube on the partitions for dimensions $d+1$ to *numDims* (line 12). Note that for a full cube (i.e., where minimum support in the **having** clause is 1), the minimum support condition is always satisfied. Thus, the recursive call descends one level deeper into the lattice. Upon return from the recursive call, we continue with the next partition for d. After all the partitions have been processed, the entire process is repeated for each of the remaining dimensions.

We explain how BUC works with the following example.

Example 4.5 **BUC construction of an iceberg cube.** Consider the iceberg cube expressed in SQL as follows:

> **compute cube** iceberg_cube **as**
> **select** A, B, C, D, **count(*)**
> **from** R
> **cube by** A, B, C, D
> **having count(*)** $>=3$

Let's see how BUC constructs the iceberg cube for the dimensions A, B, C, and D, where the minimum support count is 3. Suppose that dimension A has four distinct values, a_1, a_2, a_3, a_4; B has four distinct values, b_1, b_2, b_3, b_4; C has two distinct values, c_1, c_2; and D has two distinct values, d_1, d_2. If we consider each group-by to be a *partition*, then we must compute every combination of the grouping attributes that satisfy minimum support (i.e., that have 3 tuples).

Figure 4.7 illustrates how the input is partitioned first according to the different attribute values of dimension A, and then B, C, and D. To do so, BUC scans the input, aggregating the tuples to obtain a count for **all**, corresponding to the cell $(*, *, *, *)$. Dimension A is used to split the input into four partitions, one for each distinct value of A. The number of tuples (counts) for each distinct value of A is recorded in *dataCount*.

BUC uses the Apriori property to save time while searching for tuples that satisfy the iceberg condition. Starting with A dimension value, a_1, the a_1 partition is aggregated, creating one tuple for the A group-by, corresponding to the cell $(a_1, *, *, *)$. Suppose $(a_1, *, *, *)$ satisfies the minimum support, in which case a recursive call is made on the partition for a_1. BUC partitions a_1 on the dimension B. It checks the count of $(a_1, b_1, *, *)$ to see if it satisfies the minimum support. If it does, it outputs the aggregated tuple to the AB group-by and recurses on $(a_1, b_1, *, *)$ to partition on C, starting with c_1. Suppose the cell count for $(a_1, b_1, c_1, *)$ is 2, which does not satisfy the minimum support. According to the Apriori property, if a cell does not satisfy minimum support, then neither can any of its descendants. Therefore, BUC prunes any further exploration of $(a_1, b_1, c_1, *)$. That is, it avoids partitioning this cell on dimension D. It backtracks to the a_1, b_1 partition and recurses on $(a_1, b_1, c_2, *)$, and so on. By checking the iceberg condition each time before performing a recursive call, BUC saves a great deal of processing time whenever a cell's count does not satisfy the minimum support.

The partition process is facilitated by a linear sorting method, CountingSort. CountingSort is fast because it does not perform any key comparisons to find partition boundaries. In addition, the counts computed during the sort can be reused to compute the group-by's in BUC. Line 2 is an optimization for partitions having a count of 1, such as

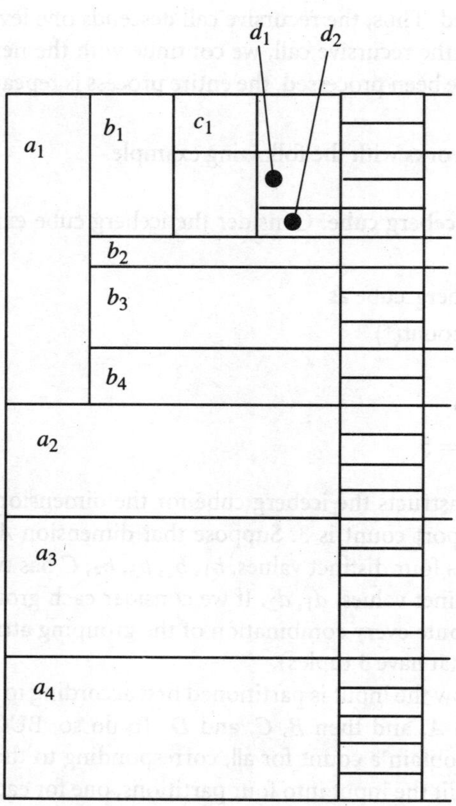

Figure 4.7 Snapshot of BUC partitioning given an example 4-D data set.

$(a_1, b_2, *, *)$ in our example. To save on partitioning costs, the count is written to each of the tuple's ancestor group-by's. This is particularly useful since, in practice, many partitions have a single tuple. ■

The performance of BUC is sensitive to the order of the dimensions and to skew in the data. Ideally, the most discriminating dimensions should be processed first. Dimensions should be processed in order of decreasing cardinality. The higher the cardinality is, the smaller the partitions are, and thus, the more partitions there will be, thereby providing BUC with greater opportunity for pruning. Similarly, the more uniform a dimension is (i.e., having less skew), the better it is for pruning.

BUC's major contribution is the idea of sharing partitioning costs. However, unlike MultiWay, it does not share the computation of aggregates between parent and child group-by's. For example, the computation of cuboid *AB* does not help that of *ABC*. The latter needs to be computed essentially from scratch.

4.1.4 Star-Cubing: Computing Iceberg Cubes Using a Dynamic Star-tree Structure

In this section, we describe the **Star-Cubing** algorithm for computing iceberg cubes. Star-Cubing combines the strengths of the other methods we have studied up to this point. It integrates top-down and bottom-up cube computation and explores both multidimensional aggregation (similar to MultiWay) and Apriori-like pruning (similar to BUC). It operates from a data structure called a star-tree, which performs lossless data compression, thereby reducing the computation time and memory requirements.

The Star-Cubing algorithm explores both the bottom-up and top-down computation models as follows: On the global computation order, it uses the bottom-up model. However, it has a sublayer underneath based on the top-down model, which explores the notion of *shared dimensions*, as we shall see below. This integration allows the algorithm to aggregate on multiple dimensions while still partitioning parent group-by's and pruning child group-by's that do not satisfy the iceberg condition.

Star-Cubing's approach is illustrated in Figure 4.8 for the computation of a 4-D data cube. If we were to follow only the bottom-up model (similar to Multiway), then the cuboids marked as pruned by Star-Cubing would still be explored. Star-Cubing is able to prune the indicated cuboids because it considers shared dimensions. *ACD*/*A* means cuboid *ACD* has shared dimension *A*, *ABD*/*AB* means cuboid *ABD* has shared dimension *AB*, *ABC*/*ABC* means cuboid *ABC* has shared dimension *ABC*, and so on. This comes from the generalization that all the cuboids in the subtree rooted at *ACD* include dimension *A*, all those rooted at *ABD* include dimensions *AB*, and all those rooted at *ABC* include dimensions *ABC* (even though there is only one such cuboid). We call these common dimensions the **shared dimensions** of those particular subtrees.

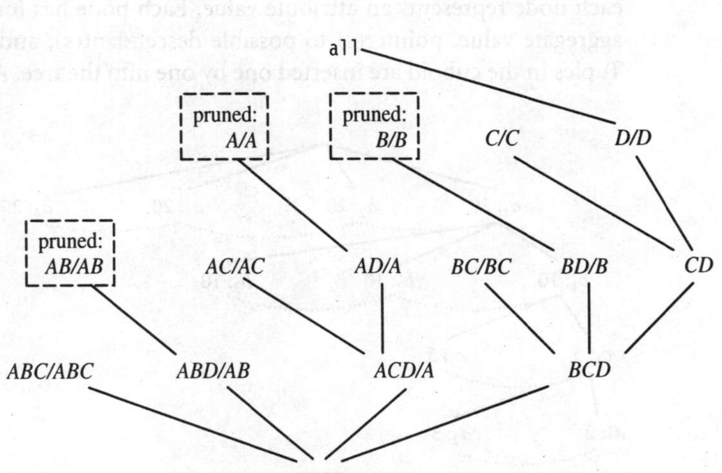

Figure 4.8 Star-Cubing: Bottom-up computation with top-down expansion of shared dimensions.

The introduction of shared dimensions facilitates shared computation. Because the shared dimensions are identified early on in the tree expansion, we can avoid recomputing them later. For example, cuboid *AB* extending from *ABD* in Figure 4.8 would actually be pruned because *AB* was already computed in *ABD*/*AB*. Similarly, cuboid *A* extending from *AD* would also be pruned because it was already computed in *ACD*/*A*.

Shared dimensions allow us to do Apriori-like pruning if the measure of an iceberg cube, such as *count*, is antimonotonic; that is, if the aggregate value on a shared dimension does not satisfy the iceberg condition, then *all of the cells descending from this shared dimension cannot satisfy the iceberg condition either*. Such cells and all of their descendants can be pruned, because these descendant cells are, by definition, more specialized (i.e., contain more dimensions) than those in the shared dimension(s). The number of tuples covered by the descendant cells will be less than or equal to the number of tuples covered by the shared dimensions. Therefore, if the aggregate value on a shared dimension fails the iceberg condition, the descendant cells cannot satisfy it either.

Example 4.6 **Pruning shared dimensions.** If the value in the shared dimension *A* is a_1 and it fails to satisfy the iceberg condition, then the whole subtree rooted at a_1CD/a_1 (including a_1C/a_1C, a_1D/a_1, a_1/a_1) can be pruned because they are all more specialized versions of a_1. ■

To explain how the Star-Cubing algorithm works, we need to explain a few more concepts, namely, *cuboid trees*, *star-nodes*, and *star-trees*.

We use trees to represent individual cuboids. Figure 4.9 shows a fragment of the **cuboid tree** of the base cuboid, *ABCD*. Each level in the tree represents a dimension, and each node represents an attribute value. Each node has four fields: the attribute value, aggregate value, pointer(s) to possible descendant(s), and pointer to possible sibling. Tuples in the cuboid are inserted one by one into the tree. A path from the root to a leaf

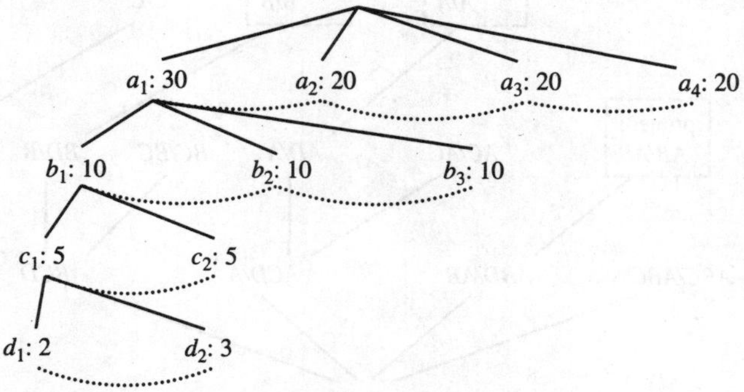

Figure 4.9 A fragment of the base cuboid tree.

node represents a tuple. For example, node c_2 in the tree has an aggregate (count) value of 5, which indicates that there are five cells of value $(a_1, b_1, c_2, *)$. This representation collapses the common prefixes to save memory usage and allows us to aggregate the values at internal nodes. With aggregate values at internal nodes, we can prune based on shared dimensions. For example, the cuboid tree of *AB* can be used to prune possible cells in *ABD*.

If the single dimensional aggregate on an attribute value *p* does not satisfy the iceberg condition, it is useless to distinguish such nodes in the iceberg cube computation. Thus the node *p* can be replaced by $*$ so that the cuboid tree can be further compressed. We say that the node *p* in an attribute *A* is a **star-node** if the single dimensional aggregate on *p* does not satisfy the iceberg condition; otherwise, *p* is a *non-star-node*. A cuboid tree that is compressed using star-nodes is called a **star-tree**.

The following is an example of star-tree construction.

Example 4.7 **Star-tree construction.** A base cuboid table is shown in Table 4.1. There are 5 tuples and 4 dimensions. The cardinalities for dimensions *A*, *B*, *C*, *D* are 2, 4, 4, 4, respectively. The one-dimensional aggregates for all attributes are shown in Table 4.2. Suppose *min_sup* = 2 in the iceberg condition. Clearly, only attribute values a_1, a_2, b_1, c_3, d_4 satisfy the condition. All the other values are below the threshold and thus become star-nodes. By collapsing star-nodes, the reduced base table is Table 4.3. Notice that the table contains two fewer rows and also fewer distinct values than Table 4.1.

We use the reduced base table to construct the cuboid tree because it is smaller. The resultant star-tree is shown in Figure 4.10. To help identify which nodes are star-nodes, a

Table 4.1 Base (Cuboid) Table: Before star reduction.

A	B	C	D	count
a_1	b_1	c_1	d_1	1
a_1	b_1	c_4	d_3	1
a_1	b_2	c_2	d_2	1
a_2	b_3	c_3	d_4	1
a_2	b_4	c_3	d_4	1

Table 4.2 One-Dimensional Aggregates.

Dimension	count = 1	count ≥ 2
A	—	$a_1(3), a_2(2)$
B	b_2, b_3, b_4	$b_1(2)$
C	c_1, c_2, c_4	$c_3(2)$
D	d_1, d_2, d_3	$d_4(2)$

Table 4.3 Compressed Base Table: After star reduction.

A	*B*	*C*	*D*	count
a_1	b_1	$*$	$*$	2
a_1	$*$	$*$	$*$	1
a_2	$*$	c_3	d_4	2

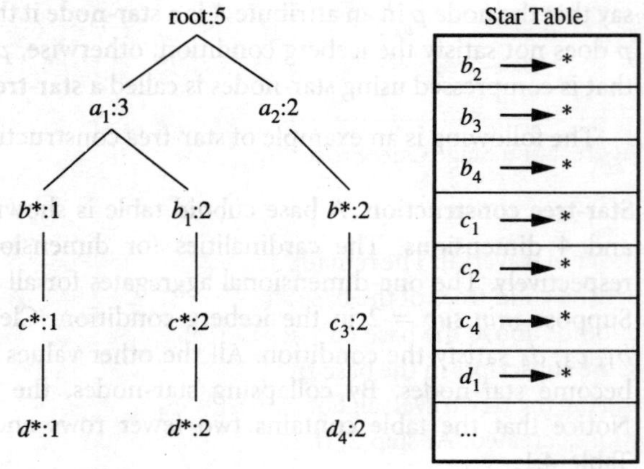

Figure 4.10 Star-tree and star-table.

star-table is constructed for each star-tree. Figure 4.10 also shows the corresponding star-table for the star-tree (where only the star-nodes are shown in the star-table). In actual implementation, a bit-vector or hash table could be used to represent the star-table for fast lookup. ■

By collapsing star-nodes, the star-tree provides a *lossless* compression of the original data. It provides a good improvement in memory usage, yet the time required to search for nodes or tuples in the tree is costly. To reduce this cost, the nodes in the star-tree are sorted in alphabetic order for each dimension, with the star-nodes appearing first. In general, nodes are sorted in the order $*, p_1, p_2, \ldots, p_n$ at each level.

Now, let's see how the Star-Cubing algorithm uses star-trees to compute an iceberg cube. The algorithm is given in Figure 4.13.

Example 4.8 **Star-Cubing.** Using the star-tree generated in Example 4.7 (Figure 4.10), we start the process of aggregation by traversing in a bottom-up fashion. Traversal is depth-first. The first stage (i.e., the processing of the first branch of the tree) is shown in Figure 4.11. The leftmost tree in the figure is the base star-tree. Each attribute value is shown with its corresponding aggregate value. In addition, subscripts by the nodes in the tree show the

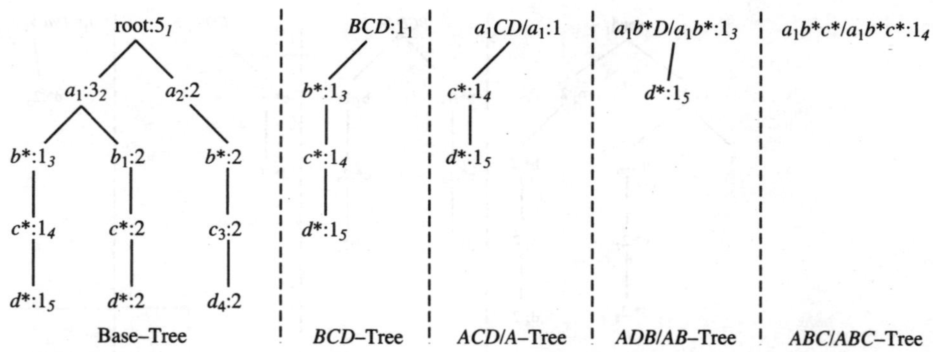

Figure 4.11 Aggregation Stage One: Processing of the left-most branch of BaseTree.

order of traversal. The remaining four trees are $BCD, ACD/A, ABD/AB, ABC/ABC$. They are the child trees of the base star-tree, and correspond to the level of three-dimensional cuboids above the base cuboid in Figure 4.8. The subscripts in them correspond to the same subscripts in the base tree—they denote the step or order in which they are created during the tree traversal. For example, when the algorithm is at step 1, the *BCD* child tree root is created. At step 2, the ACD/A child tree root is created. At step 3, the ABD/AB tree root and the $b*$ node in *BCD* are created.

When the algorithm has reached step 5, the trees in memory are exactly as shown in Figure 4.11. Because the depth-first traversal has reached a leaf at this point, it starts backtracking. Before traversing back, the algorithm notices that all possible nodes in the base dimension (*ABC*) have been visited. This means the ABC/ABC tree is complete, so the count is output and the tree is destroyed. Similarly, upon moving back from $d*$ to $c*$ and seeing that $c*$ has no siblings, the count in ABD/AB is also output and the tree is destroyed.

When the algorithm is at $b*$ during the back-traversal, it notices that there exists a sibling in b_1. Therefore, it will keep ACD/A in memory and perform a depth-first search on b_1 just as it did on $b*$. This traversal and the resultant trees are shown in Figure 4.12. The child trees ACD/A and ABD/AB are created again but now with the new values from the b_1 subtree. For example, notice that the aggregate count of $c*$ in the ACD/A tree has increased from 1 to 3. The trees that remained intact during the last traversal are reused and the new aggregate values are added on. For instance, another branch is added to the *BCD* tree.

Just like before, the algorithm will reach a leaf node at $d*$ and traverse back. This time, it will reach a_1 and notice that there exists a sibling in a_2. In this case, all child trees except *BCD* in Figure 4.12 are destroyed. Afterward, the algorithm will perform the same traversal on a_2. *BCD* continues to grow while the other subtrees start fresh with a_2 instead of a_1. ■

A node must satisfy two conditions in order to generate child trees: (1) the measure of the node must satisfy the iceberg condition; and (2) the tree to be generated must

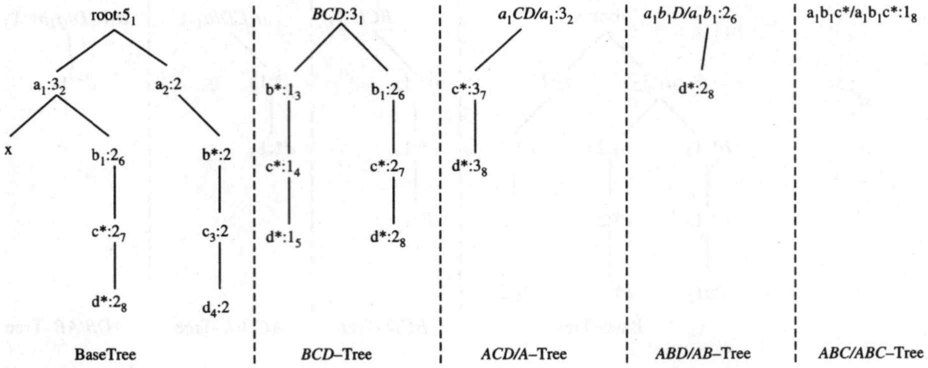

Figure 4.12 Aggregation Stage Two: Processing of the second branch of BaseTree.

include at least one non-star (i.e., nontrivial) node. This is because if all the nodes were star-nodes, then none of them would satisfy *min_sup*. Therefore, it would be a complete waste to compute them. This pruning is observed in Figures 4.11 and 4.12. For example, the left subtree extending from node a_1 in the base-tree in Figure 4.11 does not include any non-star-nodes. Therefore, the a_1CD/a_1 subtree should not have been generated. It is shown, however, for illustration of the child tree generation process.

Star-Cubing is sensitive to the ordering of dimensions, as with other iceberg cube construction algorithms. For best performance, the dimensions are processed in order of decreasing cardinality. This leads to a better chance of early pruning, because the higher the cardinality, the smaller the partitions, and therefore the higher possibility that the partition will be pruned.

Star-Cubing can also be used for full cube computation. When computing the full cube for a dense data set, Star-Cubing's performance is comparable with MultiWay and is much faster than BUC. If the data set is sparse, Star-Cubing is significantly faster than MultiWay and faster than BUC, in most cases. For iceberg cube computation, Star-Cubing is faster than BUC, where the data are skewed and the speedup factor increases as *min_sup* decreases.

4.1.5 Precomputing Shell Fragments for Fast High-Dimensional OLAP

Recall the reason that we are interested in precomputing data cubes: Data cubes facilitate fast on-line analytical processing (OLAP) in a multidimensional data space. However, a full data cube of high dimensionality needs massive storage space and unrealistic computation time. Iceberg cubes provide a more feasible alternative, as we have seen, wherein the iceberg condition is used to specify the computation of only a subset of the full cube's cells. However, although an iceberg cube is smaller and requires less computation time than its corresponding full cube, it is not an ultimate solution. For one, the computation and storage of the iceberg cube can still be costly. For example, if the

```
Algorithm: Star-Cubing. Compute iceberg cubes by Star-Cubing.
Input:
  ■ R: a relational table
  ■ min_support: minimum support threshold for the iceberg condition (taking count as the measure).
Output: The computed iceberg cube.
Method: Each star-tree corresponds to one cuboid tree node, and vice versa.
BEGIN
    scan R twice, create star-table S and star-tree T;
    output count of T.root;
    call starcubing(T, T.root);
END

procedure starcubing(T, cnode)// cnode: current node
{
for each non-null child C of T's cuboid tree
      insert or aggregate cnode to the corresponding
          position or node in C's star-tree;
if (cnode.count ≥ min_support) then {
      if (cnode ≠ root) then
          output cnode.count;
      if (cnode is a leaf) then
          output cnode.count;
      else { // initiate a new cuboid tree
          create C_C as a child of T's cuboid tree;
          let T_C be C_C's star-tree;
          T_C.root's count = cnode.count;
      }
}
if (cnode is not a leaf) then
      starcubing(T, cnode.first_child);
if (C_C is not null) then {
      starcubing(T_C, T_C.root);
      remove C_C from T's cuboid tree; }
if (cnode has sibling) then
      starcubing(T, cnode.sibling);
remove T;
}
```

Figure 4.13 The Star-Cubing algorithm.

base cuboid cell, $(a_1, a_2, \ldots, a_{60})$, passes minimum support (or the iceberg threshold), it will generate 2^{60} iceberg cube cells. Second, it is difficult to determine an appropriate iceberg threshold. Setting the threshold too low will result in a huge cube, whereas setting the threshold too high may invalidate many useful applications. Third, an iceberg cube cannot be incrementally updated. Once an aggregate cell falls below the iceberg threshold and is pruned, its measure value is lost. Any incremental update would require recomputing the cells from scratch. This is extremely undesirable for large real-life applications where incremental appending of new data is the norm.

One possible solution, which has been implemented in some commercial data warehouse systems, is to compute a thin **cube shell**. For example, we could compute all cuboids with three dimensions or less in a 60-dimensional data cube, resulting in cube shell of size 3. The resulting set of cuboids would require much less computation and storage than the full 60-dimensional data cube. However, there are two disadvantages of this approach. First, we would still need to compute $\binom{60}{3}+\binom{60}{2}+60=36{,}050$ cuboids, each with many cells. Second, such a cube shell does not support high-dimensional OLAP because (1) it does not support OLAP on four or more dimensions, and (2) it cannot even support drilling along three dimensions, such as, say, (A_4, A_5, A_6), *on a subset of data* selected based on the constants provided in three *other* dimensions, such as (A_1, A_2, A_3). This requires the computation of the corresponding six-dimensional cuboid.

Instead of computing a cube shell, we can compute only portions or fragments of it. This section discusses the *shell fragment* approach for OLAP query processing. It is based on the following key observation about OLAP in high-dimensional space. Although a data cube may contain many dimensions, *most OLAP operations are performed on only a small number of dimensions at a time.* In other words, an OLAP query is likely to ignore many dimensions (i.e., treating them as irrelevant), fix some dimensions (e.g., using query constants as instantiations), and leave only a few to be manipulated (for drilling, pivoting, etc.). This is because it is neither realistic nor fruitful for anyone to comprehend the changes of thousands of cells involving tens of dimensions simultaneously in a high-dimensional space at the same time. Instead, it is more natural to first locate some cuboids of interest and then drill along one or two dimensions to examine the changes of a few related dimensions. Most analysts will only need to examine, at any one moment, the combinations of a small number of dimensions. This implies that if multidimensional aggregates can be computed quickly on a *small number of dimensions inside a high-dimensional space*, we may still achieve fast OLAP without materializing the original high-dimensional data cube. Computing the full cube (or, often, even an iceberg cube or shell cube) can be excessive. Instead, a *semi-on-line computation model with certain preprocessing* may offer a more feasible solution. Given a base cuboid, some quick preparation computation can be done first (i.e., off-line). After that, a query can then be computed on-line using the preprocessed data.

The shell fragment approach follows such a semi-on-line computation strategy. It involves two algorithms: one for computing shell fragment cubes and one for query processing with the fragment cubes. The shell fragment approach can handle databases of extremely high dimensionality and can quickly compute small local cubes on-line. It explores the *inverted index* data structure, which is popular in information retrieval and Web-based information systems. The basic idea is as follows. Given a high-dimensional data set, we partition the dimensions into a set of disjoint dimension *fragments*, convert each fragment into its corresponding inverted index representation, and then construct *shell fragment cubes* while keeping the inverted indices associated with the cube cells. Using the precomputed shell fragment cubes, we can dynamically assemble and compute cuboid cells of the required data cube on-line. This is made efficient by set intersection operations on the inverted indices.

To illustrate the shell fragment approach, we use the tiny database of Table 4.4 as a running example. Let the cube measure be count(). Other measures will be discussed later. We first look at how to construct the inverted index for the given database.

Example 4.9 **Construct the inverted index.** For each attribute value in each dimension, list the tuple identifiers (*TIDs*) of all the tuples that have that value. For example, attribute value a_2 appears in tuples 4 and 5. The TIDlist for a_2 then contains exactly two items, namely 4 and 5. The resulting inverted index table is shown in Table 4.5. It retains all of the information of the original database. It uses exactly the same amount of memory as the original database. ■

"How do we compute shell fragments of a data cube?" The shell fragment computation algorithm, **Frag-Shells**, is summarized in Figure 4.14. We first partition all the dimensions of the given data set into independent groups of dimensions, called **fragments** (line 1). We scan the base cuboid and construct an inverted index for each attribute (lines 2 to 6). Line 3 is for when the measure is other than the tuple **count()**, which will

Table 4.4 The original database.

TID	*A*	*B*	*C*	*D*	*E*
1	a_1	b_1	c_1	d_1	e_1
2	a_1	b_2	c_1	d_2	e_1
3	a_1	b_2	c_1	d_1	e_2
4	a_2	b_1	c_1	d_1	e_2
5	a_2	b_1	c_1	d_1	e_3

Table 4.5 The inverted index.

Attribute Value	*Tuple ID List*	*List Size*
a_1	$\{1, 2, 3\}$	3
a_2	$\{4, 5\}$	2
b_1	$\{1, 4, 5\}$	3
b_2	$\{2, 3\}$	2
c_1	$\{1, 2, 3, 4, 5\}$	5
d_1	$\{1, 3, 4, 5\}$	4
d_2	$\{2\}$	1
e_1	$\{1, 2\}$	2
e_2	$\{3, 4\}$	2
e_3	$\{5\}$	1

Algorithm: Frag-Shells. Compute shell fragments on a given high-dimensional base table (i.e., base cuboid).

Input: A base cuboid, B, of n dimensions, namely, $(A_1, \ldots, A_n)$.

Output:

- a set of fragment partitions, $\{P_1, \ldots P_k\}$, and their corresponding (local) fragment cubes, $\{S_1, \ldots, S_k\}$, where P_i represents some set of dimension(s) and $P_1 \cup \ldots \cup P_k$ make up all the n dimensions
- an *ID_measure* array if the measure is not the tuple count, count()

Method:

(1) partition the set of dimensions $(A_1, \ldots, A_n)$ into
      a set of k fragments $P_1, \ldots, P_k$ (based on data & query distribution)
(2) scan base cuboid, B, once and do the following {
(3)   insert each ⟨*TID, measure*⟩ into *ID_measure* array
(4)   for each attribute value a_j of each dimension A_i
(5)   build an inverted index entry: ⟨a_j, *TIDlist*⟩
(6) }
(7) for each fragment partition P_i
(8)   build a local fragment cube, S_i, by intersecting their
      corresponding TIDlists and computing their measures

Figure 4.14 Algorithm for shell fragment computation.

be described later. For each fragment, we compute the full *local* (i.e., fragment-based) data cube while retaining the inverted indices (lines 7 to 8). Consider a database of 60 dimensions, namely, $A_1, A_2, \ldots, A_{60}$. We can first partition the 60 dimensions into 20 fragments of size 3: $(A_1, A_2, A_3), (A_4, A_5, A_6), \ldots, (A_{58}, A_{59}, A_{60})$. For each fragment, we compute its full data cube while recording the inverted indices. For example, in fragment (A_1, A_2, A_3), we would compute seven cuboids: $A_1, A_2, A_3, A_1A_2, A_2A_3, A_1A_3, A_1A_2A_3$. Furthermore, an inverted index is retained for each cell in the cuboids. That is, for each cell, its associated TIDlist is recorded.

The benefit of computing local cubes of each shell fragment instead of computing the complete cube shell can be seen by a simple calculation. For a base cuboid of 60 dimensions, there are only $7 \times 20 = 140$ cuboids to be computed according to the above shell fragment partitioning. This is in contrast to the 36,050 cuboids computed for the cube shell of size 3 described earlier! Notice that the above fragment partitioning is based simply on the grouping of consecutive dimensions. A more desirable approach would be to partition based on popular dimension groupings. Such information can be obtained from domain experts or the past history of OLAP queries.

Let's return to our running example to see how shell fragments are computed.

Example 4.10 **Compute shell fragments.** Suppose we are to compute the shell fragments of size 3. We first divide the five dimensions into two fragments, namely (A, B, C) and (D, E). For each fragment, we compute the full local data cube by intersecting the TIDlists in Table 4.5 in a top-down depth-first order in the cuboid lattice. For example, to compute the cell

Table 4.6 Cuboid *AB*.

Cell	*Intersection*	*Tuple ID List*	*List Size*
(a_1, b_1)	$\{1, 2, 3\} \cap \{1, 4, 5\}$	$\{1\}$	1
(a_1, b_2)	$\{1, 2, 3\} \cap \{2, 3\}$	$\{2, 3\}$	2
(a_2, b_1)	$\{4, 5\} \cap \{1, 4, 5\}$	$\{4, 5\}$	2
(a_2, b_2)	$\{4, 5\} \cap \{2, 3\}$	$\{\}$	0

Table 4.7 Cuboid *DE*.

Cell	*Intersection*	*Tuple ID List*	*List Size*
(d_1, e_1)	$\{1, 3, 4, 5\} \cap \{1, 2\}$	$\{1\}$	1
(d_1, e_2)	$\{1, 3, 4, 5\} \cap \{3, 4\}$	$\{3, 4\}$	2
(d_1, e_3)	$\{1, 3, 4, 5\} \cap \{5\}$	$\{5\}$	1
(d_2, e_1)	$\{2\} \cap \{1, 2\}$	$\{2\}$	1

$(a_1, b_2, *)$, we intersect the tuple ID lists of a_1 and b_2 to obtain a new list of $\{2, 3\}$. Cuboid *AB* is shown in Table 4.6.

After computing cuboid *AB*, we can then compute cuboid *ABC* by intersecting all pairwise combinations between Table 4.6 and the row c_1 in Table 4.5. Notice that because cell (a_2, b_2) is empty, it can be effectively discarded in subsequent computations, based on the Apriori property. The same process can be applied to compute fragment (D, E), which is completely independent from computing (A, B, C). Cuboid *DE* is shown in Table 4.7. ■

If the measure in the iceberg condition is **count()** (as in tuple counting), there is no need to reference the original database for this because the *length* of the TIDlist is equivalent to the tuple count. *"Do we need to reference the original database if computing other measures, such as average()?"* Actually, we can build and reference an *ID_measure* array instead, which stores what we need to compute other measures. For example, to compute **average()**, we let the *ID_measure* array hold three elements, namely, (*TID*, **item_count, sum**), for each cell (line 3 of the shell computation algorithm). The **average()** measure for each aggregate cell can then be computed by accessing only this *ID_measure* array, using **sum()/item_count()**. Considering a database with 10^6 tuples, each taking 4 bytes each for *TID*, **item_count**, and **sum**, the *ID_measure* array requires 12 MB, whereas the corresponding database of 60 dimensions will require $(60+3) \times 4 \times 10^6 = 252$ MB (assuming each attribute value takes 4 bytes). Obviously, *ID_measure* array is a more compact data structure and is more likely to fit in memory than the corresponding high-dimensional database.

To illustrate the design of the *ID_measure* array, let's look at the following example.

Example 4.11 **Computing cubes with the average() measure.** Suppose that Table 4.8 shows an example sales database where each tuple has two associated values, such as **item_count** and **sum**, where **item_count** is the count of items sold.

To compute a data cube for this database with the measure **average()**, we need to have a TIDlist for each cell: $\{TID_1, \ldots, TID_n\}$. Because each TID is uniquely associated with a particular set of measure values, all future computations just need to fetch the measure values associated with the tuples in the list. In other words, by keeping an *ID_measure* array in memory for on-line processing, we can handle complex algebraic measures, such as average, variance, and standard deviation. Table 4.9 shows what exactly should be kept for our example, which is substantially smaller than the database itself. ■

The shell fragments are negligible in both storage space and computation time in comparison with the full data cube. Note that we can also use the Frag-Shells algorithm to compute the full data cube by including all of the dimensions as a single fragment. Because the order of computation with respect to the cuboid lattice is top-down and depth-first (similar to that of BUC), the algorithm can perform Apriori pruning if applied to the construction of iceberg cubes.

"Once we have computed the shell fragments, how can they be used to answer OLAP queries?" Given the precomputed shell fragments, we can view the cube space as a virtual cube and perform OLAP queries related to the cube on-line. In general, there are two types of queries: (1) *point query* and (2) *subcube query*.

Table 4.8 A database with two measure values.

TID	*A*	*B*	*C*	*D*	*E*	*item_count*	*sum*
1	a_1	b_1	c_1	d_1	e_1	5	70
2	a_1	b_2	c_1	d_2	e_1	3	10
3	a_1	b_2	c_1	d_1	e_2	8	20
4	a_2	b_1	c_1	d_1	e_2	5	40
5	a_2	b_1	c_1	d_1	e_3	2	30

Table 4.9 *ID_measure* array of Table 4.8.

TID	*item_count*	*sum*
1	5	70
2	3	10
3	8	20
4	5	40
5	2	30

In a **point query**, all of the *relevant* dimensions in the cube have been instantiated (that is, there are no *inquired* dimensions in the relevant set of dimensions). For example, in an n-dimensional data cube, $A_1A_2\ldots A_n$, a point query could be in the form of $\langle A_1, A_5, A_9 : M?\rangle$, where $A_1 = \{a_{11}, a_{18}\}, A_5 = \{a_{52}, a_{55}, a_{59}\}, A_9 = a_{94}$, and M is the inquired measure for each corresponding cube cell. For a cube with a small number of dimensions, we can use "*" to represent a "don't care" position where the corresponding dimension is *irrelevant*, that is, neither inquired nor instantiated. For example, in the query $\langle a_2,\ b_1,\ c_1,\ d_1,\ * : \textbf{count()}?\rangle$ for the database in Table 4.4, the first four dimension values are instantiated to a_2, b_1, c_1, and d_1, respectively, while the last dimension is irrelevant, and **count()** (which is the tuple count by context) is the inquired measure.

In a **subcube query**, at least one of the *relevant* dimensions in the cube is *inquired*. For example, in an n-dimensional data cube $A_1A_2\ldots A_n$, a subcube query could be in the form $\langle A_1, A_5?, A_9, A_{21}? : M?\rangle$, where $A_1 = \{a_{11}, a_{18}\}$ and $A_9 = a_{94}$, A_5 and A_{21} are the inquired dimensions, and M is the inquired measure. For a cube with a small number of dimensions, we can use "*" for an irrelevant dimension and "?" for an inquired one. For example, in the query $\langle a_2,\ ?,\ c_1,\ *,\ ? : \textbf{count()}?\rangle$ we see that the first and third dimension values are instantiated to a_2 and c_1, respectively, while the fourth is irrelevant, and the second and the fifth are inquired. *A subcube query computes all possible value combinations of the inquired dimensions.* It essentially returns a local data cube consisting of the inquired dimensions.

"How can we use shell fragments to answer a point query?" Because a point query explicitly provides the set of instantiated variables on the set of relevant dimensions, we can make maximal use of the precomputed shell fragments by finding the *best fitting* (that is, *dimension-wise completely matching*) fragments to fetch and intersect the associated TIDlists.

Let the point query be of the form $\langle \alpha_i, \alpha_j, \alpha_k, \alpha_p : M?\rangle$, where α_i represents a set of instantiated values of dimension A_i, and so on for α_j, α_k, and α_p. First, we check the shell fragment schema to determine which dimensions among A_i, A_j, A_k, and A_p are in the same fragment(s). Suppose A_i and A_j are in the same fragment, while A_k and A_p are in two other fragments. We fetch the corresponding TIDlists on the precomputed 2-D fragment for dimensions A_i and A_j using the instantiations α_i and α_j, and fetch the TIDlists on the 1-D fragments for dimensions A_k and A_p using the instantiations α_k and α_p, respectively. The obtained TIDlists are intersected to derive the TIDlist table. This table is then used to derive the specified measure (e.g., by taking the length of the TIDlists for tuple **count()**, or by fetching **item_count()** and **sum()** from the *ID_measure* array to compute **average()**) for the final set of cells.

Example 4.12 Point query. Suppose a user wants to compute the point query, $\langle a_2,\ b_1,\ c_1,\ d_1,\ *: \textbf{count()}?\rangle$, for our database in Table 4.4 and that the shell fragments for the partitions (A, B, C) and (D, E) are precomputed as described in Example 4.10. The query is broken down into two subqueries based on the precomputed fragments: $\langle a_2,\ b_1,\ c_1,\ *,\ *\rangle$ and $\langle *,\ *,\ *,\ d_1,\ *\rangle$. The best fit precomputed shell fragments for the two subqueries are ABC and D. The fetch of the TIDlists for the two subqueries returns two lists: $\{4, 5\}$ and

{1, 3, 4, 5}. Their intersection is the list {4, 5}, which is of size 2. Thus the final answer is count() = 2. ■

A subcube query returns a local data cube based on the instantiated and inquired dimensions. Such a data cube needs to be aggregated in a multidimensional way so that on-line analytical processing (such as drilling, dicing, pivoting, etc.) can be made available to users for flexible manipulation and analysis. Because instantiated dimensions usually provide highly selective constants that dramatically reduce the size of the valid TIDlists, we should make maximal use of the precomputed shell fragments by finding the fragments that best fit the set of instantiated dimensions, and fetching and intersecting the associated TIDlists to derive the reduced TIDlist. This list can then be used to intersect the best-fitting shell fragments consisting of the inquired dimensions. This will generate the relevant and inquired base cuboid, which can then be used to compute the relevant subcube on the fly using an efficient on-line cubing algorithm.

Let the subcube query be of the form $\langle \alpha_i, \alpha_j, A_k?, \alpha_p, A_q? : M? \rangle$, where α_i, α_j, and α_p represent a set of instantiated values of dimension A_i, A_j, and A_p, respectively, and A_k and A_q represent two inquired dimensions. First, we check the shell fragment schema to determine which dimensions among (1) A_i, A_j, and A_p, and (2) among A_k and A_q are in the same fragment partition. Suppose A_i and A_j belong to the same fragment, as do A_k and A_q, but that A_p is in a different fragment. We fetch the corresponding TIDlists in the precomputed 2-D fragment for A_i and A_j using the instantiations α_i and α_j, then fetch the TIDlist on the precomputed 1-D fragment for A_p using instantiation α_p, and then fetch the TIDlists on the precomputed 1-D fragments for A_k and A_q, respectively, using no instantiations (i.e., all possible values). The obtained TIDlists are intersected to derive the final TIDlists, which are used to fetch the corresponding measures from the *ID_measure* array to derive the "base cuboid" of a 2-D subcube for two dimensions (A_k, A_q). A fast cube computation algorithm can be applied to compute this 2-D cube based on the derived base cuboid. The computed 2-D cube is then ready for OLAP operations.

Example 4.13 Subcube query. Suppose a user wants to compute the subcube query, $\langle a_2, b_1, ?, *, ? :$ count()?$\rangle$, for our database in Table 4.4, and that the shell fragments have been precomputed as described in Example 4.10. The query can be broken into three best-fit fragments according to the instantiated and inquired dimensions: *AB*, *C*, and *E*, where *AB* has the instantiation (a_2, b_1). The fetch of the TIDlists for these partitions returns: (a_2, b_1):{4, 5}, (c_1):{1, 2, 3, 4, 5}, and $\{(e_1$:{1, 2}$)$, $(e_2$:{3, 4}$)$, $(e_3$:{5}$)\}$, respectively. The intersection of these corresponding TIDlists contains a cuboid with two tuples: $\{(c_1, e_2)$:{4}[5], (c_1, e_3):{5}$\}$. This base cuboid can be used to compute the 2-D data cube, which is trivial. ■

[5] That is, the intersection of the TIDlists for (a_2, b_1), (c_1), and (e_2) is {4}.

For large data sets, a fragment size of 2 or 3 typically results in reasonable storage requirements for the shell fragments and for fast query response time. Querying with shell fragments is substantially faster than answering queries using precomputed data cubes that are stored on disk. In comparison to full cube computation, Frag-Shells is recommended if there are less than four inquired dimensions. Otherwise, more efficient algorithms, such as Star-Cubing, can be used for fast on-line cube computation. Frag-Shells can easily be extended to allow incremental updates, the details of which are left as an exercise.

4.1.6 Computing Cubes with Complex Iceberg Conditions

The iceberg cubes we have discussed so far contain only simple iceberg conditions, such as *count* ≥ 50 or *price_sum* ≥ 1000 (specified in the **having** clause). Such conditions have a nice property: *if the condition is violated for some cell c, then every descendant of c will also violate that condition.* For example, if the quantity of an item I sold in a region R_1 is less than 50, then the same item I sold in a subregion of R_1 can never satisfy the condition *count* ≥ 50. Conditions that obey this property are known as antimonotonic.

Not all iceberg conditions are antimonotonic. For example, the condition *avg(price)* ≥ 800 is not antimonotonic. This is because if the average price of an item, such as, say, "*TV*", in region R_1, is less than \$800, then a descendant of the cell representing "*TV*" and R_1, such as "*TV*" in a subregion of R_1, can still have an average price of over \$800.

"Can we still push such an iceberg condition deep into the cube computation process for improved efficiency?" To answer this question, we first look at an example.

Example 4.14 **Iceberg cube with the average measure.** Consider the *salesInfo* table given in Table 4.10, which registers sales related to month, day, city, customer group, item, and price.

Suppose, as data analysts, we have the following query: *Find groups of sales that contain at least 50 items and whose average item price is at least \$800, grouped by month, city, and/or customer group.* We can specify an iceberg cube, *sales_avg_iceberg*, to answer the query, as follows:

Table 4.10 A *salesInfo* table.

month	*day*	*city*	*cust_group*	*item*	*price*
Jan	10	Chicago	Education	HP Printer	485
Jan	15	Chicago	Household	Sony TV	1,200
Jan	20	New York	Education	Canon Camera	1,280
Feb	20	New York	Business	IBM Laptop	2,500
Mar	4	Vancouver	Education	Seagate HD	520
...	...	...	...	...	...

```
compute cube sales_avg_iceberg as
select month, city, customer_group, avg(price), count(*)
from salesInfo
cube by month, city, customer_group
having avg(price) >= 800 and count(*) >= 50
```

Here, the iceberg condition involves the measure *average*, which is not antimonotonic. This implies that if a cell, c, cannot satisfy the iceberg condition, "$average(c) \geq v$", we cannot prune away the descendants of c because it is possible that the average value for some of them may satisfy the condition. ■

"How can we compute sales_avg_iceberg?" It would be highly inefficient to first materialize the full data cube and then select the cells satisfying the **having** clause of the iceberg condition. We have seen that a cube with an antimonotonic iceberg condition can be computed efficiently by exploring the Apriori property. However, because this iceberg cube involves a non-antimonotonic iceberg condition, Apriori pruning cannot be applied. *"Can we transform the non-antimonotonic condition to a somewhat weaker but antimonotonic one so that we can still take advantage of pruning?"*

The answer is "yes." Here we examine one interesting such method. A cell c is said to have n base cells if it covers n nonempty descendant base cells. The **top-k average** of c, denoted as $avg^k(c)$, is the average value (i.e., price) of the *top-k base cells* of c (i.e., the first k cells when all the base cells in c are sorted in value-descending order) if $k \leq n$; or $-\infty$ if $k > n$. With this notion of top-k average, we can transform the original iceberg condition "**avg(**$price$**)** $\geq v$ **and count(*)** $\geq k$" into the weaker but antimonotonic condition "$avg^k(c) \geq v$". The reasoning is that if the average of the top-k nonempty descendant base cells of a cell c is less than v, there exists no subset from this set of base cells that can contain k or more base cells and have a bigger average value than v. Thus, it is safe to prune away the cell c.

It is costly to sort and keep the top-k base cell values for each aggregated cell. For efficient implementation, we can use only a few records to register some aggregated values to facilitate similar pruning. For example, we could use one record, r_0, to keep the sum and count of the cells whose value is no less than v, and a few records, such as r_1, r_2, and r_3, to keep the sum and count of the cells whose price falls into the range of $[0.8 - 1.0)$, $[0.6 - 0.8)$, $[0.4 - 0.6)$ of v, respectively. If the counts of r_0 and r_1 are no less than k but the average of the two is less than v, there is no hope of finding any descendants of c that can satisfy the iceberg condition. Thus c and its descendants can be pruned off in iceberg cube computation.

Similar transformation methods can be applied to many other iceberg conditions, such as those involving *average* on a set of positive and negative values, *range, variance*, and *standard deviation*. Details of the transformation methods are left as an exercise for interested readers.

4.2 Further Development of Data Cube and OLAP Technology

In this section, we study further developments of data cube and OLAP technology. Section 4.2.1 describes data mining by *discovery-driven exploration of data cubes*, where anomalies in the data are automatically detected and marked for the user with visual cues. Section 4.2.2 describes *multifeature cubes* for complex data mining queries involving multiple dependent aggregates at multiple granularity. Section 4.2.3 presents methods for *constrained gradient analysis* in data cubes, which identifies cube cells that have dramatic changes in value in comparison with their siblings, ancestors, or descendants.

4.2.1 Discovery-Driven Exploration of Data Cubes

As studied in previous sections, a data cube may have a large number of cuboids, and each cuboid may contain a large number of (aggregate) cells. With such an overwhelmingly large space, it becomes a burden for users to even just browse a cube, let alone think of exploring it thoroughly. Tools need to be developed to assist users in intelligently exploring the huge aggregated space of a data cube.

Discovery-driven exploration is such a cube exploration approach. In discovery-driven exploration, precomputed measures indicating data exceptions are used to guide the user in the data analysis process, at all levels of aggregation. We hereafter refer to these measures as *exception indicators*. Intuitively, an **exception** is a data cube cell value that is significantly different from the value anticipated, based on a statistical model. The model considers variations and patterns in the measure value across *all of the dimensions* to which a cell belongs. For example, if the analysis of *item-sales* data reveals an increase in sales in December in comparison to all other months, this may seem like an exception in the time dimension. However, it is not an exception if the item dimension is considered, since there is a similar increase in sales for other items during December. The model considers exceptions hidden at all aggregated group-by's of a data cube. Visual cues such as background color are used to reflect the degree of exception of each cell, based on the precomputed exception indicators. Efficient algorithms have been proposed for cube construction, as discussed in Section 4.1. The computation of exception indicators can be overlapped with cube construction, so that the overall construction of data cubes for discovery-driven exploration is efficient.

Three measures are used as exception indicators to help identify data anomalies. These measures indicate the degree of surprise that the quantity in a cell holds, with respect to its expected value. The measures are computed and associated with every cell, for all levels of aggregation. They are as follows:

- **SelfExp**: This indicates the degree of surprise of the cell value, relative to other cells at the same level of aggregation.

- **InExp**: This indicates the degree of surprise somewhere beneath the cell, if we were to drill down from it.
- **PathExp**: This indicates the degree of surprise for each drill-down path from the cell.

The use of these measures for discovery-driven exploration of data cubes is illustrated in the following example.

Example 4.15 **Discovery-driven exploration of a data cube.** Suppose that you would like to analyze the monthly sales at *AllElectronics* as a percentage difference from the previous month. The dimensions involved are *item*, *time*, and *region*. You begin by studying the data aggregated over all items and sales regions for each month, as shown in Figure 4.15.

To view the exception indicators, you would click on a button marked **highlight exceptions** on the screen. This translates the SelfExp and InExp values into visual cues, displayed with each cell. The background color of each cell is based on its SelfExp value. In addition, a box is drawn around each cell, where the thickness and color of the box are a function of its InExp value. Thick boxes indicate high InExp values. In both cases, the darker the color, the greater the degree of exception. For example, the dark, thick boxes for sales during July, August, and September signal the user to explore the lower-level aggregations of these cells by drilling down.

Drill-downs can be executed along the aggregated *item* or *region* dimensions. *"Which path has more exceptions?"* you wonder. To find this out, you select a cell of interest and trigger a **path exception** module that colors each dimension based on the PathExp value of the cell. This value reflects the degree of surprise of that path. Suppose that the path along *item* contains more exceptions.

A drill-down along *item* results in the cube slice of Figure 4.16, showing the sales over time for each item. At this point, you are presented with many different sales values to analyze. By clicking on the **highlight exceptions** button, the visual cues are displayed, bringing focus toward the exceptions. Consider the sales difference of 41% for *"Sony b/w printers"* in September. This cell has a dark background, indicating a high SelfExp value, meaning that the cell is an exception. Consider now the sales difference of −15% for *"Sony b/w printers"* in November, and of −11% in December. The −11% value for December is marked as an exception, while the −15% value is not, even though −15% is a bigger deviation than −11%. This is because the exception indicators consider all of the dimensions that a cell is in. Notice that the December sales of most of the other items have a large positive value, while the November sales do not. Therefore, by considering the

Sum of sales	Month											
	Jan	Feb	Mar	Apr	May	Jun	Jul	Aug	Sep	Oct	Nov	Dec
Total		1%	−1%	0%	1%	3%	−1%	−9%	−1%	2%	−4%	3%

Figure 4.15 Change in sales over time.

Avg. sales						*Month*						
Item	Jan	Feb	Mar	Apr	May	Jun	Jul	Aug	Sep	Oct	Nov	Dec
Sony b/w printer		9%	−8%	2%	−5%	14%	−4%	0%	41%	−13%	−15%	[illegible]
Sony color printer		0%	0%	3%	2%	4%	−10%	−13%	0%	4%	−6%	4%
HP b/w printer		−2%	1%	2%	3%	8%	0%	−12%	−9%	3%	−3%	6%
HP color printer		0%	0%	−2%	1%	0%	−1%	−7%	−2%	1%	−4%	1%
IBM desktop computer		1%	−2%	−1%	−1%	3%	3%	−10%	4%	1%	−4%	−1%
IBM laptop computer		0%	0%	−1%	3%	4%	2%	−10%	−2%	0%	−9%	3%
Toshiba desktop computer		−2%	−5%	1%	1%	−1%	1%	5%	−3%	−5%	−1%	−1%
Toshiba laptop computer		1%	0%	3%	0%	−2%	−2%	−5%	3%	2%	−1%	0%
Logitech mouse		3%	−2%	−1%	0%	4%	6%	−11%	2%	1%	−4%	0%
Ergo-way mouse		0%	0%	2%	3%	1%	−2%	−2%	−5%	0%	−5%	8%

Figure 4.16 Change in sales for each *item-time* combination.

Avg. sales						*Month*						
Region	Jan	Feb	Mar	Apr	May	Jun	Jul	Aug	Sep	Oct	Nov	Dec
North		−1%	−3%	−1%	0%	3%	4%	−7%	1%	0%	−3%	−3%
South		−1%	1%	−9%	6%	−1%	−39%	9%	[illegible]	4%	1%	7%
East		−1%	−2%	2%	−3%	1%	18%	−2%	11%	−3%	−2%	−1%
West		4%	0%	−1%	−3%	5%	1%	−18%	8%	5%	−8%	1%

Figure 4.17 Change in sales for the item *IBM desktop computer* per region.

position of the cell in the cube, the sales difference for *"Sony b/w printers"* in December is exceptional, while the November sales difference of this item is not.

The InExp values can be used to indicate exceptions at lower levels that are not visible at the current level. Consider the cells for *"IBM desktop computers"* in July and September. These both have a dark, thick box around them, indicating high InExp values. You may decide to further explore the sales of *"IBM desktop computers"* by drilling down along *region*. The resulting sales difference by *region* is shown in Figure 4.17, where the **highlight exceptions** option has been invoked. The visual cues displayed make it easy to instantly notice an exception for the sales of *"IBM desktop computers"* in the southern region, where such sales have decreased by −39% and −34% in July and September, respectively. These detailed exceptions were far from obvious when we were viewing the data as an *item-time* group-by, aggregated over *region* in Figure 4.16. Thus, the InExp value is useful for searching for exceptions at lower-level cells of the cube. Because no other cells in Figure 4.17 have a high InExp value, you may roll up back to the data of Figure 4.16 and choose another cell from which to drill down. In this way, the exception indicators can be used to guide the discovery of interesting anomalies in the data. ■

"How are the exception values computed?" The SelfExp, InExp, and PathExp measures are based on a statistical method for table analysis. They take into account all of the group-by's (aggregations) in which a given cell value participates. A cell value is considered an exception based on how much it differs from its expected value, where its expected value is determined with a statistical model described below. The difference between a given cell value and its expected value is called a **residual**. Intuitively, the larger the residual, the more the given cell value is an exception. The comparison of residual values requires us to scale the values based on the expected standard deviation associated with the residuals. A cell value is therefore considered an exception if its scaled residual value exceeds a prespecified threshold. The SelfExp, InExp, and PathExp measures are based on this scaled residual.

The expected value of a given cell is a function of the higher-level group-by's of the given cell. For example, given a cube with the three dimensions *A*, *B*, and *C*, the expected value for a cell at the *i*th position in *A*, the *j*th position in *B*, and the *k*th position in *C* is a function of γ, γ_i^A, γ_j^B, γ_k^C, γ_{ij}^{AB}, γ_{ik}^{AC}, and γ_{jk}^{BC}, which are coefficients of the statistical model used. The coefficients reflect how different the values at more detailed levels are, based on generalized impressions formed by looking at higher-level aggregations. In this way, the exception quality of a cell value is based on the exceptions of the values below it. Thus, when seeing an exception, it is natural for the user to further explore the exception by drilling down.

"How can the data cube be efficiently constructed for discovery-driven exploration?" This computation consists of three phases. The first step involves the computation of the aggregate values defining the cube, such as sum or count, over which exceptions will be found. The second phase consists of model fitting, in which the coefficients mentioned above are determined and used to compute the standardized residuals. This phase can be overlapped with the first phase because the computations involved are similar. The third phase computes the SelfExp, InExp, and PathExp values, based on the standardized residuals. This phase is computationally similar to phase 1. Therefore, the computation of data cubes for discovery-driven exploration can be done efficiently.

4.2.2 Complex Aggregation at Multiple Granularity: Multifeature Cubes

Data cubes facilitate the answering of data mining queries as they allow the computation of aggregate data at multiple levels of granularity. In this section, you will learn about *multifeature cubes*, which compute complex queries involving multiple dependent aggregates at multiple granularity. These cubes are very useful in practice. Many complex data mining queries can be answered by multifeature cubes without any significant increase in computational cost, in comparison to cube computation for simple queries with standard data cubes.

All of the examples in this section are from the Purchases data of *AllElectronics*, where an *item* is purchased in a sales *region* on a business day (*year, month, day*). The shelf life in months of a given item is stored in *shelf*. The item price and sales (in dollars) at a given region are stored in *price* and *sales*, respectively. To aid in our study of multifeature cubes, let's first look at an example of a simple data cube.

Example 4.16 Query 1: A simple data cube query. Find the total sales in 2004, broken down by *item*, *region*, and *month*, with subtotals for each dimension.

To answer Query 1, a data cube is constructed that aggregates the total sales at the following eight different levels of granularity: {(*item, region, month*), (*item, region*), (*item, month*), (*month, region*), (*item*), (*month*), (*region*), ()}, where () represents **all**. Query 1 uses a typical data cube like that introduced in the previous chapter. We call such a data cube a simple data cube because it does not involve any dependent aggregates. ■

"*What is meant by 'dependent aggregates'?*" We answer this by studying the following example of a complex query.

Example 4.17 Query 2: A complex query. Grouping by all subsets of {*item, region, month*}, find the maximum *price* in 2004 for each group and the total *sales* among all maximum price tuples.

The specification of such a query using standard SQL can be long, repetitive, and difficult to optimize and maintain. Alternatively, Query 2 can be specified concisely using an extended SQL syntax as follows:

```
select     item, region, month, max(price), sum(R.sales)
from       Purchases
where      year = 2004
cube by    item, region, month: R
such that  R.price = max(price)
```

The tuples representing purchases in 2004 are first selected. The **cube by** clause computes aggregates (or group-by's) for all possible combinations of the attributes *item*, *region*, and *month*. It is an *n*-dimensional generalization of the **group by** clause. The attributes specified in the **cube by** clause are the **grouping attributes**. Tuples with the same value on all grouping attributes form one group. Let the groups be $g_1, \ldots, g_r$. For each group of tuples g_i, the maximum price max_{g_i} among the tuples forming the group is computed. The variable R is a **grouping variable**, ranging over all tuples in group g_i whose price is equal to max_{g_i} (as specified in the **such that** clause). The sum of sales of the tuples in g_i that R ranges over is computed and returned with the values of the grouping attributes of g_i. The resulting cube is a **multifeature cube** in that it supports complex data mining queries for which multiple dependent aggregates are computed at a variety of granularities. For example, the sum of sales returned in Query 2 is dependent on the set of maximum price tuples for each group. ■

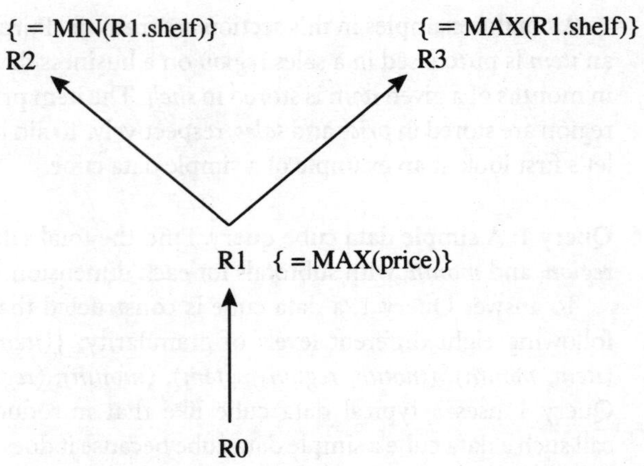

Figure 4.18 A multifeature cube graph for Query 3.

Let's look at another example.

Example 4.18 Query 3: **An even more complex query.** Grouping by all subsets of {*item, region, month*}, find the maximum *price* in 2004 for each group. Among the maximum price tuples, find the minimum and maximum item *shelf lives*. Also find the fraction of the total *sales* due to tuples that have minimum shelf life within the set of all maximum price tuples, and the fraction of the total *sales* due to tuples that have maximum shelf life within the set of all maximum price tuples.

The **multifeature cube graph** of Figure 4.18 helps illustrate the aggregate dependencies in the query. There is one node for each grouping variable, plus an additional initial node, R0. Starting from node R0, the set of maximum price tuples in 2004 is first computed (node R1). The graph indicates that grouping variables R2 and R3 are "dependent" on R1, since a directed line is drawn from R1 to each of R2 and R3. In a multifeature cube graph, a directed line from grouping variable R_i to R_j means that R_j always ranges over a subset of the tuples that R_i ranges over. When expressing the query in extended SQL, we write "R_j **in** R_i" as shorthand to refer to this case. For example, the minimum shelf life tuples at R2 range over the maximum price tuples at R1, that is, "**R2 in R1**." Similarly, the maximum shelf life tuples at R3 range over the maximum price tuples at R1, that is, "**R3 in R1**."

From the graph, we can express Query 3 in extended SQL as follows:

```
select    item, region, month, max(price), min(R1.shelf), max(R1.shelf),
          sum(R1.sales), sum(R2.sales), sum(R3.sales)
from      Purchases
where     year = 2004
cube by   item, region, month: R1, R2, R3
```

such that R1.price = **max**(price) **and**
R2 **in** R1 **and** R2.shelf = **min**(R1.shelf) **and**
R3 **in** R1 **and** R3.shelf = **max**(R1.shelf)

■

"How can multifeature cubes be computed efficiently?" The computation of a multifeature cube depends on the types of aggregate functions used in the cube. In Chapter 3, we saw that aggregate functions can be categorized as either distributive, algebraic, or holistic. Multifeature cubes can be organized into the same categories and computed efficiently by minor extension of the previously studied cube computation methods.

4.2.3 Constrained Gradient Analysis in Data Cubes

Many data cube applications need to analyze the *changes of complex measures* in multidimensional space. For example, in real estate, we may want to ask what are the *changes* of the *average* house price in the Vancouver area in the year 2004 compared against 2003, and the answer could be "the average price for those sold to professionals in the West End went down by 20%, while those sold to business people in Metrotown went up by 10%, etc." Expressions such as "professionals in the West End" correspond to cuboid cells and describe *sectors* of the business modeled by the data cube.

The problem of mining *changes* of *complex measures* in a multidimensional space was first proposed by Imielinski, Khachiyan, and Abdulghani [IKA02] as the **cubegrade** problem, which can be viewed as a generalization of association rules[6] and data cubes. It studies how changes in a set of measures (aggregates) of interest are associated with changes in the underlying characteristics of sectors, where changes in sector characteristics are expressed in terms of dimensions of the cube and are limited to *specialization* (drill-down), *generalization* (roll-up), and *mutation* (a change in one of the cube's dimensions). For example, we may want to ask "what kind of sector characteristics are associated with major changes in average house price in the Vancouver area in 2004?" The answer will be *pairs of sectors*, associated with major changes in average house price, including, for example, "the sector of professional buyers in the West End area of Vancouver" versus "the sector of all buyers in the entire area of Vancouver" as a specialization (or generalization). The cubegrade problem is significantly more expressive than association rules, because it captures data trends and handles complex measures, not just **count**, as association rules do. The problem has broad applications, from trend analysis to answering "what-if" questions and discovering exceptions or outliers.

The curse of dimensionality and the need for understandable results pose serious challenges for finding an efficient and scalable solution to the cubegrade problem. Here we examine a confined but interesting version of the cubegrade problem, called

[6] Association rules were introduced in Chapter 1. They are often used in market basket analysis to find associations between items purchased in transactional sales databases. Association rule mining is described in detail in Chapter 5.

constrained multidimensional gradient analysis, which reduces the search space and derives interesting results. It incorporates the following types of constraints:

1. **Significance constraint:** This ensures that we examine only the cells that have certain "statistical significance" in the data, such as containing at least a specified number of base cells or at least a certain total sales. In the data cube context, this constraint acts as the iceberg condition, which prunes a huge number of trivial cells from the answer set.

2. **Probe constraint:** This selects a subset of cells (called **probe cells**) from all of the possible cells as starting points for examination. Because the cubegrade problem needs to compare each cell in the cube with other cells that are either specializations, generalizations, or mutations of the given cell, it extracts pairs of similar cell characteristics associated with big changes in measure in a data cube. Given three cells, a, b, and c, if a is a specialization of b, then we say it is a **descendant** of b, in which case, b is a generalization or **ancestor** of a. Cell c is a mutation of a if the two have identical values in all but one dimension, where the dimension for which they vary cannot have a value of "*". Cells a and c are considered **siblings.** Even when considering only iceberg cubes, a large number of pairs may still be generated. Probe constraints allow the user to specify a subset of cells that are of interest for the analysis task. In this way, the study is focused only on these cells and their relationships with corresponding ancestors, descendants, and siblings.
3. **Gradient constraint:** This specifies the user's range of interest on the gradient (measure change). A user is typically interested in only certain types of changes between the cells (sectors) under comparison. For example, we may be interested in only those cells whose average profit increases by more than 40% compared to that of the probe cells. Such changes can be specified as a threshold in the form of either a ratio or a difference between certain measure values of the cells under comparison. A cell that captures the change from the probe cell is referred to as a **gradient cell.**

The following example illustrates each of the above types of constraints.

Example 4.19 Constrained average gradient analysis. The base table, D, for *AllElectronics* sales has the schema

sales(year, city, customer_group, item_group, count, avg_price).

Attributes *year, city, customer_group*, and *item_group* are the *dimensional attributes*; *count* and *avg_price* are the *measure attributes*. Table 4.11 shows a set of base and aggregate cells. Tuple c_1 is a base cell, while tuples c_2, c_3, and c_4 are aggregate cells. Tuple c_3 is a sibling of c_2, c_4 is an ancestor of c_2, and c_1 is a descendant of c_2.

Suppose that the significance constraint, C_{sig}, is $(count \geq 100)$, meaning that a cell with *count* no less than 100 is regarded as significant. Suppose that the probe constraint, C_{prb}, is *(city = "Vancouver," customer_group = "Business," item_group = *)*. This means

Table 4.11 A set of base and aggregate cells.

c_1	(2000, *Vancouver, Business, PC*, 300, \$2100)
c_2	(∗, *Vancouver, Business, PC*, 2800, \$1900)
c_3	(∗, *Toronto, Business, PC*, 7900, \$2350)
c_4	(∗, ∗, *Business, PC*, 58600, \$2250)

that the set of *probe cells*, *P*, is the set of aggregate tuples regarding the sales of the Business customer group in Vancouver, *for every product group*, provided the *count* in the tuple is greater than or equal to 100. It is easy to see that $c_2 \in P$.

Let the gradient constraint, $C_{grad}(c_g, c_p)$, be $(avg\_price(c_g)/avg\_price(c_p) \geq 1.4)$. The constrained gradient analysis problem is thus to find all pairs, (c_g, c_p), where c_p is a probe cell in *P*; c_g is a sibling, ancestor, or descendant of c_p; c_g is a significant cell, and c_g's average price is at least 40% more than c_p's. ■

If a data cube is fully materialized, the query posed in Example 4.19 becomes a relatively simple retrieval of the pairs of computed cells that satisfy the constraints. Unfortunately, the number of aggregate cells is often too huge to be precomputed and stored. Typically, only the base table or cuboid is available, so that the task then becomes how to efficiently compute the gradient-probe pairs from it.

One rudimentary approach to computing such gradients is to conduct a search for the gradient cells, once per probe cell. This approach is inefficient because it would involve a large amount of repeated work for different probe cells. A suggested method is a set-oriented approach that starts with a set of probe cells, utilizes constraints early on during search, and explores pruning, when possible, during progressive computation of pairs of cells. With each gradient cell, the set of all possible probe cells that might co-occur in interesting gradient-probe pairs are associated with some descendants of the gradient cell. These probe cells are considered "live probe cells." This set is used to search for future gradient cells, while considering significance constraints and gradient constraints to reduce the search space as follows:

1. The significance constraints can be used directly for pruning: If a cell, *c*, cannot satisfy the significance constraint, then *c* and its descendants can be pruned because none of them can be significant, and
2. Because the gradient constraint may specify a complex measure (such as **avg** $\geq v$), the incorporation of both the significance constraint and the gradient constraint can be used for pruning in a manner similar to that discussed in Section 4.1.6 on computing cubes with complex iceberg conditions. That is, we can explore a weaker but antimonotonic form of the constraint, such as the *top-k average*, $avg^k(c) \geq v$, where *k* is the significance constraint (such as 100 in Example 4.19), and *v* is derived from the gradient constraint based on $v = c_g \times v_p$, where c_g is the *gradient_contraint_threshold*, and v_p is the value of the corresponding probe cell. That is, if the current cell, *c*, cannot

satisfy this constraint, further exploration of its descendants will be useless and thus can be pruned.

The *constrained cube gradient analysis* has been shown to be effective at exploring the significant changes among related cube cells in multidimensional space.

4.3 Attribute-Oriented Induction—An Alternative Method for Data Generalization and Concept Description

Data generalization summarizes data by replacing relatively low-level values (such as numeric values for an attribute *age*) with higher-level concepts (such as *young*, *middle-aged*, and *senior*). Given the large amount of data stored in databases, it is useful to be able to describe concepts in concise and succinct terms at generalized (rather than low) levels of abstraction. Allowing data sets to be generalized at multiple levels of abstraction facilitates users in examining the general behavior of the data. Given the *AllElectronics* database, for example, instead of examining individual customer transactions, sales managers may prefer to view the data generalized to higher levels, such as summarized by customer groups according to geographic regions, frequency of purchases per group, and customer income.

This leads us to the notion of *concept description*, which is a form of data generalization. A concept typically refers to a collection of data such as *frequent_buyers*, *graduate_students*, and so on. As a data mining task, concept description is not a simple enumeration of the data. Instead, **concept description** generates descriptions for the *characterization* and *comparison* of the data. It is sometimes called **class description**, when the concept to be described refers to a class of objects. **Characterization** provides a concise and succinct summarization of the given collection of data, while concept or class **comparison** (also known as **discrimination**) provides descriptions comparing two or more collections of data.

Up to this point, we have studied data cube (or OLAP) approaches to concept description using multidimensional, multilevel data generalization in data warehouses. *"Is data cube technology sufficient to accomplish all kinds of concept description tasks for large data sets?"* Consider the following cases.

- **Complex data types and aggregation**: Data warehouses and OLAP tools are based on a multidimensional data model that views data in the form of a data cube, consisting of dimensions (or attributes) and measures (aggregate functions). However, many current OLAP systems confine dimensions to nonnumeric data and measures to numeric data. In reality, the database can include attributes of various data types, including numeric, nonnumeric, spatial, text, or image, which ideally should be included in the concept description. Furthermore, the aggregation of attributes in a database may include sophisticated data types, such as the collection of nonnumeric data, the merging of spatial regions, the composition of images, the integration of texts, and the grouping of object pointers. Therefore, OLAP, with its restrictions on the possible dimension and measure types, represents a simplified model for data analysis. Concept description should handle complex data types of the attributes and their aggregations, as necessary.

- **User-control versus automation:** On-line analytical processing in data warehouses is a user-controlled process. The selection of dimensions and the application of OLAP operations, such as drill-down, roll-up, slicing, and dicing, are primarily directed and controlled by the users. Although the control in most OLAP systems is quite user-friendly, users do require a good understanding of the role of each dimension. Furthermore, in order to find a satisfactory description of the data, users may need to specify a long sequence of OLAP operations. It is often desirable to have a more automated process that helps users determine which dimensions (or attributes) should be included in the analysis, and the degree to which the given data set should be generalized in order to produce an interesting summarization of the data.

This section presents an alternative method for concept description, called *attribute-oriented induction*, which works for complex types of data and relies on a data-driven generalization process.

4.3.1 Attribute-Oriented Induction for Data Characterization

The **attribute-oriented induction (AOI)** approach to concept description was first proposed in 1989, a few years before the introduction of the data cube approach. The data cube approach is essentially based on *materialized views* of the data, which typically have been precomputed in a data warehouse. In general, it performs off-line aggregation before an OLAP or data mining query is submitted for processing. On the other hand, the attribute-oriented induction approach is basically a *query-oriented*, generalization-based, on-line data analysis technique. Note that there is no inherent barrier distinguishing the two approaches based on on-line aggregation versus off-line precomputation. Some aggregations in the data cube can be computed on-line, while off-line precomputation of multidimensional space can speed up attribute-oriented induction as well.

The general idea of attribute-oriented induction is to first collect the task-relevant data using a database query and then perform generalization based on the examination of the number of distinct values of each attribute in the relevant set of data. The generalization is performed by either *attribute removal* or *attribute generalization.* Aggregation is performed by merging identical generalized tuples and accumulating their respective counts. This reduces the size of the generalized data set. The resulting generalized relation can be mapped into different forms for presentation to the user, such as charts or rules.

The following examples illustrate the process of attribute-oriented induction. We first discuss its use for characterization. The method is extended for the mining of class comparisons in Section 4.3.4.

Example 4.20 **A data mining query for characterization.** Suppose that a user would like to describe the general characteristics of graduate students in the *Big University* database, given the attributes *name, gender, major, birth_place, birth_date, residence, phone# (telephone number),* and *gpa (grade_point_average).* A data mining query for this characterization can be expressed in the data mining query language, DMQL, as follows:

> **use** Big_University_DB
> **mine characteristics as** "Science_Students"
> **in relevance to** name, gender, major, birth_place, birth_date, residence, phone#, gpa
> **from** student
> **where** status in "graduate"

We will see how this example of a typical data mining query can apply attribute-oriented induction for mining characteristic descriptions.

First, **data focusing** should be performed *before* attribute-oriented induction. This step corresponds to the specification of the task-relevant data (i.e., data for analysis). The data are collected based on the information provided in the data mining query. Because a data mining query is usually relevant to only a portion of the database, selecting the relevant set of data not only makes mining more efficient, but also derives more meaningful results than mining the entire database.

Specifying the set of relevant attributes (i.e., attributes for mining, as indicated in DMQL with the **in relevance to** clause) may be difficult for the user. A user may select only a few attributes that he or she feels may be important, while missing others that could also play a role in the description. For example, suppose that the dimension *birth_place* is defined by the attributes *city, province_or_state,* and *country.* Of these attributes, let's say that the user has only thought to specify *city.* In order to allow generalization on the *birth_place* dimension, the other attributes defining this dimension should also be included. In other words, having the system automatically include *province_or_state* and *country* as relevant attributes allows *city* to be generalized to these higher conceptual levels during the induction process.

At the other extreme, suppose that the user may have introduced too many attributes by specifying all of the possible attributes with the clause "**in relevance to** ∗". In this case, all of the attributes in the relation specified by the **from** clause would be included in the analysis. Many of these attributes are unlikely to contribute to an interesting description. A correlation-based (Section 2.4.1) or entropy-based (Section 2.6.1) analysis method can be used to perform attribute *relevance analysis* and filter out statistically irrelevant or weakly relevant attributes from the descriptive mining process. Other approaches, such as attribute subset selection, are also described in Chapter 2.

*"What does the '***where** *status* in *"graduate"' clause mean?"* This **where** clause implies that a concept hierarchy exists for the attribute *status.* Such a concept hierarchy organizes primitive-level data values for *status,* such as *"M.Sc."*, *"M.A."*, *"M.B.A."*, *"Ph.D."*, *"B.Sc."*, *"B.A."*, into higher conceptual levels, such as *"graduate"* and *"undergraduate."* This use

Table 4.12 Initial working relation: a collection of task-relevant data.

name	*gender*	*major*	*birth_place*	*birth_date*	*residence*	*phone#*	*gpa*
Jim Woodman	M	CS	Vancouver, BC, Canada	8-12-76	3511 Main St., Richmond	687-4598	3.67
Scott Lachance	M	CS	Montreal, Que, Canada	28-7-75	345 1st Ave., Richmond	253-9106	3.70
Laura Lee	F	physics	Seattle, WA, USA	25-8-70	125 Austin Ave., Burnaby	420-5232	3.83
...	...	...	...	...	...	...	...

of concept hierarchies does not appear in traditional relational query languages, yet is likely to become a common feature in data mining query languages.

The data mining query presented above is transformed into the following relational query for the collection of the task-relevant set of data:

> **use** Big_University_DB
> **select** name, gender, major, birth_place, birth_date, residence, phone#, gpa
> **from** student
> **where** status in {*"M.Sc."*, *"M.A."*, *"M.B.A."*, *"Ph.D."*}

The transformed query is executed against the relational database, *Big_University_DB*, and returns the data shown in Table 4.12. This table is called the (task-relevant) **initial working relation.** It is the data on which induction will be performed. Note that each tuple is, in fact, a conjunction of attribute-value pairs. Hence, we can think of a tuple within a relation as a rule of conjuncts, and of induction on the relation as the generalization of these rules. ■

"Now that the data are ready for attribute-oriented induction, how is attribute-oriented induction performed?" The essential operation of attribute-oriented induction is *data generalization*, which can be performed in either of two ways on the initial working relation: *attribute removal* and *attribute generalization*.

Attribute removal is based on the following rule: *If there is a large set of distinct values for an attribute of the initial working relation, but either (1) there is no generalization operator on the attribute (e.g., there is no concept hierarchy defined for the attribute), or (2) its higher-level concepts are expressed in terms of other attributes, then the attribute should be removed from the working relation.*

Let's examine the reasoning behind this rule. An attribute-value pair represents a conjunct in a generalized tuple, or rule. The removal of a conjunct eliminates a constraint and thus generalizes the rule. If, as in case 1, there is a large set of distinct values for an attribute but there is no generalization operator for it, the attribute should be removed because it cannot be generalized, and preserving it would imply keeping a large number of disjuncts, which contradicts the goal of generating concise rules. On the other hand, consider case 2, where the higher-level concepts of the attribute are expressed in terms of other attributes. For example, suppose that the attribute in question is *street*, whose higher-level concepts are represented by the attributes ⟨*city, province_or_state, country*⟩.

The removal of *street* is equivalent to the application of a generalization operator. This rule corresponds to the generalization rule known as *dropping conditions* in the machine learning literature on *learning from examples*.

Attribute generalization is based on the following rule: *If there is a large set of distinct values for an attribute in the initial working relation, and there exists a set of generalization operators on the attribute, then a generalization operator should be selected and applied to the attribute.* This rule is based on the following reasoning. Use of a generalization operator to generalize an attribute value within a tuple, or rule, in the working relation will make the rule cover more of the original data tuples, thus generalizing the concept it represents. This corresponds to the generalization rule known as *climbing generalization trees* in *learning from examples*, or *concept tree ascension*.

Both rules, *attribute removal* and *attribute generalization*, claim that if there is a *large* set of distinct values for an attribute, further generalization should be applied. This raises the question: how large is "*a large set of distinct values for an attribute*" considered to be?

Depending on the attributes or application involved, a user may prefer some attributes to remain at a rather low abstraction level while others are generalized to higher levels. The control of how high an attribute should be generalized is typically quite subjective. The control of this process is called **attribute generalization control**. If the attribute is generalized "too high," it may lead to overgeneralization, and the resulting rules may not be very informative. On the other hand, if the attribute is not generalized to a "sufficiently high level," then undergeneralization may result, where the rules obtained may not be informative either. Thus, a balance should be attained in attribute-oriented generalization.

There are many possible ways to control a generalization process. We will describe two common approaches and then illustrate how they work with an example.

The first technique, called **attribute generalization threshold control**, either sets one generalization threshold for all of the attributes, or sets one threshold for each attribute. If the number of distinct values in an attribute is greater than the attribute threshold, further attribute removal or attribute generalization should be performed. Data mining systems typically have a default attribute threshold value generally ranging from 2 to 8 and should allow experts and users to modify the threshold values as well. If a user feels that the generalization reaches too high a level for a particular attribute, the threshold can be increased. This corresponds to drilling down along the attribute. Also, to further generalize a relation, the user can reduce the threshold of a particular attribute, which corresponds to rolling up along the attribute.

The second technique, called **generalized relation threshold control**, sets a threshold for the generalized relation. If the number of (distinct) tuples in the generalized relation is greater than the threshold, further generalization should be performed. Otherwise, no further generalization should be performed. Such a threshold may also be preset in the data mining system (usually within a range of 10 to 30), or set by an expert or user, and should be adjustable. For example, if a user feels that the generalized relation is too small, he or she can increase the threshold, which implies drilling down. Otherwise, to further generalize a relation, the threshold can be reduced, which implies rolling up.

These two techniques can be applied in sequence: first apply the attribute threshold control technique to generalize each attribute, and then apply relation threshold control to further reduce the size of the generalized relation. No matter which generalization control technique is applied, the user should be allowed to adjust the generalization thresholds in order to obtain interesting concept descriptions.

In many database-oriented induction processes, users are interested in obtaining quantitative or statistical information about the data at different levels of abstraction. Thus, it is important to accumulate count and other aggregate values in the induction process. Conceptually, this is performed as follows. The aggregate function, **count**, is associated with each database tuple. Its value for each tuple in the initial working relation is initialized to 1. Through attribute removal and attribute generalization, tuples within the initial working relation may be generalized, resulting in groups of *identical tuples*. In this case, all of the identical tuples forming a group should be merged into one tuple. The count of this new, generalized tuple is set to the total number of tuples from the initial working relation that are represented by (i.e., were merged into) the new generalized tuple. For example, suppose that by attribute-oriented induction, 52 data tuples from the initial working relation are all generalized to the same tuple, T. That is, the generalization of these 52 tuples resulted in 52 identical instances of tuple T. These 52 identical tuples are merged to form one instance of T, whose count is set to 52. Other popular aggregate functions that could also be associated with each tuple include **sum** and **avg**. For a given generalized tuple, **sum** contains the sum of the values of a given numeric attribute for the initial working relation tuples making up the generalized tuple. Suppose that tuple T contained **sum**(*units_sold*) as an aggregate function. The sum value for tuple T would then be set to the total number of units sold for each of the 52 tuples. The aggregate **avg** (average) is computed according to the formula, **avg** = **sum/count**.

Example 4.21 **Attribute-oriented induction.** Here we show how attribute-oriented induction is performed on the initial working relation of Table 4.12. For each attribute of the relation, the generalization proceeds as follows:

1. *name:* Since there are a large number of distinct values for *name* and there is no generalization operation defined on it, this attribute is removed.
2. *gender:* Since there are only two distinct values for *gender*, this attribute is retained and no generalization is performed on it.
3. *major:* Suppose that a concept hierarchy has been defined that allows the attribute *major* to be generalized to the values {*arts&science, engineering, business*}. Suppose also that the attribute generalization threshold is set to 5, and that there are more than 20 distinct values for *major* in the initial working relation. By attribute generalization and attribute generalization control, *major* is therefore generalized by climbing the given concept hierarchy.
4. *birth_place:* This attribute has a large number of distinct values; therefore, we would like to generalize it. Suppose that a concept hierarchy exists for *birth_place*, defined

as "*city* < *province_or_state* < *country*". If the number of distinct values for *country* in the initial working relation is greater than the attribute generalization threshold, then *birth_place* should be removed, because even though a generalization operator exists for it, the generalization threshold would not be satisfied. If instead, the number of distinct values for *country* is less than the attribute generalization threshold, then *birth_place* should be generalized to *birth_country*.

5. *birth_date:* Suppose that a hierarchy exists that can generalize *birth_date* to *age*, and *age* to *age_range*, and that the number of age ranges (or intervals) is small with respect to the attribute generalization threshold. Generalization of *birth_date* should therefore take place.

6. *residence:* Suppose that *residence* is defined by the attributes *number, street, residence_city, residence_province_or_state*, and *residence_country*. The number of distinct values for *number* and *street* will likely be very high, since these concepts are quite low level. The attributes *number* and *street* should therefore be removed, so that *residence* is then generalized to *residence_city*, which contains fewer distinct values.

7. *phone#:* As with the attribute *name* above, this attribute contains too many distinct values and should therefore be removed in generalization.

8. *gpa:* Suppose that a concept hierarchy exists for *gpa* that groups values for grade point average into numerical intervals like {3.75–4.0, 3.5–3.75,...}, which in turn are grouped into descriptive values, such as {*excellent, very good*,...}. The attribute can therefore be generalized.

The generalization process will result in groups of identical tuples. For example, the first two tuples of Table 4.12 both generalize to the same identical tuple (namely, the first tuple shown in Table 4.13). Such identical tuples are then merged into one, with their **counts** accumulated. This process leads to the generalized relation shown in Table 4.13.

Based on the vocabulary used in OLAP, we may view **count** as a *measure*, and the remaining attributes as *dimensions*. Note that aggregate functions, such as **sum**, may be applied to numerical attributes, like *salary* and *sales*. These attributes are referred to as *measure attributes*. ■

Implementation techniques and methods of presenting the derived generalization are discussed in the following subsections.

Table 4.13 A generalized relation obtained by attribute-oriented induction on the data of Table 4.12.

gender	*major*	*birth_country*	*age_range*	*residence_city*	*gpa*	*count*
M	Science	Canada	20–25	Richmond	very_good	16
F	Science	Foreign	25–30	Burnaby	excellent	22
...	...	...	...	...	...	...

4.3.2 Efficient Implementation of Attribute-Oriented Induction

"How is attribute-oriented induction actually implemented?" The previous subsection provided an introduction to attribute-oriented induction. The general procedure is summarized in Figure 4.19. The efficiency of this algorithm is analyzed as follows:

- Step 1 of the algorithm is essentially a relational query to collect the task-relevant data into the **working relation**, W. Its processing efficiency depends on the query processing methods used. Given the successful implementation and commercialization of database systems, this step is expected to have good performance.

Algorithm: Attribute oriented induction. Mining generalized characteristics in a relational database given a user's data mining request.

Input:

- *DB*, a relational database;
- *DMQuery*, a data mining query;
- *a_list*, a list of attributes (containing attributes, a_i);
- $Gen(a_i)$, a set of concept hierarchies or generalization operators on attributes, a_i;
- $a\_gen\_thresh(a_i)$, attribute generalization thresholds for each a_i.

Output: P, a *Prime_generalized_relation*.

Method:

1. $W \leftarrow$ **get_task_relevant_data** (*DMQuery*, *DB*); // Let W, the working relation, hold the task-relevant data.
2. **prepare_for_generalization** (W); // This is implemented as follows.
   (a) Scan W and collect the distinct values for each attribute, a_i. (Note: If W is very large, this may be done by examining a sample of W.)
   (b) For each attribute a_i, determine whether a_i should be removed, and if not, compute its minimum desired level L_i based on its given or default attribute threshold, and determine the mapping-pairs (v, v'), where v is a distinct value of a_i in W, and v' is its corresponding generalized value at level L_i.
3. $P \leftarrow$ **generalization** (W),
   The *Prime_generalized_relation*, P, is derived by replacing each value v in W by its corresponding v' in the mapping while accumulating **count** and computing any other aggregate values.
   This step can be implemented efficiently using either of the two following variations:
   (a) For each generalized tuple, insert the tuple into a sorted prime relation P by a binary search: if the tuple is already in P, simply increase its **count** and other aggregate values accordingly; otherwise, insert it into P.
   (b) Since in most cases the number of distinct values at the prime relation level is small, the prime relation can be coded as an m-dimensional array where m is the number of attributes in P, and each dimension contains the corresponding generalized attribute values. Each array element holds the corresponding **count** and other aggregation values, if any. The insertion of a generalized tuple is performed by measure aggregation in the corresponding array element.

Figure 4.19 Basic algorithm for attribute-oriented induction.

- Step 2 collects statistics on the working relation. This requires scanning the relation at most once. The cost for computing the minimum desired level and determining the mapping pairs, (v, v'), for each attribute is dependent on the number of distinct values for each attribute and is smaller than N, the number of tuples in the initial relation.

- Step 3 derives the **prime relation,** P. This is performed by inserting generalized tuples into P. There are a total of N tuples in W and p tuples in P. For each tuple, t, in W, we substitute its attribute values based on the derived mapping-pairs. This results in a generalized tuple, t'. If variation (a) is adopted, each t' takes $O(\log p)$ to find the location for count increment or tuple insertion. Thus the total time complexity is $O(N \times \log p)$ for all of the generalized tuples. If variation (b) is adopted, each t' takes $O(1)$ to find the tuple for count increment. Thus the overall time complexity is $O(N)$ for all of the generalized tuples.

Many data analysis tasks need to examine a good number of dimensions or attributes. This may involve *dynamically* introducing and testing additional attributes rather than just those specified in the mining query. Moreover, a user with little knowledge of the *truly* relevant set of data may simply specify "**in relevance to** $*$" in the mining query, which includes all of the attributes into the analysis. Therefore, an advanced concept description mining process needs to perform attribute relevance analysis on large sets of attributes to select the most relevant ones. Such analysis may employ correlation or entropy measures, as described in Chapter 2 on data preprocessing.

4.3.3 Presentation of the Derived Generalization

"Attribute-oriented induction generates one or a set of generalized descriptions. How can these descriptions be visualized?" The descriptions can be presented to the user in a number of different ways. Generalized descriptions resulting from attribute-oriented induction are most commonly displayed in the form of a **generalized relation** (or **table**).

Example 4.22 **Generalized relation (table).** Suppose that attribute-oriented induction was performed on a *sales* relation of the *AllElectronics* database, resulting in the generalized description of Table 4.14 for sales in 2004. The description is shown in the form of a generalized relation. Table 4.13 of Example 4.21 is another example of a generalized relation. ■

Descriptions can also be visualized in the form of **cross-tabulations,** or **crosstabs.** In a two-dimensional crosstab, each row represents a value from an attribute, and each column represents a value from another attribute. In an n-dimensional crosstab (for $n > 2$), the columns may represent the values of more than one attribute, with subtotals shown for attribute-value groupings. This representation is similar to *spreadsheets.* It is easy to map directly from a data cube structure to a crosstab.

Example 4.23 **Cross-tabulation.** The generalized relation shown in Table 4.14 can be transformed into the 3-D cross-tabulation shown in Table 4.15. ■

Table 4.14 A generalized relation for the sales in 2004.

location	*item*	*sales (in million dollars)*	*count (in thousands)*
Asia	TV	15	300
Europe	TV	12	250
North_America	TV	28	450
Asia	computer	120	1000
Europe	computer	150	1200
North_America	computer	200	1800

Table 4.15 A crosstab for the sales in 2004.

	item					
	TV		*computer*		*both_items*	
location	sales	count	sales	count	sales	count
Asia	15	300	120	1000	135	1300
Europe	12	250	150	1200	162	1450
North_America	28	450	200	1800	228	2250
all_regions	45	1000	470	4000	525	5000

Generalized data can be presented graphically, using bar charts, pie charts, and curves. Visualization with graphs is popular in data analysis. Such graphs and curves can represent 2-D or 3-D data.

Example 4.24 **Bar chart and pie chart.** The sales data of the crosstab shown in Table 4.15 can be transformed into the bar chart representation of Figure 4.20 and the pie chart representation of Figure 4.21. ■

Finally, a 3-D generalized relation or crosstab can be represented by a 3-D data cube, which is useful for browsing the data at different levels of generalization.

Example 4.25 **Cube view.** Consider the data cube shown in Figure 4.22 for the dimensions *item, location*, and *cost*. This is the same kind of data cube that we have seen so far, although it is presented in a slightly different way. Here, the *size* of a cell (displayed as a tiny cube) represents the count of the corresponding cell, while the *brightness* of the cell can be used to represent another measure of the cell, such as sum (*sales*). Pivoting, drilling, and slicing-and-dicing operations can be performed on the data cube browser by mouse clicking. ■

A generalized relation may also be represented in the form of logic rules. Typically, each generalized tuple represents a rule disjunct. Because data in a large database usually span a diverse range of distributions, a single generalized tuple is unlikely to *cover*, or

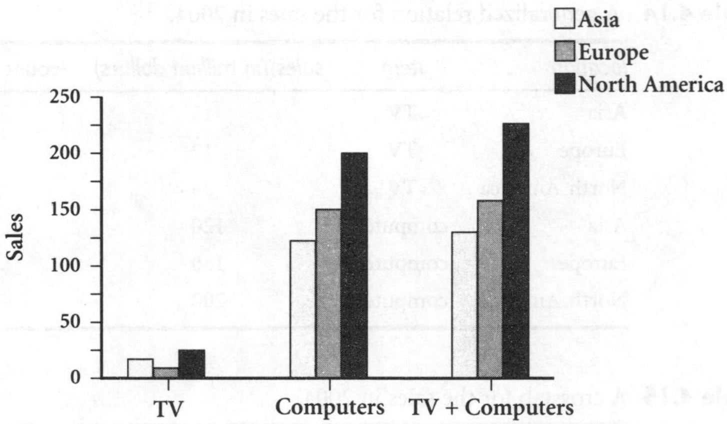

Figure 4.20 Bar chart representation of the sales in 2004.

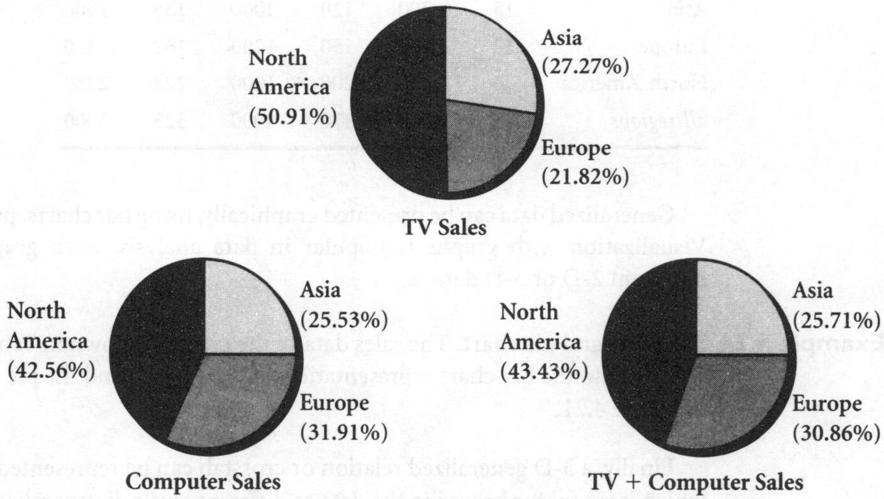

Figure 4.21 Pie chart representation of the sales in 2004.

represent, 100% of the initial working relation tuples, or *cases*. Thus, quantitative information, such as the percentage of data tuples that satisfy the left- and right-hand side of the rule, should be associated with each rule. A logic rule that is associated with quantitative information is called a **quantitative rule**.

To define a quantitative characteristic rule, we introduce the **t-weight** as an interestingness measure that describes the *typicality* of each *disjunct* in the rule, or of each *tuple*

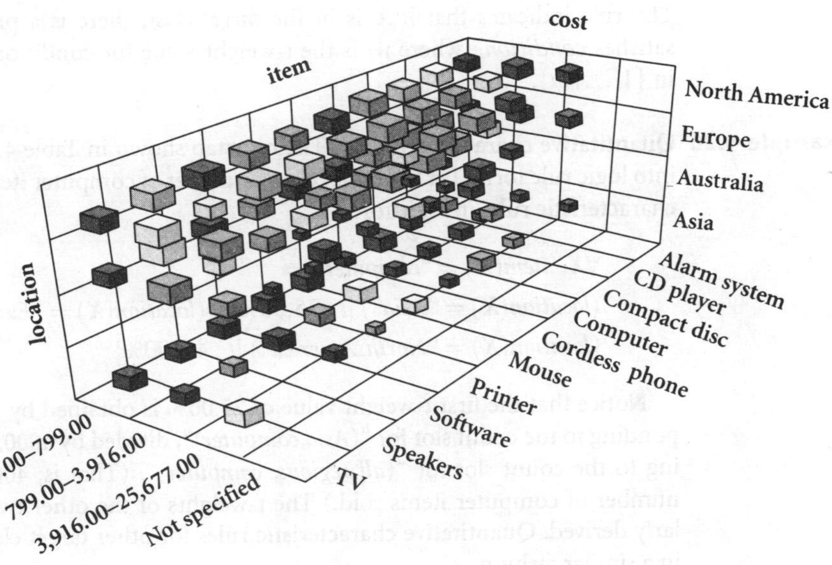

Figure 4.22 A 3-D cube view representation of the sales in 2004.

in the corresponding generalized relation. The measure is defined as follows. Let the class of objects that is to be characterized (or described by the rule) be called the *target class.* Let q_a be a generalized tuple describing the target class. The **t-weight** for q_a is the percentage of tuples of the target class from the initial working relation that are covered by q_n. Formally, we have

$$t\_weight = \text{count}(q_a)/\Sigma_{i=1}^{n}\text{count}(q_a), \tag{4.1}$$

where n is the number of tuples for the target class in the generalized relation; $q_1, \ldots, q_n$ are tuples for the target class in the generalized relation; and q_a is in $q_1, \ldots, q_n$. Obviously, the range for the t-weight is [0.0, 1.0] or [0%, 100%].

A **quantitative characteristic rule** can then be represented either (1) in logic form by associating the corresponding t-weight value with each disjunct covering the target class, or (2) in the relational table or crosstab form by changing the **count** values in these tables for tuples of the target class to the corresponding t-weight values.

Each disjunct of a quantitative characteristic rule represents a condition. In general, the disjunction of these conditions forms a *necessary* condition of the target class, since the condition is derived based on all of the cases of the target class; that is, all tuples of the target class must satisfy this condition. However, the rule may not be a *sufficient* condition of the target class, since a tuple satisfying the same condition could belong to another class. Therefore, the rule should be expressed in the form

$$\forall X,\ target\_class(X) \Rightarrow condition_1(X)[t : w_1] \vee \cdots \vee condition_m(X)[t : w_m]. \tag{4.2}$$

The rule indicates that if X is in the *target_class*, there is a probability of w_i that X satisfies *condition*$_i$, where w_i is the t-weight value for condition or disjunct i, and i is in $\{1,\ldots,m\}$.

Example 4.26 **Quantitative characteristic rule.** The crosstab shown in Table 4.15 can be transformed into logic rule form. Let the target class be the set of computer items. The corresponding characteristic rule, in logic form, is

$$\begin{aligned}&\forall X,\ item(X) = \text{“computer”} \Rightarrow\\&(location(X) = \text{“Asia”})\ [t: 25.00\%] \vee (location(X) = \text{“Europe”})\ [t: 30.00\%] \vee\\&(location(X) = \text{“North\_America”})\ [t: 45, 00\%]\end{aligned}$$

Notice that the first t-weight value of 25.00% is obtained by 1000, the value corresponding to the count slot for "(*Asia,computer*)", divided by 4000, the value corresponding to the count slot for "(*all_regions, computer*)". (That is, 4000 represents the total number of computer items sold.) The t-weights of the other two disjuncts were similarly derived. Quantitative characteristic rules for other target classes can be computed in a similar fashion. ■

"How can the t-weight and interestingness measures in general be used by the data mining system to display only the concept descriptions that it objectively evaluates as interesting?" A threshold can be set for this purpose. For example, if the t-weight of a generalized tuple is lower than the threshold, then the tuple is considered to represent only a negligible portion of the database and can therefore be ignored as uninteresting. Ignoring such negligible tuples does not mean that they should be removed from the intermediate results (i.e., the prime generalized relation, or the data cube, depending on the implementation) because they may contribute to subsequent further exploration of the data by the user via interactive rolling up or drilling down of other dimensions and levels of abstraction. Such a threshold may be referred to as a **significance threshold** or **support threshold**, where the latter term is commonly used in association rule mining.

4.3.4 Mining Class Comparisons: Discriminating between Different Classes

In many applications, users may not be interested in having a single class (or concept) described or characterized, but rather would prefer to mine a description that compares or distinguishes one class (or concept) from other comparable classes (or concepts). Class discrimination or comparison (hereafter referred to as **class comparison**) mines descriptions that distinguish a target class from its contrasting classes. Notice that the target and contrasting classes must be *comparable* in the sense that they share similar dimensions and attributes. For example, the three classes, *person, address*, and *item*, are not comparable. However, the sales in the last three years are comparable classes, and so are computer science students versus physics students.

Our discussions on class characterization in the previous sections handle multilevel data summarization and characterization in a single class. The techniques developed can be extended to handle class comparison across several comparable classes. For example, the attribute generalization process described for class characterization can be modified so that the generalization is performed *synchronously* among all the classes compared. This allows the attributes in all of the classes to be generalized to the *same* levels of abstraction. Suppose, for instance, that we are given the *AllElectronics* data for sales in 2003 and sales in 2004 and would like to compare these two classes. Consider the dimension *location* with abstractions at the *city*, *province_or_state*, and *country* levels. Each class of data should be generalized to the same *location* level. That is, they are synchronously all generalized to either the *city* level, or the *province_or_state* level, or the *country* level. Ideally, this is more useful than comparing, say, the sales in Vancouver in 2003 with the sales in the United States in 2004 (i.e., where each set of sales data is generalized to a different level). The users, however, should have the option to overwrite such an automated, synchronous comparison with their own choices, when preferred.

"How is class comparison performed?" In general, the procedure is as follows:

1. **Data collection:** The set of relevant data in the database is collected by query processing and is partitioned respectively into a *target class* and one or a set of *contrasting class(es)*.

2. **Dimension relevance analysis:** If there are many dimensions, then dimension relevance analysis should be performed on these classes to select only the highly relevant dimensions for further analysis. Correlation or entropy-based measures can be used for this step (Chapter 2).

3. **Synchronous generalization:** Generalization is performed on the target class to the level controlled by a user- or expert-specified dimension threshold, which results in a **prime target class relation.** The concepts in the contrasting class(es) are generalized to the same level as those in the prime target class relation, forming the **prime contrasting class(es) relation.**

4. **Presentation of the derived comparison:** The resulting class comparison description can be visualized in the form of tables, graphs, and rules. This presentation usually includes a "contrasting" measure such as **count%** (percentage count) that reflects the comparison between the target and contrasting classes. The user can adjust the comparison description by applying drill-down, roll-up, and other OLAP operations to the target and contrasting classes, as desired.

The above discussion outlines a general algorithm for mining comparisons in databases. In comparison with characterization, the above algorithm involves synchronous generalization of the target class with the contrasting classes, so that classes are simultaneously compared at the same levels of abstraction.

The following example mines a class comparison describing the graduate students and the undergraduate students at *Big University*.

Example 4.27 **Mining a class comparison.** Suppose that you would like to compare the general properties between the graduate students and the undergraduate students at *Big University*, given the attributes *name, gender, major, birth_place, birth_date, residence, phone#,* and *gpa*.

This data mining task can be expressed in DMQL as follows:

```
use Big_University_DB
mine comparison as "grad_vs_undergrad_students"
in relevance to name, gender, major, birth_place, birth_date, residence,
        phone#, gpa
for "graduate_students"
where status in "graduate"
versus "undergraduate_students"
where status in "undergraduate"
analyze count%
from student
```

Let's see how this typical example of a data mining query for mining comparison descriptions can be processed.

First, the query is transformed into two relational queries that collect two sets of task-relevant data: one for the *initial target class working relation*, and the other for the *initial contrasting class working relation*, as shown in Tables 4.16 and 4.17. This can also be viewed as the construction of a data cube, where the status {*graduate, undergraduate*} serves as one dimension, and the other attributes form the remaining dimensions.

Table 4.16 Initial working relations: the *target class* (graduate students)

name	gender	major	birth_place	birth_date	residence	phone#	gpa
Jim Woodman	M	CS	Vancouver, BC, Canada	8-12-76	3511 Main St., Richmond	687-4598	3.67
Scott Lachance	M	CS	Montreal, Que, Canada	28-7-75	345 1st Ave., Vancouver	253-9106	3.70
Laura Lee	F	Physics	Seattle, WA, USA	25-8-70	125 Austin Ave., Burnaby	420-5232	3.83
...	...	...	...	...	...	...	...

Table 4.17 Initial working relations: the *contrasting class* (undergraduate students)

name	gender	major	birth_place	birth_date	residence	phone#	gpa
Bob Schumann	M	Chemistry	Calgary, Alt, Canada	10-1-78	2642 Halifax St., Burnaby	294-4291	2.96
Amy Eau	F	Biology	Golden, BC, Canada	30-3-76	463 Sunset Cres., Vancouver	681-5417	3.52
...	...	...	...	...	...	...	...

Second, dimension relevance analysis can be performed, when necessary, on the two classes of data. After this analysis, irrelevant or weakly relevant dimensions, such as *name, gender, birth_place, residence*, and *phone#*, are removed from the resulting classes. Only the highly relevant attributes are included in the subsequent analysis.

Third, synchronous generalization is performed: Generalization is performed on the target class to the levels controlled by user- or expert-specified dimension thresholds, forming the *prime target class relation*. The contrasting class is generalized to the same levels as those in the prime target class relation, forming the *prime contrasting class(es) relation*, as presented in Tables 4.18 and 4.19. In comparison with undergraduate students, graduate students tend to be older and have a higher GPA, in general.

Finally, the resulting class comparison is presented in the form of tables, graphs, and/or rules. This visualization includes a contrasting measure (such as **count%**) that compares between the target class and the contrasting class. For example, 5.02% of the graduate students majoring in Science are between 26 and 30 years of age and have a "good" GPA, while only 2.32% of undergraduates have these same characteristics. Drilling and other OLAP operations may be performed on the target and contrasting classes as deemed necessary by the user in order to adjust the abstraction levels of the final description. ■

"How can class comparison descriptions be presented?" As with class characterizations, class comparisons can be presented to the user in various forms, including

Table 4.18 Prime generalized relation for the *target class* (graduate students)

major	*age_range*	*gpa*	count%
Science	21...25	good	5.53%
Science	26...30	good	5.02%
Science	over_30	very_good	5.86%
...	...	...	...
Business	over_30	excellent	4.68%

Table 4.19 Prime generalized relation for the *contrasting class* (undergraduate students)

major	*age_range*	*gpa*	count%
Science	16...20	fair	5.53%
Science	16...20	good	4.53%
...	...	...	...
Science	26...30	good	2.32%
...	...	...	...
Business	over_30	excellent	0.68%

generalized relations, crosstabs, bar charts, pie charts, curves, cubes, and rules. With the exception of logic rules, these forms are used in the same way for characterization as for comparison. In this section, we discuss the visualization of class comparisons in the form of discriminant rules.

As is similar with characterization descriptions, the discriminative features of the target and contrasting classes of a comparison description can be described quantitatively by a *quantitative discriminant rule*, which associates a statistical interestingness measure, *d-weight*, with each generalized tuple in the description.

Let q_a be a generalized tuple, and C_j be the target class, where q_a covers some tuples of the target class. Note that it is possible that q_a also covers some tuples of the contrasting classes, particularly since we are dealing with a comparison description. The **d-weight** for q_a is the ratio of the number of tuples from the initial target class working relation that are covered by q_a to the total number of tuples in both the initial target class and contrasting class working relations that are covered by q_a. Formally, the d-weight of q_a for the class C_j is defined as

$$d\_weight = \mathrm{count}(q_a \in C_j)/\Sigma_{i=1}^{m}\mathrm{count}(q_a \in C_i), \tag{4.3}$$

where m is the total number of the target and contrasting classes, C_j is in $\{C_1, \ldots, C_m\}$, and $\mathrm{count}\ (q_a \in C_i)$ is the number of tuples of class C_i that are covered by q_a. The range for the d-weight is [0.0, 1.0] (or [0%, 100%]).

A high d-weight in the target class indicates that the concept represented by the generalized tuple is primarily derived from the target class, whereas a low d-weight implies that the concept is primarily derived from the contrasting classes. A threshold can be set to control the display of interesting tuples based on the d-weight or other measures used, as described in Section 4.3.3.

Example 4.28 **Computing the d-weight measure.** In Example 4.27, suppose that the count distribution for the generalized tuple, *major* = *"Science" AND age_range* = *"21...25" AND gpa* = *"good"*, from Tables 4.18 and 4.19 is as shown in Table 20.

The d-weight for the given generalized tuple is 90/(90 + 210) = 30% with respect to the target class, and 210/(90 + 210) = 70% with respect to the contrasting class. That is, *if a student majoring in Science is 21 to 25 years old and has a "good" gpa, then based on the data, there is a 30% probability that she is a graduate student, versus a 70% probability that*

Table 4.20 Count distribution between graduate and undergraduate students for a generalized tuple.

status	*major*	*age_range*	*gpa*	count
graduate	Science	21...25	good	90
undergraduate	Science	21...25	good	210

she is an undergraduate student. Similarly, the d-weights for the other generalized tuples in Tables 4.18 and 4.19 can be derived. ■

A **quantitative discriminant rule** for the target class of a given comparison description is written in the form

$$\forall X,\ target\_class(X) \Leftarrow condition(X)\ \ [d{:}d\_weight], \tag{4.4}$$

where the condition is formed by a generalized tuple of the description. This is different from rules obtained in class characterization, where the arrow of implication is from left to right.

Example 4.29 **Quantitative discriminant rule.** Based on the generalized tuple and count distribution in Example 4.28, a quantitative discriminant rule for the target class *graduate_student* can be written as follows:

$$\begin{aligned}\forall X,\ Status(X) = \text{``}graduate\_student\text{''} \Leftarrow \\ major(X) = \text{``}Science\text{''} \wedge age\_range(X) = \text{``21...25''} \\ \wedge\ gpa(X) = \text{``}good\text{''}[d: 30\%].\end{aligned} \tag{4.5}$$

■

Notice that a discriminant rule provides a *sufficient* condition, but not a *necessary* one, for an object (or tuple) to be in the target class. For example, Rule (4.6) implies that if X satisfies the condition, then the probability that X is a graduate student is 30%. However, it does not imply the probability that X meets the condition, given that X is a graduate student. This is because although the tuples that meet the condition are in the target class, other tuples that do not necessarily satisfy this condition may also be in the target class, because the rule may not cover *all* of the examples of the target class in the database. Therefore, the condition is sufficient, but not necessary.

4.3.5 Class Description: Presentation of Both Characterization and Comparison

"Because class characterization and class comparison are two aspects forming a class description, can we present both in the same table or in the same rule?" Actually, as long as we have a clear understanding of the meaning of the t-weight and d-weight measures and can interpret them correctly, there is no additional difficulty in presenting both aspects in the same table. Let's examine an example of expressing both class characterization and class comparison in the same crosstab.

Example 4.30 **Crosstab for class characterization and class comparison.** Let Table 4.21 be a crosstab showing the total number (in thousands) of TVs and computers sold at *AllElectronics* in 2004.

Table 4.21 A crosstab for the total number (count) of TVs and computers sold in thousands in 2004.

	item		
location	*TV*	*computer*	*both_items*
Europe	80	240	320
North_America	120	560	680
both_regions	200	800	1000

Table 4.22 The same crosstab as in Table 4.21, but here the t-weight and d-weight values associated with each class are shown.

	item								
	TV			*computer*			*both_items*		
location	count	t-weight	d-weight	count	t-weight	d-weight	count	t-weight	d-weight
Europe	80	25%	40%	240	75%	30%	320	100%	32%
North_America	120	17.65%	60%	560	82.35%	70%	680	100%	68%
both_regions	200	20%	100%	800	80%	100%	1000	100%	100%

Let *Europe* be the target class and *North_America* be the contrasting class. The t-weights and d-weights of the sales distribution between the two classes are presented in Table 4.22. According to the table, the t-weight of a generalized tuple or object (e.g., *item* = "*TV*") for a given class (e.g., the target class *Europe*) shows how typical the tuple is of the given class (e.g., what proportion of these sales in Europe are for TVs?). The d-weight of a tuple shows how distinctive the tuple is in the given (target or contrasting) class in comparison with its rival class (e.g., how do the TV sales in Europe compare with those in North America?).

For example, the t-weight for "*(Europe, TV)*" is 25% because the number of TVs sold in Europe (80,000) represents only 25% of the European sales for both items (320,000). The d-weight for "*(Europe, TV)*" is 40% because the number of TVs sold in Europe (80,000) represents 40% of the number of TVs sold in both the target and the contrasting classes of Europe and North America, respectively (which is 200,000). ■

Notice that the **count** measure in the crosstab of Table 4.22 obeys the general property of a crosstab (i.e., the **count** values per row and per column, when totaled, match the corresponding totals in the *both_items* and *both_regions* slots, respectively). However, this property is not observed by the t-weight and d-weight measures, because the semantic meaning of each of these measures is different from that of **count**, as we explained in Example 4.30.

"Can a quantitative characteristic rule and a quantitative discriminant rule be expressed together in the form of one rule?" The answer is yes—a quantitative characteristic rule and a quantitative discriminant rule for the same class can be combined to form a *quantitative description rule* for the class, which displays the t-weights *and* d-weights associated with the corresponding characteristic and discriminant rules. To see how this is done, let's quickly review how quantitative characteristic and discriminant rules are expressed.

As discussed in Section 4.3.3, a quantitative characteristic rule provides a necessary condition for the given target class since it presents a probability measurement for each property that can occur in the target class. Such a rule is of the form

$$\forall X,\ target\_class(X) \Rightarrow condition_1(X)[t : w_1] \vee \cdots \vee condition_m(X)[t : w_m], \qquad (4.6)$$

where each condition represents a property of the target class. The rule indicates that if X is in the *target_class*, the probability that X satisfies $condition_i$ is the value of the t-weight, w_i, where i is in $\{1, \ldots, m\}$.

As previously discussed in Section 4.3.4, a quantitative discriminant rule provides a sufficient condition for the target class since it presents a quantitative measurement of the properties that occur in the target class versus those that occur in the contrasting classes. Such a rule is of the form

$$\forall X,\ target\_class(X) \Leftarrow condition_1(X)[d : w_1] \wedge \cdots \wedge condition_m(X)[d : w_m]. \qquad (4.7)$$

The rule indicates that if X satisfies $condition_i$, there is a probability of w_i (the d-weight value) that X is in the *target_class*, where i is in $\{1, \ldots, m\}$.

A quantitative characteristic rule and a quantitative discriminant rule for a given class can be combined as follows to form a **quantitative description rule**: (1) For each condition, show both the associated t-weight and d-weight, and (2) a bidirectional arrow should be used between the given class and the conditions. That is, a quantitative description rule is of the form

$$\begin{aligned} \forall X,\ target\_class(X) \Leftrightarrow\ & condition_1(X)[t : w_1, d : w'_1] \\ & \theta \cdots \theta\ condition_m(X)[t : w_m, d : w'_m], \end{aligned} \qquad (4.8)$$

where θ represents a logical disjunction/conjuction. (That is, if we consider the rule as a characteristic rule, the conditions are ORed to from a disjunct. Otherwise, if we consider the rule as a discriminant rule, the conditions are ANDed to form a conjunct). The rule indicates that for i from 1 to m, if X is in the *target_class*, there is a probability of w_i that X satisfies $condition_i$; and if X satisfies $condition_i$, there is a probability of w'_i that X is in the *target_class*.

Example 4.31 Quantitative description rule. It is straightforward to transform the crosstab of Table 4.22 in Example 4.30 into a class description in the form of quantitative description rules. For example, the quantitative description rule for the target class, *Europe*, is

$$\forall X,\ location(X) = \text{"}Europe\text{"} \Leftrightarrow (item(X) = \text{"}TV\text{"})\ [t: 25\%, d: 40\%]\ \theta\ (item(X) = \text{"}computer\text{"})\ [t: 75\%, d: 30\%]. \tag{4.9}$$

For the sales of TVs and computers at *AllElectronics* in 2004, the rule states that if the sale of one of these items occurred in Europe, then the probability of the item being a TV is 25%, while that of being a computer is 75%. On the other hand, if we compare the sales of these items in Europe and North America, then 40% of the TVs were sold in Europe (and therefore we can deduce that 60% of the TVs were sold in North America). Furthermore, regarding computer sales, 30% of these sales took place in Europe. ■

4.4 Summary

- **Data generalization** is a process that abstracts a large set of task-relevant data in a database from a relatively low conceptual level to higher conceptual levels. Data generalization approaches include data cube–based data aggregation and attribute-oriented induction.
- From a data analysis point of view, data generalization is a form of *descriptive data mining*. **Descriptive data mining** describes data in a concise and summarative manner and presents interesting general properties of the data. This is different from **predictive data mining**, which analyzes data in order to construct one or a set of models, and attempts to predict the behavior of new data sets. This chapter focused on methods for descriptive data mining.
- A data cube consists of a **lattice of cuboids**. Each cuboid corresponds to a different degree of summarization of the given multidimensional data.
- **Full materialization** refers to the computation of all of the cuboids in a data cube lattice. **Partial materialization** refers to the selective computation of a subset of the cuboid cells in the lattice. Iceberg cubes and shell fragments are examples of partial materialization. An **iceberg cube** is a data cube that stores only those cube cells whose aggregate value (e.g., count) is above some minimum support threshold. For **shell fragments** of a data cube, only some cuboids involving a small number of dimensions are computed. Queries on additional combinations of the dimensions can be computed on the fly.
- There are several efficient **data cube computation methods**. In this chapter, we discussed in depth four cube computation methods: (1) **MultiWay** array aggregation for materializing full data cubes in sparse-array-based, bottom-up, shared computation; (2) **BUC** for computing iceberg cubes by exploring ordering and sorting for efficient top-down computation; (3) **Star-Cubing** for integration of top-down and bottom-up computation using a star-tree structure; and (4) high-dimensional

OLAP by precomputing only the partitioned shell fragments (thus called *minimal cubing*).

- There are several methods for effective and efficient exploration of data cubes, including *discovery-driven cube exploration, multifeature data cubes,* and *constrained cube gradient analysis.* **Discovery-driven exploration** of data cubes uses precomputed measures and visual cues to indicate data exceptions at all levels of aggregation, guiding the user in the data analysis process. **Multifeature cubes** compute complex queries involving multiple dependent aggregates at multiple granularity. **Constrained cube gradient analysis** explores *significant changes in measures* in a multidimensional space, based on a given set of probe cells, where changes in sector characteristics are expressed in terms of dimensions of the cube and are limited to *specialization* (drill-down), *generalization* (roll-up), and *mutation* (a change in one of the cube's dimensions).
- **Concept description** is the most basic form of descriptive data mining. It describes a given set of task-relevant data in a concise and summarative manner, presenting interesting general properties of the data. Concept (or class) description consists of **characterization** and **comparison** (or **discrimination**). The former summarizes and describes a collection of data, called the **target class**, whereas the latter summarizes and distinguishes one collection of data, called the **target class**, from other collection(s) of data, collectively called the **contrasting class(es)**.
- **Concept characterization** can be implemented using **data cube (OLAP-based) approaches** and the **attribute-oriented induction approach**. These are attribute- or dimension-based generalization approaches. The **attribute-oriented induction approach** consists of the following techniques: *data focusing, data generalization by attribute removal or attribute generalization, count and aggregate value accumulation, attribute generalization control,* and *generalization data visualization*.
- **Concept comparison** can be performed using the attribute-oriented induction or data cube approaches in a manner similar to concept characterization. Generalized tuples from the target and contrasting classes can be quantitatively compared and contrasted.
- Characterization and comparison descriptions (which form a concept description) can both be presented in the *same* generalized relation, crosstab, or quantitative rule form, although they are displayed with different interestingness measures. These measures include the **t-weight** (for tuple typicality) and **d-weight** (for tuple discriminability).

Exercises

4.1 Assume a base cuboid of 10 dimensions contains only three base cells: (1) $(a_1, d_2, d_3, d_4, \ldots, d_9, d_{10})$, (2) $(d_1, b_2, d_3, d_4, \ldots, d_9, d_{10})$, and (3) $(d_1, d_2, c_3, d_4, \ldots, d_9, d_{10})$, where $a_1 \neq d_1$, $b_2 \neq d_2$, and $c_3 \neq d_3$. The measure of the cube is *count*.

(a) How many *nonempty* cuboids will a full data cube contain?

(b) How many *nonempty* aggregate (i.e., nonbase) cells will a full cube contain?

(c) How many *nonempty* aggregate cells will an iceberg cube contain if the condition of the iceberg cube is "*count* ≥ 2"?

(d) A cell, *c*, is a *closed cell* if there exists no cell, *d*, such that *d* is a specialization of cell *c* (i.e., *d* is obtained by replacing a $*$ in *c* by a non-$*$ value) and *d* has the same measure value as *c*. A *closed cube* is a data cube consisting of only closed cells. How many closed cells are in the full cube?

4.2 There are several typical cube computation methods, such as *Multiway array computation* (MultiWay) [ZDN97], *BUC* (bottom-up computation) [BR99], and *Star-Cubing* [XHLW03].

Briefly describe these three methods (i.e., use one or two lines to outline the key points), and compare their feasibility and performance under the following conditions:

(a) Computing a dense full cube of low dimensionality (e.g., less than 8 dimensions)

(b) Computing an iceberg cube of around 10 dimensions with a highly skewed data distribution

(c) Computing a sparse iceberg cube of high dimensionality (e.g., over 100 dimensions)

4.3 [*Contributed by Chen Chen*] Suppose a data cube, *C*, has *D* dimensions, and the base cuboid contains *k* distinct tuples.

(a) Present a formula to calculate the minimum number of cells that the cube, *C*, may contain.

(b) Present a formula to calculate the maximum number of cells that *C* may contain.

(c) Answer parts (a) and (b) above as if the count in each cube cell must be no less than a threshold, *v*.

(d) Answer parts (a) and (b) above as if only closed cells are considered (with the minimum count threshold, *v*).

4.4 Suppose that a base cuboid has three dimensions, *A*, *B*, *C*, with the following number of cells: $|A| = 1,000,000$, $|B| = 100$, and $|C| = 1000$. Suppose that each dimension is evenly partitioned into 10 portions for *chunking*.

(a) Assuming each dimension has only one level, draw the complete lattice of the cube.

(b) If each cube cell stores one measure with 4 bytes, what is the total size of the computed cube if the cube is *dense*?

(c) State the order for computing the chunks in the cube that requires the least amount of space, and compute the total amount of main memory space required for computing the 2-D planes.

4.5 Often, the aggregate measure value of many cells in a large data cuboid is zero, resulting in a huge, yet sparse, multidimensional matrix.

(a) Design an implementation method that can elegantly overcome this sparse matrix problem. Note that you need to explain your data structures in detail and discuss the space needed, as well as how to retrieve data from your structures.

(b) Modify your design in (a) to handle *incremental data updates.* Give the reasoning behind your new design.

4.6 When computing a cube of high dimensionality, we encounter the inherent *curse of dimensionality* problem: there exists a huge number of subsets of combinations of dimensions.

(a) Suppose that there are only two base cells, $\{(a_1, a_2, a_3, \ldots, a_{100}), (a_1, a_2, b_3, \ldots, b_{100})\}$, in a 100-dimensional base cuboid. Compute the number of nonempty aggregate cells. Comment on the storage space and time required to compute these cells.

(b) Suppose we are to compute an iceberg cube from the above. If the minimum support count in the iceberg condition is two, how many aggregate cells will there be in the iceberg cube? Show the cells.

(c) Introducing iceberg cubes will lessen the burden of computing trivial aggregate cells in a data cube. However, even with iceberg cubes, we could still end up having to compute a large number of trivial uninteresting cells (i.e., with small counts). Suppose that a database has 20 tuples that map to (or cover) the two following base cells in a 100-dimensional base cuboid, each with a cell count of 10: $\{(a_1, a_2, a_3, \ldots, a_{100}) : 10, (a_1, a_2, b_3, \ldots, b_{100}) : 10\}$.

i. Let the minimum support be 10. How many distinct aggregate cells will there be like the following: $\{(a_1, a_2, a_3, a_4, \ldots, a_{99}, *) : 10, \ldots, (a_1, a_2, *, a_4, \ldots, a_{99}, a_{100}) : 10, \ldots, (a_1, a_2, a_3, *, \ldots, *, *) : 10\}$?

ii. If we ignore all the aggregate cells that can be obtained by replacing some constants with $*$'s while keeping the same measure value, how many distinct cells are left? What are the cells?

4.7 Propose an algorithm that computes *closed iceberg cubes* efficiently.

4.8 Suppose that we would like to compute an iceberg cube for the dimensions, A, B, C, D, where we wish to materialize all cells that satisfy a minimum support count of at least v, and where *cardinality(A) <cardinality(B) <cardinality(C) <cardinality(D)*. Show the BUC processing tree (which shows the order in which the BUC algorithm explores the lattice of a data cube, starting from **all**) for the construction of the above iceberg cube.

4.9 Discuss how you might extend the *Star-Cubing* algorithm to compute iceberg cubes where the iceberg condition tests for an **avg** that is no bigger than some value, v.

4.10 A flight data warehouse for a travel agent consists of six dimensions: *traveler, departure (city), departure_time, arrival, arrival_time,* and *flight*; and two measures: *count*, and *avg_fare*, where *avg_fare* stores the concrete fare at the lowest level but average fare at other levels.

(a) Suppose the cube is fully materialized. Starting with the *base cuboid [traveller, departure, departure_time, arrival, arrival_time, flight]*, what *specific OLAP operations* (e.g., roll-up *flight* to *airline*) should one perform in order to list the average fare per month for *each business traveler* who flies American Airlines (*AA*) from L.A. in the year 2004?

(b) Suppose we want to compute a data cube where the condition is that the minimum number of records is 10 and the average fare is over $500. Outline an efficient cube computation method (based on common sense about flight data distribution).

4.11 (Implementation project) There are four typical data cube computation methods: MultiWay [ZDN97], BUC [BR99], H-cubing [HPDW01], and Star-Cubing [XHLW03].

(a) Implement any one of these cube computation algorithms and describe your implementation, experimentation, and performance. Find another student who has implemented a different algorithm on the same platform (e.g., C++ on Linux) and compare your algorithm performance with his/hers.
Input:
   i. An n-dimensional base cuboid table (for $n < 20$), which is essentially a relational table with n attributes
   ii. An iceberg condition: *count* $(C) \geq k$ where k is a positive integer as a parameter

Output:
   i. The set of computed cuboids that satisfy the iceberg condition, in the order of your output generation
   ii. Summary of the set of cuboids in the form of "*cuboid ID*: the number of nonempty cells", sorted in alphabetical order of cuboids, e.g., *A*:155, *AB*: 120, *ABC*: 22, *ABCD*: 4, *ABCE*: 6, *ABD*: 36, where the number after ":" represents the number of nonempty cells. (this is used to quickly check the correctness of your results)

(b) Based on your implementation, discuss the following:
   i. What challenging computation problems are encountered as the number of dimensions grows large?
   ii. How can iceberg cubing solve the problems of part (a) for some data sets (and characterize such data sets)?
   iii. Give one simple example to show that sometimes iceberg cubes cannot provide a good solution.

(c) Instead of computing a data cube of high dimensionality, we may choose to materialize the cuboids that have only a small number of dimension combinations. For example, for a 30-dimensional data cube, we may only compute the 5-dimensional cuboids for every possible 5-dimensional combination. The resulting cuboids form a *shell cube*. Discuss how easy or hard it is to modify your cube computation algorithm to facilitate such computation.

4.12 Consider the following *multifeature cube* query: Grouping by all subsets of {*item, region, month*}, find the minimum shelf life in 2004 for each group and the fraction of the total sales due to tuples whose price is less than $100 and whose shelf life is between 1.25 and 1.5 of the minimum shelf life.

(a) Draw the multifeature cube graph for the query.

(b) Express the query in extended SQL.

(c) Is this a *distributive* multifeature cube? Why or why not?

4.13 For *class characterization*, what are the major differences between a data cube–based implementation and a relational implementation such as attribute-oriented induction? Discuss which method is most efficient and under what conditions this is so.

4.14 Suppose that the following table is derived by *attribute-oriented induction*.

class	*birth_place*	count
Programmer	USA	180
	others	120
DBA	USA	20
	others	80

(a) Transform the table into a crosstab showing the associated t-weights and d-weights.

(b) Map the class *Programmer* into a (bidirectional) *quantitative descriptive rule*, for example,

$$\forall X, Programmer(X) \Leftrightarrow (birth\_place(X) = \text{"}USA\text{"} \wedge \ldots)$$
$$[t : x\%, d : y\%] \ldots \theta\ (\ldots)[t : w\%, d : z\%].$$

4.15 Discuss why *relevance analysis* is beneficial and how it can be performed and integrated into the characterization process. Compare the result of two induction methods: (1) with relevance analysis and (2) without relevance analysis.

4.16 Given a generalized relation, *R*, derived from a database, *DB*, suppose that a set, $\triangle DB$, of tuples needs to be deleted from *DB*. Outline an *incremental* updating procedure for applying the necessary deletions to *R*.

4.17 Outline a data cube–based *incremental* algorithm for mining class comparisons.

Bibliographic Notes

Gray, Chauduri, Bosworth, et al. [GCB+97] proposed the data cube as a relational aggregation operator generalizing group-by, crosstabs, and subtotals. Harinarayan, Rajaraman, and Ullman [HRU96] proposed a greedy algorithm for the partial materialization of cuboids in the computation of a data cube. Sarawagi and Stonebraker [SS94] developed a chunk-based computation technique for the efficient organization of large multidimensional arrays. Agarwal, Agrawal, Deshpande, et al. [AAD+96] proposed several methods for the efficient computation of multidimensional aggregates for ROLAP servers. The chunk-based MultiWay array aggregation method for data cube computation in MOLAP was proposed in Zhao, Deshpande, and Naughton [ZDN97]. Ross and Srivastava [RS97] developed a method for computing sparse data cubes. Iceberg queries were first described in Fang, Shivakumar, Garcia-Molina, et al. [FSGM+98]. BUC, a scalable method that computes iceberg cubes from the apex cuboid, downward, was introduced by Beyer and Ramakrishnan [BR99]. Han, Pei, Dong, and Wang [HPDW01] introduced an H-cubing method for computing iceberg cubes with complex measures using an H-tree structure. The Star-cubing method for computing iceberg cubes with a dynamic star-tree structure was introduced by Xin, Han, Li, and Wah [XHLW03]. MMCubing, an efficient iceberg cube computation method that factorizes the lattice space, was developed by Shao, Han, and Xin [SHX04]. The shell-fragment-based minimal cubing approach for efficient high-dimensional OLAP introduced in this chapter was proposed by Li, Han, and Gonzalez [LHG04].

Aside from computing iceberg cubes, another way to reduce data cube computation is to materialize condensed, dwarf, or quotient cubes, which are variants of closed cubes. Wang, Feng, Lu, and Yu proposed computing a reduced data cube, called a *condensed cube* [WLFY02]. Sismanis, Deligiannakis, Roussopoulos, and Kotids proposed computing a compressed data cube, called a *dwarf cube*. Lakshmanan, Pei, and Han proposed a *quotient cube* structure to summarize the semantics of a data cube [LPH02], which was further extended to a *qc-tree structure* by Lakshmanan, Pei, and Zhao [LPZ03]. Xin, Han, Shao, and Liu [Xin+06] developed C-Cubing (i.e., *Closed-Cubing*), an *aggregation-based* approach that performs efficient closed-cube computation using a new algebraic measure called *closedness*.

There are also various studies on the computation of compressed data cubes by approximation, such as quasi-cubes by Barbara and Sullivan [BS97a], wavelet cubes by Vitter, Wang, and Iyer [VWI98], compressed cubes for query approximation on continuous dimensions by Shanmugasundaram, Fayyad, and Bradley [SFB99], and using log-linear models to compress data cubes by Barbara and Wu [BW00]. Computation of stream data "cubes" for multidimensional regression analysis has been studied by Chen, Dong, Han, et al. [CDH+02].

For works regarding the selection of materialized cuboids for efficient OLAP query processing, see Chaudhuri and Dayal [CD97], Harinarayan, Rajaraman, and Ullman [HRU96], Sristava, Dar, Jagadish, and Levy [SDJL96], Gupta [Gup97], Baralis, Paraboschi, and Teniente [BPT97], and Shukla, Deshpande, and Naughton [SDN98]. Methods for cube size estimation can be found in Deshpande, Naughton, Ramasamy, et al. [DNR+97], Ross and Srivastava [RS97], and Beyer and Ramakrishnan [BR99]. Agrawal, Gupta, and Sarawagi [AGS97] proposed operations for modeling multidimensional databases.

The discovery-driven exploration of OLAP data cubes was proposed by Sarawagi, Agrawal, and Megiddo [SAM98]. Further studies on the integration of OLAP with data mining capabilities include the proposal of DIFF and RELAX operators for intelligent exploration of multidimensional OLAP data by Sarawagi and Sathe [SS00, SS01]. The construction of multifeature data cubes is described in Ross, Srivastava, and Chatziantoniou [RSC98]. Methods for answering queries quickly by on-line aggregation are described in Hellerstein, Haas, and Wang [HHW97] and Hellerstein, Avnur, Chou, et al. [HAC+99]. A cube-gradient analysis problem, called *cubegrade*, was first proposed by Imielinski, Khachiyan, and Abdulghani [IKA02]. An efficient method for multidimensional constrained gradient analysis in data cubes was studied by Dong, Han, Lam, et al. [DHL+01].

Generalization and concept description methods have been studied in the statistics literature long before the onset of computers. Good summaries of statistical descriptive data mining methods include Cleveland [Cle93] and Devore [Dev95]. Generalization-based induction techniques, such as learning from examples, were proposed and studied in the machine learning literature before data mining became active. A theory and methodology of inductive learning was proposed by Michalski [Mic83]. The learning-from-examples method was proposed by Michalski [Mic83]. Version space was proposed by Mitchell [Mit77, Mit82]. The method of factoring the version space was presented by Subramanian and Feigenbaum [SF86b]. Overviews of machine learning techniques can be found in Dietterich and Michalski [DM83], Michalski, Carbonell, and Mitchell [MCM86], and Mitchell [Mit97].

Database-oriented methods for concept description explore scalable and efficient techniques for describing large sets of data. The attribute-oriented induction method described in this chapter was first proposed by Cai, Cercone, and Han [CCH91] and further extended by Han, Cai, and Cercone [HCC93], Han and Fu [HF96], Carter and Hamilton [CH98], and Han, Nishio, Kawano, and Wang [HNKW98].

5 Mining Frequent Patterns, Associations, and Correlations

Frequent patterns are patterns (such as itemsets, subsequences, or substructures) that appear in a data set frequently. For example, a set of items, such as milk and bread, that appear frequently together in a transaction data set is a *frequent itemset*. A subsequence, such as buying first a PC, then a digital camera, and then a memory card, if it occurs frequently in a shopping history database, is a *(frequent) sequential pattern*. A *substructure* can refer to different structural forms, such as subgraphs, subtrees, or sublattices, which may be combined with itemsets or subsequences. If a substructure occurs frequently, it is called a *(frequent) structured pattern*. Finding such frequent patterns plays an essential role in mining associations, correlations, and many other interesting relationships among data. Moreover, it helps in data classification, clustering, and other data mining tasks as well. Thus, frequent pattern mining has become an important data mining task and a focused theme in data mining research.

In this chapter, we introduce the concepts of frequent patterns, associations, and correlations, and study how they can be mined efficiently. The topic of frequent pattern mining is indeed rich. This chapter is dedicated to methods of *frequent itemset mining*. We delve into the following questions: How can we find frequent itemsets from large amounts of data, where the data are either transactional or relational? How can we mine association rules in multilevel and multidimensional space? Which association rules are the most interesting? How can we help or guide the mining procedure to discover interesting associations or correlations? How can we take advantage of user preferences or constraints to speed up the mining process? The techniques learned in this chapter may also be extended for more advanced forms of frequent pattern mining, such as from sequential and structured data sets, as we will study in later chapters.

5.1 Basic Concepts and a Road Map

Frequent pattern mining searches for recurring relationships in a given data set. This section introduces the basic concepts of frequent pattern mining for the discovery of interesting associations and correlations between itemsets in transactional and relational databases. We begin in Section 5.1.1 by presenting an example of market basket analysis, the earliest form of frequent pattern mining for association rules. The basic concepts of mining frequent patterns and associations are given in Section 5.1.2. Section 5.1.3 presents a road map to the different kinds of frequent patterns, association rules, and correlation rules that can be mined.

5.1.1 Market Basket Analysis: A Motivating Example

Frequent itemset mining leads to the discovery of associations and correlations among items in large transactional or relational data sets. With massive amounts of data continuously being collected and stored, many industries are becoming interested in mining such patterns from their databases. The discovery of interesting correlation relationships among huge amounts of business transaction records can help in many business decision-making processes, such as catalog design, cross-marketing, and customer shopping behavior analysis.

A typical example of frequent itemset mining is **market basket analysis.** This process analyzes customer buying habits by finding associations between the different items that customers place in their "shopping baskets" (Figure 5.1). The discovery of such associations can help retailers develop marketing strategies by gaining insight into which items are frequently purchased together by customers. For instance, if customers are buying

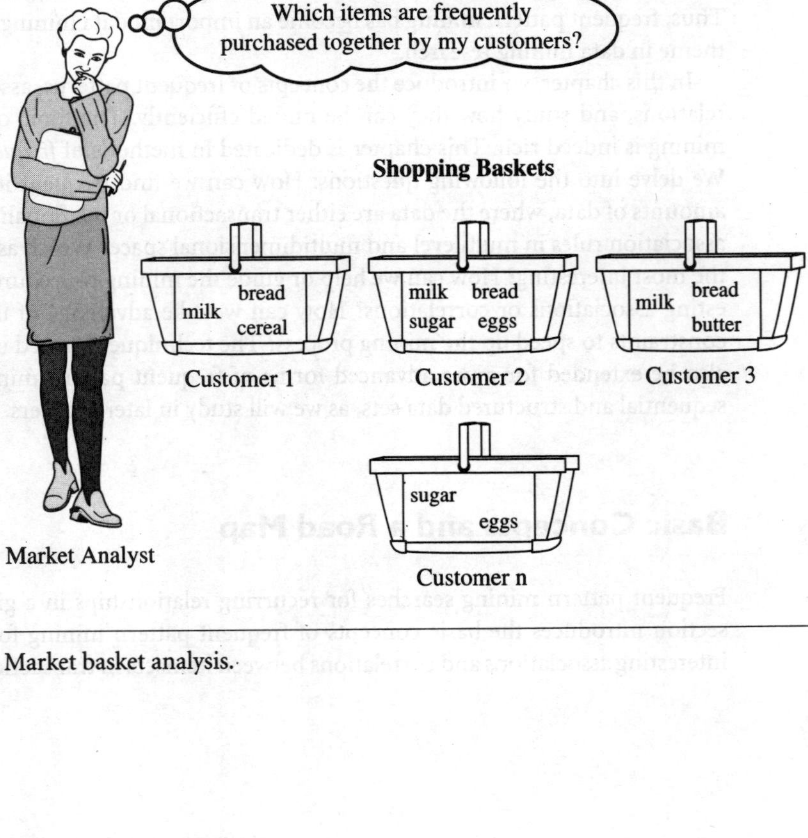

Figure 5.1 Market basket analysis.

milk, how likely are they to also buy bread (and what kind of bread) on the same trip to the supermarket? Such information can lead to increased sales by helping retailers do selective marketing and plan their shelf space.

Let's look at an example of how market basket analysis can be useful.

Example 5.1 **Market basket analysis.** Suppose, as manager of an *AllElectronics* branch, you would like to learn more about the buying habits of your customers. Specifically, you wonder, *"Which groups or sets of items are customers likely to purchase on a given trip to the store?"* To answer your question, market basket analysis may be performed on the retail data of customer transactions at your store. You can then use the results to plan marketing or advertising strategies, or in the design of a new catalog. For instance, market basket analysis may help you design different store layouts. In one strategy, items that are frequently purchased together can be placed in proximity in order to further encourage the sale of such items together. If customers who purchase computers also tend to buy antivirus software at the same time, then placing the hardware display close to the software display may help increase the sales of both items. In an alternative strategy, placing hardware and software at opposite ends of the store may entice customers who purchase such items to pick up other items along the way. For instance, after deciding on an expensive computer, a customer may observe security systems for sale while heading toward the software display to purchase antivirus software and may decide to purchase a home security system as well. Market basket analysis can also help retailers plan which items to put on sale at reduced prices. If customers tend to purchase computers and printers together, then having a sale on printers may encourage the sale of printers *as well as* computers. ■

If we think of the universe as the set of items available at the store, then each item has a Boolean variable representing the presence or absence of that item. Each basket can then be represented by a Boolean vector of values assigned to these variables. The Boolean vectors can be analyzed for buying patterns that reflect items that are frequently *associated* or purchased together. These patterns can be represented in the form of **association rules**. For example, the information that customers who purchase computers also tend to buy antivirus software at the same time is represented in Association Rule (5.1) below:

$$computer \Rightarrow antivirus\_software\ [support = 2\%, confidence = 60\%] \qquad (5.1)$$

Rule **support** and **confidence** are two measures of rule interestingness. They respectively reflect the usefulness and certainty of discovered rules. A support of 2% for Association Rule (5.1) means that 2% of all the transactions under analysis show that computer and antivirus software are purchased together. A confidence of 60% means that 60% of the customers who purchased a computer also bought the software. Typically, association rules are considered interesting if they satisfy both a **minimum support threshold** and a **minimum confidence threshold**. Such thresholds can be set by users or domain experts. Additional analysis can be performed to uncover interesting statistical correlations between associated items.

5.1.2 Frequent Itemsets, Closed Itemsets, and Association Rules

Let $\mathcal{I} = \{I_1, I_2, \ldots, I_m\}$ be a set of items. Let D, the task-relevant data, be a set of database transactions where each transaction T is a set of items such that $T \subseteq \mathcal{I}$. Each transaction is associated with an identifier, called TID. Let A be a set of items. A transaction T is said to contain A if and only if $A \subseteq T$. An association rule is an implication of the form $A \Rightarrow B$, where $A \subset \mathcal{I}$, $B \subset \mathcal{I}$, and $A \cap B = \phi$. The rule $A \Rightarrow B$ holds in the transaction set D with **support** s, where s is the percentage of transactions in D that contain $A \cup B$ (i.e., the *union* of sets A and B, or say, both A and B). This is taken to be the probability, $P(A \cup B)$.[1] The rule $A \Rightarrow B$ has **confidence** c in the transaction set D, where c is the percentage of transactions in D containing A that also contain B. This is taken to be the conditional probability, $P(B|A)$. That is,

$$support(A \Rightarrow B) = P(A \cup B) \tag{5.2}$$

$$confidence(A \Rightarrow B) = P(B|A). \tag{5.3}$$

Rules that satisfy both a minimum support threshold (*min_sup*) and a minimum confidence threshold (*min_conf*) are called **strong**. By convention, we write support and confidence values so as to occur between 0% and 100%, rather than 0 to 1.0.

A set of items is referred to as an **itemset**.[2] An itemset that contains k items is a **k-itemset**. The set {*computer, antivirus_software*} is a 2-itemset. The **occurrence frequency of an itemset** is the number of transactions that contain the itemset. This is also known, simply, as the **frequency**, **support count**, or **count** of the itemset. Note that the itemset support defined in Equation (5.2) is sometimes referred to as *relative support*, whereas the occurrence frequency is called the **absolute support**. If the relative support of an itemset I satisfies a prespecified **minimum support threshold** (i.e., the absolute support of I satisfies the corresponding **minimum support count threshold**), then I is a **frequent** itemset.[3] The set of frequent k-itemsets is commonly denoted by L_k.[4]

From Equation (5.3), we have

$$confidence(A \Rightarrow B) = P(B|A) = \frac{support(A \cup B)}{support(A)} = \frac{support\_count(A \cup B)}{support\_count(A)}. \tag{5.4}$$

Equation (5.4) shows that the confidence of rule $A \Rightarrow B$ can be easily derived from the support counts of A and $A \cup B$. That is, once the support counts of A, B, and $A \cup B$ are

[1] Notice that the notation $P(A \cup B)$ indicates the probability that a transaction contains the *union* of set A and set B (i.e., it contains every item in A and in B). This should not be confused with $P(A \text{ or } B)$, which indicates the probability that a transaction contains either A or B.

[2] In the data mining research literature, "itemset" is more commonly used than "item set."

[3] In early work, itemsets satisfying minimum support were referred to as **large**. This term, however, is somewhat confusing as it has connotations to the number of items in an itemset rather than the frequency of occurrence of the set. Hence, we use the more recent term **frequent**.

[4] Although the term **frequent** is preferred over **large**, for historical reasons frequent k-itemsets are still denoted as L_k.

found, it is straightforward to derive the corresponding association rules $A \Rightarrow B$ and $B \Rightarrow A$ and check whether they are strong. Thus the problem of mining association rules can be reduced to that of mining frequent itemsets.

In general, association rule mining can be viewed as a two-step process:

1. **Find all frequent itemsets:** By definition, each of these itemsets will occur at least as frequently as a predetermined minimum support count, *min_sup*.
2. **Generate strong association rules from the frequent itemsets:** By definition, these rules must satisfy minimum support and minimum confidence.

Additional interestingness measures can be applied for the discovery of correlation relationships between associated items, as will be discussed in Section 5.4. Because the second step is much less costly than the first, the overall performance of mining association rules is determined by the first step.

A major challenge in mining frequent itemsets from a large data set is the fact that such mining often generates a huge number of itemsets satisfying the minimum support (*min_sup*) threshold, especially when *min_sup* is set low. This is because if an itemset is frequent, each of its subsets is frequent as well. A long itemset will contain a combinatorial number of shorter, frequent sub-itemsets. For example, a frequent itemset of length 100, such as $\{a_1, a_2, \ldots, a_{100}\}$, contains $\binom{100}{1} = 100$ frequent 1-itemsets: $a_1, a_2, \ldots, a_{100}$, $\binom{100}{2}$ frequent 2-itemsets: $(a_1, a_2), (a_1, a_3), \ldots, (a_{99}, a_{100})$, and so on. The total number of frequent itemsets that it contains is thus,

$$\binom{100}{1} + \binom{100}{2} + \cdots + \binom{100}{100} = 2^{100} - 1 \approx 1.27 \times 10^{30}. \tag{5.5}$$

This is too huge a number of itemsets for any computer to compute or store. To overcome this difficulty, we introduce the concepts of *closed frequent itemset* and *maximal frequent itemset*.

An itemset X is **closed** in a data set S if there exists no proper super-itemset[5] Y such that Y has the same support count as X in S. An itemset X is a **closed frequent itemset** in set S if X is both closed and frequent in S. An itemset X is a **maximal frequent itemset** (or **max-itemset**) in set S if X is frequent, and there exists no super-itemset Y such that $X \subset Y$ and Y is frequent in S.

Let C be the set of closed frequent itemsets for a data set S satisfying a minimum support threshold, *min_sup*. Let $\mathcal{M}$ be the set of maximal frequent itemsets for S satisfying *min_sup*. Suppose that we have the support count of each itemset in C and $\mathcal{M}$. Notice that C and its count information can be used to derive the whole set of frequent itemsets. Thus we say that C contains complete information regarding its corresponding frequent itemsets. On the other hand, $\mathcal{M}$ registers only the support of the maximal itemsets.

[5] Y is a proper super-itemset of X if X is a proper sub-itemset of Y, that is, if $X \subset Y$. In other words, every item of X is contained in Y but there is at least one item of Y that is not in X.

It usually does not contain the complete support information regarding its corresponding frequent itemsets. We illustrate these concepts with the following example.

Example 5.2 **Closed and maximal frequent itemsets.** Suppose that a transaction database has only two transactions: $\{\langle a_1, a_2, \ldots, a_{100}\rangle; \langle a_1, a_2, \ldots, a_{50}\rangle\}$. Let the minimum support count threshold be $min\_sup = 1$. We find two closed frequent itemsets and their support counts, that is, $C = \{\{a_1, a_2, \ldots, a_{100}\} : 1; \{a_1, a_2, \ldots, a_{50}\} : 2\}$. There is one maximal frequent itemset: $\mathcal{M} = \{\{a_1, a_2, \ldots, a_{100}\} : 1\}$. (We cannot include $\{a_1, a_2, \ldots, a_{50}\}$ as a maximal frequent itemset because it has a frequent super-set, $\{a_1, a_2, \ldots, a_{100}\}$.) Compare this to the above, where we determined that there are $2^{100} - 1$ frequent itemsets, which is too huge a set to be enumerated!

The set of closed frequent itemsets contains complete information regarding the frequent itemsets. For example, from C, we can derive, say, (1) $\{a_2, a_{45} : 2\}$ since $\{a_2, a_{45}\}$ is a sub-itemset of the itemset $\{a_1, a_2, \ldots, a_{50} : 2\}$; and (2) $\{a_8, a_{55} : 1\}$ since $\{a_8, a_{55}\}$ is not a sub-itemset of the previous itemset but of the itemset $\{a_1, a_2, \ldots, a_{100} : 1\}$. However, from the maximal frequent itemset, we can only assert that both itemsets ($\{a_2, a_{45}\}$ and $\{a_8, a_{55}\}$) are frequent, but we cannot assert their actual support counts. ■

5.1.3 Frequent Pattern Mining: A Road Map

Market basket analysis is just one form of frequent pattern mining. In fact, there are many kinds of frequent patterns, association rules, and correlation relationships. Frequent pattern mining can be classified in various ways, based on the following criteria:

- **Based on the *completeness* of patterns to be mined:** As we discussed in the previous subsection, we can mine the **complete set of frequent itemsets**, the **closed frequent itemsets**, and the **maximal frequent itemsets**, given a minimum support threshold. We can also mine **constrained frequent itemsets** (i.e., those that satisfy a set of user-defined constraints), **approximate frequent itemsets** (i.e., those that derive only approximate support counts for the mined frequent itemsets), **near-match frequent itemsets** (i.e., those that tally the support count of the near or almost matching itemsets), **top-*k* frequent itemsets** (i.e., the *k* most frequent itemsets for a user-specified value, *k*), and so on.

  Different applications may have different requirements regarding the completeness of the patterns to be mined, which in turn can lead to different evaluation and optimization methods. In this chapter, our study of mining methods focuses on mining the *complete set of frequent itemsets*, *closed frequent itemsets*, and *constrained frequent itemsets*. We leave the mining of frequent itemsets under other completeness requirements as an exercise.

- **Based on the *levels of abstraction* involved in the rule set:** Some methods for association rule mining can find rules at differing levels of abstraction. For example, suppose that a set of association rules mined includes the following rules where X is a variable representing a customer:

$$buys(X, \text{"computer"}) \Rightarrow buys(X, \text{"HP\_printer"}) \tag{5.6}$$

$$buys(X, \text{"laptop\_computer"}) \Rightarrow buys(X, \text{"HP\_printer"}) \quad (5.7)$$

In Rules (5.6) and (5.7), the items bought are referenced at different levels of abstraction (e.g., "*computer*" is a higher-level abstraction of "*laptop computer*"). We refer to the rule set mined as consisting of **multilevel association rules.** If, instead, the rules within a given set do not reference items or attributes at different levels of abstraction, then the set contains **single-level association rules.**

- **Based on the *number of data dimensions* involved in the rule:** If the items or attributes in an association rule reference only one dimension, then it is a **single-dimensional association rule.** Note that Rule (5.1), for example, could be rewritten as Rule (5.8):

$$buys(X, \text{"computer"}) \Rightarrow buys(X, \text{"antivirus\_software"}) \quad (5.8)$$

Rules (5.6), (5.7), and (5.8) are single-dimensional association rules because they each refer to only one dimension, *buys*.[6]

If a rule references two or more dimensions, such as the dimensions *age, income*, and *buys*, then it is a **multidimensional association rule.** The following rule is an example of a multidimensional rule:

$$age(X, \text{"30...39"}) \wedge income(X, \text{"42K...48K"}) \Rightarrow buys(X, \text{"high resolution TV"}). \quad (5.9)$$

- **Based on the *types of values* handled in the rule:** If a rule involves associations between the presence or absence of items, it is a **Boolean association rule.** For example, Rules (5.1), (5.6), and (5.7) are Boolean association rules obtained from market basket analysis.

  If a rule describes associations between quantitative items or attributes, then it is a **quantitative association rule.** In these rules, quantitative values for items or attributes are partitioned into intervals. Rule (5.9) is also considered a quantitative association rule. Note that the quantitative attributes, *age* and *income*, have been discretized.

- **Based on the *kinds of rules* to be mined:** Frequent pattern analysis can generate various kinds of rules and other interesting relationships. **Association rules** are the most popular kind of rules generated from frequent patterns. Typically, such mining can generate a large number of rules, many of which are redundant or do not indicate a correlation relationship among itemsets. Thus, the discovered associations can be further analyzed to uncover statistical correlations, leading to **correlation rules.**

  We can also mine **strong gradient relationships** among itemsets, where a gradient is the ratio of the measure of an item when compared with that of its parent (a generalized itemset), its child (a specialized itemset), or its sibling (a comparable itemset). One such example is: "*The average sales from Sony_Digital_Camera increase over 16% when sold together with Sony_Laptop_Computer*": both Sony_Digital_Camera and Sony_Laptop_Computer are siblings, where the parent itemset is Sony.

[6] Following the terminology used in multidimensional databases, we refer to each distinct predicate in a rule as a *dimension*.

- **Based on the *kinds of patterns* to be mined:** Many kinds of frequent patterns can be mined from different kinds of data sets. For this chapter, our focus is on **frequent itemset mining**, that is, the mining of frequent itemsets (sets of items) from transactional or relational data sets. However, other kinds of frequent patterns can be found from other kinds of data sets. **Sequential pattern mining** searches for frequent *subsequences* in a *sequence data set*, where a sequence records an ordering of events. For example, with sequential pattern mining, we can study the order in which items are frequently purchased. For instance, customers may tend to first buy a PC, followed by a digital camera, and then a memory card. **Structured pattern mining** searches for frequent *substructures* in a *structured data set*. Notice that *structure* is a general concept that covers many different kinds of structural forms, such as graphs, lattices, trees, sequences, sets, single items, or combinations of such structures. Single items are the simplest form of structure. Each element of an itemset may contain a subsequence, a subtree, and so on, and such containment relationships can be defined recursively. Therefore, structured pattern mining can be considered as the most general form of frequent pattern mining.

In the next section, we will study efficient methods for mining the basic (i.e., single-level, single-dimensional, Boolean) frequent itemsets from transactional databases, and show how to generate association rules from such itemsets. The extension of this scope of mining to multilevel, multidimensional, and quantitative rules is discussed in Section 5.3. The mining of strong correlation relationships is studied in Section 5.4. Constraint-based mining is studied in Section 5.5. We address the more advanced topic of mining sequence and structured patterns in later chapters. Nevertheless, most of the methods studied here can be easily extended for mining more complex kinds of patterns.

5.2 Efficient and Scalable Frequent Itemset Mining Methods

In this section, you will learn methods for mining the simplest form of frequent patterns—*single-dimensional, single-level, Boolean frequent itemsets*, such as those discussed for market basket analysis in Section 5.1.1. We begin by presenting **Apriori**, the basic algorithm for finding frequent itemsets (Section 5.2.1). In Section 5.2.2, we look at how to generate strong association rules from frequent itemsets. Section 5.2.3 describes several variations to the Apriori algorithm for improved efficiency and scalability. Section 5.2.4 presents methods for mining frequent itemsets that, unlike Apriori, do not involve the generation of "candidate" frequent itemsets. Section 5.2.5 presents methods for mining frequent itemsets that take advantage of vertical data format. Methods for mining closed frequent itemsets are discussed in Section 5.2.6.

5.2.1 The Apriori Algorithm: Finding Frequent Itemsets Using Candidate Generation

Apriori is a seminal algorithm proposed by R. Agrawal and R. Srikant in 1994 for mining frequent itemsets for Boolean association rules. The name of the algorithm is based on the fact that the algorithm uses *prior knowledge* of frequent itemset properties, as we shall see following. Apriori employs an iterative approach known as a *level-wise* search, where k-itemsets are used to explore $(k+1)$-itemsets. First, the set of frequent 1-itemsets is found by scanning the database to accumulate the count for each item, and collecting those items that satisfy minimum support. The resulting set is denoted L_1. Next, L_1 is used to find L_2, the set of frequent 2-itemsets, which is used to find L_3, and so on, until no more frequent k-itemsets can be found. The finding of each L_k requires one full scan of the database.

To improve the efficiency of the level-wise generation of frequent itemsets, an important property called the **Apriori property**, presented below, is used to reduce the search space. We will first describe this property, and then show an example illustrating its use.

Apriori property: *All nonempty subsets of a frequent itemset must also be frequent.*

The Apriori property is based on the following observation. By definition, if an itemset I does not satisfy the minimum support threshold, *min_sup*, then I is not frequent; that is, $P(I) < min\_sup$. If an item A is added to the itemset I, then the resulting itemset (i.e., $I \cup A$) cannot occur more frequently than I. Therefore, $I \cup A$ is not frequent either; that is, $P(I \cup A) < min\_sup$.

This property belongs to a special category of properties called **antimonotone** in the sense that *if a set cannot pass a test, all of its supersets will fail the same test as well.* It is called *antimonotone* because the property is monotonic in the context of failing a test.[7]

"How is the Apriori property used in the algorithm?" To understand this, let us look at how L_{k-1} is used to find L_k for $k \geq 2$. A two-step process is followed, consisting of **join** and **prune** actions.

1. **The join step**: To find L_k, a set of **candidate** k-itemsets is generated by joining L_{k-1} with itself. This set of candidates is denoted C_k. Let l_1 and l_2 be itemsets in L_{k-1}. The notation $l_i[j]$ refers to the jth item in l_i (e.g., $l_1[k-2]$ refers to the second to the last item in l_1). By convention, Apriori assumes that items within a transaction or itemset are sorted in lexicographic order. For the $(k-1)$-itemset, l_i, this means that the items are sorted such that $l_i[1] < l_i[2] < \ldots < l_i[k-1]$. The join, $L_{k-1} \bowtie L_{k-1}$, is performed, where members of L_{k-1} are joinable if their first $(k-2)$ items are in common. That is, members l_1 and l_2 of L_{k-1} are joined if $(l_1[1] = l_2[1]) \land (l_1[2] = l_2[2]) \land \ldots \land (l_1[k-2] = l_2[k-2]) \land (l_1[k-1] < l_2[k-1])$. The condition $l_1[k-1] < l_2[k-1]$ simply ensures that no duplicates are generated. The resulting itemset formed by joining l_1 and l_2 is $l_1[1], l_1[2], \ldots, l_1[k-2], l_1[k-1], l_2[k-1]$.

2. **The prune step**: C_k is a superset of L_k, that is, its members may or may not be frequent, but all of the frequent k-itemsets are included in C_k. A scan of the database to determine the count of each candidate in C_k would result in the determination of L_k (i.e., all candidates having a count no less than the minimum support count are frequent by definition, and therefore belong to L_k). C_k, however, can be huge, and so this could

[7]The Apriori property has many applications. It can also be used to prune search during data cube computation (Chapter 4).

Table 5.1 Transactional data for an *AllElectronics* branch.

TID	*List of item_IDs*
T100	I1, I2, I5
T200	I2, I4
T300	I2, I3
T400	I1, I2, I4
T500	I1, I3
T600	I2, I3
T700	I1, I3
T800	I1, I2, I3, I5
T900	I1, I2, I3

involve heavy computation. To reduce the size of C_k, the Apriori property is used as follows. Any $(k-1)$-itemset that is not frequent cannot be a subset of a frequent k-itemset. Hence, if any $(k-1)$-subset of a candidate k-itemset is not in L_{k-1}, then the candidate cannot be frequent either and so can be removed from C_k. This **subset testing** can be done quickly by maintaining a hash tree of all frequent itemsets.

Example 5.3 **Apriori.** Let's look at a concrete example, based on the *AllElectronics* transaction database, D, of Table 5.1. There are nine transactions in this database, that is, $|D| = 9$. We use Figure 5.2 to illustrate the Apriori algorithm for finding frequent itemsets in D.

1. In the first iteration of the algorithm, each item is a member of the set of candidate 1-itemsets, C_1. The algorithm simply scans all of the transactions in order to count the number of occurrences of each item.
2. Suppose that the minimum support count required is 2, that is, *min_sup* = 2. (Here, we are referring to *absolute* support because we are using a support count. The corresponding relative support is 2/9 = 22%). The set of frequent 1-itemsets, L_1, can then be determined. It consists of the candidate 1-itemsets satisfying minimum support. In our example, all of the candidates in C_1 satisfy minimum support.
3. To discover the set of frequent 2-itemsets, L_2, the algorithm uses the join $L_1 \bowtie L_1$ to generate a candidate set of 2-itemsets, C_2.[8] C_2 consists of $\binom{|L_1|}{2}$ 2-itemsets. Note that no candidates are removed from C_2 during the prune step because each subset of the candidates is also frequent.

[8] $L_1 \bowtie L_1$ is equivalent to $L_1 \times L_1$, since the definition of $L_k \bowtie L_k$ requires the two joining itemsets to share $k-1=0$ items.

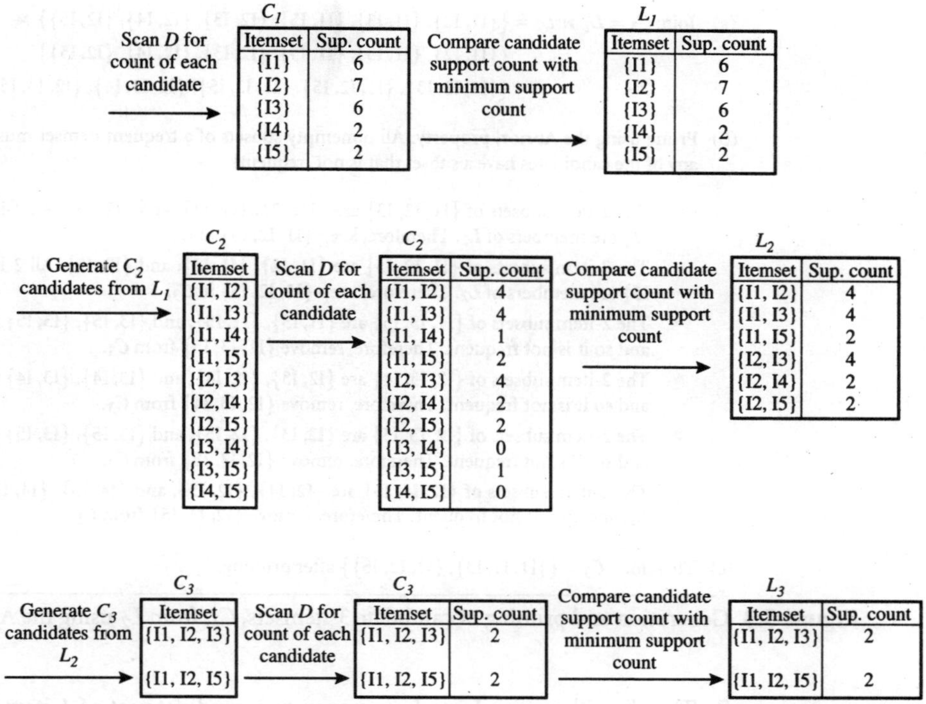

Figure 5.2 Generation of candidate itemsets and frequent itemsets, where the minimum support count is 2.

4. Next, the transactions in D are scanned and the support count of each candidate itemset in C_2 is accumulated, as shown in the middle table of the second row in Figure 5.2.

5. The set of frequent 2-itemsets, L_2, is then determined, consisting of those candidate 2-itemsets in C_2 having minimum support.

6. The generation of the set of candidate 3-itemsets, C_3, is detailed in Figure 5.3. From the join step, we first get $C_3 = L_2 \bowtie L_2 = \{\{I1, I2, I3\}, \{I1, I2, I5\}, \{I1, I3, I5\}, \{I2, I3, I4\}, \{I2, I3, I5\}, \{I2, I4, I5\}\}$. Based on the Apriori property that all subsets of a frequent itemset must also be frequent, we can determine that the four latter candidates cannot possibly be frequent. We therefore remove them from C_3, thereby saving the effort of unnecessarily obtaining their counts during the subsequent scan of D to determine L_3. Note that when given a candidate k-itemset, we only need to check if its $(k-1)$-subsets are frequent since the Apriori algorithm uses a level-wise search strategy. The resulting pruned version of C_3 is shown in the first table of the bottom row of Figure 5.2.

7. The transactions in D are scanned in order to determine L_3, consisting of those candidate 3-itemsets in C_3 having minimum support (Figure 5.2).

(a) Join: $C_3 = L_2 \bowtie L_2 = \{\{I1, I2\}, \{I1, I3\}, \{I1, I5\}, \{I2, I3\}, \{I2, I4\}, \{I2, I5\}\} \bowtie \{\{I1, I2\}, \{I1, I3\}, \{I1, I5\}, \{I2, I3\}, \{I2, I4\}, \{I2, I5\}\}$
$= \{\{I1, I2, I3\}, \{I1, I2, I5\}, \{I1, I3, I5\}, \{I2, I3, I4\}, \{I2, I3, I5\}, \{I2, I4, I5\}\}$.

(b) Prune using the Apriori property: All nonempty subsets of a frequent itemset must also be frequent. Do any of the candidates have a subset that is not frequent?

- The 2-item subsets of {I1, I2, I3} are {I1, I2}, {I1, I3}, and {I2, I3}. All 2-item subsets of {I1, I2, I3} are members of L_2. Therefore, keep {I1, I2, I3} in C_3.
- The 2-item subsets of {I1, I2, I5} are {I1, I2}, {I1, I5}, and {I2, I5}. All 2-item subsets of {I1, I2, I5} are members of L_2. Therefore, keep {I1, I2, I5} in C_3.
- The 2-item subsets of {I1, I3, I5} are {I1, I3}, {I1, I5}, and {I3, I5}. {I3, I5} is not a member of L_2, and so it is not frequent. Therefore, remove {I1, I3, I5} from C_3.
- The 2-item subsets of {I2, I3, I4} are {I2, I3}, {I2, I4}, and {I3, I4}. {I3, I4} is not a member of L_2, and so it is not frequent. Therefore, remove {I2, I3, I4} from C_3.
- The 2-item subsets of {I2, I3, I5} are {I2, I3}, {I2, I5}, and {I3, I5}. {I3, I5} is not a member of L_2, and so it is not frequent. Therefore, remove {I2, I3, I5} from C_3.
- The 2-item subsets of {I2, I4, I5} are {I2, I4}, {I2, I5}, and {I4, I5}. {I4, I5} is not a member of L_2, and so it is not frequent. Therefore, remove {I2, I4, I5} from C_3.

(c) Therefore, $C_3 = \{\{I1, I2, I3\}, \{I1, I2, I5\}\}$ after pruning.

Figure 5.3 Generation and pruning of candidate 3-itemsets, C_3, from L_2 using the Apriori property.

8. The algorithm uses $L_3 \bowtie L_3$ to generate a candidate set of 4-itemsets, C_4. Although the join results in {{I1, I2, I3, I5}}, this itemset is pruned because its subset {{I2, I3, I5}} is not frequent. Thus, $C_4 = \phi$, and the algorithm terminates, having found all of the frequent itemsets. ■

Figure 5.4 shows pseudo-code for the Apriori algorithm and its related procedures. Step 1 of Apriori finds the frequent 1-itemsets, L_1. In steps 2 to 10, L_{k-1} is used to generate candidates C_k in order to find L_k for $k \geq 2$. The apriori_gen procedure generates the candidates and then uses the Apriori property to eliminate those having a subset that is not frequent (step 3). This procedure is described below. Once all of the candidates have been generated, the database is scanned (step 4). For each transaction, a subset function is used to find all subsets of the transaction that are candidates (step 5), and the count for each of these candidates is accumulated (steps 6 and 7). Finally, all of those candidates satisfying minimum support (step 9) form the set of frequent itemsets, L (step 11). A procedure can then be called to generate association rules from the frequent itemsets. Such a procedure is described in Section 5.2.2.

The apriori_gen procedure performs two kinds of actions, namely, **join** and **prune**, as described above. In the join component, L_{k-1} is joined with L_{k-1} to generate potential candidates (steps 1 to 4). The prune component (steps 5 to 7) employs the Apriori property to remove candidates that have a subset that is not frequent. The test for infrequent subsets is shown in procedure has_infrequent_subset.

Algorithm: Apriori. Find frequent itemsets using an iterative level-wise approach based on candidate generation.

Input:

- D, a database of transactions;
- *min_sup*, the minimum support count threshold.

Output: L, frequent itemsets in D.

Method:

```
L1 = find_frequent_1-itemsets(D);
for (k = 2; L_{k-1} ≠ φ; k++) {
    C_k = apriori_gen(L_{k-1});
    for each transaction t ∈ D { // scan D for counts
        C_t = subset(C_k, t); // get the subsets of t that are candidates
        for each candidate c ∈ C_t
            c.count++;
    }
    L_k = {c ∈ C_k | c.count ≥ min_sup}
}
return L = ∪_k L_k;

procedure apriori_gen(L_{k-1}:frequent (k − 1)-itemsets)
    for each itemset l1 ∈ L_{k-1}
        for each itemset l2 ∈ L_{k-1}
            if (l1[1] = l2[1]) ∧ (l1[2] = l2[2]) ∧ ... ∧ (l1[k−2] = l2[k−2]) ∧ (l1[k−1] < l2[k−1]) then {
                c = l1 ⋈ l2; // join step: generate candidates
                if has_infrequent_subset(c, L_{k-1}) then
                    delete c; // prune step: remove unfruitful candidate
                else add c to C_k;
            }
    return C_k;

procedure has_infrequent_subset(c: candidate k-itemset;
            L_{k-1}: frequent (k − 1)-itemsets); // use prior knowledge
    for each (k − 1)-subset s of c
        if s ∉ L_{k-1} then
            return TRUE;
    return FALSE;
```

Figure 5.4 The Apriori algorithm for discovering frequent itemsets for mining Boolean association rules.

5.2.2 Generating Association Rules from Frequent Itemsets

Once the frequent itemsets from transactions in a database D have been found, it is straightforward to generate strong association rules from them (where *strong* association rules satisfy both minimum support and minimum confidence). This can be done using Equation (5.4) for confidence, which we show again here for completeness:

$$confidence(A \Rightarrow B) = P(B|A) = \frac{support\_count(A \cup B)}{support\_count(A)}.$$

The conditional probability is expressed in terms of itemset support count, where $support\_count(A \cup B)$ is the number of transactions containing the itemsets $A \cup B$, and $support\_count(A)$ is the number of transactions containing the itemset A. Based on this equation, association rules can be generated as follows:

- For each frequent itemset l, generate all nonempty subsets of l.
- For every nonempty subset s of l, output the rule "$s \Rightarrow (l - s)$" if $\frac{support\_count(l)}{support\_count(s)} \geq min\_conf$, where min_conf is the minimum confidence threshold.

Because the rules are generated from frequent itemsets, each one automatically satisfies minimum support. Frequent itemsets can be stored ahead of time in hash tables along with their counts so that they can be accessed quickly.

Example 5.4 **Generating association rules.** Let's try an example based on the transactional data for *AllElectronics* shown in Table 5.1. Suppose the data contain the frequent itemset l = {I1, I2, I5}. What are the association rules that can be generated from l? The nonempty subsets of l are {I1, I2}, {I1, I5}, {I2, I5}, {I1}, {I2}, and {I5}. The resulting association rules are as shown below, each listed with its confidence:

$$
\begin{array}{ll}
I1 \wedge I2 \Rightarrow I5, & confidence = 2/4 = 50\% \\
I1 \wedge I5 \Rightarrow I2, & confidence = 2/2 = 100\% \\
I2 \wedge I5 \Rightarrow I1, & confidence = 2/2 = 100\% \\
I1 \Rightarrow I2 \wedge I5, & confidence = 2/6 = 33\% \\
I2 \Rightarrow I1 \wedge I5, & confidence = 2/7 = 29\% \\
I5 \Rightarrow I1 \wedge I2, & confidence = 2/2 = 100\%
\end{array}
$$

If the minimum confidence threshold is, say, 70%, then only the second, third, and last rules above are output, because these are the only ones generated that are strong. Note that, unlike conventional classification rules, association rules can contain more than one conjunct in the right-hand side of the rule. ■

5.2.3 Improving the Efficiency of Apriori

"How can we further improve the efficiency of Apriori-based mining?" Many variations of the Apriori algorithm have been proposed that focus on improving the efficiency of the original algorithm. Several of these variations are summarized as follows:

Hash-based technique (hashing itemsets into corresponding buckets): A hash-based technique can be used to reduce the size of the candidate k-itemsets, C_k, for $k > 1$. For example, when scanning each transaction in the database to generate the frequent 1-itemsets, L_1, from the candidate 1-itemsets in C_1, we can generate all of the 2-itemsets for each transaction, hash (i.e., map) them into the different *buckets* of a *hash table* structure, and increase the corresponding bucket counts (Figure 5.5). A 2-itemset whose corresponding bucket count in the hash table is below the support

Create hash table H_2 using hash function $h(x, y) = ((order\ of\ x) \times 10 + (order\ of\ y))\ mod\ 7$ →

H_2

bucket address	0	1	2	3	4	5	6
bucket count	2	2	4	2	2	4	4
bucket contents	{I1, I4}	{I1, I5}	{I2, I3}	{I2, I4}	{I2, I5}	{I1, I2}	{I1, I3}
	{I3, I5}	{I1, I5}	{I2, I3}	{I2, I4}	{I2, I5}	{I1, I2}	{I1, I3}
			{I2, I3}			{I1, I2}	{I1, I3}
			{I2, I3}			{I1, I2}	{I1, I3}

Figure 5.5 Hash table, H_2, for candidate 2-itemsets: This hash table was generated by scanning the transactions of Table 5.1 while determining L_1 from C_1. If the minimum support count is, say, 3, then the itemsets in buckets 0, 1, 3, and 4 cannot be frequent and so they should not be included in C_2.

threshold cannot be frequent and thus should be removed from the candidate set. Such a hash-based technique may substantially reduce the number of the candidate k-itemsets examined (especially when $k = 2$).

Transaction reduction (reducing the number of transactions scanned in future iterations): A transaction that does not contain any frequent k-itemsets cannot contain any frequent $(k+1)$-itemsets. Therefore, such a transaction can be marked or removed from further consideration because subsequent scans of the database for j-itemsets, where $j > k$, will not require it.

Partitioning (partitioning the data to find candidate itemsets): A partitioning technique can be used that requires just two database scans to mine the frequent itemsets (Figure 5.6). It consists of two phases. In Phase I, the algorithm subdivides the transactions of D into n nonoverlapping partitions. If the minimum support threshold for transactions in D is *min_sup*, then the minimum support count for a partition is *min_sup* $\times$ *the number of transactions in that partition*. For each partition, all frequent itemsets within the partition are found. These are referred to as **local frequent itemsets**. The procedure employs a special data structure that, for each itemset, records the TIDs of the transactions containing the items in the itemset. This allows it to find all of the local frequent k-itemsets, for $k = 1, 2, \ldots$, in just one scan of the database.

A local frequent itemset may or may not be frequent with respect to the entire database, D. *Any itemset that is potentially frequent with respect to D must occur as a frequent itemset in at least one of the partitions.* Therefore, all local frequent itemsets are candidate itemsets with respect to D. The collection of frequent itemsets from all partitions forms the **global candidate itemsets** with respect to D. In Phase II, a second scan of D is conducted in which the actual support of each candidate is assessed in order to determine the global frequent itemsets. Partition size and the number of partitions are set so that each partition can fit into main memory and therefore be read only once in each phase.

Sampling (mining on a subset of the given data): The basic idea of the sampling approach is to pick a random sample S of the given data D, and then search for frequent itemsets in S instead of D. In this way, we trade off some degree of accuracy

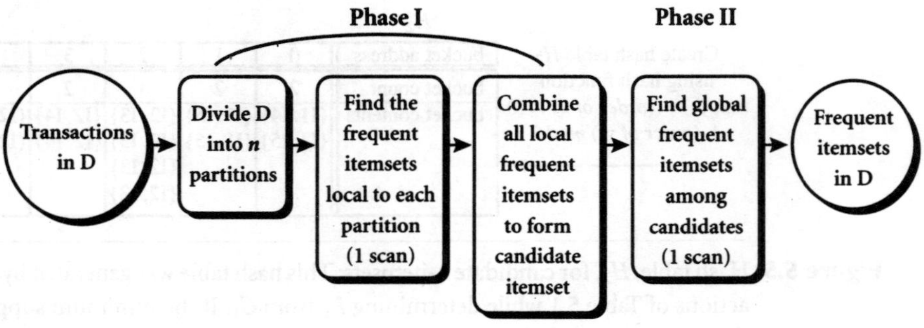

Figure 5.6 Mining by partitioning the data.

against efficiency. The sample size of S is such that the search for frequent itemsets in S can be done in main memory, and so only one scan of the transactions in S is required overall. Because we are searching for frequent itemsets in S rather than in D, it is possible that we will miss some of the global frequent itemsets. To lessen this possibility, we use a lower support threshold than minimum support to find the frequent itemsets local to S (denoted L^S). The rest of the database is then used to compute the actual frequencies of each itemset in L^S. A mechanism is used to determine whether all of the global frequent itemsets are included in L^S. If L^S actually contains all of the frequent itemsets in D, then only one scan of D is required. Otherwise, a second pass can be done in order to find the frequent itemsets that were missed in the first pass. The sampling approach is especially beneficial when efficiency is of utmost importance, such as in computationally intensive applications that must be run frequently.

Dynamic itemset counting (adding candidate itemsets at different points during a scan): A dynamic itemset counting technique was proposed in which the database is partitioned into blocks marked by start points. In this variation, new candidate itemsets can be added at any start point, unlike in Apriori, which determines new candidate itemsets only immediately before each complete database scan. The technique is dynamic in that it estimates the support of all of the itemsets that have been counted so far, adding new candidate itemsets if all of their subsets are estimated to be frequent. The resulting algorithm requires fewer database scans than Apriori.

Other variations involving the mining of multilevel and multidimensional association rules are discussed in the rest of this chapter. The mining of associations related to spatial data and multimedia data are discussed in Chapter 10.

5.2.4 Mining Frequent Itemsets without Candidate Generation

As we have seen, in many cases the Apriori candidate generate-and-test method significantly reduces the size of candidate sets, leading to good performance gain. However, it can suffer from two nontrivial costs:

- *It may need to generate a huge number of candidate sets.* For example, if there are 10^4 frequent 1-itemsets, the Apriori algorithm will need to generate more than 10^7 candidate 2-itemsets. Moreover, to discover a frequent pattern of size 100, such as $\{a_1, \ldots, a_{100}\}$, it has to generate at least $2^{100} - 1 \approx 10^{30}$ candidates in total.
- *It may need to repeatedly scan the database and check a large set of candidates by pattern matching.* It is costly to go over each transaction in the database to determine the support of the candidate itemsets.

"Can we design a method that mines the complete set of frequent itemsets without candidate generation?" An interesting method in this attempt is called **frequent-pattern growth,** or simply **FP-growth**, which adopts a *divide-and-conquer* strategy as follows. First, it compresses the database representing frequent items into a **frequent-pattern tree,** or **FP-tree,** which retains the itemset association information. It then divides the compressed database into a set of *conditional databases* (a special kind of projected database), each associated with one frequent item or "pattern fragment," and mines each such database separately. You'll see how it works with the following example.

Example 5.5 **FP-growth (finding frequent itemsets without candidate generation).** We re-examine the mining of transaction database, *D*, of Table 5.1 in Example 5.3 using the frequent-pattern growth approach.

The first scan of the database is the same as Apriori, which derives the set of frequent items (1-itemsets) and their support counts (frequencies). Let the minimum support count be 2. The set of frequent items is sorted in the order of descending support count. This resulting set or *list* is denoted *L*. Thus, we have *L* = {{I2: 7}, {I1: 6}, {I3: 6}, {I4: 2}, {I5: 2}}.

An FP-tree is then constructed as follows. First, create the root of the tree, labeled with "null." Scan database *D* a second time. The items in each transaction are processed in *L* order (i.e., sorted according to descending support count), and a branch is created for each transaction. For example, the scan of the first transaction, "T100: I1, I2, I5," which contains three items (I2, I1, I5 in *L* order), leads to the construction of the first branch of the tree with three nodes, ⟨I2: 1⟩, ⟨I1:1⟩, and ⟨I5: 1⟩, where I2 is linked as a child of the root, I1 is linked to I2, and I5 is linked to I1. The second transaction, T200, contains the items I2 and I4 in *L* order, which would result in a branch where I2 is linked to the root and I4 is linked to I2. However, this branch would share a common **prefix**, I2, with the existing path for T100. Therefore, we instead increment the count of the I2 node by 1, and create a new node, ⟨I4: 1⟩, which is linked as a child of ⟨I2: 2⟩. In general, when considering the branch to be added for a transaction, the count of each node along a common prefix is incremented by 1, and nodes for the items following the prefix are created and linked accordingly.

To facilitate tree traversal, an item header table is built so that each item points to its occurrences in the tree via a chain of **node-links.** The tree obtained after scanning all of the transactions is shown in Figure 5.7 with the associated node-links. In this way, the problem of mining frequent patterns in databases is transformed to that of mining the FP-tree.

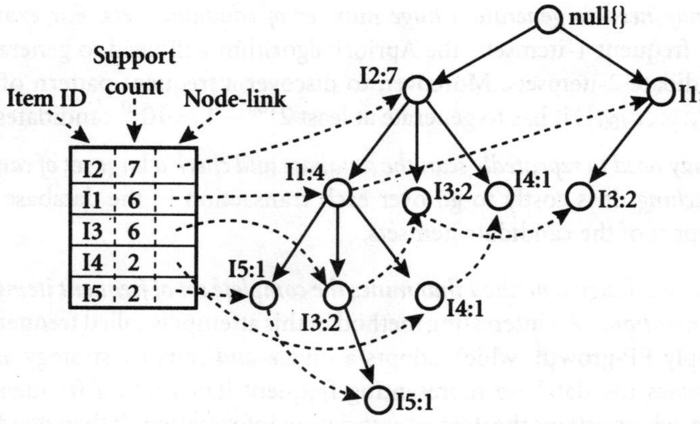

Figure 5.7 An FP-tree registers compressed, frequent pattern information.

Table 5.2 Mining the FP-tree by creating conditional (sub-)pattern bases.

Item	*Conditional Pattern Base*	*Conditional FP-tree*	*Frequent Patterns Generated*
I5	{{I2, I1: 1}, {I2, I1, I3: 1}}	⟨I2: 2, I1: 2⟩	{I2, I5: 2}, {I1, I5: 2}, {I2, I1, I5: 2}
I4	{{I2, I1: 1}, {I2: 1}}	⟨I2: 2⟩	{I2, I4: 2}
I3	{{I2, I1: 2}, {I2: 2}, {I1: 2}}	⟨I2: 4, I1: 2⟩, ⟨I1: 2⟩	{I2, I3: 4}, {I1, I3: 4}, {I2, I1, I3: 2}
I1	{{I2: 4}}	⟨I2: 4⟩	{I2, I1: 4}

The FP-tree is mined as follows. Start from each frequent length-1 pattern (as an initial **suffix pattern**), construct its **conditional pattern base** (a "subdatabase," which consists of the set of *prefix paths* in the FP-tree co-occurring with the suffix pattern), then construct its (*conditional*) FP-tree, and perform mining recursively on such a tree. The pattern growth is achieved by the concatenation of the suffix pattern with the frequent patterns generated from a conditional FP-tree.

Mining of the FP-tree is summarized in Table 5.2 and detailed as follows. We first consider I5, which is the last item in L, rather than the first. The reason for starting at the end of the list will become apparent as we explain the FP-tree mining process. I5 occurs in two branches of the FP-tree of Figure 5.7. (The occurrences of I5 can easily be found by following its chain of node-links.) The paths formed by these branches are ⟨I2, I1, I5: 1⟩ and ⟨I2, I1, I3, I5: 1⟩. Therefore, considering I5 as a suffix, its corresponding two prefix paths are ⟨I2, I1: 1⟩ and ⟨I2, I1, I3: 1⟩, which form its conditional pattern base. Its conditional FP-tree contains only a single path, ⟨I2: 2, I1: 2⟩; I3 is not included because its support count of 1 is less than the minimum support count. The single path generates all the combinations of frequent patterns: {I2, I5: 2}, {I1, I5: 2}, {I2, I1, I5: 2}.

For I4, its two prefix paths form the conditional pattern base, {{I2 I1: 1}, {I2: 1}}, which generates a single-node conditional FP-tree, ⟨I2: 2⟩, and derives one frequent

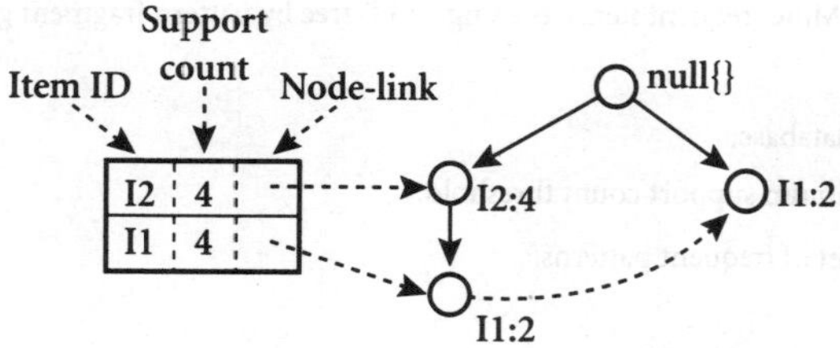

Figure 5.8 The conditional FP-tree associated with the conditional node I3.

pattern, {I2, I1: 2}. Notice that although I5 follows I4 in the first branch, there is no need to include I5 in the analysis here because any frequent pattern involving I5 is analyzed in the examination of I5.

Similar to the above analysis, I3's conditional pattern base is {{I2, I1: 2}, {I2: 2}, {I1: 2}}. Its conditional FP-tree has two branches, ⟨I2: 4, I1: 2⟩ and ⟨I1: 2⟩, as shown in Figure 5.8, which generates the set of patterns, {{I2, I3: 4}, {I1, I3: 4}, {I2, I1, I3: 2}}. Finally, I1's conditional pattern base is {{I2: 4}}, whose FP-tree contains only one node, ⟨I2: 4⟩, which generates one frequent pattern, {I2, I1: 4}. This mining process is summarized in Figure 5.9. ■

The FP-growth method transforms the problem of finding long frequent patterns to searching for shorter ones recursively and then concatenating the suffix. It uses the least frequent items as a suffix, offering good selectivity. The method substantially reduces the search costs.

When the database is large, it is sometimes unrealistic to construct a main memory-based FP-tree. An interesting alternative is to first partition the database into a set of projected databases, and then construct an FP-tree and mine it in each projected database. Such a process can be recursively applied to any projected database if its FP-tree still cannot fit in main memory.

A study on the performance of the FP-growth method shows that it is efficient and scalable for mining both long and short frequent patterns, and is about an order of magnitude faster than the Apriori algorithm. It is also faster than a Tree-Projection algorithm, which recursively projects a database into a tree of projected databases.

5.2.5 Mining Frequent Itemsets Using Vertical Data Format

Both the Apriori and FP-growth methods mine frequent patterns from a set of transactions in *TID-itemset* format (that is, $\{TID : itemset\}$), where *TID* is a transaction-id and *itemset* is the set of items bought in transaction *TID*. This data format is known as **horizontal data format**. Alternatively, data can also be presented in *item-TID_set* format (that is, $\{item : TID\_set\}$), where *item* is an item name, and *TID_set* is the set of transaction identifiers containing the item. This format is known as **vertical data format**.

In this section, we look at how frequent itemsets can also be mined efficiently using vertical data format, which is the essence of the ECLAT (Equivalence CLASS Transformation) algorithm developed by Zaki [Zak00].

Algorithm: FP_growth. Mine frequent itemsets using an FP-tree by pattern fragment growth.

Input:

- *D*, a transaction database;
- *min_sup*, the minimum support count threshold.

Output: The complete set of frequent patterns.

Method:

1. The FP-tree is constructed in the following steps:

   (a) Scan the transaction database *D* once. Collect *F*, the set of frequent items, and their support counts. Sort *F* in support count descending order as *L*, the *list* of frequent items.

   (b) Create the root of an FP-tree, and label it as "null." For each transaction *Trans* in *D* do the following. Select and sort the frequent items in *Trans* according to the order of *L*. Let the sorted frequent item list in *Trans* be $[p|P]$, where *p* is the first element and *P* is the remaining list. Call insert_tree($[p|P]$, *T*), which is performed as follows. If *T* has a child *N* such that *N.item-name* = *p.item-name*, then increment *N*'s count by 1; else create a new node *N*, and let its count be 1, its parent link be linked to *T*, and its node-link to the nodes with the same *item-name* via the node-link structure. If *P* is nonempty, call insert_tree(*P*, *N*) recursively.

2. The FP-tree is mined by calling FP_growth(*FP_tree, null*), which is implemented as follows.

```
procedure FP_growth(Tree, α)
    if Tree contains a single path P then
        for each combination (denoted as β) of the nodes in the path P
            generate pattern β ∪ α with support_count = minimum support count of nodes in β;
    else for each a_i in the header of Tree {
        generate pattern β = a_i ∪ α with support_count = a_i.support_count;
        construct β's conditional pattern base and then β's conditional FP_tree Tree_β;
        if Tree_β ≠ ∅ then
            call FP_growth(Tree_β, β); }
```

Figure 5.9 The FP-growth algorithm for discovering frequent itemsets without candidate generation.

Table 5.3 The vertical data format of the transaction data set *D* of Table 5.1.

itemset	*TID_set*
I1	{T100, T400, T500, T700, T800, T900}
I2	{T100, T200, T300, T400, T600, T800, T900}
I3	{T300, T500, T600, T700, T800, T900}
I4	{T200, T400}
I5	{T100, T800}

Example 5.6 Mining frequent itemsets using vertical data format. Consider the horizontal data format of the transaction database, *D*, of Table 5.1 in Example 5.3. This can be transformed into the vertical data format shown in Table 5.3 by scanning the data set once.

Mining can be performed on this data set by intersecting the TID_sets of every pair of frequent single items. The minimum support count is 2. Because every single item is frequent in Table 5.3, there are 10 intersections performed in total, which lead to 8 nonempty 2-itemsets as shown in Table 5.4. Notice that because the itemsets {I1, I4} and {I3, I5} each contain only one transaction, they do not belong to the set of frequent 2-itemsets.

Based on the Apriori property, a given 3-itemset is a candidate 3-itemset only if every one of its 2-itemset subsets is frequent. The candidate generation process here will generate only two 3-itemsets: {I1, I2, I3} and {I1, I2, I5}. By intersecting the TID_sets of any two corresponding 2-itemsets of these candidate 3-itemsets, it derives Table 5.5, where there are only two frequent 3-itemsets: {I1, I2, I3: 2} and {I1, I2, I5: 2}. ■

Example 5.6 illustrates the process of mining frequent itemsets by exploring the vertical data format. First, we transform the horizontally formatted data to the vertical format by scanning the data set once. The support count of an itemset is simply the length of the TID_set of the itemset. Starting with $k = 1$, the frequent k-itemsets can be used to construct the candidate $(k+1)$-itemsets based on the Apriori property. The computation is done by intersection of the TID_sets of the frequent k-itemsets to compute the TID_sets of the corresponding $(k+1)$-itemsets. This process repeats, with k incremented by 1 each time, until no frequent itemsets or no candidate itemsets can be found.

Besides taking advantage of the Apriori property in the generation of candidate $(k+1)$-itemset from frequent k-itemsets, another merit of this method is that there is no need to scan the database to find the support of $(k+1)$ itemsets (for $k \geq 1$). This

Table 5.4 The 2-itemsets in vertical data format.

itemset	*TID_set*
{I1, I2}	{T100, T400, T800, T900}
{I1, I3}	{T500, T700, T800, T900}
{I1, I4}	{T400}
{I1, I5}	{T100, T800}
{I2, I3}	{T300, T600, T800, T900}
{I2, I4}	{T200, T400}
{I2, I5}	{T100, T800}
{I3, I5}	{T800}

Table 5.5 The 3-itemsets in vertical data format.

itemset	*TID_set*
{I1, I2, I3}	{T800, T900}
{I1, I2, I5}	{T100, T800}

is because the TID_set of each k-itemset carries the complete information required for counting such support. However, the TID_sets can be quite long, taking substantial memory space as well as computation time for intersecting the long sets.

To further reduce the cost of registering long TID_sets, as well as the subsequent costs of intersections, we can use a technique called *diffset*, which keeps track of only the differences of the TID_sets of a $(k+1)$-itemset and a corresponding k-itemset. For instance, in Example 5.6 we have {I1} = {T100, T400, T500, T700, T800, T900} and {I1, I2} = {T100, T400, T800, T900}. The *diffset* between the two is *diffset*({I1, I2}, {I1}) = {T500, T700}. Thus, rather than recording the four TIDs that make up the intersection of {I1} and {I2}, we can instead use diffset to record just two TIDs indicating the difference between {I1} and {I1, I2}. Experiments show that in certain situations, such as when the data set contains many dense and long patterns, this technique can substantially reduce the total cost of vertical format mining of frequent itemsets.

5.2.6 Mining Closed Frequent Itemsets

In Section 5.1.2 we saw how frequent itemset mining may generate a huge number of frequent itemsets, especially when the *min_sup* threshold is set low or when there exist long patterns in the data set. Example 5.2 showed that closed frequent itemsets[9] can substantially reduce the number of patterns generated in frequent itemset mining while preserving the complete information regarding the set of frequent itemsets. That is, from the set of closed frequent itemsets, we can easily derive the set of frequent itemsets and their support. Thus in practice, it is more desirable to mine the set of closed frequent itemsets rather than the set of all frequent itemsets in most cases.

"How can we mine closed frequent itemsets?" A naïve approach would be to first mine the complete set of frequent itemsets and then remove every frequent itemset that is a proper subset of, and carries the same support as, an existing frequent itemset. However, this is quite costly. As shown in Example 5.2, this method would have to first derive $2^{100}-1$ frequent itemsets in order to obtain a length-100 frequent itemset, all before it could begin to eliminate redundant itemsets. This is prohibitively expensive. In fact, there exist only a very small number of closed frequent itemsets in the data set of Example 5.2.

A recommended methodology is to search for closed frequent itemsets directly during the mining process. This requires us to prune the search space as soon as we can identify the case of closed itemsets during mining. Pruning strategies include the following:

Item merging: *If every transaction containing a frequent itemset X also contains an itemset Y but not any proper superset of Y, then $X \cup Y$ forms a frequent closed itemset and there is no need to search for any itemset containing X but no Y.*

For example, in Table 5.2 of Example 5.5, the projected conditional database for prefix itemset {I5:2} is {{I2, I1},{I2, I1, I3}}, from which we can see that each of

[9]Remember that X is a *closed frequent* itemset in a data set S if there exists no proper super-itemset Y such that Y has the same support count as X in S, and X satisfies minimum support.

its transactions contains itemset {I2, I1} but no proper superset of {I2, I1}. Itemset {I2, I1} can be merged with {I5} to form the closed itemset, {I5, I2, I1: 2}, and we do not need to mine for closed itemsets that contain I5 but not {I2, I1}.

Sub-itemset pruning: *If a frequent itemset X is a proper subset of an already found frequent closed itemset Y and support_count(X) = support_count(Y), then X and all of X's descendants in the set enumeration tree cannot be frequent closed itemsets and thus can be pruned.*

Similar to Example 5.2, suppose a transaction database has only two transactions: $\{\langle a_1, a_2, \ldots, a_{100}\rangle, \langle a_1, a_2, \ldots, a_{50}\rangle\}$, and the minimum support count is $min\_sup = 2$. The projection on the first item, a_1, derives the frequent itemset, $\{a_1, a_2, \ldots, a_{50}: 2\}$, based on the *itemset merging* optimization. Because support($\{a_2\}$) = support ($\{a_1, a_2, \ldots, a_{50}\}$) = 2, and $\{a_2\}$ is a proper subset of $\{a_1, a_2, \ldots, a_{50}\}$, there is no need to examine a_2 and its projected database. Similar pruning can be done for $a_3, \ldots, a_{50}$ as well. Thus the mining of closed frequent itemsets in this data set terminates after mining a_1's projected database.

Item skipping: *In the depth-first mining of closed itemsets, at each level, there will be a prefix itemset X associated with a header table and a projected database. If a local frequent item p has the same support in several header tables at different levels, we can safely prune p from the header tables at higher levels.*

Consider, for example, the transaction database above having only two transactions: $\{\langle a_1, a_2, \ldots, a_{100}\rangle, \langle a_1, a_2, \ldots, a_{50}\rangle\}$, where $min\_sup = 2$. Because a_2 in a_1's projected database has the same support as a_2 in the global header table, a_2 can be pruned from the global header table. Similar pruning can be done for $a_3, \ldots, a_{50}$. There is no need to mine anything more after mining a_1's projected database.

Besides pruning the search space in the closed itemset mining process, another important optimization is to perform efficient checking of a newly derived frequent itemset to see whether it is closed, because the mining process cannot ensure that every generated frequent itemset is closed.

When a new frequent itemset is derived, it is necessary to perform two kinds of closure checking: (1) *superset checking*, which checks if this new frequent itemset is a superset of some already found closed itemsets with the same support, and (2) *subset checking*, which checks whether the newly found itemset is a subset of an already found closed itemset with the same support.

If we adopt the *item merging* pruning method under a divide-and-conquer framework, then the superset checking is actually built-in and there is no need to explicitly perform superset checking. This is because if a frequent itemset $X \cup Y$ is found later than itemset X, and carries the same support as X, it must be in X's projected database and must have been generated during itemset merging.

To assist in subset checking, a compressed **pattern-tree** can be constructed to maintain the set of closed itemsets mined so far. The pattern-tree is similar in structure to the FP-tree except that all of the closed itemsets found are stored explicitly in the corresponding tree branches. For efficient subset checking, we can use the following property: *If the* *current itemset S_c can be subsumed by another already found closed itemset S_a, then (1) S_c and S_a have the same support, (2) the length of S_c is smaller than that of S_a, and (3) all of the items in S_c are contained in S_a.* Based on this property, a **two-level hash index structure** can be built for fast accessing of the pattern-tree: The first level uses the identifier of the last item in S_c as a hash key (since this identifier must be within the branch of S_c), and the second level uses the support of S_c as a hash key (since S_c and S_a have the same support). This will substantially speed up the subset checking process.

The above discussion illustrates methods for efficient mining of closed frequent itemsets. *"Can we extend these methods for efficient mining of maximal frequent itemsets?"* Because maximal frequent itemsets share many similarities with closed frequent itemsets, many of the optimization techniques developed here can be extended to mining maximal frequent itemsets. However, we leave this method as an exercise for interested readers.

5.3 Mining Various Kinds of Association Rules

We have studied efficient methods for mining frequent itemsets and association rules. In this section, we consider additional application requirements by extending our scope to include mining multilevel association rules, multidimensional association rules, and quantitative association rules in transactional and/or relational databases and data warehouses. *Multilevel association rules* involve concepts at different levels of abstraction. *Multidimensional association rules* involve more than one dimension or predicate (e.g., rules relating what a customer *buys* as well as the customer's *age.*) *Quantitative association rules* involve numeric attributes that have an implicit ordering among values (e.g., *age*).

5.3.1 Mining Multilevel Association Rules

For many applications, it is difficult to find strong associations among data items at low or primitive levels of abstraction due to the sparsity of data at those levels. Strong associations discovered at high levels of abstraction may represent commonsense knowledge. Moreover, what may represent common sense to one user may seem novel to another. Therefore, data mining systems should provide capabilities for mining association rules at multiple levels of abstraction, with sufficient flexibility for easy traversal among different abstraction spaces.

Let's examine the following example.

Example 5.7 **Mining multilevel association rules.** Suppose we are given the task-relevant set of transactional data in Table 5.6 for sales in an *AllElectronics* store, showing the items purchased for each transaction. The concept hierarchy for the items is shown in Figure 5.10. A concept hierarchy defines a sequence of mappings from a set of low-level concepts to higher-level, more general concepts. Data can be generalized by replacing low-level concepts within the data by their higher-level concepts, or *ancestors*, from a concept hierarchy.

Table 5.6 Task-relevant data, *D*.

TID	*Items Purchased*
T100	IBM-ThinkPad-T40/2373, HP-Photosmart-7660
T200	Microsoft-Office-Professional-2003, Microsoft-Plus!-Digital-Media
T300	Logitech-MX700-Cordless-Mouse, Fellowes-Wrist-Rest
T400	Dell-Dimension-XPS, Canon-PowerShot-S400
T500	IBM-ThinkPad-R40/P4M, Symantec-Norton-Antivirus-2003
...	...

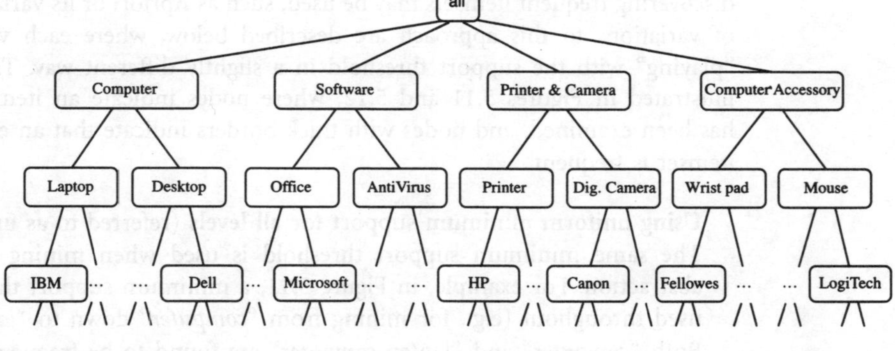

Figure 5.10 A concept hierarchy for *AllElectronics* computer items.

The concept hierarchy of Figure 5.10 has five levels, respectively referred to as levels 0 to 4, starting with level 0 at the root node for all (the most general abstraction level). Here, level 1 includes *computer, software, printer&camera,* and *computer accessory*, level 2 includes *laptop computer, desktop computer, office software, antivirus software,* ..., and level 3 includes *IBM desktop computer,* ..., *Microsoft office software*, and so on. Level 4 is the most specific abstraction level of this hierarchy. It consists of the raw data values. Concept hierarchies for categorical attributes are often implicit within the database schema, in which case they may be automatically generated using methods such as those described in Chapter 2. For our example, the concept hierarchy of Figure 5.10 was generated from data on product specifications. Concept hierarchies for numerical attributes can be generated using discretization techniques, many of which were introduced in Chapter 2. Alternatively, concept hierarchies may be specified by users familiar with the data, such as store managers in the case of our example.

The items in Table 5.6 are at the lowest level of the concept hierarchy of Figure 5.10. It is difficult to find interesting purchase patterns at such raw or primitive-level data. For instance, if *"IBM-ThinkPad-R40/P4M"* or *"Symantec-Norton-Antivirus-2003"* each occurs in a very small fraction of the transactions, then it can be difficult to find strong associations involving these specific items. Few people may buy these items together, making it unlikely that the itemset will satisfy minimum support. However, we would expect that it is easier to find strong associations between generalized abstractions of these items, such as between "*IBM laptop computer*" and "*antivirus software.*" ■

Association rules generated from mining data at multiple levels of abstraction are called **multiple-level** or **multilevel association rules**. Multilevel association rules can be mined efficiently using concept hierarchies under a support-confidence framework. In general, a top-down strategy is employed, where counts are accumulated for the calculation of frequent itemsets at each concept level, starting at the concept level 1 and working downward in the hierarchy toward the more specific concept levels, until no more frequent itemsets can be found. For each level, any algorithm for discovering frequent itemsets may be used, such as Apriori or its variations. A number of variations to this approach are described below, where each variation involves "playing" with the support threshold in a slightly different way. The variations are illustrated in Figures 5.11 and 5.12, where nodes indicate an item or itemset that has been examined, and nodes with thick borders indicate that an examined item or itemset is frequent.

- **Using uniform minimum support for all levels** (referred to as **uniform support**): The same minimum support threshold is used when mining at each level of abstraction. For example, in Figure 5.11, a minimum support threshold of 5% is used throughout (e.g., for mining from "*computer*" down to "*laptop computer*"). Both "*computer*" and "*laptop computer*" are found to be frequent, while "*desktop computer*" is not.

  When a uniform minimum support threshold is used, the search procedure is simplified. The method is also simple in that users are required to specify only one minimum support threshold. An Apriori-like optimization technique can be adopted, based on the knowledge that an ancestor is a superset of its descendants: The search avoids examining itemsets containing any item whose ancestors do not have minimum support.

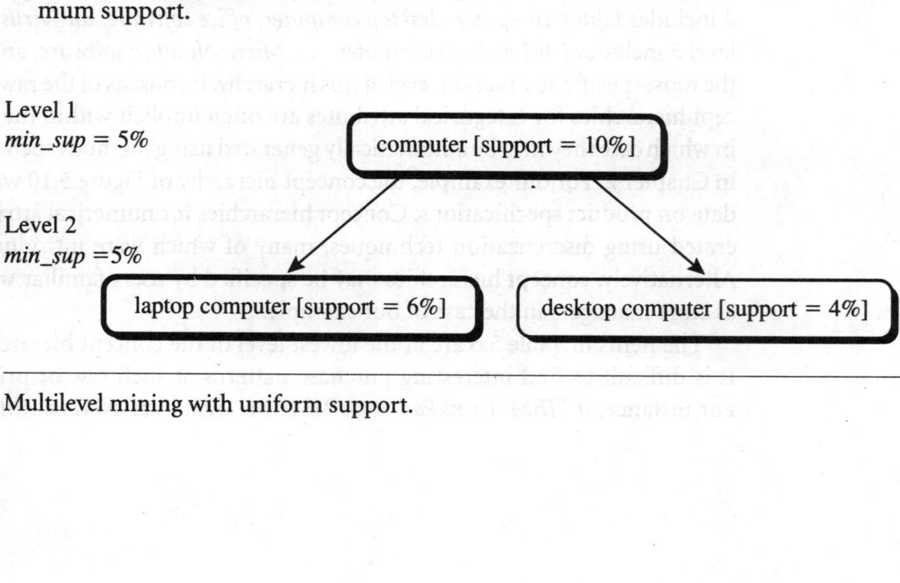

Figure 5.11 Multilevel mining with uniform support.

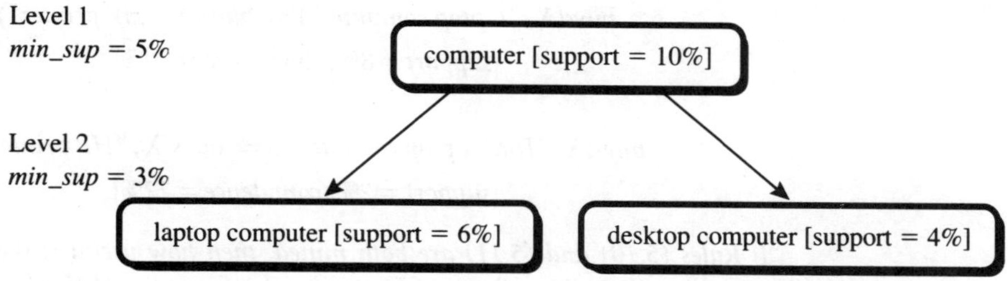

Figure 5.12 Multilevel mining with reduced support.

The uniform support approach, however, has some difficulties. It is unlikely that items at lower levels of abstraction will occur as frequently as those at higher levels of abstraction. If the minimum support threshold is set too high, it could miss some meaningful associations occurring at low abstraction levels. If the threshold is set too low, it may generate many uninteresting associations occurring at high abstraction levels. This provides the motivation for the following approach.

Using reduced minimum support at lower levels (referred to as **reduced support**): Each level of abstraction has its own minimum support threshold. The deeper the level of abstraction, the smaller the corresponding threshold is. For example, in Figure 5.12, the minimum support thresholds for levels 1 and 2 are 5% and 3%, respectively. In this way, *"computer,"* *"laptop computer,"* and *"desktop computer"* are all considered frequent.

Using item or group-based minimum support (referred to as group-based support): Because users or experts often have insight as to which groups are more important than others, it is sometimes more desirable to set up user-specific, item, or group-based minimal support thresholds when mining multilevel rules. For example, a user could set up the minimum support thresholds based on product price, or on items of interest, such as by setting particularly low support thresholds for *laptop computers* and *flash drives* in order to pay particular attention to the association patterns containing items in these categories.

Notice that the Apriori property may not always hold uniformly across all of the items when mining under reduced support and group-based support. However, efficient methods can be developed based on the extension of the property. The details are left as an exercise for interested readers.

A serious side effect of mining multilevel association rules is its generation of many redundant rules across multiple levels of abstraction due to the "ancestor" relationships among items. For example, consider the following rules where *"laptop computer"* is an ancestor of *"IBM laptop computer"* based on the concept hierarchy of Figure 5.10, and where X is a variable representing customers who purchased items in *AllElectronics* transactions.

$$buys(X, \text{"laptop computer"}) \Rightarrow buys(X, \text{"HP printer"})$$
$$[support = 8\%, confidence = 70\%] \quad (5.10)$$

$$buys(X, \text{"IBM laptop computer"}) \Rightarrow buys(X, \text{"HP printer"})$$
$$[support = 2\%, confidence = 72\%] \quad (5.11)$$

"If Rules (5.10) and (5.11) are both mined, then how useful is the latter rule?" you may wonder. *"Does it really provide any novel information?"* If the latter, less general rule does not provide new information, then it should be removed. Let's look at how this may be determined. A rule $R1$ is an **ancestor** of a rule $R2$, if $R1$ can be obtained by replacing the items in $R2$ by their ancestors in a concept hierarchy. For example, Rule (5.10) is an ancestor of Rule (5.11) because *"laptop computer"* is an ancestor of *"IBM laptop computer."* Based on this definition, a rule can be considered redundant if its support and confidence are close to their "expected" values, based on an ancestor of the rule. As an illustration, suppose that Rule (5.10) has a 70% confidence and 8% support, and that about one-quarter of all *"laptop computer"* sales are for *"IBM laptop computers."* We may expect Rule (5.11) to have a confidence of around 70% (since all data samples of *"IBM laptop computer"* are also samples of *"laptop computer"*) and a support of around 2% (i.e., $8\% \times \frac{1}{4}$). If this is indeed the case, then Rule (5.11) is not interesting because it does not offer any additional information and is less general than Rule (5.10).

5.3.2 Mining Multidimensional Association Rules from Relational Databases and Data Warehouses

So far in this chapter, we have studied association rules that imply a single predicate, that is, the predicate *buys*. For instance, in mining our *AllElectronics* database, we may discover the Boolean association rule

$$buys(X, \text{"digital camera"}) \Rightarrow buys(X, \text{"HP printer"}). \quad (5.12)$$

Following the terminology used in multidimensional databases, we refer to each distinct predicate in a rule as a dimension. Hence, we can refer to Rule (5.12) as a **single-dimensional** or **intradimensional association rule** because it contains a single distinct predicate (e.g., *buys*) with multiple occurrences (i.e., the predicate occurs more than once within the rule). As we have seen in the previous sections of this chapter, such rules are commonly mined from transactional data.

Suppose, however, that rather than using a transactional database, sales and related information are stored in a relational database or data warehouse. Such data stores are multidimensional, by definition. For instance, in addition to keeping track of the items purchased in sales transactions, a relational database may record other attributes associated with the items, such as the quantity purchased or the price, or the branch location of the sale. Additional relational information regarding the customers who purchased the items, such as customer age, occupation, credit rating, income, and address, may also be stored. Considering each database attribute or warehouse dimension as a predicate, we can therefore mine association rules containing *multiple* predicates, such as

$$age(X, \text{“20...29”}) \wedge occupation(X, \text{“student”}) \Rightarrow buys(X, \text{“laptop”}). \quad (5.13)$$

Association rules that involve two or more dimensions or predicates can be referred to as **multidimensional association rules.** Rule (5.13) contains three predicates (*age, occupation,* and *buys*), each of which occurs *only once* in the rule. Hence, we say that it has **no repeated predicates.** Multidimensional association rules with no repeated predicates are called **interdimensional association rules.** We can also mine multidimensional association rules with repeated predicates, which contain multiple occurrences of some predicates. These rules are called **hybrid-dimensional association rules.** An example of such a rule is the following, where the predicate *buys* is repeated:

$$age(X, \text{“20...29”}) \wedge buys(X, \text{“laptop”}) \Rightarrow buys(X, \text{“HP printer”}) \quad (5.14)$$

Note that database attributes can be categorical or quantitative. **Categorical** attributes have a finite number of possible values, with no ordering among the values (e.g., *occupation, brand, color*). Categorical attributes are also called **nominal** attributes, because their values are “names of things.” **Quantitative** attributes are numeric and have an implicit ordering among values (e.g., *age, income, price*). Techniques for mining multidimensional association rules can be categorized into two basic approaches regarding the treatment of quantitative attributes.

In the first approach, *quantitative attributes are discretized using predefined concept hierarchies.* This discretization occurs before mining. For instance, a concept hierarchy for *income* may be used to replace the original numeric values of this attribute by interval labels, such as “0...20K”, “21K ...30K”, “31K ...40K”, and so on. Here, discretization is *static* and predetermined. Chapter 2 on data preprocessing gave several techniques for discretizing numeric attributes. The discretized numeric attributes, with their interval labels, can then be treated as categorical attributes (where each interval is considered a category). We refer to this as **mining multidimensional association rules using static discretization of quantitative attributes.**

In the second approach, *quantitative attributes are discretized or clustered into “bins” based on the distribution of the data.* These bins may be further combined during the mining process. The discretization process is *dynamic* and established so as to satisfy some mining criteria, such as maximizing the confidence of the rules mined. Because this strategy treats the numeric attribute values as quantities rather than as predefined ranges or categories, association rules mined from this approach are also referred to as **(dynamic) quantitative association rules.**

Let’s study each of these approaches for mining multidimensional association rules. For simplicity, we confine our discussion to interdimensional association rules. Note that rather than searching for frequent itemsets (as is done for single-dimensional association rule mining), in multidimensional association rule mining we search for frequent *predicate sets.* A ***k*-predicate set** is a set containing k conjunctive predicates. For instance, the set of predicates $\{age, occupation, buys\}$ from Rule (5.13) is a 3-predicate set. Similar to the notation used for itemsets, we use the notation L_k to refer to the set of frequent k-predicate sets.

Mining Multidimensional Association Rules Using Static Discretization of Quantitative Attributes

Quantitative attributes, in this case, are discretized before mining using predefined concept hierarchies or data discretization techniques, where numeric values are replaced by interval labels. Categorical attributes may also be generalized to higher conceptual levels if desired. If the resulting task-relevant data are stored in a relational table, then any of the frequent itemset mining algorithms we have discussed can be modified easily so as to find all frequent predicate sets rather than frequent itemsets. In particular, instead of searching on only one attribute like *buys*, we need to search through all of the relevant attributes, treating each attribute-value pair as an itemset.

Alternatively, the transformed multidimensional data may be used to construct a *data cube*. Data cubes are well suited for the mining of multidimensional association rules: They store aggregates (such as counts), in multidimensional space, which is essential for computing the support and confidence of multidimensional association rules. An overview of data cube technology was presented in Chapter 3. Detailed algorithms for data cube computation were given in Chapter 4. Figure 5.13 shows the lattice of cuboids defining a data cube for the dimensions *age*, *income*, and *buys*. The cells of an n-dimensional cuboid can be used to store the support counts of the corresponding

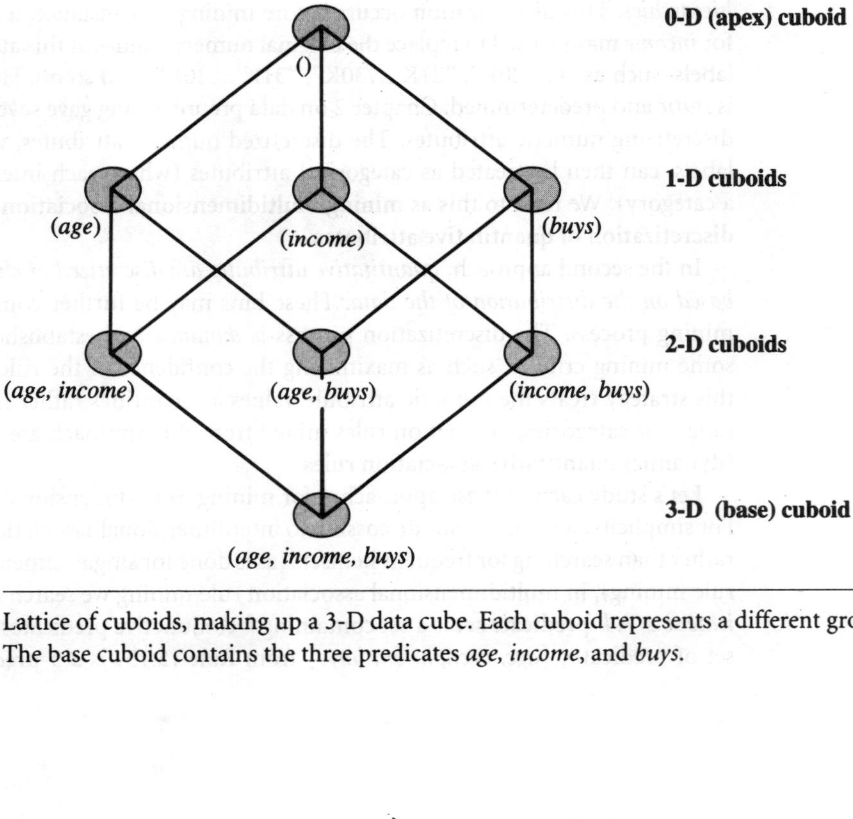

Figure 5.13 Lattice of cuboids, making up a 3-D data cube. Each cuboid represents a different group-by. The base cuboid contains the three predicates *age, income,* and *buys*.

n-predicate sets. The base cuboid aggregates the task-relevant data by *age, income*, and *buys*; the 2-D cuboid, (*age, income*), aggregates by *age* and *income*, and so on; the 0-D (apex) cuboid contains the total number of transactions in the task-relevant data.

Due to the ever-increasing use of data warehouse and OLAP technology, it is possible that a data cube containing the dimensions that are of interest to the user may already exist, fully materialized. If this is the case, we can simply fetch the corresponding aggregate values and return the rules needed using a rule generation algorithm (Section 5.2.2). Notice that even in this case, the Apriori property can still be used to prune the search space. If a given *k*-predicate set has support *sup*, which does not satisfy minimum support, then further exploration of this set should be terminated. This is because any more specialized version of the *k*-itemset will have support no greater that *sup* and, therefore, will not satisfy minimum support either. In cases where no relevant data cube exists for the mining task, we must create one on the fly. This becomes an iceberg cube computation problem, where the minimum support threshold is taken as the iceberg condition (Chapter 4).

Mining Quantitative Association Rules

Quantitative association rules are multidimensional association rules in which the numeric attributes are *dynamically* discretized during the mining process so as to satisfy some mining criteria, such as maximizing the confidence or compactness of the rules mined. In this section, we focus specifically on how to mine quantitative association rules having two quantitative attributes on the left-hand side of the rule and one categorical attribute on the right-hand side of the rule. That is,

$$A_{quan1} \wedge A_{quan2} \Rightarrow A_{cat}$$

where A_{quan1} and A_{quan2} are tests on quantitative attribute intervals (where the intervals are dynamically determined), and A_{cat} tests a categorical attribute from the task-relevant data. Such rules have been referred to as **two-dimensional quantitative association rules,** because they contain two quantitative dimensions. For instance, suppose you are curious about the association relationship between pairs of quantitative attributes, like customer age and income, and the type of television (such as *high-definition TV*, i.e., *HDTV*) that customers like to buy. An example of such a 2-D quantitative association rule is

$$age(X, \text{"30...39"}) \wedge income(X, \text{"42K...48K"}) \Rightarrow buys(X, \text{"HDTV"}) \quad (5.15)$$

"How can we find such rules?" Let's look at an approach used in a system called **ARCS** (Association Rule Clustering System), which borrows ideas from image processing. Essentially, this approach maps pairs of quantitative attributes onto a 2-D grid for tuples satisfying a given categorical attribute condition. The grid is then searched for clusters of points from which the association rules are generated. The following steps are involved in ARCS:

Binning: Quantitative attributes can have a very wide range of values defining their domain. Just think about how big a 2-D grid would be if we plotted *age* and *income* as axes, where each possible value of *age* was assigned a unique position on one axis, and similarly, each possible value of *income* was assigned a unique position on the other axis! To keep grids down to a manageable size, we instead partition the ranges of quantitative attributes into intervals. These intervals are dynamic in that they may later be further combined during the mining process. The partitioning process is referred to as **binning**, that is, where the intervals are considered "bins." Three common binning strategies area as follows:

- **Equal-width binning**, where the interval size of each bin is the same
- **Equal-frequency binning**, where each bin has approximately the same number of tuples assigned to it,
- **Clustering-based binning**, where clustering is performed on the quantitative attribute to group *neighboring points* (judged based on various distance measures) into the same bin

ARCS uses equal-width binning, where the bin size for each quantitative attribute is input by the user. A 2-D array for each possible bin combination involving both quantitative attributes is created. Each array cell holds the corresponding count distribution for each possible class of the categorical attribute of the rule right-hand side. By creating this data structure, the task-relevant data need only be scanned once. The same 2-D array can be used to generate rules for any value of the categorical attribute, based on the same two quantitative attributes. Binning is also discussed in Chapter 2.

Finding frequent predicate sets: Once the 2-D array containing the count distribution for each category is set up, it can be scanned to find the frequent predicate sets (those satisfying minimum support) that also satisfy minimum confidence. Strong association rules can then be generated from these predicate sets, using a rule generation algorithm like that described in Section 5.2.2.

Clustering the association rules: The strong association rules obtained in the previous step are then mapped to a 2-D grid. Figure 5.14 shows a 2-D grid for 2-D quantitative association rules predicting the condition *buys*(*X*, "*HDTV*") on the rule right-hand side, given the quantitative attributes *age* and *income*. The four Xs correspond to the rules

$$age(X, 34) \wedge income(X, \text{"}31K...40K\text{"}) \Rightarrow buys(X, \text{"}HDTV\text{"}) \quad (5.16)$$

$$age(X, 35) \wedge income(X, \text{"}31K...40K\text{"}) \Rightarrow buys(X, \text{"}HDTV\text{"}) \quad (5.17)$$

$$age(X, 34) \wedge income(X, \text{"}41K...50K\text{"}) \Rightarrow buys(X, \text{"}HDTV\text{"}) \quad (5.18)$$

$$age(X, 35) \wedge income(X, \text{"}41K...50K\text{"}) \Rightarrow buys(X, \text{"}HDTV\text{"}). \quad (5.19)$$

"Can we find a simpler rule to replace the above four rules?" Notice that these rules are quite "close" to one another, forming a rule cluster on the grid. Indeed, the four rules can be combined or "clustered" together to form the following simpler rule, which subsumes and replaces the above four rules:

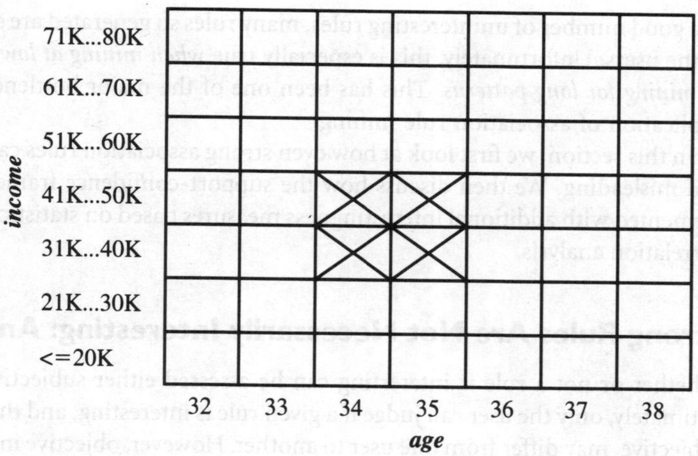

Figure 5.14 A 2-D grid for tuples representing customers who purchase high-definition TVs.

$$age(X, \text{“}34...35\text{”}) \wedge income(X, \text{“}31K...50K\text{”}) \Rightarrow buys(X, \text{“}HDTV\text{”}) \quad ($$

ARCS employs a clustering algorithm for this purpose. The algorithm scan grid, searching for rectangular clusters of rules. In this way, bins of the quan tive attributes occurring within a rule cluster may be further combined, and l further dynamic discretization of the quantitative attributes occurs.

The grid-based technique described here assumes that the initial association can be clustered into rectangular regions. Before performing the clustering, smoo techniques can be used to help remove noise and outliers from the data. Recta clusters may oversimplify the data. Alternative approaches have been proposed, ba other shapes of regions that tend to better fit the data, yet require greater compu effort.

A non-grid-based technique has been proposed to find quantitative associatior that are more general, where any number of quantitative and categorical attribut appear on either side of the rules. In this technique, quantitative attributes are dy cally partitioned using equal-frequency binning, and the partitions are combined on a measure of *partial completeness,* which quantifies the information lost due to tioning. For references on these alternatives to ARCS, see the bibliographic notes.

From Association Mining to Correlation Analysis

Most association rule mining algorithms employ a support-confidence framev Often, many interesting rules can be found using low support thresholds. Alth minimum support and confidence thresholds *help* weed out or exclude the explor of a good number of uninteresting rules, many rules so generated are still not interesting to the users. Unfortunately, this is especially true *when mining at low support thresholds or mining for long patterns.* This has been one of the major bottlenecks for successful application of association rule mining.

In this section, we first look at how even strong association rules can be uninteresting and misleading. We then discuss how the support-confidence framework can be supplemented with additional interestingness measures based on statistical significance and correlation analysis.

5.4.1 Strong Rules Are Not Necessarily Interesting: An Example

Whether or not a rule is interesting can be assessed either subjectively or objectively. Ultimately, only the user can judge if a given rule is interesting, and this judgment, being subjective, may differ from one user to another. However, objective interestingness measures, based on the statistics "behind" the data, can be used as one step toward the goal of weeding out uninteresting rules from presentation to the user.

"How can we tell which strong association rules are really interesting?" Let's examine the following example.

Example 5.8 **A misleading "strong" association rule.** Suppose we are interested in analyzing transactions at *AllElectronics* with respect to the purchase of computer games and videos. Let *game* refer to the transactions containing computer games, and *video* refer to those containing videos. Of the 10,000 transactions analyzed, the data show that 6,000 of the customer transactions included computer games, while 7,500 included videos, and 4,000 included both computer games and videos. Suppose that a data mining program for discovering association rules is run on the data, using a minimum support of, say, 30% and a minimum confidence of 60%. The following association rule is discovered:

$$buys(X, \text{"computer games"}) \Rightarrow buys(X, \text{"videos"}) \; [support = 40\%, confidence = 66\%] \tag{5.21}$$

Rule (5.21) is a strong association rule and would therefore be reported, since its support value of $\frac{4{,}000}{10{,}000} = 40\%$ and confidence value of $\frac{4{,}000}{6{,}000} = 66\%$ satisfy the minimum support and minimum confidence thresholds, respectively. However, Rule (5.21) is misleading because the probability of purchasing videos is 75%, which is even larger than 66%. In fact, computer games and videos are negatively associated because the purchase of one of these items actually decreases the likelihood of purchasing the other. Without fully understanding this phenomenon, we could easily make unwise business decisions based on Rule (5.21). ■

The above example also illustrates that the confidence of a rule $A \Rightarrow B$ can be deceiving in that it is only an *estimate* of the conditional probability of itemset B given itemset A. It does not measure the real strength (or lack of strength) of the correlation and implication between A and B. Hence, alternatives to the support-confidence framework can be useful in mining interesting data relationships.

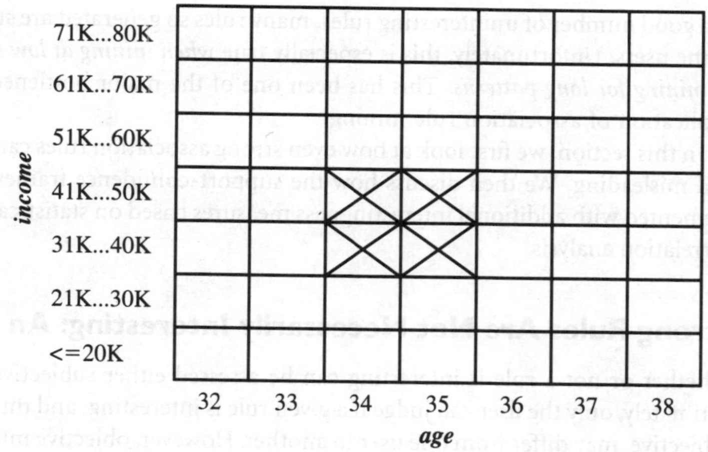

Figure 5.14 A 2-D grid for tuples representing customers who purchase high-definition TVs.

$$age(X, \text{“34...35”}) \wedge income(X, \text{“31}K\text{...50}K\text{”}) \Rightarrow buys(X, \text{“}HDTV\text{”}) \quad (5.20)$$

ARCS employs a clustering algorithm for this purpose. The algorithm scans the grid, searching for rectangular clusters of rules. In this way, bins of the quantitative attributes occurring within a rule cluster may be further combined, and hence further dynamic discretization of the quantitative attributes occurs.

The grid-based technique described here assumes that the initial association rules can be clustered into rectangular regions. Before performing the clustering, smoothing techniques can be used to help remove noise and outliers from the data. Rectangular clusters may oversimplify the data. Alternative approaches have been proposed, based on other shapes of regions that tend to better fit the data, yet require greater computation effort.

A non-grid-based technique has been proposed to find quantitative association rules that are more general, where any number of quantitative and categorical attributes can appear on either side of the rules. In this technique, quantitative attributes are dynamically partitioned using equal-frequency binning, and the partitions are combined based on a measure of *partial completeness*, which quantifies the information lost due to partitioning. For references on these alternatives to ARCS, see the bibliographic notes.

From Association Mining to Correlation Analysis

Most association rule mining algorithms employ a support-confidence framework. Often, many interesting rules can be found using low support thresholds. Although minimum support and confidence thresholds *help* weed out or exclude the exploration of a good number of uninteresting rules, many rules so generated are still not interesting to the users. Unfortunately, this is especially true *when mining at low support thresholds or mining for long patterns*. This has been one of the major bottlenecks for successful application of association rule mining.

In this section, we first look at how even strong association rules can be uninteresting and misleading. We then discuss how the support-confidence framework can be supplemented with additional interestingness measures based on statistical significance and correlation analysis.

5.4.1 Strong Rules Are Not Necessarily Interesting: An Example

Whether or not a rule is interesting can be assessed either subjectively or objectively. Ultimately, only the user can judge if a given rule is interesting, and this judgment, being subjective, may differ from one user to another. However, objective interestingness measures, based on the statistics "behind" the data, can be used as one step toward the goal of weeding out uninteresting rules from presentation to the user.

"How can we tell which strong association rules are really interesting?" Let's examine the following example.

Example 5.8 **A misleading "strong" association rule.** Suppose we are interested in analyzing transactions at *AllElectronics* with respect to the purchase of computer games and videos. Let *game* refer to the transactions containing computer games, and *video* refer to those containing videos. Of the 10,000 transactions analyzed, the data show that 6,000 of the customer transactions included computer games, while 7,500 included videos, and 4,000 included both computer games and videos. Suppose that a data mining program for discovering association rules is run on the data, using a minimum support of, say, 30% and a minimum confidence of 60%. The following association rule is discovered:

$$buys(X, \text{"computer games"}) \Rightarrow buys(X, \text{"videos"}) \;\; [support = 40\%, confidence = 66\%] \tag{5.21}$$

Rule (5.21) is a strong association rule and would therefore be reported, since its support value of $\frac{4,000}{10,000} = 40\%$ and confidence value of $\frac{4,000}{6,000} = 66\%$ satisfy the minimum support and minimum confidence thresholds, respectively. However, Rule (5.21) is misleading because the probability of purchasing videos is 75%, which is even larger than 66%. In fact, computer games and videos are negatively associated because the purchase of one of these items actually decreases the likelihood of purchasing the other. Without fully understanding this phenomenon, we could easily make unwise business decisions based on Rule (5.21). ■

The above example also illustrates that the confidence of a rule $A \Rightarrow B$ can be deceiving in that it is only an *estimate* of the conditional probability of itemset B given itemset A. It does not measure the real strength (or lack of strength) of the correlation and implication between A and B. Hence, alternatives to the support-confidence framework can be useful in mining interesting data relationships.

5.4.2 From Association Analysis to Correlation Analysis

As we have seen above, the support and confidence measures are insufficient at filtering out uninteresting association rules. To tackle this weakness, a correlation measure can be used to augment the support-confidence framework for association rules. This leads to *correlation rules* of the form

$$A \Rightarrow B \text{ [}support, confidence. correlation\text{]}. \tag{5.22}$$

That is, a correlation rule is measured not only by its support and confidence but also by the correlation between itemsets A and B. There are many different correlation measures from which to choose. In this section, we study various correlation measures to determine which would be good for mining large data sets.

Lift is a simple correlation measure that is given as follows. The occurrence of itemset A is **independent** of the occurrence of itemset B if $P(A \cup B) = P(A)P(B)$; otherwise, itemsets A and B are **dependent** and **correlated** as events. This definition can easily be extended to more than two itemsets. The **lift** between the occurrence of A and B can be measured by computing

$$lift(A, B) = \frac{P(A \cup B)}{P(A)P(B)}. \tag{5.23}$$

If the resulting value of Equation (5.23) is less than 1, then the occurrence of A is *negatively correlated with* the occurrence of B. If the resulting value is greater than 1, then A and B are *positively correlated*, meaning that the occurrence of one implies the occurrence of the other. If the resulting value is equal to 1, then A and B are *independent* and there is no correlation between them.

Equation (5.23) is equivalent to $P(B|A)/P(B)$, or $conf(A \Rightarrow B)/sup(B)$, which is also referred as the *lift* of the association (or correlation) rule $A \Rightarrow B$. In other words, it assesses the degree to which the occurrence of one "lifts" the occurrence of the other. For example, if A corresponds to the sale of computer games and B corresponds to the sale of videos, then given the current market conditions, the sale of games is said to increase or "lift" the likelihood of the sale of videos by a factor of the value returned by Equation (5.23).

Let's go back to the computer game and video data of Example 5.8.

Example 5.9 **Correlation analysis using lift.** To help filter out misleading "strong" associations of the form $A \Rightarrow B$ from the data of Example 5.8, we need to study how the two itemsets, A and B, are correlated. Let $\overline{game}$ refer to the transactions of Example 5.8 that do not contain computer games, and $\overline{video}$ refer to those that do not contain videos. The transactions can be summarized in a *contingency table*, as shown in Table 5.7. From the table, we can see that the probability of purchasing a computer game is $P(\{game\}) = 0.60$, the probability of purchasing a video is $P(\{video\}) = 0.75$, and the probability of purchasing both is $P(\{game, video\}) = 0.40$. By Equation (5.23), the lift of Rule (5.21) is $P(\{game, video\})/(P(\{game\}) \times P(\{video\})) = 0.40/(0.60 \times 0.75) = 0.89$. Because this value is less than 1, there is a negative correlation between the occurrence of $\{game\}$ and $\{video\}$. The numerator is the likelihood of a customer purchasing both, while the

Table 5.7 A 2 × 2 contingency table summarizing the transactions with respect to game and video purchases.

	game	$\overline{game}$	Σ_{row}
video	4,000	3,500	7,500
$\overline{video}$	2,000	500	2,500
Σ_{col}	6,000	4,000	10,000

Table 5.8 The above contingency table, now shown with the expected values.

	game	$\overline{game}$	Σ_{row}
video	4,000 (4,500)	3,500 (3,000)	7,500
$\overline{video}$	2,000 (1,500)	500 (1,000)	2,500
Σ_{col}	6,000	4,000	10,000

denominator is what the likelihood would have been if the two purchases were completely independent. Such a negative correlation cannot be identified by a support-confidence framework. ■

The second correlation measure that we study is the χ^2 measure, which was introduced in Chapter 2 (Equation 2.9). To compute the χ^2 value, we take the squared difference between the observed and expected value for a slot (A and B pair) in the contingency table, divided by the expected value. This amount is summed for all slots of the contingency table. Let's perform a χ^2 analysis of the above example.

Example 5.10 **Correlation analysis using χ^2.** To compute the correlation using χ^2 analysis, we need the observed value and expected value (displayed in parenthesis) for each slot of the contingency table, as shown in Table 5.8. From the table, we can compute the χ^2 value as follows:

$$\chi^2 = \Sigma\frac{(observed\text{ - }expected)^2}{expected} = \frac{(4{,}000-4{,}500)^2}{4{,}500} + \frac{(3{,}500-3{,}000)^2}{3{,}000} + \frac{(2{,}000-1{,}500)^2}{1{,}500} + \frac{(500-1{,}000)^2}{1{,}000} = 555.6.$$

Because the χ^2 value is greater than one, and the observed value of the slot (*game, video*) = 4,000, which is less than the expected value 4,500, *buying game* and *buying video* are *negatively correlated*. This is consistent with the conclusion derived from the analysis of the *lift* measure in Example 5.9. ■

Let's examine two other correlation measures, *all_confidence* and *cosine*, as defined below.

Given an itemset $X = \{i_1, i_2, \ldots, i_k\}$, the **all_confidence** of X is defined as

$$all\_conf(X) = \frac{sup(X)}{max\_item\_sup(X)} = \frac{sup(X)}{max\{sup(i_j)|\forall i_j \in X\}}, \tag{5.24}$$

where $max\{sup(i_j)|\forall i_j \in X\}$ is the maximum (single) item support of all the items in X, and hence is called the **max_item_sup** of the itemset X. The *all_confidence* of X is the minimal confidence among the set of rules $i_j \rightarrow X - i_j$, where $i_j \in X$.

Given two itemsets A and B, the **cosine** measure of A and B is defined as

$$cosine(A, B) = \frac{P(A \cup B)}{\sqrt{P(A) \times P(B)}} = \frac{sup(A \cup B)}{\sqrt{sup(A) \times sup(B)}}. \tag{5.25}$$

The *cosine* measure can be viewed as a harmonized *lift* measure: the two formulae are similar except that for cosine, the *square root* is taken on the product of the probabilities of A and B. This is an important difference, however, because by taking the square root, the cosine value is only influenced by the supports of A, B, and $A \cup B$, and not by the total number of transactions.

"Are these two measures better than lift and χ^2 in assessing the correlation relationship?" To answer this question, we first look at some other typical data sets before returning to our running example.

Example 5.11 **Comparison of four correlation measures on typical data sets.** The correlation relationships between the purchases of two items, *milk* and *coffee*, can be examined by summarizing their purchase history in the form of Table 5.9, a 2×2 contingency table, where an entry such as mc represents the number of transactions containing both milk and coffee. For the derivation of *all_confidence*, we let itemset $X = \{m, c\}$ so that $sup(X) = mc$ in Equation (5.24).

Table 5.10 shows a set of transactional data sets with their corresponding contingency tables and values for each of the four correlation measures. From the table, we see that m and c are positively correlated in A_1 through A_4, independent in B_1, and negatively correlated in C_1 through C_3. All four measures are good indicators for the independent case, B_1. *Lift* and χ^2 are poor indicators of the other relationships, whereas *all_confidence* and *cosine* are good indicators. Another interesting fact is that between *all_confidence* and *cosine*, *cosine* is the better indicator when $\overline{m}c$ and $m\overline{c}$ are not balanced. This is because *cosine* considers the supports of both A and B, whereas *all_confidence* considers only the

Table 5.9 A 2×2 contingency table for two items.

	milk	$\overline{milk}$	Σ_{row}
coffee	mc	$\overline{m}c$	c
$\overline{coffee}$	$m\overline{c}$	$\overline{mc}$	$\overline{c}$
Σ_{col}	m	$\overline{m}$	Σ

Table 5.10 Comparison of four correlation measures using contingency tables for different data sets.

Data Set	*mc*	$\overline{m}c$	$m\overline{c}$	$\overline{mc}$	*all_conf.*	*cosine*	*lift*	χ^2
A_1	1,000	100	100	100,000	0.91	0.91	83.64	83,452.6
A_2	1,000	100	100	10,000	0.91	0.91	9.26	9,055.7
A_3	1,000	100	100	1,000	0.91	0.91	1.82	1,472.7
A_4	1,000	100	100	0	0.91	0.91	0.99	9.9
B_1	1,000	1,000	1,000	1,000	0.50	0.50	1.00	0.0
C_1	100	1,000	1,000	100,000	0.09	0.09	8.44	670.0
C_2	1,000	100	10,000	100,000	0.09	0.29	9.18	8,172.8
C_3	1	1	100	10,000	0.01	0.07	50.0	48.5

maximal support. Such a difference can be seen by comparing C_1 and C_2. C_1 should be more negatively correlated for *m* and *c* than C_2 because *mc* is the smallest among the three counts, *mc*, $\overline{m}c$, and $m\overline{c}$, in C_1. However, this can only be seen by checking the *cosine* measure because the *all_confidence* values are identical in C_1 and C_2.

"Why are lift and χ^2 *so poor at distinguishing correlation relationships in the above transactional data sets?"* To answer this, we have to consider the *null-transactions.* A **null-transaction** is a transaction that does not contain any of the itemsets being examined. In our example, $\overline{mc}$ represents the number of null-transactions. Lift and χ^2 have difficulty distinguishing correlation relationships because they are both strongly influenced by $\overline{mc}$. Typically, the number of null-transactions can outweigh the number of individual purchases, because many people may buy neither milk nor coffee. On the other hand, *all_confidence* and *cosine* values are good indicators of correlation because their definitions remove the influence of $\overline{mc}$ (i.e., they are not influenced by the number of null-transactions). ■

A measure is **null-invariant** if its value is free from the influence of null-transactions. Null-invariance is an important property for measuring correlations in large transaction databases. Among the four above measures, *all_confidence* and *cosine* are null-invariant measures.

"Are all_confidence and cosine the best at assessing correlation in all cases?" Let's examine the game-and-video examples again.

Example 5.12 **Comparison of four correlation meaures on game-and-video data.** We revisit Examples 5.4.1 to 5.4.2. Let D_1 be the original game (*g*) and video (*v*) data set from Table 5.7. We add two more data sets, D_0 and D_2, where D_0 has zero null-transactions, and D_2 has 10,000 null-transactions (instead of only 500 as in D_1). The values of all four correlation measures are shown in Table 5.11.

In Table 5.11, *gv*, $\overline{g}v$, and $g\overline{v}$ remain the same in D_0, D_1, and D_2. However, lift and χ^2 change from rather negative to rather positive correlations, whereas *all_confidence* and *cosine* have the nice null-invariant property, and their values remain the same in

Table 5.11 Comparison of the four correlation measures for game-and-video data sets.

Data Set	*gv*	$\overline{g}v$	$g\overline{v}$	$\overline{g}\overline{v}$	*all_conf.*	*cosine*	*lift*	χ^2
D_0	4,000	3,500	2,000	0	0.53	0.60	0.84	1,477.8
D_1	4,000	3,500	2,000	500	0.53	0.60	0.89	555.6
D_2	4,000	3,500	2,000	10,000	0.53	0.60	1.73	2,913.0

all cases. Unfortunately, we cannot precisely assert that a set of items are positively or negatively correlated when the value of *all_confidence* or *cosine* is around 0.5. Strictly based on whether the value is greater than 0.5, we will claim that g and v are positively correlated in D_1; however, it has been shown that they are negatively correlated by the lift and χ^2 analysis. Therefore, a good strategy is to perform the *all_confidence* or *cosine* analysis first, and when the result shows that they are *weakly* postively/negatively correlated, other analyses can be performed to assist in obtaining a more complete picture. ■

Besides null-invariance, another nice feature of the *all_confidence* measure is that it has the Apriori-like *downward closure* property. That is, if a pattern is *all-confident* (i.e., passing a minimal *all_confidence* threshold), so is every one of its subpatterns. In other words, if a pattern is not all-confident, further growth (or specialization) of this pattern will never satisfy the minimal *all_confidence* threshold. This is obvious since according to Equation (5.24), adding any item into an itemset X will never increase $sup(X)$, never decrease $max\_item\_sup(X)$, and thus never increase $all\_conf(X)$. This property makes Apriori-like pruning possible: we can prune any patterns that cannot satisfy the minimal *all_confidence* threshold during the growth of all-confident patterns in mining.

In summary, the use of only support and confidence measures to mine associations results in the generation of a large number of rules, most of which are uninteresting to the user. Instead, we can augment the support-confidence framework with a correlation measure, resulting in the mining of *correlation rules*. The added measure substantially reduces the number of rules generated, and leads to the discovery of more meaningful rules. However, there seems to be no single correlation measure that works well for all cases. Besides those introduced in this section, many other interestingness measures have been studied in the literature. Unfortunately, most such measures do not have the null-invariance property. Because large data sets typically have many null-transactions, it is important to consider the null-invariance property when selecting appropriate interestingness measures in the correlation analysis. Our analysis shows that both *all_confidence* and *cosine* are good correlation measures for large applications, although it is wise to augment them with additional tests, such as *lift*, when the test result is not conclusive.

5.5 Constraint-Based Association Mining

A data mining process may uncover thousands of rules from a given set of data, most of which end up being unrelated or uninteresting to the users. Often, users have a good sense of which "direction" of mining may lead to interesting patterns and the "form" of the patterns or rules they would like to find. Thus, a good heuristic is to have the users specify such intuition or expectations as *constraints* to confine the search space. This strategy is known as **constraint-based mining**. The constraints can include the following:

- **Knowledge type constraints:** These specify the type of knowledge to be mined, such as association or correlation.
- **Data constraints:** These specify the set of task-relevant data.
- **Dimension/level constraints:** These specify the desired dimensions (or attributes) of the data, or levels of the concept hierarchies, to be used in mining.
- **Interestingness constraints:** These specify thresholds on statistical measures of rule interestingness, such as support, confidence, and correlation.
- **Rule constraints:** These specify the form of rules to be mined. Such constraints may be expressed as metarules (rule templates), as the maximum or minimum number of predicates that can occur in the rule antecedent or consequent, or as relationships among attributes, attribute values, and/or aggregates.

The above constraints can be specified using a high-level declarative data mining query language and user interface.

The first four of the above types of constraints have already been addressed in earlier parts of this book and chapter. In this section, we discuss the use of *rule constraints* to focus the mining task. This form of constraint-based mining allows users to describe the rules that they would like to uncover, thereby making the data mining process more *effective*. In addition, a sophisticated mining query optimizer can be used to exploit the constraints specified by the user, thereby making the mining process more *efficient*. Constraint-based mining encourages interactive exploratory mining and analysis. In Section 5.5.1, you will study metarule-guided mining, where syntactic rule constraints are specified in the form of rule templates. Section 5.5.2 discusses the use of additional rule constraints, specifying set/subset relationships, constant initiation of variables, and aggregate functions. For ease of discussion, we assume that the user is searching for association rules. The procedures presented can easily be extended to the mining of correlation rules by adding a correlation measure of interestingness to the support-confidence framework, as described in the previous section.

5.5.1 Metarule-Guided Mining of Association Rules

"How are metarules useful?" Metarules allow users to specify the syntactic form of rules that they are interested in mining. The rule forms can be used as constraints to help improve the efficiency of the mining process. Metarules may be based on the analyst's experience, expectations, or intuition regarding the data or may be automatically generated based on the database schema.

Example 5.13 **Metarule-guided mining.** Suppose that as a market analyst for *AllElectronics*, you have access to the data describing customers (such as customer age, address, and credit rating) as well as the list of customer transactions. You are interested in finding associations between customer traits and the items that customers buy. However, rather than finding *all* of the association rules reflecting these relationships, you are particularly interested only in determining which pairs of customer traits promote the sale of office software. A metarule can be used to specify this information describing the form of rules you are interested in finding. An example of such a metarule is

$$P_1(X, Y) \wedge P_2(X, W) \Rightarrow buys(X, \text{"office software"}), \tag{5.26}$$

where P_1 and P_2 are **predicate variables** that are instantiated to attributes from the given database during the mining process, X is a variable representing a customer, and Y and W take on values of the attributes assigned to P_1 and P_2, respectively. Typically, a user will specify a list of attributes to be considered for instantiation with P_1 and P_2. Otherwise, a default set may be used.

In general, a metarule forms a hypothesis regarding the relationships that the user is interested in probing or confirming. The data mining system can then search for rules that match the given metarule. For instance, Rule (5.27) matches or **complies with** Metarule (5.26).

$$age(X, \text{"30...39"}) \wedge income(X, \text{"41K...60K"}) \Rightarrow buys(X, \text{"office software"}) \tag{5.27}$$

■

"How can metarules be used to guide the mining process?" Let's examine this problem closely. Suppose that we wish to mine interdimensional association rules, such as in the example above. A metarule is a rule template of the form

$$P_1 \wedge P_2 \wedge \cdots \wedge P_l \Rightarrow Q_1 \wedge Q_2 \wedge \cdots \wedge Q_r, \tag{5.28}$$

where P_i $(i = 1, \ldots, l)$ and Q_j $(j = 1, \ldots, r)$ are either instantiated predicates or predicate variables. Let the number of predicates in the metarule be $p = l + r$. In order to find interdimensional association rules satisfying the template,

- We need to find all frequent p-predicate sets, L_p.
- We must also have the support or count of the l-predicate subsets of L_p in order to compute the confidence of rules derived from L_p.

This is a typical case of mining multidimensional association rules, which was discussed in Section 5.3.2. By extending such methods using techniques described in the following section, we can derive efficient methods for metarule-guided mining.

5.5.2 Constraint Pushing: Mining Guided by Rule Constraints

Rule constraints specify expected set/subset relationships of the variables in the mined rules, constant initiation of variables, and aggregate functions. Users typically employ their knowledge of the application or data to specify rule constraints for the mining task. These rule constraints may be used together with, or as an alternative to, metarule-guided mining. In this section, we examine rule constraints as to how they can be used to make the mining process more efficient. Let's study an example where rule constraints are used to mine hybrid-dimensional association rules.

Example 5.14 **A closer look at mining guided by rule constraints.** Suppose that *AllElectronics* has a sales multidimensional database with the following interrelated relations:

- *sales(customer_name, item_name, TID)*
- *lives_in(customer_name, region, city)*
- *item(item_name, group, price)*
- *transaction(TID, day, month, year)*

where *lives_in, item,* and *transaction* are three dimension tables, linked to the fact table *sales* via three keys, *customer_name, item_name,* and *TID (transaction_id)*, respectively.

Our association mining query is to *"Find the sales of which cheap items (where the sum of the prices is less than $100) may promote the sales of which expensive items (where the minimum price is $500) of the same group for Chicago customers in 2004."* This can be expressed in the DMQL data mining query language as follows, where each line of the query has been enumerated to aid in our discussion:

(1) **mine associations as**
(2) $lives\_in(C, \_, \text{"Chicago"}) \wedge sales^{+}(C, ?\{I\}, \{S\}) \Rightarrow sales^{+}(C, ?\{J\}, \{T\})$
(3) **from** sales
(4) **where** S.year = 2004 **and** T.year = 2004 **and** I.group = J.group
(5) **group by** C, I.group
(6) **having** sum(I.price) < 100 **and** min(J.price) ≥ 500
(7) **with support threshold** = 1%
(8) **with confidence threshold** = 50%

Before we discuss the rule constraints, let's look at the above query. Line 1 is a knowledge type constraint, where association patterns are to be discovered. Line 2 specifies a metarule. This is an abbreviated form for the following metarule for hybrid-dimensional association rules (multidimensional association rules where the repeated predicate here is *sales*):

$$\begin{aligned} &lives\_in(C, \_, \text{"Chicago"}) \\ &\quad \wedge sales(C, ?I_1, S_1) \wedge \ldots \wedge sales(C, ?I_k, S_k) \wedge I = \{I_1, \ldots, I_k\} \wedge S = \{S_1, \ldots, S_k\} \\ &\quad \Rightarrow sales(C, ?J_1, T_1) \wedge \ldots \wedge sales(C, ?J_m, T_m) \wedge J = \{J_1, \ldots, J_m\} \wedge T = \{T_1, \ldots, T_m\} \end{aligned}$$

which means that one or more *sales* records in the form of "$sales(C, ?I_1, S_1) \wedge \ldots sales(C, ?I_k, S_k)$" will reside at the rule antecedent (left-hand side), and the question mark "?"

means that only *item_name*, $I_1, \ldots, I_k$ need be printed out. "$I = \{I_1, \ldots, I_k\}$" means that all the *I*s at the antecedent are taken from a set *I*, obtained from the SQL-like **where** clause of line 4. Similar notational conventions are used at the consequent (right-hand side).

The metarule may allow the generation of association rules like the following:

$$lives\_in(C, \_, \text{"Chicago"}) \wedge sales(C, \text{"Census\_CD"}, \_) \wedge$$
$$sales(C, \text{"MS/Office"}, \_) \Rightarrow sales(C, \text{"MS/SQLServer"}, \_) \;\; [1.5\%, 68\%], \quad (5.29)$$

which means that if a customer in Chicago bought "Census_CD" and "MS/Office," it is likely (with a probability of 68%) that the customer also bought "MS/SQLServer," and 1.5% of all of the customers bought all three.

Data constraints are specified in the "*lives_in(C, _, "Chicago")*" portion of the metarule (i.e., all the customers who live in Chicago) and in line 3, which specifies that only the fact table, *sales*, need be explicitly referenced. In such a multidimensional database, variable reference is simplified. For example, "*S.year = 2004*" is equivalent to the SQL statement "**from** *sales S, transaction T* **where** *S.TID = T.TID* **and** *T.year =2004.*" All three dimensions (*lives_in, item,* and *transaction*) are used. Level constraints are as follows: for *lives_in*, we consider just *customer_name* since *region* is not referenced and *city = "Chicago"* is only used in the selection; for *item*, we consider the levels *item_name* and *group* since they are used in the query; and for *transaction*, we are only concerned with *TID* since *day* and *month* are not referenced and *year* is used only in the selection.

Rule constraints include most portions of the **where** (line 4) and **having** (line 6) clauses, such as "*S.year = 2004,*" "*T.year = 2004,*" "*I.group = J.group,*" "*sum(I.price) ≤ 100,*" and "*min(J.price) ≥ 500.*" Finally, lines 7 and 8 specify two interestingness constraints (i.e., thresholds), namely, a minimum support of 1% and a minimum confidence of 50%. ■

Dimension/level constraints and interestingness constraints can be applied after mining to filter out discovered rules, although it is generally more efficient and less expensive to use them *during* mining, to help prune the search space. Dimension/level constraints were discussed in Section 5.3, and interestingness constraints have been discussed throughout this chapter. Let's focus now on rule constraints.

"How can we use rule constraints to prune the search space? More specifically, what kind of rule constraints can be 'pushed' deep into the mining process and still ensure the completeness of the answer returned for a mining query?"

Rule constraints can be classified into the following five categories with respect to frequent itemset mining: (1) *antimonotonic,* (2) *monotonic,* (3) *succinct,* (4) *convertible,* and (5) *inconvertible.* For each category, we will use an example to show its characteristics and explain how such kinds of constraints can be used in the mining process.

The first category of constraints is **antimonotonic**. Consider the rule constraint "$sum(I.price) \leq 100$" of Example 5.14. Suppose we are using the Apriori framework, which at each iteration *k* explores itemsets of size *k*. If the price summation of the items in an itemset is no less than 100, this itemset can be pruned from the search space, since adding more items into the set will only make it more expensive and thus will never satisfy the constraint. In other words, if an itemset does not satisfy this rule constraint, none of its supersets can satisfy the constraint. If a rule constraint obeys this property, it is **antimonotonic.** Pruning by antimonotonic constraints can be applied at each iteration of Apriori-style algorithms to help improve the efficiency of the overall mining process while guaranteeing completeness of the data mining task.

The Apriori property, which states that all nonempty subsets of a frequent itemset must also be frequent, is antimonotonic. If a given itemset does not satisfy minimum support, none of its supersets can. This property is used at each iteration of the Apriori algorithm to reduce the number of candidate itemsets examined, thereby reducing the search space for association rules.

Other examples of antimonotonic constraints include "$min(J.price) \geq 500$," "$count(I) \leq 10$," and so on. Any itemset that violates either of these constraints can be discarded since adding more items to such itemsets can never satisfy the constraints. Note that a constraint such as "$avg(I.price) \leq 100$" is not antimonotonic. For a given itemset that does not satisfy this constraint, a superset created by adding some (cheap) items may result in satisfying the constraint. Hence, pushing this constraint inside the mining process will not guarantee completeness of the data mining task. A list of SQL-primitives-based constraints is given in the first column of Table 5.12. The antimonotonicity of the constraints is indicated in the second column of the table. To simplify our discussion, only existence operators (e.g., $=$, $\in$, but not $\neq$, $\notin$) and comparison (or containment) operators with equality (e.g., $\leq$, $\subseteq$) are given.

The second category of constraints is **monotonic.** If the rule constraint in Example 5.14 were "$sum(I.price) \geq 100$," the constraint-based processing method would be quite different. If an itemset I satisfies the constraint, that is, the sum of the prices in the set is no less than 100, further addition of more items to I will increase cost and will always satisfy the constraint. Therefore, further testing of this constraint on itemset I becomes redundant. In other words, if an itemset satisfies this rule constraint, so do all of its supersets. If a rule constraint obeys this property, it is **monotonic.** Similar rule monotonic constraints include "$min(I.price) \leq 10$," "$count(I) \geq 10$," and so on. The monotonicity of the list of SQL-primitives-based constraints is indicated in the third column of Table 5.12.

The third category is **succinct constraints.** For this category of constraints, we can *enumerate all and only those sets that are guaranteed to satisfy the constraint.* That is, if a rule constraint is **succinct**, we can directly generate precisely the sets that satisfy it, even before support counting begins. This avoids the substantial overhead of the generate-and-test paradigm. In other words, such constraints are *precounting prunable.* For example, the constraint "$min(J.price) \geq 500$" in Example 5.14 is succinct, because we can explicitly and precisely generate all the sets of items satisfying the constraint. Specifically, such a set must contain at least one item whose price is no less than \$500. It is of the form $S_1 \cup S_2$, where $S_1 \neq \emptyset$ is a subset of the set of all those items with prices no less than \$500, and S_2, possibly empty, is a subset of the set of all those items with prices no greater than \$500. Because there is a precise "formula" for generating all of the sets satisfying a succinct constraint, there is no need to

Table 5.12 Characterization of commonly used SQL-based constraints.

Constraint	*Antimonotonic*	*Monotonic*	*Succinct*
$v \in S$	no	yes	yes
$S \supseteq V$	no	yes	yes
$S \subseteq V$	yes	no	yes
$min(S) \leq v$	no	yes	yes
$min(S) \geq v$	yes	no	yes
$max(S) \leq v$	yes	no	yes
$max(S) \geq v$	no	yes	yes
$count(S) \leq v$	yes	no	weakly
$count(S) \geq v$	no	yes	weakly
$sum(S) \leq v \ (\forall a \in S, a \geq 0)$	yes	no	no
$sum(S) \geq v \ (\forall a \in S, a \geq 0)$	no	yes	no
$range(S) \leq v$	yes	no	no
$range(S) \geq v$	no	yes	no
$avg(S)\ \theta\ v, \theta \in \{\leq, \geq\}$	convertible	convertible	no
$support(S) \geq \xi$	yes	no	no
$support(S) \leq \xi$	no	yes	no
$all\_confidence(S) \geq \xi$	yes	no	no
$all\_confidence(S) \leq \xi$	no	yes	no

iteratively check the rule constraint during the mining process. The succinctness of the list of SQL-primitives-based constraints is indicated in the fourth column of Table 5.12.[10]

The fourth category is **convertible constraints.** Some constraints belong to none of the above three categories. However, if the items in the itemset are arranged in a particular order, the constraint may become monotonic or antimonotonic with regard to the frequent itemset mining process. For example, the constraint "$avg(I.price) \leq 100$" is neither antimonotonic nor monotonic. However, if items in a transaction are added to an itemset in price-ascending order, the constraint becomes *antimonotonic,* because if an itemset I violates the constraint (i.e., with an average price greater than \$100), then further addition of more expensive items into the itemset will never make it satisfy the constraint. Similarly, if items in a transaction are added to an itemset in price-descending order, it becomes *monotonic,* because if the itemset satisfies the constraint (i.e., with an average price no

[10] For constraint $count(S) \leq v$ (and similarly for $count(S) \geq v$), we can have a member generation function based on a cardinality constraint (i.e., $\{X \mid X \subseteq Itemset \wedge |X| \leq v\}$). Member generation in this manner takes a different flavor and thus is called *weakly succinct.*

greater than \$100), then adding cheaper items into the current itemset will still make the average price no greater than \$100. Aside from "$avg(S) \leq v$," and "$avg(S) \geq v$," given in Table 5.12, there are many other convertible constraints, such as "$variance(S) \geq v$," "$standard\_deviation(S) \geq v$," and so on.

Note that the above discussion does not imply that every constraint is convertible. For example, "$sum(S)\,\theta v$," where $\theta \in \{\leq, \geq\}$ and each element in S could be of any real value, is not convertible. Therefore, there is yet a fifth category of constraints, called **inconvertible constraints.** The good news is that although there still exist some tough constraints that are not convertible, most simple SQL expressions with built-in SQL aggregates belong to one of the first four categories to which efficient constraint mining methods can be applied.

5.6 Summary

- The discovery of frequent patterns, association, and correlation relationships among huge amounts of data is useful in selective marketing, decision analysis, and business management. A popular area of application is **market basket analysis**, which studies the buying habits of customers by searching for sets of items that are frequently purchased together (or in sequence). **Association rule mining** consists of first finding **frequent itemsets** (set of items, such as A and B, satisfying a *minimum support threshold*, or percentage of the task-relevant tuples), from which **strong** association rules in the form of $A \Rightarrow B$ are generated. These rules also satisfy a *minimum confidence threshold* (a prespecified probability of satisfying B under the condition that A is satisfied). Associations can be further analyzed to uncover **correlation rules**, which convey statistical correlations between itemsets A and B.
- **Frequent pattern mining** can be categorized in many different ways according to various criteria, such as the following:

  1. Based on the **completeness** of patterns to be mined, categories of frequent pattern mining include mining the *complete set of frequent itemsets*, the *closed frequent itemsets*, the *maximal frequent itemsets*, and *constrained frequent itemsets*.
  2. Based on the **levels** and **dimensions** of data involved in the rule, categories can include the mining of *single-level association rules*, *multilevel association rules*, *single-dimensional association rules*, and *multidimensional association rules*.
  3. Based on the **types of values** handled in the rule, the categories can include mining *Boolean association rules* and *quantitative association rules*.
  4. Based on the **kinds of rules** to be mined, categories include mining *association rules* and *correlation rules*.
  5. Based on the **kinds of patterns** to be mined, frequent pattern mining can be classified into *frequent itemset mining*, *sequential pattern mining*, *structured pattern mining*, and so on. This chapter has focused on frequent itemset mining.

- Many efficient and scalable algorithms have been developed for **frequent itemset mining**, from which association and correlation rules can be derived. These algorithms can be classified into three categories: (1) *Apriori-like algorithms*, (2) *frequent-pattern growth*-based algorithms, such as FP-growth, and (3) *algorithms that use the vertical data format*.
- **The Apriori algorithm** is a seminal algorithm for mining frequent itemsets for Boolean association rules. It explores the level-wise mining Apriori property that *all nonempty subsets of a frequent itemset must also be frequent*. At the kth iteration (for $k \geq 2$), it forms frequent k-itemset candidates based on the frequent $(k-1)$-itemsets, and scans the database once to find the *complete* set of frequent k-itemsets, L_k.

  Variations involving hashing and transaction reduction can be used to make the procedure more efficient. Other variations include partitioning the data (mining on each partition and then combining the results) and sampling the data (mining on a subset of the data). These variations can reduce the number of data scans required to as little as two or one.
- **Frequent pattern growth (FP-growth)** is a method of mining frequent itemsets without candidate generation. It constructs a highly compact data structure (an *FP-tree*) to compress the original transaction database. Rather than employing the generate-and-test strategy of Apriori-like methods, it focuses on frequent pattern (fragment) growth, which avoids costly candidate generation, resulting in greater efficiency.
- **Mining frequent itemsets using vertical data format (ECLAT)** is a method that transforms a given data set of transactions in the horizontal data format of *TID-itemset* into the vertical data format of *item-TID_set*. It mines the transformed data set by TID_set intersections based on the Apriori property and additional optimization techniques, such as *diffset*.
- Methods for mining frequent itemsets can be extended for the mining of **closed frequent itemsets** (from which the set of frequent itemsets can easily be derived). These incorporate additional optimization techniques, such as *item merging, sub-itemset pruning*, and *item skipping*, as well as efficient *subset checking* of generated itemsets in a *pattern-tree*.
- Mining frequent itemsets and associations has been **extended in various ways** to include mining *multilevel association rules* and *multidimensional association rules*.
- **Multilevel association rules** can be mined using several strategies, based on how minimum support thresholds are defined at each level of abstraction, such as *uniform support, reduced support*, and *group-based support*. Redundant multilevel (descendant) association rules can be eliminated if their support and confidence are close to their expected values, based on their corresponding ancestor rules.
- Techniques for mining **multidimensional association rules** can be categorized according to their treatment of quantitative attributes. First, quantitative attributes may be *discretized statically*, based on predefined concept hierarchies. Data cubes are well suited to this approach, because both the data cube and quantitative attributes can

use concept hierarchies. Second, **quantitative association rules** can be mined where quantitative attributes are discretized dynamically based on binning and/or clustering, where "adjacent" association rules may be further combined by clustering to generate concise and meaningful rules.

- Not all strong association rules are interesting. It is more effective to mine items that are statistically correlated. Therefore, association rules should be augmented with a correlation measure to generate more meaningful **correlation rules**. There are several correlation measures to choose from, including **lift**, χ^2, **all_confidence**, and **cosine**. A measure is **null-invariant** if its value is free from the influence of **null-transactions** (i.e., *transactions that do not contain any of the itemsets being examined*). Because large databases typically have numerous null-transactions, a null-invariant correlation measure should be used, such as *all_confidence* or *cosine*. When interpreting correlation measure values, it is important to understand their implications and limitations.

- **Constraint-based rule mining** allows users to focus the search for rules by providing metarules (i.e., pattern templates) and additional mining constraints. Such mining is facilitated with the use of a declarative data mining query language and user interface, and poses great challenges for mining query optimization. Rule constraints can be classified into five categories: **antimonotonic, monotonic, succinct, convertible,** and **inconvertible.** Constraints belonging to the first four of these categories can be used during frequent itemset mining to guide the process, leading to more efficient and effective mining.

- **Association rules should not be used directly for prediction** without further analysis or domain knowledge. They do not necessarily indicate causality. They are, however, a helpful starting point for further exploration, making them a popular tool for understanding data. The application of frequent patterns to classification, cluster analysis, and other data mining tasks will be discussed in subsequent chapters.

Exercises

5.1 The Apriori algorithm uses *prior knowledge* of subset support properties.

(a) Prove that all nonempty subsets of a frequent itemset must also be frequent.

(b) Prove that the support of any nonempty subset s' of itemset s must be at least as great as the support of s.

(c) Given frequent itemset l and subset s of l, prove that the confidence of the rule "$s' \Rightarrow (l - s')$" cannot be more than the confidence of "$s \Rightarrow (l - s)$", where s' is a subset of s.

(d) A *partitioning* variation of Apriori subdivides the transactions of a database D into n nonoverlapping partitions. Prove that any itemset that is frequent in D must be frequent in at least one partition of D.

5.2 Section 5.2.2 describes a method for *generating association rules* from frequent itemsets. Propose a more efficient method. Explain why it is more efficient than the one proposed in Section 5.2.2. (*Hint:* Consider incorporating the properties of Exercise 5.1(b) and 5.1(c) into your design.)

5.3 A database has five transactions. Let $min\_sup = 60\%$ and $min\_conf = 80\%$.

TID	*items_bought*
T100	{M, O, N, K, E, Y}
T200	{D, O, N, K, E, Y }
T300	{M, A, K, E}
T400	{M, U, C, K, Y}
T500	{C, O, O, K, I ,E}

(a) Find all frequent itemsets using Apriori and FP-growth, respectively. Compare the efficiency of the two mining processes.

(b) List all of the *strong* association rules (with support *s* and confidence *c*) matching the following metarule, where *X* is a variable representing customers, and $item_i$ denotes variables representing items (e.g., "*A*", "*B*", etc.):

$$\forall x \in transaction,\ buys(X, item_1) \wedge buys(X, item_2) \Rightarrow buys(X, item_3) \quad [s, c]$$

5.4 (**Implementation project**) Implement three *frequent itemset mining* algorithms introduced in this chapter: (1) Apriori [AS94b], (2) FP-growth [HPY00], and (3) ECLAT [Zak00] (mining using vertical data format), using a programming language that you are familiar with, such as C++ or Java. Compare the performance of each algorithm with various kinds of large data sets. Write a report to analyze the situations (such as data size, data distribution, minimal support threshold setting, and pattern density) where one algorithm may perform better than the others, and state why.

5.5 A database has four transactions. Let $min\_sup = 60\%$ and $min\_conf = 80\%$.

cust_ID	*TID*	*items_bought* (in the form of *brand-item_category*)
01	T100	{King's-Crab, Sunset-Milk, Dairyland-Cheese, Best-Bread}
02	T200	{Best-Cheese, Dairyland-Milk, Goldenfarm-Apple, Tasty-Pie, Wonder-Bread}
01	T300	{Westcoast-Apple, Dairyland-Milk, Wonder-Bread, Tasty-Pie}
03	T400	{Wonder-Bread, Sunset-Milk, Dairyland-Cheese}

(a) At the granularity of *item_category* (e.g., $item_i$ could be "*Milk*"), for the following rule template,

$$\forall X \in transaction,\ buys(X, item_1) \wedge buys(X, item_2) \Rightarrow buys(X, item_3) \quad [s, c]$$

list the frequent k-itemset for the largest k, and *all* of the *strong* association rules (with their support s and confidence c) containing the frequent k-itemset for the largest k.

(b) At the granularity of *brand-item_category* (e.g., $item_i$ could be "*Sunset-Milk*"), for the following rule template

$$\forall X \in customer,\ buys(X, item_1) \wedge buys(X, item_2) \Rightarrow buys(X, item_3),$$

list the frequent k-itemset for the largest k (but do not print any rules).

5.6 Suppose that a large store has a transaction database that is *distributed* among four locations. Transactions in each component database have the same format, namely $T_j : \{i_1, \ldots, i_m\}$, where T_j is a transaction identifier, and i_k $(1 \leq k \leq m)$ is the identifier of an item purchased in the transaction. Propose an efficient algorithm to mine global association rules (without considering multilevel associations). You may present your algorithm in the form of an outline. Your algorithm should not require shipping all of the data to one site and should not cause excessive network communication overhead.

5.7 Suppose that frequent itemsets are saved for a large transaction database, *DB*. Discuss how to efficiently mine the (global) association rules under the same minimum support threshold if a set of new transactions, denoted as ΔDB, is (incrementally) added in?

5.8 [*Contributed by Tao Cheng*] Most frequent pattern mining algorithms consider only distinct items in a transaction. However, multiple occurrences of an item in the same shopping basket, such as four cakes and three jugs of milk, can be important in transaction data analysis. How can one mine frequent itemsets efficiently considering multiple occurrences of items? Propose modifications to the well-known algorithms, such as Apriori and FP-growth, to adapt to such a situation.

5.9 **(Implementation project)** Implement three *closed frequent itemset mining* methods (1) A-Close [PBTL99] (based on an extension of Apriori [AS94b]), (2) CLOSET+ [WHP03] (based on an extension of FP-growth [HPY00]), and (3) CHARM [ZH02] (based on an extension of ECLAT [Zak00]). Compare their performance with various kinds of large data sets. Write a report to answer the following questions:

(a) Why is mining the set of closed frequent itemsets often more desirable than mining the complete set of frequent itemsets (based on your experiments on the same data set as Exercise 5.4)?

(b) Analyze in which situations (such as data size, data distribution, minimal support threshold setting, and pattern density) and why one algorithm performs better than the others.

5.10 Suppose that a data relation describing students at *Big University* has been generalized to the generalized relation R in Table 5.13.

Let the concept hierarchies be as follows:

$$
\begin{aligned}
\textit{status}: \quad & \{\textit{freshman, sophomore, junior, senior}\} \in \textit{undergraduate}. \\
& \{\textit{M.Sc., M.A., Ph.D.}\} \in \textit{graduate}. \\
\textit{major}: \quad & \{\textit{physics, chemistry, math}\} \in \textit{science}. \\
& \{\textit{cs, engineering}\} \in \textit{appl\_sciences}. \\
& \{\textit{French, philosophy}\} \in \textit{arts}. \\
\textit{age}: \quad & \{16...20, 21...25\} \in \textit{young}. \\
& \{26...30, \textit{over\_30}\} \in \textit{old}. \\
\textit{nationality}: \quad & \{\textit{Asia, Europe, Latin\_America}\} \in \textit{foreign}. \\
& \{\textit{U.S.A., Canada}\} \in \textit{North\_America}.
\end{aligned}
$$

Table 5.13 Generalized relation for Exercise 5.9.

major	*status*	*age*	*nationality*	*gpa*	*count*
French	M.A	over_30	Canada	2.8_3.2	3
cs	junior	16...20	Europe	3.2_3.6	29
physics	M.S	26...30	Latin_America	3.2_3.6	18
engineering	Ph.D	26...30	Asia	3.6_4.0	78
philosophy	Ph.D	26...30	Europe	3.2_3.6	5
French	senior	16...20	Canada	3.2_3.6	40
chemistry	junior	21...25	USA	3.6_4.0	25
cs	senior	16...20	Canada	3.2_3.6	70
philosophy	M.S	over_30	Canada	3.6_4.0	15
French	junior	16...20	USA	2.8_3.2	8
philosophy	junior	26...30	Canada	2.8_3.2	9
philosophy	M.S	26...30	Asia	3.2_3.6	9
French	junior	16...20	Canada	3.2_3.6	52
math	senior	16...20	USA	3.6_4.0	32
cs	junior	16...20	Canada	3.2_3.6	76
philosophy	Ph.D	26...30	Canada	3.6_4.0	14
philosophy	senior	26...30	Canada	2.8_3.2	19
French	Ph.D	over_30	Canada	2.8_3.2	1
engineering	junior	21...25	Europe	3.2_3.6	71
math	Ph.D	26...30	Latin_America	3.2_3.6	7
chemistry	junior	16...20	USA	3.6_4.0	46
engineering	junior	21...25	Canada	3.2_3.6	96
French	M.S	over_30	Latin_America	3.2_3.6	4
philosophy	junior	21...25	USA	2.8_3.2	8
math	junior	16...20	Canada	3.6_4.0	59

Let the minimum support threshold be 20% and the minimum confidence threshold be 50% (at each of the levels).

(a) Draw the concept hierarchies for *status, major, age,* and *nationality*.

(b) Write a program to find the set of strong multilevel association rules in R using *uniform support* for all levels, for the following rule template,

$$\forall S \in R, P(S,x) \wedge Q(S,y) \Rightarrow gpa(S,z) \quad [s,c]$$

where $P, Q \in \{status, major, age, nationality\}$.

(c) Use the program to find the set of strong multilevel association rules in R using *level-cross filtering by single items*. In this strategy, an item at the ith level is examined if and only if its parent node at the $(i-1)$th level in the concept hierarchy is frequent. That is, if a node is frequent, its children will be examined; otherwise, its descendants are pruned from the search. Use a reduced support of 10% for the lowest abstraction level, for the preceding rule template.

5.11 Propose and outline a **level-shared mining** approach to mining multilevel association rules in which each item is encoded by its level position, and an initial scan of the database collects the count for each item *at each concept level*, identifying frequent and subfrequent items. Comment on the processing cost of mining multilevel associations with this method in comparison to mining single-level associations.

5.12 **(Implementation project)** Many techniques have been proposed to further improve the performance of frequent-itemset mining algorithms. Taking FP-tree-based frequent pattern-growth algorithms, such as FP-growth, as an example, implement one of the following optimization techniques, and compare the performance of your new implementation with the one that does not incorporate such optimization.

(a) The previously proposed frequent pattern mining with FP-tree generates conditional pattern bases using a bottom-up projection technique (i.e., project on the prefix path of an item p). However, one can develop a **top-down projection** technique (i.e., project on the suffix path of an item p in the generation of a conditional pattern-base). Design and implement such a top-down FP-tree mining method and compare your performance with the bottom-up projection method.

(b) Nodes and pointers are used uniformly in FP-tree in the design of the FP-growth algorithm. However, such a structure may consume a lot of space when the data are sparse. One possible alternative design is to explore **array- and pointer-based hybrid implementation,** where a node may store multiple items when it contains no splitting point to multiple subbranches. Develop such an implementation and compare it with the original one.

(c) It is time and space-consuming to generate numerous conditional pattern bases during pattern-growth mining. One interesting alternative is to **push right** the branches that have been mined for a particular item p, that is, to push them to the remaining branch(es) of the FP-tree. This is done so that fewer conditional pattern bases have to be generated and additional sharing can be explored when mining the remaining branches of the FP-tree. Design and implement such a method and conduct a performance study on it.

5.13 Give a short example to show that items in a strong association rule may actually be *negatively correlated.*

5.14 The following contingency table summarizes supermarket transaction data, where *hot dogs* refers to the transactions containing hot dogs, $\overline{hot\ dogs}$ refers to the transactions that do not contain hot dogs, *hamburgers* refers to the transactions containing hamburgers, and $\overline{hamburgers}$ refers to the transactions that do not contain hamburgers.

	hot dogs	$\overline{hot\ dogs}$	Σ_{row}
hamburgers	2,000	500	2,500
$\overline{hamburgers}$	1,000	1,500	2,500
Σ_{col}	3,000	2,000	5,000

(a) Suppose that the association rule "*hot dogs* ⇒ *hamburgers*" is mined. Given a minimum support threshold of 25% and a minimum confidence threshold of 50%, is this association rule strong?

(b) Based on the given data, is the purchase of *hot dogs* independent of the purchase of *hamburgers*? If not, what kind of *correlation* relationship exists between the two?

5.15 In multidimensional data analysis, it is interesting to extract pairs of *similar* cell characteristics associated with substantial changes in measure in a data cube, where cells are considered *similar* if they are related by roll-up (i.e., *ancestors*), drill-down (i.e., *descendants*), or one-dimensional mutation (i.e., *siblings*) operations. Such an analysis is called **cube gradient analysis.** Suppose the cube measure is *average.* A user poses a set of *probe cells* and would like to find their corresponding sets of *gradient cells,* each of which satisfies a certain gradient threshold. For example, find the set of corresponding gradient cells whose average sale price is greater than 20% of that of the given probe cells. Develop an algorithm than mines the set of constrained gradient cells efficiently in a large data cube.

5.16 Association rule mining often generates a large number of rules. Discuss effective methods that can be used to reduce the number of rules generated while still preserving most of the interesting rules.

5.17 Sequential patterns can be mined in methods similar to the mining of association rules. Design an efficient algorithm to mine **multilevel sequential patterns** from a transaction database. An example of such a pattern is the following: "*A customer who buys a PC will buy Microsoft software within three months,*" on which one may drill down to find a more refined version of the pattern, such as "*A customer who buys a Pentium PC will buy Microsoft Office within three months.*"

5.18 Prove that each entry in the following table correctly characterizes its corresponding rule constraint for frequent itemset mining.

	Rule constraint	Antimonotonic	Monotonic	Succinct
a)	$v \in S$	no	yes	yes
b)	$S \subseteq V$	yes	no	yes
c)	$min(S) \leq v$	no	yes	yes
d)	$range(S) \leq v$	yes	no	no

5.19 The price of each item in a store is nonnegative. The store manager is only interested in rules of the form: "*one free item may trigger \$200 total purchases in the same transaction.*" State how to mine such rules *efficiently*.

5.20 The price of each item in a store is nonnegative. For each of the following cases, identify the kinds of constraint they represent and briefly discuss how to mine such association rules *efficiently*.

(a) Containing at least one Nintendo game

(b) Containing items the sum of whose prices is less than \$150

(c) Containing one free item and other items the sum of whose prices is at least \$200

(d) Where the average price of all the items is between \$100 and \$500

Bibliographic Notes

Association rule mining was first proposed by Agrawal, Imielinski, and Swami [AIS93]. The Apriori algorithm discussed in Section 5.2.1 for frequent itemset mining was presented in Agrawal and Srikant [AS94b]. A variation of the algorithm using a similar pruning heuristic was developed independently by Mannila, Tiovonen, and Verkamo [MTV94]. A joint publication combining these works later appeared in Agrawal, Mannila, Srikant, Toivonen, and Verkamo [AMS+96]. A method for generating association rules from frequent itemsets is described in Agrawal and Srikant [AS94a].

References for the variations of Apriori described in Section 5.2.3 include the following. The use of hash tables to improve association mining efficiency was studied by Park, Chen, and Yu [PCY95a]. Transaction reduction techniques are described in Agrawal and Srikant [AS94b], Han and Fu [HF95], and Park, Chen, and Yu [PCY95a]. The partitioning technique was proposed by Savasere, Omiecinski, and Navathe [SON95]. The sampling approach is discussed in Toivonen [Toi96]. A dynamic itemset counting approach is given in Brin, Motwani, Ullman, and Tsur [BMUT97]. An efficient incremental updating of mined association rules was proposed by Cheung, Han, Ng, and Wong [CHNW96]. Parallel and distributed association data mining under the Apriori framework was studied by Park, Chen, and Yu [PCY95b], Agrawal and Shafer [AS96], and Cheung, Han, Ng, et al. [CHN+96]. Another parallel association mining method, which explores itemset clustering using a vertical database layout, was proposed in Zaki, Parthasarathy, Ogihara, and Li [ZPOL97].

Other scalable frequent itemset mining methods have been proposed as alternatives to the Apriori-based approach. FP-growth, a pattern-growth approach for mining frequent itemsets without candidate generation, was proposed by Han, Pei, and Yin [HPY00] (Section 5.2.4). An exploration of hyperstructure mining of frequent patterns, called H-Mine, was proposed by Pei, Han, Lu, Nishio, Tang, and Yang [PHMA+01]. OP, a method that integrates top-down and bottom-up traversal of FP-trees in pattern-growth mining, was proposed by Liu, Pan, Wang, and Han [LPWH02]. An array-based implementation of prefix-tree-structure for efficient pattern growth mining was proposed by Grahne and Zhu [GZ03b]. ECLAT, an approach for mining frequent itemsets by exploring the vertical data format, was proposed by Zaki [Zak00]. A depth-first generation of frequent itemsets was proposed by Agarwal, Aggarwal, and Prasad [AAP01].

The mining of frequent closed itemsets was proposed in Pasquier, Bastide, Taouil, and Lakhal [PBTL99], where an Apriori-based algorithm called A-Close for such mining was presented. CLOSET, an efficient closed itemset mining algorithm based on the frequent-pattern growth method, was proposed by Pei, Han, and Mao [PHM00], and further refined as CLOSET+ in Wang, Han, and Pei [WHP03]. FPClose, a prefix-tree-based algorithm for mining closed itemsets using the pattern-growth approach, was proposed by Grahne and Zhu [GZ03b]. An extension for mining closed frequent itemsets with the vertical data format, called CHARM, was proposed by Zaki and Hsiao [ZH02]. Mining max-patterns was first studied by Bayardo [Bay98]. Another efficient method for mining maximal frequent itemsets using vertical data format, called MAFIA, was proposed by Burdick, Calimlim, and Gehrke [BCG01]. AFOPT, a method that explores a *right push* operation on FP-trees during the mining process, was proposed by Liu, Lu, Lou, and Yu [LLLY03]. Pan, Cong, Tung, et al. [PCT+03] proposed CARPENTER, a method for finding closed patterns in long biological datasets, which integrates the advantages of row-enumeration and pattern-growth methods. A FIMI (Frequent Itemset Mining Implementation) workshop dedicated to the implementation methods of frequent itemset mining was reported by Goethals and Zaki [GZ03a].

Frequent itemset mining has various extensions, including sequential pattern mining (Agrawal and Srikant [AS95]), episodes mining (Mannila, Toivonen, and Verkamo [MTV97]), spatial association rule mining (Koperski and Han [KH95]), cyclic association rule mining (Ozden, Ramaswamy, and Silberschatz [ORS98]), negative association rule mining (Savasere, Omiecinski, and Navathe [SON98]), intertransaction association rule mining (Lu, Han, and Feng [LHF98]), and calendric market basket analysis (Ramaswamy, Mahajan, and Silberschatz [RMS98]). Multilevel association mining was studied in Han and Fu [HF95], and Srikant and Agrawal [SA95]. In Srikant and Agrawal [SA95], such mining was studied in the context of *generalized association rules*, and an R-interest measure was proposed for removing redundant rules. A non-grid-based technique for mining quantitative association rules, which uses a measure of partial completeness, was proposed by Srikant and Agrawal [SA96]. The ARCS system for mining quantitative association rules based on rule clustering was proposed by Lent, Swami, and Widom [LSW97]. Techniques for mining quantitative rules based on x-monotone and rectilinear regions were presented by Fukuda, Morimoto, Morishita, and Tokuyama [FMMT96], and Yoda, Fukuda, Morimoto, et al. [YFM+97]. Mining multidimensional association rules using static discretization of quantitative attributes and data cubes was studied by Kamber, Han, and Chiang [KHC97]. Mining (distance-based) association rules over interval data was proposed by Miller and Yang [MY97]. Mining quantitative association rules based on a statistical theory to present only those that deviate substantially from normal data was studied by Aumann and Lindell [AL99].

The problem of mining interesting rules has been studied by many researchers. The statistical independence of rules in data mining was studied by Piatetski-Shapiro [PS91b]. The interestingness problem of strong association rules is discussed in Chen, Han, and Yu [CHY96], Brin, Motwani, and Silverstein [BMS97], and Aggarwal and Yu [AY99], which cover several interestingness measures including *lift*. An efficient method for generalizing associations to correlations is given in Brin, Motwani, and Silverstein [BMS97]. Other alternatives to the support-confidence framework for assessing the interestingness of association rules are proposed in Brin, Motwani, Ullman, and Tsur [BMUT97] and Ahmed, El-Makky, and Taha [AEMT00]. A method for mining strong gradient relationships among itemsets was proposed by Imielinski, Khachiyan, and Abdulghani [IKA02]. Silverstein, Brin, Motwani, and Ullman [SBMU98] studied the problem of mining causal structures over transaction databases. Some comparative studies of different interestingness measures were done by Hilderman and Hamilton [HH01] and by Tan, Kumar, and Srivastava [TKS02]. The use of *all_confidence* as a correlation measure for generating interesting association rules was studied by Omiecinski [Omi03] and by Lee, Kim, Cai, and Han [LKCH03].

To reduce the huge set of frequent patterns generated in data mining, recent studies have been working on mining compressed sets of frequent patterns. Mining closed patterns can be viewed as lossless compression of frequent patterns. Lossy compression of patterns include maximal patterns by Bayardo [Bay98]), top-*k* patterns by Wang, Han, Lu, and Tsvetkov [WHLT05], and error-tolerant patterns by Yang, Fayyad, and Bradley [YFB01]. Afrati, Gionis, and Mannila [AGM04] proposed to use *K* itemsets to cover a collection of frequent itemsets. Yan, Cheng, Xin, and Han proposed a profile-based approach [YCXH05], and Xin, Han, Yan, and Cheng proposed a clustering-based approach [XHYC05] for frequent itemset compression.

The use of metarules as syntactic or semantic filters defining the form of interesting single-dimensional association rules was proposed in Klemettinen, Mannila, Ronkainen, et al. [KMR+94]. Metarule-guided mining, where the metarule consequent specifies an action (such as Bayesian clustering or plotting) to be applied to the data satisfying the metarule antecedent, was proposed in Shen, Ong, Mitbander, and Zaniolo [SOMZ96]. A relation-based approach to metarule-guided mining of association rules was studied in Fu and Han [FH95]. Methods for constraint-based association rule mining discussed in this chapter were studied by Ng, Lakshmanan, Han, and Pang [NLHP98], Lakshmanan, Ng, Han, and Pang [LNHP99], and Pei, Han, and Lakshmanan [PHL01]. An efficient method for mining constrained correlated sets was given in Grahne, Lakshmanan, and Wang [GLW00]. A dual mining approach was proposed by Bucila, Gehrke, Kifer, and White [BGKW03]. Other ideas involving the use of templates or predicate constraints in mining have been discussed in [AK93], [DT93], [HK91], [LHC97], [ST96], and [SVA97].

The association mining language presented in this chapter was based on an extension of the data mining query language, DMQL, proposed in Han, Fu, Wang, et al. [HFW+96], by incorporation of the spirit of the SQL-like operator for mining single-dimensional association rules proposed by Meo, Psaila, and Ceri [MPC96]. MSQL, a query language for mining flexible association rules, was proposed by Imielinski and Virmani [IV99]. *OLE DB for Data Mining (DM)*, a data mining query language that includes association mining modules, was proposed by Microsoft Corporation [Cor00].

6 Classification and Prediction

Databases are rich with hidden information that can be used for intelligent decision making. Classification and prediction are two forms of data analysis that can be used to extract models describing important data classes or to predict future data trends. Such analysis can help provide us with a better understanding of the data at large. Whereas *classification* predicts categorical (discrete, unordered) labels, *prediction* models continuous-valued functions. For example, we can build a classification model to categorize bank loan applications as either safe or risky, or a prediction model to predict the expenditures in dollars of potential customers on computer equipment given their income and occupation. Many classification and prediction methods have been proposed by researchers in machine learning, pattern recognition, and statistics. Most algorithms are memory resident, typically assuming a small data size. Recent data mining research has built on such work, developing scalable classification and prediction techniques capable of handling large disk-resident data.

In this chapter, you will learn basic techniques for data classification, such as how to build decision tree classifiers, Bayesian classifiers, Bayesian belief networks, and rule-based classifiers. Backpropagation (a neural network technique) is also discussed, in addition to a more recent approach to classification known as support vector machines. Classification based on association rule mining is explored. Other approaches to classification, such as *k*-nearest-neighbor classifiers, case-based reasoning, genetic algorithms, rough sets, and fuzzy logic techniques, are introduced. Methods for prediction, including linear regression, nonlinear regression, and other regression-based models, are briefly discussed. Where applicable, you will learn about extensions to these techniques for their application to classification and prediction in *large* databases. Classification and prediction have numerous applications, including fraud detection, target marketing, performance prediction, manufacturing, and medical diagnosis.

6.1 What Is Classification? What Is Prediction?

A bank loans officer needs analysis of her data in order to learn which loan applicants are "safe" and which are "risky" for the bank. A marketing manager at *AllElectronics* needs data analysis to help guess whether a customer with a given profile will buy a new computer. A medical researcher wants to analyze breast cancer data in order to predict which one of three specific treatments a patient should receive. In each of these examples, the data analysis task is **classification**, where a model or **classifier** is constructed to predict *categorical labels*, such as "safe" or "risky" for the loan application data; "yes" or "no" for the marketing data; or "treatment A," "treatment B," or "treatment C" for the medical data. These categories can be represented by discrete values, where the ordering among values has no meaning. For example, the values 1, 2, and 3 may be used to represent treatments A, B, and C, where there is no ordering implied among this group of treatment regimes.

Suppose that the marketing manager would like to predict how much a given customer will spend during a sale at *AllElectronics*. This data analysis task is an example of **numeric prediction**, where the model constructed predicts a *continuous-valued function*, or *ordered value*, as opposed to a categorical label. This model is a **predictor. Regression analysis** is a statistical methodology that is most often used for numeric prediction, hence the two terms are often used synonymously. We do not treat the two terms as synonyms, however, because several other methods can be used for numeric prediction, as we shall see later in this chapter. Classification and numeric prediction are the two major types of **prediction problems**. For simplicity, when there is no ambiguity, we will use the shortened term of *prediction* to refer to *numeric prediction*.

"How does classification work? **Data classification** is a two-step process, as shown for the loan application data of Figure 6.1. (The data are simplified for illustrative purposes. In reality, we may expect many more attributes to be considered.) In the first step, a classifier is built describing a predetermined set of data classes or concepts. This is the **learning step** (or training phase), where a classification algorithm builds the classifier by analyzing or "learning from" a **training set** made up of database tuples and their associated class labels. A tuple, $\boldsymbol{X}$, is represented by an n-dimensional **attribute vector,** $\boldsymbol{X} = (x_1, x_2, \ldots, x_n)$, depicting n measurements made on the tuple from n database attributes, respectively, $A_1, A_2, \ldots, A_n$.[1] Each tuple, $\boldsymbol{X}$, is assumed to belong to a predefined class as determined by another database attribute called the **class label attribute.** The class label attribute is discrete-valued and unordered. It is *categorical* in that each value serves as a category or class. The individual tuples making up the training set are referred to as **training tuples** and are selected from the database under analysis. In the context of classification, data tuples can be referred to as *samples, examples, instances, data points,* or *objects.*[2]

Because the class label of each training tuple *is provided*, this step is also known as **supervised learning** (i.e., the learning of the classifier is "supervised" in that it is told

[1]Each attribute represents a "feature" of $\boldsymbol{X}$. Hence, the pattern recognition literature uses the term *feature vector* rather than *attribute vector*. Since our discussion is from a database perspective, we propose the term "attribute vector." In our notation, any variable representing a vector is shown in bold italic font; measurements depicting the vector are shown in italic font, e.g., $\boldsymbol{X} = (x_1, x_2, x_3)$.

[2]In the machine learning literature, training tuples are commonly referred to as *training samples*. Throughout this text, we prefer to use the term *tuples* instead of *samples,* since we discuss the theme of classification from a database-oriented perspective.

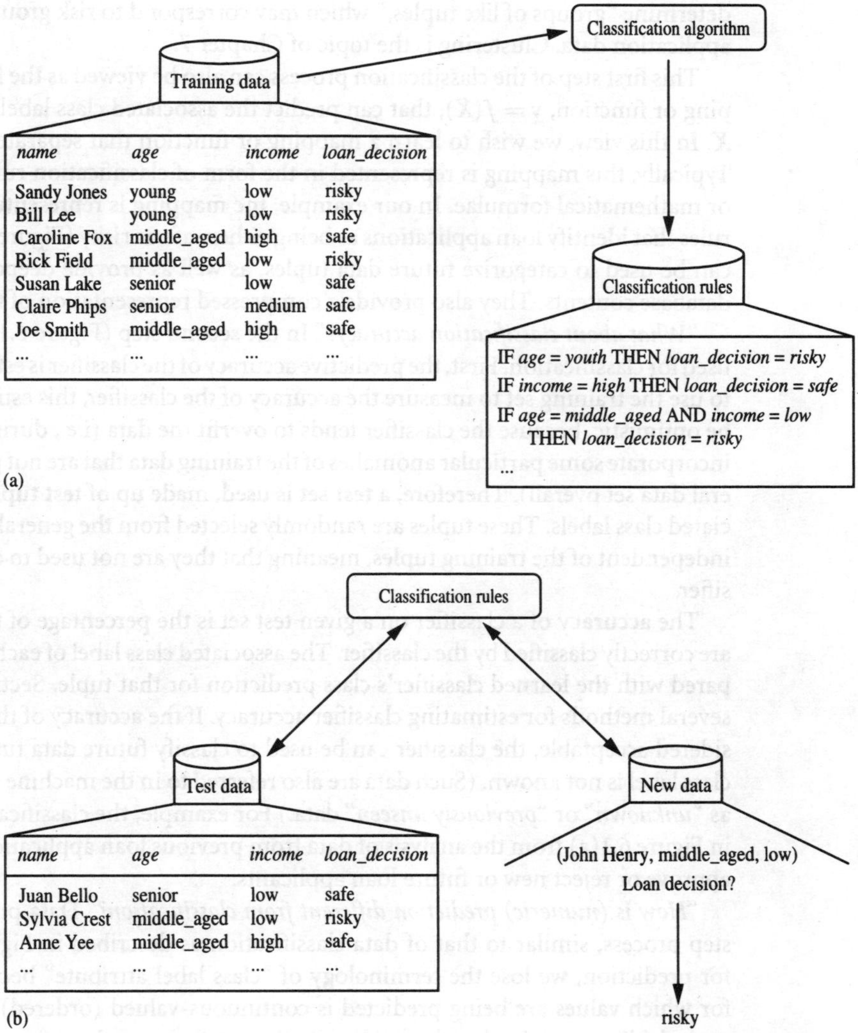

Figure 6.1 The data classification process: (a) *Learning*: Training data are analyzed by a classification algorithm. Here, the class label attribute is *loan_decision*, and the learned model or classifier is represented in the form of classification rules. (b) *Classification*: Test data are used to estimate the accuracy of the classification rules. If the accuracy is considered acceptable, the rules can be applied to the classification of new data tuples.

to which class each training tuple belongs). It contrasts with **unsupervised learning** (or **clustering**), in which the class label of each training tuple is not known, and the number or set of classes to be learned may not be known in advance. For example, if we did not have the *loan_decision* data available for the training set, we could use clustering to try to determine "groups of like tuples," which may correspond to risk groups within the loan application data. Clustering is the topic of Chapter 7.

This first step of the classification process can also be viewed as the learning of a mapping or function, $y = f(X)$, that can predict the associated class label y of a given tuple X. In this view, we wish to learn a mapping or function that separates the data classes. Typically, this mapping is represented in the form of classification rules, decision trees, or mathematical formulae. In our example, the mapping is represented as classification rules that identify loan applications as being either safe or risky (Figure 6.1(a)). The rules can be used to categorize future data tuples, as well as provide deeper insight into the database contents. They also provide a compressed representation of the data.

"What about classification accuracy?" In the second step (Figure 6.1(b)), the model is used for classification. First, the predictive accuracy of the classifier is estimated. If we were to use the training set to measure the accuracy of the classifier, this estimate would likely be optimistic, because the classifier tends to **overfit** the data (i.e., during learning it may incorporate some particular anomalies of the training data that are not present in the general data set overall). Therefore, a **test set** is used, made up of **test tuples** and their associated class labels. These tuples are randomly selected from the general data set. They are independent of the training tuples, meaning that they are not used to construct the classifier.

The **accuracy** of a classifier on a given test set is the percentage of test set tuples that are correctly classified by the classifier. The associated class label of each test tuple is compared with the learned classifier's class prediction for that tuple. Section 6.13 describes several methods for estimating classifier accuracy. If the accuracy of the classifier is considered acceptable, the classifier can be used to classify future data tuples for which the class label is not known. (Such data are also referred to in the machine learning literature as *"unknown"* or *"previously unseen"* data.) For example, the classification rules learned in Figure 6.1(a) from the analysis of data from previous loan applications can be used to approve or reject new or future loan applicants.

"How is (numeric) prediction different from classification?" Data prediction is a two-step process, similar to that of data classification as described in Figure 6.1. However, for prediction, we lose the terminology of "class label attribute" because the attribute for which values are being predicted is continuous-valued (ordered) rather than categorical (discrete-valued and unordered). The attribute can be referred to simply as the **predicted attribute.**[3] Suppose that, in our example, we instead wanted to predict the amount (in dollars) that would be "safe" for the bank to loan an applicant. The data mining task becomes prediction, rather than classification. We would replace the categorical attribute, *loan_decision*, with the continuous-valued *loan_amount* as the predicted attribute, and build a predictor for our task.

Note that prediction can also be viewed as a mapping or function, $y = f(X)$, where X is the input (e.g., a tuple describing a loan applicant), and the output y is a continuous or

[3]We could also use this term for classification, although for that task the term "class label attribute" is more descriptive.

ordered value (such as the predicted amount that the bank can safely loan the applicant); That is, we wish to learn a mapping or function that models the relationship between ***X*** and *y*.

Prediction and classification also differ in the methods that are used to build their respective models. As with classification, the training set used to build a predictor should not be used to assess its accuracy. An independent test set should be used instead. The accuracy of a predictor is estimated by computing an error based on the difference between the predicted value and the actual known value of *y* for each of the test tuples, ***X***. There are various predictor error measures (Section 6.12.2). General methods for error estimation are discussed in Section 6.13.

6.2 Issues Regarding Classification and Prediction

This section describes issues regarding preprocessing the data for classification and prediction. Criteria for the comparison and evaluation of classification methods are also described.

6.2.1 Preparing the Data for Classification and Prediction

The following preprocessing steps may be applied to the data to help improve the accuracy, efficiency, and scalability of the classification or prediction process.

- **Data cleaning:** This refers to the preprocessing of data in order to remove or reduce *noise* (by applying smoothing techniques, for example) and the treatment of *missing values* (e.g., by replacing a missing value with the most commonly occurring value for that attribute, or with the most probable value based on statistics). Although most classification algorithms have some mechanisms for handling noisy or missing data, this step can help reduce confusion during learning.
- **Relevance analysis:** Many of the attributes in the data may be *redundant*. **Correlation analysis** can be used to identify whether any two given attributes are statistically related. For example, a strong correlation between attributes A_1 and A_2 would suggest that one of the two could be removed from further analysis. A database may also contain *irrelevant* attributes. **Attribute subset selection**[4] can be used in these cases to find a reduced set of attributes such that the resulting probability distribution of the data classes is as close as possible to the original distribution obtained using all attributes. Hence, relevance analysis, in the form of correlation analysis and attribute subset selection, can be used to detect attributes that do not contribute to the classification or prediction task. Including such attributes may otherwise slow down, and possibly mislead, the learning step.

[4]In machine learning, this is known as *feature subset selection*.

Ideally, the time spent on relevance analysis, when added to the time spent on learning from the resulting "reduced" attribute (or feature) subset, should be less than the time that would have been spent on learning from the original set of attributes. Hence, such analysis can help improve classification efficiency and scalability.

- **Data transformation and reduction:** The data may be transformed by normalization, particularly when neural networks or methods involving distance measurements are used in the learning step. **Normalization** involves scaling all values for a given attribute so that they fall within a small specified range, such as -1.0 to 1.0, or 0.0 to 1.0. In methods that use distance measurements, for example, this would prevent attributes with initially large ranges (like, say, *income*) from outweighing attributes with initially smaller ranges (such as binary attributes).

  The data can also be transformed by *generalizing* it to higher-level concepts. Concept hierarchies may be used for this purpose. This is particularly useful for continuous-valued attributes. For example, numeric values for the attribute *income* can be generalized to discrete ranges, such as *low, medium*, and *high*. Similarly, categorical attributes, like *street*, can be generalized to higher-level concepts, like *city*. Because generalization compresses the original training data, fewer input/output operations may be involved during learning.

  Data can also be reduced by applying many other methods, ranging from wavelet transformation and principle components analysis to discretization techniques, such as binning, histogram analysis, and clustering.

Data cleaning, relevance analysis (in the form of correlation analysis and attribute subset selection), and data transformation are described in greater detail in Chapter 2 of this book.

6.2.2 Comparing Classification and Prediction Methods

Classification and prediction methods can be compared and evaluated according to the following criteria:

- **Accuracy: The accuracy of a classifier** refers to the ability of a given classifier to correctly predict the class label of new or previously unseen data (i.e., tuples without class label information). Similarly, the **accuracy of a predictor** refers to how well a given predictor can guess the value of the predicted attribute for new or previously unseen data. Accuracy measures are given in Section 6.12. Accuracy can be estimated using one or more test sets that are independent of the training set. Estimation techniques, such as cross-validation and bootstrapping, are described in Section 6.13. Strategies for improving the accuracy of a model are given in Section 6.14. Because the accuracy computed is only an estimate of how well the classifier or predictor will do on new data tuples, confidence limits can be computed to help gauge this estimate. This is discussed in Section 6.15.

- **Speed:** This refers to the computational costs involved in generating and using the given classifier or predictor.
- **Robustness:** This is the ability of the classifier or predictor to make correct predictions given noisy data or data with missing values.
- **Scalability:** This refers to the ability to construct the classifier or predictor efficiently given large amounts of data.
- **Interpretability:** This refers to the level of understanding and insight that is provided by the classifier or predictor. Interpretability is subjective and therefore more difficult to assess. We discuss some work in this area, such as the extraction of classification rules from a "black box" neural network classifier called backpropagation (Section 6.6.4).

These issues are discussed throughout the chapter with respect to the various classification and prediction methods presented. Recent data mining research has contributed to the development of scalable algorithms for classification and prediction. Additional contributions include the exploration of mined "associations" between attributes and their use for effective classification. Model selection is discussed in Section 6.15.

6.3 Classification by Decision Tree Induction

Decision tree induction is the learning of decision trees from class-labeled training tuples. A **decision tree** is a flowchart-like tree structure, where each **internal node** (nonleaf node) denotes a test on an attribute, each **branch** represents an outcome of the test, and each **leaf node** (or *terminal node*) holds a class label. The topmost node in a tree is the **root** node.

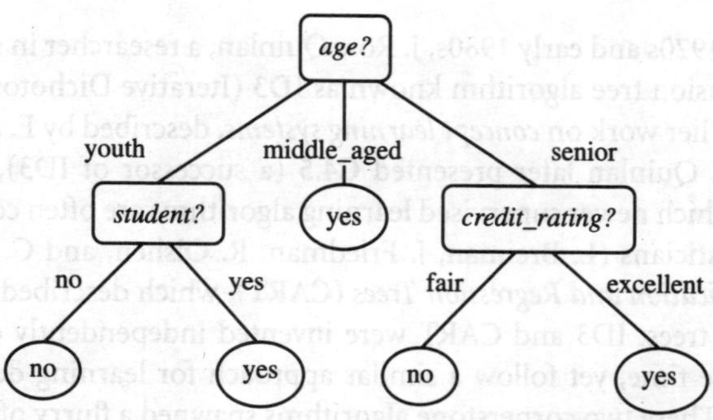

Figure 6.2 A decision tree for the concept *buys_computer*, indicating whether a customer at *AllElectronics* is likely to purchase a computer. Each internal (nonleaf) node represents a test on an attribute. Each leaf node represents a class (either *buys_computer* = *yes* or *buys_computer* = *no*).

A typical decision tree is shown in Figure 6.2. It represents the concept *buys_computer*, that is, it predicts whether a customer at *AllElectronics* is likely to purchase a computer. Internal nodes are denoted by rectangles, and leaf nodes are denoted by ovals. Some decision tree algorithms produce only *binary* trees (where each internal node branches to exactly two other nodes), whereas others can produce nonbinary trees.

"How are decision trees used for classification?" Given a tuple, ***X***, for which the associated class label is unknown, the attribute values of the tuple are tested against the decision tree. A path is traced from the root to a leaf node, which holds the class prediction for that tuple. Decision trees can easily be converted to classification rules.

"Why are decision tree classifiers so popular?" The construction of decision tree classifiers does not require any domain knowledge or parameter setting, and therefore is appropriate for exploratory knowledge discovery. Decision trees can handle high dimensional data. Their representation of acquired knowledge in tree form is intuitive and generally easy to assimilate by humans. The learning and classification steps of decision tree induction are simple and fast. In general, decision tree classifiers have good accuracy. However, successful use may depend on the data at hand. Decision tree induction algorithms have been used for classification in many application areas, such as medicine, manufacturing and production, financial analysis, astronomy, and molecular biology. Decision trees are the basis of several commercial rule induction systems.

In Section 6.3.1, we describe a basic algorithm for learning decision trees. During tree construction, *attribute selection measures* are used to select the attribute that best partitions the tuples into distinct classes. Popular measures of attribute selection are given in Section 6.3.2. When decision trees are built, many of the branches may reflect noise or outliers in the training data. *Tree pruning* attempts to identify and remove such branches, with the goal of improving classification accuracy on unseen data. Tree pruning is described in Section 6.3.3. Scalability issues for the induction of decision trees from large databases are discussed in Section 6.3.4.

6.3.1 Decision Tree Induction

During the late 1970s and early 1980s, J. Ross Quinlan, a researcher in machine learning, developed a decision tree algorithm known as **ID3** (Iterative Dichotomiser). This work expanded on earlier work on *concept learning systems*, described by E. B. Hunt, J. Marin, and P. T. Stone. Quinlan later presented **C4.5** (a successor of ID3), which became a benchmark to which newer supervised learning algorithms are often compared. In 1984, a group of statisticians (L. Breiman, J. Friedman, R. Olshen, and C. Stone) published the book *Classification and Regression Trees* (**CART**), which described the generation of binary decision trees. ID3 and CART were invented independently of one another at around the same time, yet follow a similar approach for learning decision trees from training tuples. These two cornerstone algorithms spawned a flurry of work on decision tree induction.

ID3, C4.5, and CART adopt a greedy (i.e., nonbacktracking) approach in which decision trees are constructed in a top-down recursive divide-and-conquer manner. Most algorithms for decision tree induction also follow such a top-down approach, which

Algorithm: Generate_decision_tree. Generate a decision tree from the training tuples of data partition *D*.

Input:

- Data partition, *D*, which is a set of training tuples and their associated class labels;
- *attribute_list*, the set of candidate attributes;
- *Attribute_selection_method*, a procedure to determine the splitting criterion that "best" partitions the data tuples into individual classes. This criterion consists of a *splitting_attribute* and, possibly, either a *split point* or *splitting subset*.

Output: A decision tree.

Method:

```
(1)  create a node N;
(2)  if tuples in D are all of the same class, C then
(3)      return N as a leaf node labeled with the class C;
(4)  if attribute_list is empty then
(5)      return N as a leaf node labeled with the majority class in D; // majority voting
(6)  apply Attribute_selection_method(D, attribute_list) to find the "best" splitting_criterion;
(7)  label node N with splitting_criterion;
(8)  if splitting_attribute is discrete-valued and
         multiway splits allowed then // not restricted to binary trees
(9)      attribute_list ← attribute_list − splitting_attribute; // remove splitting_attribute
(10) for each outcome j of splitting_criterion
     // partition the tuples and grow subtrees for each partition
(11)     let D_j be the set of data tuples in D satisfying outcome j; // a partition
(12)     if D_j is empty then
(13)         attach a leaf labeled with the majority class in D to node N;
(14)     else attach the node returned by Generate_decision_tree(D_j, attribute_list) to node N;
     endfor
(15) return N;
```

Figure 6.3 Basic algorithm for inducing a decision tree from training tuples.

starts with a training set of tuples and their associated class labels. The training set is recursively partitioned into smaller subsets as the tree is being built. A basic decision tree algorithm is summarized in Figure 6.3. At first glance, the algorithm may appear long, but fear not! It is quite straightforward. The strategy is as follows.

- The algorithm is called with three parameters: *D*, *attribute_list*, and *Attribute_selection_method*. We refer to *D* as a data partition. Initially, it is the complete set of training tuples and their associated class labels. The parameter *attribute_list* is a list of attributes describing the tuples. *Attribute_selection_method* specifies a heuristic procedure for selecting the attribute that "best" discriminates the given tuples according to class. This procedure employs an attribute selection measure, such as information gain or the gini index. Whether the tree is strictly binary is generally driven by the attribute selection measure. Some attribute selection measures, such as the gini index, enforce the resulting tree to be binary. Others, like information gain, do not, therein allowing multiway splits (i.e., two or more branches to be grown from a node).

- The tree starts as a single node, N, representing the training tuples in D (step 1).[5]
- If the tuples in D are all of the same class, then node N becomes a leaf and is labeled with that class (steps 2 and 3). Note that steps 4 and 5 are terminating conditions. All of the terminating conditions are explained at the end of the algorithm.
- Otherwise, the algorithm calls *Attribute_selection_method* to determine the **splitting criterion.** The splitting criterion tells us which attribute to test at node N by determining the "best" way to separate or partition the tuples in D into individual classes (step 6). The splitting criterion also tells us which branches to grow from node N with respect to the outcomes of the chosen test. More specifically, the splitting criterion indicates the **splitting attribute** and may also indicate either a **split-point** or a **splitting subset.** The splitting criterion is determined so that, ideally, the resulting partitions at each branch are as "pure" as possible. A partition is **pure** if all of the tuples in it belong to the same class. In other words, if we were to split up the tuples in D according to the mutually exclusive outcomes of the splitting criterion, we hope for the resulting partitions to be as pure as possible.
- The node N is labeled with the splitting criterion, which serves as a test at the node (step 7). A branch is grown from node N for each of the outcomes of the splitting criterion. The tuples in D are partitioned accordingly (steps 10 to 11). There are three possible scenarios, as illustrated in Figure 6.4. Let A be the splitting attribute. A has v distinct values, $\{a_1, a_2, \ldots, a_v\}$, based on the training data.

1. *A is discrete-valued*: In this case, the outcomes of the test at node N correspond directly to the known values of A. A branch is created for each known value, a_j, of A and labeled with that value (Figure 6.4(a)). Partition D_j is the subset of class-labeled tuples in D having value a_j of A. Because all of the tuples in a given partition have the same value for A, then A need not be considered in any future partitioning of the tuples. Therefore, it is removed from *attribute_list* (steps 8 to 9).
2. *A is continuous-valued*: In this case, the test at node N has two possible outcomes, corresponding to the conditions $A \leq$ *split_point* and $A >$ *split_point*, respectively,

[5] The partition of class-labeled training tuples at node N is the set of tuples that follow a path from the root of the tree to node N when being processed by the tree. This set is sometimes referred to in the literature as the *family* of tuples at node N. We have referred to this set as the "tuples represented at node N," "the tuples that reach node N," or simply "the tuples at node N." Rather than storing the actual tuples at a node, most implementations store pointers to these tuples.

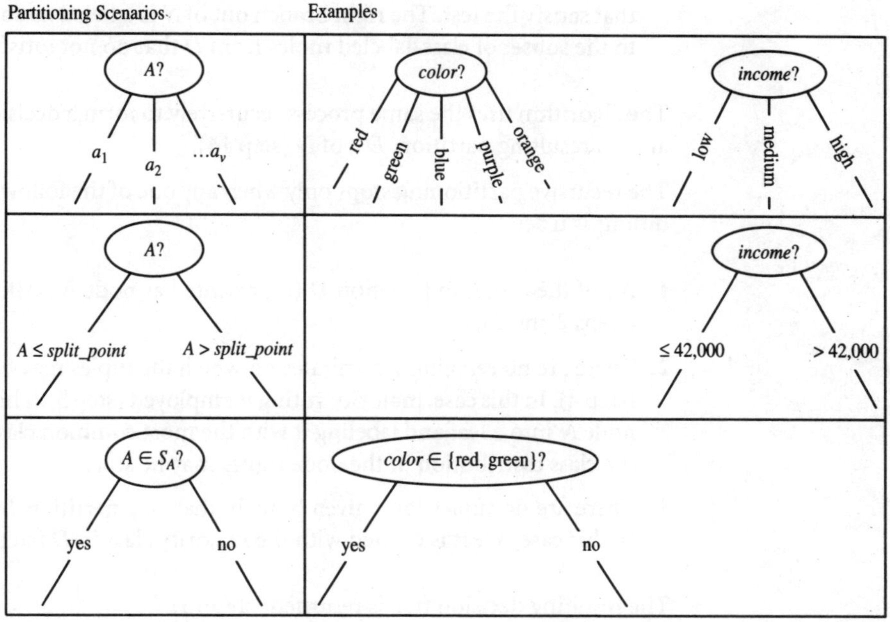

Figure 6.4 Three possibilities for partitioning tuples based on the splitting criterion, shown with examples. Let A be the splitting attribute. (a) If A is discrete-valued, then one branch is grown for each known value of A. (b) If A is continuous-valued, then two branches are grown, corresponding to $A \leq split\_point$ and $A > split\_point$. (c) If A is discrete-valued and a binary tree must be produced, then the test is of the form $A \in S_A$, where S_A is the splitting subset for A.

where *split_point* is the split-point returned by *Attribute_selection_method* as part of the splitting criterion. (In practice, the split-point, a, is often taken as the midpoint of two known adjacent values of A and therefore may not actually be a pre-existing value of A from the training data.) Two branches are grown from N and labeled according to the above outcomes (Figure 6.4(b)). The tuples are partitioned such that D_1 holds the subset of class-labeled tuples in D for which $A \leq split\_point$, while D_2 holds the rest.

3. *A is discrete-valued* and a *binary tree* must be produced (as dictated by the attribute selection measure or algorithm being used): The test at node N is of the form "$A \in S_A$?". S_A is the splitting subset for A, returned by *Attribute_selection_method* as part of the splitting criterion. It is a subset of the known values of A. If a given tuple has value a_j of A and if $a_j \in S_A$, then the test at node N is satisfied. Two branches are grown from N (Figure 6.4(c)). By convention, the left branch out of N is labeled *yes* so that D_1 corresponds to the subset of class-labeled tuples in D

that satisfy the test. The right branch out of N is labeled *no* so that D_2 corresponds to the subset of class-labeled tuples from D that do not satisfy the test.

- The algorithm uses the same process recursively to form a decision tree for the tuples at each resulting partition, D_j, of D (step 14).
- The recursive partitioning stops only when any one of the following terminating conditions is true:

  1. All of the tuples in partition D (represented at node N) belong to the same class (steps 2 and 3), or
  2. There are no remaining attributes on which the tuples may be further partitioned (step 4). In this case, **majority voting** is employed (step 5). This involves converting node N into a leaf and labeling it with the most common class in D. Alternatively, the class distribution of the node tuples may be stored.
  3. There are no tuples for a given branch, that is, a partition D_j is empty (step 12). In this case, a leaf is created with the majority class in D (step 13).

- The resulting decision tree is returned (step 15).

The computational complexity of the algorithm given training set D is $O(n \times |D| \times log(|D|))$, where n is the number of attributes describing the tuples in D and $|D|$ is the number of training tuples in D. This means that the computational cost of growing a tree grows at most $n \times |D| \times log(|D|)$ with $|D|$ tuples. The proof is left as an exercise for the reader.

Incremental versions of decision tree induction have also been proposed. When given new training data, these restructure the decision tree acquired from learning on previous training data, rather than relearning a new tree from scratch.

Differences in decision tree algorithms include how the attributes are selected in creating the tree (Section 6.3.2) and the mechanisms used for pruning (Section 6.3.3). The basic algorithm described above requires one pass over the training tuples in D for each level of the tree. This can lead to long training times and lack of available memory when dealing with large databases. Improvements regarding the scalability of decision tree induction are discussed in Section 6.3.4. A discussion of strategies for extracting rules from decision trees is given in Section 6.5.2 regarding rule-based classification.

6.3.2 Attribute Selection Measures

An **attribute selection measure** is a heuristic for selecting the splitting criterion that "best" separates a given data partition, D, of class-labeled training tuples into individual classes. If we were to split D into smaller partitions according to the outcomes of the splitting criterion, ideally each partition would be pure (i.e., all of the tuples that fall into a given partition would belong to the same class). Conceptually, the "best" splitting criterion is the one that most closely results in such a scenario. Attribute selection measures are also known as **splitting rules** because they determine how the tuples at a given node are to be split. The attribute selection measure provides a ranking for each attribute describing the given training tuples. The attribute having the best score for the measure[6] is chosen as the *splitting attribute* for the given tuples. If the splitting attribute is continuous-valued or if we are restricted to binary trees then, respectively, either a *split point* or a *splitting subset* must also be determined as part of the splitting criterion. The tree node created for partition D is labeled with the splitting criterion, branches are grown for each outcome of the criterion, and the tuples are partitioned accordingly. This section describes three popular attribute selection measures—*information gain, gain ratio,* and *gini index*.

The notation used herein is as follows. Let D, the data partition, be a training set of class-labeled tuples. Suppose the class label attribute has m distinct values defining m distinct classes, C_i (for $i = 1, \ldots, m$). Let $C_{i,D}$ be the set of tuples of class C_i in D. Let $|D|$ and $|C_{i,D}|$ denote the number of tuples in D and $C_{i,D}$, respectively.

Information gain

ID3 uses **information gain** as its attribute selection measure. This measure is based on pioneering work by Claude Shannon on information theory, which studied the value or "information content" of messages. Let node N represent or hold the tuples of partition D. The attribute with the highest information gain is chosen as the splitting attribute for node N. This attribute minimizes the information needed to classify the tuples in the resulting partitions and reflects the least randomness or "impurity" in these partitions. Such an approach minimizes the expected number of tests needed to classify a given tuple and guarantees that a simple (but not necessarily the simplest) tree is found.

The expected information needed to classify a tuple in D is given by

$$Info(D) = -\sum_{i=1}^{m} p_i \log_2(p_i), \tag{6.1}$$

where p_i is the probability that an arbitrary tuple in D belongs to class C_i and is estimated by $|C_{i,D}|/|D|$. A log function to the base 2 is used, because the information is encoded in bits. *Info(D)* is just the average amount of information needed to identify the class label of a tuple in D. Note that, at this point, the information we have is based solely on the proportions of tuples of each class. *Info(D)* is also known as the **entropy** of D.

Now, suppose we were to partition the tuples in D on some attribute A having v distinct values, $\{a_1, a_2, \ldots, a_v\}$, as observed from the training data. If A is discrete-valued, these values correspond directly to the v outcomes of a test on A. Attribute A can be used to split D into v partitions or subsets, $\{D_1, D_2, \ldots, D_v\}$, where D_j contains those tuples in D that have outcome a_j of A. These partitions would correspond to the branches grown from node N. Ideally, we would like this partitioning to produce an exact classification

[6] Depending on the measure, either the highest or lowest score is chosen as the best (i.e., some measures strive to maximize while others strive to minimize).

of the tuples. That is, we would like for each partition to be pure. However, it is quite likely that the partitions will be impure (e.g., where a partition may contain a collection of tuples from different classes rather than from a single class). How much more information would we still need (after the partitioning) in order to arrive at an exact classification? This amount is measured by

$$Info_A(D) = \sum_{j=1}^{v} \frac{|D_j|}{|D|} \times Info(D_j). \tag{6.2}$$

The term $\frac{|D_j|}{|D|}$ acts as the weight of the jth partition. $Info_A(D)$ is the expected information required to classify a tuple from D based on the partitioning by A. The smaller the expected information (still) required, the greater the purity of the partitions.

Information gain is defined as the difference between the original information requirement (i.e., based on just the proportion of classes) and the new requirement (i.e., obtained after partitioning on A). That is,

$$Gain(A) = Info(D) - Info_A(D). \tag{6.3}$$

In other words, *Gain(A)* tells us how much would be gained by branching on A. It is the expected reduction in the information requirement caused by knowing the value of A. The attribute A with the highest information gain, ($Gain(A)$), is chosen as the splitting attribute at node N. This is equivalent to saying that we want to partition on the attribute A that would do the "best classification," so that the amount of information still required to finish classifying the tuples is minimal (i.e., minimum $Info_A(D)$).

Example 6.1 **Induction of a decision tree using information gain.** Table 6.1 presents a training set, D, of class-labeled tuples randomly selected from the *AllElectronics* customer database. (The data are adapted from [Qui86]. In this example, each attribute is discrete-valued. Continuous-valued attributes have been generalized.) The class label attribute, *buys_computer*, has two distinct values (namely, {*yes*, *no*}); therefore, there are two distinct classes (that is, $m = 2$). Let class C_1 correspond to *yes* and class C_2 correspond to *no*. There are nine tuples of class *yes* and five tuples of class *no*. A (root) node N is created for the tuples in D. To find the splitting criterion for these tuples, we must compute the information gain of each attribute. We first use Equation (6.1) to compute the expected information needed to classify a tuple in D:

$$Info(D) = -\frac{9}{14}\log_2\left(\frac{9}{14}\right) - \frac{5}{14}\log_2\left(\frac{5}{14}\right) = 0.940 \text{ bits.}$$

Next, we need to compute the expected information requirement for each attribute. Let's start with the attribute *age*. We need to look at the distribution of *yes* and *no* tuples for each category of *age*. For the *age* category *youth*, there are two *yes* tuples and three *no* tuples. For the category *middle_aged*, there are four *yes* tuples and zero *no* tuples. For the category *senior*, there are three *yes* tuples and two *no* tuples. Using Equation (6.2),

Table 6.1 Class-labeled training tuples from the *AllElectronics* customer database.

RID	*age*	*income*	*student*	*credit_rating*	*Class: buys_computer*
1	youth	high	no	fair	no
2	youth	high	no	excellent	no
3	middle_aged	high	no	fair	yes
4	senior	medium	no	fair	yes
5	senior	low	yes	fair	yes
6	senior	low	yes	excellent	no
7	middle_aged	low	yes	excellent	yes
8	youth	medium	no	fair	no
9	youth	low	yes	fair	yes
10	senior	medium	yes	fair	yes
11	youth	medium	yes	excellent	yes
12	middle_aged	medium	no	excellent	yes
13	middle_aged	high	yes	fair	yes
14	senior	medium	no	excellent	no

the expected information needed to classify a tuple in D if the tuples are partitioned according to *age* is

$$\begin{aligned}Info_{age}(D) &= \frac{5}{14} \times (-\frac{2}{5}\log_2\frac{2}{5} - \frac{3}{5}\log_2\frac{3}{5}) \\ &+ \frac{4}{14} \times (-\frac{4}{4}\log_2\frac{4}{4} - \frac{0}{4}\log_2\frac{0}{4}) \\ &+ \frac{5}{14} \times (-\frac{3}{5}\log_2\frac{3}{5} - \frac{2}{5}\log_2\frac{2}{5}) \\ &= 0.694 \text{ bits.}\end{aligned}$$

Hence, the gain in information from such a partitioning would be

$$Gain(age) = Info(D) - Info_{age}(D) = 0.940 - 0.694 = 0.246 \text{ bits.}$$

Similarly, we can compute $Gain(income) = 0.029$ bits, $Gain(student) = 0.151$ bits, and $Gain(credit\_rating) = 0.048$ bits. Because *age* has the highest information gain among the attributes, it is selected as the splitting attribute. Node N is labeled with *age*, and branches are grown for each of the attribute's values. The tuples are then partitioned accordingly, as shown in Figure 6.5. Notice that the tuples falling into the partition for *age* = *middle_aged* all belong to the same class. Because they all belong to class *"yes,"* a leaf should therefore be created at the end of this branch and labeled with *"yes."* The final decision tree returned by the algorithm is shown in Figure 6.2. ■

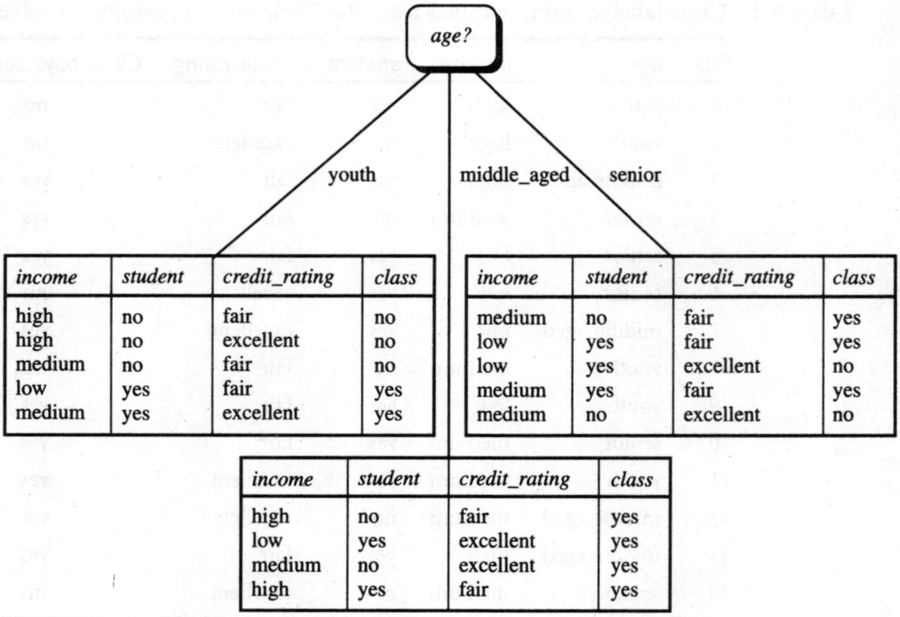

income	*student*	*credit_rating*	*class*
high	no	fair	no
high	no	excellent	no
medium	no	fair	no
low	yes	fair	yes
medium	yes	excellent	yes

income	*student*	*credit_rating*	*class*
high	no	fair	yes
low	yes	excellent	yes
medium	no	excellent	yes
high	yes	fair	yes

income	*student*	*credit_rating*	*class*
medium	no	fair	yes
low	yes	fair	yes
low	yes	excellent	no
medium	yes	fair	yes
medium	no	excellent	no

Figure 6.5 The attribute *age* has the highest information gain and therefore becomes the splitting attribute at the root node of the decision tree. Branches are grown for each outcome of *age*. The tuples are shown partitioned accordingly.

"But how can we compute the information gain of an attribute that is continuous-valued, unlike above?" Suppose, instead, that we have an attribute A that is continuous-valued, rather than discrete-valued. (For example, suppose that instead of the discretized version of *age* above, we instead have the raw values for this attribute.) For such a scenario, we must determine the "best" **split-point** for A, where the split-point is a threshold on A. We first sort the values of A in increasing order. Typically, the midpoint between each pair of adjacent values is considered as a possible split-point. Therefore, given v values of A, then $v-1$ possible splits are evaluated. For example, the midpoint between the values a_i and a_{i+1} of A is

$$\frac{a_i + a_{i+1}}{2}. \tag{6.4}$$

If the values of A are sorted in advance, then determining the best split for A requires only one pass through the values. For each possible split-point for A, we evaluate $Info_A(D)$, where the number of partitions is two, that is $v = 2$ (or $j = 1, 2$) in Equation (6.2). The point with the minimum expected information requirement for A is selected as the *split_point* for A. D_1 is the set of tuples in D satisfying $A \leq split\_point$, and D_2 is the set of tuples in D satisfying $A > split\_point$.

Gain ratio

The information gain measure is biased toward tests with many outcomes. That is, it prefers to select attributes having a large number of values. For example, consider an attribute that acts as a unique identifier, such as *product_ID*. A split on *product_ID* would result in a large number of partitions (as many as there are values), each one containing just one tuple. Because each partition is pure, the information required to classify data set D based on this partitioning would be $Info_{product\_ID}(D) = 0$. Therefore, the information gained by partitioning on this attribute is maximal. Clearly, such a partitioning is useless for classification.

C4.5, a successor of ID3, uses an extension to information gain known as *gain ratio*, which attempts to overcome this bias. It applies a kind of normalization to information gain using a "split information" value defined analogously with $Info(D)$ as

$$SplitInfo_A(D) = -\sum_{j=1}^{v} \frac{|D_j|}{|D|} \times \log_2\left(\frac{|D_j|}{|D|}\right). \tag{6.5}$$

This value represents the potential information generated by splitting the training data set, D, into v partitions, corresponding to the v outcomes of a test on attribute A. Note that, for each outcome, it considers the number of tuples having that outcome with respect to the total number of tuples in D. It differs from information gain, which measures the information with respect to classification that is acquired based on the same partitioning. The gain ratio is defined as

$$GainRatio(A) = \frac{Gain(A)}{SplitInfo(A)}. \tag{6.6}$$

The attribute with the maximum gain ratio is selected as the splitting attribute. Note, however, that as the split information approaches 0, the ratio becomes unstable. A constraint is added to avoid this, whereby the information gain of the test selected must be large—at least as great as the average gain over all tests examined.

Example 6.2 Computation of gain ratio for the attribute *income*. A test on *income* splits the data of Table 6.1 into three partitions, namely *low*, *medium*, and *high*, containing four, six, and four tuples, respectively. To compute the gain ratio of *income*, we first use Equation (6.5) to obtain

$$SplitInfo_A(D) = -\frac{4}{14} \times \log_2\left(\frac{4}{14}\right) - \frac{6}{14} \times \log_2\left(\frac{6}{14}\right) - \frac{4}{14} \times \log_2\left(\frac{4}{14}\right).$$

$$= 0.926.$$

From Example 6.1, we have $Gain(income) = 0.029$. Therefore, $GainRatio(income) = 0.029/0.926 = 0.031$. ■

Gini index

The Gini index is used in CART. Using the notation described above, the Gini index measures the impurity of D, a data partition or set of training tuples, as

$$Gini(D) = 1 - \sum_{i=1}^{m} p_i^2, \tag{6.7}$$

where p_i is the probability that a tuple in D belongs to class C_i and is estimated by $|C_{i,D}|/|D|$. The sum is computed over m classes.

The Gini index considers a binary split for each attribute. Let's first consider the case where A is a discrete-valued attribute having v distinct values, $\{a_1, a_2, \ldots, a_v\}$, occurring in D. To determine the best binary split on A, we examine all of the possible subsets that can be formed using known values of A. Each subset, S_A, can be considered as a binary test for attribute A of the form "$A \in S_A$?". Given a tuple, this test is satisfied if the value of A for the tuple is among the values listed in S_A. If A has v possible values, then there are 2^v possible subsets. For example, if *income* has three possible values, namely {*low, medium, high*}, then the possible subsets are {*low, medium, high*}, {*low, medium*}, {*low, high*}, {*medium, high*}, {*low*}, {*medium*}, {*high*}, and {}. We exclude the power set, {*low, medium, high*}, and the empty set from consideration since, conceptually, they do not represent a split. Therefore, there are $2^v - 2$ possible ways to form two partitions of the data, D, based on a binary split on A.

When considering a binary split, we compute a weighted sum of the impurity of each resulting partition. For example, if a binary split on A partitions D into D_1 and D_2, the gini index of D given that partitioning is

$$Gini_A(D) = \frac{|D_1|}{|D|} Gini(D_1) + \frac{|D_2|}{|D|} Gini(D_2). \tag{6.8}$$

For each attribute, each of the possible binary splits is considered. For a discrete-valued attribute, the subset that gives the minimum gini index for that attribute is selected as its splitting subset.

For continuous-valued attributes, each possible split-point must be considered. The strategy is similar to that described above for information gain, where the midpoint between each pair of (sorted) adjacent values is taken as a possible split-point. The point giving the minimum Gini index for a given (continuous-valued) attribute is taken as the split-point of that attribute. Recall that for a possible split-point of A, D_1 is the set of tuples in D satisfying $A \leq split\_point$, and D_2 is the set of tuples in D satisfying $A > split\_point$.

The reduction in impurity that would be incurred by a binary split on a discrete- or continuous-valued attribute A is

$$\Delta Gini(A) = Gini(D) - Gini_A(D). \tag{6.9}$$

The attribute that maximizes the reduction in impurity (or, equivalently, has the minimum Gini index) is selected as the splitting attribute. This attribute and either its splitting subset (for a discrete-valued splitting attribute) or split-point (for a continuous-valued splitting attribute) together form the splitting criterion.

Example 6.3 **Induction of a decision tree using gini index.** Let D be the training data of Table 6.1 where there are nine tuples belonging to the class *buys_computer* = *yes* and the remaining five tuples belong to the class *buys_computer* = *no*. A (root) node N is created for the tuples in D. We first use Equation (6.7) for Gini index to compute the impurity of D:

$$Gini(D) = 1 - \left(\frac{9}{14}\right)^2 - \left(\frac{5}{14}\right)^2 = 0.459.$$

To find the splitting criterion for the tuples in D, we need to compute the gini index for each attribute. Let's start with the attribute *income* and consider each of the possible splitting subsets. Consider the subset {*low, medium*}. This would result in 10 tuples in partition D_1 satisfying the condition "*income* ∈ {*low, medium*}." The remaining four tuples of D would be assigned to partition D_2. The Gini index value computed based on this partitioning is

$$\begin{aligned}
& Gini_{income \in \{low, medium\}}(D) \\
& = \frac{10}{14} Gini(D_1) + \frac{4}{14} Gini(D_2) \\
& = \frac{10}{14}\left(1 - \left(\frac{6}{10}\right)^2 - \left(\frac{4}{10}\right)^2\right) + \frac{4}{14}\left(1 - \left(\frac{1}{4}\right)^2 - \left(\frac{3}{4}\right)^2\right) \\
& = 0.450 \\
& = Gini_{income \in \{high\}}(D).
\end{aligned}$$

Similarly, the Gini index values for splits on the remaining subsets are: 0.315 (for the subsets {*low, high*} and {*medium*}) and 0.300 (for the subsets {*medium, high*} and {*low*}). Therefore, the best binary split for attribute *income* is on {*medium, high*} (or {*low*}) because it minimizes the gini index. Evaluating the attribute, we obtain {*youth, senior*} (or {*middle_aged*}) as the best split for *age* with a Gini index of 0.375; the attributes {*student*} and {*credit_rating*} are both binary, with Gini index values of 0.367 and 0.429, respectively.

The attribute *income* and splitting subset {*medium, high*} therefore give the minimum gini index overall, with a reduction in impurity of 0.459 − 0.300 = 0.159. The binary split "*income* ∈ {*medium, high*}" results in the maximum reduction in impurity of the tuples in D and is returned as the splitting criterion. Node N is labeled with the criterion, two branches are grown from it, and the tuples are partitioned accordingly. Hence, the Gini index has selected *income* instead of *age* at the root node, unlike the (nonbinary) tree created by information gain (Example 6.1). ■

This section on attribute selection measures was not intended to be exhaustive. We have shown three measures that are commonly used for building decision trees. These measures are not without their biases. Information gain, as we saw, is biased toward multivalued attributes. Although the gain ratio adjusts for this bias, it tends to prefer unbalanced splits in which one partition is much smaller than the others. The Gini index is biased toward multivalued attributes and has difficulty when the number of classes is large. It also tends to favor tests that result in equal-sized partitions and purity in both partitions. Although biased, these measures give reasonably good results in practice.

Many other attribute selection measures have been proposed. CHAID, a decision tree algorithm that is popular in marketing, uses an attribute selection measure that is based on the statistical χ^2 test for independence. Other measures include C-SEP (which performs better than information gain and Gini index in certain cases) and G-statistic (an information theoretic measure that is a close approximation to χ^2 distribution).

Attribute selection measures based on the **Minimum Description Length (MDL)** principle have the least bias toward multivalued attributes. MDL-based measures use encoding techniques to define the "best" decision tree as the one that requires the fewest number of bits to both (1) encode the tree and (2) encode the exceptions to the tree (i.e., cases that are not correctly classified by the tree). Its main idea is that the simplest of solutions is preferred.

Other attribute selection measures consider **multivariate splits** (i.e., where the partitioning of tuples is based on a *combination* of attributes, rather than on a single attribute). The CART system, for example, can find multivariate splits based on a linear combination of attributes. Multivariate splits are a form of **attribute** (or feature) **construction,** where new attributes are created based on the existing ones. (Attribute construction is also discussed in Chapter 2, as a form of data transformation.) These other measures mentioned here are beyond the scope of this book. Additional references are given in the Bibliographic Notes at the end of this chapter.

"*Which attribute selection measure is the best?*" All measures have some bias. It has been shown that the time complexity of decision tree induction generally increases exponentially with tree height. Hence, measures that tend to produce shallower trees (e.g., with multiway rather than binary splits, and that favor more balanced splits) may be preferred. However, some studies have found that shallow trees tend to have a large number of leaves and higher error rates. Despite several comparative studies, no one attribute selection measure has been found to be significantly superior to others. Most measures give quite good results.

6.3.3 Tree Pruning

When a decision tree is built, many of the branches will reflect anomalies in the training data due to noise or outliers. Tree pruning methods address this problem of *overfitting* the data. Such methods typically use statistical measures to remove the least reliable branches. An unpruned tree and a pruned version of it are shown in Figure 6.6. Pruned trees tend to be smaller and less complex and, thus, easier to comprehend. They are usually faster and better at correctly classifying independent test data (i.e., of previously unseen tuples) than unpruned trees.

"*How does tree pruning work?*" There are two common approaches to tree pruning: *prepruning* and *postpruning*.

In the **prepruning** approach, a tree is "pruned" by halting its construction early (e.g., by deciding not to further split or partition the subset of training tuples at a given node).

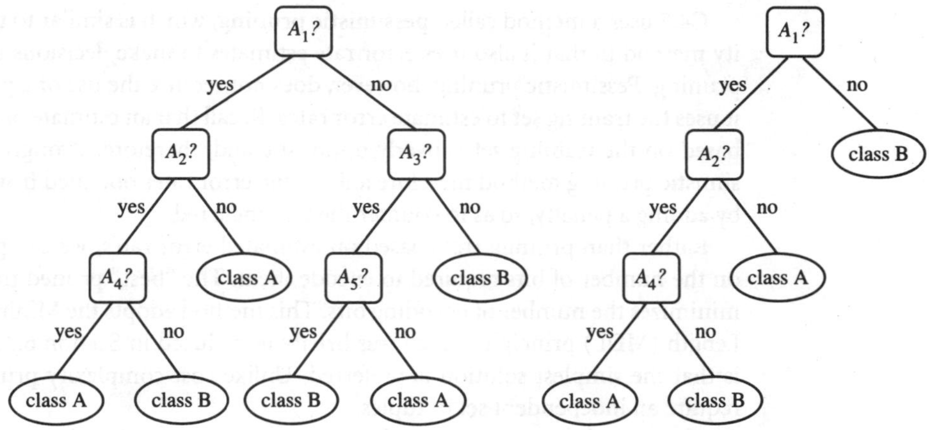

Figure 6.6 An unpruned decision tree and a pruned version of it.

Upon halting, the node becomes a leaf. The leaf may hold the most frequent class among the subset tuples or the probability distribution of those tuples.

When constructing a tree, measures such as statistical significance, information gain, Gini index, and so on can be used to assess the goodness of a split. If partitioning the tuples at a node would result in a split that falls below a prespecified threshold, then further partitioning of the given subset is halted. There are difficulties, however, in choosing an appropriate threshold. High thresholds could result in oversimplified trees, whereas low thresholds could result in very little simplification.

The second and more common approach is **postpruning**, which removes subtrees from a "fully grown" tree. A subtree at a given node is pruned by removing its branches and replacing it with a leaf. The leaf is labeled with the most frequent class among the subtree being replaced. For example, notice the subtree at node "A_3?" in the unpruned tree of Figure 6.6. Suppose that the most common class within this subtree is "*class B.*" In the pruned version of the tree, the subtree in question is pruned by replacing it with the leaf "*class B.*"

The **cost complexity** pruning algorithm used in CART is an example of the postpruning approach. This approach considers the cost complexity of a tree to be a function of the number of leaves in the tree and the error rate of the tree (where the **error rate** is the percentage of tuples misclassified by the tree). It starts from the bottom of the tree. For each internal node, N, it computes the cost complexity of the subtree at N, and the cost complexity of the subtree at N if it were to be pruned (i.e., replaced by a leaf node). The two values are compared. If pruning the subtree at node N would result in a smaller cost complexity, then the subtree is pruned. Otherwise, it is kept. A **pruning set** of class-labeled tuples is used to estimate cost complexity. This set is independent of the training set used to build the unpruned tree and of any test set used for accuracy estimation. The algorithm generates a set of progressively pruned trees. In general, the smallest decision tree that minimizes the cost complexity is preferred.

C4.5 uses a method called **pessimistic pruning**, which is similar to the cost complexity method in that it also uses error rate estimates to make decisions regarding subtree pruning. Pessimistic pruning, however, does not require the use of a prune set. Instead, it uses the training set to estimate error rates. Recall that an estimate of accuracy or error based on the training set is overly optimistic and, therefore, strongly biased. The pessimistic pruning method therefore adjusts the error rates obtained from the training set by adding a penalty, so as to counter the bias incurred.

Rather than pruning trees based on estimated error rates, we can prune trees based on the number of bits required to encode them. The "best" pruned tree is the one that minimizes the number of encoding bits. This method adopts the Minimum Description Length (MDL) principle, which was briefly introduced in Section 6.3.2. The basic idea is that the simplest solution is preferred. Unlike cost complexity pruning, it does not require an independent set of tuples.

Alternatively, prepruning and postpruning may be interleaved for a combined approach. Postpruning requires more computation than prepruning, yet generally leads to a more reliable tree. No single pruning method has been found to be superior over all others. Although some pruning methods do depend on the availability of additional data for pruning, this is usually not a concern when dealing with large databases.

Although pruned trees tend to be more compact than their unpruned counterparts, they may still be rather large and complex. Decision trees can suffer from *repetition* and *replication* (Figure 6.7), making them overwhelming to interpret. **Repetition** occurs when an attribute is repeatedly tested along a given branch of the tree (such as "*age* $<$ *60?*", followed by "*age* $<$ *45*"?, and so on). In **replication**, duplicate subtrees exist within the tree. These situations can impede the accuracy and comprehensibility of a decision tree. The use of multivariate splits (splits based on a combination of attributes) can prevent these problems. Another approach is to use a different form of knowledge representation, such as rules, instead of decision trees. This is described in Section 6.5.2, which shows how a *rule-based classifier* can be constructed by extracting IF-THEN rules from a decision tree.

6.3.4 Scalability and Decision Tree Induction

"What if D, the disk-resident training set of class-labeled tuples, does not fit in memory? In other words, how scalable is decision tree induction?" The efficiency of existing decision tree algorithms, such as ID3, C4.5, and CART, has been well established for relatively small data sets. Efficiency becomes an issue of concern when these algorithms are applied to the mining of very large real-world databases. The pioneering decision tree algorithms that we have discussed so far have the restriction that the training tuples should reside *in memory*. In data mining applications, very large training sets of millions of tuples are common. Most often, the training data will not fit in memory! Decision tree construction therefore becomes inefficient due to swapping of the training tuples in and out of main and cache memories. More scalable approaches, capable of handling training data that are too large to fit in memory, are required. Earlier strategies to "save space" included discretizing continuous-valued attributes and sampling data at each node. These techniques, however, still assume that the training set can fit in memory.

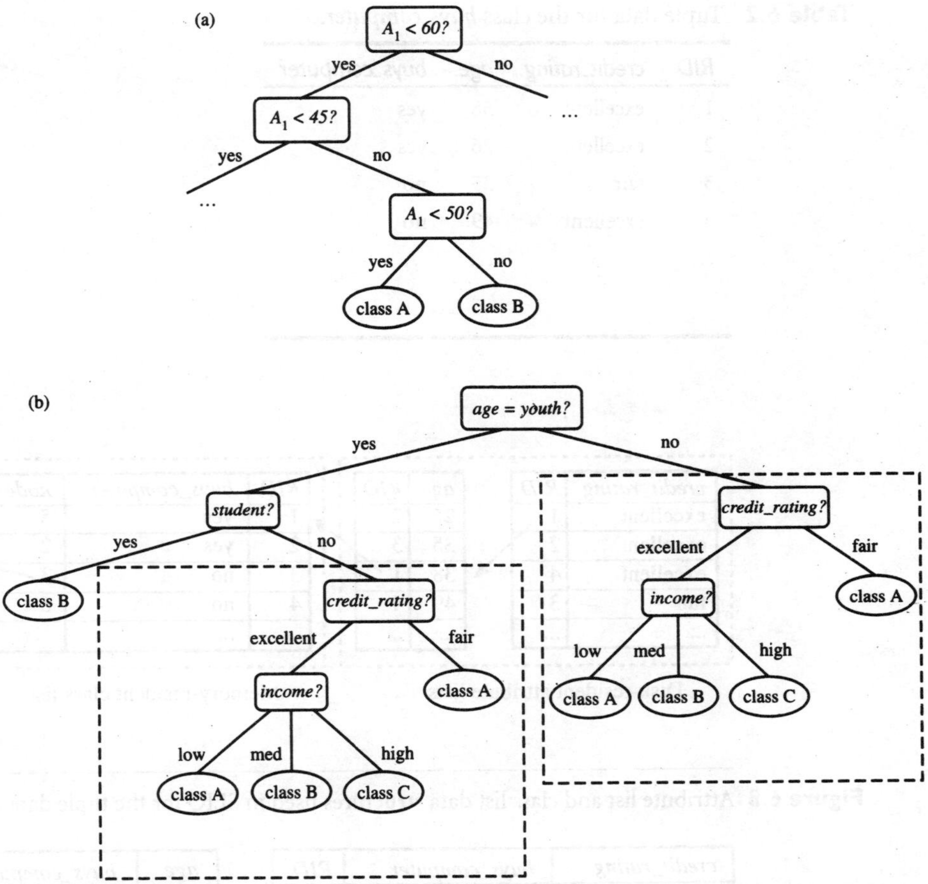

Figure 6.7 An example of subtree (a) **repetition** (where an attribute is repeatedly tested along a given branch of the tree, e.g., *age*) and (b) **replication** (where duplicate subtrees exist within a tree, such as the subtree headed by the node "*credit_rating?*").

More recent decision tree algorithms that address the scalability issue have been proposed. Algorithms for the induction of decision trees from very large training sets include SLIQ and SPRINT, both of which can handle categorical and continuous-valued attributes. Both algorithms propose presorting techniques on disk-resident data sets that are too large to fit in memory. Both define the use of new data structures to facilitate the tree construction. SLIQ employs disk-resident *attribute lists* and a single memory-resident *class list*. The attribute lists and class list generated by SLIQ for the tuple data of Table 6.2 are shown in Figure 6.8. Each attribute has an associated attribute list, indexed by *RID* (a record identifier). Each tuple is represented by a linkage of one entry from each attribute list to an entry in the class list (holding the class label of the given tuple), which in turn is linked to its corresponding leaf node

Table 6.2 Tuple data for the class *buys_computer*.

RID	*credit_rating*	*age*	*buys_computer*
1	excellent	38	yes
2	excellent	26	yes
3	fair	35	no
4	excellent	49	no
...	...	...	...

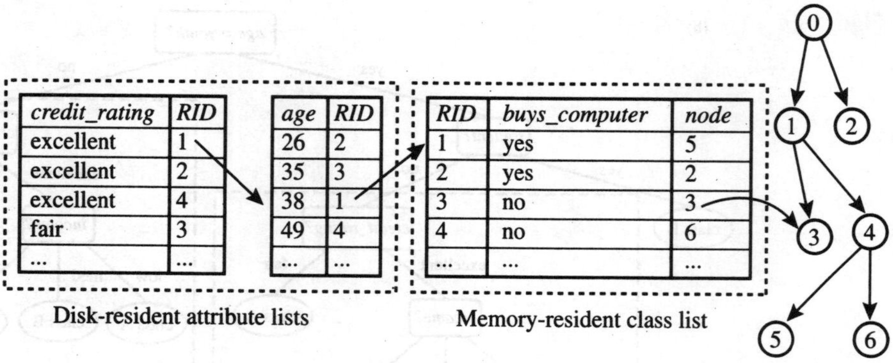

Figure 6.8 Attribute list and class list data structures used in SLIQ for the tuple data of Table 6.2.

credit_rating	*buys_computer*	*RID*
excellent	yes	1
excellent	yes	2
excellent	no	4
fair	no	3
...	...	...

age	*buys_computer*	*RID*
26	yes	2
35	no	3
38	yes	1
49	no	4
...	...	...

Figure 6.9 Attribute list data structure used in SPRINT for the tuple data of Table 6.2.

in the decision tree. The class list remains in memory because it is often accessed and modified in the building and pruning phases. The size of the class list grows proportionally with the number of tuples in the training set. When a class list cannot fit into memory, the performance of SLIQ decreases.

SPRINT uses a different *attribute list* data structure that holds the class and *RID* information, as shown in Figure 6.9. When a node is split, the attribute lists are partitioned and distributed among the resulting child nodes accordingly. When a list is

age	*buys_computer*	
	yes	no
youth	2	3
middle_aged	4	0
senior	3	2

income	*buys_computer*	
	yes	no
low	3	1
medium	4	2
high	2	2

student	*buys_computer*	
	yes	no
yes	6	1
no	3	4

credit_rating	*buys_computer*	
	yes	no
fair	6	2
excellent	3	3

Figure 6.10 The use of data structures to hold aggregate information regarding the training data (such as these AVC-sets describing the data of Table 6.1) are one approach to improving the scalability of decision tree induction.

partitioned, the order of the records in the list is maintained. Hence, partitioning lists does not require resorting. SPRINT was designed to be easily parallelized, further contributing to its scalability.

While both SLIQ and SPRINT handle disk-resident data sets that are too large to fit into memory, the scalability of SLIQ is limited by the use of its memory-resident data structure. SPRINT removes all memory restrictions, yet requires the use of a hash tree proportional in size to the training set. This may become expensive as the training set size grows.

To further enhance the scalability of decision tree induction, a method called RainForest was proposed. It adapts to the amount of main memory available and applies to any decision tree induction algorithm. The method maintains an **AVC-set** (where AVC stands for "Attribute-Value, Classlabel") for each attribute, at each tree node, describing the training tuples at the node. The AVC-set of an attribute A at node N gives the class label counts for each value of A for the tuples at N. Figure 6.10 shows AVC-sets for the tuple data of Table 6.1. The set of all AVC-sets at a node N is the **AVC-group** of N. The size of an AVC-set for attribute A at node N depends only on the number of distinct values of A and the number of classes in the set of tuples at N. Typically, this size should fit in memory, even for real-world data. RainForest has techniques, however, for handling the case where the AVC-group does not fit in memory. RainForest can use any attribute selection measure and was shown to be more efficient than earlier approaches employing aggregate data structures, such as SLIQ and SPRINT.

BOAT (Bootstrapped Optimistic Algorithm for Tree Construction) is a decision tree algorithm that takes a completely different approach to scalability—it is not based on the use of any special data structures. Instead, it uses a statistical technique known as "bootstrapping" (Section 6.13.3) to create several smaller samples (or subsets) of the given training data, each of which fits in memory. Each subset is used to construct a tree, resulting in several trees. The trees are examined and used to construct a new tree, T', that turns out to be "very close" to the tree that would have been generated if all of the original training data had fit in memory. BOAT can use any attribute selection measure that selects binary splits and that is based on the notion of purity of partitions, such as the gini index. BOAT uses a lower bound on the attribute selection measure in order to detect if this "very good" tree, T', is different from the "real" tree, T, that would have been generated using the entire data. It refines T' in order to arrive at T.

BOAT usually requires only two scans of D. This is quite an improvement, even in comparison to traditional decision tree algorithms (such as the basic algorithm in Figure 6.3), which require one scan per level of the tree! BOAT was found to be two to three times faster than RainForest, while constructing exactly the same tree. An additional advantage of BOAT is that it can be used for incremental updates. That is, BOAT can take new insertions and deletions for the training data and update the decision tree to reflect these changes, without having to reconstruct the tree from scratch.

6.4 Bayesian Classification

"What are Bayesian classifiers?" Bayesian classifiers are statistical classifiers. They can predict class membership probabilities, such as the probability that a given tuple belongs to a particular class.

Bayesian classification is based on Bayes' theorem, described below. Studies comparing classification algorithms have found a simple Bayesian classifier known as the *naive Bayesian classifier* to be comparable in performance with decision tree and selected neural network classifiers. Bayesian classifiers have also exhibited high accuracy and speed when applied to large databases.

Naïve Bayesian classifiers assume that the effect of an attribute value on a given class is independent of the values of the other attributes. This assumption is called *class conditional independence*. It is made to simplify the computations involved and, in this sense, is considered "naïve." *Bayesian belief networks* are graphical models, which unlike naïve Bayesian classifiers, allow the representation of dependencies among subsets of attributes. Bayesian belief networks can also be used for classification.

Section 6.4.1 reviews basic probability notation and Bayes' theorem. In Section 6.4.2 you will learn how to do naïve Bayesian classification. Bayesian belief networks are described in Section 6.4.3.

6.4.1 Bayes' Theorem

Bayes' theorem is named after Thomas Bayes, a nonconformist English clergyman who did early work in probability and decision theory during the 18th century. Let X be a data tuple. In Bayesian terms, X is considered "evidence." As usual, it is described by measurements made on a set of n attributes. Let H be some hypothesis, such as that the data tuple X belongs to a specified class C. For classification problems, we want to determine $P(H|X)$, the probability that the hypothesis H holds given the "evidence" or observed data tuple X. In other words, we are looking for the probability that tuple X belongs to class C, given that we know the attribute description of X.

$P(H|X)$ is the **posterior probability**, or *a posteriori probability*, of H conditioned on X. For example, suppose our world of data tuples is confined to customers described by the attributes *age* and *income*, respectively, and that X is a 35-year-old customer with an income of \$40,000. Suppose that H is the hypothesis that our customer will buy a computer. Then $P(H|X)$ reflects the probability that customer X will buy a computer given that we know the customer's age and income.

In contrast, $P(H)$ is the **prior probability**, or *a priori probability*, of H. For our example, this is the probability that any given customer will buy a computer, regardless of age, income, or any other information, for that matter. The posterior probability, $P(H|X)$, is based on more information (e.g., customer information) than the prior probability, $P(H)$, which is independent of X.

Similarly, $P(X|H)$ is the posterior probability of X conditioned on H. That is, it is the probability that a customer, X, is 35 years old and earns \$40,000, given that we know the customer will buy a computer.

$P(X)$ is the prior probability of X. Using our example, it is the probability that a person from our set of customers is 35 years old and earns \$40,000.

"How are these probabilities estimated?" $P(H)$, $P(X|H)$, and $P(X)$ may be estimated from the given data, as we shall see below. **Bayes' theorem** is useful in that it provides a way of calculating the posterior probability, $P(H|X)$, from $P(H)$, $P(X|H)$, and $P(X)$. Bayes' theorem is

$$P(H|X) = \frac{P(X|H)P(H)}{P(X)}. \tag{6.10}$$

Now that we've got that out of the way, in the next section, we will look at how Bayes' theorem is used in the naive Bayesian classifier.

6.4.2 Naïve Bayesian Classification

The **naïve Bayesian** classifier, or **simple Bayesian** classifier, works as follows:

1. Let D be a training set of tuples and their associated class labels. As usual, each tuple is represented by an n-dimensional attribute vector, $X = (x_1, x_2, \ldots, x_n)$, depicting n measurements made on the tuple from n attributes, respectively, $A_1, A_2, \ldots, A_n$.

2. Suppose that there are m classes, $C_1, C_2, \ldots, C_m$. Given a tuple, X, the classifier will predict that X belongs to the class having the highest posterior probability, conditioned on X. That is, the naïve Bayesian classifier predicts that tuple X belongs to the class C_i if and only if

$$P(C_i|X) > P(C_j|X) \quad \text{for } 1 \le j \le m, j \ne i.$$

Thus we maximize $P(C_i|X)$. The class C_i for which $P(C_i|X)$ is maximized is called the *maximum posteriori hypothesis*. By Bayes' theorem (Equation (6.10)),

$$P(C_i|X) = \frac{P(X|C_i)P(C_i)}{P(X)}. \tag{6.11}$$

3. As $P(X)$ is constant for all classes, only $P(X|C_i)P(C_i)$ need be maximized. If the class prior probabilities are not known, then it is commonly assumed that the classes are

equally likely, that is, $P(C_1) = P(C_2) = \cdots = P(C_m)$, and we would therefore maximize $P(X|C_i)$. Otherwise, we maximize $P(X|C_i)P(C_i)$. Note that the class prior probabilities may be estimated by $P(C_i) = |C_{i,D}|/|D|$, where $|C_{i,D}|$ is the number of training tuples of class C_i in D.

4. Given data sets with many attributes, it would be extremely computationally expensive to compute $P(X|C_i)$. In order to reduce computation in evaluating $P(X|C_i)$, the naive assumption of **class conditional independence** is made. This presumes that the values of the attributes are conditionally independent of one another, given the class label of the tuple (i.e., that there are no dependence relationships among the attributes). Thus,

$$P(X|C_i) = \prod_{k=1}^{n} P(x_k|C_i) = P(x_1|C_i) \times P(x_2|C_i) \times \cdots \times P(x_n|C_i). \tag{6.12}$$

We can easily estimate the probabilities $P(x_1|C_i), P(x_2|C_i), \ldots, P(x_n|C_i)$ from the training tuples. Recall that here x_k refers to the value of attribute A_k for tuple X. For each attribute, we look at whether the attribute is categorical or continuous-valued. For instance, to compute $P(X|C_i)$, we consider the following:

(a) If A_k is categorical, then $P(x_k|C_i)$ is the number of tuples of class C_i in D having the value x_k for A_k, divided by $|C_{i,D}|$, the number of tuples of class C_i in D.

(b) If A_k is continuous-valued, then we need to do a bit more work, but the calculation is pretty straightforward. A continuous-valued attribute is typically assumed to have a Gaussian distribution with a mean μ and standard deviation σ, defined by

$$g(x, \mu, \sigma) = \frac{1}{\sqrt{2\pi}\sigma} e^{-\frac{(x-\mu)^2}{2\sigma^2}}, \tag{6.13}$$

so that

$$P(x_k|C_i) = g(x_k, \mu_{C_i}, \sigma_{C_i}). \tag{6.14}$$

These equations may appear daunting, but hold on! We need to compute μ_{C_i} and σ_{C_i}, which are the mean (i.e., average) and standard deviation, respectively, of the values of attribute A_k for training tuples of class C_i. We then plug these two quantities into Equation (6.13), together with x_k, in order to estimate $P(x_k|C_i)$. For example, let X = (35, \$40,000), where A_1 and A_2 are the attributes *age* and *income*, respectively. Let the class label attribute be *buys_computer*. The associated class label for X is *yes* (i.e., *buys_computer = yes*). Let's suppose that *age* has not been discretized and therefore exists as a continuous-valued attribute. Suppose that from the training set, we find that customers in D who buy a computer are 38 ± 12 years of age. In other words, for attribute *age* and this class, we have μ = 38 years and $\sigma = 12$. We can plug these quantities, along with $x_1 = 35$ for our tuple X into Equation (6.13) in order to estimate $P(age = 35|buys\_computer = yes)$. For a quick review of mean and standard deviation calculations, please see Section 2.2.

5. In order to predict the class label of X, $P(X|C_i)P(C_i)$ is evaluated for each class C_i. The classifier predicts that the class label of tuple X is the class C_i if and only if

$$P(X|C_i)P(C_i) > P(X|C_j)P(C_j) \quad \text{for } 1 \le j \le m, j \ne i. \tag{6.15}$$

In other words, the predicted class label is the class C_i for which $P(X|C_i)P(C_i)$ is the maximum.

"How effective are Bayesian classifiers?" Various empirical studies of this classifier in comparison to decision tree and neural network classifiers have found it to be comparable in some domains. In theory, Bayesian classifiers have the minimum error rate in comparison to all other classifiers. However, in practice this is not always the case, owing to inaccuracies in the assumptions made for its use, such as class conditional independence, and the lack of available probability data.

Bayesian classifiers are also useful in that they provide a theoretical justification for other classifiers that do not explicitly use Bayes' theorem. For example, under certain assumptions, it can be shown that many neural network and curve-fitting algorithms output the *maximum posteriori* hypothesis, as does the naïve Bayesian classifier.

Example 6.4 **Predicting a class label using naïve Bayesian classification.** We wish to predict the class label of a tuple using naïve Bayesian classification, given the same training data as in Example 6.3 for decision tree induction. The training data are in Table 6.1. The data tuples are described by the attributes *age, income, student,* and *credit_rating.* The class label attribute, *buys_computer*, has two distinct values (namely, {*yes, no*}). Let C_1 correspond to the class *buys_computer* = *yes* and C_2 correspond to *buys_computer* = *no.* The tuple we wish to classify is

$$X = (age = youth, income = medium, student = yes, credit\_rating = fair)$$

We need to maximize $P(X|C_i)P(C_i)$, for $i = 1, 2$. $P(C_i)$, the prior probability of each class, can be computed based on the training tuples:

$$P(buys\_computer = yes) = 9/14 = 0.643$$
$$P(buys\_computer = no) = 5/14 = 0.357$$

To compute $PX|C_i)$, for $i = 1, 2$, we compute the following conditional probabilities:

$$P(age = youth \mid buys\_computer = yes) = 2/9 = 0.222$$
$$P(age = youth \mid buys\_computer = no) = 3/5 = 0.600$$
$$P(income = medium \mid buys\_computer = yes) = 4/9 = 0.444$$
$$P(income = medium \mid buys\_computer = no) = 2/5 = 0.400$$
$$P(student = yes \mid buys\_computer = yes) = 6/9 = 0.667$$
$$P(student = yes \mid buys\_computer = no) = 1/5 = 0.200$$
$$P(credit\_rating = fair \mid buys\_computer = yes) = 6/9 = 0.667$$
$$P(credit\_rating = fair \mid buys\_computer = no) = 2/5 = 0.400$$

Using the above probabilities, we obtain

$$P(X|buys\_computer = yes) = P(age = youth \mid buys\_computer = yes) \times$$
$$P(income = medium \mid buys\_computer = yes) \times$$
$$P(student = yes \mid buys\_computer = yes) \times$$
$$P(credit\_rating = fair \mid buys\_computer = yes)$$
$$= 0.222 \times 0.444 \times 0.667 \times 0.667 = 0.044.$$

Similarly,

$$P(X|buys\_computer = no) = 0.600 \times 0.400 \times 0.200 \times 0.400 = 0.019.$$

To find the class, C_i, that maximizes $P(X|C_i)P(C_i)$, we compute

$$P(X|buys\_computer = yes)P(buys\_computer = yes) = 0.044 \times 0.643 = 0.028$$
$$P(X|buys\_computer = no)P(buys\_computer = no) = 0.019 \times 0.357 = 0.007$$

Therefore, the naïve Bayesian classifier predicts *buys_computer* = *yes* for tuple X. ■

"What if I encounter probability values of zero?" Recall that in Equation (6.12), we estimate $P(X|C_i)$ as the product of the probabilities $P(x_1|C_i), P(x_2|C_i), \ldots, P(x_n|C_i)$, based on the assumption of class conditional independence. These probabilities can be estimated from the training tuples (step 4). We need to compute $P(X|C_i)$ for *each* class ($i = 1, 2, \ldots, m$) in order to find the class C_i for which $P(X|C_i)P(C_i)$ is the maximum (step 5). Let's consider this calculation. For each attribute-value pair (i.e., $A_k = x_k$, for $k = 1, 2, \ldots, n$) in tuple X, we need to count the number of tuples having that attribute-value pair, per class (i.e., per C_i, for $i = 1, \ldots, m$). In Example 6.4, we have two classes ($m = 2$), namely *buys_computer* = *yes* and *buys_computer* = *no*. Therefore, for the attribute-value pair *student* = *yes* of X, say, we need two counts—the number of customers who are students and for which *buys_computer* = *yes* (which contributes to $P(X|buys\_computer = yes)$) and the number of customers who are students and for which *buys_computer* = *no* (which contributes to $P(X|buys\_computer = no)$). But what if, say, there are no training tuples representing students for the class *buys_computer* = *no*, resulting in $P(student = yes|buys\_computer = no) = 0$? In other words, what happens if we should end up with a probability value of zero for some $P(x_k|C_i)$? Plugging this zero value into Equation (6.12) would return a zero probability for $P(X|C_i)$, even though, without the zero probability, we may have ended up with a high probability, suggesting that X belonged to class C_i! A zero probability cancels the effects of all of the other (posteriori) probabilities (on C_i) involved in the product.

There is a simple trick to avoid this problem. We can assume that our training database, D, is so large that adding one to each count that we need would only make a negligible difference in the estimated probability value, yet would conveniently avoid the case of probability values of zero. This technique for probability estimation is known as the **Laplacian correction** or **Laplace estimator**, named after Pierre Laplace, a French mathematician who lived from 1749 to 1827. If we have, say, q counts to which we each add one, then we must remember to add q to the corresponding denominator used in the probability calculation. We illustrate this technique in the following example.

Example 6.5 **Using the Laplacian correction to avoid computing probability values of zero.** Suppose that for the class *buys_computer* = *yes* in some training database, *D*, containing 1,000 tuples, we have 0 tuples with *income* = *low*, 990 tuples with *income* = *medium*, and 10 tuples with *income* = *high*. The probabilities of these events, without the Laplacian correction, are 0, 0.990 (from 999/1000), and 0.010 (from 10/1,000), respectively. Using the Laplacian correction for the three quantities, we pretend that we have 1 more tuple for each income-value pair. In this way, we instead obtain the following probabilities (rounded up to three decimal places):

$$\frac{1}{1{,}003} = 0.001, \frac{991}{1{,}003} = 0.988, \text{ and } \frac{11}{1{,}003} = 0.011,$$

respectively. The "corrected" probability estimates are close to their "uncorrected" counterparts, yet the zero probability value is avoided. ■

6.4.3 Bayesian Belief Networks

The naïve Bayesian classifier makes the assumption of class conditional independence, that is, given the class label of a tuple, the values of the attributes are assumed to be conditionally independent of one another. This simplifies computation. When the assumption holds true, then the naïve Bayesian classifier is the most accurate in comparison with all other classifiers. In practice, however, dependencies can exist between variables. **Bayesian belief networks** specify joint conditional probability distributions. They allow class conditional independencies to be defined between subsets of variables. They provide a graphical model of causal relationships, on which learning can be performed. Trained Bayesian belief networks can be used for classification. Bayesian belief networks are also known as **belief networks, Bayesian networks,** and **probabilistic networks.** For brevity, we will refer to them as belief networks.

A belief network is defined by two components—a *directed acyclic graph* and a set of *conditional probability tables* (Figure 6.11). Each node in the directed acyclic graph represents a random variable. The variables may be discrete or continuous-valued. They may correspond to actual attributes given in the data or to "hidden variables" believed to form a relationship (e.g., in the case of medical data, a hidden variable may indicate a syndrome, representing a number of symptoms that, together, characterize a specific disease). Each arc represents a probabilistic dependence. If an arc is drawn from a node *Y* to a node *Z*, then *Y* is a **parent** or **immediate predecessor** of *Z*, and *Z* is a **descendant** of *Y*. *Each variable is conditionally independent of its nondescendants in the graph, given its parents.*

Figure 6.11 is a simple belief network, adapted from [RBKK95] for six Boolean variables. The arcs in Figure 6.11(a) allow a representation of causal knowledge. For example, having lung cancer is influenced by a person's family history of lung cancer, as well as whether or not the person is a smoker. Note that the variable *PositiveXRay* is independent of whether the patient has a family history of lung cancer or is a smoker, given that we know the patient has lung cancer. In other words, once we know the outcome of the variable *LungCancer*, then the variables *FamilyHistory* and *Smoker* do not provide

(a)

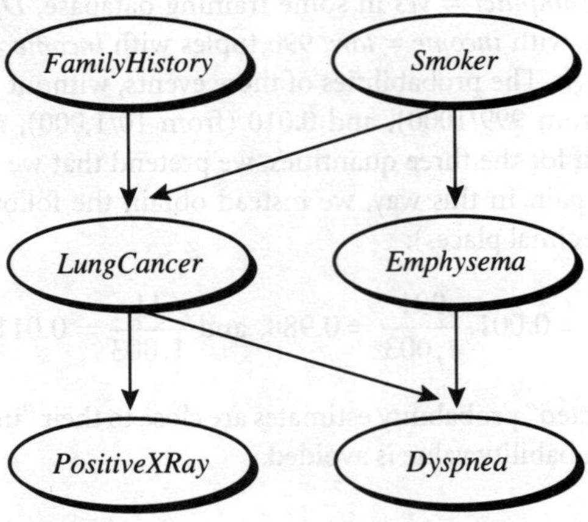

(b)

	FH, S	*FH, ~S*	*~FH, S*	*~FH, ~S*
LC	0.8	0.5	0.7	0.1
~LC	0.2	0.5	0.3	0.9

Figure 6.11 A simple Bayesian belief network: (a) A proposed causal model, represented by a directed acyclic graph. (b) The conditional probability table for the values of the variable *LungCancer (LC)* showing each possible combination of the values of its parent nodes, *FamilyHistory (FH)* and *Smoker (S)*. Figure is adapted from [RBKK95].

any additional information regarding *PositiveXRay*. The arcs also show that the variable *LungCancer* is conditionally independent of *Emphysema*, given its parents, *FamilyHistory* and *Smoker*.

A belief network has one **conditional probability table (CPT)** for each variable. The CPT for a variable Y specifies the conditional distribution $P(Y|Parents(Y))$, where $Parents(Y)$ are the parents of Y. Figure 6.11(b) shows a CPT for the variable *LungCancer*. The conditional probability for each known value of *LungCancer* is given for each possible combination of values of its parents. For instance, from the upper leftmost and bottom rightmost entries, respectively, we see that

$$P(LungCancer = yes \mid FamilyHistory = yes, Smoker = yes) = 0.8$$

$$P(LungCancer = no \mid FamilyHistory = no, Smoker = no) = 0.9$$

Let $\mathbf{X} = (x_1, \ldots, x_n)$ be a data tuple described by the variables or attributes $Y_1, \ldots, Y_n$, respectively. Recall that each variable is conditionally independent of its nondescendants in the network graph, given its parents. This allows the network to provide a complete representation of the existing joint probability distribution with the following equation:

$$P(x_1, \ldots, x_n) = \prod_{i=1}^{n} P(x_i|Parents(Y_i)), \tag{6.16}$$

where $P(x_1, \ldots, x_n)$ is the probability of a particular combination of values of $\mathbf{X}$, and the values for $P(x_i|Parents(Y_i))$ correspond to the entries in the CPT for Y_i.

A node within the network can be selected as an "output" node, representing a class label attribute. There may be more than one output node. Various algorithms for learning can be applied to the network. Rather than returning a single class label, the classification process can return a probability distribution that gives the probability of each class.

6.4.4 Training Bayesian Belief Networks

"*How does a Bayesian belief network learn?*" In the learning or training of a belief network, a number of scenarios are possible. The network **topology** (or "layout" of nodes and arcs) may be given in advance or inferred from the data. The network variables may be *observable* or *hidden* in all or some of the training tuples. The case of hidden data is also referred to as *missing values* or *incomplete data*.

Several algorithms exist for learning the network topology from the training data given observable variables. The problem is one of discrete optimization. For solutions, please see the bibliographic notes at the end of this chapter. Human experts usually have a good grasp of the direct conditional dependencies that hold in the domain under analysis, which helps in network design. Experts must specify conditional probabilities for the nodes that participate in direct dependencies. These probabilities can then be used to compute the remaining probability values.

If the network topology is known and the variables are observable, then training the network is straightforward. It consists of computing the CPT entries, as is similarly done when computing the probabilities involved in naive Bayesian classification.

When the network topology is given and some of the variables are hidden, there are various methods to choose from for training the belief network. We will describe a promising method of gradient descent. For those without an advanced math background, the description may look rather intimidating with its calculus-packed formulae. However, packaged software exists to solve these equations, and the general idea is easy to follow.

Let D be a training set of data tuples, $\mathbf{X_1}, \mathbf{X_2}, \ldots, \mathbf{X}_{|D|}$. Training the belief network means that we must learn the values of the CPT entries. Let w_{ijk} be a CPT entry for the variable $Y_i = y_{ij}$ having the parents $U_i = u_{ik}$, where $w_{ijk} \equiv P(Y_i = y_{ij}|U_i = u_{ik})$. For example, if w_{ijk} is the upper leftmost CPT entry of Figure 6.11(b), then Y_i is *LungCancer*; y_{ij} is its value, "*yes*"; U_i lists the parent nodes of Y_i, namely, {*FamilyHistory, Smoker*}; and u_{ik} lists the values of the parent nodes, namely, {"*yes*", "*yes*"}. The w_{ijk} are viewed as weights, analogous to the weights in hidden units of neural networks (Section 6.6). The set of weights is collectively referred to as $\mathbf{W}$. The weights are initialized to random probability values. A *gradient descent* strategy performs greedy hill-climbing. At each iteration, the weights are updated and will eventually converge to a local optimum solution.

A **gradient descent** strategy is used to search for the w_{ijk} values that best model the data, based on the assumption that each possible setting of w_{ijk} is equally likely. Such a strategy is iterative. It searches for a solution along the negative of the gradient (i.e., steepest descent) of a criterion function. We want to find the set of weights, $\mathbf{W}$, that maximize this function. To start with, the weights are initialized to random probability values.

The gradient descent method performs greedy hill-climbing in that, at each iteration or step along the way, the algorithm moves toward what appears to be the best solution at the moment, without backtracking. The weights are updated at each iteration. Eventually, they converge to a local optimum solution.

For our problem, we maximize $P_w(D) = \prod_{d=1}^{|D|} P_w(X_d)$. This can be done by following the gradient of $\ln P_w(S)$, which makes the problem simpler. Given the network topology and initialized w_{ijk}, the algorithm proceeds as follows:

1. **Compute the gradients:** For each i, j, k, compute

$$\frac{\partial \ln P_w(D)}{\partial w_{ijk}} = \sum_{d=1}^{|D|} \frac{P(Y_i = y_{ij}, U_i = u_{ik}|X_d)}{w_{ijk}}. \tag{6.17}$$

The probability in the right-hand side of Equation (6.17) is to be calculated for each training tuple, X_d, in D. For brevity, let's refer to this probability simply as p. When the variables represented by Y_i and U_i are hidden for some X_d, then the corresponding probability p can be computed from the observed variables of the tuple using standard algorithms for Bayesian network inference such as those available in the commercial software package HUGIN (*http://www.hugin.dk*).

2. **Take a small step in the direction of the gradient:** The weights are updated by

$$w_{ijk} \leftarrow w_{ijk} + (l)\frac{\partial \ln P_w(D)}{\partial w_{ijk}}, \tag{6.18}$$

where l is the **learning rate** representing the step size and $\frac{\partial \ln P_w(D)}{\partial w_{ijk}}$ is computed from Equation (6.17). The learning rate is set to a small constant and helps with convergence.

3. **Renormalize the weights:** Because the weights w_{ijk} are probability values, they must be between 0.0 and 1.0, and $\sum_j w_{ijk}$ must equal 1 for all i, k. These criteria are achieved by renormalizing the weights after they have been updated by Equation (6.18).

Algorithms that follow this form of learning are called *Adaptive Probabilistic Networks*. Other methods for training belief networks are referenced in the bibliographic notes at the end of this chapter. Belief networks are computationally intensive. Because belief networks provide explicit representations of causal structure, a human expert can provide prior knowledge to the training process in the form of network topology and/or conditional probability values. This can significantly improve the learning rate.

6.5 Rule-Based Classification

In this section, we look at rule-based classifiers, where the learned model is represented as a set of IF-THEN rules. We first examine how such rules are used for classification.

We then study ways in which they can be generated, either from a decision tree or directly from the training data using a *sequential covering algorithm.*

6.5.1 Using IF-THEN Rules for Classification

Rules are a good way of representing information or bits of knowledge. A **rule-based classifier** uses a set of IF-THEN rules for classification. An IF-THEN rule is an expression of the form

IF *condition* THEN *conclusion*.

An example is rule $R1$,

R1: IF $age = youth$ AND $student = yes$ THEN $buys\_computer = yes$.

The "IF"-part (or left-hand side) of a rule is known as the **rule antecedent** or **precondition.** The "THEN"-part (or right-hand side) is the **rule consequent.** In the rule antecedent, the condition consists of one or more *attribute tests* (such as $age = youth$, and $student = yes$) that are logically ANDed. The rule's consequent contains a class prediction (in this case, we are predicting whether a customer will buy a computer). $R1$ can also be written as

R1: $(age = youth) \wedge (student = yes) \Rightarrow (buys\_computer = yes)$.

If the condition (that is, all of the attribute tests) in a rule antecedent holds true for a given tuple, we say that the rule antecedent is **satisfied** (or simply, that the rule is satisfied) and that the rule **covers** the tuple.

A rule R can be assessed by its coverage and accuracy. Given a tuple, X, from a class-labeled data set, D, let n_{covers} be the number of tuples covered by R; $n_{correct}$ be the number of tuples correctly classified by R; and $|D|$ be the number of tuples in D. We can define the **coverage** and **accuracy** of R as

$$coverage(R) = \frac{n_{covers}}{|D|} \tag{6.19}$$

$$accuracy(R) = \frac{n_{correct}}{n_{covers}}. \tag{6.20}$$

That is, a rule's coverage is the percentage of tuples that are covered by the rule (i.e., whose attribute values hold true for the rule's antecedent). For a rule's accuracy, we look at the tuples that it covers and see what percentage of them the rule can correctly classify.

Example 6.6 **Rule accuracy and coverage.** Let's go back to our data of Table 6.1. These are class-labeled tuples from the *AllElectronics* customer database. Our task is to predict whether a customer will buy a computer. Consider rule $R1$ above, which covers 2 of the 14 tuples. It can correctly classify both tuples. Therefore, $coverage(R1) = 2/14 = 14.28\%$ and $accuracy$ $(R1) = 2/2 = 100\%$. ■

Let's see how we can use rule-based classification to predict the class label of a given tuple, ***X***. If a rule is satisfied by ***X***, the rule is said to be **triggered**. For example, suppose we have

$$X = (age = youth,\ income = medium,\ student = yes,\ credit\_rating = fair).$$

We would like to classify ***X*** according to *buys_computer*. ***X*** satisfies *R*1, which triggers the rule.

If *R*1 is the only rule satisfied, then the rule **fires** by returning the class prediction for ***X***. Note that triggering does not always mean firing because there may be more than one rule that is satisfied! If more than one rule is triggered, we have a potential problem. What if they each specify a different class? Or what if no rule is satisfied by ***X***?

We tackle the first question. If more than one rule is triggered, we need a **conflict resolution strategy** to figure out which rule gets to fire and assign its class prediction to ***X***. There are many possible strategies. We look at two, namely *size ordering* and *rule ordering*.

The **size ordering** scheme assigns the highest priority to the triggering rule that has the "toughest" requirements, where toughness is measured by the rule antecedent *size*. That is, the triggering rule with the most attribute tests is fired.

The **rule ordering** scheme prioritizes the rules beforehand. The ordering may be *class-based* or *rule-based*. With **class-based ordering**, the classes are sorted in order of decreasing "importance," such as by decreasing *order of prevalence*. That is, all of the rules for the most prevalent (or most frequent) class come first, the rules for the next prevalent class come next, and so on. Alternatively, they may be sorted based on the misclassification cost per class. Within each class, the rules are not ordered—they don't have to be because they all predict the same class (and so there can be no class conflict!). With **rule-based ordering**, the rules are organized into one long priority list, according to some measure of rule quality such as accuracy, coverage, or size (number of attribute tests in the rule antecedent), or based on advice from domain experts. When rule ordering is used, the rule set is known as a **decision list**. With rule ordering, the triggering rule that appears earliest in the list has highest priority, and so it gets to fire its class prediction. Any other rule that satisfies ***X*** is ignored. Most rule-based classification systems use a class-based rule-ordering strategy.

Note that in the first strategy, overall the rules are *unordered*. They can be applied in any order when classifying a tuple. That is, a disjunction (logical OR) is implied between each of the rules. Each rule represents a stand-alone nugget or piece of knowledge. This is in contrast to the rule-ordering (decision list) scheme for which rules must be applied in the prescribed order so as to avoid conflicts. Each rule in a decision list implies the negation of the rules that come before it in the list. Hence, rules in a decision list are more difficult to interpret.

Now that we have seen how we can handle conflicts, let's go back to the scenario where there is no rule satisfied by ***X***. How, then, can we determine the class label of ***X***? In this case, a fallback or **default rule** can be set up to specify a default class, based on a training set. This may be the class in majority or the majority class of the tuples that were not covered by any rule. The default rule is evaluated at the end, if and only if no other rule covers X. The condition in the default rule is empty. In this way, the rule fires when no other rule is satisfied.

In the following sections, we examine how to build a rule-based classifier.

6.5.2 Rule Extraction from a Decision Tree

In Section 6.3, we learned how to build a decision tree classifier from a set of training data. Decision tree classifiers are a popular method of classification—it is easy to understand how decision trees work and they are known for their accuracy. Decision trees can become large and difficult to interpret. In this subsection, we look at how to build a rule-based classifier by extracting IF-THEN rules from a decision tree. In comparison with a decision tree, the IF-THEN rules may be easier for humans to understand, particularly if the decision tree is very large.

To extract rules from a decision tree, one rule is created for each path from the root to a leaf node. Each splitting criterion along a given path is logically ANDed to form the rule antecedent ("IF" part). The leaf node holds the class prediction, forming the rule consequent ("THEN" part).

Example 6.7 **Extracting classification rules from a decision tree.** The decision tree of Figure 6.2 can be converted to classification IF-THEN rules by tracing the path from the root node to each leaf node in the tree. The rules extracted from Figure 6.2 are

$R1$: IF $age = youth$ AND $student = no$ THEN $buys\_computer = no$
$R2$: IF $age = youth$ AND $student = yes$ THEN $buys\_computer = yes$
$R3$: IF $age = middle\_aged$ THEN $buys\_computer = yes$
$R4$: IF $age = senior$ AND $credit\_rating = excellent$ THEN $buys\_computer = yes$
$R5$: IF $age = senior$ AND $credit\_rating = fair$ THEN $buys\_computer = no$

■

A disjunction (logical OR) is implied between each of the extracted rules. Because the rules are extracted directly from the tree, they are **mutually exclusive and exhaustive.** By *mutually exclusive*, this means that we cannot have rule conflicts here because no two rules will be triggered for the same tuple. (We have one rule per leaf, and any tuple can map to only one leaf.) By *exhaustive*, there is one rule for each possible attribute-value combination, so that this set of rules does not require a default rule. Therefore, the order of the rules does not matter—they are *unordered*.

Since we end up with one rule per leaf, the set of extracted rules is not much simpler than the corresponding decision tree! The extracted rules may be even more difficult to interpret than the original trees in some cases. As an example, Figure 6.7 showed decision trees that suffer from subtree repetition and replication. The resulting set of rules extracted can be large and difficult to follow, because some of the attribute tests may be irrelevant or redundant. So, the plot thickens. Although it is easy to extract rules from a decision tree, we may need to do some more work by pruning the resulting rule set.

"How can we prune the rule set?" For a given rule antecedent, any condition that does not improve the estimated accuracy of the rule can be pruned (i.e., removed), thereby generalizing the rule. C4.5 extracts rules from an unpruned tree, and then prunes the rules using a pessimistic approach similar to its tree pruning method. The training tuples and their associated class labels are used to estimate rule accuracy. However, because this would result in an optimistic estimate, alternatively, the estimate is adjusted to compensate for the bias, resulting in a pessimistic estimate. In addition, any rule that does not contribute to the overall accuracy of the entire rule set can also be pruned.

Other problems arise during rule pruning, however, as the rules *will no longer be* mutually exclusive and exhaustive. For conflict resolution, C4.5 adopts a **class-based ordering scheme**. It groups all rules for a single class together, and then determines a ranking of these class rule sets. Within a rule set, the rules are not ordered. C4.5 orders the class rule sets so as to minimize the number of *false-positive errors* (i.e., where a rule predicts a class, C, but the actual class is not C). The class rule set with the least number of false positives is examined first. Once pruning is complete, a final check is done to remove any duplicates. When choosing a default class, C4.5 does not choose the majority class, because this class will likely have many rules for its tuples. Instead, it selects the class that contains the most training tuples that were not covered by any rule.

6.5.3 Rule Induction Using a Sequential Covering Algorithm

IF-THEN rules can be extracted directly from the training data (i.e., without having to generate a decision tree first) using a **sequential covering algorithm**. The name comes from the notion that the rules are learned *sequentially* (one at a time), where each rule for a given class will ideally *cover* many of the tuples of that class (and hopefully none of the tuples of other classes). Sequential covering algorithms are the most widely used approach to mining disjunctive sets of classification rules, and form the topic of this subsection. Note that in a newer alternative approach, classification rules can be generated using *associative classification algorithms*, which search for attribute-value pairs that occur frequently in the data. These pairs may form association rules, which can be analyzed and used in classification. Since this latter approach is based on association rule mining (Chapter 5), we prefer to defer its treatment until later, in Section 6.8.

There are many sequential covering algorithms. Popular variations include AQ, CN2, and the more recent, RIPPER. The general strategy is as follows. Rules are learned one at a time. Each time a rule is learned, the tuples covered by the rule are removed, and the process repeats on the remaining tuples. This sequential learning of rules is in contrast to decision tree induction. Because the path to each leaf in a decision tree corresponds to a rule, we can consider decision tree induction as learning a set of rules *simultaneously*.

A basic sequential covering algorithm is shown in Figure 6.12. Here, rules are learned for one class at a time. Ideally, when learning a rule for a class, C_i, we would like the rule to cover all (or many) of the training tuples of class C and none (or few) of the tuples from other classes. In this way, the rules learned should be of high accuracy. The rules need not necessarily be of high coverage. This is because we can have more than one

Algorithm: Sequential covering. Learn a set of IF-THEN rules for classification.

Input:

- *D*, a data set class-labeled tuples;
- *Att_vals*, the set of all attributes and their possible values.

Output: A set of IF-THEN rules.

Method:

```
Rule_set = {}; // initial set of rules learned is empty
for each class c do
    repeat
        Rule = Learn_One_Rule(D, Att_vals, c);
        remove tuples covered by Rule from D;
    until terminating condition;
    Rule_set = Rule_set + Rule; // add new rule to rule set
endfor
return Rule_Set;
```

Figure 6.12 Basic sequential covering algorithm.

rule for a class, so that different rules may cover different tuples within the same class. The process continues until the terminating condition is met, such as when there are no more training tuples or the quality of a rule returned is below a user-specified threshold. The *Learn_One_Rule* procedure finds the "best" rule for the current class, given the current set of training tuples.

"*How are rules learned?*" Typically, rules are grown in a *general-to-specific* manner (Figure 6.13). We can think of this as a beam search, where we start off with an empty rule and then gradually keep appending attribute tests to it. We append by adding the attribute test as a logical conjunct to the existing condition of the rule antecedent. Suppose our training set, *D*, consists of loan application data. Attributes regarding each applicant include their age, income, education level, residence, credit rating, and the term of the loan. The classifying attribute is *loan_decision*, which indicates whether a loan is accepted (considered safe) or rejected (considered risky). To learn a rule for the class "accept," we start off with the most general rule possible, that is, the condition of the rule antecedent is empty. The rule is:

IF THEN *loan_decision* = *accept*.

We then consider each possible attribute test that may be added to the rule. These can be derived from the parameter *Att_vals*, which contains a list of attributes with their associated values. For example, for an attribute-value pair (*att*, *val*), we can consider

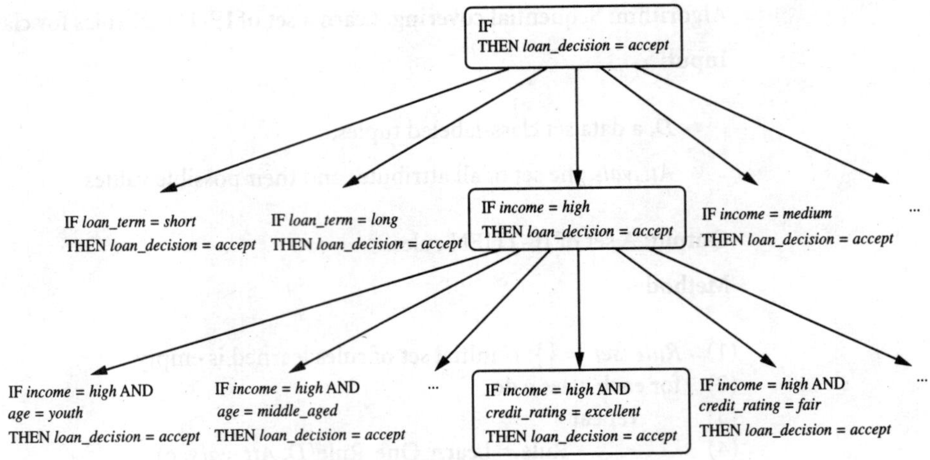

Figure 6.13 A general-to-specific search through rule space.

attribute tests such as $att = val$, $att \leq val$, $att > val$, and so on. Typically, the training data will contain many attributes, each of which may have several possible values. Finding an optimal rule set becomes computationally explosive. Instead, *Learn_One_Rule* adopts a greedy depth-first strategy. Each time it is faced with adding a new attribute test (conjunct) to the current rule, it picks the one that most improves the rule quality, based on the training samples. We will say more about rule quality measures in a minute. For the moment, let's say we use rule accuracy as our quality measure. Getting back to our example with Figure 6.13, suppose *Learn_One_Rule* finds that the attribute test *income* = *high* best improves the accuracy of our current (empty) rule. We append it to the condition, so that the current rule becomes

IF *income* = *high* THEN *loan_decision* = *accept*.

Each time we add an attribute test to a rule, the resulting rule should cover more of the "accept" tuples. During the next iteration, we again consider the possible attribute tests and end up selecting *credit_rating* = *excellent*. Our current rule grows to become

IF *income* = *high* AND *credit_rating* = *excellent* THEN *loan_decision* = *accept*.

The process repeats, where at each step, we continue to greedily grow rules until the resulting rule meets an acceptable quality level.

Greedy search does not allow for backtracking. At each step, we *heuristically* add what appears to be the best choice at the moment. What if we unknowingly made a poor choice along the way? To lessen the chance of this happening, instead of selecting the best attribute test to append to the current rule, we can select the best *k* attribute tests. In this way, we perform a beam search of width k wherein we maintain the k best candidates overall at each step, rather than a single best candidate.

Rule Quality Measures

Learn_One_Rule needs a measure of rule quality. Every time it considers an attribute test, it must check to see if appending such a test to the current rule's condition will result in an improved rule. Accuracy may seem like an obvious choice at first, but consider the following example.

Example 6.8 Choosing between two rules based on accuracy. Consider the two rules as illustrated in Figure 6.14. Both are for the class *loan_decision* = *accept*. We use "*a*" to represent the tuples of class "*accept*" and "*r*" for the tuples of class "*reject*." Rule *R*1 correctly classifies 38 of the 40 tuples it covers. Rule *R*2 covers only two tuples, which it correctly classifies. Their respective accuracies are 95% and 100%. Thus, *R*2 has greater accuracy than *R*1, but it is not the better rule because of its small coverage. ■

From the above example, we see that accuracy on its own is not a reliable estimate of rule quality. Coverage on its own is not useful either—for a given class we could have a rule that covers many tuples, most of which belong to other classes! Thus, we seek other measures for evaluating rule quality, which may integrate aspects of accuracy and coverage. Here we will look at a few, namely *entropy*, another based on *information gain*, and a *statistical test* that considers coverage. For our discussion, suppose we are learning rules for the class *c*. Our current rule is *R*: IF *condition* THEN *class* = *c*. We want to see if logically ANDing a given attribute test to *condition* would result in a better rule. We call the new condition, *condition*′, where *R*′: IF *condition*′ THEN *class* = *c* is our potential new rule. In other words, we want to see if *R*′ is any better than *R*.

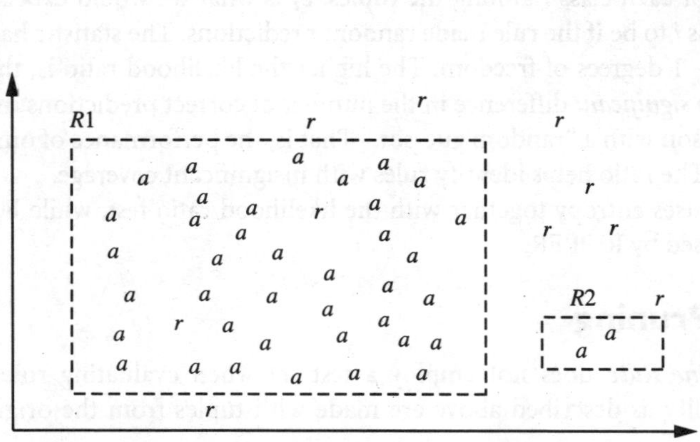

Figure 6.14 Rules for the class *loan_decision* = *accept*, showing *accept* (*a*) and *reject* (*r*) tuples.

We have already seen entropy in our discussion of the information gain measure used for attribute selection in decision tree induction (Section 6.3.2, Equation 6.1). It is also known as the *expected information* needed to classify a tuple in data set, D. Here, D is the set of tuples covered by $condition'$ and p_i is the probability of class C_i in D. The lower the entropy, the better $condition'$ is. Entropy prefers conditions that cover a large number of tuples of a single class and few tuples of other classes.

Another measure is based on information gain and was proposed in **FOIL** (First Order Inductive Learner), a sequential covering algorithm that learns first-order logic rules. Learning first-order rules is more complex because such rules contain variables, whereas the rules we are concerned with in this section are propositional (i.e., variable-free).[7] In machine learning, the tuples of the class for which we are learning rules are called *positive* tuples, while the remaining tuples are *negative*. Let *pos* (*neg*) be the number of positive (negative) tuples covered by R. Let pos' (neg') be the number of positive (negative) tuples covered by R'. FOIL assesses the information gained by extending *condition* as

$$FOIL\_Gain = pos' \times \left(\log_2 \frac{pos'}{pos' + neg'} - log_2 \frac{pos}{pos + neg}\right). \tag{6.21}$$

It favors rules that have high accuracy and cover many positive tuples.

We can also use a statistical test of significance to determine if the apparent effect of a rule is not attributed to chance but instead indicates a genuine correlation between attribute values and classes. The test compares the observed distribution among classes of tuples covered by a rule with the expected distribution that would result if the rule made predictions at random. We want to assess whether any observed differences between these two distributions may be attributed to chance. We can use the **likelihood ratio statistic**,

$$Likelihood\_Ratio = 2 \sum_{i=1}^{m} f_i \log\left(\frac{f_i}{e_i}\right), \tag{6.22}$$

where m is the number of classes. For tuples satisfying the rule, f_i is the observed frequency of each class i among the tuples. e_i is what we would expect the frequency of each class i to be if the rule made random predictions. The statistic has a χ^2 distribution with $m - 1$ degrees of freedom. The higher the likelihood ratio is, the more likely that there is a *significant* difference in the number of correct predictions made by our rule in comparison with a "random guessor." That is, the performance of our rule is not due to chance. The ratio helps identify rules with insignificant coverage.

CN2 uses entropy together with the likelihood ratio test, while FOIL's information gain is used by RIPPER.

Rule Pruning

Learn_One_Rule does not employ a test set when evaluating rules. Assessments of rule quality as described above are made with tuples from the original training data.

[7]Incidentally, FOIL was also proposed by Quinlan, the father of ID3.

Such assessment is optimistic because the rules will likely overfit the data. That is, the rules may perform well on the training data, but less well on subsequent data. To compensate for this, we can prune the rules. A rule is pruned by removing a conjunct (attribute test). We choose to prune a rule, *R*, if the pruned version of *R* has greater quality, as assessed on an independent set of tuples. As in decision tree pruning, we refer to this set as a *pruning set.* Various pruning strategies can be used, such as the pessimistic pruning approach described in the previous section. FOIL uses a simple yet effective method. Given a rule, *R*,

$$FOIL\_Prune(R) = \frac{pos - neg}{pos + neg}, \tag{6.23}$$

where *pos* and *neg* are the number of positive and negative tuples covered by *R*, respectively. This value will increase with the accuracy of *R* on a pruning set. Therefore, if the *FOIL_Prune* value is higher for the pruned version of *R*, then we prune *R*. By convention, RIPPER starts with the most recently added conjunct when considering pruning. Conjuncts are pruned one at a time as long as this results in an improvement.

6.6 Classification by Backpropagation

"What is backpropagation?" Backpropagation is a neural network learning algorithm. The field of neural networks was originally kindled by psychologists and neurobiologists who sought to develop and test computational analogues of neurons. Roughly speaking, a **neural network** is a set of connected input/output units in which each connection has a weight associated with it. During the learning phase, the network learns by adjusting the weights so as to be able to predict the correct class label of the input tuples. Neural network learning is also referred to as **connectionist learning** due to the connections between units.

Neural networks involve long training times and are therefore more suitable for applications where this is feasible. They require a number of parameters that are typically best determined empirically, such as the network topology or "structure." Neural networks have been criticized for their poor interpretability. For example, it is difficult for humans to interpret the symbolic meaning behind the learned weights and of "hidden units" in the network. These features initially made neural networks less desirable for data mining.

Advantages of neural networks, however, include their high tolerance of noisy data as well as their ability to classify patterns on which they have not been trained. They can be used when you may have little knowledge of the relationships between attributes and classes. They are well-suited for continuous-valued inputs *and outputs*, unlike most decision tree algorithms. They have been successful on a wide array of real-world data, including handwritten character recognition, pathology and laboratory medicine, and training a computer to pronounce English text. Neural network algorithms are inherently parallel; parallelization techniques can be used to speed up the computation process. In addition, several techniques have recently been developed for the extraction of rules from trained neural networks. These factors contribute toward the usefulness of neural networks for classification and prediction in data mining.

There are many different kinds of neural networks and neural network algorithms. The most popular neural network algorithm is *backpropagation*, which gained repute in the 1980s. In Section 6.6.1 you will learn about multilayer feed-forward networks, the type of neural network on which the backpropagation algorithm performs. Section 6.6.2 discusses defining a network topology. The backpropagation algorithm is described in Section 6.6.3. Rule extraction from trained neural networks is discussed in Section 6.6.4.

6.6.1 A Multilayer Feed-Forward Neural Network

The backpropagation algorithm performs learning on a *multilayer feed-forward* neural network. It iteratively learns a set of weights for prediction of the class label of tuples. A **multilayer feed-forward** neural network consists of an *input layer*, one or more *hidden layers*, and an *output layer*. An example of a multilayer feed-forward network is shown in Figure 6.15.

Each layer is made up of units. The inputs to the network correspond to the attributes measured for each training tuple. The inputs are fed simultaneously into the units making up the **input layer**. These inputs pass through the input layer and are then weighted and fed simultaneously to a second layer of "neuronlike" units, known as a **hidden layer**. The outputs of the hidden layer units can be input to another hidden layer, and so on. The number of hidden layers is arbitrary, although in practice, usually only one is used. The weighted outputs of the last hidden layer are input to units making up the **output layer**, which emits the network's prediction for given tuples.

The units in the input layer are called **input units**. The units in the hidden layers and output layer are sometimes referred to as **neurodes**, due to their symbolic biological basis, or as **output units**. The multilayer neural network shown in Figure 6.15 has two layers

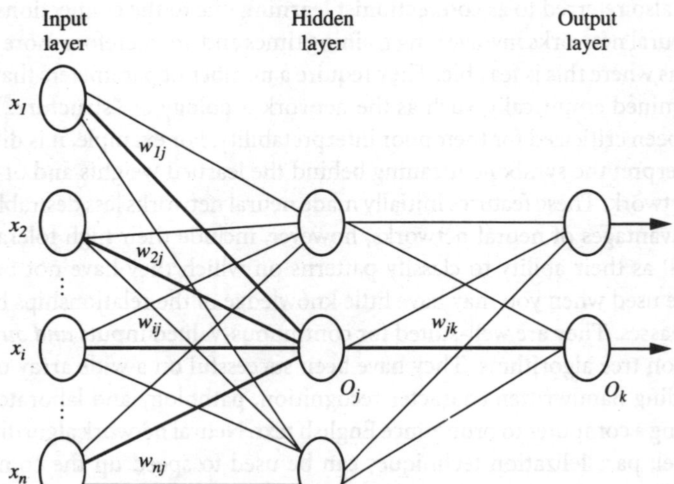

Figure 6.15 A multilayer feed-forward neural network.

of output units. Therefore, we say that it is a **two-layer** neural network. (The input layer is not counted because it serves only to pass the input values to the next layer.) Similarly, a network containing two hidden layers is called a *three-layer* neural network, and so on. The network is **feed-forward** in that none of the weights cycles back to an input unit or to an output unit of a previous layer. It is **fully connected** in that each unit provides input to each unit in the next forward layer.

Each output unit takes, as input, a weighted sum of the outputs from units in the previous layer (see Figure 6.17). It applies a nonlinear (activation) function to the weighted input. Multilayer feed-forward neural networks are able to model the class prediction as a nonlinear combination of the inputs. From a statistical point of view, they perform nonlinear regression. *Multilayer feed-forward networks, given enough hidden units and enough training samples, can closely approximate any function.*

6.6.2 Defining a Network Topology

"How can I design the topology of the neural network?" Before training can begin, the user must decide on the network topology by specifying the number of units in the input layer, the number of hidden layers (if more than one), the number of units in each hidden layer, and the number of units in the output layer.

Normalizing the input values for each attribute measured in the training tuples will help speed up the learning phase. Typically, input values are normalized so as to fall between 0.0 and 1.0. Discrete-valued attributes may be encoded such that there is one input unit per domain value. For example, if an attribute A has three possible or known values, namely $\{a_0, a_1, a_2\}$, then we may assign three input units to represent A. That is, we may have, say, I_0, I_1, I_2 as input units. Each unit is initialized to 0. If $A = a_0$, then I_0 is set to 1. If $A = a_1$, I_1 is set to 1, and so on. Neural networks can be used for both classification (to predict the class label of a given tuple) or prediction (to predict a continuous-valued output). For classification, one output unit may be used to represent two classes (where the value 1 represents one class, and the value 0 represents the other). If there are more than two classes, then one output unit per class is used.

There are no clear rules as to the "best" number of hidden layer units. Network design is a trial-and-error process and may affect the accuracy of the resulting trained network. The initial values of the weights may also affect the resulting accuracy. Once a network has been trained and its accuracy is not considered acceptable, it is common to repeat the training process with a different network topology or a different set of initial weights. Cross-validation techniques for accuracy estimation (described in Section 6.13) can be used to help decide when an acceptable network has been found. A number of automated techniques have been proposed that search for a "good" network structure. These typically use a hill-climbing approach that starts with an initial structure that is selectively modified.

6.6.3 Backpropagation

"How does backpropagation work?" Backpropagation learns by iteratively processing a data set of training tuples, comparing the network's prediction for each tuple with the

actual known *target* value. The target value may be the known class label of the training tuple (for classification problems) or a continuous value (for prediction). For each training tuple, the weights are modified so as to minimize the mean squared error between the network's prediction and the actual target value. These modifications are made in the "backwards" direction, that is, from the output layer, through each hidden layer down to the first hidden layer (hence the name *backpropagation*). Although it is not guaranteed, in general the weights will eventually converge, and the learning process stops. The algorithm is summarized in Figure 6.16. The steps involved are expressed in terms of inputs, outputs, and errors, and may seem awkward if this is your first look at neural network learning. However, once you become familiar with the process, you will see that each step is inherently simple. The steps are described below.

Algorithm: Backpropagation. Neural network learning for classification or prediction, using the backpropagation algorithm.

Input:

- D, a data set consisting of the training tuples and their associated target values;
- l, the learning rate;
- *network*, a multilayer feed-forward network.

Output: A trained neural network.

Method:

```
Initialize all weights and biases in network;
while terminating condition is not satisfied {
    for each training tuple X in D {
        // Propagate the inputs forward:
        for each input layer unit j {
            O_j = I_j; // output of an input unit is its actual input value
        for each hidden or output layer unit j {
            I_j = Σ_i w_ij O_i + θ_j; //compute the net input of unit j with respect to the
                previous layer, i
            O_j = 1/(1+e^(-I_j)); } // compute the output of each unit j
        // Backpropagate the errors:
        for each unit j in the output layer
            Err_j = O_j(1 − O_j)(T_j − O_j); // compute the error
        for each unit j in the hidden layers, from the last to the first hidden layer
            Err_j = O_j(1 − O_j) Σ_k Err_k w_jk; // compute the error with respect to the
                next higher layer, k
        for each weight w_ij in network {
            Δw_ij = (l)Err_j O_i; // weight increment
            w_ij = w_ij + Δw_ij; } // weight update
        for each bias θ_j in network {
            Δθ_j = (l)Err_j; // bias increment
            θ_j = θ_j + Δθ_j; } // bias update
        }}
```

Figure 6.16 Backpropagation algorithm.

Initialize the weights: The weights in the network are initialized to small random numbers (e.g., ranging from -1.0 to 1.0, or -0.5 to 0.5). Each unit has a *bias* associated with it, as explained below. The biases are similarly initialized to small random numbers.

Each training tuple, X, is processed by the following steps.

Propagate the inputs forward: First, the training tuple is fed to the input layer of the network. The inputs pass through the input units, unchanged. That is, for an input unit, j, its output, O_j, is equal to its input value, I_j. Next, the net input and output of each unit in the hidden and output layers are computed. The net input to a unit in the hidden or output layers is computed as a linear combination of its inputs. To help illustrate this point, a hidden layer or output layer unit is shown in Figure 6.17. Each such unit has a number of inputs to it that are, in fact, the outputs of the units connected to it in the previous layer. Each connection has a weight. To compute the net input to the unit, each input connected to the unit is multiplied by its corresponding weight, and this is summed. Given a unit j in a hidden or output layer, the net input, I_j, to unit j is

$$I_j = \sum_i w_{ij} O_i + \theta_j, \tag{6.24}$$

where w_{ij} is the weight of the connection from unit i in the previous layer to unit j; O_i is the output of unit i from the previous layer; and θ_j is the **bias** of the unit. The bias acts as a threshold in that it serves to vary the activity of the unit.

Each unit in the hidden and output layers takes its net input and then applies an **activation** function to it, as illustrated in Figure 6.17. The function symbolizes the activation

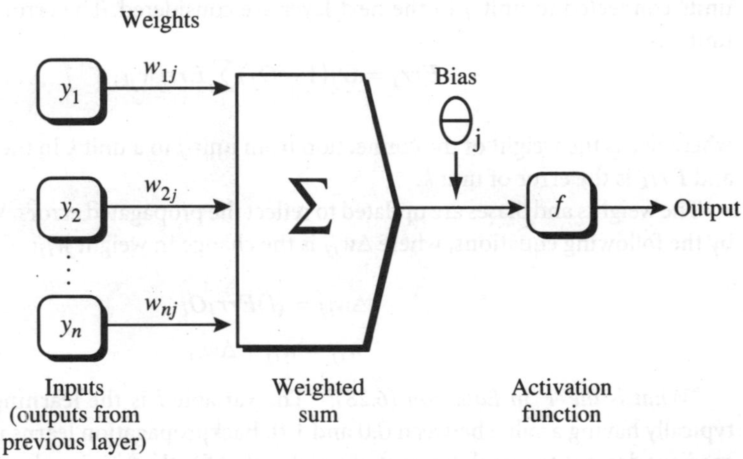

Figure 6.17 A hidden or output layer unit j: The inputs to unit j are outputs from the previous layer. These are multiplied by their corresponding weights in order to form a weighted sum, which is added to the bias associated with unit j. A nonlinear activation function is applied to the net input. (For ease of explanation, the inputs to unit j are labeled $y_1, y_2, \ldots, y_n$. If unit j were in the first hidden layer, then these inputs would correspond to the input tuple $(x_1, x_2, \ldots, x_n)$.)

of the neuron represented by the unit. The logistic, or **sigmoid,** function is used. Given the net input I_j to unit j, then O_j, the output of unit j, is computed as

$$O_j = \frac{1}{1+e^{-I_j}}. \tag{6.25}$$

This function is also referred to as a *squashing function*, because it maps a large input domain onto the smaller range of 0 to 1. The logistic function is nonlinear and differentiable, allowing the backpropagation algorithm to model classification problems that are linearly inseparable.

We compute the output values, O_j, for each hidden layer, up to and including the output layer, which gives the network's prediction. In practice, it is a good idea to cache (i.e., save) the intermediate output values at each unit as they are required again later, when backpropagating the error. This trick can substantially reduce the amount of computation required.

Backpropagate the error: The error is propagated backward by updating the weights and biases to reflect the error of the network's prediction. For a unit j in the output layer, the error Err_j is computed by

$$Err_j = O_j(1-O_j)(T_j-O_j), \tag{6.26}$$

where O_j is the actual output of unit j, and T_j is the known target value of the given training tuple. Note that $O_j(1-O_j)$ is the derivative of the logistic function.

To compute the error of a hidden layer unit j, the weighted sum of the errors of the units connected to unit j in the next layer are considered. The error of a hidden layer unit j is

$$Err_j = O_j(1-O_j)\sum_k Err_k w_{jk}, \tag{6.27}$$

where w_{jk} is the weight of the connection from unit j to a unit k in the next higher layer, and Err_k is the error of unit k.

The weights and biases are updated to reflect the propagated errors. Weights are updated by the following equations, where Δw_{ij} is the change in weight w_{ij}:

$$\Delta w_{ij} = (l)Err_j O_i \tag{6.28}$$

$$w_{ij} = w_{ij} + \Delta w_{ij} \tag{6.29}$$

"What is the 'l' in Equation (6.28)?" The variable l is the **learning rate**, a constant typically having a value between 0.0 and 1.0. Backpropagation learns using a method of gradient descent to search for a set of weights that fits the training data so as to minimize the mean squared distance between the network's class prediction and the known target value of the tuples.[8] The learning rate helps avoid getting stuck at a local minimum

[8]A method of gradient descent was also used for training Bayesian belief networks, as described in Section 6.4.4.

in decision space (i.e., where the weights appear to converge, but are not the optimum solution) and encourages finding the global minimum. If the learning rate is too small, then learning will occur at a very slow pace. If the learning rate is too large, then oscillation between inadequate solutions may occur. A rule of thumb is to set the learning rate to $1/t$, where t is the number of iterations through the training set so far.

Biases are updated by the following equations below, where $\Delta\theta_j$ is the change in bias θ_j:

$$\Delta\theta_j = (l)Err_j \tag{6.30}$$

$$\theta_j = \theta_j + \Delta\theta_j \tag{6.31}$$

Note that here we are updating the weights and biases after the presentation of each tuple. This is referred to as **case updating**. Alternatively, the weight and bias increments could be accumulated in variables, so that the weights and biases are updated after all of the tuples in the training set have been presented. This latter strategy is called **epoch updating**, where one iteration through the training set is an **epoch**. In theory, the mathematical derivation of backpropagation employs epoch updating, yet in practice, case updating is more common because it tends to yield more accurate results.

Terminating condition: Training stops when

- All Δw_{ij} in the previous epoch were so small as to be below some specified threshold, or
- The percentage of tuples misclassified in the previous epoch is below some threshold, or
- A prespecified number of epochs has expired.

In practice, several hundreds of thousands of epochs may be required before the weights will converge.

"How efficient is backpropagation?" The computational efficiency depends on the time spent training the network. Given $|D|$ tuples and w weights, each epoch requires $O(|D| \times w)$ time. However, in the worst-case scenario, the number of epochs can be exponential in n, the number of inputs. In practice, the time required for the networks to converge is highly variable. A number of techniques exist that help speed up the training time. For example, a technique known as *simulated annealing* can be used, which also ensures convergence to a global optimum.

Example 6.9 **Sample calculations for learning by the backpropagation algorithm.** Figure 6.18 shows a multilayer feed-forward neural network. Let the learning rate be 0.9. The initial weight and bias values of the network are given in Table 6.3, along with the first training tuple, $X = (1, 0, 1)$, whose class label is 1.

This example shows the calculations for backpropagation, given the first training tuple, X. The tuple is fed into the network, and the net input and output of each unit are computed. These values are shown in Table 6.4. The error of each unit is computed

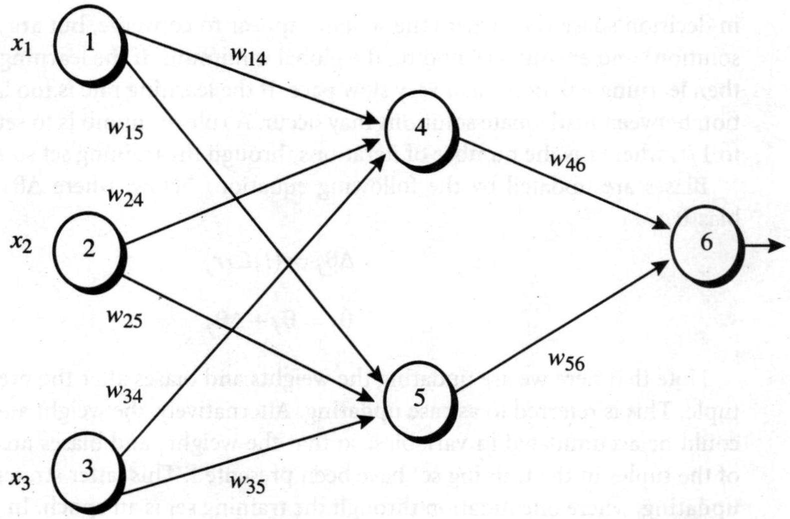

Figure 6.18 An example of a multilayer feed-forward neural network.

Table 6.3 Initial input, weight, and bias values.

x_1	x_2	x_3	w_{14}	w_{15}	w_{24}	w_{25}	w_{34}	w_{35}	w_{46}	w_{56}	θ_4	θ_5	θ_6
1	0	1	0.2	−0.3	0.4	0.1	−0.5	0.2	−0.3	−0.2	−0.4	0.2	0.1

Table 6.4 The net input and output calculations.

Unit j	*Net input,* I_j	*Output,* O_j
4	$0.2+0-0.5-0.4=-0.7$	$1/(1+e^{0.7})=0.332$
5	$-0.3+0+0.2+0.2=0.1$	$1/(1+e^{-0.1})=0.525$
6	$(-0.3)(0.332)-(0.2)(0.525)+0.1=-0.105$	$1/(1+e^{0.105})=0.474$

and propagated backward. The error values are shown in Table 6.5. The weight and bias updates are shown in Table 6.6. ■

Several variations and alternatives to the backpropagation algorithm have been proposed for classification in neural networks. These may involve the dynamic adjustment of the network topology and of the learning rate or other parameters, or the use of different error functions.

6.6.4 Inside the Black Box: Backpropagation and Interpretability

"Neural networks are like a black box. How can I 'understand' what the backpropagation network has learned?" A major disadvantage of neural networks lies in their knowledge

Table 6.5 Calculation of the error at each node.

Unit j	Err_j
6	$(0.474)(1-0.474)(1-0.474) = 0.1311$
5	$(0.525)(1-0.525)(0.1311)(-0.2) = -0.0065$
4	$(0.332)(1-0.332)(0.1311)(-0.3) = -0.0087$

Table 6.6 Calculations for weight and bias updating.

Weight or bias	*New value*
w_{46}	$-0.3 + (0.9)(0.1311)(0.332) = -0.261$
w_{56}	$-0.2 + (0.9)(0.1311)(0.525) = -0.138$
w_{14}	$0.2 + (0.9)(-0.0087)(1) = 0.192$
w_{15}	$-0.3 + (0.9)(-0.0065)(1) = -0.306$
w_{24}	$0.4 + (0.9)(-0.0087)(0) = 0.4$
w_{25}	$0.1 + (0.9)(-0.0065)(0) = 0.1$
w_{34}	$-0.5 + (0.9)(-0.0087)(1) = -0.508$
w_{35}	$0.2 + (0.9)(-0.0065)(1) = 0.194$
θ_6	$0.1 + (0.9)(0.1311) = 0.218$
θ_5	$0.2 + (0.9)(-0.0065) = 0.194$
θ_4	$-0.4 + (0.9)(-0.0087) = -0.408$

representation. Acquired knowledge in the form of a network of units connected by weighted links is difficult for humans to interpret. This factor has motivated research in extracting the knowledge embedded in trained neural networks and in representing that knowledge symbolically. Methods include extracting rules from networks and sensitivity analysis.

Various algorithms for the extraction of rules have been proposed. The methods typically impose restrictions regarding procedures used in training the given neural network, the network topology, and the discretization of input values.

Fully connected networks are difficult to articulate. Hence, often the first step toward extracting rules from neural networks is **network pruning**. This consists of simplifying the network structure by removing weighted links that have the least effect on the trained network. For example, a weighted link may be deleted if such removal does not result in a decrease in the classification accuracy of the network.

Once the trained network has been pruned, some approaches will then perform link, unit, or activation value clustering. In one method, for example, clustering is used to find the set of common activation values for each hidden unit in a given trained two-layer neural network (Figure 6.19). The combinations of these activation values for each hidden unit are analyzed. Rules are derived relating combinations of activation values with corresponding output unit values. Similarly, the sets of input

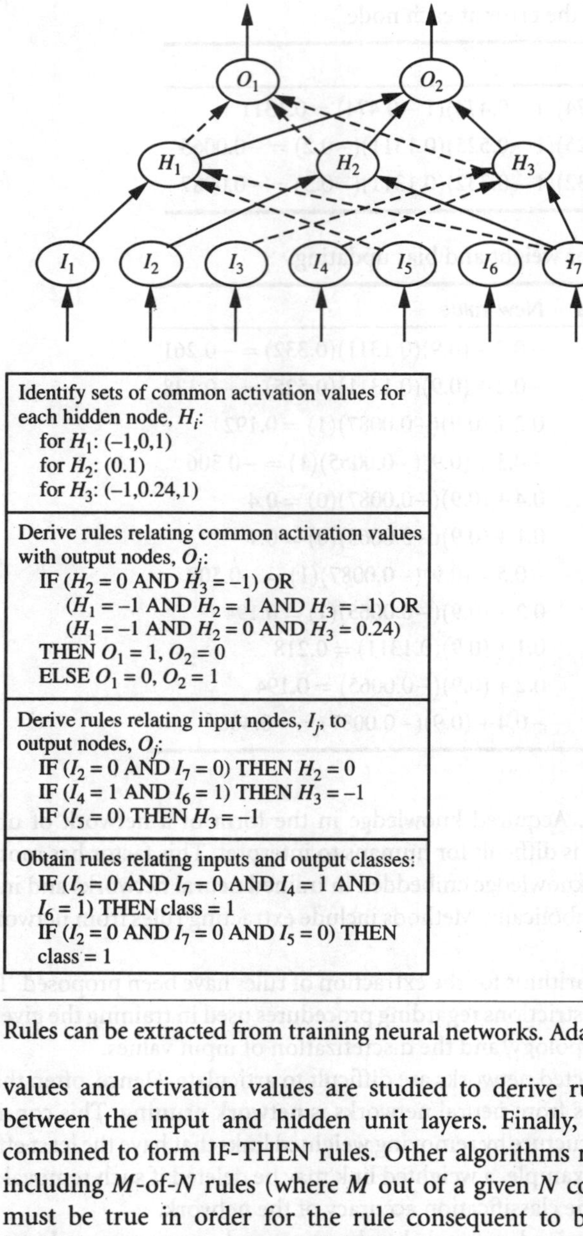

Figure 6.19 Rules can be extracted from training neural networks. Adapted from [LSL95].

values and activation values are studied to derive rules describing the relationship between the input and hidden unit layers. Finally, the two sets of rules may be combined to form IF-THEN rules. Other algorithms may derive rules of other forms, including *M*-of-*N* rules (where *M* out of a given *N* conditions in the rule antecedent must be true in order for the rule consequent to be applied), decision trees with *M*-of-*N* tests, fuzzy rules, and finite automata.

Sensitivity analysis is used to assess the impact that a given input variable has on a network output. The input to the variable is varied while the remaining input variables are fixed at some value. Meanwhile, changes in the network output are monitored. The knowledge gained from this form of analysis can be represented in rules such as "*IF X decreases 5% THEN Y increases 8%.*"

6.7 Support Vector Machines

In this section, we study **Support Vector Machines**, a promising new method for the classification of both linear and nonlinear data. In a nutshell, a support vector machine (or SVM) is an algorithm that works as follows. It uses a nonlinear mapping to transform the original training data into a higher dimension. Within this new dimension, it searches for the linear optimal separating hyperplane (that is, a "decision boundary" separating the tuples of one class from another). With an appropriate nonlinear mapping to a sufficiently high dimension, data from two classes can always be separated by a hyperplane. The SVM finds this hyperplane using *support vectors* ("essential" training tuples) and *margins* (defined by the support vectors). We will delve more into these new concepts further below.

"I've heard that SVMs have attracted a great deal of attention lately. Why?" The first paper on support vector machines was presented in 1992 by Vladimir Vapnik and colleagues Bernhard Boser and Isabelle Guyon, although the groundwork for SVMs has been around since the 1960s (including early work by Vapnik and Alexei Chervonenkis on statistical learning theory). Although the training time of even the fastest SVMs can be extremely slow, they are highly accurate, owing to their ability to model complex nonlinear decision boundaries. They are much less prone to overfitting than other methods. The support vectors found also provide a compact description of the learned model. SVMs can be used for prediction as well as classification. They have been applied to a number of areas, including handwritten digit recognition, object recognition, and speaker identification, as well as benchmark time-series prediction tests.

6.7.1 The Case When the Data Are Linearly Separable

To explain the mystery of SVMs, let's first look at the simplest case—a two-class problem where the classes are linearly separable. Let the data set D be given as $(\boldsymbol{X}_1, y_1)$, $(\boldsymbol{X}_2, y_2), \ldots, (\boldsymbol{X}_{|D|}, y_{|D|})$, where $\boldsymbol{X}_i$ is the set of training tuples with associated class labels, y_i. Each y_i can take one of two values, either $+1$ or -1 (i.e., $y_i \in \{+1, -1\}$), corresponding to the classes *buys_computer = yes* and *buys_computer = no*, respectively. To aid in visualization, let's consider an example based on two input attributes, A_1 and A_2, as shown in Figure 6.20. From the graph, we see that the 2-D data are **linearly separable** (or "linear," for short) because a straight line can be drawn to separate all of the tuples of class $+1$ from all of the tuples of class -1. There are an infinite number of separating lines that could be drawn. We want to find the "best" one, that is, one that (we hope) will have the minimum classification error on previously unseen tuples. How can we find this best line? Note that if our data were 3-D (i.e., with three attributes), we would want to find the best separating *plane*. Generalizing to n dimensions, we want to find the best *hyperplane*. We will use the term "hyperplane" to refer to the decision boundary that we are seeking, regardless of the number of input attributes. So, in other words, how can we find the best hyperplane?

An SVM approaches this problem by searching for the **maximum marginal hyperplane**. Consider Figure 6.21, which shows two possible separating hyperplanes and

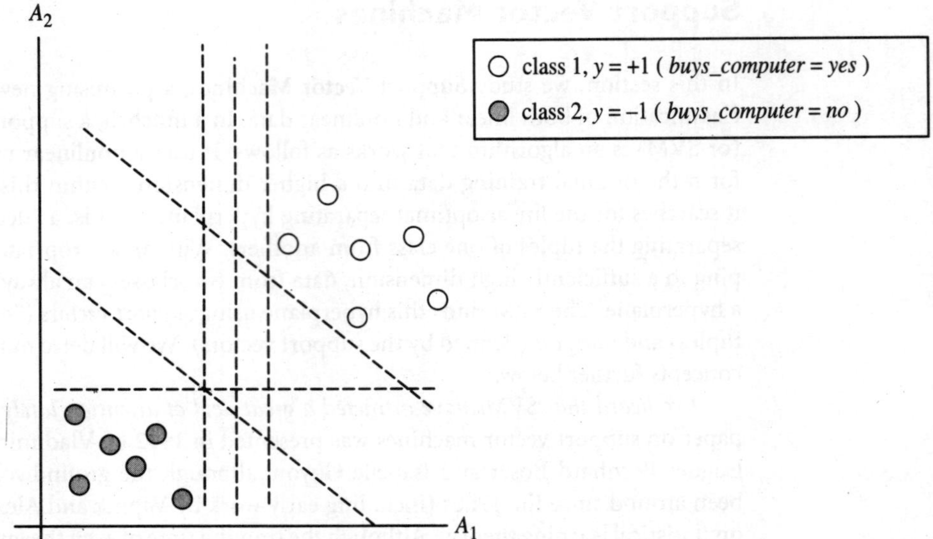

Figure 6.20 The 2-D training data are linearly separable. There are an infinite number of (possible) separating hyperplanes or "decision boundaries." Which one is best?

their associated margins. Before we get into the definition of margins, let's take an intuitive look at this figure. Both hyperplanes can correctly classify all of the given data tuples. Intuitively, however, we expect the hyperplane with the larger margin to be more accurate at classifying future data tuples than the hyperplane with the smaller margin. This is why (during the learning or training phase), the SVM searches for the hyperplane with the largest margin, that is, the *maximum marginal hyperplane* (MMH). The associated margin gives the largest separation between classes. Getting to an informal definition of **margin**, we can say that the shortest distance from a hyperplane to one side of its margin is equal to the shortest distance from the hyperplane to the other side of its margin, where the "sides" of the margin are parallel to the hyperplane. When dealing with the MMH, this distance is, in fact, the shortest distance from the MMH to the closest training tuple of either class.

A separating hyperplane can be written as

$$\boldsymbol{W} \cdot \boldsymbol{X} + b = 0, \tag{6.32}$$

where $\boldsymbol{W}$ is a weight vector, namely, $\boldsymbol{W} = \{w_1, w_2, \ldots, w_n\}$; n is the number of attributes; and b is a scalar, often referred to as a bias. To aid in visualization, let's consider two input attributes, A_1 and A_2, as in Figure 6.21(b). Training tuples are 2-D, e.g., $\boldsymbol{X} = (x_1, x_2)$, where x_1 and x_2 are the values of attributes A_1 and A_2, respectively, for $\boldsymbol{X}$. If we think of b as an additional weight, w_0, we can rewrite the above separating hyperplane as

$$w_0 + w_1x_1 + w_2x_2 = 0. \tag{6.33}$$

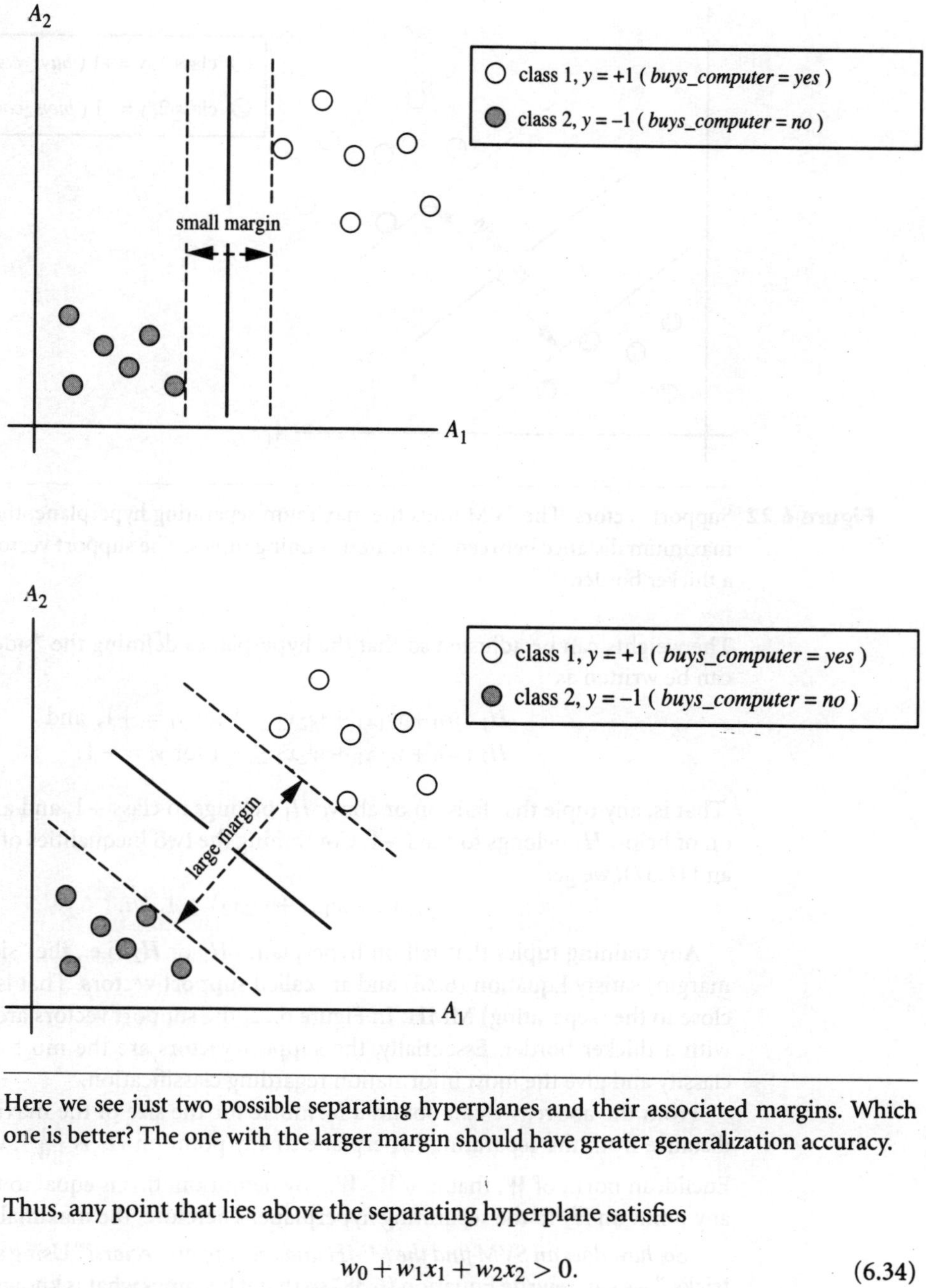

Figure 6.21 Here we see just two possible separating hyperplanes and their associated margins. Which one is better? The one with the larger margin should have greater generalization accuracy.

Thus, any point that lies above the separating hyperplane satisfies

$$w_0 + w_1x_1 + w_2x_2 > 0. \tag{6.34}$$

Similarly, any point that lies below the separating hyperplane satisfies

$$w_0 + w_1x_1 + w_2x_2 < 0. \tag{6.35}$$

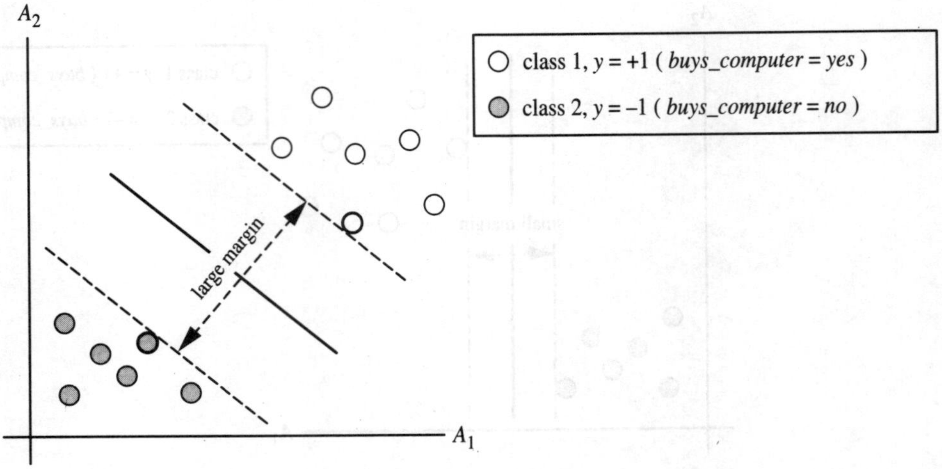

Figure 6.22 Support vectors. The SVM finds the maximum separating hyperplane, that is, the one with maximum distance between the nearest training tuples. The support vectors are shown with a thicker border.

The weights can be adjusted so that the hyperplanes defining the "sides" of the margin can be written as

$$H_1 : w_0 + w_1x_1 + w_2x_2 \geq 1 \text{ for } y_i = +1, \text{ and} \quad (6.36)$$

$$H_2 : w_0 + w_1x_1 + w_2x_2 \leq -1 \text{ for } y_i = -1. \quad (6.37)$$

That is, any tuple that falls on or above H_1 belongs to class $+1$, and any tuple that falls on or below H_2 belongs to class -1. Combining the two inequalities of Equations (6.36) and (6.37), we get

$$y_i(w_0 + w_1x_1 + w_2x_2) \geq 1, \ \forall i. \quad (6.38)$$

Any training tuples that fall on hyperplanes H_1 or H_2 (i.e., the "sides" defining the margin) satisfy Equation (6.38) and are called **support vectors.** That is, they are equally close to the (separating) MMH. In Figure 6.22, the support vectors are shown encircled with a thicker border. Essentially, the support vectors are the most difficult tuples to classify and give the most information regarding classification.

From the above, we can obtain a formulae for the size of the maximal margin. The distance from the separating hyperplane to any point on H_1 is $\frac{1}{||W||}$, where $||W||$ is the Euclidean norm of $\boldsymbol{W}$, that is $\sqrt{\boldsymbol{W} \cdot \boldsymbol{W}}$.[9] By definition, this is equal to the distance from any point on H_2 to the separating hyperplane. Therefore, the maximal margin is $\frac{2}{||W||}$.

"So, how does an SVM find the MMH and the support vectors?" Using some "fancy math tricks," we can rewrite Equation (6.38) so that it becomes what is known as a constrained

[9] If $\boldsymbol{W} = \{w_1, w_2, \ldots, w_n\}$ then $\sqrt{\boldsymbol{W} \cdot \boldsymbol{W}} = \sqrt{w_1^2 + w_2^2 + \cdots + w_n^2}$.

(convex) quadratic optimization problem. Such fancy math tricks are beyond the scope of this book. Advanced readers may be interested to note that the tricks involve rewriting Equation (6.38) using a Lagrangian formulation and then solving for the solution using Karush-Kuhn-Tucker (KKT) conditions. Details can be found in references at the end of this chapter. If the data are small (say, less than 2,000 training tuples), any optimization software package for solving constrained convex quadratic problems can then be used to find the support vectors and MMH. For larger data, special and more efficient algorithms for training SVMs can be used instead, the details of which exceed the scope of this book. Once we've found the support vectors and MMH (note that the support vectors define the MMH!), we have a trained support vector machine. The MMH is a linear class boundary, and so the corresponding SVM can be used to classify linearly separable data. We refer to such a trained SVM as a *linear SVM*.

"Once I've got a trained support vector machine, how do I use it to classify test (i.e., new) tuples?" Based on the Lagrangian formulation mentioned above, the MMH can be rewritten as the decision boundary

$$d(\boldsymbol{X}^T) = \sum_{i=1}^{l} y_i \alpha_i \boldsymbol{X}_i \boldsymbol{X}^T + b_0, \tag{6.39}$$

where y_i is the class label of support vector $\boldsymbol{X}_i$; $\boldsymbol{X}^T$ is a test tuple; α_i and b_0 are numeric parameters that were determined automatically by the optimization or SVM algorithm above; and l is the number of support vectors.

Interested readers may note that the α_i are Lagrangian multipliers. For linearly separable data, the support vectors are a subset of the actual training tuples (although there will be a slight twist regarding this when dealing with nonlinearly separable data, as we shall see below).

Given a test tuple, $\boldsymbol{X}^T$, we plug it into Equation (6.39), and then check to see the sign of the result. This tells us on which side of the hyperplane the test tuple falls. If the sign is positive, then $\boldsymbol{X}^T$ falls on or above the MMH, and so the SVM predicts that $\boldsymbol{X}^T$ belongs to class $+1$ (representing *buys_computer* = *yes*, in our case). If the sign is negative, then $\boldsymbol{X}^T$ falls on or below the MMH and the class prediction is -1 (representing *buys_computer* = *no*).

Notice that the Lagrangian formulation of our problem (Equation (6.39)) contains a dot product between support vector $\boldsymbol{X}_i$ and test tuple $\boldsymbol{X}^T$. This will prove very useful for finding the MMH and support vectors for the case when the given data are nonlinearly separable, as described further below.

Before we move on to the nonlinear case, there are two more important things to note. The complexity of the learned classifier is characterized by the number of support vectors rather than the dimensionality of the data. Hence, SVMs tend to be less prone to overfitting than some other methods. The support vectors are the essential or critical training tuples—they lie closest to the decision boundary (MMH). If all other training tuples were removed and training were repeated, the same separating hyperplane would be found. Furthermore, the number of support vectors found can be used to compute an (upper) bound on the expected error rate of the SVM classifier, which is independent of the data dimensionality. An SVM with a small number of support vectors can have good generalization, even when the dimensionality of the data is high.

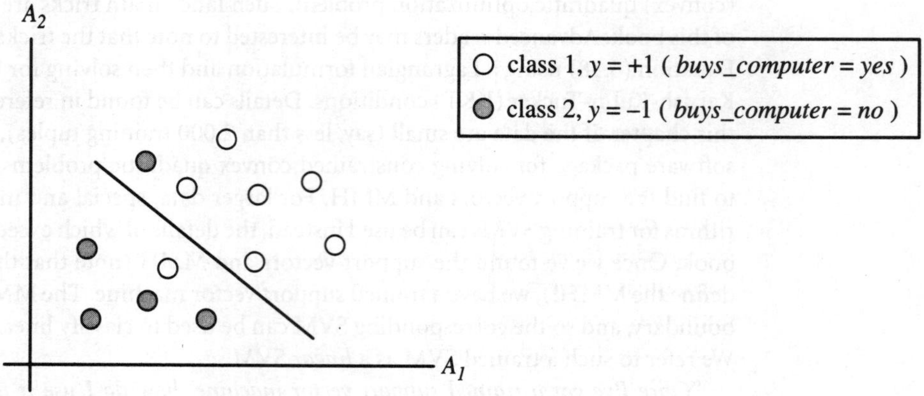

Figure 6.23 A simple 2-D case showing linearly inseparable data. Unlike the linear separable data of Figure 6.20, here it is not possible to draw a straight line to separate the classes. Instead, the decision boundary is nonlinear.

6.7.2 The Case When the Data Are Linearly Inseparable

In Section 6.7.1 we learned about linear SVMs for classifying linearly separable data, but what if the data are not linearly separable, as in Figure 6.23? In such cases, no straight line can be found that would separate the classes. The linear SVMs we studied would not be able to find a feasible solution here. Now what?

The good news is that the approach described for linear SVMs can be extended to create *nonlinear SVMs* for the classification of *linearly inseparable data* (also called *nonlinearly separable data*, or *nonlinear data*, for short). Such SVMs are capable of finding nonlinear decision boundaries (i.e., nonlinear hypersurfaces) in input space.

"So," you may ask, "how can we extend the linear approach?" We obtain a nonlinear SVM by extending the approach for linear SVMs as follows. There are two main steps. In the first step, we transform the original input data into a higher dimensional space using a nonlinear mapping. Several common nonlinear mappings can be used in this step, as we will describe further below. Once the data have been transformed into the new higher space, the second step searches for a linear separating hyperplane in the new space. We again end up with a quadratic optimization problem that can be solved using the linear SVM formulation. The maximal marginal hyperplane found in the new space corresponds to a nonlinear separating hypersurface in the original space.

Example 6.10 **Nonlinear transformation of original input data into a higher dimensional space.** Consider the following example. A 3D input vector $\boldsymbol{X} = (x_1, x_2, x_3)$ is mapped into a 6D space, $\boldsymbol{Z}$, using the mappings $\phi_1(\boldsymbol{X}) = x_1$, $\phi_2(\boldsymbol{X}) = x_2$, $\phi_3(\boldsymbol{X}) = x_3$, $\phi_4(\boldsymbol{X}) = (x_1)^2$, $\phi_5(\boldsymbol{X}) = x_1x_2$, and $\phi_6(\boldsymbol{X}) = x_1x_3$. A decision hyperplane in the new space is $d(\boldsymbol{Z}) = \boldsymbol{WZ} + b$, where $\boldsymbol{W}$ and $\boldsymbol{Z}$ are vectors. This is linear. We solve for $\boldsymbol{W}$ and b and then substitute back so that the linear decision hyperplane in the new (Z) space corresponds to a nonlinear second-order polynomial in the original 3-D input space,

$$d(Z) = w_1x_1 + w_2x_2 + w_3x_3 + w_4(x_1)^2 + w_5x_1x_2 + w_6x_1x_3 + b$$
$$= w_1z_1 + w_2z_2 + w_3z_3 + w_4z_4 + w_5z_5 + w_6z_6 + b$$ ■

But there are some problems. First, how do we choose the nonlinear mapping to a higher dimensional space? Second, the computation involved will be costly. Refer back to Equation (6.39) for the classification of a test tuple, X^T. Given the test tuple, we have to compute its dot product with every one of the support vectors.[10] In training, we have to compute a similar dot product several times in order to find the MMH. This is especially expensive. Hence, the dot product computation required is very heavy and costly. We need another trick!

Luckily, we can use another math trick. It so happens that in solving the quadratic optimization problem of the linear SVM (i.e., when searching for a linear SVM in the new higher dimensional space), the training tuples appear only in the form of dot products, $\phi(X_i) \cdot \phi(X_j)$, where $\phi(X)$ is simply the nonlinear mapping function applied to transform the training tuples. Instead of computing the dot product on the transformed data tuples, it turns out that it is mathematically equivalent to instead apply a *kernel function*, $K(X_i, X_j)$, to the original input data. That is,

$$K(X_i, X_j) = \phi(X_i) \cdot \phi(X_j). \tag{6.40}$$

In other words, everywhere that $\phi(X_i) \cdot \phi(X_j)$ appears in the training algorithm, we can replace it with $K(X_i, X_j)$. In this way, all calculations are made in the original input space, which is of potentially much lower dimensionality! We can safely avoid the mapping—it turns out that we don't even have to know what the mapping is! We will talk more later about what kinds of functions can be used as kernel functions for this problem.

After applying this trick, we can then proceed to find a maximal separating hyperplane. The procedure is similar to that described in Section 6.7.1, although it involves placing a user-specified upper bound, C, on the Lagrange multipliers, α_i. This upper bound is best determined experimentally.

"What are some of the kernel functions that could be used?" Properties of the kinds of kernel functions that could be used to replace the dot product scenario described above have been studied. Three admissible kernel functions include:

$$\textbf{Polynomial kernel of degree } h: \quad K(X_i, X_j) = (X_i \cdot X_j + 1)^h \tag{6.41}$$

$$\textbf{Gaussian radial basis function kernel}: \quad K(X_i, X_j) = e^{-\|X_i - X_j\|^2/2\sigma^2} \tag{6.42}$$

$$\textbf{Sigmoid kernel}: \quad K(X_i, X_j) = \tanh(\kappa X_i \cdot X_j - \delta) \tag{6.43}$$

[10] The dot product of two vectors, $X^T = (x_1^T, x_2^T, \ldots, x_n^T)$ and $X_i = (x_{i1}, x_{i2}, \ldots, x_{in})$ is $x_1^T x_{i1} + x_2^T x_{i2} + \cdots + x_n^T x_{in}$. Note that this involves one multiplication and one addition for each of the n dimensions.

Each of these results in a different nonlinear classifier in (the original) input space. Neural network aficionados will be interested to note that the resulting decision hyperplanes found for nonlinear SVMs are the same type as those found by other well-known neural network classifiers. For instance, an SVM with a Gaussian radial basis function (RBF) gives the same decision hyperplane as a type of neural network known as a radial basis function (RBF) network. An SVM with a sigmoid kernel is equivalent to a simple two-layer neural network known as a multilayer perceptron (with no hidden layers). There are no golden rules for determining which admissible kernel will result in the most accurate SVM. In practice, the kernel chosen does not generally make a large difference in resulting accuracy. SVM training always finds a global solution, unlike neural networks such as backpropagation, where many local minima usually exist (Section 6.6.3).

So far, we have described linear and nonlinear SVMs for binary (i.e., two-class) classification. SVM classifiers can be combined for the multiclass case. A simple and effective approach, given *m* classes, trains *m* classifiers, one for each class (where classifier *j* learns to return a positive value for class *j* and a negative value for the rest). A test tuple is assigned the class corresponding to the largest positive distance.

Aside from classification, SVMs can also be designed for linear and nonlinear regression. Here, instead of learning to predict discrete class labels (like the $y_i \in \{+1, -1\}$ above), SVMs for regression attempt to learn the input-output relationship between input training tuples, $\mathbf{X}_i$, and their corresponding continuous-valued outputs, $y_i \in \mathcal{R}$. An approach similar to SVMs for classification is followed. Additional user-specified parameters are required.

A major research goal regarding SVMs is to improve the speed in training and testing so that SVMs may become a more feasible option for very large data sets (e.g., of millions of support vectors). Other issues include determining the best kernel for a given data set and finding more efficient methods for the multiclass case.

6.8 Associative Classification: Classification by Association Rule Analysis

Frequent patterns and their corresponding association or correlation rules characterize interesting relationships between attribute conditions and class labels, and thus have been recently used for effective classification. Association rules show strong associations between attribute-value pairs (or *items*) that occur frequently in a given data set. Association rules are commonly used to analyze the purchasing patterns of customers in a store. Such analysis is useful in many decision-making processes, such as product placement, catalog design, and cross-marketing. The discovery of association rules is based on *frequent itemset mining*. Many methods for frequent itemset mining and the generation of association rules were described in Chapter 5. In this section, we look at **associative classification**, where association rules are generated and analyzed for use in classification. The general idea is that we can search for strong associations between frequent patterns (conjunctions of attribute-value pairs) and class labels. Because association rules explore highly confident associations among multiple attributes, this approach may overcome some constraints introduced by decision-tree induction, which considers only one attribute at a time. In many studies, associative classification has been found to be more accurate than some traditional classification methods, such as C4.5. In particular, we study three main methods: CBA, CMAR, and CPAR.

Before we begin, let's look at association rule mining, in general. Association rules are mined in a two-step process consisting of *frequent itemset mining*, followed by *rule generation*. The first step searches for patterns of attribute-value pairs that occur repeatedly in a data set, where each attribute-value pair is considered an *item*. The resulting attribute-value pairs form *frequent itemsets*. The second step analyzes the frequent itemsets in order to generate association rules. All association rules must satisfy certain criteria regarding their "accuracy" (or *confidence*) and the proportion of the data set that they actually represent (referred to as *support*). For example, the following is an association rule mined from a data set, D, shown with its confidence and support.

$$age = youth \wedge credit = OK \Rightarrow buys\_computer = yes \ \ [support = 20\%, confidence = 93\%] \tag{6.44}$$

where "$\wedge$" represents a logical "AND." We will say more about confidence and support in a minute.

More formally, let D be a data set of tuples. Each tuple in D is described by n attributes, $A_1, A_2, \ldots, A_n$, and a class label attribute, A_{class}. All continuous attributes are discretized and treated as categorical attributes. An **item**, p, is an attribute-value pair of the form (A_i, v), where A_i is an attribute taking a value, v. A data tuple $X = (x_1, x_2, \ldots, x_n)$ satisfies an item, $p = (A_i, v)$, if and only if $x_i = v$, where x_i is the value of the ith attribute of X. Association rules can have any number of items in the rule antecedent (left-hand side) and any number of items in the rule consequent (right-hand side). However, when mining association rules for use in classification, we are only interested in association rules of the form $p_1 \wedge p_2 \wedge \ldots p_l \Rightarrow A_{class} = C$ where the rule antecedent is a conjunction of items, $p_1, p_2, \ldots, p_l$ $(l \leq n)$, associated with a class label, C. For a given rule, R, the percentage of tuples in D satisfying the rule antecedent that also have the class label C is called the **confidence** of R. From a classification point of view, this is akin to rule accuracy. For example, a confidence of 93% for Association Rule (6.44) means that 93% of the customers in D who are young and have an OK credit rating belong to the class *buys_computer = yes*. The percentage of tuples in D satisfying the rule antecedent and having class label C is called the **support** of R. A support of 20% for Association Rule (6.44) means that 20% of the customers in D are young, have an OK credit rating, and belong to the class *buys_computer = yes*.

Methods of associative classification differ primarily in the approach used for frequent itemset mining and in how the derived rules are analyzed and used for classification. We now look at some of the various methods for associative classification.

One of the earliest and simplest algorithms for associative classification is **CBA** (Classification-Based Association). CBA uses an iterative approach to frequent itemset mining, similar to that described for Apriori in Section 5.2.1, where multiple passes are made over the data and the derived frequent itemsets are used to generate and test longer itemsets. In general, the number of passes made is equal to the length of the longest rule found. The complete set of rules satisfying minimum confidence and minimum support thresholds are found and then analyzed for inclusion in the classifier. CBA uses a heuristic method to construct the classifier, where the rules are organized according to decreasing precedence based on their confidence and support. If a set of rules has the same antecedent, then the rule with the highest confidence is selected to represent the set. When classifying a new tuple, the first rule satisfying the tuple is used to classify it. The classifier also contains a default rule, having lowest precedence, which specifies a default class for any new tuple that is not satisfied by any other rule in the classifier. In this way, the set of rules making up the classifier form a *decision list*. In general, CBA was empirically found to be more accurate than C4.5 on a good number of data sets.

CMAR (Classification based on Multiple Association Rules) differs from CBA in its strategy for frequent itemset mining and its construction of the classifier. It also employs several rule pruning strategies with the help of a tree structure for efficient storage and retrieval of rules. CMAR adopts a variant of the *FP-growth* algorithm to find the complete set of rules satisfying the minimum confidence and minimum support thresholds. FP-growth was described in Section 5.2.4. FP-growth uses a tree structure, called an *FP-tree*, to register all of the frequent itemset information contained in the given data set, *D*. This requires only two scans of *D*. The frequent itemsets are then mined from the FP-tree. CMAR uses an enhanced FP-tree that maintains the distribution of class labels among tuples satisfying each frequent itemset. In this way, it is able to combine rule generation together with frequent itemset mining in a single step.

CMAR employs another tree structure to store and retrieve rules efficiently and to prune rules based on confidence, correlation, and database coverage. Rule pruning strategies are triggered whenever a rule is inserted into the tree. For example, given two rules, $R1$ and $R2$, if the antecedent of $R1$ is more general than that of $R2$ and $conf(R1) \geq conf(R2)$, then $R2$ is pruned. The rationale is that highly specialized rules with low confidence can be pruned if a more generalized version with higher confidence exists. CMAR also prunes rules for which the rule antecedent and class are not positively correlated, based on a χ^2 test of statistical significance.

As a classifier, CMAR operates differently than CBA. Suppose that we are given a tuple **X** to classify and that only one rule satisfies or matches **X**.[11] This case is trivial—we simply assign the class label of the rule. Suppose, instead, that more than one rule satisfies **X**. These rules form a set, *S*. Which rule would we use to determine the class label of **X**? CBA would assign the class label of the most confident rule among the rule set, *S*. CMAR instead considers multiple rules when making its class prediction. It divides the rules into groups according to class labels. All rules within a group share the same class label and each group has a distinct class label. CMAR uses a weighted χ^2 measure to find the "strongest" group of rules, based on the statistical correlation of rules within a group. It then assigns **X** the class label of the strongest group. In this way it considers multiple

[11] If the antecedent of a rule satisfies or matches **X**, then we say that the rule satisfies **X**.

rules, rather than a single rule with highest confidence, when predicting the class label of a new tuple. On experiments, CMAR had slightly higher average accuracy in comparison with CBA. Its runtime, scalability, and use of memory were found to be more efficient.

CBA and CMAR adopt methods of frequent itemset mining to generate *candidate* association rules, which include all conjunctions of attribute-value pairs (items) satisfying minimum support. These rules are then examined, and a subset is chosen to represent the classifier. However, such methods generate quite a large number of rules. CPAR takes a different approach to rule generation, based on a rule generation algorithm for classification known as FOIL (Section 6.5.3). FOIL builds rules to distinguish positive tuples (say, having class *buys_computer* = *yes*) from negative tuples (such as *buys_computer* = *no*). For multiclass problems, FOIL is applied to each class. That is, for a class, *C*, all tuples of class *C* are considered positive tuples, while the rest are considered negative tuples. Rules are generated to distinguish *C* tuples from all others. Each time a rule is generated, the positive samples it satisfies (or *covers*) are removed until all the positive tuples in the data set are covered. CPAR relaxes this step by allowing the covered tuples to remain under consideration, but reducing their weight. The process is repeated for each class. The resulting rules are merged to form the classifier rule set.

During classification, CPAR employs a somewhat different multiple rule strategy than CMAR. If more than one rule satisfies a new tuple, ***X***, the rules are divided into groups according to class, similar to CMAR. However, CPAR uses the best *k* rules of each group to predict the class label of ***X***, based on expected accuracy. By considering the best *k* rules rather than all of the rules of a group, it avoids the influence of lower ranked rules. The accuracy of CPAR on numerous data sets was shown to be close to that of CMAR. However, since CPAR generates far fewer rules than CMAR, it shows much better efficiency with large sets of training data.

In summary, associative classification offers a new alternative to classification schemes by building rules based on conjunctions of attribute-value pairs that occur frequently in data.

6.9 Lazy Learners (or Learning from Your Neighbors)

The classification methods discussed so far in this chapter—decision tree induction, Bayesian classification, rule-based classification, classification by backpropagation, support vector machines, and classification based on association rule mining—are all examples of *eager learners.* **Eager learners**, when given a set of training tuples, will construct a generalization (i.e., classification) model before receiving new (e.g., test) tuples to classify. We can think of the learned model as being ready and eager to classify previously unseen tuples.

Imagine a contrasting lazy approach, in which the learner instead waits until the last minute before doing any model construction in order to classify a given test tuple. That is, when given a training tuple, a **lazy learner** simply stores it (or does only a little minor processing) and waits until it is given a test tuple. Only when it sees the test tuple does it perform generalization in order to classify the tuple based on its similarity to the stored training tuples. Unlike eager learning methods, lazy learners do less work when a training tuple is presented and more work when making a classification or prediction. Because lazy learners store the training tuples or "instances," they are also referred to as **instance-based learners**, even though all learning is essentially based on instances.

When making a classification or prediction, lazy learners can be computationally expensive. They require efficient storage techniques and are well-suited to implementation on parallel hardware. They offer little explanation or insight into the structure of the data. Lazy learners, however, naturally support incremental learning. They are able to model complex decision spaces having hyperpolygonal shapes that may not be as easily describable by other learning algorithms (such as hyper-rectangular shapes modeled by decision trees). In this section, we look at two examples of lazy learners: *k-nearest-neighbor classifiers* and *case-based reasoning classifiers.*

6.9.1 *k*-Nearest-Neighbor Classifiers

The *k*-nearest-neighbor method was first described in the early 1950s. The method is labor intensive when given large training sets, and did not gain popularity until the 1960s when increased computing power became available. It has since been widely used in the area of pattern recognition.

Nearest-neighbor classifiers are based on learning by analogy, that is, by comparing a given test tuple with training tuples that are similar to it. The training tuples are described by *n* attributes. Each tuple represents a point in an *n*-dimensional space. In this way, all of the training tuples are stored in an *n*-dimensional pattern space. When given an unknown tuple, a ***k*-nearest-neighbor classifier** searches the pattern space for the *k* training tuples that are closest to the unknown tuple. These *k* training tuples are the *k* "nearest neighbors" of the unknown tuple.

"Closeness" is defined in terms of a distance metric, such as Euclidean distance. The Euclidean distance between two points or tuples, say, $X_1 = (x_{11}, x_{12}, \ldots, x_{1n})$ and $X_2 = (x_{21}, x_{22}, \ldots, x_{2n})$, is

$$dist(X_1, X_2) = \sqrt{\sum_{i=1}^{n} (x_{1i} - x_{2i})^2}. \qquad (6.45)$$

In other words, for each numeric attribute, we take the difference between the corresponding values of that attribute in tuple X_1 and in tuple X_2, square this difference, and accumulate it. The square root is taken of the total accumulated distance count. Typically, we normalize the values of each attribute before using Equation (6.45). This helps prevent attributes with initially large ranges (such as *income*) from outweighing attributes with initially smaller ranges (such as binary attributes). Min-max normalization, for example, can be used to transform a value v of a numeric attribute A to v' in the range [0, 1] by computing

$$v' = \frac{v - min_A}{max_A - min_A}, \qquad (6.46)$$

where min_A and max_A are the minimum and maximum values of attribute A. Chapter 2 describes other methods for data normalization as a form of data transformation.

For k-nearest-neighbor classification, the unknown tuple is assigned the most common class among its k nearest neighbors. When $k = 1$, the unknown tuple is assigned the class of the training tuple that is closest to it in pattern space. Nearest-neighbor classifiers can also be used for prediction, that is, to return a real-valued prediction for a given unknown tuple. In this case, the classifier returns the average value of the real-valued labels associated with the k nearest neighbors of the unknown tuple.

"But how can distance be computed for attributes that not numeric, but categorical, such as color?" The above discussion assumes that the attributes used to describe the tuples are all numeric. For categorical attributes, a simple method is to compare the corresponding value of the attribute in tuple X_1 with that in tuple X_2. If the two are identical (e.g., tuples X_1 and X_2 both have the color blue), then the difference between the two is taken as 0. If the two are different (e.g., tuple X_1 is blue but tuple X_2 is red), then the difference is considered to be 1. Other methods may incorporate more sophisticated schemes for differential grading (e.g., where a larger difference score is assigned, say, for blue and white than for blue and black).

"What about missing values?" In general, if the value of a given attribute A is missing in tuple X_1 and/or in tuple X_2, we assume the maximum possible difference. Suppose that each of the attributes have been mapped to the range [0, 1]. For categorical attributes, we take the difference value to be 1 if either one or both of the corresponding values of A are missing. If A is numeric and missing from both tuples X_1 and X_2, then the difference is also taken to be 1. If only one value is missing and the other (which we'll call v') is present and normalized, then we can take the difference to be either $|1 - v'|$ or $|0 - v'|$ (i.e., $1 - v'$ or v'), whichever is greater.

"How can I determine a good value for k, the number of neighbors?" This can be determined experimentally. Starting with $k = 1$, we use a test set to estimate the error rate of the classifier. This process can be repeated each time by incrementing k to allow for one more neighbor. The k value that gives the minimum error rate may be selected. In general, the larger the number of training tuples is, the larger the value of k will be (so that classification and prediction decisions can be based on a larger portion of the stored tuples). As the number of training tuples approaches infinity and $k = 1$, the error rate can be no worse then twice the Bayes error rate (the latter being the theoretical minimum). If k also approaches infinity, the error rate approaches the Bayes error rate.

Nearest-neighbor classifiers use distance-based comparisons that intrinsically assign equal weight to each attribute. They therefore can suffer from poor accuracy when given noisy or irrelevant attributes. The method, however, has been modified to incorporate attribute weighting and the pruning of noisy data tuples. The choice of a distance metric can be critical. The Manhattan (city block) distance (Section 7.2.1), or other distance measurements, may also be used.

Nearest-neighbor classifiers can be extremely slow when classifying test tuples. If D is a training database of $|D|$ tuples and $k = 1$, then $O(|D|)$ comparisons are required in order to classify a given test tuple. By presorting and arranging the stored tuples into search trees, the number of comparisons can be reduced to $O(log(|D|)$. Parallel implementation can reduce the running time to a constant, that is $O(1)$, which is independent of $|D|$. Other techniques to speed up classification time include the use of *partial distance* calculations and *editing* the stored tuples. In the **partial distance** method, we compute the distance based on a subset of the n attributes. If this distance exceeds a threshold, then further computation for the given stored tuple is halted, and the process moves on to the next stored tuple. The **editing** method removes training tuples that prove useless. This method is also referred to as **pruning** or **condensing** because it reduces the total number of tuples stored.

6.9.2 Case-Based Reasoning

Case-based reasoning (CBR) classifiers use a database of problem solutions to solve new problems. Unlike nearest-neighbor classifiers, which store training tuples as points in Euclidean space, CBR stores the tuples or "cases" for problem solving as complex symbolic descriptions. Business applications of CBR include problem resolution for customer service help desks, where cases describe product-related diagnostic problems. CBR has also been applied to areas such as engineering and law, where cases are either technical designs or legal rulings, respectively. Medical education is another area for CBR, where patient case histories and treatments are used to help diagnose and treat new patients.

When given a new case to classify, a case-based reasoner will first check if an identical training case exists. If one is found, then the accompanying solution to that case is returned. If no identical case is found, then the case-based reasoner will search for training cases having components that are similar to those of the new case. Conceptually, these training cases may be considered as neighbors of the new case. If cases are represented as graphs, this involves searching for subgraphs that are similar to subgraphs within the new case. The case-based reasoner tries to combine the solutions of the neighboring training cases in order to propose a solution for the new case. If incompatibilities arise with the individual solutions, then backtracking to search for other solutions may be necessary. The case-based reasoner may employ background knowledge and problem-solving strategies in order to propose a feasible combined solution.

Challenges in case-based reasoning include finding a good similarity metric (e.g., for matching subgraphs) and suitable methods for combining solutions. Other challenges include the selection of salient features for indexing training cases and the development of efficient indexing techniques. A trade-off between accuracy and efficiency evolves as the number of stored cases becomes very large. As this number increases, the case-based reasoner becomes more intelligent. After a certain point, however, the efficiency of the system will suffer as the time required to search for and process relevant cases increases. As with nearest-neighbor classifiers, one solution is to edit the training database. Cases that are redundant or that have not proved useful may be discarded for the sake of improved performance. These decisions, however, are not clear-cut and their automation remains an active area of research.

6.10 Other Classification Methods

In this section, we give a brief description of several other classification methods, including genetic algorithms, rough set approach, and fuzzy set approaches. In general, these methods are less commonly used for classification in commercial data mining systems than the methods described earlier in this chapter. However, these methods do show their strength in certain applications, and hence it is worthwhile to include them here.

6.10.1 Genetic Algorithms

Genetic algorithms attempt to incorporate ideas of natural evolution. In general, genetic learning starts as follows. An initial **population** is created consisting of randomly generated rules. Each rule can be represented by a string of bits. As a simple example, suppose that samples in a given training set are described by two Boolean attributes, A_1 and A_2, and that there are two classes, C_1 and C_2. The rule "*IF* A_1 *AND NOT* A_2 *THEN* C_2" can be encoded as the bit string "100," where the two leftmost bits represent attributes A_1 and A_2, respectively, and the rightmost bit represents the class. Similarly, the rule "*IF NOT* A_1 *AND NOT* A_2 *THEN* C_1" can be encoded as "001." If an attribute has k values, where $k > 2$, then k bits may be used to encode the attribute's values. Classes can be encoded in a similar fashion.

Based on the notion of survival of the fittest, a new population is formed to consist of the *fittest* rules in the current population, as well as *offspring* of these rules. Typically, the **fitness** of a rule is assessed by its classification accuracy on a set of training samples.

Offspring are created by applying genetic operators such as crossover and mutation. In **crossover**, substrings from pairs of rules are swapped to form new pairs of rules. In **mutation**, randomly selected bits in a rule's string are inverted.

The process of generating new populations based on prior populations of rules continues until a population, P, evolves where each rule in P satisfies a prespecified fitness threshold.

Genetic algorithms are easily parallelizable and have been used for classification as well as other optimization problems. In data mining, they may be used to evaluate the fitness of other algorithms.

6.10.2 Rough Set Approach

Rough set theory can be used for classification to discover structural relationships within imprecise or noisy data. It applies to discrete-valued attributes. Continuous-valued attributes must therefore be discretized before its use.

Rough set theory is based on the establishment of **equivalence classes** within the given training data. All of the data tuples forming an equivalence class are indiscernible, that is, the samples are identical with respect to the attributes describing the data. Given real-world data, it is common that some classes cannot be distinguished in terms of the available attributes. Rough sets can be used to approximately or "roughly" define such classes. A rough set definition for a given class, C, is approximated by two sets—a **lower**

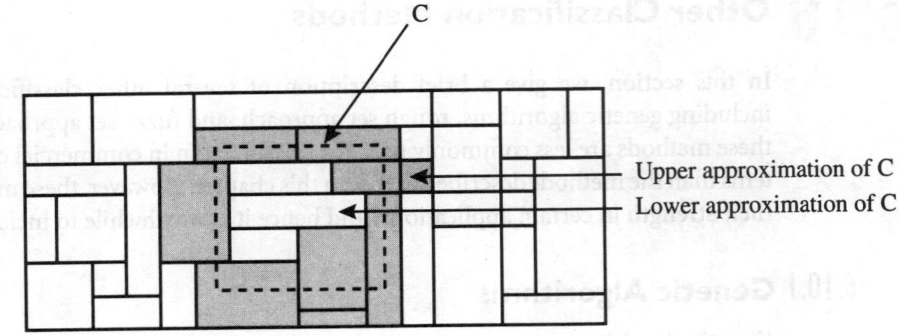

Figure 6.24 A rough set approximation of the set of tuples of the class C using lower and upper approximation sets of C. The rectangular regions represent equivalence classes.

approximation of C and an **upper approximation** of C. The lower approximation of C consists of all of the data tuples that, based on the knowledge of the attributes, are certain to belong to C without ambiguity. The upper approximation of C consists of all of the tuples that, based on the knowledge of the attributes, cannot be described as not belonging to C. The lower and upper approximations for a class C are shown in Figure 6.24, where each rectangular region represents an equivalence class. Decision rules can be generated for each class. Typically, a decision table is used to represent the rules.

Rough sets can also be used for attribute subset selection (or feature reduction, where attributes that do not contribute toward the classification of the given training data can be identified and removed) and relevance analysis (where the contribution or significance of each attribute is assessed with respect to the classification task). The problem of finding the minimal subsets (**reducts**) of attributes that can describe all of the concepts in the given data set is NP-hard. However, algorithms to reduce the computation intensity have been proposed. In one method, for example, a **discernibility matrix** is used that stores the differences between attribute values for each pair of data tuples. Rather than searching on the entire training set, the matrix is instead searched to detect redundant attributes.

6.10.3 Fuzzy Set Approaches

Rule-based systems for classification have the disadvantage that they involve sharp cutoffs for continuous attributes. For example, consider the following rule for customer credit application approval. The rule essentially says that applications for customers who have had a job for two or more years and who have a high income (i.e., of at least \$50,000) are approved:

$$IF\ (years\_employed \geq 2)\ AND\ (income \geq 50K)\ THEN\ credit = approved. \quad (6.47)$$

By Rule (6.47), a customer who has had a job for at least two years will receive credit if her income is, say, \$50,000, but not if it is \$49,000. Such harsh thresholding may seem unfair.

Instead, we can discretize *income* into categories such as {*low_income, medium_income, high_income*}, and then apply **fuzzy logic** to allow "fuzzy" thresholds or boundaries to be defined for each category (Figure 6.25). Rather than having a precise cutoff between categories, fuzzy logic uses truth values between 0.0 and 1.0 to represent the degree of membership that a certain value has in a given category. Each category then represents a **fuzzy set**. Hence, with fuzzy logic, we can capture the notion that an income of $49,000 is, more or less, high, although not as high as an income of $50,000. Fuzzy logic systems typically provide graphical tools to assist users in converting attribute values to fuzzy truth values.

Fuzzy set theory is also known as **possibility theory**. It was proposed by Lotfi Zadeh in 1965 as an alternative to traditional two-value logic and probability theory. It lets us work at a high level of abstraction and offers a means for dealing with imprecise measurement of data. Most important, fuzzy set theory allows us to deal with vague or inexact facts. For example, being a member of a set of high incomes is inexact (e.g., if $50,000 is high, then what about $49,000? Or $48,000?) Unlike the notion of traditional "crisp" sets where an element either belongs to a set *S* or its complement, in fuzzy set theory, elements can belong to more than one fuzzy set. For example, the income value $49,000 belongs to both the *medium* and *high* fuzzy sets, but to differing degrees. Using fuzzy set notation and following Figure 6.25, this can be shown as

$$m_{medium\_income}(\$49K) = 0.15 \; and \; m_{high\_income}(\$49K) = 0.96,$$

where *m* denotes the membership function, operating on the fuzzy sets of *medium_income* and *high_income*, respectively. In fuzzy set theory, membership values for a given element, *x*, (e.g., such as for $49,000) do not have to sum to 1. This is unlike traditional probability theory, which is constrained by a summation axiom.

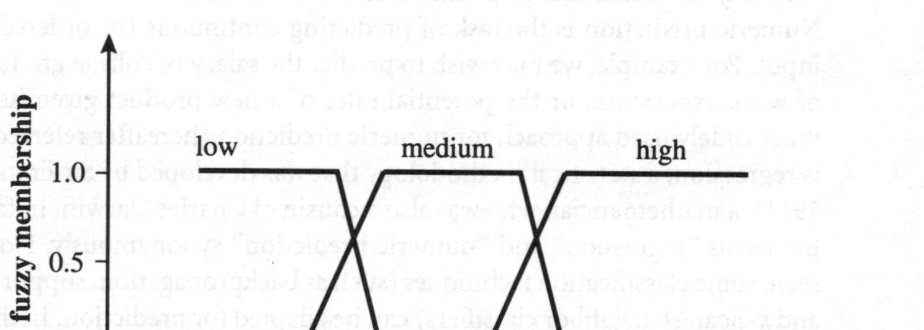

Figure 6.25 Fuzzy truth values for *income*, representing the degree of membership of *income* values with respect to the categories {*low, medium, high*}. Each category represents a fuzzy set. Note that a given income value, *x*, can have membership in more than one fuzzy set. The membership values of *x* in each fuzzy set do not have to total to 1.

Fuzzy set theory is useful for data mining systems performing rule-based classification. It provides operations for combining fuzzy measurements. Suppose that in addition to the fuzzy sets for *income*, we defined the fuzzy sets *junior_employee* and *senior_employee* for the attribute *years_employed*. Suppose also that we have a rule that, say, tests *high_income* and *senior_employee* in the rule antecedent (IF part) for a given employee, *x*. If these two fuzzy measures are ANDed together, the minimum of their measure is taken as the measure of the rule. In other words,

$$m_{(high\_income\ AND\ senior\_employee)}(x) = min(m_{high\_income}(x), m_{senior\_employee}(x)).$$

This is akin to saying that a chain is as strong as its weakest link. If the two measures are ORed, the maximum of their measure is taken as the measure of the rule. In other words,

$$m_{(high\_income\ OR\ senior\_employee)}(x) = max(m_{high\_income}(x), m_{senior\_employee}(x)).$$

Intuitively, this is like saying that a rope is as strong as its strongest strand.

Given a tuple to classify, more than one fuzzy rule may apply. Each applicable rule contributes a vote for membership in the categories. Typically, the truth values for each predicted category are summed, and these sums are combined. Several procedures exist for translating the resulting fuzzy output into a *defuzzified* or crisp value that is returned by the system.

Fuzzy logic systems have been used in numerous areas for classification, including market research, finance, health care, and environmental engineering.

6.11 Prediction

"What if we would like to predict a continuous value, rather than a categorical label?" Numeric prediction is the task of predicting continuous (or ordered) values for given input. For example, we may wish to predict the salary of college graduates with 10 years of work experience, or the potential sales of a new product given its price. By far, the most widely used approach for numeric prediction (hereafter referred to as prediction) is **regression**, a statistical methodology that was developed by Sir Frances Galton (1822–1911), a mathematician who was also a cousin of Charles Darwin. In fact, many texts use the terms "regression" and "numeric prediction" synonymously. However, as we have seen, some classification techniques (such as backpropagation, support vector machines, and *k*-nearest-neighbor classifiers) can be adapted for prediction. In this section, we discuss the use of regression techniques for prediction.

Regression analysis can be used to model the relationship between one or more *independent* or **predictor** variables and a *dependent* or **response** variable (which is continuous-valued). In the context of data mining, the predictor variables are the attributes of interest describing the tuple (i.e., making up the attribute vector). In general, the values of the predictor variables are known. (Techniques exist for handling cases where such values may be missing.) The response variable is what we want to predict—it is what we referred to in Section 6.1 as the predicted attribute. Given a tuple described by predictor variables, we want to predict the associated value of the response variable.

Regression analysis is a good choice when all of the predictor variables are continuous-valued as well. Many problems can be solved by *linear regression*, and even more can be tackled by applying transformations to the variables so that a nonlinear problem can be converted to a linear one. For reasons of space, we cannot give a fully detailed treatment of regression. Instead, this section provides an intuitive introduction to the topic. Section 6.11.1 discusses straight-line regression analysis (which involves a single predictor variable) and multiple linear regression analysis (which involves two or more predictor variables). Section 6.11.2 provides some pointers on dealing with nonlinear regression. Section 6.11.3 mentions other regression-based methods, such as generalized linear models, Poisson regression, log-linear models, and regression trees.

Several software packages exist to solve regression problems. Examples include SAS (*www.sas.com*), SPSS (*www.spss.com*), and S-Plus (*www.insightful.com*). Another useful resource is the book *Numerical Recipes in C*, by Press, Flannery, Teukolsky, and Vetterling, and its associated source code.

6.11.1 Linear Regression

Straight-line regression analysis involves a response variable, y, and a single predictor variable, x. It is the simplest form of regression, and models y as a linear function of x. That is,

$$y = b + wx, \tag{6.48}$$

where the variance of y is assumed to be constant, and b and w are **regression coefficients** specifying the Y-intercept and slope of the line, respectively. The regression coefficients, w and b, can also be thought of as weights, so that we can equivalently write,

$$y = w_0 + w_1 x. \tag{6.49}$$

These coefficients can be solved for by the **method of least squares**, which estimates the best-fitting straight line as the one that minimizes the error between the actual data and the estimate of the line. Let D be a training set consisting of values of predictor variable, x, for some population and their associated values for response variable, y. The training set contains $|D|$ data points of the form $(x_1, y_1), (x_2, y_2), \ldots, (x_{|D|}, y_{|D|})$.[12] The regression coefficients can be estimated using this method with the following equations:

$$w_1 = \frac{\sum_{i=1}^{|D|}(x_i - \bar{x})(y_i - \bar{y})}{\sum_{i=1}^{|D|}(x_i - \bar{x})^2} \tag{6.50}$$

[12]Note that earlier, we had used the notation $(\mathbf{X}_i, y_i)$ to refer to training tuple i having associated class label y_i, where $\mathbf{X}_i$ was an attribute (or feature) *vector* (that is, $\mathbf{X}_i$ was described by more than one attribute). Here, however, we are dealing with just one predictor variable. Since the $\mathbf{X}_i$ here are one-dimensional, we use the notation x_i over $\mathbf{X}_i$ in this case.

$$w_0 = \bar{y} - w_1\bar{x} \tag{6.51}$$

where $\bar{x}$ is the mean value of $x_1, x_2, \ldots, x_{|D|}$, and $\bar{y}$ is the mean value of $y_1, y_2, \ldots, y_{|D|}$. The coefficients w_0 and w_1 often provide good approximations to otherwise complicated regression equations.

Example 6.11 **Straight-line regression using the method of least squares.** Table 6.7 shows a set of paired data where x is the number of years of work experience of a college graduate and y is the

Table 6.7 Salary data.

x years experience	*y salary (in \$1000s)*
3	30
8	57
9	64
13	72
3	36
6	43
11	59
21	90
1	20
16	83

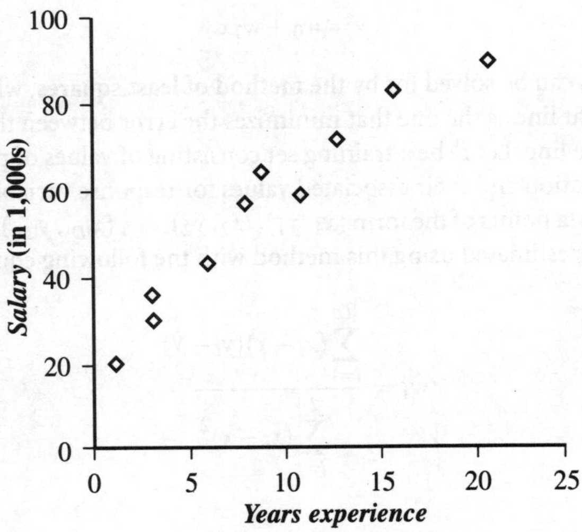

Figure 6.26 Plot of the data in Table 6.7 for Example 6.11. Although the points do not fall on a straight line, the overall pattern suggests a linear relationship between x (*years experience*) and y (*salary*).

corresponding salary of the graduate. The 2-D data can be graphed on a *scatter plot*, as in Figure 6.26. The plot suggests a linear relationship between the two variables, x and y. We model the relationship that salary may be related to the number of years of work experience with the equation $y = w_0 + w_1 x$.

Given the above data, we compute $\bar{x} = 9.1$ and $\bar{y} = 55.4$. Substituting these values into Equations (6.50) and (6.51), we get

$$w_1 = \frac{(3-9.1)(30-55.4)+(8-9.1)(57-55.4)+\cdots+(16-9.1)(83-55.4)}{(3-9.1)^2+(8-9.1)^2+\cdots+(16-9.1)^2} = 3.5$$

$$w_0 = 55.4-(3.5)(9.1) = 23.6$$

Thus, the equation of the least squares line is estimated by $y = 23.6 + 3.5x$. Using this equation, we can predict that the salary of a college graduate with, say, 10 years of experience is \$58,600. ■

Multiple linear regression is an extension of straight-line regression so as to involve more than one predictor variable. It allows response variable y to be modeled as a linear function of, say, n predictor variables or attributes, $A_1, A_2, \ldots, A_n$, describing a tuple, $\boldsymbol{X}$. (That is, $\boldsymbol{X} = (x_1, x_2, \ldots, x_n)$.) Our training data set, D, contains data of the form $(\boldsymbol{X_1}, y_1), (\boldsymbol{X_2}, y_2), \ldots, (\boldsymbol{X_{|D|}}, y_{|D|})$, where the $\boldsymbol{X_i}$ are the n-dimensional training tuples with associated class labels, y_i. An example of a multiple linear regression model based on two predictor attributes or variables, A_1 and A_2, is

$$y = w_0 + w_1 x_1 + w_2 x_2, \tag{6.52}$$

where x_1 and x_2 are the values of attributes A_1 and A_2, respectively, in $\boldsymbol{X}$. The method of least squares shown above can be extended to solve for w_0, w_1, and w_2. The equations, however, become long and are tedious to solve by hand. Multiple regression problems are instead commonly solved with the use of statistical software packages, such as SAS, SPSS, and S-Plus (see references above.)

6.11.2 Nonlinear Regression

"How can we model data that does not show a linear dependence? For example, what if a given response variable and predictor variable have a relationship that may be modeled by a polynomial function?" Think back to the straight-line linear regression case above where dependent response variable, y, is modeled as a linear function of a single independent predictor variable, x. What if we can get a more accurate model using a nonlinear model, such as a parabola or some other higher-order polynomial? **Polynomial regression** is often of interest when there is just one predictor variable. It can be modeled by adding polynomial terms to the basic linear model. By applying transformations to the variables, we can convert the nonlinear model into a linear one that can then be solved by the method of least squares.

Example 6.12 **Transformation of a polynomial regression model to a linear regression model.** Consider a cubic polynomial relationship given by

$$y = w_0 + w_1 x + w_2 x^2 + w_3 x^3. \tag{6.53}$$

To convert this equation to linear form, we define new variables:

$$x_1 = x \qquad x_2 = x^2 \qquad x_3 = x^3 \tag{6.54}$$

Equation (6.53) can then be converted to linear form by applying the above assignments, resulting in the equation $y = w_0 + w_1 x_1 + w_2 x_2 + w_3 x_3$, which is easily solved by the method of least squares using software for regression analysis. Note that polynomial regression is a special case of multiple regression. That is, the addition of high-order terms like x^2, x^3, and so on, which are simple functions of the single variable, x, can be considered equivalent to adding new independent variables. ■

In Exercise 15, you are asked to find the transformations required to convert a nonlinear model involving a power function into a linear regression model.

Some models are intractably nonlinear (such as the sum of exponential terms, for example) and cannot be converted to a linear model. For such cases, it may be possible to obtain least square estimates through extensive calculations on more complex formulae.

Various statistical measures exist for determining how well the proposed model can predict y. These are described in Section 6.12.2. Obviously, the greater the number of predictor attributes is, the slower the performance is. Before applying regression analysis, it is common to perform attribute subset selection (Section 2.5.2) to eliminate attributes that are unlikely to be good predictors for y. In general, regression analysis is accurate for prediction, except when the data contain outliers. Outliers are data points that are highly inconsistent with the remaining data (e.g., they may be way out of the expected value range). Outlier detection is discussed in Chapter 7. Such techniques must be used with caution, however, so as not to remove data points that are valid, although they may vary greatly from the mean.

6.11.3 Other Regression-Based Methods

Linear regression is used to model continuous-valued functions. It is widely used, owing largely to its simplicity. *"Can it also be used to predict categorical labels?"* **Generalized linear models** represent the theoretical foundation on which linear regression can be applied to the modeling of categorical response variables. In generalized linear models, the variance of the response variable, y, is a function of the mean value of y, unlike in linear regression, where the variance of y is constant. Common types of generalized linear models include **logistic regression** and **Poisson regression.** Logistic regression models the probability of some event occurring as a linear function of a set of predictor variables. Count data frequently exhibit a Poisson distribution and are commonly modeled using Poisson regression.

Log-linear models approximate *discrete* multidimensional probability distributions. They may be used to estimate the probability value associated with data cube cells. For example, suppose we are given data for the attributes *city, item, year*, and *sales*. In the log-linear method, all attributes must be categorical; hence continuous-valued attributes (like *sales*) must first be discretized. The method can then be used to estimate the probability of each cell in the 4-D base cuboid for the given attributes, based on the 2-D cuboids for *city* and *item*, *city* and *year*, *city* and *sales*, and the 3-D cuboid for *item*, *year*, and *sales*. In this way, an iterative technique can be used to build higher-order data cubes from lower-order ones. The technique scales up well to allow for many dimensions. Aside from prediction, the log-linear model is useful for data compression (since the smaller-order cuboids together typically occupy less space than the base cuboid) and data smoothing (since cell estimates in the smaller-order cuboids are less subject to sampling variations than cell estimates in the base cuboid).

Decision tree induction can be adapted so as to predict continuous (ordered) values, rather than class labels. There are two main types of trees for prediction—*regression trees* and *model trees*. **Regression trees** were proposed as a component of the CART learning system. (Recall that the acronym CART stands for *Classification and Regression Trees*.) Each regression tree leaf stores a continuous-valued prediction, which is actually the average value of the predicted attribute for the training tuples that reach the leaf. Since the terms "regression" and "numeric prediction" are used synonymously in statistics, the resulting trees were called "regression trees," even though they did not use any regression equations. By contrast, in **model trees**, each leaf holds a regression model—a multivariate linear equation for the predicted attribute. Regression and model trees tend to be more accurate than linear regression when the data are not represented well by a simple linear model.

6.12 Accuracy and Error Measures

Now that you may have trained a classifier or predictor, there may be many questions going through your mind. For example, suppose you used data from previous sales to train a classifier to predict customer purchasing behavior. You would like an estimate of how accurately the classifier can predict the purchasing behavior of future customers, that is, future customer data on which the classifier has not been trained. You may even have tried different methods to build more than one classifier (or predictor) and now wish to compare their accuracy. But what is accuracy? How can we estimate it? Are there strategies for increasing the accuracy of a learned model? These questions are addressed in the next few sections. Section 6.12.1 describes measures for computing classifier accuracy. Predictor error measures are given in Section 6.12.2. We can use these measures in techniques for accuracy estimation, such as the *holdout, random subsampling, k-fold cross-validation*, and *bootstrap* methods (Section 6.13). In Section 6.14, we'll learn some tricks for increasing model accuracy, such as *bagging* and *boosting*. Finally, Section 6.15 discusses **model selection** (i.e., choosing one classifier or predictor over another).

Classes	*buys_computer = yes*	*buys_computer = no*	*Total*	*Recognition (%)*
buys_computer = yes	6,954	46	7,000	99.34
buys_computer = no	412	2,588	3,000	86.27
Total	7,366	2,634	10,000	95.52

Figure 6.27 A confusion matrix for the classes *buys_computer = yes* and *buys_computer = no,* where an entry is row *i* and column *j* shows the number of tuples of class *i* that were labeled by the classifier as class *j*. Ideally, the nondiagonal entries should be zero or close to zero.

6.12.1 Classifier Accuracy Measures

Using training data to derive a classifier or predictor and then to estimate the accuracy of the resulting learned model can result in misleading overoptimistic estimates due to overspecialization of the learning algorithm to the data. (We'll say more on this in a moment!) Instead, accuracy is better measured on a test set consisting of class-labeled tuples that were not used to train the model. The **accuracy** of a classifier on a given test set is the percentage of test set tuples that are correctly classified by the classifier. In the pattern recognition literature, this is also referred to as the overall **recognition rate** of the classifier, that is, it reflects how well the classifier recognizes tuples of the various classes.

We can also speak of the **error rate or misclassification rate** of a classifier, M, which is simply $1 - Acc(M)$, where $Acc(M)$ is the accuracy of M. If we were to use the training set to estimate the error rate of a model, this quantity is known as the **resubstitution error.** This error estimate is optimistic of the true error rate (and similarly, the corresponding accuracy estimate is optimistic) because the model is not tested on any samples that it has not already seen.

The *confusion matrix* is a useful tool for analyzing how well your classifier can recognize tuples of different classes. A confusion matrix for two classes is shown in Figure 6.27. Given m classes, a **confusion matrix** is a table of at least size m by m. An entry, $CM_{i,\,j}$ in the first m rows and m columns indicates the number of tuples of class i that were labeled by the classifier as class j. For a classifier to have good accuracy, ideally most of the tuples would be represented along the diagonal of the confusion matrix, from entry $CM_{1,\,1}$ to entry $CM_{m,\,m}$, with the rest of the entries being close to zero. The table may have additional rows or columns to provide totals or recognition rates per class.

Given two classes, we can talk in terms of **positive tuples** (tuples of the main class of interest, e.g., *buys_computer = yes*) versus **negative tuples** (e.g., *buys_computer = no*).[13] **True positives** refer to the positive tuples that were correctly labeled by the classifier, while **true negatives** are the negative tuples that were correctly labeled by the classifier. **False positives** are the negative tuples that were incorrectly labeled (e.g., tuples of class *buys_computer = no* for which the classifier predicted *buys_computer = yes*). Similarly,

[13]In the machine learning and pattern recognition literature, these are referred to as *positive samples* and *negatives samples*, respectively.

		Predicted class	
		C_1	C_2
Actual class	C_1	true positives	false negatives
	C_2	false positives	true negatives

Figure 6.28 A confusion matrix for positive and negative tuples.

false negatives are the positive tuples that were incorrectly labeled (e.g., tuples of class *buys_computer = yes* for which the classifier predicted *buys_computer = no*). These terms are useful when analyzing a classifier's ability and are summarized in Figure 6.28.

"Are there alternatives to the accuracy measure?" Suppose that you have trained a classifier to classify medical data tuples as either *"cancer"* or *"not_cancer."* An accuracy rate of, say, 90% may make the classifier seem quite accurate, but what if only, say, 3–4% of the training tuples are actually *"cancer"*? Clearly, an accuracy rate of 90% may not be acceptable—the classifier could be correctly labelling only the *"not_cancer"* tuples, for instance. Instead, we would like to be able to access how well the classifier can recognize *"cancer"* tuples (the positive tuples) and how well it can recognize *"not_cancer"* tuples (the negative tuples). The **sensitivity** and **specificity** measures can be used, respectively, for this purpose. Sensitivity is also referred to as the *true positive (recognition) rate* (that is, the proportion of positive tuples that are correctly identified), while specificity is the *true negative rate* (that is, the proportion of negative tuples that are correctly identified). In addition, we may use **precision** to access the percentage of tuples labeled as *"cancer"* that actually are *"cancer"* tuples. These measures are defined as

$$sensitivity = \frac{t\_pos}{pos} \tag{6.55}$$

$$specificity = \frac{t\_neg}{neg} \tag{6.56}$$

$$precision = \frac{t\_pos}{(t\_pos + f\_pos)} \tag{6.57}$$

where *t_pos* is the number of true positives (*"cancer"* tuples that were correctly classified as such), *pos* is the number of positive (*"cancer"*) tuples, *t_neg* is the number of true negatives (*"not_cancer"* tuples that were correctly classified as such), *neg* is the number of negative (*"not_cancer"*) tuples, and *f_pos* is the number of false positives (*"not_cancer"* tuples that were incorrectly labeled as *"cancer"*). It can be shown that accuracy is a function of sensitivity and specificity:

$$accuracy = sensitivity\frac{pos}{(pos + neg)} + specificity\frac{neg}{(pos + neg)}. \tag{6.58}$$

The true positives, true negatives, false positives, and false negatives are also useful in assessing the **costs and benefits** (or risks and gains) associated with a classification model. The cost associated with a false negative (such as, incorrectly predicting that a cancerous patient is not cancerous) is far greater than that of a false positive (incorrectly yet conservatively labeling a noncancerous patient as cancerous). In such cases, we can outweigh one type of error over another by assigning a different cost to each. These costs may consider the danger to the patient, financial costs of resulting therapies, and other hospital costs. Similarly, the benefits associated with a true positive decision may be different than that of a true negative. Up to now, to compute classifier accuracy, we have assumed equal costs and essentially divided the sum of true positives and true negatives by the total number of test tuples. Alternatively, we can incorporate costs and benefits by instead computing the average cost (or benefit) per decision. Other applications involving cost-benefit analysis include loan application decisions and target marketing mailouts. For example, the cost of loaning to a defaulter greatly exceeds that of the lost business incurred by denying a loan to a nondefaulter. Similarly, in an application that tries to identify households that are likely to respond to mailouts of certain promotional material, the cost of mailouts to numerous households that do not respond may outweigh the cost of lost business from not mailing to households that would have responded. Other costs to consider in the overall analysis include the costs to collect the data and to develop the classification tool.

"Are there other cases where accuracy may not be appropriate?" In classification problems, it is commonly assumed that all tuples are uniquely classifiable, that is, that each training tuple can belong to only one class. Yet, owing to the wide diversity of data in large databases, it is not always reasonable to assume that all tuples are uniquely classifiable. Rather, it is more probable to assume that each tuple may belong to more than one class. How then can the accuracy of classifiers on large databases be measured? The accuracy measure is not appropriate, because it does not take into account the possibility of tuples belonging to more than one class.

Rather than returning a class label, it is useful to return a probability class distribution. Accuracy measures may then use a **second guess** heuristic, whereby a class prediction is judged as correct if it agrees with the first or second most probable class. Although this does take into consideration, to some degree, the nonunique classification of tuples, it is not a complete solution.

6.12.2 Predictor Error Measures

"How can we measure predictor accuracy?" Let D^T be a test set of the form $(\mathbf{X_1}, y_1)$, $(\mathbf{X_2}, y_2), \ldots, (\mathbf{X_d}, y_d)$, where the $\mathbf{X_i}$ are the n-dimensional test tuples with associated known values, y_i, for a response variable, y, and d is the number of tuples in D^T. Since predictors return a continuous value rather than a categorical label, it is difficult to say *exactly* whether the predicted value, y'_i, for $\mathbf{X_i}$ is correct. Instead of focusing on whether y'_i is an "exact" match with y_i, we instead look at how far off the predicted value is from the actual known value. **Loss functions** measure the error between y_i and the predicted value, y'_i. The most common loss functions are:

$$\textbf{Absolute error}: \quad |y_i - y'_i| \tag{6.59}$$

$$\textbf{Squared error}: \quad (y_i - y'_i)^2 \tag{6.60}$$

Based on the above, the test error (rate), or **generalization error**, is the average loss over the test set. Thus, we get the following error rates.

$$\textbf{Mean absolute error:} \quad \frac{\sum_{i=1}^{d} |y_i - y_i'|}{d} \tag{6.61}$$

$$\textbf{Mean squared error:} \quad \frac{\sum_{i=1}^{d} (y_i - y_i')^2}{d} \tag{6.62}$$

The mean squared error exaggerates the presence of outliers, while the mean absolute error does not. If we were to take the square root of the mean squared error, the resulting error measure is called the **root mean squared error**. This is useful in that it allows the error measured to be of the same magnitude as the quantity being predicted.

Sometimes, we may want the error to be relative to what it would have been if we had just predicted $\bar{y}$, the mean value for y from the training data, D. That is, we can normalize the total loss by dividing by the total loss incurred from always predicting the mean. Relative measures of error include:

$$\textbf{Relative absolute error:} \quad \frac{\sum_{i=1}^{d} |y_i - y_i'|}{\sum_{i=1}^{d} |y_i - \bar{y}|} \tag{6.63}$$

$$\textbf{Relative squared error:} \quad \frac{\sum_{i=1}^{d} (y_i - y_i')^2}{\sum_{i=1}^{d} (y_i - \bar{y})^2} \tag{6.64}$$

where $\bar{y}$ is the mean value of the y_i's of the training data, that is $\bar{y} = \frac{\sum_{i=1}^{t} y_i}{d}$. We can take the root of the relative squared error to obtain the **root relative squared error** so that the resulting error is of the same magnitude as the quantity predicted.

In practice, the choice of error measure does not greatly affect prediction model selection.

6.13 Evaluating the Accuracy of a Classifier or Predictor

How can we use the above measures to obtain a reliable estimate of classifier accuracy (or predictor accuracy in terms of error)? Holdout, random subsampling, cross-validation, and the bootstrap are common techniques for assessing accuracy based on

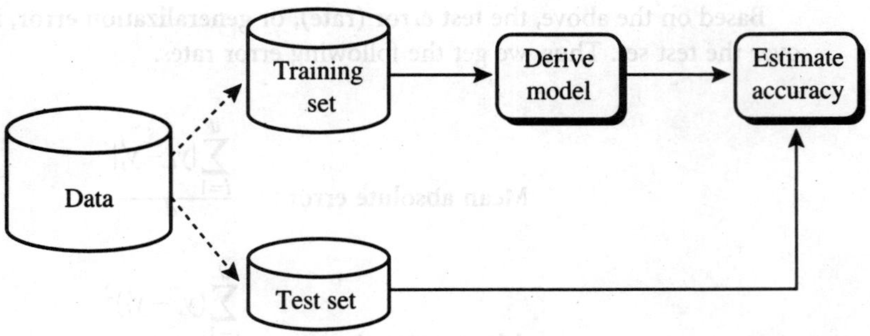

Figure 6.29 Estimating accuracy with the holdout method.

randomly sampled partitions of the given data. The use of such techniques to estimate accuracy increases the overall computation time, yet is useful for model selection.

6.13.1 Holdout Method and Random Subsampling

The **holdout** method is what we have alluded to so far in our discussions about accuracy. In this method, the given data are randomly partitioned into two independent sets, a *training set* and a *test set*. Typically, two-thirds of the data are allocated to the training set, and the remaining one-third is allocated to the test set. The training set is used to derive the model, whose accuracy is estimated with the test set (Figure 6.29). The estimate is pessimistic because only a portion of the initial data is used to derive the model.

Random subsampling is a variation of the holdout method in which the holdout method is repeated k times. The overall accuracy estimate is taken as the average of the accuracies obtained from each iteration. (For prediction, we can take the average of the predictor error rates.)

6.13.2 Cross-validation

In **k-fold cross-validation**, the initial data are randomly partitioned into k mutually exclusive subsets or "folds," $D_1, D_2, \ldots, D_k$, each of approximately equal size. Training and testing is performed k times. In iteration i, partition D_i is reserved as the test set, and the remaining partitions are collectively used to train the model. That is, in the first iteration, subsets $D_2, \ldots, D_k$ collectively serve as the training set in order to obtain a first model, which is tested on D_1; the second iteration is trained on subsets $D_1, D_3, \ldots, D_k$ and tested on D_2; and so on. Unlike the holdout and random subsampling methods above, here, each sample is used the same number of times for training and once for testing. For classification, the accuracy estimate is the overall number of correct classifications from the k iterations, divided by the total number of tuples in the initial data. For prediction, the error estimate can be computed as the total loss from the k iterations, divided by the total number of initial tuples.

Leave-one-out is a special case of k-fold cross-validation where k is set to the number of initial tuples. That is, only one sample is "left out" at a time for the test set. In **stratified cross-validation,** the folds are stratified so that the class distribution of the tuples in each fold is approximately the same as that in the initial data.

In general, stratified 10-fold cross-validation is recommended for estimating accuracy (even if computation power allows using more folds) due to its relatively low bias and variance.

6.13.3 Bootstrap

Unlike the accuracy estimation methods mentioned above, the **bootstrap method** samples the given training tuples uniformly *with replacement.* That is, each time a tuple is selected, it is equally likely to be selected again and readded to the training set. For instance, imagine a machine that randomly selects tuples for our training set. In *sampling with replacement,* the machine is allowed to select the same tuple more than once.

There are several bootstrap methods. A commonly used one is the **.632 bootstrap,** which works as follows. Suppose we are given a data set of d tuples. The data set is sampled d times, with replacement, resulting in a *bootstrap sample* or training set of d samples. It is very likely that some of the original data tuples will occur more than once in this sample. The data tuples that did not make it into the training set end up forming the test set. Suppose we were to try this out several times. As it turns out, on average, 63.2% of the original data tuples will end up in the bootstrap, and the remaining 36.8% will form the test set (hence, the name, .632 bootstrap.)

"Where does the figure, 63.2%, come from?" Each tuple has a probability of $1/d$ of being selected, so the probability of not being chosen is $(1-1/d)$. We have to select d times, so the probability that a tuple will not be chosen during this whole time is $(1-1/d)^d$. If d is large, the probability approaches $e^{-1} = 0.368$.[14] Thus, 36.8% of tuples will not be selected for training and thereby end up in the test set, and the remaining 63.2% will form the training set.

We can repeat the sampling procedure k times, where in each iteration, we use the current test set to obtain an accuracy estimate of the model obtained from the current bootstrap sample. The overall accuracy of the model is then estimated as

$$Acc(M) = \sum_{i=1}^{k}(0.632 \times Acc(M_i)_{test\_set} + 0.368 \times Acc(M_i)_{train\_set}), \tag{6.65}$$

where $Acc(M_i)_{test\_set}$ is the accuracy of the model obtained with bootstrap sample i when it is applied to test set i. $Acc(M_i)_{train\_set}$ is the accuracy of the model obtained with bootstrap sample i when it is applied to the original set of data tuples. The bootstrap method works well with small data sets.

[14] e is the base of natural logarithms, that is, $e = 2.718$.

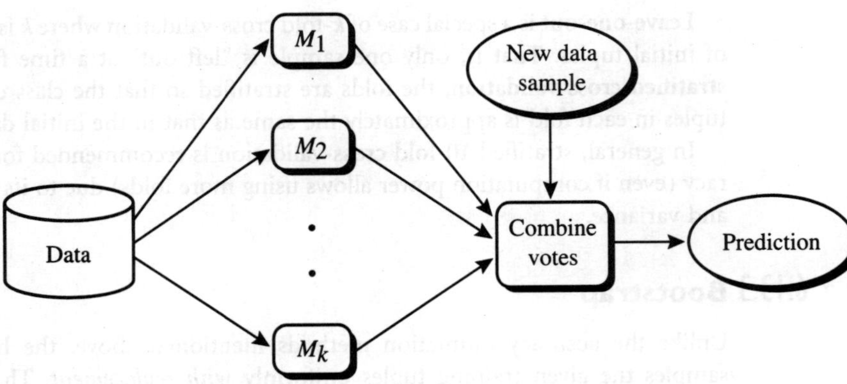

Figure 6.30 Increasing model accuracy: Bagging and boosting each generate a set of classification or prediction models, $M_1, M_2, \ldots, M_k$. Voting strategies are used to combine the predictions for a given unknown tuple.

6.14 Ensemble Methods—Increasing the Accuracy

In Section 6.3.3, we saw how pruning can be applied to decision tree induction to help improve the accuracy of the resulting decision trees. Are there *general* strategies for improving classifier and predictor accuracy?

The answer is yes. *Bagging* and *boosting* are two such techniques (Figure 6.30). They are examples of **ensemble methods**, or methods that use a *combination* of models. Each combines a series of k learned models (classifiers or predictors), $M_1, M_2, \ldots, M_k$, with the aim of creating an improved composite model, $M*$. Both bagging and boosting can be used for classification as well as prediction.

6.14.1 Bagging

We first take an intuitive look at how bagging works as a method of increasing accuracy. For ease of explanation, we will assume at first that our model is a classifier. Suppose that you are a patient and would like to have a diagnosis made based on your symptoms. Instead of asking one doctor, you may choose to ask several. If a certain diagnosis occurs more than any of the others, you may choose this as the final or best diagnosis. That is, the final diagnosis is made based on a majority vote, where each doctor gets an equal vote. Now replace each doctor by a classifier, and you have the basic idea behind bagging. Intuitively, a majority vote made by a large group of doctors may be more reliable than a majority vote made by a small group.

Given a set, D, of d tuples, **bagging** works as follows. For iteration i ($i = 1, 2, \ldots, k$), a training set, D_i, of d tuples is sampled with replacement from the original set of tuples, D. Note that the term bagging stands for *bootstrap aggregation*. Each training set is a bootstrap sample, as described in Section 6.13.3. Because sampling with replacement is used, some

Algorithm: Bagging. The bagging algorithm—create an ensemble of models (classifiers or predictors) for a learning scheme where each model gives an equally-weighted prediction.

Input:

- D, a set of d training tuples;
- k, the number of models in the ensemble;
- a learning scheme (e.g., decision tree algorithm, backpropagation, etc.)

Output: A composite model, $M*$.

Method:

```
(1) for i = 1 to k do // create k models:
(2)     create bootstrap sample, D_i, by sampling D with replacement;
(3)     use D_i to derive a model, M_i;
(4) endfor
```

To use the composite model on a tuple, X:

```
(1) if classification then
(2)     let each of the k models classify X and return the majority vote;
(3) if prediction then
(4)     let each of the k models predict a value for X and return the average predicted value;
```

Figure 6.31 Bagging.

of the original tuples of D may not be included in D_i, whereas others may occur more than once. A classifier model, M_i, is learned for each training set, D_i. To classify an unknown tuple, X, each classifier, M_i, returns its class prediction, which counts as one vote. The bagged classifier, $M*$, counts the votes and assigns the class with the most votes to X. Bagging can be applied to the prediction of continuous values by taking the average value of each prediction for a given test tuple. The algorithm is summarized in Figure 6.31.

The bagged classifier often has significantly greater accuracy than a single classifier derived from D, the original training data. It will not be considerably worse and is more robust to the effects of noisy data. The increased accuracy occurs because the composite model reduces the variance of the individual classifiers. For prediction, it was theoretically proven that a bagged predictor will *always* have improved accuracy over a single predictor derived from D.

6.14.2 Boosting

We now look at the ensemble method of boosting. As in the previous section, suppose that as a patient, you have certain symptoms. Instead of consulting one doctor, you choose to consult several. Suppose you assign weights to the value or worth of each doctor's diagnosis, based on the accuracies of previous diagnoses they have made. The final diagnosis is then a combination of the weighted diagnoses. This is the essence behind boosting.

In **boosting**, weights are assigned to each training tuple. A series of k classifiers is iteratively learned. After a classifier M_i is learned, the weights are updated to allow the subsequent classifier, M_{i+1}, to "pay more attention" to the training tuples that were misclassified by M_i. The final boosted classifier, $M*$, combines the votes of each individual classifier, where the weight of each classifier's vote is a function of its accuracy. The boosting algorithm can be extended for the prediction of continuous values.

Adaboost is a popular boosting algorithm. Suppose we would like to boost the accuracy of some learning method. We are given D, a data set of d class-labeled tuples, $(\boldsymbol{X_1}, y_1)$, $(\boldsymbol{X_2}, y_2), \ldots, (\boldsymbol{X_d}, y_d)$, where y_i is the class label of tuple $\boldsymbol{X_i}$. Initially, Adaboost assigns each training tuple an equal weight of $1/d$. Generating k classifiers for the ensemble requires k rounds through the rest of the algorithm. In round i, the tuples from D are sampled to form a training set, D_i, of size d. Sampling with replacement is used—the same tuple may be selected more than once. Each tuple's chance of being selected is based on its weight. A classifier model, M_i, is derived from the training tuples of D_i. Its error is then calculated using D_i as a test set. The weights of the training tuples are then adjusted according to how they were classified. If a tuple was incorrectly classified, its weight is increased. If a tuple was correctly classified, its weight is decreased. A tuple's weight reflects how hard it is to classify—the higher the weight, the more often it has been misclassified. These weights will be used to generate the training samples for the classifier of the next round. The basic idea is that when we build a classifier, we want it to focus more on the misclassified tuples of the previous round. Some classifiers may be better at classifying some "hard" tuples than others. In this way, we build a series of classifiers that complement each other. The algorithm is summarized in Figure 6.32.

Now, let's look at some of the math that's involved in the algorithm. To compute the error rate of model M_i, we sum the weights of each of the tuples in D_i that M_i misclassified. That is,

$$error(M_i) = \sum_{j}^{d} w_j \times err(\boldsymbol{X_j}), \tag{6.66}$$

where $err(\boldsymbol{X_j})$ is the misclassification error of tuple $\boldsymbol{X_j}$: If the tuple was misclassified, then $err(\boldsymbol{X_j})$ is 1. Otherwise, it is 0. If the performance of classifier M_i is so poor that its error exceeds 0.5, then we abandon it. Instead, we try again by generating a new D_i training set, from which we derive a new M_i.

The error rate of M_i affects how the weights of the training tuples are updated. If a tuple in round i was correctly classified, its weight is multiplied by $error(M_i)/(1 - error(M_i))$. Once the weights of all of the correctly classified tuples are updated, the weights for all tuples (including the misclassified ones) are normalized so that their sum remains the same as it was before. To normalize a weight, we multiply it by the sum of the old weights, divided by the sum of the new weights. As a result, the weights of misclassified tuples are increased and the weights of correctly classified tuples are decreased, as described above.

"Once boosting is complete, how is the ensemble of classifiers used to predict the class label of a tuple, X?" Unlike bagging, where each classifier was assigned an equal vote,

Algorithm: Adaboost. A boosting algorithm—create an ensemble of classifiers. Each one gives a weighted vote.

Input:

- D, a set of d class-labeled training tuples;
- k, the number of rounds (one classifier is generated per round);
- a classification learning scheme.

Output: A composite model.

Method:

(1) initialize the weight of each tuple in D to $1/d$;
(2) **for** $i = 1$ to k **do** // for each round:
(3)   sample D with replacement according to the tuple weights to obtain D_i;
(4)   use training set D_i to derive a model, M_i;
(5)   compute $error(M_i)$, the error rate of M_i (Equation 6.66)
(6)   **if** $error(M_i) > 0.5$ **then**
(7)   reinitialize the weights to $1/d$
(8)   go back to step 3 and try again;
(9)   **endif**
(10)   **for each** tuple in D_i that was correctly classified **do**
(11)   multiply the weight of the tuple by $error(M_i)/(1 - error(M_i))$; // update weights
(12)   normalize the weight of each tuple;
(13) **endfor**

To use the composite model to classify tuple, X:

(1) initialize weight of each class to 0;
(2) **for** $i = 1$ to k **do** // for each classifier:
(3) $w_i = log\frac{1-error(M_i)}{error(M_i)}$; // weight of the classifier's vote
(4) $c = M_i(X)$; // get class prediction for X from M_i
(5)   add w_i to weight for class c
(6) **endfor**
(7) return the class with the largest weight;

Figure 6.32 Adaboost, a boosting algorithm.

boosting assigns a weight to each classifier's vote, based on how well the classifier performed. The lower a classifier's error rate, the more accurate it is, and therefore, the higher its weight for voting should be. The weight of classifier M_i's vote is

$$log\frac{1-error(M_i)}{error(M_i)} \tag{6.67}$$

For each class, c, we sum the weights of each classifier that assigned class c to $\boldsymbol{X}$. The class with the highest sum is the "winner" and is returned as the class prediction for tuple $\boldsymbol{X}$.

"How does boosting compare with bagging?" Because of the way boosting focuses on the misclassified tuples, it risks overfitting the resulting composite model to such data. Therefore, sometimes the resulting "boosted" model may be less accurate than a single model derived from the same data. Bagging is less susceptible to model overfitting. While both can significantly improve accuracy in comparison to a single model, boosting tends to achieve greater accuracy.

6.15 Model Selection

Suppose that we have generated two models, M_1 and M_2 (for either classification or prediction), from our data. We have performed 10-fold cross-validation to obtain a mean error rate for each. How can we determine which model is best? It may seem intuitive to select the model with the lowest error rate, however, the mean error rates are just *estimates* of error on the true population of future data cases. There can be considerable variance between error rates within any given 10-fold cross-validation experiment. Although the mean error rates obtained for M_1 and M_2 may appear different, that difference may not be statistically significant. What if any difference between the two may just be attributed to chance? This section addresses these questions.

6.15.1 Estimating Confidence Intervals

To determine if there is any "real" difference in the mean error rates of two models, we need to employ a *test of statistical significance*. In addition, we would like to obtain some confidence limits for our mean error rates so that we can make statements like *"any observed mean will not vary by +/− two standard errors 95% of the time for future samples"* or *"one model is better than the other by a margin of error of +/− 4%."*

What do we need in order to perform the statistical test? Suppose that for each model, we did 10-fold cross-validation, say, 10 times, each time using a different 10-fold partitioning of the data. Each partitioning is independently drawn. We can average the 10 error rates obtained each for M_1 and M_2, respectively, to obtain the mean error rate for each model. For a given model, the individual error rates calculated in the cross-validations may be considered as different, independent samples from a probability distribution. In general, they follow a *t distribution with k-1 degrees of freedom* where, here, $k = 10$. (This distribution looks very similar to a normal, or Gaussian, distribution even though the functions defining the two are quite different. Both are unimodal, symmetric, and bell-shaped.) This allows us to do hypothesis testing where the significance test used is the ***t*-test**, or **Student's *t*-test**. Our hypothesis is that the two models are the same, or in other words, that the difference in mean error rate between the two is zero. If we can reject this hypothesis (referred to as the *null hypothesis*), then we can conclude that the difference between the two models is statistically significant, in which case we can select the model with the lower error rate.

In data mining practice, we may often employ a single test set, that is, the same test set can be used for both M_1 and M_2. In such cases, we do a **pairwise comparison** of the two models *for each* 10-fold cross-validation round. That is, for the ith round of 10-fold cross-validation, the same cross-validation partitioning is used to obtain an error rate for M_1 and an error rate for M_2. Let $err(M_1)_i$ (or $err(M_2)_i$) be the error rate of model M_1 (or M_2) on round i. The error rates for M_1 are averaged to obtain a mean error rate for M_1, denoted $\overline{err}(M_1)$. Similarly, we can obtain $\overline{err}(M_2)$. The variance of the difference between the two models is denoted $var(M_1 - M_2)$. The t-test computes the *t-statistic with* $k-1$ *degrees of freedom* for k samples. In our example we have $k = 10$ since, here, the k samples are our error rates obtained from ten 10-fold cross-validations for each model. The t-statistic for pairwise comparison is computed as follows:

$$t = \frac{\overline{err}(M_1) - \overline{err}(M_2)}{\sqrt{var(M_1 - M_2)/k}}, \tag{6.68}$$

where

$$var(M_1 - M_2) = \frac{1}{k}\sum_{i=1}^{k}\left[err(M_1)_i - err(M_2)_i - (\overline{err}(M_1) - \overline{err}(M_2))\right]^2. \tag{6.69}$$

To determine whether M_1 and M_2 are significantly different, we compute t and select a significance level, sig. In practice, a significance level of 5% or 1% is typically used. We then consult a table for the t distribution, available in standard textbooks on statistics. This table is usually shown arranged by degrees of freedom as rows and significance levels as columns. Suppose we want to ascertain whether the difference between M_1 and M_2 is significantly different for 95% of the population, that is, $sig = 5\%$ or 0.05. We need to find the t distribution value corresponding to $k-1$ degrees of freedom (or 9 degrees of freedom for our example) from the table. However, because the t distribution is symmetric, typically only the upper percentage points of the distribution are shown. Therefore, we look up the table value for $z = sig/2$, which in this case is 0.025, where z is also referred to as a confidence limit. If $t > z$ or $t < -z$, then our value of t lies in the rejection region, within the tails of the distribution. This means that we can reject the null hypothesis that the means of M_1 and M_2 are the same and conclude that there is a statistically significant difference between the two models. Otherwise, if we cannot reject the null hypothesis, we then conclude that any difference between M_1 and M_2 can be attributed to chance.

If two test sets are available instead of a single test set, then a nonpaired version of the t-test is used, where the variance between the means of the two models is estimated as

$$var(M_1 - M_2) = \sqrt{\frac{var(M_1)}{k_1} + \frac{var(M_2)}{k_2}}, \tag{6.70}$$

and k_1 and k_2 are the number of cross-validation samples (in our case, 10-fold cross-validation rounds) used for M_1 and M_2, respectively. When consulting the table of t distribution, the number of degrees of freedom used is taken as the minimum number of degrees of the two models.

6.15.2 ROC Curves

ROC curves are a useful visual tool for comparing two classification models. The name ROC stands for *Receiver Operating Characteristic*. ROC curves come from signal detection theory that was developed during World War II for the analysis of radar images. An ROC curve shows the trade-off between the true positive rate or sensitivity (proportion of positive tuples that are correctly identified) and the false-positive rate (proportion of negative tuples that are incorrectly identified as positive) for a given model. That is, given a two-class problem, it allows us to visualize the trade-off between the rate at which the model can accurately recognize 'yes' cases versus the rate at which it mistakenly identifies 'no' cases as 'yes' for different "portions" of the test set. Any increase in the true positive rate occurs at the cost of an increase in the false-positive rate. The area under the ROC curve is a measure of the accuracy of the model.

In order to plot an ROC curve for a given classification model, *M*, the model must be able to return a probability or ranking for the predicted class of each test tuple. That is, we need to rank the test tuples in decreasing order, where the one the classifier thinks is most likely to belong to the positive or 'yes' class appears at the top of the list. Naive Bayesian and backpropagation classifiers are appropriate, whereas others, such as decision tree classifiers, can easily be modified so as to return a class probability distribution for each prediction. The vertical axis of an ROC curve represents the true positive rate. The horizontal axis represents the false-positive rate. An ROC curve for *M* is plotted as follows. Starting at the bottom left-hand corner (where the true positive rate and false-positive rate are both 0), we check the actual class label of the tuple at the top of the list. If we have a true positive (that is, a positive tuple that was correctly classified), then on the ROC curve, we move up and plot a point. If, instead, the tuple really belongs to the 'no' class, we have a false positive. On the ROC curve, we move right and plot a point. This process is repeated for each of the test tuples, each time moving up on the curve for a true positive or toward the right for a false positive.

Figure 6.33 shows the ROC curves of two classification models. The plot also shows a diagonal line where for every true positive of such a model, we are just as likely to encounter a false positive. Thus, the closer the ROC curve of a model is to the diagonal line, the less accurate the model. If the model is really good, initially we are more likely to encounter true positives as we move down the ranked list. Thus, the curve would move steeply up from zero. Later, as we start to encounter fewer and fewer true positives, and more and more false positives, the curve cases off and becomes more horizontal.

To assess the accuracy of a model, we can measure the area under the curve. Several software packages are able to perform such calculation. The closer the area is to 0.5, the less accurate the corresponding model is. A model with perfect accuracy will have an area of 1.0.

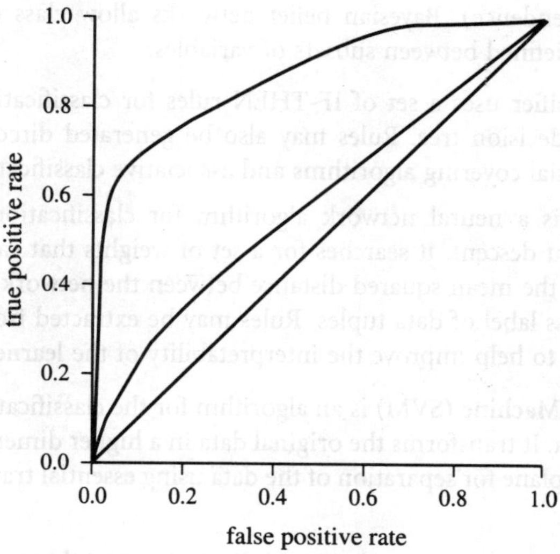

Figure 6.33 The ROC curves of two classification models.

6.16 Summary

- Classification and prediction are two forms of data analysis that can be used to extract models describing important data classes or to predict future data trends. While classification predicts categorical labels (classes), **prediction** models continuous-valued functions.
- Preprocessing of the data in preparation for classification and prediction can involve **data cleaning** to reduce noise or handle missing values, **relevance analysis** to remove irrelevant or redundant attributes, and **data transformation**, such as generalizing the data to higher-level concepts or normalizing the data.
- Predictive accuracy, computational speed, robustness, scalability, and interpretability are five **criteria** for the evaluation of classification and prediction methods.
- ID3, C4.5, and CART are greedy algorithms for the induction of **decision trees**. Each algorithm uses an attribute selection measure to select the attribute tested for each nonleaf node in the tree. **Pruning** algorithms attempt to improve accuracy by removing tree branches reflecting noise in the data. Early decision tree algorithms typically assume that the data are memory resident—a limitation to data mining on large databases. Several scalable algorithms, such as **SLIQ, SPRINT,** and **RainForest**, have been proposed to address this issue.
- **Naïve Bayesian classification** and **Bayesian belief networks** are based on Bayes, theorem of posterior probability. Unlike naïve Bayesian classification (which assumes class

conditional independence), Bayesian belief networks allow class conditional independencies to be defined between subsets of variables.

- A **rule-based classifier** uses a set of IF-THEN rules for classification. Rules can be extracted from a decision tree. Rules may also be generated directly from training data using sequential covering algorithms and associative classification algorithms.

- **Backpropagation** is a neural network algorithm for classification that employs a method of gradient descent. It searches for a set of weights that can model the data so as to minimize the mean squared distance between the network's class prediction and the actual class label of data tuples. Rules may be extracted from trained neural networks in order to help improve the interpretability of the learned network.

- A **Support Vector Machine (SVM)** is an algorithm for the classification of both linear and nonlinear data. It transforms the original data in a higher dimension, from where it can find a hyperplane for separation of the data using essential training tuples called **support vectors.**

- **Associative classification** uses association mining techniques that search for frequently occurring patterns in large databases. The patterns may generate rules, which can be analyzed for use in classification.

- Decision tree classifiers, Bayesian classifiers, classification by backpropagation, support vector machines, and classification based on association are all examples of **eager learners** in that they use training tuples to construct a generalization model and in this way are ready for classifying new tuples. This contrasts with **lazy learners** or **instance-based** methods of classification, such as nearest-neighbor classifiers and case-based reasoning classifiers, which store all of the training tuples in pattern space and wait until presented with a test tuple before performing generalization. Hence, lazy learners require efficient indexing techniques.

- In **genetic algorithms**, populations of rules "evolve" via operations of crossover and mutation until all rules within a population satisfy a specified threshold. **Rough set theory** can be used to approximately define classes that are not distinguishable based on the available attributes. **Fuzzy set** approaches replace "brittle" threshold cutoffs for continuous-valued attributes with degree of membership functions.

- Linear, nonlinear, and generalized linear models of **regression** can be used for prediction. Many nonlinear problems can be converted to linear problems by performing transformations on the predictor variables. Unlike decision trees, regression trees and model trees are used for prediction. In regression trees, each leaf stores a continuous-valued prediction. In model trees, each leaf holds a regression model.

- **Stratified *k*-fold cross-validation** is a recommended method for accuracy estimation. **Bagging** and **boosting** methods can be used to increase overall accuracy by learning and combining a series of individual models. For classifiers, **sensitivity, specificity,** and **precision** are useful alternatives to the accuracy measure, particularly when the main class of interest is in the minority. There are many measures of predictor error, such as the **mean squared error**, the **mean absolute error**, the **relative squared error**, and the **relative absolute error**. **Significance tests** and **ROC curves** are useful for model selection.

- There have been numerous comparisons of the different classification and prediction methods, and the matter remains a research topic. No single method has been found to be superior over all others for all data sets. Issues such as accuracy, training time, robustness, interpretability, and scalability must be considered and can involve trade-offs, further complicating the quest for an overall superior method. Empirical studies show that the accuracies of many algorithms are sufficiently similar that their differences are statistically insignificant, while training times may differ substantially. For classification, most neural network and statistical methods involving splines tend to be more computationally intensive than most decision tree methods.

Exercises

6.1 Briefly outline the major steps of *decision tree classification*.

6.2 Why is *tree pruning* useful in decision tree induction? What is a drawback of using a separate set of tuples to evaluate pruning?

6.3 Given a decision tree, you have the option of (a) converting the decision tree to rules and then pruning the resulting rules, or (b) pruning the decision tree and then converting the pruned tree to rules. What advantage does (a) have over (b)?

6.4 It is important to calculate the worst-case computational complexity of the decision tree algorithm. Given data set D, the number of attributes n, and the number of training tuples $|D|$, show that the computational cost of growing a tree is at most $n \times |D| \times log(|D|)$.

6.5 Why is *naïve Bayesian classification* called "naïve"? Briefly outline the major ideas of naïve Bayesian classification.

6.6 Given a 5 GB data set with 50 attributes (each containing 100 distinct values) and 512 MB of main memory in your laptop, outline an efficient method that constructs decision trees in such large data sets. Justify your answer by rough calculation of your main memory usage.

6.7 RainForest is an interesting scalable algorithm for decision tree induction. Develop a scalable naive Bayesian classification algorithm that requires just a single scan of the entire data set for most databases. Discuss whether such an algorithm can be refined to incorporate *boosting* to further enhance its classification accuracy.

6.8 Compare the advantages and disadvantages of *eager* classification (e.g., decision tree, Bayesian, neural network) versus *lazy* classification (e.g., *k*-nearest neighbor, case-based reasoning).

6.9 Design an efficient method that performs effective naïve Bayesian classification over an *infinite* data stream (i.e., you can scan the data stream only once). If we wanted to discover the *evolution* of such classification schemes (e.g., comparing the classification scheme at this moment with earlier schemes, such as one from a week ago), what modified design would you suggest?

6.10 What is *associative classification*? Why is associative classification able to achieve higher classification accuracy than a classical decision tree method? Explain how associative classification can be used for text document classification.

6.11 The following table consists of training data from an employee database. The data have been generalized. For example, "31 ... 35" for *age* represents the age range of 31 to 35. For a given row entry, *count* represents the number of data tuples having the values for *department, status, age,* and *salary* given in that row.

department	*status*	*age*	*salary*	*count*
sales	senior	31...35	46K...50K	30
sales	junior	26...30	26K...30K	40
sales	junior	31...35	31K...35K	40
systems	junior	21...25	46K...50K	20
systems	senior	31...35	66K...70K	5
systems	junior	26...30	46K...50K	3
systems	senior	41...45	66K...70K	3
marketing	senior	36...40	46K...50K	10
marketing	junior	31...35	41K...45K	4
secretary	senior	46...50	36K...40K	4
secretary	junior	26...30	26K...30K	6

Let *status* be the class label attribute.

(a) How would you modify the basic decision tree algorithm to take into consideration the *count* of each generalized data tuple (i.e., of each row entry)?

(b) Use your algorithm to construct a decision tree from the given data.

(c) Given a data tuple having the values *"systems," "26...30,"* and *"46–50K"* for the attributes *department, age,* and *salary*, respectively, what would a naive Bayesian classification of the *status* for the tuple be?

(d) Design a multilayer feed-forward neural network for the given data. Label the nodes in the input and output layers.

(e) Using the multilayer feed-forward neural network obtained above, show the weight values after one iteration of the backpropagation algorithm, given the training instance *"(sales, senior, 31...35, 46K...50K)."* Indicate your initial weight values and biases, and the learning rate used.

6.12 The *support vector machine (SVM)* is a highly accurate classification method. However, SVM classifiers suffer from slow processing when training with a large set of data tuples. Discuss how to overcome this difficulty and develop a scalable SVM algorithm for efficient SVM classification in large datasets.

6.13 Write an algorithm for *k-nearest-neighbor classification* given *k* and *n*, the number of attributes describing each tuple.

6.14 The following table shows the midterm and final exam grades obtained for students in a database course.

x *Midterm exam*	*y* *Final exam*
72	84
50	63
81	77
74	78
94	90
86	75
59	49
83	79
65	77
33	52
88	74
81	90

(a) Plot the data. Do *x* and *y* seem to have a linear relationship?

(b) Use the *method of least squares* to find an equation for the prediction of a student's final exam grade based on the student's midterm grade in the course.

(c) Predict the final exam grade of a student who received an 86 on the midterm exam.

6.15 Some *nonlinear regression* models can be converted to linear models by applying transformations to the predictor variables. Show how the nonlinear regression equation $y = \alpha X^{\beta}$ can be converted to a linear regression equation solvable by the method of least squares.

6.16 What is *boosting*? State why it may improve the accuracy of decision tree induction.

6.17 Show that accuracy is a function of *sensitivity* and *specificity*, that is, prove Equation (6.58).

6.18 Suppose that we would like to select between two prediction models, M_1 and M_2. We have performed 10 rounds of 10-fold cross-validation on each model, where the same data partitioning in round *i* is used for both M_1 and M_2. The error rates obtained for M_1 are 30.5, 32.2, 20.7, 20.6, 31.0, 41.0, 27.7, 26.0, 21.5, 26.0. The error rates for M_2 are 22.4, 14.5, 22.4, 19.6, 20.7, 20.4, 22.1, 19.4, 16.2, 35.0. Comment on whether one model is significantly better than the other considering a significance level of 1%.

6.19 It is difficult to assess classification *accuracy* when individual data objects may belong to more than one class at a time. In such cases, comment on what criteria you would use to compare different classifiers modeled after the same data.

Bibliographic Notes

Classification from machine learning, statistics, and pattern recognition perspectives has been described in many books, such as Weiss and Kulikowski [WK91], Michie, Spiegelhalter, and Taylor [MST94], Russel and Norvig [RN95], Langley [Lan96], Mitchell [Mit97], Hastie, Tibshirani, and Friedman [HTF01], Duda, Hart, and Stork [DHS01], Alpaydin [Alp04], Tan, Steinbach, and Kumar [TSK05], and Witten and Frank [WF05]. Many of these books describe each of the basic methods of classification discussed in this chapter, as well as practical techniques for the evaluation of classifier performance. Edited collections containing seminal articles on machine learning can be found in Michalski, Carbonell, and Mitchell [MCM83,MCM86], Kodratoff and Michalski [KM90], Shavlik and Dietterich [SD90], and Michalski and Tecuci [MT94]. For a presentation of machine learning with respect to data mining applications, see Michalski, Bratko, and Kubat [MBK98].

The C4.5 algorithm is described in a book by Quinlan [Qui93]. The CART system is detailed in *Classification and Regression Trees* by Breiman, Friedman, Olshen, and Stone [BFOS84]. Both books give an excellent presentation of many of the issues regarding decision tree induction. C4.5 has a commercial successor, known as C5.0, which can be found at *www.rulequest.com*. ID3, a predecessor of C4.5, is detailed in Quinlan [Qui86]. It expands on pioneering work on concept learning systems, described by Hunt, Marin, and Stone [HMS66]. Other algorithms for decision tree induction include FACT (Loh and Vanichsetakul [LV88]), QUEST (Loh and Shih [LS97]), PUBLIC (Rastogi and Shim [RS98]), and CHAID (Kass [Kas80] and Magidson [Mag94]). INFERULE (Uthurusamy, Fayyad, and Spangler [UFS91]) learns decision trees from inconclusive data, where probabilistic rather than categorical classification rules are obtained. KATE (Manago and Kodratoff [MK91]) learns decision trees from complex structured data. Incremental versions of ID3 include ID4 (Schlimmer and Fisher [SF86a]) and ID5 (Utgoff [Utg88]), the latter of which is extended in Utgoff, Berkman, and Clouse [UBC97]. An incremental version of CART is described in Crawford [Cra89]. BOAT (Gehrke, Ganti, Ramakrishnan, and Loh [GGRL99]), a decision tree algorithm that addresses the scalabilty issue in data mining, is also incremental. Other decision tree algorithms that address scalability include SLIQ (Mehta, Agrawal, and Rissanen [MAR96]), SPRINT (Shafer, Agrawal, and Mehta [SAM96]), RainForest (Gehrke, Ramakrishnan, and Ganti [GRG98]), and earlier approaches, such as Catlet [Cat91], and Chan and Stolfo [CS93a, CS93b]. The integration of attribution-oriented induction with decision tree induction is proposed in Kamber, Winstone, Gong, et al. [KWG+97]. For a comprehensive survey of many salient issues relating to decision tree induction, such as attribute selection and pruning, see Murthy [Mur98].

For a detailed discussion on attribute selection measures, see Kononenko and Hong [KH97]. Information gain was proposed by Quinlan [Qui86] and is based on pioneering work on information theory by Shannon and Weaver [SW49]. The gain ratio, proposed as an extension to information gain, is described as part of C4.5 [Qui93]. The Gini index was proposed for CART [BFOS84]. The G-statistic, based on information theory, is given in Sokal and Rohlf [SR81]. Comparisons of attribute selection measures include Buntine and Niblett [BN92], Fayyad and Irani [FI92], Kononenko [Kon95], Loh and Shih [LS97], and Shih [Shi99]. Fayyad and Irani [FI92] show limitations of impurity-based measures such as information gain and Gini index. They propose a class of attribute selection measures called C-SEP (Class SEParation), which outperform impurity-based measures in certain cases. Kononenko [Kon95] notes that attribute selection measures based on the minimum description length principle have the least bias toward multivalued attributes. Martin and Hirschberg [MH95] proved that the time complexity of decision tree induction increases exponentially with respect to tree height in the worst case, and under fairly general conditions in the average case. Fayad and Irani [FI90] found that shallow decision trees tend to have many leaves and higher error rates for a large variety of domains. Attribute (or feature) construction is described in Liu and Motoda [LM98, Le98]. Examples of systems with attribute construction include BACON by Langley, Simon, Bradshaw, and Zytkow [LSBZ87], Stagger by Schlimmer [Sch86], FRINGE by Pagallo [Pag89], and AQ17-DCI by Bloedorn and Michalski [BM98].

There are numerous algorithms for decision tree pruning, including cost complexity pruning (Breiman, Friedman, Olshen, and Stone [BFOS84]), reduced error pruning (Quinlan [Qui87]), and pessimistic pruning (Quinlan [Qui86]). PUBLIC (Rastogi and Shim [RS98]) integrates decision tree construction with tree pruning. MDL-based pruning methods can be found in Quinlan and Rivest [QR89], Mehta, Agrawal, and Rissanen [MRA95], and Rastogi and Shim [RS98]. Other methods include Niblett and Bratko [NB86], and Hosking, Pednault, and Sudan [HPS97]. For an empirical comparison of pruning methods, see Mingers [Min89] and Malerba, Floriana, and Semeraro [MFS95]. For a survey on simplifying decision trees, see Breslow and Aha [BA97].

There are several examples of rule-based classifiers. These include AQ15 (Hong, Mozetic, and Michalski [HMM86]), CN2 (Clark and Niblett [CN89]), ITRULE (Smyth and Goodman [SG92]), RISE (Domingos [Dom94]), IREP (Furnkranz and Widmer [FW94]), RIPPER (Cohen [Coh95]), FOIL (Quinlan and Cameron-Jones [Qui90, QCJ93]), and Swap-1 (Weiss and Indurkhya [WI98]). For the extraction of rules from decision trees, see Quinlan [Qui87, Qui93]. Rule refinement strategies that identify the most interesting rules among a given rule set can be found in Major and Mangano [MM95].

Thorough presentations of Bayesian classification can be found in Duda, Hart, and Stork [DHS01], Weiss and Kulikowski [WK91], and Mitchell [Mit97]. For an analysis of the predictive power of naïve Bayesian classifiers when the class conditional independence assumption is violated, see Domingos and Pazzani [DP96]. Experiments with kernel density estimation for continuous-valued attributes, rather than Gaussian estimation, have been reported for naïve Bayesian classifiers in John [Joh97]. For an introduction to Bayesian belief networks, see Heckerman [Hec96]. For a thorough presentation of probabilistic networks, see Pearl [Pea88]. Solutions for learning the belief network structure from training data given observable variables are proposed in Cooper and Herskovits [CH92], Buntine [Bun94], and Heckerman, Geiger, and Chickering [HGC95]. Algorithms for inference on belief networks can be found in Russell and Norvig [RN95] and Jensen [Jen96]. The method of gradient descent, described in Section 6.4.4 for training Bayesian belief networks, is given in Russell, Binder, Koller, and Kanazawa [RBKK95]. The example given in Figure 6.11 is adapted from Russell et al. [RBKK95]. Alternative strategies for learning belief networks with hidden variables include application of Dempster, Laird, and Rubin's [DLR77] EM (Expectation Maximization) algorithm (Lauritzen [Lau95]) and methods based on the minimum description length principle (Lam [Lam98]). Cooper [Coo90] showed that the general problem of inference in unconstrained belief networks is NP-hard. Limitations of belief networks, such as their large computational complexity (Laskey and Mahoney [LM97]), have prompted the exploration of hierarchical and composable Bayesian models (Pfeffer, Koller, Milch, and Takusagawa [PKMT99] and Xiang, Olesen, and Jensen [XOJ00]). These follow an object-oriented approach to knowledge representation.

The perceptron is a simple neural network, proposed in 1958 by Rosenblatt [Ros58], which became a landmark in early machine learning history. Its input units are randomly connected to a single layer of output linear threshold units. In 1969, Minsky and Papert [MP69] showed that perceptrons are incapable of learning concepts that are linearly inseparable. This limitation, as well as limitations on hardware at the time, dampened enthusiasm for research in computational neuronal modeling for nearly 20 years. Renewed interest was sparked following presentation of the backpropagation algorithm in 1986 by Rumelhart, Hinton, and Williams [RHW86], as this algorithm can learn concepts that are linearly inseparable. Since then, many variations for backpropagation have been proposed, involving, for example, alternative error functions (Hanson and Burr [HB88]), dynamic adjustment of the network topology (Mézard and Nadal [MN89], Fahlman and Lebiere [FL90], Le Cun, Denker, and Solla [LDS90], and Harp, Samad, and Guha [HSG90]), and dynamic adjustment of the learning rate and momentum parameters (Jacobs [Jac88]). Other variations are discussed in Chauvin and Rumelhart [CR95]. Books on neural networks include Rumelhart and McClelland [RM86], Hecht-Nielsen [HN90], Hertz, Krogh, and Palmer [HKP91], Bishop [Bis95], Ripley [Rip96], and Haykin [Hay99]. Many books on machine learning, such as [Mit97, RN95], also contain good explanations of the backpropagation algorithm. There are several techniques for extracting rules from neural networks, such as [SN88, Gal93, TS93, Avn95, LSL95, CS96b, LGT97]. The method of rule extraction described in Section 6.6.4 is based on Lu, Setiono, and Liu [LSL95]. Critiques of techniques for rule extraction from neural networks can be found in Craven and Shavlik [CS97]. Roy [Roy00] proposes that the theoretical foundations of neural networks are flawed with respect to assumptions made regarding how connectionist learning models the brain. An extensive survey of applications of neural networks in industry, business, and science is provided in Widrow, Rumelhart, and Lehr [WRL94].

Support Vector Machines (SVMs) grew out of early work by Vapnik and Chervonenkis on statistical learning theory [VC71]. The first paper on SVMs was presented by Boser,

Guyon, and Vapnik [BGV92]. More detailed accounts can be found in books by Vapnik [Vap95, Vap98]. Good starting points include the tutorial on SVMs by Burges [Bur98] and textbook coverage by Kecman [Kec01]. For methods for solving optimization problems, see Fletcher [Fle87] and Nocedal and Wright [NW99]. These references give additional details alluded to as "fancy math tricks" in our text, such as transformation of the problem to a Lagrangian formulation and subsequent solving using Karush-Kuhn-Tucker (KKT) conditions. For the application of SVMs to regression, see Schlkopf, Bartlett, Smola, and Williamson [SBSW99], and Drucker, Burges, Kaufman, Smola, and Vapnik [DBK+97]. Approaches to SVM for large data include the sequential minimal optimization algorithm by Platt [Pla98], decomposition approaches such as in Osuna, Freund, and Girosi [OFG97], and CB-SVM, a microclustering-based SVM algorithm for large data sets, by Yu, Yang, and Han [YYH03].

Many algorithms have been proposed that adapt association rule mining to the task of classification. The CBA algorithm for associative classification was proposed by Liu, Hsu, and Ma [LHM98]. A classifier, using emerging patterns, was proposed by Dong and Li [DL99] and Li, Dong, and Ramamohanarao [LDR00]. CMAR (Classification based on Multiple Association Rules) was presented in Li, Han, and Pei [LHP01]. CPAR (Classification based on Predictive Association Rules) was proposed in Yin and Han [YH03b]. Cong, Tan, Tung, and Xu proposed a method for mining top-*k* covering rule groups for classifying gene expression data with high accuracy [CTTX05]. Lent, Swami, and Widom [LSW97] proposed the ARCS system, which was described in Section 5.3 on mining multidimensional association rules. It combines ideas from association rule mining, clustering, and image processing, and applies them to classification. Meretakis and Wüthrich [MW99] proposed to construct a naïve Bayesian classifier by mining long itemsets.

Nearest-neighbor classifiers were introduced in 1951 by Fix and Hodges [FH51]. A comprehensive collection of articles on nearest-neighbor classification can be found in Dasarathy [Das91]. Additional references can be found in many texts on classification, such as Duda et al. [DHS01] and James [Jam85], as well as articles by Cover and Hart [CH67] and Fukunaga and Hummels [FH87]. Their integration with attribute-weighting and the pruning of noisy instances is described in Aha [Aha92]. The use of search trees to improve nearest-neighbor classification time is detailed in Friedman, Bentley, and Finkel [FBF77]. The partial distance method was proposed by researchers in vector quantization and compression. It is outlined in Gersho and Gray [GG92]. The editing method for removing "useless" training tuples was first proposed by Hart [Har68]. The computational complexity of nearest-neighbor classifiers is described in Preparata and Shamos [PS85]. References on case-based reasoning (CBR) include the texts Riesbeck and Schank [RS89] and Kolodner [Kol93], as well as Leake [Lea96] and Aamodt and Plazas [AP94]. For a list of business applications, see Allen [All94]. Examples in medicine include CASEY by Koton [Kot88] and PROTOS by Bareiss, Porter, and Weir [BPW88], while Rissland and Ashley [RA87] is an example of CBR for law. CBR is available in several commercial software products. For texts on genetic algorithms, see Goldberg [Gol89], Michalewicz [Mic92], and Mitchell [Mit96]. Rough sets were introduced in Pawlak [Paw91]. Concise summaries of rough set theory in data mining include Ziarko [Zia91], and Cios, Pedrycz, and Swiniarski [CPS98]. Rough sets have been used for feature reduction and expert system design in many applications, including Ziarko [Zia91], Lenarcik and Piasta [LP97], and Swiniarski [Swi98]. Algorithms to reduce the computation intensity in finding reducts have been proposed in Skowron and Rauszer [SR92]. Fuzzy set theory was proposed by Zadeh in [Zad65, Zad83]. Additional descriptions can be found in [YZ94, Kec01].

Many good textbooks cover the techniques of regression. Examples include James [Jam85], Dobson [Dob01], Johnson and Wichern [JW02], Devore [Dev95], Hogg and Craig [HC95], Neter, Kutner, Nachtsheim, and Wasserman [NKNW96], and Agresti [Agr96]. The book by Press, Teukolsky, Vetterling, and Flannery [PTVF96] and accompanying source code contain many statistical procedures, such as the method of least squares for both linear and multiple regression. Recent nonlinear regression models include projection pursuit and MARS (Friedman [Fri91]). Log-linear models are also known in the computer science literature as *multiplicative models*. For log-linear models from a computer science perspective, see Pearl [Pea88]. Regression trees (Breiman, Friedman, Olshen, and Stone [BFOS84]) are often comparable in performance with other regression methods, particularly when there exist many higher-order dependencies among the predictor variables. For model trees, see Quinlan [Qui92].

Methods for data cleaning and data transformation are discussed in Kennedy, Lee, Van Roy, et al. [KLV+98], Weiss and Indurkhya [WI98], Pyle [Pyl99], and Chapter 2 of this book. Issues involved in estimating classifier accuracy are described in Weiss and Kulikowski [WK91] and Witten and Frank [WF05]. The use of stratified 10-fold cross-validation for estimating classifier accuracy is recommended over the holdout, cross-validation, leave-one-out (Stone [Sto74]) and bootstrapping (Efron and Tibshirani [ET93]) methods, based on a theoretical and empirical study by Kohavi [Koh95]. Bagging is proposed in Breiman [Bre96]. The boosting technique of Freund and Schapire [FS97] has been applied to several different classifiers, including decision tree induction (Quinlan [Qui96]) and naive Bayesian classification (Elkan [Elk97]). Sensitivity, specificity, and precision are discussed in Frakes and Baeza-Yates [FBY92]. For ROC analysis, see Egan [Ega75] and Swets [Swe88].

The University of California at Irvine (UCI) maintains a Machine Learning Repository of data sets for the development and testing of classification algorithms. It also maintains a Knowledge Discovery in Databases (KDD) Archive, an online repository of large data sets that encompasses a wide variety of data types, analysis tasks, and application areas. For information on these two repositories, see *www.ics.uci.edu/~mlearn/MLRepository.html* and *http://kdd.ics.uci.edu.*

No classification method is superior over all others for all data types and domains. Empirical comparisons of classification methods include [Qui88, SMT91, BCP93, CM94, MST94, BU95], and [LLS00].

7 Cluster Analysis

Imagine that you are given a set of data objects for analysis where, unlike in classification, the class label of each object is not known. This is quite common in large databases, because assigning class labels to a large number of objects can be a very costly process. *Clustering* is the process of grouping the data into classes or *clusters*, so that objects within a cluster have high similarity in comparison to one another but are very dissimilar to objects in other clusters. Dissimilarities are assessed based on the attribute values describing the objects. Often, distance measures are used. Clustering has its roots in many areas, including data mining, statistics, biology, and machine learning.

In this chapter, we study the requirements of clustering methods for large amounts of data. We explain how to compute dissimilarities between objects represented by various attribute or variable types. We examine several clustering techniques, organized into the following categories: *partitioning methods, hierarchical methods, density-based methods, grid-based methods, model-based methods, methods for high-dimensional data* (such as *frequent pattern–based methods*), and *constraint-based clustering*. Clustering can also be used for *outlier detection*, which forms the final topic of this chapter.

7.1 What Is Cluster Analysis?

The process of grouping a set of physical or abstract objects into classes of *similar* objects is called **clustering**. A cluster is a collection of data objects that are *similar* to one another within the same cluster and are *dissimilar* to the objects in other clusters. A cluster of data objects can be treated collectively as one group and so may be considered as a form of data compression. Although classification is an effective means for distinguishing groups or classes of objects, it requires the often costly collection and labeling of a large set of training tuples or patterns, which the classifier uses to model each group. It is often more desirable to proceed in the reverse direction: First partition the set of data into groups based on data similarity (e.g., using clustering), and then assign labels to the relatively small number of groups. Additional advantages of such a clustering-based process are that it is adaptable to changes and helps single out useful features that distinguish different groups.

Cluster analysis is an important human activity. Early in childhood, we learn how to distinguish between cats and dogs, or between animals and plants, by continuously improving subconscious clustering schemes. By automated clustering, we can identify dense and sparse regions in object space and, therefore, discover overall distribution patterns and interesting correlations among data attributes. Cluster analysis has been widely used in numerous applications, including market research, pattern recognition, data analysis, and image processing. In business, clustering can help marketers discover distinct groups in their customer bases and characterize customer groups based on purchasing patterns. In biology, it can be used to derive plant and animal taxonomies, categorize genes with similar functionality, and gain insight into structures inherent in populations. Clustering may also help in the identification of areas of similar land use in an earth observation database and in the identification of groups of houses in a city according to house type, value, and geographic location, as well as the identification of groups of automobile insurance policy holders with a high average claim cost. It can also be used to help classify documents on the Web for information discovery.

Clustering is also called **data segmentation** in some applications because clustering partitions large data sets into groups according to their *similarity*. Clustering can also be used for **outlier detection**, where outliers (values that are "far away" from any cluster) may be more interesting than common cases. Applications of outlier detection include the detection of credit card fraud and the monitoring of criminal activities in electronic commerce. For example, exceptional cases in credit card transactions, such as very expensive and frequent purchases, may be of interest as possible fraudulent activity. As a data mining function, cluster analysis can be used as a stand-alone tool to gain insight into the distribution of data, to observe the characteristics of each cluster, and to focus on a particular set of clusters for further analysis. Alternatively, it may serve as a preprocessing step for other algorithms, such as characterization, attribute subset selection, and classification, which would then operate on the detected clusters and the selected attributes or features.

Data clustering is under vigorous development. Contributing areas of research include data mining, statistics, machine learning, spatial database technology, biology, and marketing. Owing to the huge amounts of data collected in databases, cluster analysis has recently become a highly active topic in data mining research.

As a branch of statistics, cluster analysis has been extensively studied for many years, focusing mainly on *distance-based cluster analysis*. Cluster analysis tools based on *k*-means, *k*-medoids, and several other methods have also been built into many statistical analysis software packages or systems, such as S-Plus, SPSS, and SAS. In machine learning, clustering is an example of **unsupervised learning**. Unlike classification, clustering and unsupervised learning do not rely on predefined classes and class-labeled training examples. For this reason, clustering is a form of **learning by observation**, rather than *learning by examples*. In data mining, efforts have focused on finding methods for efficient and effective cluster analysis in *large databases*. Active themes of research focus on the *scalability* of clustering methods, the effectiveness of methods for clustering *complex shapes and types of data, high-dimensional* clustering techniques, and methods for clustering *mixed numerical and categorical data* in large databases.

Clustering is a challenging field of research in which its potential applications pose their own special requirements. The following are typical requirements of clustering in data mining:

- **Scalability:** Many clustering algorithms work well on small data sets containing fewer than several hundred data objects; however, a large database may contain millions of objects. Clustering on a *sample* of a given large data set may lead to biased results. Highly scalable clustering algorithms are needed.
- **Ability to deal with different types of attributes:** Many algorithms are designed to cluster interval-based (numerical) data. However, applications may require clustering other types of data, such as binary, categorical (nominal), and ordinal data, or mixtures of these data types.
- **Discovery of clusters with arbitrary shape:** Many clustering algorithms determine clusters based on Euclidean or Manhattan distance measures. Algorithms based on such distance measures tend to find spherical clusters with similar size and density. However, a cluster could be of any shape. It is important to develop algorithms that can detect clusters of arbitrary shape.
- **Minimal requirements for domain knowledge to determine input parameters:** Many clustering algorithms require users to input certain parameters in cluster analysis (such as the number of desired clusters). The clustering results can be quite sensitive to input parameters. Parameters are often difficult to determine, especially for data sets containing high-dimensional objects. This not only burdens users, but it also makes the quality of clustering difficult to control.
- **Ability to deal with noisy data:** Most real-world databases contain outliers or missing, unknown, or erroneous data. Some clustering algorithms are sensitive to such data and may lead to clusters of poor quality.
- **Incremental clustering and insensitivity to the order of input records:** Some clustering algorithms cannot incorporate newly inserted data (i.e., database updates) into existing clustering structures and, instead, must determine a new clustering from scratch. Some clustering algorithms are sensitive to the order of input data. That is, given a set of data objects, such an algorithm may return dramatically different clusterings depending on the order of presentation of the input objects. It is important to develop incremental clustering algorithms and algorithms that are insensitive to the order of input.
- **High dimensionality:** A database or a data warehouse can contain several dimensions or attributes. Many clustering algorithms are good at handling low-dimensional data, involving only two to three dimensions. Human eyes are good at judging the quality of clustering for up to three dimensions. Finding clusters of data objects in high-dimensional space is challenging, especially considering that such data can be sparse and highly skewed.

- **Constraint-based clustering:** Real-world applications may need to perform clustering under various kinds of constraints. Suppose that your job is to choose the locations for a given number of new automatic banking machines (ATMs) in a city. To decide upon this, you may cluster households while considering constraints such as the city's rivers and highway networks, and the type and number of customers per cluster. A challenging task is to find groups of data with good clustering behavior that satisfy specified constraints.

- **Interpretability and usability:** Users expect clustering results to be interpretable, comprehensible, and usable. That is, clustering may need to be tied to specific semantic interpretations and applications. It is important to study how an application goal may influence the selection of clustering features and methods.

With these requirements in mind, our study of cluster analysis proceeds as follows. First, we study different types of data and how they can influence clustering methods. Second, we present a general categorization of clustering methods. We then study each clustering method in detail, including partitioning methods, hierarchical methods, density-based methods, grid-based methods, and model-based methods. We also examine clustering in high-dimensional space, constraint-based clustering, and outlier analysis.

7.2 Types of Data in Cluster Analysis

In this section, we study the types of data that often occur in cluster analysis and how to preprocess them for such an analysis. Suppose that a data set to be clustered contains n objects, which may represent persons, houses, documents, countries, and so on. Main memory-based clustering algorithms typically operate on either of the following two data structures.

- **Data matrix** (or *object-by-variable structure*): This represents n objects, such as persons, with p variables (also called *measurements* or *attributes*), such as age, height, weight, gender, and so on. The structure is in the form of a relational table, or n-by-p matrix (n objects $\times p$ variables):

$$\begin{bmatrix} x_{11} & \cdots & x_{1f} & \cdots & x_{1p} \\ \cdots & \cdots & \cdots & \cdots & \cdots \\ x_{i1} & \cdots & x_{if} & \cdots & x_{ip} \\ \cdots & \cdots & \cdots & \cdots & \cdots \\ x_{n1} & \cdots & x_{nf} & \cdots & x_{np} \end{bmatrix} \tag{7.1}$$

- **Dissimilarity matrix** (or *object-by-object structure*): This stores a collection of proximities that are available for all pairs of n objects. It is often represented by an n-by-n table:

$$\begin{bmatrix} 0 & & & & \\ d(2,1) & 0 & & & \\ d(3,1) & d(3,2) & 0 & & \\ \vdots & \vdots & \vdots & & \\ d(n,1) & d(n,2) & \cdots & \cdots & 0 \end{bmatrix} \tag{7.2}$$

where $d(i, j)$ is the measured **difference** or **dissimilarity** between objects i and j. In general, $d(i, j)$ is a nonnegative number that is close to 0 when objects i and j are highly similar or "near" each other, and becomes larger the more they differ. Since $d(i, j) = d(j, i)$, and $d(i, i) = 0$, we have the matrix in (7.2). Measures of dissimilarity are discussed throughout this section.

The rows and columns of the data matrix represent different entities, while those of the dissimilarity matrix represent the same entity. Thus, the data matrix is often called a **two-mode** matrix, whereas the dissimilarity matrix is called a **one-mode** matrix. Many clustering algorithms operate on a dissimilarity matrix. If the data are presented in the form of a data matrix, it can first be transformed into a dissimilarity matrix before applying such clustering algorithms.

In this section, we discuss how object dissimilarity can be computed for objects described by *interval-scaled* variables; by *binary* variables; by *categorical, ordinal,* and *ratio-scaled* variables; or combinations of these variable types. Nonmetric similarity between complex objects (such as documents) is also described. The dissimilarity data can later be used to compute clusters of objects.

7.2.1 Interval-Scaled Variables

This section discusses *interval-scaled variables* and their standardization. It then describes distance measures that are commonly used for computing the dissimilarity of objects described by such variables. These measures include the *Euclidean, Manhattan,* and *Minkowski distances.*

"What are interval-scaled variables?" **Interval-scaled variables** are continuous measurements of a roughly linear scale. Typical examples include weight and height, latitude and longitude coordinates (e.g., when clustering houses), and weather temperature.

The measurement unit used can affect the clustering analysis. For example, changing measurement units from meters to inches for height, or from kilograms to pounds for weight, may lead to a very different clustering structure. In general, expressing a variable in smaller units will lead to a larger range for that variable, and thus a larger effect on the resulting clustering structure. To help avoid dependence on the choice of measurement units, the data should be standardized. Standardizing measurements attempts to give all variables an equal weight. This is particularly useful when given no prior knowledge of the data. However, in some applications, users may intentionally want to give more weight to a certain set of variables than to others. For example, when clustering basketball player candidates, we may prefer to give more weight to the variable height.

"How can the data for a variable be standardized?" To standardize measurements, one choice is to convert the original measurements to unitless variables. Given measurements for a variable f, this can be performed as follows.

1. Calculate the **mean absolute deviation**, s_f:

$$s_f = \frac{1}{n}(|x_{1f} - m_f| + |x_{2f} - m_f| + \cdots + |x_{nf} - m_f|), \tag{7.3}$$

where $x_{1f}, \ldots, x_{nf}$ are n measurements of f, and m_f is the *mean* value of f, that is, $m_f = \frac{1}{n}(x_{1f} + x_{2f} + \cdots + x_{nf})$.

2. Calculate the **standardized measurement**, or **z-score**:

$$z_{if} = \frac{x_{if} - m_f}{s_f}. \tag{7.4}$$

The mean absolute deviation, s_f, is more robust to outliers than the standard deviation, σ_f. When computing the mean absolute deviation, the deviations from the mean (i.e., $|x_{if} - m_f|$) are not squared; hence, the effect of outliers is somewhat reduced. There are more robust measures of dispersion, such as the *median absolute deviation*. However, the advantage of using the mean absolute deviation is that the z-scores of outliers do not become too small; hence, the outliers remain detectable.

Standardization may or may not be useful in a particular application. Thus the choice of whether and how to perform standardization should be left to the user. Methods of standardization are also discussed in Chapter 2 under normalization techniques for data preprocessing.

After standardization, or without standardization in certain applications, the dissimilarity (or similarity) between the objects described by interval-scaled variables is typically computed based on the distance between each pair of objects. The most popular distance measure is **Euclidean distance**, which is defined as

$$d(i,j) = \sqrt{(x_{i1} - x_{j1})^2 + (x_{i2} - x_{j2})^2 + \cdots + (x_{in} - x_{jn})^2}, \tag{7.5}$$

where $i = (x_{i1}, x_{i2}, \ldots, x_{in})$ and $j = (x_{j1}, x_{j2}, \ldots, x_{jn})$ are two n-dimensional data objects.

Another well-known metric is **Manhattan** (or **city block**) **distance**, defined as

$$d(i,j) = |x_{i1} - x_{j1}| + |x_{i2} - x_{j2}| + \cdots + |x_{in} - x_{jn}|. \tag{7.6}$$

Both the Euclidean distance and Manhattan distance satisfy the following mathematic requirements of a distance function:

1. $d(i, j) \geq 0$: Distance is a nonnegative number.
2. $d(i, i) = 0$: The distance of an object to itself is 0.
3. $d(i, j) = d(j, i)$: Distance is a symmetric function.
4. $d(i, j) \leq d(i, h) + d(h, j)$: Going directly from object i to object j in space is no more than making a detour over any other object h (*triangular inequality*).

Example 7.1 Euclidean distance and Manhattan distance. Let $x_1 = (1,2)$ and $x_2 = (3,5)$ represent two objects as in Figure 7.1. The Euclidean distance between the two is $\sqrt{(2^2+3^2)} = 3.61$. The Manhattan distance between the two is $2+3=5$. ■

Minkowski distance is a generalization of both Euclidean distance and Manhattan distance. It is defined as

$$d(i, j) = (|x_{i1} - x_{j1}|^p + |x_{i2} - x_{j2}|^p + \cdots + |x_{in} - x_{jn}|^p)^{1/p}, \quad (7.7)$$

where p is a positive integer. Such a distance is also called L_p norm, in some literature. It represents the Manhattan distance when $p = 1$ (i.e., L_1 norm) and Euclidean distance when $p = 2$ (i.e., L_2 norm).

If each variable is assigned a weight according to its perceived importance, the weighted Euclidean distance can be computed as

$$d(i, j) = \sqrt{w_1|x_{i1} - x_{j1}|^2 + w_2|x_{i2} - x_{j2}|^2 + \cdots + w_m|x_{in} - x_{jn}|^2}. \quad (7.8)$$

Weighting can also be applied to the Manhattan and Minkowski distances.

7.2.2 Binary Variables

Let us see how to compute the dissimilarity between objects described by either *symmetric* or *asymmetric binary variables*.

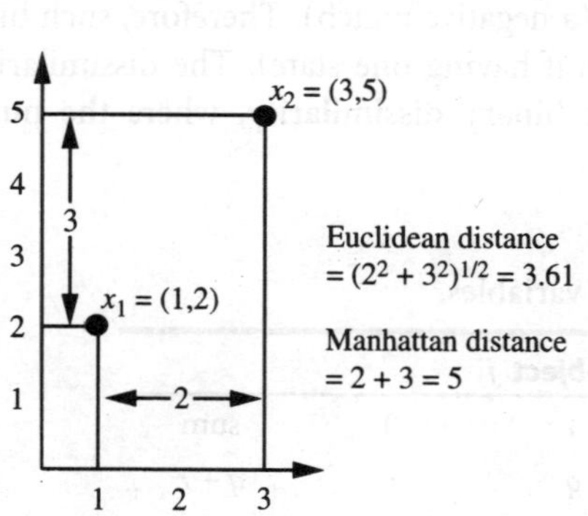

Figure 7.1 Euclidean and Manhattan distances between two objects.

A **binary variable** has only two states: 0 or 1, where 0 means that the variable is absent, and 1 means that it is present. Given the variable *smoker* describing a patient, for instance, 1 indicates that the patient smokes, while 0 indicates that the patient does not. Treating binary variables as if they are interval-scaled can lead to misleading clustering results. Therefore, methods specific to binary data are necessary for computing dissimilarities.

"So, how can we compute the dissimilarity between two binary variables?" One approach involves computing a dissimilarity matrix from the given binary data. If all binary variables are thought of as having the same weight, we have the 2-by-2 contingency table of Table 7.1, where q is the number of variables that equal 1 for both objects i and j, r is the number of variables that equal 1 for object i but that are 0 for object j, s is the number of variables that equal 0 for object i but equal 1 for object j, and t is the number of variables that equal 0 for both objects i and j. The total number of variables is p, where $p = q+r+s+t$.

"What is the difference between symmetric and asymmetric binary variables?" A binary variable is **symmetric** if both of its states are equally valuable and carry the same weight; that is, there is no preference on which outcome should be coded as 0 or 1. One such example could be the attribute *gender* having the states *male* and *female.* Dissimilarity that is based on symmetric binary variables is called **symmetric binary dissimilarity.** Its dissimilarity (or distance) measure, defined in Equation (7.9), can be used to assess the dissimilarity between objects i and j.

$$d(i, j) = \frac{r+s}{q+r+s+t}. \tag{7.9}$$

A binary variable is **asymmetric** if the outcomes of the states are not equally important, such as the *positive* and *negative* outcomes of a disease *test.* By convention, we shall code the most important outcome, which is usually the rarest one, by 1 (e.g., *HIV positive*) and the other by 0 (e.g., *HIV negative*). Given two asymmetric binary variables, the agreement of two 1s (a positive match) is then considered more significant than that of two 0s (a negative match). Therefore, such binary variables are often considered "monary" (as if having one state). The dissimilarity based on such variables is called **asymmetric binary dissimilarity,** where the number of negative

Table 7.1 A contingency table for binary variables.

		object j		
		1	0	sum
	1	q	r	$q+r$
object i	0	s	t	$s+t$
	sum	$q+s$	$r+t$	p

matches, t, is considered unimportant and thus is ignored in the computation, as shown in Equation (7.10).

$$d(i, j) = \frac{r+s}{q+r+s}. \tag{7.10}$$

Complementarily, we can measure the distance between two binary variables based on the notion of *similarity* instead of *dissimilarity*. For example, the **asymmetric binary similarity** between the objects i and j, or $sim(i, j)$, can be computed as,

$$sim(i, j) = \frac{q}{q+r+s} = 1 - d(i, j). \tag{7.11}$$

The coefficient $sim(i, j)$ is called the **Jaccard coefficient**, which is popularly referenced in the literature.

When both symmetric and asymmetric binary variables occur in the same data set, the mixed variables approach described in Section 7.2.4 can be applied.

Example 7.2 **Dissimilarity between binary variables.** Suppose that a patient record table (Table 7.2) contains the attributes *name, gender, fever, cough, test-1, test-2, test-3,* and *test-4,* where *name* is an object identifier, *gender* is a symmetric attribute, and the remaining attributes are asymmetric binary.

For asymmetric attribute values, let the values Y (*yes*) and P (*positive*) be set to 1, and the value N (*no* or *negative*) be set to 0. Suppose that the distance between objects (patients) is computed based only on the asymmetric variables. According to Equation (7.10), the distance between each pair of the three patients, Jack, Mary, and Jim, is

$$\begin{aligned} d(Jack, Mary) &= \tfrac{0+1}{2+0+1} = 0.33 \\ d(Jack, Jim) &= \tfrac{1+1}{1+1+1} = 0.67 \\ d(Mary, Jim) &= \tfrac{1+2}{1+1+2} = 0.75 \end{aligned}$$

Table 7.2 A relational table where patients are described by binary attributes.

name	*gender*	*fever*	*cough*	*test-1*	*test-2*	*test-3*	*test-4*
Jack	M	Y	N	P	N	N	N
Mary	F	Y	N	P	N	P	N
Jim	M	Y	Y	N	N	N	N
⋮	⋮	⋮	⋮	⋮	⋮	⋮	⋮

These measurements suggest that Mary and Jim are unlikely to have a similar disease because they have the highest dissimilarity value among the three pairs. Of the three patients, Jack and Mary are the most likely to have a similar disease. ■

7.2.3 Categorical, Ordinal, and Ratio-Scaled Variables

"How can we compute the dissimilarity between objects described by categorical, ordinal, and ratio-scaled variables?"

Categorical Variables

A **categorical variable** is a generalization of the binary variable in that it can take on more than two states. For example, *map_color* is a categorical variable that may have, say, five states: *red, yellow, green, pink,* and *blue.*

Let the number of states of a categorical variable be M. The states can be denoted by letters, symbols, or a set of integers, such as $1, 2, \ldots, M$. Notice that such integers are used just for data handling and do not represent any specific ordering.

"How is dissimilarity computed between objects described by categorical variables?" The dissimilarity between two objects i and j can be computed based on the ratio of mismatches:

$$d(i, j) = \frac{p - m}{p}, \tag{7.12}$$

where m is the number of *matches* (i.e., the number of variables for which i and j are in the same state), and p is the total number of variables. Weights can be assigned to increase the effect of m or to assign greater weight to the matches in variables having a larger number of states.

Example 7.3 **Dissimilarity between categorical variables.** Suppose that we have the sample data of Table 7.3, except that only the *object-identifier* and the variable (or attribute) *test-1* are available, where *test-1* is categorical. (We will use *test-2* and *test-3* in later examples.) Let's compute the dissimilarity matrix (7.2), that is,

Table 7.3 A sample data table containing variables of mixed type.

object identifier	*test-1 (categorical)*	*test-2 (ordinal)*	*test-3 (ratio-scaled)*
1	code-A	excellent	445
2	code-B	fair	22
3	code-C	good	164
4	code-A	excellent	1,210

$$\begin{bmatrix} 0 & & & \\ d(2,1) & 0 & & \\ d(3,1) & d(3,2) & 0 & \\ d(4,1) & d(4,2) & d(4,3) & 0 \end{bmatrix}$$

Since here we have one categorical variable, *test-1*, we set $p = 1$ in Equation (7.12) so that $d(i, j)$ evaluates to 0 if objects i and j match, and 1 if the objects differ. Thus, we get

$$\begin{bmatrix} 0 & & & \\ 1 & 0 & & \\ 1 & 1 & 0 & \\ 0 & 1 & 1 & 0 \end{bmatrix}$$

■

Categorical variables can be encoded by asymmetric binary variables by creating a new binary variable for each of the M states. For an object with a given state value, the binary variable representing that state is set to 1, while the remaining binary variables are set to 0. For example, to encode the categorical variable *map_color*, a binary variable can be created for each of the five colors listed above. For an object having the color *yellow*, the *yellow* variable is set to 1, while the remaining four variables are set to 0. The dissimilarity coefficient for this form of encoding can be calculated using the methods discussed in Section 7.2.2.

Ordinal Variables

A **discrete ordinal variable** resembles a categorical variable, except that the M states of the ordinal value are ordered in a meaningful sequence. Ordinal variables are very useful for registering subjective assessments of qualities that cannot be measured objectively. For example, professional ranks are often enumerated in a sequential order, such as *assistant*, *associate*, and *full* for professors. A **continuous ordinal variable** looks like a set of continuous data of an unknown scale; that is, the relative ordering of the values is essential but their actual magnitude is not. For example, the relative ranking in a particular sport (e.g., gold, silver, bronze) is often more essential than the actual values of a particular measure. Ordinal variables may also be obtained from the discretization of interval-scaled quantities by splitting the value range into a finite number of classes. The values of an ordinal variable can be mapped to *ranks*. For example, suppose that an ordinal variable f has M_f states. These ordered states define the ranking $1, \ldots, M_f$.

"How are ordinal variables handled?" The treatment of ordinal variables is quite similar to that of interval-scaled variables when computing the dissimilarity between objects. Suppose that f is a variable from a set of ordinal variables describing

n objects. The dissimilarity computation with respect to f involves the following steps:

1. The value of f for the ith object is x_{if}, and f has M_f ordered states, representing the ranking $1, \ldots, M_f$. Replace each x_{if} by its corresponding rank, $r_{if} \in \{1, \ldots, M_f\}$.
2. Since each ordinal variable can have a different number of states, it is often necessary to map the range of each variable onto [0.0,1.0] so that each variable has equal weight. This can be achieved by replacing the rank r_{if} of the ith object in the fth variable by

$$z_{if} = \frac{r_{if} - 1}{M_f - 1}. \tag{7.13}$$

3. Dissimilarity can then be computed using any of the distance measures described in Section 7.2.1 for interval-scaled variables, using z_{if} to represent the f value for the ith object.

Example 7.4 **Dissimilarity between ordinal variables.** Suppose that we have the sample data of Table 7.3, except that this time only the *object-identifier* and the continuous ordinal variable, *test*-2, are available. There are three states for *test*-2, namely *fair*, *good*, and *excellent*, that is $M_f = 3$. For step 1, if we replace each value for *test*-2 by its rank, the four objects are assigned the ranks 3, 1, 2, and 3, respectively. Step 2 normalizes the ranking by mapping rank 1 to 0.0, rank 2 to 0.5, and rank 3 to 1.0. For step 3, we can use, say, the Euclidean distance (Equation (7.5)), which results in the following dissimilarity matrix:

$$\begin{bmatrix} 0 & & & \\ 1 & 0 & & \\ 0.5 & 0.5 & 0 & \\ 0 & 1.0 & 0.5 & 0 \end{bmatrix}$$

■

Ratio-Scaled Variables

A **ratio-scaled variable** makes a positive measurement on a nonlinear scale, such as an exponential scale, approximately following the formula

$$Ae^{Bt} \text{ or } Ae^{-Bt} \tag{7.14}$$

where A and B are positive constants, and t typically represents time. Common examples include the growth of a bacteria population or the decay of a radioactive element.

"How can I compute the dissimilarity between objects described by ratio-scaled variables?" There are three methods to handle ratio-scaled variables for computing the dissimilarity between objects.

- Treat ratio-scaled variables like interval-scaled variables. This, however, is not usually a good choice since it is likely that the scale may be distorted.
- Apply **logarithmic transformation** to a ratio-scaled variable f having value x_{if} for object i by using the formula $y_{if} = \log(x_{if})$. The y_{if} values can be treated as interval-valued, as described in Section 7.2.1. Notice that for some ratio-scaled variables, log-log or other transformations may be applied, depending on the variable's definition and the application.
- Treat x_{if} as continuous ordinal data and treat their ranks as interval-valued.

The latter two methods are the most effective, although the choice of method used may depend on the given application.

Example 7.5 **Dissimilarity between ratio-scaled variables.** This time, we have the sample data of Table 7.3, except that only the *object-identifier* and the ratio-scaled variable, *test-3*, are available. Let's try a logarithmic transformation. Taking the *log* of *test-3* results in the values 2.65, 1.34, 2.21, and 3.08 for the objects 1 to 4, respectively. Using the Euclidean distance (Equation (7.5)) on the transformed values, we obtain the following dissimilarity matrix:

$$\begin{bmatrix} 0 & & & \\ 1.31 & 0 & & \\ 0.44 & 0.87 & 0 & \\ 0.43 & 1.74 & 0.87 & 0 \end{bmatrix}$$

■

7.2.4 Variables of Mixed Types

Sections 7.2.1 to 7.2.3 discussed how to compute the dissimilarity between objects described by variables of the same type, where these types may be either *interval-scaled, symmetric binary, asymmetric binary, categorical, ordinal,* or *ratio-scaled.* However, in many real databases, objects are described by a *mixture* of variable types. In general, a database can contain all of the six variable types listed above.

"So, how can we compute the dissimilarity between objects of mixed variable types?" One approach is to group each kind of variable together, performing a separate cluster analysis for each variable type. This is feasible if these analyses derive compatible results. However, in real applications, it is unlikely that a separate cluster analysis per variable type will generate compatible results.

A more preferable approach is to process all variable types together, performing a single cluster analysis. One such technique combines the different variables into a single dissimilarity matrix, bringing all of the meaningful variables onto a common scale of the interval [0.0,1.0].

Suppose that the data set contains p variables of mixed type. The dissimilarity $d(i, j)$ between objects i and j is defined as

$$d(i, j) = \frac{\sum_{f=1}^{p} \delta_{ij}^{(f)} d_{ij}^{(f)}}{\sum_{f=1}^{p} \delta_{ij}^{(f)}}, \tag{7.15}$$

where the indicator $\delta_{ij}^{(f)} = 0$ if either (1) x_{if} or x_{jf} is missing (i.e., there is no measurement of variable f for object i or object j), or (2) $x_{if} = x_{jf} = 0$ and variable f is asymmetric binary; otherwise, $\delta_{ij}^{(f)} = 1$. The contribution of variable f to the dissimilarity between i and j, that is, $d_{ij}^{(f)}$, is computed dependent on its type:

- If f is interval-based: $d_{ij}^{(f)} = \frac{|x_{if} - x_{jf}|}{max_h x_{hf} - min_h x_{hf}}$, where h runs over all nonmissing objects for variable f.
- If f is binary or categorical: $d_{ij}^{(f)} = 0$ if $x_{if} = x_{jf}$; otherwise $d_{ij}^{(f)} = 1$.
- If f is ordinal: compute the ranks r_{if} and $z_{if} = \frac{r_{if} - 1}{M_f - 1}$, and treat z_{if} as interval-scaled.
- If f is ratio-scaled: either perform logarithmic transformation and treat the transformed data as interval-scaled; or treat f as continuous ordinal data, compute r_{if} and z_{if}, and then treat z_{if} as interval-scaled.

The above steps are identical to what we have already seen for each of the individual variable types. The only difference is for interval-based variables, where here we normalize so that the values map to the interval [0.0,1.0]. Thus, the dissimilarity between objects can be computed even when the variables describing the objects are of different types.

Example 7.6 **Dissimilarity between variables of mixed type.** Let's compute a dissimilarity matrix for the objects of Table 7.3. Now we will consider *all* of the variables, which are of different types. In Examples 7.3 to 7.5, we worked out the dissimilarity matrices for each of the individual variables. The procedures we followed for *test*-1 (which is categorical) and *test*-2 (which is ordinal) are the same as outlined above for processing variables of mixed types. Therefore, we can use the dissimilarity matrices obtained for *test*-1 and *test*-2 later when we compute Equation (7.15). First, however, we need to complete some work for *test*-3 (which is ratio-scaled). We have already applied a logarithmic transformation to its values. Based on the transformed values of 2.65, 1.34, 2.21, and 3.08 obtained for the objects 1 to 4, respectively, we let $max_h x_h = 3.08$ and $min_h x_h = 1.34$. We then normalize the values in the dissimilarity matrix obtained in Example 7.5 by dividing each one by $(3.08 - 1.34) = 1.74$. This results in the following dissimilarity matrix for *test*-3:

$$\begin{bmatrix} 0 & & & \\ 0.75 & 0 & & \\ 0.25 & 0.50 & 0 & \\ 0.25 & 1.00 & 0.50 & 0 \end{bmatrix}$$

We can now use the dissimilarity matrices for the three variables in our computation of Equation (7.15). For example, we get $d(2,1) = \frac{1(1)+1(1)+1(0.75)}{3} = 0.92$. The resulting dissimilarity matrix obtained for the data described by the three variables of mixed types is:

$$\begin{bmatrix} 0 & & & \\ 0.92 & 0 & & \\ 0.58 & 0.67 & 0 & \\ 0.08 & 1.00 & 0.67 & 0 \end{bmatrix}$$

If we go back and look at Table 7.3, we can intuitively guess that objects 1 and 4 are the most similar, based on their values for *test*-1 and *test*-2. This is confirmed by the dissimilarity matrix, where $d(4,1)$ is the lowest value for any pair of different objects. Similarly, the matrix indicates that objects 2 and 4 are the least similar. ■

7.2.5 Vector Objects

In some applications, such as information retrieval, text document clustering, and biological taxonomy, we need to compare and cluster complex objects (such as documents) containing a large number of symbolic entities (such as keywords and phrases). To measure the distance between complex objects, it is often desirable to abandon traditional metric distance computation and introduce a nonmetric similarity function.

There are several ways to define such a similarity function, $s(\boldsymbol{x}, \boldsymbol{y})$, to compare two vectors $\boldsymbol{x}$ and $\boldsymbol{y}$. One popular way is to define the similarity function as a **cosine measure** as follows:

$$s(\boldsymbol{x}, \boldsymbol{y}) = \frac{\boldsymbol{x}^t \cdot \boldsymbol{y}}{||\boldsymbol{x}||\,||\boldsymbol{y}||}, \tag{7.16}$$

where $\boldsymbol{x}^t$ is a transposition of vector $\boldsymbol{x}$, $||\boldsymbol{x}||$ is the Euclidean norm of vector $\boldsymbol{x}$,[1] $||\boldsymbol{y}||$ is the Euclidean norm of vector $\boldsymbol{y}$, and s is essentially the cosine of the angle between vectors $\boldsymbol{x}$ and $\boldsymbol{y}$. This value is invariant to rotation and dilation, but it is not invariant to translation and general linear transformation.

[1]The Euclidean normal of vector $\boldsymbol{x} = (x_1, x_2, \ldots, x_p)$ is defined as $\sqrt{x_1^2 + x_2^2 + \ldots + x_p^2}$. Conceptually, it is the length of the vector.

When variables are binary-valued (0 or 1), the above similarity function can be interpreted in terms of shared features and attributes. Suppose an object x possesses the ith attribute if $x_i = 1$. Then $x^t \cdot y$ is the number of attributes possessed by both x and y, and $|x||y|$ is the geometric mean of the number of attributes possessed by x and the number possessed by y. Thus $s(x, y)$ is a measure of relative possession of common attributes.

Example 7.7 **Nonmetric similarity between two objects using cosine.** Suppose we are given two vectors, $x = (1, 1, 0, 0)$ and $y = (0, 1, 1, 0)$. By Equation (7.16), the similarity between x and y is $s(x, y) = \frac{(0+1+0+0)}{\sqrt{2}\sqrt{2}} = 0.5$. ■

A simple variation of the above measure is

$$s(x, y) = \frac{x^t \cdot y}{x^t \cdot x + y^t \cdot y - x^t \cdot y} \tag{7.17}$$

which is the ratio of the number of attributes shared by x and y to the number of attributes possessed by x or y. This function, known as the **Tanimoto coefficient** or **Tanimoto distance**, is frequently used in information retrieval and biology taxonomy.

Notice that there are many ways to select a particular similarity (or distance) function or normalize the data for cluster analysis. There is no universal standard to guide such selection. The appropriate selection of such measures will heavily depend on the given application. One should bear this in mind and refine the selection of such measures to ensure that the clusters generated are meaningful and useful for the application at hand.

7.3 A Categorization of Major Clustering Methods

Many clustering algorithms exist in the literature. It is difficult to provide a crisp categorization of clustering methods because these categories may overlap, so that a method may have features from several categories. Nevertheless, it is useful to present a relatively organized picture of the different clustering methods.

In general, the major clustering methods can be classified into the following categories.

Partitioning methods: Given a database of n objects or data tuples, a partitioning method constructs k partitions of the data, where each partition represents a cluster and $k \leq n$. That is, it classifies the data into k groups, which together satisfy the following requirements: (1) each group must contain at least one object, and (2) each object must belong to exactly one group. Notice that the second requirement can be relaxed in some fuzzy partitioning techniques. References to such techniques are given in the bibliographic notes.

Given k, the number of partitions to construct, a partitioning method creates an initial partitioning. It then uses an **iterative relocation technique** that attempts to improve the partitioning by moving objects from one group to another. The general criterion of a good partitioning is that objects in the same cluster are "close" or related to each other, whereas objects of different clusters are "far apart" or very different. There are various kinds of other criteria for judging the quality of partitions.

To achieve global optimality in partitioning-based clustering would require the exhaustive enumeration of all of the possible partitions. Instead, most applications adopt one of a few popular heuristic methods, such as (1) the *k-means* algorithm, where each cluster is represented by the mean value of the objects in the cluster, and (2) the *k-medoids* algorithm, where each cluster is represented by one of the objects located near the center of the cluster. These heuristic clustering methods work well for finding spherical-shaped clusters in small to medium-sized databases. To find clusters with complex shapes and for clustering very large data sets, partitioning-based methods need to be extended. Partitioning-based clustering methods are studied in depth in Section 7.4.

Hierarchical methods: A hierarchical method creates a hierarchical decomposition of the given set of data objects. A hierarchical method can be classified as being either *agglomerative* or *divisive*, based on how the hierarchical decomposition is formed. The *agglomerative approach*, also called the *bottom-up* approach, starts with each object forming a separate group. It successively merges the objects or groups that are close to one another, until all of the groups are merged into one (the topmost level of the hierarchy), or until a termination condition holds. The *divisive approach*, also called the *top-down* approach, starts with all of the objects in the same cluster. In each successive iteration, a cluster is split up into smaller clusters, until eventually each object is in one cluster, or until a termination condition holds.

Hierarchical methods suffer from the fact that once a step (merge or split) is done, it can never be undone. This rigidity is useful in that it leads to smaller computation costs by not having to worry about a combinatorial number of different choices. However, such techniques cannot correct erroneous decisions. There are two approaches to improving the quality of hierarchical clustering: (1) perform careful analysis of object "linkages" at each hierarchical partitioning, such as in Chameleon, or (2) integrate hierarchical agglomeration and other approaches by first using a hierarchical agglomerative algorithm to group objects into *microclusters*, and then performing *macroclustering* on the microclusters using another clustering method such as iterative relocation, as in BIRCH. Hierarchical clustering methods are studied in Section 7.5.

Density-based methods: Most partitioning methods cluster objects based on the distance between objects. Such methods can find only spherical-shaped clusters and encounter difficulty at discovering clusters of arbitrary shapes. Other clustering methods have been developed based on the notion of *density*. Their general idea is to continue growing the given cluster as long as the density (number of objects or data points) in the "neighborhood" exceeds some threshold; that is, for each data point within a given cluster, the neighborhood of a given radius has to contain at least a minimum number of points. Such a method can be used to filter out noise (outliers) and discover clusters of arbitrary shape.

DBSCAN and its extension, OPTICS, are typical density-based methods that grow clusters according to a density-based connectivity analysis. DENCLUE is a method that clusters objects based on the analysis of the value distributions of density functions. Density-based clustering methods are studied in Section 7.6.

Grid-based methods: Grid-based methods quantize the object space into a finite number of cells that form a grid structure. All of the clustering operations are performed on the grid structure (i.e., on the quantized space). The main advantage of this approach is its fast processing time, which is typically independent of the number of data objects and dependent only on the number of cells in each dimension in the quantized space.

STING is a typical example of a grid-based method. WaveCluster applies wavelet transformation for clustering analysis and is both grid-based and density-based. Grid-based clustering methods are studied in Section 7.7.

Model-based methods: Model-based methods hypothesize a model for each of the clusters and find the best fit of the data to the given model. A model-based algorithm may locate clusters by constructing a density function that reflects the spatial distribution of the data points. It also leads to a way of automatically determining the number of clusters based on standard statistics, taking "noise" or outliers into account and thus yielding robust clustering methods.

EM is an algorithm that performs expectation-maximization analysis based on statistical modeling. COBWEB is a conceptual learning algorithm that performs probability analysis and takes *concepts* as a model for clusters. SOM (or self-organizing feature map) is a neural network-based algorithm that clusters by mapping high-dimensional data into a 2-D or 3-D feature map, which is also useful for data visualization. Model-based clustering methods are studied in Section 7.8.

The choice of clustering algorithm depends both on the type of data available and on the particular purpose of the application. If cluster analysis is used as a descriptive or exploratory tool, it is possible to try several algorithms on the same data to see what the data may disclose.

Some clustering algorithms integrate the ideas of several clustering methods, so that it is sometimes difficult to classify a given algorithm as uniquely belonging to only one clustering method category. Furthermore, some applications may have clustering criteria that require the integration of several clustering techniques.

Aside from the above categories of clustering methods, there are two classes of clustering tasks that require special attention. One is *clustering high-dimensional data*, and the other is *constraint-based clustering*.

Clustering high-dimensional data is a particularly important task in cluster analysis because many applications require the analysis of objects containing a large number of features or dimensions. For example, text documents may contain thousands of terms or keywords as features, and DNA microarray data may provide information on the expression levels of thousands of genes under hundreds of conditions. Clustering high-dimensional data is challenging due to the curse of dimensionality. Many dimensions may not be relevant. As the number of dimensions increases, the data become increasingly sparse so that the distance measurement between pairs of points become meaningless and the average density of points anywhere in the data is likely to be low. Therefore, a different clustering methodology needs to be developed for high-dimensional data. CLIQUE and PROCLUS are two influential *subspace clustering methods*, which search for clusters in subspaces (or subsets of dimensions) of the data, rather than over the entire data space. **Frequent pattern–based clustering**, another clustering methodology, extracts *distinct frequent patterns* among subsets of dimensions that occur frequently. It uses such patterns to group objects and generate meaningful clusters. pCluster is an example of frequent pattern–based clustering that groups objects based on their pattern similarity. High-dimensional data clustering methods are studied in Section 7.9.

Constraint-based clustering is a clustering approach that performs clustering by incorporation of user-specified or application-oriented constraints. A constraint expresses a user's expectation or describes "properties" of the desired clustering results, and provides an effective means for communicating with the clustering process. Various kinds of constraints can be specified, either by a user or as per application requirements. Our focus of discussion will be on *spatial clustering* with the existence of obstacles and clustering under user-specified constraints. In addition, *semi-supervised clustering* is described, which employs, for example, pairwise constraints (such as pairs of instances labeled as belonging to the same or different clusters) in order to improve the quality of the resulting clustering. Constraint-based clustering methods are studied in Section 7.10.

In the following sections, we examine each of the above clustering methods in detail. We also introduce algorithms that integrate the ideas of several clustering methods. Outlier analysis, which typically involves clustering, is described in Section 7.11. In general, the notation used in these sections is as follows. Let D be a data set of n objects to be clustered. An **object** is described by d variables (attributes or dimensions) and therefore may also be referred to as a *point* in d-dimensional object space. Objects are represented in bold italic font (e.g., $\boldsymbol{p}$).

7.4 Partitioning Methods

Given D, a data set of n objects, and k, the number of clusters to form, a **partitioning algorithm** organizes the objects into k partitions ($k \leq n$), where each partition represents a cluster. The clusters are formed to optimize an objective partitioning criterion, such as a dissimilarity function based on distance, so that the objects within a cluster are "similar," whereas the objects of different clusters are "dissimilar" in terms of the data set attributes.

7.4.1 Classical Partitioning Methods: *k*-Means and *k*-Medoids

The most well-known and commonly used partitioning methods are *k-means*, *k-medoids*, and their variations.

Centroid-Based Technique: The *k*-Means Method

The ***k*-means algorithm** takes the input parameter, k, and partitions a set of n objects into k clusters so that the resulting intracluster similarity is high but the intercluster similarity is low. Cluster similarity is measured in regard to the *mean* value of the objects in a cluster, which can be viewed as the cluster's *centroid* or *center of gravity*.

"How does the k-means algorithm work?" The k-means algorithm proceeds as follows. First, it randomly selects k of the objects, each of which initially represents a cluster mean or center. For each of the remaining objects, an object is assigned to the cluster to which it is the most similar, based on the distance between the object and the cluster mean. It then computes the new mean for each cluster. This process iterates until the criterion function converges. Typically, the **square-error criterion** is used, defined as

$$E = \sum_{i=1}^{k} \sum_{\boldsymbol{p} \in C_i} |\boldsymbol{p} - \boldsymbol{m}_i|^2, \tag{7.18}$$

where E is the sum of the square error for all objects in the data set; $\boldsymbol{p}$ is the point in space representing a given object; and $\boldsymbol{m}_i$ is the mean of cluster C_i (both $\boldsymbol{p}$ and $\boldsymbol{m}_i$ are multidimensional). In other words, for each object in each cluster, the distance from the object to its cluster center is squared, and the distances are summed. This criterion tries to make the resulting k clusters as compact and as separate as possible. The k-means procedure is summarized in Figure 7.2.

Example 7.8 **Clustering by *k*-means partitioning.** Suppose that there is a set of objects located in space as depicted in the rectangle shown in Figure 7.3(a). Let $k = 3$; that is, the user would like the objects to be partitioned into three clusters.

According to the algorithm in Figure 7.2, we arbitrarily choose three objects as the three initial cluster centers, where cluster centers are marked by a "+". Each object is distributed to a cluster based on the cluster center to which it is the nearest. Such a distribution forms silhouettes encircled by dotted curves, as shown in Figure 7.3(a).

Next, the cluster centers are updated. That is, the mean value of each cluster is recalculated based on the current objects in the cluster. Using the new cluster centers, the objects are redistributed to the clusters based on which cluster center is the nearest. Such a redistribution forms new silhouettes encircled by dashed curves, as shown in Figure 7.3(b).

This process iterates, leading to Figure 7.3(c). The process of iteratively reassigning objects to clusters to improve the partitioning is referred to as *iterative relocation*. Eventually, no redistribution of the objects in any cluster occurs, and so the process terminates. The resulting clusters are returned by the clustering process. ■

The algorithm attempts to determine k partitions that minimize the square-error function. It works well when the clusters are compact clouds that are rather well

Algorithm: *k*-means. The *k*-means algorithm for partitioning, where each cluster's center is represented by the mean value of the objects in the cluster.

Input:

- k: the number of clusters,
- D: a data set containing n objects.

Output: A set of k clusters.

Method:

```
(1) arbitrarily choose k objects from D as the initial cluster centers;
(2) repeat
(3)     (re)assign each object to the cluster to which the object is the most similar,
            based on the mean value of the objects in the cluster;
(4)     update the cluster means, i.e., calculate the mean value of the objects for
            each cluster;
(5) until no change;
```

Figure 7.2 The *k*-means partitioning algorithm.

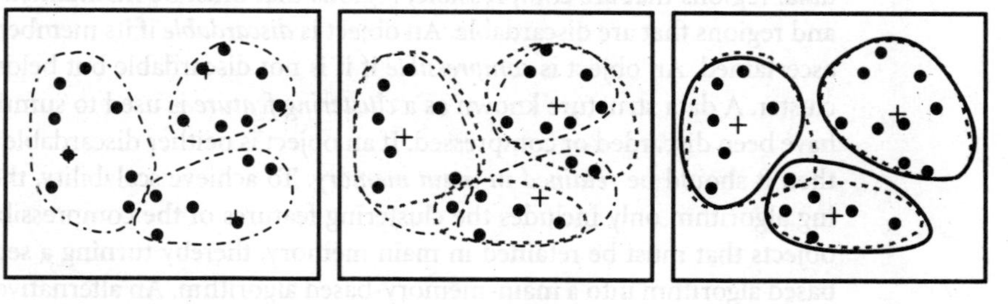

(a) (b) (c)

Figure 7.3 Clustering of a set of objects based on the *k*-means method. (The mean of each cluster is marked by a "+".)

separated from one another. The method is relatively scalable and efficient in processing large data sets because the computational complexity of the algorithm is $O(nkt)$, where n is the total number of objects, k is the number of clusters, and t is the number of iterations. Normally, $k \ll n$ and $t \ll n$. The method often terminates at a local optimum.

The *k*-means method, however, can be applied only when the mean of a cluster is defined. This may not be the case in some applications, such as when data with categorical attributes are involved. The necessity for users to specify k, the number of clusters, in advance can be seen as a disadvantage. The *k*-means method is not suitable for discovering clusters with nonconvex shapes or clusters of very different size. Moreover, it is sensitive to noise and outlier data points because a small number of such data can substantially influence the mean value.

There are quite a few variants of the k-means method. These can differ in the selection of the initial k means, the calculation of dissimilarity, and the strategies for calculating cluster means. An interesting strategy that often yields good results is to first apply a hierarchical agglomeration algorithm, which determines the number of clusters and finds an initial clustering, and then use iterative relocation to improve the clustering.

Another variant to k-means is the **k-modes method,** which extends the k-means paradigm to cluster categorical data by replacing the means of clusters with modes, using new dissimilarity measures to deal with categorical objects and a frequency-based method to update modes of clusters. The k-means and the k-modes methods can be integrated to cluster data with mixed numeric and categorical values.

The **EM (Expectation-Maximization)** algorithm (which will be further discussed in Section 7.8.1) extends the k-means paradigm in a different way. Whereas the k-means algorithm assigns each object to a cluster, in EM each object is assigned to *each* cluster according to a weight representing its probability of membership. In other words, there are no strict boundaries between clusters. Therefore, new means are computed based on weighted measures.

"How can we make the k-means algorithm more scalable?" A recent approach to scaling the k-means algorithm is based on the idea of identifying three kinds of regions in data: regions that are compressible, regions that must be maintained in main memory, and regions that are discardable. An object is *discardable* if its membership in a cluster is ascertained. An object is *compressible* if it is not discardable but belongs to a tight subcluster. A data structure known as a *clustering feature* is used to summarize objects that have been discarded or compressed. If an object is neither discardable nor compressible, then it should be *retained in main memory*. To achieve scalability, the iterative clustering algorithm only includes the clustering features of the compressible objects and the objects that must be retained in main memory, thereby turning a secondary-memory-based algorithm into a main-memory-based algorithm. An alternative approach to scaling the k-means algorithm explores the microclustering idea, which first groups nearby objects into "microclusters" and then performs k-means clustering on the microclusters. Microclustering is further discussed in Section 7.5.

Representative Object-Based Technique: The k-Medoids Method

The k-means **algorithm** is sensitive to outliers because an object with an extremely large value may substantially distort the distribution of data. This effect is particularly exacerbated due to the use of the *square*-error function (Equation (7.18)).

"How might the algorithm be modified to diminish such sensitivity?" Instead of taking the mean value of the objects in a cluster as a reference point, we can pick actual objects to represent the clusters, using one representative object per cluster. Each remaining object is clustered with the representative object to which it is the most similar. The partitioning method is then performed based on the principle of minimizing the sum of

the dissimilarities between each object and its corresponding reference point. That is, an **absolute-error criterion** is used, defined as

$$E = \sum_{j=1}^{k} \sum_{p \in C_j} |p - o_j|, \tag{7.19}$$

where E is the sum of the absolute error for all objects in the data set; p is the point in space representing a given object in cluster C_j; and o_j is the representative object of C_j. In general, the algorithm iterates until, eventually, each representative object is actually the **medoid**, or most centrally located object, of its cluster. This is the basis of the **k-medoids method** for grouping n objects into k clusters.

Let's look closer at k-medoids clustering. The initial representative objects (or seeds) are chosen arbitrarily. The iterative process of replacing representative objects by nonrepresentative objects continues as long as the quality of the resulting clustering is improved. This quality is estimated using a cost function that measures the average dissimilarity between an object and the representative object of its cluster. To determine whether a nonrepresentative object, o_{random}, is a good replacement for a current representative object, o_j, the following four cases are examined for each of the nonrepresentative objects, p, as illustrated in Figure 7.4.

- **Case 1:** p currently belongs to representative object, o_j. If o_j is replaced by o_{random} as a representative object and p is closest to one of the other representative objects, o_i, $i \neq j$, then p is reassigned to o_i.
- **Case 2:** p currently belongs to representative object, o_j. If o_j is replaced by o_{random} as a representative object and p is closest to o_{random}, then p is reassigned to o_{random}.
- **Case 3:** p currently belongs to representative object, o_i, $i \neq j$. If o_j is replaced by o_{random} as a representative object and p is still closest to o_i, then the assignment does not change.

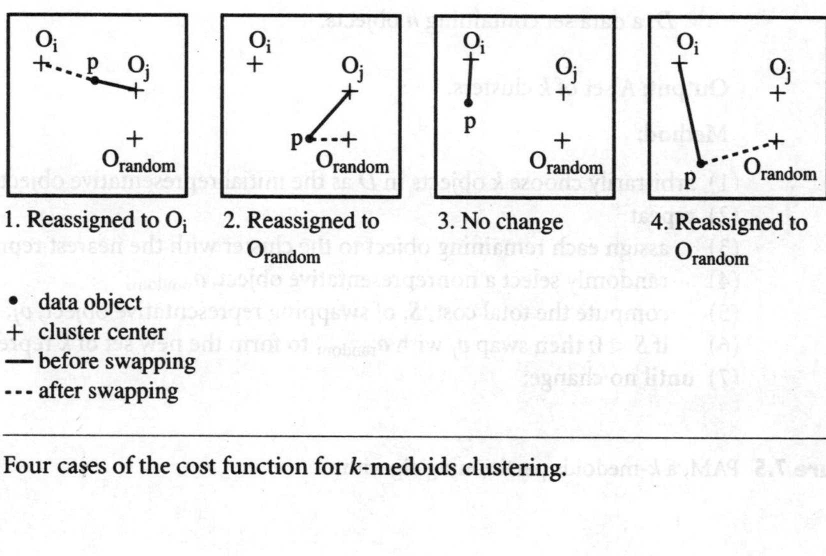

Figure 7.4 Four cases of the cost function for k-medoids clustering.

- **Case 4:** p currently belongs to representative object, o_i, $i \neq j$. If o_j is replaced by o_{random} as a representative object and p is closest to o_{random}, then p is reassigned to o_{random}.

Each time a reassignment occurs, a difference in absolute error, E, is contributed to the cost function. Therefore, the cost function calculates the *difference* in absolute-error value if a current representative object is replaced by a nonrepresentative object. The total cost of swapping is the sum of costs incurred by all nonrepresentative objects. If the total cost is negative, then o_j is replaced or swapped with o_{random} since the actual absolute error E would be reduced. If the total cost is positive, the current representative object, o_j, is considered acceptable, and nothing is changed in the iteration.

PAM (Partitioning Around Medoids) was one of the first k-medoids algorithms introduced (Figure 7.5). It attempts to determine k partitions for n objects. After an initial random selection of k representative objects, the algorithm repeatedly tries to make a better choice of cluster representatives. All of the possible pairs of objects are analyzed, where one object in each pair is considered a representative object and the other is not. The quality of the resulting clustering is calculated for each such combination. An object, o_j, is replaced with the object causing the greatest reduction in error. The set of best objects for each cluster in one iteration forms the representative objects for the next iteration. The final set of representative objects are the respective medoids of the clusters. The complexity of each iteration is $O(k(n-k)^2)$. For large values of n and k, such computation becomes very costly.

Algorithm: k-**medoids.** PAM, a k-medoids algorithm for partitioning based on medoid or central objects.

Input:

- k: the number of clusters,
- D: a data set containing n objects.

Output: A set of k clusters.

Method:

(1) arbitrarily choose k objects in D as the initial representative objects or seeds;
(2) **repeat**
(3) assign each remaining object to the cluster with the nearest representative object;
(4) randomly select a nonrepresentative object, o_{random};
(5) compute the total cost, S, of swapping representative object, o_j, with o_{random};
(6) **if** $S < 0$ **then** swap o_j with o_{random} to form the new set of k representative objects;
(7) **until** no change;

Figure 7.5 PAM, a k-medoids partitioning algorithm.

"Which method is more robust—k-means or k-medoids?" The *k*-medoids method is more robust than *k*-means in the presence of noise and outliers, because a medoid is less influenced by outliers or other extreme values than a mean. However, its processing is more costly than the *k*-means method. Both methods require the user to specify *k*, the number of clusters.

Aside from using the mean or the medoid as a measure of cluster center, other alternative measures are also commonly used in partitioning clustering methods. The *median* can be used, resulting in the *k-median* method, where the median or "middle value" is taken for each ordered attribute. Alternatively, in the *k-modes* method, the most frequent value for each attribute is used.

7.4.2 Partitioning Methods in Large Databases: From *k*-Medoids to CLARANS

"How efficient is the k-medoids algorithm on large data sets?" A typical *k*-medoids partitioning algorithm like PAM works effectively for small data sets, but does not scale well for large data sets. To deal with larger data sets, a *sampling*-based method, called CLARA (Clustering LARge Applications), can be used.

The idea behind CLARA is as follows: Instead of taking the whole set of data into consideration, a small portion of the actual data is chosen as a representative of the data. Medoids are then chosen from this sample using PAM. If the sample is selected in a fairly random manner, it should closely represent the original data set. The representative objects (medoids) chosen will likely be similar to those that would have been chosen from the whole data set. CLARA draws multiple samples of the data set, applies PAM on each sample, and returns its best clustering as the output. As expected, CLARA can deal with larger data sets than PAM. The complexity of each iteration now becomes $O(ks^2 + k(n-k))$, where s is the size of the sample, k is the number of clusters, and n is the total number of objects.

The effectiveness of CLARA depends on the sample size. Notice that PAM searches for the best k medoids among a given data set, whereas CLARA searches for the best k medoids among the *selected sample* of the data set. CLARA cannot find the best clustering if any of the best sampled medoids is not among the best k medoids. That is, if an object o_i is one of the best k medoids but is not selected during sampling, CLARA will never find the best clustering. This is, therefore, a trade-off for efficiency. A good clustering based on sampling will not necessarily represent a good clustering of the whole data set if the sample is biased.

"How might we improve the quality and scalability of CLARA?" A *k*-medoids type algorithm called CLARANS (Clustering Large Applications based upon RANdomized Search) was proposed, which combines the sampling technique with PAM. However, unlike CLARA, CLARANS does not confine itself to any sample at any given time. While CLARA has a fixed sample at each stage of the search, CLARANS draws a sample with some randomness in each step of the search. Conceptually, the clustering process can be viewed as a search through a graph, where each node is a potential solution (a set of k medoids). Two nodes are *neighbors* (that is, connected by an arc in

the graph) if their sets differ by only one object. Each node can be assigned a cost that is defined by the total dissimilarity between every object and the medoid of its cluster. At each step, PAM examines all of the neighbors of the current node in its search for a minimum cost solution. The current node is then replaced by the neighbor with the largest descent in costs. Because CLARA works on a sample of the entire data set, it examines fewer neighbors and restricts the search to subgraphs that are smaller than the original graph. While CLARA draws a sample of nodes at the beginning of a search, CLARANS dynamically draws a random sample of neighbors in each step of a search. The number of neighbors to be randomly sampled is restricted by a user-specified parameter. In this way, CLARANS does not confine the search to a localized area. If a better neighbor is found (i.e., having a lower error), CLARANS moves to the neighbor's node and the process starts again; otherwise, the current clustering produces a local minimum. If a local minimum is found, CLARANS starts with new randomly selected nodes in search for a new local minimum. Once a user-specified number of local minima has been found, the algorithm outputs, as a solution, the best local minimum, that is, the local minimum having the lowest cost.

CLARANS has been experimentally shown to be more effective than both PAM and CLARA. It can be used to find the most "natural" number of clusters using a *silhouette coefficient*—a property of an object that specifies how much the object truly belongs to the cluster. CLARANS also enables the detection of outliers. However, the computational complexity of CLARANS is about $O(n^2)$, where n is the number of objects. Furthermore, its clustering quality is dependent on the sampling method used. The ability of CLARANS to deal with data objects that reside on disk can be further improved by focusing techniques that explore spatial data structures, such as R*-trees.

7.5 Hierarchical Methods

A hierarchical clustering method works by grouping data objects into a tree of clusters. Hierarchical clustering methods can be further classified as either *agglomerative* or *divisive*, depending on whether the hierarchical decomposition is formed in a bottom-up (merging) or top-down (splitting) fashion. The quality of a pure hierarchical clustering method suffers from its inability to perform adjustment once a merge or split decision has been executed. That is, if a particular merge or split decision later turns out to have been a poor choice, the method cannot backtrack and correct it. Recent studies have emphasized the integration of hierarchical agglomeration with iterative relocation methods.

7.5.1 Agglomerative and Divisive Hierarchical Clustering

In general, there are two types of hierarchical clustering methods:

- **Agglomerative hierarchical clustering:** This bottom-up strategy starts by placing each object in its own cluster and then merges these atomic clusters into larger and larger clusters, until all of the objects are in a single cluster or until certain termination conditions are satisfied. Most hierarchical clustering methods belong to this category. They differ only in their definition of intercluster similarity.

- **Divisive hierarchical clustering:** This top-down strategy does the reverse of agglomerative hierarchical clustering by starting with all objects in one cluster. It subdivides the cluster into smaller and smaller pieces, until each object forms a cluster on its own or until it satisfies certain termination conditions, such as a desired number of clusters is obtained or the diameter of each cluster is within a certain threshold.

Example 7.9 **Agglomerative versus divisive hierarchical clustering.** Figure 7.6 shows the application of AGNES (AGglomerative NESting), an agglomerative hierarchical clustering method, and DIANA (DIvisive ANAlysis), a divisive hierarchical clustering method, to a data set of five objects, $\{a, b, c, d, e\}$. Initially, AGNES places each object into a cluster of its own. The clusters are then merged step-by-step according to some criterion. For example, clusters C_1 and C_2 may be merged if an object in C_1 and an object in C_2 form the minimum Euclidean distance between any two objects from different clusters. This is a **single-linkage** approach in that each cluster is represented by all of the objects in the cluster, and the similarity between two clusters is measured by the similarity of the *closest* pair of data points belonging to different clusters. The cluster merging process repeats until all of the objects are eventually merged to form one cluster.

In DIANA, all of the objects are used to form one initial cluster. The cluster is split according to some principle, such as the maximum Euclidean distance between the closest neighboring objects in the cluster. The cluster splitting process repeats until, eventually, each new cluster contains only a single object. ■

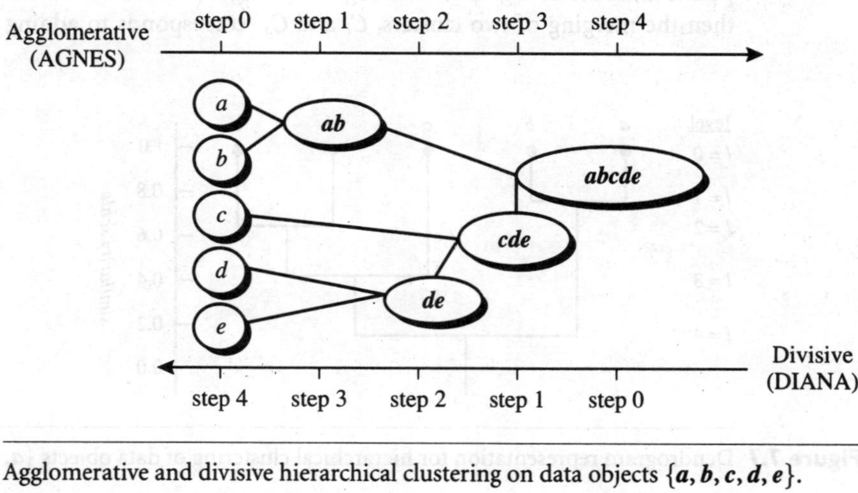

Figure 7.6 Agglomerative and divisive hierarchical clustering on data objects $\{a, b, c, d, e\}$.

In either agglomerative or divisive hierarchical clustering, the user can specify the desired number of clusters as a termination condition.

A tree structure called a **dendrogram** is commonly used to represent the process of hierarchical clustering. It shows how objects are grouped together step by step. Figure 7.7 shows a dendrogram for the five objects presented in Figure 7.6, where $l = 0$ shows the five objects as singleton clusters at level 0. At $l = 1$, objects $\boldsymbol{a}$ and $\boldsymbol{b}$ are grouped together to form the first cluster, and they stay together at all subsequent levels. We can also use a vertical axis to show the similarity scale between clusters. For example, when the similarity of two groups of objects, $\{a, b\}$ and $\{c, d, e\}$, is roughly 0.16, they are merged together to form a single cluster.

Four widely used measures for distance between clusters are as follows, where $|\boldsymbol{p} - \boldsymbol{p}'|$ is the distance between two objects or points, $\boldsymbol{p}$ and $\boldsymbol{p}'$; $\boldsymbol{m_i}$ is the mean for cluster, C_i; and n_i is the number of objects in C_i.

$$\text{Minimum distance}: \quad d_{min}(C_i, C_j) = \min_{p \in C_i, p' \in C_j} |\boldsymbol{p} - \boldsymbol{p}'| \tag{7.20}$$

$$\text{Maximum distance}: \quad d_{max}(C_i, C_j) = \max_{p \in C_i, p' \in C_j} |\boldsymbol{p} - \boldsymbol{p}'| \tag{7.21}$$

$$\text{Mean distance}: \quad d_{mean}(C_i, C_j) = |\boldsymbol{m_i} - \boldsymbol{m_j}| \tag{7.22}$$

$$\text{Average distance}: \quad d_{avg}(C_i, C_j) = \frac{1}{n_i n_j} \sum_{p \in C_i} \sum_{p' \in C_j} |\boldsymbol{p} - \boldsymbol{p}'| \tag{7.23}$$

When an algorithm uses the *minimum distance*, $d_{min}(C_i, C_j)$, to measure the distance between clusters, it is sometimes called a **nearest-neighbor clustering algorithm.** Moreover, if the clustering process is terminated when the distance between nearest clusters exceeds an arbitrary threshold, it is called a **single-linkage algorithm.** If we view the data points as nodes of a graph, with edges forming a path between the nodes in a cluster, then the merging of two clusters, C_i and C_j, corresponds to adding an edge between

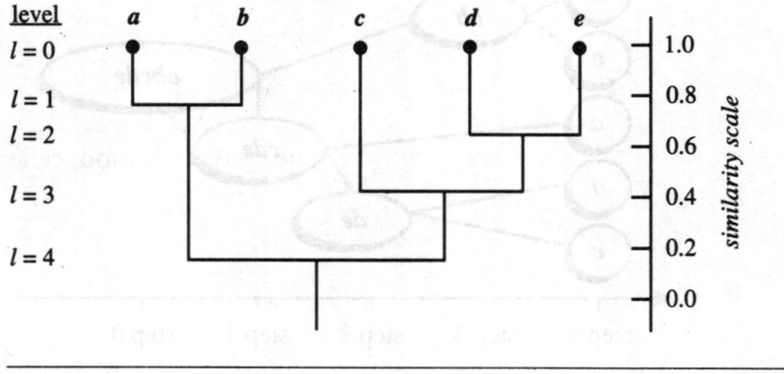

Figure 7.7 Dendrogram representation for hierarchical clustering of data objects $\{a, b, c, d, e\}$.

the nearest pair of nodes in C_i and C_j. Because edges linking clusters always go between distinct clusters, the resulting graph will generate a tree. Thus, an agglomerative hierarchical clustering algorithm that uses the minimum distance measure is also called a **minimal spanning tree algorithm.**

When an algorithm uses the *maximum distance*, $d_{max}(C_i, C_j)$, to measure the distance between clusters, it is sometimes called a **farthest-neighbor clustering algorithm.** If the clustering process is terminated when the maximum distance between nearest clusters exceeds an arbitrary threshold, it is called a **complete-linkage algorithm.** By viewing data points as nodes of a graph, with edges linking nodes, we can think of each cluster as a *complete* subgraph, that is, with edges connecting all of the nodes in the clusters. The distance between two clusters is determined by the most distant nodes in the two clusters. Farthest-neighbor algorithms tend to minimize the increase in diameter of the clusters at each iteration as little as possible. If the true clusters are rather compact and approximately equal in size, the method will produce high-quality clusters. Otherwise, the clusters produced can be meaningless.

The above minimum and maximum measures represent two extremes in measuring the distance between clusters. They tend to be overly sensitive to outliers or noisy data. The use of *mean* or *average distance* is a compromise between the minimum and maximum distances and overcomes the outlier sensitivity problem. Whereas the *mean distance* is the simplest to compute, the *average distance* is advantageous in that it can handle categoric as well as numeric data.[2] The computation of the mean vector for categoric data can be difficult or impossible to define.

"What are some of the difficulties with hierarchical clustering?" The hierarchical clustering method, though simple, often encounters difficulties regarding the selection of merge or split points. Such a decision is critical because once a group of objects is merged or split, the process at the next step will operate on the newly generated clusters. It will neither undo what was done previously nor perform object swapping between clusters. Thus merge or split decisions, if not well chosen at some step, may lead to low-quality clusters. Moreover, the method does not scale well, because each decision to merge or split requires the examination and evaluatation of a good number of objects or clusters.

One promising direction for improving the clustering quality of hierarchical methods is to integrate hierarchical clustering with other clustering techniques, resulting in multiple-phase clustering. Three such methods are introduced in the following subsections. The first, called BIRCH, begins by partitioning objects hierarchically using tree structures, where the leaf or low-level nonleaf nodes can be viewed as "microclusters" depending on the scale of resolution. It then applies other clustering algorithms to perform macroclustering on the microclusters. The second method, called ROCK, merges clusters based on their interconnectivity. The third method, called Chameleon, explores dynamic modeling in hierarchical clustering.

[2]To handle categoric data, dissimilarity measures such as those described in Sections 7.2.2 and 7.2.3 can be used to replace $|\boldsymbol{p}-\boldsymbol{p}'|$ with $d(\boldsymbol{p},\boldsymbol{p}')$ in Equation (7.23).

7.5.2 BIRCH: Balanced Iterative Reducing and Clustering Using Hierarchies

BIRCH is designed for clustering a large amount of numerical data by integration of hierarchical clustering (at the initial *microclustering* stage) and other clustering methods such as iterative partitioning (at the later *macroclustering* stage). It overcomes the two difficulties of agglomerative clustering methods: (1) scalability and (2) the inability to undo what was done in the previous step.

BIRCH introduces two concepts, *clustering feature* and *clustering feature tree* (*CF tree*), which are used to summarize cluster representations. These structures help the clustering method achieve good speed and scalability in large databases and also make it effective for incremental and dynamic clustering of incoming objects.

Let's look closer at the above-mentioned structures. Given n d-dimensional data objects or points in a cluster, we can define the centroid x_0, radius R, and diameter D of the cluster as follows:

$$x_0 = \frac{\sum_{i=1}^{n} x_i}{n} \tag{7.24}$$

$$R = \sqrt{\frac{\sum_{i=1}^{n}(x_i - x_0)^2}{n}} \tag{7.25}$$

$$D = \sqrt{\frac{\sum_{i=1}^{n}\sum_{j=1}^{n}(x_i - x_j)^2}{n(n-1)}} \tag{7.26}$$

where R is the average distance from member objects to the centroid, and D is the average pairwise distance within a cluster. Both R and D reflect the tightness of the cluster around the centroid. A clustering feature (CF) is a three-dimensional vector summarizing information about clusters of objects. Given n d-dimensional objects or points in a cluster, $\{x_i\}$, then the CF of the cluster is defined as

$$CF = \langle n, LS, SS \rangle, \tag{7.27}$$

where n is the number of points in the cluster, LS is the linear sum of the n points (i.e., $\sum_{i=1}^{n} x_i$), and SS is the square sum of the data points (i.e., $\sum_{i=1}^{n} x_i^2$).

A clustering feature is essentially a summary of the statistics for the given cluster: the zeroth, first, and second moments of the cluster from a statistical point of view. Clustering features are *additive*. For example, suppose that we have two disjoint clusters, C_1 and C_2, having the clustering features, CF_1 and CF_2, respectively. The clustering feature for the cluster that is formed by merging C_1 and C_2 is simply $CF_1 + CF_2$.

Clustering features are sufficient for calculating all of the measurements that are needed for making clustering decisions in BIRCH. BIRCH thus utilizes storage efficiently by employing the clustering features to summarize information about the clusters of objects, thereby bypassing the need to store all objects.

Example 7.10 **Clustering feature.** Suppose that there are three points, (2, 5), (3, 2), and (4, 3), in a cluster, C_1. The clustering feature of C_1 is

$$CF_1 = \langle 3, (2+3+4, 5+2+3), (2^2+3^2+4^2, 5^2+2^2+3^2)\rangle = \langle 3, (9, 10), (29, 38)\rangle.$$

Suppose that C_1 is disjoint to a second cluster, C_2, where $CF_2 = \langle 3, (35, 36), (417, 440)\rangle$. The clustering feature of a new cluster, C_3, that is formed by merging C_1 and C_2, is derived by adding CF_1 and CF_2. That is,

$$CF_3 = \langle 3+3, (9+35, 10+36), (29+417, 38+440)\rangle = \langle 6, (44, 46), (446, 478)\rangle. \quad \blacksquare$$

A **CF tree** is a height-balanced tree that stores the clustering features for a hierarchical clustering. An example is shown in Figure 7.8. By definition, a nonleaf node in a tree has descendants or "children." The nonleaf nodes store sums of the CFs of their children, and thus summarize clustering information about their children. A CF tree has two parameters: *branching factor*, *B*, and *threshold*, *T*. The branching factor specifies the maximum number of children per nonleaf node. The threshold parameter specifies the maximum diameter of subclusters stored at the leaf nodes of the tree. These two parameters influence the size of the resulting tree.

BIRCH tries to produce the best clusters with the available resources. Given a limited amount of main memory, an important consideration is to minimize the time required for I/O. BIRCH applies a *multiphase* clustering technique: a single scan of the data set yields a basic good clustering, and one or more additional scans can (optionally) be used to further improve the quality. The primary phases are:

- **Phase 1:** BIRCH scans the database to build an initial in-memory CF tree, which can be viewed as a multilevel compression of the data that tries to preserve the inherent clustering structure of the data.

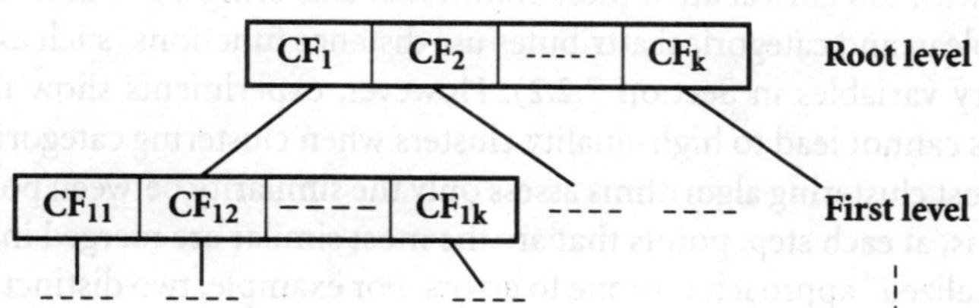

Figure 7.8 A CF tree structure.

- **Phase 2:** BIRCH applies a (selected) clustering algorithm to cluster the leaf nodes of the CF tree, which removes sparse clusters as outliers and groups dense clusters into larger ones.

For Phase 1, the CF tree is built dynamically as objects are inserted. Thus, the method is incremental. An object is inserted into the closest leaf entry (subcluster). If the diameter of the subcluster stored in the leaf node after insertion is larger than the threshold value, then the leaf node and possibly other nodes are split. After the insertion of the new object, information about it is passed toward the root of the tree. The size of the CF tree can be changed by modifying the threshold. If the size of the memory that is needed for storing the CF tree is larger than the size of the main memory, then a smaller threshold value can be specified and the CF tree is rebuilt. The rebuild process is performed by building a new tree from the leaf nodes of the old tree. Thus, the process of rebuilding the tree is done without the necessity of rereading all of the objects or points. This is similar to the insertion and node split in the construction of B+-trees. Therefore, for building the tree, data has to be read just once. Some heuristics and methods have been introduced to deal with outliers and improve the quality of CF trees by additional scans of the data. Once the CF tree is built, any clustering algorithm, such as a typical partitioning algorithm, can be used with the CF tree in Phase 2.

"How effective is BIRCH?" The computation complexity of the algorithm is $O(n)$, where n is the number of objects to be clustered. Experiments have shown the linear scalability of the algorithm with respect to the number of objects and good quality of clustering of the data. However, since each node in a CF tree can hold only a limited number of entries due to its size, a CF tree node does not always correspond to what a user may consider a natural cluster. Moreover, if the clusters are not spherical in shape, BIRCH does not perform well, because it uses the notion of radius or diameter to control the boundary of a cluster.

7.5.3 ROCK: A Hierarchical Clustering Algorithm for Categorical Attributes

ROCK (RObust Clustering using linKs) is a hierarchical clustering algorithm that explores the concept of *links* (the number of *common neighbors* between two objects) for data with categorical attributes. Traditional clustering algorithms for clustering data with Boolean and categorical attributes use distance functions (such as those introduced for binary variables in Section 7.2.2). However, experiments show that such distance measures cannot lead to high-quality clusters when clustering categorical data. Furthermore, most clustering algorithms assess only the similarity between points when clustering; that is, at each step, points that are the most similar are merged into a single cluster. This "localized" approach is prone to errors. For example, two distinct clusters may have a few points or outliers that are close; therefore, relying on the similarity between points to make clustering decisions could cause the two clusters to be merged. ROCK takes a more global approach to clustering by considering the *neighborhoods* of individual pairs of points. If two similar points also have similar neighborhoods, then the two points likely belong to the same cluster and so can be merged.

More formally, two points, p_i and p_j, are **neighbors** if $sim(p_i, p_j) \geq \theta$, where *sim* is a similarity function and θ is a user-specified threshold. We can choose *sim* to be a distance metric or even a nonmetric (provided by a domain expert or as in Section 7.2.5) that is normalized so that its values fall between 0 and 1, with larger values indicating that the points are more similar. The number of **links** between p_i and p_j is defined as the number of common neighbors between p_i and p_j. If the number of links between two points is large, then it is more likely that they belong to the same cluster. By considering neighboring data points in the relationship between individual pairs of points, ROCK is more robust than standard clustering methods that focus only on point similarity.

A good example of data containing categorical attributes is *market basket data* (Chapter 5). Such data consists of a database of transactions, where each transaction is a set of items. Transactions are considered records with Boolean attributes, each corresponding to an individual item, such as bread or cheese. In the record for a transaction, the attribute corresponding to an item is *true* if the transaction contains the item; otherwise, it is *false*. Other data sets with categorical attributes can be handled in a similar manner. ROCK's concepts of neighbors and links are illustrated in the following example, where the similarity between two "points" or transactions, T_i and T_j, is defined with the **Jaccard coefficient** as

$$sim(T_i, T_j) = \frac{|T_i \cap T_j|}{|T_i \cup T_j|}. \qquad (7.28)$$

Example 7.11 **Using neighborhood *link* information together with point similarity.** Suppose that a market basket database contains transactions regarding the items $a, b, \ldots, g$. Consider two clusters of transactions, C_1 and C_2. C_1, which references the items $\langle a, b, c, d, e\rangle$, contains the transactions $\{a, b, c\}, \{a, b, d\}, \{a, b, e\}, \{a, c, d\}, \{a, c, e\}, \{a, d, e\}, \{b, c, d\}$, $\{b, c, e\}$, $\{b, d, e\}$, $\{c, d, e\}$. C_2 references the items $\langle a, b, f, g\rangle$. It contains the transactions $\{a, b, f\}$, $\{a, b, g\}$, $\{a, f, g\}$, $\{b, f, g\}$. Suppose, first, that we consider only the similarity between points while ignoring neighborhood information. The Jaccard coefficient between the transactions $\{a, b, c\}$ and $\{b, d, e\}$ of C_1 is $\frac{1}{5} = 0.2$. In fact, the Jaccard coefficient between any pair of transactions in C_1 ranges from 0.2 to 0.5 (e.g., $\{a, b, c\}$ and $\{a, b, d\}$). The Jaccard coefficient between transactions belonging to different clusters may also reach 0.5 (e.g., $\{a, b, c\}$ of C_1 with $\{a, b, f\}$ or $\{a, b, g\}$ of C_2). Clearly, by using the Jaccard coefficient on its own, we cannot obtain the desired clusters.

On the other hand, the link-based approach of ROCK can successfully separate the transactions into the appropriate clusters. As it turns out, for each transaction, the transaction with which it has the most links is always another transaction from the same cluster. For example, let $\theta = 0.5$. Transaction $\{a, b, f\}$ of C_2 has five links with transaction $\{a, b, g\}$ of the same cluster (due to common neighbors $\{a, b, c\}$, $\{a, b, d\}$, $\{a, b, e\}$, $\{a, f, g\}$, and $\{b, f, g\}$). However, transaction $\{a, b, f\}$ of C_2 has only three links with $\{a, b, c\}$ of C_1 (due to $\{a, b, d\}$, $\{a, b, e\}$, and $\{a, b, g\}$). Similarly, transaction $\{a, f, g\}$ of C_2 has two links with every other transaction in C_2, and zero links with each transaction in C_1. Thus, the link-based approach, which considers neighborhood information in addition to object similarity, can correctly distinguish the two clusters of transactions. ■

Based on these ideas, ROCK first constructs a sparse graph from a given data similarity matrix using a similarity threshold and the concept of shared neighbors. It then performs agglomerative hierarchical clustering on the sparse graph. A goodness measure is used to evaluate the clustering. Random sampling is used for scaling up to large data sets. The worst-case time complexity of ROCK is $O(n^2 + nm_m m_a + n^2 logn)$, where m_m and m_a are the maximum and average number of neighbors, respectively, and n is the number of objects.

In several real-life data sets, such as the congressional voting data set and the mushroom data set at UC-Irvine Machine Learning Repository, ROCK has demonstrated its power at deriving much more meaningful clusters than the traditional hierarchical clustering algorithms.

7.5.4 Chameleon: A Hierarchical Clustering Algorithm Using Dynamic Modeling

Chameleon is a hierarchical clustering algorithm that uses dynamic modeling to determine the similarity between pairs of clusters. It was derived based on the observed weaknesses of two hierarchical clustering algorithms: ROCK and CURE. ROCK and related schemes emphasize cluster interconnectivity while ignoring information regarding cluster proximity. CURE and related schemes consider cluster proximity yet ignore cluster interconnectivity. In Chameleon, cluster similarity is assessed based on how well-connected objects are within a cluster *and* on the proximity of clusters. That is, two clusters are merged if their *interconnectivity* is high and they are *close together*. Thus, Chameleon does not depend on a static, user-supplied model and can automatically adapt to the internal characteristics of the clusters being merged. The merge process facilitates the discovery of natural and homogeneous clusters and applies to all types of data as long as a similarity function can be specified.

"How does Chameleon work?" The main approach of Chameleon is illustrated in Figure 7.9. Chameleon uses a k-nearest-neighbor graph approach to construct a sparse graph, where each vertex of the graph represents a data object, and there exists an edge between two vertices (objects) if one object is among the k-most-similar objects of the other. The edges are weighted to reflect the similarity between objects. Chameleon uses a graph partitioning algorithm to partition the k-nearest-neighbor graph into a large number of relatively small subclusters. It then uses an agglomerative hierarchical clustering algorithm that repeatedly merges subclusters based on their similarity. To determine the pairs of most similar subclusters, it takes into account both the interconnectivity as well as the closeness of the clusters. We will give a mathematical definition for these criteria shortly.

Note that the k-nearest-neighbor graph captures the concept of neighborhood dynamically: the neighborhood radius of an object is determined by the *density* of the region in which the object resides. In a dense region, the neighborhood is defined narrowly; in a

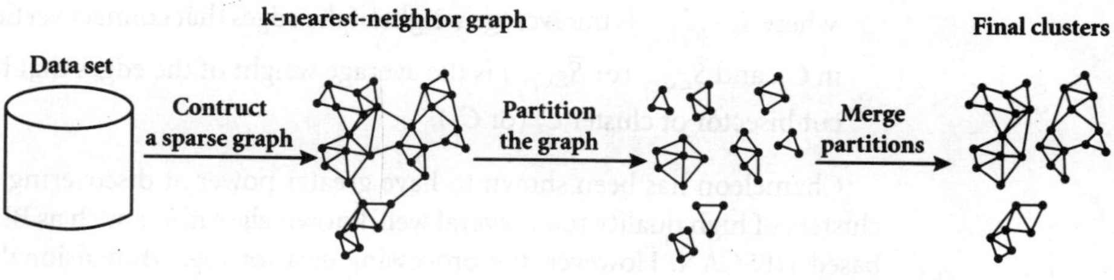

Figure 7.9 Chameleon: Hierarchical clustering based on k-nearest neighbors and dynamic modeling. Based on [KHK99].

sparse region, it is defined more widely. This tends to result in more natural clusters, in comparison with density-based methods like DBSCAN (described in Section 7.6.1) that instead use a *global* neighborhood. Moreover, the density of the region is recorded as the weight of the edges. That is, the edges of a dense region tend to weigh more than that of a sparse region.

The graph-partitioning algorithm partitions the k-nearest-neighbor graph such that it minimizes the **edge cut**. That is, a cluster C is partitioned into subclusters C_i and C_j so as to minimize the *weight of the edges* that would be cut should C be bisected into C_i and C_j. Edge cut is denoted $EC(C_i, C_j)$ and assesses the ***absolute*** interconnectivity between clusters C_i and C_j.

Chameleon determines the similarity between each pair of clusters C_i and C_j according to their *relative interconnectivity*, $RI(C_i, C_j)$, and their *relative closeness*, $RC(C_i, C_j)$:

- The **relative interconnectivity**, $RI(C_i, C_j)$, between two clusters, C_i and C_j, is defined as the absolute interconnectivity between C_i and C_j, normalized with respect to the internal interconnectivity of the two clusters, C_i and C_j. That is,

$$RI(C_i, C_j) = \frac{|EC_{\{C_i, C_j\}}|}{\frac{1}{2}(|EC_{C_i}| + |EC_{C_j}|)}, \tag{7.29}$$

where $EC_{\{C_i, C_j\}}$ is the edge cut, defined as above, for a cluster containing both C_i and C_j. Similarly, EC_{C_i} (or EC_{C_j}) is the minimum sum of the cut edges that partition C_i (or C_j) into two roughly equal parts.

- The **relative closeness**, $RC(C_i, C_j)$, between a pair of clusters, C_i and C_j, is the absolute closeness between C_i and C_j, normalized with respect to the internal closeness of the two clusters, C_i and C_j. It is defined as

$$RC(C_i, C_j) = \frac{\overline{S}_{EC_{\{C_i, C_j\}}}}{\frac{|C_i|}{|C_i|+|C_j|}\overline{S}_{EC_{C_i}} + \frac{|C_j|}{|C_i|+|C_j|}\overline{S}_{EC_{C_j}}}, \tag{7.30}$$

where $\overline{S}_{EC_{\{C_i,C_j\}}}$ is the average weight of the edges that connect vertices in C_i to vertices in C_j, and $\overline{S}_{EC_{C_i}}$ (or $\overline{S}_{EC_{C_j}}$) is the average weight of the edges that belong to the min-cut bisector of cluster C_i (or C_j).

Chameleon has been shown to have greater power at discovering arbitrarily shaped clusters of high quality than several well-known algorithms such as BIRCH and density-based DBSCAN. However, the processing cost for high-dimensional data may require $O(n^2)$ time for n objects in the worst case.

7.6 Density-Based Methods

To discover clusters with arbitrary shape, density-based clustering methods have been developed. These typically regard clusters as dense regions of objects in the data space that are separated by regions of low density (representing noise). DBSCAN grows clusters according to a density-based connectivity analysis. OPTICS extends DBSCAN to produce a *cluster ordering* obtained from a wide range of parameter settings. DENCLUE clusters objects based on a set of density distribution functions.

7.6.1 DBSCAN: A Density-Based Clustering Method Based on Connected Regions with Sufficiently High Density

DBSCAN (Density-Based Spatial Clustering of Applications with Noise) is a density-based clustering algorithm. The algorithm grows regions with sufficiently high density into clusters and discovers clusters of arbitrary shape in spatial databases with noise. It defines a cluster as a maximal set of *density-connected* points.

The basic ideas of density-based clustering involve a number of new definitions. We intuitively present these definitions, and then follow up with an example.

- The neighborhood within a radius ε of a given object is called the **ε-neighborhood** of the object.
- If the ε-neighborhood of an object contains at least a minimum number, *MinPts*, of objects, then the object is called a **core object**.
- Given a set of objects, D, we say that an object $\boldsymbol{p}$ is **directly density-reachable** from object $\boldsymbol{q}$ if $\boldsymbol{p}$ is within the ε-neighborhood of $\boldsymbol{q}$, and $\boldsymbol{q}$ is a core object.
- An object $\boldsymbol{p}$ is **density-reachable** from object $\boldsymbol{q}$ with respect to ε and *MinPts* in a set of objects, D, if there is a chain of objects $\boldsymbol{p}_1, \ldots, \boldsymbol{p}_n$, where $\boldsymbol{p}_1 = \boldsymbol{q}$ and $\boldsymbol{p}_n = \boldsymbol{p}$ such that $\boldsymbol{p}_{i+1}$ is directly density-reachable from $\boldsymbol{p}_i$ with respect to ε and *MinPts*, for $1 \le i \le n$, $\boldsymbol{p}_i \in D$.
- An object $\boldsymbol{p}$ is **density-connected** to object $\boldsymbol{q}$ with respect to ε and *MinPts* in a set of objects, D, if there is an object $\boldsymbol{o} \in D$ such that both $\boldsymbol{p}$ and $\boldsymbol{q}$ are density-reachable from $\boldsymbol{o}$ with respect to ε and *MinPts*.

Density reachability is the transitive closure of direct density reachability, and this relationship is asymmetric. Only core objects are mutually density reachable. Density connectivity, however, is a symmetric relation.

Example 7.12 **Density-reachability and density connectivity.** Consider Figure 7.10 for a given ε represented by the radius of the circles, and, say, let *MinPts* = 3. Based on the above definitions:

- Of the labeled points, ***m***, ***p***, ***o***, and ***r*** are core objects because each is in an ε-neighborhood containing at least three points.
- ***q*** is directly density-reachable from ***m***. ***m*** is directly density-reachable from ***p*** and vice versa.
- ***q*** is (indirectly) density-reachable from ***p*** because ***q*** is directly density-reachable from ***m*** and ***m*** is directly density-reachable from ***p***. However, ***p*** is not density-reachable from ***q*** because ***q*** is not a core object. Similarly, ***r*** and ***s*** are density-reachable from ***o***, and ***o*** is density-reachable from ***r***.
- ***o***, ***r***, and ***s*** are all density-connected. ■

A **density-based cluster** is a set of density-connected objects that is maximal with respect to density-reachability. Every object not contained in any cluster is considered to be *noise*.

"How does DBSCAN find clusters?" DBSCAN searches for clusters by checking the ε-neighborhood of each point in the database. If the ε-neighborhood of a point ***p*** contains more than *MinPts*, a new cluster with ***p*** as a core object is created. DBSCAN then iteratively collects directly density-reachable objects from these core objects, which may involve the merge of a few density-reachable clusters. The process terminates when no new point can be added to any cluster.

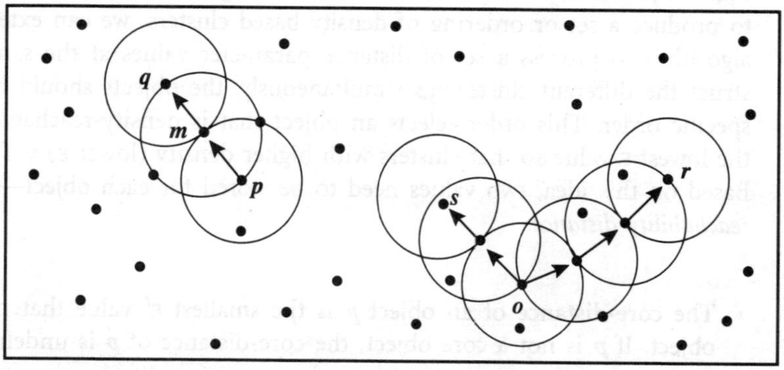

Figure 7.10 Density reachability and density connectivity in density-based clustering. Based on [EKSX96].

If a spatial index is used, the computational complexity of DBSCAN is $O(n\log n)$, where n is the number of database objects. Otherwise, it is $O(n^2)$. With appropriate settings of the user-defined parameters ε and *MinPts*, the algorithm is effective at finding arbitrary-shaped clusters.

7.6.2 OPTICS: Ordering Points to Identify the Clustering Structure

Although DBSCAN can cluster objects given input parameters such as ε and *MinPts*, it still leaves the user with the responsibility of selecting parameter values that will lead to the discovery of acceptable clusters. Actually, this is a problem associated with many other clustering algorithms. Such parameter settings are usually empirically set and difficult to determine, especially for real-world, high-dimensional data sets. Most algorithms are very sensitive to such parameter values: slightly different settings may lead to very different clusterings of the data. Moreover, high-dimensional real data sets often have very skewed distributions, such that their intrinsic clustering structure may not be characterized by *global* density parameters.

To help overcome this difficulty, a cluster analysis method called **OPTICS** was proposed. Rather than produce a data set clustering explicitly, OPTICS computes an augmented *cluster ordering* for automatic and interactive cluster analysis. This ordering represents the density-based clustering structure of the data. It contains information that is equivalent to density-based clustering obtained from a wide range of parameter settings. The cluster ordering can be used to extract basic clustering information (such as cluster centers or arbitrary-shaped clusters) as well as provide the intrinsic clustering structure.

By examining DBSCAN, we can easily see that for a constant *MinPts* value, density-based clusters with respect to a higher density (i.e., a lower value for ε) are *completely contained* in density-connected sets obtained with respect to a lower density. Recall that the parameter ε is a distance—it is the neighborhood radius. Therefore, in order to produce a set or ordering of density-based clusters, we can extend the DBSCAN algorithm to process a set of distance parameter values at the same time. To construct the different clusterings simultaneously, the objects should be processed in a specific order. This order selects an object that is density-reachable with respect to the lowest ε value so that clusters with higher density (lower ε) will be finished first. Based on this idea, two values need to be stored for each object—*core-distance* and *reachability-distance*:

- The **core-distance** of an object $\boldsymbol{p}$ is the smallest ε' value that makes $\{p\}$ a core object. If $\boldsymbol{p}$ is not a core object, the core-distance of $\boldsymbol{p}$ is undefined.
- The **reachability-distance** of an object $\boldsymbol{q}$ with respect to another object $\boldsymbol{p}$ is the greater value of the core-distance of $\boldsymbol{p}$ and the Euclidean distance between $\boldsymbol{p}$ and $\boldsymbol{q}$. If $\boldsymbol{p}$ is not a core object, the reachability-distance between $\boldsymbol{p}$ and $\boldsymbol{q}$ is undefined.

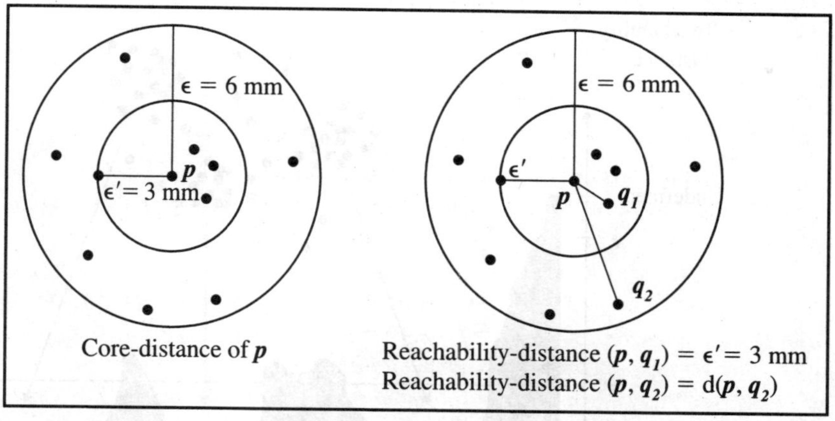

Figure 7.11 OPTICS terminology. Based on [ABKS99].

Example 7.13 **Core-distance and reachability-distance.** Figure 7.11 illustrates the concepts of core-distance and reachability-distance. Suppose that $\varepsilon = 6$ mm and $MinPts = 5$. The core-distance of $\boldsymbol{p}$ is the distance, ε', between $\boldsymbol{p}$ and the fourth closest data object. The reachability-distance of $\boldsymbol{q_1}$ with respect to $\boldsymbol{p}$ is the core-distance of $\boldsymbol{p}$ (i.e., $\varepsilon' = 3$ mm) because this is greater than the Euclidean distance from $\boldsymbol{p}$ to $\boldsymbol{q_1}$. The reachability-distance of $\boldsymbol{q_2}$ with respect to $\boldsymbol{p}$ is the Euclidean distance from $\boldsymbol{p}$ to $\boldsymbol{q_2}$ because this is greater than the core-distance of $\boldsymbol{p}$. ■

"How are these values used?" The OPTICS algorithm creates an ordering of the objects in a database, additionally storing the core-distance and a suitable reachability-distance for each object. An algorithm was proposed to extract clusters based on the ordering information produced by OPTICS. Such information is sufficient for the extraction of all density-based clusterings with respect to any distance ε' that is smaller than the distance ε used in generating the order.

The cluster ordering of a data set can be represented graphically, which helps in its understanding. For example, Figure 7.12 is the reachability plot for a simple two-dimensional data set, which presents a general overview of how the data are structured and clustered. The data objects are plotted in cluster order (horizontal axis) together with their respective reachability-distance (vertical axis). The three Gaussian "bumps" in the plot reflect three clusters in the data set. Methods have also been developed for viewing clustering structures of high-dimensional data at various levels of detail.

Because of the structural equivalence of the OPTICS algorithm to DBSCAN, the OPTICS algorithm has the same runtime complexity as that of DBSCAN, that is, $O(n \log n)$ if a spatial index is used, where n is the number of objects.

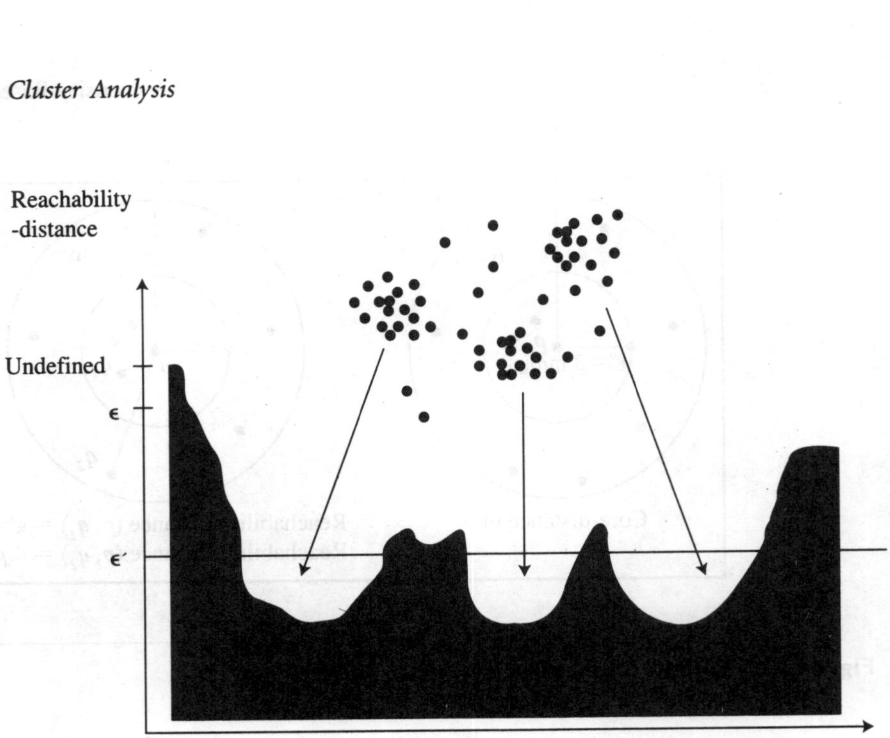

Figure 7.12 Cluster ordering in OPTICS. Figure is based on [ABKS99].

7.6.3 DENCLUE: Clustering Based on Density Distribution Functions

DENCLUE (DENsity-based CLUstEring) is a clustering method based on a set of density distribution functions. The method is built on the following ideas: (1) the influence of each data point can be formally modeled using a mathematical function, called an *influence function*, which describes the impact of a data point within its neighborhood; (2) the overall density of the data space can be modeled analytically as the sum of the influence function applied to all data points; and (3) clusters can then be determined mathematically by identifying *density attractors*, where density attractors are local maxima of the overall density function.

Let x and y be objects or points in F^d, a d-dimensional input space. The **influence function** of data object y on x is a function, $f_B^y : F^d \rightarrow R_0^+$, which is defined in terms of a basic influence function f_B:

$$f_B^y(x) = f_B(x, y). \tag{7.31}$$

This reflects the impact of y on x. In principle, the influence function can be an arbitrary function that can be determined by the distance between two objects in a neighborhood. The distance function, $d(x, y)$, should be reflexive and symmetric, such as the Euclidean distance function (Section 7.2.1). It can be used to compute a *square wave influence function*,

$$f_{Square}(\boldsymbol{x},\boldsymbol{y}) = \begin{cases} 0 & if\ d(\boldsymbol{x},\boldsymbol{y}) > \sigma \\ 1 & otherwise, \end{cases} \tag{7.32}$$

or a *Gaussian influence function,*

$$f_{Gauss}(\boldsymbol{x},\boldsymbol{y}) = e^{-\frac{d(\boldsymbol{x},\boldsymbol{y})^2}{2\sigma^2}}. \tag{7.33}$$

To help understand the concept of influence function, the following example offers some additional insight.

Example 7.14 **Influence function.** Consider the square wave influence function of Equation (7.32). If objects $\boldsymbol{x}$ and $\boldsymbol{y}$ are far apart from one another in the d-dimensional space, then the distance, $d(\boldsymbol{x},\boldsymbol{y})$, will be above some threshold, σ. In this case, the influence function returns a 0, representing the lack of influence between distant points. On the other hand, if $\boldsymbol{x}$ and $\boldsymbol{y}$ are "close" (where closeness is determined by the parameter σ), a value of 1 is returned, representing the notion that one influences the other. ∎

The **density function** at an object or point $\boldsymbol{x} \in F^d$ is defined as the sum of influence functions of all data points. That is, it is the total influence on $\boldsymbol{x}$ of all of the data points. Given n data objects, $D = \{\boldsymbol{x}_1, \ldots, \boldsymbol{x}_n\} \subset F^d$, the density function at $\boldsymbol{x}$ is defined as

$$f_B^D(\boldsymbol{x}) = \sum_{i=1}^{n} f_B^{\boldsymbol{x}_i}(\boldsymbol{x}) = f_B^{\boldsymbol{x}_1}(\boldsymbol{x}) + f_B^{\boldsymbol{x}_2}(\boldsymbol{x}) + \cdots + f_B^{\boldsymbol{x}_n}(\boldsymbol{x}). \tag{7.34}$$

For example, the density function that results from the Gaussian influence function (7.33) is

$$f_{Gauss}^D(\boldsymbol{x}) = \sum_{i=1}^{n} e^{-\frac{d(\boldsymbol{x},\boldsymbol{x}_i)^2}{2\sigma^2}}. \tag{7.35}$$

Figure 7.13 shows a 2-D data set together with the corresponding overall density functions for a square wave and a Gaussian influence function.

From the density function, we can define the *gradient* of the function and the *density attractor*, the local maxima of the overall density function. A point $\boldsymbol{x}$ is said to be *density attracted* to a density attractor $\boldsymbol{x}^*$ if there exists a set of points $\boldsymbol{x}_0, \boldsymbol{x}_1 \ldots, \boldsymbol{x}_k$ such that $\boldsymbol{x}_0 = \boldsymbol{x}$, $\boldsymbol{x}_k = \boldsymbol{x}^*$ and the *gradient* of $\boldsymbol{x}_{i-1}$ is in the direction of $\boldsymbol{x}_i$ for $0 < i < k$. Intuitively, a density attractor influences many other points. For a continuous and differentiable influence function, a hill-climbing algorithm guided by the gradient can be used to determine the density attractor of a set of data points.

In general, points that are density attracted to $\boldsymbol{x}^*$ may form a cluster. Based on the above notions, both *center-defined cluster* and *arbitrary-shape cluster* can be formally defined. A **center-defined cluster** for a density attractor, $\boldsymbol{x}^*$, is a subset of points, $C \subseteq D$, that are *density-attracted* by $\boldsymbol{x}^*$, and where the density function at $\boldsymbol{x}^*$ is no less than a

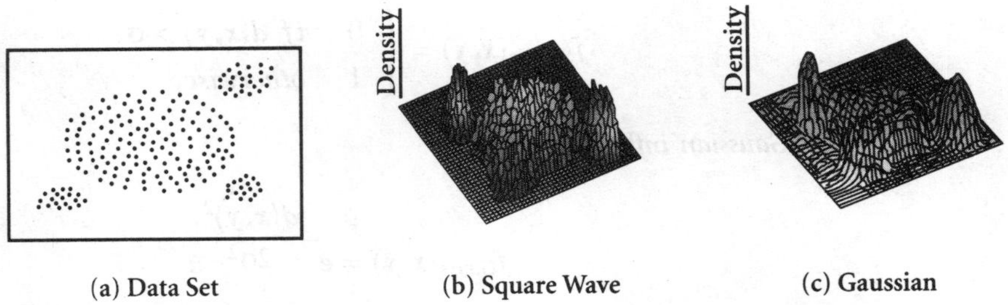

Figure 7.13 Possible density functions for a 2-D data set. From [HK98].

threshold, ξ. Points that are density-attracted by $\boldsymbol{x}^*$, but for which the density function value is less than ξ, are considered outliers. That is, intuitively, points in a cluster are influenced by many points, but outliers are not. An **arbitrary-shape cluster** for a set of density attractors is a set of *C*s, each being density-attracted to its respective density-attractor, where (1) the density function value at each density-attractor is no less than a threshold, ξ, and (2) there exists a path, P, from each density-attractor to another, where the density function value for each point along the path is no less than ξ. Examples of center-defined and arbitrary-shape clusters are shown in Figure 7.14.

"What major advantages does DENCLUE have in comparison with other clustering algorithms?" There are several: (1) it has a solid mathematical foundation and generalizes various clustering methods, including partitioning, hierarchical, and density-based methods; (2) it has good clustering properties for data sets with large amounts of noise; (3) it allows a compact mathematical description of arbitrarily shaped clusters in high-dimen sional data sets; and (4) it uses grid cells, yet only keeps information about grid cells that actually contain data points. It manages these cells in a tree-based access structure, and thus is significantly faster than some influential algorithms, such as DBSCAN. However, the method requires careful selection of the density parameter σ and noise threshold ξ, as the selection of such parameters may significantly influence the quality of the clustering results.

7.7 Grid-Based Methods

The grid-based clustering approach uses a multiresolution grid data structure. It quantizes the object space into a finite number of cells that form a grid structure on which all of the operations for clustering are performed. The main advantage of the approach is its fast processing time, which is typically independent of the number of data objects, yet dependent on only the number of cells in each dimension in the quantized space.

Some typical examples of the grid-based approach include STING, which explores statistical information stored in the grid cells; WaveCluster, which clusters objects using a wavelet transform method; and CLIQUE, which represents a grid-and density-based approach for clustering in high-dimensional data space that will be introduced in Section 7.9.

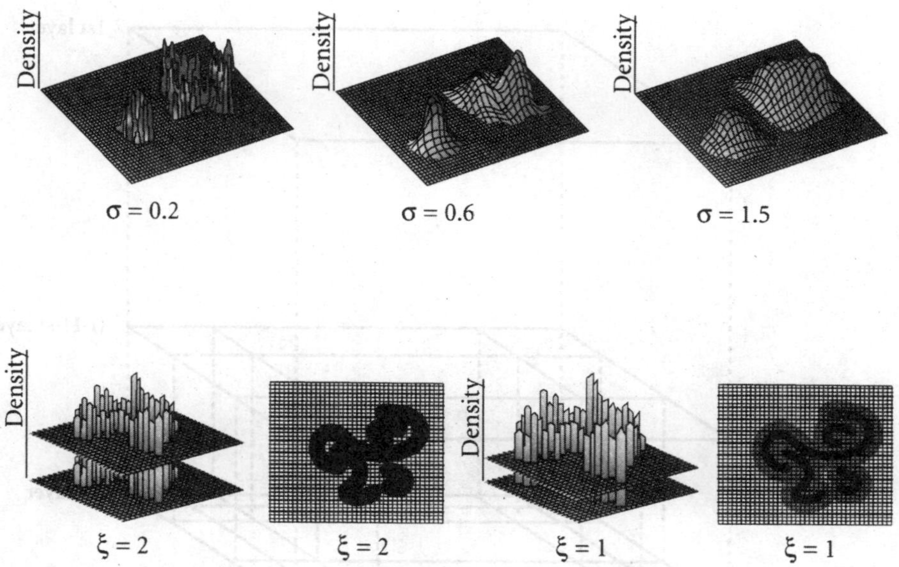

Figure 7.14 Examples of center-defined clusters (top row) and arbitrary-shape clusters (bottom row).

7.7.1 STING: STatistical INformation Grid

STING is a grid-based multiresolution clustering technique in which the spatial area is divided into rectangular cells. There are usually several levels of such rectangular cells corresponding to different levels of resolution, and these cells form a hierarchical structure: each cell at a high level is partitioned to form a number of cells at the next lower level. Statistical information regarding the attributes in each grid cell (such as the mean, maximum, and minimum values) is precomputed and stored. These statistical parameters are useful for query processing, as described below.

Figure 7.15 shows a hierarchical structure for STING clustering. Statistical parameters of higher-level cells can easily be computed from the parameters of the lower-level cells. These parameters include the following: the attribute-independent parameter, *count*; the attribute-dependent parameters, *mean*, *stdev* (standard deviation), *min* (minimum), *max* (maximum); and the type of *distribution* that the attribute value in the cell follows, such as *normal*, *uniform*, *exponential*, or *none* (if the distribution is unknown). When the data are loaded into the database, the parameters *count*, *mean*, *stdev*, *min*, and *max* of the bottom-level cells are calculated directly from the data. The value of *distribution* may either be assigned by the user if the distribution type is known beforehand or obtained by hypothesis tests such as the χ^2 test. The type of distribution of a higher-level cell can be computed based on the majority of distribution types of its corresponding lower-level cells in conjunction with a threshold filtering process. If the distributions of the lower-level cells disagree with each other and fail the threshold test, the distribution type of the high-level cell is set to *none*.

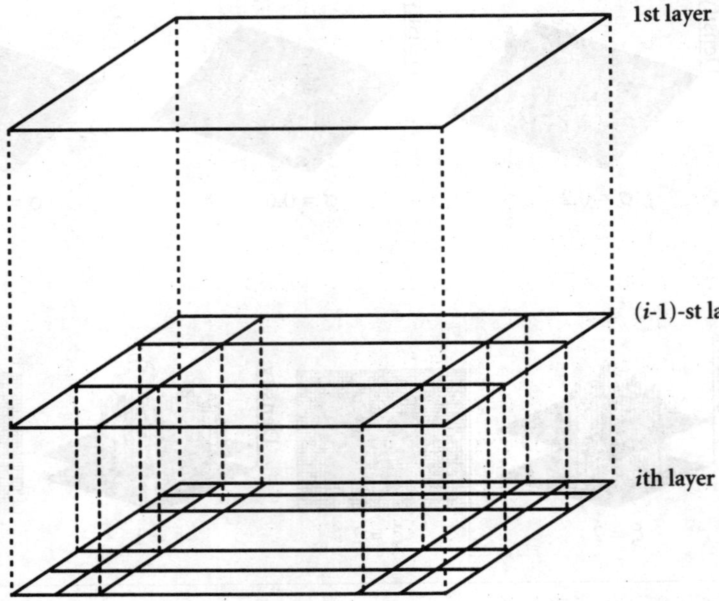

Figure 7.15 A hierarchical structure for STING clustering.

"How is this statistical information useful for query answering?" The statistical parameters can be used in a top-down, grid-based method as follows. First, a layer within the hierarchical structure is determined from which the query-answering process is to start. This layer typically contains a small number of cells. For each cell in the current layer, we compute the confidence interval (or estimated range of probability) reflecting the cell's relevancy to the given query. The irrelevant cells are removed from further consideration. Processing of the next lower level examines only the remaining relevant cells. This process is repeated until the bottom layer is reached. At this time, if the query specification is met, the regions of relevant cells that satisfy the query are returned. Otherwise, the data that fall into the relevant cells are retrieved and further processed until they meet the requirements of the query.

"What advantages does STING offer over other clustering methods?" STING offers several advantages: (1) the grid-based computation is *query-independent*, because the statistical information stored in each cell represents the summary information of the data in the grid cell, independent of the query; (2) the grid structure facilitates parallel processing and incremental updating; and (3) the method's efficiency is a major advantage: STING goes through the database once to compute the statistical parameters of the cells, and hence the time complexity of generating clusters is $O(n)$, where n is the total number of objects. After generating the hierarchical structure, the query processing time is $O(g)$, where g is the total number of grid cells at the lowest level, which is usually much smaller than n.

Because STING uses a multiresolution approach to cluster analysis, the quality of STING clustering depends on the granularity of the lowest level of the grid structure. If the granularity is very fine, the cost of processing will increase substantially; however, if the bottom level of the grid structure is too coarse, it may reduce the quality of cluster analysis. Moreover, STING does not consider the spatial relationship between the children and their neighboring cells for construction of a parent cell. As a result, the shapes of the resulting clusters are isothetic; that is, all of the cluster boundaries are either horizontal or vertical, and no diagonal boundary is detected. This may lower the quality and accuracy of the clusters despite the fast processing time of the technique.

7.7.2 WaveCluster: Clustering Using Wavelet Transformation

WaveCluster is a multiresolution clustering algorithm that first summarizes the data by imposing a multidimensional grid structure onto the data space. It then uses a *wavelet transformation* to transform the original feature space, finding dense regions in the transformed space.

In this approach, each grid cell summarizes the information of a group of points that map into the cell. This summary information typically fits into main memory for use by the multiresolution wavelet transform and the subsequent cluster analysis.

A **wavelet transform** is a signal processing technique that decomposes a signal into different frequency subbands. The wavelet model can be applied to d-dimensional signals by applying a one-dimensional wavelet transform d times. In applying a wavelet transform, data are transformed so as to preserve the relative distance between objects at different levels of resolution. This allows the natural clusters in the data to become more distinguishable. Clusters can then be identified by searching for dense regions in the new domain. Wavelet transforms are also discussed in Chapter 2, where they are used for data reduction by compression. Additional references to the technique are given in the bibliographic notes.

"Why is wavelet transformation useful for clustering?" It offers the following advantages:

- *It provides unsupervised clustering.* It uses hat-shaped filters that emphasize regions where the points cluster, while suppressing weaker information outside of the cluster boundaries. Thus, dense regions in the original feature space act as attractors for nearby points and as inhibitors for points that are further away. This means that the clusters in the data automatically stand out and "clear" the regions around them. Thus, another advantage is that wavelet transformation can automatically result in the removal of outliers.

- *The multiresolution property of wavelet transformations can help detect clusters at varying levels of accuracy.* For example, Figure 7.16 shows a sample of two-dimensional feature space, where each point in the image represents the attribute or feature values of one object in the spatial data set. Figure 7.17 shows the resulting wavelet transformation at different resolutions, from a fine scale (scale 1) to a coarse scale (scale 3). At each level, the four subbands into which the original data are decomposed are shown. The subband shown in the upper-left quadrant emphasizes the average neighborhood around each data point. The subband in the upper-right quadrant emphasizes the horizontal edges of the data. The subband in the lower-left quadrant emphasizes the vertical edges, while the subband in the lower-right quadrant emphasizes the corners.

- *Wavelet-based clustering is very fast*, with a computational complexity of $O(n)$, where n is the number of objects in the database. The algorithm implementation can be made parallel.

WaveCluster is a grid-based and density-based algorithm. It conforms with many of the requirements of a good clustering algorithm: It handles large data sets efficiently, discovers clusters with arbitrary shape, successfully handles outliers, is insensitive to the order of input, and does not require the specification of input parameters such as the

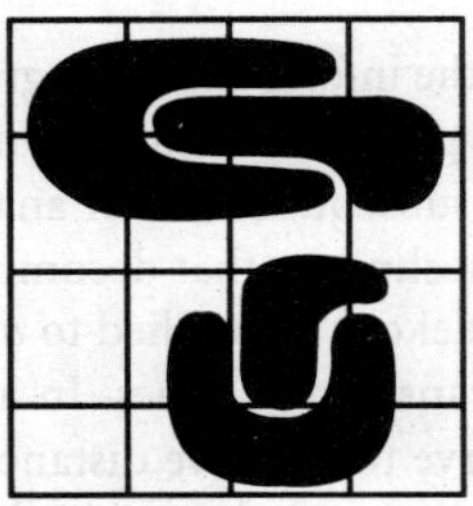

Figure 7.16 A sample of two-dimensional feature space. From [SCZ98].

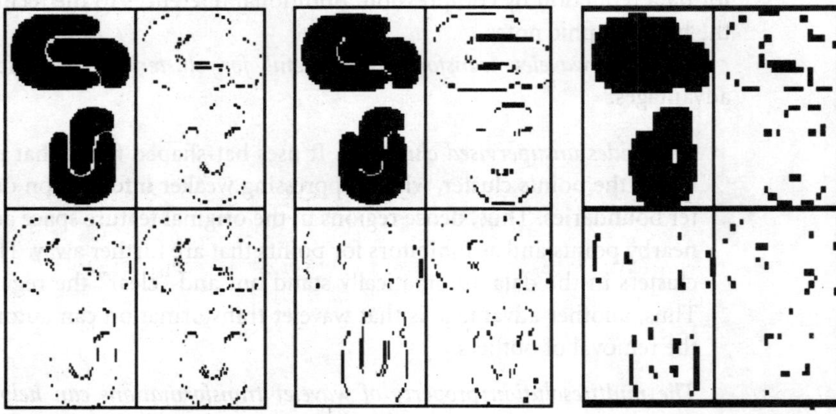

(a) (b) (c)

Figure 7.17 Multiresolution of the feature space in Figure 7.16 at (a) scale 1 (high resolution); (b) scale 2 (medium resolution); and (c) scale 3 (low resolution). From [SCZ98].

number of clusters or a neighborhood radius. In experimental studies, WaveCluster was found to outperform BIRCH, CLARANS, and DBSCAN in terms of both efficiency and clustering quality. The study also found WaveCluster capable of handling data with up to 20 dimensions.

7.8 Model-Based Clustering Methods

Model-based clustering methods attempt to optimize the fit between the given data and some mathematical model. Such methods are often based on the assumption that the data are generated by a mixture of underlying probability distributions. In this section, we describe three examples of model-based clustering. Section 7.8.1 presents an extension of the k-means partitioning algorithm, called Expectation-Maximization. Conceptual clustering is discussed in Section 7.8.2. A neural network approach to clustering is given in Section 7.8.3.

7.8.1 Expectation-Maximization

In practice, each cluster can be represented mathematically by a parametric probability distribution. The entire data is a *mixture* of these distributions, where each individual distribution is typically referred to as a *component distribution*. We can therefore cluster the data using a finite **mixture density model** of k probability distributions, where each distribution represents a cluster. The problem is to estimate the parameters of the probability distributions so as to best fit the data. Figure 7.18 is an example of a simple finite mixture density model. There are two clusters. Each follows a normal or Gaussian distribution with its own mean and standard deviation.

The **EM (Expectation-Maximization)** algorithm is a popular iterative refinement algorithm that can be used for finding the parameter estimates. It can be viewed as an extension of the k-means paradigm, which assigns an object to the cluster with which it is most similar, based on the cluster mean (Section 7.4.1). Instead of assigning each object to a dedicated cluster, EM assigns each object to a cluster according to a weight representing the probability of membership. In other words, there are no strict boundaries between clusters. Therefore, new means are computed based on weighted measures.

EM starts with an initial estimate or "guess" of the parameters of the mixture model (collectively referred to as the *parameter vector*). It iteratively rescores the objects against the mixture density produced by the parameter vector. The rescored objects are then used to update the parameter estimates. Each object is assigned a probability that it would possess a certain set of attribute values given that it was a member of a given cluster. The algorithm is described as follows:

1. Make an initial guess of the parameter vector: This involves randomly selecting k objects to represent the cluster means or centers (as in k-means partitioning), as well as making guesses for the additional parameters.

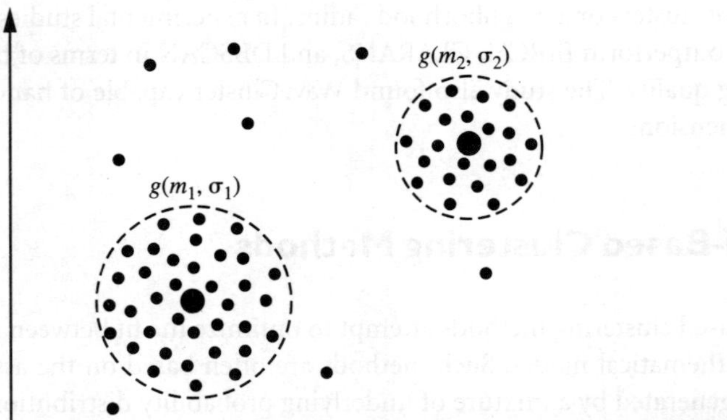

Figure 7.18 Each cluster can be represented by a probability distribution, centered at a mean, and with a standard deviation. Here, we have two clusters, corresponding to the Gaussian distributions $g(m_1, \sigma_1)$ and $g(m_2, \sigma_2)$, respectively, where the dashed circles represent the first standard deviation of the distributions.

2. Iteratively refine the parameters (or clusters) based on the following two steps:

(a) **Expectation Step:** Assign each object $\boldsymbol{x}_i$ to cluster C_k with the probability

$$P(\boldsymbol{x}_i \in C_k) = p(C_k|\boldsymbol{x}_i) = \frac{p(C_k)p(\boldsymbol{x}_i|C_k)}{p(\boldsymbol{x}_i)}, \tag{7.36}$$

where $p(\boldsymbol{x}_i|C_k) = N(m_k, E_k(\boldsymbol{x}_i))$ follows the normal (i.e., Gaussian) distribution around mean, m_k, with expectation, E_k. In other words, this step calculates the probability of cluster membership of object $\boldsymbol{x}_i$, for each of the clusters. These probabilities are the "expected" cluster memberships for object $\boldsymbol{x}_i$.

(b) **Maximization Step:** Use the probability estimates from above to re-estimate (or refine) the model parameters. For example,

$$m_k = \frac{1}{n}\sum_{i=1}^{n}\frac{\boldsymbol{x}_i P(\boldsymbol{x}_i \in C_k)}{\sum_j P(\boldsymbol{x}_i \in C_j)}. \tag{7.37}$$

This step is the "maximization" of the likelihood of the distributions given the data.

The EM algorithm is simple and easy to implement. In practice, it converges fast but may not reach the global optima. Convergence is guaranteed for certain forms of optimization functions. The computational complexity is linear in d (the number of input features), n (the number of objects), and t (the number of iterations).

Bayesian clustering methods focus on the computation of class-conditional probability density. They are commonly used in the statistics community. In industry,

AutoClass is a popular Bayesian clustering method that uses a variant of the EM algorithm. The best clustering maximizes the ability to predict the attributes of an object given the correct cluster of the object. AutoClass can also estimate the number of clusters. It has been applied to several domains and was able to discover a new class of stars based on infrared astronomy data. Further references are provided in the bibliographic notes.

7.8.2 Conceptual Clustering

Conceptual clustering is a form of clustering in machine learning that, given a set of unlabeled objects, produces a classification scheme over the objects. Unlike conventional clustering, which primarily identifies groups of like objects, conceptual clustering goes one step further by also finding characteristic descriptions for each group, where each group represents a concept or class. Hence, conceptual clustering is a two-step process: clustering is performed first, followed by characterization. Here, clustering quality is not solely a function of the individual objects. Rather, it incorporates factors such as the generality and simplicity of the derived concept descriptions.

Most methods of conceptual clustering adopt a statistical approach that uses probability measurements in determining the concepts or clusters. Probabilistic descriptions are typically used to represent each derived concept.

COBWEB is a popular and simple method of incremental conceptual clustering. Its input objects are described by categorical attribute-value pairs. COBWEB creates a hierarchical clustering in the form of a **classification tree**.

"But what is a classification tree? Is it the same as a decision tree?" Figure 7.19 shows a classification tree for a set of animal data. A classification tree differs from a decision tree. Each node in a classification tree refers to a concept and contains a probabilistic description of that concept, which summarizes the objects classified under the node. The probabilistic description includes the probability of the concept and conditional probabilities of the form $P(A_i = v_{ij}|C_k)$, where $A_i = v_{ij}$ is an attribute-value pair (that is, the ith attribute takes its jth possible value) and C_k is the concept class. (Counts are accumulated and stored at each node for computation of the probabilities.) This is unlike decision trees, which label branches rather than nodes and use logical rather than probabilistic descriptors.[3] The sibling nodes at a given level of a classification tree are said to form a *partition*. To classify an object using a classification tree, a partial matching function is employed to descend the tree along a path of "best" matching nodes.

COBWEB uses a heuristic evaluation measure called *category utility* to guide construction of the tree. **Category utility** (CU) is defined as

$$\frac{\sum_{k=1}^{n} P(C_k)[\sum_i \sum_j P(A_i = v_{ij}|C_k)^2 - \sum_i \sum_j P(A_i = v_{ij})^2]}{n}, \tag{7.38}$$

where n is the number of nodes, concepts, or "categories" forming a partition, $\{C_1, C_2, \ldots, C_n\}$, at the given level of the tree. In other words, category utility is the

[3]Decision trees are described in Chapter 6.

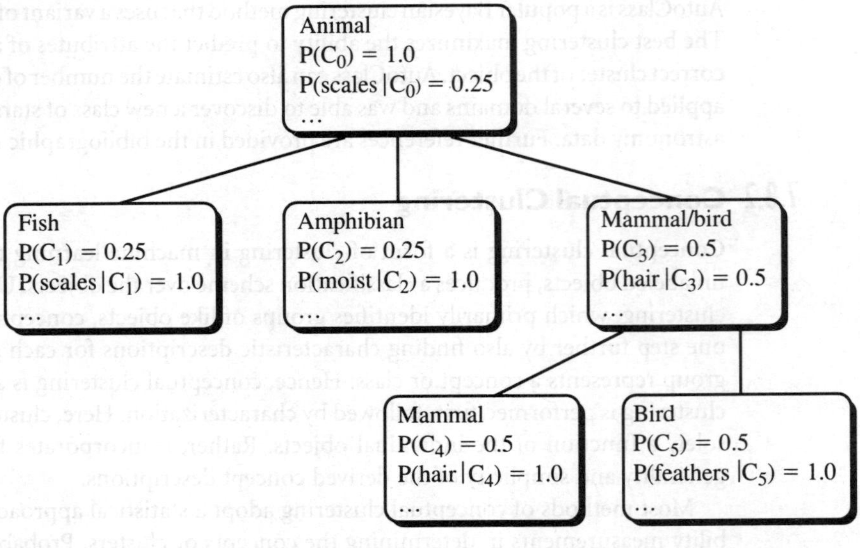

Figure 7.19 A classification tree. Figure is based on [Fis87].

increase in the expected number of attribute values that can be correctly guessed given a partition (where this expected number corresponds to the term $P(C_k)\Sigma_i\Sigma_j P(A_i = v_{ij}|C_k)^2$) over the expected number of correct guesses with no such knowledge (corresponding to the term $\Sigma_i\Sigma_j P(A_i = v_{ij})^2$). Although we do not have room to show the derivation, category utility rewards intraclass similarity and interclass dissimilarity, where:

- **Intraclass similarity** is the probability $P(A_i = v_{ij}|C_k)$. The larger this value is, the greater the proportion of class members that share this attribute-value pair and the more predictable the pair is of class members.
- **Interclass dissimilarity** is the probability $P(C_k|A_i = v_{ij})$. The larger this value is, the fewer the objects in contrasting classes that share this attribute-value pair and the more predictive the pair is of the class.

Let's look at how COBWEB works. COBWEB incrementally incorporates objects into a classification tree.

"Given a new object, how does COBWEB decide where to incorporate it into the classification tree?" COBWEB descends the tree along an appropriate path, updating counts along the way, in search of the "best host" or node at which to classify the object. This decision is based on temporarily placing the object in each node and computing the category utility of the resulting partition. The placement that results in the highest category utility should be a good host for the object.

"What if the object does not really belong to any of the concepts represented in the tree so far? What if it is better to create a new node for the given object?" That is a good point. In fact, COBWEB also computes the category utility of the partition that would result if a new node were to be created for the object. This is compared to the above computation based on the existing nodes. The object is then placed in an existing class, or a new class is created for it, based on the partition with the highest category utility value. Notice that COBWEB has the ability to automatically adjust the number of classes in a partition. It does not need to rely on the user to provide such an input parameter.

The two operators mentioned above are highly sensitive to the input order of the object. COBWEB has two additional operators that help make it less sensitive to input order. These are **merging** and **splitting**. When an object is incorporated, the two best hosts are considered for merging into a single class. Furthermore, COBWEB considers splitting the children of the best host among the existing categories. These decisions are based on category utility. The merging and splitting operators allow COBWEB to perform a bidirectional search—for example, a merge can undo a previous split.

COBWEB has a number of limitations. First, it is based on the assumption that probability distributions on separate attributes are statistically independent of one another. This assumption is, however, not always true because correlation between attributes often exists. Moreover, the probability distribution representation of clusters makes it quite expensive to update and store the clusters. This is especially so when the attributes have a large number of values because the time and space complexities depend not only on the number of attributes, but also on the number of values for each attribute. Furthermore, the classification tree is not height-balanced for skewed input data, which may cause the time and space complexity to degrade dramatically.

CLASSIT is an extension of COBWEB for incremental clustering of continuous (or real-valued) data. It stores a continuous normal distribution (i.e., mean and standard deviation) for each individual attribute in each node and uses a modified category utility measure that is an integral over continuous attributes instead of a sum over discrete attributes as in COBWEB. However, it suffers similar problems as COBWEB and thus is not suitable for clustering large database data.

Conceptual clustering is popular in the machine learning community. However, the method does not scale well for large data sets.

7.8.3 Neural Network Approach

The neural network approach is motivated by biological neural networks.[4] Roughly speaking, a neural network is a set of connected input/output units, where each connection has a weight associated with it. Neural networks have several properties that make them popular for clustering. First, neural networks are inherently parallel and distributed processing architectures. Second, neural networks learn by adjusting their interconnection weights so as to best fit the data. This allows them to "normalize" or "prototype"

[4]Neural networks were also introduced in Chapter 6 on classification and prediction.

the patterns and act as feature (or attribute) extractors for the various clusters. Third, neural networks process numerical vectors and require object patterns to be represented by quantitative features only. Many clustering tasks handle only numerical data or can transform their data into quantitative features if needed.

The neural network approach to clustering tends to represent each cluster as an *exemplar*. An exemplar acts as a "prototype" of the cluster and does not necessarily have to correspond to a particular data example or object. New objects can be distributed to the cluster whose exemplar is the most similar, based on some distance measure. The attributes of an object assigned to a cluster can be predicted from the attributes of the cluster's exemplar.

Self-organizing feature maps (SOMs) are one of the most popular neural network methods for cluster analysis. They are sometimes referred to as *Kohonen self-organizing feature maps*, after their creator, Teuvo Kohonon, or as *topologically ordered maps*. SOMs' goal is to represent all points in a high-dimensional source space by points in a low-dimensional (usually 2-D or 3-D) target space, such that the distance and proximity relationships (hence the topology) are preserved as much as possible. The method is particularly useful when a nonlinear mapping is inherent in the problem itself.

SOMs can also be viewed as a constrained version of *k-means* clustering, in which the cluster centers tend to lie in a low-dimensional manifold in the feature or attribute space. With SOMs, clustering is performed by having several units competing for the current object. The unit whose weight vector is closest to the current object becomes the winning or active unit. So as to move even closer to the input object, the weights of the winning unit are adjusted, as well as those of its nearest neighbors. SOMs assume that there is some topology or ordering among the input objects and that the units will eventually take on this structure in space. The organization of units is said to form a **feature map**. SOMs are believed to resemble processing that can occur in the brain and are useful for visualizing high-dimensional data in 2-D or 3-D space.

The SOM approach has been used successfully for Web document clustering. The left graph of Figure 7.20 shows the result of clustering 12,088 Web articles from the usenet newsgroup comp.ai.neural-nets using the SOM approach, while the right graph of the figure shows the result of drilling down on the keyword: "mining."

The neural network approach to clustering has strong theoretical links with actual brain processing. Further research is required to make it more effective and scalable in large databases due to long processing times and the intricacies of complex data.

7.9 Clustering High-Dimensional Data

Most clustering methods are designed for clustering low-dimensional data and encounter challenges when the dimensionality of the data grows really high (say, over 10 dimensions, or even over thousands of dimensions for some tasks). This is because when the dimensionality increases, usually only a small number of dimensions are relevant to

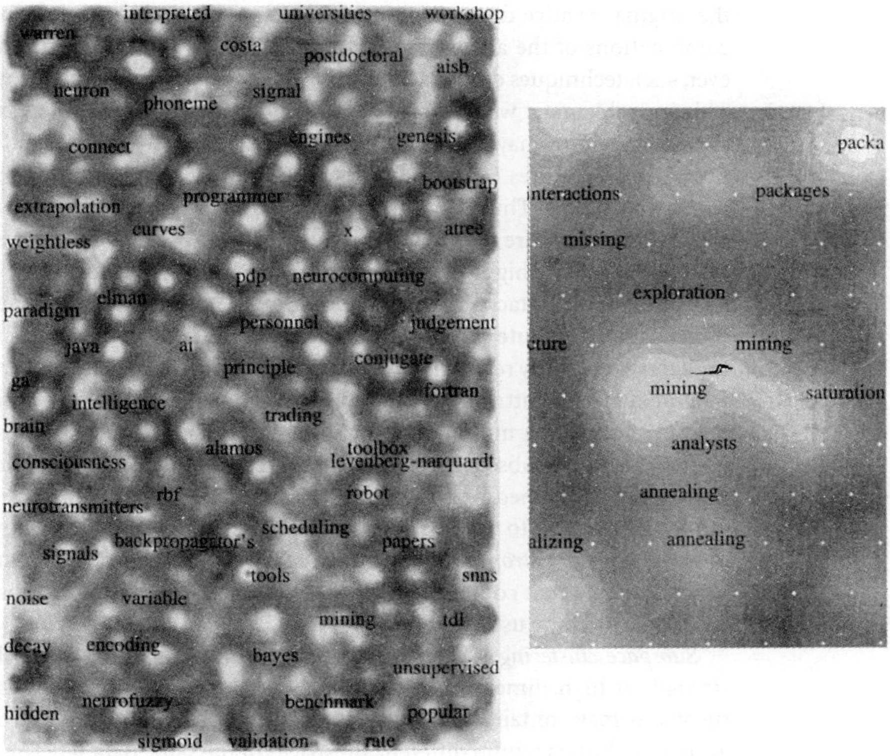

Figure 7.20 The result of SOM clustering of 12,088 Web articles on comp.ai.neural-nets (left), and of drilling down on the keyword: "mining" (right). Based on *http://websom.hut.fi/websom/comp.ai.neural-nets-new/html/root.html.*

certain clusters, but data in the irrelevant dimensions may produce much noise and mask the real clusters to be discovered. Moreover, when dimensionality increases, data usually become increasingly sparse because the data points are likely located in different dimensional subspaces. When the data become really sparse, data points located at different dimensions can be considered as all equally distanced, and the distance measure, which is essential for cluster analysis, becomes meaningless.

To overcome this difficulty, we may consider using *feature* (or *attribute*) *transformation* and *feature* (or *attribute*) *selection* techniques.

Feature transformation methods, such as *principal component analysis*[5] and *singular value decomposition*,[6] transform the data onto a smaller space while generally preserving

[5]Principal component analysis was introduced in Chapter 2 as a method of dimensionality reduction.
[6]Singular value decomposition is discussed in Chapter 8.

the original relative distance between objects. They summarize data by creating linear combinations of the attributes, and may discover hidden structures in the data. However, such techniques do not actually remove any of the original attributes from analysis. This is problematic when there are a large number of irrelevant attributes. The irrelevant information may mask the real clusters, even after transformation. Moreover, the transformed features (attributes) are often difficult to interpret, making the clustering results less useful. Thus, feature transformation is only suited to data sets where most of the dimensions are relevant to the clustering task. Unfortunately, real-world data sets tend to have many highly correlated, or redundant, dimensions.

Another way of tackling the curse of dimensionality is to try to remove some of the dimensions. **Attribute subset selection** (or **feature subset selection**[7]) is commonly used for *data reduction* by removing irrelevant or redundant dimensions (or attributes). Given a set of attributes, attribute subset selection finds the subset of attributes that are most relevant to the data mining task. Attribute subset selection involves searching through various attribute subsets and evaluating these subsets using certain criteria. It is most commonly performed by supervised learning—the most relevant set of attributes are found with respect to the given class labels. It can also be performed by an unsupervised process, such as *entropy analysis*, which is based on the property that entropy tends to be low for data that contain tight clusters. Other evaluation functions, such as category utility, may also be used.

Subspace clustering is an extension to attribute subset selection that has shown its strength at high-dimensional clustering. It is based on the observation that different subspaces may contain different, meaningful clusters. **Subspace clustering** searches for groups of clusters within different subspaces of the same data set. The problem becomes how to find such subspace clusters effectively and efficiently.

In this section, we introduce three approaches for effective clustering of high-dimensional data: *dimension-growth subspace clustering*, represented by CLIQUE, *dimension-reduction projected clustering*, represented by PROCLUS, and *frequent pattern-based clustering*, represented by pCluster.

7.9.1 CLIQUE: A Dimension-Growth Subspace Clustering Method

CLIQUE (CLustering In QUEst) was the first algorithm proposed for dimension-growth subspace clustering in high-dimensional space. In **dimension-growth subspace clustering**, the clustering process starts at single-dimensional subspaces and grows upward to higher-dimensional ones. Because CLIQUE partitions each dimension like a grid structure and determines whether a cell is dense based on the number of points it contains, it can also be viewed as an integration of density-based and grid-based clustering methods. However, its overall approach is typical of subspace clustering for high-dimensional space, and so it is introduced in this section.

[7] Attribute subset selection is known in the machine learning literature as feature subset selection. It was discussed in Chapter 2.

The ideas of the CLIQUE clustering algorithm are outlined as follows.

- Given a large set of multidimensional data points, the data space is usually not uniformly occupied by the data points. CLIQUE's clustering identifies the sparse and the "crowded" *areas in space* (or **units**), thereby discovering the overall distribution patterns of the data set.
- A unit is **dense** if the fraction of total data points contained in it exceeds an input model parameter. In CLIQUE, a cluster is defined as a maximal set of *connected dense units*.

"How does CLIQUE work?" CLIQUE performs multidimensional clustering in two steps.

In the first step, CLIQUE partitions the d-dimensional data space into nonoverlapping rectangular units, identifying the dense units among these. This is done (in 1-D) for each dimension. For example, Figure 7.21 shows dense rectangular units found with respect to *age* for the dimensions *salary* and (number of weeks of) *vacation*. The subspaces representing these dense units are intersected to form a *candidate* search space in which dense units of higher dimensionality may exist.

"Why does CLIQUE confine its search for dense units of higher dimensionality to the intersection of the dense units in the subspaces?" The identification of the candidate search space is based on the *Apriori property* used in association rule mining.[8] In general, the property employs prior knowledge of items in the search space so that portions of the space can be pruned. The property, adapted for CLIQUE, states the following: *If a k-dimensional unit is dense, then so are its projections in $(k-1)$-dimensional space.* That is, given a k-dimensional candidate dense unit, if we check its $(k-1)$-th projection units and find any that are not dense, then we know that the kth dimensional unit cannot be dense either. Therefore, we can generate potential or candidate dense units in k-dimensional space from the dense units found in $(k-1)$-dimensional space. In general, the resulting space searched is much smaller than the original space. The dense units are then examined in order to determine the clusters.

In the second step, CLIQUE generates a minimal description for each cluster as follows. For each cluster, it determines the maximal region that covers the cluster of connected dense units. It then determines a minimal cover (logic description) for each cluster.

"How effective is CLIQUE?" CLIQUE automatically finds subspaces of the highest dimensionality such that high-density clusters exist in those subspaces. It is insensitive to the order of input objects and does not presume any canonical data distribution. It scales linearly with the size of input and has good scalability as the number of dimensions in the data is increased. However, obtaining meaningful clustering results is dependent on

[8]Association rule mining is described in detail in Chapter 5. In particular, the Apriori property is described in Section 5.2.1. The Apriori property can also be used for cube computation, as described in Chapter 4.

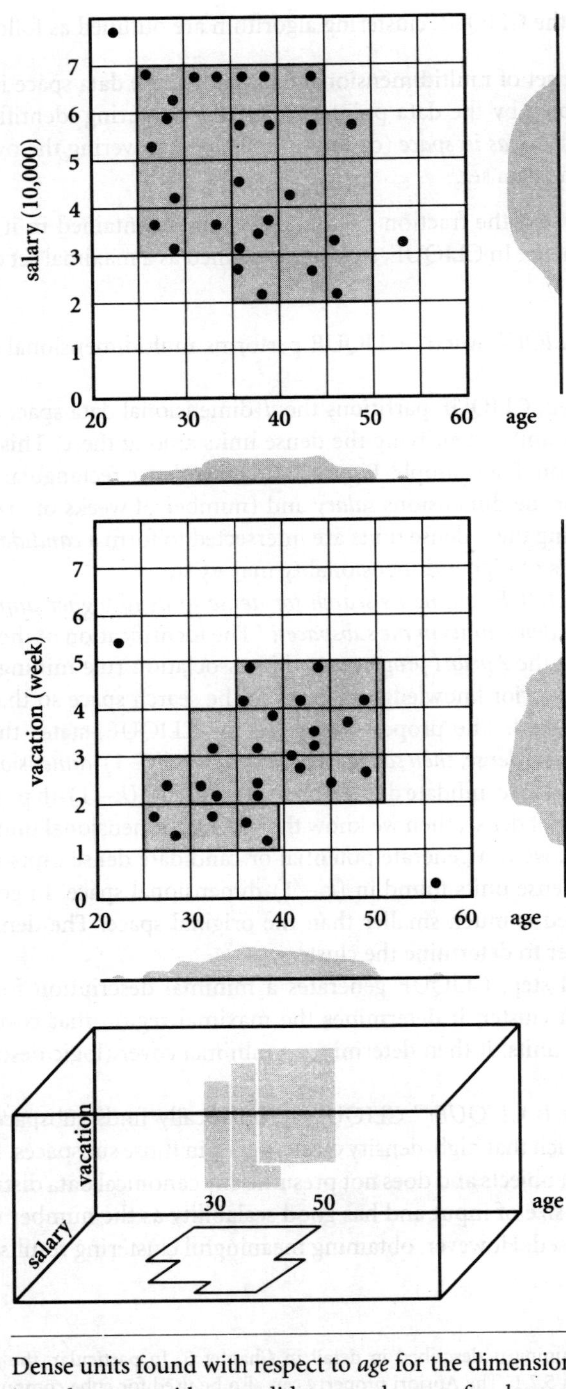

Figure 7.21 Dense units found with respect to *age* for the dimensions *salary* and *vacation* are intersected in order to provide a candidate search space for dense units of higher dimensionality.

proper tuning of the grid size (which is a stable structure here) and the density threshold. This is particularly difficult because the grid size and density threshold are used across all combinations of dimensions in the data set. Thus, the accuracy of the clustering results may be degraded at the expense of the simplicity of the method. Moreover, for a given dense region, all projections of the region onto lower-dimensionality subspaces will also be dense. This can result in a large overlap among the reported dense regions. Furthermore, it is difficult to find clusters of rather different density within different dimensional subspaces.

Several extensions to this approach follow a similar philosophy. For example, let's think of a grid as a set of fixed bins. Instead of using fixed bins for each of the dimensions, we can use an adaptive, data-driven strategy to dynamically determine the bins for each dimension based on data distribution statistics. Alternatively, instead of using a density threshold, we would use entropy (Chapter 6) as a measure of the quality of subspace clusters.

7.9.2 PROCLUS: A Dimension-Reduction Subspace Clustering Method

PROCLUS (PROjected CLUStering) is a typical **dimension-reduction subspace clustering method.** That is, instead of starting from single-dimensional spaces, it starts by finding an initial approximation of the clusters in the high-dimensional attribute space. Each dimension is then assigned a weight for each cluster, and the updated weights are used in the next iteration to regenerate the clusters. This leads to the exploration of dense regions in all subspaces of some desired dimensionality and avoids the generation of a large number of overlapped clusters in projected dimensions of lower dimensionality.

PROCLUS finds the best set of medoids by a hill-climbing process similar to that used in CLARANS, but generalized to deal with projected clustering. It adopts a distance measure called *Manhattan segmental distance*, which is the Manhattan distance on a set of relevant dimensions. The PROCLUS algorithm consists of three phases: *initialization, iteration*, and *cluster refinement*. In the *initialization* phase, it uses a greedy algorithm to select a set of initial medoids that are far apart from each other so as to ensure that each cluster is represented by at least one object in the selected set. More concretely, it first chooses a random sample of data points proportional to the number of clusters we wish to generate, and then applies the greedy algorithm to obtain an even smaller final subset for the next phase. The *iteration* phase selects a random set of k medoids from this reduced set (of medoids), and replaces "bad" medoids with randomly chosen new medoids if the clustering is improved. For each medoid, a set of dimensions is chosen whose average distances are small compared to statistical expectation. The total number of dimensions associated to medoids must be $k \times l$, where l is an input parameter that selects the average dimensionality of cluster subspaces. The *refinement* phase computes new dimensions for each medoid based on the clusters found, reassigns points to medoids, and removes outliers.

Experiments on PROCLUS show that the method is efficient and scalable at finding high-dimensional clusters. Unlike CLIQUE, which outputs many overlapped clusters, PROCLUS finds nonoverlapped partitions of points. The discovered clusters may help better understand the high-dimensional data and facilitate other subsequence analyses.

7.9.3 Frequent Pattern–Based Clustering Methods

This section looks at how methods of *frequent pattern mining* can be applied to clustering, resulting in **frequent pattern–based cluster analysis.** Frequent pattern mining, as the name implies, searches for patterns (such as sets of items or objects) that occur frequently in large data sets. Frequent pattern mining can lead to the discovery of interesting associations and correlations among data objects. Methods for frequent pattern mining were introduced in Chapter 5. The idea behind frequent pattern–based cluster analysis is that the frequent patterns discovered may also indicate clusters. Frequent pattern–based cluster analysis is well suited to high-dimensional data. It can be viewed as an extension of the dimension-growth subspace clustering approach. However, the boundaries of different dimensions are not obvious, since here they are represented by sets of frequent itemsets. That is, rather than growing the clusters dimension by dimension, we grow sets of frequent itemsets, which eventually lead to cluster descriptions. Typical examples of frequent pattern–based cluster analysis include the clustering of text documents that contain thousands of distinct keywords, and the analysis of microarray data that contain tens of thousands of measured values or "features." In this section, we examine two forms of frequent pattern–based cluster analysis: *frequent term–based text clustering* and *clustering by pattern similarity in microarray data analysis.*

In **frequent term–based text clustering,** text documents are clustered based on the frequent terms they contain. Using the vocabulary of text document analysis, a **term** is any sequence of characters separated from other terms by a delimiter. A term can be made up of a single word or several words. In general, we first remove nontext information (such as HTML tags and punctuation) and stop words. Terms are then extracted. A *stemming algorithm* is then applied to reduce each term to its basic *stem.* In this way, each document can be represented as a set of terms. Each set is typically large. Collectively, a large set of documents will contain a very large set of distinct terms. If we treat each term as a dimension, the dimension space will be of very high dimensionality! This poses great challenges for document cluster analysis. The dimension space can be referred to as *term vector space,* where each document is represented by a term vector.

This difficulty can be overcome by *frequent term–based analysis.* That is, by using an efficient frequent itemset mining algorithm introduced in Section 5.2, we can mine a set of frequent terms from the set of text documents. Then, instead of clustering on high-dimensional term vector space, we need only consider the low-dimensional frequent term sets as "cluster candidates." Notice that a frequent term set is not a cluster but rather the description of a cluster. The corresponding cluster consists of the set of documents containing all of the terms of the frequent term set. A *well-selected subset* of the set of all frequent term sets can be considered as a clustering.

"How, then, can we select a good subset of the set of all frequent term sets?" This step is critical because such a selection will determine the quality of the resulting clustering. Let F_i be a set of frequent term sets and $cov(F_i)$ be the set of documents covered by F_i. That is, $cov(F_i)$ refers to the documents that contain all of the terms in F_i. The general principle for finding a well-selected subset, $F_1, \ldots, F_k$, of the set of all frequent term sets is to ensure that (1) $\Sigma_{i=1}^{k} cov(F_i) = D$ (i.e., the selected subset should cover all of the documents to be clustered); and (2) the overlap between any two partitions, F_i and F_j (for $i \neq j$), should be minimized. An overlap measure based on entropy[9] is used to assess cluster overlap by measuring the distribution of the documents supporting some cluster over the remaining cluster candidates.

An advantage of frequent term–based text clustering is that it automatically generates a description for the generated clusters in terms of their frequent term sets. Traditional clustering methods produce only clusters—a description for the generated clusters requires an additional processing step.

Another interesting approach for clustering high-dimensional data is based on pattern similarity among the objects on a subset of dimensions. Here we introduce the **pCluster** method, which performs **clustering by pattern similarity in microarray data analysis.** In DNA microarray analysis, the expression levels of two genes may rise and fall synchronously in response to a set of environmental stimuli or conditions. Under the pCluster model, two objects are similar if they exhibit a *coherent pattern on a subset of dimensions.* Although the magnitude of their expression levels may not be close, the patterns they exhibit can be very much alike. This is illustrated in Example 7.15. Discovery of such clusters of genes is essential in revealing significant connections in gene regulatory networks.

Example 7.15 **Clustering by pattern similarity in DNA microarray analysis.** Figure 7.22 shows a fragment of microarray data containing only three genes (taken as "objects" here) and ten attributes (columns a to j). No patterns among the three objects are visibly explicit. However, if two subsets of attributes, $\{b, c, h, j, e\}$ and $\{f, d, a, g, i\}$, are selected and plotted as in Figure 7.23(a) and (b) respectively, it is easy to see that they form some interesting patterns: Figure 7.23(a) forms a **shift pattern**, where the three curves are similar to each other with respect to a shift operation along the y-axis; while Figure 7.23(b) forms a **scaling pattern**, where the three curves are similar to each other with respect to a scaling operation along the y-axis. ■

Let us first examine how to discover shift patterns. In DNA microarray data, each row corresponds to a gene and each column or attribute represents a condition under which the gene is developed. The usual Euclidean distance measure cannot capture pattern similarity, since the y values of different curves can be quite far apart. Alternatively, we could first transform the data to derive new attributes, such as $A_{ij} = v_i - v_j$ (where v_i and

[9] Entropy is a measure from information theory. It was introduced in Chapter 2 regarding data discretization and is also described in Chapter 6 regarding decision tree construction.

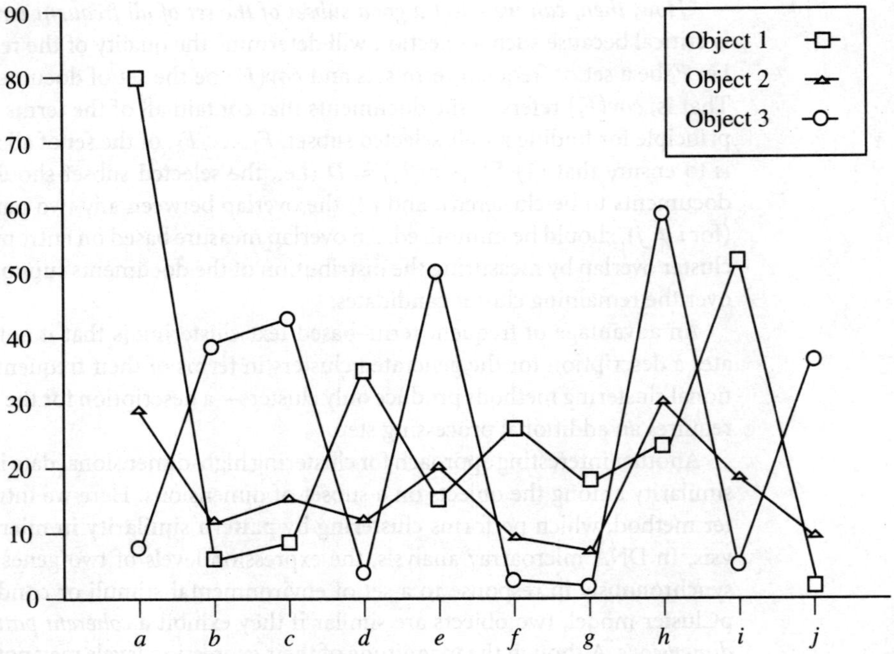

Figure 7.22 Raw data from a fragment of microarray data containing only 3 objects and 10 attributes.

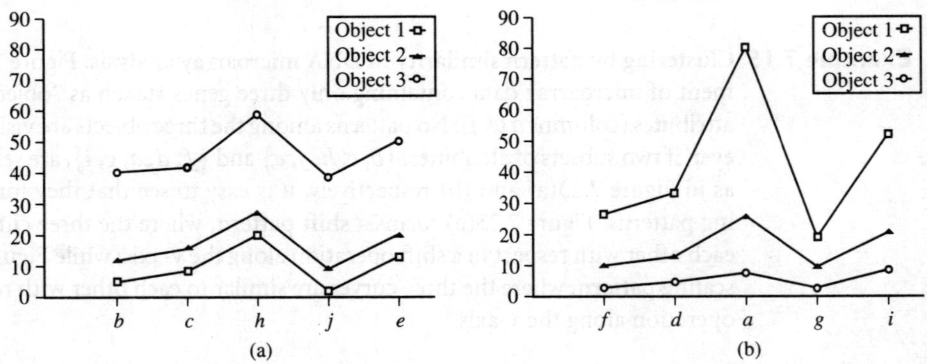

Figure 7.23 Objects in Figure 7.22 form (a) a *shift pattern* in subspace $\{b, c, h, j, e\}$, and (b) a *scaling pattern* in subspace $\{f, d, a, g, i\}$.

v_j are object values for attributes A_i and A_j, respectively), and then cluster on the derived attributes. However, this would introduce $d(d-1)/2$ dimensions for a d-dimensional data set, which is undesirable for a nontrivial d value. A **biclustering** method was proposed in an attempt to overcome these difficulties. It introduces a new measure, the **mean**

squared residue score, which measures the coherence of the genes and conditions in a submatrix of a DNA array. Let $I \subset X$ and $J \subset Y$ be subsets of genes, X, and conditions, Y, respectively. The pair, (I, J), specifies a submatrix, A_{IJ}, with the mean squared residue score defined as

$$H(IJ) = \frac{1}{|I||J|} \sum_{i \in I,\, j \in J} (d_{ij} - d_{iJ} - d_{Ij} + d_{IJ})^2, \tag{7.39}$$

where d_{ij} is the measured value of gene i for condition j, and

$$d_{iJ} = \frac{1}{|J|} \sum_{j \in J} d_{ij}, \quad d_{Ij} = \frac{1}{|I|} \sum_{i \in I} d_{ij}, \quad d_{IJ} = \frac{1}{|I||J|} \sum_{i \in I, j \in J} d_{ij}, \tag{7.40}$$

where d_{iJ} and d_{Ij} are the row and column means, respectively, and d_{IJ} is the mean of the subcluster matrix, A_{IJ}. A submatrix, A_{IJ}, is called a **δ-bicluster** if $H(I, J) \leq \delta$ for some $\delta > 0$. A randomized algorithm is designed to find such clusters in a DNA array. There are two major limitations of this method. First, a submatrix of a δ-bicluster is not necessarily a δ-bicluster, which makes it difficult to design an efficient pattern growth–based algorithm. Second, because of the averaging effect, a δ-bicluster may contain some undesirable outliers yet still satisfy a rather small δ threshold.

To overcome the problems of the biclustering method, a *pCluster* model was introduced as follows. Given objects $\boldsymbol{x}, \boldsymbol{y} \in O$ and attributes $a, b \in T$, *pScore* is defined by a 2×2 matrix as

$$pScore\left(\begin{bmatrix} d_{xa} & d_{xb} \\ d_{ya} & d_{yb} \end{bmatrix}\right) = |(d_{xa} - d_{xb}) - (d_{ya} - d_{yb})|, \tag{7.41}$$

where d_{xa} is the value of object (or gene) $\boldsymbol{x}$ for attribute (or condition) a, and so on. A pair, (O, T), forms a **δ-pCluster** if, for any 2×2 matrix, X, in (O, T), we have $pScore(X) \leq \delta$ for some $\delta > 0$. Intuitively, this means that the change of values on the two attributes between the two objects is confined by δ for every pair of objects in O and every pair of attributes in T.

It is easy to see that δ-pCluster has the downward closure property; that is, if (O, T) forms a δ-pCluster, then any of its submatrices is also a δ-pCluster. Moreover, because a pCluster requires that every two objects and every two attributes conform with the inequality, the clusters modeled by the pCluster method are more homogeneous than those modeled by the bicluster method.

In frequent itemset mining, itemsets are considered frequent if they satisfy a minimum support threshold, which reflects their frequency of occurrence. Based on the definition of pCluster, the problem of mining pClusters becomes one of mining frequent patterns in which each pair of objects and their corresponding features must satisfy the specified δ threshold. A frequent pattern–growth method can easily be extended to mine such patterns efficiently.

Now, let's look into how to discover scaling patterns. Notice that the original *pScore* definition, though defined for shift patterns in Equation (7.41), can easily be extended for scaling by introducing a new inequality,

$$\frac{d_{xa}/d_{ya}}{d_{xb}/d_{yb}} \leq \delta'. \tag{7.42}$$

This can be computed efficiently because Equation (7.41) is a logarithmic form of Equation (7.42). That is, the same pCluster model can be applied to the data set after converting the data to the logarithmic form. Thus, the efficient derivation of δ-pClusters for shift patterns can naturally be extended for the derivation of δ-pClusters for scaling patterns.

The pCluster model, though developed in the study of microarray data cluster analysis, can be applied to many other applications that require finding similar or coherent patterns involving a subset of numerical dimensions in large, high-dimensional data sets.

7.10 Constraint-Based Cluster Analysis

In the above discussion, we assume that cluster analysis is an automated, algorithmic computational process, based on the evaluation of similarity or distance functions among a set of objects to be clustered, *with little user guidance or interaction*. However, users often have a clear view of the application requirements, which they would ideally like to use to guide the clustering process and influence the clustering results. Thus, in many applications, it is desirable to have the clustering process take user preferences and constraints into consideration. Examples of such information include the expected number of clusters, the minimal or maximal cluster size, weights for different objects or dimensions, and other desirable characteristics of the resulting clusters. Moreover, when a clustering task involves a rather high-dimensional space, it is very difficult to generate meaningful clusters by relying solely on the clustering parameters. User input regarding important dimensions or the desired results will serve as crucial hints or meaningful constraints for effective clustering. In general, we contend that knowledge discovery would be most effective if one could develop an environment for human-centered, exploratory mining of data, that is, where the human user is allowed to play a key role in the process. Foremost, a user should be allowed to specify a *focus*—directing the mining algorithm toward the kind of "knowledge" that the user is interested in finding. Clearly, user-guided mining will lead to more desirable results and capture the application semantics.

Constraint-based clustering finds clusters that satisfy user-specified preferences or constraints. Depending on the nature of the constraints, constraint-based clustering may adopt rather different approaches. Here are a few categories of constraints.

1. **Constraints on individual objects:** We can specify constraints on the objects to be clustered. In a real estate application, for example, one may like to spatially cluster only

those luxury mansions worth over a million dollars. This constraint confines the set of objects to be clustered. It can easily be handled by preprocessing (e.g., performing selection using an SQL query), after which the problem reduces to an instance of unconstrained clustering.

2. **Constraints on the selection of clustering parameters:** A user may like to set a desired range for each clustering parameter. Clustering parameters are usually quite specific to the given clustering algorithm. Examples of parameters include k, the desired number of clusters in a k-means algorithm; or ε (the radius) and *MinPts* (the minimum number of points) in the DBSCAN algorithm. Although such user-specified parameters may strongly influence the clustering results, they are usually confined to the algorithm itself. Thus, their fine tuning and processing are usually not considered a form of constraint-based clustering.

3. **Constraints on distance or similarity functions:** We can specify different distance or similarity functions for specific attributes of the objects to be clustered, or different distance measures for specific pairs of objects. When clustering sportsmen, for example, we may use different weighting schemes for height, body weight, age, and skill level. Although this will likely change the mining results, it may not alter the clustering process per se. However, in some cases, such changes may make the evaluation of the distance function nontrivial, especially when it is tightly intertwined with the clustering process. This can be seen in the following example.

Example 7.16 **Clustering with obstacle objects.** A city may have rivers, bridges, highways, lakes, and mountains. We do not want to swim across a river to reach an automated banking machine. Such *obstacle objects* and their effects can be captured by redefining the distance functions among objects. Clustering with obstacle objects using a partitioning approach requires that the distance between each object and its corresponding cluster center be reevaluated at each iteration whenever the cluster center is changed. However, such reevaluation is quite expensive with the existence of obstacles. In this case, efficient new methods should be developed for clustering with obstacle objects in large data sets. ■

4. **User-specified constraints on the properties of individual clusters:** A user may like to specify desired characteristics of the resulting clusters, which may strongly influence the clustering process. Such constraint-based clustering arises naturally in practice, as in Example 7.17.

Example 7.17 **User-constrained cluster analysis.** Suppose a package delivery company would like to determine the locations for k service stations in a city. The company has a database of customers that registers the customers' names, locations, length of time since the customers began using the company's services, and average monthly charge. We may formulate this location selection problem as an instance of unconstrained clustering using a distance function computed based on customer location. However, a smarter approach is to partition the customers into two classes: *high-value* customers (who need frequent, regular service) and *ordinary* customers (who require occasional service). In order to save costs and provide good service, the manager adds the following constraints: (1) each station should serve at least 100 high-value customers; and (2) each station should serve at least 5,000 ordinary customers. Constraint-based clustering will take such constraints into consideration during the clustering process. ■

5. **Semi-supervised clustering based on "partial" supervision:** The quality of unsupervised clustering can be significantly improved using some weak form of supervision. This may be in the form of pairwise constraints (i.e., pairs of objects labeled as belonging to the same or different cluster). Such a constrained clustering process is called *semi-supervised clustering*.

In this section, we examine how efficient constraint-based clustering methods can be developed for large data sets. Since cases 1 and 2 above are trivial, we focus on cases 3 to 5 as typical forms of constraint-based cluster analysis.

7.10.1 Clustering with Obstacle Objects

Example 7.16 introduced the problem of clustering with obstacle objects regarding the placement of automated banking machines. The machines should be easily accessible to the bank's customers. This means that during clustering, we must take obstacle objects into consideration, such as rivers, highways, and mountains. Obstacles introduce constraints on the distance function. The straight-line distance between two points is meaningless if there is an obstacle in the way. As pointed out in Example 7.16, we do not want to have to swim across a river to get to a banking machine!

"How can we approach the problem of clustering with obstacles?" A partitioning clustering method is preferable because it minimizes the distance between objects and their cluster centers. If we choose the *k*-means method, a cluster center may not be accessible given the presence of obstacles. For example, the cluster mean could turn out to be in the middle of a lake. On the other hand, the *k*-medoids method chooses an object within the cluster as a center and thus guarantees that such a problem cannot occur. Recall that every time a new medoid is selected, the distance between each object and its newly selected cluster center has to be recomputed. Because there could be obstacles between two objects, the distance between two objects may have to be derived by geometric computations (e.g., involving triangulation). The computational cost can get very high if a large number of objects and obstacles are involved.

The clustering with obstacles problem can be represented using a graphical notation. First, a point, p, is **visible** from another point, q, in the region, R, if the straight line joining p and q does not intersect any obstacles. A **visibility graph** is the graph, $VG = (V, E)$, such that each vertex of the obstacles has a corresponding node in V and two nodes, v_1 and v_2, in V are joined by an edge in E if and only if the corresponding vertices they represent are visible to each other. Let $VG' = (V', E')$ be a visibility graph created from VG by adding two additional points, p and q, in

V'. E' contains an edge joining two points in V' if the two points are mutually visible. The shortest path between two points, $\boldsymbol{p}$ and $\boldsymbol{q}$, will be a subpath of VG' as shown in Figure 7.24(a). We see that it begins with an edge from $\boldsymbol{p}$ to either $\boldsymbol{v}_1, \boldsymbol{v}_2$, or $\boldsymbol{v}_3$, goes through some path in VG, and then ends with an edge from either $\boldsymbol{v}_4$ or $\boldsymbol{v}_5$ to $\boldsymbol{q}$.

To reduce the cost of distance computation between any two pairs of objects or points, several preprocessing and optimization techniques can be used. One method groups points that are close together into microclusters. This can be done by first triangulating the region R into triangles, and then grouping nearby points in the same triangle into microclusters, using a method similar to BIRCH or DBSCAN, as shown in Figure 7.24(b). By processing microclusters rather than individual points, the overall computation is reduced. After that, precomputation can be performed to build two kinds of join indices based on the computation of the shortest paths: (1) *VV indices*, for any pair of obstacle vertices, and (2) *MV indices*, for any pair of microcluster and obstacle vertex. Use of the indices helps further optimize the overall performance.

With such precomputation and optimization, the distance between any two points (at the granularity level of microcluster) can be computed efficiently. Thus, the clustering process can be performed in a manner similar to a typical efficient k-medoids algorithm, such as CLARANS, and achieve good clustering quality for large data sets. Given a large set of points, Figure 7.25(a) shows the result of clustering a large set of points without considering obstacles, whereas Figure 7.25(b) shows the result with consideration of obstacles. The latter represents rather different but more desirable clusters. For example, if we carefully compare the upper left-hand corner of the two graphs, we see that Figure 7.25(a) has a cluster center on an obstacle (making the center inaccessible), whereas all cluster centers in Figure 7.25(b) are accessible. A similar situation has occurred with respect to the bottom right-hand corner of the graphs.

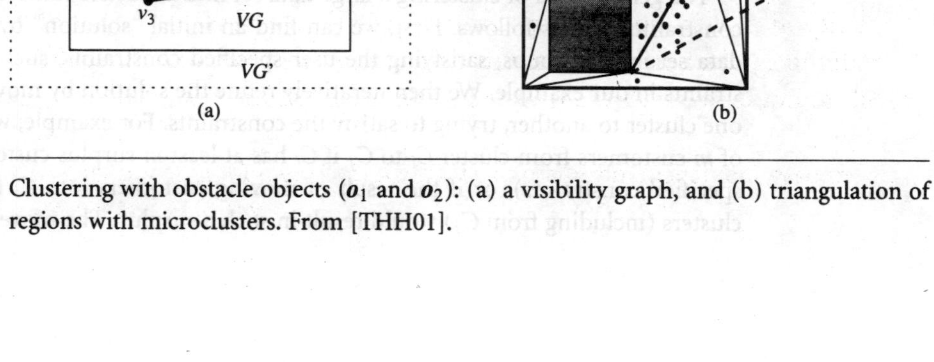

Figure 7.24 Clustering with obstacle objects (o_1 and o_2): (a) a visibility graph, and (b) triangulation of regions with microclusters. From [THH01].

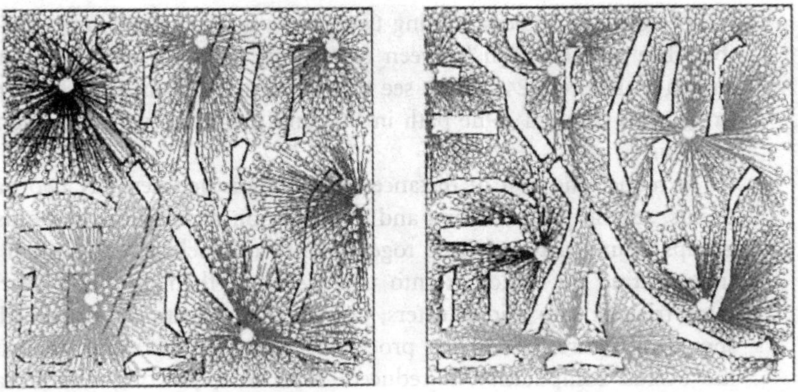

Figure 7.25 Clustering results obtained without and with consideration of obstacles (where rivers and inaccessible highways or city blocks are represented by polygons): (a) clustering without considering obstacles, and (b) clustering with obstacles.

7.10.2 User-Constrained Cluster Analysis

Let's examine the problem of relocating package delivery centers, as illustrated in Example 7.17. Specifically, a package delivery company with n customers would like to determine locations for k service stations so as to minimize the traveling distance between customers and service stations. The company's customers are regarded as either *high-value* customers (requiring frequent, regular services) or *ordinary* customers (requiring occasional services). The manager has stipulated two constraints: each station should serve (1) at least 100 high-value customers and (2) at least 5,000 ordinary customers.

This can be considered as a constrained optimization problem. We could consider using a mathematical programming approach to handle it. However, such a solution is difficult to scale to large data sets. To cluster n customers into k clusters, a mathematical programming approach will involve at least $k \times n$ variables. As n can be as large as a few million, we could end up having to solve a few million simultaneous equations—a very expensive feat. A more efficient approach is proposed that explores the idea of microclustering, as illustrated below.

The general idea of clustering a large data set into k clusters satisfying user-specified constraints goes as follows. First, we can find an initial "solution" by partitioning the data set into k groups, satisfying the user-specified constraints, such as the two constraints in our example. We then iteratively refine the solution by moving objects from one cluster to another, trying to satisfy the constraints. For example, we can move a set of m customers from cluster C_i to C_j if C_i has at least m surplus customers (under the specified constraints), or if the result of moving customers into C_i from some other clusters (including from C_j) would result in such a surplus. The movement is desirable if the total sum of the distances of the objects to their corresponding cluster centers is reduced. Such movement can be directed by selecting promising points to be moved, such as objects that are currently assigned to some cluster, C_i, but that are actually closer to a representative (e.g., centroid) of some other cluster, C_j. We need to watch out for and handle deadlock situations (where a constraint is impossible to satisfy), in which case, a deadlock resolution strategy can be employed.

To increase the clustering efficiency, data can first be preprocessed using the micro-clustering idea to form microclusters (groups of points that are close together), thereby avoiding the processing of all of the points individually. Object movement, deadlock detection, and constraint satisfaction can be tested at the microcluster level, which reduces the number of points to be computed. Occasionally, such microclusters may need to be broken up in order to resolve deadlocks under the constraints. This methodology ensures that the effective clustering can be performed in large data sets under the user-specified constraints with good efficiency and scalability.

7.10.3 Semi-Supervised Cluster Analysis

In comparison with supervised learning, clustering lacks guidance from users or classifiers (such as class label information), and thus may not generate highly desirable clusters. The quality of unsupervised clustering can be significantly improved using some weak form of supervision, for example, in the form of pairwise constraints (i.e., pairs of objects labeled as belonging to the same or different clusters). Such a clustering process based on user feedback or guidance constraints is called **semi-supervised clustering.**

Methods for semi-supervised clustering can be categorized into two classes: *constraint-based semi-supervised clustering* and *distance-based semi-supervised clustering.* **Constraint-based semi-supervised clustering** relies on *user-provided labels or constraints* to guide the algorithm toward a more appropriate data partitioning. This includes modifying the objective function based on constraints, or initializing and constraining the clustering process based on the labeled objects. **Distance-based semi-supervised clustering** employs an adaptive distance measure that is trained to satisfy the labels or constraints in the supervised data. Several different adaptive distance measures have been used, such as string-edit distance trained using Expectation-Maximization (EM), and Euclidean distance modified by a shortest distance algorithm.

An interesting clustering method, called **CLTree** (CLustering based on decision TREEs), integrates unsupervised clustering with the idea of supervised classification. It is an example of constraint-based semi-supervised clustering. It transforms a clustering task into a classification task by viewing the set of points to be clustered as belonging to one class, labeled as "Y," and adds a set of relatively uniformly distributed, "nonexistence points" with a different class label, "N." The problem of partitioning the data space into data (dense) regions and empty (sparse) regions can then be transformed into a classification problem. For example, Figure 7.26(a) contains a set of data points to be clustered. These points can be viewed as a set of "Y" points. Figure 7.26(b) shows the addition of a set of uniformly distributed "N" points, represented by the "∘" points. The original

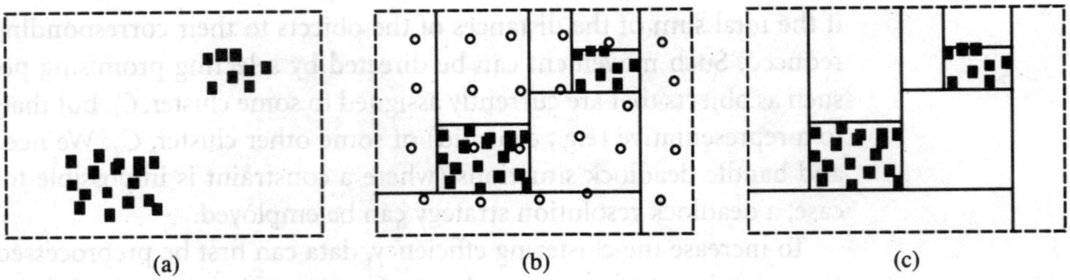

Figure 7.26 Clustering through decision tree construction: (a) the set of data points to be clustered, viewed as a set of "*Y*" points, (b) the addition of a set of uniformly distributed "*N*" points, represented by "o", and (c) the clustering result with "*Y*" points only.

clustering problem is thus transformed into a classification problem, which works out a scheme that distinguishes "*Y*" and "*N*" points. A decision tree induction method can be applied[10] to partition the two-dimensional space, as shown in Figure 7.26(c). Two clusters are identified, which are from the "*Y*" points only.

Adding a large number of "*N*" points to the original data may introduce unnecessary overhead in computation. Furthermore, it is unlikely that any points added would truly be uniformly distributed in a very high-dimensional space as this would require an exponential number of points. To deal with this problem, we do not physically add any of the "*N*" points, but only *assume* their existence. This works because the decision tree method does not actually require the points. Instead, it only needs the *number* of "*N*" points at each decision tree node. This number can be computed when needed, without having to add points to the original data. Thus, CLTree can achieve the results in Figure 7.26(c) without actually adding any "*N*" points to the original data. Again, two clusters are identified.

The question then is how many (*virtual*) "*N*" points should be added in order to achieve good clustering results. The answer follows this simple rule: *At the root node, the number of inherited "N" points is 0. At any current node, E, if the number of "N" points inherited from the parent node of E is less than the number of "Y" points in E, then the number of "N" points for E is increased to the number of "Y" points in E. (That is, we set the number of "N" points to be as big as the number of "Y" points.)* Otherwise, the number of inherited "*N*" points is used in *E*. The basic idea is to use an equal number of "*N*" points to the number of "*Y*" points.

Decision tree classification methods use a measure, typically based on information gain, to select the attribute test for a decision node (Section 6.3.2). The data are then split or partitioned according the test or "cut." Unfortunately, with clustering, this can lead to the fragmentation of some clusters into scattered regions. To address this problem, methods were developed that use information gain, but allow the ability to look ahead.

[10]Decision tree induction was described in Chapter 6 on classification.

That is, CLTree first finds initial cuts and then looks ahead to find better partitions that cut less into cluster regions. It finds those cuts that form regions with a very low relative density. The idea is that we want to split at the cut point that may result in a big empty ("*N*") region, which is more likely to separate clusters. With such tuning, CLTree can perform high-quality clustering in high-dimensional space. It can also find subspace clusters as the decision tree method normally selects only a subset of the attributes. An interesting by-product of this method is the empty (sparse) regions, which may also be useful in certain applications. In marketing, for example, clusters may represent different segments of existing customers of a company, while empty regions reflect the profiles of noncustomers. Knowing the profiles of noncustomers allows the company to tailor their services or marketing to target these potential customers.

7.11 Outlier Analysis

"*What is an outlier?*" Very often, there exist data objects that do not comply with the general behavior or model of the data. Such data objects, which are grossly different from or inconsistent with the remaining set of data, are called **outliers**.

Outliers can be caused by measurement or execution error. For example, the display of a person's age as −999 could be caused by a program default setting of an unrecorded age. Alternatively, outliers may be the result of inherent data variability. The salary of the chief executive officer of a company, for instance, could naturally stand out as an outlier among the salaries of the other employees in the firm.

Many data mining algorithms try to minimize the influence of outliers or eliminate them all together. This, however, could result in the loss of important hidden information because *one person's noise could be another person's signal.* In other words, the outliers may be of particular interest, such as in the case of fraud detection, where outliers may indicate fraudulent activity. Thus, outlier detection and analysis is an interesting data mining task, referred to as **outlier mining**.

Outlier mining has wide applications. As mentioned previously, it can be used in fraud detection, for example, by detecting unusual usage of credit cards or telecommunication services. In addition, it is useful in customized marketing for identifying the spending behavior of customers with extremely low or extremely high incomes, or in medical analysis for finding unusual responses to various medical treatments.

Outlier mining can be described as follows: Given a set of n data points or objects and k, the expected number of outliers, find the top k objects that are considerably dissimilar, exceptional, or inconsistent with respect to the remaining data. The outlier mining problem can be viewed as two subproblems: (1) define what data can be considered as inconsistent in a given data set, and (2) find an efficient method to mine the outliers so defined.

The problem of defining outliers is nontrivial. If a regression model is used for data modeling, analysis of the residuals can give a good estimation for data "extremeness." The task becomes tricky, however, when finding outliers in time-series data, as they may be hidden in trend, seasonal, or other cyclic changes. When multidimensional data are analyzed, not any particular one but rather a *combination* of dimension values may be extreme. For nonnumeric (i.e., categorical) data, the definition of outliers requires special consideration.

"What about using data visualization methods for outlier detection?" This may seem like an obvious choice, since human eyes are very fast and effective at noticing data inconsistencies. However, this does not apply to data containing cyclic plots, where values that appear to be outliers could be perfectly valid values in reality. Data visualization methods are weak in detecting outliers in data with many categorical attributes or in data of high dimensionality, since human eyes are good at visualizing numeric data of only two to three dimensions.

In this section, we instead examine computer-based methods for outlier detection. These can be categorized into four approaches: the *statistical approach*, the *distance-based approach*, the *density-based local outlier approach*, and the *deviation-based approach*, each of which are studied here. Notice that while clustering algorithms discard outliers as noise, they can be modified to include outlier detection as a by-product of their execution. In general, users must check that each outlier discovered by these approaches is indeed a "real" outlier.

7.11.1 Statistical Distribution-Based Outlier Detection

The statistical distribution-based approach to outlier detection assumes a distribution or probability model for the given data set (e.g., a normal or Poisson distribution) and then identifies outliers with respect to the model using a *discordancy test*. Application of the test requires knowledge of the data set parameters (such as the assumed data distribution), knowledge of distribution parameters (such as the mean and variance), and the expected number of outliers.

"How does the discordancy testing work?" A statistical discordancy test examines two hypotheses: a *working hypothesis* and an *alternative hypothesis*. A **working hypothesis**, H, is a statement that the entire data set of n objects comes from an initial distribution model, F, that is,

$$H : \boldsymbol{o}_i \in F, \quad \text{where } i = 1, 2, \ldots, n. \tag{7.43}$$

The hypothesis is retained if there is no statistically significant evidence supporting its rejection. A **discordancy test** verifies whether an object, $\boldsymbol{o}_i$, is significantly large (or small) in relation to the distribution F. Different test statistics have been proposed for use as a discordancy test, depending on the available knowledge of the data. Assuming that some statistic, T, has been chosen for discordancy testing, and the value of the statistic for object $\boldsymbol{o}_i$ is v_i, then the distribution of T is constructed. Significance probability, $SP(v_i) = Prob(T > v_i)$, is evaluated. If $SP(v_i)$ is sufficiently small, then $\boldsymbol{o}_i$ is discordant and the working hypothesis is rejected. An **alternative hypothesis**, $\overline{H}$, which states that $\boldsymbol{o}_i$ comes from another distribution model, G, is adopted. The result is very much dependent on which model F is chosen because $\boldsymbol{o}_i$ may be an outlier under one model and a perfectly valid value under another.

The alternative distribution is very important in determining the power of the test, that is, the probability that the working hypothesis is rejected when $\boldsymbol{o}_i$ is really an outlier. There are different kinds of alternative distributions.

- **Inherent alternative distribution:** In this case, the working hypothesis that all of the objects come from distribution F is rejected in favor of the alternative hypothesis that all of the objects arise from another distribution, G:

$$\overline{H}: \boldsymbol{o}_i \in G, \quad \text{where } i = 1, 2, \ldots, n. \tag{7.44}$$

  F and G may be different distributions or differ only in parameters of the same distribution. There are constraints on the form of the G distribution in that it must have potential to produce outliers. For example, it may have a different mean or dispersion, or a longer tail.

- **Mixture alternative distribution:** The mixture alternative states that discordant values are not outliers in the F population, but contaminants from some other population, G. In this case, the alternative hypothesis is

$$\overline{H}: \boldsymbol{o}_i \in (1-\lambda)F + \lambda G, \quad \text{where } i = 1, 2, \ldots, n. \tag{7.45}$$

- **Slippage alternative distribution:** This alternative states that all of the objects (apart from some prescribed small number) arise independently from the initial model, F, with its given parameters, whereas the remaining objects are independent observations from a modified version of F in which the parameters have been shifted.

There are two basic types of procedures for detecting outliers:

- **Block procedures:** In this case, either all of the suspect objects are treated as outliers or all of them are accepted as consistent.
- **Consecutive (or sequential) procedures:** An example of such a procedure is the *inside-out* procedure. Its main idea is that the object that is least "likely" to be an outlier is tested first. If it is found to be an outlier, then all of the more extreme values are also considered outliers; otherwise, the next most extreme object is tested, and so on. This procedure tends to be more effective than block procedures.

"How effective is the statistical approach at outlier detection?" A major drawback is that most tests are for single attributes, yet many data mining problems require finding outliers in multidimensional space. Moreover, the statistical approach requires knowledge about parameters of the data set, such as the data distribution. However, in many cases, the data distribution may not be known. Statistical methods do not guarantee that all outliers will be found for the cases where no specific test was developed, or where the observed distribution cannot be adequately modeled with any standard distribution.

7.11.2 Distance-Based Outlier Detection

The notion of distance-based outliers was introduced to counter the main limitations imposed by statistical methods. An object, $\boldsymbol{o}$, in a data set, D, is a **distance-based (DB) outlier** with parameters *pct* and *dmin*,[11] that is, a $\boldsymbol{DB(pct, dmin)}$**-outlier**, if at least a fraction, *pct*, of the objects in D lie at a distance greater than *dmin* from $\boldsymbol{o}$. In other words, rather than relying on statistical tests, we can think of distance-based outliers as those objects that do not have "enough" neighbors, where neighbors are defined based on distance from the given object. In comparison with statistical-based methods, distance-based outlier detection generalizes the ideas behind discordancy testing for various standard distributions. Distance-based outlier detection avoids the excessive computation that can be associated with fitting the observed distribution into some standard distribution and in selecting discordancy tests.

For many discordancy tests, it can be shown that if an object, $\boldsymbol{o}$, is an outlier according to the given test, then $\boldsymbol{o}$ is also a $DB(pct, dmin)$-outlier for some suitably defined *pct* and *dmin*. For example, if objects that lie three or more standard deviations from the mean are considered to be outliers, assuming a normal distribution, then this definition can be generalized by a $DB(0.9988, 0.13\sigma)$ outlier.[12]

Several efficient algorithms for mining distance-based outliers have been developed. These are outlined as follows.

Index-based algorithm: Given a data set, the index-based algorithm uses multidimensional indexing structures, such as R-trees or k-d trees, to search for neighbors of each object $\boldsymbol{o}$ within radius *dmin* around that object. Let M be the maximum number of objects within the *dmin*-neighborhood of an outlier. Therefore, once $M+1$ neighbors of object $\boldsymbol{o}$ are found, it is clear that $\boldsymbol{o}$ is not an outlier. This algorithm has a worst-case complexity of $O(n^2k)$, where n is the number of objects in the data set and k is the dimensionality. The index-based algorithm scales well as k increases. However, this complexity evaluation takes only the search time into account, even though the task of building an index in itself can be computationally intensive.

Nested-loop algorithm: The nested-loop algorithm has the same computational complexity as the index-based algorithm but avoids index structure construction and tries to minimize the number of I/Os. It divides the memory buffer space into two halves and the data set into several logical blocks. By carefully choosing the order in which blocks are loaded into each half, I/O efficiency can be achieved.

[11] The parameter *dmin* is the neighborhood radius around object $\boldsymbol{o}$. It corresponds to the parameter ε in Section 7.6.1.

[12] The parameters *pct* and *dmin* are computed using the normal curve's probability density function to satisfy the probability condition $(P|\boldsymbol{x}-3| \leq dmin) < 1-pct$, i.e., $P(3-dmin \leq \boldsymbol{x} \leq 3+dmin) < -pct$, where $\boldsymbol{x}$ is an object. (Note that the solution may not be unique.) A *dmin*-neighborhood of radius 0.13 indicates a spread of ± 0.13 units around the 3 σ mark (i.e., [2.87, 3.13]). For a complete proof of the derivation, see [KN97].

Cell-based algorithm: To avoid $O(n^2)$ computational complexity, a cell-based algorithm was developed for memory-resident data sets. Its complexity is $O(c^k + n)$, where c is a constant depending on the number of cells and k is the dimensionality. In this method, the data space is partitioned into cells with a side length equal to $\frac{dmin}{2\sqrt{k}}$. Each cell has two *layers* surrounding it. The first layer is one cell thick, while the second is $\lceil 2\sqrt{k} - 1 \rceil$ cells thick, rounded up to the closest integer. The algorithm counts outliers on a *cell-by-cell* rather than an object-by-object basis. For a given cell, it accumulates three counts—the number of objects in the cell, in the cell and the first layer together, and in the cell and both layers together. Let's refer to these counts as *cell_count*, *cell_+_1_layer_count*, and *cell_+_2_layers_count*, respectively.

"How are outliers determined in this method?" Let M be the maximum number of outliers that can exist in the *dmin*-neighborhood of an outlier.

- An object, $\boldsymbol{o}$, in the current cell is considered an outlier only if *cell_+_1_layer_count* is less than or equal to M. If this condition does not hold, then all of the objects in the cell can be removed from further investigation as they cannot be outliers.
- If *cell_+_2_layers_count* is less than or equal to M, then *all* of the objects in the cell are considered outliers. Otherwise, if this number is more than M, then it is possible that some of the objects in the cell may be outliers. To detect these outliers, object-by-object processing is used where, for each object, $\boldsymbol{o}$, in the cell, objects in the second layer of $\boldsymbol{o}$ are examined. For objects in the cell, only those objects having no more than M points in their *dmin*-neighborhoods are outliers. The *dmin*-neighborhood of an object consists of the object's cell, all of its first layer, and some of its second layer.

A variation to the algorithm is linear with respect to n and guarantees that no more than three passes over the data set are required. It can be used for large disk-resident data sets, yet does not scale well for high dimensions.

Distance-based outlier detection requires the user to set both the *pct* and *dmin* parameters. Finding suitable settings for these parameters can involve much trial and error.

7.11.3 Density-Based Local Outlier Detection

Statistical and distance-based outlier detection both depend on the overall or "global" distribution of the given set of data points, D. However, data are usually not uniformly distributed. These methods encounter difficulties when analyzing data with rather different density distributions, as illustrated in the following example.

Example 7.18 **Necessity for density-based local outlier detection.** Figure 7.27 shows a simple 2-D data set containing 502 objects, with two obvious clusters. Cluster C_1 contains 400 objects. Cluster C_2 contains 100 objects. Two additional objects, $\boldsymbol{o}_1$ and $\boldsymbol{o}_2$ are clearly outliers. However, by distance-based outlier detection (which generalizes many notions from

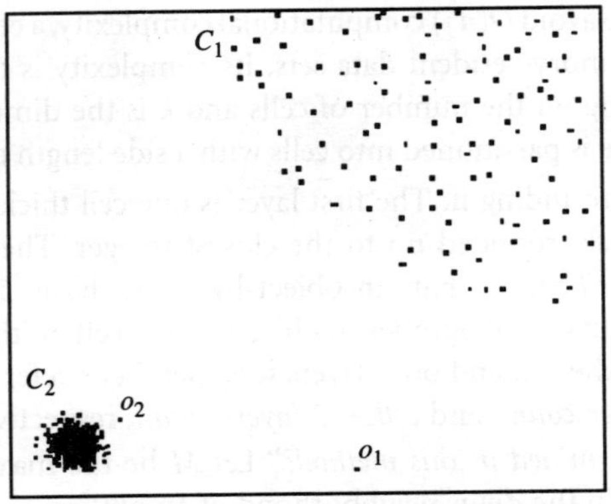

Figure 7.27 The necessity of density-based local outlier analysis. From [BKNS00].

statistical-based outlier detection), only o_1 is a reasonable $DB(pct, dmin)$-outlier, because if $dmin$ is set to be less than the minimum distance between o_2 and C_2, then all 501 objects are further away from o_2 than $dmin$. Thus, o_2 would be considered a $DB(pct, dmin)$-outlier, but so would all of the objects in C_1! On the other hand, if $dmin$ is set to be greater than the minimum distance between o_2 and C_2, then even when o_2 is not regarded as an outlier, some points in C_1 may still be considered outliers. ■

This brings us to the notion of *local outliers*. An object is a **local outlier** if it is outlying *relative to its local neighborhood*, particulary with respect to the density of the neighborhood. In this view, o_2 of Example 7.18 is a local outlier relative to the density of C_2. Object o_1 is an outlier as well, and no objects in C_1 are mislabeled as outliers. This forms the basis of **density-based local outlier detection.** Another key idea of this approach to outlier detection is that, unlike previous methods, it does not consider being an outlier as a binary property. Instead, it assesses the *degree* to which an object is an outlier. This degree of "outlierness" is computed as the **local outlier factor (LOF)** of an object. It is local in the sense that the degree depends on how isolated the object is with respect to the surrounding neighborhood. This approach can detect both global and local outliers.

To define the local outlier factor of an object, we need to introduce the concepts of k-distance, k-distance neighborhood, reachability distance,[13] and local reachability density. These are defined as follows:

- The $\boldsymbol{k}$**-distance** of an object $\boldsymbol{p}$ is the maximal distance that $\boldsymbol{p}$ gets from its k-nearest neighbors. This distance is denoted as k-*distance*$(\boldsymbol{p})$. It is defined as the distance, $d(\boldsymbol{p}, \boldsymbol{o})$, between $\boldsymbol{p}$ and an object $\boldsymbol{o} \in D$, such that (1) for at least k objects, $\boldsymbol{o}' \in D$, it

[13] The reachability distance here is similar to the reachability distance defined for OPTICS in Section 7.6.2, although it is given in a somewhat different context.

holds that $d(\boldsymbol{p}, \boldsymbol{o}') \leq d(\boldsymbol{p}, \boldsymbol{o})$. That is, there are at least k objects in D that are as close as or closer to $\boldsymbol{p}$ than $\boldsymbol{o}$, and (2) for at most $k-1$ objects, $\boldsymbol{o}'' \in D$, it holds that $d(\boldsymbol{p}, \boldsymbol{o}'') < d(\boldsymbol{p}, \boldsymbol{o})$. That is, there are at most $k-1$ objects that are closer to $\boldsymbol{p}$ than $\boldsymbol{o}$. You may be wondering at this point how k is determined. The LOF method links to density-based clustering in that it sets k to the parameter *MinPts*, which specifies the minimum number of points for use in identifying clusters based on density (Sections 7.6.1 and 7.6.2). Here, *MinPts* (as k) is used to define the local neighborhood of an object, $\boldsymbol{p}$.

- The **k-distance neighborhood** of an object $\boldsymbol{p}$ is denoted $N_{k\_distance(\boldsymbol{p})}(\boldsymbol{p})$, or $N_k(\boldsymbol{p})$ for short. By setting k to *MinPts*, we get $N_{MinPts}(\boldsymbol{p})$. It contains the *MinPts*-nearest neighbors of $\boldsymbol{p}$. That is, it contains every object whose distance is not greater than the *MinPts*-distance of $\boldsymbol{p}$.

- The **reachability distance** of an object $\boldsymbol{p}$ with respect to object $\boldsymbol{o}$ (where $\boldsymbol{o}$ is within the *MinPts*-nearest neighbors of $\boldsymbol{p}$), is defined as $reach\_dist_{MinPts}(\boldsymbol{p}, \boldsymbol{o}) = max\{MinPts\text{-}distance(\boldsymbol{o}), d(\boldsymbol{p}, \boldsymbol{o})\}$. Intuitively, if an object $\boldsymbol{p}$ is far away from $\boldsymbol{o}$, then the reachability distance between the two is simply their actual distance. However, if they are "sufficiently" close (i.e., where $\boldsymbol{p}$ is within the *MinPts*-distance neighborhood of $\boldsymbol{o}$), then the actual distance is replaced by the *MinPts*-distance of $\boldsymbol{o}$. This helps to significantly reduce the statistical fluctuations of $d(\boldsymbol{p}, \boldsymbol{o})$ for all of the $\boldsymbol{p}$ close to $\boldsymbol{o}$. The higher the value of *MinPts* is, the more similar is the reachability distance for objects within the same neighborhood.

- Intuitively, the **local reachability density** of $\boldsymbol{p}$ is the inverse of the average reachability density based on the *MinPts*-nearest neighbors of $\boldsymbol{p}$. It is defined as

$$lrd_{MinPts}(\boldsymbol{p}) = \frac{|N_{MinPts}(\boldsymbol{p})|}{\Sigma_{\boldsymbol{o} \in N_{MinPts}(\boldsymbol{p})} reach\_dist_{MinPts}(\boldsymbol{p}, \boldsymbol{o})}. \tag{7.46}$$

- The **local outlier factor** (LOF) of $\boldsymbol{p}$ captures the degree to which we call $\boldsymbol{p}$ an outlier. It is defined as

$$LOF_{MinPts}(\boldsymbol{p}) = \frac{\Sigma_{\boldsymbol{o} \in N_{MinPts}(\boldsymbol{p})} \frac{lrd_{MinPts}(\boldsymbol{o})}{lrd_{MinPts}(\boldsymbol{p})}}{|N_{MinPts}(\boldsymbol{p})|}. \tag{7.47}$$

It is the average of the ratio of the local reachability density of $\boldsymbol{p}$ and those of $\boldsymbol{p}$'s *MinPts*-nearest neighbors. It is easy to see that the lower $\boldsymbol{p}$'s local reachability density is, and the higher the local reachability density of $\boldsymbol{p}$'s *MinPts*-nearest neighbors are, the higher $LOF(\boldsymbol{p})$ is.

From this definition, if an object $\boldsymbol{p}$ is not a local outlier, $LOF(\boldsymbol{p})$ is close to 1. The more that $\boldsymbol{p}$ is qualified to be a local outlier, the higher $LOF(\boldsymbol{p})$ is. Therefore, we can determine whether a point $\boldsymbol{p}$ is a local outlier based on the computation of $LOF(\boldsymbol{p})$. Experiments based on both synthetic and real-world large data sets have demonstrated the power of *LOF* at identifying local outliers.

7.11.4 Deviation-Based Outlier Detection

Deviation-based outlier detection does not use statistical tests or distance-based measures to identify exceptional objects. Instead, it identifies outliers by examining the main characteristics of objects in a group. Objects that "deviate" from this description are considered outliers. Hence, in this approach the term *deviations* is typically used to refer to outliers. In this section, we study two techniques for deviation-based outlier detection. The first sequentially compares objects in a set, while the second employs an OLAP data cube approach.

Sequential Exception Technique

The sequential exception technique simulates the way in which humans can distinguish unusual objects from among a series of supposedly like objects. It uses implicit redundancy of the data. Given a data set, D, of n objects, it builds a sequence of subsets, $\{D_1, D_2, \ldots, D_m\}$, of these objects with $2 \le m \le n$ such that

$$D_{j-1} \subset D_j, \quad \text{where } D_j \subseteq D. \tag{7.48}$$

Dissimilarities are assessed between subsets in the sequence. The technique introduces the following key terms.

- **Exception set:** This is the set of deviations or outliers. It is defined as the smallest subset of objects whose removal results in the greatest reduction of dissimilarity in the residual set.[14]
- **Dissimilarity function:** This function does not require a metric distance between the objects. It is any function that, if given a set of objects, returns a low value if the objects are similar to one another. The greater the dissimilarity among the objects, the higher the value returned by the function. The dissimilarity of a subset is incrementally computed based on the subset prior to it in the sequence. Given a subset of n numbers, $\{x_1, \ldots, x_n\}$, a possible dissimilarity function is the variance of the numbers in the set, that is,

$$\frac{1}{n}\sum_{i=1}^{n}(x_i - \bar{x})^2, \tag{7.49}$$

  where $\bar{x}$ is the mean of the n numbers in the set. For character strings, the dissimilarity function may be in the form of a pattern string (e.g., containing wildcard characters) that is used to cover all of the patterns seen so far. The dissimilarity increases when the pattern covering all of the strings in D_{j-1} does not cover any string in D_j that is not in D_{j-1}.

[14]For interested readers, this is equivalent to the greatest reduction in *Kolmogorov complexity* for the amount of data discarded.

- **Cardinality function:** This is typically the count of the number of objects in a given set.
- **Smoothing factor:** This function is computed for each subset in the sequence. It assesses how much the dissimilarity can be reduced by removing the subset from the original set of objects. This value is scaled by the cardinality of the set. The subset whose smoothing factor value is the largest is the exception set.

The general task of finding an exception set can be NP-hard (i.e., intractable). A sequential approach is computationally feasible and can be implemented using a linear algorithm.

"How does this technique work?" Instead of assessing the dissimilarity of the current subset with respect to its complementary set, the algorithm selects a sequence of subsets from the set for analysis. For every subset, it determines the dissimilarity difference of the subset with respect to the *preceding* subset in the sequence.

"Can't the order of the subsets in the sequence affect the results?" To help alleviate any possible influence of the input order on the results, the above process can be repeated several times, each with a different random ordering of the subsets. The subset with the largest smoothing factor value, among all of the iterations, becomes the exception set.

OLAP Data Cube Technique

An OLAP approach to deviation detection uses data cubes to identify regions of anomalies in large multidimensional data. This technique was described in detail in Chapter 4. For added efficiency, the deviation detection process is overlapped with cube computation. The approach is a form of *discovery-driven exploration*, in which precomputed measures indicating data exceptions are used to guide the user in data analysis, at all levels of aggregation. A cell value in the cube is considered an exception if it is significantly different from the expected value, based on a statistical model. The method uses visual cues such as background color to reflect the degree of exception of each cell. The user can choose to drill down on cells that are flagged as exceptions. The measure value of a cell may reflect exceptions occurring at more detailed or *lower levels* of the cube, where these exceptions are not visible from the current level.

The model considers variations and patterns in the measure value across *all of the dimensions* to which a cell belongs. For example, suppose that you have a data cube for sales data and are viewing the sales summarized per month. With the help of the visual cues, you notice an increase in sales in December in comparison to all other months. This may seem like an exception in the time dimension. However, by drilling down on the month of December to reveal the sales per item in that month, you note that there is a similar increase in sales for other items during December. Therefore, an increase in total sales in December is not an exception if the item dimension is considered. The model considers exceptions hidden at all aggregated group-by's of a data cube. Manual detection of such exceptions is difficult because the search space is typically very large, particularly when there are many dimensions involving concept hierarchies with several levels.

7.12 Summary

- A **cluster** is a collection of data objects that are *similar* to one another within the same cluster and are *dissimilar* to the objects in other clusters. The process of grouping a set of physical or abstract objects into classes of *similar* objects is called **clustering.**

- Cluster analysis has wide **applications**, including market or customer segmentation, pattern recognition, biological studies, spatial data analysis, Web document classification, and many others. Cluster analysis can be used as a stand-alone data mining tool to gain insight into the data distribution or can serve as a preprocessing step for other data mining algorithms operating on the detected clusters.

- The quality of clustering can be assessed based on a measure of **dissimilarity** of objects, which can be computed for **various types of data**, including *interval-scaled, binary, categorical, ordinal,* and *ratio-scaled* variables, or combinations of these variable types. For nonmetric vector data, the *cosine measure* and the *Tanimoto coefficient* are often used in the assessment of similarity.

- Clustering is a dynamic field of research in data mining. Many clustering algorithms have been developed. These can be **categorized** into *partitioning methods, hierarchical methods, density-based methods, grid-based methods, model-based methods, methods for high-dimensional data* (including *frequent pattern–based methods*), and *constraint-based methods.* Some algorithms may belong to more than one category.

- A **partitioning method** first creates an initial set of k partitions, where parameter k is the number of partitions to construct. It then uses an *iterative relocation technique* that attempts to improve the partitioning by moving objects from one group to another. Typical partitioning methods include k-means, k-medoids, CLARANS, and their improvements.

- A **hierarchical method** creates a hierarchical decomposition of the given set of data objects. The method can be classified as being either *agglomerative* (*bottom-up*) or *divisive* (*top-down*), based on how the hierarchical decomposition is formed. To compensate for the rigidity of *merge* or *split*, the quality of hierarchical agglomeration can be improved by analyzing object linkages at each hierarchical partitioning (such as in ROCK and Chameleon), or by first performing *microclustering* (that is, grouping objects into "microclusters") and then operating on the microclusters with other clustering techniques, such as iterative relocation (as in BIRCH).

- A **density-based method** clusters objects based on the notion of density. It either grows clusters according to the density of neighborhood objects (such as in DBSCAN) or according to some density function (such as in DENCLUE). OPTICS is a density-based method that generates an augmented ordering of the clustering structure of the data.

- A **grid-based method** first quantizes the object space into a finite number of cells that form a grid structure, and then performs clustering on the grid structure. STING is a typical example of a grid-based method based on statistical information stored in grid cells. WaveCluster and CLIQUE are two clustering algorithms that are both grid-based and density-based.

- A **model-based method** hypothesizes a model for each of the clusters and finds the best fit of the data to that model. Examples of model-based clustering include the EM algorithm (which uses a mixture density model), conceptual clustering (such as COBWEB), and neural network approaches (such as self-organizing feature maps).
- **Clustering high-dimensional data** is of crucial importance, because in many advanced applications, data objects such as text documents and microarray data are high-dimensional in nature. There are three typical methods to handle high-dimensional data sets: *dimension-growth subspace clustering*, represented by CLIQUE, *dimension-reduction projected clustering*, represented by PROCLUS, and *frequent pattern–based clustering*, represented by pCluster.
- A **constraint-based clustering method** groups objects based on application-dependent or user-specified constraints. For example, clustering with the existence of obstacle objects and clustering under user-specified constraints are typical methods of constraint-based clustering. Typical examples include clustering with the existence of obstacle objects, clustering under user-specified constraints, and semi-supervised clustering based on "weak" supervision (such as pairs of objects labeled as belonging to the same or different cluster).
- *One person's noise could be another person's signal.* **Outlier detection and analysis** are very useful for fraud detection, customized marketing, medical analysis, and many other tasks. Computer-based outlier analysis methods typically follow either a *statistical distribution-based approach*, a *distance-based approach*, a *density-based local outlier detection approach*, or a *deviation-based approach*.

Exercises

7.1 Briefly outline how to compute the *dissimilarity* between objects described by the following types of variables:

(a) Numerical (interval-scaled) variables
(b) Asymmetric binary variables
(c) Categorical variables
(d) Ratio-scaled variables
(e) Nonmetric vector objects

7.2 Given the following measurements for the variable *age*:

18, 22, 25, 42, 28, 43, 33, 35, 56, 28,

standardize the variable by the following:

(a) Compute the mean absolute deviation of *age*.

(b) Compute the z-score for the first four measurements.

7.3 Given two objects represented by the tuples (22, 1, 42, 10) and (20, 0, 36, 8):

(a) Compute the *Euclidean distance* between the two objects.

(b) Compute the *Manhattan distance* between the two objects.

(c) Compute the *Minkowski distance* between the two objects, using $q = 3$.

7.4 Section 7.2.3 gave a method wherein a categorical variable having M states can be encoded by M *asymmetric binary variables*. Propose a more efficient encoding scheme and state why it is more efficient.

7.5 Briefly describe the following approaches to clustering: *partitioning* methods, *hierarchical* methods, *density-based* methods, *grid-based* methods, *model-based* methods, methods for *high-dimensional data*, and *constraint-based* methods. Give examples in each case.

7.6 Suppose that the data mining task is to cluster the following eight points (with (x, y) representing location) into three clusters:

$$A_1(2, 10), A_2(2, 5), A_3(8, 4), B_1(5, 8), B_2(7, 5), B_3(6, 4), C_1(1, 2), C_2(4, 9).$$

The distance function is Euclidean distance. Suppose initially we assign A_1, B_1, and C_1 as the center of each cluster, respectively. Use the *k-means* algorithm to show *only*

(a) The three cluster centers after the first round execution

(b) The final three clusters

7.7 Both *k-means* and *k-medoids* algorithms can perform effective clustering. Illustrate the strength and weakness of *k-means* in comparison with the *k-medoids* algorithm. Also, illustrate the strength and weakness of these schemes in comparison with a hierarchical clustering scheme (such as AGNES).

7.8 Use a diagram to illustrate how, for a constant *MinPts* value, *density-based clusters* with respect to a higher density (i.e., a lower value for ε, the neighborhood radius) are completely contained in density-connected sets obtained with respect to a lower density.

7.9 Why is it that *BIRCH* encounters difficulties in finding clusters of arbitrary shape but *OPTICS* does not? Can you propose some modifications to BIRCH to help it find clusters of arbitrary shape?

7.10 Present conditions under which *density-based* clustering is more suitable than partitioning-based clustering and hierarchical clustering. Given some application examples to support your argument.

7.11 Give an example of how specific clustering methods may be *integrated*, for example, where one clustering algorithm is used as a preprocessing step for another. In addition, provide reasoning on why the integration of two methods may sometimes lead to improved clustering quality and efficiency.

7.12 Clustering has been popularly recognized as an important data mining task with broad applications. Give one application example for each of the following cases:

(a) An application that takes clustering as a major *data mining function*

(b) An application that takes clustering as a *preprocessing tool* for data preparation for other data mining tasks

7.13 *Data cubes* and *multidimensional databases* contain categorical, ordinal, and numerical data in hierarchical or aggregate forms. Based on what you have learned about the clustering methods, design a clustering method that finds clusters in large data cubes effectively and efficiently.

7.14 *Subspace clustering* is a methodology for finding interesting clusters in high-dimensional space. This methodology can be applied to cluster any kind of data. Outline an efficient algorithm that may extend density connectivity-based clustering for finding clusters of arbitrary shapes in projected dimensions in a high-dimensional data set.

7.15 [*Contributed by Alex Kotov*] Describe each of the following clustering algorithms in terms of the following criteria: (i) shapes of clusters that can be determined; (ii) input parameters that must be specified; and (iii) limitations.

(a) *k*-means

(b) *k*-medoids

(c) CLARA

(d) BIRCH

(e) ROCK

(f) Chameleon

(g) DBSCAN

7.16 [*Contributed by Tao Cheng*] Many clustering algorithms handle either only numerical data, such as BIRCH, or only categorical data, such as ROCK, but not both. Analyze why this is the case. Note, however, that the EM clustering algorithm can easily be extended to handle data with both numerical and categorical attributes. Briefly explain why it can do so and how.

7.17 Human eyes are fast and effective at judging the quality of clustering methods for two-dimensional data. Can you design a *data visualization* method that may help humans visualize data clusters and judge the clustering quality for three-dimensional data? What about for even higher-dimensional data?

7.18 Suppose that you are to allocate a number of automatic teller machines (ATMs) in a given region so as to satisfy a number of constraints. Households or places of work may be clustered so that typically one ATM is assigned per cluster. The clustering, however, may be constrained by two factors: (1) obstacle objects (i.e., there are bridges, rivers, and highways that can affect ATM accessibility), and (2) additional user-specified constraints, such as each ATM should serve at least 10,000 households. How can a clustering algorithm such as *k*-means be modified for quality clustering under *both* constraints?

7.19 For *constraint-based clustering*, aside from having the minimum number of customers in each cluster (for ATM allocation) as a constraint, there could be many other kinds of constraints. For example, a constraint could be in the form of the maximum number of customers per cluster, average income of customers per cluster, maximum distance between every two clusters, and so on. Categorize the kinds of constraints that can be imposed on the clusters produced and discuss how to perform clustering efficiently under such kinds of constraints.

7.20 Design a *privacy-preserving clustering* method so that a data owner would be able to ask a third party to mine the data for quality clustering without worrying about the potential inappropriate disclosure of certain private or sensitive information stored in the data.

7.21 Why is outlier mining important? Briefly describe the different approaches behind *statistical-based outlier detection, distanced-based outlier detection, density-based local outlier detection*, and *deviation-based outlier detection.*

7.22 *Local outlier factor* (LOF) is an interesting notion for the discovery of local outliers in an environment where data objects are distributed rather unevenly. However, its performance should be further improved in order to efficiently discover local outliers. Can you propose an efficient method for effective discovery of local outliers in large data sets?

Bibliographic Notes

Clustering has been studied extensively for more then 40 years and across many disciplines due to its broad applications. Most books on pattern classification and machine learning contain chapters on cluster analysis or unsupervised learning. Several textbooks are dedicated to the methods of cluster analysis, including Hartigan [Har75], Jain and Dubes [JD88], Kaufman and Rousseeuw [KR90], and Arabie, Hubert, and De Sorte [AHS96]. There are also many survey articles on different aspects of clustering methods. Recent ones include Jain, Murty, and Flynn [JMF99] and Parsons, Haque, and Liu [PHL04].

Methods for combining variables of different types into a single dissimilarity matrix were introduced by Kaufman and Rousseeuw [KR90].

For partitioning methods, the *k*-means algorithm was first introduced by Lloyd [Llo57] and then MacQueen [Mac67]. The *k*-medoids algorithms of PAM and CLARA were proposed by Kaufman and Rousseeuw [KR90]. The *k*-modes (for clustering categorical data) and *k*-prototypes (for clustering hybrid data) algorithms were proposed by Huang [Hua98]. The *k*-modes clustering algorithm was also proposed independently by Chaturvedi, Green, and Carroll [CGC94, CGC01].

The CLARANS algorithm was proposed by Ng and Han [NH94]. Ester, Kriegel, and Xu [EKX95] proposed techniques for further improvement of the performance of CLARANS using efficient spatial access methods, such as R*-tree and focusing techniques. A *k*-means–based scalable clustering algorithm was proposed by Bradley, Fayyad, and Reina [BFR98].

An early survey of agglomerative hierarchical clustering algorithms was conducted by Day and Edelsbrunner [DE84]. Agglomerative hierarchical clustering, such as AGNES, and divisive hierarchical clustering, such as DIANA, were introduced by Kaufman and Rousseeuw [KR90]. An interesting direction for improving the clustering quality of hierarchical clustering methods is to integrate hierarchical clustering with distance-based iterative relocation or other nonhierarchical clustering methods. For example, BIRCH, by Zhang, Ramakrishnan, and Livny [ZRL96], first performs hierarchical clustering with a CF-tree before applying other techniques. Hierarchical clustering can also be performed by sophisticated linkage analysis, transformation, or nearest-neighbor analysis, such as CURE by Guha, Rastogi, and Shim [GRS98], ROCK (for clustering categorical attributes) by Guha, Rastogi, and Shim [GRS99b], and Chameleon by Karypis, Han, and Kumar [KHK99].

For density-based clustering methods, DBSCAN was proposed by Ester, Kriegel, Sander, and Xu [EKSX96]. Ankerst, Breunig, Kriegel, and Sander [ABKS99] developed OPTICS, a cluster-ordering method that facilitates density-based clustering without worrying about parameter specification. The DENCLUE algorithm, based on a set of density distribution functions, was proposed by Hinneburg and Keim [HK98].

A grid-based multiresolution approach called STING, which collects statistical information in grid cells, was proposed by Wang, Yang, and Muntz [WYM97]. WaveCluster, developed by Sheikholeslami, Chatterjee, and Zhang [SCZ98], is a multiresolution clustering approach that transforms the original feature space by wavelet transform.

For model-based clustering, the EM (Expectation-Maximization) algorithm was developed by Dempster, Laird, and Rubin [DLR77]. AutoClass is a Bayesian statistics-based method for model-based clustering by Cheeseman and Stutz [CS96a] that uses a variant of the EM algorithm. There are many other extensions and applications of EM, such as Lauritzen [Lau95]. For a set of seminal papers on conceptual clustering, see Shavlik and Dietterich [SD90]. Conceptual clustering was first introduced by Michalski and Stepp [MS83]. Other examples of the conceptual clustering approach include COBWEB by Fisher [Fis87], and CLASSIT by Gennari, Langley, and Fisher [GLF89]. Studies of the neural network approach [He99] include SOM (self-organizing feature maps) by Kohonen [Koh82], [Koh89], by Carpenter and Grossberg [Ce91], and by Kohonen, Kaski, Lagus, et al. [KKL+00], and competitive learning by Rumelhart and Zipser [RZ85].

Scalable methods for clustering categorical data were studied by Gibson, Kleinberg, and Raghavan [GKR98], Guha, Rastogi, and Shim [GRS99b], and Ganti, Gehrke, and Ramakrishnan [GGR99]. There are also many other clustering paradigms. For example, fuzzy clustering methods are discussed in Kaufman and Rousseeuw [KR90], Bezdek [Bez81], and Bezdek and Pal [BP92].

For high-dimensional clustering, an Apriori-based dimension-growth subspace clustering algorithm called CLIQUE was proposed by Agrawal, Gehrke, Gunopulos, and

Raghavan [AGGR98]. It integrates density-based and grid-based clustering methods. A sampling-based, dimension-reduction subspace clustering algorithm called PROCLUS, and its extension, ORCLUS, were proposed by Aggarwal et al. [APW+99] and by Aggarwal and Yu [AY00], respectively. An entropy-based subspace clustering algorithm for mining numerical data, called ENCLUS, was proposed by Cheng, Fu, and Zhang [CFZ99]. For a frequent pattern–based approach to handling high-dimensional data, Beil, Ester, and Xu [BEX02] proposed a method for frequent term–based text clustering. H. Wang, W. Wang, Yang, and Yu proposed pCluster, a pattern similarity–based clustering method [WWYY02].

Recent studies have proceeded to clustering stream data, as in Babcock, Babu, Datar, et al. [BBD+02]. A *k*-median-based data stream clustering algorithm was proposed by Guha, Mishra, Motwani, and O'Callaghan [GMMO00], and by O'Callaghan, Mishra, Meyerson, et al. [OMM+02]. A method for clustering evolving data streams was proposed by Aggarwal, Han, Wang, and Yu [AHWY03]. A framework for projected clustering of high-dimensional data streams was proposed by Aggarwal, Han, Wang, and Yu [AHWY04a].

A framework for constraint-based clustering based on user-specified constraints was built by Tung, Han, Lakshmanan, and Ng [THLN01]. An efficient method for constraint-based spatial clustering in the existence of physical obstacle constraints was proposed by Tung, Hou, and Han [THH01]. The quality of unsupervised clustering can be significantly improved using supervision in the form of pairwise constraints (i.e., pairs of instances labeled as belonging to the same or different clustering). Such a process is considered semi-supervised clustering. A probabilistic framework for semi-supervised clustering was proposed by Basu, Bilenko, and Mooney [BBM04]. The CLTree method, which transforms the clustering problem into a classification problem and then uses decision tree induction for cluster analysis, was proposed by Liu, Xia, and Yu [LXY01].

Outlier detection and analysis can be categorized into four approaches: the statistical approach, the distance-based approach, the density-based local outlier detection, and the deviation-based approach. The statistical approach and discordancy tests are described in Barnett and Lewis [BL94]. Distance-based outlier detection is described in Knorr and Ng [KN97, KN98]. The detection of density-based local outliers was proposed by Breunig, Kriegel, Ng, and Sander [BKNS00]. Outlier detection for high-dimensional data is studied by Aggarwal and Yu [AY01]. The sequential problem approach to deviation-based outlier detection was introduced in Arning, Agrawal, and Raghavan [AAR96]. Sarawagi, Agrawal, and Megiddo [SAM98] introduced a discovery-driven method for identifying exceptions in large multidimensional data using OLAP data cubes. Jagadish, Koudas, and Muthukrishnan [JKM99] introduced an efficient method for mining deviants in time-series databases.

8 Mining Stream, Time-Series, and Sequence Data

Our previous chapters introduced the basic concepts and techniques of data mining. The techniques studied, however, were for simple and structured data sets, such as data in relational databases, transactional databases, and data warehouses. The growth of data in various *complex forms* (e.g., semi-structured and unstructured, spatial and temporal, hypertext and multimedia) has been explosive owing to the rapid progress of data collection and advanced database system technologies, and the World Wide Web. Therefore, an increasingly important task in data mining is to mine complex types of data. Furthermore, many data mining applications need to mine patterns that are more sophisticated than those discussed earlier, including sequential patterns, subgraph patterns, and features in interconnected networks. We treat such tasks as advanced topics in data mining.

In the following chapters, we examine how to further develop the essential data mining techniques (such as characterization, association, classification, and clustering) and how to develop new ones to cope with complex types of data. We start off, in this chapter, by discussing the mining of stream, time-series, and sequence data. Chapter 9 focuses on the mining of graphs, social networks, and multirelational data. Chapter 10 examines mining object, spatial, multimedia, text, and Web data. Research into such mining is fast evolving. Our discussion provides a broad introduction. We expect that many new books dedicated to the mining of complex kinds of data will become available in the future.

As this chapter focuses on the mining of stream data, time-series data, and sequence data, let's look at each of these areas.

Imagine a satellite-mounted remote sensor that is constantly generating data. The data are massive (e.g., terabytes in volume), temporally ordered, fast changing, and potentially infinite. This is an example of *stream data*. Other examples include telecommunications data, transaction data from the retail industry, and data from electric power grids. Traditional OLAP and data mining methods typically require multiple scans of the data and are therefore infeasible for stream data applications. In Section 8.1, we study advanced mining methods for the analysis of such constantly flowing data.

A *time-series database* consists of sequences of values or events obtained over repeated measurements of time. Suppose that you are given time-series data relating to stock market prices. How can the data be analyzed to identify trends? Given such data for two different stocks, can we find any similarities between the two? These questions are explored in Section 8.2. Other applications involving time-series data include economic and sales forecasting, utility studies, and the observation of natural phenomena (such as atmosphere, temperature, and wind).

A *sequence database* consists of sequences of ordered elements or events, recorded with or without a concrete notion of time. *Sequential pattern mining* is the discovery of frequently occurring ordered events or subsequences as patterns. An example of a sequential pattern is "*Customers who buy a Canon digital camera are likely to buy an HP color printer within a month.*" Periodic patterns, which recur in regular periods or durations, are another kind of pattern related to sequences. Section 8.3 studies methods of sequential pattern mining.

Recent research in bioinformatics has resulted in the development of numerous methods for the analysis of biological sequences, such as DNA and protein sequences. Section 8.4 introduces several popular methods, including biological *sequence alignment algorithms* and the *hidden Markov model.*

8.1 Mining Data Streams

Tremendous and potentially infinite volumes of *data streams* are often generated by real-time surveillance systems, communication networks, Internet traffic, on-line transactions in the financial market or retail industry, electric power grids, industry production processes, scientific and engineering experiments, remote sensors, and other dynamic environments. Unlike traditional data sets, **stream data** flow in and out of a computer system *continuously* and with varying update rates. They are *temporally ordered, fast changing, massive, and potentially infinite*. It may be impossible to store an entire data stream or to scan through it multiple times due to its tremendous volume. Moreover, stream data tend to be of a rather low level of abstraction, whereas most analysts are interested in relatively high-level dynamic changes, such as trends and deviations. To discover knowledge or patterns from data streams, it is necessary to develop single-scan, on-line, multilevel, multidimensional stream processing and analysis methods.

Such single-scan, on-line data analysis methodology should not be confined to only stream data. It is also critically important for processing nonstream data that are massive. With data volumes mounting by terabytes or even petabytes, stream data nicely capture our data processing needs of today: even when the complete set of data is collected and can be stored in massive data storage devices, single scan (as in data stream systems) instead of random access (as in database systems) may still be the most realistic processing mode, because it is often too expensive to scan such a data set multiple times.

In this section, we introduce several on-line stream data analysis and mining methods. Section 8.1.1 introduces the basic methodologies for stream data processing and querying. Multidimensional analysis of stream data, encompassing stream data cubes and multiple granularities of time, is described in Section 8.1.2. Frequent-pattern mining and classification are presented in Sections 8.1.3 and 8.1.4, respectively. The clustering of dynamically evolving data streams is addressed in Section 8.1.5.

8.1.1 Methodologies for Stream Data Processing and Stream Data Systems

As seen from the previous discussion, it is impractical to scan through an entire data stream more than once. Sometimes we cannot even "look" at every element of a stream because the stream flows in so fast and changes so quickly. The gigantic size of such data sets also implies that we generally cannot store the entire stream data set in main memory or even on disk. The problem is not just that there is a lot of data, it is that the universes that we are keeping track of are relatively large, where a *universe* is the domain of possible values for an attribute. For example, if we were tracking the ages of millions of people, our universe would be relatively small, perhaps between zero and one hundred and twenty. We could easily maintain exact summaries of such data. In contrast, the universe corresponding to the set of all pairs of IP addresses on the Internet is very large, which makes exact storage intractable. A reasonable way of thinking about data streams is to actually think of a physical stream of water. Heraclitus once said that you can never step in the same stream twice,[1] and so it is with stream data.

For effective processing of stream data, new data structures, techniques, and algorithms are needed. Because we do not have an infinite amount of space to store stream data, we often trade off between accuracy and storage. That is, we generally are willing to settle for approximate rather than exact answers. **Synopses** allow for this by providing *summaries* of the data, which typically can be used to return approximate answers to queries. Synopses use *synopsis data structures*, which are any data structures that are substantially *smaller* than their base data set (in this case, the stream data). From the algorithmic point of view, we want our algorithms to be efficient in both space and time. Instead of storing all or most elements seen so far, using $O(N)$ space, we often want to use polylogarithmic space, $O(\log^k N)$, where N is the number of elements in the stream data. We may relax the requirement that our answers are exact, and ask for approximate answers within a small error range with high probability. That is, many data stream–based algorithms compute an approximate answer within a factor ε of the actual answer, with high probability. Generally, as the approximation factor $(1+\varepsilon)$ goes down, the space requirements go up. In this section, we examine some common synopsis data structures and techniques.

Random Sampling

Rather than deal with an entire data stream, we can think of *sampling* the stream at periodic intervals. *"To obtain an unbiased sampling of the data, we need to know the length of the stream in advance. But what can we do if we do not know this length in advance?"* In this case, we need to modify our approach.

[1] Plato citing Heraclitus: "Heraclitus somewhere says that all things are in process and nothing stays still, and likening existing things to the stream of a river he says you would not step twice into the same river."

A technique called **reservoir sampling** can be used to select an unbiased random sample of s elements without replacement. The idea behind reservoir sampling is relatively simple. We maintain a sample of size at least s, called the "reservoir," from which a random sample of size s can be generated. However, generating this sample from the reservoir can be costly, especially when the reservoir is large. To avoid this step, we maintain a set of s *candidates* in the reservoir, which form a true random sample of the elements seen so far in the stream. As the data stream flows, every new element has a certain probability of replacing an old element in the reservoir. Let's say we have seen N elements thus far in the stream. The probability that a new element replaces an old one, chosen at random, is then s/N. This maintains the invariant that the set of s candidates in our reservoir forms a random sample of the elements seen so far.

Sliding Windows

Instead of sampling the data stream randomly, we can use the **sliding window model** to analyze stream data. The basic idea is that rather than running computations on all of the data seen so far, or on some sample, we can make decisions based only on *recent data*. More formally, at every time t, a new data element arrives. This element "expires" at time $t+w$, where w is the window "size" or length. The sliding window model is useful for stocks or sensor networks, where only recent events may be important. It also reduces memory requirements because only a small window of data is stored.

Histograms

The histogram is a synopsis data structure that can be used to approximate the frequency distribution of element values in a data stream. A **histogram** partitions the data into a set of contiguous *buckets*. Depending on the partitioning rule used, the *width* (bucket value range) and *depth* (number of elements per bucket) can vary. The equal-width partitioning rule is a simple way to construct histograms, where the range of each bucket is the same. Although easy to implement, this may not sample the probability distribution function well. A better approach is to use V-Optimal histograms (see Section 2.5.4). Similar to clustering, V-Optimal histograms define bucket sizes that minimize the frequency variance within each bucket, which better captures the distribution of the data. These histograms can then be used to approximate query answers rather than using sampling techniques.

Multiresolution Methods

A common way to deal with a large amount of data is through the use of *data reduction methods* (see Section 2.5). A popular data reduction method is the use of divide-and-conquer strategies such as multiresolution data structures. These allow a program to trade off between accuracy and storage, but also offer the ability to understand a data stream at multiple levels of detail.

A concrete example is a *balanced binary tree*, where we try to maintain this balance as new data come in. Each level of the tree provides a different resolution. The farther away we are from the tree root, the more detailed is the level of resolution.

A more sophisticated way to form multiple resolutions is to use a clustering method to organize stream data into a hierarchical structure of trees. For example, we can use a typical hierarchical clustering data structure like CF-tree in BIRCH (see Section 7.5.2) to form a hierarchy of *microclusters*. With dynamic stream data flowing in and out, summary statistics of data streams can be incrementally updated over time in the hierarchy of microclusters. Information in such microclusters can be aggregated into larger *macroclusters* depending on the application requirements to derive general data statistics at multiresolution.

Wavelets (Section 2.5.3), a technique from signal processing, can be used to build a multiresolution hierarchy structure over an input signal, in this case, the stream data. Given an input signal, we would like to break it down or rewrite it in terms of simple, orthogonal basis functions. The simplest basis is the Haar wavelet. Using this basis corresponds to recursively performing averaging and differencing at multiple levels of resolution. Haar wavelets are easy to understand and implement. They are especially good at dealing with spatial and multimedia data. Wavelets have been used as approximations to histograms for query optimization. Moreover, wavelet-based histograms can be dynamically maintained over time. Thus, wavelets are a popular multiresolution method for data stream compression.

Sketches

Synopses techniques mainly differ by how exactly they trade off accuracy for storage. Sampling techniques and sliding window models focus on a small part of the data, whereas other synopses try to summarize the entire data, often at multiple levels of detail. Some techniques require multiple passes over the data, such as histograms and wavelets, whereas other methods, such as *sketches*, can operate in a single pass.

Suppose that, ideally, we would like to maintain the full histogram over the universe of objects or elements in a data stream, where the universe is $U = \{1, 2, \ldots, v\}$ and the stream is $A = \{a_1, a_2, \ldots, a_N\}$. That is, for each value i in the universe, we want to maintain the frequency or number of occurrences of i in the sequence A. If the universe is large, this structure can be quite large as well. Thus, we need a smaller representation instead.

Let's consider the **frequency moments** of A. These are the numbers, F_k, defined as

$$F_k = \sum_{i=1}^{v} m_i^k, \tag{8.1}$$

where v is the universe or domain size (as above), m_i is the frequency of i in the sequence, and $k \geq 0$. In particular, F_0 is the number of distinct elements in the sequence. F_1 is the length of the sequence (that is, N, here). F_2 is known as the *self-join size*, the repeat rate, or as Gini's index of homogeneity. The frequency moments of a data set provide useful information about the data for database applications, such as query answering. In addition, they indicate the degree of *skew* or asymmetry in the data (Section 2.2.1), which is useful in parallel database applications for determining an appropriate partitioning algorithm for the data.

When the amount of memory available is smaller than v, we need to employ a synopsis. The estimation of the frequency moments can be done by synopses that are known as **sketches.** These build a small-space summary for a distribution vector (e.g., histogram) using randomized linear projections of the underlying data vectors. Sketches provide probabilistic guarantees on the quality of the approximate answer (e.g., the answer to the given query is 12 ± 1 with a probability of 0.90). Given N elements and a universe U of v values, such sketches can approximate F_0, F_1, and F_2 in $O(\log v + \log N)$ space. The basic idea is to hash every element uniformly at random to either $z_i \in \{-1, +1\}$, and then maintain a random variable, $X = \sum_i m_i z_i$. It can be shown that X^2 is a good estimate for F_2. To explain why this works, we can think of hashing elements to -1 or $+1$ as assigning each element value to an arbitrary side of a tug of war. When we sum up to get X, we can think of measuring the displacement of the rope from the center point. By squaring X, we square this displacement, capturing the data skew, F_2.

To get an even better estimate, we can maintain multiple random variables, X_i. Then by choosing the median value of the square of these variables, we can increase our confidence that the estimated value is close to F_2.

From a database perspective, **sketch partitioning** was developed to improve the performance of sketching on data stream query optimization. Sketch partitioning uses coarse statistical information on the base data to *intelligently* partition the domain of the underlying attributes in a way that provably tightens the error guarantees.

Randomized Algorithms

Randomized algorithms, in the form of random sampling and sketching, are often used to deal with massive, high-dimensional data streams. The use of randomization often leads to simpler and more efficient algorithms in comparison to known deterministic algorithms.

If a randomized algorithm always returns the right answer but the running times vary, it is known as a **Las Vegas** algorithm. In contrast, a **Monte Carlo** algorithm has bounds on the running time but may not return the correct result. We mainly consider Monte Carlo algorithms. One way to think of a randomized algorithm is simply as a probability distribution over a set of deterministic algorithms.

Given that a randomized algorithm returns a random variable as a result, we would like to have bounds on the tail probability of that random variable. This tells us that the probability that a random variable deviates from its expected value is small. One basic tool is **Chebyshev's Inequality**. Let X be a random variable with mean μ and standard deviation σ (variance σ^2). Chebyshev's inequality says that

$$P(|X - \mu| > k) \le \frac{\sigma^2}{k^2} \tag{8.2}$$

for any given positive real number, k. This inequality can be used to bound the variance of a random variable.

In many cases, multiple random variables can be used to boost the confidence in our results. As long as these random variables are fully independent, **Chernoff bounds** can be used. Let $X_1, X_2, \ldots, X_n$ be independent Poisson trials. In a Poisson trial, the probability of success varies from trial to trial. If X is the sum of X_1 to X_n, then a weaker version of the Chernoff bound tells us that

$$\Pr[X < (1+\delta)\mu] < e^{-\mu\delta^2/4} \tag{8.3}$$

where $\delta \in (0, 1]$. This shows that the probability decreases exponentially as we move from the mean, which makes poor estimates much more unlikely.

Data Stream Management Systems and Stream Queries

In traditional database systems, data are stored in finite and persistent databases. However, stream data are infinite and impossible to store fully in a database. In a **Data Stream Management System (DSMS)**, there may be multiple data streams. They arrive on-line and are continuous, temporally ordered, and potentially infinite. Once an element from a data stream has been processed, it is discarded or archived, and it cannot be easily retrieved unless it is explicitly stored in memory.

A stream data query processing architecture includes three parts: *end user, query processor*, and *scratch space* (which may consist of main memory and disks). An end user issues a query to the DSMS, and the query processor takes the query, processes it using the information stored in the scratch space, and returns the results to the user.

Queries can be either *one-time queries* or *continuous queries*. A **one-time query** is evaluated once over a point-in-time snapshot of the data set, with the answer returned to the user. A **continuous query** is evaluated continuously as data streams continue to arrive. The answer to a continuous query is produced over time, always reflecting the stream data seen so far. A continuous query can act as a watchdog, as in "*sound the alarm if the power consumption for Block 25 exceeds a certain threshold.*" Moreover, a query can be **predefined** (i.e., supplied to the data stream management system before any relevant data have arrived) or **ad hoc** (i.e., issued on-line after the data streams have already begun). A predefined query is generally a continuous query, whereas an ad hoc query can be either one-time or continuous.

Stream Query Processing

The special properties of stream data introduce new challenges in query processing. In particular, data streams may grow unboundedly, and it is possible that queries may require unbounded memory to produce an exact answer. How can we distinguish between queries that can be answered exactly using a given bounded amount of memory and queries that must be approximated? Actually, without knowing the size of the input data streams, it is impossible to place a limit on the memory requirements for most common queries, such as those involving joins, unless the domains of the attributes involved in the query are restricted. This is because without domain restrictions, an unbounded number of attribute values must be remembered because they might turn out to join with tuples that arrive in the future.

Providing an exact answer to a query may require unbounded main memory; therefore a more realistic solution is to provide an approximate answer to the query. *Approximate query answering* relaxes the memory requirements and also helps in handling system load, because streams can come in too fast to process exactly. In addition, ad hoc queries need approximate history to return an answer. We have already discussed common synopses that are useful for approximate query answering, such as random sampling, sliding windows, histograms, and sketches.

As this chapter focuses on stream data mining, we will not go into any further details of stream query processing methods. For additional discussion, interested readers may consult the literature recommended in the bibliographic notes of this chapter.

8.1.2 Stream OLAP and Stream Data Cubes

Stream data are generated continuously in a dynamic environment, with huge volume, infinite flow, and fast-changing behavior. It is impossible to store such data streams completely in a data warehouse. Most stream data represent low-level information, consisting of various kinds of detailed temporal and other features. To find interesting or unusual patterns, it is essential to perform *multidimensional analysis* on aggregate measures (such as sum and average). This would facilitate the discovery of critical changes in the data at higher levels of abstraction, from which users can drill down to examine more detailed levels, when needed. Thus multidimensional OLAP analysis is still needed in stream data analysis, but how can we implement it?

Consider the following motivating example.

Example 8.1 **Multidimensional analysis for power supply stream data.** A power supply station generates infinite streams of power usage data. Suppose *individual_user, street_address*, and *second* are the attributes at the lowest level of granularity. Given a large number of users, it is only realistic to analyze the fluctuation of power usage at certain high levels, such as by city or street district and by quarter (of an hour), making timely power supply adjustments and handling unusual situations.

Conceptually, for multidimensional analysis, we can view such stream data as a *virtual* data cube, consisting of one or a few measures and a set of dimensions, including one *time* dimension, and a few other dimensions, such as *location*, *user-category*, and so on. However, in practice, it is impossible to materialize such a data cube, because the materialization requires a huge amount of data to be computed and stored. Some efficient methods must be developed for systematic analysis of such data. ■

Data warehouse and OLAP technology is based on the integration and consolidation of data in multidimensional space to facilitate powerful and fast on-line data analysis. A fundamental difference in the analysis of stream data from that of relational and warehouse data is that the stream data are generated in huge volume, flowing in and out dynamically and changing rapidly. Due to limited memory, disk space, and processing power, it is impossible to register completely the detailed level of data and compute a fully materialized cube. A realistic design is to explore several data compression techniques, including (1) *tilted time frame* on the time dimension, (2) storing data only at some *critical layers*, and (3) exploring efficient computation of a *very partially materialized data cube*. The (partial) stream data cubes so constructed are much smaller than those constructed from the raw stream data but will still be effective for multidimensional stream data analysis. We examine such a design in more detail.

Time Dimension with Compressed Time Scale: Tilted Time Frame

In stream data analysis, people are usually interested in recent changes at a fine scale but in long-term changes at a coarse scale. Naturally, we can register time at different levels of granularity. The most recent time is registered at the finest granularity; the more distant time is registered at a coarser granularity; and the level of coarseness depends on the application requirements and on how old the time point is (from the current time). Such a time dimension model is called a **tilted time frame.** This model is sufficient for many analysis tasks and also ensures that the total amount of data to retain in memory or to be stored on disk is small.

There are many possible ways to design a titled time frame. Here we introduce three models, as illustrated in Figure 8.1: (1) *natural tilted time frame model*, (2) *logarithmic tilted time frame model*, and (3) *progressive logarithmic tilted time frame model*.

A **natural tilted time frame model** is shown in Figure 8.1(a), where the time frame (or window) is structured in multiple granularities based on the "natural" or usual time scale: the most recent 4 quarters (15 minutes), followed by the last 24 hours, then 31 days, and then 12 months (the actual scale used is determined by the application). Based on this model, we can compute frequent itemsets in the last hour with the precision of a quarter of an hour, or in the last day with the precision of an hour, and

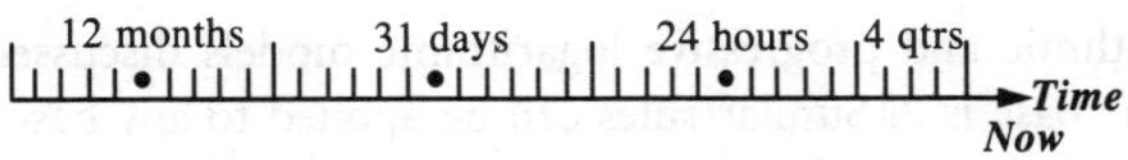

(a) A natural tilted time frame model.

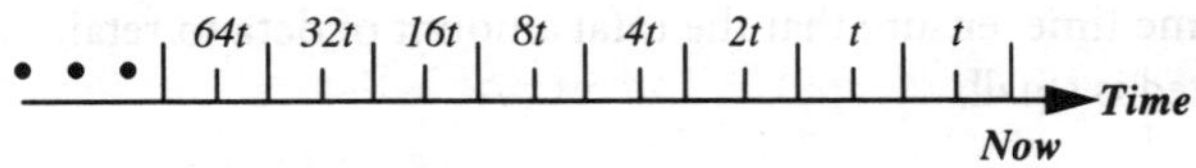

(b) A logarithmic tilted time frame model.

Frame no.	Snapshots (by clock time)
0	69 67 65
1	66 62 58
2	68 60 52
3	56 40 24
4	48 16
5	64 32

(c) A progressive logarithmic tilted time frame table.

Figure 8.1 Three models for tilted time frames.

so on until the whole year with the precision of a month.[2] This model registers only $4+24+31+12=71$ units of time for a year instead of $365 \times 24 \times 4 = 35{,}040$ units, with an acceptable trade-off of the grain of granularity at a distant time.

The second model is the **logarithmic tilted time frame model**, as shown in Figure 8.1(b), where the time frame is structured in multiple granularities according to a logarithmic scale. Suppose that the most recent slot holds the transactions of the current quarter. The remaining slots are for the last quarter, the next two quarters (ago), 4 quarters, 8 quarters, 16 quarters, and so on, growing at an exponential rate. According to this model, with one year of data and the finest precision at a quarter, we would need $\log_2(365 \times 24 \times 4)+1 = 16.1$ units of time instead of $365 \times 24 \times 4 = 35{,}040$ units. That is, we would just need 17 time frames to store the compressed information.

The third method is the **progressive logarithmic tilted time frame model**, where snapshots are stored at differing levels of granularity depending on the recency. Let T be the clock time elapsed since the beginning of the stream. Snapshots are classified into different *frame numbers*, which can vary from 0 to *max_frame*, where $\log_2(T) - max\_capacity \leq max\_frame \leq \log_2(T)$, and *max_capacity* is the maximal number of snapshots held in each frame.

Each snapshot is represented by its timestamp. The rules for insertion of a snapshot t (at time t) into the snapshot frame table are defined as follows: (1) if $(t \bmod 2^i) = 0$ but $(t \bmod 2^{i+1}) \neq 0$, t is inserted into *frame_number* i if $i \leq max\_frame$; otherwise (i.e., $i > max\_frame$), t is inserted into *max_frame*; and (2) each slot has a *max_capacity*. At the insertion of t into *frame_number* i, if the slot already reaches its *max_capacity*, the oldest snapshot in this frame is removed and the new snapshot inserted.

Example 8.2 Progressive logarithmic tilted time frame. Consider the snapshot frame table of Figure 8.1(c), where *max_frame* is 5 and *max_capacity* is 3. Let's look at how timestamp 64 was inserted into the table. We know $(64 \bmod 2^6) = 0$ but $(64 \bmod 2^7) \neq 0$, that is, $i = 6$. However, since this value of i exceeds *max_frame*, 64 was inserted into frame 5 instead of frame 6. Suppose we now need to insert a timestamp of 70. At time 70, since $(70 \bmod 2^1) = 0$ but $(70 \bmod 2^2) \neq 0$, we would insert 70 into *frame_number* 1. This would knock out the oldest snapshot of 58, given the slot capacity of 3. From the table, we see that the closer a timestamp is to the current time, the denser are the snapshots stored. ■

In the logarithmic and progressive logarithmic models discussed above, we have assumed that the base is 2. Similar rules can be applied to any base α, where α is an integer and $\alpha > 1$. All three tilted time frame models provide a natural way for incremental insertion of data and for gradually fading out older values.

The tilted time frame models shown are sufficient for typical time-related queries, and at the same time, ensure that the total amount of data to retain in memory and/or to be computed is small.

[2] We align the time axis with the natural calendar time. Thus, for each granularity level of the tilted time frame, there might be a partial interval, which is less than a full unit at that level.

Depending on the given application, we can provide different fading factors in the titled time frames, such as by placing more weight on the more recent time frames. We can also have flexible alternative ways to design the tilted time frames. For example, suppose that we are interested in comparing the stock average from each day of the current week with the corresponding averages from the same weekdays last week, last month, or last year. In this case, we can single out Monday to Friday instead of compressing them into the whole week as one unit.

Critical Layers

Even with the *tilted time frame* model, it can still be too costly to dynamically compute and store a materialized cube. Such a cube may have quite a few dimensions, each containing multiple levels with many distinct values. Because stream data analysis has only limited memory space but requires fast response time, we need additional strategies that work in conjunction with the tilted time frame model. One approach is to compute and store only some mission-critical cuboids of the full data cube.

In many applications, it is beneficial to dynamically and incrementally compute and store two critical cuboids (or **layers**), which are determined based on their conceptual and computational importance in stream data analysis. The first layer, called the **minimal interest layer**, is the minimally interesting layer that an analyst would like to study. It is necessary to have such a layer because it is often neither cost effective nor interesting in practice to examine the minute details of stream data. The second layer, called the **observation layer**, is the layer at which an analyst (or an automated system) would like to continuously study the data. This can involve making decisions regarding the signaling of exceptions, or drilling down along certain paths to lower layers to find cells indicating data exceptions.

Example 8.3 **Critical layers for a power supply stream data cube.** Let's refer back to Example 8.1 regarding the multidimensional analysis of stream data for a power supply station. Dimensions at the lowest level of granularity (i.e., the raw data layer) included *individual_user, street_address*, and *second*. At the minimal interest layer, these three dimensions are *user_group, street_block*, and *minute*, respectively. Those at the observation layer are $*$ (meaning **all** *user*), *city*, and *quarter*, respectively, as shown in Figure 8.2.

Based on this design, we would not need to compute any cuboids that are lower than the minimal interest layer because they would be beyond user interest. Thus, to compute our base cuboid, representing the cells of minimal interest, we need to compute and store the (three-dimensional) aggregate cells for the (*user_group, street_block, minute*) group-by. This can be done by aggregations on the dimensions *user* and *address* by rolling up from *individual_user* to *user_group* and from *street_address* to *street_block*, respectively, and by rolling up on the *time* dimension from *second* to *minute*.

Similarly, the cuboids at the observation layer should be computed dynamically, taking the tilted time frame model into account as well. This is the layer that an analyst takes as an observation deck, watching the current stream data by examining the slope of changes at this layer to make decisions. This layer can be obtained by rolling up the

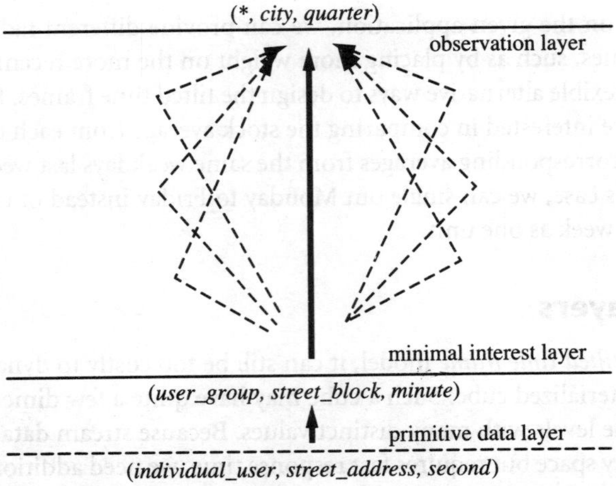

Figure 8.2 Two critical layers in a "power supply station" stream data cube.

cube along the *user* dimension to $*$ (for all *user*), along the *address* dimension to *city*, and along the *time* dimension to *quarter*. If something unusual is observed, the analyst can investigate by drilling down to lower levels to find data exceptions. ■

Partial Materialization of a Stream Cube

"What if a user needs a layer that would be between the two critical layers?" Materializing a cube at only two critical layers leaves much room for how to compute the cuboids in between. These cuboids can be precomputed fully, partially, or not at all (i.e., leave everything to be computed on the fly). An interesting method is **popular path cubing**, which rolls up the cuboids from the minimal interest layer to the observation layer by following one popular drilling path, materializes only the layers along the path, and leaves other layers to be computed only when needed. This method achieves a reasonable trade-off between space, computation time, and flexibility, and has quick incremental aggregation time, quick drilling time, and small space requirements.

To facilitate efficient computation and storage of the popular path of the stream cube, a compact data structure needs to be introduced so that the space taken in the computation of aggregations is minimized. A hyperlinked tree structure called *H-tree* is revised and adopted here to ensure that a compact structure is maintained in memory for efficient computation of multidimensional and multilevel aggregations.

Each branch of the H-tree is organized in the same order as the specified popular path. The aggregate cells are stored in the nonleaf nodes of the H-tree, forming the computed cuboids along the popular path. Aggregation for each corresponding slot in the tilted time frame is performed from the minimal interest layer all the way up to the observation layer by aggregating along the popular path. The step-by-step aggregation is performed while inserting the new generalized tuples into the corresponding time slots.

The H-tree ordering is based on the popular drilling path given by users or experts. This ordering facilitates the computation and storage of the cuboids along the path. The aggregations along the drilling path from the minimal interest layer to the observation layer are performed during the generalizing of the stream data to the minimal interest layer, which takes only one scan of stream data. Because all the cells to be computed are the cuboids along the popular path, and the cuboids to be computed are the nonleaf nodes associated with the H-tree, both space and computation overheads are minimized.

Although it is impossible to materialize all the cells of a stream cube, the stream data cube so designed facilitates fast on-line drilling along any single dimension or along combinations of a small number of dimensions. The H-tree-based architecture facilitates incremental updating of stream cubes as well.

8.1.3 Frequent-Pattern Mining in Data Streams

As discussed in Chapter 5, frequent-pattern mining finds a set of patterns that occur frequently in a data set, where a pattern can be a set of items (called an *itemset*), a subsequence, or a substructure. A pattern is considered frequent if its count satisfies a *minimum support*. Scalable methods for mining frequent patterns have been extensively studied for static data sets. However, mining such patterns in dynamic data streams poses substantial new challenges. Many existing frequent-pattern mining algorithms require the system to scan the whole data set more than once, but this is unrealistic for infinite data streams. How can we perform incremental updates of frequent itemsets for stream data since an infrequent itemset can become frequent later on, and hence cannot be ignored? Moreover, a frequent itemset can become infrequent as well. The number of infrequent itemsets is exponential and so it is impossible to keep track of all of them.

To overcome this difficulty, there are two possible approaches. One is to keep track of only a predefined, limited set of items and itemsets. This method has very limited usage and expressive power because it requires the system to confine the scope of examination to only the set of predefined itemsets beforehand. The second approach is to derive an *approximate* set of answers. In practice, approximate answers are often sufficient. A number of approximate item or itemset counting algorithms have been developed in recent research. Here we introduce one such algorithm: the Lossy Counting algorithm. It approximates the frequency of items or itemsets within a user-specified error bound, ε. This concept is illustrated as follows.

Example 8.4 **Approximate frequent items.** A router is interested in all items whose frequency is at least 1% (*min_support*) of the entire traffic stream seen so far. It is felt that 1/10 of *min_support* (i.e., $\varepsilon = 0.1\%$) is an acceptable margin of error. This means that all frequent items with a support of at least *min_support* will be output, but that some items with a support of at least (*min_support* $- \varepsilon$) will also be output. ∎

Lossy Counting Algorithm

We first introduce the Lossy Counting algorithm for frequent items. This algorithm is fairly simple but quite efficient. We then look at how the method can be extended to find approximate frequent itemsets.

"How does the Lossy Counting algorithm find frequent items?" A user first provides two input parameters: (1) the *min_support* threshold, σ, and (2) the error bound mentioned previously, denoted as ε. The incoming stream is conceptually divided into buckets of width $w = \lceil 1/\varepsilon \rceil$. Let N be the current *stream length*, that is, the number of items seen so far. The algorithm uses a frequency-list data structure for all items with frequency greater than 0. For each item, the list maintains f, the approximate frequency count, and Δ, the maximum possible error of f.

The algorithm processes buckets of items as follows. When a new bucket comes in, the items in the bucket are added to the frequency list. If a given item already exists in the list, we simply increase its frequency count, f. Otherwise, we insert it into the list with a frequency count of 1. If the new item is from the bth bucket, we set Δ, the maximum possible error on the frequency count of the item, to be $b-1$. Based on our discussion so far, the item frequency counts hold the actual frequencies rather than approximations. They become approximates, however, because of the next step. Whenever a bucket "boundary" is reached (that is, N has reached a multiple of width w, such as w, $2w$, $3w$, etc.), the frequency list is examined. Let b be the current bucket number. An item entry is deleted if, for that entry, $f + \Delta \leq b$. In this way, the algorithm aims to keep the frequency list small so that it may fit in main memory. The frequency count stored for each item will either be the true frequency of the item or an *underestimate* of it.

"By how much can a frequency count be underestimated?" One of the most important factors in approximation algorithms is the approximation ratio (or error bound). Let's look at the case where an item is deleted. This occurs when $f + \Delta \leq b$ for an item, where b is the current bucket number. We know that $b \leq N/w$, that is, $b \leq \varepsilon N$. The actual frequency of an item is at most $f + \Delta$. Thus, the most that an item can be underestimated is εN. If the actual support of this item is σ (this is the minimum support or lower bound for it to be considered frequent), then the actual frequency is σN, and the frequency, f, on the frequency list should be at least $(\sigma N - \varepsilon N)$. Thus, if we output all of the items in the frequency list having an f value of at least $(\sigma N - \varepsilon N)$, then all of the frequent items will be output. In addition, some subfrequent items (with an actual frequency of at least $\sigma N - \varepsilon N$ but less than σN) will be output, too.

The Lossy Counting algorithm has three nice properties: (1) there are no false negatives, that is, there is no true frequent item that is not output; (2) false positives are quite "positive" as well, since the output items will have a frequency of at least $\sigma N - \varepsilon N$; and (3) the frequency of a frequent item can be underestimated by at most εN. For frequent items, this underestimation is only a small fraction of its true frequency, so this approximation is acceptable.

"How much space is needed to save the frequency list?" It has been shown that the algorithm takes at most $\frac{1}{\varepsilon}\log(\varepsilon N)$ entries in computation, where N is the stream length so far. If we assume that elements with very low frequency tend to occur

more or less uniformly at random, then it has been shown that Lossy Counting requires no more than $\frac{7}{\varepsilon}$ space. Thus, the space requirement for this algorithm is reasonable.

It is much more difficult to find frequent itemsets than to find frequent items in data streams, because the number of possible itemsets grows exponentially with that of different items. As a consequence, there will be many more frequent itemsets. If we still process the data bucket by bucket, we will probably run out of memory. An alternative is to process as many buckets as we can at a time.

To find frequent itemsets, transactions are still divided by buckets with bucket size, $w = \lceil 1/\varepsilon \rceil$. However, this time, we will read as many buckets as possible into main memory. As before, we maintain a frequency list, although now it pertains to itemsets rather than items. Suppose we can read β buckets into main memory. After that, we update the frequency list by all these buckets as follows. If a given itemset already exists in the frequency list, we update f by counting the occurrences of the itemset among the current batch of β buckets. If the updated entry satisfies $f + \Delta \leq b$, where b is the current bucket number, we delete the entry. If an itemset has frequency $f \geq \beta$ and does not appear in the list, it is inserted as a new entry where Δ is set to $b - \beta$ as the maximum error of f.

In practice, β will be large, such as greater than 30. This approach will save memory because all itemsets with frequency less than β will not be recorded in the frequency list anymore. For smaller values of β (such as 1 for the frequent item version of the algorithm described earlier), more spurious subsets will find their way into the frequency list. This would drastically increase the average size and refresh rate of the frequency list and harm the algorithm's efficiency in both time and space.

In general, Lossy Counting is a simple but effective algorithm for finding frequent items and itemsets approximately. Its limitations lie in three aspects: (1) the space bound is insufficient because the frequency list may grow infinitely as the stream goes on; (2) for frequent itemsets, the algorithm scans each transaction many times and the size of main memory will greatly impact the efficiency of the algorithm; and (3) the output is based on all of the previous data, although users can be more interested in recent data than that in the remote past. A tilted time frame model with different time granularities can be integrated with Lossy Counting in order to emphasize the recency of the data.

8.1.4 Classification of Dynamic Data Streams

In Chapter 6, we studied several methods for the classification of static data. Classification is a two-step process consisting of *learning*, or *model construction* (where a model is constructed based on class-labeled tuples from a training data set), and *classification*, or *model usage* (where the model is used to predict the class labels of tuples from new data sets). The latter lends itself to stream data, as new examples are immediately classified by the model as they arrive.

"So, does this mean we can apply traditional classification methods to stream data as well?" In a traditional setting, the training data reside in a relatively static database. Many

classification methods will scan the training data multiple times. Therefore, the first step of model construction is typically performed off-line as a batch process. With data streams, however, there is typically no off-line phase. The data flow in so quickly that storage and multiple scans are infeasible.

To further illustrate how traditional classification methods are inappropriate for stream data, consider the practice of constructing decision trees as models. Most decision tree algorithms tend to follow the same basic top-down, recursive strategy, yet differ in the statistical measure used to choose an optimal splitting attribute. To review, a decision tree consists of internal (nonleaf) nodes, branches, and leaf nodes. An attribute selection measure is used to select the *splitting attribute* for the current node. This is taken to be the attribute that best discriminates the training tuples according to class. In general, branches are grown for each possible value of the splitting attribute, the training tuples are partitioned accordingly, and the process is recursively repeated at each branch. However, in the stream environment, it is neither possible to collect the complete set of data nor realistic to rescan the data, thus such a method has to be re-examined.

Another distinguishing characteristic of data streams is that they are time-varying, as opposed to traditional database systems, where only the current state is stored. This change in the nature of the data takes the form of changes in the target classification model over time and is referred to as **concept drift**. Concept drift is an important consideration when dealing with stream data.

Several methods have been proposed for the classification of stream data. We introduce four of them in this subsection. The first three, namely the *Hoeffding tree algorithm*, *Very Fast Decision Tree (VFDT)*, and *Concept-adapting Very Fast Decision Tree (CVFDT)*, extend traditional decision tree induction. The fourth uses a *classifier ensemble* approach, in which multiple classifiers are considered using a voting method.

Hoeffding Tree Algorithm

The **Hoeffding tree algorithm** is a decision tree learning method for stream data classification. It was initially used to track Web clickstreams and construct models to predict which Web hosts and Web sites a user is likely to access. It typically runs in sublinear time and produces a nearly identical decision tree to that of traditional batch learners. It uses *Hoeffding trees*, which exploit the idea that a small sample can often be enough to choose an optimal splitting attribute. This idea is supported mathematically by the *Hoeffding bound* (or *additive Chernoff bound*). Suppose we make N independent observations of a random variable r with range R, where r is an attribute selection measure. (For a probability, R is one, and for an information gain, it is $\log c$, where c is the number of classes.) In the case of Hoeffding trees, r is information gain. If we compute the mean, $\bar{r}$, of this sample, the **Hoeffding bound** states that the true mean of r is at least $\bar{r} - \varepsilon$, with probability $1 - \delta$, where δ is user-specified and

$$\varepsilon = \sqrt{\frac{R^2 ln(1/\delta)}{2N}}. \tag{8.4}$$

The Hoeffding tree algorithm uses the Hoeffding bound to determine, with high probability, the smallest number, N, of examples needed at a node when selecting a splitting attribute. This attribute would be the same as that chosen using infinite examples! We'll see how this is done shortly. The Hoeffding bound is independent of the probability distribution, unlike most other bound equations. This is desirable, as it may be impossible to know the probability distribution of the information gain, or whichever attribute selection measure is used.

"How does the Hoeffding tree algorithm use the Hoeffding bound?" The algorithm takes as input a sequence of training examples, S, described by attributes A, and the accuracy parameter, δ. In addition, the evaluation function $G(A_i)$ is supplied, which could be information gain, gain ratio, Gini index, or some other attribute selection measure. At each node in the decision tree, we need to maximize $G(A_i)$ for one of the remaining attributes, A_i. Our goal is to find the smallest number of tuples, N, for which the Hoeffding bound is satisfied. For a given node, let A_a be the attribute that achieves the highest G, and A_b be the attribute that achieves the second highest G. If $G(A_a) - G(A_b) > \varepsilon$, where ε is calculated from Equation (8.4), we can confidently say that this difference is larger than zero. We select A_a as the best splitting attribute with confidence $1 - \delta$.

The only statistics that must be maintained in the Hoeffding tree algorithm are the counts n_{ijk} for the value v_j of attribute A_i with class label y_k. Therefore, if d is the number of attributes, v is the maximum number of values for any attribute, c is the number of classes, and l is the maximum depth (or number of levels) of the tree, then the total memory required is $O(ldvc)$. This memory requirement is very modest compared to other decision tree algorithms, which usually store the entire training set in memory.

"How does the Hoeffding tree compare with trees produced by traditional decision trees algorithms that run in batch mode?" The Hoeffding tree becomes asymptotically close to that produced by the batch learner. Specifically, the expected disagreement between the Hoeffding tree and a decision tree with infinite examples is at most δ/p, where p is the leaf probability, or the probability that an example will fall into a leaf. If the two best splitting attributes differ by 10% (i.e., $\varepsilon/R = 0.10$), then by Equation (8.4), it would take 380 examples to ensure a desired accuracy of 90% (i.e., $\delta = 0.1$). For $\delta = 0.0001$, it would take only 725 examples, demonstrating an exponential improvement in δ with only a linear increase in the number of examples. For this latter case, if $p = 1\%$, the expected disagreement between the trees would be at most $\delta/p = 0.01\%$, with only 725 examples per node.

In addition to high accuracy with a small sample, Hoeffding trees have other attractive properties for dealing with stream data. First, multiple scans of the same data are never performed. This is important because data streams often become too large to store. Furthermore, the algorithm is incremental, which can be seen in Figure 8.3 (adapted from [GGR02]). The figure demonstrates how new examples are integrated into the tree as they stream in. This property contrasts with batch learners, which wait until the data are accumulated before constructing the model. Another advantage of incrementally building the tree is that we can use it to classify data even while it is being built. The tree will continue to grow and become more accurate as more training data stream in.

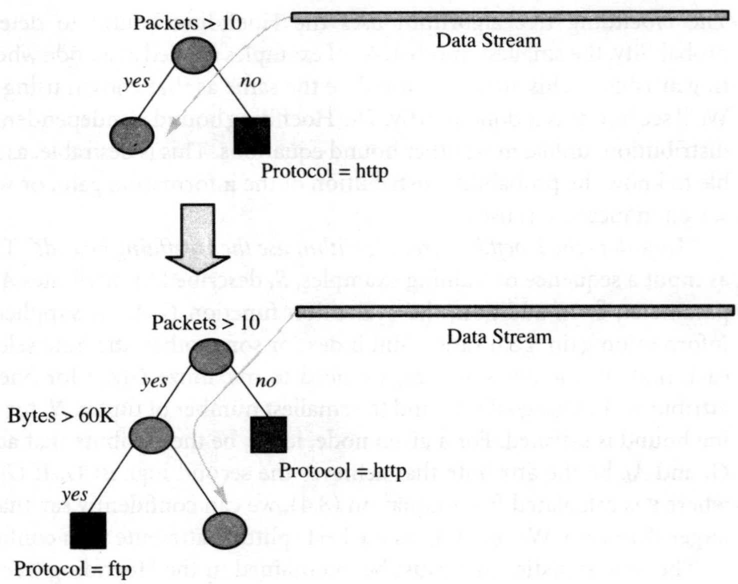

Figure 8.3 The nodes of the Hoeffding tree are created incrementally as more samples stream in.

There are, however, weaknesses to the Hoeffding tree algorithm. For example, the algorithm spends a great deal of time with attributes that have nearly identical splitting quality. In addition, the memory utilization can be further optimized. Finally, the algorithm cannot handle concept drift, because once a node is created, it can never change.

Very Fast Decision Tree (VFDT) and Concept-adapting Very Fast Decision Tree (CVFDT)

The VFDT (Very Fast Decision Tree) algorithm makes several modifications to the Hoeffding tree algorithm to improve both speed and memory utilization. The modifications include breaking near-ties during attribute selection more aggressively, computing the G function after a number of training examples, deactivating the least promising leaves whenever memory is running low, dropping poor splitting attributes, and improving the initialization method. VFDT works well on stream data and also compares extremely well to traditional classifiers in both speed and accuracy. However, it still cannot handle concept drift in data streams.

"What can we do to manage concept drift?" Basically, we need a way to identify in a timely manner those elements of the stream that are no longer consistent with the current concepts. A common approach is to use a *sliding window*. The intuition behind it is to incorporate new examples yet eliminate the effects of old ones. We

can repeatedly apply a traditional classifier to the examples in the sliding window. As new examples arrive, they are inserted into the beginning of the window; a corresponding number of examples is removed from the end of the window, and the classifier is reapplied. This technique, however, is sensitive to the window size, *w*. If *w* is too large, the model will not accurately represent the concept drift. On the other hand, if *w* is too small, then there will not be enough examples to construct an accurate model. Moreover, it will become very expensive to continually construct a new classifier model.

To adapt to concept-drifting data streams, the VFDT algorithm was further developed into the **Concept-adapting Very Fast Decision Tree algorithm (CVFDT)**. CVFDT also uses a sliding window approach; however, it does not construct a new model from scratch each time. Rather, it updates statistics at the nodes by incrementing the counts associated with new examples and decrementing the counts associated with old ones. Therefore, if there is a concept drift, some nodes may no longer pass the Hoeffding bound. When this happens, an alternate subtree will be grown, with the new best splitting attribute at the root. As new examples stream in, the alternate subtree will continue to develop, without yet being used for classification. Once the alternate subtree becomes more accurate than the existing one, the old subtree is replaced.

Empirical studies show that CVFDT achieves better accuracy than VFDT with time-changing data streams. In addition, the size of the tree in CVFDT is much smaller than that in VFDT, because the latter accumulates many outdated examples.

A Classifier Ensemble Approach to Stream Data Classification

Let's look at another approach to classifying concept drifting data streams, where we instead use a *classifier ensemble*. The idea is to train an ensemble or group of classifiers (using, say, C4.5, or naïve Bayes) from sequential chunks of the data stream. That is, whenever a new chunk arrives, we build a new classifier from it. The individual classifiers are weighted based on their expected classification accuracy in a time-changing environment. Only the top-*k* classifiers are kept. The decisions are then based on the weighted votes of the classifiers.

"Why is this approach useful?" There are several reasons for involving more than one classifier. Decision trees are not necessarily the most natural method for handling concept drift. Specifically, if an attribute near the root of the tree in CVFDT no longer passes the Hoeffding bound, a large portion of the tree must be regrown. Many other classifiers, such as naïve Bayes, are not subject to this weakness. In addition, naïve Bayesian classifiers also supply relative probabilities along with the class labels, which expresses the confidence of a decision. Furthermore, CVFDT's automatic elimination of old examples may not be prudent. Rather than keeping only the most up-to-date examples, the ensemble approach discards the least accurate classifiers. Experimentation shows that the ensemble approach achieves greater accuracy than any one of the single classifiers.

8.1.5 Clustering Evolving Data Streams

Imagine a huge amount of dynamic stream data. Many applications require the automated clustering of such data into groups based on their similarities. Examples include applications for network intrusion detection, analyzing Web clickstreams, and stock market analysis. Although there are many powerful methods for clustering static data sets (Chapter 7), clustering data streams places additional constraints on such algorithms. As we have seen, the data stream model of computation requires algorithms to make a single pass over the data, with bounded memory and limited processing time, whereas the stream may be highly dynamic and evolving over time.

For effective clustering of stream data, several new methodologies have been developed, as follows:

- **Compute and store summaries of past data:** Due to limited memory space and fast response requirements, compute summaries of the previously seen data, store the relevant results, and use such summaries to compute important statistics when required.
- **Apply a divide-and-conquer strategy:** Divide data streams into chunks based on order of arrival, compute summaries for these chunks, and then merge the summaries. In this way, larger models can be built out of smaller building blocks.
- **Incremental clustering of incoming data streams:** Because stream data enter the system continuously and incrementally, the clusters derived must be incrementally refined.
- **Perform microclustering as well as macroclustering analysis:** Stream clusters can be computed in two steps: (1) compute and store summaries at the *microcluster* level, where microclusters are formed by applying a hierarchical bottom-up clustering algorithm (Section 7.5.1), and (2) compute *macroclusters* (such as by using another clustering algorithm to group the microclusters) at the user-specified level. This two-step computation effectively compresses the data and often results in a smaller margin of error.
- **Explore multiple time granularity for the analysis of cluster evolution:** Because the more recent data often play a different role from that of the remote (i.e., older) data in stream data analysis, use a tilted time frame model to store snapshots of summarized data at different points in time.
- **Divide stream clustering into on-line and off-line processes:** While data are streaming in, basic summaries of data snapshots should be computed, stored, and incrementally updated. Therefore, an on-line process is needed to maintain such dynamically changing clusters. Meanwhile, a user may pose queries to ask about past, current, or evolving clusters. Such analysis can be performed off-line or as a process independent of on-line cluster maintenance.

Several algorithms have been developed for clustering data streams. Two of them, namely, STREAM and CluStream, are introduced here.

STREAM: A *k*-Medians-based Stream Clustering Algorithm

Given a data stream model of points, $X_1, \ldots, X_N$, with timestamps, $T_1, \ldots, T_N$, the objective of stream clustering is to maintain a consistently good clustering of the sequence seen so far using a small amount of memory and time.

STREAM is a single-pass, constant factor approximation algorithm that was developed for the *k-medians problem*. The k-medians problem is to cluster N data points into k clusters or groups such that the sum squared error (SSQ) between the points and the cluster center to which they are assigned is minimized. The idea is to assign similar points to the same cluster, where these points are dissimilar from points in other clusters.

Recall that in the stream data model, data points can only be seen once, and memory and time are limited. To achieve high-quality clustering, the STREAM algorithm processes data streams in buckets (or batches) of m points, with each bucket fitting in main memory. For each bucket, b_i, STREAM clusters the bucket's points into k clusters. It then summarizes the bucket information by retaining only the information regarding the k centers, with each cluster center being weighted by the number of points assigned to its cluster. STREAM then discards the points, retaining only the center information. Once enough centers have been collected, the weighted centers are again clustered to produce another set of $O(k)$ cluster centers. This is repeated so that at every level, at most m points are retained. This approach results in a one-pass, $O(kN)$-time, $O(N^{\varepsilon})$-space (for some constant $\varepsilon < 1$), constant-factor approximation algorithm for data stream k-medians.

STREAM derives quality k-medians clusters with limited space and time. However, it considers neither the evolution of the data nor time granularity. The clustering can become dominated by the older, outdated data of the stream. In real life, the nature of the clusters may vary with both the moment at which they are computed, as well as the time horizon over which they are measured. For example, a user may wish to examine clusters occurring last week, last month, or last year. These may be considerably different. Therefore, a data stream clustering algorithm should also provide the flexibility to compute clusters over user-defined time periods in an interactive manner. The following algorithm, CluStream, addresses these concerns.

CluStream: Clustering Evolving Data Streams

CluStream is an algorithm for the clustering of evolving data streams based on user-specified, on-line clustering queries. It divides the clustering process into on-line and off-line components. The on-line component computes and stores summary statistics about the data stream using *microclusters*, and performs incremental on-line computation and maintenance of the microclusters. The off-line component does macroclustering and answers various user questions using the stored summary statistics, which are based on the tilted time frame model.

To cluster evolving data streams based on both historical and current stream data information, the tilted time frame model (such as a progressive logarithmic model) is adopted, which stores the snapshots of a set of microclusters at different levels of granularity depending on recency. The intuition here is that more information will be needed for more recent events as opposed to older events. The stored information can be used for processing history-related, user-specific clustering queries.

A microcluster in CluStream is represented as a *clustering feature*. CluStream extends the concept of the clustering feature developed in BIRCH (see Section 7.5.2) to include the temporal domain. As a *temporal extension of the clustering feature*, a microcluster for a set of d-dimensional points, $X_1, \ldots, X_n$, with timestamps, $T_1, \ldots, T_n$, is defined as the $(2d+3)$ tuple $(CF2^x, CF1^x, CF2^t, CF1^t, n)$, wherein $CF2^x$ and $CF1^x$ are d-dimensional vectors while $CF2^t$, $CF1^t$, and n are scalars. $CF2^x$ maintains the sum of the squares of the data values per dimension, that is, $\sum_{i=1}^{n} X_i^2$. Similarly, for each dimension, the sum of the data values is maintained in $CF1^x$. From a statistical point of view, $CF2^x$ and $CF1^x$ represent the second- and first-order moments (Section 8.1.1) of the data, respectively. The sum of squares of the timestamps is maintained in $CF2^t$. The sum of the timestamps is maintained in $CF1^t$. Finally, the number of data points in the microcluster is maintained in n.

Clustering features have additive and subtractive properties that make them very useful for data stream cluster analysis. For example, two microclusters can be merged by adding their respective clustering features. Furthermore, a large number of microclusters can be maintained without using a great deal of memory. Snapshots of these microclusters are stored away at key points in time based on the tilted time frame.

The on-line microcluster processing is divided into two phases: (1) statistical data collection and (2) updating of microclusters. In the first phase, a total of q microclusters, $M_1, \ldots, M_q$, are maintained, where q is usually significantly larger than the number of natural clusters and is determined by the amount of available memory. In the second phase, microclusters are updated. Each new data point is added to either an existing cluster or a new one. To decide whether a new cluster is required, a maximum boundary for each cluster is defined. If the new data point falls within the boundary, it is added to the cluster; otherwise, it is the first data point in a new cluster. When a data point is added to an existing cluster, it is "absorbed" because of the additive property of the microclusters. When a data point is added to a new cluster, the least recently used existing cluster has to be removed or two existing clusters have to be merged, depending on certain criteria, in order to create memory space for the new cluster.

The off-line component can perform user-directed macroclustering or cluster evolution analysis. Macroclustering allows a user to explore the stream clusters over different time horizons. A **time horizon**, h, is a history of length h of the stream. Given a user-specified time horizon, h, and the number of desired macroclusters, k, macroclustering finds k high-level clusters over h. This is done as follows: First, the snapshot at time $t_c - h$ is subtracted from the snapshot at the current time, t_c. Clusters older than the beginning of the horizon are not included. The microclusters in the horizon are considered as weighted pseudo-points and are reclustered in order to determine higher-level clusters. Notice that the clustering process is similar to the method used in STREAM but requires only two snapshots (the beginning and end of the horizon) and is more flexible over a range of user queries.

"What if a user wants to see how clusters have changed over, say, the last quarter or the last year?" Cluster evolution analysis looks at how clusters change over time. Given a

user-specified time horizon, h, and two clock times, t_1 and t_2 (where $t_1 < t_2$), **cluster evolution analysis** examines the evolving nature of the data arriving between $(t_2 - h, t_2)$ and that arriving between $(t_1 - h, t_1)$. This involves answering questions like whether new clusters in the data at time t_1 were not present at time t_2, or whether some of the original clusters were lost. This also involves analyzing whether some of the original clusters at time t_1 shifted in position and nature. With the available microcluster information, this can be done by computing the net snapshots of the microclusters, $N(t_1, h)$ and $N(t_2, h)$, and then computing the snapshot changes over time. Such evolution analysis of the data over time can be used for network intrusion detection to identify new types of attacks within the network.

CluStream was shown to derive high-quality clusters, especially when the changes are dramatic. Moreover, it offers rich functionality to the user because it registers the essential historical information with respect to cluster evolution. The tilted time frame along with the microclustering structure allow for better accuracy and efficiency on real data. Finally, it maintains scalability in terms of stream size, dimensionality, and the number of clusters.

In general, stream data mining is still a fast-evolving research field. With the massive amount of data streams populating many applications, it is expected that many new stream data mining methods will be developed, especially for data streams containing additional semantic information, such as time-series streams, spatiotemporal data streams, and video and audio data streams.

8.2 Mining Time-Series Data

"What is a time-series database?" A **time-series database** consists of sequences of values or events obtained over repeated measurements of time. The values are typically measured at equal time intervals (e.g., hourly, daily, weekly). Time-series databases are popular in many applications, such as stock market analysis, economic and sales forecasting, budgetary analysis, utility studies, inventory studies, yield projections, workload projections, process and quality control, observation of natural phenomena (such as atmosphere, temperature, wind, earthquake), scientific and engineering experiments, and medical treatments. A time-series database is also a sequence database. However, a **sequence database** is any database that consists of sequences of ordered events, with or without concrete notions of time. For example, Web page traversal sequences and customer shopping transaction sequences are sequence data, but they may not be time-series data. The mining of sequence data is discussed in Section 8.3.

With the growing deployment of a large number of sensors, telemetry devices, and other on-line data collection tools, the amount of time-series data is increasing rapidly, often in the order of gigabytes per day (such as in stock trading) or even per minute (such as from NASA space programs). How can we find correlation relationships within time-series data? How can we analyze such huge numbers of time series to find similar or regular patterns, trends, bursts (such as sudden sharp changes), and outliers, with fast or even on-line real-time response? This has become an increasingly important and challenging problem. In this section, we examine several aspects of mining time-series databases, with a focus on trend analysis and similarity search.

8.2.1 Trend Analysis

A time series involving a variable Y, representing, say, the daily closing price of a share in a stock market, can be viewed as a function of time t, that is, $Y = F(t)$. Such a function can be illustrated as a time-series graph, as shown in Figure 8.4, which describes a point moving with the passage of time.

"How can we study time-series data?" In general, there are two goals in time-series analysis: (1) *modeling time series* (i.e., to gain insight into the mechanisms or underlying forces that generate the time series), and (2) *forecasting time series* (i.e., to predict the future values of the time-series variables).

Trend analysis consists of the following four major **components** or **movements** for characterizing time-series data:

- **Trend or long-term movements:** These indicate the general direction in which a time-series graph is moving over a long interval of time. This movement is displayed by a **trend curve,** or a **trend line.** For example, the trend curve of Figure 8.4 is indicated by a dashed curve. Typical methods for determining a trend curve or trend line include the *weighted moving average method* and the *least squares method*, discussed later.
- **Cyclic movements or cyclic variations:** These refer to the *cycles*, that is, the long-term oscillations about a trend line or curve, which may or may not be periodic. That is, the cycles need not necessarily follow exactly similar patterns after equal intervals of time.

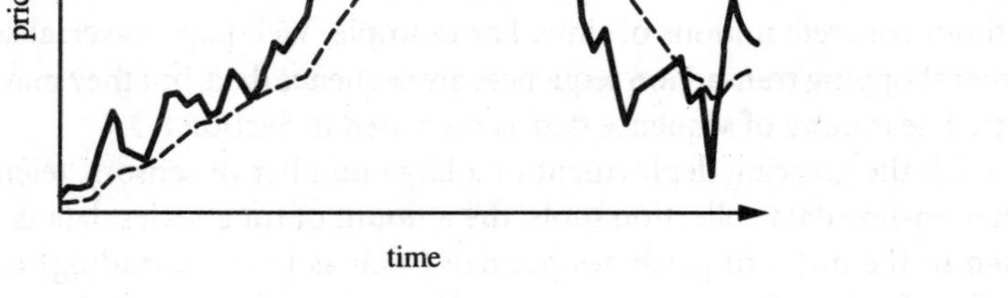

Figure 8.4 Time-series data of the stock price of *AllElectronics* over time. The *trend* is shown with a dashed curve, calculated by a moving average.

- **Seasonal movements or seasonal variations:** These are systematic or calendar related. Examples include events that recur annually, such as the sudden increase in sales of chocolates and flowers before Valentine's Day or of department store items before Christmas. The observed increase in water consumption in summer due to warm weather is another example. In these examples, seasonal movements are the identical or nearly identical patterns that a time series appears to follow during corresponding months of successive years.
- **Irregular or random movements:** These characterize the sporadic motion of time series due to random or chance events, such as labor disputes, floods, or announced personnel changes within companies.

Note that *regression analysis* has been a popular tool for modeling time series, finding trends and outliers in such data sets. Regression is a fundamental topic in statistics and is described in many textbooks. Thus, we will not spend much time on this theme.[3] However, pure regression analysis cannot capture all of the four movements described above that occur in real-world applications. Hence, our discussion of trend analysis and modeling time series focuses on the above movements.

The trend, cyclic, seasonal, and irregular movements are represented by the variables T, C, S, I, respectively. Time-series modeling is also referred to as the **decomposition** of a time series into these four basic movements. The time-series variable Y can be modeled as either the product of the four variables (i.e., $Y = T \times C \times S \times I$) or their sum. This choice is typically empirical.

"Given a sequence of values for Y *(i.e.,* $y_1, y_2, y_3, \ldots$*) for analysis, how can we adjust the data for seasonal fluctuations?"* This can be performed by estimating and then removing from the time series the influences of the data that are systematic or calendar related. In many business transactions, for example, there are expected regular seasonal fluctuations, such as higher sales volumes during the Christmas season. Such fluctuations can conceal both the true underlying movement of the series as well as certain nonseasonal characteristics that may be of interest. Therefore, it is important to identify such seasonal variations and "deseasonalize" the data. For this purpose, the concept of **seasonal index** is introduced, as a set of numbers showing the relative values of a variable during the months of a year. For example, if the sales during October, November, and December are 80%, 120%, and 140% of the average monthly sales for the whole year, respectively, then 80, 120, and 140 are the **seasonal index numbers** for the year. If the original monthly data are divided by the corresponding seasonal index numbers, the resulting data are said to be **deseasonalized**, or *adjusted for seasonal variations*. Such data still include trend, cyclic, and irregular movements.

To detect seasonal patterns, we can also look for correlations between each ith element of the series and $(i-k)$th element (where k is referred to as the **lag**) using **autocorrelation analysis**. For example, we can measure the correlation in sales for every twelfth month,

[3] A simple introduction to regression is included in Chapter 6: Classification and Prediction.

where here, $k = 12$. The correlation coefficient given in Chapter 2 (Equation (2.8)) can be used. Let $\langle y_1, y_2, \ldots, y_N \rangle$ be the time series. To apply Equation (2.8), the two attributes in the equation respectively refer to the two random variables representing the time series viewed with lag k. These times series are $\langle y_1, y_2, \ldots, y_{N-k} \rangle$ and $\langle y_{k+1}, y_{k+2}, \ldots, y_N \rangle$. A zero value indicates that there is no correlation relationship. A positive value indicates a positive correlation, that is, both variables increase together. A negative value indicates a negative correlation, that is, one variable increases as the other decreases. The higher the positive (or negative) value is, the greater is the positive (or negative) correlation relationship.

"How can we determine the trend of the data?" A common method for determining trend is to calculate a **moving average of order** n as the following sequence of arithmetic means:

$$\frac{y_1 + y_2 + \cdots + y_n}{n}, \frac{y_2 + y_3 + \cdots + y_{n+1}}{n}, \frac{y_3 + y_4 + \cdots + y_{n+2}}{n}, \cdots \tag{8.5}$$

A moving average tends to reduce the amount of variation present in the data set. Thus the process of replacing the time series by its moving average eliminates unwanted fluctuations and is therefore also referred to as the **smoothing of time series.** If weighted arithmetic means are used in Sequence (8.5), the resulting sequence is called a **weighted moving average of order** n.

Example 8.5 **Moving averages.** Given a sequence of nine values, we can compute its moving average of order 3, and its weighted moving average of order 3 using the weights (1, 4, 1). This information can be displayed in tabular form, where each value in the moving average is the mean of the three values immediately above it, and each value in the weighted moving average is the weighted average of the three values immediately above it.

Original data:	3	7	2	0	4	5	9	7	2
Moving average of order 3:		4	3	2	3	6	7	6	
Weighted (1, 4, 1) moving average of order 3:		5.5	2.5	1	3.5	5.5	8	6.5	

Using the first equation in Sequence 8.5, we calculate the first moving average as $\frac{3+7+2}{3} = 4$. The first weighted average value is calculated as $\frac{1\times3+4\times7+1\times2}{1+4+1} = 5.5$. The weighted average typically assigns greater weights to the central elements in order to offset the smoothing effect. ■

A moving average loses the data at the beginning and end of a series; may sometimes generate cycles or other movements that are not present in the original data; and may be strongly affected by the presence of extreme values. Notice that the influence of extreme values can be reduced by employing a weighted moving average with appropriate weights as shown in Example 8.5. An appropriate moving average can help smooth out irregular variations in the data. In general, small deviations tend to occur with large frequency, whereas large deviations tend to occur with small frequency, following a normal distribution.

"Are there other ways to estimate the trend?" Yes, one such method is the **freehand method,** where an approximate curve or line is drawn to fit a set of data based on the

user's own judgment. This method is costly and barely reliable for any large-scale data mining. An alternative is the **least squares method**,[4] where we consider the best-fitting curve C as the *least squares curve*, that is, the curve having the minimum of $\sum_{i=1}^{n} d_i^2$, where the *deviation* or *error*, d_i, is the difference between the value y_i of a point (x_i, y_i) and the corresponding value as determined from the curve C.

The data can then be adjusted for trend by dividing the data by their corresponding trend values. As mentioned earlier, an appropriate moving average will smooth out the irregular variations. This leaves us with only cyclic variations for further analysis. If periodicity or approximate periodicity of cycles occurs, **cyclic indexes** can be constructed in a manner similar to that for seasonal indexes.

In practice, it is useful to first graph the time series and qualitatively estimate the presence of long-term trends, seasonal variations, and cyclic variations. This may help in selecting a suitable method for analysis and in comprehending its results.

Time-series forecasting finds a mathematical formula that will approximately generate the historical patterns in a time series. It is used to make long-term or short-term predictions of future values. There are several models for forecasting: **ARIMA (Auto-Regressive Integrated Moving Average)**, also known as the Box-Jenkins methodology (after its creators), is a popular example. It is powerful yet rather complex to use. The quality of the results obtained may depend on the user's level of experience. Interested readers may consult the bibliographic notes for references to the technique.

8.2.2 Similarity Search in Time-Series Analysis

"What is a similarity search?" Unlike normal database queries, which find data that match the given query *exactly*, a **similarity search** finds data sequences that *differ only slightly* from the given query sequence. Given a set of time-series sequences, S, there are two types of similarity searches: *subsequence matching* and *whole sequence matching*. **Subsequence matching** finds the sequences in S that contain subsequences that are similar to a given query sequence x, while **whole sequence matching** finds a set of sequences in S that are similar to each other (as a whole). Subsequence matching is a more frequently encountered problem in applications. Similarity search in time-series analysis is useful for financial market analysis (e.g., stock data analysis), medical diagnosis (e.g., cardiogram analysis), and in scientific or engineering databases (e.g., power consumption analysis).

Data Reduction and Transformation Techniques

Due to the tremendous size and high-dimensionality of time-series data, *data reduction* often serves as the first step in time-series analysis. Data reduction leads to not only much smaller storage space but also much faster processing. As discussed in Chapter 2, major

[4]The least squares method was introduced in Section 6.11.1 under the topic of linear regression.

strategies for data reduction include *attribute subset selection* (which removes irrelevant or redundant attributes or dimensions), *dimensionality reduction* (which typically employs signal processing techniques to obtain a reduced version of the original data), and *numerosity reduction* (where data are replaced or estimated by alternative, smaller representations, such as histograms, clustering, and sampling). Because time series can be viewed as data of very high dimensionality where each point of time can be viewed as a dimension, dimensionality reduction is our major concern here. For example, to compute correlations between two time-series curves, the reduction of the time series from length (i.e., dimension) n to k may lead to a reduction from $O(n)$ to $O(k)$ in computational complexity. If $k \ll n$, the complexity of the computation will be greatly reduced.

Several dimensionality reduction techniques can be used in time-series analysis. Examples include (1) the *discrete Fourier transform (DFT)* as the classical data reduction technique, (2) more recently developed *discrete wavelet transforms (DWT)*, (3) Singular Value Decomposition (SVD) based on Principle Components Analysis (PCA),[5] and (4) random projection-based sketch techniques (as discussed in Section 8.1.1), which can also give a good-quality synopsis of data. Because we have touched on these topics earlier in this book, and because a thorough explanation is beyond our scope, we will not go into great detail here. The first three techniques listed are signal processing techniques. A given time series can be considered as a finite sequence of real values (or *coefficients*), recorded over time in some *object space*. The data or *signal* is transformed (using a specific transformation function) into a signal in a *transformed space*. A small subset of the "strongest" transformed coefficients are saved as *features*. These features form a *feature space*, which is simply a projection of the transformed space. This representation is sparse so that operations that can take advantage of data sparsity are computationally very fast if performed in feature space. The features can be transformed back into object space, resulting in a compressed approximation of the original data.

Many techniques for signal analysis require the data to be in the *frequency domain*. Therefore, **distance-preserving orthonormal transformations** are often used to transform the data from the time domain to the frequency domain. Usually, a data-independent transformation is applied, where the transformation matrix is determined a priori, independent of the input data. Because the distance between two signals in the time domain is the same as their Euclidean distance in the frequency domain, the DFT does a good job of preserving essentials in the first few coefficients. By keeping only the first few (i.e., "strongest") coefficients of the DFT, we can compute the lower bounds of the actual distance.

Indexing Methods for Similarity Search

"Once the data are transformed by, say, a DFT, how can we provide support for efficient search in time-series data?" For efficient accessing, a *multidimensional index* can be

[5]The Discrete Fourier transform, wavelet transforms, and principal components analysis are briefly introduced in Section 2.5.3.

constructed using the first few Fourier coefficients. When a similarity query is submitted to the system, the index can be used to retrieve the sequences that are at most a certain small distance away from the query sequence. Postprocessing is then performed by computing the actual distance between sequences in the time domain and discarding any false matches.

For subsequence matching, each sequence can be broken down into a set of "pieces" of *windows* with length w. In one approach, the features of the subsequence inside each window are then extracted. Each sequence is mapped to a "trail" in the feature space. The trail of each sequence is divided into "subtrails," each represented by a minimum bounding rectangle. A multipiece assembly algorithm can then be used to search for longer sequence matches.

Various kinds of indexing methods have been explored to speed up the similarity search. For example, *R-trees* and *R*-trees* have been used to store the minimal bounding rectangles mentioned above. In addition, the *ε-kdB tree* has been developed for faster spatial similarity joins on high-dimensional points, and *suffix trees* have also been explored. References are given in the bibliographic notes.

Similarity Search Methods

The above trail-based approach to similarity search was pioneering, yet has a number of limitations. In particular, it uses the Euclidean distance as a similarity measure, which is sensitive to outliers. Furthermore, what if there are differences in the baseline and scale of the two time series being compared? What if there are gaps? Here, we discuss an approach that addresses these issues.

For similarity analysis of time-series data, Euclidean distance is typically used as a similarity measure. Here, the smaller the distance between two sets of time-series data, the more similar are the two series. However, we cannot directly apply the Euclidean distance. Instead, we need to consider differences in the *baseline* and *scale* (or amplitude) of our two series. For example, one stock's value may have a baseline of around $20 and fluctuate with a relatively large amplitude (such as between $15 and $25), while another could have a baseline of around $100 and fluctuate with a relatively small amplitude (such as between $90 and $110). The distance from one baseline to another is referred to as the **offset**.

A straightforward approach to solving the baseline and scale problem is to apply a **normalization transformation**. For example, a sequence $X = \langle x_1, x_2, \ldots, x_n \rangle$ can be replaced by a normalized sequence $X' = \langle x'_1, x'_2, \ldots, x'_n \rangle$, using the following formula,

$$x'_i = \frac{x_i - \mu}{\sigma} \tag{8.6}$$

where μ is the mean value of the sequence X and σ is the standard deviation of X. We can transform other sequences using the same formula, and then compare them for similarity.

Most real-world applications do not require the matching subsequences to be perfectly aligned along the time axis. In other words, we should allow for pairs of subsequences to match if they are of the *same shape*, but differ due to the presence of **gaps** within a sequence (where one of the series may be missing some of the values that exist in the other) or differences in offsets or amplitudes. This is particularly useful in many similar sequence analyses, such as stock market analysis and cardiogram analysis.

"How can subsequence matching be performed to allow for such differences?" Users or experts can specify parameters such as a sliding window size, the width of an envelope for similarity, the maximum gap, a matching fraction, and so on. Figure 8.5 illustrates the process involved, starting with two sequences in their original form. First, gaps are removed. The resulting sequences are normalized with respect to offset translation (where one time series is adjusted to align with the other by shifting the baseline or phase) and amplitude scaling. For this normalization, techniques such

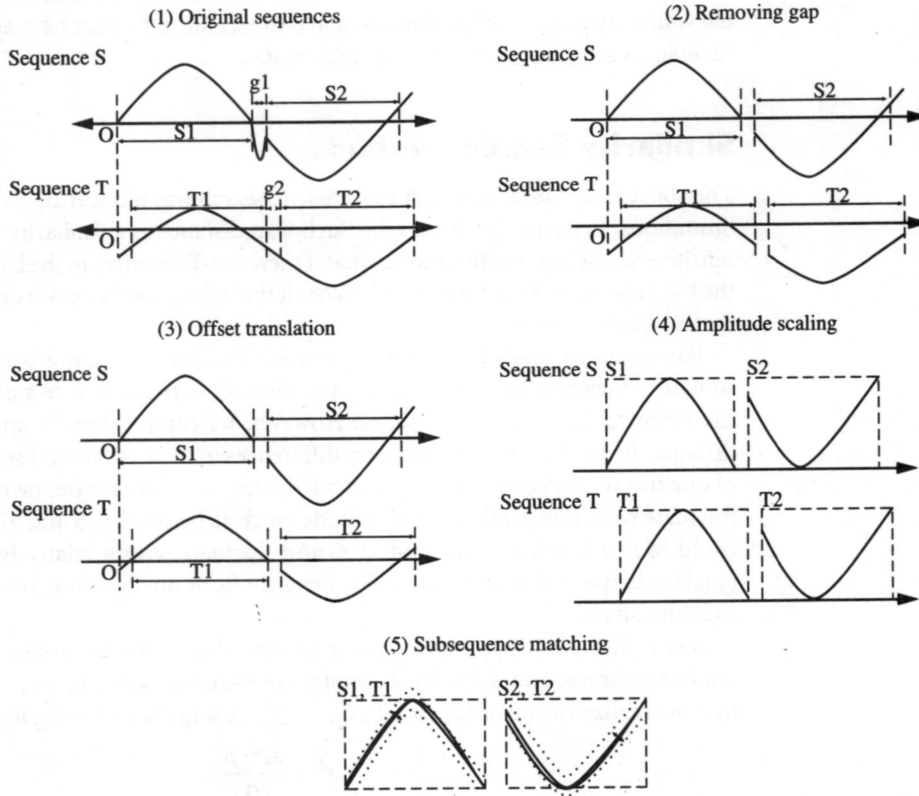

Figure 8.5 Subsequence matching in time-series data: The original sequences are of the same shape, yet adjustments need to be made to deal with differences in gaps, offsets, and amplitudes. These adjustments allow subsequences to be matched within an envelope of width ε. Based on [ALSS95].

as those described in Section 2.4.2 may be used. Two subsequences are considered *similar* and can be matched if one lies within an envelope of ε width around the other (where ε is a small number, specified by a user or expert), ignoring outliers. Two sequences are *similar* if they have enough nonoverlapping time-ordered pairs of similar subsequences.

Based on the above, a similarity search that handles gaps and differences in offsets and amplitudes can be performed by the following steps:

1. **Atomic matching**: Normalize the data. Find all pairs of gap-free windows of a small length that are similar.
2. **Window stitching**: Stitch similar windows to form pairs of large similar subsequences, allowing gaps between atomic matches.
3. **Subsequence ordering**: Linearly order the subsequence matches to determine whether enough similar pieces exist.

With such processing, sequences of similar shape but with gaps or differences in offsets or amplitudes can be found to match each other or to match query templates.

Query Languages for Time Sequences

"How can I specify the similarity search to be performed?" We need to design and develop powerful query languages to facilitate the specification of similarity searches in time sequences. A **time-sequence query language** should be able to specify not only simple similarity queries like *"Find all of the sequences similar to a given subsequence Q,"* but also sophisticated queries like *"Find all of the sequences that are similar to some sequence in class C_1, but not similar to any sequence in class C_2."* Moreover, it should be able to support various kinds of queries, such as range queries and nearest-neighbor queries.

An interesting kind of time-sequence query language is a **shape definition language**. It allows users to define and query the *overall shape* of time sequences using human-readable series of sequence transitions or macros, while ignoring the specific details.

Example 8.6 **Using a shape definition language.** The pattern *up, Up, UP* can be used to describe increasing degrees of rising slopes. A macro, such as *spike*, can denote a sequence like (*SteepUps, flat, SteepDowns*), where *SteepUps* is defined as ({*Up, UP*}, {*Up, UP*}, {*Up, UP*}), which means that one *SteepUps* consists of three steep up-slopes, each corresponding to either *Up* or *UP*. *SteepDowns* is similarly defined. ■

Such a shape definition language increases the users' flexibility at specifying queries of desired shapes for sequence similarity search.

8.3 Mining Sequence Patterns in Transactional Databases

A **sequence database** consists of sequences of ordered elements or events, recorded with or without a concrete notion of time. There are many applications involving sequence data. Typical examples include customer shopping sequences, Web clickstreams, biological sequences, sequences of events in science and engineering, and in natural and social developments. In this section, we study *sequential pattern mining* in transactional databases. In particular, we start with the basic concepts of sequential pattern mining in Section 8.3.1. Section 8.3.2 presents several scalable methods for such mining. Constraint-based sequential pattern mining is described in Section 8.3.3. Periodicity analysis for sequence data is discussed in Section 8.3.4. Specific methods for mining sequence patterns in biological data are addressed in Section 8.4.

8.3.1 Sequential Pattern Mining: Concepts and Primitives

"What is sequential pattern mining?" **Sequential pattern mining** is the mining of frequently occurring ordered events or subsequences as patterns. An example of a sequential pattern is *"Customers who buy a Canon digital camera are likely to buy an HP color printer within a month."* For retail data, sequential patterns are useful for shelf placement and promotions. This industry, as well as telecommunications and other businesses, may also use sequential patterns for targeted marketing, customer retention, and many other tasks. Other areas in which sequential patterns can be applied include Web access pattern analysis, weather prediction, production processes, and network intrusion detection. Notice that most studies of sequential pattern mining concentrate on *categorical* (or *symbolic*) *patterns*, whereas numerical curve analysis usually belongs to the scope of trend analysis and forecasting in statistical time-series analysis, as discussed in Section 8.2.

The sequential pattern mining problem was first introduced by Agrawal and Srikant in 1995 [AS95] based on their study of customer purchase sequences, as follows: "*Given a set of sequences, where each sequence consists of a list of events (or elements) and each event consists of a set of items, and given a user-specified minimum support threshold of min_sup, sequential pattern mining finds all **frequent** subsequences, that is, the subsequences whose occurrence frequency in the set of sequences is no less than min_sup.*"

Let's establish some vocabulary for our discussion of sequential pattern mining. Let $\mathcal{I} = \{I_1, I_2, \ldots, I_p\}$ be the set of all *items*. An **itemset** is a nonempty set of items. A **sequence** is an ordered list of **events**. A sequence s is denoted $\langle e_1 e_2 e_3 \cdots e_l \rangle$, where event e_1 occurs before e_2, which occurs before e_3, and so on. Event e_j is also called an **element** of s. In the case of customer purchase data, an event refers to a shopping trip in which a customer bought items at a certain store. The event is thus an itemset, that is, an unordered list of items that the customer purchased during the trip. The itemset (or event) is denoted $(x_1 x_2 \cdots x_q)$, where x_k is an item. For brevity, the brackets are omitted if an element has only one item, that is, element (x) is written as x. Suppose that a customer made several shopping trips to the store. These ordered events form a sequence for the customer. That is, the customer first bought the items in s_1, then later bought the items in s_2, and so on. An item can occur at most once in an event of a sequence, but can occur multiple times in different events of a sequence. The number of instances of items in a sequence is called the **length** of the sequence. A sequence with length l is called an **l-sequence**. A sequence $\alpha = \langle a_1 a_2 \cdots a_n \rangle$ is called a **subsequence** of another sequence $\beta = \langle b_1 b_2 \cdots b_m \rangle$, and β is a **supersequence** of α, denoted as $\alpha \sqsubseteq \beta$, if there exist integers $1 \leq j_1 < j_2 < \cdots < j_n \leq m$ such that $a_1 \subseteq b_{j_1}, a_2 \subseteq b_{j_2}, \ldots, a_n \subseteq b_{j_n}$. For example, if $\alpha = \langle (ab), d \rangle$ and $\beta = \langle (abc), (de) \rangle$, where a, b, c, d, and e are items, then α is a subsequence of β and β is a supersequence of α.

A **sequence database**, S, is a set of tuples, $\langle SID, s \rangle$, where SID is a *sequence_ID* and s is a sequence. For our example, S contains sequences for all customers of the store. A tuple $\langle SID, s \rangle$ is said to **contain** a sequence α, if α is a subsequence of s. The **support** of a sequence α in a sequence database S is the number of tuples in the database containing α, that is, $support_S(\alpha) = |\{\langle SID, s \rangle | (\langle SID, s \rangle \in S) \wedge (\alpha \sqsubseteq s)\}|$. It can be denoted as $support(\alpha)$ if the sequence database is clear from the context. Given a positive integer min_sup as the **minimum support threshold**, a sequence α is **frequent** in sequence database S if $support_S(\alpha) \geq min\_sup$. That is, for sequence α to be frequent, it must occur at least min_sup times in S. *A frequent sequence is called a* **sequential pattern**. A sequential pattern with length l is called an **l-pattern**. The following example illustrates these concepts.

Example 8.7 **Sequential patterns.** Consider the sequence database, S, given in Table 8.1, which will be used in examples throughout this section. Let $min\_sup = 2$. The set of *items* in the database is $\{a, b, c, d, e, f, g\}$. The database contains four sequences.

Let's look at *sequence* 1, which is $\langle a(abc)(ac)d(cf) \rangle$. It has five *events*, namely (a), (abc), (ac), (d), and (cf), which occur in the order listed. Items a and c each appear more than once in different events of the sequence. There are nine instances of items in sequence 1; therefore, it has a *length* of nine and is called a *9-sequence*. Item a occurs three times in sequence 1 and so contributes three to the length of the sequence. However, the entire sequence contributes only one to the *support* of $\langle a \rangle$. Sequence $\langle a(bc)df \rangle$ is a *subsequence* of sequence 1 since the events of the former are each subsets of events in sequence 1, and the order of events is preserved. Consider subsequence $s = \langle (ab)c \rangle$. Looking at the sequence database, S, we see that sequences 1 and 3 are the only ones that *contain* the subsequence s. The support of s is thus 2, which satisfies minimum support.

Table 8.1 A sequence database

Sequence_ID	*Sequence*
1	$\langle a(abc)(ac)d(cf) \rangle$
2	$\langle (ad)c(bc)(ae) \rangle$
3	$\langle (ef)(ab)(df)cb \rangle$
4	$\langle eg(af)cbc \rangle$

Therefore, s is frequent, and so we call it a *sequential pattern*. It is a 3-*pattern* since it is a sequential pattern of length three. ■

This model of sequential pattern mining is an abstraction of customer-shopping sequence analysis. Scalable methods for sequential pattern mining on such data are described in Section 8.3.2, which follows. Many other sequential pattern mining applications may not be covered by this model. For example, when analyzing Web clickstream sequences, gaps between clicks become important if one wants to predict what the next click might be. In DNA sequence analysis, *approximate* patterns become useful since DNA sequences may contain (symbol) insertions, deletions, and mutations. Such diverse requirements can be viewed as *constraint relaxation* or *enforcement*. In Section 8.3.3, we discuss how to extend the basic sequential mining model to *constrained* sequential pattern mining in order to handle these cases.

8.3.2 Scalable Methods for Mining Sequential Patterns

Sequential pattern mining is computationally challenging because such mining may generate and/or test a combinatorially explosive number of intermediate subsequences.

"*How can we develop efficient and scalable methods for sequential pattern mining?*" Recent developments have made progress in two directions: (1) efficient methods for mining the *full set* of sequential patterns, and (2) efficient methods for mining only the *set of closed* sequential patterns, where a sequential pattern s is closed if there exists no sequential pattern s' where s' is a proper supersequence of s, and s' has the same (frequency) support as s.[6] Because all of the subsequences of a frequent sequence are also frequent, mining the set of closed sequential patterns may avoid the generation of unnecessary subsequences and thus lead to more compact results as well as more efficient methods than mining the full set. We will first examine methods for mining the full set and then study how they can be extended for mining the closed set. In addition, we discuss modifications for mining multilevel, multidimensional sequential patterns (i.e., with multiple levels of granularity).

The major approaches for mining the full set of sequential patterns are similar to those introduced for frequent itemset mining in Chapter 5. Here, we discuss three such approaches for sequential pattern mining, represented by the algorithms GSP, SPADE, and PrefixSpan, respectively. GSP adopts a *candidate generate-and-test* approach using *horizonal data format* (where the data are represented as ⟨*sequence_ID* : *sequence_of_itemsets*⟩, as usual, where each itemset is an event). SPADE adopts a candidate generate-and-test approach using *vertical data format* (where the data are represented as ⟨*itemset* : (*sequence_ID*, *event_ID*)⟩). The vertical data format can be obtained by transforming from a horizontally formatted sequence database in just one scan. PrefixSpan is a *pattern growth* method, which does not require candidate generation.

[6]Closed frequent itemsets were introduced in Chapter 5. Here, the definition is applied to sequential patterns.

All three approaches either directly or indirectly explore the **Apriori property**, stated as follows: *every nonempty subsequence of a sequential pattern is a sequential pattern.* (Recall that for a pattern to be called sequential, it must be frequent. That is, it must satisfy minimum support.) The Apriori property is antimonotonic (or downward-closed) in that, if a sequence cannot pass a test (e.g., regarding minimum support), all of its supersequences will also fail the test. Use of this property to prune the search space can help make the discovery of sequential patterns more efficient.

GSP: A Sequential Pattern Mining Algorithm Based on Candidate Generate-and-Test

GSP (Generalized Sequential Patterns) is a sequential pattern mining method that was developed by Srikant and Agrawal in 1996. It is an extension of their seminal algorithm for frequent itemset mining, known as Apriori (Section 5.2). GSP uses the downward-closure property of sequential patterns and adopts a multiple-pass, candidate generate-and-test approach. The algorithm is outlined as follows. In the first scan of the database, it finds all of the frequent items, that is, those with minimum support. Each such item yields a 1-event frequent sequence consisting of that item. Each subsequent pass starts with a *seed set* of sequential patterns—the set of sequential patterns found in the previous pass. This seed set is used to generate new potentially frequent patterns, called *candidate sequences*. Each candidate sequence contains one more item than the seed sequential pattern from which it was generated (where each event in the pattern may contain one or multiple items). Recall that the number of instances of items in a sequence is the *length* of the sequence. So, all of the candidate sequences in a given pass will have the same length. We refer to a sequence with length k as a k-sequence. Let C_k denote the set of candidate k-sequences. A pass over the database finds the support for each candidate k-sequence. The candidates in C_k with at least *min_sup* form L_k, the set of all *frequent* k-sequences. This set then becomes the seed set for the next pass, $k+1$. The algorithm terminates when no new sequential pattern is found in a pass, or no candidate sequence can be generated.

The method is illustrated in the following example.

Example 8.8 **GSP: Candidate generate-and-test (using horizontal data format).** Suppose we are given the same sequence database, S, of Table 8.1 from Example 8.7, with $min\_sup = 2$. Note that the data are represented in horizontal data format. In the first scan ($k = 1$), GSP collects the support for each item. The set of candidate 1-sequences is thus (shown here in the form of "*sequence:support*"): $\langle a \rangle : 4$, $\langle b \rangle : 4$, $\langle c \rangle : 3$, $\langle d \rangle : 3$, $\langle e \rangle : 3$, $\langle f \rangle : 3$, $\langle g \rangle : 1$.

The sequence $\langle g \rangle$ has a support of only 1 and is the only sequence that does not satisfy minimum support. By filtering it out, we obtain the first seed set, $L_1 = \{\langle a \rangle, \langle b \rangle, \langle c \rangle, \langle d \rangle, \langle e \rangle, \langle f \rangle\}$. Each member in the set represents a 1-event sequential pattern. Each subsequent pass starts with the seed set found in the previous pass and uses it to generate new candidate sequences, which are potentially frequent.

Using L_1 as the seed set, this set of six length-1 sequential patterns generates a set of $6 \times 6 + \frac{6 \times 5}{2} = 51$ candidate sequences of length 2, $C_2 = \{\langle aa \rangle, \langle ab \rangle, \ldots, \langle af \rangle, \langle ba \rangle, \langle bb \rangle, \ldots, \langle ff \rangle, \langle (ab) \rangle, \langle (ac) \rangle, \ldots, \langle (ef) \rangle\}$.

In general, the set of candidates is generated by a self-join of the sequential patterns found in the previous pass (see Section 5.2.1 for details). GSP applies the Apriori property to prune the set of candidates as follows. In the k-th pass, a sequence is a candidate only if each of its length-$(k-1)$ subsequences is a sequential pattern found at the $(k-1)$-th pass. A new scan of the database collects the support for each candidate sequence and finds a new set of sequential patterns, L_k. This set becomes the seed for the next pass. The algorithm terminates when no sequential pattern is found in a pass or when no candidate sequence is generated. Clearly, the number of scans is at least the maximum length of sequential patterns. GSP needs one more scan if the sequential patterns obtained in the last scan still generate new candidates (none of which are found to be frequent).

Although GSP benefits from the Apriori pruning, it still generates a large number of candidates. In this example, six length-1 sequential patterns generate 51 length-2 candidates; 22 length-2 sequential patterns generate 64 length-3 candidates; and so on. Some candidates generated by GSP may not appear in the database at all. In this example, 13 out of 64 length-3 candidates do not appear in the database, resulting in wasted time. ■

The example shows that although an Apriori-like sequential pattern mining method, such as GSP, reduces search space, it typically needs to scan the database multiple times. It will likely generate a huge set of candidate sequences, especially when mining long sequences. There is a need for more efficient mining methods.

SPADE: An Apriori-Based Vertical Data Format Sequential Pattern Mining Algorithm

The Apriori-like sequential pattern mining approach (based on candidate generate-and-test) can also be explored by mapping a sequence database into vertical data format. In **vertical data format**, the database becomes a set of tuples of the form $\langle itemset : (sequence\_ID, event\_ID) \rangle$. That is, for a given itemset, we record the sequence identifier and corresponding event identifier for which the itemset occurs. The **event identifier** serves as a timestamp within a sequence. The *event_ID* of the ith itemset (or event) in a sequence is i. Note than an itemset can occur in more than one sequence. The set of (*sequence_ID*, *event_ID*) pairs for a given itemset forms the **ID_list** of the itemset. The mapping from horizontal to vertical format requires one scan of the database. A major advantage of using this format is that we can determine the support of any k-sequence by simply joining the ID_lists of any two of its $(k-1)$-length subsequences. The length of the resulting ID_list (i.e., unique *sequence_ID* values) is equal to the support of the k-sequence, which tells us whether the sequence is frequent.

SPADE (Sequential PAttern Discovery using Equivalent classes) is an Apriori-based sequential pattern mining algorithm that uses vertical data format. As with GSP, SPADE requires one scan to find the frequent 1-sequences. To find candidate 2-sequences, we join all pairs of single items if they are frequent (therein, it applies the Apriori property), if they share the same sequence identifier, and if their event identifiers follow a sequential ordering. That is, the first item in the pair must occur as an event before the second item, where both occur in the same sequence. Similarly, we can grow the length of itemsets from length 2 to length 3, and so on. The procedure stops when no frequent sequences can be found or no such sequences can be formed by such joins. The following example helps illustrate the process.

Example 8.9 **SPADE: Candidate generate-and-test using vertical data format.** Let $min\_sup = 2$. Our running example sequence database, S, of Table 8.1 is in horizonal data format. SPADE first scans S and transforms it into vertical format, as shown in Figure 8.6(a). Each itemset (or event) is associated with its ID_list, which is the set of *SID* (*sequence_ID*) and *EID* (*event_ID*) pairs that contain the itemset. The ID_list for individual items, a, b, and so on, is shown in Figure 8.6(b). For example, the ID_list for item b consists of the following (*SID*, *EID*) pairs: $\{(1, 2), (2, 3), (3, 2), (3, 5), (4, 5)\}$, where the entry (1, 2) means that b occurs in sequence 1, event 2, and so on. Items a and b are frequent. They can be joined to form the length-2 sequence, $\langle a, b\rangle$. We find the support of this sequence as follows. We join the ID_lists of a and b by joining on the same *sequence_ID* wherever, according to the *event_IDs*, a occurs before b. That is, the join must preserve the temporal order of the events involved. The result of such a join for a and b is shown in the ID_list for ab of Figure 8.6(c). For example, the ID_list for 2-sequence ab is a set of triples, (*SID*, *EID*(a), *EID*(b)), namely $\{(1, 1, 2), (2, 1, 3), (3, 2, 5), (4, 3, 5)\}$. The entry (2, 1, 3), for example, shows that both a and b occur in sequence 2, and that a (event 1 of the sequence) occurs before b (event 3), as required. Furthermore, the frequent 2-sequences can be joined (while considering the Apriori pruning heuristic that the (k-1)-subsequences of a candidate k-sequence must be frequent) to form 3-sequences, as in Figure 8.6(d), and so on. The process terminates when no frequent sequences can be found or no candidate sequences can be formed. Additional details of the method can be found in Zaki [Zak01]. ■

The use of vertical data format, with the creation of ID_lists, reduces scans of the sequence database. The ID_lists carry the information necessary to find the support of candidates. As the length of a frequent sequence increases, the size of its ID_list decreases, resulting in very fast joins. However, the basic search methodology of SPADE and GSP is breadth-first search (e.g., exploring 1-sequences, then 2-sequences, and so on) and Apriori pruning. Despite the pruning, both algorithms have to generate large sets of candidates in breadth-first manner in order to grow longer sequences. Thus, most of the difficulties suffered in the GSP algorithm recur in SPADE as well.

PrefixSpan: Prefix-Projected Sequential Pattern Growth

Pattern growth is a method of frequent-pattern mining that does not require candidate generation. The technique originated in the FP-growth algorithm for transaction databases, presented in Section 5.2.4. The general idea of this approach is as follows: it finds the frequent single items, then compresses this information into a *frequent-pattern*

SID	*EID*	*itemset*
1	1	a
1	2	abc
1	3	ac
1	4	d
1	5	cf
2	1	ad
2	2	c
2	3	bc
2	4	ae
3	1	ef
3	2	ab
3	3	df
3	4	c
3	5	b
4	1	e
4	2	g
4	3	af
4	4	c
4	5	b
4	6	c

(a) vertical format database

a		b		…
SID	*EID*	*SID*	*EID*	…
1	1	1	2	
1	2	2	3	
1	3	3	2	
2	1	3	5	
2	4	4	5	
3	2			
4	3			

(b) ID_lists for some 1-sequences

ab			ba			…
SID	*EID(a)*	*EID(b)*	*SID*	*EID(b)*	*EID(a)*	…
1	1	2	1	2	3	
2	1	3	2	3	4	
3	2	5				
4	3	5				

(c) ID_lists for some 2-sequences

aba				…
SID	*EID(a)*	*EID(b)*	*EID(a)*	…
1	1	2	3	
2	1	3	4	

(d) ID_lists for some 3-sequences

Figure 8.6 The SPADE mining process: (a) vertical format database; (b) to (d) show fragments of the ID_lists for 1-sequences, 2-sequences, and 3-sequences, respectively.

tree, or *FP-tree*. The FP-tree is used to generate a set of projected databases, each associated with one frequent item. Each of these databases is mined separately. The algorithm builds prefix patterns, which it concatenates with suffix patterns to find frequent patterns, avoiding candidate generation. Here, we look at PrefixSpan, which extends the pattern-growth approach to instead mine sequential patterns.

Suppose that all the items within an event are listed alphabetically. For example, instead of listing the items in an event as, say, (*bac*), we list them as (*abc*) without loss of generality. Given a sequence $\alpha = \langle e_1 e_2 \cdots e_n \rangle$ (where each e_i corresponds to a frequent event in a sequence database, S), a sequence $\beta = \langle e'_1 e'_2 \cdots e'_m \rangle$ $(m \leq n)$ is called a prefix of α if and only if (1) $e'_i = e_i$ for $(i \leq m-1)$; (2) $e'_m \subseteq e_m$; and (3) all the frequent items in $(e_m - e'_m)$ are alphabetically after those in e'_m. Sequence $\gamma = \langle e''_m e_{m+1} \cdots e_n \rangle$ is called the **suffix** of α with respect to prefix β, denoted as $\gamma = \alpha/\beta$, where $e''_m = (e_m - e'_m)$.[7] We also denote $\alpha = \beta \cdot \gamma$. Note if β is not a subsequence of α, the suffix of α with respect to β is empty.

We illustrate these concepts with the following example.

Example 8.10 **Prefix and suffix.** Let sequence $s = \langle a(abc)(ac)d(cf)\rangle$, which corresponds to sequence 1 of our running example sequence database. $\langle a\rangle$, $\langle aa\rangle$, $\langle a(ab)\rangle$, and $\langle a(abc)\rangle$ are four prefixes of s. $\langle (abc)(ac)d(cf)\rangle$ is the suffix of s with respect to the prefix $\langle a\rangle$; $\langle (\_bc)(ac)d(cf)\rangle$ is its suffix with respect to the prefix $\langle aa\rangle$; and $\langle (\_c)(ac)d(cf)\rangle$ is its suffix with respect to the prefix $\langle a(ab)\rangle$. ■

Based on the concepts of prefix and suffix, the problem of mining sequential patterns can be decomposed into a set of subproblems as shown:

1. Let $\{\langle x_1\rangle, \langle x_2\rangle, \ldots, \langle x_n\rangle\}$ be the complete set of length-1 sequential patterns in a sequence database, S. The complete set of sequential patterns in S can be partitioned into n disjoint subsets. The ith subset $(1 \le i \le n)$ is the set of sequential patterns with prefix $\langle x_i\rangle$.
2. Let α be a length-l sequential pattern and $\{\beta_1, \beta_2, \ldots, \beta_m\}$ be the set of all length-$(l+1)$ sequential patterns with prefix α. The complete set of sequential patterns with prefix α, except for α itself, can be partitioned into m disjoint subsets. The jth subset $(1 \le j \le m)$ is the set of sequential patterns prefixed with β_j.

Based on this observation, the problem can be partitioned recursively. That is, each subset of sequential patterns can be further partitioned when necessary. This forms a *divide-and-conquer* framework. To mine the subsets of sequential patterns, we construct corresponding *projected databases* and mine each one recursively.

Let's use our running example to examine how to use the prefix-based projection approach for mining sequential patterns.

Example 8.11 **PrefixSpan: A pattern-growth approach.** Using the same sequence database, S, of Table 8.1 with $min\_sup = 2$, sequential patterns in S can be mined by a prefix-projection method in the following steps.

1. *Find length-1 sequential patterns.* Scan S once to find all of the frequent items in sequences. Each of these frequent items is a length-1 sequential pattern. They are $\langle a\rangle : 4$, $\langle b\rangle : 4$, $\langle c\rangle : 4$, $\langle d\rangle : 3$, $\langle e\rangle : 3$, and $\langle f\rangle : 3$, where the notation "$\langle pattern\rangle : count$" represents the pattern and its associated support count.

[7] If e''_m is not empty, the suffix is also denoted as $\langle (\_ \text{ items in } e''_m) e_{m+1} \cdots e_n\rangle$.

Table 8.2 Projected databases and sequential patterns

prefix	*projected database*	*sequential patterns*
$\langle a \rangle$	$\langle (abc)(ac)d(cf) \rangle$, $\langle (\_d)c(bc)(ae) \rangle$, $\langle (\_b)(df)eb \rangle$, $\langle (\_f)cbc \rangle$	$\langle a \rangle$, $\langle aa \rangle$, $\langle ab \rangle$, $\langle a(bc) \rangle$, $\langle a(bc)a \rangle$, $\langle aba \rangle$, $\langle abc \rangle$, $\langle (ab) \rangle$, $\langle (ab)c \rangle$, $\langle (ab)d \rangle$, $\langle (ab)f \rangle$, $\langle (ab)dc \rangle$, $\langle ac \rangle$, $\langle aca \rangle$, $\langle acb \rangle$, $\langle acc \rangle$, $\langle ad \rangle$, $\langle adc \rangle$, $\langle af \rangle$
$\langle b \rangle$	$\langle (\_c)(ac)d(cf) \rangle$, $\langle (\_c)(ae) \rangle$, $\langle (df)cb \rangle$, $\langle c \rangle$	$\langle b \rangle$, $\langle ba \rangle$, $\langle bc \rangle$, $\langle (bc) \rangle$, $\langle (bc)a \rangle$, $\langle bd \rangle$, $\langle bdc \rangle$, $\langle bf \rangle$
$\langle c \rangle$	$\langle (ac)d(cf) \rangle$, $\langle (bc)(ae) \rangle$, $\langle b \rangle$, $\langle bc \rangle$	$\langle c \rangle$, $\langle ca \rangle$, $\langle cb \rangle$, $\langle cc \rangle$
$\langle d \rangle$	$\langle (cf) \rangle$, $\langle c(bc)(ae) \rangle$, $\langle (\_f)cb \rangle$	$\langle d \rangle$, $\langle db \rangle$, $\langle dc \rangle$, $\langle dcb \rangle$
$\langle e \rangle$	$\langle (\_f)(ab)(df)cb \rangle$, $\langle (af)cbc \rangle$	$\langle e \rangle$, $\langle ea \rangle$, $\langle eab \rangle$, $\langle eac \rangle$, $\langle eacb \rangle$, $\langle eb \rangle$, $\langle ebc \rangle$, $\langle ec \rangle$, $\langle ecb \rangle$, $\langle ef \rangle$, $\langle efb \rangle$, $\langle efc \rangle$, $\langle efcb \rangle$.
$\langle f \rangle$	$\langle (ab)(df)cb \rangle$, $\langle cbc \rangle$	$\langle f \rangle$, $\langle fb \rangle$, $\langle fbc \rangle$, $\langle fc \rangle$, $\langle fcb \rangle$

2. *Partition the search space.* The complete set of sequential patterns can be partitioned into the following six subsets according to the six prefixes: (1) the ones with prefix $\langle a \rangle$, (2) the ones with prefix $\langle b \rangle, \ldots$, and (6) the ones with prefix $\langle f \rangle$.

3. *Find subsets of sequential patterns.* The subsets of sequential patterns mentioned in step 2 can be mined by constructing corresponding *projected databases* and mining each recursively. The projected databases, as well as the sequential patterns found in them, are listed in Table 8.2, while the mining process is explained as follows:

   (a) *Find sequential patterns with prefix $\langle a \rangle$.* Only the sequences containing $\langle a \rangle$ should be collected. Moreover, in a sequence containing $\langle a \rangle$, only the subsequence prefixed with the first occurrence of $\langle a \rangle$ should be considered. For example, in sequence $\langle (ef)(ab)(df)cb \rangle$, only the subsequence $\langle (\_b)(df)cb \rangle$ should be considered for mining sequential patterns prefixed with $\langle a \rangle$. Notice that $(\_b)$ means that the last event in the prefix, which is a, together with b, form one event.
   The sequences in S containing $\langle a \rangle$ are projected with respect to $\langle a \rangle$ to form the $\langle a \rangle$*-projected database*, which consists of four suffix sequences: $\langle (abc)(ac)d(cf) \rangle$, $\langle (\_d)c(bc)(ae) \rangle$, $\langle (\_b)(df)cb \rangle$, and $\langle (\_f)cbc \rangle$.
   By scanning the $\langle a \rangle$-projected database once, its locally frequent items are identified as $a : 2$, $b : 4$, $\_b : 2$, $c : 4$, $d : 2$, and $f : 2$. Thus all the length-2 sequential patterns prefixed with $\langle a \rangle$ are found, and they are: $\langle aa \rangle : 2$, $\langle ab \rangle : 4$, $\langle (ab) \rangle : 2$, $\langle ac \rangle : 4$, $\langle ad \rangle : 2$, and $\langle af \rangle : 2$.

Recursively, all sequential patterns with prefix $\langle a\rangle$ can be partitioned into six subsets: (1) those prefixed with $\langle aa\rangle$, (2) those with $\langle ab\rangle, \ldots$, and finally, (6) those with $\langle af\rangle$. These subsets can be mined by constructing respective projected databases and mining each recursively as follows:

i. The $\langle aa\rangle$-projected database consists of two nonempty (suffix) subsequences prefixed with $\langle aa\rangle$: $\{\langle(\_bc)(ac)d(cf)\rangle, \{\langle(\_e)\rangle\}$. Because there is no hope of generating any frequent subsequence from this projected database, the processing of the $\langle aa\rangle$-projected database terminates.

ii. The $\langle ab\rangle$-projected database consists of three suffix sequences: $\langle(\_c)(ac)d(cf)\rangle$, $\langle(\_c)a\rangle$, and $\langle c\rangle$. Recursively mining the $\langle ab\rangle$-projected database returns four sequential patterns: $\langle(\_c)\rangle$, $\langle(\_c)a\rangle$, $\langle a\rangle$, and $\langle c\rangle$ (i.e., $\langle a(bc)\rangle$, $\langle a(bc)a\rangle$, $\langle aba\rangle$, and $\langle abc\rangle$.) They form the complete set of sequential patterns prefixed with $\langle ab\rangle$.

iii. The $\langle(ab)\rangle$-projected database contains only two sequences: $\langle(\_c)(ac)\,d(cf)\rangle$ and $\langle(df)cb\rangle$, which leads to the finding of the following sequential patterns prefixed with $\langle(ab)\rangle$: $\langle c\rangle$, $\langle d\rangle$, $\langle f\rangle$, and $\langle dc\rangle$.

iv. The $\langle ac\rangle$-, $\langle ad\rangle$-, and $\langle af\rangle$- projected databases can be constructed and recursively mined in a similar manner. The sequential patterns found are shown in Table 8.2.

(b) *Find sequential patterns with prefix $\langle b\rangle$, $\langle c\rangle$, $\langle d\rangle$, $\langle e\rangle$, and $\langle f\rangle$, respectively*. This can be done by constructing the $\langle b\rangle$-, $\langle c\rangle$-, $\langle d\rangle$-, $\langle e\rangle$-, and $\langle f\rangle$-projected databases and mining them respectively. The projected databases as well as the sequential patterns found are also shown in Table 8.2.

4. *The set of sequential patterns is the collection of patterns found in the above recursive mining process.* ■

The method described above generates no candidate sequences in the mining process. However, it may generate many projected databases, one for each frequent prefix-subsequence. Forming a large number of projected databases recursively may become the major cost of the method, if such databases have to be generated physically. An important optimization technique is **pseudo-projection**, which registers the index (or identifier) of the corresponding sequence and the starting position of the projected suffix in the sequence instead of performing physical projection. That is, a physical projection of a sequence is replaced by registering a sequence identifier and the projected position index point. Pseudo-projection reduces the cost of projection substantially when such projection can be done in main memory. However, it may not be efficient if the pseudo-projection is used for disk-based accessing because random access of disk space is costly. The suggested approach is that if the original sequence database or the projected databases are too big to fit in memory, the physical projection should be applied; however, the execution should be swapped to pseudo-projection once the projected databases can fit in memory. This methodology is adopted in the PrefixSpan implementation.

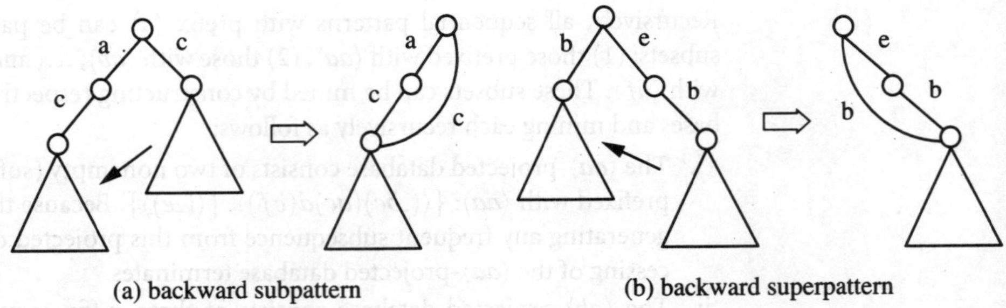

Figure 8.7 A backward subpattern and a backward superpattern.

A performance comparison of GSP, SPADE, and PrefixSpan shows that PrefixSpan has the best overall performance. SPADE, although weaker than PrefixSpan in most cases, outperforms GSP. Generating huge candidate sets may consume a tremendous amount of memory, thereby causing candidate generate-and-test algorithms to become very slow. The comparison also found that when there is a large number of frequent subsequences, all three algorithms run slowly. This problem can be partially solved by closed sequential pattern mining.

Mining Closed Sequential Patterns

Because mining the complete set of frequent subsequences can generate a huge number of sequential patterns, an interesting alternative is to mine frequent *closed subsequences* only, that is, those containing no supersequence with the same support. Mining closed sequential patterns can produce a significantly less number of sequences than the full set of sequential patterns. Note that the full set of frequent subsequences, together with their supports, can easily be derived from the closed subsequences. Thus, closed subsequences have the same expressive power as the corresponding full set of subsequences. Because of their compactness, they may also be quicker to find.

CloSpan is an efficient closed sequential pattern mining method. The method is based on a property of sequence databases, called **equivalence of projected databases**, stated as follows: *Two projected sequence databases,* $S|_\alpha = S|_\beta$,[8] $\alpha \sqsubseteq \beta$ *(i.e.,* α *is a subsequence of* β*), are equivalent if and only if the total number of items in* $S|_\alpha$ *is equal to the total number of items in* $S|_\beta$.

Based on this property, CloSpan can prune the nonclosed sequences from further consideration during the mining process. That is, whenever we find two prefix-based projected databases that are exactly the same, we can stop growing one of them. This can be used to prune *backward subpatterns* and *backward superpatterns* as indicated in Figure 8.7.

[8] In $S|_\alpha$, a sequence database S is projected with respect to sequence (e.g., prefix) α. The notation $S|_\beta$ can be similarly defined.

After such pruning and mining, a postprocessing step is still required in order to delete nonclosed sequential patterns that may exist in the derived set. A later algorithm called BIDE (which performs a bidirectional search) can further optimize this process to avoid such additional checking.

Empirical results show that CloSpan often derives a much smaller set of sequential patterns in a shorter time than PrefixSpan, which mines the complete set of sequential patterns.

Mining Multidimensional, Multilevel Sequential Patterns

Sequence identifiers (representing individual customers, for example) and sequence items (such as products bought) are often associated with additional pieces of information. Sequential pattern mining should take advantage of such additional information to discover interesting patterns in multidimensional, multilevel information space. Take customer shopping transactions, for instance. In a sequence database for such data, the additional information associated with sequence IDs could include customer age, address, group, and profession. Information associated with items could include item category, brand, model type, model number, place manufactured, and manufacture date. Mining *multidimensional, multilevel* sequential patterns is the discovery of interesting patterns in such a broad dimensional space, at different levels of detail.

Example 8.12 **Multidimensional, multilevel sequential patterns.** The discovery that "*Retired customers who purchase a digital camera are likely to purchase a color printer within a month*" and that "*Young adults who purchase a laptop are likely to buy a flash drive within two weeks*" are examples of multidimensional, multilevel sequential patterns. By grouping customers into "*retired customers*" and "*young adults*" according to the values in the age dimension, and by generalizing items to, say, "*digital camera*" rather than a specific model, the patterns mined here are associated with additional dimensions and are at a higher level of granularity. ■

"*Can a typical sequential pattern algorithm such as PrefixSpan be extended to efficiently mine multidimensional, multilevel sequential patterns?*" One suggested modification is to associate the multidimensional, multilevel information with the *sequence_ID* and *item_ID*, respectively, which the mining method can take into consideration when finding frequent subsequences. For example, (*Chicago, middle_aged, business*) can be associated with *sequence_ID_1002* (for a given customer), whereas (*Digital_camera, Canon, Supershot, SD*400, *Japan*, 2005) can be associated with *item_ID_543005* in the sequence. A sequential pattern mining algorithm will use such information in the mining process to find sequential patterns associated with multidimensional, multilevel information.

8.3.3 Constraint-Based Mining of Sequential Patterns

As shown in our study of frequent-pattern mining in Chapter 5, mining that is performed without user- or expert-specified constraints may generate numerous patterns that are of no interest. Such unfocused mining can reduce both the efficiency and usability of frequent-pattern mining. Thus, we promote **constraint-based mining**, which incorporates user-specified constraints to reduce the search space and derive only patterns that are of interest to the user.

Constraints can be expressed in many forms. They may specify desired relationships between attributes, attribute values, or aggregates within the resulting patterns mined. Regular expressions can also be used as constraints in the form of "pattern templates," which specify the desired form of the patterns to be mined. The general concepts introduced for constraint-based frequent pattern mining in Section 5.5.1 apply to constraint-based sequential pattern mining as well. The key idea to note is that these kinds of constraints can be used *during* the mining process to confine the search space, thereby improving (1) the efficiency of the mining and (2) the interestingness of the resulting patterns found. This idea is also referred to as *"pushing the constraints deep into the mining process."*

We now examine some typical examples of constraints for sequential pattern mining. First, constraints can be related to the **duration**, T, of a sequence. The duration may be the maximal or minimal length of the sequence in the database, or a user-specified duration related to time, such as the year 2005. Sequential pattern mining can then be confined to the data within the specified duration, T.

Constraints relating to the maximal or minimal length (duration) can be treated as *antimonotonic* or *monotonic* constraints, respectively. For example, the constraint $T \leq 10$ is **antimonotonic** since, if a sequence does not satisfy this constraint, then neither will any of its supersequences (which are, obviously, longer). The constraint $T > 10$ is **monotonic**. This means that if a sequence satisfies the constraint, then all of its supersequences will also satisfy the constraint. We have already seen several examples in this chapter of how antimonotonic constraints (such as those involving minimum support) can be pushed deep into the mining process to prune the search space. Monotonic constraints can be used in a way similar to its frequent-pattern counterpart as well.

Constraints related to a specific duration, such as a particular year, are considered *succinct* constraints. A constraint is **succinct** if we can enumerate all and only those sequences that are guaranteed to satisfy the constraint, even before support counting begins. Suppose, here, $T = 2005$. By selecting the data for which $year = 2005$, we can enumerate all of the sequences *guaranteed to satisfy* the constraint before mining begins. In other words, we don't need to generate and test. Thus, such constraints contribute toward efficiency in that they avoid the substantial overhead of the generate-and-test paradigm.

Durations may also be defined as being related to sets of partitioned sequences, such as every year, or every month after stock dips, or every two weeks before and after an earthquake. In such cases, *periodic patterns* (Section 8.3.4) can be discovered.

Second, the constraint may be related to an **event folding window**, w. A set of events occurring within a specified period can be viewed as occurring together. If w is set to be as long as the duration, T, it finds time-insensitive frequent patterns—these are essentially frequent patterns, such as "*In 1999, customers who bought a PC bought a digital camera as well*" (i.e., without bothering about which items were bought first). If w is set to 0 (i.e., no event sequence folding), sequential patterns are found where each event occurs at a distinct time instant, such as "*A customer who bought a PC and then a digital camera is likely to buy an SD memory chip in a month.*" If w is set to be something in between (e.g., for transactions occurring within the same month or within a sliding window of 24 hours), then these transactions are considered as occurring within the same period, and such sequences are "folded" in the analysis.

Third, a desired (time) **gap** between events in the discovered patterns may be specified as a constraint. Possible cases are: (1) $gap = 0$ (no gap is allowed), which is to find strictly consecutive sequential patterns like $a_{i-1}a_ia_{i+1}$. For example, if the event folding window is set to a week, this will find frequent patterns occurring in consecutive weeks; (2) $min\_gap \leq gap \leq max\_gap$, which is to find patterns that are separated by at least min_gap but at most max_gap, such as "*If a person rents movie A, it is likely she will rent movie B within 30 days*" implies $gap \leq 30$ (days); and (3) $gap = c \neq 0$, which is to find patterns with an exact gap, c. It is straightforward to push gap constraints into the sequential pattern mining process. With minor modifications to the mining process, it can handle constraints with approximate gaps as well.

Finally, a user can specify constraints on the kinds of sequential patterns by providing "pattern templates" in the form of *serial episodes* and *parallel episodes* using *regular expressions*. A **serial episode** is a set of events that occurs in a total order, whereas a **parallel episode** is a set of events whose occurrence ordering is trivial. Consider the following example.

Example 8.13 Specifying serial episodes and parallel episodes with regular expressions. Let the notation (E, t) represent *event type E* at *time t*. Consider the data $(A, 1)$, $(C, 2)$, and $(B, 5)$ with an event folding window width of $w = 2$, where the serial episode $A \rightarrow B$ and the parallel episode A & C both occur in the data. The user can specify constraints in the form of a regular expression, such as $(A|B)C * (D|E)$, which indicates that the user would like to find patterns where event A and B first occur (but they are parallel in that their relative ordering is unimportant), followed by one or a set of events C, followed by the events D and E (where D can occur either before or after E). Other events can occur in between those specified in the regular expression. ■

A regular expression constraint may be neither antimonotonic nor monotonic. In such cases, we cannot use it to prune the search space in the same ways as described above. However, by modifying the PrefixSpan-based pattern-growth approach, such constraints can be handled elegantly. Let's examine one such example.

Example 8.14 Constraint-based sequential pattern mining with a regular expression constraint. Suppose that our task is to mine sequential patterns, again using the sequence database, S, of Table 8.1. This time, however, we are particularly interested in patterns that match the regular expression constraint, $C = \langle a \star \{bb|(bc)d|dd\}\rangle$, with minimum support.

Such a regular expression constraint is neither antimonotonic, nor monotonic, nor succinct. Therefore, it cannot be pushed deep into the mining process. Nonetheless, this constraint can easily be integrated with the pattern-growth mining process as follows.

First, only the $\langle a \rangle$-projected database, $S|_{\langle a \rangle}$, needs to be mined, since the regular expression constraint C starts with a. Retain only the sequences in $S|_{\langle a \rangle}$ that contain items within the set $\{b, c, d\}$. Second, the remaining mining can proceed from the suffix. This is essentially the *SuffixSpan* algorithm, which is symmetric to PrefixSpan in that it grows suffixes from the end of the sequence forward. The growth should match the suffix as the constraint, $\langle \{bb|(bc)d|dd\} \rangle$. For the projected databases that match these suffixes, we can grow sequential patterns either in prefix- or suffix-expansion manner to find all of the remaining sequential patterns. ■

Thus, we have seen several ways in which constraints can be used to improve the efficiency and usability of sequential pattern mining.

8.3.4 Periodicity Analysis for Time-Related Sequence Data

"What is periodicity analysis?" Periodicity analysis is the mining of periodic patterns, that is, the search for recurring patterns in time-related sequence data. Periodicity analysis can be applied to many important areas. For example, seasons, tides, planet trajectories, daily power consumptions, daily traffic patterns, and weekly TV programs all present certain periodic patterns. Periodicity analysis is often performed over time-series data, which consists of sequences of values or events typically measured at equal time intervals (e.g., hourly, daily, weekly). It can also be applied to other time-related sequence data where the value or event may occur at a nonequal time interval or at any time (e.g., on-line transactions). Moreover, the items to be analyzed can be numerical data, such as daily temperature or power consumption fluctuations, or categorical data (events), such as purchasing a product or watching a game.

The problem of mining periodic patterns can be viewed from different perspectives. Based on the coverage of the pattern, we can categorize periodic patterns into *full* versus *partial* periodic patterns:

- A **full periodic pattern** is a pattern where every point in time contributes (precisely or approximately) to the cyclic behavior of a time-related sequence. For example, all of the days in the year *approximately* contribute to the season cycle of the year.
- A **partial periodic pattern** specifies the periodic behavior of a time-related sequence at some but not all of the points in time. For example, Sandy reads the *New York Times* from 7:00 to 7:30 every weekday morning, but her activities at other times do not have much regularity. Partial periodicity is a looser form of periodicity than full periodicity and occurs more commonly in the real world.

Based on the precision of the periodicity, a pattern can be either *synchronous* or *asynchronous*, where the former requires that an event occur at a relatively fixed offset in each "stable" period, such as 3 p.m. every day, whereas the latter allows that the event fluctuates in a somewhat loosely defined period. A pattern can also be either *precise* or *approximate*, depending on the data value or the offset within a period. For example, if

Sandy reads the newspaper at 7:00 on some days, but at 7:10 or 7:15 on others, this is an approximate periodic pattern.

Techniques for full periodicity analysis for numerical values have been studied in signal analysis and statistics. Methods like FFT (Fast Fourier Transformation) are commonly used to transform data from the time domain to the frequency domain in order to facilitate such analysis.

Mining partial, categorical, and asynchronous periodic patterns poses more challenging problems in regards to the development of efficient data mining solutions. This is because most statistical methods or those relying on time-to-frequency domain transformations are either inapplicable or expensive at handling such problems.

Take mining partial periodicity as an example. Because partial periodicity mixes periodic events and nonperiodic events together in the same period, a time-to-frequency transformation method, such as FFT, becomes ineffective because it treats the time series as an inseparable flow of values. Certain periodicity detection methods can uncover some partial periodic patterns, but only if the period, length, and timing of the segment (subsequence of interest) in the partial patterns have certain behaviors and are explicitly specified. For the newspaper reading example, we need to explicitly specify details such as "Find the regular activities of Sandy during the half-hour after 7:00 for a period of 24 hours." A naïve adaptation of such methods to the partial periodic pattern mining problem would be prohibitively expensive, requiring their application to a huge number of possible combinations of the three parameters of period, length, and timing.

Most of the studies on mining partial periodic patterns apply the Apriori property heuristic and adopt some variations of Apriori-like mining methods. Constraints can also be pushed deep into the mining process. Studies have also been performed on the efficient mining of partially periodic event patterns or asynchronous periodic patterns with unknown or with approximate periods.

Mining partial periodicity may lead to the discovery of **cyclic or periodic association rules**, which are rules that associate a set of events that occur periodically. An example of a periodic association rule is "*Based on day-to-day transactions, if afternoon tea is well received between 3:00 to 5:00 p.m., dinner will sell well between 7:00 to 9:00 p.m. on weekends.*"

Due to the diversity of applications of time-related sequence data, further development of efficient algorithms for mining various kinds of periodic patterns in sequence databases is desired.

8.4 Mining Sequence Patterns in Biological Data

Bioinformatics is a promising young field that applies computer technology in molecular biology and develops algorithms and methods to manage and analyze biological data. Because DNA and protein sequences are essential biological data and exist in huge volumes as well, it is important to develop effective methods to compare and align biological sequences and discover biosequence patterns.

Before we get into further details, let's look at the type of data being analyzed. DNA and proteins sequences are long linear chains of chemical components. In the case of DNA, these components or "building blocks" are four **nucleotides** (also called *bases*), namely adenine (A), cytosine (C), guanine (G), and thymine (T). In the case of proteins, the components are 20 **amino acids**, denoted by 20 different letters of the alphabet. A gene is a sequence of typically hundreds of individual nucleotides arranged in a particular order. A **genome** is the complete set of genes of an organism. When proteins are needed, the corresponding genes are transcribed into RNA. RNA is a chain of nucleotides. DNA directs the synthesis of a variety of RNA molecules, each with a unique role in cellular function.

"*Why is it useful to compare and align biosequences?*" The alignment is based on the fact that all living organisms are related by evolution. This implies that the nucleotide (DNA, RNA) and proteins sequences of the species that are closer to each other in evolution should exhibit more similarities. An **alignment** is the process of lining up sequences to achieve a maximal level of identity, which also expresses the degree of similarity between sequences. Two sequences are **homologous** if they share a common ancestor. The degree of similarity obtained by sequence alignment can be useful in determining the possibility of homology between two sequences. Such an alignment also helps determine the relative positions of multiple species in an evolution tree, which is called a **phylogenetic tree.**

In Section 8.4.1, we first study methods for *pairwise alignment* (i.e., the alignment of two biological sequences). This is followed by methods for *multiple sequence alignment.* Section 8.4.2 introduces the popularly used Hidden Markov Model (HMM) for biological sequence analysis.

8.4.1 Alignment of Biological Sequences

The problem of alignment of biological sequences can be described as follows: *Given two or more input biological sequences, identify similar sequences with long conserved subsequences.* If the number of sequences to be aligned is exactly two, it is called **pairwise sequence alignment**; otherwise, it is **multiple sequence alignment**. The sequences to be compared and aligned can be either nucleotides (DNA/RNA) or amino acids (proteins). For nucleotides, two symbols align if they are identical. However, for amino acids, two symbols align if they are identical, or if one can be derived from the other by substitutions that are likely to occur in nature. There are two kinds of alignments: *local alignments* versus *global alignments*. The former means that only portions of the sequences are aligned, whereas the latter requires alignment over the entire length of the sequences.

For either nucleotides or amino acids, insertions, deletions, and substitutions occur in nature with different probabilities. **Substitution matrices** are used to represent the probabilities of substitutions of nucleotides or amino acids and probabilities of insertions and deletions. Usually, we use the gap character, "−", to indicate positions where it is preferable not to align two symbols. To evaluate the quality of alignments, a *scoring* mechanism is typically defined, which usually counts identical or similar symbols as positive scores and gaps as negative ones. The algebraic sum of the scores is taken as the alignment measure. The goal of alignment is to achieve the maximal score among all the possible alignments. However, it is very expensive (more exactly, an NP-hard problem) to find optimal alignment. Therefore, various heuristic methods have been developed to find suboptimal alignments.

Pairwise Alignment

Example 8.15 Pairwise alignment. Suppose we have two amino acid sequences as follows, and the substitution matrix of amino acids for pairwise alignment is shown in Table 8.3.

Suppose the penalty for initiating a gap (called the *gap penalty*) is −8 and that for extending a gap (i.e., *gap extension penalty*) is also −8. We can then compare two potential sequence alignment candidates, as shown in Figure 8.8 (a) and (b) by calculating their total alignment scores.

The total score of the alignment for Figure 8.8(a) is $(-2)+(-8)+(5)+(-8)+(-8)+(15)+(-8)+(10)+(6)+(-8)+(6)=0$, whereas that for Figure 8.8(b) is

Table 8.3 The substitution matrix of amino acids.

HEAGAWGHEE

PAWHEAE

	A	*E*	*G*	*H*	*W*
A	5	−1	0	−2	−3
E	−1	6	−3	0	−3
H	−2	0	−2	10	−3
P	−1	−1	−2	−2	−4
W	−3	−3	−3	−3	15

```
H E A G A W G H E − E
    |     |   | |   |
P − A − − W − H E A E
```

(*a*)

```
H E A G A W G H E − E
        | |   | |   |
− − P − A W − H E A E
```

(*b*)

Figure 8.8 Scoring two potential pairwise alignments, (*a*) and (*b*), of amino acids.

$(-8)+(-8)+(-1)+(-8)+(5)+(15)+(-8)+(10)+(6)+(-8)+(6) = 1$. Thus the alignment of Figure 8.8(b) is slightly better than that in Figure 8.8(a). ■

Biologists have developed 20 × 20 triangular matrices that provide the weights for comparing identical and different amino acids as well as the penalties that should be attributed to gaps. Two frequently used matrices are PAM (Percent Accepted Mutation) and BLOSUM (BlOcks SUbstitution Matrix). These substitution matrices represent the weights obtained by comparing the amino acid substitutions that have occurred through evolution.

For global pairwise sequence alignment, two influential algorithms have been proposed: the *Needleman-Wunsch Algorithm* and the *Smith-Waterman Algorithm*. The former uses weights for the outmost edges that encourage the best overall global alignment, whereas the latter favors the contiguity of segments being aligned. Both build up "optimal" alignment from "optimal" alignments of subsequences. Both use the methodology of dynamic programming. Since these algorithms use recursion to fill in an intermediate results table, it takes $O(mn)$ space and $O(n^2)$ time to execute them. Such computational complexity could be feasible for moderate-sized sequences but is not feasible for aligning large sequences, especially for entire genomes, where a *genome* is the complete set of genes of an organism. Another approach called *dot matrix plot* uses Boolean matrices to represent possible alignments that can be detected visually. The method is simple and facilitates easy visual inspection. However, it still takes $O(n^2)$ in time and space to construct and inspect such matrices.

To reduce the computational complexity, heuristic alignment algorithms have been proposed. Heuristic algorithms speed up the alignment process at the price of possibly missing the best scoring alignment. There are two influential heuristic alignment programs: (1) BLAST (Basic Local Alignment Search Tool), and (2) FASTA (Fast Alignment Tool). Both find high-scoring local alignments between a query sequence and a target database. Their basic idea is to first locate high-scoring short stretches and then extend them to achieve suboptimal alignments. Because the BLAST algorithm has been very popular in biology and bioinformatics research, we examine it in greater detail here.

The BLAST Local Alignment Algorithm

The BLAST algorithm was first developed by Altschul, Gish, Miller, et al. around 1990 at the National Center for Biotechnology Information (NCBI). The software, its tutorials, and a wealth of other information can be accessed at *www.ncbi.nlm.nih.gov/BLAST/*. BLAST finds regions of local similarity between biosequences. The program compares nucleotide or protein sequences to sequence databases and calculates the statistical significance of matches. BLAST can be used to infer functional and evolutionary relationships between sequences as well as to help identify members of gene families.

The NCBI website contains many common BLAST databases. According to their content, they are grouped into nucleotide and protein databases. NCBI also provides specialized BLAST databases such as the vector screening database, a variety of genome databases for different organisms, and trace databases.

BLAST applies a heuristic method to find the highest local alignments between a query sequence and a database. BLAST improves the overall speed of search by breaking the sequences to be compared into sequences of fragments (referred to as **words**) and initially seeking matches between these words. In BLAST, the words are considered as k-tuples. For DNA nucleotides, a word typically consists of 11 bases (nucleotides), whereas for proteins, a word typically consists of 3 amino acids. BLAST first creates a hash table of neighborhood (i.e., closely matching) words, while the threshold for "closeness" is set based on statistics. It starts from exact matches to neighborhood words. Because good alignments should contain many close matches, we can use statistics to determine which matches are significant. By hashing, we can find matches in $O(n)$ (linear) time. By extending matches in both directions, the method finds high-quality alignments consisting of many high-scoring and maximum segment pairs.

There are many versions and extensions of the BLAST algorithms. For example, MEGABLAST, Discontiguous MEGABLAST, and BLASTN all can be used to identify a nucleotide sequence. MEGABLAST is specifically designed to efficiently find long alignments between very similar sequences, and thus is the best tool to use to find the identical match to a query sequence. Discontiguous MEGABLAST is better at finding nucleotide sequences that are similar, but not identical (i.e., gapped alignments), to a nucleotide query. One of the important parameters governing the sensitivity of BLAST searches is the length of the initial words, or *word size*. The word size is adjustable in BLASTN and can be reduced from the default value to a minimum of 7 to increase search sensitivity. Thus BLASTN is better than MEGABLAST at finding alignments to related nucleotide sequences from other organisms. For protein searches, BLASTP, PSI-BLAST, and PHI-BLAST are popular. Standard protein-protein BLAST (BLASTP) is used for both identifying a query amino acid sequence and for finding similar sequences in protein databases. Position-Specific Iterated (PSI)-BLAST is designed for more sensitive protein-protein similarity searches. It is useful for finding very distantly related proteins. Pattern-Hit Initiated (PHI)-BLAST can do a restricted protein pattern search. It is designed to search for proteins that contain a pattern specified by the user and are similar to the query sequence in the vicinity of the pattern. This dual requirement is intended to reduce the number of database hits that contain the pattern, but are likely to have no true homology to the query.

Multiple Sequence Alignment Methods

Multiple sequence alignment is usually performed on a set of sequences of amino acids that are believed to have similar structures. The goal is to find common patterns that are conserved among all the sequences being considered.

The alignment of multiple sequences has many applications. First, such an alignment may assist in the identification of highly conserved residues (amino acids), which are likely to be essential sites for structure and function. This will guide or help pairwise alignment as well. Second, it will help build gene or protein families using conserved regions, forming a basis for phylogenetic analysis (i.e., the inference of evolutionary relationships between genes). Third, conserved regions can be used to develop primers for amplifying DNA sequences and probes for DNA microarray analysis.

From the computational point of view, it is more challenging to align multiple sequences than to perform pairwise alignment of two sequences. This is because multisequence alignment can be considered as a multidimensional alignment problem, and there are many more possibilities for approximate alignments of subsequences in multiple dimensions.

There are two major approaches for approximate multiple sequence alignment. The first method reduces a multiple alignment to a series of pairwise alignments and then combines the result. The popular **Feng-Doolittle alignment** method belongs to this approach. Feng-Doolittle alignment first computes all of the possible pairwise alignments by dynamic programming and converts or normalizes alignment scores to distances. It then constructs a "guide tree" by clustering and performs progressive alignment based on the guide tree in a bottom-up manner. Following this approach, a multiple alignment tool, Clustal W, and its variants have been developed as software packages for multiple sequence alignments. The software handles a variety of input/output formats and provides displays for visual inspection.

The second multiple sequence alignment method uses hidden Markov models (HMMs). Due to the extensive use and popularity of hidden Markov models, we devote an entire section to this approach. It is introduced in Section 8.4.2, which follows.

From the above discussion, we can see that several interesting methods have been developed for multiple sequence alignment. Due to its computational complexity, the development of effective and scalable methods for multiple sequence alignment remains an active research topic in biological data mining.

8.4.2 Hidden Markov Model for Biological Sequence Analysis

Given a biological sequence, such as a DNA sequence or an amino acid (protein), biologists would like to analyze what that sequence represents. For example, is a given DNA sequence a gene or not? Or, to which family of proteins does a particular amino acid sequence belong? In general, given sequences of symbols from some alphabet, we would like to represent the structure or statistical regularities of classes of sequences. In this section, we discuss *Markov chains* and *hidden Markov models*—probabilistic models that are well suited for this type of task. Other areas of research, such as speech and pattern recognition, are faced with similar sequence analysis tasks.

To illustrate our discussion of Markov chains and hidden Markov models, we use a classic problem in biological sequence analysis—that of finding *CpG islands* in a DNA sequence. Here, the alphabet consists of four **nucleotides**, namely, A (adenine), C (cytosine), G (guanine), and T (thymine). **CpG** denotes a pair (or subsequence) of nucleotides, where G appears immediately after C along a DNA strand. The C in a CpG pair is often modified by a process known as *methylation* (where the C is replaced by methyl-C, which tends to mutate to T). As a result, CpG pairs occur infrequently in the human genome. However, methylation is often suppressed around *promotors* or "start" regions of many genes. These areas contain a relatively high concentration of CpG pairs, collectively referred to along a chromosome as **CpG islands**, which typically vary in length from a few hundred to a few thousand nucleotides long. CpG islands are very useful in genome mapping projects.

Two important questions that biologists have when studying DNA sequences are (1) given a short sequence, is it from a CpG island or not? and (2) given a long sequence, can we find all of the CpG islands within it? We start our exploration of these questions by introducing Markov chains.

Markov Chain

A **Markov chain** is a model that generates sequences in which the probability of a symbol depends only on the previous symbol. Figure 8.9 is an example Markov chain model. A Markov chain model is defined by (a) a set of *states*, Q, which emit symbols and (b) a set of *transitions* between states. States are represented by circles and transitions are represented by arrows. Each transition has an associated **transition probability,** a_{ij}, which represents the conditional probability of going to state j in the next step, given that the current state is i. The sum of all transition probabilities from a given state must equal 1, that is, $\sum_{j \in Q} a_{ij} = 1$ for all $j \in Q$. If an arc is not shown, it is assumed to have a 0 probability. The transition probabilities can also be written as a *transition matrix*, $A = \{a_{ij}\}$.

Example 8.16 **Markov chain.** The Markov chain in Figure 8.9 is a probabilistic model for CpG islands. The states are A, C, G, and T. For readability, only some of the transition probabilities are shown. For example, the transition probability from state G to state T is 0.14, that is, $P(x_i = \mathrm{T}|x_{i-1} = \mathrm{G}) = 0.14$. Here, the emitted symbols are understood. For example, the symbol C is emitted when transitioning from state C. In speech recognition, the symbols emitted could represent spoken words or phrases. ■

Given some sequence x of length L, how probable is x given the model? If x is a DNA sequence, we could use our Markov chain model to determine how probable it is that x is from a CpG island. To do so, we look at the probability of x as a *path*, $x_1x_2 \ldots x_L$, in the chain. This is the probability of starting in the first state, x_1, and making successive transitions to x_2, x_3, and so on, to x_L. In a Markov chain model, the probability of x_L

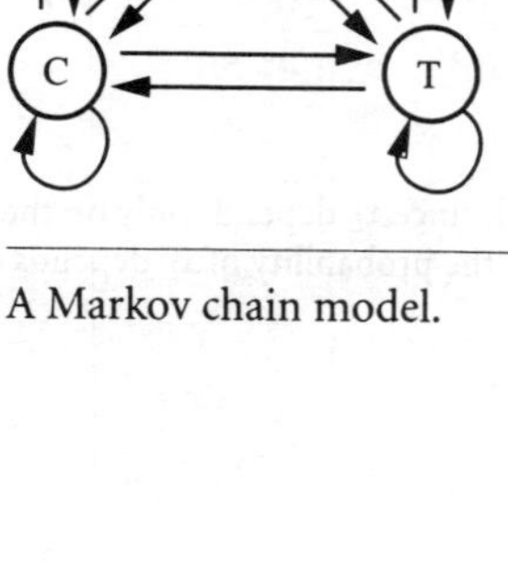

Figure 8.9 A Markov chain model.

depends on the value of only the *previous one state*, x_{L-1}, not on the entire previous sequence.[9] This characteristic is known as the **Markov property**, which can be written as

$$P(x) = P(x_L|x_{L-1})P(x_{L-1}|x_{L-2})\cdots P(x_2|x_1)P(x_1)$$
$$= P(x_1)\prod_{i=2}^{L} P(x_i|x_{i-1}). \tag{8.7}$$

That is, the Markov chain can only "remember" the previous one state of its history. Beyond that, it is "memoryless."

In Equation (8.7), we need to specify $P(x_1)$, the probability of the starting state. For simplicity, we would like to model this as a transition too. This can be done by adding a *begin* state, denoted 0, so that the starting state becomes $x_0 = 0$. Similarly, we can add an *end* state, also denoted as 0. Note that $P(x_i|x_{i-1})$ is the transition probability, $a_{x_{i-1}x_i}$. Therefore, Equation (8.7) can be rewritten as

$$P(x) = \prod_{i=1}^{L} a_{x_{i-1}x_i}, \tag{8.8}$$

which computes the probability that sequence x belongs to the given Markov chain model, that is, $P(x|model)$. Note that the begin and end states are silent in that they do not emit symbols in the path through the chain.

We can use the Markov chain model for classification. Suppose that we want to distinguish CpG islands from other "non-CpG" sequence regions. Given training sequences from CpG islands (labeled "+") and from non-CpG islands (labeled "−"), we can construct two Markov chain models—the first, denoted "+", to represent CpG islands, and the second, denoted "−", to represent non-CpG islands. Given a sequence, x, we use the respective models to compute $P(x|+)$, the probability that x is from a CpG island, and $P(x|-)$, the probability that it is from a non-CpG island. The *log-odds ratio* can then be used to classify x based on these two probabilities.

"But first, how can we estimate the transition probabilities for each model?" Before we can compute the probability of x being from either of the two models, we need to estimate the transition probabilities for the models. Given the CpG (+) training sequences, we can estimate the transition probabilities for the CpG island model as

$$a^+_{ij} = \frac{c^+_{ij}}{\sum_k c^+_{ik}}, \tag{8.9}$$

where c^+_{ij} is the number of times that nucleotide j follows nucleotide i in the given sequences labeled "+". For the non-CpG model, we use the non-CpG island sequences (labeled "−") in a similar way to estimate a^-_{ij}.

[9]This is known as a **first-order Markov chain model**, since x_L depends only on the previous state, x_{L-1}. In general, for the ***k*-th-order Markov chain model**, the probability of x_L depends on the values of only the *previous k* states.

To determine whether x is from a CpG island or not, we compare the models using the **logs-odds ratio**, defined as

$$log\frac{P(x|+)}{P(x|-)} = \sum_{i=1}^{L} log\frac{a^{+}_{x_{i-1}x_i}}{a^{-}_{x_{i-1}x_i}}. \tag{8.10}$$

If this ratio is greater than 0, then we say that x is from a CpG island.

Example 8.17 **Classification using a Markov chain.** Our model for CpG islands and our model for non-CpG islands both have the same structure, as shown in our example Markov chain of Figure 8.9. Let CpG^{+} be the transition matrix for the CpG island model. Similarly, CpG^{-} is the transition matrix for the non-CpG island model. These are (adapted from Durbin, Eddy, Krogh, and Mitchison [DEKM98]):

$$CpG^{+} = \begin{bmatrix} & A & C & G & T \\ A & 0.20 & 0.26 & 0.44 & 0.10 \\ C & 0.16 & 0.36 & 0.28 & 0.20 \\ G & 0.15 & 0.35 & 0.36 & 0.14 \\ T & 0.09 & 0.37 & 0.36 & 0.18 \end{bmatrix} \tag{8.11}$$

$$CpG^{-} = \begin{bmatrix} & A & C & G & T \\ A & 0.27 & 0.19 & 0.31 & 0.23 \\ C & 0.33 & 0.31 & 0.08 & 0.28 \\ G & 0.26 & 0.24 & 0.31 & 0.19 \\ T & 0.19 & 0.25 & 0.28 & 0.28 \end{bmatrix} \tag{8.12}$$

Notice that the transition probability $a^{+}_{CG} = 0.28$ is higher than $a^{-}_{CG} = 0.08$. Suppose we are given the sequence x = CGCG. The log-odds ratio of x is

$$log\frac{0.28}{0.08} + log\frac{0.35}{0.24} + log\frac{0.28}{0.08} = 1.25 > 0.$$

Thus, we say that x is from a CpG island. ■

In summary, we can use a Markov chain model to determine if a DNA sequence, x, is from a CpG island. This was the first of our two important questions mentioned at the beginning of this section. To answer the second question, that of finding all of the CpG islands in a given sequence, we move on to hidden Markov models.

Hidden Markov Model

Given a long DNA sequence, how can we find all CpG islands within it? We could try the Markov chain method above, using a sliding window. For each window, we could compute the log-odds ratio. CpG islands within intersecting windows could be merged to determine CpG islands within the long sequence. This approach has some difficulties: It is not clear what window size to use, and CpG islands tend to vary in length.

What if, instead, we merge the two Markov chains from above (for CpG islands and non-CpG islands, respectively) and add transition probabilities between the two chains? The result is a *hidden Markov model*, as shown in Figure 8.10. The states are renamed by adding "+" and "−" labels to distinguish them. For readability, only the transitions between "+" and "−" states are shown, in addition to those for the begin and end states. Let $\pi = \pi_1\pi_2 \ldots \pi_L$ be a path of states that generates a sequence of symbols, $x = x_1x_2 \ldots x_L$. In a Markov chain, the path through the chain for x is unique. With a hidden Markov model, however, different paths can generate the same sequence. For example, the states C^+ and C^- both emit the symbol C. Therefore, we say the model is "hidden" in that we do not know for sure which states were visited in generating the sequence. The transition probabilities between the original two models can be determined using training sequences containing transitions between CpG islands and non-CpG islands.

A Hidden Markov Model (HMM) is defined by

- a set of states, Q
- a set of transitions, where transition probability $a_{kl} = P(\pi_i = l|\pi_{i-1} = k)$ is the probability of transitioning from state k to state l for $k, l \in Q$
- an **emission probability**, $e_k(b) = P(x_i = b|\pi_i = k)$, for each state, k, and each symbol, b, where $e_k(b)$ is the probability of seeing symbol b in state k. The sum of all emission probabilities at a given state must equal 1, that is, $\sum_b e_k = 1$ for each state, k.

Example 8.18 **A hidden Markov model.** The transition matrix for the hidden Markov model of Figure 8.10 is larger than that of Example 8.16 for our earlier Markov chain example.

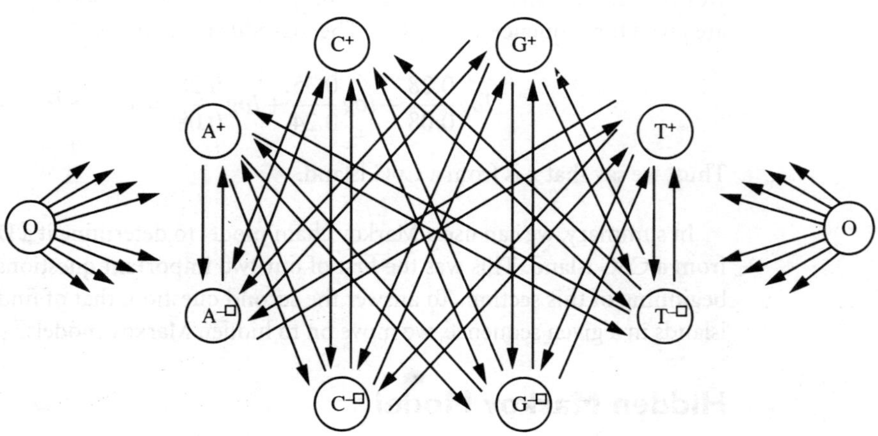

Figure 8.10 A hidden Markov model.

It contains the states A$^+$, C$^+$, G$^+$, T$^+$, A$^-$, C$^-$, G$^-$, T$^-$ (not shown). The transition probabilities between the "+" states are as before. Similarly, the transition probabilities between the "−" states are as before. The transition probabilities between "+" and "−" states can be determined as mentioned above, using training sequences containing known transitions from CpG islands to non-CpG islands, and vice versa. The emission probabilities are $e_{A^+}(A) = 1$, $e_{A^+}(C) = 0$, $e_{A^+}(G) = 0$, $e_{A^+}(T) = 0$, $e_{A^-}(A) = 1$, $e_{A^-}(C) = 0$, $e_{A^-}(G) = 0$, $e_{A^-}(T) = 0$, and so on. Although here the probability of emitting a symbol at a state is either 0 or 1, in general, emission probabilities need not be zero-one. ■

Tasks using hidden Markov models include:

- *Evaluation*: Given a sequence, x, determine the probability, $P(x)$, of obtaining x in the model.
- *Decoding:* Given a sequence, determine the most probable path through the model that produced the sequence.
- *Learning*: Given a model and a set of training sequences, find the model parameters (i.e., the transition and emission probabilities) that explain the training sequences with relatively high probability. The goal is to find a model that generalizes well to sequences we have not seen before.

Evaluation, decoding, and learning can be handled using the forward algorithm, Viterbi algorithm, and Baum-Welch algorithm, respectively. These algorithms are discussed in the following sections.

Forward Algorithm

What is the probability, $P(x)$, that sequence x was generated by a given hidden Markov model (where, say, the model represents a sequence class)? This problem can be solved using the **forward algorithm**.

Let $x = x_1x_2 \ldots x_L$ be our sequence of symbols. A path is a sequence of states. Many paths can generate x. Consider one such path, which we denote $\pi = \pi_1\pi_2 \ldots \pi_L$. If we incorporate the begin and end states, denoted as 0, we can write π as $\pi_0 = 0, \pi_1\pi_2 \ldots \pi_L$, $\pi_{L+1} = 0$. The probability that the model generated sequence x using path π is

$$\begin{aligned} P(x, \pi) &= a_{0\pi_1} e_{\pi_1}(x_1) \cdot a_{\pi_1\pi_2} e_{\pi_2}(x_2) \cdots a_{\pi_{L-1}\pi_L} e_{\pi_L}(x_L) \cdot a_{\pi_L 0} \\ &= a_{0\pi_1} \prod_{i=1}^{L} e_{\pi_i}(x_i) a_{\pi_i\pi_{i+1}} \end{aligned} \quad (8.13)$$

where $\pi_{L+1} = 0$. We must, however, consider all of the paths that can generate x. Therefore, the probability of x given the model is

$$P(x) = \sum_{\pi} P(x, \pi). \quad (8.14)$$

That is, we add the probabilities of all possible paths for x.

Algorithm: Forward algorithm. Find the probability, $P(x)$, that sequence x was generated by the given hidden Markov model.

Input:

- A hidden Markov model, defined by a set of states, Q, that emit symbols, and by transition and emission probabilities;
- x, a sequence of symbols.

Output: Probability, $P(x)$.

Method:

(1) Initialization ($i = 0$): $f_0(0) = 1$, $f_k(0) = 0$ for $k > 0$
(2) Recursion ($i = 1 \ldots L$): $f_l(i) = e_l(x_i)\sum_k f_k(i-1)a_{kl}$
(3) Termination: $P(x) = \sum_k f_k(L)a_{k0}$

Figure 8.11 Forward algorithm.

Unfortunately, the number of paths can be exponential with respect to the length, L, of x, so brute force evaluation by enumerating all paths is impractical. The forward algorithm exploits a dynamic programming technique to solve this problem. It defines **forward variables,** $f_k(i)$, to be the probability of being in state k having observed the first i symbols of sequence x. We want to compute $f_{\pi_{L+1}=0}(L)$, the probability of being in the end state having observed all of sequence x.

The forward algorithm is shown in Figure 8.11. It consists of three steps. In step 1, the forward variables are initialized for all states. Because we have not viewed any part of the sequence at this point, the probability of being in the start state is 1 (i.e., $f_0(0) = 1$), and the probability of being in any other state is 0. In step 2, the algorithm sums over all the probabilities of all the paths leading from one state emission to another. It does this recursively for each move from state to state. Step 3 gives the termination condition. The whole sequence (of length L) has been viewed, and we enter the end state, 0. We end up with the summed-over probability of generating the required sequence of symbols.

Viterbi Algorithm

Given a sequence, x, what is the most probable path in the model that generates x? This problem of decoding can be solved using the **Viterbi algorithm.**

Many paths can generate x. We want to find the most probable one, $\pi^\star$, that is, the path that maximizes the probability of having generated x. This is $\pi^\star = argmax_\pi P(\pi|x)$.[10] It so happens that this is equal to $argmax_\pi P(x, \pi)$. (The proof is left as an exercise for the reader.) We saw how to compute $P(x, \pi)$ in Equation (8.13). For a sequence of length L, there are $|Q|^L$ possible paths, where $|Q|$ is the number of states in the model. It is

[10] In mathematics, *argmax* stands for the argument of the maximum. Here, this means that we want the path, π, for which $P(\pi|x)$ attains its maximum value.

infeasible to enumerate all of these possible paths! Once again, we resort to a dynamic programming technique to solve the problem.

At each step along the way, the Viterbi algorithm tries to find the most probable path leading from one symbol of the sequence to the next. We define $v_l(i)$ to be the probability of the most probable path accounting for the first i symbols of x and ending in state l. To find π^*, we need to compute $max_k v_k(L)$, the probability of the most probable path accounting for all of the sequence and ending in the end state. The probability, $v_l(i)$, is

$$v_l(i) = e_l(x_i) \cdot max_k(v_l(k)a_{kl}), \tag{8.15}$$

which states that the most probable path that generates $x_1 \dots x_i$ and ends in state l has to emit x_i in state x_l (hence, the emission probability, $e_l(x_i)$) and has to contain the most probable path that generates $x_1 \dots x_{i-1}$ and ends in state k, followed by a transition from state k to state l (hence, the transition probability, a_{kl}). Thus, we can compute $v_k(L)$ for any state, k, recursively to obtain the probability of the most probable path.

The Viterbi algorithm is shown in Figure 8.12. Step 1 performs initialization. Every path starts at the begin state (0) with probability 1. Thus, for $i = 0$, we have $v_0(0) = 1$, and the probability of starting at any other state is 0. Step 2 applies the *recurrence formula* for $i = 1$ to L. At each iteration, we assume that we know the most likely path for $x_1 \dots x_{i-1}$ that ends in state k, for all $k \in Q$. To find the most likely path to the i-th state from there, we maximize $v_k(i-1)a_{kl}$ over all predecessors $k \in Q$ of l. To obtain $v_l(i)$, we multiply by $e_l(x_i)$ since we have to emit x_i from l. This gives us the first formula in step 2. The values $v_k(i)$ are stored in a $Q \times L$ dynamic programming matrix. We keep pointers (*ptr*) in this matrix so that we can obtain the path itself. The algorithm terminates in step 3, where finally, we have $max_k v_k(L)$. We enter the end state of 0 (hence, the transition probability, a_{k0}) but do not emit a symbol. The Viterbi algorithm runs in $O(|Q|^2|L|)$ time. It is more efficient than the forward algorithm because it investigates only the most probable path and avoids summing over all possible paths.

Algorithm: Viterbi algorithm. Find the most probable path that emits the sequence of symbols, x.

Input:

- A hidden Markov model, defined by a set of states, Q, that emit symbols, and by transition and emission probabilities;
- x, a sequence of symbols.

Output: The most probable path, π^*.

Method:

(1) Initialization ($i = 0$): $v_0(0) = 1$, $v_k(0) = 0$ for $k > 0$

(2) Recursion ($i = 1 \dots L$): $v_l(i) = e_l(x_i) max_k(v_k(i-1)a_{kl})$
$ptr_i(l) = argmax_k(v_k(i-1)a_{kl})$

(3) Termination: $P(x, \pi^*) = max_k(v_k(L)a_{k0})$
$\pi^*_L = argmax_k(v_k(L)a_{k0})$

Figure 8.12 Viterbi (decoding) algorithm.

Baum-Welch Algorithm

Given a training set of sequences, how can we determine the parameters of a hidden Markov model that will best explain the sequences? In other words, we want to learn or adjust the transition and emission probabilities of the model so that it can predict the path of future sequences of symbols. If we know the state path for each training sequence, learning the model parameters is simple. We can compute the percentage of times each particular transition or emission is used in the set of training sequences to determine a_{kl}, the transition probabilities, and $e_k(b)$, the emission probabilities.

When the paths for the training sequences are unknown, there is no longer a direct closed-form equation for the estimated parameter values. An iterative procedure must be used, like the **Baum-Welch algorithm.** The Baum-Welch algorithm is a special case of the EM algorithm (Section 7.8.1), which is a family of algorithms for learning probabilistic models in problems that involve hidden states.

The Baum-Welch algorithm is shown in Figure 8.13. The problem of finding the optimal transition and emission probabilities is intractable. Instead, the Baum-Welch algorithm finds a locally optimal solution. In step 1, it initializes the probabilities to an arbitrary estimate. It then continuously re-estimates the probabilities (step 2) until convergence (i.e., when there is very little change in the probability values between iterations). The re-estimation first calculates the expected transmission and emission probabilities. The transition and emission probabilities are then updated to maximize the likelihood of the expected values.

In summary, Markov chains and hidden Markov models are probabilistic models in which the probability of a state depends only on that of the previous state. They are particularly useful for the analysis of biological sequence data, whose tasks include evaluation, decoding, and learning. We have studied the forward, Viterbi, and Baum-Welch algorithms. The algorithms require multiplying many probabilities, resulting in very

Algorithm: Baum-Welch algorithm. Find the model parameters (transition and emission probabilities) that best explain the training set of sequences.

Input:

- A training set of sequences.

Output:

- Transition probabilities, a_{kl};
- Emission probabilities, $e_k(b)$;

Method:

(1) initialize the transmission and emission probabilities;
(2) iterate until convergence
  (2.1) calculate the expected number of times each transition or emission is used
  (2.2) adjust the parameters to maximize the likelihood of these expected values

Figure 8.13 Baum-Welch (learning) algorithm.

small numbers that can cause underflow arithmetic errors. A way around this is to use the logarithms of the probabilities.

8.5 Summary

- **Stream data** flow in and out of a computer system *continuously* and with varying update rates. They are *temporally ordered, fast changing, massive* (e.g., gigabytes to terabytes in volume), and *potentially infinite*. Applications involving stream data include telecommunications, financial markets, and satellite data processing.
- **Synopses** provide *summaries* of stream data, which typically can be used to return *approximate* answers to queries. Random sampling, sliding windows, histograms, multiresolution methods (e.g., for data reduction), sketches (which operate in a single pass), and randomized algorithms are all forms of synopses.
- The **tilted time frame** model allows data to be stored at multiple granularities of time. The most recent time is registered at the finest granularity. The most distant time is at the coarsest granularity.
- A **stream data cube** can store compressed data by (1) using the tilted time frame model on the time dimension, (2) storing data at only some **critical layers**, which reflect the levels of data that are of most interest to the analyst, and (3) performing *partial materialization* based on "popular paths" through the critical layers.
- Traditional methods of **frequent itemset mining, classification,** and **clustering** tend to scan the data multiple times, making them infeasible for stream data. Stream-based versions of such mining instead try to find approximate answers within a user-specified error bound. Examples include the Lossy Counting algorithm for frequent itemset stream mining; the Hoeffding tree, VFDT, and CVFDT algorithms for stream data classification; and the STREAM and CluStream algorithms for stream data clustering.
- A **time-series database** consists of sequences of values or events changing with time, typically measured at equal time intervals. Applications include stock market analysis, economic and sales forecasting, cardiogram analysis, and the observation of weather phenomena.
- **Trend analysis** decomposes time-series data into the following: *trend* (long-term) *movements, cyclic movements, seasonal movements* (which are systematic or calendar related), and *irregular movements* (due to random or chance events).
- **Subsequence matching** is a form of *similarity search* that finds subsequences that are similar to a given query sequence. Such methods match subsequences that have the same shape, while accounting for gaps (missing values) and differences in baseline/offset and scale.
- A **sequence database** consists of sequences of ordered elements or events, recorded with or without a concrete notion of time. Examples of sequence data include customer shopping sequences, Web clickstreams, and biological sequences.

- **Sequential pattern mining** is the mining of frequently occurring ordered events or subsequences as patterns. Given a sequence database, any sequence that satisfies minimum support is **frequent** and is called a **sequential pattern.** An example of a sequential pattern is "*Customers who buy a Canon digital camera are likely to buy an HP color printer within a month.*" Algorithms for sequential pattern mining include GSP, SPADE, and PrefixSpan, as well as CloSpan (which mines closed sequential patterns).

- **Constraint-based mining** of sequential patterns incorporates user-specified constraints to reduce the search space and derive only patterns that are of interest to the user. Constraints may relate to the *duration* of a sequence, to an *event folding window* (where events occurring within such a window of time can be viewed as occurring together), and to *gaps* between events. *Pattern templates* may also be specified as a form of constraint using regular expressions.

- **Periodicity analysis** is the mining of periodic patterns, that is, the search for recurring patterns in time-related sequence databases. *Full periodic* and *partial periodic* patterns can be mined, as well as *periodic association rules.*

- **Biological sequence analysis** compares, aligns, indexes, and analyzes biological sequences, which can be either sequences of nucleotides or of amino acids. Biosequence analysis plays a crucial role in bioinformatics and modern biology. Such analysis can be partitioned into two essential tasks: **pairwise sequence alignment** and **multiple sequence alignment**. The dynamic programming approach is commonly used for sequence alignments. Among many available analysis packages, BLAST (Basic Local Alignment Search Tool) is one of the most popular tools in biosequence analysis.

- **Markov chains** and **hidden Markov models** are probabilistic models in which the probability of a state depends only on that of the previous state. They are particularly useful for the analysis of biological sequence data. Given a sequence of symbols, x, the forward algorithm finds the probability of obtaining x in the model, whereas the Viterbi algorithm finds the most probable path (corresponding to x) through the model. The Baum-Welch algorithm learns or adjusts the model parameters (*transition* and *emission* probabilities) so as to best explain a set of training sequences.

Exercises

8.1 A *stream data cube* should be relatively stable in size with respect to infinite data streams. Moreover, it should be incrementally updateable with respect to infinite data streams. Show that the stream cube proposed in Section 8.1.2 satisfies these two requirements.

8.2 In stream data analysis, we are often interested in only the nontrivial or exceptionally large cube cells. These can be formulated as *iceberg conditions.* Thus, it may seem that the iceberg cube [BR99] is a likely model for stream cube architecture. Unfortunately, this is not the case because iceberg cubes cannot accommodate the incremental updates required due to the constant arrival of new data. Explain why.

8.3 An important task in stream data analysis is to *detect outliers* in a multidimensional environment. An example is the detection of unusual power surges, where the dimensions include *time* (i.e., comparing with the normal duration), *region* (i.e., comparing with surrounding regions), *sector* (i.e., university, residence, government), and so on. Outline an efficient stream OLAP method that can detect outliers in data streams. Provide reasons as to why your design can ensure such quality.

8.4 *Frequent itemset mining in data streams* is a challenging task. It is too costly to keep the frequency count for every itemset. However, because a currently infrequent itemset may become frequent, and a currently frequent one may become infrequent in the future, it is important to keep as much frequency count information as possible. Given a fixed amount of memory, can you work out a good mechanism that may maintain high-quality approximation of itemset counting?

8.5 For the above approximate frequent itemset counting problem, it is interesting to incorporate the notion of *tilted time frame*. That is, we can put less weight on more remote itemsets when counting frequent itemsets. Design an efficient method that may obtain high-quality approximation of itemset frequency in data streams in this case.

8.6 A classification model may change dynamically along with the changes of training data streams. This is known as *concept drift*. Explain why decision tree induction may not be a suitable method for such dynamically changing data sets. Is naïve Bayesian a better method on such data sets? Comparing with the naïve Bayesian approach, is lazy evaluation (such as the *k*-nearest-neighbor approach) even better? Explain your reasoning.

8.7 The concept of microclustering has been popular for on-line maintenance of clustering information for data streams. By exploring the power of microclustering, design an effective *density-based* clustering method for clustering evolving data streams.

8.8 Suppose that a power station stores data regarding power consumption levels by time and by region, in addition to power usage information per customer in each region. Discuss how to solve the following problems in such a *time-series database*:

(a) Find similar power consumption curve fragments for a given region on Fridays.

(b) Every time a power consumption curve rises sharply, what may happen within the next 20 minutes?

(c) How can we find the most influential features that distinguish a stable power consumption region from an unstable one?

8.9 Regression is commonly used in trend analysis for *time-series data sets*. An item in a time-series database is usually associated with properties in multidimensional space. For example, an electric power consumer may be associated with consumer location, category, and time of usage (weekdays vs. weekends). In such a multidimensional space, it is often necessary to perform *regression analysis in an OLAP manner* (i.e., drilling and rolling along any dimension combinations that a user desires). Design an efficient mechanism so that regression analysis can be performed efficiently in multidimensional space.

8.10 Suppose that a restaurant chain would like to mine customers' consumption behavior relating to major sport events, such as "*Every time there is a major sport event on TV, the sales of Kentucky Fried Chicken will go up 20% one hour before the match.*"

(a) For this problem, there are multiple sequences (each corresponding to one restaurant in the chain). However, each sequence is long and contains multiple occurrences of a (sequential) pattern. Thus this problem is different from the setting of sequential pattern mining problem discussed in this chapter. Analyze what are the differences in the two problem definitions and how such differences may influence the development of mining algorithms.

(b) Develop a method for finding such patterns efficiently.

8.11 **(Implementation project)** The sequential pattern mining algorithm introduced by Srikant and Agrawal [SA96] finds sequential patterns among a set of sequences. Although there have been interesting follow-up studies, such as the development of the algorithms SPADE (Zaki [Zak01]), PrefixSpan (Pei, Han, Mortazavi-Asl, et al. [PHMA+01]), and CloSpan (Yan, Han, and Afshar [YHA03]), the basic definition of "sequential pattern" has not changed. However, suppose we would like to find frequently occurring subsequences (i.e., *sequential patterns) within one given sequence*, where, say, gaps are not allowed. (That is, we do not consider AG to be a subsequence of the sequence ATG.) For example, the string ATGCTCGAGCT contains a substring GCT with a support of 2. Derive an efficient algorithm that finds the complete set of subsequences satisfying a minimum support threshold. Explain how your algorithm works using a small example, and show some performance results for your implementation.

8.12 Suppose frequent subsequences have been mined from a sequence database, with a given (relative) minimum support, *min_sup*. The database can be updated in two cases: (i) adding new sequences (e.g., new customers buying items), and (ii) appending new subsequences to some existing sequences (e.g., existing customers buying new items). For *each case*, work out an efficient *incremental mining* method that derives the complete subsequences satisfying *min_sup*, without mining the whole sequence database from scratch.

8.13 Closed sequential patterns can be viewed as a lossless compression of a large set of sequential patterns. However, the set of closed sequential patterns may still be too large for effective analysis. There should be some mechanism for *lossy compression* that may further reduce the set of sequential patterns derived from a sequence database.

(a) Provide a good definition of lossy compression of sequential patterns, and reason why such a definition may lead to effective compression with minimal information loss (i.e., high compression quality).

(b) Develop an efficient method for such pattern compression.

(c) Develop an efficient method that mines such compressed patterns directly from a sequence database.

8.14 As discussed in Section 8.3.4, mining partial periodic patterns will require a user to specify the length of the period. This may burden the user and reduces the effectiveness of mining. Propose a method that will *automatically mine the minimal period of a pattern* without requiring a predefined period. Moreover, extend the method to find *approximate periodicity* where the period will not need to be precise (i.e., it can fluctuate within a specified small range).

8.15 There are several major differences between *biological sequential patterns* and *transactional sequential patterns.* First, in transactional sequential patterns, the gaps between two events are usually nonessential. For example, the pattern "*purchasing a digital camera two months after purchasing a PC*" does not imply that the two purchases are consecutive. However, for biological sequences, gaps play an important role in patterns. Second, patterns in a transactional sequence are usually precise. However, a biological pattern can be quite imprecise, allowing insertions, deletions, and mutations. Discuss how the mining methodologies in these two domains are influenced by such differences.

8.16 BLAST is a typical heuristic alignment method for *pairwise sequence alignment.* It first locates high-scoring short stretches and then extends them to achieve suboptimal alignments. When the sequences to be aligned are really long, BLAST may run quite slowly. Propose and discuss some enhancements to improve the scalability of such a method.

8.17 The Viterbi algorithm uses the equality, $argmax_{\pi}P(\pi|x) = argmax_{\pi}P(x, \pi)$, in its search for the most probable path, π^*, through a *hidden Markov model* for a given sequence of symbols, x. Prove the equality.

8.18 **(Implementation project)** A *dishonest casino* uses a fair die most of the time. However, it switches to a loaded die with a probability of 0.05, and switches back to the fair die with a probability 0.10. The fair die has a probability of $\frac{1}{6}$ of rolling any number. The loaded die has $P(1) = P(2) = P(3) = P(4) = P(5) = 0.10$ and $P(6) = 0.50$.

(a) Draw a hidden Markov model for the dishonest casino problem using two states, Fair (F) and Loaded (L). Show all transition and emission probabilities.

(b) Suppose you pick up a die at random and roll a 6. What is the probability that the die is loaded, that is, find $P(6|D_L)$? What is the probability that it is fair, that is, find $P(6|D_F)$? What is the probability of rolling a 6 from the die you picked up? If you roll a sequence of 666, what is the probability that the die is loaded?

(c) Write a program that, given a sequence of rolls (e.g., $x = 5114362366\ldots$), predicts when the fair die was used and when the loaded die was used. (Hint: This is similar to detecting CpG islands and non-CPG islands in a given long sequence.) Use the Viterbi algorithm to get the most probable path through the model. Describe your implementation in report form, showing your code and some examples.

Bibliographic Notes

Stream data mining research has been active in recent years. Popular surveys on stream data systems and stream data processing include Babu and Widom [BW01], Babcock, Babu, Datar, et al. [BBD+02], Muthukrishnan [Mut03], and the tutorial by Garofalakis, Gehrke, and Rastogi [GGR02].

There have been extensive studies on stream data management and the processing of continuous queries in stream data. For a description of synopsis data structures for stream data, see Gibbons and Matias [GM98]. Vitter introduced the notion of reservoir sampling as a way to select an unbiased random sample of n elements without replacement from a larger ordered set of size N, where N is unknown [Vit85]. Stream query or aggregate processing methods have been proposed by Chandrasekaran and Franklin [CF02], Gehrke, Korn, and Srivastava [GKS01], Dobra, Garofalakis, Gehrke, and Rastogi [DGGR02], and Madden, Shah, Hellerstein, and Raman [MSHR02]. A one-pass summary method for processing approximate aggregate queries using wavelets was proposed by Gilbert, Kotidis, Muthukrishnan, and Strauss [GKMS01]. Statstream, a statistical method for the monitoring of thousands of data streams in real time, was developed by Zhu and Shasha [ZS02, SZ04].

There are also many stream data projects. Examples include Aurora by Zdonik, Cetintemel, Cherniack, et al. [ZCC+02], which is targeted toward stream monitoring applications; STREAM, developed at Stanford University by Babcock, Babu, Datar, et al., aims at developing a general-purpose Data Stream Management System (DSMS) [BBD+02]; and an early system called Tapestry by Terry, Goldberg, Nichols, and Oki [TGNO92], which used continuous queries for content-based filtering over an append-only database of email and bulletin board messages. A restricted subset of SQL was used as the query language in order to provide guarantees about efficient evaluation and append-only query results.

A multidimensional stream cube model was proposed by Chen, Dong, Han, et al. [CDH+02] in their study of multidimensional regression analysis of time-series data streams. MAIDS (Mining Alarming Incidents from Data Streams), a stream data mining system built on top of such a stream data cube, was developed by Cai, Clutter, Pape, et al. [CCP+04].

For mining frequent items and itemsets on stream data, Manku and Motwani proposed sticky sampling and lossy counting algorithms for approximate frequency counts over data streams [MM02]. Karp, Papadimitriou, and Shenker proposed a counting algorithm for finding frequent elements in data streams [KPS03]. Giannella, Han, Pei, et al. proposed a method for mining frequent patterns in data streams at multiple time granularities [GHP+04]. Metwally, Agrawal, and El Abbadi proposed a memory-efficient method for computing frequent and top-k elements in data streams [MAA05].

For stream data classification, Domingos and Hulten proposed the VFDT algorithm, based on their Hoeffding tree algorithm [DH00]. CVFDT, a later version of VFDT, was developed by Hulten, Spencer, and Domingos [HSD01] to handle concept drift in time-changing data streams. Wang, Fan, Yu, and Han proposed an ensemble classifier to mine concept-drifting data streams [WFYH03]. Aggarwal, Han, Wang, and Yu developed a k-nearest-neighbor-based method for classify evolving data streams [AHWY04b].

Several methods have been proposed for clustering data streams. The k-median-based STREAM algorithm was proposed by Guha, Mishra, Motwani, and O'Callaghan [GMMO00] and by O'Callaghan, Mishra, Meyerson, et al. [OMM+02]. Aggarwal, Han, Wang, and Yu proposed CluStream, a framework for clustering evolving data streams

[AHWY03], and HPStream, a framework for projected clustering of high-dimensional data streams [AHWY04a].

Statistical methods for time-series analysis have been proposed and studied extensively in statistics, such as in Chatfield [Cha03], Brockwell and Davis [BD02], and Shumway and Stoffer [SS05]. StatSoft's Electronic Textbook (*www.statsoft.com/textbook/ stathome.html*) is a useful online resource that includes a discussion on time-series data analysis. The ARIMA forecasting method is described in Box, Jenkins, and Reinsel [BJR94]. Efficient similarity search in sequence databases was studied by Agrawal, Faloutsos, and Swami [AFS93]. A fast subsequence matching method in time-series databases was presented by Faloutsos, Ranganathan, and Manolopoulos [FRM94]. Agrawal, Lin, Sawhney, and Shim [ALSS95] developed a method for fast similarity search in the presence of noise, scaling, and translation in time-series databases. Language primitives for querying shapes of histories were proposed by Agrawal, Psaila, Wimmers, and Zait [APWZ95]. Other work on similarity-based search of time-series data includes Rafiei and Mendelzon [RM97], and Yi, Jagadish, and Faloutsos [YJF98]. Yi, Sidiropoulos, Johnson, Jagadish, et al. [YSJ+00] introduced a method for on-line mining for co-evolving time sequences. Chen, Dong, Han, et al. [CDH+02] proposed a multidimensional regression method for analysis of multidimensional time-series data. Shasha and Zhu present a state-of-the-art overview of the methods for high-performance discovery in time series [SZ04].

The problem of mining sequential patterns was first proposed by Agrawal and Srikant [AS95]. In the Apriori-based GSP algorithm, Srikant and Agrawal [SA96] generalized their earlier notion to include time constraints, a sliding time window, and user-defined taxonomies. Zaki [Zak01] developed a vertical-format-based sequential pattern mining method called SPADE, which is an extension of vertical-format-based frequent itemset mining methods, like Eclat and Charm [Zak98, ZH02]. PrefixSpan, a pattern growth approach to sequential pattern mining, and its predecessor, FreeSpan, were developed by Pei, Han, Mortazavi-Asl, et al. [HPMA+00, PHMA+01, PHMA+04]. The CloSpan algorithm for mining closed sequential patterns was proposed by Yan, Han, and Afshar [YHA03]. BIDE, a bidirectional search for mining frequent closed sequences, was developed by Wang and Han [WH04].

The studies of sequential pattern mining have been extended in several different ways. Mannila, Toivonen, and Verkamo [MTV97] consider frequent episodes in sequences, where episodes are essentially acyclic graphs of events whose edges specify the temporal before-and-after relationship but without timing-interval restrictions. Sequence pattern mining for plan failures was proposed in Zaki, Lesh, and Ogihara [ZLO98]. Garofalakis, Rastogi, and Shim [GRS99a] proposed the use of regular expressions as a flexible constraint specification tool that enables user-controlled focus to be incorporated into the sequential pattern mining process. The embedding of multidimensional, multilevel information into a transformed sequence database for sequential pattern mining was proposed by Pinto, Han, Pei, et al. [PHP+01]. Pei, Han, and Wang studied issues regarding constraint-based sequential pattern mining [PHW02]. CLUSEQ is a sequence clustering algorithm, developed by Yang and Wang [YW03]. An incremental sequential pattern mining algorithm, IncSpan, was proposed by Cheng, Yan, and Han [CYH04]. SeqIndex, efficient sequence indexing by frequent and discriminative analysis of sequential patterns, was studied by Cheng, Yan, and Han [CYH05]. A method for parallel mining of closed sequential patterns was proposed by Cong, Han, and Padua [CHP05].

Data mining for periodicity analysis has been an interesting theme in data mining. Özden, Ramaswamy, and Silberschatz [ORS98] studied methods for mining periodic or cyclic association rules. Lu, Han, and Feng [LHF98] proposed intertransaction association rules, which are implication rules whose two sides are totally ordered episodes with timing-interval restrictions (on the events in the episodes and on the two sides). Bettini, Wang, and Jajodia [BWJ98] consider a generalization of intertransaction association rules. The notion of mining partial periodicity was first proposed by Han, Dong, and Yin, together with a max-subpattern hit set method [HDY99]. Ma and Hellerstein [MH01a] proposed a method for mining partially periodic event patterns with unknown periods. Yang, Wang, and Yu studied mining asynchronous periodic patterns in time-series data [YWY03].

Methods for the analysis of biological sequences have been introduced in many textbooks, such as Waterman [Wat95], Setubal and Meidanis [SM97], Durbin, Eddy, Krogh, and Mitchison [DEKM98], Baldi and Brunak [BB01], Krane and Raymer [KR03], Jones and Pevzner [JP04], and Baxevanis and Ouellette [BO04]. BLAST was developed by Altschul, Gish, Miller, et al. [AGM$^+$90]. Information about BLAST can be found at the NCBI Web site *www.ncbi.nlm.nih.gov/BLAST/*. For a systematic introduction of the BLAST algorithms and usages, see the book "BLAST" by Korf, Yandell, and Bedell [KYB03].

For an introduction to Markov chains and hidden Markov models from a biological sequence perspective, see Durbin, Eddy, Krogh, and Mitchison [DEKM98] and Jones and Pevzner [JP04]. A general introduction can be found in Rabiner [Rab89]. Eddy and Krogh have each respectively headed the development of software packages for hidden Markov models for protein sequence analysis, namely HMMER (pronounced "hammer," available at *http://hmmer.wustl.edu/*) and SAM (*www.cse.ucsc.edu/research/ compbio/sam.html*).

9 Graph Mining, Social Network Analysis, and Multirelational Data Mining

We have studied frequent-itemset mining in Chapter 5 and sequential-pattern mining in Section 3 of Chapter 8. Many scientific and commercial applications need patterns that are more complicated than frequent itemsets and sequential patterns and require extra effort to discover. Such sophisticated patterns go beyond *sets* and *sequences*, toward *trees, lattices, graphs, networks*, and *other complex structures.*

As a general data structure, *graphs* have become increasingly important in modeling sophisticated structures and their interactions, with broad applications including chemical informatics, bioinformatics, computer vision, video indexing, text retrieval, and Web analysis. *Mining frequent subgraph patterns* for further characterization, discrimination, classification, and cluster analysis becomes an important task. Moreover, graphs that link many nodes together may form different kinds of networks, such as telecommunication networks, computer networks, biological networks, and Web and social community networks. Because such networks have been studied extensively in the context of social networks, their analysis has often been referred to as *social network analysis.* Furthermore, in a relational database, objects are semantically linked across multiple relations. Mining in a relational database often requires mining across multiple interconnected relations, which is similar to mining in connected graphs or networks. Such kind of mining across data relations is considered *multirelational data mining.*

In this chapter, we study knowledge discovery in such interconnected and complex structured data. Section 9.1 introduces graph mining, where the core of the problem is mining frequent subgraph patterns over a collection of graphs. Section 9.2 presents concepts and methods for social network analysis. Section 9.3 examines methods for multirelational data mining, including both cross-relational classification and user-guided multirelational cluster analysis.

9.1 Graph Mining

Graphs become increasingly important in modeling complicated structures, such as circuits, images, chemical compounds, protein structures, biological networks, social networks, the Web, workflows, and XML documents. Many graph search algorithms have been developed in chemical informatics, computer vision, video indexing, and text retrieval. With the increasing demand on the analysis of large amounts of structured data, graph mining has become an active and important theme in data mining.

Among the various kinds of graph patterns, *frequent substructures* are the very basic patterns that can be discovered in a collection of graphs. They are useful for characterizing graph sets, discriminating different groups of graphs, classifying and clustering graphs, building graph indices, and facilitating similarity search in graph databases. Recent studies have developed several graph mining methods and applied them to the discovery of interesting patterns in various applications. For example, there have been reports on the discovery of active chemical structures in HIV-screening datasets by contrasting the support of frequent graphs between different classes. There have been studies on the use of frequent structures as features to classify chemical compounds, on the frequent graph mining technique to study protein structural families, on the detection of considerably large frequent subpathways in metabolic networks, and on the use of frequent graph patterns for graph indexing and similarity search in graph databases. Although graph mining may include mining frequent subgraph patterns, graph classification, clustering, and other analysis tasks, in this section we focus on mining frequent subgraphs. We look at various methods, their extensions, and applications.

9.1.1 Methods for Mining Frequent Subgraphs

Before presenting graph mining methods, it is necessary to first introduce some preliminary concepts relating to frequent graph mining.

We denote the **vertex set** of a graph g by $V(g)$ and the **edge set** by $E(g)$. A label function, L, maps a vertex or an edge to a label. A graph g is a **subgraph** of another graph g' if there exists a subgraph isomorphism from g to g'. Given a labeled graph data set, $D = \{G_1, G_2, \ldots, G_n\}$, we define $support(g)$ (or $frequency(g)$) as the percentage (or number) of graphs in D where g is a subgraph. A **frequent graph** is a graph whose support is no less than a minimum support threshold, *min_sup*.

Example 9.1 **Frequent subgraph.** Figure 9.1 shows a sample set of chemical structures. Figure 9.2 depicts two of the frequent subgraphs in this data set, given a minimum support of 66.6%. ■

"How can we discover frequent substructures?" The discovery of frequent substructures usually consists of two steps. In the first step, we generate frequent substructure candidates. The frequency of each candidate is checked in the second step. Most studies on frequent substructure discovery focus on the optimization of the first step, because the second step involves a subgraph isomorphism test whose computational complexity is excessively high (i.e., NP-complete).

In this section, we look at various methods for frequent substructure mining. In general, there are two basic approaches to this problem: an Apriori-based approach and a pattern-growth approach.

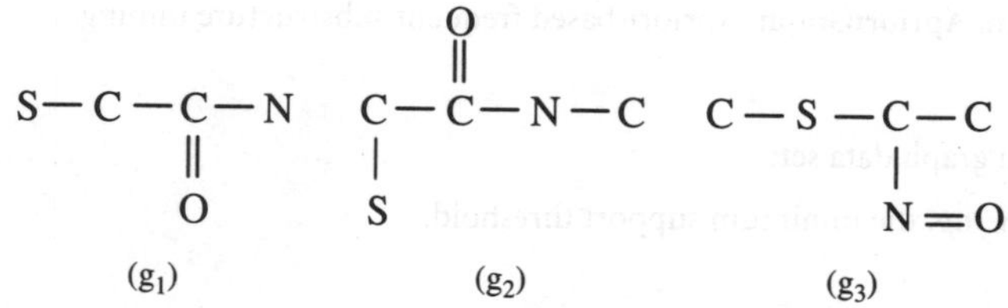

Figure 9.1 A sample graph data set.

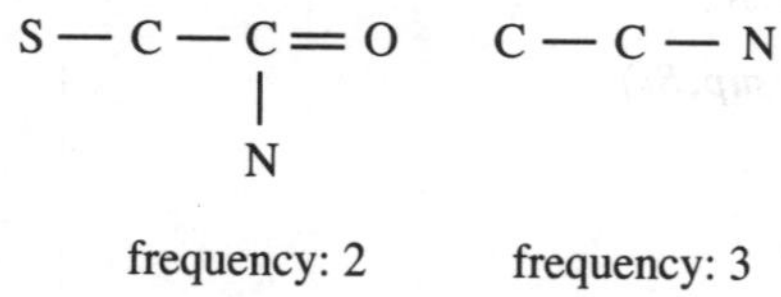

Figure 9.2 Frequent graphs.

Apriori-based Approach

Apriori-based frequent substructure mining algorithms share similar characteristics with Apriori-based frequent itemset mining algorithms (Chapter 5). The search for frequent graphs starts with graphs of small "size," and proceeds in a bottom-up manner by generating candidates having an extra vertex, edge, or path. The definition of graph size depends on the algorithm used.

The general framework of Apriori-based methods for frequent substructure mining is outlined in Figure 9.3. We refer to this algorithm as AprioriGraph. S_k is the frequent substructure set of size k. We will clarify the definition of graph size when we describe specific Apriori-based methods further below. AprioriGraph adopts a *level-wise* mining methodology. At each iteration, the size of newly discovered frequent substructures is increased by one. These new substructures are first generated by joining two similar but slightly different frequent subgraphs that were discovered in the previous call to AprioriGraph. This candidate generation procedure is outlined on line 4. The frequency of the newly formed graphs is then checked. Those found to be frequent are used to generate larger candidates in the next round.

The main design complexity of Apriori-based substructure mining algorithms is the candidate generation step. The candidate generation in frequent itemset mining is straightforward. For example, suppose we have two frequent itemsets of size-3: (abc) and (bcd). The frequent itemset candidate of size-4 generated from them is simply $(abcd)$, derived from a join. However, the candidate generation problem in frequent substructure mining is harder than that in frequent itemset mining, because there are many ways to join two substructures.

Algorithm: AprioriGraph. Apriori-based frequent substructure mining.

Input:

- D, a graph data set;
- *min_sup*, the minimum support threshold.

Output:

- S_k, the frequent substructure set.

Method:

```
S_1 ← frequent single-elements in the data set;
Call AprioriGraph(D, min_sup, S_1);

procedure AprioriGraph(D, min_sup, S_k)
    S_{k+1} ← ∅;
    for each frequent g_i ∈ S_k do
        for each frequent g_j ∈ S_k do
            for each size (k+1) graph g formed by the merge of g_i and g_j do
                if g is frequent in D and g ∉ S_{k+1} then
                    insert g into S_{k+1};
    if s_{k+1} ≠ ∅ then
        AprioriGraph(D, min_sup, S_{k+1});
    return;
```

Figure 9.3 AprioriGraph.

Recent Apriori-based algorithms for frequent substructure mining include AGM, FSG, and a path-join method. AGM shares similar characteristics with Apriori-based itemset mining. FSG and the path-join method explore edges and connections in an Apriori-based fashion. Each of these methods explores various candidate generation strategies.

The AGM algorithm uses a *vertex-based candidate generation* method that increases the substructure size by one vertex at each iteration of AprioriGraph. Two size-k frequent graphs are joined only if they have the same size-$(k-1)$ subgraph. Here, *graph size* is the number of vertices in the graph. The newly formed candidate includes the size-$(k-1)$ subgraph in common and the additional two vertices from the two size-k patterns. Because it is undetermined whether there is an edge connecting the additional two vertices, we actually can form two substructures. Figure 9.4 depicts the two substructures joined by two chains (where a chain is a sequence of connected edges).

The FSG algorithm adopts an *edge-based candidate generation* strategy that increases the substructure size by one edge in each call of AprioriGraph. Two size-k patterns are

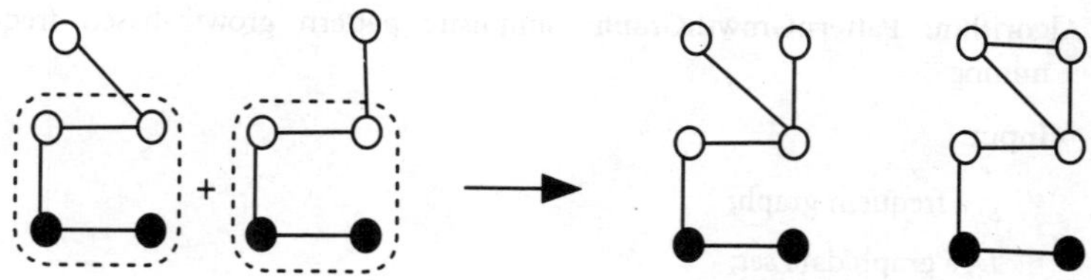

Figure 9.4 AGM: Two substructures joined by two chains.

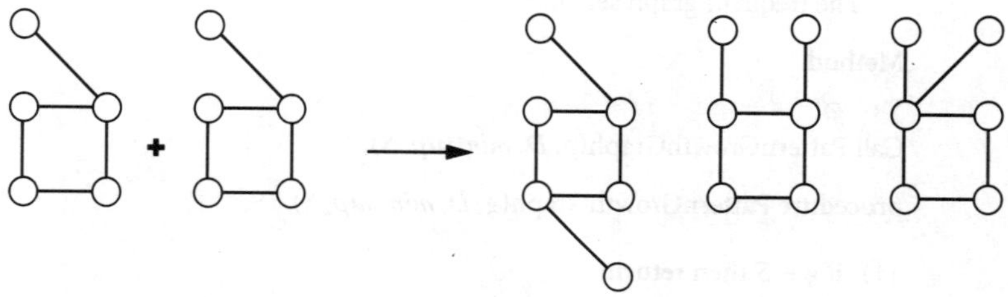

Figure 9.5 FSG: Two substructure patterns and their potential candidates.

merged if and only if they share the same subgraph having $k-1$ edges, which is called the **core**. Here, *graph size* is taken to be the number of edges in the graph. The newly formed candidate includes the core and the additional two edges from the size-k patterns. Figure 9.5 shows potential candidates formed by two structure patterns. Each candidate has one more edge than these two patterns. This example illustrates the complexity of joining two structures to form a large pattern candidate.

In the third Apriori-based approach, an *edge-disjoint path method* was proposed, where graphs are classified by the number of disjoint paths they have, and two paths are edge-disjoint if they do not share any common edge. A substructure pattern with $k+1$ disjoint paths is generated by joining substructures with k disjoint paths.

Apriori-based algorithms have considerable overhead when joining two size-k frequent substructures to generate size-$(k+1)$ graph candidates. In order to avoid such overhead, non-Apriori-based algorithms have recently been developed, most of which adopt the pattern-growth methodology. This methodology tries to extend patterns directly from a single pattern. In the following, we introduce the pattern-growth approach for frequent subgraph mining.

Pattern-Growth Approach

The Apriori-based approach has to use the breadth-first search (BFS) strategy because of its level-wise candidate generation. In order to determine whether a size-$(k+1)$ graph is frequent, it must check all of its corresponding size-k subgraphs to obtain an upper bound of its frequency. Thus, before mining any size-$(k+1)$ subgraph, the Apriori-like

Algorithm: PatternGrowthGraph. Simplistic pattern growth-based frequent substructure mining.

Input:

- g, a frequent graph;
- D, a graph data set;
- min_sup, minimum support threshold.

Output:

- The frequent graph set, S.

Method:

$S \leftarrow \varnothing$;
Call PatternGrowthGraph(g, D, min_sup, S);

procedure PatternGrowthGraph(g, D, min_sup, S)

(1) **if** $g \in S$ **then return;**
(2) **else** insert g into S;
(3) scan D once, find all the edges e such that g can be extended to $g \diamond_x e$;
(4) **for each** frequent $g \diamond_x e$ **do**
(5) *PatternGrowthGraph*($g \diamond_x e$, D, min_sup, S);
(6) **return;**

Figure 9.6 PatternGrowthGraph.

approach usually has to complete the mining of size-k subgraphs. Therefore, BFS is necessary in the Apriori-like approach. In contrast, the *pattern-growth approach* is more flexible regarding its search method. It can use breadth-first search as well as depth-first search (DFS), the latter of which consumes less memory.

A graph g can be *extended* by adding a new edge e. The newly formed graph is denoted by $g \diamond_x e$. Edge e may or may not introduce a new vertex to g. If e introduces a new vertex, we denote the new graph by $g \diamond_{xf} e$, otherwise, $g \diamond_{xb} e$, where f or b indicates that the extension is in a *forward* or *backward* direction.

Figure 9.6 illustrates a general framework for pattern growth–based frequent substructure mining. We refer to the algorithm as PatternGrowthGraph. For each discovered graph g, it performs extensions recursively until all the frequent graphs with g embedded are discovered. The recursion stops once no frequent graph can be generated.

PatternGrowthGraph is simple, but not efficient. The bottleneck is at the inefficiency of extending a graph. The same graph can be discovered many times. For example, there may exist n different $(n-1)$-edge graphs that can be extended to the same n-edge graph. The repeated discovery of the same graph is computationally inefficient. We call a graph that is discovered a second time a **duplicate graph.** Although line 1 of PatternGrowthGraph gets rid of duplicate graphs, the generation and detection of duplicate graphs may increase the workload. In order to reduce the

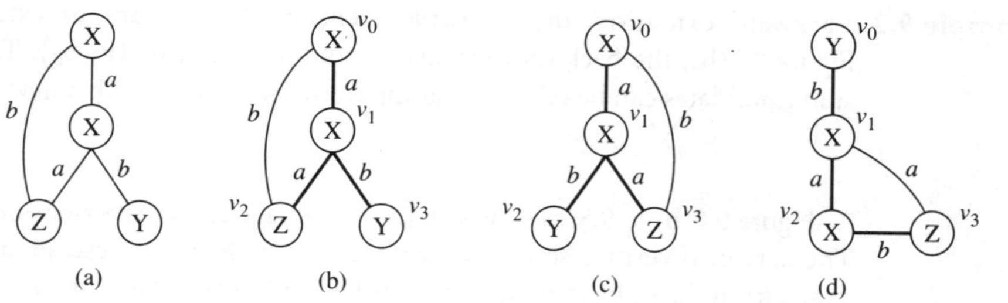

Figure 9.7 DFS subscripting.

generation of duplicate graphs, each frequent graph should be extended as conservatively as possible. This principle leads to the design of several new algorithms. A typical such example is the gSpan algorithm, as described below.

The gSpan algorithm is designed to reduce the generation of duplicate graphs. It need not search previously discovered frequent graphs for duplicate detection. It does not extend any duplicate graph, yet still guarantees the discovery of the complete set of frequent graphs.

Let's see how the gSpan algorithm works. To traverse graphs, it adopts a depth-first search. Initially, a starting vertex is randomly chosen and the vertices in a graph are marked so that we can tell which vertices have been visited. The visited vertex set is expanded repeatedly until a full depth-first search (DFS) tree is built. One graph may have various DFS trees depending on how the depth-first search is performed (i.e., the vertex visiting order). The darkened edges in Figure 9.7(b) to 9.7(d) show three DFS trees for the same graph of Figure 9.7(a). The vertex labels are x, y, and z; the edge labels are a and b. Alphabetic order is taken as the default order in the labels. When building a DFS tree, the visiting sequence of vertices forms a linear order. We use subscripts to record this order, where $i < j$ means v_i is visited before v_j when the depth-first search is performed. A graph G subscripted with a DFS tree T is written as G_T. T is called a **DFS subscripting** of G.

Given a DFS tree T, we call the starting vertex in T, v_0, the *root*. The last visited vertex, v_n, is called the *right-most vertex*. The straight path from v_0 to v_n is called the *right-most path*. In Figure 9.7(b) to 9.7(d), three different subscriptings are generated based on the corresponding DFS trees. The right-most path is (v_0, v_1, v_3) in Figure 9.7(b) and 9.7(c), and (v_0, v_1, v_2, v_3) in Figure 9.7(d).

PatternGrowth extends a frequent graph in every possible position, which may generate a large number of duplicate graphs. The gSpan algorithm introduces a more sophisticated extension method. The new method restricts the extension as follows: Given a graph G and a DFS tree T in G, a new edge e can be added between the right-most vertex and another vertex on the right-most path (*backward extension*); or it can introduce a new vertex and connect to a vertex on the right-most path (*forward extension*). Because both kinds of extensions take place on the right-most path, we call them *right-most extension*, denoted by $G \diamond_r e$ (for brevity, T is omitted here).

Example 9.2 **Backward extension and forward extension.** If we want to extend the graph in Figure 9.7(b), the backward extension candidates can be (v_3, v_0). The forward extension candidates can be edges extending from v_3, v_1, or v_0 with a new vertex introduced. ■

Figure 9.8(b) to 9.8(g) shows all the potential right-most extensions of Figure 9.8(a). The darkened vertices show the right-most path. Among these, Figure 9.8(b) to 9.8(d) grows from the right-most vertex while Figure 9.8(e) to 9.8(g) grows from other vertices on the right-most path. Figure 9.8(b.0) to 9.8(b.4) are children of Figure 9.8(b), and Figure 9.8(f.0) to 9.8(f.3) are children of Figure 9.8(f). In summary, backward extension only takes place on the right-most vertex, while forward extension introduces a new edge from vertices on the right-most path.

Because many DFS trees/subscriptings may exist for the same graph, we choose one of them as the *base subscripting* and only conduct right-most extension on that DFS tree/subscripting. Otherwise, right-most extension cannot reduce the generation of duplicate graphs because we would have to extend the same graph for every DFS subscripting.

We transform each subscripted graph to an edge sequence, called a **DFS code**, so that we can build an order among these sequences. The goal is to select the subscripting that generates the minimum sequence as its base subscripting. There are two kinds of orders in this transformation process: (1) *edge order*, which maps edges in a subscripted graph into a sequence; and (2) *sequence order*, which builds an order among edge sequences (i.e., graphs).

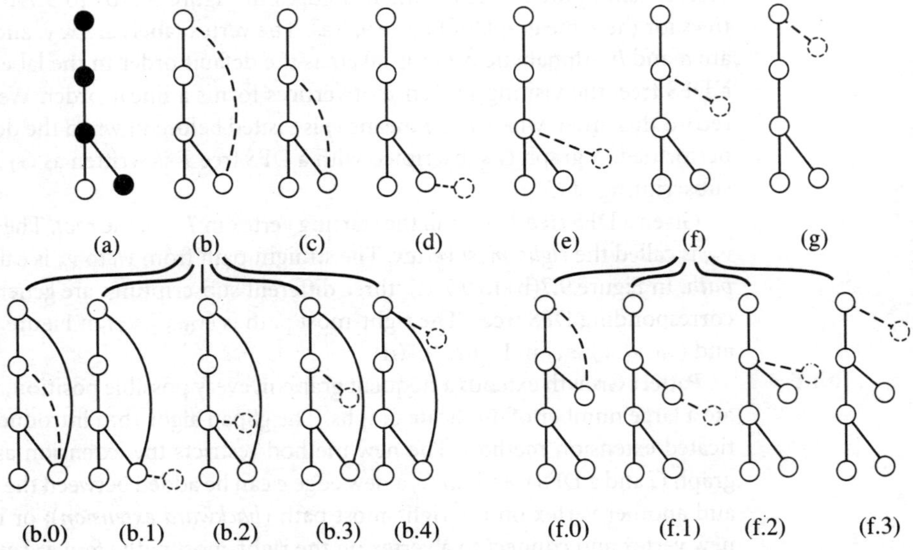

Figure 9.8 Right-most extension.

First, we introduce edge order. Intuitively, DFS tree defines the discovery order of forward edges. For the graph shown in Figure 9.7(b), the forward edges are visited in the order of $(0,1),(1,2),(1,3)$. Now we put backward edges into the order as follows. Given a vertex v, all of its backward edges should appear just before its forward edges. If v does not have any forward edge, we put its backward edges after the forward edge, where v is the second vertex. For vertex v_2 in Figure 9.7(b), its backward edge $(2,0)$ should appear after $(1,2)$ because v_2 does not have any forward edge. Among the backward edges from the same vertex, we can enforce an order. Assume that a vertex v_i has two backward edges, (i,j_1) and (i,j_2). If $j_1 < j_2$, then edge (i,j_1) will appear before edge (i,j_2). So far, we have completed the ordering of the edges in a graph. Based on this order, a graph can be transformed into an edge sequence. A complete sequence for Figure 9.7(b) is $(0,1),(1,2),(2,0),(1,3)$.

Based on this ordering, three different DFS codes, γ_0, γ_1, and γ_2, generated by DFS subscriptings in Figure 9.7(b), 9.7(c), and 9.7(d), respectively, are shown in Table 9.1. An edge is represented by a 5-tuple, $(i,j,l_i,l_{(i,j)},l_j)$; l_i and l_j are the labels of v_i and v_j, respectively, and $l_{(i,j)}$ is the label of the edge connecting them.

Through DFS coding, a one-to-one mapping is built between a subscripted graph and a DFS code (a one-to-many mapping between a graph and DFS codes). When the context is clear, we treat a subscripted graph and its DFS code as the same. All the notations on subscripted graphs can also be applied to DFS codes. The graph represented by a DFS code α is written G_α.

Second, we define an order among edge sequences. Since one graph may have several DFS codes, we want to build an order among these codes and select one code to represent the graph. Because we are dealing with labeled graphs, the label information should be considered as one of the ordering factors. The labels of vertices and edges are used to break the tie when two edges have the exact same subscript, but different labels. Let the edge order relation $\prec_T$ take the first priority, the vertex label l_i take the second priority, the edge label $l_{(i,j)}$ take the third, and the vertex label l_j take the fourth to determine the order of two edges. For example, the first edge of the three DFS codes in Table 9.1 is $(0,1,X,a,X)$, $(0,1,X,a,X)$, and $(0,1,Y,b,X)$, respectively. All of them share the same subscript $(0,1)$. So relation $\prec_T$ cannot tell the difference among them. But using label information, following the order of first vertex label, edge label, and second vertex label, we have $(0,1,X,a,X) < (0,1,Y,b,X)$. The ordering based on the above rules is called

Table 9.1 DFS code for Figure 9.7(b), 9.7(c), and 9.7(d).

edge	γ_0	γ_1	γ_2
e_0	$(0,1,X,a,X)$	$(0,1,X,a,X)$	$(0,1,Y,b,X)$
e_1	$(1,2,X,a,Z)$	$(1,2,X,b,Y)$	$(1,2,X,a,X)$
e_2	$(2,0,Z,b,X)$	$(1,3,X,a,Z)$	$(2,3,X,b,Z)$
e_3	$(1,3,X,b,Y)$	$(3,0,Z,b,X)$	$(3,1,Z,a,X)$

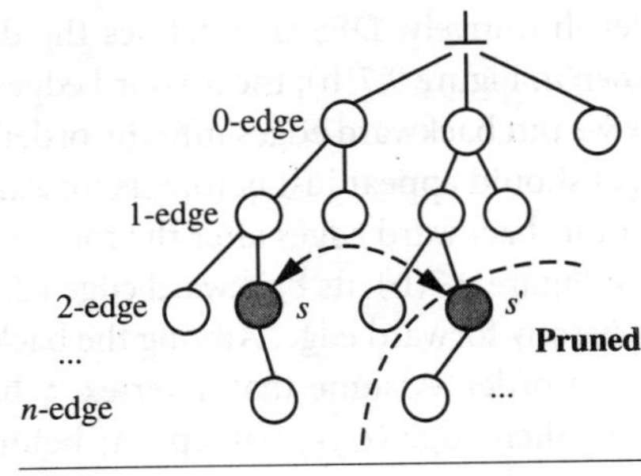

Figure 9.9 Lexicographic search tree.

DFS Lexicographic Order. According to this ordering, we have $\gamma_0 < \gamma_1 < \gamma_2$ for the DFS codes listed in Table 9.1.

Based on the DFS lexicographic ordering, the *minimum DFS code* of a given graph G, written as $\mathsf{dfs}(G)$, is the minimal one among all the DFS codes. For example, code γ_0 in Table 9.1 is the minimum DFS code of the graph in Figure 9.7(a). The subscripting that generates the minimum DFS code is called the *base subscripting.*

We have the following important relationship between the minimum DFS code and the isomorphism of the two graphs: *Given two graphs G and G', G is isomorphic to G' if and only if* $\mathsf{dfs}(G) = \mathsf{dfs}(G')$. Based on this property, what we need to do for mining frequent subgraphs is to perform only the right-most extensions on the minimum DFS codes, since such an extension will guarantee the completeness of mining results.

Figure 9.9 shows how to arrange all DFS codes in a search tree through right-most extensions. The root is an empty code. Each node is a DFS code encoding a graph. Each edge represents a right-most extension from a $(k-1)$-length DFS code to a k-length DSF code. The tree itself is ordered: left siblings are smaller than right siblings in the sense of DFS lexicographic order. Because any graph has at least one DFS code, the search tree can enumerate all possible subgraphs in a graph data set. However, one graph may have several DFS codes, minimum and nonminimum. The search of nonminimum DFS codes does not produce useful results. *"Is it necessary to perform right-most extension on nonminimum DFS codes?"* The answer is "*no.*" If codes s and s' in Figure 9.9 encode the same graph, the search space under s' can be safely pruned.

The details of gSpan are depicted in Figure 9.10. gSpan is called recursively to extend graph patterns so that their frequent descendants are found until their support is lower than min_sup or its code is not minimum any more. The difference between gSpan and PatternGrowth is at the right-most extension and extension termination of nonminimum DFS codes (lines 1-2). We replace the existence judgement in lines 1-2 of PatternGrowth with the inequation $s \neq dfs(s)$. Actually, $s \neq dfs(s)$ is more efficient to calculate. Line 5 requires exhaustive enumeration of s in D in order to count the frequency of all the possible right-most extensions of s.

The algorithm of Figure 9.10 implements a depth-first search version of gSpan. Actually, breadth-first search works too: for each newly discovered frequent subgraph

Algorithm: gSpan. Pattern growth-based frequent substructure mining that reduces duplicate graph generation.

Input:

- *s*, a DFS code;
- *D*, a graph data set;
- *min_sup*, the minimum support threshold.

Output:

- The frequent graph set, *S*.

Method:

$S \leftarrow \varnothing$;

Call gSpan(*s*, *D*, *min_sup*, *S*);

procedure PatternGrowthGraph(*s*, *D*, *min_sup*, *S*)

(1) **if** $s \neq dfs(s)$, **then**

(2)   **return;**

(3) insert *s* into *S*;

(4) set *C* to $\varnothing$;

(5) scan *D* once, find all the edges *e* such that *s* can be *right-most* extended to $s \diamond_r e$; insert $s \diamond_r e$ into *C* and count its frequency;

(6) sort *C* in DFS lexicographic order;

(7) **for each** frequent $s \diamond_r e$ in *C* **do**

(8)   *gSpan*($s \diamond_r e$, *D*, *min_sup*, *S*);

(9) **return;**

Figure 9.10 gSpan: A pattern-growth algorithm for frequent substructure mining.

in line 8, instead of directly calling gSpan, we insert it into a global first-in-first-out queue *Q*, which records all subgraphs that have not been extended. We then "gSpan" each subgraph in *Q* one by one. The performance of a breadth-first search version of gSpan is very close to that of the depth-first search, although the latter usually consumes less memory.

9.1.2 Mining Variant and Constrained Substructure Patterns

The frequent subgraph mining discussed in the previous section handles only one special kind of graphs: *labeled, undirected, connected simple graphs without any specific constraints*. That is, we assume that the database to be mined contains a set of graphs, each consisting of a set of labeled vertices and labeled but undirected edges, with no other constraints. However, many applications or users may need to enforce various kinds of *constraints* on the patterns to be mined or seek *variant substructure patterns*. For example, we may like to mine patterns, each of which contains certain specific vertices/edges, or where the total number of vertices/edges is within a specified range. Or what if we seek patterns where the average density of the graph patterns is above a threshold? Although it is possible to develop customized algorithms for each such case, there are too many variant cases to consider. Instead, a general framework is needed—one that can classify constraints on the graph patterns. Efficient constraint-based methods can then be developed for mining substructure patterns and their variants. In this section, we study several variants and constrained substructure patterns and look at how they can be mined.

Mining Closed Frequent Substructures

The first important variation of a frequent substructure is the **closed frequent substructure.** Take mining frequent subgraphs as an example. As with frequent itemset mining and sequential pattern mining, mining graph patterns may generate an explosive number of patterns. This is particularly true for dense data sets, because all of the subgraphs of a frequent graph are also frequent. This is an inherent problem, because according to the Apriori property, all the subgraphs of a frequent substructure must be frequent. A large graph pattern may generate an exponential number of frequent subgraphs. For example, among 423 confirmed active chemical compounds in an AIDS antiviral screen data set, there are nearly 1 million frequent graph patterns whose support is at least 5%. This renders the further analysis on frequent graphs nearly impossible.

One way to alleviate this problem is to mine only frequent closed graphs, where a frequent graph G is **closed** if and only if there is no proper supergraph G' that has the same support as G. Alternatively, we can mine maximal subgraph patterns where a frequent pattern G is **maximal** if and only if there is no frequent super-pattern of G. A set of closed subgraph patterns has the same expressive power as the full set of subgraph patterns under the same minimum support threshold, because the latter can be generated by the derived set of closed graph patterns. On the other hand, the maximal pattern set is a subset of the closed pattern set. It is usually more compact than the closed pattern set. However, we cannot use it to reconstruct the entire set of frequent patterns—the support information of a pattern is lost if it is a proper subpattern of a maximal pattern, yet carries a different support.

Example 9.3 **Maximal frequent graph.** The two graphs in Figure 9.2 are closed frequent graphs, but only the first graph is a maximal frequent graph. The second graph is not maximal because it has a frequent supergraph. ■

Mining closed graphs leads to a complete but more compact representation. For example, for the AIDS antiviral data set mentioned above, among the 1 million frequent graphs, only about 2,000 are closed frequent graphs. If further analysis, such as classification or clustering, is performed on closed frequent graphs instead of frequent graphs, it will achieve similar accuracy with less redundancy and higher efficiency.

An efficient method, called CloseGraph, was developed for mining closed frequent graphs by extension of the gSpan algorithm. Experimental study has shown that CloseGraph often generates far fewer graph patterns and runs more efficiently than gSpan, which mines the full pattern set.

Extension of Pattern-Growth Approach: Mining Alternative Substructure Patterns

A typical pattern-growth graph mining algorithm, such as gSpan or CloseGraph, mines *labeled, connected, undirected* frequent or closed subgraph patterns. Such a graph mining framework can easily be extended for mining *alternative substructure patterns.* Here we discuss a few such alternatives.

First, the method can be extended for **mining unlabeled or partially labeled graphs.** Each vertex and each edge in our previously discussed graphs contain labels. Alternatively, if none of the vertices and edges in a graph are labeled, the graph is **unlabeled.** A graph is **partially labeled** if only some of the edges and/or vertices are labeled. To handle such cases, we can build a label set that contains the original label set and a new empty label, ϕ. Label ϕ is assigned to vertices and edges that do not have labels. Notice that label ϕ may match with any label or with ϕ only, depending on the application semantics. With this transformation, gSpan (and CloseGraph) can directly mine unlabeled or partially labeled graphs.

Second, we examine whether gSpan can be extended to **mining nonsimple graphs.** A **nonsimple graph** may have a *self-loop* (i.e., an edge joins a vertex to itself) and *multiple edges* (i.e., several edges connecting two of the same vertices). In gSpan, we always first grow backward edges and then forward edges. In order to accommodate self-loops, the growing order should be changed to *backward edges, self-loops, and forward edges.* If we allow sharing of the same vertices in two neighboring edges in a DFS code, the definition of DFS lexicographic order can handle multiple edges smoothly. Thus gSpan can mine nonsimple graphs efficiently, too.

Third, we see how gSpan can be extended to handle **mining directed graphs.** In a directed graph, each edge of the graph has a defined direction. If we use a 5-tuple, $(i, j, l_i, l_{(i,j)}, l_j)$, to represent an undirected edge, then for directed edges, a new state is introduced to form a 6-tuple, $(i, j, d, l_i, l_{(i,j)}, l_j)$, where d represents the direction of an edge. Let $d = +1$ be the direction from i (v_i) to j (v_j), whereas $d = -1$ is that from j (v_j) to i (v_i). Notice that the sign of d is not related to the forwardness or backwardness of an edge. When extending a graph with one more edge, this edge may have two choices of d, which only introduces a new state in the growing procedure and need not change the framework of gSpan.

Fourth, the method can also be extended to **mining disconnected graphs.** There are two cases to be considered: (1) the graphs in the data set may be disconnected, and (2) the graph patterns may be disconnected. For the first case, we can transform the original data set by adding a virtual vertex to connect the disconnected graphs in each graph. We then apply gSpan on the new graph data set. For the second case, we redefine the DFS code. A disconnected graph pattern can be viewed as a set of connected graphs, $r = \{g_0, g_1, \ldots, g_m\}$, where g_i is a connected graph, $0 \leq i \leq m$. Because each graph can be mapped to a minimum DFS code, a disconnected graph r can be translated into a code, $\gamma = (s_0, s_1, \ldots, s_m)$, where s_i is the minimum DFS code of g_i. The order of g_i in r is irrelevant. Thus, we enforce an order in $\{s_i\}$ such that $s_0 \leq s_1 \leq \ldots \leq s_m$. γ can be extended by either adding one-edge s_{m+1} ($s_m \leq s_{m+1}$) or by extending s_m, ..., and s_0. When checking the frequency of γ in the graph data set, make sure that $g_0, g_1, \ldots,$ and g_m are disconnected with each other.

Finally, if we view a tree as a degenerated graph, it is straightforward to extend the method to **mining frequent subtrees**. In comparison with a general graph, a tree can be considered as a degenerated direct graph that does not contain any edges that can go back to its parent or ancestor nodes. Thus if we consider that our traversal always starts at the root (because the tree does not contain any backward edges), gSpan is ready to mine tree structures. Based on the mining efficiency of the pattern growth–based approach, it is expected that gSpan can achieve good performance in tree-structure mining.

Constraint-Based Mining of Substructure Patterns

As we have seen in previous chapters, various kinds of constraints can be associated with a user's mining request. Rather than developing many case-specific substructure mining algorithms, it is more appropriate to set up a general framework of constraint-based substructure mining so that systematic strategies can be developed to push constraints deep into the mining process.

Constraint-based mining of frequent substructures can be developed systematically, similar to the constraint-based mining of frequent patterns and sequential patterns introduced in Chapters 5 and 8. Take graph mining as an example. As with the constraint-based frequent pattern mining framework outlined in Chapter 5, graph constraints can be classified into a few categories, including *antimonotonic*, *monotonic*, and *succinct*. Efficient constraint-based mining methods can be developed in a similar way by extending efficient graph-pattern mining algorithms, such as gSpan and CloseGraph.

Example 9.4 **Constraint-based substructure mining.** Let's examine a few commonly encountered classes of constraints to see how the constraint-pushing technique can be integrated into the pattern-growth mining framework.

1. **Element, set, or subgraph containment constraint.** Suppose a user requires that the mined patterns contain a particular set of subgraphs. This is a **succinct constraint**, which can be pushed deep into the beginning of the mining process. That is, we can take the given set of subgraphs as a query, perform selection first using the constraint, and then mine on the selected data set by growing (i.e., extending) the patterns from the given set of subgraphs. A similar strategy can be developed if we require that the mined graph pattern must contain a particular set of edges or vertices.

2. **Geometric constraint.** A geometric constraint can be that the angle between each pair of connected edges must be within a range, written as "$C_G = min\_angle \leq angle(e_1, e_2, v, v_1, v_2) \leq max\_angle$," where two edges e_1 and e_2 are connected at vertex v with the two vertices at the other ends as v_1 and v_2, respectively. C_G is an **antimonotonic constraint** because if one angle in a graph formed by two edges does not satisfy C_G, further growth on the graph will never satisfy C_G. Thus C_G can be pushed deep into the edge growth process and reject any growth that does not satisfy C_G.
3. **Value-sum constraint.** For example, such a constraint can be that the sum of (positive) weights on the edges, Sum_e, be within a range *low* and *high*. This constraint can be split into two constraints, $Sum_e \geq low$ and $Sum_e \leq high$. The former is a **monotonic constraint**, because once it is satisfied, further "growth" on the graph by adding more edges will always satisfy the constraint. The latter is an **antimonotonic constraint,** because once the condition is not satisfied, further growth of Sum_e will never satisfy it. The constraint pushing strategy can then be easily worked out. ■

Notice that a graph-mining query may contain multiple constraints. For example, we may want to mine graph patterns that satisfy constraints on both the geometric and minimal sum of edge weights. In such cases, we should try to push multiple constraints simultaneously, exploring a method similar to that developed for frequent itemset mining. For the multiple constraints that are difficult to push in simultaneously, customized constraint-based mining algorithms should be developed accordingly.

Mining Approximate Frequent Substructures

An alternative way to reduce the number of patterns to be generated is to mine approximate frequent substructures, which allow slight structural variations. With this technique, we can represent several slightly different frequent substructures using one approximate substructure.

The principle of *minimum description length* (Chapter 6) is adopted in a substructure discovery system called SUBDUE, which mines approximate frequent substructures. It looks for a substructure pattern that can best compress a graph set based on the Minimum Description Length (MDL) principle, which essentially states that the simplest representation is preferred. SUBDUE adopts a constrained beam search method. It grows a single vertex incrementally by expanding a node in it. At each expansion, it searches for the best total description length: the description length of the pattern and the description length of the graph set with all the instances of the pattern condensed into single nodes. SUBDUE performs approximate matching to allow slight variations of substructures, thus supporting the discovery of approximate substructures.

There should be many different ways to mine approximate substructure patterns. Some may lead to a better representation of the entire set of substructure patterns, whereas others may lead to more efficient mining techniques. More research is needed in this direction.

Mining Coherent Substructures

A frequent substructure G is a **coherent subgraph** if the mutual information between G and each of its own subgraphs is above some threshold. The number of coherent substructures is significantly smaller than that of frequent substructures. Thus, mining coherent substructures can efficiently prune redundant patterns (i.e., patterns that are similar to each other and have similar support). A promising method was developed for mining such substructures. Its experiments demonstrate that in mining spatial motifs from protein structure graphs, the discovered coherent substructures are usually statistically significant. This indicates that coherent substructure mining selects a small subset of features that have high distinguishing power between protein classes.

Mining Dense Substructures

In the analysis of graph pattern mining, researchers have found that there exists a specific kind of graph structure, called a **relational graph**, where each node label is used only once per graph. The relational graph is widely used in modeling and analyzing massive networks (e.g., biological networks, social networks, transportation networks, and the World Wide Web). In biological networks, nodes represent objects like genes, proteins, and enzymes, whereas edges encode the relationships, such as control, reaction, and correlation, between these objects. In social networks, each node represents a unique entity, and an edge describes a kind of relationship between entities. One particular interesting pattern is the **frequent highly connected** or **dense** subgraph in large relational graphs. In social networks, this kind of pattern can help identify groups where people are strongly associated. In computational biology, a highly connected subgraph could represent a set of genes within the same functional module (i.e., a set of genes participating in the same biological pathways).

This may seem like a simple constraint-pushing problem using the minimal or average degree of a vertex, where the **degree** of a vertex v is the number of edges that connect v. Unfortunately, things are not so simple. Although average degree and minimum degree display some level of connectivity in a graph, they cannot guarantee that the graph is connected in a balanced way. Figure 9.11 shows an example where some part of a graph may be loosely connected even if its average degree and minimum degree are both high. The removal of edge e_1 would make the whole graph fall apart. We may enforce the

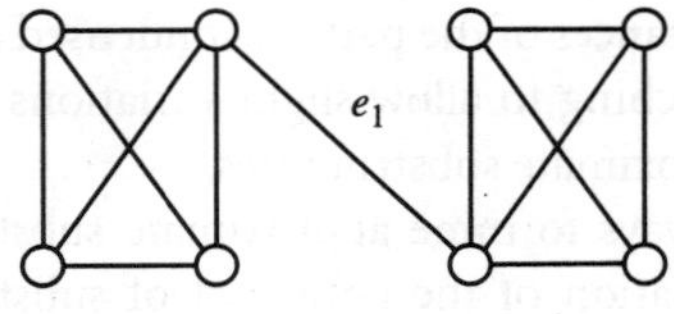

Figure 9.11 Average Degree: 3.25, Minimum Degree: 3.

following downward closure constraint: a graph is highly connected if and only if each of its connected subgraphs is highly connected. However, some global tightly connected graphs may not be locally well connected. It is too strict to have this downward closure constraint. Thus, we adopt the concept of *edge connectivity*, as follows: Given a graph G, an **edge cut** is a set of edges E_c such that $E(G) - E_c$ is disconnected. A **minimum cut** is the smallest set in all edge cuts. The **edge connectivity** of G is the size of a minimum cut. A graph is **dense** if its edge connectivity is no less than a specified minimum cut threshold.

Now the problem becomes how to mine closed frequent dense relational graphs that satisfy a user-specified connectivity constraint. There are two approaches to mining such closed dense graphs efficiently: a pattern-growth approach called Close-Cut and a pattern-reduction approach called Splat. We briefly outline their ideas as follows.

Similar to pattern-growth frequent itemset mining, **CloseCut** first starts with a small frequent candidate graph and extends it as much as possible by adding new edges until it finds the largest supergraph with the same support (i.e., its closed supergraph). The discovered graph is decomposed to extract subgraphs satisfying the connectivity constraint. It then extends the candidate graph by adding new edges, and repeats the above operations until no candidate graph is frequent.

Instead of enumerating graphs from small ones to large ones, **Splat** directly intersects relational graphs to obtain highly connected graphs. Let pattern g be a highly connected graph in relational graphs $G_{i_1}, G_{i_2}, \ldots$, and G_{i_l} $(i_1 < i_2 < \ldots < i_l)$. In order to mine patterns in a larger set $\{G_{i_1}, G_{i_2}, \ldots, G_{i_l}, G_{i_{l+1}}\}$, Splat intersects g with graph $G_{i_{l+1}}$. Let $g' = g \cap G_{i_{l+1}}$. Some edges in g may be removed because they do not exist in graph $G_{i_{l+1}}$. Thus, the connectivity of the new graph g' may no longer satisfy the constraint. If so, g' is decomposed into smaller highly connected subgraphs. We progressively reduce the size of candidate graphs by intersection and decomposition operations. We call this approach a **pattern-reduction approach.**

Both methods have shown good scalability in large graph data sets. CloseCut has better performance on patterns with high support and low connectivity. On the contrary, Splat can filter frequent graphs with low connectivity in the early stage of mining, thus achieving better performance for the high-connectivity constraints. Both methods are successfully used to extract interesting patterns from multiple biological networks.

9.1.3 Applications: Graph Indexing, Similarity Search, Classification, and Clustering

In the previous two sections, we discussed methods for mining various kinds of frequent substructures. There are many interesting applications of the discovered structured patterns. These include building graph indices in large graph databases, performing similarity search in such data sets, characterizing structure data sets, and classifying and clustering the complex structures. We examine such applications in this section.

Graph Indexing with Discriminative Frequent Substructures

Indexing is essential for efficient search and query processing in database and information systems. Technology has evolved from single-dimensional to multidimensional indexing, claiming a broad spectrum of successful applications, including relational database systems and spatiotemporal, time-series, multimedia, text-, and Web-based information systems. However, the traditional indexing approach encounters challenges in databases involving complex objects, like graphs, because a graph may contain an exponential number of subgraphs. It is ineffective to build an index based on vertices or edges, because such features are nonselective and unable to distinguish graphs. On the other hand, building index structures based on subgraphs may lead to an explosive number of index entries.

Recent studies on graph indexing have proposed a *path-based indexing* approach, which takes the *path* as the basic indexing unit. This approach is used in the GraphGrep and Daylight systems. The general idea is to enumerate all of the existing paths in a database up to *maxL* length and index them, where a path is a vertex sequence, $v_1, v_2, \ldots, v_k$, such that, $\forall 1 \leq i \leq k-1$, (v_i, v_{i+1}) is an edge. The method uses the index to identify every graph, g_i, that contains all of the paths (up to *maxL* length) in query q. Even though paths are easier to manipulate than trees and graphs, and the index space is predefined, the path-based approach may not be suitable for complex graph queries, because the set of paths in a graph database is usually huge. The structural information in the graph is lost when a query graph is broken apart. It is likely that many false-positive answers will be returned. This can be seen from the following example.

Example 9.5 **Difficulty with the path-based indexing approach.** Figure 9.12 is a sample chemical data set extracted from an AIDS antiviral screening database.[1] For simplicity, we ignore the bond type. Figure 9.13 shows a sample query: 2,3-dimethylbutane. Assume that this query is posed to the sample database. Although only graph (c) in Figure 9.12 is the answer, graphs (a) and (b) cannot be pruned because both of them contain all of the paths existing in the query graph: c, $c-c$, $c-c-c$, and $c-c-c-c$. In this case, carbon chains (up to length 3) are not discriminative enough to distinguish the sample graphs. This indicates that the path may not be a good structure to serve as an index feature. ■

A method called gIndex was developed to build a compact and effective graph index structure. It takes frequent and discriminative substructures as index features. Frequent substructures are ideal candidates because they explore the shared structures in the data and are relatively stable to database updates. To reduce the *index size* (i.e., the number of frequent substructures that are used in the indices), the concept of discriminative

[1] *http://dtp.nci.nih.gov/docs/aids/aids_data.html.*

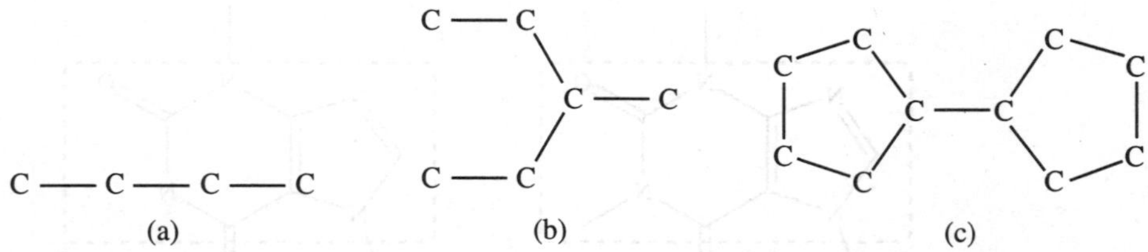

Figure 9.12 A sample chemical data set.

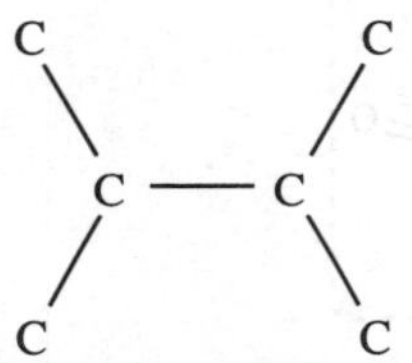

Figure 9.13 A sample query.

frequent substructure is introduced. A frequent substructure is *discriminative* if its support cannot be well approximated by the intersection of the graph sets that contain one of its subgraphs. The experiments on the AIDS antiviral data sets and others show that this method leads to far smaller index structures. In addition, it achieves similar performance in comparison with the other indexing methods, such as the path index and the index built directly on frequent substructures.

Substructure Similarity Search in Graph Databases

Bioinformatics and chem-informatics applications involve query-based search in massive, complex structural data. Even with a graph index, such search can encounter challenges because it is often too restrictive to search for an exact match of an index entry. Efficient *similarity search of complex structures* becomes a vital operation. Let's examine a simple example.

Example 9.6 **Similarity search of chemical structures.** Figure 9.14 is a chemical data set with three molecules. Figure 9.15 shows a substructure query. Obviously, no match exists for this query graph. If we relax the query by taking out one edge, then caffeine and thesal in Figure 9.14(a) and 9.14(b) will be good matches. If we relax the query further, the structure in Figure 9.14(c) could also be an answer. ■

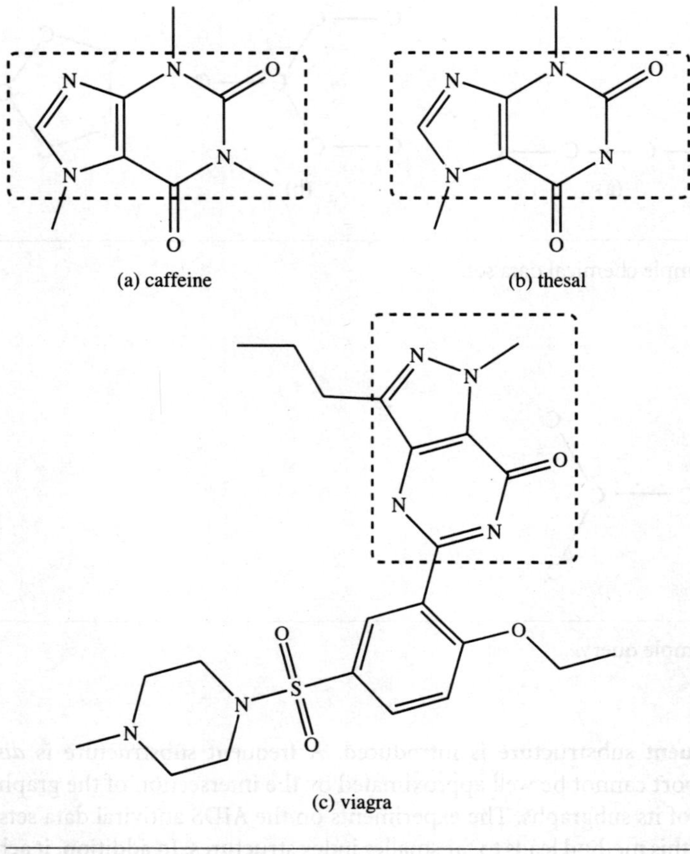

(a) caffeine (b) thesal

(c) viagra

Figure 9.14 A chemical database.

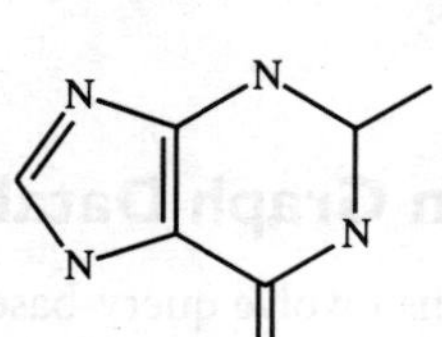

Figure 9.15 A query graph.

A naïve solution to this similarity search problem is to form a set of subgraph queries with one or more edge deletions and then use the exact substructure search. This does not work when the number of deletions is more than 1. For example, if we allow three edges to be deleted in a 20-edge query graph, it may generate $\binom{20}{3} = 1140$ substructure queries, which are too expensive to check.

A feature-based structural filtering algorithm, called Grafil (Graph Similarity Filtering), was developed to filter graphs efficiently in large-scale graph databases. Grafil models each query graph as a set of features and transforms the edge deletions into "feature misses" in the query graph. It is shown that using too many features will not leverage the filtering performance. Therefore, a multifilter composition strategy is developed, where each filter uses a distinct and complementary subset of the features. The filters are constructed by a hierarchical, one-dimensional clustering algorithm that groups features with similar selectivity into a *feature set*. Experiments have shown that the multifilter strategy can significantly improve performance for a moderate relaxation ratio.

Classification and Cluster Analysis Using Graph Patterns

"Can we apply the discovered patterns to classification and cluster analysis? If so, how?" The discovered frequent graph patterns and/or their variants can be used as features for graph classification. First, we mine frequent graph patterns in the training set. The features that are frequent in one class but rather infrequent in the other class(es) should be considered as highly discriminative features. Such features will then be used for model construction. To achieve high-quality classification, we can adjust the thresholds on frequency, discriminativeness, and graph connectivity based on the data, the number and quality of the features generated, and the classification accuracy. Various classification approaches, including support vector machines, naïve Bayesian, and associative classification, can be used in such graph-based classification.

Similarly, cluster analysis can be explored with mined graph patterns. The set of graphs that share a large set of similar graph patterns should be considered as highly similar and should be grouped into similar clusters. Notice that the concept of graph connectivity (or minimal cuts) introduced in the section for mining frequent dense graphs can be used as an important measure to group similar graphs into clusters. In addition, the minimal support threshold can be used as a way to adjust the number of frequent clusters or generate hierarchical clusters. The graphs that do not belong to any cluster or that are far away from the derived clusters can be considered as *outliers*. Thus outliers can be considered as a by-product of cluster analysis.

Many different kinds of graphs can be discovered in graph pattern mining, especially when we consider the possibilities of setting different kinds of thresholds. Different graph patterns may likely lead to different classification and clustering results, thus it is important to consider mining graph patterns and graph classification/clustering as an intertwined process rather than a two-step process. That is, the qualities of graph classification and clustering can be improved by exploring alternative methods and thresholds when mining graph patterns.

9.2 Social Network Analysis

The notion of social networks, where relationships between entities are represented as *links* in a graph, has attracted increasing attention in the past decades. Thus social network analysis, from a data mining perspective, is also called *link analysis* or *link mining*. In this section, we introduce the concept of social networks in Section 9.2.1, and study the characteristics of social networks in Section 9.2.2. In Section 9.2.3, we look at the tasks and challenges involved in link mining, and finally, explore exemplar forms of mining on social networks in Section 9.2.4.

9.2.1 What Is a Social Network?

From the point of view of data mining, a **social network** is a *heterogeneous* and *multirelational* data set represented by a graph. The graph is typically very large, with **nodes** corresponding to *objects* and **edges** corresponding to *links* representing relationships or interactions between objects. Both nodes and links have *attributes*. Objects may have class labels. Links can be one-directional and are not required to be binary.

Social networks need not be social in context. There are many real-world instances of technological, business, economic, and biologic social networks. Examples include electrical power grids, telephone call graphs, the spread of computer viruses, the World Wide Web, and coauthorship and citation networks of scientists. Customer networks and collaborative filtering problems (where product recommendations are made based on the preferences of other customers) are other examples. In biology, examples range from epidemiological networks, cellular and metabolic networks, and food webs, to the neural network of the nematode worm *Caenorhabditis elegans* (the only creature whose neural network has been completely mapped). The exchange of e-mail messages within corporations, newsgroups, chat rooms, friendships, sex webs (linking sexual partners), and the quintessential "old-boy" network (i.e., the overlapping boards of directors of the largest companies in the United States) are examples from sociology.

Small world (social) networks have received considerable attention as of late. They reflect the concept of "small worlds," which originally focused on networks among individuals. The phrase captures the initial surprise between two strangers ("What a small world!") when they realize that they are indirectly linked to one another through mutual acquaintances. In 1967, Harvard sociologist, Stanley Milgram, and his colleagues conducted experiments in which people in Kansas and Nebraska were asked to direct letters to strangers in Boston by forwarding them to friends who they thought might know the strangers in Boston. Half of the letters were successfully delivered through no more than five intermediaries. Additional studies by Milgram and others, conducted between other cities, have shown that there appears to be a universal "six degrees of separation" between any two individuals in the world. Examples of small world networks are shown in Figure 9.16. **Small world networks** have been characterized as having a high degree of local clustering for a small fraction of the nodes (i.e., these nodes are interconnected with one another), which at the same time are no more than a few degrees of separation from the remaining nodes. It is believed that many social, physical, human-designed, and biological networks exhibit such small world characteristics. These characteristics are further described and modeled in Section 9.2.2.

"Why all this interest in small world networks and social networks, in general? What is the interest in characterizing networks and in mining them to learn more about their structure?"

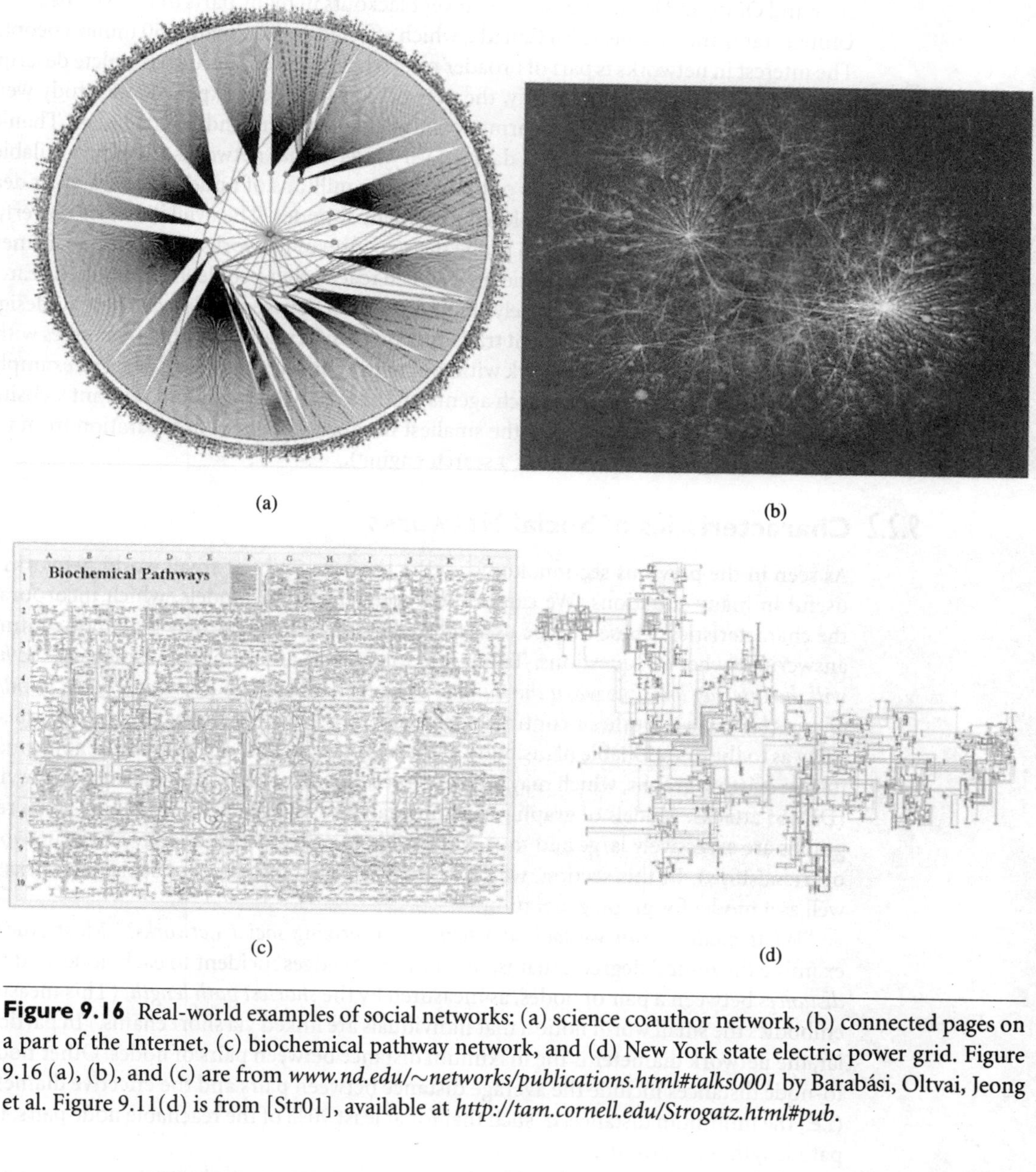

(a) (b) (c) (d)

Figure 9.16 Real-world examples of social networks: (a) science coauthor network, (b) connected pages on a part of the Internet, (c) biochemical pathway network, and (d) New York state electric power grid. Figure 9.16 (a), (b), and (c) are from *www.nd.edu/~networks/publications.html#talks0001* by Barabási, Oltvai, Jeong et al. Figure 9.11(d) is from [Str01], available at *http://tam.cornell.edu/Strogatz.html#pub.*

The reason is that structure always affects function. For example, the topology of social networks affects the spread of infectious disease through a structured population. The topology of a power grid affects the stability and robustness of its power transmission. For instance, a power failure in Cleveland, Ohio, on August 14, 2003, triggered, through an interconnecting grid system, the shutting down of nuclear power plants in New York state and Ohio, and led to widespread power blackouts in many parts of the Northeastern United States and Southeastern Canada, which affected approximately 50 million people. The interest in networks is part of broader research in the accurate and complete description of *complex systems*. Previously, the networks available for experimental study were small and few, with very little information available regarding individual nodes. Thanks to the Internet, huge amounts of data on very large social networks are now available. These typically contain from tens of thousands to millions of nodes. Often, a great deal of information is available at the level of individual nodes. The availability of powerful computers has made it possible to probe the structure of networks. Searching social networks can help us better understand how we can reach other people. In addition, research on small worlds, with their relatively small separation between nodes, can help us design networks that facilitate the efficient transmission of information or other resources without having to overload the network with too many redundant connections. For example, it may help us design smarter search agents on the Web, which can find relevant websites in response to a query, all within the smallest number of degrees of separation from the initial website (which is, typically, a search engine).

9.2.2 Characteristics of Social Networks

As seen in the previous section, knowing the characteristics of small world networks is useful in many situations. We can build graph generation models, which incorporate the characteristics. These may be used to predict how a network may look in the future, answering "what-if" questions. Taking the Internet as an example, we may ask *"What will the Internet look like when the number of nodes doubles?"* and *"What will the number of edges be?"*. If a hypothesis contradicts the generally accepted characteristics, this raises a flag as to the questionable plausibility of the hypothesis. This can help detect abnormalities in existing graphs, which may indicate fraud, spam, or Distributed Denial of Service (DDoS) attacks. Models of graph generation can also be used for simulations when real graphs are excessively large and thus, impossible to collect (such as a very large network of friendships). In this section, we study the basic characteristics of social networks as well as a model for graph generation.

"What qualities can we look at when characterizing social networks?" Most studies examine the **nodes' degrees**, that is, the number of edges incident to each node, and the *distances* between a pair of nodes, as measured by the *shortest path length*. (This measure embodies the small world notion that individuals are linked via short chains.) In particular, the **network diameter** is the maximum distance between pairs of nodes. Other node-to-node distances include the **average distance** between pairs and the **effective diameter** (i.e., the minimum distance, d, such that for at least 90% of the reachable node pairs, the path length is at most d).

Social networks are rarely static. Their graph representations evolve as nodes and edges are added or deleted over time. In general, social networks tend to exhibit the following phenomena:

1. **Densification power law:** Previously, it was believed that as a network evolves, the number of degrees grows linearly in the number of nodes. This was known as the

constant average degree assumption. However, extensive experiments have shown that, on the contrary, networks become increasingly *dense* over time with the average degree increasing (and hence, the number of edges growing superlinearly in the number of nodes). The densification follows the **densification power law (or growth power law)**, which states

$$e(t) \propto n(t)^a, \tag{9.1}$$

where $e(t)$ and $n(t)$, respectively, represent the number of edges and nodes of the graph at time t, and the exponent a generally lies strictly between 1 and 2. Note that if $a = 1$, this corresponds to constant average degree over time, whereas $a = 2$ corresponds to an extremely dense graph where each node has edges to a constant fraction of all nodes.

2. **Shrinking diameter:** It has been experimentally shown that the effective diameter tends to *decrease* as the network grows. This contradicts an earlier belief that the diameter slowly increases as a function of network size. As an intuitive example, consider a citation network, where nodes are papers and a citation from one paper to another is indicated by a directed edge. The out-links of a node, v (representing the papers cited by v), are "frozen" at the moment it joins the graph. The decreasing distances between pairs of nodes consequently appears to be the result of subsequent papers acting as "bridges" by citing earlier papers from other areas.

3. **Heavy-tailed out-degree and in-degree distributions:** The number of out-degrees for a node tends to follow a heavy-tailed distribution by observing the **power law**, $1/n^a$, where n is the rank of the node in the order of decreasing out-degrees and typically, $0 < a < 2$ (Figure 9.17). The smaller the value of a, the heavier the tail. This phenomena is represented in the **preferential attachment model**, where each new node attaches to an existing network by a constant number of out-links, following a

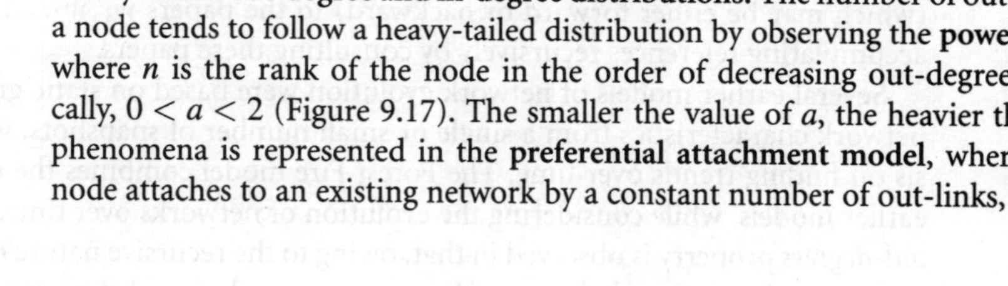

Figure 9.17 The number of out-degrees (y-axis) for a node tends to follow a heavy-tailed distribution. The node rank (x-axis) is defined as the order of deceasing out-degrees of the node.

"rich-get-richer" rule. The in-degrees also follow a heavy-tailed distribution, although it tends be more skewed than the out-degrees distribution.

A **Forest Fire model** for graph generation was proposed, which captures these characteristics of graph evolution over time. It is based on the notion that new nodes attach to the network by "burning" through existing edges in epidemic fashion. It uses two parameters, *forward burning probability*, p, and *backward burning ratio*, r, which are described below. Suppose a new node, v, arrives at time t. It attaches to G_t, the graph constructed so far, in the following steps:

1. It chooses an *ambassador node*, w, at random, and forms a link to w.
2. It selects x links incident to w, where x is a random number that is binomially distributed with mean $(1-p)^{-1}$. It chooses from out-links and in-links of w but selects in-links with probability r times lower than out-links. Let $w_1, w_2, \ldots, w_x$ denote the nodes at the other end of the selected edges.
3. Our new node, v, forms out-links to $w_1, w_2, \ldots, w_x$ and then applies step 2 recursively to each of $w_1, w_2, \ldots, w_x$. Nodes cannot be visited a second time so as to prevent the construction from cycling. The process continues until it dies out.

For an intuitive feel of the model, we return to our example of a citation network. The author of a new paper, v, initially consults w, and follows a subset of its references (which may be either forward or backward) to the papers $w_1, w_2, \ldots, w_x$. It continues accumulating references recursively by consulting these papers.

Several earlier models of network evolution were based on static graphs, identifying network characteristics from a single or small number of snapshots, with little emphasis on finding trends over time. The Forest Fire model combines the essence of several earlier models, while considering the evolution of networks over time. The *heavy-tailed out-degrees* property is observed in that, owing to the recursive nature of link formation, new nodes have a good chance of burning many edges and thus producing large out-degrees. The *heavy-tailed in-degrees* property is preserved in that Forest Fire follows the "rich-get-richer" rule: highly linked nodes can easily be reached by a new node, regardless of which ambassador the new node starts from. The flavor of a model known as the *copying model* is also observed in that a new node copies many of the neighbors of its ambassador. The *densification power law* is upheld in that a new node will have many links near the community of its ambassador, a few links beyond this, and much fewer farther away. Rigorous empirical studies found that the *shrinking diameter* property was upheld. Nodes with heavy-tailed out-degrees may serve as "bridges" that connect formerly disparate parts of the network, decreasing the network diameter.

9.2.3 Link Mining: Tasks and Challenges

"How can we mine social networks?" Traditional methods of machine learning and data mining, taking, as input, a random sample of homogenous objects from a single

relation, may not be appropriate here. The data comprising social networks tend to be heterogeneous, multirelational, and semi-structured. As a result, a new field of research has emerged called **link mining.** Link mining is a confluence of research in social networks, link analysis, hypertext and Web mining, graph mining, relational learning, and inductive logic programming. It embodies descriptive and predictive modeling. By considering links (the relationships between objects), more information is made available to the mining process. This brings about several new tasks. Here, we list these tasks with examples from various domains:

1. **Link-based object classification.** In traditional classification methods, objects are classified based on the attributes that describe them. Link-based classification predicts the category of an object based not only on its attributes, but also on its links, and on the attributes of linked objects.

   Web page classification is a well-recognized example of link-based classification. It predicts the category of a Web page based on word occurrence (words that occur on the page) and *anchor text* (the hyperlink words, that is, the words you click on when you click on a link), both of which serve as attributes. In addition, classification is based on links between pages and other attributes of the pages and links. In the *bibliography domain*, objects include papers, authors, institutions, journals, and conferences. A classification task is to predict the topic of a paper based on word occurrence, citations (other papers that cite the paper), and cocitations (other papers that are cited within the paper), where the citations act as links. An example from *epidemiology* is the task of predicting the disease type of a patient based on characteristics (e.g., symptoms) of the patient, and on characteristics of other people with whom the patient has been in contact. (These other people are referred to as the patients' *contacts.*)

2. **Object type prediction.** This predicts the type of an object, based on its attributes and its links, and on the attributes of objects linked to it. In the bibliographic domain, we may want to predict the venue type of a publication as either conference, journal, or workshop. In the *communication domain*, a similar task is to predict whether a communication contact is by e-mail, phone call, or mail.

3. **Link type prediction.** This predicts the type or purpose of a link, based on properties of the objects involved. Given epidemiological data, for instance, we may try to predict whether two people who know each other are family members, coworkers, or acquaintances. In another example, we may want to predict whether there is an advisor-advisee relationship between two coauthors. Given Web page data, we can try to predict whether a link on a page is an advertising link or a navigational link.

4. **Predicting link existence.** Unlike link type prediction, where we know a connection exists between two objects and we want to predict its type, instead we may want to predict whether a link exists between two objects. Examples include predicting whether there will be a link between two Web pages, and whether a paper will cite

another paper. In epidemiology, we can try to predict with whom a patient came in contact.

5. **Link cardinality estimation.** There are two forms of link cardinality estimation. First, we may predict the number of links to an object. This is useful, for instance, in predicting the authoritativeness of a Web page based on the number of links to it (in-links). Similarly, the number of out-links can be used to identify Web pages that act as *hubs*, where a hub is one or a set of Web pages that point to many authoritative pages of the same topic. In the bibliographic domain, the number of citations in a paper may indicate the impact of the paper—the more citations the paper has, the more influential it is likely to be. In epidemiology, predicting the number of links between a patient and his or her contacts is an indication of the potential for disease transmission.
   A more difficult form of link cardinality estimation predicts the number of objects reached along a path from an object. This is important in estimating the number of objects that will be returned by a query. In the Web page domain, we may predict the number of pages that would be retrieved by crawling a site (where *crawling* refers to a methodological, automated search through the Web, mainly to create a copy of all of the visited pages for later processing by a search engine). Regarding citations, we can also use link cardinality estimation to predict the number of citations of a specific author in a given journal.

6. **Object reconciliation.** In object reconciliation, the task is to predict whether two objects are, in fact, the same, based on their attributes and links. This task is common in information extraction, duplication elimination, object consolidation, and citation matching, and is also known as *record linkage* or *identity uncertainty*. Examples include predicting whether two websites are mirrors of each other, whether two citations actually refer to the same paper, and whether two apparent disease strains are really the same.

7. **Group detection.** Group detection is a clustering task. It predicts when a set of objects belong to the same group or cluster, based on their attributes as well as their link structure. An area of application is the identification of *Web communities*, where a Web community is a collection of Web pages that focus on a particular theme or topic. A similar example in the bibliographic domain is the identification of research communities.

8. **Subgraph detection.** Subgraph identification finds characteristic subgraphs within networks. This is a form of graph search and was described in Section 9.1. An example from biology is the discovery of subgraphs corresponding to protein structures. In chemistry, we can search for subgraphs representing chemical substructures.

9. **Metadata mining.** Metadata are data about data. Metadata provide semi-structured data about unstructured data, ranging from text and Web data to multimedia databases. It is useful for data integration tasks in many domains. Metadata mining can be used for *schema mapping* (where, say, the attribute *customer_id* from one database is mapped to *cust_number* from another database because they both refer to the

same entity); *schema discovery*, which generates schema from semi-structured data; and *schema reformulation*, which refines the schema based on the mined metadata. Examples include matching two bibliographic sources, discovering schema from unstructured or semi-structured data on the Web, and mapping between two medical ontologies.

In summary, the exploitation of link information between objects brings on additional tasks for link mining in comparison with traditional mining approaches. The implementation of these tasks, however, invokes many challenges. We examine several of these challenges here:

1. **Logical versus statistical dependencies.** Two types of dependencies reside in the graph—*link structures* (representing the logical relationship between objects) and *probabilistic dependencies* (representing statistical relationships, such as correlation between attributes of objects where, typically, such objects are logically related). The coherent handling of these dependencies is also a challenge for multirelational data mining, where the data to be mined exist in multiple tables. We must search over the different possible logical relationships between objects, in addition to the standard search over probabilistic dependencies between attributes. This takes a huge search space, which further complicates finding a plausible mathematical model. Methods developed in inductive logic programming may be applied here, which focus on search over logical relationships.
2. **Feature construction.** In link-based classification, we consider the attributes of an object as well as the attributes of objects linked to it. In addition, the links may also have attributes. The goal of *feature construction* is to construct a single feature representing these attributes. This can involve feature selection and feature aggregation. In *feature selection*, only the most discriminating features are included.[2] *Feature aggregation* takes a multiset of values over the set of related objects and returns a summary of it. This summary may be, for instance, the mode (most frequently occurring value); the mean value of the set (if the values are numerical); or the median or "middle" value (if the values are ordered). However, in practice, this method is not always appropriate.
3. **Instances versus classes.** This alludes to whether the model refers explicitly to individuals or to classes (generic categories) of individuals. An advantage of the former model is that it may be used to connect particular individuals with high probability. An advantage of the latter model is that it may be used to generalize to new situations, with different individuals.
4. **Collective classification and collective consolidation.** Consider training a model for classification, based on a set of class-labeled objects. Traditional classification

[2] Feature (or attribute) selection was introduced in Chapter 2.

methods consider only the attributes of the objects. After training, suppose we are given a new set of unlabeled objects. Use of the model to infer the class labels for the new objects is complicated due to possible correlations between objects—the labels of linked objects may be correlated. Classification should therefore involve an additional iterative step that updates (or consolidates) the class label of each object based on the labels of objects linked to it. In this sense, classification is done *collectively* rather than independently.

5. **Effective use of labeled and unlabeled data.** A recent strategy in learning is to incorporate a mix of both labeled and unlabeled data. Unlabeled data can help infer the object attribute distribution. Links between unlabeled (test) data allow us to use attributes of linked objects. Links between labeled (training) data and unlabeled (test) data induce dependencies that can help make more accurate inferences.

6. **Link prediction.** A challenge in link prediction is that the prior probability of a particular link between objects is typically extremely low. Approaches to link prediction have been proposed based on a number of measures for analyzing the proximity of nodes in a network. Probabilistic models have been proposed as well. For large data sets, it may be more effective to model links at a higher level.

7. **Closed versus open world assumption.** Most traditional approaches assume that we know all the potential entities in the domain. This "closed world" assumption is unrealistic in real-world applications. Work in this area includes the introduction of a language for specifying probability distributions over relational structures that involve a varying set of objects.

8. **Community mining from multirelational networks.** Typical work on social network analysis includes the discovery of groups of objects that share similar properties. This is known as *community mining*. Web page linkage is an example, where a discovered community may be a set of Web pages on a particular topic. Most algorithms for community mining assume that there is only one social network, representing a relatively homogenous relationship. In reality, there exist multiple, heterogeneous social networks, representing various relationships. A new challenge is the mining of hidden communities on such heterogeneous social networks, which is also known as *community mining on multirelational social networks.*

These challenges will continue to stimulate much research in link mining.

9.2.4 Mining on Social Networks

In this section, we explore exemplar areas of mining on social networks, namely, link prediction, mining customer networks for viral marketing, mining newsgroups using networks, and community mining from multirelational networks. Other exemplars include characteristic subgraph detection (discussed in Section 9.1) and mining link structures on the Web (addressed in Chapter 10 on text and Web mining). Pointers to research on link-based classification and clustering are given in the bibliographic notes and exercises.

Link Prediction: What Edges Will Be Added to the Network?

Social networks are dynamic. New links appear, indicating new interactions between objects. In the **link prediction problem**, we are given a snapshot of a social network at time t and wish to *predict the edges that will be added to the network during the interval from time t to a given future time, t′*. In essence, we seek to uncover the extent to which the evolution of a social network can be modeled using features intrinsic to the model itself. As an example, consider a social network of coauthorship among scientists. Intuitively, we may predict that two scientists who are "close" in the network may be likely to collaborate in the future. Hence, link prediction can be thought of as a contribution to the study of social network evolution models.

Approaches to link prediction have been proposed based on several measures for analyzing the "proximity" of nodes in a network. Many measures originate from techniques in graph theory and social network analysis. The general methodology is as follows: All methods assign a connection weight, $score(X, Y)$, to pairs of nodes, X and Y, based on the given proximity measure and input graph, G. A ranked list in decreasing order of $score(X, Y)$ is produced. This gives the predicted new links in decreasing order of confidence. The predictions can be evaluated based on real observations on experimental data sets.

The simplest approach ranks pairs, $\langle X, Y\rangle$, by the length of their *shortest path* in G. This embodies the small world notion that all individuals are linked through short chains. (Since the convention is to rank all pairs in order of *decreasing* score, here, $score(X, Y)$ is defined as the negative of the shortest path length.) Several measures use neighborhood information. The simplest such measure is *common neighbors*—the greater the number of neighbors that X and Y have in common, the more likely X and Y are to form a link in the future. Intuitively, if authors X and Y have never written a paper together but have many colleagues in common, the more likely they are to collaborate in the future. Other measures are based on the *ensemble of all paths* between two nodes. The *Katz* measure, for example, computes a weighted sum over all paths between X and Y, where shorter paths are assigned heavier weights. All of the measures can be used in conjunction with higher-level approaches, such as *clustering*. For instance, the link prediction method can be applied to a cleaned-up version of the graph, in which spurious edges have been removed.

In experiments conducted on bibliographic citation data sets, no one method is superior to all others. Several methods significantly outperform a random predictor, which suggests that network topology can provide useful information for link prediction. The Katz measure, and variations of it based on clustering, performed consistently well, although the accuracy of prediction is still very low. Future work on link prediction may focus on finding better ways to use network topology information, as well as to improve the efficiency of node distance calculations such as by approximation.

Mining Customer Networks for Viral Marketing

Viral marketing is an application of social network mining that explores how individuals can influence the buying behavior of others. Traditionally, companies have employed **direct marketing** (where the decision to market to a particular individual is based solely on her characteristics) or **mass marketing** (where individuals are targeted based on the population segment to which they belong). These approaches, however, neglect the influence that customers can have on the purchasing decisions of others. For example, consider a person who decides to see a particular movie and persuades a group of friends to see the same film. **Viral marketing** aims to optimize the positive word-of-mouth effect among customers. It can choose to spend more money marketing to an individual if that person has many social connections. Thus, by considering the interactions between customers, viral marketing may obtain higher profits than traditional marketing, which ignores such interactions.

The growth of the Internet over the past two decades has led to the availability of many social networks that can be mined for the purposes of viral marketing. Examples include e-mail mailing lists, UseNet groups, on-line forums, instant relay chat (IRC), instant messaging, collaborative filtering systems, and knowledge-sharing sites. **Knowledge-sharing sites** (such as Epinions at *www.epinions.com*) allow users to offer advice or rate products to help others, typically for free. Users can rate the usefulness or "trustworthiness" of a review, and may possibly rate other reviewers as well. In this way, a network of trust relationships between users (known as a "web of trust") evolves, representing a social network for mining.

The **network value** of a customer is the expected increase in sales to *others* that results from marketing to that customer. In the example given, if our customer convinces others to see a certain movie, then the movie studio is justified in spending more money on promoting the film to her. If, instead, our customer typically listens to others when deciding what movie to see, then marketing spent on her may be a waste of resources. Viral marketing considers a customer's network value. Ideally, we would like to mine a customer's network (e.g., of friends and relatives) to predict how probable she is to buy a certain product based not only on the characteristics of the customer, but also on the influence of the customer's neighbors in the network. If we market to a particular set of customers then, through viral marketing, we may query the *expected profit from the entire network*, after the influence of those customers has propagated throughout. This would allow us to search for the optimal set of customers to which to market. Considering the network value of customers (which is overlooked by traditional direct marketing), this may result in an improved marketing plan.

Given a set of n potential customers, let X_i be a Boolean variable that is set to 1 if customer i purchases the product being marketed, and 0 otherwise. The neighbors of X_i are the customers who directly influence X_i. M_i is defined as the *marketing action* that is taken for customer i. M_i could be Boolean (such as, set to 1 if the customer is sent a coupon, and 0 otherwise) or categoric (indicating which of several possible actions is taken). Alternatively, M_i may be continuous-valued (indicating the size of the discount offered, for example). We would like to find the marketing plan that maximizes profit.

A probabilistic model was proposed that optimizes M_i as a continuous value. That is, it optimizes the amount of marketing money spent on each customer, rather than just making a binary decision on whether to target the customer.

The model considers the following factors that influence a customer's network value. First, the customer should have high connectivity in the network and also give the product a good rating. If a highly-connected customer gives a negative review, her network value can be negative, in which case, marketing to her is not recommended. Second, the customer should have more influence on others (preferably, much more) than they have on her. Third, the *recursive* nature of this word-of-mouth type of influence should be considered. A customer may influence acquaintances, who in turn, may like the product and influence other people, and so on, until the whole network is reached. The model also incorporates another important consideration: it may pay to lose money on some customers if they are influential enough in a positive way. For example, giving a product for free to a well-selected customer may pay off many times in sales to other customers. This is a big twist from traditional direct marketing, which will only offer a customer a discount if the expected profits from the customer alone exceed the cost of the offer. The model takes into consideration the fact that we have only partial knowledge of the network and that gathering such knowledge can have an associated cost.

The task of finding the optimal set of customers is formalized as a well-defined optimization problem: *find the set of customers that maximizes the net profits*. This problem is known to be NP-hard (intractable); however, it can be approximated within 63% of the optimal using a simple hill-climbing search procedure. Customers are added to the set as long as this improves overall profit. The method was found to be robust in the presence of incomplete knowledge of the network.

Viral marketing techniques may be applied to other areas that require a large social outcome with only limited resources. Reducing the spread of HIV, combatting teenage smoking, and grass-roots political initiative are some examples. The application of viral marketing techniques to the Web domain, and vice versa, is an area of further research.

Mining Newsgroups Using Networks

Web-based social network analysis is closely related to Web mining, a topic to be studied in the next chapter. There we will introduce two popular Web page ranking algorithms, PageRank and HITS, which are proposed based on the fact that a link of Web page *A* to *B* usually indicates the endorsement of *B* by *A*.

The situation is rather different in newsgroups on topic discussions. A typical newsgroup posting consists of one or more quoted lines from another posting followed by the opinion of the author. Such quoted responses form "quotation links" and create a network in which the vertices represent individuals and the links "responded-to" relationships. An interesting phenomenon is that people more frequently respond to a message when they *disagree* than when they *agree*. This behavior exists in many newsgroups and is in sharp contrast to the Web page link graph, where linkage is an indicator of agreement or common interest. Based on this behavior, one can effectively classify and partition authors in the newsgroup into *opposite camps* by analyzing the graph structure of the responses.

This newsgroup classification process can be performed using a graph-theoretic approach. The *quotation network* (or *graph)* can be constructed by building a quotation link between person i and person j if i has quoted from an earlier posting written by j. We can consider any bipartition of the vertices into two sets: F represents those *for* an issue and A represents those *against* it. If most edges in a newsgroup graph represent disagreements, then the optimum choice is to maximize the number of edges across these two sets. Because it is known that theoretically the *max-cut problem* (i.e., maximizing the number of edges to cut so that a graph is partitioned into two disconnected subgraphs) is an NP-hard problem, we need to explore some alternative, practical solutions. In particular, we can exploit two additional facts that hold in our situation: (1) rather than being a general graph, our instance is largely a bipartite graph with some noise edges added, and (2) neither side of the bipartite graph is much smaller than the other. In such situations, we can transform the problem into a minimum-weight, approximately balanced cut problem, which in turn can be well approximated by computationally simple spectral methods. Moreover, to further enhance the classification accuracy, we can first manually categorize a small number of prolific posters and tag the corresponding vertices in the graph. This information can then be used to bootstrap a better overall partitioning by enforcing the constraint that those classified on one side by human effort should remain on that side during the algorithmic partitioning of the graph.

Based on these ideas, an efficient algorithm was proposed. Experiments with some newsgroup data sets on several highly debatable social topics, such as abortion, gun control, and immigration, demonstrate that links carry less noisy information than text. Methods based on linguistic and statistical analysis of text yield lower accuracy on such newsgroup data sets than that based on the link analysis shown earlier because the vocabulary used by the opponent sides tends to be largely identical, and many newsgroup postings consist of too-brief text to facilitate reliable linguistic analysis.

Community Mining from Multirelational Networks

With the growth of the Web, *community mining* has attracted increasing attention. A great deal of such work has focused on mining implicit communities of Web pages, of scientific literature from the Web, and of document citations. In principle, a community can be defined as a group of objects sharing some common properties. Community mining can be thought of as subgraph identification. For example, in Web page linkage, two Web pages (objects) are related if there is a hyperlink between them. A graph of Web page linkages can be mined to identify a community or set of Web pages on a particular topic.

Most techniques for graph mining and community mining are based on a homogenous graph, that is, they assume only one kind of relationship exists between the objects. However, in real social networks, there are always various kinds of relationships between the objects. Each relation can be viewed as a **relation network.** In this sense, the multiple relations form a **multirelational social network** (also referred to as a **heterogeneous social network**). Each kind of relation may play a distinct role in a particular task. Here, the different relation graphs can provide us with different communities.

To find a community with certain properties, we first need to identify which relation plays an important role in such a community. Such a relation might not exist explicitly, that is, we may need to first discover such a *hidden relation* before finding the community on such a relation network. Different users may be interested in different relations within a network. Thus, if we mine networks by assuming only one kind of relation, we may end up missing out on a lot of valuable hidden community information, and such mining may not be adaptable to the diverse information needs of various users. This brings us to the problem of *multirelational community mining*, which involves the mining of hidden communities on heterogeneous social networks.

Let us consider a simple example. In a typical human community, there may exist many relations: some people work at the same place; some share the same interests; some go to the same hospital, and so on. Mathematically, this community can be characterized by a large graph in which the nodes represent people and the edges evaluate their relation strength. Because there are different kinds of relations, the edges of this graph should be heterogeneous. For some tasks, we can also model this community using several homogeneous graphs. Each graph reflects one kind of relation. Suppose an infectious disease breaks out, and the government tries to find those most likely to be infected. Obviously, the existing relationships among people cannot play an equivalent role. It seems reasonable to assume that under such a situation the relation "*works at the same place*" or "*lives together*" should play a critical role. The question becomes: "*How can we select the relation that is most relevant to the disease spreading? Is there a hidden relation (based on the explicit relations) that best reveals the spread path of the disease?*"

These questions can be modeled mathematically as **relation selection and extraction** in *multirelational social network analysis*. The problem of relation extraction can be simply stated as follows: In a heterogeneous social network, based on some labeled examples (e.g., provided by a user as queries), how can we evaluate the importance of different relations? In addition, how can we obtain a combination of the existing relations, which best matches the relation of labeled examples?

As an example, consider the network in Figure 9.18, which has three different relations, shown as (a), (b), and (c), respectively. Suppose a user requires that the four colored objects belong to the same community and specifies this with a query. Clearly, the relative importance of each of the three relations differs with respect to the user's information need. Of the three relations, we see that (a) is the most relevant to the user's need and is thus the most important, while (b) comes in second. Relation (c) can be seen as noise in regards to the user's information need. Traditional social network analysis does not distinguish these relations. The different relations are treated equally. They are simply combined together for describing the structure between objects. Unfortunately, in this example, relation (c) has a negative effect for this purpose. However, if we combine these relations according to their importance, relation (c) can be easily excluded,

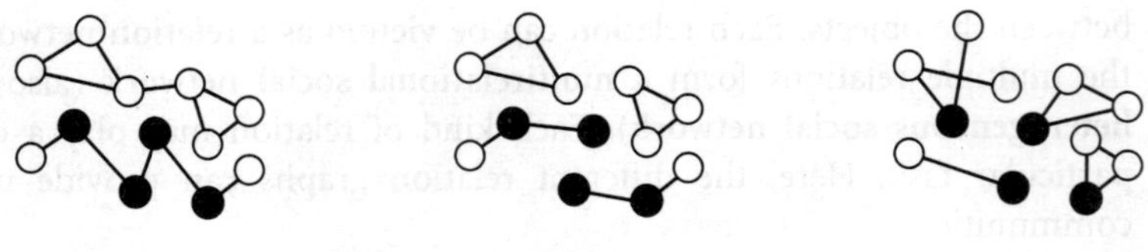

Figure 9.18 There are three relations in the network. The four colored objects are required to belong to the same community, according to a user query.

leaving relations (a) and (b) to be used to discover the community structure, which is consistent with the user's requirement.

A user might submit a more complex query in some situations. For example, a user may specify that, say, the two upper colored objects and the two lower colored objects should belong to different communities. In this situation, the importance of the three relations of Figure 9.18 changes. Relation (b) becomes the most important, while relation (a) becomes useless (and even has a negative effect with regards to the query). Thus, in a multirelational social network, community mining should be dependent on the user's query (or information need). A user's query can be very flexible. Earlier techniques focus on only a *single* relational network and are independent of the user's query and thus cannot cope with such a complex situation.

An algorithm for relation extraction and selection was proposed, which models the task as an optimization problem. The problem can be mathematically defined as follows. Given are a set of objects and a set of relations, which can be represented by a set of graphs $G_i(V,E_i)$, $i = 1,\ldots,n$, where n is the number of relations, V is the set of nodes (objects), and E_i is the set of edges with respect to the i-th relation. The weights on the edges can be naturally defined according to the relation strength of two objects. The algorithm characterizes each relation by a graph with a weight matrix. Let M_i denote the **weight matrix** associated with G_i, $i = 1,\ldots,n$. Each element in the matrix reflects the relation strength between a pair of objects in the relation. Suppose a *hidden relation* is represented by a graph $\widehat{G}(V,\widehat{E})$, and $\widehat{M}$ denotes the weight matrix associated with $\widehat{G}$. A user specifies her information need as a query in the form of a set of labeled objects $\mathbf{X} = [\mathbf{x}_1,\cdots,\mathbf{x}_m]$ and $\mathbf{y} = [y_1,\cdots,y_m]$, where y_j is the label of $\mathbf{x}_j$ (such labeled objects indicate partial information of the hidden relation $\widehat{G}$). The algorithm aims at finding a linear combination of these weight matrices that can best approximate $\widehat{G}$ (the weight matrix associated with the labeled examples.) The obtained combination is more likely to meet the user's information need, so it leads to better performance in community mining.

The algorithm was tested on bibliographic data. Naturally, multiple relations exist between authors. Authors can publish papers in thousands of different conferences, and each conference can be considered as a relation, resulting in a multirelational social network. Given some user-provided examples (like a group of authors), the algorithm can extract a new relation using the examples and find all other groups in that relation. The extracted relation can be interpreted as the groups of authors that share certain kinds of similar interests.

9.3 Multirelational Data Mining

Relational databases are the most popular repository for *structured* data. In a relational database, multiple relations are linked together via entity-relationship links (Chapter 1). Many classification approaches (such as neural networks and support vector machines) can only be applied to data represented in single, "flat" relational form—that is, they expect data in a single table. However, many real-world applications, such as credit card fraud detection, loan applications, and biological data analysis, involve decision-making processes based on information stored in multiple relations in a relational database. Thus, multirelational data mining has become a field of strategic importance.

9.3.1 What Is Multirelational Data Mining?

Multirelational data mining (MRDM) methods search for patterns that involve multiple tables (relations) from a relational database. Consider the multirelational schema of Figure 9.19, which defines a financial database. Each table or relation represents an entity or a relationship, described by a set of attributes. Links between relations show the relationship between them. One method to apply traditional data mining methods (which assume that the data reside in a single table) is propositionalization, which converts multiple relational data into a single flat data relation, using joins and aggregations. This, however, could lead to the generation of a huge, undesirable "universal relation" (involving all of the attributes). Furthermore, it can result in the loss of information, including essential semantic information represented by the links in the database design.

Multirelational data mining aims to discover knowledge directly from relational data. There are different multirelational data mining tasks, including multirelational classification, clustering, and frequent pattern mining. Multirelational classification aims to build a classification model that utilizes information in different relations. Multirelational clustering aims to group tuples into clusters using their own attributes as well as tuples related to them in different relations. Multirelational frequent pattern mining aims at finding patterns involving interconnected items in different relations. We first use multirelational classification as an example to illustrate the purpose and procedure of multirelational data mining. We then introduce multirelational classification and multirelational clustering in detail in the following sections.

In a database for multirelational classification, there is one **target relation,** R_t, whose tuples are called **target tuples** and are associated with class labels. The other relations are *nontarget relations.* Each relation may have one *primary key* (which uniquely identifies tuples in the relation) and several *foreign keys* (where a primary key in one relation can

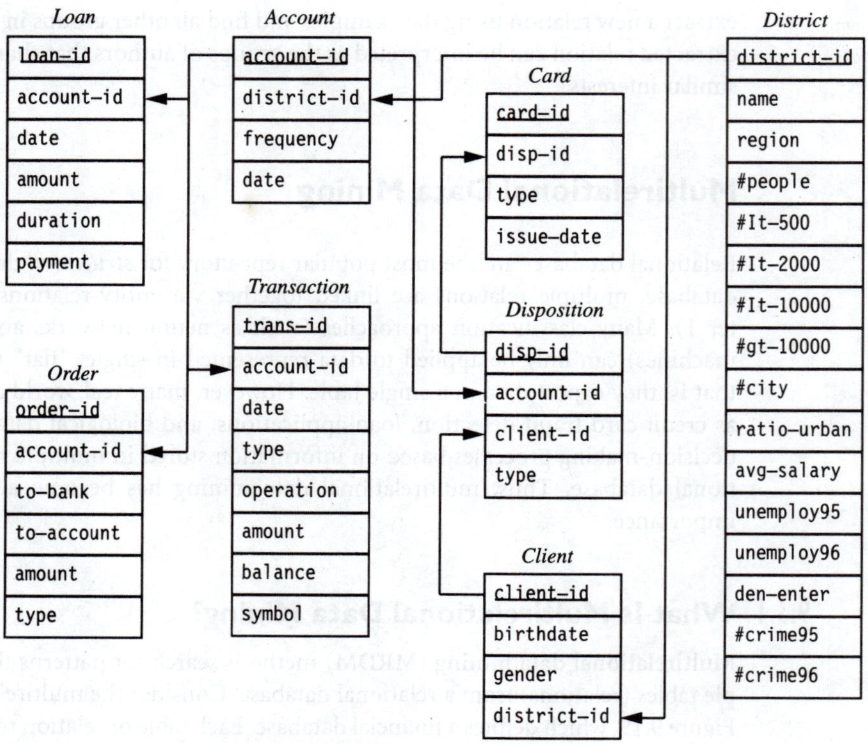

Figure 9.19 A financial database (from [PKDD CUP 99]).

be linked to the foreign key in another). If we assume a two-class problem, then we pick one class as the **positive** class and the other as the **negative** class. The most important task for building an accurate multirelational classifier is to find relevant features in different relations that help distinguish *positive* and *negative* target tuples.

Example 9.7 **A database for multirelational classification.** Consider the relational database of Figure 9.19. Arrows go from primary keys to corresponding foreign keys. Suppose the target relation is *Loan*. Each target tuple is either positive or negative, indicating whether the loan is paid on time. The task of multirelational classification is to build a hypothesis to distinguish positive and negative target tuples, using information in different relations. ■

For classification, in general, we search for hypotheses that help distinguish positive and negative target tuples. The most popular form of hypotheses for multirelational classification is sets of rules. Each rule is a list (*logical* conjunct) of *predicates*, associated with

Loan					
loan_ID	*account_ID*	*amount*	*duration*	*payment*	*class*
1	124	1000	12	120	+
2	124	4000	12	350	+
3	108	10000	24	500	−
4	45	12000	36	400	−
5	45	2000	24	90	+

Account		
account_ID	*frequency*	*date*
124	monthly	960227
108	weekly	950923
45	monthly	941209
67	weekly	950101

Figure 9.20 An example database (the last column of the *Loan* relation contains the class labels.)

a class label. A **predicate** is a constraint on an attribute in a relation. A predicate is often defined based on a certain join path, as illustrated in Example 9.8. A target tuple **satisfies** a rule if and only if it satisfies every predicate of the rule.

Example 9.8 Predicates and rules. *Predicate* "$p_1 = Loan(L, \_, \_, \_, payment >= 12, \_)$" means that the *duration* of loan *L* is no less than 12 months. It is an example of a **numerical predicate**. Predicate "$p_2 = Loan(L, A, \_, \_, \_, \_), Account(A, \_, frequency = monthly, \_)$" is defined on the *join path*, *Loan* ⋈ *Account*, which means that the associated account of a loan has *frequency* "*monthly.*" It is a **categorical predicate**. Suppose that a rule for positive (+) target tuples is "$r = Loan(L, +) : - Loan(L, A, \_, \_, \_, \_), Account(A, \_, frequency = monthly, \_)$." We say a tuple, *t*, in *Loan* satisfies *r* if and only if **any** tuple in *Account* that is joinable with *t* has the value "monthly" in the *frequency* attribute of *Account*. Consider the example database of Figure 9.20. Two such tuples (namely, with *account_IDs* of 124 and 45) in *Account* satisfy the predicate $Account(A, \_, frequency = monthly, \_)$. Therefore, four tuples (with *loan_IDs* of 1, 2, 4, and 5) in *Loan* satisfy the rule. ■

Given the training data that contain a target relation and a set of nontarget relations, a rule-based multirelational classification approach will build a model consisting of a set of rules. When predicting the class label of a target tuple *t*, it will make the prediction based on all rules satisfied by *t*. For example, it may predict *t*'s class label based on the rule with highest accuracy on the training set.

9.3.2 ILP Approach to Multirelational Classification

Inductive Logic Programming (ILP) is the most widely used category of approaches to multirelational classification. There are many ILP approaches. In general, they aim to find hypotheses of a certain format that can predict the class labels of target tuples, based on background knowledge (i.e., the information stored in all relations). The ILP problem is defined as follows: *Given background knowledge B, a set of positive examples P, and a set of negative examples N, find a hypothesis H such that: (1)* $\forall t \in P : H \cup B \models t$ *(completeness), and (2)* $\forall t \in N : H \cup B \not\models t$ *(consistency), where* $\models$ *stands for logical implication.*

Well-known ILP systems include FOIL, Golem, and Progol. FOIL is a top-down learner, which builds rules that cover many positive examples and few negative ones. Golem is a bottom-up learner, which performs generalizations from the most specific rules. Progol uses a combined search strategy. Recent approaches, like TILDE, Mr-SMOTI, and RPTs, use the idea of C4.5 and inductively construct decision trees from relational data.

Although many ILP approaches achieve good classification accuracy, most of them are not highly scalable with respect to the number of relations in the database. The target relation can usually join with each nontarget relation via multiple join paths. Thus, in a database with reasonably complex schema, a large number of join paths will need to be explored. In order to identify good features, many ILP approaches repeatedly join the relations along different join paths and evaluate features based on the joined relation. This is time consuming, especially when the joined relation contains many more tuples than the target relation.

We look at FOIL as a typical example of ILP approaches. FOIL is a sequential *covering algorithm* that builds rules one at a time. After building a rule, all positive target tuples satisfying that rule are removed, and FOIL will focus on tuples that have not been covered by any rule. When building each rule, predicates are added one by one. At each step, every possible predicate is evaluated, and the best one is appended to the current rule.

To evaluate a predicate p, FOIL temporarily appends it to the current rule. This forms the rule $r+p$. FOIL constructs a new data set, which contains all target tuples satisfying $r+p$, together with the relevant nontarget tuples on the join path specified by $r+p$. Predicate p is evaluated based on the number of positive and negative target tuples satisfying $r+p$, using the *foil gain* measure, which is defined as follows: Let $P(r)$ and $N(r)$ denote the number of positive and negative tuples satisfying a rule r, respectively. Suppose the current rule is r. The *foil gain* of p is computed as follows:

$$I(r) = -\log \frac{P(r)}{P(r)+N(r)} \tag{9.2}$$

$$foil\_gain(p) = P(r+p) \cdot [I(r) - I(r+p)] \tag{9.3}$$

Intuitively, *foil_gain*(p) represents the total number of bits saved in representing positive tuples by appending p to the current rule. It indicates how much the predictive power of the rule can be increased by appending p to it. The best predicate found is the one with the highest foil gain.

Example 9.9 **Search for predicates by joins.** Consider the example database of Figure 9.20. Our task is to learn rules to distinguish positive (+) and negative (−) target tuples. In order to compute the foil gain of predicates in a nontarget relation like *Account*, FOIL needs to first create a joined relation of *Loan* and *Account*, as in Figure 9.21. For each predicate p in *Account*, FOIL needs to find all positive and negative tuples satisfying $r+p$, where r is the current rule.

Loan ⋈ Account							
loan_ID	*account_ID*	*amount*	*duration*	*payment*	*frequency*	*date*	*class*
1	124	1000	12	120	monthly	960227	+
2	124	4000	12	350	monthly	960227	+
3	108	10000	24	500	weekly	950923	−
4	45	12000	36	400	monthly	941209	−
5	45	2000	24	90	monthly	941209	+

Figure 9.21 The joined relation of *Loan* and *Account*.

The foil gain of all predicates on a certain attribute can be computed by scanning the corresponding column in the joined relation once. It can also find the best predicate in a continuous attribute, by first sorting that column and then iterating from the smallest value to the largest one to compute the foil gain, using each value as the splitting point. ■

Many ILP approaches for multirelational classification use similar methods to evaluate predicates. For databases with complex schema, the search space is huge, and there are many possible predicates at each step. For example, in the database in Figure 9.19, *Loan* can join with *Account*, *Order*, *Transaction*, and *Disposition*, each of which can join with several other relations. To build rules, FOIL needs to repeatedly construct many joined relations by physical joins to find good predicates. This procedure becomes very time consuming for databases with reasonably complex schemas.

9.3.3 Tuple ID Propagation

Tuple ID propagation is a technique for performing virtual join, which greatly improves efficiency of multirelational classification. Instead of physically joining relations, they are virtually joined by attaching the IDs of target tuples to tuples in nontarget relations. In this way the predicates can be evaluated as if a physical join were performed. Tuple ID propagation is flexible and efficient, because IDs can easily be propagated between any two relations, requiring only small amounts of data transfer and extra storage space. By doing so, predicates in different relations can be evaluated with little redundant computation.

Suppose that the primary key of the target relation is an attribute of integers, which represents the ID of each target tuple (we can create such a primary key if there isn't one). Suppose two relations, R_1 and R_2, can be joined by attributes $R_1.A$ and $R_2.A$. In tuple ID propagation, each tuple t in R_1 is associated with a set of IDs in the target relation, represented by ***IDset***(t). For each tuple u in R_2, we set $IDset(u) = \bigcup_{t \in R_1, t.A = u.A} IDset(t)$. That is, the tuple IDs in the *IDset* for tuple t of R_1 are propagated to each tuple, u, in R_2 that is joinable with t on attribute A.

Loan			
loan_ID	*account_ID*	···	*class*
1	124		+
2	124		+
3	108		−
4	45		+
5	45		+

Account				
account_ID	*frequency*	*date*	*ID set*	*class labels*
124	monthly	960227	1, 2	2+, 0−
108	weekly	950923	3	0+, 1−
45	monthly	941209	4, 5	1+, 1−
67	weekly	950101	–	0+, 0−

Figure 9.22 Example of tuple ID propagation (some attributes in *Loan* are not shown).

Example 9.10 **Tuple ID propagation.** Consider the example database shown in Figure 9.22, which has the same schema as in Figure 9.20. The relations are joinable on the attribute *account_ID*. Instead of performing a physical join, the IDs and class labels of target (*Loan*) tuples can be propagated to the *Account* relation. For example, the first two tuples in *Loan* are joinable with the first tuple in *Account*, thus their tuple IDs ({1,2}) are propagated to the first tuple in *Account*. The other tuple IDs are propagated in the same way. ■

To further illustrate tuple ID propagation, let's see how it can be used to compute the foil gain of predicates without having to perform physical joins. Given relations R_1 and R_2 as above, suppose that R_1 is the target relation, and all tuples in R_1 satisfy the current rule (others have been eliminated). For convenience, let the current rule contain a predicate on $R_1.A$, which enables the join of R_1 with R_2. For each tuple u of R_2, $IDset(u)$ represents all target tuples joinable with u, using the join path specified in the current rule. If tuple IDs are propagated from R_1 to R_2, then the foil gain of every predicate in R_2 can be computed using the propagated IDs on R_2.

Example 9.11 **Computing foil gain using tuple ID propagation (IDsets).** Suppose the current rule, r, is "$Loan(L,+) :- Loan(L, A, \_, \_, \_, \_)$." From Figure 9.22, we note that three positive and two negative target tuples satisfy r. Therefore, $P(r) = 3$ and $N(r) = 2$. (This would have been determined during the process of building the current rule.) To evaluate predicate p = "$Account(A, \_, frequency = monthly, \_)$," we need to find the tuples in the *Account* relation that satisfy p. There are two such tuples, namely, {124, 45}. We find the IDs of target tuples that can be joined with these two tuples by taking the union of their corresponding *IDsets*. This results in $\{1, 2, 4, 5\}$. Among these, there are three positive and one negative target tuples. Thus, $P(r+p) = 3$ and $N(r+p) = 1$. The foil gain of predicate p can easily be computed from Equations 9.2 and 9.3. That is, $foil\_gain(p) = 3 \cdot [-\log_2(3/5) + \log_2(3/4)] = 0.966$. Thus, with tuple propagation, we are able to compute the foil gain without having to perform any physical joins. ■

Besides propagating IDs from the target relation to relations directly joinable with it, we can also propagate IDs transitively from one nontarget relation to another. Suppose two nontarget relations, R_2 and R_3, can be joined by attributes $R_2.A$ and $R_3.A$. For each tuple v in R_2, $IDset(v)$ represents the target tuples joinable with v (using the join path specified by the current rule). By propagating IDs from R_2 to R_3 through the join $R_2.A = R_3.A$, for each tuple u in R_3, $IDset(u)$ represents target tuples that can be joined with u (using the join path in the current rule, plus the join $R_2.A = R_3.A$). Thus, by tuple ID propagation between nontarget relations, we can also compute the foil gain based on the propagated IDs.

Tuple ID propagation, although valuable, should be enforced with certain constraints. There are two cases where such propagation could be counterproductive: (1) propagation via large fan-outs, and (2) propagation via long, weak links. The first case occurs when, after propagating the IDs to a relation R, it is found that every tuple in R is joined with many target tuples and every target tuple is joined with many tuples in R. The semantic link between R and the target relation is then typically very weak because the link is unselective. For example, propagation among people via birth-country links may not be productive. The second case occurs when the propagation goes through long links (e.g., linking a student with his car dealer's pet may not be productive, either). From the sake of efficiency and accuracy, propagation via such links is discouraged.

9.3.4 Multirelational Classification Using Tuple ID Propagation

In this section we introduce **CrossMine**, an approach that uses tuple ID propagation for multirelational classification. To better integrate the information of ID propagation, CrossMine uses *complex predicates* as elements of rules. A complex predicate, p, contains two parts:

1. *prop-path*: This indicates how to propagate IDs. For example, the path "*Loan.account_ID* → *Account.account_ID*" indicates propagating IDs from *Loan* to *Account* using *account_ID*. If no ID propagation is involved, *prop-path* is empty.
2. *constraint*: This is a predicate indicating the constraint on the relation to which the IDs are propagated. It can be either categorical or numerical.

A complex predicate is usually equivalent to two conventional predicates. For example, the rule "$Loan(L,+) :- Loan(L, A, \_, \_, \_, \_), Account(A, \_, frequent = monthly, \_)$" can be represented by "$Loan(+) : -[Loan.account\_ID \rightarrow Account.account\_ID, Account.frequency = monthly]$."

CrossMine builds a classifier containing a set of rules, each containing a list of complex predicates and a class label. The algorithm of CrossMine is shown in Figure 9.23. CrossMine is also a sequential covering algorithm like FOIL. It builds rules one at a time. After a rule r is built, all positive target tuples satisfying r are removed from the data

Algorithm: CrossMine. Rule-based classification across multiple relations.

Input:

- D, a relational database;
- R_t a target relation.

Output:

- A set of rules for predicting class labels of target tuples.

Method:

```
rule set R ← ∅;
while (true)
    rule r ← empty-rule;
    set R_t to active;
    repeat
        Complex predicate p ← the predicate with highest foil gain;
        if foil_gain(p) < MIN_FOIL_GAIN then
            break;
        else
            r ← r + p; // append predicate, increasing rule length by 1
            remove all target tuples not satisfying r;
            update IDs on every active relation;
            if p.constraint is on an inactive relation then
                set that relation active;
        endif
    until (r.length = MAX_RULE_LENGTH)
    if r = empty-rule then break;
    R ← R ∪ {r};
    remove all positive target tuples satisfying r;
    set all relations inactive;
endwhile
return R;
```

Figure 9.23 Algorithm CrossMine.

set. To build a rule, CrossMine repeatedly searches for the best complex predicate and appends it to the current rule, until the stop criterion is met. A relation is active if it appears in the current rule. Before searching for the next best predicate, each active relation is required to have the *IDset* of propagated IDs for each of its tuples. When searching for a predicate, CrossMine evaluates all of the possible predicates on any active relation or any relation that is joinable with an active relation. When there are more than two classes of target tuples, CrossMine builds a set of rules for each class.

"How does CrossMine find the best predicate to append to the current rule?" At each step, CrossMine uses tuple ID propagation to search for the best predicate in all of the active relations, or relations that are joinable with any active relation. In our example, at first only the *Loan* relation is active. If the first best predicate is found in, say, the *Account* relation, *Account* becomes active as well. CrossMine tries to propagate the tuple IDs from *Loan* or *Account* to other relations to find the next best predicate. In this way, the search range is gradually expanded along promising directions reflecting strong semantic links between entities. This avoids aimless search in the huge hypothesis space.

Suppose that CrossMine is searching for the best predicate on a categorical attribute, A_c, in a relation, R. CrossMine evaluates all possible predicates and selects the best one. For each value a_i of A_c, a predicate $p_i = [R.A_c = a_i]$ is built. CrossMine scans the values of each tuple on A_c to find the numbers of positive and negative target tuples satisfying each predicate, p_i. The foil gain of each p_i can then be computed to find the best predicate. For numerical predicates, it uses the method described in Section 9.3.2.

The above algorithm may fail to find good predicates in databases containing relations that are only used to join with other relations. For example, in the database of Figure 9.24, there is no useful attribute in the *Has_Loan* relation. Therefore, the rules built will not involve any predicates on the *Client* and *District* relations. CrossMine adopts a *look-one-ahead* method to solve this problem. After IDs have been propagated to a relation $\bar{R}$ (such as *Has_Loan*), if $\bar{R}$ contains a foreign key referencing the primary key of a relation $\bar{R}'$ (such as *client_ID* of *Client*), then IDs are propagated from $\bar{R}$ to $\bar{R}'$, and used

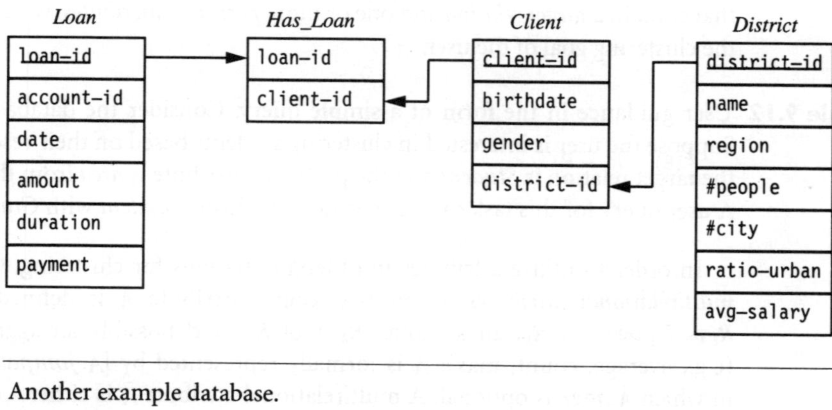

Figure 9.24 Another example database.

to search for good predicates in R'. By this method, in the example of Figure 9.24, we can find rules like "*Loan*(+) : −[*Loan.loan_ID* → *Has_Loan.loan_ID*, *Has_Loan.client_ID* → *Client.client_ID*, *Client.birthdate* < 01/01/60]."

After generating a classifier, CrossMine needs to predict the class labels of unlabeled target tuples. Suppose there is a rule, $r = R_t(+) : -p_1, p_2, \ldots, p_k$, where each p_i is a complex predicate. CrossMine propagates the IDs of target tuples along the *prop-path* of each predicate, and prunes all IDs of target tuples not satisfying the constraint of p_i. In this way it can easily find all target tuples satisfying each rule. For each target tuple t, the most accurate rule that is satisfied by t is used to predict the class label of t.

"How does CrossMine fare in terms of scalability and accuracy?" Experiments have shown that CrossMine is highly scalable compared with traditional ILP approaches and also achieves high accuracy. These features make it attractive for multirelational classification in real-world databases.

9.3.5 Multirelational Clustering with User Guidance

Multirelational clustering is the process of partitioning data objects into a set of clusters based on their similarity, utilizing information in multiple relations. In this section we will introduce **CrossClus** (Cross-relational Clustering with user guidance), an algorithm for multirelational clustering that explores how to utilize user guidance in clustering and tuple ID propagation to avoid physical joins.

One major challenge in multirelational clustering is that there are too many attributes in different relations, and usually only a small portion of them are relevant to a specific clustering task. Consider the computer science department database of Figure 9.25. In order to cluster students, attributes cover many different aspects of information, such as courses taken by students, publications of students, advisors and research groups of students, and so on. A user is usually interested in clustering students using a certain aspect of information (e.g., clustering students by their research areas). Users often have a good grasp of their application's requirements and data semantics. Therefore, a user's guidance, even in the form of a simple query, can be used to improve the efficiency and quality of high-dimensional multirelational clustering. CrossClus accepts user queries that contain a *target relation* and one or more *pertinent attributes*, which together specify the clustering goal of the user.

Example 9.12 **User guidance in the form of a simple query.** Consider the database of Figure 9.25. Suppose the user is interested in clustering students based on their research areas. Here, the target relation is *Student* and the pertinent attribute is *area* from the *Group* relation. A user query for this task can be specified as "cluster *Student* with *Group.area*." ■

In order to utilize attributes in different relations for clustering, CrossClus defines *multirelational attributes*. A **multirelational attribute** $\tilde{A}$ is defined by a join path $R_t \bowtie R_1 \bowtie \cdots \bowtie R_k$, an attribute $R_k.A$ of R_k, and possibly an aggregation operator (e.g., average, count, max). $\tilde{A}$ is formally represented by $[\tilde{A}.joinpath, \tilde{A}.attr, \tilde{A}.aggr]$, in which $\tilde{A}.aggr$ is optional. A multirelational attribute $\tilde{A}$ is either a *categorical feature*

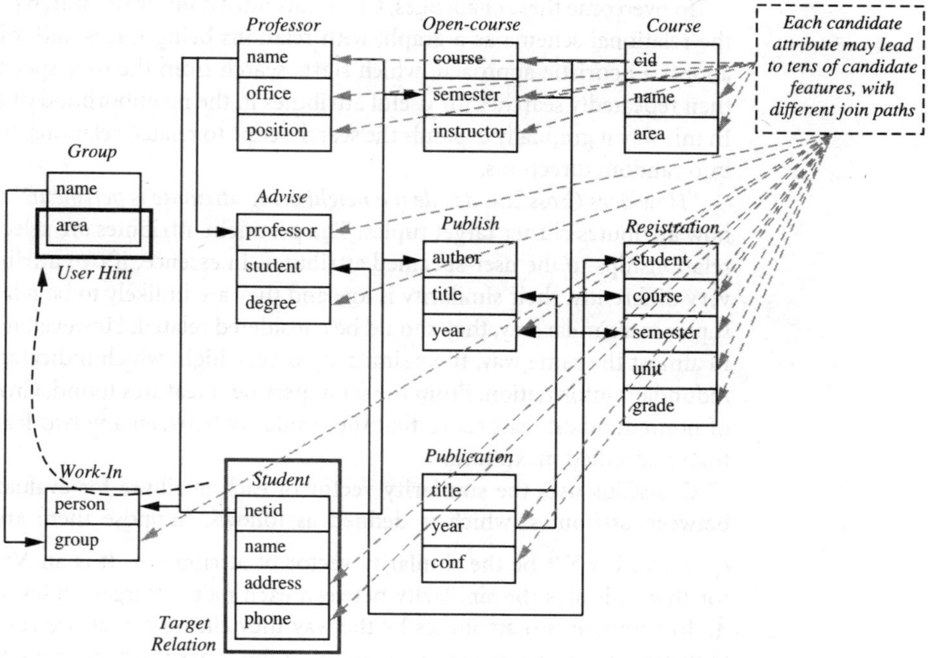

Figure 9.25 Schema of a computer science department database.

or a *numerical one*, depending on whether $R_k.A$ is categorical or numerical. If $\tilde{A}$ is a categorical feature, then for a target tuple t, $t.\tilde{A}$ represents the distribution of values among tuples in R_k that are joinable with t. For example, suppose $\tilde{A} = [\textit{Student} \bowtie \textit{Register} \bowtie \textit{OpenCourse} \bowtie \textit{Course}, \textit{area}]$ (areas of courses taken by each student). If a student t_1 takes four courses in database and four courses in AI, then $t_1.\tilde{A} =$ (database:0.5, AI:0.5). If $\tilde{A}$ is numerical, then it has a certain aggregation operator (average, count, max, ...), and $t.\tilde{A}$ is the aggregated value of tuples in R_k that are joinable with t.

In the multirelational clustering process, CrossClus needs to search pertinent attributes across multiple relations. CrossClus must address two major challenges in the searching process. First, the target relation, R_t, can usually join with each nontarget relation, R, via many different join paths, and each attribute in R can be used as a multirelational attribute. It is impossible to perform any kind of exhaustive search in this huge search space. Second, among the huge number of attributes, some are pertinent to the user query (e.g., a student's advisor is related to her research area), whereas many others are irrelevant (e.g., a student's classmates' personal information). How can we identify pertinent attributes while avoiding aimless search in irrelevant regions in the attribute space?

To overcome these challenges, CrossClus must confine the search process. It considers the relational schema as a graph, with relations being nodes and joins being edges. It adopts a heuristic approach, which starts search from the user-specified attribute, and then repeatedly searches for useful attributes in the neighborhood of existing attributes. In this way it gradually expands the search scope to related relations, but will not go deep into random directions.

"How does CrossClus decide if a neighboring attribute is pertinent?" CrossClus looks at how attributes cluster target tuples. The pertinent attributes are selected based on their relationships to the user-specified attributes. In essence, if two attributes cluster tuples very differently, their similarity is low and they are unlikely to be related. If they cluster tuples in a similar way, they should be considered related. However, if they cluster tuples in almost the same way, their similarity is very high, which indicates that they contain redundant information. From the set of pertinent features found, CrossClus selects a set of nonredundant features so that the similarity between any two features is no greater than a specified maximum.

CrossClus uses the **similarity vector** of each attribute for evaluating the similarity between attributes, which is defined as follows. Suppose there are N target tuples, $t_1, \ldots, t_N$. Let $\mathbf{V}^{\tilde{A}}$ be the similarity vector of attribute $\tilde{A}$. It is an N^2-dimensional vector that indicates the similarity between each pair of target tuples, t_i and t_j, based on $\tilde{A}$. To compare two attributes by the way they cluster tuples, we can look at how alike their similarity vectors are, by computing the inner product of the two similarity vectors. However, this is expensive to compute. Many applications cannot even afford to store N^2-dimensional vectors. Instead, CrossClus converts the hard problem of computing the similarity between similarity vectors to an easier problem of computing *similarities between attribute values*, which can be solved in linear time.

Example 9.13 Multirelational search for pertinent attributes. Let's look at how CrossClus proceeds in answering the query of Example 9.12, where the user has specified her desire to cluster students by their research areas. To create the initial multirelational attribute for this query, CrossClus searches for the shortest join path from the target relation, *Student*, to the relation *Group*, and creates a multirelational attribute $\tilde{A}$ using this path. We simulate the procedure of attribute searching, as shown in Figure 9.26. An initial pertinent multirelational attribute [*Student* $\bowtie$ *WorkIn* $\bowtie$ *Group*, *area*] is created for this query (step 1 in the figure). At first CrossClus considers attributes in the following relations that are joinable with either the target relation or the relation containing the initial pertinent attribute: *Advise*, *Publish*, *Registration*, *WorkIn*, and *Group*. Suppose the best attribute is [*Student* $\bowtie$ *Advise*, *professor*], which corresponds to the student's advisor (step 2). This brings the *Professor* relation into consideration in further search. CrossClus will search for additional pertinent features until most tuples are sufficiently covered. CrossClus uses tuple ID propagation (Section 9.3.3) to virtually join different relations, thereby avoiding expensive physical joins during its search. ■

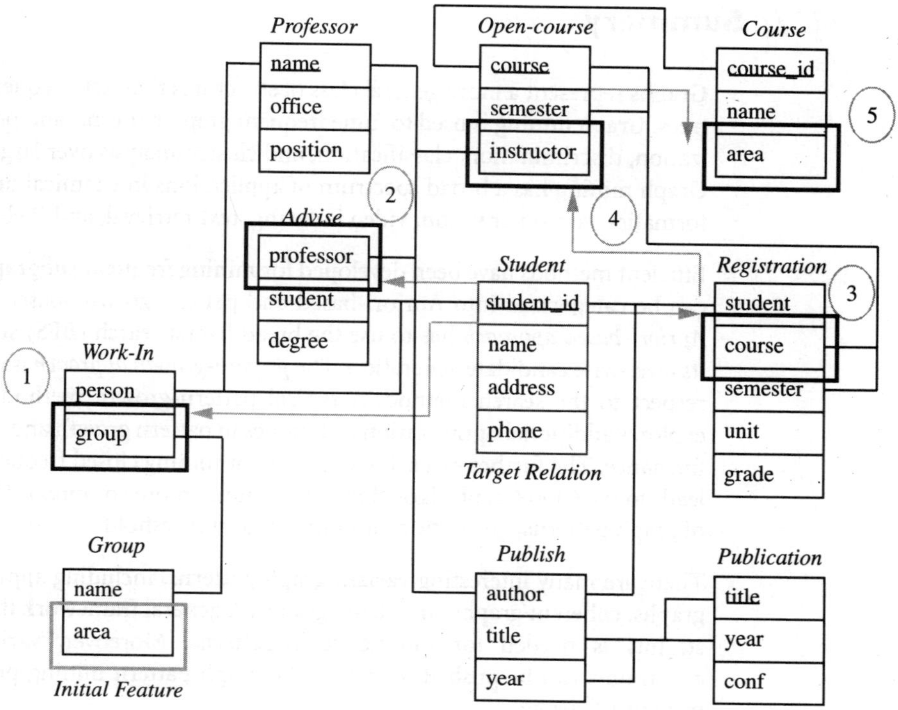

Figure 9.26 Search for pertinent attributes in CrossClus.

Now that we have an intuitive idea of how CrossClus employs user guidance to search for attributes that are highly pertinent to the user's query, the next question is, how does it perform the actual clustering? With the potentially large number of target tuples, an efficient and scalable clustering algorithm is needed. Because the multirelational attributes do not form a Euclidean space, the *k*-medoids method (Section 7.4.1) was chosen, which requires only a distance measure between tuples. In particular, CLARANS (Section 7.4.2), an efficient *k*-medoids algorithm for large databases, was used. The main idea of CLARANS is to consider the whole space of all possible clusterings as a graph and to use randomized search to find good clusterings in this graph. It starts by randomly selecting *k* tuples as the initial medoids (or cluster representatives), from which it constructs *k* clusters. In each step, an existing medoid is replaced by a new randomly selected medoid. If the replacement leads to better clustering, the new medoid is kept. This procedure is repeated until the clusters remain stable.

CrossClus provides the clustering results to the user, together with information about each attribute. From the attributes of multiple relations, their join paths, and aggregation operators, the user learns the meaning of each cluster, and thus gains a better understanding of the clustering results.

9.4 Summary

- **Graphs** represent a more general class of structures than sets, sequences, lattices, and trees. **Graph mining** is used to mine frequent graph patterns, and perform characterization, discrimination, classification, and cluster analysis over large graph data sets. Graph mining has a broad spectrum of applications in chemical informatics, bioinformatics, computer vision, video indexing, text retrieval, and Web analysis.

- Efficient methods have been developed for **mining frequent subgraph patterns.** They can be categorized into Apriori-based and pattern growth–based approaches. The *Apriori-based approach* has to use the breadth-first search (BFS) strategy because of its level-wise candidate generation. The *pattern-growth approach* is more flexible with respect to the search method. A typical pattern-growth method is gSpan, which explores additional optimization techniques in pattern growth and achieves high performance. The further extension of gSpan for mining closed frequent graph patterns leads to the CloseGraph algorithm, which mines more compressed but complete sets of graph patterns, given the minimum support threshold.

- There are many interesting **variant graph patterns**, including approximate frequent graphs, coherent graphs, and dense graphs. A general framework that considers constraints is needed for mining such patterns. Moreover, various user-specific constraints can be pushed deep into the graph pattern mining process to improve mining efficiency.

- Application development of graph mining has led to the generation of compact and effective **graph index structures** using frequent and discriminative graph patterns. **Structure similarity search** can be achieved by exploration of multiple graph features. **Classification and cluster analysis of graph data sets** can be explored by their integration with the graph pattern mining process.

- A **social network** is a *heterogeneous* and *multirelational* data set represented by a graph, which is typically very large, with *nodes* corresponding to *objects*, and *edges* (or *links*) representing relationships between objects.

- **Small world networks** reflect the concept of small worlds, which originally focused on networks among individuals. They have been characterized as having a high degree of local clustering for a small fraction of the nodes (i.e., these nodes are interconnected with one another), while being no more than a few degrees of separation from the remaining nodes.

- Social networks exhibit certain characteristics. They tend to follow the **densification power law**, which states that networks become increasingly *dense* over time. **Shrinking diameter** is another characteristic, where the effective diameter often *decreases* as the network grows. Node *out-degrees* and *in-degrees* typically follow a **heavy-tailed distribution.** A **Forest Fire model** for graph generation was proposed, which incorporates these characteristics.

- **Link mining** is a confluence of research in social networks, link analysis, hypertext and Web mining, graph mining, relational learning, and inductive logic programming. Link mining tasks include *link-based object classification*, *object type prediction*, *link type prediction*, *link existence prediction*, *link cardinality estimation*, *object reconciliation* (which predicts whether two objects are, in fact, the same), and *group detection* (which clusters objects). Other tasks include *subgraph identification* (which finds characteristic subgraphs within networks) and *metadata mining* (which uncovers schema-type information regarding unstructured data).

- In **link prediction**, measures for analyzing the proximity of network nodes can be used to predict and rank new links. Examples include the *shortest path* (which ranks node pairs by their shortest path in the network) and *common neighbors* (where the greater the number of neighbors that two nodes share, the more likely they are to form a link). Other measures may be based on the *ensemble* of all paths between two nodes.

- **Viral marketing** aims to optimize the positive word-of-mouth effect among customers. By considering the interactions between customers, it can choose to spend more money marketing to an individual if that person has many social connections.

- Newsgroup discussions form a kind of network based on the "responded-to" relationships. Because people generally respond more frequently to a message when they *disagree* than when they *agree*, graph partitioning algorithms can be used to **mine newsgroups** based on such a network to effectively classify authors in the newsgroup into *opposite camps*.

- Most community mining methods assume that there is only one kind of relation in the network, and moreover, the mining results are independent of the users' information needs. In reality, there may be multiple relations between objects, which collectively form a **multirelational social network** (or *heterogeneous social network*). *Relation selection and extraction* in such networks evaluates the importance of the different relations with respect to user information provided as queries. In addition, it searches for a combination of the existing relations that may reveal a *hidden community* within the multirelational network.

- **Multirelational data mining (MRDM)** methods search for patterns that involve *multiple tables* (relations) from a relational database.

- **Inductive Logic Programming (ILP)** is the most widely used category of approaches to multirelational classification. It finds hypotheses of a certain format that can predict the class labels of target tuples, based on background knowledge. Although many ILP approaches achieve good classification accuracy, most are not highly scalable due to the computational expense of repeated joins.

- **Tuple ID propagation** is a method for virtually joining different relations by attaching the IDs of target tuples to tuples in nontarget relations. It is much less costly than physical joins, in both time and space.

- CrossMine and CrossClus are methods for **multirelational classification** and **multirelational clustering**, respectively. Both use tuple ID propagation to avoid physical joins. In addition, CrossClus employs user guidance to constrain the search space.

Exercises

9.1 Given two predefined sets of graphs, *contrast patterns* are substructures that are frequent in one set but infrequent in the other. Discuss how to mine contrast patterns efficiently in large graph data sets.

9.2 Multidimensional information can be associated with the vertices and edges of each graph. Study how to develop efficient methods for mining *multidimensional graph patterns*.

9.3 *Constraints* often play an important role in efficient graph mining. There are many potential constraints based on users' requests in graph mining. For example, one may want graph patterns containing or excluding certain vertices (or edges), with minimal or maximal size, containing certain subgraphs, with certain summation values, and so on. Based on how a constraint behaves in graph mining, give a systematic classification of constraints and work out rules on how to maximally use such constraints in efficient graph mining.

9.4 Our discussion of frequent graph pattern mining was confined to graph transactions (i.e., considering each graph in a graph database as a single "transaction" in a transactional database). In many applications, one needs to mine frequent subgraphs in a *large single graph* (such as the Web or a large social network). Study how to develop efficient methods for mining frequent and closed graph patterns in such data sets.

9.5 What are the challenges for *classification in a large social network* in comparison with classification in a single data relation? Suppose each node in a network represents a paper, associated with certain properties, such as author, research topic, and so on, and each directed edge from node *A* to node *B* indicates that paper *A* cites paper *B*. Design an effective classification scheme that may effectively build a model for highly regarded papers on a particular topic.

9.6 A group of students are linked to each other in a social network via advisors, courses, research groups, and friendship relationships. Present a *clustering* method that may partition students into different groups according to their research interests.

9.7 Many diseases spread via people's physical contacts in public places, such as offices, classrooms, buses, shopping centers, hotels, and restaurants. Suppose a database registers the concrete movement of many people (e.g., location, time, duration, and activity). Design a method that can be used to rank the "not visited" places during a virus-spreading season.

9.8 Design an effective method that discovers *hierarchical clusters in a social network*, such as a hierarchical network of friends.

9.9 Social networks evolve with time. Suppose the history of a social network is kept. Design a method that may discover the *trend of evolution* of the network.

9.10 There often exist *multiple social networks* linking a group of objects. For example, a student could be in a class, a research project group, a family member, member of a neighborhood, and so on. It is often beneficial to consider their joint effects or interactions. Design an efficient method in social network analysis that may incorporate multiple social networks in data mining.

9.11 Outline an efficient method that may find strong *correlation rules* in a large, multirelational database.

9.12 It is important to take a user's advice to cluster objects across multiple relations, because many features among these relations could be relevant to the objects. A user may select a sample set of objects and claim that some should be in the same cluster but some cannot. Outline an effective clustering method with such *user guidance*.

9.13 As a result of the close relationships among multiple departments or enterprises, it is necessary to perform data mining across multiple but interlinked databases. In comparison with multirelational data mining, one major difficulty with mining across multiple databases is *semantic heterogeneity* across databases. For example, "William Nelson" in one database could be "Bill Nelson" or "B. Nelson" in another one. Design a data mining method that may consolidate such objects by exploring object linkages among multiple databases.

9.14 Outline an effective method that performs *classification* across multiple heterogeneous databases.

Bibliographic Notes

Research into graph mining has developed many frequent subgraph mining methods. Washio and Motoda [WM03] performed a survey on graph-based data mining. Many well-known pairwise isomorphism testing algorithms were developed, such as Ullmann's Backtracking [Ull76] and McKay's Nauty [McK81]. Dehaspe, Toivonen, and King [DTK98] applied inductive logic programming to predict chemical carcinogenicity by mining frequent substructures. Several Apriori-based frequent substructure mining algorithms have been proposed, including AGM by Inokuchi, Washio, and Motoda [IWM98], FSG by Kuramochi and Karypis [KK01], and an edge-disjoint path-join algorithm by Vanetik, Gudes, and Shimony [VGS02]. Pattern-growth-based graph pattern mining algorithms include gSpan by Yan and Han [YH02], MoFa by Borgelt and Berthold [BB02], FFSM and SPIN by Huan, Wang, and Prins [HWP03] and Prins, Yang, Huan, and Wang [PYHW04], respectively, and Gaston by Nijssen and Kok [NK04]. These algorithms were inspired by PrefixSpan [PHMA$^+$01] for mining sequences, and TreeMinerV [Zak02] and FREQT [AAK$^+$02] for mining trees. A disk-based frequent graph mining method was proposed by Wang, Wang, Pei, et al. [WWP$^+$04].

Mining closed graph patterns was studied by Yan and Han [YH03], with the proposal of the algorithm, CloseGraph, as an extension of gSpan and CloSpan [YHA03]. Holder, Cook, and Djoko [HCD9] proposed SUBDUE for approximate substructure pattern discovery based on minimum description length and background knowledge. Mining coherent subgraphs was studied by Huan, Wang, Bandyopadhyay, et al. [HWB+04]. For mining relational graphs, Yan, Zhou, and Han [YZH05] proposed two algorithms, CloseCut and Splat, to discover exact dense frequent substructures in a set of relational graphs.

Many studies have explored the applications of mined graph patterns. Path-based graph indexing approaches are used in GraphGrep, developed by Shasha, Wang, and Giugno [SWG02], and in Daylight, developed by James, Weininger, and Delany [JWD03]. Frequent graph patterns were used as graph indexing features in the gIndex and Grafil methods proposed by Yan, Yu, and Han [YYH04, YYH05] to perform fast graph search and structure similarity search. Borgelt and Berthold [BB02] illustrated the discovery of active chemical structures in an HIV-screening data set by contrasting the support of frequent graphs between different classes. Deshpande, Kuramochi, and Karypis [DKK02] used frequent structures as features to classify chemical compounds. Huan, Wang, Bandyopadhyay, et al. [HWB+04] successfully applied the frequent graph mining technique to study protein structural families. Koyuturk, Grama, and Szpankowski [KGS04] proposed a method to detect frequent subgraphs in biological networks. Hu, Yan, Yu, et al. [HYY+05] developed an algorithm called CoDense to find dense subgraphs across multiple biological networks.

There has been a great deal of research on social networks. For texts on social network analysis, see Wasserman and Faust [WF94], Degenne and Forse [DF99], Scott [Sco05], Watts [Wat03a], Barabási [Bar03], and Carrington, Scott, and Wasserman [CSW05]. For a survey of work on social network analysis, see Newman [New03]. Barabási, Oltvai, Jeong, et al. have several comprehensive tutorials on the topic, available at *www.nd.edu/~networks/publications.htm#talks0001*. Books on small world networks include Watts [Wat03b] and Buchanan [Buc03]. Milgram's "six degrees of separation" experiment is presented in [Mil67].

The *Forest Fire model* for network generation was proposed in Leskovec, Kleinberg, and Faloutsos [LKF05]. The *preferential attachment model* was studied in Albert and Barbasi [AB99] and Cooper and Frieze [CF03]. The *copying model* was explored in Kleinberg, Kumar, Raghavan, et al. [KKR+99] and Kumar, Raghavan, Rajagopalan, et al. [KRR+00].

Link mining tasks and challenges were overviewed by Getoor [Get03]. A link-based classification method was proposed in Lu and Getoor [LG03]. Iterative classification and inference algorithms have been proposed for hypertext classification by Chakrabarti, Dom, and Indyk [CDI98] and Oh, Myaeng, and Lee [OML00]. Bhattacharya and Getoor [BG04] proposed a method for clustering linked data, which can be used to solve the data mining tasks of entity deduplication and group discovery. A method for group discovery was proposed by Kubica, Moore, and Schneider [KMS03]. Approaches to link prediction, based on measures for analyzing the "proximity" of nodes in a network, were described in Liben-Nowell and Kleinberg [LNK03]. The Katz measure was presented in Katz [Kat53]. A probabilistic model for learning link structure was given in Getoor, Friedman, Koller, and Taskar [GFKT01]. Link prediction for counterterrorism was proposed by Krebs [Kre02]. Viral marketing was described by Domingos [Dom05] and his work with Richardson [DR01, RD02]. BLOG (Bayesian LOGic), a language for reasoning with unknown objects, was proposed by Milch, Marthi, Russell, et al. [MMR05] to address the closed world assumption problem. Mining newsgroups to partition discussion participants into opposite camps using quotation networks was proposed by Agrawal, Rajagopalan, Srikant, and Xu [ARSX04]. The relation selection and extraction approach to community mining from multirelational networks was described in Cai, Shao, He, et al. [CSH$^+$05].

Multirelational data mining has been investigated extensively in the Inductive Logic Programming (ILP) community. Lavrac and Dzeroski [LD94] and Muggleton [Mug95] provided comprehensive introductions to Inductive Logic Programming (ILP). An overview of multirelational data mining was given by Dzeroski [Dze03]. Well-known ILP systems include FOIL by Quinlan and Cameron-Jones [QCJ93], Golem by Muggleton and Feng [MF90], and Progol by Muggleton [Mug95]. More recent systems include TILDE by Blockeel, De Raedt, and Ramon [BRR98], Mr-SMOTI by Appice, Ceci, and Malerba [ACM03], and RPTs by Neville, Jensen, Friedland, and Hay [NJFH03], which inductively construct decision trees from relational data. Probabilistic approaches to multirelational classification include probabilistic relational models by Getoor, Friedman, Koller, and Taskar [GFKT01] and by Taskar, Segal, and Koller [TSK01]. Popescul, Ungar, Lawrence, and Pennock [PULP02] proposed an approach to integrate ILP and statistical modeling for document classification and retrieval. The CrossMine approach was described in Yin, Han, Yang, and Yu [YHYY04]. The look-one-ahead method used in CrossMine was developed by Blockeel, De Raedt, and Ramon [BRR98]. Multirelational clustering was explored by Gartner, Lloyd, and Flach [GLF04], and Kirsten and Wrobel [KW98, KW00]. CrossClus performs multirelational clustering with user guidance and was proposed by Yin, Han, and Yu [YHY05].

10 Mining Object, Spatial, Multimedia, Text, and Web Data

Our previous chapters on advanced data mining discussed how to uncover knowledge from stream, time-series, sequence, graph, social network, and multirelational data. In this chapter, we examine data mining methods that handle object, spatial, multimedia, text, and Web data. These kinds of data are commonly encountered in many social, economic, scientific, engineering, and governmental applications, and pose new challenges in data mining. We first examine how to perform multidimensional analysis and descriptive mining of complex data objects in Section 10.1. We then study methods for mining spatial data (Section 10.2), multimedia data (Section 10.3), text (Section 10.4), and the World Wide Web (Section 10.5) in sequence.

10.1 Multidimensional Analysis and Descriptive Mining of Complex Data Objects

Many advanced, data-intensive applications, such as scientific research and engineering design, need to store, access, and analyze complex but relatively structured data objects. These objects cannot be represented as simple and uniformly structured records (i.e., tuples) in data relations. Such application requirements have motivated the design and development of *object-relational* and *object-oriented* database systems. Both kinds of systems deal with the efficient storage and access of vast amounts of disk-based **complex structured data objects**. These systems organize a large set of complex data objects into *classes*, which are in turn organized into *class/subclass* hierarchies. Each **object** in a class is associated with (1) an *object-identifier*, (2) a *set of attributes* that may contain sophisticated data structures, set- or list-valued data, class composition hierarchies, multimedia data, and (3) a *set of methods* that specify the computational routines or rules associated with the object class. There has been extensive research in the field of database systems on how to efficiently index, store, access, and manipulate complex objects in object-relational and object-oriented database systems. Technologies handling these issues are discussed in many books on database systems, especially on object-oriented and object-relational database systems.

One step beyond the storage and access of massive-scaled, complex object data is the systematic analysis and mining of such data. This includes two major tasks: (1) construct multidimensional data warehouses for complex object data and perform online analytical processing (OLAP) in such data warehouses, and (2) develop effective and scalable methods for mining knowledge from object databases and/or data warehouses. The second task is largely covered by the mining of specific kinds of data (such as spatial, temporal, sequence, graph- or tree-structured, text, and multimedia data), since these data form the major new kinds of complex data objects. As in Chapters 8 and 9, in this chapter we continue to study methods for mining complex data. Thus, our focus in this section will be mainly on how to construct object data warehouses and perform OLAP analysis on data warehouses for such data.

A major limitation of many commercial data warehouse and OLAP tools for multidimensional database analysis is their restriction on the allowable data types for dimensions and measures. Most data cube implementations confine dimensions to nonnumeric data, and measures to simple, aggregated values. To introduce data mining and multidimensional data analysis for complex objects, this section examines how to perform generalization on complex structured objects and construct object cubes for OLAP and mining in object databases.

To facilitate generalization and induction in object-relational and object-oriented databases, it is important to study how each component of such databases can be generalized, and how the generalized data can be used for multidimensional data analysis and data mining.

10.1.1 Generalization of Structured Data

An important feature of object-relational and object-oriented databases is their capability of storing, accessing, and modeling **complex structure-valued data**, such as set- and list-valued data and data with nested structures.

"How can generalization be performed on such data?" Let's start by looking at the generalization of set-valued, list-valued, and sequence-valued attributes.

A **set-valued attribute** may be of homogeneous or heterogeneous type. Typically, set-valued data can be generalized by (1) *generalization of each value in the set to its corresponding higher-level concept*, or (2) *derivation of the general behavior of the set*, such as the number of elements in the set, the types or value ranges in the set, the weighted average for numerical data, or the major clusters formed by the set. Moreover, generalization can be performed by *applying different generalization operators to explore alternative generalization paths*. In this case, the result of generalization is a heterogeneous set.

Example 10.1 **Generalization of a set-valued attribute.** Suppose that the *hobby* of a person is a set-valued attribute containing the set of values {*tennis, hockey, soccer, violin, SimCity*}. This set can be generalized to a set of high-level concepts, such as {*sports, music, computer_games*} or into the number 5 (i.e., the number of hobbies in the set). Moreover, a *count* can be associated with a generalized value to indicate how many elements are generalized to that value, as in {*sports(3), music(1), computer_games(1)*}, where *sports(3)* indicates *three kinds of sports*, and so on. ■

A set-valued attribute may be generalized to a set-valued or a single-valued attribute; a single-valued attribute may be generalized to a set-valued attribute if the values form a lattice or "hierarchy" or if the generalization follows different paths. Further generalizations on such a generalized set-valued attribute should follow the generalization path of each value in the set.

List-valued attributes and **sequence-valued attributes** can be *generalized in a manner similar to that for set-valued attributes except that the order of the elements in the list or sequence should be preserved in the generalization.* Each value in the list can be generalized into its corresponding higher-level concept. Alternatively, a list can be generalized according to its general behavior, such as the length of the list, the type of list elements, the value range, the weighted average value for numerical data, or by dropping unimportant elements in the list. A list may be generalized into a list, a set, or a single value.

Example 10.2 **Generalization of list-valued attributes.** Consider the following list or sequence of data for a person's education record: "*((B.Sc. in Electrical Engineering, U.B.C., Dec., 1998), (M.Sc. in Computer Engineering, U. Maryland, May, 2001), (Ph.D. in Computer Science, UCLA, Aug., 2005))*". This can be generalized by dropping less important descriptions (attributes) of each tuple in the list, such as by dropping the *month* attribute to obtain "*((B.Sc., U.B.C., 1998), ...)*", and/or by retaining only the most important tuple(s) in the list, e.g., "*(Ph.D. in Computer Science, UCLA, 2005)*". ■

A **complex structure-valued attribute** may contain sets, tuples, lists, trees, records, and their combinations, where one structure may be *nested* in another at any level. In general, a structure-valued attribute can be generalized in several ways, such as (1) generalizing each attribute in the structure while maintaining the shape of the structure, (2) flattening the structure and generalizing the flattened structure, (3) summarizing the low-level structures by high-level concepts or aggregation, and (4) returning the type or an overview of the structure.

In general, statistical analysis and cluster analysis may help toward deciding on the directions and degrees of generalization to perform, since most generalization processes are to retain main features and remove noise, outliers, or fluctuations.

10.1.2 Aggregation and Approximation in Spatial and Multimedia Data Generalization

Aggregation and approximation are another important means of generalization. They are especially useful for generalizing attributes with large sets of values, complex structures, and spatial or multimedia data.

Let's take **spatial data** as an example. We would like to generalize detailed geographic points into clustered regions, such as business, residential, industrial, or agricultural areas, according to land usage. Such generalization often requires the merge of a set of geographic areas by spatial operations, such as spatial union or spatial clustering methods. Aggregation and approximation are important techniques for this form of generalization. In a **spatial merge**, it is necessary to not only merge the regions of similar types within the same general class but also to compute the total areas, average density, or other aggregate functions while ignoring some scattered regions with different types if they are unimportant to the study. Other spatial operators, such as *spatial-union, spatial-overlapping,* and *spatial-intersection* (which may require the merging of scattered small regions into large, clustered regions) can also use spatial aggregation and approximation as data generalization operators.

Example 10.3 **Spatial aggregation and approximation.** Suppose that we have different pieces of land for various purposes of agricultural usage, such as the planting of vegetables, grains, and fruits. These pieces can be merged or *aggregated* into one large piece of agricultural land by a spatial merge. However, such a piece of agricultural land may contain highways, houses, and small stores. If the majority of the land is used for agriculture, the scattered regions for other purposes can be ignored, and the whole region can be claimed as an agricultural area by *approximation.* ■

A **multimedia database** may contain complex texts, graphics, images, video fragments, maps, voice, music, and other forms of audio/video information. Multimedia data are typically stored as sequences of bytes with variable lengths, and segments of data are linked together or indexed in a multidimensional way for easy reference.

Generalization on multimedia data can be performed by recognition and extraction of the essential features and/or general patterns of such data. There are many ways to extract such information. For an *image*, the size, color, shape, texture, orientation, and relative positions and structures of the contained objects or regions in the image can be extracted by aggregation and/or approximation. For a segment of *music*, its melody can be summarized based on the approximate patterns that repeatedly occur in the segment, while its style can be summarized based on its tone, tempo, or the major musical instruments played. For an *article*, its abstract or general organizational structure (e.g., the table of contents, the subject and index terms that frequently occur in the article, etc.) may serve as its generalization.

In general, it is a challenging task to generalize spatial data and multimedia data in order to extract interesting knowledge implicitly stored in the data. Technologies developed in spatial databases and multimedia databases, such as spatial data accessing and analysis techniques, pattern recognition, image analysis, text analysis, content-based image/text retrieval and multidimensional indexing methods, should be integrated with data generalization and data mining techniques to achieve satisfactory results. Techniques for mining such data are further discussed in the following sections.

10.1.3 Generalization of Object Identifiers and Class/Subclass Hierarchies

"How can object identifiers be generalized?" At first glance, it may seem impossible to generalize an object identifier. It remains unchanged even after structural reorganization of the data. However, since objects in an object-oriented database are

organized into classes, which in turn are organized into class/subclass hierarchies, the generalization of an object can be performed by referring to its associated hierarchy. Thus, an object identifier can be generalized as follows. First, the object identifier is generalized to the identifier of the *lowest subclass* to which the object belongs. The identifier of this subclass can then, in turn, be generalized to a higher-level class/subclass identifier by *climbing up* the class/subclass hierarchy. Similarly, a class or a subclass can be generalized to its corresponding superclass(es) by climbing up its associated class/subclass hierarchy.

"Can inherited properties of objects be generalized?" Since object-oriented databases are organized into class/subclass hierarchies, some attributes or methods of an object class are not explicitly specified in the class but are inherited from higher-level classes of the object. Some object-oriented database systems allow **multiple inheritance,** where properties can be inherited from more than one superclass when the class/subclass "hierarchy" is organized in the shape of a lattice. The inherited properties of an object can be derived by query processing in the object-oriented database. From the data generalization point of view, it is unnecessary to distinguish which data are stored within the class and which are inherited from its superclass. As long as the set of relevant data are collected by query processing, the data mining process will treat the inherited data in the same manner as the data stored in the object class, and perform generalization accordingly.

Methods are an important component of object-oriented databases. They can also be inherited by objects. Many behavioral data of objects can be derived by the application of methods. Since a method is usually defined by a computational procedure/function or by a set of deduction rules, it is impossible to perform generalization on the method itself. However, generalization can be performed on *the data derived* by application of the method. That is, once the set of task-relevant data is derived by application of the method, generalization can then be performed on these data.

10.1.4 Generalization of Class Composition Hierarchies

An attribute of an object may be composed of or described by another object, some of whose attributes may be in turn composed of or described by other objects, thus forming a **class composition hierarchy**. Generalization on a class composition hierarchy can be viewed as generalization on a set of nested structured data (which are possibly infinite, if the nesting is recursive).

In principle, the reference to a composite object may traverse via a long sequence of references along the corresponding class composition hierarchy. However, in most cases, the longer the sequence of references traversed, the weaker the semantic linkage between the original object and the referenced composite object. For example, an attribute *vehicles_owned* of an object class *student* could refer to another object class *car*, which may contain an attribute *auto_dealer*, which may refer to attributes describing the dealer's *manager* and *children*. Obviously, it is unlikely that any interesting general regularities exist between a student and her car dealer's manager's children. Therefore, generalization on a class of objects should be performed on the descriptive attribute values and methods of the class, with limited reference to its closely related components via its closely related linkages in the class composition hierarchy. That is, in order to discover interesting knowledge, generalization should be performed on the objects in the class composition hierarchy that are *closely related in semantics* to the currently focused class(es), but not on those that have only remote and rather weak semantic linkages.

10.1.5 Construction and Mining of Object Cubes

In an object database, data generalization and multidimensional analysis are not applied to individual objects but to classes of objects. Since a set of objects in a class may share many attributes and methods, and the generalization of each attribute and method may apply a sequence of generalization operators, the major issue becomes how to make the generalization processes cooperate among different attributes and methods in the class(es).

"So, how can class-based generalization be performed for a large set of objects?" For class-based generalization, the *attribute-oriented induction method* developed in Chapter 4 for mining characteristics of relational databases can be extended to mine data characteristics in object databases. Consider that a generalization-based data mining process can be viewed as the application of a sequence of class-based generalization operators on different attributes. Generalization can continue until the resulting class contains a small number of generalized objects that can be summarized as a concise, generalized rule in high-level terms. For efficient implementation, the generalization of multidimensional attributes of a complex object class can be performed by examining each attribute (or dimension), generalizing each attribute to simple-valued data, and constructing a multidimensional data cube, called an **object cube**. Once an object cube is constructed, multidimensional analysis and data mining can be performed on it in a manner similar to that for relational data cubes.

Notice that from the application point of view, it is not always desirable to generalize a set of values to single-valued data. Consider the attribute *keyword*, which may contain a set of keywords describing a book. It does not make much sense to generalize this set of keywords to one single value. In this context, it is difficult to construct an object cube containing the *keyword* dimension. We will address some progress in this direction in the next section when discussing spatial data cube construction. However, it remains a challenging research issue to develop techniques for handling set-valued data effectively in object cube construction and object-based multidimensional analysis.

10.1.6 Generalization-Based Mining of Plan Databases by Divide-and-Conquer

To show how generalization can play an important role in mining complex databases, we examine a case of mining significant patterns of successful actions in a plan database using a divide-and-conquer strategy.

A **plan** consists of a variable sequence of *actions*. A **plan database**, or simply a **planbase**, is a large collection of plans. **Plan mining** is the task of mining significant patterns or knowledge from a planbase. Plan mining can be used to discover travel patterns of business passengers in an air flight database or to find significant patterns from the sequences of actions in the repair of automobiles. Plan mining is different from sequential pattern mining, where a large number of frequently occurring sequences are mined at a very detailed level. Instead, plan mining is the extraction of important or significant *generalized* (sequential) patterns from a planbase.

Let's examine the plan mining process using an air travel example.

Example 10.4 **An air flight planbase.** Suppose that the air travel planbase shown in Table 10.1 stores customer flight sequences, where each record corresponds to an *action* in a sequential database, and a *sequence* of records sharing the same plan number is considered as one plan with a sequence of actions. The columns *departure* and *arrival* specify the codes of the airports involved. Table 10.2 stores information about each airport.

There could be many patterns mined from a planbase like Table 10.1. For example, we may discover that most flights from cities in the Atlantic United States to Midwestern cities have a stopover at ORD in Chicago, which could be because ORD is the principal hub for several major airlines. Notice that the airports that act as airline hubs (such as LAX in Los Angeles, ORD in Chicago, and JFK in New York) can easily be derived from Table 10.2 based on *airport_size*. However, there could be hundreds of hubs in a travel database. Indiscriminate mining may result in a large number of "rules" that lack substantial support, without providing a clear overall picture.

Table 10.1 A database of travel plans: a travel planbase.

plan#	*action#*	*departure*	*departure_time*	*arrival*	*arrival_time*	*airline*	...
1	1	ALB	800	JFK	900	TWA	...
1	2	JFK	1000	ORD	1230	UA	...
1	3	ORD	1300	LAX	1600	UA	...
1	4	LAX	1710	SAN	1800	DAL	...
2	1	SPI	900	ORD	950	AA	...
⋮	⋮	⋮	⋮	⋮	⋮	⋮	⋮

Table 10.2 An airport information table.

airport_code	*city*	*state*	*region*	*airport_size*	...
ORD	Chicago	Illinois	Mid-West	100000	...
SPI	Springfield	Illinois	Mid-West	10000	...
LAX	Los Angeles	California	Pacific	80000	...
ALB	Albany	New York	Atlantic	20000	...
⋮	⋮	⋮	⋮	⋮	⋮

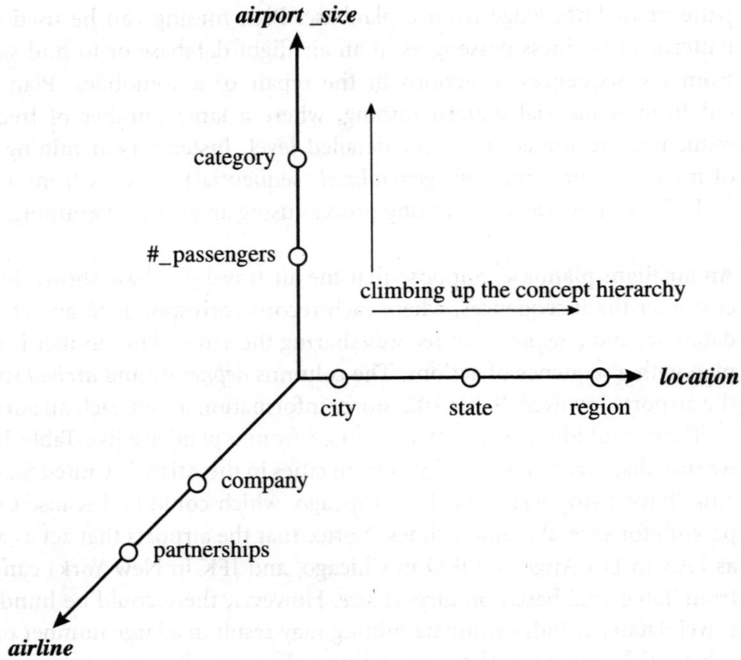

Figure 10.1 A multidimensional view of a database.

"So, how should we go about mining a planbase?" We would like to find a small number of general (sequential) patterns that cover a substantial portion of the plans, and then we can divide our search efforts based on such mined sequences. The key to mining such patterns is to generalize the plans in the planbase to a sufficiently high level. A multidimensional database model, such as the one shown in Figure 10.1 for the air flight planbase, can be used to facilitate such plan generalization. Since low-level information may never share enough commonality to form succinct plans, we should do the following: (1) generalize the planbase in different directions using the multidimensional model; (2) observe when the generalized plans share common, interesting, sequential patterns with substantial support; and (3) derive high-level, concise plans.

Let's examine this planbase. By combining tuples with the same plan number, the sequences of actions (shown in terms of airport codes) may appear as follows:

ALB - JFK - ORD - LAX - SAN
SPI - ORD - JFK - SYR

...

Table 10.3 Multidimensional generalization of a planbase.

plan#	*loc_seq*	*size_seq*	*state_seq*	*region_seq*	...
1	ALB-JFK-ORD-LAX-SAN	S-L-L-L-S	N-N-I-C-C	E-E-M-P-P	...
2	SPI-ORD-JFK-SYR	S-L-L-S	I-I-N-N	M-M-E-E	...
⋮	⋮	⋮	⋮	⋮	⋮

Table 10.4 Merging consecutive, identical actions in plans.

plan#	*size_seq*	*state_seq*	*region_seq*	...
1	S-L^+-S	N^+-I-C^+	E^+-M-P^+	...
2	S-L^+-S	I^+-N^+	M^+-E^+	...
⋮	⋮	⋮	⋮	⋮

These sequences may look very different. However, they can be generalized in multiple dimensions. When they are generalized based on the *airport_size* dimension, we observe some interesting sequential patterns, like *S-L-L-S*, where *L* represents a large airport (i.e., a hub), and *S* represents a relatively small regional airport, as shown in Table 10.3.

The generalization of a large number of air travel plans may lead to some rather general but highly regular patterns. This is often the case if the **merge** and **optional** operators are applied to the generalized sequences, where the former merges (and collapses) consecutive identical symbols into one using the transitive closure notation "+" to represent a sequence of actions of the same type, whereas the latter uses the notation "[ ]" to indicate that the object or action inside the square brackets "[ ]" is optional. Table 10.4 shows the result of applying the *merge* operator to the plans of Table 10.3.

By merging and collapsing similar actions, we can derive generalized sequential patterns, such as Pattern (10.1):

$$[S]-L^{+}-[S] \qquad [98.5\%] \tag{10.1}$$

The pattern states that 98.5% of travel plans have the pattern $[S]-L^{+}-[S]$, where $[S]$ indicates that action S is optional, and L^{+} indicates one or more repetitions of L. In other words, the travel pattern consists of flying first from possibly a small airport, hopping through one to many large airports, and finally reaching a large (or possibly, a small) airport.

After a sequential pattern is found with sufficient support, it can be used to partition the planbase. We can then mine each partition to find common characteristics. For example, from a partitioned planbase, we may find

$$flight(x,y) \wedge airport\_size(x,S) \wedge airport\_size(y,L) \Rightarrow region(x) = region(y) \ [75\%], \tag{10.2}$$

which means that for a direct flight from a small airport x to a large airport y, there is a 75% probability that x and y belong to the same region. ■

This example demonstrates a *divide-and-conquer strategy*, which first finds interesting, high-level concise sequences of plans by multidimensional generalization of a planbase, and then partitions the planbase based on mined patterns to discover the corresponding characteristics of subplanbases. This mining approach can be applied to many other applications. For example, in Weblog mining, we can study general access patterns from the Web to identify popular Web portals and common paths before digging into detailed subordinate patterns.

The plan mining technique can be further developed in several aspects. For instance, a *minimum support threshold* similar to that in association rule mining can be used to determine the level of generalization and ensure that a pattern covers a sufficient number of cases. Additional operators in plan mining can be explored, such as *less_than*. Other variations include extracting associations from subsequences, or mining sequence patterns involving multidimensional attributes—for example, the patterns involving both airport size and location. Such dimension-combined mining also requires the generalization of each dimension to a high level before examination of the combined sequence patterns.

10.2 Spatial Data Mining

A **spatial database** stores a large amount of space-related data, such as maps, preprocessed remote sensing or medical imaging data, and VLSI chip layout data. Spatial databases have many features distinguishing them from relational databases. They carry topological and/or distance information, usually organized by sophisticated, multidimensional spatial indexing structures that are accessed by spatial data access methods and often require spatial reasoning, geometric computation, and spatial knowledge representation techniques.

Spatial data mining refers to the extraction of knowledge, spatial relationships, or other interesting patterns not explicitly stored in spatial databases. Such mining demands an integration of data mining with spatial database technologies. It can be used for understanding spatial data, discovering spatial relationships and relationships between spatial and nonspatial data, constructing spatial knowledge bases, reorganizing spatial databases, and optimizing spatial queries. It is expected to have wide applications in geographic information systems, geomarketing, remote sensing, image database exploration, medical imaging, navigation, traffic control, environmental studies, and many other areas where spatial data are used. A crucial challenge to spatial data mining is the exploration of *efficient* spatial data mining techniques due to the huge amount of spatial data and the complexity of spatial data types and spatial access methods.

"What about using statistical techniques for spatial data mining?" Statistical spatial data analysis has been a popular approach to analyzing spatial data and exploring geographic information. The term *geostatistics* is often associated with continuous geographic space,

whereas the term *spatial statistics* is often associated with discrete space. In a statistical model that handles nonspatial data, one usually assumes statistical independence among different portions of data. However, different from traditional data sets, there is no such independence among spatially distributed data because in reality, spatial objects are often interrelated, or more exactly spatially *co-located*, in the sense that *the closer the two objects are located, the more likely they share similar properties*. For example, nature resource, climate, temperature, and economic situations are likely to be similar in geographically closely located regions. People even consider this as the first law of geography: "*Everything is related to everything else, but nearby things are more related than distant things.*" Such a property of close interdependency across nearby space leads to the notion of **spatial autocorrelation.** Based on this notion, spatial statistical modeling methods have been developed with good success. Spatial data mining will further develop spatial statistical analysis methods and extend them for huge amounts of spatial data, with more emphasis on efficiency, scalability, cooperation with database and data warehouse systems, improved user interaction, and the discovery of new types of knowledge.

10.2.1 Spatial Data Cube Construction and Spatial OLAP

"*Can we construct a spatial data warehouse?*" Yes, as with relational data, we can integrate spatial data to construct a data warehouse that facilitates spatial data mining. A **spatial data warehouse** is a *subject-oriented, integrated, time-variant*, and *nonvolatile* collection of both spatial and nonspatial data in support of spatial data mining and spatial-data-related decision-making processes.

Let's look at the following example.

Example 10.5 **Spatial data cube and spatial OLAP.** There are about 3,000 weather probes distributed in British Columbia (BC), Canada, each recording daily temperature and precipitation for a designated small area and transmitting signals to a provincial weather station. With a spatial data warehouse that supports spatial OLAP, a user can view weather patterns on a map by month, by region, and by different combinations of temperature and precipitation, and can dynamically drill down or roll up along any dimension to explore desired patterns, such as "wet and hot regions in the Fraser Valley in Summer 1999." ■

There are several challenging issues regarding the construction and utilization of spatial data warehouses. The first challenge is the integration of spatial data from heterogeneous sources and systems. Spatial data are usually stored in different industry firms and government agencies using various data formats. Data formats are not only structure-specific (e.g., raster- vs. vector-based spatial data, object-oriented vs. relational models, different spatial storage and indexing structures), but also vendor-specific (e.g., ESRI, MapInfo, Intergraph). There has been a great deal of work on the integration and exchange of heterogeneous spatial data, which has paved the way for spatial data integration and spatial data warehouse construction.

The second challenge is the realization of fast and flexible on-line analytical processing in spatial data warehouses. The star schema model introduced in Chapter 3 is a good choice for modeling spatial data warehouses because it provides a concise and organized warehouse structure and facilitates OLAP operations. However, in a spatial warehouse, both dimensions and measures may contain spatial components.

There are three types of *dimensions* in a spatial data cube:

- A **nonspatial dimension** contains only nonspatial data. Nonspatial dimensions *temperature* and *precipitation* can be constructed for the warehouse in Example 10.5, since each contains nonspatial data whose generalizations are nonspatial (such as "*hot*" for *temperature* and "*wet*" for *precipitation*).
- A **spatial-to-nonspatial dimension** is a dimension whose primitive-level data are spatial but whose generalization, starting at a certain high level, becomes nonspatial. For example, the spatial dimension *city* relays geographic data for the U.S. map. Suppose that the dimension's spatial representation of, say, Seattle is generalized to the string "*pacific_northwest.*" Although "*pacific_northwest*" is a spatial concept, its representation is not spatial (since, in our example, it is a string). It therefore plays the role of a nonspatial dimension.
- A **spatial-to-spatial dimension** is a dimension whose primitive level and all of its high-level generalized data are spatial. For example, the dimension *equi_temperature_region* contains spatial data, as do all of its generalizations, such as with regions covering *0-5_degrees* (Celsius), *5-10_degrees*, and so on.

We distinguish two types of *measures* in a spatial data cube:

- A **numerical measure** contains only numerical data. For example, one measure in a spatial data warehouse could be the *monthly_revenue* of a region, so that a roll-up may compute the total revenue by year, by county, and so on. Numerical measures can be further classified into *distributive*, *algebraic*, and *holistic*, as discussed in Chapter 3.
- A **spatial measure** contains a collection of pointers to spatial objects. For example, in a generalization (or roll-up) in the spatial data cube of Example 10.5, the regions with the same range of *temperature* and *precipitation* will be grouped into the same cell, and the measure so formed contains a collection of pointers to those regions.

A nonspatial data cube contains only nonspatial dimensions and numerical measures. If a spatial data cube contains spatial dimensions but no spatial measures, its OLAP operations, such as drilling or pivoting, can be implemented in a manner similar to that for nonspatial data cubes.

"But what if I need to use spatial measures in a spatial data cube?" This notion raises some challenging issues on efficient implementation, as shown in the following example.

Example 10.6 **Numerical versus spatial measures.** A star schema for the *BC_weather* warehouse of Example 10.5 is shown in Figure 10.2. It consists of four dimensions: *region temperature*, *time*, and *precipitation*, and three measures: *region_map*, *area*, and *count*. A concept hierarchy for each dimension can be created by users or experts, or generated automatically by data clustering analysis. Figure 10.3 presents hierarchies for each of the dimensions in the *BC_weather* warehouse.

Of the three measures, *area* and *count* are *numerical* measures that can be computed similarly as for nonspatial data cubes; *region_map* is a *spatial* measure that represents a collection of spatial pointers to the corresponding regions. Since different spatial OLAP operations result in different collections of spatial objects in *region_map*, it is a major challenge to compute the merges of a large number of regions flexibly and dynamically. For example, two different roll-ups on the BC weather map data (Figure 10.2) may produce two different generalized region maps, as shown in Figure 10.4, each being the result of merging a large number of small (probe) regions from Figure 10.2. ■

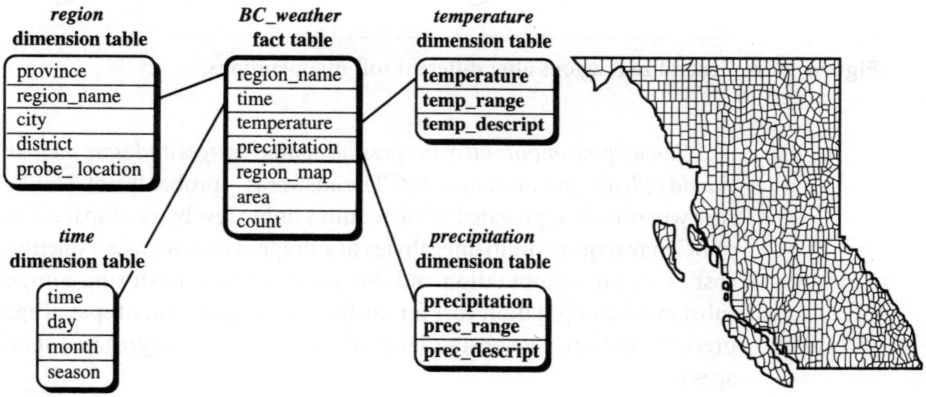

Figure 10.2 A star schema of the *BC_weather* spatial data warehouse and corresponding BC weather probes map.

region_name dimension:
probe_location < *district* < *city* < *region* < *province*

time dimension:
hour < *day* < *month* < *season*

temperature dimension:
(*cold, mild, hot*) $\subset$ all(*temperature*)
(*below_−20*, −20...−11, −10...0) $\subset$ *cold*
(0...10, 11...15, 16...20) $\subset$ *mild*
(20...25, 26...30, 31...35, *above_35*) $\subset$ *hot*

precipitation dimension:
(*dry, fair, wet*) $\subset$ all(*precipitation*)
(0...0.05, 0.06...0.2) $\subset$ *dry*
(0.2...0.5, 0.6...1.0, 1.1...1.5) $\subset$ *fair*
(1.5...2.0, 2.1...3.0, 3.1...5.0, *above_5.0*) $\subset$ *wet*

Figure 10.3 Hierarchies for each dimension of the *BC_weather* data warehouse.

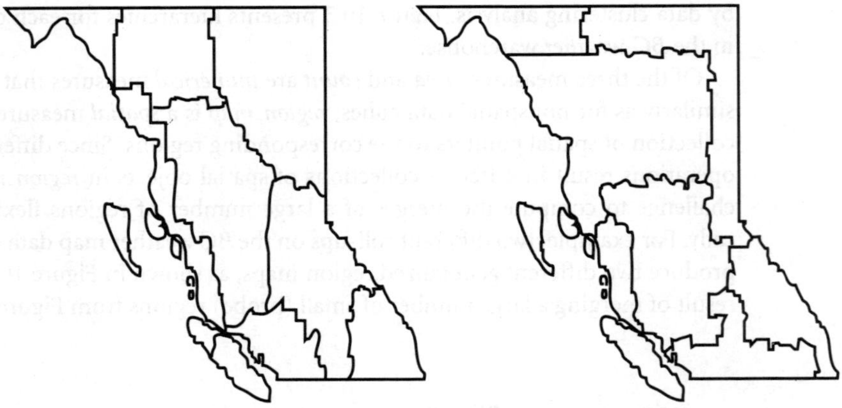

Figure 10.4 Generalized regions after different roll-up operations.

"Can we precompute all of the possible spatial merges and store them in the corresponding cuboid cells of a spatial data cube?" The answer is—probably not. Unlike a numerical measure where each aggregated value requires only a few bytes of space, a merged region map of BC may require multi-megabytes of storage. Thus, we face a dilemma in balancing the cost of on-line computation and the space overhead of storing computed measures: the substantial computation cost for on-the-fly computation of spatial aggregations calls for precomputation, yet substantial overhead for storing aggregated spatial values discourages it.

There are at least three possible choices in regard to the computation of spatial measures in spatial data cube construction:

- *Collect and store the corresponding spatial object pointers but do not perform precomputation of spatial measures in the spatial data cube.* This can be implemented by storing, in the corresponding cube cell, a pointer to a collection of spatial object pointers, and invoking and performing the spatial merge (or other computation) of the corresponding spatial objects, when necessary, on the fly. This method is a good choice if only spatial display is required (i.e., no real spatial merge has to be performed), or if there are not many regions to be merged in any pointer collection (so that the on-line merge is not very costly), or if on-line spatial merge computation is fast (recently, some efficient spatial merge methods have been developed for fast spatial OLAP). Since OLAP results are often used for on-line spatial analysis and mining, it is still recommended to precompute some of the spatially connected regions to speed up such analysis.
- *Precompute and store a rough approximation of the spatial measures in the spatial data cube.* This choice is good for a rough view or coarse estimation of spatial merge results under the assumption that it requires little storage space. For example, a **minimum bounding rectangle (MBR)**, represented by two points, can be taken as a rough estimate

of a merged region. Such a precomputed result is small and can be presented quickly to users. If higher precision is needed for specific cells, the application can either fetch precomputed high-quality results, if available, or compute them on the fly.

- *Selectively precompute some spatial measures in the spatial data cube.* This can be a smart choice. The question becomes, "Which portion of the cube should be selected for materialization?" The selection can be performed at the cuboid level, that is, either precompute and store *each* set of mergeable spatial regions for *each* cell of a selected cuboid, or precompute none if the cuboid is not selected. Since a cuboid usually consists of a large number of spatial objects, it may involve precomputation and storage of a large number of mergeable spatial objects, some of which may be rarely used. Therefore, it is recommended to perform selection at a finer granularity level: examining each group of mergeable spatial objects in a cuboid to determine whether such a merge should be precomputed. The decision should be based on the utility (such as access frequency or access priority), shareability of merged regions, and the balanced overall cost of space and on-line computation.

With efficient implementation of spatial data cubes and spatial OLAP, generalization-based descriptive spatial mining, such as spatial characterization and discrimination, can be performed efficiently.

10.2.2 Mining Spatial Association and Co-location Patterns

Similar to the mining of association rules in transactional and relational databases, *spatial association rules* can be mined in spatial databases. A **spatial association rule** is of the form $A \Rightarrow B\ [s\%, c\%]$, where A and B are sets of spatial or nonspatial predicates, $s\%$ is the support of the rule, and $c\%$ is the confidence of the rule. For example, the following is a spatial association rule:

$$is\_a(X, \text{“}school\text{”}) \wedge close\_to(X, \text{“}sports\_center\text{”}) \Rightarrow close\_to(X, \text{“}park\text{”}) \quad [0.5\%, 80\%].$$

This rule states that 80% of schools that are close to sports centers are also close to parks, and 0.5% of the data belongs to such a case.

Various kinds of spatial predicates can constitute a spatial association rule. Examples include distance information (such as *close_to* and *far_away*), topological relations (like *intersect, overlap*, and *disjoint*), and spatial orientations (like *left_of* and *west_of*).

Since spatial association mining needs to evaluate multiple spatial relationships among a large number of spatial objects, the process could be quite costly. An interesting mining optimization method called **progressive refinement** can be adopted in spatial association analysis. The method first mines large data sets *roughly* using a fast algorithm and then improves the quality of mining in a pruned data set using a more expensive algorithm.

To ensure that the pruned data set covers the complete set of answers when applying the high-quality data mining algorithms at a later stage, an important requirement for the rough mining algorithm applied in the early stage is the **superset coverage property**: that is, it preserves all of the potential answers. In other words, it should allow a *false-positive* *test*, which might include some data sets that do not belong to the answer sets, but it should not allow a *false-negative test*, which might exclude some potential answers.

For mining spatial associations related to the spatial predicate *close_to*, we can first collect the candidates that pass the minimum support threshold by

- Applying certain rough spatial evaluation algorithms, for example, using an MBR structure (which registers only two spatial points rather than a set of complex polygons), and
- Evaluating the relaxed spatial predicate, *g_close_to*, which is a generalized *close_to* covering a broader context that includes *close_to, touch*, and *intersect*.

If two spatial objects are closely located, their enclosing MBRs must be closely located, matching *g_close_to*. However, the reverse is not always true: if the enclosing MBRs are closely located, the two spatial objects may or may not be located so closely. Thus, the MBR pruning is a false-positive testing tool for closeness: only those that pass the *rough* test need to be further examined using more expensive spatial computation algorithms. With this preprocessing, only the patterns that are frequent at the approximation level will need to be examined by more detailed and finer, yet more expensive, spatial computation.

Besides mining spatial association rules, one may like to identify groups of particular features that appear frequently close to each other in a geospatial map. Such a problem is essentially the problem of mining **spatial co-locations**. Finding spatial co-locations can be considered as a special case of mining spatial associations. However, based on the property of spatial autocorrelation, interesting features likely coexist in closely located regions. Thus spatial co-location can be just what one really wants to explore. Efficient methods can be developed for mining spatial co-locations by exploring the methodologies like Aprori and progressive refinement, similar to what has been done for mining spatial association rules.

10.2.3 Spatial Clustering Methods

Spatial data clustering identifies clusters, or densely populated regions, according to some distance measurement in a large, multidimensional data set. Spatial clustering methods were thoroughly studied in Chapter 7 since cluster analysis usually considers spatial data clustering in examples and applications. Therefore, readers interested in spatial clustering should refer to Chapter 7.

10.2.4 Spatial Classification and Spatial Trend Analysis

Spatial classification analyzes spatial objects to derive classification schemes in relevance to certain spatial properties, such as the *neighborhood* of a district, highway, or river.

Example 10.7 **Spatial classification.** Suppose that you would like to classify regions in a province into *rich* versus *poor* according to the average family income. In doing so, you would like to identify the important spatial-related factors that determine a region's classification.

Many properties are associated with spatial objects, such as hosting a university, containing interstate highways, being near a lake or ocean, and so on. These properties can be used for relevance analysis and to find interesting classification schemes. Such classification schemes may be represented in the form of decision trees or rules, for example, as described in Chapter 6. ■

Spatial trend analysis deals with another issue: the detection of changes and trends along a spatial dimension. Typically, trend analysis detects changes with time, such as the changes of temporal patterns in time-series data. Spatial trend analysis replaces time with space and studies the trend of nonspatial or spatial data changing with space. For example, we may observe the trend of changes in economic situation when moving away from the center of a city, or the trend of changes of the climate or vegetation with the increasing distance from an ocean. For such analyses, regression and correlation analysis methods are often applied by utilization of spatial data structures and spatial access methods.

There are also many applications where patterns are changing with *both space and time*. For example, traffic flows on highways and in cities are both time and space related. Weather patterns are also closely related to both time and space. Although there have been a few interesting studies on spatial classification and spatial trend analysis, the investigation of spatiotemporal data mining is still in its early stage. More methods and applications of spatial classification and trend analysis, especially those associated with time, need to be explored.

10.2.5 Mining Raster Databases

Spatial database systems usually handle vector data that consist of points, lines, polygons (regions), and their compositions, such as networks or partitions. Typical examples of such data include maps, design graphs, and 3-D representations of the arrangement of the chains of protein molecules. However, a huge amount of space-related data are in **digital raster (image) forms**, such as satellite images, remote sensing data, and computer tomography. It is important to explore data mining in raster or image databases. Methods for mining raster and image data are examined in the following section regarding the mining of multimedia data.

10.3 Multimedia Data Mining

"What is a multimedia database?" A **multimedia database system** stores and manages a large collection of *multimedia data*, such as audio, video, image, graphics, speech, text, document, and hypertext data, which contain text, text markups, and linkages. Multimedia database systems are increasingly common owing to the popular use of audio-video equipment, digital cameras, CD-ROMs, and the Internet. Typical multimedia database systems include NASA's EOS (Earth Observation System), various kinds of image and audio-video databases, and Internet databases.

In this section, our study of multimedia data mining focuses on image data mining. Mining text data and mining the World Wide Web are studied in the two subsequent sections. Here we introduce multimedia data mining methods, including similarity search in multimedia data, multidimensional analysis, classification and prediction analysis, and mining associations in multimedia data.

10.3.1 Similarity Search in Multimedia Data

"When searching for similarities in multimedia data, can we search on either the data description or the data content?" That is correct. For similarity searching in multimedia data, we consider two main families of multimedia indexing and retrieval systems: (1) **description-based retrieval** systems, which build indices and perform object retrieval based on image descriptions, such as keywords, captions, size, and time of creation; and (2) **content-based retrieval** systems, which support retrieval based on the image content, such as color histogram, texture, pattern, image topology, and the shape of objects and their layouts and locations within the image. Description-based retrieval is labor-intensive if performed manually. If automated, the results are typically of poor quality. For example, the assignment of keywords to images can be a tricky and arbitrary task. Recent development of Web-based image clustering and classification methods has improved the quality of description-based Web image retrieval, because imagesurrounded text information as well as Web linkage information can be used to extract proper description and group images describing a similar theme together. Content-based retrieval uses visual features to index images and promotes object retrieval based on feature similarity, which is highly desirable in many applications.

In a content-based image retrieval system, there are often two kinds of queries: *image-sample-based queries* and *image feature specification queries*. **Image-sample-based queries** find all of the images that are similar to the given image sample. This search compares the **feature vector** (or **signature**) extracted from the sample with the feature vectors of images that have already been extracted and indexed in the image database. Based on this comparison, images that are close to the sample image are returned. **Image feature specification queries** specify or sketch image features like color, texture, or shape, which are translated into a feature vector to be matched with the feature vectors of the images in the database. Content-based retrieval has wide applications, including medical diagnosis, weather prediction, TV production, Web search engines for images, and e-commerce. Some systems, such as *QBIC* (*Query By Image Content*), support both sample-based and image feature specification queries. There are also systems that support both content-based and description-based retrieval.

Several approaches have been proposed and studied for similarity-based retrieval in image databases, based on image signature:

- **Color histogram–based signature**: In this approach, the signature of an image includes color histograms based on the color composition of an image regardless of its scale or orientation. This method does not contain any information about shape, image topology, or texture. Thus, two images with similar color composition but that contain very different shapes or textures may be identified as similar, although they could be completely unrelated semantically.

- **Multifeature composed signature:** In this approach, the signature of an image includes a composition of multiple features: color histogram, shape, image topology, and texture. The extracted image features are stored as metadata, and images are indexed based on such metadata. Often, separate distance functions can be defined for each feature and subsequently combined to derive the overall results. Multidimensional content-based search often uses one or a few probe features to search for images containing such (similar) features. It can therefore be used to search for similar images. This is the most popularly used approach in practice.
- **Wavelet-based signature:** This approach uses the dominant wavelet coefficients of an image as its signature. Wavelets capture shape, texture, and image topology information in a single unified framework.[1] This improves efficiency and reduces the need for providing multiple search primitives (unlike the second method above). However, since this method computes a single signature for an entire image, it may fail to identify images containing similar objects where the objects *differ* in location or size.
- **Wavelet-based signature with region-based granularity:** In this approach, the computation and comparison of signatures are at the granularity of regions, not the entire image. This is based on the observation that similar images may contain similar regions, but a region in one image could be a translation or scaling of a matching region in the other. Therefore, a similarity measure between the query image Q and a target image T can be defined in terms of the fraction of the area of the two images covered by matching pairs of regions from Q and T. Such a region-based similarity search can find images containing similar objects, where these objects may be translated or scaled.

10.3.2 Multidimensional Analysis of Multimedia Data

"Can we construct a data cube for multimedia data analysis?" To facilitate the multidimensional analysis of large multimedia databases, multimedia data cubes can be designed and constructed in a manner similar to that for traditional data cubes from relational data. A **multimedia data cube** can contain additional dimensions and measures for multimedia information, such as color, texture, and shape.

Let's examine a multimedia data mining system prototype called MultiMediaMiner, which extends the DBMiner system by handling multimedia data. The example database tested in the MultiMediaMiner system is constructed as follows. Each image contains two descriptors: a *feature descriptor* and a *layout descriptor*. The original image is not stored directly in the database; only its descriptors are stored. The description information encompasses fields like image file name, image URL, image type (e.g., gif, tiff, jpeg, mpeg, bmp, avi), a list of all known Web pages referring to the image (i.e., parent URLs), a list of keywords, and a thumbnail used by the user interface for image and video browsing. The **feature descriptor** is a set of vectors for each visual characteristic. The main

[1] Wavelet analysis was introduced in Section 2.5.3.

vectors are a color vector containing the color histogram quantized to 512 colors ($8 \times 8 \times 8$ for $R \times G \times B$), an MFC (Most Frequent Color) vector, and an MFO (Most Frequent Orientation) vector. The MFC and MFO contain five color centroids and five edge orientation centroids for the five most frequent colors and five most frequent orientations, respectively. The edge orientations used are 0°, 22.5°, 45°, 67.5°, 90°, and so on. The **layout descriptor** contains a color layout vector and an edge layout vector. Regardless of their original size, all images are assigned an 8×8 grid. The most frequent color for each of the 64 cells is stored in the color layout vector, and the number of edges for each orientation in each of the cells is stored in the edge layout vector. Other sizes of grids, like 4×4, 2×2, and 1×1, can easily be derived.

The *Image Excavator* component of MultiMediaMiner uses image contextual information, like HTML tags in Web pages, to derive keywords. By traversing on-line directory structures, like the Yahoo! directory, it is possible to create hierarchies of keywords mapped onto the directories in which the image was found. These graphs are used as concept hierarchies for the dimension *keyword* in the multimedia data cube.

"*What kind of dimensions can a multimedia data cube have?*" A multimedia data cube can have many dimensions. The following are some examples: the size of the image or video in bytes; the width and height of the frames (or pictures), constituting two dimensions; the date on which the image or video was created (or last modified); the format type of the image or video; the frame sequence duration in seconds; the image or video Internet domain; the Internet domain of pages referencing the image or video (parent URL); the keywords; a color dimension; an edge-orientation dimension; and so on. Concept hierarchies for many numerical dimensions may be automatically defined. For other dimensions, such as for Internet domains or color, predefined hierarchies may be used.

The construction of a multimedia data cube will facilitate multidimensional analysis of multimedia data primarily based on visual content, and the mining of multiple kinds of knowledge, including summarization, comparison, classification, association, and clustering. The *Classifier* module of MultiMediaMiner and its output are presented in Figure 10.5.

The multimedia data cube seems to be an interesting model for multidimensional analysis of multimedia data. However, we should note that it is difficult to implement a data cube efficiently given a large number of dimensions. This curse of dimensionality is especially serious in the case of multimedia data cubes. We may like to model color, orientation, texture, keywords, and so on, as multiple dimensions in a multimedia data cube. However, many of these attributes are set-oriented instead of single-valued. For example, one image may correspond to a set of keywords. It may contain a set of objects, each associated with a set of colors. If we use each keyword as a dimension or each detailed color as a dimension in the design of the data cube, it will create a huge number of dimensions. On the other hand, not doing so may lead to the modeling of an image at a rather rough, limited, and imprecise scale. More research is needed on how to design a multimedia data cube that may strike a balance between efficiency and the power of representation.

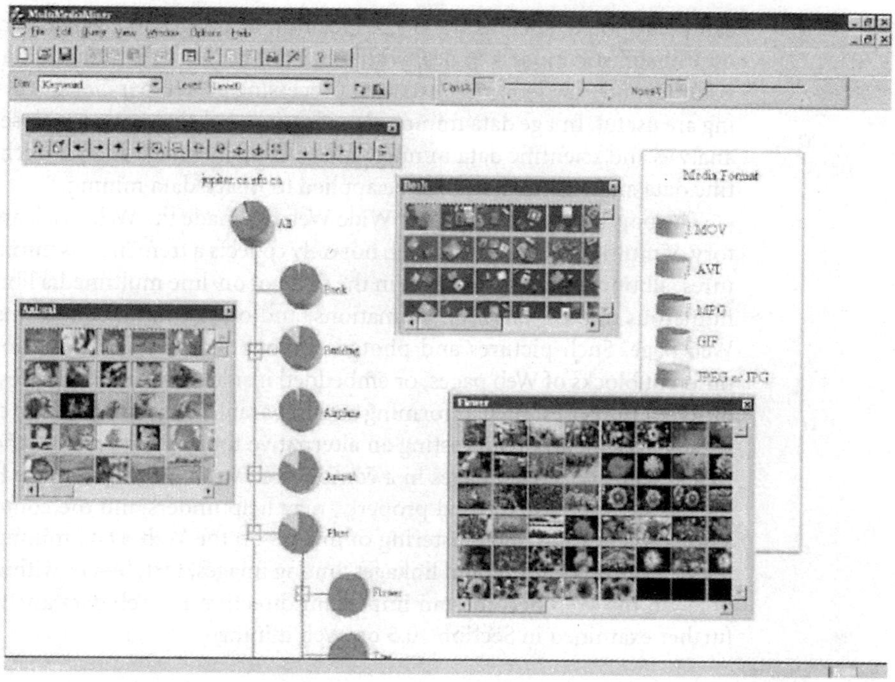

Figure 10.5 An output of the *Classifier* module of MultiMediaMiner.

10.3.3 Classification and Prediction Analysis of Multimedia Data

Classification and predictive modeling have been used for mining multimedia data, especially in scientific research, such as astronomy, seismology, and geoscientific research. In general, all of the classification methods discussed in Chapter 6 can be used in image analysis and pattern recognition. Moreover, in-depth statistical pattern analysis methods are popular for distinguishing subtle features and building high-quality models.

Example 10.8 **Classification and prediction analysis of astronomy data.** Taking sky images that have been carefully classified by astronomers as the training set, we can construct models for the recognition of galaxies, stars, and other stellar objects, based on properties like magnitudes, areas, intensity, image moments, and orientation. A large number of sky images taken by telescopes or space probes can then be tested against the constructed models in order to identify new celestial bodies. Similar studies have successfully been performed to identify volcanoes on Venus. ■

Data preprocessing is important when mining image data and can include data cleaning, data transformation, and feature extraction. Aside from standard methods used in pattern recognition, such as edge detection and Hough transformations, techniques can be explored, such as the decomposition of images to eigenvectors or the adoption of probabilistic models to deal with uncertainty. Since the image data are often in huge volumes and may require substantial processing power, parallel and distributed processing are useful. Image data mining classification and clustering are closely linked to image analysis and scientific data mining, and thus many image analysis techniques and scientific data analysis methods can be applied to image data mining.

The popular use of the World Wide Web has made the Web a rich and gigantic repository of multimedia data. The Web not only collects a tremendous number of photos, pictures, albums, and video images in the form of on-line multimedia libraries, but also has numerous photos, pictures, animations, and other multimedia forms on almost every Web page. Such pictures and photos, surrounded by text descriptions, located at the different blocks of Web pages, or embedded inside news or text articles, may serve rather different purposes, such as forming an inseparable component of the content, serving as an advertisement, or suggesting an alternative topic. Furthermore, these Web pages are linked with other Web pages in a complicated way. Such text, image location, and Web linkage information, if used properly, may help understand the contents of the text or assist classification and clustering of images on the Web. Data mining by making good use of relative locations and linkages among images, text, blocks within a page, and page links on the Web becomes an important direction in Web data analysis, which will be further examined in Section 10.5 on Web mining.

10.3.4 Mining Associations in Multimedia Data

"*What kinds of associations can be mined in multimedia data?*" Association rules involving multimedia objects can be mined in image and video databases. At least three categories can be observed:

- **Associations between image content and nonimage content features:** A rule like "*If at least 50% of the upper part of the picture is blue, then it is likely to represent sky*" belongs to this category since it links the image content to the keyword *sky.*
- **Associations among image contents that are not related to spatial relationships:** A rule like "*If a picture contains two blue squares, then it is likely to contain one red circle as well*" belongs to this category since the associations are all regarding image contents.
- **Associations among image contents related to spatial relationships:** A rule like "*If a red triangle is between two yellow squares, then it is likely a big oval-shaped object is underneath*" belongs to this category since it associates objects in the image with spatial relationships.

To mine associations among multimedia objects, we can treat each image as a transaction and find frequently occurring patterns among different images.

"*What are the differences between mining association rules in multimedia databases versus in transaction databases?*" There are some subtle differences. First, an image may contain multiple objects, each with many features such as color, shape, texture, keyword, and spatial location, so there could be many possible associations. In many cases, a feature may be considered as the same in two images at a certain level of resolution, but different at a finer resolution level. Therefore, it is essential to promote a **progressive resolution refinement** approach. That is, we can first mine frequently occurring patterns at a relatively rough resolution level, and then focus only on those that have passed the minimum support threshold when mining at a finer resolution level. This is because the patterns that are not frequent at a rough level cannot be frequent at finer resolution levels. Such a multiresolution mining strategy substantially reduces the overall data mining cost without loss of the quality and completeness of data mining results. This leads to an efficient methodology for mining frequent itemsets and associations in large multimedia databases.

Second, because a picture containing multiple recurrent objects is an important feature in image analysis, recurrence of the same objects should not be ignored in association analysis. For example, a picture containing two golden circles is treated quite differently from that containing only one. This is quite different from that in a transaction database, where the fact that a person buys one gallon of milk or two may often be treated the same as "*buys_milk*." Therefore, the definition of multimedia association and its measurements, such as support and confidence, should be adjusted accordingly.

Third, there often exist important spatial relationships among multimedia objects, such as *above*, *beneath*, *between*, *nearby*, *left-of*, and so on. These features are very useful for exploring object associations and correlations. Spatial relationships together with other content-based multimedia features, such as color, shape, texture, and keywords, may form interesting associations. Thus, spatial data mining methods and properties of topological spatial relationships become important for multimedia mining.

10.3.5 Audio and Video Data Mining

Besides still images, an incommensurable amount of audiovisual information is becoming available in digital form, in digital archives, on the World Wide Web, in broadcast data streams, and in personal and professional databases. This amount is rapidly growing. There are great demands for effective content-based retrieval and data mining methods for audio and video data. Typical examples include searching for and multimedia editing of particular video clips in a TV studio, detecting suspicious persons or scenes in surveillance videos, searching for particular events in a personal multimedia repository such as MyLifeBits, discovering patterns and outliers in weather radar recordings, and finding a particular melody or tune in your MP3 audio album.

To facilitate the recording, search, and analysis of audio and video information from multimedia data, industry and standardization committees have made great strides toward developing a set of standards for multimedia information description and compression. For example, MPEG-*k* (developed by MPEG: *Moving Picture Experts Group*) and JPEG are typical video compression schemes. The most recently released MPEG-7, formally named "*Multimedia Content Description Interface*," is a standard for describing the multimedia content data. It supports some degree of interpretation of the information meaning, which can be passed onto, or accessed by, a device or a computer.

MPEG-7 is not aimed at any one application in particular; rather, the elements that MPEG-7 standardizes support as broad a range of applications as possible. The audiovisual data description in MPEG-7 includes still pictures, video, graphics, audio, speech, three-dimensional models, and information about how these data elements are combined in the multimedia presentation.

The MPEG committee standardizes the following elements in MPEG-7: (1) a set of *descriptors*, where each descriptor defines the syntax and semantics of a feature, such as color, shape, texture, image topology, motion, or title; (2) a set of *descriptor schemes*, where each scheme specifies the structure and semantics of the relationships between its components (descriptors or description schemes); (3) a set of *coding schemes* for the descriptors, and (4) a *description definition language* (DDL) to specify schemes and descriptors. Such standardization greatly facilitates content-based video retrieval and video data mining.

It is unrealistic to treat a video clip as a long sequence of individual still pictures and analyze each picture since there are too many pictures, and most adjacent images could be rather similar. In order to capture the story or event structure of a video, it is better to treat each video clip as a collection of actions and events in time and first temporarily segment them into video shots. A *shot* is a group of frames or pictures where the video content from one frame to the adjacent ones does not change abruptly. Moreover, the most representative frame in a video shot is considered the *key frame* of the shot. Each key frame can be analyzed using the image feature extraction and analysis methods studied above in the content-based image retrieval. The sequence of key frames will then be used to define the sequence of the events happening in the video clip. Thus the detection of shots and the extraction of key frames from video clips become the essential tasks in video processing and mining.

Video data mining is still in its infancy. There are still a lot of research issues to be solved before it becomes general practice. Similarity-based preprocessing, compression, indexing and retrieval, information extraction, redundancy removal, frequent pattern discovery, classification, clustering, and trend and outlier detection are important data mining tasks in this domain.

10.4 Text Mining

Most previous studies of data mining have focused on structured data, such as relational, transactional, and data warehouse data. However, in reality, a substantial portion of the available information is stored in **text databases** (or **document databases**), which consist of large collections of documents from various sources, such as news articles, research papers, books, digital libraries, e-mail messages, and Web pages. Text databases are rapidly growing due to the increasing amount of information available in electronic form, such as electronic publications, various kinds of electronic documents, e-mail, and the World Wide Web (which can also be viewed as a huge, interconnected, dynamic text database). Nowadays most of the information in government, industry, business, and other institutions are stored electronically, in the form of text databases.

Data stored in most text databases are *semistructured data* in that they are neither completely unstructured nor completely structured. For example, a document may contain a few structured fields, such as *title*, *authors*, *publication_date*, *category*, and so on, but also contain some largely unstructured text components, such as *abstract* and *contents*. There have been a great deal of studies on the modeling and implementation of semistructured data in recent database research. Moreover, information retrieval techniques, such as text indexing methods, have been developed to handle unstructured documents.

Traditional information retrieval techniques become inadequate for the increasingly vast amounts of text data. Typically, only a small fraction of the many available documents will be relevant to a given individual user. Without knowing what could be in the documents, it is difficult to formulate effective queries for analyzing and extracting useful information from the data. Users need tools to compare different documents, rank the importance and relevance of the documents, or find patterns and trends across multiple documents. Thus, text mining has become an increasingly popular and essential theme in data mining.

10.4.1 Text Data Analysis and Information Retrieval

"What is information retrieval?" **Information retrieval** (IR) is a field that has been developing in parallel with database systems for many years. Unlike the field of database systems, which has focused on query and transaction processing of structured data, information retrieval is concerned with the organization and retrieval of information from a large number of text-based documents. Since information retrieval and database systems each handle different kinds of data, some database system problems are usually not present in information retrieval systems, such as concurrency control, recovery, transaction management, and update. Also, some common information retrieval problems are usually not encountered in traditional database systems, such as unstructured documents, approximate search based on keywords, and the notion of relevance.

Due to the abundance of text information, information retrieval has found many applications. There exist many information retrieval systems, such as on-line library catalog systems, on-line document management systems, and the more recently developed Web search engines.

A typical information retrieval problem is to locate relevant documents in a document collection based on a user's query, which is often some keywords describing an information need, although it could also be an example relevant document. In such a search problem, a user takes the initiative to "pull" the relevant information out from the collection; this is most appropriate when a user has some ad hoc (i.e., short-term) information need, such as finding information to buy a used car. When a user has a long-term information need (e.g., a researcher's interests), a retrieval system may also take the initiative to "push" any newly arrived information item to a user if the item is judged as being relevant to the user's information need. Such an information access process is called *information filtering*, and the corresponding systems are often called *filtering systems* or *recommender systems*. From a technical viewpoint, however, search and filtering share many common techniques. Below we briefly discuss the major techniques in information retrieval with a focus on search techniques.

Basic Measures for Text Retrieval: Precision and Recall

"Suppose that a text retrieval system has just retrieved a number of documents for me based on my input in the form of a query. How can we assess how accurate or correct the system was?" Let the set of documents relevant to a query be denoted as $\{Relevant\}$, and the set of documents retrieved be denoted as $\{Retrieved\}$. The set of documents that are both relevant and retrieved is denoted as $\{Relevant\} \cap \{Retrieved\}$, as shown in the Venn diagram of Figure 10.6. There are two basic measures for assessing the quality of text retrieval:

- **Precision:** This is the percentage of retrieved documents that are in fact relevant to the query (i.e., "correct" responses). It is formally defined as

$$precision = \frac{|\{Relevant\} \cap \{Retrieved\}|}{|\{Retrieved\}|}.$$

- **Recall:** This is the percentage of documents that are relevant to the query and were, in fact, retrieved. It is formally defined as

$$recall = \frac{|\{Relevant\} \cap \{Retrieved\}|}{|\{Relevant\}|}.$$

An information retrieval system often needs to trade off recall for precision or vice versa. One commonly used trade-off is the **F-score**, which is defined as the harmonic mean of recall and precision:

$$F\_score = \frac{recall \times precision}{(recall + precision)/2}.$$

The harmonic mean discourages a system that sacrifices one measure for another too drastically.

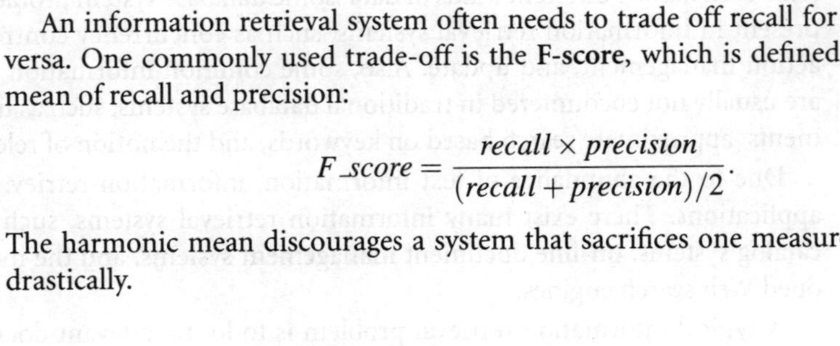

Figure 10.6 Relationship between the set of relevant documents and the set of retrieved documents.

Precision, recall, and F-score are the basic measures of a retrieved set of documents. These three measures are not directly useful for comparing two ranked lists of documents because they are not sensitive to the internal ranking of the documents in a retrieved set. In order to measure the quality of a ranked list of documents, it is common to compute an average of precisions at all the ranks where a new relevant document is returned. It is also common to plot a graph of precisions at many different levels of recall; a higher curve represents a better-quality information retrieval system. For more details about these measures, readers may consult an information retrieval textbook, such as [BYRN99].

Text Retrieval Methods

"What methods are there for information retrieval?" Broadly speaking, retrieval methods fall into two categories: They generally either view the retrieval problem as a *document selection problem* or as a *document ranking problem.*

In **document selection** methods, the query is regarded as specifying constraints for selecting relevant documents. A typical method of this category is the **Boolean retrieval model**, in which a document is represented by a set of keywords and a user provides a Boolean expression of keywords, such as *"car* **and** *repair shops," "tea* **or** *coffee,"* or *"database systems* **but not** *Oracle."* The retrieval system would take such a Boolean query and return documents that satisfy the Boolean expression. Because of the difficulty in prescribing a user's information need exactly with a Boolean query, the Boolean retrieval method generally only works well when the user knows a lot about the document collection and can formulate a good query in this way.

Document ranking methods use the query to rank all documents in the order of relevance. For ordinary users and exploratory queries, these methods are more appropriate than document selection methods. Most modern information retrieval systems present a ranked list of documents in response to a user's keyword query. There are many different ranking methods based on a large spectrum of mathematical foundations, including algebra, logic, probability, and statistics. The common intuition behind all of these methods is that we may match the keywords in a query with those in the documents and score each document based on how well it matches the query. The goal is to approximate the *degree of relevance* of a document with a score computed based on information such as the frequency of words in the document and the whole collection. Notice that it is inherently difficult to provide a precise measure of the degree of relevance between a set of keywords. For example, it is difficult to quantify the distance between *data mining* and *data analysis.* Comprehensive empirical evaluation is thus essential for validating any retrieval method.

A detailed discussion of all of these retrieval methods is clearly out of the scope of this book. Following we briefly discuss the most popular approach—the *vector space model.* For other models, readers may refer to information retrieval textbooks, as referenced in the bibliographic notes. Although we focus on the vector space model, some steps discussed are not specific to this particular approach.

The basic idea of the vector space model is the following: We represent a document and a query both as vectors in a high-dimensional space corresponding to all the keywords and use an appropriate similarity measure to compute the similarity between the query vector and the document vector. The similarity values can then be used for ranking documents.

"How do we tokenize text?" The first step in most retrieval systems is to identify keywords for representing documents, a preprocessing step often called **tokenization.** To avoid indexing useless words, a text retrieval system often associates a *stop list* with a set of documents. A **stop list** is a set of words that are deemed "irrelevant." For example, *a, the, of, for, with,* and so on are **stop words,** even though they may appear frequently. Stop lists may vary per document set. For example, *database systems* could be an important keyword in a newspaper. However, it may be considered as a stop word in a set of research papers presented in a database systems conference.

A group of different words may share the same **word stem.** A text retrieval system needs to identify groups of words where the words in a group are small syntactic variants of one another and collect only the common word stem per group. For example, the group of words *drug, drugged,* and *drugs,* share a common word stem, *drug,* and can be viewed as different occurrences of the same word.

"How can we model a document to facilitate information retrieval?" Starting with a set of d documents and a set of t terms, we can model each document as a vector v in the t dimensional space $\mathcal{R}^t$, which is why this method is called the **vector-space model.** Let the **term frequency** be the number of occurrences of term t in the document d, that is, $freq(d,t)$. The (weighted) **term-frequency matrix** $TF(d,t)$ measures the association of a term t with respect to the given document d: it is generally defined as 0 if the document does not contain the term, and nonzero otherwise. There are many ways to define the term-weighting for the nonzero entries in such a vector. For example, we can simply set $TF(d,t) = 1$ if the term t occurs in the document d, or use the term frequency $freq(d,t)$, or the **relative term frequency**, that is, the term frequency versus the total number of occurrences of all the terms in the document. There are also other ways to normalize the term frequency. For example, the Cornell SMART system uses the following formula to compute the (normalized) term frequency:

$$TF(d,t) = \begin{cases} 0 & \textit{if } freq(d,t) = 0 \\ 1 + \log(1 + \log(freq(d,t))) & \textit{otherwise.} \end{cases} \tag{10.3}$$

Besides the term frequency measure, there is another important measure, called **inverse document frequency (IDF),** that represents the scaling factor, or the importance, of a term t. If a term t occurs in many documents, its importance will be scaled down due to its reduced discriminative power. For example, the term *database systems* may likely be less important if it occurs in many research papers in a database system conference. According to the same Cornell SMART system, $IDF(t)$ is defined by the following formula:

$$IDF(t) = \log \frac{1 + |d|}{|d_t|}, \tag{10.4}$$

where d is the document collection, and d_t is the set of documents containing term t. If $|d_t| \ll |d|$, the term t will have a large IDF scaling factor and vice versa.

In a complete vector-space model, TF and IDF are combined together, which forms the **TF-IDF measure**:

$$TF\text{-}IDF(d,t) = TF(d,t) \times IDF(t). \tag{10.5}$$

Let us examine how to compute similarity among a set of documents based on the notions of term frequency and inverse document frequency.

Example 10.9 **Term frequency and inverse document frequency.** Table 10.5 shows a term frequency matrix where each row represents a document vector, each column represents a term, and each entry registers $freq(d_i,t_j)$, the number of occurrences of term t_j in document d_i. Based on this table we can calculate the TF-IDF value of a term in a document. For example, for t_6 in d_4, we have

$$TF(d_4,t_6) = 1+\log(1+\log(15)) = 1.3377$$

$$IDF(t_6) = \log\frac{1+5}{3} = 0.301.$$

■

Therefore,

$$TF\text{-}IDF(d_4,t_6) = 1.3377 \times 0.301 = 0.403$$

"How can we determine if two documents are similar?" Since similar documents are expected to have similar relative term frequencies, we can measure the similarity among a set of documents or between a document and a query (often defined as a set of keywords), based on similar relative term occurrences in the frequency table. Many metrics have been proposed for measuring document similarity based on relative term occurrences or document vectors. A representative metric is the **cosine measure**, defined as follows. Let v_1 and v_2 be two document vectors. Their cosine similarity is defined as

$$sim(v_1,v_2) = \frac{v_1 \cdot v_2}{|v_1||v_2|}, \tag{10.6}$$

where the inner product $v_1 \cdot v_2$ is the standard vector dot product, defined as $\Sigma_{i=1}^{t} v_{1i}v_{2i}$, and the norm $|v_1|$ in the denominator is defined as $|v_1| = \sqrt{v_1 \cdot v_1}$.

Table 10.5 A term frequency matrix showing the frequency of terms per document.

document/term	t_1	t_2	t_3	t_4	t_5	t_6	t_7
d_1	0	4	10	8	0	5	0
d_2	5	19	7	16	0	0	32
d_3	15	0	0	4	9	0	17
d_4	22	3	12	0	5	15	0
d_5	0	7	0	9	2	4	12

Text Indexing Techniques

There are several popular text retrieval indexing techniques, including *inverted indices* and *signature files.*

An **inverted index** is an index structure that maintains two hash indexed or B+-tree indexed tables: *document_table* and *term_table*, where

- *document_table* consists of a set of document records, each containing two fields: *doc_id* and *posting_list*, where *posting_list* is a list of terms (or pointers to terms) that occur in the document, sorted according to some relevance measure.
- *term_table* consists of a set of term records, each containing two fields: *term_id* and *posting_list*, where *posting_list* specifies a list of document identifiers in which the term appears.

With such organization, it is easy to answer queries like "*Find all of the documents associated with a given set of terms,*" or "*Find all of the terms associated with a given set of documents.*" For example, to find all of the documents associated with a set of terms, we can first find a list of document identifiers in *term_table* for each term, and then intersect them to obtain the set of relevant documents. Inverted indices are widely used in industry. They are easy to implement. The *posting_lists* could be rather long, making the storage requirement quite large. They are easy to implement, but are not satisfactory at handling *synonymy* (where two very different words can have the same meaning) and *polysemy* (where an individual word may have many meanings).

A **signature file** is a file that stores a *signature* record for each document in the database. Each signature has a fixed size of b bits representing terms. A simple encoding scheme goes as follows. Each bit of a document signature is initialized to 0. A bit is set to 1 if the term it represents appears in the document. A signature S_1 matches another signature S_2 if each bit that is set in signature S_2 is also set in S_1. Since there are usually more terms than available bits, multiple terms may be mapped into the same bit. Such multiple-to-one mappings make the search expensive because a document that matches the signature of a query does not necessarily contain the set of keywords of the query. The document has to be retrieved, parsed, stemmed, and checked. Improvements can be made by first performing frequency analysis, stemming, and by filtering stop words, and then using a hashing technique and superimposed coding technique to encode the list of terms into bit representation. Nevertheless, the problem of multiple-to-one mappings still exists, which is the major disadvantage of this approach.

Readers can refer to [WMB99] for more detailed discussion of indexing techniques, including how to compress an index.

Query Processing Techniques

Once an inverted index is created for a document collection, a retrieval system can answer a keyword query quickly by looking up which documents contain the query keywords. Specifically, we will maintain a score accumulator for each document and update these accumulators as we go through each query term. For each query term, we will fetch all of the documents that match the term and increase their scores. More sophisticated query processing techniques are discussed in [WMB99].

When examples of relevant documents are available, the system can learn from such examples to improve retrieval performance. This is called *relevance feedback* and has proven to be effective in improving retrieval performance. When we do not have such relevant examples, a system can *assume* the top few retrieved documents in some initial retrieval results to be relevant and extract more related keywords to expand a query. Such feedback is called *pseudo-feedback* or *blind feedback* and is essentially a process of mining useful keywords from the top retrieved documents. Pseudo-feedback also often leads to improved retrieval performance.

One major limitation of many existing retrieval methods is that they are based on exact keyword matching. However, due to the complexity of natural languages, keyword-based retrieval can encounter two major difficulties. The first is the **synonymy problem**: two words with identical or similar meanings may have very different surface forms. For example, a user's query may use the word "automobile," but a relevant document may use "vehicle" instead of "automobile." The second is the **polysemy problem**: the same keyword, such as *mining*, or *Java*, may mean different things in different contexts.

We now discuss some advanced techniques that can help solve these problems as well as reduce the index size.

10.4.2 Dimensionality Reduction for Text

With the similarity metrics introduced in Section 10.4.1, we can construct similarity-based indices on text documents. Text-based queries can then be represented as vectors, which can be used to search for their nearest neighbors in a document collection. However, for any nontrivial document database, the number of terms T and the number of documents D are usually quite large. Such high dimensionality leads to the problem of inefficient computation, since the resulting frequency table will have size $T \times D$. Furthermore, the high dimensionality also leads to very sparse vectors and increases the difficulty in detecting and exploiting the relationships among terms (e.g., synonymy). To overcome these problems, dimensionality reduction techniques such as *latent semantic indexing*, *probabilistic latent semantic analysis*, and *locality preserving indexing* can be used.

We now briefly introduce these methods. To explain the basic idea beneath latent semantic indexing and locality preserving indexing, we need to use some matrix and vector notations. In the following part, we use $\mathbf{x}_1, \ldots, \mathbf{x}_{tn} \in \mathbb{R}^m$ to represent the n documents with m features (words). They can be represented as a term-document matrix $X = [\mathbf{x}_1, \mathbf{x}_2, \ldots, \mathbf{x}_n]$.

Latent Semantic Indexing

Latent semantic indexing (LSI) is one of the most popular algorithms for document dimensionality reduction. It is fundamentally based on SVD (singular value decomposition). Suppose the *rank* of the term-document X is r, then LSI decomposes X using SVD as follows:

$$X = U\Sigma V^T, \tag{10.7}$$

where $\Sigma = diag(\sigma_1, \ldots, \sigma_r)$ and $\sigma_1 \geq \sigma_2 \geq \cdots \geq \sigma_r$ are the singular values of X, $U = [\boldsymbol{a}_1, \ldots, \boldsymbol{a}_r]$ and $\boldsymbol{a}_i$ is called the *left singular vector*, and $V = [\boldsymbol{v}_1, \ldots, \boldsymbol{v}_r]$, and $\boldsymbol{v}_i$ is called the *right singular vector*. LSI uses the first k vectors in U as the transformation matrix to embed the original documents into a k-dimensional subspace. It can be easily checked that the column vectors of U are the eigenvectors of XX^T. The basic idea of LSI is to extract the most representative features, and at the same time the reconstruction error can be minimized. Let $\boldsymbol{a}$ be the transformation vector. The objective function of LSI can be stated as follows:

$$\boldsymbol{a}_{opt} = \arg\min_{\boldsymbol{a}} \|X - \boldsymbol{a}\boldsymbol{a}^T X\|^2 = \arg\max_{\boldsymbol{a}} \boldsymbol{a}^T XX^T \boldsymbol{a}, \tag{10.8}$$

with the constraint,

$$\boldsymbol{a}^T \boldsymbol{a} = 1. \tag{10.9}$$

Since XX^T is symmetric, the basis functions of LSI are orthogonal.

Locality Preserving Indexing

Different from LSI, which aims to extract the most representative features, Locality Preserving Indexing (LPI) aims to extract the most discriminative features. The basic idea of LPI is to preserve the locality information (i.e., if two documents are near each other in the original document space, LPI tries to keep these two documents close together in the reduced dimensionality space). Since the neighboring documents (data points in high-dimensional space) probably relate to the same topic, LPI is able to map the documents related to the same semantics as close to each other as possible.

Given the document set $\boldsymbol{x}_1, \ldots, \boldsymbol{x}_n \in \mathbb{R}^m$, LPI constructs a similarity matrix $S \in \mathbb{R}^{n\times n}$. The transformation vectors of LPI can be obtained by solving the following minimization problem:

$$\boldsymbol{a}_{opt} = \arg\min_{\boldsymbol{a}} \sum_{i,j} \left(\boldsymbol{a}^T \boldsymbol{x}_i - \boldsymbol{a}^T \boldsymbol{x}_j\right)^2 S_{ij} = \arg\min_{\boldsymbol{a}} \boldsymbol{a}^T XLX^T \boldsymbol{a}, \tag{10.10}$$

with the constraint,

$$\boldsymbol{a}^T XDX^T \boldsymbol{a} = 1, \tag{10.11}$$

where $L = D - S$ is the *Graph Laplacian* and $D_{ii} = \sum_j S_{ij}$. D_{ii} measures the local density around $\boldsymbol{x}_i$. LPI constructs the similarity matrix S as

$$S_{ij} = \begin{cases} \frac{\boldsymbol{x}_i^T \boldsymbol{x}_j}{\|\boldsymbol{x}_i^T \boldsymbol{x}_j\|}, & \text{if } \boldsymbol{x}_i \text{ is among the } p \text{ nearest neighbors of } \boldsymbol{x}_j \\ & \text{or } \boldsymbol{x}_j \text{ is among the } p \text{ nearest neighbors of } \boldsymbol{x}_i \\ 0, & \text{otherwise.} \end{cases} \tag{10.12}$$

Thus, the objective function in LPI incurs a heavy penalty if neighboring points $\boldsymbol{x}_i$ and $\boldsymbol{x}_j$ are mapped far apart. Therefore, minimizing it is an attempt to ensure that if $\boldsymbol{x}_i$ and $\boldsymbol{x}_j$ are "close" then y_i $(=\boldsymbol{a}^T\boldsymbol{x}_i)$ and y_j $(=\boldsymbol{a}^T\boldsymbol{x}_j)$ are close as well. Finally, the basis functions of LPI are the eigenvectors associated with the smallest eigenvalues of the following generalized eigen-problem:

$$XLX^T\boldsymbol{a} = \lambda XDX^T\boldsymbol{a}. \tag{10.13}$$

LSI aims to find the best subspace approximation to the original document space in the sense of minimizing the global reconstruction error. In other words, LSI seeks to uncover the most representative features. LPI aims to discover the local geometrical structure of the document space. Since the neighboring documents (data points in high-dimensional space) probably relate to the same topic, LPI can have more discriminating power than LSI. Theoretical analysis of LPI shows that LPI is an unsupervised approximation of the supervised Linear Discriminant Analysis (LDA). Therefore, for document clustering and document classification, we might expect LPI to have better performance than LSI. This was confirmed empirically.

Probabilistic Latent Semantic Indexing

The probabilistic latent semantic indexing (PLSI) method is similar to LSI, but achieves dimensionality reduction through a probabilistic mixture model. Specifically, we assume there are k latent common themes in the document collection, and each is characterized by a multinomial word distribution. A document is regarded as a sample of a mixture model with these theme models as components. We fit such a mixture model to all the documents, and the obtained k component multinomial models can be regarded as defining k new semantic dimensions. The mixing weights of a document can be used as a new representation of the document in the low latent semantic dimensions.

Formally, let $C = \{d_1, d_2, \ldots, d_n\}$ be a collection of n documents. Let $\theta_1, \ldots, \theta_k$ be k theme multinomial distributions. A word w in document d_i is regarded as a sample of the following mixture model.

$$p_{d_i}(w) = \sum_{j=1}^{k} [\pi_{d_i,j} p(w|\theta_j)] \tag{10.14}$$

where $\pi_{d_i,j}$ is a document-specific mixing weight for the j-th aspect theme, and $\sum_{j=1}^{k} \pi_{d_i,j} = 1$.

The log-likelihood of the collection C is

$$\log p(C|\Lambda) = \sum_{i=1}^{n} \sum_{w \in V} [c(w, d_i) \log(\sum_{j=1}^{k} (\pi_{d_i,j} p(w|\theta_j)))], \tag{10.15}$$

where V is the set of all the words (i.e., vocabulary), $c(w, d_i)$ is the count of word w in document d_i, and $\Lambda = (\{\theta_j, \{\pi_{d_i,j}\}_{i=1}^{n}\}_{j=1}^{k})$ is the set of all the theme model parameters.

The model can be estimated using the Expectation-Maximization (EM) algorithm (Chapter 7), which computes the following maximum likelihood estimate:

$$\hat{\Lambda} = argmax_{\Lambda} \log p(C|\Lambda). \tag{10.16}$$

Once the model is estimated, $\theta_1, \ldots, \theta_k$ define k new semantic dimensions and $\pi_{d_i,j}$ gives a representation of d_i in this low-dimension space.

10.4.3 Text Mining Approaches

There are many approaches to text mining, which can be classified from different perspectives, based on the inputs taken in the text mining system and the data mining tasks to be performed. In general, the major approaches, based on the kinds of data they take as input, are: (1) the **keyword-based approach**, where the input is a set of keywords or terms in the documents, (2) the **tagging approach**, where the input is a set of tags, and (3) the **information-extraction approach**, which inputs semantic information, such as events, facts, or entities uncovered by information extraction. A simple keyword-based approach may only discover relationships at a relatively shallow level, such as rediscovery of compound nouns (e.g., "database" and "systems") or co-occurring patterns with less significance (e.g., "terrorist" and "explosion"). It may not bring much deep understanding to the text. The tagging approach may rely on tags obtained by *manual tagging* (which is costly and is unfeasible for large collections of documents) or by some *automated categorization algorithm* (which may process a relatively small set of tags and require defining the categories beforehand). The information-extraction approach is more advanced and may lead to the discovery of some deep knowledge, but it requires semantic analysis of text by natural language understanding and machine learning methods. This is a challenging knowledge discovery task.

Various text mining tasks can be performed on the extracted keywords, tags, or semantic information. These include document clustering, classification, information extraction, association analysis, and trend analysis. We examine a few such tasks in the following discussion.

Keyword-Based Association Analysis

"What is keyword-based association analysis?" Such analysis collects sets of keywords or terms that occur frequently together and then finds the association or correlation relationships among them.

Like most of the analyses in text databases, association analysis first preprocesses the text data by parsing, stemming, removing stop words, and so on, and then evokes association mining algorithms. In a document database, each document can be viewed as a transaction, while a set of keywords in the document can be considered as a set of items in the transaction. That is, the database is in the format

$$\{document\_id, a\_set\_of\_keywords\}.$$

The problem of keyword association mining in document databases is thereby mapped to item association mining in transaction databases, where many interesting methods have been developed, as described in Chapter 5.

Notice that a set of frequently occurring consecutive or closely located keywords may form a *term* or a *phrase*. The association mining process can help detect **compound associations**, that is, domain-dependent terms or phrases, such as [Stanford, University] or [U.S., President, George W. Bush], or **noncompound associations**, such as [dollars, shares, exchange, total, commission, stake, securities]. Mining based on these associations is referred to as "*term-level* association mining" (as opposed to mining on individual words). Term recognition and term-level association mining enjoy two advantages in text analysis: (1) terms and phrases are automatically tagged so there is no need for human effort in tagging documents; and (2) the number of meaningless results is greatly reduced, as is the execution time of the mining algorithms.

With such term and phrase recognition, term-level mining can be evoked to find associations among a set of detected terms and keywords. Some users may like to find associations between pairs of keywords or terms from a given set of keywords or phrases, whereas others may wish to find the maximal set of terms occurring together. Therefore, based on user mining requirements, standard association mining or max-pattern mining algorithms may be evoked.

Document Classification Analysis

Automated document classification is an important text mining task because, with the existence of a tremendous number of on-line documents, it is tedious yet essential to be able to automatically organize such documents into classes to facilitate document retrieval and subsequent analysis. Document classification has been used in automated topic tagging (i.e., assigning labels to documents), topic directory construction, identification of the document writing styles (which may help narrow down the possible authors of anonymous documents), and classifying the purposes of hyperlinks associated with a set of documents.

"How can automated document classification be performed?" A general procedure is as follows: First, a set of preclassified documents is taken as the training set. The training set is then analyzed in order to derive a classification scheme. Such a classification scheme often needs to be refined with a testing process. The so-derived classification scheme can be used for classification of other on-line documents.

This process appears similar to the classification of relational data. However, there is a fundamental difference. Relational data are well structured: each tuple is defined by a set of attribute-value pairs. For example, in the tuple {*sunny*, *warm*, *dry*, *not_windy*, *play_tennis*}, the value "*sunny*" corresponds to the attribute *weather_outlook*, "*warm*" corresponds to the attribute *temperature*, and so on. The classification analysis decides which set of attribute-value pairs has the greatest discriminating power in determining whether a person is going to play tennis. On the other hand, document databases are not structured according to attribute-value pairs. That is, a set of keywords associated with a set of documents is not organized into a fixed set of attributes or dimensions. If we view each distinct keyword, term, or feature in the document as a dimension, there may be thousands of dimensions in a set of documents. Therefore, commonly used relational data-oriented classification methods, such as decision tree analysis, may not be effective for the classification of document databases.

Based on our study of a wide spectrum of classification methods in Chapter 6, here we examine a few typical classification methods that have been used successfully in text classification. These include nearest-neighbor classification, feature selection methods, Bayesian classification, support vector machines, and association-based classification.

According to the vector-space model, two documents are similar if they share similar document vectors. This model motivates the construction of the **k-nearest-neighbor classifier**, based on the intuition that similar documents are expected to be assigned the same class label. We can simply index all of the training documents, each associated with its corresponding class label. When a test document is submitted, we can treat it as a query to the IR system and retrieve from the training set k documents that are most similar to the query, where k is a tunable constant. The class label of the test document can be determined based on the class label distribution of its k nearest neighbors. Such class label distribution can also be refined, such as based on weighted counts instead of raw counts, or setting aside a portion of labeled documents for validation. By tuning k and incorporating the suggested refinements, this kind of classifier can achieve accuracy comparable with the best classifier. However, since the method needs nontrivial space to store (possibly redundant) training information and additional time for inverted index lookup, it has additional space and time overhead in comparison with other kinds of classifiers.

The vector-space model may assign large weight to rare items disregarding its class distribution characteristics. Such rare items may lead to ineffective classification. Let's examine an example in the TF-IDF measure computation. Suppose there are two terms t_1 and t_2 in two classes C_1 and C_2, each having 100 training documents. Term t_1 occurs in five documents in each class (i.e., 5% of the overall corpus), but t_2 occurs in 20 documents in class C_1 only (i.e., 10% of the overall corpus). Term t_1 will have a higher TF-IDF value because it is rarer, but it is obvious t_2 has stronger discriminative power in this case. A **feature selection**[2] process can be used to remove terms in the training documents that are statistically uncorrelated with the class labels. This will reduce the set of terms to be used in classification, thus improving both efficiency and accuracy.

After feature selection, which removes nonfeature terms, the resulting "cleansed" training documents can be used for effective classification. **Bayesian classification** is one of several popular techniques that can be used for effective document classification. Since document classification can be viewed as the calculation of the statistical distribution of documents in specific classes, a Bayesian classifier first trains the model by calculating a generative document distribution $P(d|c)$ to each class c of document d and then tests which class is most likely to generate the test document. Since both methods handle high-dimensional data sets, they can be used for effective document classification. Other classification methods have also been used in documentation classification. For example, if we represent classes by numbers and construct a direct mapping function from term space to the class variable, **support vector machines** can be used to perform effective classification since they work well in high-dimensional space. The *least-square linear regression method* is also used as a method for discriminative classification.

[2]Feature (or attribute) selection is described in Chapter 2.

Finally, we introduce **association-based classification**, which classifies documents based on a set of associated, frequently occurring text patterns. Notice that very frequent terms are likely poor discriminators. Thus only those terms that are not very frequent and that have good discriminative power will be used in document classification. Such an association-based classification method proceeds as follows: First, keywords and terms can be extracted by information retrieval and simple association analysis techniques. Second, concept hierarchies of keywords and terms can be obtained using available term classes, such as WordNet, or relying on expert knowledge, or some keyword classification systems. Documents in the training set can also be classified into class hierarchies. A term association mining method can then be applied to discover sets of associated terms that can be used to maximally distinguish one class of documents from others. This derives a set of association rules associated with each document class. Such classification rules can be ordered based on their discriminative power and occurrence frequency, and used to classify new documents. Such kind of association-based document classifier has been proven effective.

For Web document classification, the Web page linkage information can be used to further assist the identification of document classes. Web linkage analysis methods are discussed in Section 10.5.

Document Clustering Analysis

Document clustering is one of the most crucial techniques for organizing documents in an unsupervised manner. When documents are represented as term vectors, the clustering methods described in Chapter 7 can be applied. However, the document space is always of very high dimensionality, ranging from several hundreds to thousands. Due to the *curse of dimensionality*, it makes sense to first project the documents into a lower-dimensional subspace in which the semantic structure of the document space becomes clear. In the low-dimensional semantic space, the traditional clustering algorithms can then be applied. To this end, spectral clustering, mixture model clustering, clustering using Latent Semantic Indexing, and clustering using Locality Preserving Indexing are the most well-known techniques. We discuss each of these methods here.

The **spectral clustering method** first performs spectral embedding (dimensionality reduction) on the original data, and then applies the traditional clustering algorithm (e.g., k-means) on the reduced document space. Recently, work on spectral clustering shows its capability to handle highly nonlinear data (the data space has high curvature at every local area). Its strong connections to differential geometry make it capable of discovering the manifold structure of the document space. One major drawback of these spectral clustering algorithms might be that they use the nonlinear embedding (dimensionality reduction), which is only defined on "training" data. They have to use all of the data points to learn the embedding. When the data set is very large, it is computationally expensive to learn such an embedding. This restricts the application of spectral clustering on large data sets.

The **mixture model clustering method** models the text data with a mixture model, often involving multinomial component models. Clustering involves two steps: (1) estimating the model parameters based on the text data and any additional prior knowledge, and (2) inferring the clusters based on the estimated model parameters. Depending on how the mixture model is defined, these methods can cluster words and documents at the same time. Probabilistic Latent Semantic Analysis (PLSA) and Latent Dirichlet Allocation (LDA) are two examples of such techniques. One potential advantage of such clustering methods is that the clusters can be designed to facilitate comparative analysis of documents.

The **Latent Semantic Indexing** (**LSI**) and **Locality Preserving Indexing** (**LPI**) methods introduced in Section 10.4.2 are linear dimensionality reduction methods. We can acquire the transformation vectors (*embedding function*) in LSI and LPI. Such embedding functions are defined everywhere; thus, we can use part of the data to learn the embedding function and embed all of the data to low-dimensional space. With this trick, clustering using LSI and LPI can handle large document data corpus.

As discussed in the previous section, LSI aims to find the best subspace approximation to the original document space in the sense of minimizing the *global* reconstruction error. In other words, LSI seeks to uncover the most representative features rather than the most discriminative features for document representation. Therefore, LSI might not be optimal in discriminating documents with different semantics, which is the ultimate goal of clustering. LPI aims to discover the *local* geometrical structure and can have more discriminating power. Experiments show that for clustering, LPI as a dimensionality reduction method is more suitable than LSI. Compared with LSI and LPI, the PLSI method reveals the latent semantic dimensions in a more interpretable way and can easily be extended to incorporate any prior knowledge or preferences about clustering.

10.5 Mining the World Wide Web

The World Wide Web serves as a huge, widely distributed, global information service center for news, advertisements, consumer information, financial management, education, government, e-commerce, and many other information services. The Web also contains a rich and dynamic collection of hyperlink information and Web page access and usage information, providing rich sources for data mining. However, based on the following observations, the Web also poses great challenges for effective resource and knowledge discovery.

- *The Web seems to be too huge for effective data warehousing and data mining.* The size of the Web is in the order of hundreds of terabytes and is still growing rapidly. Many organizations and societies place most of their public-accessible information on the Web. It is barely possible to set up a data warehouse to replicate, store, or integrate all of the data on the Web.[3]

[3]There have been efforts to store or integrate all of the data on the Web. For example, a huge Internet archive can be accessed at *www.archive.org*.

- *The complexity of Web pages is far greater than that of any traditional text document collection.* Web pages lack a unifying structure. They contain far more authoring style and content variations than any set of books or other traditional text-based documents. The Web is considered a huge digital library; however, the tremendous number of documents in this library are not arranged according to any particular sorted order. There is no index by category, nor by title, author, cover page, table of contents, and so on. It can be very challenging to search for the information you desire in such a library!
- *The Web is a highly dynamic information source.* Not only does the Web grow rapidly, but its information is also constantly updated. News, stock markets, weather, sports, shopping, company advertisements, and numerous other Web pages are updated regularly on the Web. Linkage information and access records are also updated frequently.
- *The Web serves a broad diversity of user communities.* The Internet currently connects more than 100 million workstations, and its user community is still rapidly expanding. Users may have very different backgrounds, interests, and usage purposes. Most users may not have good knowledge of the structure of the information network and may not be aware of the heavy cost of a particular search. They can easily get lost by groping in the "darkness" of the network, or become bored by taking many access "hops" and waiting impatiently for a piece of information.
- *Only a small portion of the information on the Web is truly relevant or useful.* It is said that 99% of the Web information is useless to 99% of Web users. Although this may not seem obvious, it is true that a particular person is generally interested in only a tiny portion of the Web, while the rest of the Web contains information that is uninteresting to the user and may swamp desired search results. How can the portion of the Web that is truly relevant to your interest be determined? How can we find high-quality Web pages on a specified topic?

These challenges have promoted research into efficient and effective discovery and use of resources on the Internet.

There are many index-based **Web search engines**. These search the Web, index Web pages, and build and store huge keyword-based indices that help locate sets of Web pages containing certain keywords. With such search engines, an experienced user may be able to quickly locate documents by providing a set of tightly constrained keywords and phrases. However, a simple keyword-based search engine suffers from several deficiencies. First, a topic of any breadth can easily contain hundreds of thousands of documents. This can lead to a huge number of document entries returned by a search engine, many of which are only marginally relevant to the topic or may contain materials of poor quality. Second, many documents that are highly relevant to a topic may not contain keywords defining them. This is referred to as the *polysemy* problem, discussed in the previous section on text mining. For example, the keyword *Java* may refer to the Java programming language, or an island in Indonesia, or brewed coffee. As another example, a search based on the keyword *search engine* may not find even the most popular Web search engines like Google, Yahoo!, AltaVista, or America Online if these services do not claim to be search engines on their Web pages. This indicates that a simple keyword-based Web search engine is not sufficient for Web resource discovery.

"If a keyword-based Web search engine is not sufficient for Web resource discovery, how can we even think of doing Web mining?" Compared with keyword-based Web search, **Web mining** is a more challenging task that searches for Web structures, ranks the importance of Web contents, discovers the regularity and dynamics of Web contents, and mines Web access patterns. However, Web mining can be used to substantially enhance the power of a Web search engine since Web mining may identify authoritative Web pages, classify Web documents, and resolve many ambiguities and subtleties raised in keyword-based Web search. In general, Web mining tasks can be classified into three categories: *Web content mining, Web structure mining,* and *Web usage mining*. Alternatively, Web structures can be treated as a part of Web contents so that Web mining can instead be simply classified into *Web content mining* and *Web usage mining*.

In the following subsections, we discuss several important issues related to Web mining: *mining the Web page layout structure* (Section 10.5.1), *mining the Web's link structures* (Section 10.5.2), *mining multimedia data on the Web* (Section 10.5.3), *automatic classification of Web documents* (Section 10.5.4), and *Weblog mining* (Section 10.5.5).

10.5.1 Mining the Web Page Layout Structure

Compared with traditional plain text, a Web page has more structure. Web pages are also regarded as semi-structured data. The basic structure of a Web page is its DOM[4] (Document Object Model) structure. The **DOM structure** of a Web page is a tree structure, where every HTML tag in the page corresponds to a node in the DOM tree. The Web page can be segmented by some predefined structural tags. Useful tags include ⟨P⟩ (paragraph), ⟨TABLE⟩ (table), ⟨UL⟩ (list), ⟨H1⟩ ~ ⟨H6⟩ (heading), etc. Thus the DOM structure can be used to facilitate information extraction.

Unfortunately, due to the flexibility of HTML syntax, many Web pages do not obey the W3C HTML specifications, which may result in errors in the DOM tree structure. Moreover, the DOM tree was initially introduced for presentation in the browser rather than description of the semantic structure of the Web page. For example, even though two nodes in the DOM tree have the same parent, the two nodes might not be more semantically related to each other than to other nodes. Figure 10.7 shows an example page.[5] Figure 10.7(a) shows part of the HTML source (we only keep the backbone code), and Figure 10.7(b) shows the DOM tree of the page. Although we have surrounding description text for each image, the DOM tree structure fails to correctly identify the semantic relationships between different parts.

In the sense of human perception, people always view a Web page as different semantic objects rather than as a single object. Some research efforts show that users

[4] *www.w3c.org/DOM*

[5] *http://yahooligans.yahoo.com/content/ecards/content/ecards/category?c=133&g=16*

```
<tr>
<td><img src="t1.jpg"></td><td><img src="t2.jpg"></td>
<td><img src="t3.jpg"></td><td><img src="t4.jpg"></td>
</tr>
<tr>
<td>Timber Wolf</td><td>Giraffes</td>
<td>Elephant Sunrise</td><td>Prowling Fox</td>
</tr>
```

(a) Part of HTML source (only keep the backbone)

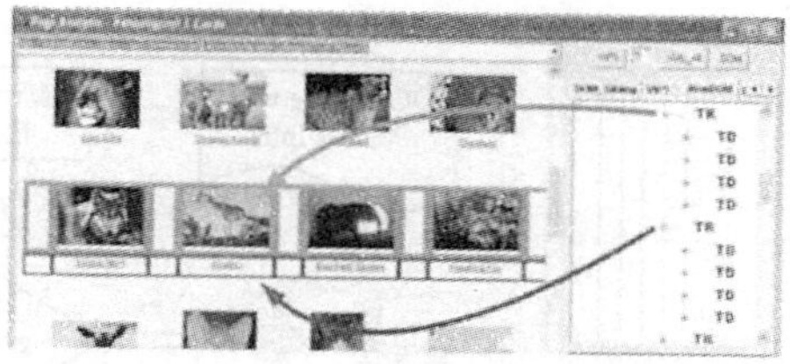

(b) The DOM tree structure (The picture area and caption area are two different TR nodes)

Figure 10.7 The HTML source and DOM tree structure of a sample page. It is difficult to extract the correct semantic content structure of the page.

always expect that certain functional parts of a Web page (e.g., navigational links or an advertisement bar) appear at certain positions on the page. Actually, when a Web page is presented to the user, the spatial and visual cues can help the user unconsciously divide the Web page into several semantic parts. Therefore, it is possible to automatically segment the Web pages by using the spatial and visual cues. Based on this observation, we can develop algorithms to extract the Web page content structure based on spatial and visual information.

Here, we introduce an algorithm called **VIsion-based Page Segmentation** (VIPS). VIPS aims to extract the semantic structure of a Web page based on its visual presentation. Such semantic structure is a tree structure: each node in the tree corresponds to a block. Each node will be assigned a value (Degree of Coherence) to indicate how coherent is the content in the block based on visual perception. The VIPS algorithm makes full use of the page layout feature. It first extracts all of the suitable blocks from the HTML DOM tree, and then it finds the separators between these blocks. Here separators denote the horizontal or vertical lines in a Web page that visually cross with no blocks. Based on these separators, the semantic tree of the Web page is constructed. A Web page can be represented as a set of blocks (leaf nodes of the semantic tree). Compared with DOM-based methods, the segments obtained by VIPS are more semantically aggregated. Noisy information, such as navigation, advertisement, and decoration can be easily removed because these elements are often placed in certain positions on a page. Contents with different topics are distinguished as separate blocks. Figure 10.8 illustrates the procedure of VIPS algorithm, and Figure 10.9 shows the partition result of the same page as in Figure 10.7.

10.5.2 Mining the Web's Link Structures to Identify Authoritative Web Pages

"What is meant by authoritative Web pages?" Suppose you would like to search for Web pages relating to a given topic, such as financial investing. In addition to retrieving pages that are relevant, you also hope that the pages retrieved will be of high quality, or *authoritative* on the topic.

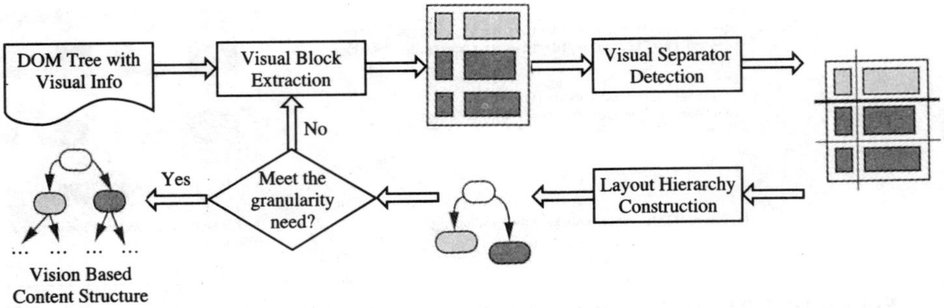

Figure 10.8 The process flow of vision-based page segmentation algorithm.

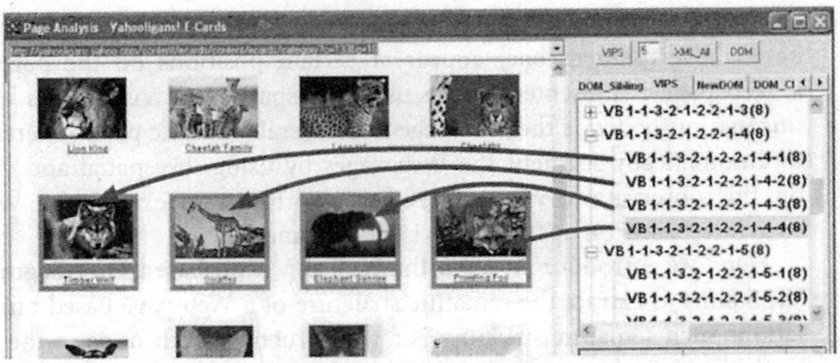

Figure 10.9 Partition using VIPS (The image with their surrounding text are accurately identified)

"But how can a search engine automatically identify authoritative Web pages for my topic?" Interestingly, the secrecy of authority is hiding in Web page linkages. The Web consists not only of pages, but also of *hyperlinks* pointing from one page to another. These hyperlinks contain an enormous amount of latent human annotation that can help automatically infer the notion of authority. When an author of a Web page creates a hyperlink pointing to another Web page, this can be considered as the author's endorsement of the other page. The collective endorsement of a given page by different authors on the Web may indicate the importance of the page and may naturally lead to the discovery of authoritative Web pages. Therefore, the tremendous amount of Web linkage information provides rich information about the relevance, the quality, and the structure of the Web's contents, and thus is a rich source for Web mining.

This idea has motivated some interesting studies on mining authoritative pages on the Web. In the 1970s, researchers in information retrieval proposed methods of using citations among journal articles to evaluate the quality of research papers. However, unlike journal citations, the Web linkage structure has some unique features. First, not every hyperlink represents the endorsement we seek. Some links are created for other purposes, such as for navigation or for paid advertisements. Yet overall, if the majority of hyperlinks are for endorsement, then the collective opinion will still dominate. Second, for commercial or competitive interests, one authority will seldom have its Web page point to its rival authorities in the same field. For example, *Coca-Cola* may prefer not to endorse its competitor *Pepsi* by not linking to *Pepsi*'s Web pages. Third, authoritative pages are seldom particularly descriptive. For example, the main Web page of Yahoo! may not contain the explicit self-description "*Web search engine.*"

These properties of Web link structures have led researchers to consider another important category of Web pages called a *hub*. A **hub** is one or a set of Web pages that provides collections of links to authorities. Hub pages may not be prominent, or there may exist few links pointing to them; however, they provide links to a collection of prominent sites on a common topic. Such pages could be lists of recommended links on individual home pages, such as recommended reference sites from a course home page, or professionally assembled resource lists on commercial sites. Hub pages play the role of implicitly conferring authorities on a focused topic. In general, a good hub is a page that points to many good authorities; a good authority is a page pointed to by many good hubs. Such a mutual reinforcement relationship between hubs and authorities helps the mining of authoritative Web pages and automated discovery of high-quality Web structures and resources.

"So, how can we use hub pages to find authoritative pages?" An algorithm using hubs, called **HITS** (Hyperlink-Induced Topic Search), was developed as follows. First, HITS uses the query terms to collect a starting set of, say, 200 pages from an index-based search engine. These pages form the **root set**. Since many of these pages are presumably relevant to the search topic, some of them should contain links to most of the prominent authorities. Therefore, the root set can be expanded into a **base set** by including all of the pages that the root-set pages link to and all of the pages that link to a page in the root set, up to a designated size cutoff such as 1,000 to 5,000 pages (to be included in the base set).

Second, a weight-propagation phase is initiated. This iterative process determines numerical estimates of hub and authority weights. Notice that links between two pages with the same Web domain (i.e., sharing the same first level in their URLs) often serve as a navigation function and thus do not confer authority. Such links are excluded from the weight-propagation analysis.

We first associate a non-negative **authority weight**, a_p, and a non-negative **hub weight**, h_p, with each page p in the base set, and initialize all a and h values to a uniform constant. The weights are normalized and an invariant is maintained that the squares of all weights sum to 1. The authority and hub weights are updated based on the following equations:

$$a_p = \Sigma_{(q \textit{ such that } q \rightarrow p)}\, h_q \tag{10.17}$$

$$h_p = \Sigma_{(q \textit{ such that } q \leftarrow p)}\, a_q \tag{10.18}$$

Equation (10.17) implies that if a page is pointed to by many good hubs, its authority weight should increase (i.e., it is the sum of the current hub weights of all of the pages pointing to it). Equation (10.18) implies that if a page is pointing to many good authorities, its hub weight should increase (i.e., it is the sum of the current authority weights of all of the pages it points to).

These equations can be written in matrix form as follows. Let us number the pages $\{1,2,\ldots,n\}$ and define their **adjacency matrix** A to be an $n \times n$ matrix where $A(i,j)$ is 1 if page i links to page j, or 0 otherwise. Similarly, we define the **authority weight vector** $\boldsymbol{a} = (a_1, a_2, \ldots, a_n)$, and the **hub weight vector** $\boldsymbol{h} = (h_1, h_2, \ldots, h_n)$. Thus, we have

$$\boldsymbol{h} = A \cdot \boldsymbol{a} \tag{10.19}$$

$$\boldsymbol{a} = A^T \cdot \boldsymbol{h}, \tag{10.20}$$

where A^T is the transposition of matrix A. Unfolding these two equations k times, we have

$$\boldsymbol{h} = A \cdot \boldsymbol{a} = AA^T\boldsymbol{h} = (AA^T)\boldsymbol{h} = (AA^T)^2\boldsymbol{h} = \cdots = (AA^T)^k\boldsymbol{h} \tag{10.21}$$

$$\boldsymbol{a} = A^T \cdot \boldsymbol{h} = A^T A\boldsymbol{a} = (A^T A)\boldsymbol{a} = (A^T A)^2\boldsymbol{a} = \cdots = (A^T A)^k\boldsymbol{a}. \tag{10.22}$$

According to linear algebra, these two sequences of iterations, when normalized, converge to the principal eigenvectors of AA^T and $A^T A$, respectively. This also proves that the authority and hub weights are intrinsic features of the linked pages collected and are not influenced by the initial weight settings.

Finally, the HITS algorithm outputs a short list of the pages with large hub weights, and the pages with large authority weights for the given search topic. Many experiments have shown that HITS provides surprisingly good search results for a wide range of queries.

Although relying extensively on links can lead to encouraging results, the method may encounter some difficulties by ignoring textual contexts. For example, HITS sometimes drifts when hubs contain multiple topics. It may also cause "topic hijacking" when many pages from a single website point to the same single popular site, giving the site too large a share of the authority weight. Such problems can be overcome by replacing the sums of Equations (10.17) and (10.18) with weighted sums, scaling down the weights of multiple links from within the same site, using *anchor text* (the text surrounding hyperlink definitions in Web pages) to adjust the weight of the links along which authority is propagated, and breaking large hub pages into smaller units.

Google's PageRank algorithm is based on a similar principle. By analyzing Web links and textual context information, it has been reported that such systems can achieve better-quality search results than those generated by term-index engines like AltaVista and those created by human ontologists such as at Yahoo!.

The above link analysis algorithms are based on the following two assumptions. First, links convey human endorsement. That is, if there exists a link from page A to page B and these two pages are authored by different people, then the link implies that the author of page A found page B valuable. Thus the importance of a page can be propagated to those pages it links to. Second, pages that are co-cited by a certain page are likely related to the same topic. However, these two assumptions may not hold in many cases. A typical example is the Web page at *http://news.yahoo.com* (Figure 10.10), which contains multiple semantics (marked with rectangles with different colors) and many links only for navigation and advertisement (the left region). In this case, the importance of each page may be miscalculated by PageRank, and *topic drift* may occur in HITS when the popular

Figure 10.10 Part of a sample Web page (*news.yahoo.com*). Clearly, this page is made up of different semantic blocks (with different color rectangles). Different blocks have different importances in the page. The links in different blocks point to the pages with different topics.

sites such as Web search engines are so close to any topic, and thus are ranked at the top regardless of the topics.

These two problems are caused by the fact that a single Web page often contains multiple semantics, and the different parts of the Web page have different importance in that page. Thus, from the perspective of semantics, a Web page should not be the smallest unit. The hyperlinks contained in different semantic blocks usually point to the pages of different topics. Naturally, it is more reasonable to regard the semantic blocks as the smallest units of information.

By using the VIPS algorithm introduced in Section 10.5.1, we can extract *page-to-block* and *block-to-page* relationships and then construct a page graph and a block graph. Based on this graph model, the new link analysis algorithms are capable of discovering the intrinsic semantic structure of the Web. The above two assumptions become reasonable in block-level link analysis algorithms. Thus, the new algorithms can improve the performance of search in Web context.

The graph model in **block-level link analysis** is induced from two kinds of relationships, that is, *block-to-page* (link structure) and *page-to-block* (page layout).

The **block-to-page relationship** is obtained from link analysis. Because a Web page generally contains several semantic blocks, different blocks are related to different topics. Therefore, it might be more reasonable to consider the hyperlinks from block to page, rather than from page to page. Let Z denote the block-to-page matrix with dimension $n \times k$. Z can be formally defined as follows:

$$Z_{ij} = \begin{cases} 1/s_i, & \text{if there is a link from block } i \text{ to page } j \\ 0, & \text{otherwise,} \end{cases} \tag{10.23}$$

where s_i is the number of pages to which block i links. Z_{ij} can also be viewed as a probability of jumping from block i to page j. The block-to-page relationship gives a more accurate and robust representation of the link structures of the Web.

The **page-to-block relationships** are obtained from page layout analysis. Let X denote the page-to-block matrix with dimension $k \times n$. As we have described, each Web page can be segmented into blocks. Thus, X can be naturally defined as follows:

$$X_{ij} = \begin{cases} f_{p_i}(b_j), & \text{if } b_j \in p_i \\ 0, & \text{otherwise,} \end{cases} \tag{10.24}$$

where f is a function that assigns to every block b in page p an importance value. Specifically, the bigger $f_p(b)$ is, the more important the block b is. Function f is empirically defined below,

$$f_p(b) = \alpha \times \frac{\text{the size of block } b}{\text{the distance between the center of } b \text{ and the center of the screen}}, \tag{10.25}$$

where α is a normalization factor to make the sum of $f_p(b)$ to be 1, that is,

$$\sum_{b \in p} f_p(b) = 1$$

Note that $f_p(b)$ can also be viewed as a probability that the user is focused on the block b when viewing the page p. Some more sophisticated definitions of f can be formulated by considering the background color, fonts, and so on. Also, f can be learned from some prelabeled data (the importance value of the blocks can be defined by people) as a regression problem by using learning algorithms, such as support vector machines and neural networks.

Based on the *block-to-page* and *page-to-block* relations, a new Web page graph that incorporates the block importance information can be defined as

$$W_{\mathcal{P}} = XZ, \tag{10.26}$$

where X is a $k \times n$ page-to-block matrix, and Z is a $n \times k$ block-to-page matrix. Thus $W_{\mathcal{P}}$ is a $k \times k$ page-to-page matrix.

The block-level PageRank can be calculated on the new Web page graph. Experiments have shown the powerfulness of block-level link analysis.

10.5.3 Mining Multimedia Data on the Web

A huge amount of multimedia data are available on the Web in different forms. These include video, audio, images, pictures, and graphs. There is an increasing demand for effective methods for organizing and retrieving such multimedia data.

Compared with the general-purpose multimedia data mining, the multimedia data on the Web bear many different properties. Web-based multimedia data are embedded on the Web page and are associated with text and link information. These texts and links can also be regarded as features of the multimedia data. Using some Web page layout mining techniques (like VIPS), a Web page can be partitioned into a set of *semantic blocks*. Thus, the block that contains multimedia data can be regarded as a whole. Searching and organizing the Web multimedia data can be referred to as searching and organizing the multimedia blocks.

Let's consider Web images as an example. Figures 10.7 and 10.9 already show that VIPS can help identify the surrounding text for Web images. Such surrounding text provides a textual description of Web images and can be used to build an image index. The Web image search problem can then be partially completed using traditional text search techniques. Many commercial Web image search engines, such as Google and Yahoo!, use such approaches.

The block-level link analysis technique described in Section 10.5.2 can be used to organize Web images. In particular, the image graph deduced from block-level link analysis can be used to achieve high-quality Web image clustering results.

To construct a Web-image graph, in addition to the *block-to-page* and *page-to-block* relations, we need to consider a new relation: **block-to-image relation**. Let Y denote the block-to-image matrix with dimension $n \times m$. For each image, at least one block contains this image. Thus, Y can be simply defined below:

$$Y_{ij} = \begin{cases} 1/s_i, & \text{if } I_j \in b_i \\ 0, & \text{otherwise,} \end{cases} \tag{10.27}$$

where s_i is the number of images contained in the image block b_i.

Now we first construct the block graph from which the image graph can be further induced. In block-level link analysis, the block graph is defined as:

$$W_{\mathcal{B}} = (1-t)ZX + tD^{-1}U, \tag{10.28}$$

where t is a suitable constant. D is a diagonal matrix, $D_{ii} = \sum_j U_{ij}$. U_{ij} is 0 if block i and block j are contained in two different Web pages; otherwise, it is set to the *DOC* (*degree of coherence*, a property of the block, which is the result of the VIPS algorithm) value of the smallest block containing both block i and block j. It is easy to check that the sum of each row of $D^{-1}U$ is 1. Thus, $W_{\mathcal{B}}$ can be viewed as a probability transition matrix such that $W_{\mathcal{B}}(a,b)$ is the probability of jumping from block a to block b.

Once the block graph is obtained, the image graph can be constructed correspondingly by noticing the fact that every image is contained in at least one block. In this way, the weight matrix of the image graph can be naturally defined as follows:

$$W_{\mathcal{I}} = Y^T W_{\mathcal{B}} Y, \tag{10.29}$$

where $W_{\mathcal{I}}$ is an $m \times m$ matrix. If two images i and j are in the same block, say b, then $W_{\mathcal{I}}(i,j) = W_{\mathcal{B}}(b,b) = 0$. However, the images in the same block are supposed to be semantically related. Thus, we get a new definition as follows:

$$W_{\mathcal{I}} = tD^{-1}Y^T Y + (1-t)Y^T W_{\mathcal{B}} Y, \tag{10.30}$$

where t is a suitable constant, and D is a diagonal matrix, $D_{ii} = \sum_j (Y^T Y)_{ij}$.

Such an image graph can better reflect the semantic relationships between the images. With this image graph, clustering and embedding can be naturally acquired. Figure 10.11(a) shows the embedding results of 1,710 images from the Yahooligans website.[6] Each data point represents an image. Each color stands for a semantic class. Clearly, the image data set was accurately clustered into six categories. Some example images of these six categories (i.e., mammal, fish, reptile, bird, amphibian, and insect) are shown in Figure 10.12.

If we use traditional link analysis methods that consider hyperlinks from page to page, the 2-D embedding result is shown in Figure 10.11(b). As can be seen, the six categories were mixed together and can hardly be separated. This comparison shows that the image graph model deduced from block-level link analysis is more powerful than traditional methods as to describing the intrinsic semantic relationships between WWW images.

10.5.4 Automatic Classification of Web Documents

In the automatic classification of Web documents, each document is assigned a class label from a set of predefined topic categories, based on a set of examples of preclassified documents. For example, Yahoo!'s taxonomy and its associated documents can be used as training and test sets in order to derive a Web document classification scheme. This scheme may then be used to classify new Web documents by assigning categories from the same taxonomy.

Keyword-based document classification methods were discussed in Section 10.4.3, as well as keyword-based association analysis. These methods can be used for Web document classification. Such a term-based classification scheme has shown good results

[6] *www.yahooligans.com/content/animals*

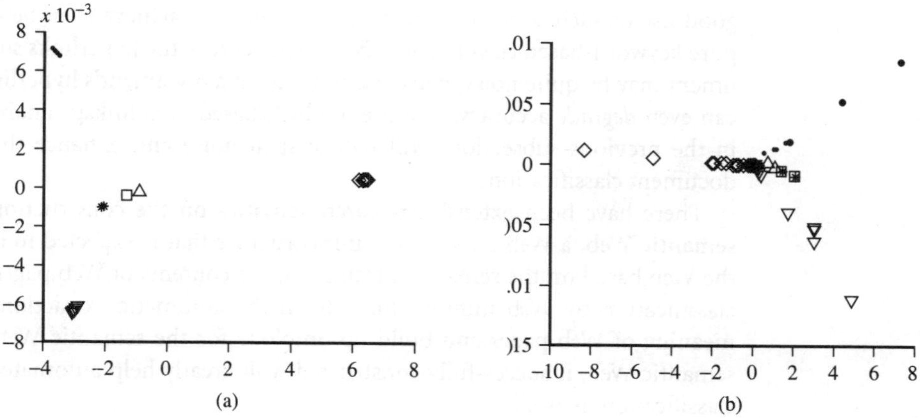

Figure 10.11 2-D embedding of the WWW images. (a) The image graph is constructed using block-level link analysis. Each color (shape) represents a semantic category. Clearly, they are well separated. (b) The image graph was constructed based on traditional perspective that the hyperlinks are considered from pages to pages. The image graph was induced from the page-to-page and page-to-image relationships.

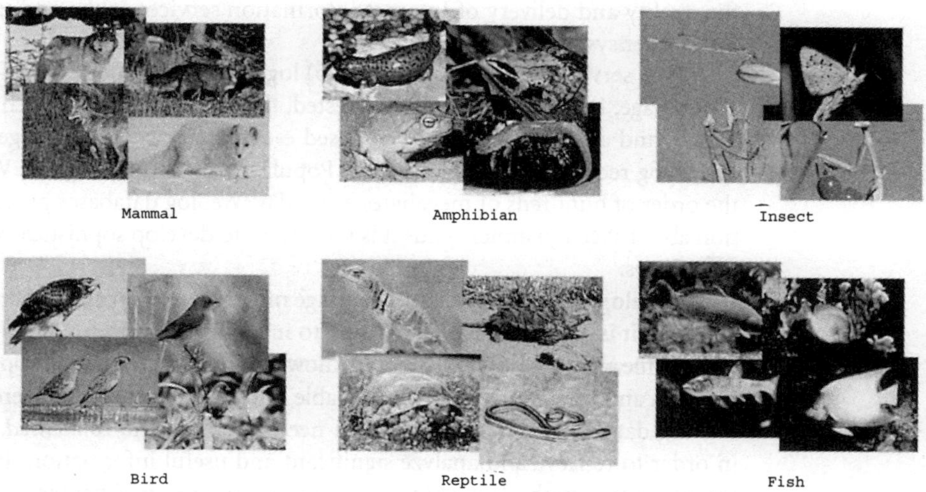

Figure 10.12 Six image categories.

in Web page classification. However, because a Web page may contain multiple themes, advertisement, and navigation information, *block-based page content analysis* may play an important role in construction of high-quality classification models. Moreover, because hyperlinks contain high-quality semantic clues to a page's topic, it is beneficial to make good use of such semantic information in order to achieve even better accuracy than pure keyword-based classification. Note that because the hyperlinks surrounding a document may be quite noisy, naïve use of terms in a document's hyperlink neighborhood can even *degrade* accuracy. The use of block-based Web linkage analysis as introduced in the previous subsections will reduce such noise and enhance the quality of Web document classification.

There have been extensive research activities on the construction and use of **the semantic Web**, a Web information infrastructure that is expected to bring structure to the Web based on the semantic meaning of the contents of Web pages. Web document classification by Web mining will help in the automatic extraction of the semantic meaning of Web pages and build up ontology for the semantic Web. Conversely, the semantic Web, if successfully constructed, will greatly help automated Web document classification as well.

10.5.5 Web Usage Mining

"*What is Web usage mining?*" Besides mining Web contents and Web linkage structures, another important task for Web mining is **Web usage mining**, which mines Weblog records to discover user access patterns of Web pages. Analyzing and exploring regularities in Weblog records can identify potential customers for electronic commerce, enhance the quality and delivery of Internet information services to the end user, and improve Web server system performance.

A Web server usually registers a (Web) log entry, or **Weblog entry**, for every access of a Web page. It includes the URL requested, the IP address from which the request originated, and a timestamp. For Web-based e-commerce servers, a huge number of Web access log records are being collected. Popular websites may register Weblog records in the order of hundreds of megabytes every day. Weblog databases provide rich information about Web dynamics. Thus it is important to develop sophisticated Weblog mining techniques.

In developing techniques for Web usage mining, we may consider the following. First, although it is encouraging and exciting to imagine the various potential applications of Weblog file analysis, it is important to know that the success of such applications depends on what and how much valid and reliable knowledge can be discovered from the large raw log data. Often, raw Weblog data need to be *cleaned, condensed, and transformed* in order to retrieve and analyze significant and useful information. In principle, these preprocessing methods are similar to those discussed in Chapter 2, although Weblog customized preprocessing is often needed.

Second, with the available URL, time, IP address, and Web page content information, a multidimensional view can be constructed on the Weblog database, and *multidimensional OLAP analysis* can be performed to find the top N users, top N accessed Web pages, most frequently accessed time periods, and so on, which will help discover potential customers, users, markets, and others.

Third, *data mining* can be performed on Weblog records to find association patterns, sequential patterns, and trends of Web accessing. For Web access pattern mining, it is often necessary to take further measures to obtain additional information of user traversal to facilitate detailed Weblog analysis. Such additional information may include user-browsing sequences of the Web pages in the Web server buffer.

With the use of such Weblog files, studies have been conducted on analyzing system performance, improving system design by Web caching, Web page prefetching, and Web page swapping; understanding the nature of Web traffic; and understanding user reaction and motivation. For example, some studies have proposed *adaptive sites*: websites that improve themselves by learning from user access patterns. Weblog analysis may also help build customized Web services for individual users.

Because Weblog data provide information about what kind of users will access what kind of Web pages, Weblog information can be integrated with Web content and Web linkage structure mining to help Web page ranking, Web document classification, and the construction of a multilayered Web information base as well. A particularly interesting application of Web usage mining is to mine a user's interaction history and search context on the client side to extract useful information for improving the ranking accuracy for the given user. For example, if a user submits a keyword query "Java" to a search engine, and then selects "Java programming language" from the returned entries for viewing, the system can infer that the displayed snippet for this Web page is interesting to the user. It can then raise the rank of pages similar to "Java programming language" and avoid presenting distracting pages about "Java Island." Hence the quality of search is improved, because search is contextualized and personalized.

10.6 Summary

- Vast amounts of data are stored in various complex forms, such as structured or unstructured, hypertext, and multimedia. Thus, **mining complex types of data**, including *object data, spatial data, multimedia data, text data*, and *Web data*, has become an increasingly important task in data mining.

- Multidimensional analysis and data mining can be performed in **object-relational and object-oriented databases**, by (1) *class-based generalization of complex objects*, including set-valued, list-valued, and other sophisticated types of data, class/subclass hierarchies, and class composition hierarchies; (2) constructing *object data cubes*; and (3) performing *generalization-based mining*. A **plan database** can be mined by a generalization-based, divide-and-conquer approach in order to find interesting general patterns at different levels of abstraction.

- **Spatial data mining** is the discovery of interesting patterns from large geospatial databases. *Spatial data cubes* that contain spatial dimensions and measures can be constructed. *Spatial OLAP* can be implemented to facilitate *multidimensional spatial data analysis*. Spatial data mining includes *mining spatial association and co-location patterns, clustering, classification*, and *spatial trend and outlier analysis*.

- **Multimedia data mining** is the discovery of interesting patterns from multimedia databases that store and manage large collections of multimedia objects, including audio data, image data, video data, sequence data, and hypertext data containing text, text markups, and linkages. Issues in multimedia data mining include *content-based retrieval and similarity search*, and *generalization and multidimensional analysis.* Multimedia data cubes contain additional dimensions and measures for multimedia information. Other topics in multimedia mining include *classification and prediction analysis, mining associations*, and *audio and video data mining.*

- A substantial portion of the available information is stored in text or document databases that consist of large collections of documents, such as news articles, technical papers, books, digital libraries, e-mail messages, and Web pages. Text information retrieval and data mining has thus become increasingly important. *Precision, recall*, and *the F-score* are three based measures from Information Retrieval (IR). Various **text retrieval methods** have been developed. These typically either focus on *document selection* (where the query is regarded as providing constraints) or *document ranking* (where the query is used to rank documents in order of relevance). The *vector-space model* is a popular example of the latter kind. Latex Sementic Indexing (LSI), Locality Preserving Indexing (LPI), and Probabilistic LSI can be used for **text dimensionality reduction. Text mining** goes one step beyond keyword-based and similarity-based information retrieval and discovers knowledge from semistructured text data using methods such as *keyword-based association analysis, document classification*, and *document clustering.*

- The World Wide Web serves as a huge, widely distributed, global information service center for news, advertisements, consumer information, financial management, education, government, e-commerce, and many other services. It also contains a rich and dynamic collection of hyperlink information, and access and usage information, providing rich sources for data mining. **Web mining** includes mining *Web linkage structures, Web contents*, and *Web access patterns*. This involves mining the *Web page layout structure*, mining the *Web's link structures* to identify *authoritative Web pages*, mining *multimedia data* on the Web, *automatic classification of Web documents*, and *Web usage mining.*

Exercises

10.1 An *object cube* can be constructed by generalization of an object-oriented or object-relational database into relatively structured data before performing multidimensional analysis. Because a set of complex data objects or properties can be generalized in multiple directions and thus derive multiple generalized features, such generalization may lead to a high-dimensional, but rather sparse (generalized) "object cube." Discuss how to perform effective online analytical processing in such an object cube.

10.2 A *heterogeneous database system* consists of multiple database systems that are defined independently, but that need to exchange and transform information among themselves and answer local and global queries. Discuss how to process a descriptive mining query in such a system using a generalization-based approach.

10.3 A *plan database* consists of a set of action sequences, such as legs of connecting flights, which can be generalized to find generalized sequence plans. Similarly, a *structure database* may consists of a set of structures, such as trees or graphs, which may also be generalized to find generalized structures. Outline a scalable method that may effectively perform such generalized structure mining.

10.4 Suppose that a city transportation department would like to perform *data analysis on highway traffic* for the planning of highway construction based on the city traffic data collected at different hours every day.

(a) Design a spatial data warehouse that stores the highway traffic information so that people can easily see the average and peak time traffic flow by highway, by time of day, and by weekdays, and the traffic situation when a major accident occurs.

(b) What information can we mine from such a spatial data warehouse to help city planners?

(c) This data warehouse contains both spatial and temporal data. Propose one mining technique that can efficiently mine interesting patterns from such a spatiotemporal data warehouse.

10.5 *Spatial association mining* can be implemented in at least two ways: (1) dynamic computation of spatial association relationships among different spatial objects, based on the mining query, and (2) precomputation of spatial distances between spatial objects, where the association mining is based on such precomputed results. Discuss (1) how to implement each approach efficiently and (2) which approach is preferable under what situation.

10.6 Traffic situations are often auto-correlated: the congestion at one highway intersection may trigger the congestion in nearby highway segments after a short period of time. Suppose we are given highway traffic history data in Chicago, including road construction segment, traffic speed associated with highway segment, direction, time, and so on. Moreover, we are given weather conditions by weather bureau in Chicago. Design a data mining method to find high-quality *spatiotemporal association rules* that may guide us to predict what could be the expected traffic situation at a given highway location.

10.7 *Similarity search in multimedia* has been a major theme in developing multimedia data retrieval systems. However, many *multimedia data mining* methods are based on the analysis of isolated simple multimedia features, such as color, shape, description, keywords, and so on.

(a) Can you show that an integration of similarity-based search with data mining may bring important progress in multimedia data mining? You may take any one mining task as an example, such as multidimensional analysis, classification, association, or clustering.

(b) Outline an implementation technique that applies a similarity-based search method to enhance the quality of clustering in multimedia data.

10.8 It is challenging but important to *discover unusual events from video data* in real time or in a very short time frame. An example is the detection of an explosion near a bus stop or a car collision at a highway junction. Outline a *video data mining* method that can be used for this purpose.

10.9 *Precision* and *recall* are two essential quality measures of an information retrieval system.

(a) Explain why it is the usual practice to trade one measure for the other. Explain why the F-score is a good measure for this purpose.

(b) Illustrate the methods that may effectively improve the F-score in an information retrieval system.

10.10 *TF-IDF* has been used as an effective measure in document classification.

(a) Give one example to show that TF-IDF may not be always a good measure in document classification.

(b) Define another measure that may overcome this difficulty.

10.11 An *e-mail database* is a database that stores a large number of electronic mail (e-mail) messages. It can be viewed as a semistructured database consisting mainly of text data. Discuss the following.

(a) How can such an e-mail database be structured so as to facilitate multidimensional search, such as by sender, by receiver, by subject, and by time?

(b) What can be mined from such an e-mail database?

(c) Suppose you have roughly classified a set of your previous e-mail messages as *junk, unimportant, normal,* or *important.* Describe how a data mining system may take this as the training set to automatically classify new e-mail messages or unclassified ones.

10.12 Junk e-mail is one of the most annoying things in Web-based business or personal communications. Design an effective scheme (which may consist of a set of methods) that can be used to *filter out junk e-mails* effectively and discuss how such methods should be evolved along with time.

10.13 It is difficult to construct a global data warehouse for the World Wide Web due to its dynamic nature and the huge amounts of data stored in it. However, it is still interesting and useful to construct data warehouses for summarized, localized, multidimensional information on the Internet. Suppose that an Internet information service company would like to set up an Internet-based data warehouse to help tourists choose local hotels and restaurants.

(a) Can you design a Web-based tourist data warehouse that would facilitate such a service?

(b) Suppose each hotel and/or restaurant contains a Web page of its own. Discuss how to locate such Web pages and what methods should be used to extract information from these Web pages in order to populate your Web-based tourist data warehouse.

(c) Discuss how to implement a mining method that may provide additional associated information, such as *"90% of customers who stay at the Downtown Hilton dine at the Emperor Garden Restaurant at least twice,"* each time a search returns a new Web page.

10.14 Each scientific or engineering discipline has its own subject index classification standard that is often used for *classifying documents* in its discipline.

(a) Design a Web document classification method that can take such a subject index to classify a set of Web documents automatically.

(b) Discuss how to use Web linkage information to improve the quality of such classification.

(c) Discuss how to use Web usage information to improve the quality of such classification.

10.15 It is interesting to *cluster* a large set of Web pages based on their similarity.

(a) Discuss what should be the similarity measure in such cluster analysis.

(b) Discuss how the block-level analysis may influence the clustering results and how to develop an efficient algorithms based on this philosophy.

(c) Since different users may like to cluster a set of Web pages differently, discuss how a user may interact with a system to influence the final clustering results, and how such a mechanism can be developed systematically.

10.16 Weblog records provide rich *Web usage information* for data mining.

(a) Mining Weblog access sequences may help prefetch certain Web pages into a Web server buffer, such as those pages that are likely to be requested in the next several clicks. Design an efficient implementation method that may help mining such access sequences.

(b) Mining Weblog access records can help cluster users into separate groups to facilitate customized marketing. Discuss how to develop an efficient implementation method that may help user clustering.

Bibliographic Notes

Mining complex types of data has been a fast-developing, popular research field, with many research papers and tutorials appearing in conferences and journals on data mining and database systems. This chapter covers a few important themes, including multidimensional analysis and mining of complex data objects, spatial data mining, multimedia data mining, text mining, and Web mining.

Zaniolo, Ceri, Faloutsos, et al. [ZCF+97] present a systematic introduction of advanced database systems for handling complex types of data. For multidimensional analysis and mining of complex data objects, Han, Nishio, Kawano, and Wang [HNKW98] proposed a method for the design and construction of object cubes by multidimensional generalization and its use for mining complex types of data in object-oriented and object-relational databases. A method for the construction of multiple-layered databases by generalization-based data mining techniques for handling semantic heterogeneity was proposed by Han, Ng, Fu, and Dao [HNFD98]. Zaki, Lesh, and Ogihara worked out a system called PlanMine, which applies sequence mining for plan failures [ZLO98]. A generalization-based method for mining plan databases by divide-and-conquer was proposed by Han, Yang, and Kim [HYK99].

Geospatial database systems and spatial data mining have been studied extensively. Some introductory materials about spatial database can be found in Maguire, Goodchild, and Rhind [MGR92], Güting [Gue94], Egenhofer [Ege89], Shekhar, Chawla, Ravada, et al. [SCR+99], Rigaux, Scholl, and Voisard [RSV01], and Shekhar and Chawla [SC03]. For geospatial data mining, a comprehensive survey on spatial data mining methods can be found in Ester, Kriegel, and Sander [EKS97] and Shekhar and Chawla [SC03]. A collection of research contributions on geographic data mining and knowledge discovery are in Miller and Han [MH01b]. Lu, Han, and Ooi [LHO93] proposed a generalization-based spatial data mining method by attribute-oriented induction. Ng and Han [NH94] proposed performing descriptive spatial data analysis based on clustering results instead of on predefined concept hierarchies. Zhou, Truffet, and Han proposed efficient polygon amalgamation methods for on-line multidimensional spatial analysis and spatial data mining [ZTH99]. Stefanovic, Han, and Koperski [SHK00] studied the problems associated with the design and construction of spatial data cubes. Koperski and Han [KH95] proposed a progressive refinement method for mining spatial association rules. Knorr and Ng [KN96] presented a method for mining aggregate proximity relationships and commonalities in spatial databases. Spatial classification and trend analysis methods have been developed by Ester, Kriegel, Sander, and Xu [EKSX97] and Ester, Frommelt, Kriegel, and Sander [EFKS98]. A two-step method for classification of spatial data was proposed by Koperski, Han, and Stefanovic [KHS98].

Spatial clustering is a highly active area of recent research into geospatial data mining. For a detailed list of references on spatial clustering methods, please see the bibliographic notes of Chapter 7. A spatial data mining system prototype, GeoMiner, was developed by Han, Koperski, and Stefanovic [HKS97]. Methods for mining spatiotemporal patterns have been studied by Tsoukatos and Gunopulos [TG01], Hadjieleftheriou, Kollios, Gunopulos, and Tsotras [HKGT03], and Mamoulis, Cao, Kollios, Hadjieleftheriou, et al. [MCK+04]. Mining spatiotemporal information related to moving objects have been studied by Vlachos, Gunopulos, and Kollios [VGK02] and Tao, Faloutsos, Papadias, and Liu [TFPL04]. A bibliography of temporal, spatial, and spatiotemporal data mining research was compiled by Roddick, Hornsby, and Spiliopoulou [RHS01].

Multimedia data mining has deep roots in image processing and pattern recognition, which has been studied extensively in computer science, with many textbooks published, such as Gonzalez and Woods [GW02], Russ [Rus02], and Duda, Hart, and Stork [DHS01]. The theory and practice of multimedia database systems have been introduced in many textbooks and surveys, including Subramanian [Sub98], Yu and Meng [YM97], Perner [Per02], and Mitra and Acharya [MA03]. The IBM QBIC

(Query by Image and Video Content) system was introduced by Flickner, Sawhney, Niblack, Ashley, et al. [FSN+95]. Faloutsos and Lin [FL95] developed a fast algorithm, FastMap, for indexing, data mining, and visualization of traditional and multimedia datasets. Natsev, Rastogi, and Shim [NRS99] developed WALRUS, a similarity retrieval algorithm for image databases that explores wavelet-based signatures with region-based granularity. Fayyad and Smyth [FS93] developed a classification method to analyze high-resolution radar images for identification of volcanoes on Venus. Fayyad, Djorgovski, and Weir [FDW96] applied decision tree methods to the classification of galaxies, stars, and other stellar objects in the Palomar Observatory Sky Survey (POSS-II) project. Stolorz and Dean [SD96] developed Quakefinder, a data mining system for detecting earthquakes from remote sensing imagery. Zaïane, Han, and Zhu [ZHZ00] proposed a progressive deepening method for mining object and feature associations in large multimedia databases. A multimedia data mining system prototype, MultiMediaMiner, was developed by Zaïane, Han, Li, et al. [ZHL+98] as an extension of the DBMiner system proposed by Han, Fu, Wang, et al. [HFW+96]. An overview of image mining methods is performed by Hsu, Lee, and Zhang [HLZ02].

Text data analysis has been studied extensively in information retrieval, with many good textbooks and survey articles, such as Salton and McGill [SM83], Faloutsos [Fal85], Salton [Sal89], van Rijsbergen [vR90], Yu and Meng [YM97], Raghavan [Rag97], Subramanian [Sub98], Baeza-Yates and Riberio-Neto [BYRN99], Kleinberg and Tomkins [KT99], Berry [Ber03], and Weiss, Indurkhya, Zhang, and Damerau [WIZD04]. The technical linkage between information filtering and information retrieval was addressed by Belkin and Croft [BC92]. The *latent semantic indexing* method for document similarity analysis was developed by Deerwester, Dumais, Furnas, et al. [DDF+90]. The *probabilistic latent semantic analysis* method was introduced to information retrieval by Hofmann [Hof98]. The *locality preserving indexing* method for document representation was developed by He, Cai, Liu, and Ma [HCLM04]. The use of signature files is described in Tsichritzis and Christodoulakis [TC83]. Feldman and Hirsh [FH98] studied methods for mining association rules in text databases. Method for automated document classification has been studied by many researchers, such as Wang, Zhou, and Liew [WZL99], Nigam, McCallum, Thrun, and Mitchell [NMTM00] and Joachims [Joa01]. An overview of text classification is given by Sebastiani [Seb02]. Document clustering by *Probabilistic Latent Semantic Analysis (PLSA)* was introduced by Hofmann [Hof98] and that using the *Latent Dirichlet Allocation (LDA)* method was proposed by Blei, Ng, and Jordan [BNJ03]. Zhai, Velivelli, and Yu [ZVY04] studied using such clustering methods to facilitate comparative analysis of documents. A comprehensive study of using dimensionality reduction methods for document clustering can be found in Cai, He, and Han [CHH05].

Web mining started in recent years together with the development of Web search engines and Web information service systems. There has been a great deal of work on Web data modeling and Web query systems, such as W3QS by Konopnicki and Shmueli [KS95], WebSQL by Mendelzon, Mihaila, and Milo [MMM97], Lorel by Abitboul, Quass, McHugh, et al. [AQM+97], Weblog by Lakshmanan, Sadri, and Subramanian [LSS96], WebOQL by Arocena and Mendelzon [AM98], and NiagraCQ by

Chen, DeWitt, Tian, and Wang [CDTW00]. Florescu, Levy, and Mendelzon [FLM98] presented a comprehensive overview of research on Web databases. An introduction to the the semantic Web was presented by Berners-Lee, Hendler, and Lassila [BLHL01].

Chakrabarti [Cha02] presented a comprehensive coverage of data mining for hypertext and the Web. Mining the Web's link structures to recognize authoritative Web pages was introduced by Chakrabarti, Dom, Kumar, et al. [CDK+99] and Kleinberg and Tomkins [KT99]. The HITS algorithm was developed by Kleinberg [Kle99]. The PageRank algorithm was developed by Brin and Page [BP98b]. Embley, Jiang, and Ng [EJN99] developed some heuristic rules based on the DOM structure to discover record boundaries within a page, which assist data extraction from the Web page. Wong and Fu [WF00] defined tag types for page segmentation and gave a label to each part of the Web page for assisting classification. Chakrabarti et al. [Cha01, CJT01] addressed the fine-grained topic distillation and disaggregated hubs into regions by analyzing DOM structure as well as intrapage text distribution. Lin and Ho [LH02] considered ⟨TABLE⟩ tag and its offspring as a content block and used an entropy-based approach to discover informative ones. Bar-Yossef and Rajagopalan [BYR02] proposed the template detection problem and presented an algorithm based on the DOM structure and the link information. Cai et al. [CYWM03, CHWM04] proposed the Vision-based Page Segmentation algorithm and developed the block-level link analysis techniques. They have also successfully applied the block-level link analysis on Web search [CYWM04] and Web image organizing and mining [CHM+04, CHL+04].

Web page classification was studied by Chakrabarti, Dom, and Indyk [CDI98] and Wang, Zhou, and Liew [WZL99]. A multilayer database approach for constructing a Web warehouse was studied by Zaïane and Han [ZH95]. Web usage mining has been promoted and implemented by many industry firms. Automatic construction of adaptive websites based on learning from Weblog user access patterns was proposed by Perkowitz and Etzioni [PE99]. The use of Weblog access patterns for exploring Web usability was studied by Tauscher and Greenberg [TG97]. A research prototype system, WebLogMiner, was reported by Zaïane, Xin, and Han [ZXH98]. Srivastava, Cooley, Deshpande, and Tan [SCDT00] presented a survey of Web usage mining and its applications. Shen, Tan, and Zhai used Weblog search history to facilitate context-sensitive information retrieval and personalized Web search [STZ05].

11 Applications and Trends in Data Mining

As a young research field, data mining has made broad and significant progress since its early beginnings in the 1980s. Today, data mining is used in a vast array of areas, and numerous commercial data mining systems are available. Many challenges, however, still remain. In this final chapter, we study applications and trends in data mining. We begin by viewing data mining applications in business and in science. We then provide tips on what to consider when purchasing a data mining software system. Additional themes in data mining are described, such as theoretical foundations of data mining, statistical techniques for data mining, visual and audio mining, and collaborative recommender systems that incorporate data mining techniques. The social impacts of data mining are discussed, including ubiquitous and invisible data mining and privacy issues. Finally, we examine current and expected data mining trends that arise in response to challenges in the field.

11.1 Data Mining Applications

In the previous chapters of this book, we have studied principles and methods for mining relational data, data warehouses, and complex types of data (including stream data, time-series and sequence data, complex structured data, spatiotemporal data, multimedia data, heterogeneous multidatabase data, text data, and Web data). Because data mining is a relatively young discipline with wide and diverse applications, there is still a nontrivial gap between general principles of data mining and application-specific, effective data mining tools. In this section, we examine a few application domains and discuss how customized data mining tools should be developed for such applications.

11.1.1 Data Mining for Financial Data Analysis

Most banks and financial institutions offer a wide variety of banking services (such as checking and savings accounts for business or individual customers), credit (such as business, mortgage, and automobile loans), and investment services (such as mutual funds). Some also offer insurance services and stock investment services.

Financial data collected in the banking and financial industry are often relatively complete, reliable, and of high quality, which facilitates systematic data analysis and data mining. Here we present a few typical cases:

- **Design and construction of data warehouses for multidimensional data analysis and data mining:** Like many other applications, data warehouses need to be constructed for banking and financial data. Multidimensional data analysis methods should be used to analyze the general properties of such data. For example, one may like to view the debt and revenue changes by month, by region, by sector, and by other factors, along with maximum, minimum, total, average, trend, and other statistical information. Data warehouses, data cubes, multifeature and discovery-driven data cubes, characterization and class comparisons, and outlier analysis all play important roles in financial data analysis and mining.
- **Loan payment prediction and customer credit policy analysis:** Loan payment prediction and customer credit analysis are critical to the business of a bank. Many factors can strongly or weakly influence loan payment performance and customer credit rating. Data mining methods, such as attribute selection and attribute relevance ranking, may help identify important factors and eliminate irrelevant ones. For example, factors related to the risk of loan payments include loan-to-value ratio, term of the loan, debt ratio (total amount of monthly debt versus the total monthly income), payment-to-income ratio, customer income level, education level, residence region, and credit history. Analysis of the customer payment history may find that, say, payment-to-income ratio is a dominant factor, while education level and debt ratio are not. The bank may then decide to adjust its loan-granting policy so as to grant loans to those customers whose applications were previously denied but whose profiles show relatively low risks according to the critical factor analysis.
- **Classification and clustering of customers for targeted marketing:** Classification and clustering methods can be used for customer group identification and targeted marketing. For example, we can use classification to identify the most crucial factors that may influence a customer's decision regarding banking. Customers with similar behaviors regarding loan payments may be identified by multidimensional clustering techniques. These can help identify customer groups, associate a new customer with an appropriate customer group, and facilitate targeted marketing.
- **Detection of money laundering and other financial crimes:** To detect money laundering and other financial crimes, it is important to integrate information from multiple databases (like bank transaction databases, and federal or state crime history databases), as long as they are potentially related to the study. Multiple data analysis tools can then be used to detect unusual patterns, such as large amounts of cash flow at certain periods, by certain groups of customers. Useful tools include data visualization tools (to display transaction activities using graphs by time and by groups of customers), linkage analysis tools (to identify links among different customers

and activities), classification tools (to filter unrelated attributes and rank the highly related ones), clustering tools (to group different cases), outlier analysis tools (to detect unusual amounts of fund transfers or other activities), and sequential pattern analysis tools (to characterize unusual access sequences). These tools may identify important relationships and patterns of activities and help investigators focus on suspicious cases for further detailed examination.

11.1.2 Data Mining for the Retail Industry

The retail industry is a major application area for data mining, since it collects huge amounts of data on sales, customer shopping history, goods transportation, consumption, and service. The quantity of data collected continues to expand rapidly, especially due to the increasing ease, availability, and popularity of business conducted on the Web, or **e-commerce**. Today, many stores also have websites where customers can make purchases on-line. Some businesses, such as Amazon.com (*www.amazon.com*), exist solely on-line, without any brick-and-mortar (i.e., physical) store locations. Retail data provide a rich source for data mining.

Retail data mining can help identify customer buying behaviors, discover customer shopping patterns and trends, improve the quality of customer service, achieve better customer retention and satisfaction, enhance goods consumption ratios, design more effective goods transportation and distribution policies, and reduce the cost of business.

A few examples of data mining in the retail industry are outlined as follows.

- **Design and construction of data warehouses based on the benefits of data mining:** Because retail data cover a wide spectrum (including sales, customers, employees, goods transportation, consumption, and services), there can be many ways to design a data warehouse for this industry. The levels of detail to include may also vary substantially. The outcome of preliminary data mining exercises can be used to help guide the design and development of data warehouse structures. This involves deciding which dimensions and levels to include and what preprocessing to perform in order to facilitate effective data mining.
- **Multidimensional analysis of sales, customers, products, time, and region:** The retail industry requires timely information regarding customer needs, product sales, trends, and fashions, as well as the quality, cost, profit, and service of commodities. It is therefore important to provide powerful multidimensional analysis and visualization tools, including the construction of sophisticated data cubes according to the needs of data analysis. The *multifeature data cube*, introduced in Chapter 4, is a useful data structure in retail data analysis because it facilitates analysis on aggregates with complex conditions.
- **Analysis of the effectiveness of sales campaigns:** The retail industry conducts sales campaigns using advertisements, coupons, and various kinds of discounts and bonuses to promote products and attract customers. Careful analysis of the effectiveness

of sales campaigns can help improve company profits. Multidimensional analysis can be used for this purpose by comparing the amount of sales and the number of transactions containing the sales items during the sales period versus those containing the same items before or after the sales campaign. Moreover, association analysis may disclose which items are likely to be purchased together with the items on sale, especially in comparison with the sales before or after the campaign.

- **Customer retention—analysis of customer loyalty:** With customer loyalty card information, one can register sequences of purchases of particular customers. Customer loyalty and purchase trends can be analyzed systematically. Goods purchased at different periods by the same customers can be grouped into sequences. Sequential pattern mining (Chapter 8) can then be used to investigate changes in customer consumption or loyalty and suggest adjustments on the pricing and variety of goods in order to help retain customers and attract new ones.
- **Product recommendation and cross-referencing of items:** By mining associations from sales records, one may discover that a customer who buys a digital camera is likely to buy another set of items. Such information can be used to form product recommendations. *Collaborative recommender systems* use data mining techniques to make personalized product recommendations during live customer transactions, based on the opinions of other customers (Section 11.3.4). Product recommendations can also be advertised on sales receipts, in weekly flyers, or on the Web to help improve customer service, aid customers in selecting items, and increase sales. Similarly, information such as "hot items this week" or attractive deals can be displayed together with the associative information in order to promote sales.

11.1.3 Data Mining for the Telecommunication Industry

The telecommunication industry has quickly evolved from offering local and long-distance telephone services to providing many other comprehensive communication services, including fax, pager, cellular phone, Internet messenger, images, e-mail, computer and Web data transmission, and other data traffic. The integration of telecommunication, computer network, Internet, and numerous other means of communication and computing is also underway. Moreover, with the deregulation of the telecommunication industry in many countries and the development of new computer and communication technologies, the telecommunication market is rapidly expanding and highly competitive. This creates a great demand for data mining in order to help understand the business involved, identify telecommunication patterns, catch fraudulent activities, make better use of resources, and improve the quality of service.

The following are a few scenarios for which data mining may improve telecommunication services:

- **Multidimensional analysis of telecommunication data:** Telecommunication data are intrinsically multidimensional, with dimensions such as calling-time, duration, location of caller, location of callee, and type of call. The multidimensional analysis of such data can be used to identify and compare the data traffic, system workload, resource usage, user group behavior, and profit. For example, analysts in the industry may wish to regularly view charts and graphs regarding calling source, destination, volume, and time-of-day usage patterns. Therefore, it is often useful to consolidate telecommunication data into large data warehouses and routinely perform multidimensional analysis using OLAP and visualization tools.

- **Fraudulent pattern analysis and the identification of unusual patterns:** Fraudulent activity costs the telecommunication industry millions of dollars per year. It is important to (1) identify potentially fraudulent users and their atypical usage patterns; (2) detect attempts to gain fraudulent entry to customer accounts; and (3) discover unusual patterns that may need special attention, such as busy-hour frustrated call attempts, switch and route congestion patterns, and periodic calls from automatic dial-out equipment (like fax machines) that have been improperly programmed. Many of these patterns can be discovered by multidimensional analysis, cluster analysis, and outlier analysis.
- **Multidimensional association and sequential pattern analysis:** The discovery of association and sequential patterns in multidimensional analysis can be used to promote telecommunication services. For example, suppose you would like to find usage patterns for a set of communication services by customer group, by month, and by time of day. The calling records may be grouped by customer in the following form:

  $$\langle customer\_ID, residence, office, time, date, service\_1, service\_2, \cdots \rangle$$

  A sequential pattern like "*If a customer in the Los Angeles area works in a city different from her residence, she is likely to first use long-distance service between two cities around 5 p.m. and then use a cellular phone for at least 30 minutes in the subsequent hour every weekday*" can be further probed by drilling up and down in order to determine whether it holds for particular pairs of cities and particular groups of persons (e.g., engineers, doctors). This can help promote the sales of specific long-distance and cellular phone combinations and improve the availability of particular services in the region.
- **Mobile telecommunication services:** Mobile telecommunication, Web and information services, and mobile computing are becoming increasingly integrated and common in our work and life. One important feature of mobile telecommunication data is its association with spatiotemporal information. Spatiotemporal data mining may become essential for finding certain patterns. For example, unusually busy mobile phone traffic at certain locations may indicate something abnormal happening in these locations. Moreover, ease of use is crucial for enticing customers to adopt new mobile services. Data mining will likely play a major role in the design of adaptive solutions enabling users to obtain useful information with relatively few keystrokes.
- **Use of visualization tools in telecommunication data analysis:** Tools for OLAP visualization, linkage visualization, association visualization, clustering, and outlier visualization have been shown to be very useful for telecommunication data analysis.

11.1.4 Data Mining for Biological Data Analysis

The past decade has seen an explosive growth in genomics, proteomics, functional genomics, and biomedical research. Examples range from the identification and comparative analysis of the genomes of human and other species (by discovering sequencing patterns, gene functions, and evolution paths) to the investigation of genetic networks and protein pathways, and the development of new pharmaceuticals and advances in cancer therapies. Biological data mining has become an essential part of a new research field called *bioinformatics*. Since the field of biological data mining is broad, rich, and dynamic, it is impossible to cover such an important and flourishing theme in one subsection. Here we outline only a few interesting topics in this field, with an emphasis on genomic and proteomic data analysis. A comprehensive introduction to biological data mining could fill several books. A good set of bioinformatics and biological data analysis books have already been published, and more are expected to come. References are provided in our bibliographic notes.

DNA sequences form the foundation of the genetic codes of all living organisms. All DNA sequences are comprised of four basic building blocks, called **nucleotides**: adenine (A), cytosine (C), guanine (G), and thymine (T). These four nucleotides (or bases) are combined to form long sequences or chains that resemble a twisted ladder. The DNA carry the information and biochemical machinery that can be copied from generation to generation. During the processes of "copying," *insertions*, *deletions*, or *mutations* (also called substitutions) of nucleotides are introduced into the DNA sequence, forming different evolution paths. A **gene** usually comprises hundreds of individual nucleotides arranged in a particular order. The nucleotides can be ordered and sequenced in an almost unlimited number of ways to form distinct genes. A **genome** is the complete set of genes of an organism. The human genome is estimated to contain around 20,000 to 25,000 genes. **Genomics** is the analysis of genome sequences.

Proteins are essential molecules for any organism. They perform life functions and make up the majority of cellular structures. The approximately 25,000 human genes give rise to about 1 million proteins through a series of translational modifications and gene splicing mechanisms. **Amino acids** (or *residues*) are the building blocks of proteins. There are 20 amino acids, denoted by 20 different letters of the alphabet. Each of the amino acids is coded for by one or more triplets of nucleotides making up DNA. The end of the chain is coded for by another set of triplets. Thus, a linear string or sequence of DNA is translated into a sequence of amino acids, forming a protein (Figure 11.1). A **proteome** is the complete set of protein molecules present in a cell, tissue, or organism. **Proteomics** is the study of proteome sequences. Proteomes are dynamic, changing from minute to minute in response to tens of thousands of intra- and extracellular environmental signals.

DNA sequence	...	*CTA*	*CAC*	*ACG*	*TGT*	*AAC*	...
amino acid sequence	...	L	H	T	C	N	...

Figure 11.1 A DNA sequence and corresponding amino acid sequence.

Chemical properties of the amino acids cause the protein chains to fold up into specific three-dimensional structures. This three-dimensional folding of the chain determines the biological function of a protein. Genes make up only about 2% of the human genome. The remainder consists of noncoding regions. Recent studies have found that a lot of noncoding DNA sequences may also have played crucial roles in protein generation and species evolution.

The identification of DNA or amino acid sequence patterns that play roles in various biological functions, genetic diseases, and evolution is challenging. This requires a great deal of research in computational algorithms, statistics, mathematical programming, data mining, machine learning, information retrieval, and other disciplines to develop effective genomic and proteomic data analysis tools.

Data mining may contribute to biological data analysis in the following aspects:

- **Semantic integration of heterogeneous, distributed genomic and proteomic databases:** Genomic and proteomic data sets are often generated at different labs and by different methods. They are distributed, heterogenous, and of a wide variety. The semantic integration of such data is essential to the cross-site analysis of biological data. Moreover, it is important to find correct linkages between research literature and their associated biological entities. Such integration and linkage analysis would facilitate the systematic and coordinated analysis of genome and biological data. This has promoted the development of integrated data warehouses and distributed federated databases to store and manage the primary and derived biological data. Data cleaning, data integration, reference reconciliation, classification, and clustering methods will facilitate the integration of biological data and the construction of data warehouses for biological data analysis.

- **Alignment, indexing, similarity search, and comparative analysis of multiple nucleotide/protein sequences:** Various biological sequence alignment methods have been developed in the past two decades. BLAST and FASTA, in particular, are tools for the systematic analysis of genomic and proteomic data. Biological sequence analysis methods differ from many sequential pattern analysis algorithms proposed in data mining research. They should allow for gaps and mismatches between a query sequence and the sequence data to be searched in order to deal with insertions, deletions, and mutations. Moreover, for protein sequences, two amino acids should also be considered a "match" if one can be derived from the other by substitutions that are likely to occur in nature. Sophisticated statistical analysis and dynamic programming methods often play a key role in the development of alignment algorithms. Indices can be constructed on such data sets so that precise and similarity searches can be performed efficiently.

  There is a combinatorial number of ways to approximately align multiple sequences. Therefore, *multiple sequence alignment* is considered a more challenging task. Methods that can help include (1) reducing a multiple alignment to a series of pairwise alignments and then combining the result, and (2) using Hidden Markov Models or HMMs (Chapter 8). However, the efficient and systematic alignment of multiple biological sequences remains an active research topic. Multiple sequence alignments can be used to identify highly conserved residues among genomes, and such conserved regions can be used to build phylogenetic trees to infer evolutionary relationships among species. Moreover, it may help disclose the secrets of evolution at the genomic level.

From the point of view of medical sciences, genomic and proteomic sequences isolated from diseased and healthy tissues can be compared to identify critical differences between them. Sequences occurring more frequently in the diseased samples may indicate the genetic factors of the disease. Those occurring more frequently only in the healthy samples may indicate mechanisms that protect the body from the disease. Although genetic analysis requires similarity search, the technique needed here is different from that used for time-series data (Chapter 8). The analysis of time series typically uses data transformation methods such as scaling, normalization, and window stitching, which are ineffective for genetic data because such data are nonnumeric. These methods do not consider the interconnections between nucleotides, which play an important role in biologic function. It is important to further develop efficient sequential pattern analysis methods for comparative analysis of biological sequences.

- **Discovery of structural patterns and analysis of genetic networks and protein pathways:** In biology, protein sequences are folded into three-dimensional structures, and such structures interact with each other based on their relative positions and the distances between them. Such complex interactions form the basis of sophisticated genetic networks and protein pathways. It is crucial to discover structural patterns and regularities among such huge but complex biological networks. To this extent, it is important to develop powerful and scalable data mining methods to discover approximate and frequent structural patterns and to study the regularities and irregularities among such interconnected biological networks.

- **Association and path analysis: identifying co-occurring gene sequences and linking genes to different stages of disease development:** Currently, many studies have focused on the comparison of one gene to another. However, most diseases are not triggered by a single gene but by a combination of genes acting together. *Association analysis* methods can be used to help determine the kinds of genes that are likely to co-occur in target samples. Such analysis would facilitate the discovery of groups of genes and the study of interactions and relationships between them.

  While a group of genes may contribute to a disease process, different genes may become active at different stages of the disease. If the sequence of genetic activities across the different stages of disease development can be identified, it may be possible to develop pharmaceutical interventions that target the different stages separately, therefore achieving more effective treatment of the disease. Such *path analysis* is expected to play an important role in genetic studies.

- **Visualization tools in genetic data analysis:** Alignments among genomic or proteomic sequences and the interactions among complex biological structures are most effectively presented in graphic forms, transformed into various kinds of easy-to-understand visual displays. Such visually appealing structures and patterns facilitate pattern understanding, knowledge discovery, and interactive data exploration. Visualization and visual data mining therefore play an important role in biological data analysis.

11.1.5 Data Mining in Other Scientific Applications

Previously, most scientific data analysis tasks tended to handle relatively small and homogeneous data sets. Such data were typically analyzed using a "formulate hypothesis, build model, and evaluate results" paradigm. In these cases, statistical techniques were appropriate and typically employed for their analysis (see Section 11.3.2). Data collection and storage technologies have recently improved, so that today, scientific data can be amassed at much higher speeds and lower costs. This has resulted in the accumulation of huge volumes of high-dimensional data, stream data, and heterogenous data, containing rich spatial and temporal information. Consequently, scientific applications are shifting from the "hypothesize-and-test" paradigm toward a "collect and store data, mine for new hypotheses, confirm with data or experimentation" process. This shift brings about new challenges for data mining.

Vast amounts of data have been collected from scientific domains (including geosciences, astronomy, and meteorology) using sophisticated telescopes, multispectral high-resolution remote satellite sensors, and global positioning systems. Large data sets are being generated due to fast numerical simulations in various fields, such as climate and ecosystem modeling, chemical engineering, fluid dynamics, and structural mechanics. Other areas requiring the analysis of large amounts of complex data include telecommunications (Section 11.1.3) and biomedical engineering (Section 11.1.4). In this section, we look at some of the challenges brought about by emerging scientific applications of data mining, such as the following:

- **Data warehouses and data preprocessing:** Data warehouses are critical for information exchange and data mining. In the area of geospatial data, however, no true geospatial data warehouse exists today. Creating such a warehouse requires finding means for resolving geographic and temporal data incompatibilities, such as reconciling semantics, referencing systems, geometry, accuracy, and precision. For scientific applications in general, methods are needed for integrating data from heterogeneous sources (such as data covering different time periods) and for identifying events. For climate and ecosystem data, for instance (which are spatial and temporal), the problem is that there are too many events in the spatial domain and too few in the temporal domain. (For example, El Niño events occur only every four to seven years, and previous data might not have been collected as systematically as today.) Methods are needed for the efficient computation of sophisticated spatial aggregates and the handling of spatial-related data streams.
- **Mining complex data types:** Scientific data sets are heterogeneous in nature, typically involving semi-structured and unstructured data, such as multimedia data and

georeferenced stream data. Robust methods are needed for handling spatiotemporal data, related concept hierarchies, and complex geographic relationships (e.g., non-Euclidian distances).

- **Graph-based mining:** It is often difficult or impossible to model several physical phenomena and processes due to limitations of existing modeling approaches. Alternatively, labeled graphs may be used to capture many of the spatial, topological, geometric, and other relational characteristics present in scientific data sets. In graph-modeling, each object to be mined is represented by a vertex in a graph, and edges between vertices represent relationships between objects. For example, graphs can be used to model chemical structures and data generated by numerical simulations, such as fluid-flow simulations. The success of graph-modeling, however, depends on improvements in the scalability and efficiency of many classical data mining tasks, such as classification, frequent pattern mining, and clustering.
- **Visualization tools and domain-specific knowledge:** High-level graphical user interfaces and visualization tools are required for scientific data mining systems. These should be integrated with existing domain-specific information systems and database systems to guide researchers and general users in searching for patterns, interpreting and visualizing discovered patterns, and using discovered knowledge in their decision making.

11.1.6 Data Mining for Intrusion Detection

The security of our computer systems and data is at continual risk. The extensive growth of the Internet and increasing availability of tools and tricks for intruding and attacking networks have prompted **intrusion detection** to become a critical component of network administration. An intrusion can be defined as any set of actions that threaten the integrity, confidentiality, or availability of a network resource (such as user accounts, file systems, system kernels, and so on).

Most commercial intrusion detection systems are limiting and do not provide a complete solution. Such systems typically employ a *misuse detection* strategy. **Misuse detection** searches for patterns of program or user behavior that match known intrusion scenarios, which are stored as *signatures.* These hand-coded signatures are laboriously provided by human experts based on their extensive knowledge of intrusion techniques. If a pattern match is found, this signals an event for which an alarm is raised. Human security analysts evaluate the alarms to decide what action to take, whether it be shutting down part of the system, alerting the relevant Internet service provider of suspicious traffic, or simply noting unusual traffic for future reference. An intrusion detection system for a large complex network can typically generate thousands or millions of alarms per day, representing an overwhelming task for the security analysts. Because systems are not static, the signatures need to be updated whenever new software versions arrive or changes in network configuration occur. An additional, major drawback is that misuse detection can only identify cases that match the signatures. That is, it is unable to detect new or previously unknown intrusion techniques.

Novel intrusions may be found by *anomaly detection* strategies. **Anomaly detection** builds models of normal network behavior (called *profiles*), which it uses to detect new patterns that significantly deviate from the profiles. Such deviations may represent actual intrusions or simply be new behaviors that need to be added to the profiles. The main advantage of anomaly detection is that it may detect novel intrusions that have not yet been observed. Typically, a human analyst must sort through the deviations to ascertain which represent real intrusions. A limiting factor of anomaly detection is the high percentage of false positives. New patterns of intrusion can be added to the set of signatures for misuse detection.

As we can see from this discussion, current traditional intrusion detection systems face many limitations. This has led to an increased interest in data mining for intrusion detection. The following are areas in which data mining technology may be applied or further developed for intrusion detection:

- **Development of data mining algorithms for intrusion detection**: Data mining algorithms can be used for misuse detection and anomaly detection. In misuse detection, training data are labeled as either "normal" or "intrusion." A classifier can then be derived to detect known intrusions. Research in this area has included the application of classification algorithms, association rule mining, and cost-sensitive modeling. Anomaly detection builds models of normal behavior and automatically detects significant deviations from it. Supervised or unsupervised learning can be used. In a supervised approach, the model is developed based on training data that are known to be "normal." In an unsupervised approach, no information is given about the training data. Anomaly detection research has included the application of classification algorithms, statistical approaches, clustering, and outlier analysis. The techniques used must be efficient and scalable, and capable of handling network data of high volume, dimensionality, and heterogeneity.

- **Association and correlation analysis, and aggregation to help select and build discriminating attributes:** Association and correlation mining can be applied to find relationships between system attributes describing the network data. Such information can provide insight regarding the selection of useful attributes for intrusion detection. New attributes derived from aggregated data may also be helpful, such as summary counts of traffic matching a particular pattern.
- **Analysis of stream data**: Due to the transient and dynamic nature of intrusions and malicious attacks, it is crucial to perform intrusion detection in the data stream environment. Moreover, an event may be normal on its own, but considered malicious if viewed as part of a sequence of events. Thus it is necessary to study what sequences of events are frequently encountered together, find sequential patterns, and identify outliers. Other data mining methods for finding evolving clusters and building dynamic classification models in data streams are also necessary for real-time intrusion detection.

- **Distributed data mining**: Intrusions can be launched from several different locations and targeted to many different destinations. Distributed data mining methods may be used to analyze network data from several network locations in order to detect these distributed attacks.

- **Visualization and querying tools:** Visualization tools should be available for viewing any anomalous patterns detected. Such tools may include features for viewing associations, clusters, and outliers. Intrusion detection systems should also have a graphical user interface that allows security analysts to pose queries regarding the network data or intrusion detection results.

In comparison to traditional intrusion detection systems, intrusion detection systems based on data mining are generally more precise and require far less manual processing and input from human experts.

11.2 Data Mining System Products and Research Prototypes

Although data mining is a relatively young field with many issues that still need to be researched in depth, many off-the-shelf data mining system products and domain-specific data mining application softwares are available. As a discipline, data mining has a relatively short history and is constantly evolving—new data mining systems appear on the market every year; new functions, features, and visualization tools are added to existing systems on a constant basis; and efforts toward the standardization of data mining language are still underway. Therefore, it is not our intention in this book to provide a detailed description of commercial data mining systems. Instead, we describe the features to consider when selecting a data mining product and offer a quick introduction to a few typical data mining systems. Reference articles, websites, and recent surveys of data mining systems are listed in the bibliographic notes.

11.2.1 How to Choose a Data Mining System

With many data mining system products available on the market, you may ask, "*What kind of system should I choose?*" Some people may be under the impression that data mining systems, like many commercial relational database systems, share the same well-defined operations and a standard query language, and behave similarly on common functionalities. If such were the case, the choice would depend more on the systems' hardware platform, compatibility, robustness, scalability, price, and service. Unfortunately, this is far from reality. Many commercial data mining systems have little in common with respect to data mining functionality or methodology and may even work with completely different kinds of data sets.

To choose a data mining system that is appropriate for your task, it is important to have a multidimensional view of data mining systems. In general, data mining systems should be assessed based on the following multiple features:

- **Data types:** Most data mining systems that are available on the market handle formatted, record-based, relational-like data with numerical, categorical, and symbolic attributes. The data could be in the form of ASCII text, relational database data, or data warehouse data. It is important to check what exact format(s) each system you are considering can handle. Some kinds of data or applications may require specialized algorithms to search for patterns, and so their requirements may not be handled by off-the-shelf, generic data mining systems. Instead, specialized data mining systems may be used, which mine either text documents, geospatial data, multimedia data, stream data, time-series data, biological data, or Web data, or are dedicated to specific applications (such as finance, the retail industry, or telecommunications). Moreover, many data mining companies offer customized data mining solutions that incorporate essential data mining functions or methodologies.

- **System issues:** A given data mining system may run on only one operating system or on several. The most popular operating systems that host data mining software are UNIX/Linux and Microsoft Windows. There are also data mining systems that run on Macintosh, OS/2, and others. Large industry-oriented data mining systems often adopt a client/server architecture, where the client could be a personal computer, and the server could be a set of powerful parallel computers. A recent trend has data mining systems providing Web-based interfaces and allowing XML data as input and/or output.

- **Data sources:** This refers to the specific data formats on which the data mining system will operate. Some systems work only on ASCII text files, whereas many others work on relational data, or data warehouse data, accessing multiple relational data sources. It is important that a data mining system supports ODBC connections or OLE DB for ODBC connections. These ensure open database connections, that is, the ability to access any relational data (including those in IBM/DB2, Microsoft SQL Server, Microsoft Access, Oracle, Sybase, etc.), as well as formatted ASCII text data.

- **Data mining functions and methodologies:** Data mining functions form the core of a data mining system. Some data mining systems provide only one data mining function, such as classification. Others may support multiple data mining functions, such as concept description, discovery-driven OLAP analysis, association mining, linkage analysis, statistical analysis, classification, prediction, clustering, outlier analysis, similarity search, sequential pattern analysis, and visual data mining. For a given data mining function (such as classification), some systems may support only one method, whereas others may support a wide variety of methods (such as decision tree analysis, Bayesian networks, neural networks, support vector machines, rule-based classification, *k*-nearest-neighbor methods, genetic algorithms, and case-based reasoning). Data mining systems that support multiple data mining functions and multiple methods per function provide the user with greater flexibility and analysis power. Many problems may require users to try a few different mining functions or incorporate several together, and different methods can be more effective than others for different kinds of data. In order to take advantage of the added flexibility, however, users may require further training and experience. Thus such systems should also provide novice users with convenient access to the most popular function and method, or to default settings.

- **Coupling data mining with database and/or data warehouse systems:** A data mining system should be coupled with a database and/or data warehouse system, where the coupled components are seamlessly integrated into a uniform information processing environment. In general, there are four forms of such coupling: *no coupling, loose coupling, semitight coupling,* and *tight coupling* (Chapter 1). Some data mining systems work only with ASCII data files and are *not coupled* with database or data warehouse systems at all. Such systems have difficulties using the data stored in database systems and handling large data sets efficiently. In data mining systems that are *loosely coupled* with database and data warehouse systems, the data are retrieved into a buffer or main memory by database or warehouse operations, and then mining functions are applied to analyze the retrieved data. These systems may not be equipped with scalable algorithms to handle large data sets when processing data mining queries. The coupling of a data mining system with a database or data warehouse system may be *semitight*, providing the efficient implementation of a few essential data mining primitives (such as sorting, indexing, aggregation, histogram analysis, multiway join, and the precomputation of some statistical measures). Ideally, a data mining system should be *tightly coupled* with a database system in the sense that the data mining and data retrieval processes are integrated by optimizing data mining queries deep into the iterative mining and retrieval process. Tight coupling of data mining with OLAP-based data warehouse systems is also desirable so that data mining and OLAP operations can be integrated to provide OLAP-mining features.
- **Scalability:** Data mining has two kinds of scalability issues: *row* (or *database size*) *scalability* and *column* (or *dimension*) *scalability*. A data mining system is considered **row scalable** if, when the number of rows is enlarged 10 times, it takes no more than 10 times to execute the same data mining queries. A data mining system is considered **column scalable** if the mining query execution time increases linearly with the number of columns (or attributes or dimensions). Due to the curse of dimensionality, it is much more challenging to make a system column scalable than row scalable.
- **Visualization tools:** *"A picture is worth a thousand words"*—this is very true in data mining. Visualization in data mining can be categorized into *data visualization, mining result visualization, mining process visualization,* and *visual data mining*, as discussed in Section 11.3.3. The variety, quality, and flexibility of visualization tools may strongly influence the usability, interpretability, and attractiveness of a data mining system.
- **Data mining query language and graphical user interface:** Data mining is an exploratory process. An easy-to-use and high-quality graphical user interface is essential in order to promote user-guided, highly interactive data mining. Most data mining systems provide user-friendly interfaces for mining. However, unlike relational database systems, where most graphical user interfaces are constructed on top of SQL (which serves as a standard, well-designed database query language), most data mining systems do not share any underlying data mining query language. Lack of a standard data mining language makes it difficult to standardize data mining products and to

ensure the interoperability of data mining systems. Recent efforts at defining and standardizing data mining query languages include Microsoft's OLE DB for Data Mining, which is described in the appendix of this book. Other standardization efforts include PMML (or Predictive Model Markup Language), part of an international consortium led by DMG (*www.dmg.org*), and CRISP-DM (or Cross-Industry Standard Process for Data Mining), described at *www.crisp-dm.org*.

11.2.2 Examples of Commercial Data Mining Systems

As mentioned earlier, due to the infancy and rapid evolution of the data mining market, it is not our intention in this book to describe any particular commercial data mining system in detail. Instead, we briefly outline a few typical data mining systems in order to give the reader an idea of what is available. We organize these systems into three groups: data mining products offered by large database or hardware vendors, those offered by vendors of statistical analysis software, and those originating from the machine learning community.

Many data mining systems specialize in one data mining function, such as classification, or just one approach for a data mining function, such as decision tree classification. Other systems provide a broad spectrum of data mining functions. Most of the systems described below provide multiple data mining functions and explore multiple knowledge discovery techniques. Website URLs for the various systems are provided in the bibliographic notes.

From database system and graphics system vendors:

- Intelligent Miner is an IBM data mining product that provides a wide range of data mining functions, including association mining, classification, regression, predictive modeling, deviation detection, clustering, and sequential pattern analysis. It also provides an application toolkit containing neural network algorithms, statistical methods, data preparation tools, and data visualization tools. Distinctive features of Intelligent Miner include the scalability of its mining algorithms and its tight integration with IBM's DB2 relational database system.
- Microsoft SQL Server 2005 is a database management system that incorporates multiple data mining functions smoothly in its relational database system and data warehouse system environments. It includes association mining, classification (using decision tree, naïve Bayes, and neural network algorithms), regression trees, sequence clustering, and time-series analysis. In addition, Microsoft SQL Server 2005 supports the integration of algorithms developed by third-party vendors and application users.
- MineSet, available from Purple Insight, was introduced by SGI in 1999. It provides multiple data mining functions, including association mining and classification, as well as advanced statistics and visualization tools. A distinguishing feature of MineSet is its set of robust graphics tools, including rule visualizer, tree visualizer, map visualizer, and (multidimensional data) scatter visualizer for the visualization of data and data mining results.

- Oracle Data Mining (ODM), an option to Oracle Database 10g Enterprise Edition, provides several data mining functions, including association mining, classification, prediction, regression, clustering, and sequence similarity search and analysis. Oracle Database 10g also provides an embedded data warehousing infrastructure for multidimensional data analysis.

From vendors of statistical analysis or data mining software:

- Clementine, from SPSS, provides an integrated data mining development environment for end users and developers. Multiple data mining functions, including association mining, classification, prediction, clustering, and visualization tools, are incorporated into the system. A distinguishing feature of Clementine is its object-oriented, extended module interface, which allows users' algorithms and utilities to be added to Clementine's visual programming environment.
- Enterprise Miner was developed by SAS Institute, Inc. It provides multiple data mining functions, including association mining, classification, regression, clustering, time-series analysis, and statistical analysis packages. A distinctive feature of Enterprise Miner is its variety of statistical analysis tools, which are built based on the long history of SAS in the market of statistical analysis.
- Insightful Miner, from Insightful Inc., provides several data mining functions, including data cleaning, classification, prediction, clustering, and statistical analysis packages, along with visualization tools. A distinguishing feature is its visual interface, which allows users to wire components together to create self-documenting programs.

Originating from the machine learning community:

- CART, available from Salford Systems, is the commercial version of the CART (Classification and Regression Trees) system discussed in Chapter 6. It creates decision trees for classification and regression trees for prediction. CART employs boosting to improve accuracy. Several attribute selection measures are available.
- See5 and C5.0, available from RuleQuest, are commercial versions of the C4.5 decision tree and rule generation method described in Chapter 6. See5 is the Windows version of C4.5, while C5.0 is its UNIX counterpart. Both incorporate boosting. The source code is also provided.
- Weka, developed at the University of Waikato in New Zealand, is open-source data mining software in Java. It contains a collection of algorithms for data mining tasks, including data preprocessing, association mining, classification, regression, clustering, and visualization.

Many other commercial data mining systems and research prototypes are also fast evolving. Interested readers may wish to consult timely surveys on data warehousing and data mining products.

11.3 Additional Themes on Data Mining

Due to the broad scope of data mining and the large variety of data mining methodologies, not all of the themes on data mining can be thoroughly covered in this book. In this section, we briefly discuss several interesting themes that were not fully addressed in the previous chapters of this book.

11.3.1 Theoretical Foundations of Data Mining

Research on the theoretical foundations of data mining has yet to mature. A solid and systematic theoretical foundation is important because it can help provide a coherent framework for the development, evaluation, and practice of data mining technology. Several theories for the basis of data mining include the following:

- **Data reduction**: In this theory, the basis of data mining is to reduce the data representation. Data reduction trades accuracy for speed in response to the need to obtain quick approximate answers to queries on very large databases. Data reduction techniques include singular value decomposition (the driving element behind principal components analysis), wavelets, regression, log-linear models, histograms, clustering, sampling, and the construction of index trees.
- **Data compression**: According to this theory, the basis of data mining is to compress the given data by encoding in terms of bits, association rules, decision trees, clusters, and so on. Encoding based on the *minimum description length principle* states that the "best" theory to infer from a set of data is the one that minimizes the length of the theory and the length of the data when encoded, using the theory as a predictor for the data. This encoding is typically in bits.
- **Pattern discovery**: In this theory, the basis of data mining is to discover patterns occurring in the database, such as associations, classification models, sequential patterns, and so on. Areas such as machine learning, neural network, association mining, sequential pattern mining, clustering, and several other subfields contribute to this theory.
- **Probability theory**: This is based on statistical theory. In this theory, the basis of data mining is to discover joint probability distributions of random variables, for example, Bayesian belief networks or hierarchical Bayesian models.
- **Microeconomic view**: The microeconomic view considers data mining as the task of finding patterns that are interesting only to the extent that they can be used in the decision-making process of some enterprise (e.g., regarding marketing strategies and production plans). This view is one of utility, in which patterns are considered interesting if they can be acted on. Enterprises are regarded as facing optimization problems, where the object is to maximize the utility or value of a decision. In this theory, data mining becomes a nonlinear optimization problem.

- **Inductive databases:** According to this theory, a database schema consists of data and patterns that are stored in the database. Data mining is therefore the problem of performing induction on databases, where the task is to query the data and the theory (i.e., patterns) of the database. This view is popular among many researchers in database systems.

These theories are not mutually exclusive. For example, pattern discovery can also be seen as a form of data reduction or data compression. Ideally, a theoretical framework should be able to model typical data mining tasks (such as association, classification, and clustering), have a probabilistic nature, be able to handle different forms of data, and consider the iterative and interactive essence of data mining. Further efforts are required toward the establishment of a well-defined framework for data mining, which satisfies these requirements.

11.3.2 Statistical Data Mining

The data mining techniques described in this book are primarily database-oriented, that is, designed for the efficient handling of huge amounts of data that are typically multidimensional and possibly of various complex types. There are, however, many well-established statistical techniques for data analysis, particularly for numeric data. These techniques have been applied extensively to some types of scientific data (e.g., data from experiments in physics, engineering, manufacturing, psychology, and medicine), as well as to data from economics and the social sciences. Some of these techniques, such as principal components analysis (Chapter 2), regression (Chapter 6), and clustering (Chapter 7), have already been addressed in this book. A thorough discussion of major statistical methods for data analysis is beyond the scope of this book; however, several methods are mentioned here for the sake of completeness. Pointers to these techniques are provided in the bibliographic notes.

- **Regression:** In general, these methods are used to predict the value of a *response* (dependent) variable from one or more *predictor* (independent) variables where the variables are numeric. There are various forms of regression, such as linear, multiple, weighted, polynomial, nonparametric, and robust (robust methods are useful when errors fail to satisfy normalcy conditions or when the data contain significant outliers).
- **Generalized linear models:** These models, and their generalization (*generalized additive models*), allow a *categorical* response variable (or some transformation of it) to be related to a set of predictor variables in a manner similar to the modeling of a numeric response variable using linear regression. Generalized linear models include logistic regression and Poisson regression.
- **Analysis of variance:** These techniques analyze experimental data for two or more populations described by a numeric response variable and one or more categorical variables (*factors*). In general, an ANOVA (single-factor analysis of variance) problem

involves a comparison of k population or treatment means to determine if at least two of the means are different. More complex ANOVA problems also exist.

- **Mixed-effect models:** These models are for analyzing grouped data—data that can be classified according to one or more grouping variables. They typically describe relationships between a response variable and some covariates in data grouped according to one or more factors. Common areas of application include multilevel data, repeated measures data, block designs, and longitudinal data.
- **Factor analysis:** This method is used to determine which variables are combined to generate a given factor. For example, for many psychiatric data, it is not possible to measure a certain factor of interest directly (such as intelligence); however, it is often possible to measure other quantities (such as student test scores) that reflect the factor of interest. Here, none of the variables are designated as dependent.
- **Discriminant analysis:** This technique is used to predict a categorical response variable. Unlike generalized linear models, it assumes that the independent variables follow a multivariate normal distribution. The procedure attempts to determine several discriminant functions (linear combinations of the independent variables) that discriminate among the groups defined by the response variable. Discriminant analysis is commonly used in social sciences.
- **Time series analysis:** There are many statistical techniques for analyzing time-series data, such as autoregression methods, univariate ARIMA (autoregressive integrated moving average) modeling, and long-memory time-series modeling.
- **Survival analysis:** Several well-established statistical techniques exist for survival analysis. These techniques originally were designed to predict the probability that a patient undergoing a medical treatment would survive at least to time t. Methods for survival analysis, however, are also commonly applied to manufacturing settings to estimate the life span of industrial equipment. Popular methods include Kaplan-Meier estimates of survival, Cox proportional hazards regression models, and their extensions.
- **Quality control:** Various statistics can be used to prepare charts for quality control, such as Shewhart charts and cusum charts (both of which display group summary statistics). These statistics include the mean, standard deviation, range, count, moving average, moving standard deviation, and moving range.

11.3.3 Visual and Audio Data Mining

Visual data mining discovers implicit and useful knowledge from large data sets using data and/or knowledge visualization techniques. The human visual system is controlled by the eyes and brain, the latter of which can be thought of as a powerful, highly parallel processing and reasoning engine containing a large knowledge base. Visual data mining essentially combines the power of these components, making it a highly attractive and effective tool for the comprehension of data distributions, patterns, clusters, and outliers in data.

Visual data mining can be viewed as an integration of two disciplines: data visualization and data mining. It is also closely related to computer graphics, multimedia systems, human computer interaction, pattern recognition, and high-performance computing. In general, data visualization and data mining can be integrated in the following ways:

- **Data visualization:** Data in a database or data warehouse can be viewed at different levels of granularity or abstraction, or as different combinations of attributes or dimensions. Data can be presented in various visual forms, such as boxplots, 3-D cubes, data distribution charts, curves, surfaces, link graphs, and so on. Figures 11.2 and 11.3 from StatSoft show data distributions in multidimensional space. Visual display can help give users a clear impression and overview of the data characteristics in a database.
- **Data mining result visualization**: Visualization of data mining results is the presentation of the results or knowledge obtained from data mining in visual forms. Such forms may include scatter plots and boxplots (obtained from descriptive data mining), as well as decision trees, association rules, clusters, outliers, generalized rules, and so on. For example, scatter plots are shown in Figure 11.4 from SAS Enterprise Miner. Figure 11.5, from MineSet, uses a plane associated with a set of pillars to

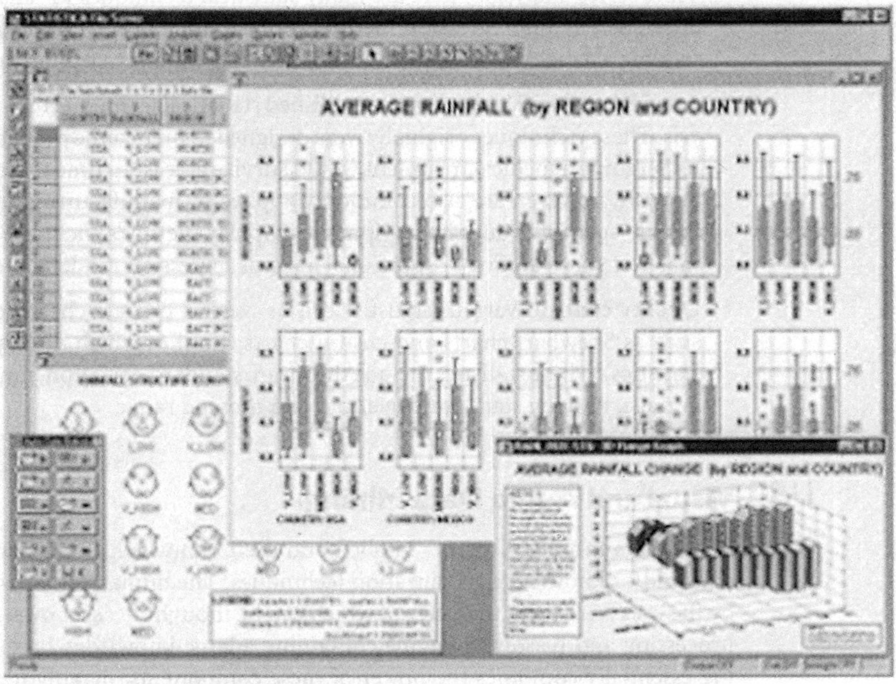

Figure 11.2 Boxplots showing multiple variable combinations in StatSoft.

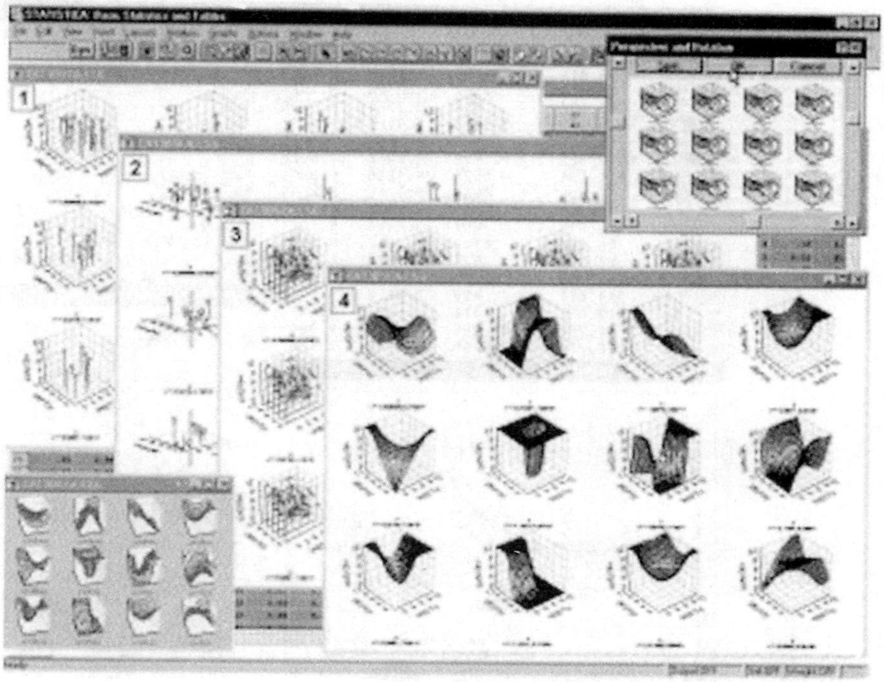

Figure 11.3 Multidimensional data distribution analysis in StatSoft.

describe a set of association rules mined from a database. Figure 11.6, also from MineSet, presents a decision tree. Figure 11.7, from IBM Intelligent Miner, presents a set of clusters and the properties associated with them.

- **Data mining process visualization**: This type of visualization presents the various processes of data mining in visual forms so that users can see how the data are extracted and from which database or data warehouse they are extracted, as well as how the selected data are cleaned, integrated, preprocessed, and mined. Moreover, it may also show which method is selected for data mining, where the results are stored, and how they may be viewed. Figure 11.8 shows a visual presentation of data mining processes by the Clementine data mining system.

- **Interactive visual data mining**: In (interactive) visual data mining, visualization tools can be used in the data mining process to help users make smart data mining decisions. For example, the data distribution in a set of attributes can be displayed using colored sectors (where the whole space is represented by a circle). This display helps users determine which sector should first be selected for classification and where a good split point for this sector may be. An example of this is shown in Figure 11.9, which is the output of a perception-based classification system (PBC) developed at the University of Munich.

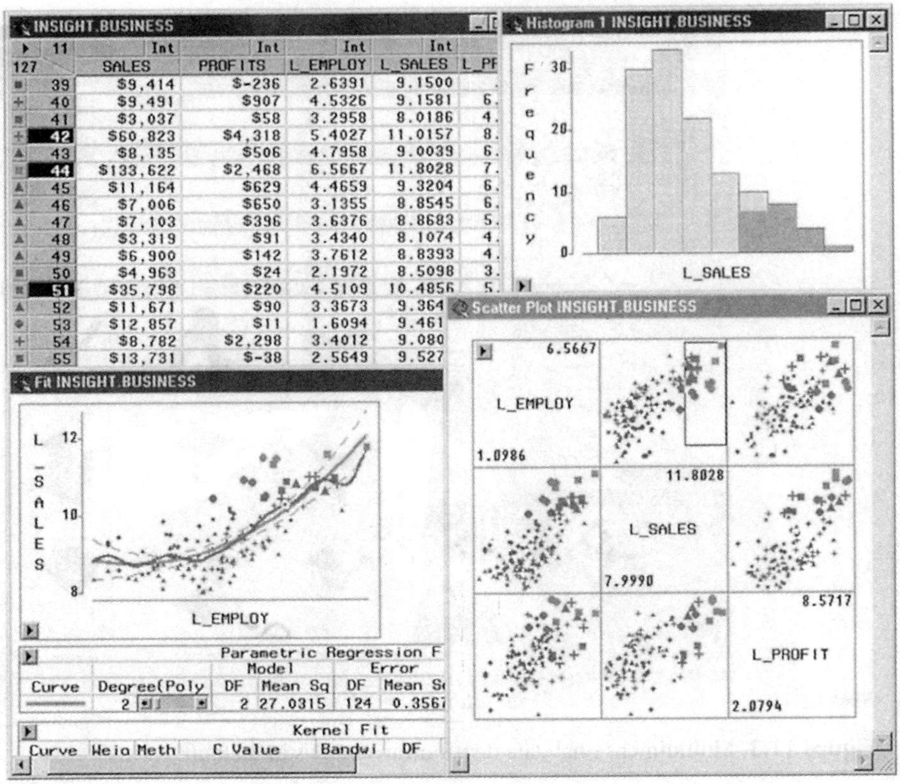

Figure 11.4 Visualization of data mining results in SAS Enterprise Miner.

Audio data mining uses audio signals to indicate the patterns of data or the features of data mining results. Although visual data mining may disclose interesting patterns using graphical displays, it requires users to concentrate on watching patterns and identifying interesting or novel features within them. This can sometimes be quite tiresome. If patterns can be transformed into sound and music, then instead of watching pictures, we can listen to pitches, rhythms, tune, and melody in order to identify anything interesting or unusual. This may relieve some of the burden of visual concentration and be more relaxing than visual mining. Therefore, audio data mining is an interesting complement to visual mining.

11.3.4 Data Mining and Collaborative Filtering

Today's consumers are faced with millions of goods and services when shopping on-line. **Recommender systems** help consumers by making product recommendations during live customer transactions. A **collaborative filtering** approach is commonly used, in which products are recommended based on the opinions of

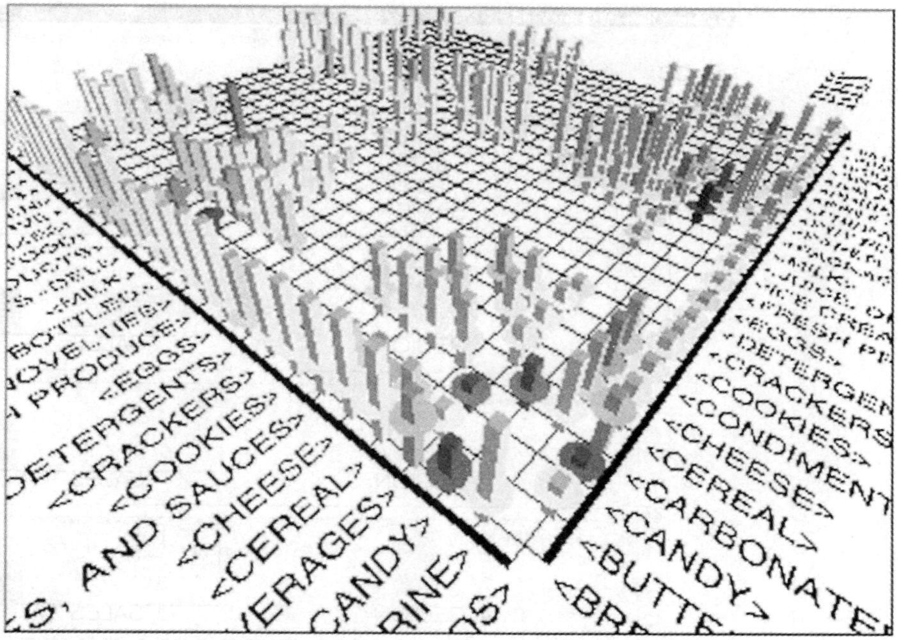

Figure 11.5 Visualization of association rules in MineSet.

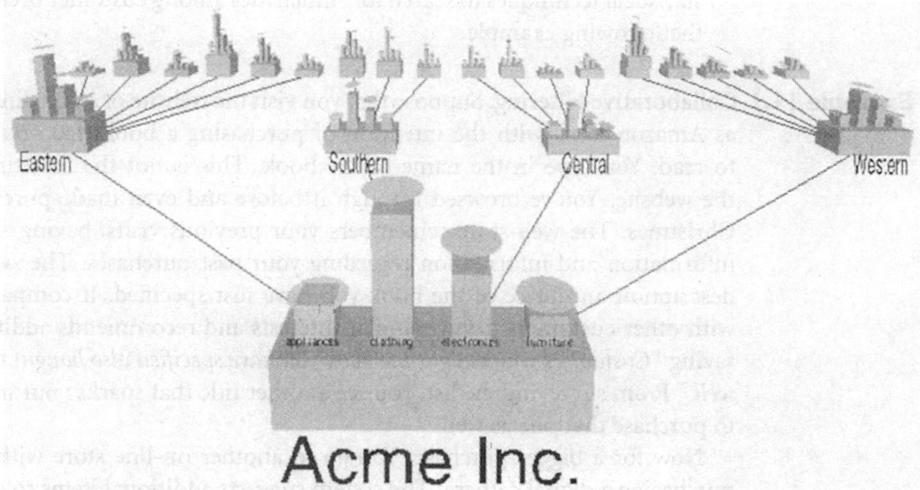

Figure 11.6 Visualization of a decision tree in MineSet.

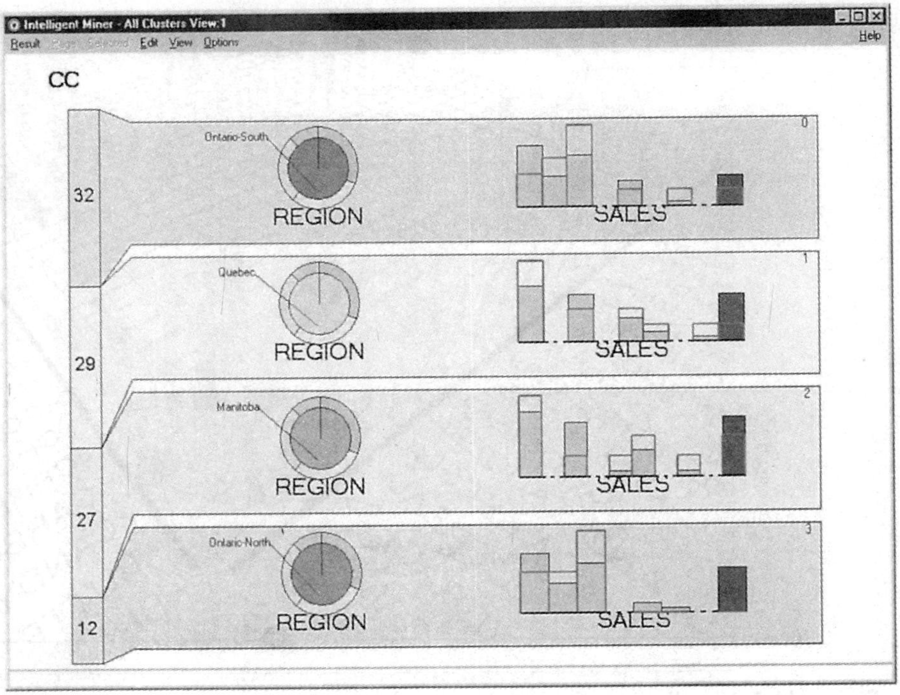

Figure 11.7 Visualization of cluster groupings in IBM Intelligent Miner.

other customers. Collaborative recommender systems may employ data mining or statistical techniques to search for similarities among customer preferences. Consider the following example.

Example 11.1 **Collaborative Filtering.** Suppose that you visit the website of an on-line bookstore (such as Amazon.com) with the intention of purchasing a book that you've been wanting to read. You type in the name of the book. This is not the first time you've visited the website. You've browsed through it before and even made purchases from it last Christmas. The web-store remembers your previous visits, having stored clickstream information and information regarding your past purchases. The system displays the description and price of the book you have just specified. It compares your interests with other customers having similar interests and recommends additional book titles, saying "*Customers who bought the book you have specified also bought these other titles as well.*" From surveying the list, you see another title that sparks your interest and decide to purchase that one as well.

Now for a bigger purchase. You go to another on-line store with the intention of purchasing a digital camera. The system suggests additional items to consider based on previously mined sequential patterns, such as "*Customers who buy this kind of digital camera are likely to buy a particular brand of printer, memory card, or photo*

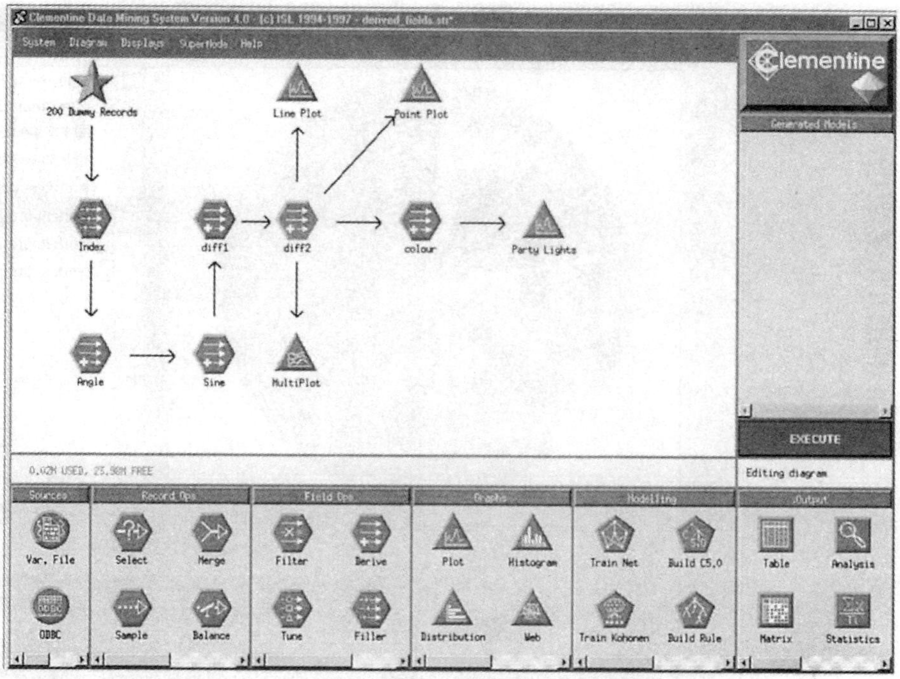

Figure 11.8 Visualization of data mining processes by Clementine.

editing software within three months." You decide to buy just the camera, without any additional items. A week later, you receive coupons from the store regarding the additional items. ■

A collaborative recommender system works by finding a set of customers, referred to as *neighbors*, that have a history of agreeing with the target customer (such as, they tend to buy similar sets of products, or give similar ratings for certain products). Collaborative recommender systems face two major challenges: scalability and ensuring quality recommendations to the consumer. Scalability is important, because e-commerce systems must be able to search through millions of potential neighbors in real time. If the site is using browsing patterns as indications of product preference, it may have thousands of data points for some of its customers. Ensuring quality recommendations is essential in order to gain consumers' trust. If consumers follow a system recommendation but then do not end up liking the product, they are less likely to use the recommender system again. As with classification systems, recommender systems can make two types of errors: false negatives and false positives. Here, *false negatives* are products that the system fails to recommend, although the consumer would like them. *False positives* are products that are recommended, but which the consumer does not like. False positives are less desirable because they can annoy or anger consumers.

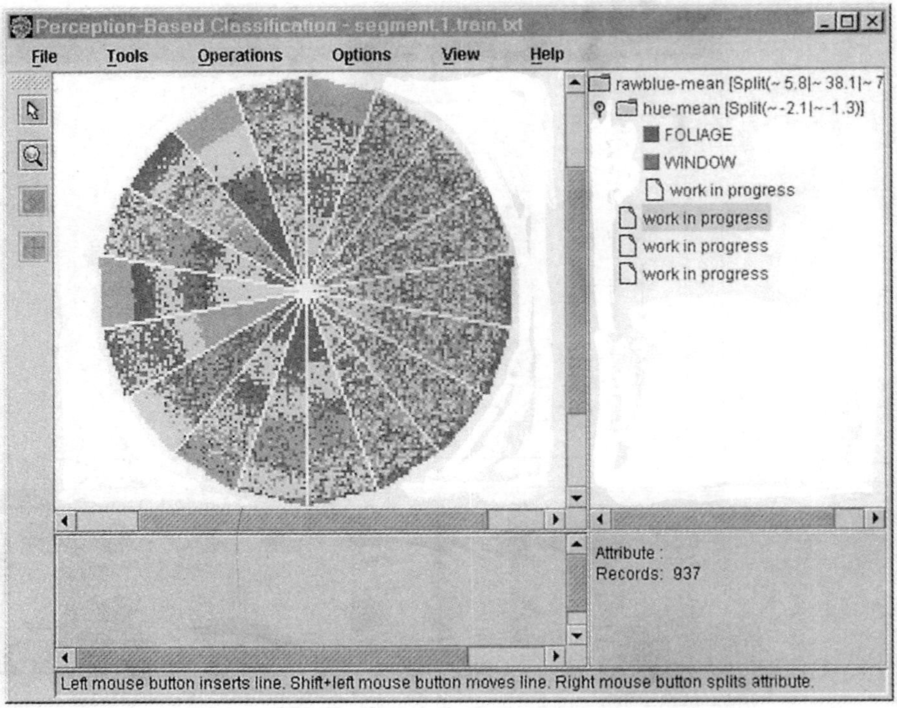

Figure 11.9 Perception-based classification (PBC): An interactive visual mining approach.

An advantage of recommender systems is that they provide *personalization* for customers of e-commerce, promoting one-to-one marketing. Amazon.com, a pioneer in the use of collaborative recommender systems, offers "a personalized store for every customer" as part of their marketing strategy. Personalization can benefit both the consumers and the company involved. By having more accurate models of their customers, companies gain a better understanding of customer needs. Serving these needs can result in greater success regarding cross-selling of related products, upselling, product affinities, one-to-one promotions, larger baskets, and customer retention.

Dimension reduction, association mining, clustering, and Bayesian learning are some of the techniques that have been adapted for collaborative recommender systems. While collaborative filtering explores the ratings of items provided by similar users, some recommender systems explore a content-based method that provides recommendations based on the similarity of the contents contained in an item. Moreover, some systems integrate both content-based and user-based methods to achieve further improved recommendations.

Collaborative recommender systems are a form of **intelligent query answering**, which consists of analyzing the intent of a query and providing generalized, neighborhood, or associated information relevant to the query. For example, rather than simply returning the book description and price in response to a customer's query, returning additional information that is related to the query but that was not explicitly asked for (such as book evaluation comments, recommendations of other books, or sales statistics) provides an intelligent answer to the same query.

11.4 Social Impacts of Data Mining

For most of us, data mining is part of our daily lives, although we may often be unaware of its presence. Section 11.4.1 looks at several examples of "ubiquitous and invisible" data mining, affecting everyday things from the products stocked at our local supermarket, to the ads we see while surfing the Internet, to crime prevention. Data mining can offer the individual many benefits by improving customer service and satisfaction, and lifestyle, in general. However, it also has serious implications regarding one's right to privacy and data security. These issues are the topic of Section 11.4.2.

11.4.1 Ubiquitous and Invisible Data Mining

Data mining is present in many aspects of our daily lives, whether we realize it or not. It affects how we shop, work, search for information, and can even influence our leisure time, health, and well-being. In this section, we look at examples of such **ubiquitous** (or ever-present) **data mining**. Several of these examples also represent **invisible data mining**, in which "smart" software, such as Web search engines, customer-adaptive Web services (e.g., using recommender algorithms), "intelligent" database systems, e-mail managers, ticket masters, and so on, incorporates data mining into its functional components, often unbeknownst to the user.

From grocery stores that print personalized coupons on customer receipts to on-line stores that recommend additional items based on customer interests, data mining has innovatively influenced what we buy, the way we shop, as well as our experience while shopping. One example is Wal-Mart, which has approximately 100 million customers visiting its more than 3,600 stores in the United States every week. Wal-Mart has 460 terabytes of point-of-sale data stored on Teradata mainframes, made by NCR. To put this into perspective, experts estimate that the Internet has less than half this amount of data. Wal-Mart allows suppliers to access data on their products and perform analyses using data mining software. This allows suppliers to identify customer buying patterns, control inventory and product placement, and identify new merchandizing opportunities. All of these affect which items (and how many) end up on the stores' shelves—something to think about the next time you wander through the aisles at Wal-Mart.

Data mining has shaped the on-line shopping experience. Many shoppers routinely turn to on-line stores to purchase books, music, movies, and toys. Section 11.3.4 discussed the use of collaborative recommender systems, which offer personalized product recommendations based on the opinions of other customers. Amazon.com was at the forefront of using such a personalized, data mining–based approach as a marketing strategy. CEO and founder Jeff Bezos had observed that in traditional brick-and-mortar stores, the hardest part is getting the customer into the store. Once the customer is there, she is likely to buy something, since the cost of going to another store is high. Therefore, the marketing for brick-and-mortar stores tends to emphasize drawing customers in, rather than the actual in-store customer experience. This is in contrast to on-line stores, where customers can "walk out" and enter another on-line store with just a click of the mouse. Amazon.com capitalized on this difference, offering a "personalized store for every customer." They use several data mining techniques to identify customer's likes and make reliable recommendations.

While we're on the topic of shopping, suppose you've been doing a lot of buying with your credit cards. Nowadays, it is not unusual to receive a phone call from one's credit card company regarding suspicious or unusual patterns of spending. Credit card companies (and long-distance telephone service providers, for that matter) use data mining to detect fraudulent usage, saving billions of dollars a year.

Many companies increasingly use data mining for **customer relationship management** (CRM), which helps provide more customized, personal service addressing individual customer's needs, in lieu of mass marketing. By studying browsing and purchasing patterns on Web stores, companies can tailor advertisements and promotions to customer profiles, so that customers are less likely to be annoyed with unwanted mass mailings or junk mail. These actions can result in substantial cost savings for companies. The customers further benefit in that they are more likely to be notified of offers that are actually of interest, resulting in less waste of personal time and greater satisfaction. This recurring theme can make its way several times into our day, as we shall see later.

Data mining has greatly influenced the ways in which people use computers, search for information, and work. Suppose that you are sitting at your computer and have just logged onto the Internet. Chances are, you have a personalized portal, that is, the initial Web page displayed by your Internet service provider is designed to have a look and feel that reflects your personal interests. Yahoo (*www.yahoo.com*) was the first to introduce this concept. Usage logs from MyYahoo are mined to provide Yahoo with valuable information regarding an individual's Web usage habits, enabling Yahoo to provide personalized content. This, in turn, has contributed to Yahoo's consistent ranking as one of the top Web search providers for years, according to *Advertising Age's BtoB* magazine's Media Power 50 (*www.btobonline.com*), which recognizes the 50 most powerful and targeted business-to-business advertising outlets each year.

After logging onto the Internet, you decide to check your e-mail. Unbeknownst to you, several annoying e-mails have already been deleted, thanks to a spam filter that uses classification algorithms to recognize spam. After processing your e-mail, you go to Google (*www.google.com*), which provides access to information from over 2 billion Web pages indexed on its server. Google is one of the most popular and widely used Internet search engines. Using Google to search for information has become a way of life for many people. Google is so popular that it has even become a new verb in the English language, meaning "to search for (something) on the Internet using the

Google search engine or, by extension, any comprehensive search engine."[1] You decide to type in some keywords for a topic of interest. Google returns a list of websites on your topic of interest, mined and organized by PageRank. Unlike earlier search engines, which concentrated solely on Web content when returning the pages relevant to a query, PageRank measures the importance of a page using structural link information from the Web graph. It is the core of Google's Web mining technology.

While you are viewing the results of your Google query, various ads pop up relating to your query. Google's strategy of tailoring advertising to match the user's interests is successful—it has increased the clicks for the companies involved by four to five times. This also makes you happier, because you are less likely to be pestered with irrelevant ads. Google was named a top-10 advertising venue by Media Power 50.

Web-wide tracking is a technology that tracks a user across each site she visits. So, while surfing the Web, information about every site you visit may be recorded, which can provide marketers with information reflecting your interests, lifestyle, and habits. DoubleClick Inc.'s DART ad management technology uses Web-wide tracking to target advertising based on behavioral or demographic attributes. Companies pay to use DoubleClick's service on their websites. The clickstream data from all of the sites using DoubleClick are pooled and analyzed for profile information regarding users who visit any of these sites. DoubleClick can then tailor advertisements to end users on behalf of its clients. In general, customer-tailored advertisements are not limited to ads placed on Web stores or company mail-outs. In the future, digital television and on-line books and newspapers may also provide advertisements that are designed and selected specifically for the given viewer or viewer group based on customer profiling information and demographics.

While you're using the computer, you remember to go to eBay (*www.ebay.com*) to see how the bidding is coming along for some items you had posted earlier this week. You are pleased with the bids made so far, implicitly assuming that they are authentic. Luckily, eBay now uses data mining to distinguish fraudulent bids from real ones.

As we have seen throughout this book, data mining and OLAP technologies can help us in our work in many ways. Business analysts, scientists, and governments can all use data mining to analyze and gain insight into their data. They may use data mining and OLAP tools, without needing to know the details of any of the underlying algorithms. All that matters to the user is the end result returned by such systems, which they can then process or use for their decision making.

Data mining can also influence our leisure time involving dining and entertainment. Suppose that, on the way home from work, you stop for some fast food. A major fast-food restaurant used data mining to understand customer behavior via market-basket and time-series analyses. Consequently, a campaign was launched to convert "drinkers" to "eaters" by offering hamburger-drink combinations for little more than the price of the drink alone. That's food for thought, the next time you order a meal combo. With a little help from data mining, it is possible that the restaurant may even know what you want to

[1] *http://open-dictionary.com.*

order before you reach the counter. Bob, an automated fast-food restaurant management system developed by HyperActive Technologies (*www.hyperactivetechnologies.com*), predicts what people are likely to order based on the type of car they drive to the restaurant, and on their height. For example, if a pick-up truck pulls up, the customer is likely to order a quarter pounder. A family car is likely to include children, which means chicken nuggets and fries. The idea is to advise the chefs of the right food to cook for incoming customers to provide faster service, better-quality food, and reduce food wastage.

After eating, you decide to spend the evening at home relaxing on the couch. Blockbuster (*www.blockbuster.com*) uses collaborative recommender systems to suggest movie rentals to individual customers. Other movie recommender systems available on the Internet include MovieLens (*www.movielens.umn.edu*) and Netflix (*www.netflix.com*). (There are even recommender systems for restaurants, music, and books that are not specifically tied to any company.) Or perhaps you may prefer to watch television instead. NBC uses data mining to profile the audiences of each show. The information gleaned contributes toward NBC's programming decisions and advertising. Therefore, the time and day of week of your favorite show may be determined by data mining.

Finally, data mining can contribute toward our health and well-being. Several pharmaceutical companies use data mining software to analyze data when developing drugs and to find associations between patients, drugs, and outcomes. It is also being used to detect beneficial side effects of drugs. The hair-loss pill Propecia, for example, was first developed to treat prostrate enlargement. Data mining performed on a study of patients found that it also promoted hair growth on the scalp. Data mining can also be used to keep our streets safe. The data mining system Clementine from SPSS is being used by police departments to identify key patterns in crime data. It has also been used by police to detect unsolved crimes that may have been committed by the same criminal. Many police departments around the world are using data mining software for crime prevention, such as the Dutch police's use of DataDetective (*www.sentient.nl*) to find patterns in criminal databases. Such discoveries can contribute toward controlling crime.

As we can see, data mining is omnipresent. For data mining to become further accepted and used as a technology, continuing research and development are needed in the many areas mentioned as challenges throughout this book—efficiency and scalability, increased user interaction, incorporation of background knowledge and visualization techniques, the evolution of a standardized data mining query language, effective methods for finding interesting patterns, improved handling of complex data types and stream data, real-time data mining, Web mining, and so on. In addition, the *integration* of data mining into existing business and scientific technologies, to provide domain-specific data mining systems, will further contribute toward the advancement of the technology. The success of data mining solutions tailored for e-commerce applications, as opposed to generic data mining systems, is an example.

11.4.2 Data Mining, Privacy, and Data Security

With more and more information accessible in electronic forms and available on the Web, and with increasingly powerful data mining tools being developed and put into use, there are increasing concerns that data mining may pose a threat to our privacy and data security. However, it is important to note that most of the major data mining applications do not even touch personal data. Prominent examples include applications involving natural resources, the prediction of floods and droughts, meteorology, astronomy, geography, geology, biology, and other scientific and engineering data. Furthermore, most studies in data mining focus on the development of scalable algorithms and also do not involve personal data. The focus of data mining technology is on the *discovery of general patterns*, not on specific information regarding individuals. In this sense, we believe that the real privacy concerns are with unconstrained access of individual records, like credit card and banking applications, for example, which *must* access privacy-sensitive information. For those data mining applications that do involve personal data, in many cases, simple methods such as removing sensitive IDs from data may protect the privacy of most individuals. Numerous data security–enhancing techniques have been developed recently. In addition, there has been a great deal of recent effort on developing *privacy-preserving* data mining methods. In this section, we look at some of the advances in protecting privacy and data security in data mining.

In 1980, the Organization for Economic Co-operation and Development (OECD) established a set of international guidelines, referred to as **fair information practices.** These guidelines aim to protect privacy and data accuracy. They cover aspects relating to data collection, use, openness, security, quality, and accountability. They include the following principles:

- **Purpose specification and use limitation:** The purposes for which personal data are collected should be specified at the time of collection, and the data collected should not exceed the stated purpose. Data mining is typically a secondary purpose of the data collection. It has been argued that attaching a disclaimer that the data may also be used for mining is generally not accepted as sufficient disclosure of intent. Due to the exploratory nature of data mining, it is impossible to know what patterns may be discovered; therefore, there is no certainty over how they may be used.
- **Openness:** There should be a general policy of openness about developments, practices, and policies with respect to personal data. Individuals have the right to know the nature of the data collected about them, the identity of the data controller (responsible for ensuring the principles), and how the data are being used.
- **Security Safeguards:** Personal data should be protected by reasonable security safeguards against such risks as loss or unauthorized access, destruction, use, modification, or disclosure of data.
- **Individual Participation:** An individual should have the right to learn whether the data controller has data relating to him or her, and if so, what that data is. The individual may also challenge such data. If the challenge is successful, the individual has the right to have the data erased, corrected, or completed. Typically, inaccurate data are only detected when an individual experiences some repercussion from it, such as the denial of credit or withholding of a payment. The organization involved usually cannot detect such inaccuracies because they lack the contextual knowledge necessary.

"How can these principles help protect customers from companies that collect personal client data?" One solution is for such companies to provide consumers with multiple **opt-out** choices, allowing consumers to specify limitations on the use of their personal data, such as (1) the consumer's personal data are not to be used at all for data mining; (2) the consumer's data can be used for data mining, but the identity of each consumer or any information that may lead to the disclosure of a person's identity should be removed; (3) the data may be used for in-house mining only; or (4) the data may be used in-house and externally as well. Alternatively, companies may provide consumers with positive consent, that is, by allowing consumers to *opt in* on the secondary use of their information for data mining. Ideally, consumers should be able to call a toll-free number or access a company website in order to opt in or out and request access to their personal data.

Counterterrorism is a new application area for data mining that is gaining interest. **Data mining for counterterrorism** may be used to detect unusual patterns, terrorist activities (including bioterrorism), and fraudulent behavior. This application area is in its infancy because it faces many challenges. These include developing algorithms for real-time mining (e.g., for building models in real time, so as to detect real-time threats such as that a building is scheduled to be bombed by 10 a.m. the next morning); for multimedia data mining (involving audio, video, and image mining, in addition to text mining); and in finding unclassified data to test such applications. While this new form of data mining raises concerns about individual privacy, it is again important to note that the data mining research is to develop a tool for the detection of abnormal patterns or activities, and the use of such tools to access certain data to uncover terrorist *patterns* or *activities* is confined only to *authorized* security agents.

"What can we do to secure the privacy of individuals while collecting and mining data?" Many **data security–enhancing techniques** have been developed to help protect data. Databases can employ a *multilevel security* model to classify and restrict data according to various security levels, with users permitted access to only their authorized level. It has been shown, however, that users executing specific queries at their authorized security level can still infer more sensitive information, and that a similar possibility can occur through data mining. Encryption is another technique in which individual data items may be encoded. This may involve *blind signatures* (which build on public key encryption), *biometric encryption* (e.g., where the image of a person's iris or fingerprint is used to encode his or her personal information), and *anonymous databases* (which permit the consolidation of various databases but limit access to personal information to only those who need to know; personal information is encrypted and stored at different locations). Intrusion detection is another active area of research that helps protect the privacy of personal data.

Privacy-preserving data mining is a new area of data mining research that is emerging in response to privacy protection during mining. It is also known as *privacy-enhanced* or *privacy-sensitive* data mining. It deals with obtaining valid data mining results without learning the underlying data values. There are two common approaches: *secure multiparty computation* and *data obscuration*. In **secure multiparty computation**, data values are encoded using simulation and cryptographic techniques so that no party can learn another's data values. This approach can be impractical when mining large databases. In **data obscuration**, the actual data are distorted by aggregation (such as using the average income for a neighborhood, rather than the actual income of residents) or by adding random noise. The original distribution of a collection of distorted data values can be approximated using a reconstruction algorithm. Mining can be performed using these approximated values, rather than the actual ones. Although a common framework for defining, measuring, and evaluating privacy is needed, many advances have been made. The field is expected to flourish.

Like any other technology, data mining may be misused. However, we must not lose sight of all the benefits that data mining research can bring, ranging from insights gained from medical and scientific applications to increased customer satisfaction by helping companies better suit their clients' needs. We expect that computer scientists, policy experts, and counterterrorism experts will continue to work with social scientists, lawyers, companies and consumers to take responsibility in building solutions to ensure data privacy protection and security. In this way, we may continue to reap the benefits of data mining in terms of time and money savings and the discovery of new knowledge.

11.5 Trends in Data Mining

The diversity of data, data mining tasks, and data mining approaches poses many challenging research issues in data mining. The development of efficient and effective data mining methods and systems, the construction of interactive and integrated data mining environments, the design of data mining languages, and the application of data mining techniques to solve large application problems are important tasks for data mining researchers and data mining system and application developers. This section describes some of the trends in data mining that reflect the pursuit of these challenges:

- **Application exploration:** Early data mining applications focused mainly on helping businesses gain a competitive edge. The exploration of data mining for businesses continues to expand as e-commerce and e-marketing have become mainstream elements of the retail industry. Data mining is increasingly used for the exploration of applications in other areas, such as financial analysis, telecommunications, biomedicine, and science. Emerging application areas include data mining for counterterrorism (including and beyond intrusion detection) and mobile (wireless) data mining. As generic data mining systems may have limitations in dealing with application-specific problems, we may see a trend toward the development of more application-specific data mining systems.

- **Scalable and interactive data mining methods:** In contrast with traditional data analysis methods, data mining must be able to handle huge amounts of data efficiently and, if possible, interactively. Because the amount of data being collected continues to increase rapidly, scalable algorithms for individual and integrated data mining functions become essential. One important direction toward improving the overall efficiency of the mining process while increasing user interaction is **constraint-based mining.** This provides users with added control by allowing the specification and use of constraints to guide data mining systems in their search for interesting patterns.

- **Integration of data mining with database systems, data warehouse systems, and Web database systems:** Database systems, data warehouse systems, and the Web have become mainstream information processing systems. It is important to ensure that data mining serves as an essential data analysis component that can be smoothly integrated into such an information processing environment. As discussed earlier, a data mining system should be tightly coupled with database and data warehouse systems. Transaction management, query processing, on-line analytical processing, and on-line analytical mining should be integrated into one unified framework. This will ensure data availability, data mining portability, scalability, high performance, and an integrated information processing environment for multidimensional data analysis and exploration.

- **Standardization of data mining language:** A standard data mining language or other standardization efforts will facilitate the systematic development of data mining solutions, improve interoperability among multiple data mining systems and functions, and promote the education and use of data mining systems in industry and society. Recent efforts in this direction include Microsoft's OLE DB for Data Mining (the appendix of this book provides an introduction), PMML, and CRISP-DM.

- **Visual data mining:** Visual data mining is an effective way to discover knowledge from huge amounts of data. The systematic study and development of visual data mining techniques will facilitate the promotion and use of data mining as a tool for data analysis.

- **New methods for mining complex types of data:** As shown in Chapters 8 to 10, mining complex types of data is an important research frontier in data mining. Although progress has been made in mining stream, time-series, sequence, graph, spatiotemporal, multimedia, and text data, there is still a huge gap between the needs for these applications and the available technology. More research is required, especially toward the integration of data mining methods with existing data analysis techniques for these types of data.

- **Biological data mining:** Although biological data mining can be considered under "application exploration" or "mining complex types of data," the unique combination of complexity, richness, size, and importance of biological data warrants special attention in data mining. Mining DNA and protein sequences, mining high-dimensional microarray data, biological pathway and network analysis, link analysis across heterogeneous biological data, and information integration of biological data by data mining are interesting topics for biological data mining research.

- **Data mining and software engineering:** As software programs become increasingly bulky in size, sophisticated in complexity, and tend to originate from the integration of multiple components developed by different software teams, it is an increasingly challenging task to ensure software robustness and reliability. The analysis of the executions of a buggy software program is essentially a data mining process—tracing the data generated during program executions may disclose important patterns and outliers that may lead to the eventual automated discovery of software bugs. We expect that the further development of data mining methodologies for software debugging will enhance software robustness and bring new vigor to software engineering.

- **Web mining:** Issues related to Web mining were also discussed in Chapter 10. Given the huge amount of information available on the Web and the increasingly important role that the Web plays in today's society, Web content mining, Weblog mining, and data mining services on the Internet will become one of the most important and flourishing subfields in data mining.
- **Distributed data mining:** Traditional data mining methods, designed to work at a centralized location, do not work well in many of the distributed computing environments present today (e.g., the Internet, intranets, local area networks, high-speed wireless networks, and sensor networks). Advances in distributed data mining methods are expected.
- **Real-time or time-critical data mining:** Many applications involving stream data (such as e-commerce, Web mining, stock analysis, intrusion detection, mobile data mining, and data mining for counterterrorism) require dynamic data mining models to be built in real time. Additional development is needed in this area.
- **Graph mining, link analysis, and social network analysis:** Graph mining, link analysis, and social network analysis are useful for capturing sequential, topological, geometric, and other relational characteristics of many scientific data sets (such as for chemical compounds and biological networks) and social data sets (such as for the analysis of hidden criminal networks). Such modeling is also useful for analyzing links in Web structure mining. The development of efficient graph and linkage models is a challenge for data mining.
- **Multirelational and multidatabase data mining:** Most data mining approaches search for patterns in a single relational table or in a single database. However, most real-world data and information are spread across multiple tables and databases. Multirelational data mining methods search for patterns involving multiple tables (relations) from a relational database. Multidatabase mining searches for patterns across multiple databases. Further research is expected in effective and efficient data mining across multiple relations and multiple databases.
- **Privacy protection and information security in data mining:** An abundance of recorded personal information available in electronic forms and on the Web, coupled with increasingly powerful data mining tools, poses a threat to our privacy and data security. Growing interest in data mining for counterterrorism also adds to the threat. Further development of privacy-preserving data mining methods is

foreseen. The collaboration of technologists, social scientists, law experts, and companies is needed to produce a rigorous definition of privacy and a formalism to prove privacy-preservation in data mining.

We look forward to the next generation of data mining technology and the further benefits that it will bring with confidence.

11.6 Summary

- Many customized data mining tools have been developed for **domain-specific applications**, including finance, the retail industry, telecommunications, bioinformatics, intrusion detection, and other science, engineering, and government data analysis. Such practice integrates domain-specific knowledge with data analysis techniques and provides mission-specific data mining solutions.
- There are many data mining systems and research prototypes to choose from. When selecting a data mining product that is appropriate for one's task, it is important to consider various **features of data mining systems** *from a multidimensional point of view*. These include data types, system issues, data sources, data mining functions and methodologies, tight coupling of the data mining system with a database or data warehouse system, scalability, visualization tools, and data mining query language and graphical user interfaces.
- Researchers have been striving to build **theoretical foundations** for data mining. Several interesting proposals have appeared, based on data reduction, data compression, pattern discovery, probability theory, microeconomic theory, and inductive databases.
- **Visual data mining** integrates data mining and data visualization in order to discover implicit and useful knowledge from large data sets. Forms of visual data mining include *data visualization, data mining result visualization, data mining process visualization*, and *interactive visual data mining*. **Audio data mining** uses audio signals to indicate data patterns or features of data mining results.
- Several well-established **statistical methods** have been proposed for data analysis, such as regression, generalized linear models, analysis of variance, mixed-effect models, factor analysis, discriminant analysis, time-series analysis, survival analysis, and quality control. Full coverage of statistical data analysis methods is beyond the scope of this book. Interested readers are referred to the statistical literature cited in the bibliographic notes for background on such statistical analysis tools.
- **Collaborative recommender systems** offer personalized product recommendations based on the opinions of other customers. They may employ data mining or statistical techniques to search for similarities among customer preferences.

- **Ubiquitous data mining** is the ever presence of data mining in many aspects of our daily lives. It can influence how we shop, work, search for information, and use a computer, as well as our leisure time, health, and well-being. In **invisible data mining**, "smart" software, such as Web search engines, customer-adaptive Web services (e.g., using recommender algorithms), e-mail managers, and so on, incorporates data mining into its functional components, often unbeknownst to the user.
- A major social concern of data mining is the issue of *privacy and data security*, particularly as the amount of data collected on individuals continues to grow. **Fair information practices** were established for privacy and data protection and cover aspects regarding the collection and use of personal data. **Data mining for counterterrorism** can benefit homeland security and save lives, yet raises additional concerns for privacy due to the possible access of personal data. Efforts towards ensuring privacy and data security include the development of **privacy-preserving data mining** (which deals with obtaining valid data mining results without learning the underlying data values) and **data security–enhancing techniques** (such as encryption).
- **Trends in data mining** include further efforts toward the exploration of new application areas, improved scalable and interactive methods (including constraint-based mining), the integration of data mining with data warehousing and database systems, the standardization of data mining languages, visualization methods, and new methods for handling complex data types. Other trends include biological data mining, mining software bugs, Web mining, distributed and real-time mining, graph mining, social network analysis, multirelational and multidatabase data mining, data privacy protection, and data security.

Exercises

11.1 Research and describe an *application of data mining* that was not presented in this chapter. Discuss how different forms of data mining can be used in the application.

11.2 Suppose that you are in the market to purchase a data mining system.

(a) Regarding the coupling of a data mining system with a database and/or data warehouse system, what are the differences between *no coupling*, *loose coupling*, *semitight coupling*, and *tight coupling*?

(b) What is the difference between *row scalability* and *column scalability*?

(c) Which feature(s) from those listed above would you look for when selecting a data mining system?

11.3 Study an existing *commercial data mining system*. Outline the major features of such a system from a multidimensional point of view, including data types handled, architecture of the system, data sources, data mining functions, data mining methodologies, coupling with database or data warehouse systems, scalability, visualization tools, and graphical user interfaces. Can you propose one improvement to such a system and outline how to realize it?

11.4 **(Research project)** Relational database query languages, like SQL, have played an essential role in the development of relational database systems. Similarly, a *data mining query language* may provide great flexibility for users to interact with a data mining system and pose various kinds of data mining queries and constraints. It is expected that different data mining query languages may be designed for mining different types of data (such as relational, text, spatiotemporal, and multimedia data) and for different kinds of applications (such as financial data analysis, biological data analysis, and social network analysis). Select an application. Based on your application requirements and the types of data to be handled, design such a data mining language and study its implementation and optimization issues.

11.5 Why is the establishment of *theoretical foundations* important for data mining? Name and describe the main theoretical foundations that have been proposed for data mining. Comment on how they each satisfy (or fail to satisfy) the requirements of an ideal theoretical framework for data mining.

11.6 **(Research project)** Building a theory for data mining is to set up a *theoretical framework* so that the major data mining functions can be explained under this framework. Take one theory as an example (e.g., data compression theory) and examine how the major data mining functions can fit into this framework. If some functions cannot fit well in the current theoretical framework, can you propose a way to extend the framework so that it can explain these functions?

11.7 There is a strong linkage between *statistical data analysis* and data mining. Some people think of data mining as automated and scalable methods for statistical data analysis. Do you agree or disagree with this perception? Present one statistical analysis method that can be automated and/or scaled up nicely by integration with the current data mining methodology.

11.8 What are the differences between *visual data mining* and *data visualization*? Data visualization may suffer from the data abundance problem. For example, it is not easy to visually discover interesting properties of network connections if a social network is huge, with complex and dense connections. Propose a data mining method that may help people see through the network topology to the interesting features of the social network.

11.9 Propose a few implementation methods for *audio data mining*. Can we integrate audio and *visual data mining* to bring fun and power to data mining? Is it possible to develop some video data mining methods? State some scenarios and your solutions to make such integrated audiovisual mining effective.

11.10 General-purpose computers and domain-independent relational database systems have become a large market in the last several decades. However, many people feel that generic data mining systems will not prevail in the data mining market. What do you think? For data mining, should we focus our efforts on developing *domain-independent* data mining tools or on developing *domain-specific* data mining solutions? Present your reasoning.

11.11 What is a *collaborative recommender system*? In what ways does it differ from a customeror product-based clustering system? How does it differ from a typical classification or predictive modeling system? Outline one method of collaborative filtering. Discuss why it works and what its limitations are in practice.

11.12 Suppose that your local bank has a data mining system. The bank has been studying your debit card usage patterns. Noticing that you make many transactions at home renovation stores, the bank decides to contact you, offering information regarding their special loans for home improvements.

(a) Discuss how this may conflict with your right to *privacy*.

(b) Describe another situation in which you feel that data mining can infringe on your privacy.

(c) Describe a *privacy-preserving data mining* method that may allow the bank to perform customer pattern analysis without infringing on customers' right to privacy.

(d) What are some examples where data mining could be used to help society? Can you think of ways it could be used that may be detrimental to society?

11.13 What are the major challenges faced in bringing data mining research to *market*? Illustrate one data mining research issue that, in your view, may have a strong impact on the market and on society. Discuss how to approach such a research issue.

11.14 Based on your view, what is the most *challenging research problem* in data mining? If you were given a number of years of time and a good number of researchers and implementors, can you work out a plan so that progress can be made toward a solution to such a problem? How?

11.15 Based on your study, suggest a possible *new frontier* in data mining that was not mentioned in this chapter.

Bibliographic Notes

Many books discuss applications of data mining. For financial data analysis and financial modeling, see Benninga and Czaczkes [BC00] and Higgins [Hig03]. For retail data mining and customer relationship management, see books by Berry and Linoff [BL04] and Berson, Smith, and Thearling [BST99], and the article by Kohavi [Koh01]. For telecommunication-related data mining, see the book by Mattison [Mat97]. Chen, Hsu, and Dayal [CHD00] reported their work on scalable telecommunication tandem traffic analysis under a data warehouse/OLAP framework. For bioinformatics and biological data analysis, there are many introductory references and textbooks. An introductory overview of bioinformatics for computer scientists was presented by Cohen [Coh04]. Recent textbooks on bioinformatics include Krane and Raymer [KR03], Jones and Pevzner [JP04], Durbin, Eddy, Krogh, and Mitchison [DEKM98], Setubal and Meidanis [SM97], Orengo, Jones, and Thornton [OJT$^+$03], and Pevzner [Pev03]. Summaries of biological data analysis methods and algorithms can also be found in many other books, such as Gusfield [Gus97], Waterman [Wat95], Baldi and Brunak [BB01], and Baxevanis and Ouellette [BO04]. There are many books on scientific data analysis, such as Grossman, Kamath, Kegelmeyer, et al. (eds.) [GKK$^+$01]. For geographic data mining, see the book edited by Miller and Han [MH01b]. Valdes-Perez [VP99] discusses the principles of human-computer collaboration for knowledge discovery in science. For intrusion detection, see Barbará [Bar02] and Northcutt and Novak [NN02].

Many data mining books contain introductions to various kinds of data mining systems and products. KDnuggets maintains an up-to-date list of data mining products at *www.kdnuggets.com/companies/products.html* and the related software at *www.kdnug gets.com/software/index.html*, respectively. For a survey of data mining and knowledge discovery software tools, see Goebel and Gruenwald [GG99]. Detailed information regarding specific data mining systems and products can be found by consulting the Web pages of the companies offering these products, the user manuals for the products in question, or magazines and journals on data mining and data warehousing. For example, the Web page URLs for the data mining systems introduced in this chapter are *www-4.ibm.com/software/data/iminer* for IBM Intelligent Miner, *www.microsoft.com/sql/evaluation/features/datamine.asp* for Microsoft SQL Server, *www.purpleinsight.com/products* for MineSet of Purple Insight, *www.oracle.com/technology/products/bi/odm* for Oracle Data Mining (ODM), *www.spss.com/clementine* for Clementine of SPSS, *www.sas.com/technologies/analytics/datamining/miner* for SAS Enterprise Miner, and *www.insightful.com/products/iminer* for Insightful Miner of Insightful Inc. CART and See5/C5.0 are available from *www.salford-systems.com* and *www.rulequest.com*, respectively. Weka is available from the University of Waikato at *www.cs.waikato.ac.nz/ml/weka*. Since data mining systems and their functions evolve rapidly, it is not our intention to provide any kind of comprehensive survey on data mining systems in this book. We apologize if your data mining systems or tools were not included.

Issues on the theoretical foundations of data mining are addressed in many research papers. Mannila presented a summary of studies on the foundations of data mining in [Man00]. The data reduction view of data mining was summarized in *The New Jersey Data Reduction Report* by Barbará, DuMouchel, Faloutos, et al. [BDF$^+$97]. The data compression view can be found in studies on the minimum description length (MDL) principle, such as Quinlan and Rivest [QR89] and Chakrabarti, Sarawagi, and Dom [CSD98]. The pattern discovery point of view of data mining is addressed in numerous machine learning and data mining studies, ranging from association mining, decision tree induction, and neural network classification to sequential pattern mining, clustering, and so on. The probability theory point of view can be seen in the statistics literature, such as in studies on Bayesian networks and hierarchical Bayesian models, as addressed in Chapter 6. Kleinberg, Papadimitriou, and Raghavan [KPR98] presented a microeconomic view, treating data mining as an optimization problem. The view of data mining as the querying of inductive databases was proposed by Imielinski and Mannila [IM96].

Statistical techniques for data analysis are described in several books, including *Intelligent Data Analysis* (2nd ed.), edited by Berthold and Hand [BH03]; *Probability and Statistics for Engineering and the Sciences* (6th ed.) by Devore [Dev03]; *Applied Linear Statistical Models with Student CD* by Kutner, Nachtsheim, Neter, and Li [KNNL04]; *An*

Introduction to Generalized Linear Models (2nd ed.) by Dobson [Dob01]; *Classification and Regression Trees* by Breiman, Friedman, Olshen, and Stone [BFOS84]; *Mixed Effects Models in S and S-PLUS* by Pinheiro and Bates [PB00]; *Applied Multivariate Statistical Analysis* (5th ed.) by Johnson and Wichern [JW02]; *Applied Discriminant Analysis* by Huberty [Hub94]; *Time Series Analysis and Its Applications* by Shumway and Stoffer [SS05]; and *Survival Analysis* by Miller [Mil98].

For visual data mining, popular books on the visual display of data and information include those by Tufte [Tuf90, Tuf97, Tuf01]. A summary of techniques for visualizing data was presented in Cleveland [Cle93]. For information about StatSoft, a statistical analysis system that allows data visualization, see *www.statsoft.inc*. A VisDB system for database exploration using multidimensional visualization methods was developed by Keim and Kriegel [KK94]. Ankerst, Elsen, Ester, and Kriegel [AEEK99] present a perception-based classification approach (PBC), for interactive visual classification. The book *Information Visualization in Data Mining and Knowledge Discovery*, edited by Fayyad, Grinstein, and Wierse [FGW01], contains a collection of articles on visual data mining methods.

There are many research papers on collaborative recommender systems. These include the GroupLens architecture for collaborative filtering by Resnick, Iacovou, Suchak, et al. [RIS$^+$94]; empirical analysis of predictive algorithms for collaborative filtering by Breese, Heckerman, and Kadie [BHK98]; its applications in information tapestry by Goldberg, Nichols, Oki, and Terry [GNOT92]; a method for learning collaborative information filters by Billsus and Pazzani [BP98a]; an algorithmic framework for performing collaborative filtering proposed by Herlocker, Konstan, Borchers, and Riedl [HKBR98]; item-based collaborative filtering recommendation algorithms by Sarwar, Karypis, Konstan, and Riedl [SKKR01] and Lin, Alvarez, and Ruiz [LAR02]; and content-boosted collaborative filtering for improved recommendations by Melville, Mooney, and Nagarajan [MMN02].

Many examples of ubiquitous and invisible data mining can be found in an insightful and entertaining article by John [Joh99], and a survey of Web mining by Srivastava, Desikan, and Kumar [SDK04]. The use of data mining at Wal-Mart was depicted in Hays [Hay04]. Bob, the automated fast food management system of HyperActive Technologies, is described at *www.hyperactivetechnologies.com*. The book *Business @ the Speed of Thought: Succeeding in the Digital Economy* by Gates [Gat00] discusses e-commerce and customer relationship management, and provides an interesting perspective on data mining in the future. For an account on the use of Clementine by police to control crime, see Beal [Bea04]. Mena [Men03] has an informative book on the use of data mining to detect and prevent crime. It covers many forms of criminal activities, including fraud detection, money laundering, insurance crimes, identity crimes, and intrusion detection.

Data mining issues regarding privacy and data security are substantially addressed in literature. One of the first papers on data mining and privacy was by Clifton and Marks [CM96]. The Fair Information Practices discussed in Section 11.4.2 were presented by the Organization for Economic Co-operation and Development (OECD) [OEC98]. Laudon [Lau96] proposed a regulated national information market that would allow personal information to be bought and sold. Cavoukian [Cav98] considered opt-out choices and data security–enhancing techniques. Data security–enhancing techniques and other issues relating to privacy were discussed in Walstrom and Roddick [WR01]. Data mining for counterterrorism and its implications for privacy were discussed in Thuraisingham [Thu04]. A survey on privacy-preserving data mining can be found in Verykios, Bertino, Fovino, and Provenza [VBFP04]. Many algorithms have been proposed, including work by Agrawal and Srikant [AS00], Evfimievski, Srikant, Agrawal, and Gehrke [ESAG02], and Vaidya and Clifton [VC03]. Agrawal and Aggarwal [AA01] proposed a metric for assessing privacy preservation, based on differential entropy. Clifton, Kantarcioğlu, and Vaidya [CKV04] discussed the need to produce a rigorous definition of privacy and a formalism to prove privacy-preservation in data mining.

Data mining standards and languages have been discussed in several forums. The new book *Data Mining with SQL Server 2005*, by Tang and MacLennan [TM05], describes Microsoft's OLE DB for Data Mining. Other efforts toward standardized data mining languages include Predictive Model Markup Language (PMML), described at *www.dmg.org*, and Cross-Industry Standard Process for Data Mining (CRISP-DM), described at *www.crisp-dm.org*.

There have been lots of discussions on trend and research directions in data mining in various forums and occasions. A recent book that collects a set of articles on trends and challenges of data mining was edited by Kargupta, Joshi, Sivakumar, and Yesha [KJSY04]. For a tutorial on distributed data mining, see Kargupta and Sivakumar [KS04]. For multirelational data mining, see the introduction by Dzeroski [Dze03], as well as work by Yin, Han, Yang, and Yu [YHYY04]. For mobile data mining, see Kargupta, Bhargava, Liu, et al. [KBL$^+$04]. Washio and Motoda [WM03] presented a survey on graph-based mining, that also covers several typical pieces of work, including Su, Cook, and Holder [SCH99], Kuramochi and Karypis [KK01], and Yan and Han [YH02]. ACM SIGKDD Explorations had special issues on several of the topics we have addressed, including DNA microarray data mining (volume 5, number 2, December 2003); constraints in data mining (volume 4, number 1, June 2002); multirelational data mining (volume 5, number 1, July 2003); and privacy and security (volume 4, number 2, December 2002).

Appendix

An Introduction to Microsoft's OLE DB for Data Mining

Most data mining products are difficult to integrate with user applications due to the lack of standardization protocols. This current state of the data mining industry can be considered similar to the database industry before the introduction of SQL. Consider, for example, a classification application that uses a decision tree package from some vendor. Later, it is decided to employ, say, a support vector machine package from another vendor. Typically, each data mining vendor has its own data mining package, which does not communicate with other products. A difficulty arises as the products from the two different vendors do not have a common interface. The application must be rebuilt from scratch. An additional problem is that most commercial data mining products do not perform mining directly on relational databases, where most data are stored. Instead, the data must be extracted from a relational database to an intermediate storage format. This requires expensive data porting and transformation operations.

A solution to these problems has been proposed in the form of Microsoft's **OLE DB for Data Mining (OLE DB for DM)**.[1] OLE DB for DM is a major step toward the standardization of data mining language primitives and aims to become the industry standard. It adopts many concepts in relational database systems and applies them to the data mining field, providing a standard programming API. It is designed to allow data mining client applications (or *data mining consumers*) to consume data mining services from a wide variety of data mining software packages (or *data mining providers*). Figure A.1 shows the basic architecture of OLE DB for DM. It allows consumer applications to communicate with different data mining providers through the same API (SQL style). This appendix provides an introduction to OLE DB for DM.

[1]OLE DB for DM API Version 1.0 was introduced in July 2000. As of late 2005, Version 2.0 has not yet been released, although its release is planned shortly. The information presented in this appendix is based on Tang, MacLennan, and Kim [TMK05] and on a draft of Chapter 3: OLE DB for Data Mining from the upcoming book, *Data Mining with SQL Server 2005*, by Z. Tang and J. MacLennan from Wiley & Sons (2005) [TM05]. For additional details not presented in this appendix, readers may refer to the book and to Microsoft's forthcoming document on Version 2.0 (see *www.Microsoft.com*).

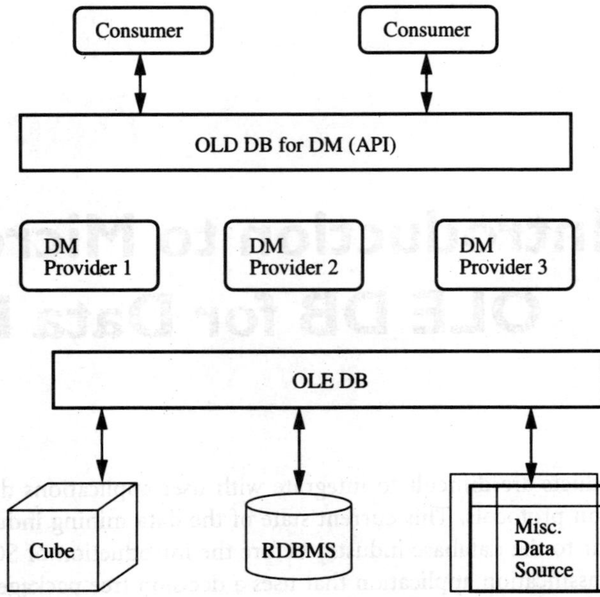

Figure A.1 Basic architecture of OLE DB for Data Mining [TMK05].

At the core of OLE DB for DM is **DMX** (Data Mining eXtensions), an SQL-like data mining query language. As an extension of OLE (Object Linking and Embedding) DB, OLE DB for DM allows the definition of a virtual object called a *Data Mining Model*. DMX statements can be used to create, modify, and work with data mining models. DMX also contains several functions that can be used to retrieve and display statistical information about the mining models. The manipulation of a data mining model is similar to that of an SQL table.

OLE DB for DM describes an abstraction of the data mining process. The three main operations performed are *model creation*, *model training*, and *model prediction and browsing*. These are described as follows:

1. **Model creation.** First, we must create a data mining model object (hereafter referred to as a data mining model), which is similar to the creation of a table in a relational database. At this point, we can think of the model as an empty table, defined by input columns, one or more *predictable* columns, and the name of the data mining algorithm to be used when the model is later trained by the data mining provider. The **create** command is used in this operation.

2. **Model training.** In this operation, data are loaded into the model and used to train it. The data mining provider uses the algorithm specified during creation of the model to search for patterns in the data. The resulting discovered patterns make up the model

content. They are stored in the data mining model, instead of the training data. The **insert** command is used in this operation.

3. **Model prediction and browsing.** A **select** statement is used to consult the data mining model content in order to make predictions and browse statistics obtained by the model.

Let's talk a bit about data. The data pertaining to a single entity (such as a customer) are referred to as a case. A simple case corresponds to a row in a table (defined by the attributes *customer_ID*, *gender*, and *age*, for example). Cases can also be nested, providing a list of information associated with a given entity. For example, if in addition to the customer attributes above, we also include the list of items purchased by the customer, this is an example of a **nested case**. A nested case contains at least one *table column*. OLE DB for DM uses table columns as defined by the Data Shaping Service included with Microsoft Data Access Components (MDAC) products.

Example A.1 A nested case of customer data. A given customer entity may be described by the columns (or attributes) *customer_ID*, *gender*, and *age*, and the table column, *item_purchases*, describing the set of items purchased by the customer (i.e., *item_name* and *item_quantity*), as follows:

customer_ID	*gender*	*age*	*item_purchases*	
			item_name	*item_quantity*
101	F	34	milk	3
			bread	2
			diapers	1

■

For the remainder of this appendix, we will study examples of each of the major data mining model operations: creation, training, and prediction and browsing.

A.1 Model Creation

A data mining model is considered as a relational table. The **create** command is used to create a mining model, as shown in the following example.

Example A.2 **Model creation.** The following statement specifies the columns of (or attributes defining) a data mining model for *home_ownership* prediction and the data mining algorithm to be used later for its training.

```
create mining model home_ownership_prediction
(
    customer_ID         long   key,
    gender              text   discrete,
    age                 long   discretized(),
    income              long   continuous,
    profession          text   discrete,
    home_ownership      text   discrete predict,
)
using Microsoft_Decision_Trees
```

The statement includes the following information. The model uses *gender, age, income,* and *profession* to predict the *home_ownership* category of the customer. Attribute *customer_ID* is of type **key**, meaning that it can uniquely identify a customer case row. Attributes gender and profession are of type **text**. Attribute *age* is continuous (of type **long**) but is to be discretized. The specification **discretized()** indicates that a default method of discretization is to be used. Alternatively, we could have used **discretized** (*method, n*), where *method* is a discretization method of the provider and *n* is the recommended number of buckets (intervals) to be used in dividing up the value range for *age*. The keyword **predict** shows that *home_ownership* is the predicted attribute for the model. Note that it is possible to have more than one predicted attribute, although, in this case, there is only one. Other attribute types not appearing above include **ordered, cyclical, sequence_time, probability, variance, stdev,** and **support**. The **using** clause specifies the decision tree algorithm to be used by the provider to later train the model. This clause may be followed by provider-specific pairs of parameter-value settings to be used by the algorithm. ■

Let's look at another example. This one includes a table column, which lists the items purchased by each customer.

Example A.3 **Model creation involving a table column (for nested cases).** Suppose that we would like to predict the items (and their associated quantity and name) that a customer may be interested in buying, based on the customer's gender, age, income, profession, home ownership status, and items already purchased by the customer. The specification for this market basket model is:

```
create mining model market_basket_prediction
(
    customer_ID         long   key,
    gender              text   discrete,
    age                 long   discretized(),
    income              long   continuous,
    profession          text   discrete,
    home_ownership      text   discrete,
item_purchases      table predict
```

```
    (
        item_name       text    key,
        item_quantity   long    normal continuous,
    )
)
using Microsoft_Decision_Trees
```

The predicted attribute *item_purchases* is actually a table column (for nested cases) defined by *item_name* (a key of *item_purchases*) and *item_quantity*. Knowledge of the distribution of continuous attributes may be used by some data mining providers. Here, *item_quantity* is known to have a normal distribution, and so this is specified. Other distribution models include uniform, lognormal, binomial, multinomial, and Poisson.

If we do not want the items already purchased to be considered by the model, we would replace the keyword **predict** by **predict_only**. This specifies that *items_purchased* is to be used only as a predictable column and not as an input column as well. ■

Creating data mining models is straightforward with the **insert** command. In the next section, we look at how to train the models.

A.2 Model Training

In model training, data are loaded into the data mining model. The data mining algorithm that was specified during model creation is now invoked. It "consumes" or analyzes the data to discover patterns among the attribute values. These patterns (such as rules, for example) or an abstraction of them are then inserted into or stored in the mining model, forming part of the *model content*. Hence, an **insert** command is used to specify model training. At the end of the command's execution, it is the discovered patterns, not the training data, that populate the mining model.

The model training syntax is

```
insert into ⟨mining_model_name⟩
    [ ⟨mapped_model_columns⟩ ]
⟨source_data_query⟩,
```

where ⟨mining_model_name⟩ specifies the model to be trained and ⟨mapped_model_columns⟩ lists the columns of the model to which input data are to be mapped. Typically, ⟨source_data_query⟩ is a **select** query from a relational database, which retrieves the training data. Most data mining providers are embedded within the relational database management system (RDBMS) containing the source data, in which case, ⟨source_data_query⟩ needs to read data from other data sources. The **openrowset** statement of OLE DB supports querying data from a data source through an OLE DB provider. The syntax is

```
openrowset('provider_name', 'provider_string', 'database query'),
```

where 'provider_name' is the name of the OLE DB provider (such as MSSQL for Microsoft SQL Server), 'provider_string' is the connection string for the provider, and 'database query' is the SQL query supported by the provider. The query returns a rowset, which is the training data. Note that the training data does not have to be loaded ahead of time and does not have to be transformed into any intermediate storage format.

If the training data contains nested cases, then the database query must use the **shape** command, provided by the Data Shaping Service defined in OLE DB. This creates a *hierarchical rowset*, that is, it loads the nested cases into the relevant table columns, as necessary.

Let's look at an example that brings all of these ideas together.

Example A.4 **Model training.** The following statement specifies the training data to be used to populate the *model_basket_prediction* model. Training the model results in populating it with the discovered patterns. The line numbers are shown only to aid in our explanation.

```
(1) insert into market_basket_prediction
(2) (  customer_ID, gender, age, income, profession, home_ownership
(3)    item_purchases (skip, item_name, item_quantity)
(4) )
(5) openrowset('sqloledb', 'myserver'; 'mylogin'; 'mypwd',
(6)    'shape
(7)        { select customer_ID, gender, age, income, profession,
                   home_ownership from Customers }
(8)        append
(9)        (   { select cust_ID, item_name, item_quantity from Purchases }
(10)       relate customer_ID to cust_ID)
(11)       as item_purchases'
(12)  )
```

Line 1 uses the **insert into** command to populate the model, with lines 2 and 3 specifying the fields in the model to be populated. The keyword **skip** in line 3 is used because the source data contains a column that is not used by the data mining model. The **openrowset** command accesses the source data. Because our model contains a table column, the **shape** command (lines 6 to 11) is used to create the nested table, *item_purchases.*

Suppose instead that we wanted to train our simpler model, *home_ownership_prediction*, which does not contain any table column. The statement would be the same as above except that lines 6 to 11 would be replaced by the line

```
'select customer_ID, gender, age, income, profession, home_ownership
    from Customers'
```

■

In summary, the manner in which the data mining model is populated is similar to that for populating an ordinary table. Note that the statement is independent of the data mining algorithm used.

A.3 Model Prediction and Browsing

A trained model can be considered a sort of "truth table," conceptually containing a row for every possible combination of values for each column (attribute) in the data mining model, including any predicted columns as well. This table is a major component of the *model content*. It can be browsed to make predictions or to look up learned statistics.

Predictions are made for a set of *test data* (containing, say, new customers for which the *home_ownership* status is not known). The test data are "joined" with the mining model (i.e., the truth table) using a special kind of join known as **prediction join**. A **select** command retrieves the resulting predictions.

In this section, we look at several examples of using a data mining model to make predictions, as well as querying and browsing the model content.

Example A.5 **Model prediction.** This statement predicts the home ownership status of customers based on the model *home_ownership_prediction*. In particular, we are only interested in the status of customers older than 35 years of age.

```
(1) select t.customer_ID, home_ownership_prediction.home_ownership
(2) from home_ownership_prediction
(3) prediction join
(4) openrowset('Provider=Microsoft.Jet.OLEDB'; 'datasource=c\:customer.db,'
(5)       'select * from Customers') as t
(6) on home_ownership_prediction.gender = t.gender and
(7)       home_ownership_prediction.age = t.age and
(8)       home_ownership_prediction.income = t.income and
(9)       home_ownership_prediction.profession = t.profession
(10) where t.age > 35
```

The **prediction join** operator joins the model's "truth table" (set of all possible cases) with the test data specified by the **openrowset** command (lines 4 to 5). The join is made on the conditions specified by the **on** clause (in lines 6 to 9), where customers must be at least 35 years old (line 10). Note that the dot operator (".") can be used to refer to a column from the scope of a nested case. The **select** command (line 1) operates on the resulting join, returning a *home_ownership* prediction for each *customer_ID*.

Note that if the column names of the input table (test cases) are exactly the same as the column names of the mining model, we can alternatively use **natural prediction join** in line 3 and omit the **on** clause (lines 6 to 9). ■

In addition, the model can be queried for various values and statistics, as shown in the following example.

Example A.6 **List distinct values for an attribute.** The set of distinct values for *profession* can be retrieved with the statement

```
select distinct profession from home_ownership_prediction
```

Similarly, the list of all items that may be purchased can be obtained with the statement

```
select distinct item_purchases.item_name from home_ownership_prediction
```

■

OLE DB for DM provides several functions that can be used to statistically describe predictions. For example, the likelihood of a predicted value can be viewed with the **PredictProbability()** function, as shown in the following example.

Example A.7 List predicted probability for each class/category or cluster. This statement returns a table with the predicted home ownership status of each customer, along with the associated probability.

```
select customer_ID, Predict(home_ownership), PredictProbability
       (home_ownership) as prob
...
```

The output is:

customer_ID	*home_ownership*	*prob*
101	owns_house	0.78
102	rents	0.85
103	owns_house	0.90
104	owns_condo	0.55
...	...	...

For each customer, the model returns the most probable class value (here, the status of *home_ownership*) and the corresponding probability. Note that, as a shortcut, we could have selected *home_ownership* directly, that is, "**select** home_ownership" is the same as "**select Predict**(home_ownership)."

If, instead, we are interested in the predicted probability of a particular home ownership status, such as *owns_house*, we can add this as a parameter of the **PredictProbability** function, as follows:

```
select customer_ID, Predict(home_ownership, 'owns_house') as prob_owns_house
...
```

This returns:

customer_ID	*prob_owns_house*
101	0.78
102	0.05
103	0.90
104	0.27
...	...

Suppose, instead, that we have a model that groups the data into clusters. The **Cluster()** and **ClusterProbability()** functions can be similarly used to view the probability associated with each cluster membership assignment, as in:

```
select customer_ID, gender, Cluster() as C, ClusterProbability() as CP
...
```

This returns:

customer_ID	*gender*	*C*	*CP*
101	F	3	0.37
102	M	5	0.26
...	...	...	...

where *C* is a cluster identifier showing the most likely cluster to which a case belongs and *CP* is the associated probability. ■

OLE DB for DM provides several other prediction functions that return a scalar (nontable) value, such as **PredictSupport()**, which returns the count of cases in support of the predicted column value; **PredictStdev()** and **PredictVariance()** for the standard deviation and variance, respectively, of the predicted attribute (generally for continuous attributes); and **PredictProbabilityStdev()** and **PredictProbabilityVariance()**. The functions **RangeMid()**, **RangeMin()**, and **RangeMax()**, respectively, return the midpoint, minimum, and maximum value of the predicted bucket for a discretized column.

The **PredictHistogram()** function can be used to return a histogram of all possible values and associated statistics for a predicted or clustered column. The histogram is in the form of a table column, which includes the columns **$Support**, **$Variance**, **$Stdev**, **$Probability**, **$ProbabilityVariance**, and **$ProbabilityStdev**.

Example A.8 List histogram with predictions. The following provides a histogram for the predicted attribute, *home_ownership*, showing the support and probability of each home ownership category:

```
select customer_ID, PredictHistogram(home_ownership) as histogram
```

customer_ID	*histogram*			
	home_ownership	*$Support*	*$Probability*	...
101	owns_house owns_condo rents	786 134 80	0.786 0.134 0.080	... ...
...	...	...	...	...

■

If the argument of PredictHistogram is **Cluster()**, then a histogram is returned for each case showing the possible cluster identifiers and associated support, probability, and so on. OLE DB for DM provides other functions that also return table columns. For example, **TopCount** can be used to view the top *k* rows in a nested table, per case, as determined according to a user-specified rank function. This is useful when the number of nested rows per case is large. **TopSum** returns the top *k* rows, per case, such that the total value for a specified reference column is at least a specified sum. Other examples include **PredictAssociation**, **PredictSequence**, and **PredictTimeSeries**. Note that some functions can take either table columns or scalar (nontable) columns as input, such as **Predict** and the latter two above.

Let's look at how we may predict associations.

Example A.9 Predict associations. The following uses the **PredictAssociation** function to produce a list of items a customer may be interested in buying, based on the items the customer has already bought. It uses our market basket model of Example A.3:

```
select customer_ID, PredictAssociation(item_purchases, exclusive)
from market_basket_prediction
prediction join
    openrowset(...)
```

The **PredictAssociation** function returns the table column, *item_purchases*.

customer_ID	*gender*	*item_purchases*	
		item_name	*item_quantity*
101	F	milk bread cereal eggs	3 2 2 1

The parameter **exclusive** specifies that any items the customer may have purchased are not to be included (i.e., only a prediction of what other items a customer is likely to buy is shown). ■

There are a few things to note regarding this example. First, the **Predict** function is special in that it knows what kind of knowledge is being predicted, based on the data mining algorithm specified for the model. Therefore, specifying **Predict**(item_purchases) in this query is equivalent to specifying **PredictAssociation**(item_purchases).

There are two alternatives to the **exclusive** parameter, namely, **inclusive** and **input_only**. We use **inclusive** if we want the prediction to contain the *complete* set of items available in the store, with associated predicted quantities. Suppose instead that we are only interested in a subset of the complete set of items (where this subset is the "input case"). Specifically, for each of these items, we want to predict the quantity that a customer may purchase, or the likelihood of purchasing the item. In this case, we would specify **input_only** as the parameter.

How do we specify that we are interested in the likelihood that the customer will purchase an item, for each item in a given input set? We add the **include_statistics** parameter to the **Predict** (or **PredictAssociation**) function. These statistics are **$Support** and **$Probability**, which are included as columns in the output for *item_purchases*. For a given item and customer combination, **$Support** is the number of similar cases (i.e., customers who bought the same item as the given customer and who have the same profile information). **$Probability** is the likelihood we mentioned earlier. That is, it is the likelihood that a customer will buy the given item. (Note that this is not the likelihood of the predicted quantity.) This results in the query:

```
select customer_ID, Predict(item_purchases, include_statistics, input_only)
from market_basket_prediction
prediction join
    openrowset(...)
```

OLE DB for DM has defined a set of *schema rowsets*, which are tables of metadata. We can access such metadata regarding the mining services available on a server (where the services may come from different providers); the parameters for each of the mining algorithms; mining models; model columns; and model content. Such information can be queried.

Example A.10 **Model content query.** The following returns the discovered patterns, represented in tabular format. (This is the "truth table" we referred to earlier.)

```
select * from home_ownership_prediction.content
```

■

The model's content may also be queried to view a set of nodes (e.g., for a decision tree), rules, formulae, or distributions. This content depends on the data mining algorithm used. The content may also be viewed by extracting an XML description of it in the form of a string. Interpretation of such a string, however, requires expertise on behalf of the client application. Navigational operations are provided for browsing model content represented as a directed graph (e.g., a decision tree). Discovered rules may also be extracted in PMML (Predictive Model Markup Language) format.

For these methods to function, the client must have certain components, namely, the OLE DB client for ADO programming or the DSO libraries for DSO programming.

However, in cases where it is not feasible to install the client components, developers can use Microsoft's XML for Analysis. XML for Analysis is a SOAP-based XML API that standardizes the interaction between clients and analytical data providers. It allows connection and interaction from any client platform without any specific client components to communicate to the server. This facilitates application deployment and allows cross-platform development.

As we have seen, OLE DB for DM is a powerful tool for creating and training data mining models and using them for predictions. It is a major step toward the standardization of a provider-independent data mining language. Together with XML for Analysis, data mining algorithms from various vendors can easily plug into consumer applications.

Bibliography

[AA01] D. Agrawal and C. C. Aggarwal. On the design and quantification of privacy preserving data mining algorithms. In *Proc. 2001 ACM SIGMOD-SIGACT-SIGART Symp. Principles of Database Systems (PODS'01)*, pages 247–255, Santa Barbara, CA, May 2001.

[AAD+96] S. Agarwal, R. Agrawal, P. M. Deshpande, A. Gupta, J. F. Naughton, R. Ramakrishnan, and S. Sarawagi. On the computation of multidimensional aggregates. In *Proc. 1996 Int. Conf. Very Large Data Bases (VLDB'96)*, pages 506–521, Bombay, India, Sept. 1996.

[AAK+02] T. Asai, K. Abe, S. Kawasoe, H. Arimura, H. Satamoto, and S. Arikawa. Efficient substructure discovery from large semi-structured data. In *Proc. 2002 SIAM Int. Conf. Data Mining (SDM'02)*, pages 158–174, Arlington, VA, April 2002.

[AAP01] R. Agarwal, C. C. Aggarwal, and V. V. V. Prasad. A tree projection algorithm for generation of frequent itemsets. *J. Parallel and Distributed Computing*, 61:350–371, 2001.

[AAR96] A. Arning, R. Agrawal, and P. Raghavan. A linear method for deviation detection in large databases. In *Proc. 1996 Int. Conf. Data Mining and Knowledge Discovery (KDD'96)*, pages 164–169, Portland, Oregon, Aug. 1996.

[AB99] R. Albert and A.-L. Barabasi. Emergence of scaling in random networks. *Science*, 286:509–512, 1999.

[ABKS99] M. Ankerst, M. Breunig, H.-P. Kriegel, and J. Sander. OPTICS: Ordering points to identify the clustering structure. In *Proc. 1999 ACM-SIGMOD Int. Conf. Management of Data (SIGMOD'99)*, pages 49–60, Philadelphia, PA, June 1999.

[ACM03] A. Appice, M. Ceci, and D. Malerba. Mining model trees: A multi-relational approach. In *Proc. 2003 Int. Conf. Inductive Logic Programming (ILP'03)*, pages 4–21, Szeged, Hungary, Sept. 2003.

[AD91] H. Almuallim and T. G. Dietterich. Learning with many irrelevant features. In *Proc. 1991 Nat. Conf. Artificial Intelligence (AAAI'91)*, pages 547–552, Anaheim, CA, July 1991.

[AEEK99] M. Ankerst, C. Elsen, M. Ester, and H.-P. Kriegel. Visual classification: An interactive approach to decision tree construction. In *Proc. 1999 Int. Conf. Knowledge Discovery and Data Mining (KDD'99)*, pages 392–396, San Diego, CA, Aug. 1999.

[AEMT00] K. M. Ahmed, N. M. El-Makky, and Y. Taha. A note on "beyond market basket: Generalizing association rules to correlations." *SIGKDD Explorations*, 1:46–48, 2000.

[AFS93] R. Agrawal, C. Faloutsos, and A. Swami. Efficient similarity search in sequence databases. In *Proc. 4th Int. Conf. Foundations of Data Organization and Algorithms*, pages 69–84, Chicago, IL, Oct. 1993.

[AGGR98] R. Agrawal, J. Gehrke, D. Gunopulos, and P. Raghavan. Automatic subspace clustering of high dimensional data for data mining applications. In *Proc. 1998 ACM-SIGMOD Int. Conf. Management of Data (SIGMOD'98)*, pages 94–105, Seattle, WA, June 1998.

[AGM+90] S. F. Altschul, W. Gish, W, Miller, E. W. Myers, and D. J. Lipman. Basic local alignment search tool. J. Mol. Biol., 215(3): 403–410, Oct 1990.

[AGM04] F. N. Afrati, A. Gionis, and H. Mannila. Approximating a collection of frequent sets. In *Proc. 2004 ACM SIGKDD Int. Conf. Knowledge Discovery in Databases (KDD'04)*, pages 12–19, Seattle, WA, Aug. 2004.

[Agr96] A. Agresti. *An Introduction to Categorical Data Analysis*. John Wiley & Sons, 1996.

[AGS97] R. Agrawal, A. Gupta, and S. Sarawagi. Modeling multidimensional databases. In *Proc. 1997 Int. Conf. Data Engineering (ICDE'97)*, pages 232–243, Birmingham, England, April 1997.

[Aha92] D. Aha. Tolerating noisy, irrelevant, and novel attributes in instance-based learning algorithms. *Int. J. Man-Machine Studies*, 36:267–287, 1992.

[AHS96] P. Arabie, L. J. Hubert, and G. De Soete. *Clustering and Classification*. World Scientific, 1996.

[AHWY03] C. C. Aggarwal, J. Han, J. Wang, and P. S. Yu. A framework for clustering evolving data streams. In *Proc. 2003 Int. Conf. Very Large Data Bases (VLDB'03)*, pages 852–863, Berlin, Germany, Sept. 2003.

[AHWY04a] C. Aggarwal, J. Han, J. Wang, and P. S. Yu. A framework for projected clustering of high dimensional data streams. In *Proc. 2004 Int. Conf. Very Large Data Bases (VLDB'04)*, pages 852–863, Toronto, Canada, Aug. 2004.

[AHWY04b] C. Aggarwal, J. Han, J. Wang, and P. S. Yu. On demand classification of data streams. In *Proc. 2004 ACM SIGKDD Int. Conf. Knowledge Discovery in Databases (KDD'04)*, pages 503–508, Seattle, WA, Aug. 2004.

[AIS93] R. Agrawal, T. Imielinski, and A. Swami. Mining association rules between sets of items in large databases. In *Proc. 1993 ACM-SIGMOD Int. Conf. Management of Data (SIGMOD'93)*, pages 207–216, Washington, DC, May 1993.

[AK93] T. Anand and G. Kahn. Opportunity explorer: Navigating large databases using knowledge discovery templates. In *Proc. AAAI-93 Workshop Knowledge Discovery in Databases*, pages 45–51, Washington, DC, July 1993.

[AL99] Y. Aumann and Y. Lindell. A statistical theory for quantitative association rules. In *Proc. 1999 Int. Conf. Knowledge Discovery and Data Mining (KDD'99)*, pages 261–270, San Diego, CA, Aug. 1999.

[All94] B. P. Allen. Case-based reasoning: Business applications. *Comm. ACM*, 37:40–42, 1994.

[Alp04] E. Alpaydin. *Introduction to Machine Learning (Adaptive Computation and Machine Learning)*. MIT Press, 2004.

[ALSS95] R. Agrawal, K.-I. Lin, H. S. Sawhney, and K. Shim. Fast similarity search in the presence of noise, scaling, and translation in time-series databases. In *Proc. 1995 Int. Conf. Very Large Data Bases (VLDB'95)*, pages 490–501, Zurich, Switzerland, Sept. 1995.

[AM98] G. Arocena and A. O. Mendelzon. WebOQL: Restructuring documents, databases, and webs. In *Proc. 1998 Int. Conf. Data Engineering (ICDE'98)*, pages 24–33, Orlando, FL, Feb. 1998.

[AMS+96] R. Agrawal, M. Mehta, J. Shafer, R. Srikant, A. Arning, and T. Bollinger. The Quest data mining system. In *Proc. 1996 Int. Conf. Data Mining and Knowledge Discovery (KDD'96)*, pages 244–249, Portland, Oregon, Aug. 1996.

[Aok98] P. M. Aoki. Generalizing "search" in generalized search trees. In *Proc. 1998 Int. Conf. Data Engineering (ICDE'98)*, pages 380–389, Orlando, FL, Feb. 1998.

[AP94] A. Aamodt and E. Plazas. Case-based reasoning: Foundational issues, methodological variations, and system approaches. *AI Comm.*, 7:39–52, 1994.

[APW+99] C. C. Aggarwal, C. Procopiuc, J. Wolf, P. S. Yu, and J.-S. Park. Fast algorithms for projected clustering. In *Proc. 1999 ACM-SIGMOD Int. Conf. Management of Data (SIGMOD'99)*, pages 61–72, Philadelphia, PA, June 1999.

[APWZ95] R. Agrawal, G. Psaila, E. L. Wimmers, and M. Zait. Querying shapes of histories. In *Proc. 1995 Int. Conf. Very Large Data Bases (VLDB'95)*, pages 502–514, Zurich, Switzerland, Sept. 1995.

[AQM+97] S. Abitboul, D. Quass, J. McHugh, J. Widom, and J. Wiener. The Lorel query language for semistructured data. *Int. J. Digital Libraries*, 1:68–88, 1997.

[ARSX04] R. Agrawal, S. Rajagopalan, R. Srikant, and Y. Xu. Mining newsgroups using networks arising from social behavior. In *Proc. 2003 Int. World Wide Web Conf. (WWW'03)*, pages 529–535, New York, NY, May 2004.

[AS94a] R. Agrawal and R. Srikant. Fast algorithm for mining association rules in large databases. In *Research Report RJ 9839*, IBM Almaden Research Center, San Jose, CA, June 1994.

[AS94b] R. Agrawal and R. Srikant. Fast algorithms for mining association rules. In *Proc. 1994 Int. Conf. Very Large Data Bases (VLDB'94)*, pages 487–499, Santiago, Chile, Sept. 1994.

[AS95] R. Agrawal and R. Srikant. Mining sequential patterns. In *Proc. 1995 Int. Conf. Data Engineering (ICDE'95)*, pages 3–14, Taipei, Taiwan, Mar. 1995.

[AS96] R. Agrawal and J. C. Shafer. Parallel mining of association rules: Design, implementation, and experience. *IEEE Trans. Knowledge and Data Engineering*, 8:962–969, 1996.

[AS00] R. Agrawal and R. Srikant. Privacy-preserving data mining. In *Proc. 2000 ACM-SIGMOD Int. Conf. Management of Data (SIGMOD'00)*, pages 439–450, Dallas, TX, May 2000.

[Avn95] S. Avner. Discovery of comprehensible symbolic rules in a neural network. In *Proc. 1995 Int. Symp. Intelligence in Neural and Biological Systems*, pages 64–67, 1995.

[AY99] C. C. Aggarwal and P. S. Yu. A new framework for itemset generation. In *Proc. 1998 ACM Symp. Principles of Database Systems (PODS'98)*, pages 18–24, Seattle, WA, June 1999.

[AY00] C. C. Aggarwal and P. S. Yu. Finding generalized projected clusters in high dimensional spaces. In *Proc. 2000 ACM-SIGMOD Int. Conf. Management of Data (SIGMOD'00)*, pages 70–81, Dallas, TX, May 2000.

[AY01] C. C. Aggarwal and P. S. Yu. Outlier detection for high dimensional data. In *Proc. 2001 ACM-SIGMOD Int. Conf. Management of Data (SIGMOD'01)*, pages 37–46, Santa Barbara, CA, May 2001.

[BA97] L. A. Breslow and D. W. Aha. Simplifying decision trees: A survey. *Knowledge Engineering Review*, 12:1–40, 1997.

[Bar02] D. Barbará. *Applications of Data Mining in Computer Security (Advances in Information Security, 6)*. Kluwer Academic Publishers, 2002.

[Bar03] A.-L. Barabasi. *Linked: How everything is connected to everything else and what it means.* Plume, 2003.

[Bay98] R. J. Bayardo. Efficiently mining long patterns from databases. In *Proc. 1998 ACM-SIGMOD Int. Conf. Management of Data (SIGMOD'98)*, pages 85–93, Seattle, WA, June 1998.

[BB01] P. Baldi and S. Brunak. *Bioinformatics: The Machine Learning Approach* (2nd ed.). MIT Press, 2001.

[BB02] C. Borgelt and M. R. Berthold. Mining molecular fragments: Finging relevant substructures of molecules. In *Proc. 2002 Int. Conf. Data Mining (ICDM'02)*, pages 211–218, Maebashi, Japan, Dec. 2002.

[BBD+02] B. Babcock, S. Babu, M. Datar, R. Motwani, and J. Widom. Models and issues in data stream systems. In *Proc. 2002 ACM Symp. Principles of Database Systems (PODS'02)*, pages 1–16, Madison, WI, June 2002.

[BBM04] S. Basu, M. Bilenko, and R. J. Mooney. A probabilistic framework for semi-supervised clustering. In *Proc. 2004 ACM SIGKDD Int. Conf. Knowledge Discovery in Databases (KDD'04)*, pages 59–68, Seattle, WA, Aug. 2004.

[BC92] N. Belkin and B. Croft. Information filtering and information retrieval: Two sides of the same coin? *Comm. ACM*, 35:29–38, 1992.

[BC00] S. Benninga and B. Czaczkes. *Financial Modeling* (2nd ed.). MIT Press, 2000.

[BCG01] D. Burdick, M. Calimlim, and J. Gehrke. MAFIA: A maximal frequent itemset algorithm for transactional databases. In *Proc. 2001 Int. Conf. Data Engineering (ICDE'01)*, pages 443–452, Heidelberg, Germany, April 2001.

[BCP93] D. E. Brown, V. Corruble, and C. L. Pittard. A comparison of decision tree classifiers with back-propagation neural networks for multimodal classification problems. *Pattern Recognition*, 26:953–961, 1993.

[BD01] P. J. Bickel and K. A. Doksum. *Mathematical Statistics: Basic Ideas and Selected Topics, Vol. 1.* Prentice Hall, 2001.

[BD02] P. J. Brockwell and R. A. Davis. *Introduction to Time Series and Forecasting* (2nd ed.). Springer, 2002.

[BDF+97] D. Barbará, W. DuMouchel, C. Faloutos, P. J. Haas, J. H. Hellerstein, Y. Ioannidis, H. V. Jagadish, T. Johnson, R. Ng, V. Poosala, K. A. Ross, and K. C. Servcik. The New Jersey data reduction report. *Bull. Technical Committee on Data Engineering*, 20:3–45, Dec. 1997.

[BDG96] A. Bruce, D. Donoho, and H.-Y. Gao. Wavelet analysis. In *IEEE Spectrum*, pages 26–35, Oct 1996.

[Bea04] B. Beal. Case study: Analytics take a bite out of crime. In *searchCRM.com (http://www.searchCRM.techtarget.com)*, Jan. 2004.

[Ber81] J. Bertin. *Graphics and Graphic Information Processing*. Berlin, 1981.

[Ber03] M. W. Berry. *Survey of Text Mining: Clustering, Classification, and Retrieval.* Springer, 2003.

[BEX02] F. Beil, M. Ester, and X. Xu. Frequent term-based text clustering. In *Proc. 2002 ACM SIGKDD Int. Conf. Knowledge Discovery in Databases (KDD'02)*, pages 436–442, Edmonton, Canada, July 2002.

[Bez81] J. C. Bezdek. *Pattern Recognition with Fuzzy Objective Function Algorithms*. Plenum Press, 1981.

[BFOS84] L. Breiman, J. Friedman, R. Olshen, and C. Stone. *Classification and Regression Trees.* Wadsworth International Group, 1984.

[BFR98] P. Bradley, U. Fayyad, and C. Reina. Scaling clustering algorithms to large databases. In *Proc. 1998 Int. Conf. Knowledge Discovery and Data Mining (KDD'98)*, pages 9–15, New York, NY, Aug. 1998.

[BG04] I. Bhattacharya and L. Getoor. Iterative record linkage for cleaning and integration. In *Proc. SIGMOD 2004 Workshop on Research Issues on Data Mining and Knowledge Discovery (DMKD'04)*, Paris, France, pages 11–18, June 2004.

[BGKW03] C. Bucila, J. Gehrke, D. Kifer, and W. White. DualMiner: A dual-pruning algorithm for itemsets with constraints. *Data Mining and Knowledge Discovery*, 7:241–272, 2003.

[BGV92] B. Boser, I. Guyon, and V. N. Vapnik. A training algorithm for optimal margin classifiers. In *Proc. Fifth Annual Workshop on Computational Learning Theory*, pages 144–152, ACM Press: San Mateo, CA, 1992.

[BH03] M. Berthold and D. J. Hand. *Intelligent Data Analysis: An Introduction* (2nd ed.). Springer-Verlag, 2003.

[BHK98] J. Breese, D. Heckerman, and C. Kadie. Empirical analysis of predictive algorithms for collaborative filtering. In *Proc. 1998 Conf. Uncertainty in Artificial Intelligence*, pages 43–52, Madison, WI, July 1998.

[Bis95] C. M. Bishop. *Neural Networks for Pattern Recognition*. Oxford University Press, 1995.

[BJR94] G. E. P. Box, G. M. Jenkins, and G. C. Reinsel. *Time Series Analysis: Forecasting and Control* (3rd ed.). Prentice-Hall, 1994.

[BKNS00] M. M. Breunig, H.-P. Kriegel, R. Ng, and J. Sander. LOF: Identifying density-based local outliers. In *Proc. 2000 ACM-SIGMOD Int. Conf. Management of Data (SIGMOD'00)*, pages 93–104, Dallas, TX, May 2000.

[BL94] V. Barnett and T. Lewis. *Outliers in Statistical Data*. John Wiley & Sons, 1994.

[BL99] M. J. A. Berry and G. Linoff. *Mastering Data Mining: The Art and Science of Customer Relationship Management*. John Wiley & Sons, 1999.

[BL04] M. J. A. Berry and G. S. Linoff. *Data Mining Techniques: For Marketing, Sales, and Customer Relationship Management*. John Wiley & Sons, 2004.

[BLHL01] T. Berners-Lee, J. Hendler, and O. Lassila. The Semantic Web. *Scientific American*, 284(5):34–43, 2001.

[BM98] E. Bloedorn and R. S. Michalski. Data-driven constructive induction: A methodology and its applications. In H. Liu, H. Motoda, editors, *Feature Selection for Knowledge Discovery and Data Mining*. Kluwer Academic Publishers, 1998.

[BMS97] S. Brin, R. Motwani, and C. Silverstein. Beyond market basket: Generalizing association rules to correlations. In *Proc. 1997 ACM-SIGMOD Int. Conf. Management of Data (SIGMOD'97)*, pages 265–276, Tucson, AZ, May 1997.

[BMUT97] S. Brin, R. Motwani, J. D. Ullman, and S. Tsur. Dynamic itemset counting and implication rules for market basket analysis. In *Proc. 1997 ACM-SIGMOD Int. Conf. Management of Data (SIGMOD'97)*, pages 255–264, Tucson, AZ, May 1997.

[BN92] W. L. Buntine and T. Niblett. A further comparison of splitting rules for decision-tree induction. *Machine Learning*, 8:75–85, 1992.

[BNJ03] D. Blei, A. Ng, and M. Jordan. Latent Dirichlet allocation. *J. Machine Learning Research*, 3:993–1022, 2003.

[BO04] A. Baxevanis and B. F. F. Ouellette. *Bioinformatics: A Practical Guide to the Analysis of Genes and Proteins* (3rd ed.). John Wiley & Sons, 2004.

[BP92] J. C. Bezdek and S. K. Pal. *Fuzzy Models for Pattern Recognition: Methods That Search for Structures in Data*. IEEE Press, 1992.

[BP97] E. Baralis and G. Psaila. Designing templates for mining association rules. *J. Intelligent Information Systems*, 9:7–32, 1997.

[BP98a] D. Billsus and M. J. Pazzani. Learning collaborative information filters. In *Proc. 1998 Int. Conf. Machine Learning (ICML'98)*, pages 46–54, Madison, WI, Aug. 1998.

[BP98b] S. Brin and L. Page. The anatomy of a large-scale hypertextual web search engine. In *Proc. 7th Int. World Wide Web Conf. (WWW'98)*, pages 107–117, Brisbane, Australia, April 1998.

[BPT97] E. Baralis, S. Paraboschi, and E. Teniente. Materialized view selection in a multidimensional database. In *Proc. 1997 Int. Conf. Very Large Data Bases (VLDB'97)*, pages 98–12, Athens, Greece, Aug. 1997.

[BPW88] E. R. Bareiss, B. W. Porter, and C. C. Weir. Protos: An exemplar-based learning apprentice. *Int. J. Man-Machine Studies*, 29:549–561, 1988.

[BR99] K. Beyer and R. Ramakrishnan. Bottom-up computation of sparse and iceberg cubes. In *Proc. 1999 ACM-SIGMOD Int. Conf. Management of Data (SIGMOD'99)*, pages 359–370, Philadelphia, PA, June 1999.

[Bre96] L. Breiman. Bagging predictors. *Machine Learning*, 24:123–140, 1996.

[BRR98] H. Blockeel, L. De Raedt, and J. Ramon. Top-down induction of logical decision trees. In *Proc. 1998 Int. Conf. Machine Learning (ICML'98)*, pages 55–63, Madison, WI, Aug. 1998.

[BS97a] D. Barbara and M. Sullivan. Quasi-cubes: Exploiting approximation in multidimensional databases. *SIGMOD Record*, 26:12–17, 1997.

[BS97b] A. Berson and S. J. Smith. *Data Warehousing, Data Mining, and OLAP*. McGraw-Hill, 1997.

[BST99] A. Berson, S. J. Smith, and K. Thearling. *Building Data Mining Applications for CRM*. McGraw-Hill, 1999.

[BT99] D. P. Ballou and G. K. Tayi. Enhancing data quality in data warehouse environments. *Comm. ACM*, 42:73–78, 1999.

[BU95] C. E. Brodley and P. E. Utgoff. Multivariate decision trees. *Machine Learning*, 19:45–77, 1995.

[Buc03] M. Buchanan. *Nexus: Small worlds and the groundbreaking theory of networks*. W. W. Norton Company, 2003.

[Bun94] W. L. Buntine. Operations for learning with graphical models. *J. Artificial Intelligence Research*, 2:159–225, 1994.

[Bur98] C. J. C. Burges. A tutorial on support vector machines for pattern recognition. *Data Mining and Knowledge Discovery*, 2:121–168, 1998.

[BW00] D. Barbará and X. Wu. Using loglinear models to compress datacube. In *Proc. 1st Int. Conf. on Web-Age Information (WAIM'2000)*, pages 311–322, 2000.

[BW01] S. Babu and J. Widom. Continuous queries over data streams. *SIGMOD Record*, 30:109–120, 2001.

[BWJ98] C. Bettini, X. Sean Wang, and S. Jajodia. Mining temporal relationships with multiple granularities in time sequences. *Data Engineering Bulletin*, 21:32–38, 1998.

[BYR02] Z. Bar-Yossef and S. Rajagopalan. Template detection via data mining and its applications. In *Proc. 2002 Int. World Wide Web Conf. (WWW'02)*, pages 580–591, Honolulu, HI, May 2002.

[BYRN99] R. A. Baeza-Yates and B. A. Ribeiro-Neto. *Modern Information Retrieval.* ACM Press/Addison-Wesley, 1999.

[Cat91] J. Catlett. *Megainduction: Machine Learning on Very Large Databases.* Ph.D. Thesis, University of Sydney, 1991.

[Cav98] A. Cavoukian. Data mining: Staking a claim on your privacy. In *Office of the Information and Privacy Commissioner, Ontario (www.ipc.on.ca/docs/datamine.pdv, viewed Mar. 2005)*, Jan. 1998.

[CCH91] Y. Cai, N. Cercone, and J. Han. Attribute-oriented induction in relational databases. In G. Piatetsky-Shapiro and W. J. Frawley, editors, *Knowledge Discovery in Databases*, pages 213–228. AAAI/MIT Press, 1991.

[CCP+04] Y. D. Cai, D. Clutter, G. Pape, J. Han, M. Welge, and L. Auvil. MAIDS: Mining alarming incidents from data streams. In *Proc. 2004 ACM-SIGMOD Int. Conf. Management of Data (SIGMOD'04)*, pages 919–920, Paris, France, June 2004.

[CCS93] E. F. Codd, S. B. Codd, and C. T. Salley. Beyond decision support. *Computer World*, 27, July 1993.

[CD88] F. Cuppens and R. Demolombe. Cooperative answering: A methodology to provide intelligent access to databases. In *Proc. 2nd Int. Conf. Expert Database Systems*, pages 621–643, Fairfax, VA, April 1988.

[CD97] S. Chaudhuri and U. Dayal. An overview of data warehousing and OLAP technology. *SIGMOD Record*, 26:65–74, 1997.

[CDH+02] Y. Chen, G. Dong, J. Han, B. W. Wah, and J. Wang. Multi-dimensional regression analysis of time-series data streams. In *Proc. 2002 Int. Conf. Very Large Data Bases (VLDB'02)*, pages 323–334, Hong Kong, China, Aug. 2002.

[CDI98] S. Chakrabarti, B. E. Dom, and P. Indyk. Enhanced hypertext classification using hyperlinks. In *Proc. 1998 ACM-SIGMOD Int. Conf. Management of Data (SIGMOD'98)*, pages 307–318, Seattle, WA, June 1998.

[CDK+99] S. Chakrabarti, B. E. Dom, S. R. Kumar, P. Raghavan, S. Rajagopalan, A. Tomkins, D. Gibson, and J. M. Kleinberg. Mining the web's link structure. *COMPUTER*, 32:60–67, 1999.

[CDTW00] J. Chen, D. DeWitt, F. Tian, and Y. Wang. NiagraCQ: A scalable continuous query system for internet databases. In *Proc. 2000 ACM-SIGMOD Int. Conf. Management of Data (SIGMOD'00)*, pages 379–390, Dallas, TX, May 2000.

[Ce91] G. A. Carpenter and S. Grossberg (eds.). *Pattern Recognition by Self-Organizing Neural Networks.* MIT Press, 1991.

[CF02] S. Chandrasekaran and M. Franklin. Streaming queries over streaming data. In *Proc. 2002 Int. Conf. Very Large Data Bases (VLDB'02)*, pages 203–214, Hong Kong, China, Aug. 2002.

[CF03] C. Cooper and A Frieze. A general model of web graphs. *Algorithms*, 22:311–335, 2003.

[CFZ99] C.-H. Cheng, A. W. Fu, and Y. Zhang. Entropy-based subspace clustering for mining numerical data. In *Proc. 1999 Int. Conf. Knowledge Discovery and Data Mining (KDD'99)*, pages 84–93, San Diego, CA, Aug. 1999.

[CGC94] A. Chaturvedi, P. Green, and J. Carroll. K-means, k-medians and k-modes: Special cases of partitioning multiway data. In *The Classification Society of North America (CSNA) Meeting Presentation*, Houston, TX, 1994.

[CGC01] A. Chaturvedi, P. Green, and J. Carroll. K-modes clustering. *J. Classification*, 18:35–55, 2001.

[CH67] T. Cover and P. Hart. Nearest neighbor pattern classification. *IEEE Trans. Information Theory*, 13:21–27, 1967.

[CH92] G. Cooper and E. Herskovits. A Bayesian method for the induction of probabilistic networks from data. *Machine Learning*, 9:309–347, 1992.

[CH98] C. Carter and H. Hamilton. Efficient attribute-oriented generalization for knowledge discovery from large databases. *IEEE Trans. Knowledge and Data Engineering*, 10:193–208, 1998.

[Cha01] S. Chakrabarti. Integrating the document object model with hyperlinks for enhanced topic distillation and information extraction. In *Proc. 2001 Int. World Wide Web Conf. (WWW'01)*, pages 211–220, Hong Kong, China, May 2001.

[Cha02] S. Chakrabarti. *Mining the Web: Statistical Analysis of Hypertext and Semi-Structured Data.* Morgan Kaufmann, 2002.

[Cha03] C. Chatfield. *The Analysis of Time Series: An Introduction* (6th ed.). Chapman and Hall, 2003.

[CHD00] Q. Chen, M. Hsu, and U. Dayal. A data-warehouse/OLAP framework for scalable telecommunication tandem traffic analysis. In *Proc. 2000 Int. Conf. Data Engineering (ICDE'00)*, pages 201–210, San Diego, CA, Feb. 2000.

[CHH05] D. Cai, X. He, and J. Han. Document clustering using locality preserving indexing. In *IEEE Trans. Knowledge and Data Engineering*, 17(12): 1624–1637, 2005.

[CHL+04] D. Cai, X. He, Z. Li, W.-Y. Ma, and J.-R. Wen. Hierarchical clustering of WWW image search results using visual, textual and link analysis. In *Proc. ACM Multimedia 2004*, pages 952–959, New York, NY, Oct. 2004.

[CHM+04] D. Cai, X. He, W.-Y. Ma, J.-R. Wen, and H.-J. Zhang. Organizing WWW images based on the analysis of page layout and web link structure. In *Proc. 2004 IEEE Int. Conf. Multimedia and EXPO (ICME'04)*, pages 113–116, Taipei, Taiwan, June 2004.

[CHN+96] D. W. Cheung, J. Han, V. Ng, A. Fu, and Y. Fu. A fast distributed algorithm for mining association rules. In *Proc. 1996 Int. Conf. Parallel and Distributed Information Systems*, pages 31–44, Miami Beach, FL, Dec. 1996.

[CHNW96] D. W. Cheung, J. Han, V. Ng, and C. Y. Wong. Maintenance of discovered association rules in large databases: An incremental updating technique. In *Proc. 1996 Int. Conf. Data Engineering (ICDE'96)*, pages 106–114, New Orleans, LA, Feb. 1996.

[CHP05] S. Cong, J. Han, and D. Padua. Parallel mining of closed sequential patterns. In *Proc. 2005 ACM SIGKDD Int. Conf. Knowledge Discovery in Databases (KDD'05)*, pages 562–567, Chicago, IL, Aug. 2005.

[CHWM04] D. Cai, X. He, J.-R. Wen, and W.-Y. Ma. Block-level link analysis. In *Proc. Int. 2004 ACM SIGIR Conf. Research and Development in Information Retrieval (SIGIR'04)*, pages 440–447, Sheffield, UK, July 2004.

[CHY96] M. S. Chen, J. Han, and P. S. Yu. Data mining: An overview from a database perspective. *IEEE Trans. Knowledge and Data Engineering*, 8:866–883, 1996.

[CJT01] S. Chakrabarti, M. Joshi, and V. Tawde. Enhanced topic distillation using text, markup tags, and hyperlinks. In *Proc. Int. 2001 ACM SIGIR Conf. Research and Development in Information Retrieval (SIGIR'01)*, pages 208–216, New Orleans, LA, Sept. 2001.

[CK98] M. Carey and D. Kossman. Reducing the braking distance of an SQL query engine. In *Proc. 1998 Int. Conf. Very Large Data Bases (VLDB'98)*, pages 158–169, New York, NY, Aug. 1998.

[CKV04] C. Clifton, M. Kantarcioğlu, and J. Vaidya. Defining privacy for data mining. In H. Kargupta, A. Joshi, K. Sivakumar, and Y. Yesha, editors, *Data Mining: Next Generation Challenges and Future Directions*, pages 255–270. AAAI/MIT Press, 2004.

[Cle93] W. Cleveland. *Visualizing Data*. Hobart Press, 1993.

[CM94] S. P. Curram and J. Mingers. Neural networks, decision tree induction and discriminant analysis: An empirical comparison. *J. Operational Research Society*, 45:440–450, 1994.

[CM96] C. Clifton and D. Marks. Security and privacy implications of data mining. In *Proc. 1996 SIGMOD'96 Workshop Research Issues on Data Mining and Knowledge Discovery (DMKD'96)*, pages 15–20, Montreal, Canada, June 1996.

[CN89] P. Clark and T. Niblett. The CN2 induction algorithm. *Machine Learning*, 3:261–283, 1989.

[Coh95] W. Cohen. Fast effective rule induction. In *Proc. 1995 Int. Conf. Machine Learning (ICML'95)*, pages 115–123, Tahoe City, CA, July 1995.

[Coh04] J. Cohen. Bioinformatics—an introduction for computer scientists. *ACM Computing Surveys*, 36:122–158, 2004.

[Coo90] G. F. Cooper. The computational complexity of probabilistic inference using Bayesian belief networks. *Artificial Intelligence*, 42:393–405, 1990.

[Cor00] Microsoft Corporation. OLEDB for Data Mining draft specification, version 0.9. In *http://www.microsoft.com/data/oledb/dm*, Feb. 2000.

[CPS98] K. Cios, W. Pedrycz, and R. Swiniarski. *Data Mining Methods for Knowledge Discovery*. Kluwer Academic Publishers, 1998.

[CR95] Y. Chauvin and D. Rumelhart. *Backpropagation: Theory, Architectures, and Applications*. Lawrence Erlbaum Assoc., 1995.

[Cra89] S. L. Crawford. Extensions to the cart algorithm. *Int. J. Man-Machine Studies*, 31:197–217, Aug. 1989.

[CS93a] P. K. Chan and S. J. Stolfo. Experiments on multistrategy learning by metalearning. In *Proc. 2nd. Int. Conf. Information and Knowledge Management*, pages 314–323, 1993.

[CS93b] P. K. Chan and S. J. Stolfo. Toward multi-strategy parallel & distributed learning in sequence analysis. In *Proc. 1st Int. Conf. Intelligent Systems for Molecular Biology (ISMB'03)*, pages 65–75, Bethesda, MD, July 1993.

[CS96a] P. Cheeseman and J. Stutz. Bayesian classification (AutoClass): Theory and results. In U. M. Fayyad, G. Piatetsky-Shapiro, P. Smyth, and R. Uthurusamy, editors, *Advances in Knowledge Discovery and Data Mining*, pages 153–180. AAAI/MIT Press, 1996.

[CS96b] M. W. Craven and J. W. Shavlik. Extracting tree-structured representations of trained networks. In D. Touretzky, M. Mozer, and M. Hasselmo, editors, *Advances in Neural Information Processing Systems*. MIT Press, 1996.

[CS97] M. W. Craven and J. W. Shavlik. Using neural networks in data mining. *Future Generation Computer Systems*, 13:211–229, 1997.

[CSD98] S. Chakrabarti, S. Sarawagi, and B. Dom. Mining surprising patterns using temporal description length. In *Proc. 1998 Int: Conf. Very Large Data Bases (VLDB'98)*, pages 606–617, New York, NY, Aug. 1998.

[CSH+05] D. Cai, Z. Shao, X. He, X. Yan, and J. Han. Community mining from multi-relational networks. In *Proc. 2005 European Conf. Principles and Practice of Knowledge Discovery in Databases (PKDD'05)*, pages 445–452, Porto, Portugal, Oct. 2005.

[CSW05] P. J. Carrington, J. Scott, and S. Wasserman. Models and methods in social network analysis. Cambridge University Press, 2005.

[CTTX05] G. Cong, K.-Lee Tan, A. K. H. Tung, and X. Xu. Mining top-k covering rule groups for gene expression data. In *Proc. 2005 ACM-SIGMOD Int. Conf. Management of Data (SIGMOD'05)*, pages 670–681, Baltimore, MD, June 2005.

[CYH04] H. Cheng, X. Yan, and J. Han. IncSpan: Incremental mining of sequential patterns in large database. In *Proc. 2004 ACM SIGKDD Int. Conf. Knowledge Discovery in Databases (KDD'04)*, pages 527–532, Seattle, WA, Aug. 2004.

[CYH05] H. Cheng, X. Yan, and J. Han. Seqindex: Indexing sequences by sequential pattern analysis. In *Proc. 2005 SIAM Int. Conf. Data Mining (SDM'05)*, pages 601–605, Newport Beach, CA, April 2005.

[CYWM03] D. Cai, S. Yu, J.-R. Wen, and W.-Y. Ma. Vips: A vision based page segmentation algorithm. In *MSR-TR-2003-79*, Microsoft Research Asia, 2003.

[CYWM04] D. Cai, S. Yu, J.-R. Wen, and W.-Y. Ma. Block-based web search. In *Proc. 2004 Int. ACM SIGIR Conf. Research and Development in Information Retrieval (SIGIR'04)*, pages 456–463, Sheffield, UK, July 2004.

[Das91] B. V. Dasarathy. *Nearest Neighbor (NN) Norms: NN Pattern Classification Techniques*. IEEE Computer Society Press, 1991.

[Dau92] I. Daubechies. *Ten Lectures on Wavelets*. Capital City Press, 1992.

[DBK+97] H. Drucker, C. J. C. Burges, L. Kaufman, A. Smola, and V. N. Vapnik. Support vector regression machines. In M. Mozer, M. Jordan, and T. Petsche, editors, *Advances in Neural Information Processing Systems 9*, pages 155–161. MIT Press, 1997.

[DDF+90] S. Deerwester, S. Dumais, G. Furnas, T. Landauer, and R. Harshman. Indexing by latent semantic analysis. *J. American Society for Information Science*, 41:391–407, 1990.

[DE84] W. H. E. Day and H. Edelsbrunner. Efficient algorithms for agglomerative hierarchical clustering methods. *J. Classification*, 1:7–24, 1984.

[De01] S. Dzeroski and N. Lavrac (eds.). *Relational Data Mining*. Springer, 2001.

[DEKM98] R. Durbin, S. Eddy, A. Krogh, and G. Mitchison. *Biological Sequence Analysis: Probability Models of Proteins and Nucleic Acids*. Cambridge University Press, 1998.

[Dev03] J. L. Devore. *Probability and Statistics for Engineering and the Sciences* (6th ed.). Duxbury Press, 2003.

[DF99] A. Degenne and M. Forse. *Introducing social networks.* Sage Publications, 1999.

[DGGR02] A. Dobra, M. Garofalakis, J. Gehrke, and R. Rastogi. Processing complex aggregate queries over data streams. In *Proc. 2002 ACM-SIGMOD Int. Conf. Management of Data (SIGMOD'02)*, pages 61–72, Madison, WI, June 2002.

[DH00] P. Domingos and G. Hulten. Mining high-speed data streams. In *Proc. 2000 ACM SIGKDD Int. Conf. Knowledge Discovery in Databases (KDD'00)*, pages 71–80, Boston, MA, Aug. 2000.

[DHL+01] G. Dong, J. Han, J. Lam, J. Pei, and K. Wang. Mining multi-dimensional constrained gradients in data cubes. In *Proc. 2001 Int. Conf. on Very Large Data Bases (VLDB'01)*, pages 321–330, Rome, Italy, Sept. 2001.

[DHS01] R. O. Duda, P. E. Hart, and D. G. Stork. *Pattern Classification* (2nd. ed.). John Wiley and Sons, 2001.

[DJ03] T. Dasu and T. Johnson. *Exploratory Data Mining and Data Cleaning.* John Wiley & Sons, 2003.

[DJMS02] T. Dasu, T. Johnson, S. Muthukrishnan, and V. Shkapenyuk. Mining database structure; or how to build a data quality browser. In *Proc. 2002 ACM-SIGMOD Int. Conf. on Management of Data (SIGMOD'02)*, pages 240–251, Madison, WI, June 2002.

[DKK02] M. Deshpande, M. Kuramochi, and G. Karypis. Automated approaches for classifying structures. In *Proc. 2002 Workshop on Data Mining in Bioinformatics (BIOKDD'02)*, pages 11–18, Edmonton, Canada, July 2002.

[DL97] M. Dash and H. Liu. Feature selection methods for classification. *Intelligent Data Analysis*, 1(3):131–156, 1997.

[DL99] G. Dong and J. Li. Efficient mining of emerging patterns: Discovering trends and differences. In *Proc. 1999 Int. Conf. Knowledge Discovery and Data Mining (KDD'99)*, pages 43–52, San Diego, CA, Aug. 1999.

[DLR77] A. Dempster, N. Laird, and D. Rubin. Maximum likelihood from incomplete data via the EM algorithm. *J. Royal Statistical Society*, 39:1–38, 1977.

[DLY97] M. Dash, H. Liu, and J. Yao. Dimensionality reduction of unsupervised data. In *Proc. 1997 IEEE Int. Conf. Tools with AI (ICTAI'97)*, pages 532–539, IEEE Computer Society, 1997.

[DM83] T. G. Dietterich and R. S. Michalski. A comparative review of selected methods for learning from examples. In Michalski et al., editors, *Machine Learning: An Artificial Intelligence Approach, Vol. 1*, pages 41–82. Morgan Kaufmann, 1983.

[DNR+97] P. Deshpande, J. Naughton, K. Ramasamy, A. Shukla, K. Tufte, and Y. Zhao. Cubing algorithms, storage estimation, and storage and processing alternatives for OLAP. *Data Engineering Bulletin*, 20:3–11, 1997.

[Dob01] A. J. Dobson. *An Introduction to Generalized Linear Models* (2nd ed.). Chapman and Hall, 2001.

[Dom94] P. Domingos. The RISE system: Conquering without separating. In *Proc. 1994 IEEE Int. Conf. Tools with Artificial Intelligence (TAI'94)*, pages 704–707, New Orleans, LA, 1994.

[Dom05] P. Domingos. Mining social networks for viral marketing. *IEEE Intelligent Systems*, 20:80–82, 2005.

[DP96] P. Domingos and M. Pazzani. Beyond independence: Conditions for the optimality of the simple Bayesian classifier. In *Proc. 1996 Int. Conf. Machine Learning (ML'96)*, pages 105–112, Bari, Italy, July 1996.

[DP97] J. Devore and R. Peck. *Statistics: The Exploration and Analysis of Data*. Duxbury Press, 1997.

[DR99] D. Donjerkovic and R. Ramakrishnan. Probabilistic optimization of top N queries. In *Proc. 1999 Int. Conf. Very Large Data Bases (VLDB'99)*, pages 411–422, Edinburgh, UK, Sept. 1999.

[DR01] P. Domingos and M. Richardson. Mining the network value of customers. In *Proc. 2001 ACM SIGKDD Int. Conf. Knowledge Discovery in Databases (KDD'01)*, pages 57–66, San Francisco, CA, Aug. 2001.

[DT93] V. Dhar and A. Tuzhilin. Abstract-driven pattern discovery in databases. *IEEE Trans. Knowledge and Data Engineering*, 5:926–938, 1993.

[DTK98] L. Dehaspe, H. Toivonen, and R. King. Finding frequent substructures in chemical compounds. In *Proc. 1998 Int. Conf. Knowledge Discovery and Data Mining (KDD'98)*, pages 30–36, New York, NY, Aug. 1998.

[Dze03] S. Dzeroski. Multirelational data mining: An introduction. *ACM SIGKDD Explorations*, 5:1–16, July 2003.

[EFKS98] M. Ester, A. Frommelt, H.-P. Kriegel, and J. Sander. Algorithms for characterization and trend detection in spatial databases. In *Proc. 1998 Int. Conf. Knowledge Discovery and Data Mining (KDD'98)*, pages 44–50, New York, NY, Aug. 1998.

[Ega75] J. P. Egan. *Signal detection theory and ROC analysis*. Academic Press, 1975.

[Ege89] M. J. Egenhofer. *Spatial Query Languages*. UMI Research Press, 1989.

[EJN99] D. W. Embley, Y. Jiang, and Y.-K. Ng. Record-boundary discovery in web documents. In *Proc. 1999 ACM-SIGMOD Int. Conf. Management of Data (SIGMOD'99)*, pages 467–478, Philadelphia, PA, June 1999.

[EKS97] M. Ester, H.-P. Kriegel, and J. Sander. Spatial data mining: A database approach. In *Proc. 1997 Int. Symp. Large Spatial Databases (SSD'97)*, pages 47–66, Berlin, Germany, July 1997.

[EKSX96] M. Ester, H.-P. Kriegel, J. Sander, and X. Xu. A density-based algorithm for discovering clusters in large spatial databases. In *Proc. 1996 Int. Conf. Knowledge Discovery and Data Mining (KDD'96)*, pages 226–231, Portland, OR, Aug. 1996.

[EKSX97] M. Ester, H.-P. Kriegel, J. Sander, and X. Xu. Density-connected sets and their application for trend detection in spatial databases. In *Proc. 1997 Int. Conf. Knowledge Discovery and Data Mining (KDD'97)*, pages 10–15, Newport Beach, CA, Aug. 1997.

[EKX95] M. Ester, H.-P. Kriegel, and X. Xu. Knowledge discovery in large spatial databases: Focusing techniques for efficient class identification. In *Proc. 1995 Int. Symp. Large Spatial Databases (SSD'95)*, pages 67–82, Portland, ME, Aug. 1995.

[Elk97] C. Elkan. Boosting and naïve Bayesian learning. In *Technical Report CS97-557*, Dept. Computer Science and Engineering, Univ. Calif. at San Diego, Sept. 1997.

[EN03] R. Elmasri and S. B. Navathe. *Fundamental of Database Systems* (4th ed.). Addison Wesley, 2003.

[Eng99] L. English. *Improving Data Warehouse and Business Information Quality: Methods for Reducing Costs and Increasing Profits*. John Wiley & Sons, 1999.

[ESAG02] A. Evfimievski, R. Srikant, R. Agrawal, and J. Gehrke. Privacy preserving mining of association rules. In *Proc. 2002 ACM SIGKDD Int. Conf. on Knowledge Discovery and Data Mining (KDD'02)*, pages 217–228, Edmonton, Canada, July 2002.

[ET93] B. Efron and R. Tibshirani. *An Introduction to the Bootstrap*. Chapman & Hall, 1993.

[Fal85] C. Faloutsos. Access methods for text. *ACM Comput. Surv.*, 17:49–74, 1985.

[FB74] R. A. Finkel and J. L. Bentley. Quad-trees: A data structure for retrieval on composite keys. *ACTA Informatica*, 4:1–9, 1974.

[FBF77] J. H. Friedman, J. L. Bentley, and R. A. Finkel. An algorithm for finding best matches in logarithmic expected time. *ACM Transactions on Math Software*, 3:209–226, 1977.

[FBY92] W. Frakes and R. Baeza-Yates. *Information Retrieval: Data Structures and Algorithms*. Prentice Hall, 1992.

[FDW96] U. M. Fayyad, S. G. Djorgovski, and N. Weir. Automating the analysis and cataloging of sky surveys. In U. M. Fayyad, G. Piatetsky-Shapiro, P. Smyth, and R. Uthurusamy, editors, *Advances in Knowledge Discovery and Data Mining*, pages 471–493. AAAI/MIT Press, 1996.

[Fe94] U. M. Fayyad and R. Uthurusamy (eds.). *Notes of AAAI'94 Workshop Knowledge Discovery in Databases (KDD'94)*. Seattle, WA, July 1994.

[Fe95] U. M. Fayyad and R. Uthurusamy (eds.). *Proc. 1995 Int. Conf. Knowledge Discovery and Data Mining (KDD'95)*. AAAI Press, Aug. 1995.

[FGW01] U. Fayyad, G. Grinstein, and A. Wierse (eds.). *Information Visualization in Data Mining and Knowledge Discovery*. Morgan Kaufmann, 2001.

[FH51] E. Fix and J. L. Hodges Jr. Discriminatory analysis, non-parametric discrimination: consistency properties. In *Technical Report 21-49-004(4)*, USAF School of Aviation Medicine, Randolph Field, Texas, 1951.

[FH87] K. Fukunaga and D. Hummels. Bayes error estimation using parzen and k-nn procedure. In *IEEE Trans. Pattern Analysis and Machine Learning*, pages 634–643, 1987.

[FH95] Y. Fu and J. Han. Meta-rule-guided mining of association rules in relational databases. In *Proc. 1995 Int. Workshop Integration of Knowledge Discovery with Deductive and Object-Oriented Databases (KDOOD'95)*, pages 39–46, Singapore, Dec. 1995.

[FH98] R. Feldman and H. Hirsh. Finding associations in collections of text. In R. S. Michalski, I. Bratko, and M. Kubat, editors, *Machine Learning and Data Mining: Methods and Applications*, pages 223–240. John Wiley & Sons, 1998.

[FI90] U. M. Fayyad and K. B. Irani. What should be minimized in a decision tree? In *Proc. 1990 Nat. Conf. Artificial Intelligence (AAAI'90)*, pages 749–754, AAAI/MIT Press, 1990.

[FI92] U. M. Fayyad and K. B. Irani. The attribute selection problem in decision tree generation. In *Proc. 1992 Nat. Conf. Artificial Intelligence (AAAI'92)*, pages 104–110, AAAI/MIT Press, 1992.

[FI93] U. Fayyad and K. Irani. Multi-interval discretization of continuous-values attributes for classification learning. In *Proc. 1993 Int. Joint Conf. Artificial Intelligence (IJCAI'93)*, pages 1022–1029, Chambery, France, 1993.

[Fis87] D. Fisher. Improving inference through conceptual clustering. In *Proc. 1987 Nat. Conf. Artificial Intelligence (AAAI'87)*, pages 461–465, Seattle, WA, July 1987.

[FL90] S. Fahlman and C. Lebiere. The cascade-correlation learning algorithm. In *Technical Report CMU-CS-90-100*, Computer Science Department, Carnegie Mellon University, Pittsburgh, PA, 1990.

[FL95] C. Faloutsos and K.-I. Lin. FastMap: A fast algorithm for indexing, data-mining and visualization of traditional and multimedia datasets. In *Proc. 1995 ACM-SIGMOD Int. Conf. Management of Data (SIGMOD'95)*, pages 163–174, San Jose, CA, May 1995.

[Fle87] R. Fletcher. *Practical Methods of Optimization*. John Wiley & Sons, 1987.

[FLM98] D. Florescu, A. Y. Levy, and A. O. Mendelzon. Database techniques for the world-wide web: A survey. *SIGMOD Record*, 27:59–74, 1998.

[FMMT96] T. Fukuda, Y. Morimoto, S. Morishita, and T. Tokuyama. Data mining using two-dimensional optimized association rules: Scheme, algorithms, and visualization. In *Proc. 1996 ACM-SIGMOD Int. Conf. Management of Data (SIGMOD'96)*, pages 13–23, Montreal, Canada, June 1996.

[FPP97] D. Freedman, R. Pisani, and R. Purves. *Statistics* (3rd ed.). W. W. Norton & Co., 1997.

[FPSSe96] U. M. Fayyad, G. Piatetsky-Shapiro, P. Smyth, and R. Uthurusamy (eds.). *Advances in Knowledge Discovery and Data Mining*. AAAI/MIT Press, 1996.

[Fri77] J. H. Friedman. A recursive partitioning decision rule for nonparametric classifiers. *IEEE Trans. on Comp.*, 26:404–408, 1977.

[Fri91] J. H. Friedman. Multivariate adaptive regression. *Annals of Statistics*, 19:1–141, 1991.

[FRM94] C. Faloutsos, M. Ranganathan, and Y. Manolopoulos. Fast subsequence matching in time-series databases. In *Proc. 1994 ACM-SIGMOD Int. Conf. Management of Data (SIGMOD'94)*, pages 419–429, Minneapolis, MN, May 1994.

[FS93] U. Fayyad and P. Smyth. Image database exploration: progress and challenges. In *Proc. AAAI'93 Workshop Knowledge Discovery in Databases (KDD'93)*, pages 14–27, Washington, DC, July 1993.

[FS97] Y. Freund and R. E. Schapire. A decision-theoretic generalization of on-line learning and an application to boosting. *J. Computer and System Sciences*, 55:119–139, 1997.

[FSGM+98] M. Fang, N. Shivakumar, H. Garcia-Molina, R. Motwani, and J. D. Ullman. Computing iceberg queries efficiently. In *Proc. 1998 Int. Conf. Very Large Data Bases (VLDB'98)*, pages 299–310, New York, NY, Aug. 1998.

[FSN+95] M. Flickner, H. Sawhney, W. Niblack, J. Ashley, B. Dom, Q. Huang, M. Gorkani, J. Hafner, D. Lee, D. Petkovic, S. Steele, and P. Yanker. Query by image and video content: The QBIC system. *IEEE Computer*, 28:23–32, 1995.

[FUe93] U. M. Fayyad, R. Uthurusamy, and G. Piatetsky-Shapiro (eds.). *Notes of AAAI'93 Workshop Knowledge Discovery in Databases (KDD'93)*. Washington, DC, July 1993.

[FW94] J. Furnkranz and G. Widmer. Incremental reduced error pruning. In *Proc. 1994 Int. Conf. Machine Learning (ICML'94)*, pages 70–77, New Brunswick, NJ, 1994.

[Gal93] S. I. Gallant. *Neural Network Learning and Expert Systems*. MIT Press, 1993.

[Gat00] B. Gates. *Business @ the Speed of Thought: Succeeding in the Digital Economy*. Warner Books, 2000.

[GCB+97] J. Gray, S. Chaudhuri, A. Bosworth, A. Layman, D. Reichart, M. Venkatrao, F. Pellow, and H. Pirahesh. Data cube: A relational aggregation operator generalizing group-by, cross-tab and sub-totals. *Data Mining and Knowledge Discovery*, 1:29–54, 1997.

[Get03] L. Getoor. Link mining: a new data mining challenge. *SIGKDD Explorations*, 5:84–89, 2003.

[GFKT01] L. Getoor, N. Friedman, D. Koller, and B. Taskar. Learning probabilistic models of relational structure. In *Proc. 2001 Int. Conf. Machine Learning (ICML'01)*, pages 170–177, Williamstown, MA, 2001.

[GFS+01] H. Galhardas, D. Florescu, D. Shasha, E. Simon, and C.-A. Saita. Declarative data cleaning: Language, model, and algorithms. In *Proc. 2001 Int. Conf. on Very Large Data Bases (VLDB'01)*, pages 371–380, Rome, Italy, Sept. 2001.

[GG92] A. Gersho and R. M. Gray. *Vector Quantization and Signal Compression*. Kluwer, 1992.

[GG98] V. Gaede and O. Günther. Multidimensional access methods. *ACM Comput. Surv.*, 30:170–231, 1998.

[GG99] M. Goebel and L. Gruenwald. A survey of data mining and knowledge discovery software tools. *SIGKDD Explorations*, 1:20–33, 1999.

[GGR99] V. Ganti, J. E. Gehrke, and R. Ramakrishnan. CACTUS—clustering categorical data using summaries. In *Proc. 1999 Int. Conf. Knowledge Discovery and Data Mining (KDD'99)*, pages 73–83, San Diego, CA, 1999.

[GGR02] M. Garofalakis, J. Gehrke, and R. Rastogi. Querying and mining data streams: You only get one look (a tutorial). In *Proc. 2002 ACM-SIGMOD Int. Conf. on Management of Data (SIGMOD'02)*, page 635, Madison, WI, June 2002.

[GGRL99] J. Gehrke, V. Ganti, R. Ramakrishnan, and W.-Y. Loh. BOAT—optimistic decision tree construction. In *Proc. 1999 ACM-SIGMOD Int. Conf. Management of Data (SIGMOD'99)*, pages 169–180, Philadelphia, PA, June 1999.

[GHP+04] C. Giannella, J. Han, J. Pei, X. Yan, and P. S. Yu. Mining frequent patterns in data streams at multiple time granularities. In H. Kargupta, A. Joshi, K. Sivakumar, and Y. Yesha, editors, *Data Mining: Next Generation Challenges and Future Directions*. AAAI/MIT Press, 2004.

[GKK+01] R. L. Grossman, C. Kamath, P. Kegelmeyer, V. Kumar, and R. R. Namburu. *Data Mining for Scientific and Engineering Applications*. Kluwer Academic Publishers, 2001.

[GKMS01] A. C. Gilbert, Y. Kotidis, S. Muthukrishnan, and M. Strauss. Surfing wavelets on streams: One-pass summaries for approximate aggregate queries. In *Proc. 2001 Int. Conf. on Very Large Data Bases (VLDB'01)*, pages 79–88, Rome, Italy, Sept. 2001.

[GKR98] D. Gibson, J. Kleinberg, and P. Raghavan. Inferring web communities from link topology. In *Proc. 9th ACM Conf. Hypertext and Hypermedia*, pages 225–234, Pittsburgh, PA, June 1998.

[GKS01] J. Gehrke, F. Korn, and D. Srivastava. On computing correlated aggregates over continuous data streams. In *Proc. 2001 ACM-SIGMOD Int. Conf. Management of Data (SIGMOD'01)*, pages 13–24, Santa Barbara, CA, May 2001.

[GLF89] J. Gennari, P. Langley, and D. Fisher. Models of incremental concept formation. *Artificial Intelligence*, 40:11–61, 1989.

[GLF04] T. Garner, J. W. Lloyd, and P. A. Flach. Kernels and distances for structured data. *Machine Learning*, 57:205–232, 2004.

[GM98] P. B. Gibbons and Y. Matias. New sampling-based summary statistics for improving approximate query answers. In *Proc. 1998 ACM-SIGMOD Int. Conf. Management of Data (SIGMOD'98)*, pages 331–342, Seattle, WA, June 1998.

[GM99] A. Gupta and I. S. Mumick. *Materialized Views: Techniques, Implementations, and Applications.* MIT Press, 1999.

[GMMO00] S. Guha, N. Mishra, R. Motwani, and L. O'Callaghan. Clustering data streams. In *Proc. 2000 Symp. Foundations of Computer Science (FOCS'00)*, pages 359–366, Redondo Beach, CA, 2000.

[GMUW02] H. Garcia-Molina, J. D. Ullman, and J. Widom. *Database Systems: The Complete Book.* Prentice Hall, 2002.

[GMV96] I. Guyon, N. Matic, and V. Vapnik. Discovering informative patterns and data cleaning. In U. M. Fayyad, G. Piatetsky-Shapiro, P. Smyth, and R. Uthurusamy, editors, *Advances in Knowledge Discovery and Data Mining*, pages 181–203. AAAI/MIT Press, 1996.

[GNOT92] D. Goldberg, D. Nichols, B. M. Oki, and D. Terry. Using collaborative filtering to weave an information tapestry. *Comm. ACM*, 35(12): 61–70, 1992.

[Gol89] D. Goldberg. *Genetic Algorithms in Search, Optimization, and Machine Learning.* Addison-Wesley, 1989.

[GRG98] J. Gehrke, R. Ramakrishnan, and V. Ganti. Rainforest: A framework for fast decision tree construction of large datasets. In *Proc. 1998 Int. Conf. Very Large Data Bases (VLDB'98)*, pages 416–427, New York, NY, Aug. 1998.

[GRS98] S. Guha, R. Rastogi, and K. Shim. Cure: An efficient clustering algorithm for large databases. In *Proc. 1998 ACM-SIGMOD Int. Conf. Management of Data (SIGMOD'98)*, pages 73–84, Seattle, WA, June 1998.

[GRS99a] M. Garofalakis, R. Rastogi, and K. Shim. SPIRIT: Sequential pattern mining with regular expression constraints. In *Proc. 1999 Int. Conf. Very Large Data Bases (VLDB'99)*, pages 223–234, Edinburgh, UK, Sept. 1999.

[GRS99b] S. Guha, R. Rastogi, and K. Shim. ROCK: A robust clustering algorithm for categorical attributes. In *Proc. 1999 Int. Conf. Data Engineering (ICDE'99)*, pages 512–521, Sydney, Australia, Mar. 1999.

[Gue94] R. H. Gueting. An introduction to spatial database systems. *The VLDB Journal*, 3:357–400, 1994.

[Gup97] H. Gupta. Selection of views to materialize in a data warehouse. In *Proc. 7th Int. Conf. Database Theory (ICDT'97)*, pages 98–112, Delphi, Greece, Jan. 1997.

[Gus97] D. Gusfield. *Algorithms on Strings, Trees and Sequences, Computer Science and Computation Biology*. Cambridge University Press, 1997.

[Gut84] A. Guttman. R-tree: A dynamic index structure for spatial searching. In *Proc. 1984 ACM-SIGMOD Int. Conf. Management of Data (SIGMOD'84)*, pages 47–57, Boston, MA, June 1984.

[GW02] R. C. Gonzalez and R. E. Woods. *Digital Image Processing* (2nd ed.). Prentice Hall, 2002.

[GZ03a] B. Goethals and M. Zaki. An introduction to workshop on frequent itemset mining implementations. In *Proc. ICDM Workshop on Frequent Itemset Mining Implementations (FIMI'03)*, Melbourne, FL, Nov. 2003.

[GZ03b] G. Grahne and J. Zhu. Efficiently using prefix-trees in mining frequent itemsets. In *Proc. ICDM'03 Int. Workshop on Frequent Itemset Mining Implementations (FIMI'03)*, Melbourne, FL, Nov. 2003.

[HAC+99] J. M. Hellerstein, R. Avnur, A. Chou, C. Hidber, C. Olston, V. Raman, T. Roth, and P. J. Haas. Interactive data analysis: The control project. *IEEE Computer*, 32:51–59, July 1999.

[Han98] J. Han. Towards on-line analytical mining in large databases. *SIGMOD Record*, 27:97–107, 1998.

[Har68] P. E. Hart. The condensed nearest neighbor rule. *IEEE Transactions on Information Theory*, 14:515–516, 1968.

[Har75] J. A. Hartigan. *Clustering Algorithms*. John Wiley & Sons, 1975.

[Hay99] S. S. Haykin. *Neural Networks: A Comprehensive Foundation*. Prentice Hall, 1999.

[Hay04] C. L. Hays. What Wal-Mart knows about customers' habits. *New York Times*, Section 3, page 1, column 1, Nov. 14, 2004.

[HB88] S. J. Hanson and D. J. Burr. Minkowski back-propagation: Learning in connectionist models with non-euclidean error signals. In *Neural Information Processing Systems*, American Institute of Physics, 1988.

[HoCr04] R. V. Hogg and A. T. Craig. *Introduction to Mathematical Statistics* (6th ed.). Prentice Hall, 2004.

[HCC93] J. Han, Y. Cai, and N. Cercone. Data-driven discovery of quantitative rules in relational databases. *IEEE Trans. Knowledge and Data Engineering*, 5:29–40, 1993.

[HCD94] L. B. Holder, D. J. Cook, and S. Djoko. Substructure discovery in the subdue system. In *Proc. AAAI'94 Workshop Knowledge Discovery in Databases (KDD'94)*, pages 169–180, Seattle, WA, July 1994.

[HCLM04] X. He, D. Cai, H. Liu, and W.-Y. Ma. Locality preserving indexing for document representation. In *Proc. 2004 Int. ACM SIGIR Conf. Research and Development in Information Retrieval (SIGIR'04)*, pages 96–103, Sheffield, UK, July 2004.

[HDY99] J. Han, G. Dong, and Y. Yin. Efficient mining of partial periodic patterns in time series database. In *Proc. 1999 Int. Conf. Data Engineering (ICDE'99)*, pages 106–115, Sydney, Australia, April 1999.

[He99] G. E. Hinton and T. J. Sejnowski (eds.). *Unsupervised Learning: Foundation of Neural Network Computation*. MIT Press, 1999.

[Hec96] D. Heckerman. Bayesian networks for knowledge discovery. In U. M. Fayyad, G. Piatetsky-Shapiro, P. Smyth, and R. Uthurusamy, editors, *Advances in Knowledge Discovery and Data Mining*, pages 273–305. MIT Press, 1996.

[HF94] J. Han and Y. Fu. Dynamic generation and refinement of concept hierarchies for knowledge discovery in databases. In *Proc. AAAI'94 Workshop Knowledge Discovery in Databases (KDD'94)*, pages 157–168, Seattle, WA, July 1994.

[HF95] J. Han and Y. Fu. Discovery of multiple-level association rules from large databases. In *Proc. 1995 Int. Conf. Very Large Data Bases (VLDB'95)*, pages 420–431, Zurich, Switzerland, Sept. 1995.

[HF96] J. Han and Y. Fu. Exploration of the power of attribute-oriented induction in data mining. In U. M. Fayyad, G. Piatetsky-Shapiro, P. Smyth, and R. Uthurusamy, editors, *Advances in Knowledge Discovery and Data Mining*, pages 399–421. AAAI/MIT Press, 1996.

[HFW$^+$96] J. Han, Y. Fu, W. Wang, J. Chiang, W. Gong, K. Koperski, D. Li, Y. Lu, A. Rajan, N. Stefanovic, B. Xia, and O. R. Zaïane. DBMiner: A system for mining knowledge in large relational databases. In *Proc. 1996 Int. Conf. Data Mining and Knowledge Discovery (KDD'96)*, pages 250–255, Portland, OR, Aug. 1996.

[HGC95] D. Heckerman, D. Geiger, and D. M. Chickering. Learning Bayesian networks: The combination of knowledge and statistical data. *Machine Learning*, 20:197–243, 1995.

[HH01] R. J. Hilderman and H. J. Hamilton. *Knowledge Discovery and Measures of Interest*. Kluwer Academic, 2001.

[HHW97] J. Hellerstein, P. Haas, and H. Wang. Online aggregation. In *Proc. 1997 ACM-SIGMOD Int. Conf. Management of Data (SIGMOD'97)*, pages 171–182, Tucson, AZ, May 1997.

[Hig03] R. C. Higgins. *Analysis for Financial Management* (7th ed.). Irwin/McGraw-Hill, 2003.

[HK91] P. Hoschka and W. Klösgen. A support system for interpreting statistical data. In G. Piatetsky-Shapiro and W. J. Frawley, editors, *Knowledge Discovery in Databases*, pages 325–346. AAAI/MIT Press, 1991.

[HK98] A. Hinneburg and D. A. Keim. An efficient approach to clustering in large multimedia databases with noise. In *Proc. 1998 Int. Conf. Knowledge Discovery and Data Mining (KDD'98)*, pages 58–65, New York, NY, Aug. 1998.

[HKBR98] J. L. Herlocker, J. A. Konstan, J. R. A. Borchers, and J. Riedl. An algorithmic framework for performing collaborative filtering. In *Proc. 1999 Int. ACM SIGIR Conf. Research and Development in Information Retrieval (SIGIR'99)*, pages 230–237, Berkeley, CA, Aug. 1998.

[HKGT03] M. Hadjieleftheriou, G. Kollios, D. Gunopulos, and V. J. Tsotras. On-line discovery of dense areas in spatio-temporal databases. In *Proc. 2003 Int. Symp. Spatial and Temporal Databases (SSTD'03)*, pages 306–324, Santorini Island, Greece, 2003.

[HKP91] J. Hertz, A. Krogh, and R. G. Palmer. *Introduction to the Theory of Neural Computation*. Addison-Wesley, 1991.

[HKS97] J. Han, K. Koperski, and N. Stefanovic. GeoMiner: A system prototype for spatial data mining. In *Proc. 1997 ACM-SIGMOD Int. Conf. Management of Data (SIGMOD'97)*, pages 553–556, Tucson, AZ, May 1997.

[HLZ02] W. Hsu, M. L. Lee, and J. Zhang. Image mining: Trends and developments. *J. Int. Info. Systems*, 19:7–23, 2002.

[HMM86] J. Hong, I. Mozetic, and R. S. Michalski. AQ15: Incremental learning of attribute-based descriptions from examples, the method and user's guide. In *Report ISG 85-5, UIUCDCS-F-86-949*, Dept. Comp. Science, University of Illinois at Urbana-Champaign, 1986.

[HMS66] E. B. Hunt, J. Marin, and P. T. Stone. *Experiments in Induction*. Academic Press, 1966.

[HMS01] D. J. Hand, H. Mannila, and P. Smyth. *Principles of Data Mining*. MIT Press, 2001.

[HN90] R. Hecht-Nielsen. *Neurocomputing*. Addison-Wesley, 1990.

[HNFD98] J. Han, R. T. Ng, Y. Fu, and S. Dao. Dealing with semantic heterogeneity by generalization-based data mining techniques. In M. P. Papazoglou and G. Schlageter (eds.), *Cooperative Information Systems: Current Trends & Directions*, pages 207–231, Academic Press, 1998.

[HNKW98] J. Han, S. Nishio, H. Kawano, and W. Wang. Generalization-based data mining in object-oriented databases using an object-cube model. *Data and Knowledge Engineering*, 25:55–97, 1998.

[Hof98] T. Hofmann. Probabilistic latent semantic indexing. In *Proc. 1999 Int. ACM SIGIR Conf. Research and Development in Information Retrieval (SIGIR'99)*, pages 50–57, Berkeley, CA, Aug. 1998.

[HPDW01] J. Han, J. Pei, G. Dong, and K. Wang. Efficient computation of iceberg cubes with complex measures. In *Proc. 2001 ACM-SIGMOD Int. Conf. Management of Data (SIGMOD'01)*, pages 1–12, Santa Barbara, CA, May 2001.

[HPMA$^+$00] J. Han, J. Pei, B. Mortazavi-Asl, Q. Chen, U. Dayal, and M.-C. Hsu. FreeSpan: Frequent pattern-projected sequential pattern mining. In *Proc. 2000 ACM SIGKDD Int. Conf. Knowledge Discovery in Databases (KDD'00)*, pages 355–359, Boston, MA, Aug. 2000.

[HPS97] J. Hosking, E. Pednault, and M. Sudan. A statistical perspective on data mining. *Future Generation Computer Systems*, 13:117–134, 1997.

[HPY00] J. Han, J. Pei, and Y. Yin. Mining frequent patterns without candidate generation. In *Proc. 2000 ACM-SIGMOD Int. Conf. Management of Data (SIGMOD'00)*, pages 1–12, Dallas, TX, May 2000.

[HRU96] V. Harinarayan, A. Rajaraman, and J. D. Ullman. Implementing data cubes efficiently. In *Proc. 1996 ACM-SIGMOD Int. Conf. Management of Data (SIGMOD'96)*, pages 205–216, Montreal, Canada, June 1996.

[HS05] J. M. Hellerstein and M. Stonebraker. *Readings in Database Systems* (4th ed.). MIT Press, 2005.

[HSD01] G. Hulten, L. Spencer, and P. Domingos. Mining time-changing data streams. In *Proc. 2001 ACM SIGKDD Int. Conf. Knowledge Discovery in Databases (KDD'01)*, San Francisco, CA, Aug. 2001.

[HSG90] S. A. Harp, T. Samad, and A. Guha. Designing application-specific neural networks using the genetic algorithm. In D. S. Touretzky, editor, *Advances in Neural Information Processing Systems II*, pages 447–454. Morgan Kaufmann, 1990.

[HSK98] J. Han, N. Stefanovic, and K. Koperski. Selective materialization: An efficient method for spatial data cube construction. In *Proc. 1998 Pacific-Asia Conf. Knowledge Discovery and Data Mining (PAKDD'98) [Lecture Notes in Artificial Intelligence, 1394, Springer Verlag, 1998]*, Melbourne, Australia, April 1998.

[HTF01] T. Hastie, R. Tibshirani, and J. Friedman. *The Elements of Statistical Learning: Data Mining, Inference, and Prediction*. Springer-Verlag, 2001.

[Hua98] Z. Huang. Extensions to the *k*-means algorithm for clustering large data sets with categorical values. *Data Mining and Knowledge Discovery*, 2:283–304, 1998.

[Hub94] C. H. Huberty. *Applied Discriminant Analysis*. John Wiley & Sons, 1994.

[Hub96] B. B. Hubbard. *The World According to Wavelets*. A. K. Peters, 1996.

[HWB$^+$04] J. Huan, W. Wang, D. Bandyopadhyay, J. Snoeyink, J. Prins, and A. Tropsha. Mining spatial motifs from protein structure graphs. In *Proc. 8th Int. Conf. Research in Computational Molecular Biology (RECOMB)*, pages 308–315, San Diego, CA, March 2004.

[HWP03] J. Huan, W. Wang, and J. Prins. Efficient mining of frequent subgraph in the presence of isomorphism. In *Proc. 2003 Int. Conf. Data Mining (ICDM'03)*, pages 549–552, Melbourne, FL, Nov. 2003.

[HYK99] J. Han, Q. Yang, and E. Kim. Plan mining by divide-and-conquer. In *Proc. 1999 SIGMOD Workshop Research Issues on Data Mining and Knowledge Discovery (DMKD'99)*, pages 8:1–8:6, Philadelphia, PA, May 1999.

[HYY$^+$05] H. Hu, X. Yan, H. Yu, J. Han, and X. J. Zhou. Mining coherent dense subgraphs across massive biological networks for functional discovery. In *Proc. 2005 Int. Conf. Intelligent Systems for Molecular Biology (ISMB'05)*, pages 213–221, Ann Arbor, MI, June 2005.

[IGG03] C. Imhoff, N. Galemmo, and J. G. Geiger. *Mastering Data Warehouse Design: Relational and Dimensional Techniques*. John Wiley & Sons, 2003.

[IKA02] T. Imielinski, L. Khachiyan, and A. Abdulghani. Cubegrades: Generalizing association rules. *Data Mining and Knowledge Discovery*, 6:219–258, 2002.

[IM96] T. Imielinski and H. Mannila. A database perspective on knowledge discovery. *Comm. ACM*, 39:58–64, 1996.

[Inm96] W. H. Inmon. *Building the Data Warehouse*. John Wiley & Sons, 1996.

[IV99] T. Imielinski and A. Virmani. MSQL: A query language for database mining. *Data Mining and Knowledge Discovery*, 3:373–408, 1999.

[IVA96] T. Imielinski, A. Virmani, and A. Abdulghani. DataMine—application programming interface and query language for KDD applications. In *Proc. 1996 Int. Conf. Data Mining and Knowledge Discovery (KDD'96)*, pages 256–261, Portland, OR, Aug. 1996.

[IWM98] A. Inokuchi, T. Washio, and H. Motoda. An apriori-based algorithm for mining frequent substructures from graph data. In *Proc. 2000 European Symp. Principle of Data Mining and Knowledge Discovery (PKDD'00)*, pages 13–23, Lyon, France, Sept. 1998.

[Jac88] R. Jacobs. Increased rates of convergence through learning rate adaptation. *Neural Networks*, 1:295–307, 1988.

[Jam85] M. James. *Classification Algorithms*. John Wiley & Sons, 1985.

[JD88] A. K. Jain and R. C. Dubes. *Algorithms for Clustering Data*. Prentice Hall, 1988.

[Jen96] F. V. Jensen. *An Introduction to Bayesian Networks*. Springer Verlag, 1996.

[JKM99] H. V. Jagadish, N. Koudas, and S. Muthukrishnan:. Mining deviants in a time series database. In *Proc. 1999 Int. Conf. Very Large Data Bases (VLDB'99)*, pages 102–113, Edinburgh, UK, Sept. 1999.

[JL96] G. H. John and P. Langley. Static versus dynamic sampling for data mining. In *Proc. 1996 Int. Conf. Knowledge Discovery and Data Mining (KDD'96)*, pages 367–370, Portland, OR, Aug. 1996.

[JMF99] A. K. Jain, M. N. Murty, and P. J. Flynn. Data clustering: A survey. *ACM Comput. Surv.*, 31:264–323, 1999.

[Joa01] T. Joachims. A statistical learning model of text classification with support vector machines. In *Proc. Int. 2001 ACM SIGIR Conf. Research and Development in Information Retrieval (SIGIR'01)*, pages 128–136, New Orleans, LA, Sept. 2001.

[Joh97] G. H. John. *Enhancements to the Data Mining Process*. Ph.D. Thesis, Computer Science Dept., Stanford University, 1997.

[Joh99] G. H. John. Behind-the-scenes data mining: A report on the KDD-98 panel. *SIGKDD Explorations*, 1:6–8, 1999.

[JP04] N. C. Jones and P. A. Pevzner. *An Introduction to Bioinformatics Algorithms*. MIT Press, 2004.

[JW02] R. A. Johnson and D. A. Wichern. *Applied Multivariate Statistical Analysis* (5th ed.). Prentice Hall, 2002.

[Kas80] G. V. Kass. An exploratory technique for investigating large quantities of categorical data. *Applied Statistics*, 29:119–127, 1980.

[Kat53] L. Katz. A new status index derived from sociometric analysis. *Psychometrika*, 18:39–43, March 1953.

[KBL+04] H. Kargupta, B. Bhargava, K. Liu, M. Powers, P. Blair, S. Bushra, J. Dull, K. Sarkar, M. Klein, M. Vasa, and D. Handy. VEDAS: A mobile and distributed data stream mining system for real-time vehicle monitoring. In *Proc. 2004 SIAM Int. Conf. Data Mining (SDM'04)*, Lake Buena Vista, FL, April 2004.

[Kec01] V. Kecman. *Learning and Soft Computing*. MIT Press, 2001.

[Ker92] R. Kerber. Discretization of numeric attributes. In *Proc. 1992 Nat. Conf. Artificial Intelligence (AAAI'92)*, pages 123–128, AAAI/MIT Press, 1992.

[KGS04] M. Koyuturk, A. Grama, and W. Szpankowski. An efficient algorithm for detecting frequent subgraphs in biological networks. *Bioinformatics*, 20:I200–I207, 2004.

[KH95] K. Koperski and J. Han. Discovery of spatial association rules in geographic information databases. In *Proc. 1995 Int. Symp. Large Spatial Databases (SSD'95)*, pages 47–66, Portland, ME, Aug. 1995.

[KH97] I. Kononenko and S. J. Hong. Attribute selection for modeling. *Future Generation Computer Systems*, 13:181–195, 1997.

[KHC97] M. Kamber, J. Han, and J. Y. Chiang. Metarule-guided mining of multi-dimensional association rules using data cubes. In *Proc. 1997 Int. Conf. Knowledge Discovery and Data Mining (KDD'97)*, pages 207–210, Newport Beach, CA, Aug. 1997.

[KHK99] G. Karypis, E.-H. Han, and V. Kumar. CHAMELEON: A hierarchical clustering algorithm using dynamic modeling. *COMPUTER*, 32:68–75, 1999.

[KHS98] K. Koperski, J. Han, and N. Stefanovic. An efficient two-step method for classification of spatial data. In *Proc. 8th Symp. Spatial Data Handling*, pages 45–55, Vancouver, Canada, 1998.

[KJ97] R. Kohavi and G. H. John. Wrappers for feature subset selection. *Artificial Intelligence*, 97:273–324, 1997.

[KJSY04] H. Kargupta, A. Joshi, K. Sivakumar, and Y. Yesha. *Data Mining: Next Generation Challenges and Future Directions*. AAAI/MIT Press, 2004.

[KK01] M. Kuramochi and G. Karypis. Frequent subgraph discovery. In *Proc. 2001 Int. Conf. Data Mining (ICDM'01)*, pages 313–320, San Jose, CA, Nov. 2001.

[KK94] D. A. Keim and H.-P. Kriegel. VisDB: Database exploration using multidimensional visualization. In *Computer Graphics and Applications*, pages 40–49, Sept. 94.

[KKL+00] T. Kohonen, S. Kaski, K. Lagus, J. Solojärvi, A. Paatero, and A. Saarela. Self-organization of massive document collection. *IEEE Trans. Neural Networks*, 11:574–585, 2000.

[KKR+99] J. M. Kleinberg, R. Kumar, P. Raghavan, S. Rajagopalan, and A. Tomkins. The Web as a graph: Measurements, models, and methods. In *Proc. Int. Conf. and Combinatorics Computing* (*COCOON*'99), pages 1–17, Tokyo, Japan, July 1999.

[Kle99] J. M. Kleinberg. Authoritative sources in a hyperlinked environment. *J. ACM*, 46:604–632, 1999.

[KLV+98] R. L. Kennedy, Y. Lee, B. Van Roy, C. D. Reed, and R. P. Lippman. *Solving Data Mining Problems Through Pattern Recognition*. Prentice Hall, 1998.

[KM90] Y. Kodratoff and R. S. Michalski. *Machine Learning, An Artificial Intelligence Approach, Vol. 3*. Morgan Kaufmann, 1990.

[KM94] J. Kivinen and H. Mannila. The power of sampling in knowledge discovery. In *Proc. 13th ACM Symp. Principles of Database Systems*, pages 77–85, Minneapolis, MN, May 1994.

[KMR+94] M. Klemettinen, H. Mannila, P. Ronkainen, H. Toivonen, and A. I. Verkamo. Finding interesting rules from large sets of discovered association rules. In *Proc. 3rd Int. Conf. Information and Knowledge Management*, pages 401–408, Gaithersburg, MD, Nov. 1994.

[KMS03] J. Kubica, A. Moore, and J. Schneider. Tractable group detection on large link data sets. In *Proc. 3rd IEEE International Conference on Data Mining*, pages 573–576, Melbourne, FL, Nov. 2003.

[KN96] E. Knorr and R. Ng. Finding aggregate proximity relationships and commonalities in spatial data mining. *IEEE Trans. Knowledge and Data Engineering*, 8:884–897, 1996.

[KN97] E. Knorr and R. Ng. A unified notion of outliers: Properties and computation. In *Proc. 1997 Int. Conf. Knowledge Discovery and Data Mining (KDD'97)*, pages 219–222, Newport Beach, CA, Aug. 1997.

[KN98] E. Knorr and R. Ng. Algorithms for mining distance-based outliers in large datasets. In *Proc. 1998 Int. Conf. Very Large Data Bases (VLDB'98)*, pages 392–403, New York, NY, Aug. 1998.

[KNNL04] M. H. Kutner, C. J. Nachtsheim, J. Neter, and W. Li. *Applied Linear Statistical Models with Student CD*. Irwin, 2004.

[Koh82] T. Kohonen. Self-organized formation of topologically correct feature maps. *Biological Cybernetics*, 43:59–69, 1982.

[Koh89] T. Kohonen. *Self-Organization and Associative Memory* (3rd ed.). Springer-Verlag, 1989.

[Koh95] R. Kohavi. A study of cross-validation and bootstrap for accuracy estimation and model selection. In *Proc. 14th Joint Int. Conf. Artificial Intelligence (IJCAI'95)*, vol. 2, pages 1137–1143, Montreal, Canada, Aug. 1995.

[Koh01] R. Kohavi. Mining e-commerce data: The good, the bad, and the ugly. In *Proc. 2001 ACM SIGKDD Int. Conf. Knowledge Discovery in Databases (KDD'01)*, pages 8–13, San Francisco, CA, Aug. 2001.

[Kol93] J. L. Kolodner. *Case-Based Reasoning*. Morgan Kaufmann, 1993.

[Kon95] I. Kononenko. On biases in estimating multi-valued attributes. In *Proc. 14th Joint Int. Conf. Artificial Intelligence (IJCAI'95)*, vol. 2, pages 1034–1040, Montreal, Canada, Aug. 1995.

[Kot88] P. Koton. Reasoning about evidence in causal explanation. In *Proc. 7th Nat. Conf. Artificial Intelligence (AAAI'88)*, pages 256–263, Aug. 1988.

[KPR98] J. M. Kleinberg, C. Papadimitriou, and P. Raghavan. A microeconomic view of data mining. *Data Mining and Knowledge Discovery*, 2:311–324, 1998.

[KPS03] R. M. Karp, C. H. Papadimitriou, and S. Shenker. A simple algorithm for finding frequent elements in streams and bags. *ACM Trans. Database Systems*, 28(1):51–55, March, 2003.

[KR90] L. Kaufman and P. J. Rousseeuw. *Finding Groups in Data: An Introduction to Cluster Analysis*. John Wiley & Sons, 1990.

[KR02] R. Kimball and M. Ross. *The Data Warehouse Toolkit: The Complete Guide to Dimensional Modeling* (2nd ed.). John Wiley & Sons, 2002.

[KR03] D. Krane and R. Raymer. *Fundamental Concepts of Bioinformatics*. Benjamin Cummings, 2003.

[Kre02] V. Krebs. Mapping networks of terrorist cells. *Connections*, 24:43–52, Winter 2002.

[KRR+00] R. Kumar, P. Raghavan, S. Rajagopalan, D. Sivakumar, A. Tomkins, and E. Upfal. Stochastic models for the web graph. In *Proc. 2000 IEEE Symp. Foundations of Computer Science (FOCS'00)*, pages 57–65, Redondo Beach, CA, Nov. 2000.

[KRRT98] R. Kimball, L. Reeves, M. Ross, and W. Thornthwaite. *The Data Warehouse Lifecycle Toolkit: Expert Methods for Designing, Developing, and Deploying Data Warehouses*. John Wiley & Sons, 1998.

[KS95] D. Konopnicki and O. Shmueli. W3QS: A query system for the world-wide-web. In *Proc. 1995 Int. Conf. Very Large Data Bases (VLDB'95)*, pages 54–65, Zurich, Switzerland, Sept. 1995.

[KS04] H. Kargupta and K. Sivakumar. Existential pleasures of distributed data mining. In H. Kargupta, A. Joshi, K. Sivakumar, and Y. Yesha, editors, *Data Mining: Next Generation Challenges and Future Directions*, pages 3–25. AAAI/MIT Press, 2004.

[KT99] J. M. Kleinberg and A. Tomkins. Application of linear algebra in information retrieval and hypertext analysis. In *Proc. 18th ACM Symp. Principles of Database Systems (PODS'99)*, pages 185–193, Philadelphia, PA, May 1999.

[KW98] M. Kirsten and S. Wrobel. Relational distance-based clustering. In *Proc. 1998 Int. Conf. Inductive Logic Programming (ILP'98)*, pages 261–270, Madison, WI, 1998.

[KW00] M. Kirsten and S. Wrobel. Extending k-means clustering to first-order representations. In *Proc. 2000 Int. Conf. Inductive Logic Programming (ILP'00)*, pages 112–129, London, UK, July 2000.

[KWG+97] M. Kamber, L. Winstone, W. Gong, S. Cheng, and J. Han. Generalization and decision tree induction: Efficient classification in data mining. In *Proc. 1997 Int. Workshop Research Issues on Data Engineering (RIDE'97)*, pages 111–120, Birmingham, England, April 1997.

[KYB03] I. Korf, M. Yandell, and J. Bedell. *BLAST*. O'Reilly, 2003.

[Lam98] W. Lam. Bayesian network refinement via machine learning approach. *IEEE Trans. Pattern Analysis and Machine Intelligence*, 20:240–252, 1998.

[Lan96] P. Langley. *Elements of Machine Learning*. Morgan Kaufmann, 1996.

[LAR02] W. Lin, S. Alvarez, and C. Ruiz. Efficient adaptive-support association rule mining for recommender systems. *Data Mining and Knowledge Discovery*, 6:83–105, 2002.

[Lau95] S. L. Lauritzen. The EM algorithm for graphical association models with missing data. *Computational Statistics and Data Analysis*, 19:191–201, 1995.

[Lau96] K. C. Laudon. Markets and privacy. *Comm. ACM*, 39:92–104, Sept. 96.

[LD94] N. Lavrac and S. Dzeroski. *Inductive Logic Programming: Techniques and Applications*. Ellis Horwood, 1994.

[LDR00] J. Li, G. Dong, and K. Ramamohanrarao. Making use of the most expressive jumping emerging patterns for classification. In *Proc. 2000 Pacific-Asia Conf. Knowledge Discovery and Data Mining (PAKDD'00)*, pages 220–232, Kyoto, Japan, April 2000.

[LDS90] Y. Le Cun, J. S. Denker, and S. A. Solla. Optimal brain damage. In D. Touretzky, editor, *Advances in Neural Information Processing Systems 2*. Morgan Kaufmann, 1990.

[Le98] H. Liu and H. Motoda (eds.). *Feature Extraction, Construction, and Selection: A Data Mining Perspective*. Kluwer Academic Publishers, 1998.

[Lea96] D. B. Leake. CBR in context: The present and future. In D. B. Leake, editor, *Case-Based Reasoning: Experiences, Lessons, and Future Directions*, pages 3–30. AAAI Press, 1996.

[LG03] Q. Lu and L. Getoor. Link-based classification. In *Proc. 2003 Int. Conf. Machine Learning (ICML'03)*, pages 496–503, Washington, DC, 2003.

[LGT97] S. Lawrence, C. L Giles, and A. C. Tsoi. Symbolic conversion, grammatical inference and rule extraction for foreign exchange rate prediction. In Y. Abu-Mostafa, A. S. Weigend, and P. N Refenes, editors, *Neural Networks in the Capital Markets*. World Scientific, 1997.

[LH02] S.-H. Lin and J.-M. Ho. Discovering informative content blocks from web documents. In *Proc. 2002 ACM SIGKDD Int. Conf. on Knowledge Discovery and Data Mining (KDD'02)*, pages 588–593, Edmonton, Canada, July 2002.

[LHC97] B. Liu, W. Hsu, and S. Chen. Using general impressions to analyze discovered classification rules. In *Proc. 1997 Int. Conf. Knowledge Discovery and Data Mining (KDD'97)*, pages 31–36, Newport Beach, CA, Aug. 1997.

[LHF98] H. Lu, J. Han, and L. Feng. Stock movement and n-dimensional inter-transaction association rules. In *Proc. 1998 SIGMOD Workshop Research Issues on Data Mining and Knowledge Discovery (DMKD'98)*, pages 12:1–12:7, Seattle, WA, June 1998.

[LHG04] X. Li, J. Han, and H. Gonzalez. High-dimensional OLAP: A minimal cubing approach. In *Proc. 2004 Int. Conf. Very Large Data Bases (VLDB'04)*, pages 528–539, Toronto, Canada, Aug. 2004.

[LHM98] B. Liu, W. Hsu, and Y. Ma. Integrating classification and association rule mining. In *Proc. 1998 Int. Conf. Knowledge Discovery and Data Mining (KDD'98)*, pages 80–86, New York, NY, Aug. 1998.

[LHO93] W. Lu, J. Han, and B. C. Ooi. Knowledge discovery in large spatial databases. In *Proc. Far East Workshop Geographic Information Systems*, pages 275–289, Singapore, June 1993.

[LHP01] W. Li, J. Han, and J. Pei. CMAR: Accurate and efficient classification based on multiple class-association rules. In *Proc. 2001 Int. Conf. Data Mining (ICDM'01)*, pages 369–376, San Jose, CA, Nov. 2001.

[LHTD02] H. Liu, F. Hussain, C. L. Tan, and M. Dash. Discretization: An enabling technique. *Data Mining and Knowledge Discovery*, 6:393–423, 2002.

[LKCH03] Y.-K. Lee, W.-Y. Kim, Y. D. Cai, and J. Han. CoMine: Efficient mining of correlated patterns. In *Proc. 2003 Int. Conf. Data Mining (ICDM'03)*, pages 581–584, Melbourne, FL, Nov. 2003.

[LKF05] J. Leskovec, J. Kleinberg, and C. Faloutsos. Graphs over time: Densification laws, shrinking diameters and possible explanations. In *Proc. 2005 ACM SIGKDD Int. Conf. on Knowledge Discovery and Data Mining (KDD'05)*, pages 177–187, Chicago, IL, Aug. 2005.

[LLLY03] G. Liu, H. Lu, W. Lou, and J. X. Yu. On computing, storing and querying frequent patterns. In *Proc. 2003 ACM SIGKDD Int. Conf. Knowledge Discovery and Data Mining (KDD'03)*, pages 607–612, Washington, D.C., Aug. 2003.

[Lloy57] S. P. Lloyd. Least Squares Quantization in PCM. *IEEE Trans. Information Theory*, 28:128–137, 1982, (original version: Technical Report, Bell Labs, 1957.)

[LLS00] T.-S. Lim, W.-Y. Loh, and Y.-S. Shih. A comparison of prediction accuracy, complexity, and training time of thirty-three old and new classification algorithms. *Machine Learning*, 40(3):203–228, Sept. 2000.

[LM97] K. Laskey and S. Mahoney. Network fragments: Representing knowledge for constructing probabilistic models. In *Proc. 13th Annual Conf. on Uncertainty in Artificial Intelligence*, pages 334–341, San Francisco, CA, Aug. 1997.

[LM98] H. Liu and H. Motoda. *Feature Selection for Knowledge Discovery and Data Mining*. Kluwer Academic Publishers, 1998.

[LNHP99] L. V. S. Lakshmanan, R. Ng, J. Han, and A. Pang. Optimization of constrained frequent set queries with 2-variable constraints. In *Proc. 1999 ACM-SIGMOD Int. Conf. Management of Data (SIGMOD'99)*, pages 157–168, Philadelphia, PA, June 1999.

[LNK03] D. Liben-Nowell and J. Kleinberg. The link prediction problem for social networks. In *Proc. 2003 Int. Conf. Information and Knowledge Management (CIKM'03)*, pages 556–559, New Orleans, LA, Nov. 2003.

[Los01] D. Loshin. *Enterprise Knowledge Management: The Data Quality Approach*. Morgan Kaufmann, 2001.

[LP97] A. Lenarcik and Z. Piasta. Probabilistic rough classifiers with mixture of discrete and continuous variables. In T. Y. Lin and N. Cercone, editors, *Rough Sets and Data Mining: Analysis for Imprecise Data*, pages 373–383. Kluwer Academic Publishers, 1997.

[LPH02] L. V. S. Lakshmanan, J. Pei, and J. Han. Quotient cube: How to summarize the semantics of a data cube. In *Proc. 2002 Int. Conf. on Very Large Data Bases (VLDB'02)*, pages 778–789, Hong Kong, China, Aug. 2002.

[LPWH02] J. Liu, Y. Pan, K. Wang, and J. Han. Mining frequent item sets by opportunistic projection. In *Proc. 2002 ACM SIGKDD Int. Conf. Knowledge Discovery in Databases (KDD'02)*, pages 239–248, Edmonton, Canada, July 2002.

[LPZ03] L. V. S. Lakshmanan, J. Pei, and Y. Zhao. QC-Trees: An efficient summary structure for semantic OLAP. In *Proc. 2003 ACM-SIGMOD Int. Conf. Management of Data (SIGMOD'03)*, pages 64–75, San Diego, CA, June 2003.

[LS95] H. Liu and R. Setiono. Chi2: Feature selection and discretization of numeric attributes. *Proc. 1995 IEEE Int. Conf. Tools with AI (ICTAI'95)*, pages 388–391, Washington, DC, Nov. 1995.

[LS97] W. Y. Loh and Y. S. Shih. Split selection methods for classification trees. *Statistica Sinica*, 7:815–840, 1997.

[LSBZ87] P. Langley, H. A. Simon, G. L. Bradshaw, and J. M. Zytkow. *Scientific Discovery: Computational Explorations of the Creative Processes*. MIT Press, 1987.

[LSL95] H. Lu, R. Setiono, and H. Liu. Neurorule: A connectionist approach to data mining. In *Proc. 1995 Int. Conf. Very Large Data Bases (VLDB'95)*, pages 478–489, Zurich, Switzerland, Sept. 1995.

[LSS96] L. V. S. Lakshmanan, F. Sadri, and S. Subramanian. A declarative query language for querying and restructuring the web. In *Proc. Int. Workshop Research Issues in Data Engineering*, pages 12–21, Tempe, AZ, 1996.

[LSW97] B. Lent, A. Swami, and J. Widom. Clustering association rules. In *Proc. 1997 Int. Conf. Data Engineering (ICDE'97)*, pages 220–231, Birmingham, England, April 1997.

[LV88] W. Y. Loh and N. Vanichsetakul. Tree-structured classificaiton via generalized discriminant analysis. *J. American Statistical Association*, 83:715–728, 1988.

[LXY01] B. Liu, Y. Xia, and P. S. Yu. Clustering through decision tree construction. In *Proc. 2000 ACM CIKM Int. Conf. Information and Knowledge Management (CIKM'00)*, pages 20–29, McLean, VA, Nov. 2001.

[MA03] S. Mitra and T. Acharya. *Data Mining: Multimedia, Soft Computing, and Bioinformatics*. John Wiley & Sons, 2003.

[MAA05] A. Metwally, D. Agrawal, and A. El Abbadi. Efficient computation of frequent and top-k elements in data streams. In *Proc. 2005 Int. Conf. Database Theory (ICDT'05)*, Edinburgh, UK, Jan. 2005.

[Mac67] J. MacQueen. Some methods for classification and analysis of multivariate observations. *Proc. 5th Berkeley Symp. Math. Statist. Prob.*, 1:281–297, 1967.

[Mag94] J. Magidson. The CHAID approach to segmentation modeling: CHI-squared automatic interaction detection. In R. P. Bagozzi, editor, *Advanced Methods of Marketing Research*, pages 118–159. Blackwell Business, 1994.

[Man00] H. Mannila. Theoretical frameworks of data mining. *SIGKDD Explorations*, 1:30–32, 2000.

[MAR96] M. Mehta, R. Agrawal, and J. Rissanen. SLIQ: A fast scalable classifier for data mining. In *Proc. 1996 Int. Conf. Extending Database Technology (EDBT'96)*, pages 18–32, Avignon, France, Mar. 1996.

[Mat97] R. Mattison. *Data Warehousing and Data Mining for Telecommunications*. Artech House, 1997.

[MBK98] R. S. Michalski, I. Brakto, and M. Kubat. *Machine Learning and Data Mining: Methods and Applications*. John Wiley & Sons, 1998.

[McK81] B. D. McKay. Practical graph isomorphism. *Congressus Numerantium*, 30:45–87, 1981.

[MCK+04] N. Mamoulis, H. Cao, G. Kollios, M. Hadjieleftheriou, Y. Tao, and D. Cheung. Mining, indexing, and querying historical spatiotemporal data. In *Proc. 2004 ACM SIGKDD Int. Conf. Knowledge Discovery in Databases (KDD'04)*, pages 236–245, Seattle, WA, Aug. 2004.

[MCM83] R. S. Michalski, J. G. Carbonell, and T. M. Mitchell. *Machine Learning, An Artificial Intelligence Approach, Vol. 1*. Morgan Kaufmann, 1983.

[MCM86] R. S. Michalski, J. G. Carbonell, and T. M. Mitchell. *Machine Learning, An Artificial Intelligence Approach, Vol. 2*. Morgan Kaufmann, 1986.

[MD88] M. Muralikrishna and D. J. DeWitt. Equi-depth histograms for extimating selectivity factors for multi-dimensional queries. In *Proc. 1988 ACM-SIGMOD Int. Conf. Management of Data (SIGMOD'88)*, pages 28–36, Chicago, IL, June 1988.

[Men03] J. Mena. *Investigative Data Mining with Security and Criminal Detection*. Butterworth-Heinemann, 2003.

[MF90] S. Muggleton and C. Feng. Efficient induction of logic programs. In *Proc. 1990 Conf. Algorithmic Learning Theory (ALT'90)*, pages 368–381, Tokyo, Japan, Oct. 1990.

[MFS95] D. Malerba, E. Floriana, and G. Semeraro. A further comparison of simplification methods for decision tree induction. In D. Fisher and H. Lenz, editors, *Learning from Data: AI and Statistics*. Springer-Verlag, 1995.

[MGR92] D. J. Maguire, M. Goodchild, and D. W. Rhind. *Geographical Information Systems: Principles and Applications*. Longman, 1992.

[MH95] J. K. Martin and D. S. Hirschberg. The time complexity of decision tree induction. In *Technical Report ICS-TR 95-27*, Dept. Information and Computer Science, Univ. California, Irvine, Aug. 1995.

[MH01a] S. Ma and J. L. Hellerstein. Mining partially periodic event patterns with unknown periods. In *Proc. 2001 Int. Conf. Data Engineering (ICDE'01)*, pages 205–214, Heidelberg, Germany, April 2001.

[MH01b] H. Miller and J. Han. *Geographic Data Mining and Knowledge Discovery*. Taylor and Francis, 2001.

[Mic83] R. S. Michalski. A theory and methodology of inductive learning. In Michalski et al., editors, *Machine Learning: An Artificial Intelligence Approach, Vol. 1*, pages 83–134. Morgan Kaufmann, 1983.

[Mic92] Z. Michalewicz. *Genetic Algorithms + Data Structures = Evolution Programs*. Springer-Verlag, 1992.

[Mil67] S. Milgram. The small world problem. *Psychology Today*, 2:60–67, 1967.

[Mil98] R. G. Miller. *Survival Analysis*. John Wiley & Sons, 1998.

[Min89] J. Mingers. An empirical comparison of pruning methods for decision-tree induction. *Machine Learning*, 4:227–243, 1989.

[Mit77] T. M. Mitchell. Version spaces: A candidate elimination approach to rule learning. In *Proc. 5th Int. Joint Conf. Artificial Intelligence*, pages 305–310, Cambridge, MA, 1977.

[Mit82] T. M. Mitchell. Generalization as search. *Artificial Intelligence*, 18:203–226, 1982.

[Mit96] M. Mitchell. *An Introduction to Genetic Algorithms*. MIT Press, 1996.

[Mit97] T. M. Mitchell. *Machine Learning*. McGraw-Hill, 1997.

[MK91] M. Manago and Y. Kodratoff. Induction of decision trees from complex structured data. In G. Piatetsky-Shapiro and W. J. Frawley, editors, *Knowledge Discovery in Databases*, pages 289–306. AAAI/MIT Press, 1991.

[MM95] J. Major and J. Mangano. Selecting among rules induced from a hurricane database. *J. Intelligent Information Systems*, 4:39–52, 1995.

[MM02] G. Manku and R. Motwani. Approximate frequency counts over data streams. In *Proc. 2002 Int. Conf. Very Large Data Bases (VLDB'02)*, pages 346–357, Hong Kong, China, Aug. 2002.

[MMM97] A. O. Mendelzon, G. A. Mihaila, and T. Milo. Querying the world-wide web. *Int. J. Digital Libraries*, 1:54–67, 1997.

[MMN02] P. Melville, R. J. Mooney, and R. Nagarajan. Content-boosted collaborative filtering for improved recommendations. In *Proc. 2002 Nat. Conf. Artificial Intelligence (AAAI'02)*, pages 187–192, Edmonton, Canada, July 2002.

[MMR04] B. Milch, B. Marthi, S. Russell, D. Sontag, D. L. Ong, and A. Kolobov. BLOG: Probabilistic Models with unknown objects. In *Proc. 19th Int. Joint Conf. on Artificial Intelligence (IJCAI'05)*, pages 1352–1359, Edinburgh, Scotland, Aug. 2005.

[MN89] M. Mézard and J.-P. Nadal. Learning in feedforward layered networks: The tiling algorithm. *J. Physics*, 22:2191–2204, 1989.

[MP69] M. L. Minsky and S. Papert. *Perceptrons: An Introduction to Computational Geometry*. MIT Press, 1969.

[MPC96] R. Meo, G. Psaila, and S. Ceri. A new SQL-like operator for mining association rules. In *Proc. 1996 Int. Conf. Very Large Data Bases (VLDB'96)*, pages 122–133, Bombay, India, Sept. 1996.

[MRA95] M. Metha, J. Rissanen, and R. Agrawal. MDL-based decision tree pruning. In *Proc. 1995 Int. Conf. Knowledge Discovery and Data Mining (KDD'95)*, pages 216–221, Montreal, Canada, Aug. 1995.

[MS83] R. S. Michalski and R. E. Stepp. Learning from observation: Conceptual clustering. In R. S. Michalski, J. G. Carbonell, and T. M. Mitchell, editors, *Machine Learning: An Artificial Intelligence Approach (Vol. 1)*. Morgan Kaufmann, 1983.

[MSHR02] S. Madden, M. Shah, J. M. Hellerstein, and V. Raman. Continuously adaptive continuous queries over streams. In *Proc. 2002 ACM-SIGMOD Int. Conf. Management of Data (SIGMOD'02)*, Madison, WI, June 2002.

[MST94] D. Michie, D. J. Spiegelhalter, and C. C. Taylor. *Machine Learning, Neural and Statistical Classification*. Ellis Horwood, 1994.

[MT94] R. S. Michalski and G. Tecuci. *Machine Learning, A Multistrategy Approach, Vol. 4*. Morgan Kaufmann, 1994.

[MTV94] H. Mannila, H. Toivonen, and A. I. Verkamo. Efficient algorithms for discovering association rules. In *Proc. AAAI'94 Workshop Knowledge Discovery in Databases (KDD'94)*, pages 181–192, Seattle, WA, July 1994.

[MTV97] H. Mannila, H Toivonen, and A. I. Verkamo. Discovery of frequent episodes in event sequences. *Data Mining and Knowledge Discovery*, 1:259–289, 1997.

[Mug95] S. Muggleton. Inverse entailment and progol. *New Generation Computing, Special issue on Inductive Logic Programming*, 3:245–286, 1995.

[Mur98] S. K. Murthy. Automatic construction of decision trees from data: A multi-disciplinary survey. *Data Mining and Knowledge Discovery*, 2:345–389, 1998.

[Mut03] S. Muthukrishnan. Data streams: algorithms and applications. In *Proc. 2003 Annual ACM-SIAM Symp. Discrete Algorithms (SODA'03)*, pages 413–413, Baltimore, MD, Jan. 2003.

[MW99] D. Meretakis and B. Wüthrich. Extending naïve Bayes classifiers using long itemsets. In *Proc. 1999 Int. Conf. Knowledge Discovery and Data Mining (KDD'99)*, pages 165–174, San Diego, CA, Aug. 1999.

[MY97] R. J. Miller and Y. Yang. Association rules over interval data. In *Proc. 1997 ACM-SIGMOD Int. Conf. Management of Data (SIGMOD'97)*, pages 452–461, Tucson, AZ, May 1997.

[NB86] T. Niblett and I. Bratko. Learning decision rules in noisy domains. In M. A. Bramer, editor, *Expert Systems '86: Research and Development in Expert Systems III*, pages 25–34. British Computer Society Specialist Group on Expert Systems, Dec. 1986.

[New03] M. E. J. Newman. The structure and function of complex networks. *SIAM Review*, 45:167–256, 2003.

[NH94] R. Ng and J. Han. Efficient and effective clustering method for spatial data mining. In *Proc. 1994 Int. Conf. Very Large Data Bases (VLDB'94)*, pages 144–155, Santiago, Chile, Sept. 1994.

[NJFH03] J. Neville, D. Jensen, L. Friedland, and M. Hay. Learning relational probability trees. In *Proc. 2003 ACM SIGKDD Int. Conf. Knowledge Discovery and Data Mining (KDD'03)*, pages 625–630, Washington, DC, Aug. 2003.

[NK04] S. Nijssen and J. Kok. A quickstart in frequent structure mining can make a difference. In *Proc. 2004 ACM SIGKDD Int. Conf. Knowledge Discovery in Databases (KDD'04)*, pages 647–652, Seattle, WA, Aug. 2004.

[NKNW96] J. Neter, M. H. Kutner, C. J. Nachtsheim, and L. Wasserman. *Applied Linear Statistical Models* (4th ed.) Irwin, 1996.

[NLHP98] R. Ng, L. V. S. Lakshmanan, J. Han, and A. Pang. Exploratory mining and pruning optimizations of constrained associations rules. In *Proc. 1998 ACM-SIGMOD Int. Conf. Management of Data (SIGMOD'98)*, pages 13–24, Seattle, WA, June 1998.

[NMTM00] K. Nigam, A. McCallum, S. Thrun, and T. Mitchell. Text classification from labeled and unlabeled documents using EM. *Machine Learning*, 39:103–134, 2000.

[NN02] S. Northcutt and J. Novak. *Network Intrusion Detection*. Sams, 2002.

[NRS99] A. Natsev, R. Rastogi, and K. Shim. Walrus: A similarity retrieval algorithm for image databases. In *Proc. 1999 ACM-SIGMOD Int. Conf. Management of Data (SIGMOD'99)*, pages 395–406, Philadelphia, PA, June 1999.

[NW99] J. Nocedal and S. J. Wright. *Numerical Optimization*. Springer-Verlag, 1999.

[OEC98] OECD. *Guidelines on the Protection of Privacy and Transborder Flows of Personal Data*. Organization for Economic Co-operation and Development, 1998.

[OFG97] E. Osuna, R. Freund, and F. Girosi. An improved training algorithm for support vector machines. In *Proc. 1997 IEEE Workshop on Neural Networks for Signal Processing (NNSP'97)*, pages 276–285, Amelia Island, FL, Sept. 1997.

[OG95] P. O'Neil and G. Graefe. Multi-table joins through bitmapped join indices. *SIGMOD Record*, 24:8–11, Sept. 1995.

[OJT+03] C. A. Orengo, D. T. Jones, and J. M. Thornton. *Bioinformatics: Genes, Proteins and Computers*. BIOS Scientific Pub., 2003.

[Ols03] J. E. Olson. *Data Quality: The Accuracy Dimension*. Morgan Kaufmann, 2003.

[Omi03] E. Omiecinski. Alternative interest measures for mining associations. *IEEE Trans. Knowledge and Data Engineering*, 15:57–69, 2003.

[OML00] H.-J. Oh, S. H. Myaeng, and M.-H. Lee. A practical hypertext categorization method using links and incrementally available class information. In *Proc. Int. 2000 ACM SIGIR Conf. Research and Development in Information Retrieval (SIGIR'00)*, pages 264–271, Athens, Greece, July 2000.

[OMM+02] L. O'Callaghan, A. Meyerson, R. Motwani, N. Mishra, and S. Guha. Streaming-data algorithms for high-quality clustering. In *Proc. 2002 Int. Conf. Data Engineering (ICDE'02)*, pages 685–696, San Francisco, CA, April 2002.

[OQ97] P. O'Neil and D. Quass. Improved query performance with variant indexes. In *Proc. 1997 ACM-SIGMOD Int. Conf. Management of Data (SIGMOD'97)*, pages 38–49, Tucson, AZ, May 1997.

[ORS98] B. Özden, S. Ramaswamy, and A. Silberschatz. Cyclic association rules. In *Proc. 1998 Int. Conf. Data Engineering (ICDE'98)*, pages 412–421, Orlando, FL, Feb. 1998.

[Pag89] G. Pagallo. Learning DNF by decision trees. In *Proc. 1989 Int. Joint Conf. Artificial Intelligence (IJCAI'89)*, pages 639–644, Morgan Kaufmann, 1989.

[Paw91] Z. Pawlak. *Rough Sets, Theoretical Aspects of Reasoning about Data*. Kluwer Academic Publishers, 1991.

[PB00] J. C. Pinheiro and D. M. Bates. *Mixed Effects Models in S and S-PLUS*. Springer-Verlag, 2000.

[PBTL99] N. Pasquier, Y. Bastide, R. Taouil, and L. Lakhal. Discovering frequent closed itemsets for association rules. In *Proc. 7th Int. Conf. Database Theory (ICDT'99)*, pages 398–416, Jerusalem, Israel, Jan. 1999.

[PCT+03] F. Pan, G. Cong, A. K. H. Tung, J. Yang, and M. Zaki. CARPENTER: Finding closed patterns in long biological datasets. In *Proc. 2003 ACM SIGKDD Int. Conf. Knowledge Discovery and Data Mining (KDD'03)*, pages 637–642, Washington, DC, Aug. 2003.

[PCY95a] J. S. Park, M. S. Chen, and P. S. Yu. An effective hash-based algorithm for mining association rules. In *Proc. 1995 ACM-SIGMOD Int. Conf. Management of Data (SIGMOD'95)*, pages 175–186, San Jose, CA, May 1995.

[PCY95b] J. S. Park, M. S. Chen, and P. S. Yu. Efficient parallel mining for association rules. In *Proc. 4th Int. Conf. Information and Knowledge Management*, pages 31–36, Baltimore, MD, Nov. 1995.

[PE99] M. Perkowitz and O. Etzioni. Adaptive web sites: Conceptual cluster mining. In *Proc. 1999 Joint Int. Conf. Artificial Intelligence (IJCAI'99)*, pages 264–269, Stockholm, Sweden, 1999.

[Pea88] J. Pearl. *Probabilistic Reasoning in Intelligent Systems.* Morgan Kauffman, 1988.

[Per02] P. Perner. *Data Mining on Multimedia Data.* Springer-Verlag, 2002.

[Pev03] J. Pevzner. *Bioinformatics and Functional Genomics.* Wiley-Liss, 2003.

[PHL01] J. Pei, J. Han, and L. V. S. Lakshmanan. Mining frequent itemsets with convertible constraints. In *Proc. 2001 Int. Conf. Data Engineering (ICDE'01)*, pages 433–332, Heidelberg, Germany, April 2001.

[PHL04] L. Parsons, E. Haque, and H. Liu. Subspace clustering for high dimensional data: A review. *SIGKDD Explorations*, 6:90–105, 2004.

[PHM00] J. Pei, J. Han, and R. Mao. CLOSET: An efficient algorithm for mining frequent closed itemsets. In *Proc. 2000 ACM-SIGMOD Int. Workshop Data Mining and Knowledge Discovery (DMKD'00)*, pages 11–20, Dallas, TX, May 2000.

[PHMA+01] J. Pei, J. Han, B. Mortazavi-Asl, H. Pinto, Q. Chen, U. Dayal, and M.-C. Hsu. PrefixSpan: Mining sequential patterns efficiently by prefix-projected pattern growth. In *Proc. 2001 Int. Conf. Data Engineering (ICDE'01)*, pages 215–224, Heidelberg, Germany, April 2001.

[PHMA+04] J. Pei, J. Han, B. Mortazavi-Asl, J. Wang, H. Pinto, Q. Chen, U. Dayal, and M.-C. Hsu. Mining sequential patterns by pattern-growth: The prefixspan approach. *IEEE Trans. Knowledge and Data Engineering*, 16:1424–1440, 2004.

[PHP+01] H. Pinto, J. Han, J. Pei, K. Wang, Q. Chen, and U. Dayal. Multi-dimensional sequential pattern mining. In *Proc. 2001 Int. Conf. Information and Knowledge Management (CIKM'01)*, pages 81–88, Atlanta, GA, Nov. 2001.

[PHW02] J. Pei, J. Han, and W. Wang. Constraint-based sequential pattern mining in large databases. In *Proc. 2002 Int. Conf. Information and Knowledge Management (CIKM'02)*, pages 18–25, McLean, VA, Nov. 2002.

[PI97] V. Poosala and Y. Ioannidis. Selectivity estimation without the attribute value independence assumption. In *Proc. 1997 Int. Conf. Very Large Data Bases (VLDB'97)*, pages 486–495, Athens, Greece, Aug. 1997.

[PKMT99] A. Pfeffer, D. Koller, B. Milch, and K. Takusagawa. SPOOK: A system for probabilistic objectoriented knowledge representation. In *Proc. 15th Annual Conf. on Uncertainty in Artificial Intelligence (UAI'99)*, pages 541–550, Stockholm, Sweden, 1999.

[Pla98] J. C. Platt. Fast training of support vector machines using sequential minimal optimization. In B. Schotolkopf, C. J. C. Burges, and A. Smola, editors, *Advances in Kernel Methods—Support Vector Learning*, pages 185–208. MIT Press, 1998.

[PS85] F. P. Preparata and M. I. Shamos. *Computational Geometry: An Introduction.* Springer-Verlag, 1985.

[PS89] G. Piatetsky-Shapiro. *Notes of IJCAI'89 Workshop Knowledge Discovery in Databases (KDD'89).* Detroit, MI, July 1989.

[PS91a] G. Piatetsky-Shapiro. Discovery, analysis, and presentation of strong rules. In G. Piatetsky-Shapiro and W. J. Frawley, editors, *Knowledge Discovery in Databases*, pages 229–238. AAAI/MIT Press, 1991.

[PS91b] G. Piatetsky-Shapiro. *Notes of AAAI'91 Workshop Knowledge Discovery in Databases (KDD'91)*. Anaheim, CA, July 1991.

[PSF91] G. Piatetsky-Shapiro and W. J. Frawley. *Knowledge Discovery in Databases*. AAAI/MIT Press, 1991.

[PTVF96] W. H. Press, S. A. Teukolosky, W. T. Vetterling, and B. P. Flannery. *Numerical Recipes in C: The Art of Scientific Computing*. Cambridge University Press, 1996.

[PULP03] A. Popescul, L. Ungar, S. Lawrence, and M. Pennock. Statistical relational learning for document mining. In *Proc. 2003 Int. Conf. Data Mining (ICDM'03)*, pages 275–282, Melbourne, FL, Nov. 2003.

[PYHW04] J. Prins, J. Yang, J. Huan, and W. Wang. Spin: Mining maximal frequent subgraphs from graph databases. In *Proc. 2004 ACM SIGKDD Int. Conf. Knowledge Discovery in Databases (KDD'04)*, pages 581–586, Seattle, WA, Aug. 2004.

[Pyl99] D. Pyle. *Data Preparation for Data Mining*. Morgan Kaufmann, 1999.

[QCJ93] J. R. Quinlan and R. M. Cameron-Jones. FOIL: A midterm report. In *Proc. 1993 European Conf. Machine Learning*, pages 3–20, Vienna, Austria, 1993.

[QR89] J. R. Quinlan and R. L. Rivest. Inferring decision trees using the minimum description length principle. *Information and Computation*, 80:227–248, Mar. 1989.

[Qui86] J. R. Quinlan. Induction of decision trees. *Machine Learning*, 1:81–106, 1986.

[Qui87] J. R. Quinlan. Simplifying decision trees. *Int. J. Man-Machine Studies*, 27:221–234, 1987.

[Qui88] J. R. Quinlan. An empirical comparison of genetic and decision-tree classifiers. In *Proc. 1988 Int. Conf. Machine Learning (ML'88)*, pages 135–141, San Mateo, CA, 1988.

[Qui89] J. R. Quinlan. Unknown attribute values in induction. In *Proc. 6th Int. Workshop Machine Learning*, pages 164–168, Ithaca, NY, June 1989.

[Qui90] J. R. Quinlan. Learning logic definitions from relations. *Machine Learning*, 5:139–166, 1990.

[Qui92] J. R. Quinlan. Learning with continuous classes. In *Proc. 1992 Australian Joint Conf. on Artificial Intelligence*, pages 343–348, Hobart, Tasmania, 1992.

[Qui93] J. R. Quinlan. *C4.5: Programs for Machine Learning*. Morgan Kaufmann, 1993.

[Qui96] J. R. Quinlan. Bagging, boosting, and C4.5. In *Proc. 1996 Nat. Conf. Artificial Intelligence (AAAI'96)*, volume 1, pages 725–730, Portland, OR, Aug. 1996.

[RA87] E. L. Rissland and K. Ashley. HYPO: A case-based system for trade secret law. In *Proc. 1st Int. Conf. on Artificial Intelligence and Law*, pages 60–66, Boston, MA, May 1987.

[Rab89] L. R. Rabiner. A tutorial on hidden markov models and selected applications in speech recognition. *Proc. IEEE*, 77:257–286, 1989.

[Rag97] P. Raghavan. Information retrieval algorithms: A survey. In *Proc. 1997 ACM-SIAM Symp. Discrete Algorithms*, pages 11–18, New Orleans, LA, 1997.

[Ras04] S. Raspl. PMML version 3.0—overview and status. In *Proc. 2004 KDD Worshop on Data Mining Standards, Services and Platforms (DM-SSP04)*, Seattle, WA, Aug. 2004.

[RBKK95] S. Russell, J. Binder, D. Koller, and K. Kanazawa. Local learning in probabilistic networks with hidden variables. In *Proc. 1995 Joint Int. Conf. Artificial Intelligence (IJCAI'95)*, pages 1146–1152, Montreal, Canada, Aug. 1995.

[RD02] M. Richardson and P. Domingos. Mining knowledge-sharing sites for viral marketing. In *Proc. 2002 ACM SIGKDD Int. Conf. Knowledge Discovery in Databases (KDD'02)*, pages 61–70, Edmonton, Canada, July 2002.

[Red92] T. Redman. *Data Quality: Management and Technology*. Bantam Books, 1992.

[Red01] T. Redman. *Data Quality: The Field Guide*. Digital Press (Elsevier), 2001.

[RG03] R. Ramakrishnan and J. Gehrke. *Database Management Systems*, (3rd ed.). McGraw-Hill, 2003.

[RH01] V. Raman and J. M. Hellerstein. Potter's wheel: An interactive data cleaning system. In *Proc. 2001 Int. Conf. on Very Large Data Bases (VLDB'01)*, pages 381–390, Rome, Italy, Sept. 2001.

[RHS01] J. F. Roddick, K. Hornsby, and M. Spiliopoulou. An updated bibliography of temporal, spatial, and spatio-temporal data mining research. In *Lecture Notes in Computer Science 2007*, pages 147–163, Springer, 2001.

[RHW86] D. E. Rumelhart, G. E. Hinton, and R. J. Williams. Learning internal representations by error propagation. In D. E. Rumelhart and J. L. McClelland, editors, *Parallel Distributed Processing*. MIT Press, 1986.

[Rip96] B. D. Ripley. *Pattern Recognition and Neural Networks*. Cambridge University Press, 1996.

[RIS+94] P. Resnick, N. Iacovou, M. Suchak, P. Bergstrom, and J. Riedl. Grouplens: An open architecture for collaborative filtering of netnews. In *Proc. 1994 Conf. Computer Supported Cooperative Work (CSCW'94)*, pages 175–186, Chapel Hill, NC, Oct. 1994.

[RM86] D. E. Rumelhart and J. L. McClelland. *Parallel Distributed Processing*. MIT Press, 1986.

[RM97] D. Rafiei and A. Mendelzon. Similarity-based queries for time series data. In *Proc. 1997 ACM-SIGMOD Int. Conf. Management of Data (SIGMOD'97)*, pages 13–25, Tucson, AZ, May 1997.

[RMS98] S. Ramaswamy, S. Mahajan, and A. Silberschatz. On the discovery of interesting patterns in association rules. In *Proc. 1998 Int. Conf. Very Large Data Bases (VLDB'98)*, pages 368–379, New York, NY, Aug. 1998.

[RN95] S. Russell and P. Norvig. *Artificial Intelligence: A Modern Approach*. Prentice Hall, 1995.

[Ros58] F. Rosenblatt. The perceptron: A probabilistic model for information storage and organization in the brain. *Psychological Review*, 65:386–498, 1958.

[RS89] C. Riesbeck and R. Schank. *Inside Case-Based Reasoning*. Lawrence Erlbaum, 1989.

[RS97] K. Ross and D. Srivastava. Fast computation of sparse datacubes. In *Proc. 1997 Int. Conf. Very Large Data Bases (VLDB'97)*, pages 116–125, Athens, Greece, Aug. 1997.

[RS98] R. Rastogi and K. Shim. Public: A decision tree classifer that integrates building and pruning. In *Proc. 1998 Int. Conf. Very Large Data Bases (VLDB'98)*, pages 404–415, New York, NY, Aug. 1998.

[RS01] F. Ramsey and D. Schafer. *The Statistical Sleuth: A Course in Methods of Data Analysis*. Duxbury Press, 2001.

[RSC98] K. A. Ross, D. Srivastava, and D. Chatziantoniou. Complex aggregation at multiple granularities. In *Proc. Int. Conf. of Extending Database Technology (EDBT'98)*, pages 263–277, Valencia, Spain, Mar. 1998.

[RSV01] P. Rigaux, M. O. Scholl, and A. Voisard. *Spatial Databases: With Application to GIS*. Morgan Kaufmann, 2001.

[Rus02] J. C. Russ. *The Image Processing Handbook, (4th ed.)*. CRC Press, 2002.

[RZ85] D. E. Rumelhart and D. Zipser. Feature discovery by competitive learning. *Cognitive Science*, 9:75–112, 1985.

[SA95] R. Srikant and R. Agrawal. Mining generalized association rules. In *Proc. 1995 Int. Conf. Very Large Data Bases (VLDB'95)*, pages 407–419, Zurich, Switzerland, Sept. 1995.

[SA96] R. Srikant and R. Agrawal. Mining sequential patterns: Generalizations and performance improvements. In *Proc. 5th Int. Conf. Extending Database Technology (EDBT'96)*, pages 3–17, Avignon, France, Mar. 1996.

[Sal89] G. Salton. *Automatic Text Processing*. Addison-Wesley, 1989.

[SAM96] J. Shafer, R. Agrawal, and M. Mehta. SPRINT: A scalable parallel classifier for data mining. In *Proc. 1996 Int. Conf. Very Large Data Bases (VLDB'96)*, pages 544–555, Bombay, India, Sept. 1996.

[SAM98] S. Sarawagi, R. Agrawal, and N. Megiddo. Discovery-driven exploration of OLAP data cubes. In *Proc. Int. Conf. of Extending Database Technology (EDBT'98)*, pages 168–182, Valencia, Spain, Mar. 1998.

[SBSW99] B. Schölkopf, P. L. Bartlett, A. Smola, and R. Williamson. Shrinking the tube: a new support vector regression algorithm. In M. S. Kearns, S. A. Solla, and D. A. Cohn, editors, *Advances in Neural Information Processing Systems 11*, pages 330–336. MIT Press, 1999.

[SC03] S. Shekhar and S. Chawla. *Spatial Databases: A Tour*. Prentice Hall, 2003.

[SCDT00] J. Srivastava, R. Cooley, M. Deshpande, and P. N. Tan. Web usage mining: Discovery and applications of usage patterns from web data. *SIGKDD Explorations*, 1:12–23, 2000.

[Sch86] J. C. Schlimmer. Learning and representation change. In *Proc. 1986 Nat. Conf. Artificial Intelligence (AAAI'86)*, pages 511–515, Philadelphia, PA, 1986.

[SCH99] S. Su, D. J. Cook, and L. B. Holder. Knowledge discovery in molecular biology: Identifying structural regularities in proteins. *Intelligent Data Analysis*, 3:413–436, 1999.

[Sco05] J. P. Scott. *Social network analysis: A handbook*. Sage Publications, 2005.

[SCR+99] S. Shekhar, S. Chawla, S. Ravada, A. Fetterer, X. Liu, and C.-T. Lu. Spatial databases—accomplishments and research needs. *IEEE Trans. Knowledge and Data Engineering*, 11:45–55, 1999.

[SCZ98] G. Sheikholeslami, S. Chatterjee, and A. Zhang. WaveCluster: A multi-resolution clustering approach for very large spatial databases. In *Proc. 1998 Int. Conf. Very Large Data Bases (VLDB'98)*, pages 428–439, New York, NY, Aug. 1998.

[SD90] J. W. Shavlik and T. G. Dietterich. *Readings in Machine Learning*. Morgan Kaufmann, 1990.

[SD96] P. Stolorz and C. Dean. Quakefinder: A scalable data mining system for detecting earthquakes from space. In *Proc. 1996 Int. Conf. Data Mining and Knowledge Discovery (KDD'96)*, pages 208–213, Portland, OR, Aug. 1996.

[SDJL96] D. Sristava, S. Dar, H. V. Jagadish, and A. V. Levy. Answering queries with aggregation using views. In *Proc. 1996 Int. Conf. Very Large Data Bases (VLDB'96)*, pages 318–329, Bombay, India, Sept. 1996.

[SDK04] J. Srivastava, P. Desikan, and V. Kumar. Web mining—concepts, applications, and research directions. In H. Kargupta, A. Joshi, K. Sivakumar, and Y. Yesha, editors, *Data Mining: Next Generation Challenges and Future Directions*, pages 405–423. AAAI/MIT Press, 2004.

[SDN98] A. Shukla, P. M. Deshpande, and J. F. Naughton. Materialized view selection for multidimensional datasets. In *Proc. 1998 Int. Conf. Very Large Data Bases (VLDB'98)*, pages 488–499, New York, NY, Aug. 1998.

[Seb02] F. Sebastiani. Machine learning in automated text categorization. *ACM Computing Surveys*, 34:1–47, 2002.

[SF86a] J. C. Schlimmer and D. Fisher. A case study of incremental concept induction. In *Proc. 1986 Nat. Conf. Artificial Intelligence (AAAI'86)*, pages 496–501, Philadelphia, PA, 1986.

[SF86b] D. Subramanian and J. Feigenbaum. Factorization in experiment generation. In *Proc. 1986 Nat. Conf. Artificial Intelligence (AAAI'86)*, pages 518–522, Philadelphia, PA, Aug. 1986.

[SFB99] J. Shanmugasundaram, U. M. Fayyad, and P. S. Bradley. Compressed data cubes for OLAP aggregate query approximation on continuous dimensions. In *Proc. 1999 Int. Conf. Knowledge Discovery and Data Mining (KDD'99)*, pages 223–232, San Diego, CA, Aug. 1999.

[SG92] P. Smyth and R. M. Goodman. An information theoretic approach to rule induction. *IEEE Trans. Knowledge and Data Engineering*, 4:301–316, 1992.

[Shi99] Y.-S. Shih. Families of splitting criteria for classification trees. In *Statistics and Computing*, 9:309–315, 1999.

[SHK00] N. Stefanovic, J. Han, and K. Koperski. Object-based selective materialization for efficient implementation of spatial data cubes. *IEEE Transactions on Knowledge and Data Engineering*, 12:938–958, 2000.

[Sho97] A. Shoshani. OLAP and statistical databases: Similarities and differences. In *Proc. 16th ACM Symp. Principles of Database Systems*, pages 185–196, Tucson, AZ, May 1997.

[Shu88] R. H. Shumway. *Applied Statistical Time Series Analysis*. Prentice Hall, 1988.

[SHX04] Z. Shao, J. Han, and D. Xin. MM-Cubing: Computing iceberg cubes by factorizing the lattice space. In *Proc. 2004 Int. Conf. on Scientific and Statistical Database Management (SSDBM'04)*, pages 213–222, Santorini Island, Greece, June 2004.

[SKKR01] B. Sarwar, G. Karypis, J. Konstan, and J. Riedl. Item-based collaborative filtering recommendation algorithms. In *Proc. 2001 Int. World Wide Web Conf. (WWW'01)*, pages 158–167, Hong Kong, China, May 2001.

[SKS02] A. Silberschatz, H. F. Korth, and S. Sudarshan. *Database System Concepts, (4th ed.)*. McGraw-Hill, 2002.

[SM83] G. Salton and M. McGill. *Introduction to Modern Information Retrieval*. McGraw-Hill, 1983.

[SM97] J. C. Setubal and J. Meidanis. *Introduction to Computational Molecular Biology*. PWS Pub Co., 1997.

[SMT91] J. W. Shavlik, R. J. Mooney, and G. G. Towell. Symbolic and neural learning algorithms: An experimental comparison. *Machine Learning*, 6:111–144, 1991.

[SN88] K. Saito and R. Nakano. Medical diagnostic expert system based on PDP model. In *Proc. 1988 IEEE International Conf. Neural Networks*, pages 225–262, San Mateo, CA, 1988.

[SOMZ96] W. Shen, K. Ong, B. Mitbander, and C. Zaniolo. Metaqueries for data mining. In U. M. Fayyad, G. Piatetsky-Shapiro, P. Smyth, and R. Uthurusamy, editors, *Advances in Knowledge Discovery and Data Mining*, pages 375–398. AAAI/MIT Press, 1996.

[SON95] A. Savasere, E. Omiecinski, and S. Navathe. An efficient algorithm for mining association rules in large databases. In *Proc. 1995 Int. Conf. Very Large Data Bases (VLDB'95)*, pages 432–443, Zurich, Switzerland, Sept. 1995.

[SON98] A. Savasere, E. Omiecinski, and S. Navathe. Mining for strong negative associations in a large database of customer transactions. In *Proc. 1998 Int. Conf. Data Engineering (ICDE'98)*, pages 494–502, Orlando, FL, Feb. 1998.

[SR81] R. Sokal and F. Rohlf. *Biometry*. Freeman, 1981.

[SR92] A. Skowron and C. Rauszer. The discernibility matrices and functions in information systems. In R. Slowinski, editor, *Intelligent Decision Support, Handbook of Applications and Advances of the Rough Set Theory*, pages 331–362. Kluwer Academic Publishers, 1992.

[SS88] W. Siedlecki and J. Sklansky. On automatic feature selection. *Int. J. Pattern Recognition and Artificial Intelligence*, 2:197–220, 1988.

[SS94] S. Sarawagi and M. Stonebraker. Efficient organization of large multidimensional arrays. In *Proc. 1994 Int. Conf. Data Engineering (ICDE'94)*, pages 328–336, Houston, TX, Feb. 1994.

[SS00] S. Sarawagi and G. Sathe. Intelligent, interactive investigation of OLAP data cubes. In *Proc. 2000 ACM-SIGMOD Int. Conf. Management of Data (SIGMOD'00)*, page 589, Dallas, TX, May 2000.

[SS01] G. Sathe and S. Sarawagi. Intelligent rollups in multidimensional OLAP data. In *Proc. 2001 Int. Conf. Very Large Data Bases (VLDB'01)*, pages 531–540, Rome, Italy, Sept. 2001.

[SS05] R. H. Shumway and D. S. Stoffer. *Time Series Analysis and Its Applications*. Springer, 2005.

[ST96] A. Silberschatz and A. Tuzhilin. What makes patterns interesting in knowledge discovery systems. *IEEE Trans. on Knowledge and Data Engineering*, 8:970–974, Dec. 1996.

[STA98] S. Sarawagi, S. Thomas, and R. Agrawal. Integrating association rule mining with relational database systems: Alternatives and implications. In *Proc. 1998 ACM-SIGMOD Int. Conf. Management of Data (SIGMOD'98)*, pages 343–354, Seattle, WA, June 1998.

[Sto74] M. Stone. Cross-validatory choice and assessment of statistical predictions. *J. Royal Statistical Society*, 36:111–147, 1974.

[STZ05] X. Shen, B. Tan, and C. Zhai. Context-sensitive information retrieval with implicit feedback. In *Proc. 2005 Int. ACM SIGIR Conf. Research and Development in Information Retrieval (SIGIR'05)*, pages 43–50, Salvador, Brazil, Aug. 2005.

[Sub98] V. S. Subrahmanian. *Principles of Multimedia Database Systems*. Morgan Kaufmann, 1998.

[SVA97] R. Srikant, Q. Vu, and R. Agrawal. Mining association rules with item constraints. In *Proc. 1997 Int. Conf. Knowledge Discovery and Data Mining (KDD'97)*, pages 67–73, Newport Beach, CA, Aug. 1997.

[SW49] C. E. Shannon and W. Weaver. *The mathematical theory of communication*. University of Illinois Press, Urbana, IL, 1949.

[Swe88] J. Swets. Measuring the accuracy of diagnostic systems. *Science*, 240:1285–1293, 1988.

[Swi98] R. Swiniarski. Rough sets and principal component analysis and their applications in feature extraction and selection, data model building and classification. In S. Pal and A. Skowron, editors, *Fuzzy Sets, Rough Sets and Decision Making Processes*. Springer-Verlag, 1998.

[SZ04] D. Shasha and Y. Zhu. *High Performance Discovery In Time Series: Techniques and Case Studies*. Springer, 2004.

[TC83] D. Tsichritzis and S. Christodoulakis. Message files. *ACM Trans. Office Information Systems*, 1:88–98, 1983.

[TFPL04] Y. Tao, C. Faloutsos, D. Papadias, and B. Liu. Prediction and indexing of moving objects with unknown motion patterns. In *Proc. 2004 ACM-SIGMOD Int. Conf. Management of Data (SIGMOD'04)*, Paris, France, June 2004.

[TG97] L. Tauscher and S. Greenberg. How people revisit web pages: Empirical findings and implications for the design of history systems. *Int. J. Human Computer Studies, Special issue on World Wide Web Usability*, 47:97–138, 1997.

[TG01] I. Tsoukatos and D. Gunopulos. Efficient mining of spatiotemporal patterns. In *Proc. 2001 Int. Symp. Spatial and Temporal Databases (SSTD'01)*, pages 425–442, Redondo Beach, CA, July 2001.

[TGNO92] D. Terry, D. Goldberg, D. Nichols, and B. Oki. Continuous queries over append-only databases. In *Proc. 1992 ACM-SIGMOD Int. Conf. Management of Data (SIGMOD'92)*, pages 321–330, 1992.

[THH01] A. K. H. Tung, J. Hou, and J. Han. Spatial clustering in the presence of obstacles. In *Proc. 2001 Int. Conf. Data Engineering (ICDE'01)*, pages 359–367, Heidelberg, Germany, April 2001.

[THLN01] A. K. H. Tung, J. Han, L. V. S. Lakshmanan, and R. T. Ng. Constraint-based clustering in large databases. In *Proc. 2001 Int. Conf. Database Theory (ICDT'01)*, pages 405–419, London, UK, Jan. 2001.

[Tho97] E. Thomsen. *OLAP Solutions: Building Multidimensional Information Systems*. John Wiley & Sons, 1997.

[Thu04] B. Thuraisingham. Data mining for counterterrorism. In H. Kargupta, A. Joshi, K. Sivakumar, and Y. Yesha, editors, *Data Mining: Next Generation Challenges and Future Directions*, pages 157–183. AAAI/MIT Press, 2004.

[TKS02] P.-N. Tan, V. Kumar, and J. Srivastava. Selecting the right interestingness measure for association patterns. In *Proc. 2002 ACM SIGKDD Int. Conf. Knowledge Discovery in Databases (KDD'02)*, pages 32–41, Edmonton, Canada, July 2002.

[TM05] Z. Tang and J. MacLennan. *Data Mining with SQL Server 2005*. John Wiley & Sons, 2005.

[TMK05] Z. Tang, J. MacLennan, and P. P. Kim. Building data mining solutions with OLE DB for DM and XML analysis. *SIGMOD Record*, 34:80–85, June 2005.

[Toi96] H. Toivonen. Sampling large databases for association rules. In *Proc. 1996 Int. Conf. Very Large Data Bases (VLDB'96)*, pages 134–145, Bombay, India, Sept. 1996.

[TS93] G. G. Towell and J. W. Shavlik. Extracting refined rules from knowledge-based neural networks. *Machine Learning*, 13:71–101, Oct. 1993.

[TSK01] B. Taskar, E. Segal, and D. Koller. Probabilistic classification and clustering in relational data. In *Proc. 2001 Int. Joint Conf. Artificial Intelligence (IJCAI'01)*, pages 870–878, Seattle, WA, 2001.

[TSK05] P. Tan, M. Steinbach, and V. Kumar. *Introduction to Data Mining*. Addison-Wesley, 2005.

[Tuf90] E. R. Tufte. *Envisioning Information*. Graphics Press, 1990.

[Tuf97] E. R. Tufte. *Visual Explanations: Images and Quantities, Evidence and Narrative*. Graphics Press, 1997.

[Tuf01] E. R. Tufte. *The Visual Display of Quantitative Information* (2nd ed.). Graphics Press, 2001.

[UBC97] P. E. Utgoff, N. C. Berkman, and J. A. Clouse. Decision tree induction based on efficient tree restructuring. *Machine Learning*, 29:5–44, 1997.

[UFS91] R. Uthurusamy, U. M. Fayyad, and S. Spangler. Learning useful rules from inconclusive data. In G. Piatetsky-Shapiro and W. J. Frawley, editors, *Knowledge Discovery in Databases*, pages 141–157. AAAI/MIT Press, 1991.

[Ull76] J. R. Ullmann. An algorithm for subgraph isomorphism. *J. ACM*, 23:31–42, 1976.

[Utg88] P. E. Utgoff. An incremental ID3. In *Proc. Fifth Int. Conf. Machine Learning*, pages 107–120, San Mateo, CA, 1988.

[Val87] P. Valduriez. Join indices. *ACM Trans. Database Systems*, 12:218–246, 1987.

[Vap95] V. N. Vapnik. *The Nature of Statistical Learning Theory*. Springer-Verlag, 1995.

[Vap98] V. N. Vapnik. *Statistical Learning Theory*. John Wiley & Sons, 1998.

[VBFP04] V. S. Verykios, E. Bertino, I. N. Fovino, and L. P. Provenza. State-of-the-art in privacy preserving data mining. *SIGMOD Record*, 33:50–57, March 2004.

[VC71] V. N. Vapnik and A. Y. Chervonenkis. On the uniform convergence of relative frequencies of events to their probabilities. *Theory of Probability and its Applications*, 16:264–280, 1971.

[VC03] J. Vaidya and C. Clifton. Privacy-preserving k-means clustering over vertically partitioned data. In *Proc. 2003 ACM SIGKDD Int. Conf. Knowledge Discovery and Data Mining (KDD'03)*, Washington, DC, Aug. 2003.

[VGK02] M. Vlachos, D. Gunopulos, and G. Kollios. Discovering similar multidimensional trajectories. In *Proc. 2002 Int. Conf. Data Engineering (ICDE'02)*, pages 673–684, San Francisco, CA, April 2002.

[VGS02] N. Vanetik, E. Gudes, and S. E. Shimony. Computing frequent graph patterns from semistructured data. In *Proc. 2002 Int. Conf. on Data Mining (ICDM'02)*, pages 458–465, Maebashi, Japan, Dec. 2002.

[Vit85] J. S. Vitter. Random sampling with a reservoir. *ACM Trans. Math. Softw.*, 11:37–57, 1985.

[VP99] P. Valdes-Perez. Principles of human-computer collaboration for knowledge-discovery in science. *Artificial Intellifence*, 107:335–346, 1999.

[VR90] C. J. van Rijsbergen. *Information Retrieval*. Butterworth, 1990.

[VWI98] J. S. Vitter, M. Wang, and B. R. Iyer. Data cube approximation and histograms via wavelets. In *Proc. 1998 Int. Conf. Information and Knowledge Management (CIKM'98)*, pages 96–104, Washington, DC, Nov. 1998.

[Wat95] M. S. Waterman. *Introduction to Computational Biology: Maps, Sequences, and Genomes (Interdisciplinary Statistics)*. CRC Press, 1995.

[Wat03a] D. J. Watts. *Six degrees: The science of a connected age*. W. W. Norton Company, 2003.

[Wat03b] D. J. Watts. *Small worlds: The dynamics of networks between order and randomness*. Princeton University Press, 2003.

[WB98] C. Westphal and T. Blaxton. *Data Mining Solutions: Methods and Tools for Solving Real-World Problems*. John Wiley & Sons, 1998.

[WF94] S. Wasserman and K. Faust. *Social Network Analysis: Methods and Applications*. Cambridge University Press, 1994.

[WF00] W. Wong and A. W. Fu. Finding structure and characteristics of web documents for classification. In *Proc. 2000 ACM-SIGMOD Int. Workshop Data Mining and Knowledge Discovery (DMKD'00)*, pages 96–105, Dallas, TX, May 2000.

[WF05] I. H. Witten and E. Frank. *Data Mining: Practical Machine Learning Tools and Techniques, (2nd ed.)*. Morgan Kaufmann, 2005.

[WFYH03] H. Wang, W. Fan, P. S. Yu, and J. Han. Mining concept-drifting data streams using ensemble classifiers. In *Proc. 2003 ACM SIGKDD Int. Conf. Knowledge Discovery and Data Mining (KDD'03)*, pages 226–235, Washington, DC, Aug. 2003.

[WH04] J. Wang and J. Han. BIDE: Efficient mining of frequent closed sequences. In *Proc. 2004 Int. Conf. Data Engineering (ICDE'04)*, pages 79–90, Boston, MA, Mar. 2004.

[WHLT05] J. Wang, J. Han, Y. Lu, and P. Tzvetkov. TFP: An efficient algorithm for mining top-k frequent closed itemsets. *IEEE Trans. Knowledge and Data Engineering*, 17:652–664, 2005.

[WHP03] J. Wang, J. Han, and J. Pei. CLOSET+: Searching for the best strategies for mining frequent closed itemsets. In *Proc. 2003 ACM SIGKDD Int. Conf. Knowledge Discovery and Data Mining (KDD'03)*, pages 236–245, Washington, DC, Aug. 2003.

[WI98] S. M. Weiss and N. Indurkhya. *Predictive Data Mining*. Morgan Kaufmann, 1998.

[Wid95] J. Widom. Research problems in data warehousing. In *Proc. 4th Int. Conf. Information and Knowledge Management*, pages 25–30, Baltimore, MD, Nov. 1995.

[WIZD04] S. Weiss, N. Indurkhya, T. Zhang, and F. Damerau. *Text Mining: Predictive Methods for Analyzing Unstructured Information*. Springer, 2004.

[WK91] S. M. Weiss and C. A. Kulikowski. *Computer Systems that Learn: Classification and Prediction Methods from Statistics, Neural Nets, Machine Learning, and Expert Systems*. Morgan Kaufmann, 1991.

[WLFY02] W. Wang, H. Lu, J. Feng, and J. X. Yu. Condensed cube: An effective approach to reducing data cube size. In *Proc. 2002 Int. Conf. Data Engineering (ICDE'02)*, pages 155–165, San Francisco, CA, April 2002.

[WM03] T. Washio and H. Motoda. State of the art of graph-based data mining. *SIGKDD Explorations*, 5:59–68, 2003.

[WMB99] I. H. Witten, A. Moffat, and T. C. Bell. *Managing Gigabytes: Compressing and Indexing Documents and Images*. Morgan Kaufmann, 1999.

[WR01] K. Wahlstrom and J. F. Roddick. On the impact of knowledge discovery and data mining. In *Selected Papers from the 2nd Australian Institute of Computer Ethics Conference (AICE2000)*, pages 22–27, Canberra, Australia, 2001.

[WRL94] B. Widrow, D. E. Rumelhart, and M. A. Lehr. Neural networks: Applications in industry, business and science. *Comm. ACM*, 37:93–105, 1994.

[WSF95] R. Wang, V. Storey, and C. Firth. A framework for analysis of data quality research. *IEEE Trans. Knowledge and Data Engineering*, 7:623–640, 1995.

[WW96] Y. Wand and R. Wang. Anchoring data quality dimensions in ontological foundations. *Comm. ACM*, 39:86–95, 1996.

[WWP+04] C. Wang, W. Wang, J. Pei, Y. Zhu, and B. Shi. Scalable mining of large disk-base graph databases. In *Proc. 2004 ACM SIGKDD Int. Conf. Knowledge Discovery in Databases (KDD'04)*, pages 316–325, Seattle, WA, Aug. 2004.

[WWYY02] H. Wang, W. Wang, J. Yang, and P. S. Yu. Clustering by pattern similarity in large data sets. In *Proc. 2002 ACM-SIGMOD Int. Conf. Management of Data (SIGMOD'02)*, pages 418–427, Madison, WI, June 2002.

[WYM97] W. Wang, J. Yang, and R. Muntz. STING: A statistical information grid approach to spatial data mining. In *Proc. 1997 Int. Conf. Very Large Data Bases (VLDB'97)*, pages 186–195, Athens, Greece, Aug. 1997.

[WZL99] K. Wang, S. Zhou, and S. C. Liew. Building hierarchical classifiers using class proximity. In *Proc. 1999 Int. Conf. Very Large Data Bases (VLDB'99)*, pages 363–374, Edinburgh, UK, Sept. 1999.

[XHLW03] D. Xin, J. Han, X. Li, and B. W. Wah. Star-cubing: Computing iceberg cubes by top-down and bottom-up integration. In *Proc. 2003 Int. Conf. Very Large Data Bases (VLDB'03)*, Berlin, Germany, pages 476–487, Sept. 2003.

[XHSLW06] D. Xin, J. Han, Z. Shao, H. Liu. C-Cubing: Efficient computation of closed cubes by aggregation-based checking, In *Proc. 2006 Int. Conf. Data Engineering (ICDE'06)*, Atlanta, Georgia, April 2006.

[XHYC05] D. Xin, J. Han, X. Yan, and H. Cheng. Mining compressed frequent-pattern sets. In *Proc. 2005 Int. Conf. Very Large Data Bases (VLDB'05)*, pages 709–720, Trondheim, Norway, Aug. 2005.

[XOJ00] Y. Xiang, K. G. Olesen, and F. V. Jensen. Practical issues in modeling large diagnostic systems with multiply sectioned Bayesian networks. *Intl. J. Pattern Recognition and Artificial Intelligence (IJPRAI)*, 14:59–71, 2000.

[YCXH05] X. Yan, H. Cheng, D. Xin, and J. Han. Summarizing itemset patterns: A profile-based approach. In *Proc. 2005 ACM SIGKDD Int. Conf. Knowledge Discovery in Databases (KDD'05)*, pages 314–323, Chicago, IL, Aug, 2005.

[YFB01] C. Yang, U. Fayyad, and P. S. Bradley. Efficient discovery of error-tolerant frequent itemsets in high dimensions. In *Proc. 2001 ACM SIGKDD Int. Conf. Knowledge Discovery in Databases (KDD'01)*, pages 194–203, San Francisco, CA, Aug. 2001.

[YFM+97] K. Yoda, T. Fukuda, Y. Morimoto, S. Morishita, and T. Tokuyama. Computing optimized rectilinear regions for association rules. In *Proc. 1997 Int. Conf. Knowledge Discovery and Data Mining (KDD'97)*, pages 96–103, Newport Beach, CA, Aug. 1997.

[YH02] X. Yan and J. Han. gSpan: Graph-based substructure pattern mining. In *Proc. 2002 Int. Conf. Data Mining (ICDM'02)*, pages 721–724, Maebashi, Japan, Dec. 2002.

[YH03a] X. Yan and J. Han. CloseGraph: Mining closed frequent graph patterns. In *Proc. 2003 ACM SIGKDD Int. Conf. Knowledge Discovery and Data Mining (KDD'03)*, pages 286–295, Washington, DC, Aug. 2003.

[YH03b] X. Yin and J. Han. CPAR: Classification based on predictive association rules. In *Proc. 2003 SIAM Int. Conf. Data Mining (SDM'03)*, pages 331–335, San Francisco, CA, May 2003.

[YHA03] X. Yan, J. Han, and R. Afshar. CloSpan: Mining closed sequential patterns in large datasets. In *Proc. 2003 SIAM Int. Conf. Data Mining (SDM'03)*, pages 166–177, San Francisco, CA, May 2003.

[YHY05] X. Yin, J. Han, and P.S. Yu. Cross-relational clustering with user's guidance. In *Proc. 2005 ACM SIGKDD Int. Conf. Knowledge Discovery in Databases (KDD'05)*, pages 344–353, Chicago, IL, Aug. 2005.

[YHYY04] X. Yin, J. Han, J. Yang, and P. S. Yu. CrossMine: Efficient classification across multiple database relations. In *Proc. 2004 Int. Conf. Data Engineering (ICDE'04)*, pages 399–410, Boston, MA, Mar. 2004.

[YJF98] B.-K. Yi, H. V. Jagadish, and C. Faloutsos. Efficient retrieval of similar time sequences under time warping. In *Proc. 1998 Int. Conf. Data Engineering (ICDE'98)*, pages 201–208, Orlando, FL, Feb. 1998.

[YM97] C. T. Yu and W. Meng. *Principles of Database Query Processing for Advanced Applications.* Morgan Kaufmann, 1997.

[YSJ+00] B.-K. Yi, N. Sidiropoulos, T. Johnson, H. V. Jagadish, C. Faloutsos, and A. Biliris. Online data mining for co-evolving time sequences. In *Proc. 2000 Int. Conf. Data Engineering (ICDE'00)*, pages 13–22, San Diego, CA, Feb. 2000.

[YW03] J. Yang and W. Wang. CLUSEQ: Efficient and effective sequence clustering. In *Proc. 2003 Int. Conf. Data Engineering (ICDE'03)*, pages 101–112, Bangalore, India, March 2003.

[YWY03] J. Yang, W. Wang, and P. S. Yu. Mining asynchronous periodic patterns in time series data. *IEEE Trans. Knowl. Data Eng.*, 15:613–628, 2003.

[YYH03] H. Yu, J. Yang, and J. Han. Classifying large data sets using SVM with hierarchical clusters. In *Proc. 2003 ACM SIGKDD Int. Conf. Knowledge Discovery and Data Mining (KDD'03)*, Washington, DC, Aug. 2003.

[YYH04] X. Yan, P. S. Yu, and J. Han. Graph indexing: A frequent structure-based approach. In *Proc. 2004 ACM-SIGMOD Int. Conf. Management of Data (SIGMOD'04)*, pages 335–346, Paris, France, June 2004.

[YYH05] X. Yan, P. S. Yu, and J. Han. Substructure similarity search in graph databases. In *Proc. 2005 ACM-SIGMOD Int. Conf. Management of Data (SIGMOD'05)*, pages 766–777, Baltimore, MD, June 2005.

[YZ94] R. R. Yager and L. A. Zadeh. *Fuzzy Sets, Neural Networks and Soft Computing*. Van Nostrand Reinhold, 1994.

[YZH05] X. Yan, X. J. Zhou, and J. Han. Mining closed relational graphs with connectivity constraints. In *Proc. 2005 ACM SIGKDD Int. Conf. Knowledge Discovery in Databases (KDD'05)*, pages 357–358, Chicago, IL, Aug. 2005.

[Zad65] L. A. Zadeh. Fuzzy sets. *Information and Control*, 8:338–353, 1965.

[Zad83] L. Zadeh. Commonsense knowledge representation based on fuzzy logic. *Computer*, 16:61–65, 1983.

[Zak98] M. J. Zaki. Efficient enumeration of frequent sequences. In *Proc. 7th Int. Conf. Information and Knowledge Management (CIKM'98)*, pages 68–75, Washington, DC, Nov. 1998.

[Zak00] M. J. Zaki. Scalable algorithms for association mining. *IEEE Trans. Knowledge and Data Engineering*, 12:372–390, 2000.

[Zak01] M. Zaki. SPADE: An efficient algorithm for mining frequent sequences. *Machine Learning*, 40:31–60, 2001.

[Zak02] M. J. Zaki. Efficiently mining frequent trees in a forest. In *Proc. 2002 ACM SIGKDD Int. Conf. Knowledge Discovery in Databases (KDD'02)*, pages 71–80, Edmonton, Canada, July 2002.

[ZCC+02] S. Zdonik, U. Cetintemel, M. Cherniack, C. Convey, S. Lee, G. Seidman, M. Stonebraker, N. Tatbul, and D. Carney. Monitoring streams—a new class of data management applications. In *Proc. 2002 Int. Conf. Very Large Data Bases (VLDB'02)*, pages 215–226, Hong Kong, China, Aug. 2002.

[ZCF+97] C. Zaniolo, S. Ceri, C. Faloutsos, R. T. Snodgrass, C. S. Subrahmanian, and R. Zicari. *Advanced Database Systems*. Morgan Kaufmann, 1997.

[ZDN97] Y. Zhao, P. M. Deshpande, and J. F. Naughton. An array-based algorithm for simultaneous multidimensional aggregates. In *Proc. 1997 ACM-SIGMOD Int. Conf. Management of Data (SIGMOD'97)*, pages 159–170, Tucson, AZ, May 1997.

[ZH95] O. R. Zaïane and J. Han. Resource and knowledge discovery in global information systems: A preliminary design and experiment. In *Proc. 1995 Int. Conf. Knowledge Discovery and Data Mining (KDD'95)*, pages 331–336, Montreal, Canada, Aug. 1995.

[ZH02] M. J. Zaki and C. J. Hsiao. CHARM: An efficient algorithm for closed itemset mining. In *Proc. 2002 SIAM Int. Conf. Data Mining (SDM'02)*, pages 457–473, Arlington, VA, April 2002.

[ZHL+98] O. R. Zaïane, J. Han, Z. N. Li, J. Y. Chiang, and S. Chee. MultiMedia-Miner: A system prototype for multimedia data mining. In *Proc. 1998 ACM-SIGMOD Int. Conf. Management of Data (SIGMOD'98)*, pages 581–583, Seattle, WA, June 1998.

[ZHZ00] O. R. Zaïane, J. Han, and H. Zhu. Mining recurrent items in multimedia with progressive resolution refinement. In *Proc. 2000 Int. Conf. Data Engineering (ICDE'00)*, pages 461–470, San Diego, CA, Feb. 2000.

[Zia91] W. Ziarko. The discovery, analysis, and representation of data dependencies in databases. In G. Piatetsky-Shapiro and W. J. Frawley, editors, *Knowledge Discovery in Databases*, pages 195–209. AAAI Press, 1991.

[ZLO98] M. J. Zaki, N. Lesh, and M. Ogihara. PLANMINE: Sequence mining for plan failures. In *Proc. 1998 Int. Conf. Knowledge Discovery and Data Mining (KDD'98)*, pages 369–373, New York, NY, Aug. 1998.

[ZPOL97] M. J. Zaki, S. Parthasarathy, M. Ogihara, and W. Li. Parallel algorithm for discovery of association rules. *Data Mining and Knowledge Discovery*, 1:343–374, 1997.

[ZRL96] T. Zhang, R. Ramakrishnan, and M. Livny. BIRCH: an efficient data clustering method for very large databases. In *Proc. 1996 ACM-SIGMOD Int. Conf. Management of Data (SIGMOD'96)*, pages 103–114, Montreal, Canada, June 1996.

[ZS02] Y. Zhu and D. Shasha. Statstream: Statistical monitoring of thousands of data streams in real time. In *Proc. 2002 Int. Conf. Very Large Data Bases (VLDB'02)*, pages 358–369, Hong Kong, China, Aug. 2002.

[ZTH99] X. Zhou, D. Truffet, and J. Han. Efficient polygon amalgamation methods for spatial OLAP and spatial data mining. In *Proc. 1999 Int. Symp. Large Spatial Databases (SSD'99)*, pages 167–187, Hong Kong, China, July 1999.

[ZVY04] C. Zhai, A. Velivelli, and B. Yu. A cross-collection mixture model for comparative text mining. In *Proc. 2004 ACM SIGKDD Int. Conf. Knowledge Discovery in Databases (KDD'04)*, pages 743–748, Seattle, WA, Aug. 2004.

[ZXH98] O. R. Zaïane, M. Xin, and J. Han. Discovering Web access patterns and trends by applying OLAP and data mining technology on Web logs. In *Proc. Advances in Digital Libraries Conf. (ADL'98)*, pages 19–29, Santa Barbara, CA, April 1998.

Index

B

C